LABOUR LAW:
TEXT AND MATERIALS

LAW IN CONTEXT

Editors: Robert Stevens (Haverford College, Pennsylvania),
William Twining (University College, London) and
Christopher McCrudden (Lincoln College, Oxford)

Labour Law:
Text and Materials ·

Second Edition

PAUL DAVIES
Fellow of Balliol College, Oxford

MARK FREEDLAND
Fellow of St John's College, Oxford
University Lecturer in Labour Law

WEIDENFELD AND NICOLSON
London

© 1979, 1984 Paul Davies and Mark Freedland
(The Acknowledgements on pp. xxxix–xl constitute
an extension of this copyright page.)

First published 1979
Second edition 1984

George Weidenfeld and Nicolson Ltd
91 Clapham High Street, London SW4 7TA

British Library Cataloguing in Publication Data

Davies, P. L. (Paul Lyndon)
 Labour law. – 2nd. – (Law in context)
 1. Labour laws and legislation – Great Britain
 I. Title II. Freedland, M. R. III. Series
 344.104′1 KD3009

ISBN 0-297-78089-1 cased
ISBN 0-297-78090-5 paperback

Photoset by Deltatype, Ellesmere Port
Printed in Great Britain by Butler & Tanner Ltd
Frome and London

To Saphié and to the memory of Lally

CONTENTS

PREFACE TO THE
SECOND EDITION

In the preface to the first edition, we stated the aim of offering in a single book some of the advantages of both a textbook and a book of cases and materials to the student reading a degree-level or equivalent course in Labour Law. This remains the aim of the second edition, in which we have been able fully to include the area of sex and race discimination in employment. It remains the case, however, that the law concerning health and safety at work is discussed only in respect of statutory consultation arrangements concerning health and safety. The material on state-provided dispute-settlement machinery, which in the first edition formed the concluding chapter, has been reduced in length and distributed among the other chapters of this edition. The principles of selection of materials and of use of comparisons with other systems of labour law are those which governed the first edition.

In detail, however, this book has been very largely rewritten. At one level, this has been made necessary by the immense extent of legislation, case-law and other developments in the field since 1979. Perhaps the most important of these have been the Employment Acts 1980 and 1982, the Transfer of Undertakings Regulations 1981, and the Equal Pay Amendment Regulations 1983. The important new cases are too numerous to list fully. They include *Jenkins* v. *Kingsgate, EEC Commission* v. *UK, Williams* v. *Compair Maxam*, the House of Lords trilogy of industrial conflict cases in 1979–80, *Hadmor* v. *Hamilton, Merkur Island Shipping* v. *Laughton, Mercury Communications* v. *Scott-Garner*, and *Dimbleby & Sons* v. *NUJ*.

There is also a deeper level at which it has been necessary to recast this book. In the preface to the first edition (written at Easter 1979) we mentioned that a general election had been called and asked the question, *Plus ça change?* That seems ironical with the hindsight of 1983, for the changes in the shape and aspect of labour law since that time have been immense, and have amounted to changes in kind as well as degree. They have meant, for instance, that our chapters on collective bargaining and industrial conflict have had to be entirely rewritten. We have also felt it appropriate to respond to changing conditions and emphases by bringing the chapter on the formation of employment to the front of the book, and by addressing more widely and directly the working of the labour market in relation to labour law, and the role of governmental measures concerned with job creation and training.

Obviously in such conditions of flux the task of being up to date at the moment of publication is more than usually difficult. We have sought to state the law as it was on 1 October 1983 and have included later developments where they could be incorporated during the production process. In one respect, however, it has been necessary to use an Appendix to ensure that the book is, as nearly as possible, up to date when published. The purpose of the Appendix is to describe the provisions of the Trade Union Bill which had just begun its passage through Parliament as the production process of this book began and has reached Report stage in the House of Commons at the time of this Preface.

As we have drawn extensively on Brown (ed.), *The Changing Contours of British Industrial Relations*, we think it worth pointing out that Daniel and Millward, *Workplace Industrial Relations*, appeared too late for us to make full use of the valuable information that it contains.

As in relation to the first edition, we are grateful to our seminar students in successive years for providing a stimulus to and a sounding-board for the development of our ideas, especially in relation to collective bargaining. Among those who have commented on parts of the text or contributed to our understanding of particular areas of law and practice, we should like to single out for particular acknowledgment Hugh Collins, Rosemary Jeffreys, John Kay and Christopher McCrudden. Among those who helped with the production of the typescript we should like to thank Mary Bugge, Frances Day, Sheila Lewis and Jean Ray. Sue Ashtiany contributed the Index and, together with Raphaela and Geoffrey Lewis, provided moral and practical support for the writing process. We are especially grateful to our publishers for their tolerance of the length of the writing process and the length of the resulting text, and finally for allowing us an Appendix in which to chronicle the most recent developments.

Paul Davies
Mark Freedland

Balliol College, Oxford and
St John's College, Oxford

St Ambrose's Day, April 1984

CASES

STATUTES

(including EEC measures, and regulations made under the European Communities Act 1972)

ACKNOWLEDGEMENTS

We are grateful to the following for allowing reproductions to be made: Basil Blackwell Publisher Ltd for the extracts from *The System of Industrial Relations in Great Britain*, 3rd edn, by H. A. Clegg, *The System of Industrial Relations in Great Britain*, edited by A. Flanders and H. A. Clegg, and *The Closed Shop in Britain* by W. E. J. McCarthy; Butterworth & Co. (Publishers) Ltd for extracts from cases reported in the *All England Law Reports*; Cambridge University Press for extracts from B. Chiplin and P. J. Sloane, *Tackling Discrimination at the Workplace* and S. Creedy, *State Pensions in Britain*; Gerald Duckworth & Co. Ltd for an extract from *Taking Rights Seriously* by Ronald Dworkin; Engineering Employers' Federation for an extract from 'Response to Green Paper on Trade Union Immunities'; Faber and Faber Ltd for extracts from *Management and Unions* by Allan Flanders and *Beyond Contract: Trust, Power and Work Relations* by Alan Fox; the Fabian Society for an extract from *Laws Against Strikes* by O. Kahn-Freund and B. Hepple; The Foundation Press Inc. for an extract from *Labor Law* by Summers and Wellington; Heinemann Educational Books Ltd for extracts from *Piecework Bargaining* by William Brown and *Governments and Trade Unions* by Denis Barnes and Eileen Reid; the Controller of Her Majesty's Stationery Office for extracts from UK official publications; Hutchinson Publishing Group Ltd for an extract from *Management by Agreement* by W. E. J. McCarthy and N. D. Ellis; Incomes Data Services Ltd for extracts from their *Studies* and *Briefs*; The Incorporated Council of Law Reporting for England and Wales for extracts from cases reported in the *Law Reports*, the *Industrial Court Reports* and the *Industrial Cases Reports*; the Industrial Law Society for extracts from articles in the *Industrial Law Journal*; the *Industrial Relations Journal* for extracts from 'A Question of Disclosure' by A. Marsh and R. Rosewell and 'Works Rules Book in the Engineering Industry' by E. O. Evans; Industrial Relations Services for extracts from cases reported in the *Industrial Relations Law Reports* and an extract from the *Health and Safety Information Bulletin* No. 33; Charles Knight & Co. Ltd for an extract from a case reported in *Knights Industrial Reports*; Kogan Page Ltd for an extract from J. Elliott, *Conflict or Cooperation?*; Longman Group Ltd for an extract from *Industrial Conflict* edited by B. Aaron and K. W. Wedderburn; Macmillan Publishing Co. Inc. for an extract from *Law in Modern Society* by R. M. Unger; the *Modern Law Review* for extracts from 'A Note on Status and Contract in British Labour Law' and a case-note by O. Kahn-Freund; Oxford University Press for extracts from *The Inequality of Pay* by E. H. Phelps Brown; Penguin Books Ltd for extracts from *Grunwick* by J. Rogaly, *The Worker and the Law*, 2nd edn, by K. W. Wedderburn, and *Wages and Salaries* by T. Lupton and A. Bowey; Routledge & Kegan Paul Ltd for an extract from *The Institutions of Private Law and their Social Functions* by K. Renner; W. Green & Son Ltd for an extract from the *Scots Law Times*; Basic Books Inc. and the Russell Sage Foundation for an extract from *Law Society and Industrial Justice* by P. Selznick; Sweet and Maxwell Ltd for extracts from *Labour and the Law* by O. Kahn-Freund; Times Newspapers Ltd for a news report appearing in *The Times*; and the Trades Union Congress for extracts from *Disputes Principles and Procedures*.

PRINCIPAL ABBREVIATIONS

We have included here only abbreviations specific to the fields of labour law and industrial relations.

(a) *Legislation*

CEA 1963	Contracts of Employment Act 1963
CEA 1972	Contracts of Employment Act 1972
CLA 1977	Criminal Law Act 1977
CPPA 1875	Conspiracy and Protection of Property Act 1875
EA 1980	Employment Act 1980
EA 1982	Employment Act 1982
EPA 1975	Employment Protection Act 1975
EPCA 1978	Employment Protection (Consolidation) Act 1978
EqPA 1970	Equal Pay Act 1970
HSWA 1974	Health and Safety at Work Act 1974
IRA 1971	Industrial Relations Act 1971
RPA 1965	Redundancy Payments Act 1965
RRA 1976	Race Relations Act 1976
SDA 1975	Sex Discrimination Act 1975
TUA 1913	Trade Union Act 1913
TULRA 1974	Trade Union and Labour Relations Act 1974
TULRA 1976	Trade Union and Labour Relations (Amendment) Act 1976
WCA 1979	Wages Councils Act 1979

(b) *Other abbreviations*

ACAS	Advisory, Conciliation and Arbitration Service
BJIR	British Journal of Industrial Relations
CAC	Central Arbitration Committee
CO	Certification Officer
DE	Department of Employment
EAT	Employment Appeal Tribunal
FWR	Fair Wages Resolution
HSC	Health and Safety Commission
IAB	Industrial Arbitration Board

ICR   Industrial Court Reports (1972–4) Industrial Cases Reports (1975–)
IDS   Incomes Data Services
ILJ   Industrial Law Journal
IRC   Independent Review Committee of the Trades Union Congress
IRJ   Industrial Relations Journal
IRLIB   Industrial Relations Legal Information Bulletin
IRLR   Industrial Relations Law Reports
IRRR   Industrial Relations Review and Report
ITR   Industrial Tribunal Reports (1966–78)
KIR   Knights Industrial Reports
MSC   Manpower Services Commission
NIRC   National Industrial Relations Court

I
Constituting the employment relationship

1 Introduction – employment and the labour market

This chapter is about the formation of the employment relationship and the law which deals with the formation of that relationship. We have made this the first topic in this book because it seems logical to begin with a subject which in many senses lays the foundations for much of what follows in later chapters. To put this argument at its lowest, it seems only sensible to begin a general account of labour law by defining, and describing the creation of, its central phenomenon, which must of course be the employment relationship itself. Despite this apparently reasonable proposition, books about labour law do not generally take the formation of the employment relationship as their starting point; indeed, this is a topic to which very little prominence is given. The reasons why so little importance has been accorded to this topic seem to us, so far from justifying the practice, to indicate good grounds for trying to ensure that the subject of constituting the employment relationship receives greater attention in the future.

Let us start with some broad propositions. It would not be a very controversial proposition today that the employment relationship is one of the centrally important social and economic relationships affecting the ordering of our society. It would also be uncontroversial to assert that, in consequence, the law concerning that relationship is centrally important law. The activities and priorities of every single post-war government of Great Britain reflect these propositions. But we have in recent years become accustomed to state these propositions in a form which puts the social and legal issues outside the area of employment law and in particular the law about the formation of the employment relationship. That is to say, we have become accustomed to refer to the importance of the formation of the employment relationship negatively, by emphasizing (understandably and rightly) the immense social and economic consequences of *unemployment*. In doing so we are really identifying the extreme importance of the level or extent of the formation and maintenance of employment relationships. It is also becoming more fully understood that the discussion of levels of employment is intimately and inseparably bound up with the question of *patterns* of employment. By patterns of employment we refer to issues such as the choices between employment and self-employment, full-time work and part-time work, permanent employment and temporary or casual employment, direct employment and agency employment, employment at a workplace or homeworking. We refer also to some demographic factors which create patterns of employment, factors such as the age, sex, marital status, nationality and racial or ethnic origins of the worker. Many of these factors have become the subject, as we shall see, of legislation or other measures concerned with discrimination in selection for employment. The significant exception is the factor of age. It is coming to be realized that questions of policy concerning the control of access to employment in terms of the age of the worker will one day have to be addressed as a matter of employment law, just as the other demographic factors referred to have been.

These questions of the levels and patterns of employment have an impact or an interaction with all the different aspects of the employment relationship with which we shall be concerned in the course of this book. It is for that reason that we can regard an account of the law relating to the formation of the employment relationship as an essential precursor to all the other aspects of labour law that we shall discuss. Let us illustrate this. In a later part of this book we discuss the content and the termination of the employment relationship, and we shall find that the changes in levels and patterns of employment have had a major impact upon the shape of the discussion. Conditions of recession, by creating an effective pressure to reduce labour costs and weakening the resistance to that pressure, have made employment protection legislation of various sorts more prominent and more vulnerable to arguments which assert that they add unduly to labour costs and by so doing operate to the ultimate disadvantage of the workforce by further curtailing already scarce opportunities for employment. This, as we shall see, has become a well-developed debate in relation to protection of the employee as regards the termination of employment; it can also be seen as shaping the development of various aspects of the law relating to the content of employment, particularly so far as the law relating to security of earnings and the law dealing with low pay are concerned.

We hope that the reader will have found potentially convincing the thesis that levels and patterns of employment have an important impact on and interaction with most aspects of labour law. Even on that assumption, however, there would not by virtue of that fact alone be sufficient justification for taking the law relating to the formation of employment out of its accustomed semi-obscurity and putting it in the prominent place in which we propose to discuss it. We have put the formation of employment first on the basis that there are a number of areas of legislative activity and governmental action which are relevant to the constituting of the employment relationship and therefore affect levels and patterns of employment but which have lain outside the traditional purview of labour law, or at least outside the areas viewed as being of central concern to labour law. We are in some sense seeking to redress that particular balance. One disclaimer is necessary before elaborating this idea. What we have said thus far might be viewed as a rationale for regarding all aspects of governmental regulation of the economy as aspects of labour law. There has indeed been a momentum in recent years towards regarding levels and patterns of employment as the central concern of the whole process of economic regulation. We do not claim to contribute to that debate nor to adrogate so large and open-ended a set of governmental activities to the province of labour law. It is in a sense unnecessary to do so, given our view that there is a smaller and more defined area which labour lawyers have been slow to recognize as of central concern to them.

We suggest that there are a number of areas of law or of governmental activity which are immediately relevant to the constituting of the employment relationship in that they affect either (1) levels of recruitment for employment, (2) the mode or criteria of selection for employment, or (3) the form in which the employment relationship is constituted. These are not watertight compartments, for a particular area of law or governmental activity might be seen as falling within more than one of these categories, and the categories might be regarded as inter-related and interacting. But they do serve to suggest a working method for the treatment of various legal topics with which we are concerned. Proceeding from the relatively familiar to the relatively unfamiliar, we shall briefly elaborate category (2) first. From a position in which decisions about selection for hiring were regarded as pre-eminently and sacrosanctly a matter within managerial prerogative except in war-time, we have seen a great growth of law controlling discrimination in selection for employment, most obviously in favour of disabled persons and by way of elimination of racial and sex discrimination. We are also witnessing a growth in the importance of controls derived from restrictions on immigration and, on the other hand, from the principle of freedom of movement of workers within the EEC. We shall also wish to develop the thesis that legal rights to reinstatement accorded to certain groups of applicants for employment (for example ex-servicemen or women after confinement) constitute an increasingly important aspect of legal control over selection for employment.

Our heads (1) and (3) can usefully be taken together, for they are crucially inter-connected. We are quite accustomed to labour law being in one sense concerned with the form in which the employment relationship is constituted, because the process of distinguishing between employment and self-employment is probably the oldest and most tradition-ridden of all the pre-occupations of labour lawyers. But that preoccupation has been largely with the proper characterization of existing relationships. We are now coming to realize what a crucial role the law has, whether by intervention or by abstention, in relation to decisions about the form in which employment shall be constituted. Questions of how far the law should encourage or discourage particular forms of employment such as labour-only subcontracting, agency working, seasonal or temporary employment, homeworking or part-time work, are looming increasingly large. These issues form an important aspect of the shaping of policies and measures concerned with levels of recruitment to employment. Thus measures such as the subsidizing of jobs, the provision of training for employment, the provision of employment recruitment services, and the conditions for social security benefits to provide income replacement where there is unemployment, all affect levels of recruitment for employment and all embody important determinants of patterns of employment. It is in that wider sense and in relation to those particular topics that we propose to discuss the constituting of the employment relationship in the present chapter.

Before we turn to the details of this discussion, it will be useful to give some description of the size and profile of the labour market whose functioning we shall be concerned with. We shall draw for this purpose on the government's annual summary and analysis of social statistics, *Social Trends*, and on the Department of Employment's monthly tables and analyses of employment statistics in the *Employment Gazette*. We start with a description and table of the extent of economic activity in mid-1979, which indicates some of the problems involved in relating the size of the actual labour force to the size of the potential labour force, and hence of gauging the extent of unemployment.

Social Trends 13 (1982), p. 51

Economic activity
The composition of the labour force is shown in the table below. Employees in employment (both full-time and part-time) plus the self-employed and members of HM Forces make up the employed labour force. The working population consists of the employed labour force plus the registered unemployed. The economically active population, or total labour force, is related to the working population by the inclusion of the unregistered unemployed, and certain other minor adjustments not shown in the table (such as for people with two or more jobs, or working students). In mid-1979 men accounted for 60 per cent of both the total and employed labour force in the United Kingdom. Three times more women than men were unregistered unemployed.

The economically inactive population is made up of full-time students and others not seeking employment – such as those who are keeping house, have retired early, or are permanently unable to work. In mid-1979 about 80 per cent of the economically inactive in the United Kingdom were women. The economically active and inactive do not sum to the population of working age as an adjustment is made for people over retirement age who are still in the labour force.

The labour force in Great Britain is estimated to have increased by over 2 million between 1961 and 1981, entirely due to the increasing participation of married women. However, data for recent years suggest that this increased participation has stopped: since 1977 the number of married women in the labour force has fallen slightly, after having increased by 77 per cent between 1961 and 1977. Among non-married women the trend was reversed – the estimated number increased between 1977 and 1981, having fallen by 15 per cent between 1961 and 1977. The number of men in the labour force has remained at around 16 million throughout the last two decades.

Labour force and population of working age, mid–1979

United Kingdom			Millions
	Males	Females	Total
Economically active			
Employees in employment[1]			
–full-time	} 13·4 {	5·8	} 22·9
–part-time		3·8	
Self-employed	1·5	0·4	1·9
H M Forces	0·3	–	0·3
Employed labour force	15·2	9·9	25·1
Registered unemployed	0·9	0·4	1·3
Unregistered unemployed[2]	0·1	0·3	0·3
Total labour force	16·2	10·5	26·7
Economically inactive			
Full-time students[3]	0·7	0·7	1·4
Others[3]	0·8	5·2	6·0
Total inactive[3]	1·5	5·9	7·4
Less persons over retirement age in labour force	0·3	0·5	0·8
Population of working age	17·4	15·9	33·3

[1] Assumes all Northern Ireland female employees work full time
[2] Estimates are based on General Household Survey and Labour Force Survey and relate only to Great Britain
[3] Persons aged over 15 and under retirement age
Source: Employment Gazette, Department of Employment, Northern Ireland Department of Manpower Services

We continue with a valuable summary of the changes in the size and structure of the labour force which were indicated by the statistics on employment set out in *Social Trends* 13 for 1982:

Pat Healy, 'Recession is Changing the Nature
of Work', *The Times*, 9 December 1982

Britain's recession is affecting not only the numbers of people able to find work, but changing the nature of their employment, according to *Social Trends*. The reduction of manufacturing jobs which began in the 1970s has accelerated in the last two years, while service industries have begun to decline, too, after a boom over the last decade.

Between June, 1979, and June, 1981, there was a 16 per cent reduction in the number of people working in manufacturing jobs, with metal manufacture experiencing the biggest drop of 27 per cent. Jobs in textiles, leather and clothing fell by 21 per cent in the same period.

The service industries expanded during the 1970s, giving jobs to 1,800,000 more people. But employment in them dropped by 3 per cent between 1979 and 1981, with only the insurance, banking and finance sector able to maintain its employment level throughout the two years.

Overall, the figures show a net reduction of 900,000 in the numbers of people employed between 1971 and 1981, with 1,700,000 losing their jobs between June, 1979 and June, 1981. Since two-thirds of the labour force work in private jobs, the private sector has been worst affected.

Attempts to reduce the numbers of civil servants and council employees led to 100,000 fewer public sector jobs in 1981, bringing the total back to its 1976 level. But 1,100,000 fewer people, including the self-employed, were working in the private sector in 1981 compared with the previous year; a reduction of 2,400,000 over the last 20 years.

Since 1961, the labour force has increased by 2,000,000, due entirely to the increasing numbers of married women taking paid jobs [see Table opposite]. That increase now seems to have stopped; an estimated 200,000 fewer married women had jobs in 1981 than in the previous year and the proportion of couples where both partners go out to work has fallen by five per cent over the last two years.

But more than half of all married couples have both partners working.

Rising unemployment is increasing the number of older men retiring prematurely: in 1971 94 per cent of men aged 45 to 64 were economically active. Ten years later the proportion was down to 88 per cent, and in April, 1982, half the men in the 60 to 64 age group on the unemployment register had been there for more than a year.

People from the ethnic minorities are disproportionately represented on the register – and also more likely to be self-employed than the host population. While 10 per cent of white men aged 16–64 are unemployed, the proportion for those from India, Pakistan and Bangladesh is 17 per cent, and from the West Indies and Guyana 21 per cent.

A similar pattern applies to women, and the over-representation of people from ethnic minorities applies to the young too. Of women aged 16 to 24, 16 per cent of the whites are unemployed, 28 per cent of West Indians, and 30 per cent from the Indian sub-continent. The proportions for men in the same age group are 19, 38 and 25 respectively.

But while only 9 per cent of white men are self-employed, 14 per cent of Asian men run their own businesses.

Labour force: estimates and projections, Great Britain

	Females				
	Married	Unmarried	All	Males	All persons
Estimates (millions)					
1961	3·9	3·9	7·7	16·1	23·8
1966	5·1	3·8	8·9	16·0	24·9
1971	5·8	3·4	9·2	15·9	25·1
1977	6·9	3·3	10·3	15·9	26·1
1979	6·8	3·5	10·3	15·8	26·0
Projections					
1981	6·6	3·7	10·3	15·7	26·0
1986	6·8	3·8	10·6	16·0	26·7

Excluding full-time students. From 1973 15-year-olds are excluded as a result of the raising of the school leaving age. Figures from 1977 therefore relate to persons aged 16 years and over. Projections based on estimates from the 1979 Labour Force Survey.
Source: Department of Employment.

It is instructive to add to those figures some details of the *Census of Employment* results for September 1981 which give some indications of the changes that had taken place in the preceding three years, in particular the changes in the place occupied by part-time female employees in the labour force:

Employment Gazette, December 1982, pp. 504, 505

First results now available from the census of employment [see Table on p. 8], relating to September 1981, show that there were 21,148,000 employees in employment, compared with 22,274,000 in June 1978 when the previous census of employment was taken. The fall in the three years was 1,126,000, the main reductions being in manufacturing industry, with a fall of 1,193,000 and in construction, down by 135,000, with service industries showing a modest rise, of 214,000.

Reflecting this industry pattern, there was a greater fall in the number of male employees, down by 965,000, than in female employees, which were lower by 161,000. The number of female employees working full time was 232,000 lower but this was partly offset by an increase of 71,000 in part time female workers, because of the opportunities in the service industries.

The overall reduction shown by the censuses between 1978 and 1981, of 1,126,000 was some 538,000 less than that in the quarterly employment series published in *Employment Gazette*. The latter are calculated by projecting forward from the previous census using information from a sample of firms and some deviation must be expected between censuses, one of the main purposes of which is to provide a periodic check of the position on a comprehensive basis.

Whilst the information from the sample of firms used in the quarterly estimates provides a good guide to trends in employment in existing businesses, it is unable to provide a comprehensive measure either of firms going out of business or of new businesses becoming established. This is particularly significant in the service industries where changes of this kind are numerous and often involve small firms; it is in these sectors where the main divergence between the census and the quarterly series has occurred. Also, associated with this, about half of the divergence was in part-time female employees.

Employees in employment

			Thousand
Great Britain	Census 1981	Census 1978	Change
All industries and services			
Male and female	21,148	22,274	−1,126
Male	12,135	13,100	−965
Female	9,013	9,173	−161
Full-time	5,254	5,486	−232
Part-time	3,759	3,688	71
Manufacturing industries			
Male and female	5,924	7,117	−1,193
Male	4,237	5,032	−795
Female	1,687	2,085	−398
Full-time	1,318	1,604	−286
Part-time	369	480	−111
Service industries			
Male and female	13,091	12,878	214
Male	6,058	6,070	−12
Female	7,033	6,808	225
Full-time	3,740	3,691	49
Part-time	3,294	3,117	177

Source: Employment Gazette, December 1982, Table 1, p. 505.

This presentation of labour statistics is concluded with a pair of graphs (see facing page) from *Employment Gazette*, April 1983, p. S5, which illustrate vividly the acceleration in recent years of the growth in unemployment, and the relatively greater speed of decline in employment in manufacturing as compared with non-manufacturing industry. In the first graph the upper line indicates the size of the working population (defined above, p. 4) and the lower line the size of the employed labour force; the shaded area between the two lines shows the number of the unemployed. It can be seen that the number of those unemployed has generally been increasing since the early 1970s, but until 1979 this was as much the result of an increase in the size of the working population as of a decline in the number of employment opportunities. Since 1979, however, the number of unemployed has increased rapidly in spite of a decline in the size of the working population – itself no doubt also attributable to the recession. The second graph (lower line) shows that the decline in employment opportunities in manufacturing was already under way at the beginning of the 1970s, although it was much more rapid after 1979. The decline in manufacturing was partly offset by an increase in employment opportunities in non-manufacturing which continued until about the middle of 1980 (cf. the analysis of the 1978 and 1981 censuses, above); since then, however, employment opportunities in this sector have also declined, to the point where the gains of the second part of the decade have been wiped out.

It is worth articulating the case for regarding data of this kind as important to the study of labour law. In a general sense they serve as a reminder of the fact that labour law is ultimately no more than an adjunct to a social reality

Working population and employed labour force: Great Britain

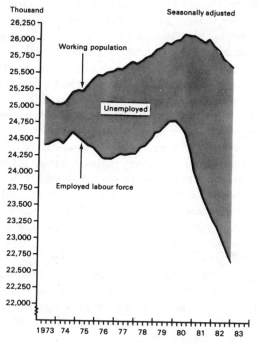

Note: Unemployment figures are on the new (claimants) basis.

Manufacturing and non-manufacturing employees in employment

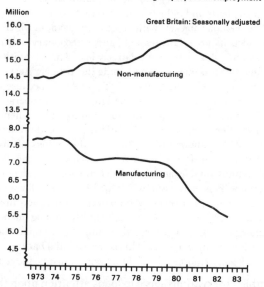

over which, as Kahn-Freund emphasized, the law exerts no more than a marginal control (see *Labour and the Law*, 2nd edn. 1977, p. 2). In a particular sense, they enable us to start to appreciate the importance of the analyses of the labour market which have been offered by labour economists in recent years. These analyses suggest that the labour market should be envisaged not as a single continuous phenomenon within which workers move freely in patterns determined by their skills and abilities, but rather as a market segmented by many social and institutional barriers to labour mobility. This segmentation is seen by many analysts as generating or perpetuating a number of social and economic problems or inequalities. The reader is referred for an admirable survey of this literature to Glen Cain, 'The challenge of segmented labour market theories to orthodox theory: a survey', *Journal of Economic Literature*, December 1976, pp. 1215 *et seq.*, and, for a study of its application in this country, to Mayhew and Rosewell, 'Labour Market Segmentation in Britain', *Oxford Bulletin of Economics and Statistics*, 1979, pp. 81 *et seq.* We shall return later to defining what we mean by the labour market and to describing how labour law impinges on it (see below, pp. 11–13); suffice it for the time being that an awareness is growing among labour lawyers that the body of law with which they are concerned has to be understood and evaluated against that particular social, economic and analytical background. The point was made with great force and clarity by Professor Hepple in his Sidney Ball Lecture in 1980 in the following terms:

Bob Hepple, 'A Right to Work?' (1981) 10 *ILJ* 65 at p. 68

The nature of the demand for labour and the inequalities of collective bargaining power within and between plants and industries has led to the often-observed phenomenon of segmented and dual labour markets with a 'primary' sector in which unions are strong and pay and job security are relatively high, and a 'secondary' sector in which unions are weak and pay and job security are relatively low. The alternative offered by [the] critics of individual rights is one of strengthening the 'primary' sector. Individuals and social groups who lack 'industrial muscle' – for example because they are black or female or work for a small employer – are designated by the operation of the primary labour market for differential access to the opportunities and benefits of employment. There is a contradiction in seeking substantial justice for those who are outside the primary segment of the labour market through the actions of disparate collective groups within that segment. It is this which has given such tremendous importance to the idea of *universal* individual legal rights, which are not dependent upon membership of a collective group. This is an issue which will be with us for some time, since the economists tell us that, with 10 per cent of the working population already unemployed, long-term unemployment is increasing particularly among men, the rate of unemployment among young people is rising and the occupational distribution of unemployment is increasingly uneven. This is the essential background against which the proposal for a legally enforceable 'right to work' must be judged.

These valuable observations serve to focus attention upon the fact that once the concerns of labour lawyers are defined in such a way as to include a broad range of measures affecting levels and patterns of employment, and once they are set in a context which takes account of the size and profile of the labour market, the law concerned with the constituting of the employment relationship assumes a primary importance for the whole of labour law. This perspective moreover throws into sharp relief a growing multiplicity of employment laws and measures which have developed to the point where they challenge the traditional assumption that the law has a marginal or minimal role in the formation of the employment relationship. The challenge to that belief should become increasingly apparent in the course of this chapter. We shall begin by developing this thesis in relation to measures affecting levels of recruitment for employment, which we think can usefully be analysed as measures controlling the size of labour supply and demand.

2 Legal controls over the size of the labour market

(a) Introduction – supply and demand in the labour market

As labour lawyers, we are accustomed to work with a very individuated model of the formation of the employment relationship; that is to say, we concentrate very much upon the making of an arrangement for employment between the particular employer and the particular worker. We are by now accustomed to assert and accept the importance of collective bargaining in relation to the making of these arrangements; but even this does not shift the focus of our attention away from the individual transaction, so that the topic tends very much to be envisaged as a multiplicity of single transactions. We think that it may be useful to look at the formation of the employment relationship and the law controlling it from a rather different perspective, that is to say a perspective from which each individual transaction is seen as a component of a larger entity, which is the functioning of the labour market. The traditional perspective reflects, and indeed reinforces, a preoccupation with the rights and obligations of the individual worker. That is a necessary preoccupation, but this different perspective may have the advantage of revealing more clearly the larger social and economic consequences of legal controls over the constituting of the employment relationship.

This argument may be made clearer by an explanation of what we mean by the functioning of the labour market. The 'labour market' is, of course, an abstract idea; it consists, like any other such notional market, in the process whereby the supply of and the demand for a particular commodity or service interact to give rise to transactions in that commodity or service. In this case the market is in labour generally; the supply is derived from the labour capacity of the working population; the demand consists in vacancies for employment; the transactions consist in the formation of employment relationships of one sort or another. In this market, excess of demand over supply is described as labour shortage, and excess of supply over demand is described as unemployment. Hence the overall functioning of the labour market is illustrated by the graph on p. 9 above, showing the relative movement of the size of the working population and the size of the employed labour force in Great Britain over the last ten years; the widening gap between the two constitutes the growing area of unemployment. Of course, vacancies, and indeed specific labour shortages, can co-exist with high and growing levels of unemployment, to the point where, as we have seen, labour economists have argued that we should think of the labour market as segmented into a number of self-contained and mutually isolated labour markets (see above, p. 10). So if we speak of the labour market as a single entity, we intend to do so only in a generic sense, and are not presupposing a continuity or flexibility of movement between its various sectors.

The foregoing description of what we mean by the labour market helps to identify the ways in which legal controls affect the size of the labour market. For this description of the meaning of the labour market makes it clear that the size of that market is a function both of the demand for and the supply of labour. Hence legal measures may affect the size of the labour market by operating either upon the supply of labour or upon the demand for it. This analysis reveals the extensiveness of the range of legal measures affecting the size of the labour market, for many legal measures demonstrably impinge on either the demand for or the supply of labour. Indeed, as we have remarked earlier, one could in this way develop a case for regarding much of the whole process of governmental regulation of the functioning of the economy as relevant to labour law. But even given that we disclaim so large an area of inquiry, there are still many relevant legal measures remaining for consideration, often nevertheless lying outside the traditional interests of labour lawyers. Thus on the supply side we see immigration rules and the work-permit system as establishing the parameters of labour supply, these parameters being in turn widened by the EEC treaty provisions for free movement of labour between member states. A number of aspects of the social security system have an impact upon labour supply (and the system has some impact also upon demand for labour). There are a number of measures in the area of job creation and training for jobs which have an impact both on the supply side and the demand side; we shall argue in relation to them that the method of analysis, adopted in this section, of distinguishing between the two types of impact is valuable because we have frequently in the past failed to appreciate the significance of this dual function that job creation and training measures may have. Finally in this catalogue of supply-side and demand-side effects, we shall examine the assertion which is often made that employment protection legislation operates to reduce the demand for labour, for instance by making it less attractive to engage employees by making it harder to dismiss them later on. In this section we shall examine in turn these different legal measures determining or at least affecting the size of the labour market.

Before we embark upon an examination of the details of the legal measures in question, there is one further general point to be made. As we pointed out in the introduction to this chapter as a whole, although we have adopted a working method of describing the relevant legal measures which distinguishes between effects upon the size of the labour market, effects upon selection for employment, and effects upon the form in which employment is constituted, it does not follow that each particular legal measure is to be regarded as important in only one of those directions. On the contrary, one cannot begin to describe the details of these measures without becoming aware of the spread of their effects among the three categories. Thus we shall find in the course of this section that many measures whose primary impact is upon the size of the labour market also have important effects upon selection for employment and the forms in which employment relationships are constituted. The reader is urged to be alert to the possibility of this multiplicity of function when considering the measures described in this section, because it is this which makes the measures concerned so especially important to an understanding of the working of labour laws. We shall attempt to draw those particular threads together at the conclusion of this section.

(b) Immigration Rules and work permits

There are more than one reason why a country may wish to prevent persons who are nationals of other countries from being admitted for the purpose of taking up employment, but the predominant reason for such restrictions, and the reason for the restrictions which operate in the UK, is the protection of the employment opportunities of the nationals of the country concerned. (Other reasons generally relate to considerations of national security, which tend to loom particularly large, for obvious reasons, during war-time and in the immediate aftermath of hostilities; compare, for instance, the restrictions on employment of aliens in the civil service currently contained in the Aliens Employment Act 1955, and the penalties attaching to the promoting of industrial unrest by aliens under the Aliens Restriction (Amendment) Act 1919.) The general acceptance of the necessity for this kind of parameter upon the labour market leads to what Blanc-Jouvan has described as 'an open, legal form of discrimination, which is based upon the objective criterion of nationality' (Folke Schmidt (ed.), *Discrimination in Employment* (Stockholm 1978), p. 257). In other words, that which is prohibited to the employer in selecting for employment as discrimination on the ground of nationality made unlawful by the RRA 1976 (see below, p. 44), is adopted, subject to certain qualifications resulting from our membership of the EEC, as a legitimate restriction placed at national level upon the size of the labour market.

Control over the entry into this country of foreign nationals for the purpose of entering into employment is exercised under the authority of a combination of two sets of administrative rules neither of which takes statutory or statutory instrument form. (We shall find that the absence of the necessity for parliamentary enactment is a common feature of legal measures affecting the size of the labour market, because, perhaps, of the extent to which they are regarded as lying within that broad area of purely governmental discretion which is concerned with the regulation of the economy; in this particular instance the measures concerned fall, in part at least, within the ambit of the traditionally untramelled prerogative of governmental control of immigration.) The first set of rules is the Immigration Rules, made under the prerogative, which lay down the practice to be followed in the administration of the Immigration Act 1971 for regulating the entry into and stay in the UK of non-patrials (that is, those without a right of abode in the UK, that right and the status of patriality being confined to certain citizens of the UK and Colonies and certain citizens of independent Commonwealth countries). The Immigration Rules are made by the Home Secretary, who is required by the Immigration Act 1971, s.3, to lay a statement of the Rules or any changes in them before Parliament where they become law unless disapproved by resolution within forty days. The current Rules are those of 1980 which further restrict the conditions on which leave to enter may be given as compared with the original Rules of 1973. We set out below the Rules relating to entry and stay for the purposes of employment or self-employment. A reading of these Rules will serve to indicate the role of work permits; we shall next examine the further rules relating to the grant of work permits. It will also indicate the crucial importance of the powers of the Home Secretary to regulate access of non-patrials to the labour market by laying down the conditions for permit-free employment and for self-employment. A most valuable account of all these provisions is provided by I. A. Macdonald in *Immigration Law and Practice* (1983).

Immigration Rules 1983

['Passenger' means any Commonwealth citizen or British protected person who requires leave to enter and any foreign national or stateless person. Special provision is made for nationals of EEC countries.]

SECTION ONE: CONTROL ON ENTRY . . .

Part III: Passengers coming for employment or business, as persons of independent means, or for marriage.

Work Permits

27   If a passenger is coming to the United Kingdom to seek employment or to take employment for which he has no work permit, and he is not eligible for admission under paragraphs 29–34 or Part IV, leave to enter is to be refused. Permits are issued by the Department of Employment in respect of a specific post with a specific employer. The possession of a work permit does not absolve the holder from complying with visa requirements.

28   The holder of a current work permit should normally be admitted for the period specified in the permit, subject to a condition permitting him to take or change employment only with the permission of the Department of Employment. The Immigration Officer is, however, to refuse leave to enter if his examination reveals good

reason for doing so. For example, leave to enter should be refused where, whether or not to the holder's knowledge, false representations were employed or material facts were not disclosed, either in writing or orally, for the purpose of obtaining the permit, or the holder's true age puts him outside the limits for employment, or he does not intend to take the employment specified, or is not capable of doing so. But if the period of validity of the permit has expired the Immigration Officer may nevertheless admit the passenger if satisfied that circumstances beyond his control prevented his arrival before the permit expired and that the job is still open to him.

Exception on grounds of United Kingdom ancestry
29   Upon proof that one of his grandparents was born in the United Kingdom and Islands, a Commonwealth citizen who wishes to take or seek employment in the United Kingdom will be granted an entry clearance for that purpose. A passenger holding an entry clearance granted in accordance with this paragraph does not need a work permit and, subject to paragraph 13, should be given indefinite leave to enter.

Permit-free employment
31   Passengers in the following categories, although coming for employment, do not need work permits and may, subject to paragraph 13, be admitted for an appropriate period not exceeding 12 months if they hold a current entry clearance granted for the purpose:
   (a) ministers of religion, missionaries and members of religious orders, if they are coming to work full-time as such and can maintain and accommodate themselves and their dependants without recourse to public funds. Members of religious orders engaged in teaching at establishments maintained by their order will not require work permits, but if they are otherwise engaged in teaching, permits will be required;
   (b) representatives of overseas firms which have no branch, subsidiary or other representative in the United Kingdom;
   (c) representatives of overseas newspapers, news agencies and broadcasting organisations, on long-term assignment to the United Kingdom.
32   Doctors and dentists coming to take up professional appointments do not need work permits and may, subject to paragraph 13, be admitted for an appropriate period not exceeding 12 months if they hold a current entry clearance granted for the purpose. Doctors eligible for hospital employment without undertaking the Department of Health and Social Security Attachment Scheme, and dentists seeking employment in or practising their profession, should be admitted without work permits for up to 6 months.
33   Passengers in the following categories, although coming for employment, do not need work permits and may, subject to paragraph 13, be admitted for an appropriate period not exceeding 12 months if they hold a current entry clearance granted for the purpose or other satisfactory documentary evidence that they do not require permits:
   (a) private servants (aged 16 and over) of members of the staff of diplomatic or consular missions or of members of the family forming part of the household of such persons;
   (b) persons coming for employment by an overseas Government or in the employment of the United Nations Organisation or other international organisation of which the United Kingdom is a member;
   (c) teachers and language assistants coming to schools in the United Kingdom

under exchange schemes approved by the Education Departments or administered by the Central Bureau for Educational Visits and Exchanges or the League
for the Exchange of Commonwealth Teachers;

(d) seamen under contract to join a ship in British waters;

(e) operational staff (but not other staff) of overseas owned airlines;

(f) seasonal workers at agricultural camps under approved schemes.

34 Doctors coming under arrangements approved by the Department of Health and
Social Security with a view to their taking up attachments under the Department's
Attachment Scheme should be admitted without work permits for up to 6 months.

Businessmen and self-employed persons

35 A passenger seeking admission for the purpose of establishing himself in the
United Kingdom in business or in self-employment, whether on his own account or in
partnership, must hold a current entry clearance issued for that purpose. A passenger
who has obtained such an entry clearance should be admitted, subject to paragraph 13,
for a period not exceeding 12 months with a condition restricting his freedom to take
employment. For an applicant to obtain an entry clearance for this purpose he will need
to satisfy the requirements of either paragraph 36 or paragraph 37. In addition he will
need to show that he will be bringing money of his own to put into the business; that his
level of financial investment will be proportional to his interest in the business; that he
will be able to bear his share of the liabilities; that he will be occupied fulltime in the
running of the business; and that there is a genuine need for his services and
investment. In no case should the amount of money to be invested by the applicant be
less than £150,000 and evidence that this amount or more is under his control and
disposable in the United Kingdom must be produced.

36 Where the applicant intends to take over, or join as a partner, an existing business,
he will need, in addition to meeting the requirements of the preceding paragraph, to
show that his share of the profits will be sufficient to maintain and accommodate him
and his dependants. Audited accounts of the business for previous years must be
produced to the entry clearance officer in order to establish the precise financial
position, together with a written statement of the terms on which he is to enter or take
over the business. There must be evidence to show that his services and investment will
create new, paid, full-time employment in the business for persons already settled here.
An entry clearance is to be refused if an applicant cannot satisfy all the relevant
requirements of this or the preceding paragraph or where it appears that the proposed
partnership or directorship amounts to disguised employment or where it seems likely
that, to obtain a livelihood, the applicant will have to supplement his business activities
by employment of any kind or by recourse to public funds.

37 If the applicant wishes to establish a new business in the United Kingdom on his
own account or to be self-employed he will need to meet the requirements of paragraph
35 and satisfy the entry clearance officer that he will be bringing into the country
sufficient funds of his own to establish an enterprise that can realistically be expected to
maintain and accommodate him and any dependants without recourse to employment
of any kind (other than his self-employment) or to public funds. He will need to show in
addition that the business will provide new, paid, full-time employment in the business
for persons already settled here. An entry clearance is to be refused if an applicant
cannot satisfy all the requirements of this paragraph and of paragraph 35. . . .

SECTION TWO: CONTROL AFTER ENTRY...

Work permit holders

116 A person coming here to work, and having a work permit issued by the Department of Employment, will normally have been admitted *for the period specified in the permit*. At the end of that period an extension of stay may be granted if the applicant is still engaged in, and the employer confirms that he wishes to continue to employ him in, the employment specified in the permit, or other employment approved by the Department of Employment. Where a permit was issued for a period of *other* than 12 months, an application for an extension of stay in the employment for which the permit was issued should be referred to the Department of Employment. Only if that Department is prepared in the particular case to approve the continued employment may an appropriate extension of stay be granted. In other cases, unless there is any exceptional reason to the contrary, this extension should be for a further 3 years. A corresponding extension should be granted to the applicant's wife and children, where appropriate and where the maintenance and accommodation requirements of paragraph 42 continue to be met. Cases where the applicant is no longer in approved employment should be considered in the light of all the relevant circumstances.

Permit-free categories

117 A person admitted in accordance with paragraphs 31–34, with the exception of crew members (see paragraph 101), may be granted extensions of stay if he is still engaged in the category of employment for which he was admitted and the employer confirms that he wishes to continue to employ him. Unless there are special reasons to the contrary the extension should be for 3 years except in the case of a teacher or language assistant under an exchange scheme, in whose case the maximum period of stay should be two years, or a seasonal worker at an agricultural camp, in whose case an extension in that capacity is not to be granted beyond 30th November in any year. A corresponding extension should be granted to an applicant's wife and children where appropriate and where the support and accommodation requirements of paragraph 42 continue to be met. A person given leave to enter or remain in some other capacity has no claim to remain for permit-free employment and applications to do so should be refused, except in the case of doctors registered with the General Medical Council, who may be granted extensions of stay for up to 3 years.

Businessmen and self-employed persons

118 People given limited leave to enter or remain in some other capacity have no claim to establish themselves here for the purpose of setting up in business whether on their own account or as partners in a new or existing business, or to be self-employed, and their applications for extension of stay or leave to remain for these purposes are to be refused.

119 In considering applications for extension of stay from people admitted with entry clearances for the purpose of setting up in business or self employment, the following factors are to be taken into account. There must be evidence that the applicant is devoting money of his own to the business proportional to his interest in it and that he is able to bear his share of any liability the business may incur. The applicant's part in the business must not amount to disguised employment; and it must be clear that he does not and will not have to supplement his business activities by employment of any kind or by recourse to public funds. In no case should his investment in the business be less

than £150,000. Evidence should be sought that the applicant is occupied full-time in the running of the business and that there is a genuine need for his services and investment. There must be evidence that his share of the profits is sufficient to maintain and accommodate him and any dependants without recourse to public funds. Audited accounts are to be produced to establish the precise financial position. There must also be evidence that his services and investments have created paid full-time employment in the business for persons already settled here. For the purposes of this paragraph business includes self-employment (other than as a writer or artist).

The regulatory powers of the Home Secretary as thus described to control entry into the country for employment or self-employment are complemented by the powers of the Secretary of State for Employment to make the arrangements for the issuing of work permits for employment. The rules for the exercise of these powers are neither set out in statutory form nor subject to parliamentary control. It is, however, the practice for the Department of Employment to make statements in Parliament describing the arrangements, and we set out below the latest such statement and the main aspects of the current arrangements as there described. It will be noted how these arrangements impinge upon the process and criteria of selection for employment, in particular by requiring the prospective employer to satisfy the Department that no suitable resident labour is available. That is a condition which the Department of Employment may obviously apply more or less rigorously in practice; of late, the tendency has been to respond to the growth of domestic unemployment by tightening this control over access by foreign nationals to the labour market.

> Work-permit arrangements: Parliamentary statement on behalf
> of the Secretary of State for Employment, 14 November 1979
> Parliamentary Debates, HC vol. 973, Written Answers col. 609

1. Except as provided in the Immigration Rules any person, other than EEC nationals, subject to immigration control coming to work in the United Kingdom is required to have a work permit. Permits are issued for employment in Great Britain by the Department of Employment and for employment in Northern Ireland by the Department of Manpower Services.

2. The arrangements described in the subsequent paragraphs are those that apply in Great Britain. The same conditions apply in Northern Ireland but references to the 'Department of Employment' and the 'Manpower Services Commission' should be read as references to the 'Department of Manpower Services' and to 'Professional and Executive Recruitment (PER)' as to 'Professional and Executive Personnel (PEP).'

3. The prospective employer must apply to the Department of Employment for a work permit for a named overseas worker and for a specific job. The permit will be issued for an initial period not exceeding 12 months. Only workers between 23 and 54 years of age are eligible for permits. A permit will not be issued if in the opinion of the Overseas Labour Section of the Department of Employment after consultation with the Manpower Services Commission suitable resident labour is available to fill the post offered nor if the wages or other conditions of employment offered are less favourable than those obtaining in the area for similar work.

4. With the exceptions referred to later, permits will be available only for workers in the following categories who can satisfy the Department that they possess the necessary qualifications and experience which should normally have been acquired outside the United Kingdom:

(a) those holding recognised professional qualifications;

(b) administrative and executive staff;

(c) highly qualified technicians having specialised experience; and

(d) other key workers with a highly scarce qualification in an industry or occupation requiring specific expert knowledge of skills.

The worker will also be expected to have an adequate command of the English language.

5. In general, an application for a work permit will be considered only if the vacancy is in an occupation serviced by the Professional and Executive Recruitment Service (PER) and which necessarily requires a worker having the qualifications referred to in paragraph 4 above. When applying for the permit the prospective employer must satisfy the Department of Employment that a genuine vacancy exists, that no suitable resident labour is available and that he has made adequate efforts to find a worker from that source and from the EEC. The employer is expected to notify the vacancy to the nearest PER office, job-centre or employment office and to allow four weeks for a suitable worker to be found. He is also expected to advertise the vacancy in the press or appropriate trade and professional journals and to undertake to pay the travelling expenses of any worker resident in this country who comes from a distance for a pre-arranged interview or to take up employment.

6. Work permits are available for highly skilled and experienced workers for senior posts in Hotel and Catering establishments who have successfully completed appropriate full-time training courses of at least two years' duration at approved schools abroad or, exceptionally, have acquired other specialised or uncommon skills and experience relevant to the industry.

7. Permits are available for entertainers and sportsmen, who meet the appropriate skills criteria (the lower age limit referred to in paragraph 3 does not apply to these permits). Professional sportsmen taking part in competitions of international standing do not normally require permits.

8. A permit may be issued to any person if in the opinion of the Secretary of State for Employment his employment is in the national interest.

9. Permits may be issued for on-the-job training or work experience with employers which can be put to use in the trainee's home country but not acquired there. This arrangement is primarily intended to benefit developing countries and their citizens. The training must be for a limited period, as far as possible agreed in advance, and extension of approval beyond one year will be given only if satisfactory progress is being maintained. Approval may also be given for employment in a super-numerary capacity, normally not lasting longer than a year, of young overseas nationals of non-EEC countries who come here to widen their occupational experience and in some cases also to improve their knowledge of English. The overseas national will not be allowed to remain here for ordinary employment at the end of the approved period of training or work experience. The age limits and the resident labour requirement referred to in paragraph 3 do not apply to these permits.

10. Overseas students who wish to take paid employment in their free time during vacations must first obtain the consent of the Department of Employment. A student

must provide satisfactory evidence from his college that employment will not interfere with his course of study. Permission will only be given where there is no suitable resident labour available and the wages and conditions of employment are not less favourable than those obtaining in the area for similar work. An overseas student is not entitled to remain in the country for employment on completion of his studies except that overseas student and pupil nurses and pupil midwives trained by NHS Authorities and needed to meet their staffing requirements may be given permission to remain in employment as State Registered Nurses, State Enrolled Nurses or State Certified Midwives provided no suitable resident labour is available. The lower age limit referred to in paragraph 3 does not apply to nurses or midwives.

11. The holder of a work permit is not permanently restricted to the particular job for which the permit was issued but will be expected to remain in the same occupation and will require the consent of the Department of Employment for any change of job. A change will only be approved if the proposed employment would have satisfied the relevant conditions for the issue of a permit to a person overseas.

12. Leave to remain may be granted by the Home Office to permit holders who continue in approved employment. After four years in approved employment they may apply to the Home Office for the removal of the time limit on their stay. If the time limit is removed they may take any employment they wish without reference to the Department of Employment.

It is important to realize that the scheme as thus described has an important impact not just upon the access of foreign workers to the labour market in an absolute sense, but also upon the terms on which they may be admitted to the labour market; in other words, as we shall find with many of the measures controlling the formation of the employment relationship, this scheme has implications for the tenure and the content of employment, in this case of foreign workers. In a study of the working of this scheme published in 1977 (6 *ILJ* 85), Daniel Duysens emphasized that the scheme, while conferring extremely wide administrative discretion upon the Department of Employment to control the entry of foreign workers into the labour market, did little to protect the job security of those who are admitted; less, indeed, than is done in other EEC countries or regarded as the goal in this respect by the EEC itself. In particular, the scheme ties the worker to a particular employer, who has to apply for the work permit yet is not bound to offer a contract of employment when permission to employ is given. The worker relies on the discretion of the Department for permission to change his job, and on the discretion of the employer to renew his job and with it his permission to stay in the country. Although after four years in the country the immigrant worker can apply for the removal of the time limit on his residence, its removal is not automatic in practice, which further increases that dependency upon one particular employer which Duysens concludes makes the system an inflexible one.

These features of the scheme have implications for the content of employment too, in the sense that the precariousness and dependency upon the employer with which this scheme endows foreign workers makes them liable to accept less than normally favourable terms and conditions of employment. Duysens described the measures taken in certain EEC countries to combat this problem and showed how, for instance, in Belgium a standard form of contract for foreign workers was insisted upon (op. cit., p. 89). The UK work-permit arrangements impose a Fair Wages type of condition for the issue of work permits, requiring that the wages and conditions of employment offered should be not less favourable than those prevailing in the area for similar work, but it is hard to be certain that this standard is effectively applied; such doubts must, moreover, be increased with the revocation of the Fair Wages Resolution itself as a protection for employees engaged on governmental or public authority contract work (see below, pp. 154 *et seq*). It was with reference to issues of this kind that Blanc-Jouvan remarked that 'in dealing with the problem of discrimination against foreign workers, we cannot really avoid a fundamental distinction between two types of questions; those which concern the right of the alien to work, and those which relate to his status as a worker' (op. cit., p. 257). In this subsection we have seen that the system of work permits and immigration, although primarily concerned with the former type of issue, nevertheless has significant implications for the status of the alien as a worker. We shall find that there is the same spread of issues involved in the special provisions relating to workers within the EEC, to which we now turn.

(c) **Free movement of workers within the EEC**
In the previous subsection, we looked at measures concerned with restricting the access of foreigners to the labour market, and considered the ramifications of such measures upon the status of foreign workers who are allowed access. In this subsection, on the other hand, we look at the requirements and consequences of a policy of positively guaranteeing access to the labour market to certain foreign nationals, namely those of EEC countries. The question will be, what kind of detailed measures are necessary to give effect to such a policy, and how far do the existing measures achieve that purpose?

The basic principle of free movement of workers within the EEC is expressed in Article 48 of the Treaty of Rome, and Article 49 requires the Council of Ministers to make the regulations and issue the directives necessary to give effect to that principle. The current legislation is the EEC Council Regulation 1612 of 1968. This Regulation confers on the nationals of a member state of the EEC the right to take up employment in other member states with the same priority as nationals of that state (Art. 1(2)). It denies application to laws and administrative practices of member states which limit this right of establishment (Art. 3(1)). It requires workers from other member states to be treated as nationals so that quotas against foreign workers shall not apply against them (Art. 4(1)). It requires that appointment to posts in member states shall not be discriminatory on grounds of nationality against nationals of other member states (Art. 6(1)). It requires equality of treatment as between nationals of the state concerned and nationals of other member states in the matters of terms and conditions of employment (Art. 7(1)) and freedom of association (Art. 8(1)). In practice Articles 7 and 8, although concerned with terms and conditions of employment, must be relevant to the formation of the contract of employment as well as to its continuing performance.

The analysis of these provisions offered by Blanc-Jouvan in the Comparative Labour Law Group symposium, *Discrimination in Employment* (op. cit., pp. 303–6), suggests a way of evaluating whether these provisions are an effective implementation of the principle of free movement of workers. He suggests that the EEC measure gives the national of an EEC country, firstly, a right of entry into any other EEC country for the purpose of employment without the need for any visa or special authorization. It is indeed the case that the Immigration Rules (see above, p. 14) relieve the nationals of other EEC countries of the need for a work permit; but Art. 48(3) and Art. 56(1) of the Treaty of Rome enable the member state to impose a condition of personal acceptability based on considerations of threats to public policy, public security or public health. In *Van Duyn* v. *Home Office* [1975] Ch. 358, the ECJ held that the Home Secretary could on that basis properly refuse entry to a Dutch national who wanted to take up employment with the Church of Scientology in the UK although employment with that organization was not specifically unlawful, and although the UK government had no corresponding control to prevent a UK citizen from taking up that employment. To that extent, the public policy exception to the requirement of freedom of movement does allow for discrimination between UK citizens and those of other EEC member states.

Blanc-Jouvan goes on to point out (at p. 304) that EEC law confers a general right to reside in the member state in which the EEC national wishes to work. This comprises a right of freedom of movement within the state concerned, and a right to residence which extends to the family of the worker, and which is a right which is not revocable upon the worker becoming unemployed, nor upon reaching the age of retirement and which continues in the surviving spouse. These further aspects of the implementation of the principle of freedom of movement of workers within the EEC are the subject of a number of further EEC regulations and directives, of which the details are conveniently set out in Grant and Martin, *Immigration Law and Practice* (1982), p. 133. The Immigration Rules make provisions to give effect to some aspects of these requirements – see Grant and Martin, op. cit., p. 136. It is, however, important to note that the implementation of the principle of free movement and the associated right of residence, are liable to be affected by case-law, some of which is of great concern for labour law generally; for instance, the decision of the ECJ in the *Unger* case (Case 75/63 [1964] CMLR 319) that the term 'worker' includes a person who has left one job and is capable of taking another, in this case a worker whose contract of employment had come to an end because she was expecting a child. Such decisions illustrate the crucial point that a measure designed to guarantee access to the labour market requires an identification of those who qualify as part of the workforce.

If an effective principle of freedom of movement of workers poses extended requirements so far as rights of residence are concerned, it is also important for labour lawyers to realize that the requirements of such a principle reach into the field of social security provision. The necessity for the latter extension is articulated in Article 51 of the Treaty of Rome, which requires the adoption of such measures in the field of social security as are necessary to provide freedom of movement for workers; in other words, to ensure that the worker is not discouraged from movement between EEC countries for the purpose of employment by adverse consequences to his social security entitlement. The principal EEC measure for giving effect to this principle is currently EEC Council Regulation 1408 of 1971. Its provisions are very clearly set out and explained in Ogus and Barendt, *The Law of Social Security* (2nd edn 1982), pp. 627 *et seq.*; suffice it to mention here that the provisions embody the principles of non-discrimination against EEC nationals in the matter of social security benefits, and aggregation of periods of insurance, employment or residence which qualify for social security benefits under the laws of other member states, and deterritoriality of rights to benefit acquired in a particular member state. Given the failure to achieve much progress towards the harmonization of social security systems of the different EEC member states which is demanded by Article 117 of the Treaty of Rome, the need for a specific social security extension of the principle of freedom of movement of workers within the EEC remains, and is a dimension of the principle which should be seen as highly relevant to control, within the ambit of labour law, over equality of access to the national labour market.

Finally in this catalogue of the different aspects of freedom of movement for EEC workers, Blanc-Jouvan points out that the principle also requires a right to work in the sense of a right to take up employment freely within each member state on the same terms as those on which it is available to the nationals of the state concerned, and, as Article 48(2) of the Treaty of Rome provides, the abolition of any discrimination based on nationality between workers of the member states as regards employment. However, Article 48(4) goes on to provide that the provisions of the Article do not apply to employment in the public service, so that the EEC provisions do not impinge upon the certification requirements for the employment of aliens in the civil service (see above, p. 13). In the private sector, the non-discrimination aspect of Article 48 is vindicated by the controls imposed by the employment provisions of the RRA 1976 upon discrimination on the ground of nationality. The principle of Article 48 would provide a criterion for assessing the adequacy of the RRA 1976 so far as workers from other EEC countries were concerned; in practice, however, issues of this kind have not been very significant because the amount of immigration into the UK for employment purposes from EEC countries has not been large. So while the measures described in this section provide an interesting illustration of the theoretical problems of legislating for an effective right for a certain group of foreign workers to have free and equal access to the national labour market, they have operated in a context in which the national labour markets of member states have remained basically compartmentalized one from the next, and the measures have not been tested under the pressures that might have applied if a supra-national labour market had offered to develop in any practical sense within the EEC.

(d) Social security and availability for work

The thesis of the present section of the present chapter is that measures having an impact on labour supply and labour demand should be regarded as relevant to labour law. As we saw earlier (above, p. 3), this could be seen as an argument for treating the whole set of mechanisms for regulation of the economy as relevant to labour law, and we disclaimed any intention of defining the thesis so broadly in this exposition of it. Equally, the same thesis could be seen as an argument for regarding the whole social security régime as relevant to labour law via its obvious impact on labour supply and its important impact on labour demand. Thus the contribution conditions for the contributory aspects of the social security scheme (including latterly the employers' National Insurance Surcharge) affect both the size and the form (e.g. employment or self-employment) of labour supply and demand, and the benefit conditions of both the contributory unemployment insurance scheme and the non-contributory supplementary benefit scheme obviously affect labour supply, influencing decisions on the part of the working population whether and on what minimum terms and in what form to seek employment; likewise the system of social security retirement pensions. There exists a well-developed discussion of and valuable literature upon this kind of strategic effect of the social security régime upon the labour market, and it would be inappropriate to try to do justice to it within the confines of this book; it is admirably summed up in Chapter 1 of Ogus and Barendt's *Law of Social Security* (2nd edn 1982). In that discussion, the attention of the labour lawyer will focus particularly upon the work-incentive aspects of earnings-related supplement to unemployment benefit and the abolition of that supplement from the beginning of 1982 onwards by s.4 of the Social Security (No. 2) Act 1980, and upon the issue of the 'poverty trap', a form of which is said to arise where the earning of an income below a certain low level, by disentitling the worker to means-tested benefits, causes him a nett loss compared with his position if unemployed – thus obviously creating a disincentive to enter the labour market within the area in which such a poverty trap operates.

Although it would not be practicable to develop in detail an account of the strategic consequences of the social security régime in the labour market, it is, however, appropriate to go into some detail in relation to certain provisions of the social security scheme which are specifically envisaged as work-incentive rules and therefore cannot properly be omitted from a discussion of legal controls over the size of the labour market. These are the rules which make availability for work a condition of entitlement both to contributory unemployment benefit under the National Insurance Scheme and to non-contributory supplementary benefit, and which until recently made registration for employment a further condition for such entitlements. Before we locate these rules in the statutory and administrative structure, it is appropriate to say something about their underlying rationale.

The policy underlying the rules which make availability for work a condition of benefit is one of confining social security support to involuntary unemployment and withholding it from voluntary unemployment. In other words, the individual who is capable of work will be protected from the consequences of being unable to get work, but not from the consequences of being unwilling to get work, or 'work-shy'. The implementation in one form or another of such a policy has been a constant feature of the development of our social security system; but it is notable that in times of high unemployment this policy comes under strain. This kind of strain has been recently and is currently visible; it consists of a tension between two competing considerations. On the one hand, the growth in the pressure on the social security system produces an increase in the demand to eliminate voluntary reliance upon the system and in some quarters an increasing willingness to explain unemployment in terms of unwillingness to work. On the other hand, it tends to be felt that it is unrealistic to insist on the notional availability of social security claimants for work when there is an increasingly chronic shortage of work for them to do. In other words – and this is the point which is of significance in labour law terms – some considerations point towards an insistence that those capable of being within the labour market remain part of the labour supply, while other considerations point towards a policy of letting some of the unemployed drop out of the labour market, thereby, superficially at least, relieving some of the social tensions associated with high levels of unemployment. The interplay of these considerations will be apparent in the recent development of the notion of availability for work, to the details of which we now briefly turn.

Availability for work is made a condition of unemployment benefit by section 17(1)(a) of the Social Security Act 1975, which makes availability for work a condition of regarding a given day as a day of unemployment. The construction placed on this condition serves to spell out what the claimant is required to do by way of keeping himself actively present in the labour market. The detailed provisions are explained by Ogus and Barendt (op. cit., pp. 101–5). Suffice it to mention that following a *Report by the National Insurance Advisory Committee on the Availability Question* in 1953 (Cmd. 8894), regulations have treated a person as unavailable for work if he has no reasonable prospects of securing work by reason of restrictions which he places on his availability unless the lack of prospects results from adverse but temporary industrial conditions or the self-imposed restrictions are reasonable in view of the claimant's physical condition or generally reasonable (currently S I 1975 No. 564, reg. 7(1)(a)). Provision is made, and was broadened in 1982, to allow claimants to take various kinds of part-time voluntary emergency relief or charitable work without thereby losing their status of availability (see now S I 1982 No. 96).

A broadly similar requirement of availability for work is made in relation to supplementary allowances by s.5 of the Supplementary Benefits Act 1976. Regulations made in 1981 (S I No. 1526) replaced the discretionary powers of the Supplementary Benefits Commission to withhold benefit with rules designed to help in the control of 'work-shyness'. These rules concentrate the requirement of availability more heavily upon one particular section of the potential labour market by making special provision for short-term disqualification on the ground of unavailability, in appropriate cases, of single persons between 18 and 45. Another very recent measure in the direction of concentrating the requirement of availability upon the central sector of the unemployed workforce has consisted in the provision relieving men over 60 of the requirement of availability as a condition for supplementary allowances – S I 1983 No. 463, reg. 4. Since the condition of availability concerns availability for, basically, full-time work as an employed earner, the effect of relieving workers in that age group of the requirement of availability is to recognize their freedom to participate in the part-time or self-employed labour market without total loss of benefit. This indicates how measures controlling the size of labour supply may operate differentially as between sections of the working population and differentially as to the form of employment involved. The significance of the policy choices which are made in this way should not be lost upon labour lawyers.

An important change has been brought about recently in the way that availability for work is in practice established. Formerly, the establishing of availability was closely linked with a requirement that claimants, both of unemployment benefit and supplementary allowances, should register for work at an Employment Office, Jobcentre or Careers Office. This requirement was administrative in the case of unemployment benefit, and statutory in the case of supplementary benefit. Following a recommendation in the Report by Sir Derek Rayner on *Payment of Benefit to Unemployed People* in 1980, registration was made voluntary for claimants aged 18 or over. (This was effected by s.38 of the Social Security and Housing Benefit Act 1982 in the case of supplementary benefit.) The immediate purpose of this change was to save money, staff and effort at Jobcentres by abolishing a procedure which was seen as a wasteful and inefficient way of testing for availability. At the same time, one associates the abolition of compulsory registration with the development of a climate in which the insistence on availability for work becomes less strict as the social and political problems of large-scale unemployment become more acute. The abolition of compulsory registration had a tangible, if indirect, effect on the way that the level of unemployment is assessed, for it became necessary to find a new basis for counting the unemployed. From early 1983 onwards the count was based instead on the numbers actually claiming benefit, which excludes those registered for work but ineligible for benefit and those eligible for benefit but not claiming it. This is thought to reduce the count by about 100,000 – see [1982] *Employment Gazette*, p. 389. The whole effect is to tend to reduce the apparent excess of labour supply over demand for labour. We now turn to measures which, on the whole, operate on the demand side of the equation.

(e) Job creation and training

This is the area where we assert most directly of all that labour lawyers have tended to underrate the significance of measures which they ought to regard as matters of central concern to them. The Employment and Training Acts, for instance, scarcely rate a mention in most accounts of labour law. Yet their practical importance comfortably exceeds that of much labour legislation, and so does their relevance to our subject. An analysis of these measures seen as measures concerned with controlling labour supply and labour demand will help to substantiate this bold claim. Again, a disclaimer is necessary. One could make out a case for including within the range of job-creation measures all the legislation and governmental provision which exists for providing financial support to commercial enterprises; one thinks here of the Industry Acts 1975 and 1981, of the European Social Fund and of the whole programme of assistance for regional development. Our claim of inclusiveness is, however, a more modest one, being limited to those measures which are specifically and directly concerned with employment creation, placing people in jobs and training them for jobs. The major pieces of legislation directed to those ends are the Industrial Training Act 1964 and the Employment and Training Acts of 1973 and 1981 (all of which are now consolidated into the Industrial Training Act 1982 so far as they relate to Industrial Training Boards), and the Employment Subsidies Act 1978. We shall examine as instruments of legal control over the labour market both these Acts and the large number of governmental schemes which have been developed in exercise of the powers conferred by those Acts.

When the current legislation was first initiated in 1964, the rate of unemployment was still relatively low, and the preoccupation of the legislators was with the quality of labour supply rather than with the size of labour demand. The Industrial Training Act 1964 sought to remedy the shortages of skilled manpower that the voluntary system had given rise to, by providing for the establishment of Industrial Training Boards, whose operation would be financed by means of a levy upon the employers in the particular industry concerned. This measure was not seen as politically contentious at the time, and labour lawyers tended to regard it as outside the mainstream of their concerns. Indeed, it has been fashionable to point as a curiosity to the fact that the industrial tribunals were first set up by this legislation (to adjudicate questions of industrial classification), with the implication that the tribunals had been slipped into legislation which was quite marginal to labour law.

Since that legislation was passed, immense changes in policy have taken place in response to conditions of growing recession and mounting un-employment. The Employment and Training Act 1973 recognized and sought to meet the need for more elaborate legislative arrangements for providing employment and training services, in response to the rapid rise in unemploy-ment which had been experienced in the early 1970s. The Act provided for the establishment of the Manpower Services Commission, the Employment Service Agency and the Training Services Agency, so providing the machinery for more intensive governmental activity in this area. The growth of a new preoccupation with increasing the size of the demand for labour was further marked by s.5 of the Act, which empowered the Secretary of State for Employment to make such arrangements as he considered appropriate for the purpose of providing temporary employment for persons in Great Britain who are without employment, including arrangements for making payments by way of grant or loan to employers for that purpose. There are two features of the system set up by the 1973 Act which are worth emphasizing before we move on to the subsequent developments. The 1973 Act brought in the dual system whereby schemes for job creation or training might emanate either from the specialist agencies or directly from the Department of Employment itself. The 1973 Act also gave some indication of the extent to which measures for job creation or training might have a bearing on selection for employment and on the form in which the employment relationship is constituted; thus s.5 of the Act tended, ironically, to favour temporary rather than permanent employment because of the political commitment which then existed to maintaining the severely temporary nature of measures for increasing, or at least arresting the decline of, labour demand by means of subsidies.

Since the 1973 Act, two somewhat conflicting policies have been at work. On the one hand, the commitment to a policy of subsidizing labour demand tended to increase with the growth in unemployment. Thus in the Employ-ment Protection Act 1975, Sch. 14, the subsidizing powers of the Department of Employment under s.5 of the 1973 Act were widened to include those of securing temporary continuation of employment for those otherwise likely to be dismissed by reason of redundancy and obtaining employment for those who would otherwise have difficulty in doing so 'because of their special circumstances and a high or increasing level of unemployment in Great Britain' (ibid., Sch. 14, para.2). The powers thus temporarily conferred were replaced by still wider powers in 1978, when s.1 of the Employment Subsidies Act provided that the Secretary of State for Employment might, if in his opinion unemployment in Great Britain continued at a high level, and with Treasury approval, set up schemes for making payments to employers 'which will enable them to retain persons in employment who would or might otherwise become unemployed, to take on new employees, and generally to maintain or enlarge their labour force'. The various powers of subsidy have continued to be very extensively used, as we shall see when we shortly come to the details of the many schemes that have been produced. On the other hand, there has latterly been a tendency back towards voluntarism and reduction of governmental activity in the matter of job creation and training, and it was this which underlay the Employment and Training Act 1981, which abolished the Employment Service Agency and the Training Services Agency, and enabled the Department of Employment to abolish Industrial Training Boards without the need for proposals to that effect from the Manpower Services Commission, thus preparing the way for a winding-down of the ITB system. Although this measure was intended to permit an absolute reduction in governmental activity in this area, it operated in an environment where more and more of such activity constantly became necessary, and so had the rather ironical effect of concentrating a greater power than before on the surviving specialist agency, the Manpower Services Commission (MSC). Against that legislative background, it will be useful to look briefly at some of the more important of the numerous job-creation or training schemes that have emanated either from the MSC or the Department of Employment in recent years. We shall begin with the schemes run by the Department and then refer to those for which the MSC is responsible.

When discussing the measures taken by the Department of Employment for creating or subsidizing jobs, we are in the very heartland of 'leaflet law', where departmental legislation of great significance to labour law is promulgated by means of leaflets describing schemes which do not require the form of statutory instruments or the substance of parliamentary scrutiny. We shall survey these measures briefly, with a view to indicating the scale on which they operate and their very considerable potential impact on patterns of selection for employment and on the forms in which the employment relationship is constituted. It will also be useful to examine how far they operate on the supply side and how far on the demand side of the labour market.

One of the first to be introduced of the schemes currently in operation was the Job Release Scheme. This is a supply-side measure which works on the principle of reducing the excess of labour supply over labour demand by paying allowances to older workers approaching the state retirement age to retire early and release their jobs to unemployed workers. Because it preceded the Employment Subsidies Act 1978 and was seen as embodying novel principles of labour subsidy, it was made the subject of special enabling legislation, namely the Job Release Act 1977. We deal with it later on as an aspect of the law concerning the termination of the employment relationship –see below, p. 567. In the three years down to April 1982, a total of 132,000 people were supported by this scheme, and at the end of that time there were 63,000 participants in the scheme. The scheme has now been supplemented by the Part-Time Job Release Scheme, which offers allowances to workers nearing retirement who change to part-time work and release part of their job to unemployed workers. This means that older workers are being encouraged to reduce the extent of their availability in the labour market so that the existing demand can be shared among a greater number of workers. This has obvious implications for the form in which employment relationships are constituted, as it encourages the creation of part-time jobs, and in particular that form of part-time employment in which a full-time job is split or shared between two workers. This in turn has potential implications for patterns of recruitment in so far as employment of that kind may be expected to be concentrated on certain particular sections of the labour market, such as older workers or married women workers.

The remaining schemes run directly by the Department of Employment operate primarily upon the demand side of the labour market by paying employers allowances for creating or maintaining jobs according to various particular sets of conditions. From the mid-1970s onwards, there was a series of schemes whereby employment subsidies were made available on a temporary basis for the purpose of averting threatened redundancies. These schemes came under pressure from the EEC Commission because of the distortion of competition brought about in the textiles, clothing and footwear industries in which they were heavily used. It seemed that these employment subsidies would be more acceptable if used to support short-time working, and so this programme was concentrated into the Temporary Short Time Working Compensation Scheme from 1979 to 1984 – see Freedland (1980) 9 *ILJ* 254. In the three years down to April 1982, nearly 895,000 jobs were supported under this scheme; at the end of that time there were 175,000 participants. We describe the working of the scheme later in this book as an aspect of security of income (see below, p. 362), but it is also appropriate to mention it at this stage as tending to encourage the operation, as an alternative to redundancy, of what is in effect a particular form of employment relationship, namely short-time working. Demand-side employment subsidies were also provided in a particular section of the labour market at that time by the Small Firms Employment Subsidy, which from 1977 to 1980 offered private-sector firms employing fewer than 200 workers subsidies for up to 26 weeks for extra full-time or part-time jobs created. More than 99,000 jobs are said to have been provided under this scheme in the last year of its operation.

In the 1980s, demand-side subsidies have been even more directly used in an effort to reduce unemployment by supporting particular patterns of employment. Thus from 1982 onwards the Young Workers Scheme provided allowances for employers for taking on workers under 18 years of age for gross wages of less than £40 per week, with reduced allowances for gross wages of between £40 and £45 per week. The scheme and its significance for collective bargaining are examined elsewhere (See Freedland (1982) 11 *ILJ* 41); suffice it to note here that the scheme had 41,500 participant workers by the end of March 1982. The tendency to use employment-subsidy schemes to reduce the numbers of unemployed persons by encouraging particular patterns of employment is even more clearly exemplified by the Job Splitting Scheme, which from the beginning of 1983 onwards offered employers allowances for creating two part-time jobs in place of an existing full-time job. This is a demand-side measure; by contrast with the Job Release Scheme for older workers (see above, p. 29), the holder of the existing full-time job is offered no allowance either for vacating that job in favour of two part-time workers or himself going from a full-time job to part of a split job. It has not hitherto proved numerically very significant; there had been only about 300 successful applications by June 1983. As a pattern of labour legislation, however, it contains a number of important features. It has an impact on the forms in which the employment relationship is constituted; in particular, it means that workers with full employment protection rights can readily be replaced by workers with reduced employment protection rights or no such rights because they work part-time (see below, pp. 100–3). There are also, as has been remarked earlier (see above, p. 30), potential problems associated with shared jobs over and above the general problems associated with part- time jobs. Moreover the scheme embodied significant restrictions upon the categories of persons who may be selected to hold the part-time jobs created under it. Selection was limited, as Leaflet PL 698 ('Job Splitting Scheme – Just What Your Company Needs') made clear in para. 7, to specific groups such as employees under notice of redundancy at the establishment concerned or wholly unemployed persons in receipt of unemployment or supplementary benefit (who are thus contributing to the count of the unemployed). It has been suggested by the Equal Opportunities Commission that these categories exclude women workers to a disproportionate extent. The rules of the Scheme were somewhat relaxed from August 1983 onwards to encourage more applications, but apparently without affecting the main points made about it here. It is at all events clear that legislation of this kind has an important bearing on the concerns of labour lawyers, and on our concerns in the present chapter, and that it should not escape attention because of the informality with which it is promulgated.

If we turn our attention from schemes for which the Department of Employment is directly responsible to schemes run by the Manpower Services Commission, we find a truly bewildering panoply of administrative measures which constitute a body of labour legislation of the greatest importance but which seems to defy description and analysis in a manner comprehensible to the student of labour law. Nevertheless, it is useful to attempt to subject these measures to analysis in terms of their impact on the supply side and the demand side of the labour market. As we have seen (above, p. 28), the role of the Manpower Services Commission in relation to the provision of training and the creation of job opportunities has been, and to an important extent still is, conceived of as basically a supply-side function concerned with improving the quality of labour supply and ensuring that the labour supply matches the demand in a qualitative sense. This would certainly be envisaged as the primary function of, for example, the MSC Training Opportunities Scheme

(TOPS) under which weekly tax-free allowances are provided for trainees attending training courses falling within the Scheme, and under which there were 61,000 completions of training courses in the 1981/2 training year. But it is clear that two important transformations of this primary function have been taking place, in response to the great growth in unemployment that has occurred in recent years. Firstly, on the supply side of the labour market, the provision of training has been increasingly directed towards the averting of unemployment as well as the improvement in the quality of labour supply. For example, the Report of the MSC for 1981/2 makes it clear (paras. 3.17 to 3.18) that the Training for Skills Programme whereby support is provided for training places both for apprentices and adults has had to be additionally funded to support apprentices threatened with redundancy. There were 35,000 participants in this scheme by March 1982.

The second great transformation which has occurred in the schemes run by the MSC has been that they have been increasingly concerned with the demand side of the labour market; that is to say, the aim of creating job vacancies in order to minimize unemployment has come to assume an increasing importance. Thus from the mid-1970s onwards there has been a series of schemes, each more extensive than the previous one, for subsidizing employers to enable them to run projects to provide temporary work for the long-term unemployed. These schemes are concerned with work of use to the community, and are directed to encouraging local authorities and voluntary organizations to act as entrepreneurs in order to create employment on an assisted basis. This was done by means of the Job Creation Programme from 1975 onwards, then by means of the Special Temporary Employment Programme from 1978 (when the Department of Employment also began to offer an Adult Employment Subsidy for the same purpose). In 1981 the STEP was replaced by the Community Enterprise Programme which was not, as STEP had been, restricted to assisted areas, thus enabling many smaller localities of high unemployment which had previously been excluded to benefit. By March 1982 there were 27,500 participants in these schemes. The successive programmes for the creation of temporary work of benefit to the community have been increasingly concerned with the problem of long-term unemployment among young people. The MSC has over the years administered funding to Community Industry, a scheme of this sort for young people established in 1972 and run under the auspices of the National Association of Youth Clubs. The latest in the succession of such schemes run by the MSC itself reflects the emphasis; from 1983 the CEP is succeeded by the Community Programme which is aimed at the 18-to-24-year-old age group of unemployed who have been out of work for at least six months and those of over 25 who have been out of work for a year. The scale of potential provision is large; the plan was to sponsor up to 130,000 jobs and to provide wages up to a maximum of £89 per week for jobs lasting up to 52 weeks. Schemes of this sort are very significant from a labour law point of view not only as affecting the size of labour demand but also as tending to concentrate employment on particular sectors of the labour supply (long-term unemployed and young workers) and particular sectors of the labour demand (community projects), and also on a particular form of employment (temporary employment).

It is in fact extremely important for labour lawyers to appreciate the extent to which this kind of governmental demand management in the labour market can bear upon their traditional concerns and preoccupations. A good example of this is to be found in the current and expanding activity of the MSC in encouraging self-employment as a means of alleviating the excess of labour supply over demand. From the beginning of the 1980s, the MSC concentrated part of its resources on providing training opportunities for self-employment and for setting up small businesses, and by 1983 was running for this purpose a New Enterprise Programme, Small Business Courses and Self-Employment Courses. From 1981, on a localized pilot basis and from 1983 on a generalized basis, the MSC administered an Enterprise Allowance Scheme to provide a weekly allowance to unemployed people engaged in setting up their own businesses. By early 1983, there were 2,000 participants in this scheme and places for a further 25,000 were to be made available. The potential impact on the form in which employment relationships are constituted does not need to be stressed.

Governmental demand management is also capable of bringing about more subtle, and perhaps more far-reaching, changes in patterns of employment and in the nature of employment relationships. The need for labour law to recognize and respond to these changes has barely been appreciated. A small illustration is provided by a decision relating to one of the schemes we have discussed. In *Greig* v. *Community Industry* [1979] ICR 356, the issue was whether the Community Industry organization acted in breach of the sex discrimination legislation (see below, p. 41 *et seq.*) by refusing to accept a young unemployed woman worker on to a team of young people doing painting and decorating work, on the ground that she would have been the only girl in the team. The EAT under the Presidency of Slynn J. decided that, given that this was in law an employment relationship, the employment provisions of the Sex Discrimination Act 1975 applied to make this a straightforward case of unlawful refusal to employ. The interesting feature of the case is that the argument which Community Industry sought to develop was that membership of a team of this sort was a social relationship of a different sort from the ordinary employment relationship, and that account should be taken of different social values which were accordingly at issue. One may take the view that this could not be accepted as a justification for what would otherwise be unlawful sex discrimination; but there is nevertheless an importance in the proposition that this should be viewed as a special kind of social relationship different from that of the ordinary employment relationship. The extent and importance of this kind of development can best be appreciated if one brings together in one place an account of the activities of the MSC in relation to youth unemployment, which we shall attempt briefly to do.

It will, we think, be clear in retrospect that one of the major changes in the framework of labour law in the last decade has been the growth of governmental demand management for the purpose of alleviating youth unemployment. From the mid-1970s onwards, the growth of unemployment among young workers and the prospect of an immense annual addition to the numbers of the unemployed from among school leavers has been a matter of increasing concern and political tension. We have seen how the programmes for creating jobs on projects of community work have been increasingly used as a means of dealing with this problem, as have the general training programmes of the MSC. There has also been a growing commitment to creating a specific labour demand for young workers by means of special schemes for job creation and training for members of that age group. In 1976 the MSC initiated the Work Experience Programme to provide employers with maintenance allowances to enable them to take on additional workers or trainees from 16 to 18 years old. The Department of Employment at that time began to offer a Recruitment Subsidy for School Leavers and a Youth Employment Subsidy for the same purposes. From 1978 onwards the MSC engaged in a more extensive set of schemes to provide unemployed young people with work experience and practical training, known collectively as the Youth Opportunities Programme. From the early 1980s the Department of Employment and the Manpower Services Commission developed between them a case for a political and practical commitment to a still more elaborate programme of this kind, which would amount to the creation of a guarantee of places either in employment or in training for all school leavers. This led to the replacement of the YOP from 1983 onwards by the Youth Training Scheme, supplemented from late 1983 onwards by the Armed Services Youth Training Scheme. The YOP had 215,000 participants by March 1982, and the YTS is of such great significance that some separate description of it is warranted. First it may be useful to refer to the sources. The policy documents leading to the creation of the Youth Training Scheme were, firstly, a paper from the MSC entitled *A New Training Initiative: An Agenda for Action* (1981). The government's response was contained in a White Paper entiled *A New Training Initiative: A Programme for Action* (Cmnd. 8455, 1981). This was followed by the MSC's Youth Task Group Report in April 1982 which developed the plan for the scheme in detail. The government's acceptance of the scheme was signified in a ministerial statement by the Secretary of State for Employment in June 1982 (Parl. Debates, HC, vol. 26, col. 22). The operating details of the scheme are described in a series of leaflets published by the MSC from January 1983 onwards. The most accessible description of the scheme is contained in a guide to it published by *Industrial Relations Review and Report* (see *IRRR* 297, June 1983, pp. 2 *et seq.*). See also (1983) 12 *ILJ* 220.

The Youth Training Scheme is described as a scheme to provide a year's programme of planned work experience integrated with work-related training or further education for young entrants into the workforce. It initially covered 16-year-old school leavers who are employed or unemployed, some 17-year-old school leavers who are unemployed in the year after leaving school, and some 18-year-old school leavers with special needs if places were available. Provision was made for there to be 460,000 entrants into this scheme in the financial year 1983/4, and the scheme had a budget of £1,100 million for 1984/5. The plan was for the MSC to secure training places for 300,000 young people with public- and private-sector employers including local authorities and voluntary organizations, and to place a further 160,000 young people in training schemes to be organized by the MSC itself. Probably the most significant feature of the scheme from a labour law point of view is the former of these two modes of arranging for training places. The method is for the MSC to contract with Managing Agents for the provision of training places and programmes by the Managing Agents, who may be employers themselves making this provision or organizers of syndicates within which this kind of provision is made. The Managing Agent is paid a per capita fee of £100 for administrative expenses for each place provided, plus an annual per capita subsidy of £1,850 for each extra trainee recruited under the scheme, and also for each trainee recruited in the normal way to the extent that a ratio of three extra trainees to two normally recruited trainees is achieved. Young persons for whom places on the scheme are provided in this way may be engaged either as employees under contracts of employment or as persons with the status of trainee, in which case they are entitled to an allowance from the Managing Agent of £25 weekly plus travel costs in excess of £4 weekly. The young person concerned may be transferred from the status of trainee to the status of employee during the year of training, but there is no obligation to employ trainees beyond their training year.

These measures have a great potential significance both for collective labour law and for individual labour law. The Youth Opportunities Programme became the subject of public controversy and attack from the trade unions because it was seen as a means by which employers could secure cheap and subsidized unskilled labour in substitution for members of the adult workforce who would otherwise have been used to meet the labour demand in question. This was asserted particularly in relation to the use of the programme in agriculture. The indications that this kind of criticism may have been justified are memorably encapsulated in a speech on the subject in the House of Commons by the MP for Truro in which he quoted from a letter of complaint about the working of the YOP from a farmer in his constituency, in which the farmer said pithily, 'Harry up the road got a free boy. Bill down the road got a free boy. Where is my free boy?' (Parl. Debates, HC, vol. 27, col. 68). The Department of Employment and the MSC have been at pains to insist that the Youth Training Scheme should not be susceptible of these criticisms because it is a training measure rather than a special employment or job-creation measure in the sense that the arrangements provide a guarantee that the quality of training will be high enough to ensure that the participants are not simply being given unskilled work to do. It remains to be seen how far this differentiation between the YOP and the YTS will be realized in practice. Much will depend on how the allocation is made between employment status and trainee status, and how the wage rates of employee trainees are determined in relation to collectively bargained terms and conditions. The underlying situation is that an increasingly dirigiste approach to labour supply and demand for young people tends to come into conflict with what we shall see in later chapters is currently a severely voluntarist approach to the determination of terms and conditions of employment generally. Until recently, it has been possible by means of the formal apprenticeship system substantially to insulate the employment of young people as trainees from the rest of the labour market. With the decline in the use of the apprenticeship system, the employment of young people as trainees assumes a greater significance in the working of the labour market generally. This is to some extent concealed by reason of an institutional tendency to treat the employment and training of young people as a compartmentalized question which is best dealt with separately from the general regulation of the labour market. This is evidenced, for example, by the creation in 1983 of a Youth Training Board to operate as a distinct body overseeing the operation of the Youth Training Scheme by the MSC. It is important that this kind of hiving-off of youth training should not deflect attention from the importance of this area to labour law generally, as will be seen when we now turn to consider the impact of the YTS on individual employment law.

The important point for individual employment law is the tendency for there to emerge a legal status of trainee which has different legal incidents from those attaching to the contract of employment but which is nevertheless a form in which substantial numbers of employment relationships are being couched. Two judicial decisions in recent years exemplify this tendency independently of the Youth Training Scheme. In *Wiltshire Police Authority* v. *Wynn* [1980] ICR 649, the Court of Appeal held that a police cadet was not an employee working under a contract of service or of apprenticeship for the purposes of the unfair dismissal legislation. Lord Denning and his colleagues took the view that the relationship displayed neither sufficient features of service to make it a contract of employment nor sufficient features of teaching to make it one of apprenticeship. This is precisely the analysis which threatens to apply to trainees under the YTS. A further powerful indication in that direction is provided by the decision of the EAT in *Daley* v. *Allied Suppliers Ltd* [1983] IRLR 14, where it was held that a young woman taking part in a work-experience scheme under the Youth Opportunities Programme was not employed under a contract of service or apprenticeship or a contract personally to execute any work or labour by the company at whose premises she was located under the scheme, so that she could not invoke the protection of the employment provisions of the Race Relations Act 1976. The EAT held that her relationship with the company was one of training and not employment, and that furthermore she had no contractual relationship at all with the MSC such as could lead to her being regarded as employed by the MSC itself. A similar analysis would seem applicable to the relationship between the trainee and the Managing Agent under the Youth Training Scheme, especially as the Managing Agent may delegate the training to another trainer (styled a Sponsor), and as the Scheme distinguishes expressly between employment status and trainee status. Apparently the standard form of contract between the MSC and the Managing Agent requires that Managing Agents and Sponsors accord rights equivalent to those of employees to trainees, and there are proposals[1] to extend the benefit of the sex and race discrimination provisions to trainees by the use of departmental powers to extend the relevant legislation; and the MSC has a policy of ensuring that trainees have rights equivalent to those of employees in the matters of disciplinary and grievance procedures and trade-union membership (see *IRRR* 297 at p. 10). But it is almost certain that YTS trainees will be subject to a substantially different legal regime from that applicable to employees under the Scheme or employees generally, and likely that their real protection in practice will be much inferior. From the standpoint of a concern with labour standards, it is an insufficient justification for this state of affairs that the trainees might be unemployed if it were not for the existence of the Scheme, and the whole development provides a very vivid illustration of the way in which measures concerned with regulation of labour supply and demand can impinge upon the more traditional concerns of labour law.

(f) Conclusion – other measures affecting the size of the labour market
In the foregoing subsections we have discussed a series of measures which we see as having a major impact on the size of labour supply or labour demand, and which we see as accordingly important to labour law. In this subsection, by way of conclusion to this theme, we shall look at some further measures which have some relevance to, or are alleged by some to be relevant to, the size of labour supply or labour demand. The measures concerned will be, firstly, the legislation concerning reinstatement in civil employment, secondly the provisions for reinstatement following maternity leave, and finally, employment protection legislation generally as a possible restraint upon labour demand. The question whether employment protection legislation does discourage employers from taking on employees has assumed a high prominence in public discussion in recent years, and has, as we shall see, played an important part in the formation of governmental policy in the area of individual employment law.

Legal control of the size of labour supply or labour demand represents a

---

[1] Implemented by departmental orders made on 21 July 1983; see also the Health and Safety (Youth Training Scheme) Regulations 1983 No. 1919.

kind of counter-voluntarism that is more likely to be accepted in war-time than in peace-time. Our system of labour law inherits from the period of the Second World War certain measures for the creation of protected labour markets for particular groups of workers which merit consideration under the heading of measures affecting the size of the labour market. The main measure for providing protected access to the post-war labour market was the legislation for reinstatement in civil employment, now contained in Part II of the National Service Act 1948 as amended or applied by the Reinstatement in Civil Employment Act 1950 and a number of other Acts, which in current conditions provide rights of reinstatement in civil employment to persons in the Reserve and Auxiliary forces who have been called out or recalled from their civilian employment for full-time service. This legislation can be regarded as controlling labour demand in so far as it gives the ex-servicemen and women in question a personal right to be taken into the employment of their former employer. The former employer's obligation, once a valid application for reinstatement has been made, is to take the applicant into employment at the first opportunity, if any, at which it is reasonable or practicable to do so. This gives less than an absolute right to the applicant to have a job provided for him, but it gives him more than a mere right to be preferred for any vacancy that may happen to arise in the ordinary course of things. The legislation has in fact been envisaged as giving a priority claim to employment not only against other applicants for a vacancy happening to arise, but also, in the absence of such a vacancy, against employees already in employment who may have to be discharged to make way for the applicant for reinstatement. The legislation specifies that the right to be reinstated does not extend to the situation where it would require the discharge of, in effect, a permanent employee with greater seniority in the employment than the applicant has even when account is taken of his pre-service employment. Although this legislation probably operated in the conditions that prevailed after the Second World War to create a protected labour market on quite a large scale for ex-servicemen, and so operated as a significant control on labour demand generally, it would be unrealistic to see it in current conditions as more than an occasionally invoked personal right to have one's job kept open, if necessary by the dismissal of one's replacement.

The latter analysis is even more obviously applicable to the other measure giving a personal right in certain circumstances to reinstatement in employment, namely the provision for reinstatement following maternity absence currently contained in ss.45–48 of the EPCA 1978 as amended by sections 11–12 of the EA 1980. Although this measure can be seen as a kind of control of demand in the labour market, designed to create a protected demand for women wishing to return to work after maternity leave or absence, it operates (on a reasonably extensive scale) as a personal right to have one's job kept open, or, in other words, as a kind of protection against dismissal extending into a period of maternity absence during which the contract of employment may have come to an end or been terminated. This analysis is borne out by an examination of the terms in which this protection is conferred. The right is to return to work in the job in which the woman concerned was orginally employed and on terms and conditions not less favourable than those which would have been applicable to her if she had not been absent (EPCA 1978, s.45(1)). The sanction is that failure to permit the exercise of the right to return to work is treated as dismissal for the purposes of the law of unfair dismissal (EPCA 1978, s.56), and the employer is provided, in effect, with a defence against a claim of unfair dismissal for dismissing a replacement employee in order to enable a woman to exercise her right to return to work (EPCA 1978, s.61). This last-mentioned provision has the significant consequence of permitting the formation of a particular kind of employment relationship, namely that of temporary employment to replace a woman employee during maternity absence, to which reduced rights attach in respect of unfair dismissal. This provision is, however, rendered largely otiose by the general extension of the qualifying period for unfair dismissal claims from six to twelve months' employment by the EA 1980 (see below, p. 508). The EA 1980 also imposed significant further conditions and restrictions upon the exercise and extent of the right to return (see ss. 11, 12), apparently in response to the view that the right to return as originally enacted placed unwarranted restrictions upon the employer's efficient use of his labour resources. The EA 1980 gave particular relief against the right to return to work to small employers with no more than five employees (EA 1981, s.12, adding new EPCA 1978, s.56A (1)), apparently on the ground that this form of employment protection measure was disproportionately burdensome to small employers. This brings us to the final topic in the present section, the argument that employment protection legislation generally operates as a constraint upon labour demand.

It was a widely held view in the mid-1970s that employment protection legislation generally, and particularly the law of unfair dismissal as re-invigorated by the Employment Protection Act of 1975, had come to operate as an indirect control upon the size of labour demand, in the sense that the legislation by attaching onerous incidents to the employment relationship discouraged employers from recruiting employees to the extent that they might otherwise have done. By the end of the 1970s, some research evidence was available in relation to the question of whether the behaviour of employers was really being influenced in this way. A general study of the impact of employment protection laws was carried out by Daniel and Stilgoe, and its results were published in 1978 ('The Impact of Employment Protection Laws', Policy Studies Institute, Vol. XLIV, No. 577). In the following summary of those findings, Daniel shows how employment protection legislation did not seem to have had the crude disincentive effect upon levels of recruitment which had often been attributed to it.

W. W. Daniel, 'The Effects of Employment Protection Laws in
Manufacturing Industry', *Department of Employment
Gazette*, June 1978, p. 660

Employment legislation and levels of recruitment

There was little sign that employment legislation in general or the EPA in particular
was inhibiting industrial recovery or contributing to the high level of unemployment by
discouraging employers from taking on new people. The crude form of that criticism,
certainly with regard to the sector of employment studied, can be unequivocally
rejected. First, there was the evidence that among employment protection measures
only unfair dismissal requirements had had a widespread impact. These provisions had
chiefly influenced disciplinary and dismissal procedures. Secondly, managers were
asked in circumstances where there was rising demand for their products but where
they were not taking on new labour, or were recruiting in smaller numbers than
previously, why this was so. Answers focused overwhelmingly on the increases in
labour productivity occurring or the spare capacity existing. Rarely was mention made
of any aspect of legislation.

Similarly, when the relative merits of different ways of increasing output were
discussed with managers, employment legislation very rarely featured as an explanation of reasons for preferring overtime, or investment in new plant or machinery, to
taking on new labour. Thirdly, at the end of the discussions the suggestion was put, that
employment protection legislation was inhibiting levels of recruitment, directly to the
sub-sample of managers to whom it was more likely to apply. All the limitations of the
question were recognized but the answers were instructive. The majority rejected the
notion as far as their plants were concerned. They said either that the legislation
represented no obstacle to the shedding of labour for the good manager, or that their
previous policies had been in advance of practices specified in the legislation. Moreover
the minority who agreed that the suggestion did make sense in relation to their plants
clearly revealed, in their explanations of how this was so, that they were generally
thinking of the quality rather than the quantity of recruits. Once again it was apparent
that to them employment protection legislation meant unfair dismissal provisions.
These, managers explained, had made them more selective in recruitment. They now
had to be certain before taking anyone on that he was suitable for the job. In
consequence recruitment and selection took longer, were more difficult and were more
costly.

While such answers clearly did not support the crude notion that employment
protection legislation was discouraging employers from taking people on where they
were needed they did suggest subtler ways in which the criticisms we examined might
have some validity. First, greater concern with the quality of recruits could mean that it
took longer to fill manpower requirements or even that they were not filled at all where
suitable candidates could not be found according to the raised standards. Secondly, the
raising of selection standards may have made it even more difficult for the hard-to-
place among the unemployed to find jobs. Thirdly, higher selection standards could
increase the costs of recruitment, feeding into the labour costs used for calculations of
the relative advantages of labour as compared with other forms of investment.

A further study on the impact of employment legislation on small firms was
carried out by Clifton and Tatton-Brown, and its results were published in
1979 ('Impact of Employment Legislation on Small Firms', Department of

Employment Research Paper No. 6, July 1979). Their conclusions were that in general the impact on the behaviour of firms of the employment protection legislation was very much what one would expect on *a priori* grounds. The legislation gave employees rights in employment, rights that might involve expense to employers. The result was that employers were more careful about whom they employed, and might look more closely at their internal labour market before taking on new labour. The evidence from the study supported the view that this would be the general direction of impact. On the other hand, it appeared that the changes in the number of employees in the small firms surveyed had not been directly influenced by the employment legislation provisions. Clifton and Tatton-Brown felt that their results countered the suggestion that the legislation had some massive and widespread effect on small firms. As we shall see in later chapters, the changes in the employment protection laws brought about by the Employment Act 1980 and other measures of that period were nevertheless to some extent dedicated to the proposition that the employment protection laws had operated as a disincentive to employment. However, from the early 1980s onwards, the massive growth in unemployment was so much more obviously attributable to conditions of economic recession than to the impact of the employment protection laws that these laws ceased on the whole to be advanced as having a disincentive effect upon employment, and the preoccupation with reducing their impact seemed to diminish as a motive for governmental action. But even if that particular suggestion of a labour-demand consequence for employment protection legislation is less current than it was, enough has been said in this section to suggest that the measures which do in fact control labour supply and demand also have a series of impacts on other aspects of the working of the employment relationship, and in particular upon the patterns of selection for employment and upon the forms in which the employment relationship is constituted. It is to the consideration of those topics that we accordingly now turn our attention.

3 Legal controls over selection for employment

(a) Introduction – sex and race discrimination in employment
The most important, or at least the most prominent, of the legal controls upon selection for employment are those provided by the employment provisions of the Sex Discrimination Act 1975 (SDA) and of the Race Relations Act 1976 (RRA). We shall deal with the other legal controls upon selection for employment at the end of this section; probably the most important of them are the measures concerning the employment of disabled workers. In this section we shall consider the employment provisions of the SDA 1975 and the RRA 1976 in some detail not only because of their immediate practical significance but also because of their importance as a model for the whole

process of controlling selection for employment. In the course of this discussion we shall aim to explain the structure of the employment provisions of those two Acts as a whole, with the consequence that their provisions relating to the content of the employment relationship and the termination of the employment relationship can be dealt with relatively briefly as an adjunct to the present discussion later on in this book (in Chapter 3, section 6 and Chapter 4, section 5, respectively). We shall analyse the provisions concerned with selection in the following way, that is to say we shall look first at the aims and policies underlying the legislation and leading to its particular formulation. We shall then consider what the judicial approaches have been to the interpretation and development of the legislation, and, on the other hand, in a separate subsection, what the social operation of the legislation has consisted of. Finally in this section we shall attempt to assess the significance of this legislation for the whole of the law concerning the constituting of the employment relationship and indeed for labour law generally.

In discussing the controls over selection for employment which have been created by the employment provisions of the SDA 1975 and RRA 1976, we shall be trying to shed some light on the following questions, which the reader is asked to bear in mind in the course of the discussion. Does the legislation represent an important but self-contained bit of human rights legislation which happens to form part of employment law? Or does it on the other hand create patterns which are of importance to labour law in a more general sense? If the latter, in what does that more general importance consist? Does this legislation open up the whole idea of controlling selection for recruitment and break down the notion of selection as wholly within managerial prerogative? Does it, on the other hand, set the pattern of legislating against the undesired effects of selection for employment as distinct from the undesired intentions in selecting? Can we see any wider impacts occurring as the result of these attributes of the legislation? Is, for example, the question of unfair selection for redundancy differently approached by reason of the patterns so established? Has the legislation shown the need for innovative approaches to problems of proof and enforcement in relation to this kind of employment law? We begin by trying to conduct this kind of inquiry in relation to the intentions of the legislators themselves.

(b) The aims of the legislation

Before we can say anything about the aims of the SDA 1975 and the RRA 1976, we must examine the relationship between them. The two statutes are in such similar terms that it would not be misleading to say that the RRA applies the provisions of the SDA *mutatis mutandis* to the problem of race discrimination. This poses the question of how so close a parallel came about. Was it that there existed a programme or aim of legislating against discrimination generally which was progressively applied first to the one kind of discrimination and then to the other? Or was it on the other hand that the original plan of legislating about sex discrimination was thought to have worked so well that it would be a good idea to apply the same formula to race discrimination? Or was the primary aim to deal with the problems of race discrimination, with the SDA as a kind of pilot scheme for this particular pattern of legislation in the field of a less politically and socially sensitive type of discrimination to control by legislation? There is a very useful account of the historical background to the SDA 1975 in a research paper on 'Equal Pay and Opportunities', by Snell, Glucklich and Povall (Department of Employment Research Paper No. 20, April 1981). They show how, from the late 1960s onwards, there was political pressure to legislate for more active promotion of equal opportunity for women in employment as well as for equal pay for women (see pp. 8–9 of their paper). In other words, the programme of complementing the Equal Pay Act 1970 with more generalized sex discrimination legislation has origins which are autonomous of those of the later race discrimination legislation, although in a broad sense both pieces of legislation no doubt have a common source in the growth of concern with all forms of discrimination, particularly in employment, at that time.

An equally informative account of the background to the RRA 1976 is provided by McCrudden in his study of 'Institutional Discrimination' which was published as a learned article in 1982 (2 *Oxford Journal of Legal Studies* 303). He shows how in the late 1960s and early 1970s there was growing awareness and criticism of the limitations of the Race Relations Acts of 1965 and 1968, in the face of a more and more pressing social problem of race discrimination (see pp. 336–7 of his article). In particular he shows that a consciousness had developed of the extent of the problem of institutional discrimination, that is to say of the extent to which the institutions of society had embedded into their structures patterns and practices with discriminatory effects, to the point where the real problems were not amenable to the kind of simple prohibitions upon direct barriers to equal opportunity with which the existing race relations legislation had been mainly concerned. In this situation, as McCrudden shows (p. 337), the movement for reform of the race discrimination legislation associated itself with the already well-developed movement towards sex discrimination legislation which would go beyond the equal pay legislation. Hence the White Paper of 1974 in which the proposals for the SDA were introduced announced an intention of harmonizing the powers and procedures for dealing with sex and race discrimination so as to secure genuine equality of opportunity in both fields (*Equality for Women*, Cmnd. 5724, 1974, para. 24). Within this framework, it was decided to harmonize the procedures, coverage and enforcement provisions of the proposed sex and race discrimination legislation, but to have two separate enforcement agencies. As McCrudden comments (p. 337), it was felt that if sex discrimination legislation was followed by race discrimination legislation in virtually identical terms, the passage of the latter would be eased in that the pattern would already have been established by the former. Hence the position that now obtains.

The main provisions of the SDA 1975 and the RRA 1976 relating to selection for and access to employment may be summarized as follows. The Acts make it unlawful to discriminate against a person in relation to employment at an establishment in Great Britain in the arrangements made for the purpose of selection for employment, in the terms on which employment is offered, by deciding not to offer employment to the person or in the way that access is afforded to opportunities for promotion, transfer or training (SDA 1975, s.6(1), (2)(a); RRA 1976, s.4(1), (2)(b)). The relevant discrimination is that between women and men, whether in favour of men or of women, or that against married persons, or that between persons distinguished by reference to their colour, race, nationality or ethnic or national origins (SDA 1975, ss.1–3; RRA 1976, s.1). Discrimination is defined for the purposes of these Acts – and this, as we shall see, is probably the most important single policy decision embodied in the legislation – as consisting of two sorts of conduct known as direct and indirect discrimination. Direct discrimination consists of treating a person less favourably than another person is or would be treated, on the ground of the first person's sex, being a married person, or colour, race, nationality or ethnic or national origins (SDA 1975, ss.1(1)(a), 2, 3; RRA 1976, ss.1(1)(a), 3(1)). Indirect discrimination consists of applying to a person a requirement or condition which applies or would apply equally to a person of the opposite sex, to an unmarried person or to a person of a different racial group but – (i) which is such that the proportion of persons of one sex, or of married persons or of persons of a particular racial group who can comply with it, is considerably smaller than the proportion of persons of the opposite sex or of unmarried persons of the same sex or of persons of a different racial group who can comply with it; and (ii) which the person applying the requirement or condition cannot show to be justified irrespective of the sex, marital status or colour, race, nationality or ethnic or national origins of the persons to whom it is applied; and (iii) which is to the detriment of the person to whom it is applied because he cannot comply with it (SDA 1975, ss.1(1)(b), 2, 3; RRA 1976, ss.1(1)(b), 3).

These provisions are made subject to an exception where being of a particular sex or of a particular racial group is a genuine occupational qualification for the job in question (SDA 1975, s.7; RRA 1976, s.5). The notion of genuine occupational qualification is defined in specific ways by the legislation; in relation to sex discrimination it is defined by reference to considerations such as reasons of physiology (other than strength and stamina) affecting the essential nature of the job, certain specific considerations concerned with decency and privacy, and the effective provision of personal welfare or educational services. In relation to race discrimination, the corresponding considerations relate mainly to authenticity in dramatic representations and other entertainments and to the most effective provision of personal welfare services to persons of a particular racial group. So the concepts of genuine occupational qualification are not open-ended ones. There is an important further exception to the non-discrimination principle in that provision is made for positive action by training bodies and employers consisting in discriminating in favour of members of a particular sex or a particular racial group in affording access to training for employment or encouraging persons to take advantage of opportunities for employment where the sex or racial group concerned has not been represented or has been under-represented in the employment in question during the previous twelve months (SDA 1975, ss.47, 48; RRA 1976, ss.37, 38).

The procedures provided for the enforcement and implementation of the employment provisions of the Acts are, briefly, as follows. There is an individual right to complain of non-compliance with the employment provisions to an industrial tribunal, which may award the remedies of (i) declaration, (ii) compensation up to the limit which applies to compensatory awards for unfair dismissal (currently £7,500 with effect from February 1983), except that damages for indirect discrimination cannot be recovered if the employer proves that the requirement or condition in question was not applied with a discriminatory intention, or (iii) a recommendation for action to remedy the discrimination, for non-compliance with which compensation may be increased up to the limit mentioned above (SDA 1975, ss.63, 65, 66(3); RRA 1976, ss.54, 56, 57(3)). In addition, agencies for the implementation and enforcement of the legislation were established – the Equal Opportunities Commission (EOC) for the sex discrimination legislation and the Commission for Racial Equality (CRE), which superseded the earlier Race Relations Board and Community Relations Commission under the race discrimination legislation (SDA 1975, Part VI; RRA 1976, Part VII). As McCrudden points out, the provisions made in respect of these agencies reflect the influence of the specialist agencies in the United States, such as the Equal Employment Opportunity Commission, upon the model on which our own institutions are based (McCrudden, op. cit., p. 303). As McCrudden puts it, in each agency to a greater or lesser extent responsibility for control of the agency lies with members appointed by government, but chosen as representatives of business, trade unions and minority groups (see SDA 1975, s.53; RRA 1976, s.43); each agency (apart from the EEOC) has a quasi-judicial power to order discrimination to cease (see SDA 1975, s.67; RRA 1976, s.58 (non-discrimination notices)); each has a quasi-legislative power to issue rules, regulations or guidelines (see SDA 1975, s.56; RRA 1976, s.47 (Codes of Practice)); each has an enforcement power to follow up findings of discrimination (see SDA 1975, ss.69, 71; RRA 1976, ss.60, 62); each has a research role (see SDA 1975, s.54; RRA 1976, s.45) and each may recommend new legislation (see SDA 1975, ss.53, 55; RRA 1976, s.43). There is in addition an important power for the EOC and the CRE to assist individual complainants in bringing proceedings under the legislation (see SDA 1975, s.75; RRA 1976, s.66) which has provided a bridge – though arguably, as we shall see, an incomplete bridge – between the at least partially collective interests protected by the legislation and the primarily individuated mechanisms for their enforcement. See, generally, Creighton, 'Enforcing the Sex Discrimination Act' (1976) 5 *ILJ* 42.

We have thus seen, in outline at least, what the main provisions of the SDA 1975 and the RRA 1976 relating to employment are. What were the aims or policies which gave the legislation the particular shape with which it emerged? The account of the development of the legislation given by McCrudden in his article to which we have referred, and even more directly the account given by Lustgarten in his article, 'The New Meaning of Discrimination' ([1978] *Public Law* 178), support a view of the legislation as embodying a series of compromises between on the one hand the aggressive approach to anti-discrimination legislation which some people wished to import from the United States, and on the other hand the approach which preferred a more conciliatory approach towards the problems of discrimination and a greater regard for the stabilities of the status quo. McCrudden shows how what we have just styled the aggressive approach to anti-discrimination legislation developed in the United States as part of a more generalized consciousness that discrimination could not be adequately explained or remedied in terms just of prejudice alone, as was the tendency until the late 1950s (McCrudden, op. cit., p. 305). It had to be understood, and ameliorated, in terms of social and economic structures having a discriminatory operation; in terms, that is, of the institutional discrimination to which we have referred earlier in this discussion. The British legislation takes up this approach in, for instance, following the United States pattern of enforcement and implement-ation by specialist administrative agencies. But Lustgarten in particular argues that this broadly positive approach is offset by various indications of hesitation and timidity in executing the grand design. For instance he sees the decision precisely to harmonize the provisions concerning race discrimination with those concerning sex discrimination as an evasion of the question whether a different social reality required different legal treatment (Lustgarten, op. cit., p. 183).

The compromise at stake in the whole of this discussion seems to be one between a perception of non-discrimination in terms simply of equality of opportunity (which is primarily a procedural concept) and a different, more obviously substantive, approach which insists that non-discrimination re-quires some degree of compensating for the cumulative consequences of inequality and tends to regard the fact of under-enjoyment by a particular group of a given advantage as powerfully indicative of the existence of discrimination against that group. Both the two writers we have referred to have reflected and elaborated upon the widely held view that the crucial decision in the British legislation in terms of these alternative approaches was the decision to define discrimination so as to include indirect discrimination. It seems to be fairly well established that this decision occurred by way of afterthought to the original conception of the legislation, an afterthought attributable to the influence of the pattern of United States legislation upon the Home Secretary of the day (see McCrudden, op. cit., p. 338; Lustgarten, op. cit., p. 180, n.8). Yet as Lustgarten especially emphasizes, it was this decision which gave the two sets of legislative provisions their basic stance and orientation. It is the inclusion of indirect discrimination which at least opens the way to the use of the legislation as a means of challenging the more deeply embedded mechanisms of institutional discrimination, and to the recognition of the group interest as distinct from the individual interest in non-discrimination. Within this framework, however, lie significant policy choices as to the way in which to formulate the notion of prohibited indirect discrimination, and it is to these that we shall now briefly refer. It will be useful at this point to set out the provision of the RRA 1976 in which direct and indirect discrimination are defined; as we have seen, the SDA 1975 used the same mode of definition (s.1(1)).

Race Relations Act 1976, s.1

1. Racial Discrimination

(1) A person discriminates against another in any circumstances relevant for the purposes of any provision of this Act if –

(*a*) on racial grounds he treats that other less favourably than he treats or would treat other persons; or

(*b*) he applies to that other a requirement or condition which he applies or would apply equally to persons not of the same racial group as that other but –

   (i) which is such that the proportion of persons of the same racial group as that other who can comply with it is considerably smaller than the proportion of persons not of that racial group who can comply with it: and

   (ii) which he cannot show to be justifiable irrespective of the colour, race, nationality or ethnic or national origins of the person to whom it is applied; and

   (iii) which is to the detriment of that other because he cannot comply with it.

(2) It is hereby declared that, for the purposes of this Act, segregating a person from other persons on racial grounds is treating him less favourably than they are treated.

Probably the most important of the policy choices that informed this definition of indirect discrimination (s.1(1)(*b*)) are embodied in the notions of the 'requirement or condition' and of the defence of justifiability. The concept of indirect discrimination is derived from the jurisprudence of the United States Supreme Court, most notably the decision in *Griggs* v. *Duke Power Company* (1971) 401 US 424. That decision confirmed a doctrine which amounts to this, that an employment practice which operates to the disadvantage of a group of persons protected by anti-discrimination legislation is to be regarded as constituting prohibited discrimination unless there is a business necessity for the practice concerned. This doctrine served to transcend the limits which circumscribed the idea of unlawful discrimination as long as that idea was envisaged in terms of a subjective intention to discriminate; and that is the role of the provision derived from that doctrine in the British legislation. But it is a limited version of that doctrine which is embodied in the notion of the application of a 'requirement or condition', since although those words are apt to cover the high-school completion and intelligence tests requirements at issue in the *Griggs* case, they are less obviously apt to cover the whole range of employment practices capable of operating to the disadvantage of the protected group. The process of intelligence testing for employment at issue in *Griggs* is less widespread and less prominent as a focus of complaint of racial discrimination in the U K than it was in the United States, and it seems probable that the British legislation was primarily directed against prohibitions on the wearing of turbans or saris and minimum height requirements. But it was important to address the question of how much wider a range of practices with a differentiatory effect should come within the legislation, especially given the relative informality, even today, of much of British personnel management and industrial relations practice: the omission to do so has, as we shall see, left a large and crucial area of interpretative discretion to the courts.

A comparably large judicial discretion is created, as we shall see, by the embodiment of the idea of business necessity in the defence of justifiability. The notion of lack of business necessity was quite integral to the doctrine . which *Griggs* represents; in effect, it was the irrelevance of the offending test or requirement to the employer's business needs which enabled such tests to be identified as mischievous in such a way as to justify legal intervention despite the absence of subjective intention to discriminate or at least the possibility of proving such an intention. It is worth noting the broad analogy with the principles of our public or administrative law, by which irrelevance of a given consideration to the implementation of an authorized purpose is increasingly seen as the fundamental basis of challenge to administrative decisions in which such a consideration has played a part. The decision on the part of those responsible for the British legislation to express this notion of relevance, which had for the most part been rendered in terms of 'necessity' in the United States case-law, in the terminology of 'justifiability', was fraught with consequence. The choice of terminology was debated during the passage of the legislation, and the indications are that perceptions differed as to which of these terms would give rise to the wider and which the narrower defence (see Lustgarten, op. cit., p. 193; McCrudden, op. cit., p. 358); but at all events it seems that the aim was to devise a defence of reasonable generosity of which the main criterion would be the irrespectiveness, of the requirement or condition in question, to the racial group to which the individual belonged. As we shall shortly see, the courts are in the course of deciding how and how rigorously to develop that kind of criterion.

These provisions effectively set the tone of the legislation; the further policy choices embodied in the employment provisions tend to carry through this tone of cautious progressiveness into the areas of implementation and enforcement. One of the most important of them is the further requirement, before a case of indirect discrimination can be made good, that the offending requirement or condition shall be to the detriment of the individual to whom it is applied because he cannot comply with it. This apparently innocuous stipulation serves in practice, as was presumably its aim, to individuate what might otherwise be a means of securing recognition of a disadvantage inflicted upon a group collectively – often with the further, though less obviously desired, consequence that the claim is incapable of being effectively proved. This emphasis upon the individual nature of the claim to non-discrimination gives shape to much of the enforcement machinery, the powers of the EOC and CRE to issue non-discrimination notices being at best only a very partial substitute for the capacity to bring class actions which has been an important feature of the anti-discrimination legislation in the United States. It is in these terms also that one must presumably account for the provisions described earlier (see above, p. 45) which effectively prevent the recovery of compensation for indirect as opposed to direct discrimination by admitting lack of intention to discriminate as a defence to claims for compensation on the ground of indirect discrimination (SDA 1975, s.66(3); RRA 1976, s.57(3)). Lustgarten sees the entrusting of the employment provisions to the forum of the industrial tribunals, which is in a sense expressive of the same emphasis on the primacy of the individual claim, as conducing to a greater sympathy for longstanding and widely agreed customs and practices than might be expected from a more remote and detached tribunal of professional judges such as the federal courts of the United States have provided (op. cit., p. 204). This gives rise to the question, with what attitudes and preferences have the British appellate courts approached the interpretation and application of these provisions, a question to which we now turn with the parting remark, on the intention of the legislators, that the cautious radicalism of their approach is thrown into sharp relief by their one venture into the generally eschewed area of positive discrimination or affirmative action, namely the provisions mentioned earlier authorizing positive action in relation to training and preparation for employment in certain defined conditions of under-representation (SDA 1975, ss.47, 48; RRA 1976, ss.37, 38). This is the exception that proves the rule that the framers of this legislation hoped that substantial and sufficient progress could be achieved by limiting particular discriminatory practices.

(c) **Judicial approaches to the legislation**
Although as we have seen the employment provisions of the sex and race discrimination legislation express a number of fairly cautious policy choices, they are nonetheless sufficiently reformist in their implications to confront the appellate courts entrusted with their interpretation with the necessity of choosing at various points whether or not to promote a purposive application of the legislation. In other words, given that this is legislation in the grand style

rather than in the formal style, the courts have to choose whether to accept that a correspondingly grand style is called for on their own part, or whether on the other hand to contain the pursuit of the purposes of the legislation within the constraints of formal interpretation. On the whole the Employment Appeal Tribunal has tended to make choices of the former sort, especially under the presidency of Phillips J. in the early days after the introduction of the SDA and the RRA. There are, however, some recent indications of the latter sort of preference, especially so far as the Court of Appeal is concerned.

The importance of judicial approaches to the legislation is well illustrated by decisions construing the various components of the concept of indirect discrimination. For example, the interpretation given to the notion of a 'requirement or condition' is one of the crucial determinants of the scope of the anti-discrimination legislation in relation to employment. For upon this interpretation depends the issue of how far the indirect discrimination concept extends beyond the control of specific bars or tests into the wider area of practices with differentiatory effects. We now have a crucial decision on this point in relation to selection for employment from the Court of Appeal in *Perera* v. *Civil Service Commission* [1983] IRLR 166. This decision had been preceded by *Clarke* v. *Eley (IMI) Kynoch Ltd* where, as we shall see later (see below, p. 523), the EAT had taken a generous view of the scope of indirect discrimination in a case concerning the legality of a rule which caused part-time workers to be selected for redundancy before full-time workers in what was otherwise a system of selection based upon seniority in the job (that is, a last-in first-out (LIFO) system). The EAT had little difficulty in accepting that the 'part-timers first' rule gave rise to a requirement or condition which disfavoured women workers.

The notion of 'requirement or condition' again received a generous construction in the case of *Watches of Switzerland* v. *Savell* [1983] IRLR 141, though this time at the cost, as we shall shortly see, of a correspondingly narrow construction of the concept of detriment. In this case the employers had a promotion procedure which was alleged to disfavour women by its vagueness, subjectivity, and scope for the operation of unconscious bias. The EAT accepted that there could be said to be a requirement or condition for promotion in that the criteria of this particular procedure had to be satisfied in order to obtain promotion. In the *Perera* case, however, there was introduced the restriction both at the level of the EAT and in the Court of Appeal that where a factor or a collection of factors taken into account by a selecting body is relied upon as a requirement or condition, that factor or collection of factors must constitute an absolute bar to selection rather than matters merely weighting the balance against the selection of a particular person. So in this case, where the factors in question were nationality, work experience in the UK and command of English, Stephenson L.J. put it thus in the Court of Appeal ([1983] IRLR 166, 170):

But in my opinion none of those factors could possibly be regarded as a requirement or a condition in the sense that the lack of it, whether of British nationality or even of the ability to communicate well in English, would be an absolute bar. The whole of the evidence indicates that a brilliant man whose personal qualities made him suitable as a legal assistant might well have been sent forward on a shortlist by the interviewing board in spite of being, perhaps, below standard on his knowledge of English and his ability to communicate in that language.

This approach could obviously operate as a significant restriction on the employment practices which can be brought within the range of the concept of indirect discrimination. The approach reflects a tendency, which we shall also encounter in relation to the unfair dismissal legislation to restrict statutory controls upon employers' decisions by applying a 'but for' test which demands that the evidence shows that the contrary decision would have been taken but for the factor whose presence is complained of. This kind of reasoning can easily be made to seem self-evidently correct; but it usually represents a choice in favour of a high requirement of causative connection between the prohibited conduct and the outcome which is complained of, a choice which in turn reflects a preference for not lightly interfering with employers' decisions and the processes by which they are reached. It is a kind of reasoning which can easily serve to give a pre-emptive answer to a question which the statute in question intended to be addressed directly and openly. Thus in this context this kind of 'but for' reasoning gives rise to the result that it is automatically acceptable for the employer to take a given collection of factors into account as long as he does not intend to discriminate, whereas the legislation if construed without the interposition of 'but for' reasoning would require it to be considered whether it was *justifiable* to take those factors into account, a question which it is surely the real point of the legislation to ask.

Somewhat parallel with these developments in judicial approaches to the notion of requirement or condition has been the interpretation accorded to the notion of ability to comply with the requirement or condition. This notion figures twice in the statutory concept of indirect discrimination: firstly in the stipulation that the proportion of the protected group who can comply with the requirement or condition in question must be considerably smaller than the proportion of the group from which that group is differentiated who can comply with it (SDA 1975, s.1(1)(b)(i); RRA 1976, s.1(1)(b)(i)); and secondly in the further stipulation that the requirement or condition must be to the detriment of the person alleged to be discriminated against because that person cannot comply with it (SDA 1975, s.1(1)(b)(iii); RRA 1976, s.1(1)(b)(iii)). The first problem in interpreting the notion of ability to comply is what respect to accord to choices on the part of the protected group or the particular member in question not to comply with a given requirement or condition with which it is physically possible for members of that group to comply. The answer given to that question determines the extent to which the legislation is effective to control practices which operate to the disadvantage of the protected group by failing or refusing to accommodate the particular customs or behaviour patterns of the group. In *Price* v. *Civil Service Commission* [1978] ICR 27, which was perhaps the classic statement of a liberal and purposive judicial approach to the construction of the discrimination legislation, the requirement complained of was that applicants for appointment as executive officers in the Civil Service should be at least 17½ and under 28 years of age. The question was whether it could be said that a considerably smaller proportion of women than of men could comply with this requirement, given that many women in their twenties do not seek employment because they are engaged in bearing and taking care of children. Phillips J. ruled that regard should be had for the spirit and intent of the Act and that accordingly (ibid., p. 31), 'It should not be said that a person "can" do something merely because it is theoretically possible for him to do so; it is necessary to see whether he can do so in practice.'

We shall return shortly to the question of how that assessment is to be made; the important point at this stage is that the question was formulated in those terms. This construction was endorsed, and applied to the parallel case of indirect discrimination against a racial group, in *Mandla* v. *Dowell Lee* [1983] ICR 385 which concerned a refusal to give a Sikh boy a place at a school because he insisted on wearing a turban at school. The House of Lords, having held that Sikhs did constitute a racial group defined by reference to ethnic origins, held that the rule against turbans applied a condition with which a Sikh could not comply in the sense that he could not do so consistently with the customs and cultural conditions of his racial group. This meant that the issue had to be resolved as one of justifiability, which is a correct implementation of the scheme of the legislation. The contrary construction of the notion of ability to comply will thus be seen to pre-empt the issue of justifiability in favour of, in our context, the employer: there would seem to be no sufficient reason for doing so.

Consistently with the approach taken in that case, it had been ruled in *Clarke* v. *Eley (IMI) Kynoch Ltd* [1983] ICR 165 that ability to comply did not include past ability to comply, so that when a worker was selected for redundancy as a part-time worker and the requirement for preferential retention was thus being a full-time worker, it was held that a given part-time worker could not be held to be able to comply with the condition merely because she could in the past have transferred to full-time work. But a rather curious contrary trend of reasoning revealed itself in the EAT in the case of *Watches of Switzerland Ltd* v. *Savell* [1983] IRLR 141. Here, as we have seen, the complaint was that the employers' promotion procedure operated according to vague, subjective criteria which left scope for subconscious bias against women. The EAT ruled that although this state of affairs could be regarded as constituting the application of a condition or requirement, there could be said to be the necessary inability to comply with that requirement only if it was shown that the complainant could not, as a woman, achieve promotion because of the procedure used in selection for promotion. As the evidence suggested that it was not impossible that a woman would be selected by this procedure, the EAT held that the necessary detriment to the complainant could not, as a matter of law, be said to have been shown. This seems to give insufficient weight to the fact that the detriment to the complainant, which the concept of indirect discrimination demands, consists of a personal inability to comply as distinct from the relative inability of the group as a whole to comply which establishes the discriminatory nature of the requirement complained of. The added requirement of personal detriment may be thought undesirable as a matter of legislative policy, but it should not present problems of the sort raised in this case. A less restrictive interpretation would say that the condition or requirement consisted in satisfying a test alleged to be arbitrary. A person who does not pass the test cannot comply with the condition, any more than a person who is five feet tall can comply with a condition requiring applicants to be six feet tall. To say otherwise is, yet again, to pre-empt the question of justifiability in the employer's favour and in a way which threatens the design of the statutory provisions.

Discussion of these various ways in which the issue of justifiability may be pre-empted brings us to the question of how the appellate courts have approached the issue of justifiability in the cases in which it has been seen as relevant. The statutory provision is that the application of a requirement or condition which satisfies the definition of indirect discrimination in other respects does not constitute indirect discrimination if it can be shown to be justifiable irrespective of the protected attribute in question, that is, sex, marital status or colour, race, nationality or ethnic or national origins as the case may be (SDA 1975, s.1(1)(*b*)(ii); RRA 1976, s.1(1)(*b*)(ii)). Our examination of the aims of the legislation suggested that the defence of justifiability was intended to have the role of confining the concept of indirect discrimination to requirements or conditions which were not related to the job in question, but that it was intended to express the notion of job-relatedness in not too restrictive a manner. Again the process of judicial construction of the legislation by the appellate courts began auspiciously with the statement by the then president of the EAT, Phillips J., of an approach to justifiability which gave firm yet measured expression to the reformist purpose of the statute. This occurred in the context of a decision about the allocation of postal rounds to postmen according to a seniority system alleged to discriminate, in its operation, against women. We shall examine the details of the decision in a later chapter (see below, p. 412); it is, however, appropriate at this point to set out the text of the EAT's approach to justifiability in that case:

Steel v. *Union of Post Office Workers*
[1978] ICR 181 at pp. 187–8

PHILLIPS J.: . . . To summarise the position so as to avoid any doubt, we are satisfied that the complainant is entitled to succeed in her claim against the Post Office under section 1(1)(*b*) and section 6(2)(*a*) unless the Post Office can show that the seniority rule was justifiable irrespective of the sex of the person to whom it is applied.

It may be helpful if we add a word of detail about what we consider to be the right approach to this question. First, the onus of proof lies upon the party asserting this proposition, in this case the Post Office. Secondly, it is a heavy onus in the sense that at the end of the day the industrial tribunal must be satisfied that the case is a genuine one where it can be said that the requirement or condition is necessary. Thirdly, in deciding whether the employer has discharged the onus the industrial tribunal should take into account all the circumstances, including the discriminatory effect of the requirement or condition if it is permitted to continue. Fourthly, it is necessary to weigh the need for the requirement or condition against that effect. Fifthly, it is right to distinguish between a requirement or condition which is necessary and one which is merely convenient, and for this purpose it is relevant to consider whether the employer can find some other and non-discriminatory method of achieving his object.

Turning to the facts of this case, it will be right to inquire whether it is necessary to allot walks by seniority or whether some other method is feasible, to consider whether the seniority rule could not be revised so as to give the women some credit for their temporary service, and to consider the extent of the disadvantage which the women suffer under the present system in terms of numbers and likely duration. Assistance may be obtained from the judgments in the Supreme Court of the United States in *Griggs* v. *Duke Power Co.* (1971) 401 US 424. Although the terms of the Act there in question are different from those of the Sex Discrimination Act 1975, it seems to us that the approach adopted by the court is relevant. In particular, the passage at p. 431 is helpful where it is said:

> Congress has now provided that tests or criteria for employment or promotion may not provide equality of opportunity merely in the sense of the fabled offer of milk to the stork and the fox. On the contrary, Congress has now required that the posture and condition of the job-seeker be taken into account. It has – to resort again to the fable – provided that the vessel in which the milk is proffered be one all seekers can use. The Act proscribes not only overt discrimination but also practices that are fair in form, but discriminatory in operation. The touchstone is business necessity. If an employment practice which operates to exclude Negroes cannot be shown to be related to job performance, the practice is prohibited.

A similar approach seems to us to be proper when applying section 1(1)(b)(ii) of the Sex Discrimination Act 1975. In other words a practice which would otherwise be discriminatory, which is the case here, is not to be licensed unless it can be shown to be justifiable, and it cannot be justifiable unless its discriminatory effect is justified by the need – not the convenience – of the business or enterprise.

The application of this approach produced findings in favour of applicants and against employers by industrial tribunals in the *Price* case (see above, p. 52: *Price* v. *Civil Service Commission (No. 2)* [1978] IRLR 3), and in the *Steel* case itself (*Steel* v. *Post Office (No. 2)* [1978] IRLR 198). It seems that the judgment of the EAT in the *Steel* case had a real practical impact in strengthening the effect of the legislation, above all by equating justifiability with necessity and need, rather than administrative convenience. Subsequent judicial interpretation has somewhat modified the rigour of that position. Thus in *Singh* v. *Rowntree MacKintosh Ltd* [1979] ICR 554, where the issue was the justifiability of a rule against beards for workers in a confectionery factory in its application to Sikhs whose religion forbids them to shave their beards, the EAT in Scotland stressed that the necessity required in the *Steel* case should be envisaged in terms of reasonable commercial necessity rather than absolute rigid necessity. This conduced to a finding that the industrial tribunal had not been wrong in law in treating the no-beards rule as justifiable. The same result occurred in *Panesar* v. *Nestlé Co. Ltd* [1980] ICR 144, where both Slynn J. presiding in the EAT and Lord Denning M.R. in the Court of Appeal stressed the factual content of the issue of justifiability as a basis for upholding the finding of the industrial tribunal in favour of the employer.

The EAT under the presidency of Browne-Wilkinson J. reasserted the primacy of the interpretation of justifiability in terms of necessity. They did so in *Hurley* v. *Mustoe* [1981] ICR 490 and in *Chiu* v. *British Aerospace plc* [1982] IRLR 56. The Court of Appeal reversed this trend, however, in *Ojutiku* v. *Manpower Services Commission* [1982] ICR 661. The justifiability issue in this case was slightly complex, because the Manpower Services Commission sought (successfully in the outcome) to justify a rule restricting access to training opportunities to applicants of certain educational qualifications and work experience, not because they regarded those as requirements for the training itself but because they thought that employers would impose those requirements when deciding whether to offer employment to the persons who had taken the training. Yet these requirements operated to the disadvantage of black applicants, and indeed it appeared that the ultimate employers whose preferences were being taken into account might be engaging in intentional discrimination in making those requirements. The Court of Appeal approached the question of justifiability in these circumstances on the footing that the criterion of justifiability was not so exacting as it would be if equated with the notion of necessity. This conduced to a finding that the requirement imposed by the Commission was justifiable, as the following passage from the judgment of Kerr L.J. demonstrates:

> *Ojutiku* v. *Manpower Services Commission*
> [1982] ICR 661 at pp. 669–71
>
> KERR L.J.: . . . It was conceded by the commission that the complainants satisfied section 1(1)(*b*)(i) and (iii). It follows that it was common ground that to this extent the requirement of previous managerial experience operates in a racially discriminatory manner to the detriment of coloured people such as the complainants. Therefore the only issue is whether there was evidence before the industrial tribunal on which it could reasonably conclude that this requirement was justifiable. This involves, first, a question of law as to the meaning of the word 'justifiable' and, secondly, if the tribunal has not misdirected itself in relation to the meaning of 'justifiable,' the issue becomes a question of fact for the tribunal. The complainants submitted that 'justifiable' in section 1(1)(*b*)(ii) means 'necessary as a matter of business' or 'something in the nature of a legitimate business necessity'; and in this connection they relied on an American judgment, *Rowe* v. *General Motors Corporation* (1972) 457 F. 2d 348, a decision of the

United States Court of Appeals, Fifth Circuit. They also relied on certain passages in the decision of the appeal tribunal in *Steel* v. *Union of Post Office Workers* [1978] I C R 181, in particular at p. 187H. So far as the American case is concerned, it should be borne in mind that the United States legislation appears to have no counterpart to the provision which is crucial in this case, section 1(1)(*b*)(ii); and it is also to be noted that in that case actual discrimination was established against the employers in question as the result of a prior practice of direct discrimination, which undoubtedly caused coloured employees to suffer by not having been able to get the same experience for the purposes of promotion as their white colleagues. For myself, I do not see how *Rowe* v. *General Motors Corporation* could in any event be applied in the context of the English legislation unless the facts were similar, which they are not in this case. In *Steel* v. *Union of Post Office Workers* the point under consideration involved the corresponding provisions in the same terms of the Sex Discrimination Act 1975. It seems to me that the appeal tribunal in that case put something of a gloss on the word 'justifiable' by suggesting that it was equivalent or close to having the same meaning as 'necessary.' But that gloss was rightly shaded, to put it no higher, by another decision of the appeal tribunal in *Singh* v. *Rowntreee MacKintosh Ltd* [1979] I C R 554, 557, in which the approach was in effect that 'justifiable' means 'reasonably necessary in all the circumstances'. In the same way as Eveleigh I.J., I decline to put any gloss on the word 'justifiable', which is a perfectly easily understandable ordinary word, except that I would say that it clearly applies a lower standard than the word 'necessary.' This is also an ordinary word which is often used in legislation, but it has not been used in this case.

It seems to me that the industrial tribunal took the right view of the meaning of the word 'justifiable' in this case. They said, in an important passage of their decision:

> In the present situation the tribunal were unanimously of the view that the respondents have made out their case under section 1(1)(*b*)(ii) of the Race Relations Act 1976. In the view of the tribunal the requirement of prior management experience is a requirement that is justified. The tribunal were unable themselves nor indeed were they able to obtain from anyone present any suggestion as to how this criterion (managerial experience) could be changed so that on the one hand the discrimination was removed and so that on the other hand the standard was maintained and that the employability after the obtaining of the qualification was also retained.

From this passage it is clear that the tribunal considered that there were two good grounds for the commission's requirement of previous managerial experience for this course. Indeed, 'advancing good grounds' is one of the dictionary definitions of the verb 'to justify.' The first ground, and to my mind by far the most important one, is that on the evidence before it the industrial tribunal was satisfied that the employment prospects of would-be managers are not in fact enhanced by such persons attaining the paper qualification of a diploma in management studies. The second ground was that they were satisfied that the requirement imposed by the commission was justifiable as maintaining the standard of the qualification sought by applicants to the commission and of the standard of the assistance and services provided by the commission itself.

In the light of the evidence to which we have been referred, it may not have been necessary for the commission to lay down the requirement of previous managerial experience. But the first of these grounds, at any rate, was to my mind clearly capable of being considered by the tribunal to be justifiable by reference to the functions of the commission under section 2(1) of the Employment and Training Act 1973. It was conceded on behalf of the complainants, in the context of this section, that the commission must be selective to some extent, because of limited funds. It cannot sponsor or assist everyone by paying for every course of training for which any applicant may be acceptable by virtue of his qualifications. The commission must be entitled to impose appropriate additional requirements to seek to ensure that its financial assistance will in fact be likely to further the applicant's actual prospects of employment, and that its assistance will not result merely in additional paper qualifications. I therefore consider that unless the commission was not entitled to rely on the practice, or the alleged practice, of employers generally, which I have explained, there was material on which the tribunal was entitled to conclude that the commission had discharged the onus of 'justifiability' under section $1(1)(b)(ii)$. I accordingly consider that the decision of the appeal tribunal is clearly entitled to be upheld on the basis of the issues which were before it.

The indications are that the decision in the *Ojutiku* case has effected a permanent if slight devaluation of the currency of justifiability. In *Clarke* v. *Eley (IMI) Kynoch Ltd* [1983] ICR 165, the President of the EAT acknowledged that the view expressed in *Ojutiku* must be viewed as having overtaken Phillips J.'s definition of justifiability in terms of necessity, and expressed some apprehension as to the direction in which the decisions of the courts were going on this issue (at p. 174). In *Mandla* v. *Dowell Lee* [1983] ICR 385, the House of Lords rejected a claim of justifiability for a no-turbans rule imposed at a school; but this was unremarkable in that the claim of justifiability asserted the desirability of being able to exclude outward manifestations of a non-Christian religion, which could hardly be accepted as a justification irrespective of the ethnic origins of the complainant. In the course of so holding, Lord Fraser indicated that he thought that justifiable meant less than 'necessary'; and that his sympathy lay with the view that this was a justifiable rule had he been free so to hold (at p. 394). The courts have not at any stage displayed comparable sympathies in the context of employment; but they have travelled quite a long way from the notion of justification as consisting in independently validated job-relatedness, which may be regarded as describing the pure milk of the doctrine as it originally developed in United States case-law.

Judicial approaches to the legislation dealing with discrimination in employment are important not only to the interpretation of its substantive concepts but also in determining the burden and quantum of proof of discrimination and the methods by which it may be proved. It is in fact an area where conceptual definition and practical problems of proof are inter-linked and continuous with each other. As we have seen, the statutory formulation of indirect discrimination is a proposition about how discrimination may be proved, as much as an abstract definition of the meaning of the term. The legislation makes no express statement about the general burden of proof of discrimination, thus leaving that burden with the complainant, except that the employer has the burden of making out a defence of justifiability to a complaint of indirect discrimination. It is widely argued that it should be made easier for a complaint of discrimination to be proved, since the achievement of the reformist purposes of the legislation depends on the possibility of establishing intentions and motivations which employers would be unlikely to accept that they possessed; see generally Lustgarten, 'Problems of Proof in Employment Discrimination Cases' (1977) 6 *ILJ* 212. The EAT under the Presidency of Phillips J. did what it could within the framework of the legislation to assist complainants with problems of proof, by maintaining that the evidential burden might be envisaged as shifting to the employer once the complainant had made out a possible case, so that a finding of no case to answer should be reserved only for the exceptional or frivolous case – *Oxford* v. *DHSS* [1977] ICR 884 – and so that, for instance, the employer's evidence ought to be taken where the complainant is shown to be better qualified or more experienced than the successful applicant for the job – *Humphreys* v. *St George's School* [1978] ICR 546. This line of development has since been pursued more actively in the Northern Ireland Court of Appeal than in the EAT; comparison may be made with the decisions in *Wallace* v. *South East Education & Library Board* [1980] IRLR 193 and *Conway* v. *Queens University Belfast* [1981] IRLR 43. The EAT and the higher appellate courts have, however, since been concerned with certain important aspects of the methods of proving discrimination, and it is to a brief consideration of those decisions that we now turn.

In order to prove discrimination, a complainant has in practice to be in a position to expose to view the process by which the employer's decision in question was reached and the data which provided the basis for the decision or which enable it to be evaluated in context. The demands for these facilities have presented the courts with some important choices of policy. One of these related to confidentiality and disclosure. The most contentious sort of demand was for the disclosure of the dossiers of the other applicants for selection or for promotion whose comparison with the complainant was the matter in issue. The question was litigated in *Science Research Council* v. *Nasse, BL Cars Ltd* v. *Vyas* [1979] ICR 921, for both the sex and the race discrimination legislation. The difference in approach between the successive appellate courts was quite marked. The EAT held that confidentiality was not a valid objection to discovery in these cases. The Court of Appeal, while not accepting confidentiality as a bar to disclosure, did accept that it was an important factor militating against disclosure, indeed a factor dictating the refusal of discovery in these two cases. Lord Denning M.R. in particular was concerned to meet the implicit challenge to the freedom with which employers might decide how to arrive at decisions about selection (see below, p. 63). The House of Lords rejected the view of the Court of Appeal that discovery of confidential documents should be ordered only in very rare cases, holding that the test was whether discovery was necessary for the fair disposal of the proceedings (which was to be determined by inspection by the chairman of the industrial tribunal). It was confirmed in the House of Lords that the rights given to individual complainants under SDA 1975, s.74, and RRA 1976, s.65, to use the special questionnaire procedure provided by the two Acts were additional to any right to apply for an order for discovery.

Access to the dossiers of competing applicants is important for the proof of direct rather than indirect discrimination. In a sense the corresponding issue for the proof of indirect discrimination is that of the extent to which statistical evidence may be used to demonstrate that the proportion of the protected group that can comply with the requirement or condition in question is considerably smaller than the proportion able to comply in the group from which the differentiation in question is being made. In one sense it can be said that the making-out of a case about proportions able to comply is in its nature a statistical case, so that the question is really what kinds of statistical case will be accepted and what kinds will be rejected. In *Price* v. *Civil Service Commission* [1978] ICR 27, Phillips J. indicated the broad acceptability of sophisticated statistical evidence provided that there was evidence from the statistician and hence the opportunity for him to be cross-examined upon the proper analysis and inferences to be drawn from the statistics (ibid., at p. 32). The EAT has since become somewhat concerned lest the making-out of an elaborate statistical case which would stand up to sophisticated cross-examination should become a pre-condition to a successful claim of indirect discrimination across a wide range of cases, and in the *Perera (No. 2)* case the court responded to this problem by leaning in favour of the complainant so far as the quantum of proof was concerned, as the following extract will show (this part of the case was not the subject of the subsequent appeal to the CA).

Perera v. *Civil Service Commission (No. 2)*
[1982] ICR 350 (EAT) at pp. 358–9

BROWNE-WILKINSON J.: . . .

3. *Application to be an administrative trainee*

In June 1979 the complainant wished to be considered for selection as an administrative trainee. The upper age limit for such applications was the age of 32: he was then aged 39. He claimed by analogy with the decision in *Price* v. *Civil Service Commission* [1978] ICR 27 that this age limit constituted indirect discrimination. He says, and it is common ground, that the age limit is a 'requirement or condition' applied to all candidates and therefore the case falls within section 1(1)(b); his ethnic group is 'coloured' and, because of the number of coloureds who immigrate into this country when adult, the proportion of coloured executive officers who can comply with that requirement is considerably smaller than the proportion of white executive officers who can so comply. Accordingly, says the complainant, the provisions of section 1(1)(b)(i) were satisfied. The Civil Service (perhaps surprisingly) has not sought to justify any requirement or condition under section 1(1)(b)(ii). As the complainant was not eligible for the appointment, he has shown detriment for the purposes of section 1(1)(b)(iii).

Therefore, the sole issue before the industrial tribunal in this case was whether the requirements of section 1(1)(b)(i) were satisfied. The complainant produced to the industrial tribunal a schedule showing that out of the 47 executive officers at the value added tax office where he worked, 22 were under the age of 32 but none of the 13 coloureds was under the age of 32. The respondents put in certain evidence as to the position at two other local offices in London. This evidence, far from conflicting with the complainant's evidence, supported it. Out of the 162 executive officers at the three offices, none of the 26 who were coloured was under the age limit of 32, whereas 110 out of 136 whites were under that age.

The majority of the industrial tribunal held that this evidence was insufficient to discharge the burden laid down by section $1(1)(b)(i)$. We find the reasons for rejecting this evidence unsatisfactory. First they point out that they had no statistics showing the proportion of coloureds and whites amongst the 60,000 executive officers in the Civil Service. This indicates an initial possible misunderstanding of what proof they were looking for. The actual number of coloureds or whites is not relevant. Nor is the ratio between the number of coloureds and the number of whites. The relevant question is what *proportion* of coloureds and what *proportion* of whites are under the age of 32. They then go on to point out that the offices may well not be typical of the Civil Service generally since, when the value added tax system was set up, there was a special scheme which admitted candidates up to an age of 55. This factor might well distort the number of both coloureds and whites who are over the age of 32 in local value added tax offices as against the rest of the Civil Service. However, so far as the coloureds are concerned it can make no difference to the proportion who can comply: however many you exclude from the 'over 32' class as being non-typical special entrants, you are still left with the fact that none of the coloureds is under 32, i.e., the proportion of coloureds who could comply remains 0 per cent. So far as the whites are concerned, by taking out non-typical late entrants, you will actually increase the percentage of the whites who are under the age of 32 and who can therefore comply with the requirements.

Next, the industrial tribunal reject the statistics as to these three offices on the grounds that they do not show at what age the coloureds came to this country. We do not understand why this is a material consideration. Finally they point out that the number of whites over 32 exceed the number of coloureds who are over 32. This is, of course, true; but again we do not understand why it is a material point: the question is the proportion of coloureds and whites respectively under the age of 32. We therefore find the reasons given by the industrial tribunal for rejecting this evidence unsatisfactory.

However, there remains the root problem that, by any normal statistical standard, the only statistical evidence laid before the industrial tribunal is in fact inadequate. It is based on a very small sample from a very small number of non-typical offices. Is it therefore right to hold that the complainant has proved his case? We have found this a very difficult point. On the one hand, the burden is on the complainant to prove his case and, viewed in isolation, the statistics produced do not prove it. On the other hand it is most undesirable that, in all cases of indirect discrimination, elaborate statistical evidence should be required before the case can be found proved. The time and expense involved in preparing and proving statistical evidence can be enormous, as experience in the United States has demonstrated. It is not good policy to require such evidence to be put forward unless it is clear that there is an issue as to whether the requirements of section $1(1)(b)(i)$ are satisfied.

With some hesitation, we have come to the conclusion that in this case the complainant has proved his case. He put forward evidence as to the Southall office alone. If the employers wished to attack that evidence, they could either themselves have put in rebutting statistics showing the true position or, without putting in such evidence, demonstrated that the statistics put forward by the complainant distorted the picture in a relevant way. In this case, they did neither. The statistical evidence they put in, far from rebutting, supported his evidence: they have not demonstrated any way in which the statistical evidence provided by the complainant, though statistically fallible, must have distorted the proportion of coloureds under the age of 32 and the proportion of whites under the age of 32. Moreover, the fact that a substantial number of coloureds are adult immigrants (which is a matter of which judicial notice can be taken) suggests that the statistical evidence, such as it is, probably gives a correct picture. In these circumstances, we hold that the complainant has proved that he has been indirectly discriminated against in relation to his application to become an administrative trainee and to that extent allow the appeal. . . .

It is, however, open to doubt whether the Court of Appeal would endorse so liberal a response to the difficulties of proof of cases depending on statistics, and the restrictive approaches that we have remarked as recently evident in relation to the issues of what is meant by requirement or condition and by detriment have the function of foreclosing the possibility of such a liberal response in the cases which are so approached. On the other hand the importance, to the reformist aims of the legislation, of the availability of statistical methods of proof is emphasized by a decision such as that of *Watches of Switzerland* v. *Savell* [1983] IRLR 141, where the misgivings of the court are all too obvious as to evidence tending to show that a promotion procedure disfavoured women by giving scope for the operation of unconscious bias against women. Yet that kind of argument is more or less the only alternative to elaborate statistical argument if indirect discrimination is to be capable of proof in any but the most open and shut cases.

So far as judicial approaches to the enforcement of the discrimination legislation are concerned, it is appropriate to deal separately with individual claims on the one hand and the enforcement activities of the EOC and CRE on the other. In relation to remedies for individual complaints, the Court of Appeal has pursued a distinctly cautious line, while there are some indications of a more liberal approach on the part of the EAT. In *Prestcold Ltd* v. *Irvine* [1981] ICR 777, the Court of Appeal upheld the EAT in the view that the power conferred upon industrial tribunals by SDA 1975, s.65(1)(c) to make recommendations for actions to remedy the discrimination in question does not include recommendations for compensation, so that in this instance the industrial tribunal had no power to recommend, as they had purported to do, that the complainant employee be paid the difference between her salary and that of the post to which she had been denied promotion by reason of discrimination. In *Skyrail Oceanic Ltd* v. *Coleman* [1981] ICR 864, the Court of Appeal (having by a majority reversed the EAT, finding the dismissal of a woman discriminatory because it was based on the assumption that her husband was the breadwinner of the family (see below, p. 522)), reduced the award of £1,000 made by the industrial tribunal for injury to feelings to £100, on the grounds that compensable injury to feelings had to result from the knowledge that it had been an act of sex discrimination that had brought about the dismissal and that in the circumstances of the present case the award of

£1,000 had been out of all proportion to the injury proved. This indicates an unwillingness on the part of the Court of Appeal to let compensation for injury to feelings serve an expressive, exemplary or punitive function in a way that those with a reformist perspective upon this legislation might regard as appropriate. We shall discover the same tension between the reformist approach and the relatively formal approach to pecuniary remedies elsewhere in the course of our account of employment protection legislation (see, for instance, below, p. 182).

This cautious approach to compensation for injury to feelings threatened, if taken to extremes, completely to undermine any kind of expressive function for the compensation awarded under the discrimination legislation. It was that extreme that the EAT sought to counteract in *Hurley* v. *Mustoe (No. 2)* [1983] ICR 422, which concerned a part-time waitress who had been dismissed when her employer had discovered that she had four children. An industrial tribunal which had rejected her complaint of sex discrimination, having been overruled in this by the EAT and directed to assess compensation, had awarded 50p compensation for injury to feelings, being partly influenced in the making of this derisory award by evidence that the complainant had been present at demonstrations held to protest against her dismissal. Among the factors which the industrial tribunal cited as tending to show that the complainant's feelings were scarcely susceptible of injury by reason of sex discrimination, they included, in a memorable phrase, 'the previous experience of the adversities of life which [she] must have gained in her employment at Dingwall's Dance Hall'. The EAT held that the industrial tribunal's power under SDA 1975, s.65, to take into account considerations of justice and equity was confined to the selection of the remedy to be given and did not extend to the quantifying of compensation, so that the tribunal was not free to reduce the award by reason of unmeritorious conduct following the dismissal complained of. Moreover the EAT found that the industrial tribunal had shown no sufficient reason for reducing the award to derisory proportions. So an agreed award of £100 was made for injury to feelings and the expressive function of the individual remedy was somewhat vindicated.

This being the faintly precarious state of individual remedies, it becomes important to examine judicial approaches to the powers of the EOC and CRE. Here we find corroboration of a fact that has been discovered in relation to other labour law institutions, namely that the principles and practice of our administrative law are on the whole hostile to the purposive pursuit of reformist goals by administrative agencies when those goals conflict with individual interests. In *CRE* v. *Amari Plastics Ltd* [1982] ICR 304, it was held both by the EAT and the Court of Appeal that a non-discrimination notice issued by the CRE under RRA 1976, s.48, was fully open to appeal on questions of fact as well as questions of law, and in particular open to appeal on the findings of fact on which the notice was based as well as findings of fact relevant to the reasonableness of the requirements made by the notice (the latter being the narrower basis of appeal for which the CRE unsuccessfully contended). In *R.* v. *CRE ex parte Prestige Group plc, The Times*, 14 February 1984, the House of Lords held (following indications emerging from the decision in *Hillingdon LBC* v. *CRE* [1982] AC 779) that the CRE did not have power to conduct a formal investigation into the activities of a named person under sections 48 and 49 of the RRA 1976, unless it had formed a belief that the person named might have committed an act made unlawful by the 1976 Act which it proposed to investigate. The stance of the judiciary is that these restrictions are firmly dictated by the legislation itself; but one wonders whether Lord Denning, for instance, who had said in the *Nasse* case of the Commission's powers of formal investigation that 'one might think we were back in the days of the Inquisition' ([1978] ICR 1124 at 1138–9), was indulging in a little irony when he concluded in the *Amari* case with the reflection that 'I am very sorry for the Commission, but they have been caught up in a spider's web spun by Parliament, from which there is little hope of their escaping' ([1982] ICR 304 at 313). Lord Fraser found it necessary in the case of *Mandla* v. *Dowell Lee* to reprove two members of the Court of Appeal for their unjustified strictures upon the CRE as oppressors and inquisitors ([1983] ICR 385 at 395), and one senses that the area of potential conflict between the EOC and CRE on the one hand and the appeal courts on the other may not yet have been fully explored.

(d) **The social operation of the discrimination legislation**
There is more information available about the social operation of the employment provisions of the discrimination legislation than about the social operation of most other aspects of labour law. This is for two reasons: firstly, the EOC and the CRE monitor the operation of their respective Acts, and secondly, the topic has been extensively surveyed by researchers. The great advantage to be derived from the possession of these sources of information is that it permits an assessment to be made of the operation of the legislation which is not solely based upon the litigation that has arisen under that legislation, for the latter often gives a false picture of the practical effect that legislation has. On the other hand, just as litigation can give a misleading view by virtue of its selectiveness, it has to be borne in mind that the EOC and the CRE are often concerned with making out a reformist case. So we shall consider separately the contributions made by the CRE and the EOC on the one hand, and by independent researchers on the other hand, to our understanding of the social operation of the two sets of provisions.

Perhaps the main insight into the operation of the provisions relating to selection for employment which is to be gained from the recent annual reports of the EOC, is that the difficulties of proof have an even more fundamental impact upon the effectiveness of the legislation than a reading of the relevant cases would suggest. The EOC made the following comments on this point in its Annual Report for 1980:

EOC Annual Report for 1980, Chapter 2, para. 3 and
Chapter 3, para. 8

3   There has been an increasing awareness of the difficulties facing many, if not the majority, of applicants in presenting individual complaints under the Sex Discrimination Act. A lack of direct evidence, which is the usual situation, requires that inferences of discrimination, where appropriate, should be drawn. The appellate courts have stated that unless appropriate inferences of discrimination can be drawn, anti-discrimination legislation will be largely defeated. The Commission is concerned that the problem identified by the appellate courts may have already sapped the resolve of many would-be complainants, which the Commission believes may have contributed substantially to the reduction of the number of individual cases under the Sex Discrimination Act. . . . As the number reduces so the level of practical awareness of the scope of the legislation is also likely to reduce, resulting in a vicious circle of decline in confidence in the effectiveness of the legislation. The Commission has reached the conclusion, therefore, that there should be a more equitable distribution of the burden of proof in sex discrimination cases, and has so recommended to the Secretary of State.
8   Complaints relating to recruitment have consistently, over the last five years, formed a substantial proportion of the enquiries coming to the Employment Section. This year they represent approximately 30% of the employment issues on which the Commission has been called upon to advise under the provisions of the Sex Discrimination Act. . . . As has been noted in previous Annual Reports, where there is not a glaring disparity between the qualifications and experience of the successful and rejected applicants, sex or marriage discrimination in recruitment can be extremely difficult to prove. This is one reason why the Commission is recommending that the burden of proof under the two Acts should be more equitably distributed between the applicant and the respondent.

In their Annual Report for 1981, the EOC reiterate their concern with difficulties of proof of discrimination in recruitment, and relate this concern to the general problem of job segregation in the sense not of formal barriers to entry into jobs for men or for women, but of acceptance of segregated patterns of entry into jobs by all concerned. The following extracts serve to make this point:

EOC Annual Report for 1981, Chapter 3, paras. 1 and 5

Job Segregation
1   The segregation of work into jobs performed traditionally by men and women is widespread, and its effect on equal opportunities far reaching: it prevents women from claiming equal pay for lack of the necessary male comparison, and it prevents them from applying for jobs in the 'male' areas because they lack the necessary experience. The work performed by women is generally low paid, with limited prospects for advancement, and it is therefore essential that any barriers to women entering non-traditional areas are removed. One case referred to the Commission which highlights all the problems involved, showed the clear acceptance throughout the organisation of 'men's jobs' and 'women's jobs', a state of *de facto* segregation recognised by the management, the trade union officials and the workforce alike. The women felt that it would be very difficult for them to undertake the so-called 'men's jobs'. In the past, if

women applied for one of these jobs, they received no encouragement from either their union or the company. This had the cumulative effect of inhibiting women so that, even when they were eligible to apply for jobs, they failed to do so because of these attitudes.

Recruitment

5   Recruitment is the major source of complaints relating to employment received by the Commission. Although the Act has been in force for six years, complaints are still received from men and women in relation to directly as well as indirectly discriminatory recruitment procedures. Discriminatory recruitment practices obviously perpetuate job segregation, but it is difficult to prove discrimination, one problem being that it is frequently necessary to have information about the other candidates in order to begin to prove a case. Access to relevant information is a major obstacle for many complainants. The House of Lords decision in the case of *Nasse* v. *SRC (1979)* set out useful guidelines on the discovery of documents but it remains difficult for the unassisted applicant to set out proving his or her case. The Commission feels that its recommendation to Government that the burden of proof under the legislation should be more equitably distributed between the applicant and the respondent (see 5th Annual Report, Appendix 5) should help individuals in seeking a remedy.

The recent Annual Reports of the CRE serve both to emphasize the extent to which racial discrimination remains a problem in relation to recruitment for employment, and to identify some specific forms of that discrimination which might not be fully identified from a reading of the case-law. One such manifestation of the problem appears from the following extract from the Report for 1980:

CRE Annual Report for 1980, section on Employment,
paras. 1–3

We continue to find evidence that many employers are still rejecting applicants for work because of their colour and some do not even acknowledge that they are discriminating. We are also finding evidence that indirect discrimination, as well as direct, is extensive and that it is largely unrecognised by those who practise it.

The results of a research study, 'Half a Chance', funded by the Commission and the Nottingham and District Community Relations Council, indicate that many firms in Nottingham were discriminating against young black applicants for white collar jobs. The method used in the study was to send three letters of application for clerical vacancies advertised in the 'Nottingham Evening Post' between 1977 and 1979. Two of the letters made it clear, for example, by the applicant's name or a reference to date of arrival in this country, that the applicant was black. In nearly half of the one hundred firms tested employers rejected black applicants in favour of white candidates whose job experience and qualifications were not better. When tests of the same type were conducted nationally by Political and Economic Planning in 1973/4, it was found that the level of discrimination against applicants for white collar vacancies was about one in three.

The Nottingham tests therefore suggest that this type of racial discrimination is increasing. When asked to comment on these findings, the Deputy Director of the Nottingham Chamber of Commerce said that, as some black people may have failed to do a good job in the past, this might be in the employer's mind and be the 'real reason for discrimination, rather than colour' (*Daily Telegraph*, 13 November 1980). This seems to suggest that it would be justifiable for a black applicant to be rejected, not on his merits, but because of stereotyped views about blacks, and if such an attitude is typical of Nottingham employers the results of the study are not surprising.

Both that Report and the CRE's Annual Report for 1981 point to word-of-mouth recruitment or recruitment by personal recommendation as a major obstacle to equality of opportunity; in the Report for 1981, reference is also made to the application of unjustifiable standards of oral and written English, and to the discriminatory consequences of the practice of giving preference to the sons or relatives of employees, particularly in the selection of apprentices. Problems of this kind are further explored in the Commission's report into its investigation of recruitment practices at the Coventry plant of the tractor manufacturers Massey Ferguson, which was published at the end of 1982. The CRE found evidence of both direct and indirect discrimination, and concluded that the main reason for the under-representation of black workers was the recruitment of hourly paid employees by reliance on unsolicited letters of application, which opened the way to the application of unjustifiable criteria related to linguistic ability and work experience, and gave disproportionate access to friends and relatives of existing predominantly white employees. The CRE Report for 1981 also urges the importance of certain types of governmental action for ensuring the effective implementation of the policies of the legislation, as the following extract will explain:

CRE Report for 1981, section 6, p. 11

EMPLOYMENT

Government Policy

Three areas of Government policy which have a strong influence on equal employment opportunities have been emphasised in previous Annual Reports: the Civil Service's employment policy, approval for our draft Code of Practice and an equal opportunity clause in Government contracts. In one of these areas there has now been some progress – our own long-standing recommendations that the Civil Service should use ethnic monitoring to assess its record on equal opportunity. In December 1981, the Home Secretary agreed that more emphasis should be placed on ethnic monitoring to help in the attack on racial disadvantage and announced that the Civil Service would hold an 'experimental census of the ethnic composition of some non-industrial grades', in order to establish a sound statistical basis for monitoring Civil Service employment. While this is a limited advance, it could pave the way to real progress if it leads to comprehensive monitoring across all Departments.

We formally transmitted our draft Code of Practice in employment to the Secretary of State for Employment at the end of 1981, following extensive consultations during previous years. In submitting the draft, the essential principle of the Code was stressed: that in addition to explaining the basic requirements of the legislation, practical guidance must be given to enable these to be translated into effective action. The draft provides such guidance for all aspects of selection and employment practice and is aimed at employers, trade unions, employees and employment agencies. We hope that the Secretary of State for Employment will ask Parliament to approve the Code without delay.

On the third issue, the Government has not undertaken any review of the equal opportunity clause in Government contracts or any assessment of compliance by contractors. This remains a crucial area in which Government action is needed and one which has long been recognised as a major aid in the United States anti-discrimination programme. Progress on this issue was called for by several black organisations during the year, as demonstrated by a resolution presented to Government after a conference co-ordinated by the Confederation of Indian Organisations.

The foregoing extract is one illustration of the fact that the CRE and EOC have, and see themselves as having, a normative role as well as a descriptive or reporting role in relation to the social operation of their respective areas of discrimination legislation. Both bodies have made use of their powers to make proposals for changes to their parent legislation. The EOC in 1980 submitted a comprehensive list of proposals for amending both the SDA 1975 and the EqPA 1970, including a recommendation for a more equitable distribution of the burden of proof in sex discrimination cases. (The proposals are summarized in Appendix 5 of the EOC's Annual Report for 1980.) The CRE in July 1983 circulated a consultative paper on recommendations for changes resulting from the review of the RRA 1976. That paper suggests alterations to the definition of direct and indirect discrimination, such as the substitution of 'practice or situation' for 'requirement or condition', the partial reallocation of the burden of proof of discrimination, the extension of the non-pecuniary heads of damage for which compensation can be awarded, the extension also of compensation for indirect discrimination to unintentional indirect discrimination, a complete revision of the formal investigation procedure, and the introduction of compulsory ethnic monitoring whereby the CRE would scrutinize records of the ethnic origins of applicants and employees that employers would be under an obligation to maintain.

The CRE and EOC have also used their powers of proposing codes of practice as a way of giving effect to their concerns about the social operation of the discrimination legislation. Early in 1983, the CRE formally submitted its proposed Code of Practice to the Secretary of State for Employment. It is to be noted that the Employment Committee of the House of Commons had reported critically upon the draft of the code that had been submitted to it, and that the CRE, while not accepting the Committee's recommendation that the code should not apply to small firms until it had been in force for three years, did revise the draft to acknowledge the less exacting applicability of the Code to small firms. The following extract from the Code, which was approved by Parliament in August 1983 and came into force in April 1984, indicates how the CRE has supplemented the legislation to deal with the problems revealed by the social operation of the provisions relating to recruitment, training and selection for employment.

Race Relations Code of Practice, SI 1983 No. 1081

Recruitment, promotion, transfer, training and dismissal

Sources of recruitment

Advertisements

1.5 When advertising job vacancies it is unlawful for employers:

to publish an advertisement which indicates, or could reasonably be understood as indicating, an intention to discriminate against applicants from a particular racial group. (For exceptions see the Race Relations Act);

1.6 It is therefore recommended that:

(a) employers should not confine advertisements unjustifiably to those areas or publications which would exclude or disproportionately reduce the numbers of applicants of a particular racial group.

(b) employers should avoid prescribing requirements such as length of residence or experience in the UK and where a particular qualification is required it should be made clear that a fully comparable qualification obtained overseas is as acceptable as a UK qualification.

1.7 In order to demonstrate their commitment to equality of opportunity it is recommended that where employers send literature to applicants, this should include a statement that they are equal opportunity employers.

Employment agencies

1.8 When recruiting through employment agencies, job centres, careers offices and schools, it is unlawful for employers:

(a) to give instructions to discriminate, for example by indicating that certain groups will or will not be preferred. (For exceptions see the Race Relations Act);

(b) to bring pressure on them to discriminate against members of a particular racial group. (For exceptions, as above).

1.9 In order to avoid indirect discrimination it is recommended that employers should not confine recruitment unjustifiably to those agencies, job centres, careers offices and schools which, because of their particular source of applicants, provide only or mainly applicants of a particular racial group.

Other sources

1.10 It is unlawful to use recruitment methods which exclude or disproportionately reduce the numbers of applicants of a particular racial group and which cannot be shown to be justifiable. It is therefore recommended that employers should not recruit through the following methods:

(a) recruitment, solely or in the first instance, through the recommendations of existing employees where the workforce concerned is wholly or predominantly white or black and the labour market is multi-racial.

(b) procedures by which applicants are mainly or wholly supplied through trade unions where this means that only members of a particular racial group, or a disproportionately high number of them, come forward.

Sources for promotion and training

1.11 It is unlawful for employers to restrict access to opportunities for promotion or training in a way which is discriminatory. It is therefore recommended that:

job and training vacancies and the application procedure should be made known to all eligible employees, and not in such a way as to exclude or disproportionately reduce the numbers of applicants from a particular racial group.

Selection for recruitment, promotion, transfer, training and dismissal

1.12 It is unlawful to discriminate, not only in recruitment, promotion, transfer and training, but also in the arrangements made for recruitment and in the ways of affording access to opportunities for promotion, transfer or training.

Selection criteria and tests

1.13 In order to avoid direct or indirect discrimination it is recommended that selection criteria and tests are examined to ensure that they are related to job requirements and are not unlawfully discriminatory (see Introduction paragraph 3.2). For example:

(a) a standard of English higher than that needed for the safe and effective performance of the job or clearly demonstrable career pattern should not be required, or a higher level of educational qualification than is needed;

(b) in particular, employers should not disqualify applicants because they are unable to complete an application form unassisted unless personal completion of the form is a valid test of the standard of English required for safe and effective performance of the job;

(c) overseas degrees, diplomas and other qualifications which are comparable with UK qualifications should be accepted as equivalents, and not simply be assumed to be of an inferior quality;

(d) selection tests which contain irrelevant questions or exercises on matters which may be unfamiliar to racial minority applicants should not be used (for example, general knowledge questions on matters more likely to be familiar to indigenous applicants);

(e) selection tests should be checked to ensure that they are related to the job's requirements, ie an individual's test markings should measure ability to do or train for the job in question.

Treatment of applicants, shortlisting, interviewing and selection

1.14 In order to avoid direct or indirect discrimination it is recommended that:

(a) Gate, reception and personnel staff should be instructed not to treat casual or formal applicants from particular racial groups less favourably than others. These instructions should be confirmed in writing.

(b) In addition, staff responsible for shortlisting, interviewing and selecting candidates should be:

clearly informed of selection criteria and of the need for their consistent application; given guidance or training on the effects which generalised assumptions and prejudices about race can have on selection decisions; made aware of the possible misunderstandings that can occur in interviews between persons of different cultural background.

(c) Wherever possible, shortlisting and interviewing should not be done by one person alone but should at least be checked at a more senior level.

Genuine occupational qualification

1.15 Selection on racial grounds is allowed in certain jobs where being of a particular racial group is a genuine occupational qualification for that job. An example is where the holder of a particular job provides persons of a racial group with personal services promoting their welfare, and those services can most effectively be provided by a person of that group.

Transfers and training

1.16 In order to avoid direct or indirect discrimination it is recommended that:

(a) staff responsible for selecting employees for transfer to other jobs should be instructed to apply selection criteria without unlawful discrimination;

(b) industry or company agreements and arrangements or custom and practice on job transfers should be examined and amended if they are found to contain requirements or conditions which appear to be indirectly discriminatory. For example if employees of a particular racial group are concentrated in particular sections, the transfer arrangements should be examined to see if they are unjustifiably and unlawfully restrictive and amended if necessary.

(c) staff responsible for selecting employees for training, whether induction, promotion or skill training should be instructed not to discriminate on racial grounds;

(d) selection criteria for training opportunities should be examined to ensure that they are not indirectly discriminatory.

The EOC has also taken steps towards proposing a code of practice, having in 1982 issued a revised consultative draft of such a code. It is interesting to compare and contrast its provisions relating to recruitment with those of the CRE code. On the whole the CRE is more specific in the guidance that it gives than the EOC code.

EOC Revised Consultative Draft Code, paras 9–21

PART I – THE ROLE OF GOOD EMPLOYMENT PRACTICES IN ELIMINATING SEX AND MARRIAGE DISCRIMINATION

9. This section of the Code describes those good employment practices which will help to eliminate discrimination. It recommends the establishment and use of consistent criteria for selection, training, promotion, redundancy and dismissal procedures which are made known to all employees. Without this consistency, decisions can be subjective and leave the way open for discrimination to occur.

Recruitment

10. The Act says:

It is unlawful for employers, unless the job is covered by an exception, to discriminate directly or indirectly on the grounds of sex or marriage
– in the arrangements they make for deciding who should be offered a job
– in any terms of employment
– by refusing or omitting to offer a person employment
[Ss.6(1)(a); 6(1)(b); 6(1)(c)]

11. It is therefore recommended that:

(a) any qualifications or requirements applied to a job which effectively restrict it to applicants of one sex or to single people, should be retained only if they are justifiable in terms of the job to be done.

(b) any age limits should be retained only if they are necessary for the job. An unjustifiable age limit could constitute unlawful indirect discrimination, for example against women who have taken time out of employment for child-rearing.

(c) where trade unions uphold such qualifications or requirements as union policy, they should amend that policy in the light of any potentially unlawful effect.

(d) each individual should be assessed according to his or her personal capability to carry out a given job. It should not be assumed that men only or women only will be able to perform certain kinds of work.

Genuine occupational qualifications (GOQs)
The Act says:

Selection on the grounds of sex is unlawful except for certain jobs when a person's sex is a genuine occupational qualification (GOQ) for that job

[Ss.7(1); 7(2); 7(3) and 7(4)]

13. There are very few instances in which a job will qualify for a GOQ on grounds of sex. Some jobs may be open to one sex exclusively for example, where considerations of privacy and decency or authenticity are involved. The Act expressly excludes strength and stamina as a GOQ. When a GOQ exists for a job, it applies also to promotion, transfer or training for that job.

14. In some instances, the GOQ will apply where some of the duties only are covered. A GOQ will not be valid, however, where members of the appropriate sex are already employed in sufficient numbers to meet the employer's likely requirements without undue inconvenience. For example, in a job where certain sales assistants may be required to undertake changing room duties, it might not be lawful to claim a GOQ, in respect of *all* the assistants on the grounds that any of them might be required to undertake changing room duties from time to time.

15. It is therefore recommended that:

– A job for which the GOQ exception was genuinely used in the past should be re-examined if the post falls vacant to see whether the GOQ still applies. Circumstances may well have changed, rendering the GOQ inapplicable.

Sources of recruitment
16. The Act says:

It is unlawful unless the job is covered by an exception:

(i) To discriminate on grounds of sex or marriage in the arrangements made for determining who should be offered employment whether recruiting by advertisements, through employment agencies, Jobcentres, or career offices.

(ii) To imply that applications from one sex or from married people will not be considered.

[S.6(1)(a)]

It is also unlawful:

To instruct or put pressure on others to omit to refer for employment people of one sex or married people unless the job is covered by an exception.

[Ss.39 and 40].

When advertising job vacancies, it is unlawful:

for employers to publish or cause to be published an advertisement which indicates or might reasonably be understood as indicating an intention to discriminate on grounds of sex or marriage.

[s.38]

17. It is therefore recommended that:

Advertising

(a) job advertising should be carried out in such a way as to encourage applications from suitable candidates of both sexes. This can be achieved both by wording of the advertisements and, for example, by placing advertisements in publications likely to reach both sexes. All advertising material and accompanying literature relating to employment or training issues should be reviewed to ensure that it avoids presenting men and women in stereotyped roles. Such stereotyping tends to perpetuate sex segregation in jobs and can also lead people of the opposite sex to believe that they would be unsuccessful in applying for particular jobs.

(b) where vacancies are filled by promotion or transfer, they should be published to all eligible employees in such a way that they do not restrict applications from both sexes.

(c) recruitment solely or primarily by word of mouth in a workforce of predominantly one sex should be avoided.

(d) where applications are supplied through trade unions and only members of one sex come forward, this should be discussed with the unions and an alternative approach adopted.

Schools

18. Employers notify vacancies to the Careers Service, but if dealing directly with single sex schools, they should ensure that both boys' and girls' schools are approached.

Selection tests

19. (a) tests should be specifically relating to the job requirements and should measure an individual's actual or inherent ability to do or train for the particular work or career.

(b) tests should be checked regularly to ensure that they remain relevant and free from any unjustifiable bias, either in content or in scoring mechanism.

Applications and interviewing

20. The Act says:

It is unlawful unless the job is covered by an exception for an employer to discriminate on grounds of sex or marriage by refusing or deliberately omitting to offer employment.

[S.6(1)(c)]

21. It is therefore recommended that:

(a) employers should ensure that personnel staff, line managers and all other employees, who may come into contact with job applicants, should be trained in the provisions of the SDA, including the fact that it is unlawful to instruct or put pressure on others to discriminate.

(b) applications from men and women should be processed in exactly the same way. For example, there should not be separate lists of male and female or married and single applicants. All those handling applications and conducting interviews should be trained in the avoidance of unlawful discrimination and records of interviews kept, where practicable, showing why applicants were rejected.

(c) questions should relate to the requirements of the job. Where it is necessary to assess whether personal circumstances will affect performance of the job (for example, where it involves unsocial hours or extensive travel) this should be discussed objectively without detailed questions based on assumptions about marital status, children, and domestic obligations. Questions about marriage plans or family intentions should not be asked, as they could be construed as showing bias against women. Information necessary for personal records can be collected after a job offer has been made.

So far as the assessments of independent researchers are concerned, we have the benefit of two extensive studies of the social operation of the employment provisions of the SDA. The first is contained in the Department of Employment Research Paper on *Equal Pay and Opportunities* by Snell, Glucklich and Povall (DE Research Paper No. 20, April 1981). The second is contained in a recent book by Chiplin and Sloane, *Tackling Discrimination at the Workplace* (1982). Snell, Glucklich and Povall reach conclusions very comparable with those emerging from the recent annual reports of the EOC about the failure of the legislation, for the most part, to have any great impact upon the fundamentals of the problem of sex discrimination in employment. They comment that when the legislation first came in, many employers, in the absence of any effective pressure to the contrary, chose to do as little as possible and to keep changes, costs and disruption to a minimum; in the organizations studied, equal pay was seen as a one-off exercise now completed, and equal opportunity was a non-event (at p. 92). They conclude that legal intervention in these kinds of issues is only really successful when supported by social attitudes, and that there should be a stronger stimulus towards equality for women at work both by voluntary and by legislative means (at pp. 97–8). Chiplin and Sloane assert that the authors of that study were expecting rather more from the legislation than it could deliver and did not seem to have taken into full consideration the many important economic forces at work, though they had succeeded in illustrating the relative ineffectiveness of the legislation (op. cit., p. 130). The general thrust of their work is towards the conclusion that the problems at issue are too deeply rooted in the economic and social structure of the labour market to be susceptible of solution by anti-discrimination legislation. The point is made in the following concluding passage of their book. The reader may usefully ask himself whether these are valid conclusions, and whether comparable conclusions would result from the same kind of study of the working of the provisions concerning racial discrimination in relation to recruitment for employment.

B. Chiplin and P. J. Sloane, *Tackling Discrimination at the Workplace* (1982), pp. 131–2

But, even if the law is 'toughened' in the ways outlined, will it make much difference? Our view is that one really must examine the more fundamental factors at work and be aware of the economic implications of these forces. It is clear to us that, in explaining the labour-market position of women, discrimination at the workplace is less significant than factors that are deep-rooted in social attitudes and behaviour and which may themselves have economic causes. We have to repeat that what happens within and to the family is to a large degree the crucial issue. Family responsibilities have widespread ramifications throughout the labour market. Indeed, if there were to be complete role-reversal, such that it was males who left work to look after children and females who had full labour-force participation over their working life, we would predict that in the long run male average earnings would be substantially lower than female average earnings and that men would be concentrated in lower-paid and lower-status jobs. This would not arise from any discrimination practised by women but simply from the value of the services supplied to the labour market. Market earnings result from the interaction of two sets of forces – those reflecting the demand side and those emanating from the supply side. Discrimination is a demand-side phenomenon and the problem in evaluating and monitoring discrimination is to determine how much of the difference between the earnings (or occupation level, hiring rate or promotion rate) of two or more groups of workers is due to differences in their supply characteristics and how much to pure discrimination by employers or members of other groups. Our own and other studies would suggest that supply-side differences are the major contributory factors. Legislation can remove the more blatant abuses, but by itself it should not be expected to produce a radical alteration in the relative position of women in the labour market. If women are to approach the earnings and occupational levels of men, it is necessary for a complete reappraisal of social attitudes to take place; and in particular there has to be a reallocation of time between housework in its broadest sense, market work and leisure between the sexes. The question still remains whether such a re-allocation would benefit the family. If it does, and as technology makes it increasingly possible, we might see a substantial improvement in the relative earnings of women over the next few decades. But it will be a slow process. On the other hand, if there really are economic advantages in the family unit as presently organised, it is likely that women in general will continue to earn substantially less than men and remain in lower-grade occupations despite the efforts of equal-opportunities legislation.

(e) The significance for labour law generally of the discrimination legislation

The foregoing discussion of the aims, interpretation and social operation of the employment provisions of the sex and race discrimination legislation may enable us to draw some conclusions about the significance of these provisions, so far as they relate to selection for employment, for labour law generally. The institutions and researchers who provided our sources of information on the social operation of the legislation were quite properly concerned with the extent to which the general aims of the legislation had been achieved or were achievable in relation to employment, rather than with the impact of this kind of legislation on our system of labour law seen as a whole. What conclusions are made possible by reversing that emphasis?

In a general sense it is clear that the discrimination legislation has served to open up the whole area of recruitment for employment to legislative control and has challenged the perception that selection for employment is for some reason not susceptible to legal control in the way, for instance, that termination of employment is seen to be. The writings of both Lustgarten and McCrudden also suggest a more particular sense in which these statutory provisions may be thought to alter the outlook of labour law, namely by introducing a new ideal pattern by reference to which employers' decisions in relation, for instance, to recruitment may be judged. Lustgarten makes the point in relation to the notion of indirect discrimination, and in particular the notion of justifiability, which should in his view be understood as demanding that employers' criteria for decisions in this area should be strictly job-related. He describes the significance of that demand in the following terms:

> L. Lustgarten, 'The New Meaning of Discrimination' [1978]
> *Public Law* 178 at p. 195

Only requirements inherent in the job may be regarded as justifiable. This seemingly abstract concept is in fact quite realistic, for it forces employers at first instance and then tribunals to make a practical appraisal of job content, cocking a sceptical eye at traditional restrictions and the more recent, albeit limited, vogue for credentials and testing. The result will surely be to eliminate many practices that have excluded able people and have been carried on primarily through habit and neglect. In numerical terms, more whites than non-whites will be the gainers. An effective anti-discrimination law is a powerful force for what is truly 'rationalisation' of industry – the clearing away of mythologies surrounding employment practices, and their replacement by prerequisites that demonstrably help select the most competent people.

Thus it will be seen that the anti-discrimination legislation tends to challenge at a fundamental level the general absence of legal control over the process of selection for hiring, and hence tends to reduce the contrast between that process and the process of termination of employment, where legal control is, as we shall see, extensive and general.

McCrudden has made a similar point in terms of the contrast between *Gesellschaft* values and *Gemeinschaft* values in relation to employment (see 'Institutional Discrimination' (1982) 2 *OJLS* (303 at 361). The two terms may best be translated (from the German) in this particular context as, respectively, commercial association and commercial community. By Gesellschaft values are meant those of achievement, efficiency, rationality and objectivity; these are contrasted with Gemeinschaft values which attach importance to intuitive judgements, humanistic considerations not susceptible of empirical verification, the preservation of tradition and local autonomy, and membership of social or ethnic groups. The suggestion is that the discrimination legislation demands compliance, or at least greater compliance than would otherwise exist, with a Gesellschaft model of the employment relationship, and that in so doing the legislation seeks to displace a Gemeinschaft-like approach to management which is thought to be widespread in British employment practice and which is thought to help to maintain and perpetuate sex and race discrimination in employment. This idea of the tension between these two contrasting sets of values is helpful to an understanding of the aims of the legislation and of the social operation of the legislation. It may also shed some light on the analysis of judicial approaches to the legislation. It is, for example, very broadly speaking possible to see the EAT as sharing the commitment of the legislators to the promotion of Gesellschaft values as a way of reducing discrimination, while it is possible to see the Court of Appeal as more reluctant to accept the challenge to Gemeinschaft values. But, above all, this type of analysis indicates the significance of this legislation to labour law generally, and sets up a kind of inquiry that will arise at a number of other points in the course of this book, most obviously, though not solely, in relation to the unfair dismissal legislation. It also helps to indicate the significance of the other types of legal control which exist in relation to formation of employment, to the consideration of which we turn in the next section of this chapter. Before doing so, we shall briefly refer to legal controls upon selection for employment other than those provided by the sex and race discrimination legislation.

(f) Conclusion – other legal controls over selection for employment

As we have indicated, the employment provisions of the sex and race discrimination legislation constitute much the most important of the legal controls over selection for employment. We have also seen from the first section of the present chapter that some of the measures which we have classified as measures concerned with the control of the size of labour supply or labour demand may also be regarded as being in part at least concerned with the control, from a certain point of view, of selection for employment. This is true, for instance, of the EEC provisions concerning freedom of movement of workers within the EEC member states (see above, p. 21). In this concluding subsection, we shall briefly draw attention to yet further areas of actual or potential legal control over selection for employment. We do this partly for the sake of descriptive completeness, but partly also with a view to indicating the variety of ways in which the law may become concerned with the control of selection for employment, and the range of methods by which such control may be exerted. We shall refer firstly to the two prominent areas of the legislation relating to disabled persons and the placement activities of the public employment service. We shall then mention other areas such as that of rehabilitation of offenders, trade-union membership or activity, and the role of trade unions in relation to selection for employment. We shall then conclude with some assessment of the total extent and importance of legal control over selection for employment, and its relation to the other aspects of the law relevant to the constituting of the employment relationship which are to be discussed later in this chapter.

An important type of control over recruitment is that provided for by the Disabled Persons (Employment) Acts 1944 and 1958, which normally require an employer of twenty persons or more to employ a quota of at least three per cent of persons registered as disabled. The legislation requires such employers not to take or offer to take into his employment any person other than one registered as disabled if, after offering such employment, the result would be that he was employing less than his quota, unless he has a permit to do so from the Department of Employment. The legislation also empowers the Secretary of State for Employment to designate classes of employment as offering specially suitable opportunities for the employment of disabled persons, and where that has been done (as it has, for instance, in relation to carpark attendants), the legislation restricts that class of employment to the registered disabled. An employer is also required not to discontinue the employment of a disabled person, except for reasonable cause, if the consequence would be that he was employing less than his quota of disabled persons. Failure to comply with these requirements may constitute an offence punishable with a fine, but the legislation does not provide remedies for the individual disabled person and does not make provisions for enforcement or policing of the legislation by an administrative agency. This, coupled with the fact that the number of persons registered as disabled has fallen considerably since the early years of the legislation, has meant that the standards set by the legislation are not in practice maintained. The Manpower Services Commission has over the years monitored the working of the legislation, and published in 1981 a review of the Quota Scheme for Disabled People. That review concluded that, with the gradual change in the nature of the social problem involved, as disablement came to consist predominantly of illness, often of a partly or entirely mental kind rather than of injuries sustained on war service, the quota system had ceased to work effectively and ought to be supplemented by general legislation and a code of practice to implement a principle of non-discrimination against disabled people in employment whether registered or unregistered. This recommendation has not yet been acted upon, but is important for the purposes of this section in so far as it amounts to a conclusion that the one piece of positive quota legislation in our labour law system could usefully be replaced by anti-discrimination legislation more comparable with the employment provisions of the sex and race discrimination legislation. To that extent it would seem that the latter legislation has come to be accepted as providing the model for legislative provision of fair opportunities for minority groups in the labour market.

Another type of indirect control over recruitment, whose importance has not been sufficiently acknowledged by labour lawyers, consists in the placement activity of the public employment service. This service of assistance with finding jobs and filling job vacancies, or job brokerage service, used to be provided by the Department of Employment, but was from 1973 entrusted to the Employment Service Agency under the general control of the Manpower Services Commission, and was from 1981 transferred to the Manpower Services Commission directly, with the abolition of its subordinate agencies (see above, p. 29). The placement activity of the public employment service used to be carried out by the employment exchanges and employment offices, but the former have been replaced by Jobcentres, and a distinct Professional and Executive Recruitment organization has been set up. The operation of the public employment service, although best considered as a control upon selection for employment, also has implications for the control of labour supply and demand, and so touches upon the concerns discussed in the second section of the present chapter. Indeed in an article on the subject in 1978 ('The Placement Activity of the Employment Service Agency', (1978) 16 *BJIR* 309), A. McGregor drew attention to the surprising lack of detailed research into the labour market effects of the placement activities now carried out by the MSC. There are certainly indications that the public employment service has an impact on the form in which employment relationships are constituted. Thus from 1981 onwards the Jobcentres began to handle self-employment opportunities and were notified of 25,000 such opportunities in the first six months of doing so. Furthermore, the *Report on the General Employment Service* prepared in 1982 as part of the Rayner review of efficiency in government organizations recommended that the public employment service should no longer advertise temporary jobs separately from other jobs and should stop using the word 'temp' while not withdrawing from that market sector. In that way, ostensibly in the pursuit of greater operational efficiency, the public employment service is steered towards a greater integration of the temporary employment market into the general labour market, with presumably a corresponding increase in the proportion of employment arranged on a temporary basis.

The most obvious impact of the placement activities of the public employment service, however, is upon patterns of selection for employment. The MSC has a generalized commitment to maintaining and facilitating equality of access to employment on the part of ethnic minorities, and it would be valuable to know what effect the operation of the placement services has in this respect. One might also expect that the placement activities might have a significant impact on the equality of opportunity of women in the labour market. The research findings so far available provide some information about the impact of the work of Jobcentres on one aspect at least of selection for employment. The recently published report of the results of a fieldwork study (Ford, Keil, Beardsworth and Bryman, 'How employers see the public employment service' (1982) *Employment Gazette* 466) suggests that the great rise in unemployment has imposed on the public employment service an increased need to screen recruits on behalf of employers if the brokerage function is to be carried out effectively, and that an increased emphasis on meeting the requirements of employers by means of screening is likely to be to the detriment of the position of the long-term unemployed.

Another form of control over discriminatory selection is exercised by the Rehabilitation of Offenders Act 1974. This makes it improper to exclude any person from an office, profession, occupation or employment on the grounds that he has a criminal conviction where that conviction is deemed by the statute to have been 'spent' (s.4(3)(*b*)). The Act does not provide any civil remedy for the rehabilitated offender who is refused employment on the grounds of his 'spent' conviction; but it makes a provision which seems to afford him the self-help remedy of giving a negative answer to the question whether he has any previous convictions (s.4(2)).

A significant omission in the area of discriminatory selection consists in the absence of any control over exclusion on the grounds of trade-union membership, non-membership or activity. It is extremely hard to account for Parliament's failure to extend the legal control over this kind of discrimination as it relates to dismissal and to action taken in the course of employment (see below, pp. 521, 405) to selection for employment. The employer may lawfully refuse to engage an employee who belongs to or wishes to take part in the activities of a trade union, or he may tacitly apply the same condition on the basis of his belief that the applicant is a trade-union member or takes part in trade-union activities. As we shall see later (below, p. 180), in *City of Birmingham* v. *Beyer* [1977] IRLR 211, the EAT made it clear that the right of freedom of association conferred by the law of unfair dismissal would not be applied in such a way as to stop up the corresponding gap in the law concerning recruitment.

Finally we may briefly consider the role of trade unions in relation to selection for employment. Such control as trade unions exercise over selection for employment will be obtained through pre-entry closed shops rather than by collective bargaining, which will be concerned with levels of recruitment rather than with selection within those levels. Under the Dock Work Scheme, trade unions acquired a statutory role in relation to recruitment by reason of their representation on dock labour boards. Indeed, it was one of the main aims of the scheme when it was introduced in 1947 to create machinery for the joint regulation of recruitment and dismissal of dock workers. Apart from this, Parliament has neither conferred any role on the trade unions in the process of selection, nor, on the other hand, sought to regulate such control over the recruitment process as trade unions may in practice acquire, except that the legislation against sex and racial discrimination and the EEC free movement rules are applied to admission to and expulsion from trade unions and to their provision of access to any benefits, facilities or services (SDA 1975, s.12; RRA 1976, s.11; Reg. 1612/68, Art. 8(1)).

Where, by reason of the existence of a pre-entry closed shop, refusal of admission to a trade union brings about exclusion from employment, the courts may regulate such exclusion on the grounds of its arbitrariness (see below, pp. 624 *et seq.*). This form of control by the union is particularly strong where the union is in a position to select employees from among its own ranks, that is where there exists a 'labour supply' shop (see below, p. 634).

By way of conclusion of this discussion of control over selection for employment, we may perhaps consider why legal control over selection for employment is relatively limited compared with legal control over dismissal from employment. The answer is to be found at various levels. At one level, the existence of an employment relationship for a certain period of time is seen as conferring upon the employee some vested interest in the continuance of his employment, whether that vested interest is expressed in contractual terms, in terms of an entitlement to protection against unfair dismissal, or in terms of a claim to continuity of obligation upon the transfer of the employing enterprise. In all these ways the claim of the existing employee comes to seem in some sense superior to those of the applicant for employment. At another level, we may observe that the claim of the existing employee not to be dismissed is seen in individual terms, whereas the claim of the applicant for employment is generally limited to his claim as a member of a certain disfavoured group. This may be seen as reflecting the difficulty of the situation of the applicant for employment. There is no pre-existing relationship between the employer and the applicant for employment by which the fairness of the employer's decision in relation to that particular applicant can be judged. The overall result is that the employee comes to acquire a heavily protected legal status not only *vis-à-vis* the employer but also in contrast to the position of the unemployed person seeking work. As that latter category becomes both larger and more centrally placed within our society, perhaps we may expect to see some shift in these relative positions.

Thus far we have considered the question of legal control over recruitment for employment as a subject distinct from that of the control of terms of employment. Yet these two topics are integrally linked because one may be free to contract with X on any terms one chooses, but with Y only on certain terms. For instance, one might be free to employ an adult male for any number of hours per week but a female under eighteen for only a certain number of hours per week. On the other hand, one may be free to employ X only if the same terms are offered as those on which Y is employed, as for instance where Y is a man and X is a woman whose circumstances are so comparable that it would be unlawful discrimination to offer her employment on different terms. We may observe in passing, for instance, how the EEC Council Regulation 1612 of 1968 deals with discrimination in selection and discrimination in terms as separate issues (see above, pp. 21–2). However, outside the province of specific legislative controls on certain types of discrimination, the employer of labour is accorded a wide freedom of choice not only as to the terms upon which he offers employment but also as to the very form in which the employment relationship is constituted. Where the terms on which employment is offered differ sufficiently widely, the difference is and should be seen as one of kind and not just degree. It has long been accepted that there is a difference of kind between the employee and the independent contractor, and it is arguable that various sub-classifications of the employment relationship itself should also be regarded as expressing differences in kind; for instance, the distinction between full-time employees and part-time employees (see below, p. 100) or the distinction between fixed-term employees and employees whose employment is terminable by notice (see below, pp. 432–5). Because we regard these differentiations between types of employment as fundamental and because we envisage them as giving rise to new problems of legal control in the future, we devote the concluding section of our discussion of control of formation of the employment relationship to a consideration of legal control of the *form* in which the employment relationship is constituted.

4 Control over the form in which the employment relationship is constituted

(a) Introduction – the choice between employment relationships

In our discussion of legal controls upon the process of recruitment we have so far addressed ourselves to the control of the labour market and to the various aspects of the employer's selection of those with whom he wishes to enter into an employment relationship. We now turn to consider the controls upon the employer's choice of form in which to contract for the supply of labour. Thus, a basic decision to be taken as to the form of the relationship is whether it is to be constituted under a contract of employment or under a contract between employer and independent contractor, that is a contract for services. Within the area of the contract of employment, we shall see in a later chapter (pp. 318 *et seq.*) how the choice of payment system can have a crucial effect on the social and economic characteristics of the relationship, in particular upon its allocation between the parties of risks connected with unavailability of work or unavailability for work. It is also possible to establish radical differentiations between types of employment relationship according to the duration of the contract – between, for instance, fixed-term employees and employees whose employment is terminable by notice, between permanent and temporary employees, between established employees and replacement employees (cf. ECPA 1978, s.61). Another differentiation can be based on the length of the employee's working hours – between, that is, full-time employees and part-time employees. There is a further differentiation, now assuming increasing importance, between the directly employed employee and the employee who is employed through an intermediary – that is to say, an agency worker. Finally, one can differentiate significantly according to the place of employment, as there is still a large and significant category of homeworkers. We now proceed to consider what influence the state exerts over the choice between the various different categories of employment relationship.

We wish to suggest that the discussion of the choice of employment relationships and the role of the law in relation thereto has come to require a new framework. The traditional discussion in this area seems to reflect an implicit acceptance of two key propositions. The first is that the choice between employment relationships comes down to a simple choice between the two alternatives of employment and self-employment, between the contract of service and the contract for services. The second is that this choice is primarily a legal choice, a choice made by lawyers or administrators in deciding what legal analysis to attribute to a given employment relationship. We wish to challenge that state of affairs by developing the following counter-propositions. Firstly, the choice between employment relationships, although it may be resoluble into a dual choice between employment and self-employment, should not be viewed solely in those terms, but rather as consisting of a choice between multiple possibilities which intersect with each other, such as those of casual or temporary employment, agency employment, part-time employment, and so forth. Secondly, this should be viewed primarily as a choice made by the parties to the relationship themselves, rather than by lawyers or administrators engaging in *post hoc* characterization of what the parties have arranged. Moreover the parties in making this choice should be viewed as making a choice primarily of a social or economic rather than a legal character. Thirdly, the role of the law in relation to that choice should not be viewed exclusively as a role of characterization, but rather as a more complex role of which characterization is only one aspect, other aspects being concerned with policy choices as to whether to encourage or discourage a particular choice of employment relationship (such as that, for instance, of labour-only subcontracting), and as to the right legal régime to be accorded to each particular kind of employment relationship. Each of these counter-propositions needs to be developed slightly further if the case against orthodoxy is to be a convincing one.

Our first counter-proposition was that the choice between employment relationships should be viewed as a multiple choice. The point is very usefully made in a recent article by George Clark ('Recent developments in working patterns' (1982) *Employment Gazette* 284), where it argued that the traditional framework of employment has undergone major moves in recent years away from full-time work towards its two main alternatives of self-employment and part-time work. This sets up as it were a triple choice between employment relationships, and the alternatives can be further multiplied. However, this proposition is a controversial one, and we propose to return to that controversy at the conclusion of this chapter when we have described the details of the choice of employment relationships as we envisage it (see below, p. 110). The second counter-proposition was that the choice is primarily a social and economic one on the part of the employer and the worker. This view is usefully substantiated by Patricia Leighton, who has devoted an interesting research project to an empirical study of how this kind of choice was actually made by a sample of employers in industries involving outwork ('Contractual Arrangements in Selected Industries', Department of Employment Research Paper No. 39, February 1983), a study which compares and contrasts the approaches of employers and workers to this choice with the theoretical approaches of the courts to the same issues when carrying out the exercise of classification of the employment relationships so formed. It is also worth pointing out there exists a debate among economists about the reasons for this kind of choice, a debate which goes to show that the categories with which lawyers work in this field are not their sole invention or their sole property. Economists have conducted their corresponding debate under headings such as that of the theory of the firm, or the principal and agent problem. The reader is referred in particular to Alchian and Demsetz, 'Production, Information Costs, and Economic Organisation' ([1972] *American Economic Review* 777) and Hallagan, 'Self-selection by contractual choice and the theory of sharecropping' ([1978] *Bell Journal of Economics* 344). Our third counter-proposition was that the role of the law in relation to this kind of choice is a more complex one than that merely of characterization. We find a substantial amount of evidence to suggest that there is an increasing legal involvement in the process of establishing special legal régimes to meet the needs of particular types of employment relationship (such as those of temporary work or homeworking). This evidence will emerge in the course of an examination of the state of the law as it relates to the different choices between employment relationships that we have referred. We now proceed to that detailed discussion, having, as we hope, indicated the scope and purpose of the inquiry.

(b) Employees and independent contractors

In relation to the distinction between employees and independent contractors, the traditional role of both the common law and statute law has been, not that of controlling the choice between these two forms of the supply of labour but, on the contrary, that of leaving the parties to make their own choice and then differentiating the consequences according to the choice they have made. Admittedly a substantial number of statutory provisions accord like treatment to contracts of service and contracts personally to execute any work or labour. This dual classification, which is undoubtedly broader than the simple concept of employment under a contract of service, is used, for instance, in relation to manual workers under the Truck Acts 1831–1940 and is often used to define the term 'workers' as in the Industrial Courts Act 1919, the Wages Council Act 1979 and the Trade Union and Labour Relations Act 1974. (See *Chitty on Contracts*, 25th edn (1983), para. 3387.) But many statutory provisions are confined to employees as such, and in particular the statutory floor of employment protection rights is confined to employees under contracts of employment (see *Chitty*, 25th edn, para. 3385). The doctrine of vicarious liability in the law of tort has long been primarily attached to contracts of employment as such, and although the new framework for statutory duties in relation to health, safety and welfare established by the Health and Safety at Work Act 1974 applies generally to 'persons at work' (s.1(1)(*a*)) which includes the self-employed (s.52(1)), within that framework certain duties are still specifically imposed on employers to their employees (s.2). In these fields and in the fields also of social security law and the law of personal taxation, important rights and liabilities are ascribed by common law and by statute according to the choice made by the parties between these two broad categories of contractual relationships.

How, then, has this crucial distinction been drawn? Victorian judges found little difficulty in conceptualizing the distinction. They were content to view the employment relationship as characterized by subordination. They viewed the independent contractor, on the other hand, as making little or no sacrifice of his personal autonomy. As they viewed both subordinated service and autonomous independent contracting as necessary and stable features of the social structure, they found it both reasonably straightforward in practice and in accordance with their social and political principles to apply this twofold distinction rigidly.

Since the Second World War, however, it has come to be recognized that the employment relationship would have to be defined, both for practical and political reasons, in terms which avoided a simple 'control' test. It was Otto Kahn-Freund who first pointed the way to a new method of definition, aware as he was that a test based on control would lead to an over-narrow view of the scope of the contract of employment.

O. Kahn-Freund, Case Note (1951) 14 *MLR*
at pp. 505–8

This distinction was based upon the social conditions of an earlier age: it assumed that the employer of labour was able to direct and instruct the labourer as to the technical methods he should use in performing his work. In a mainly agricultural society and even in the earlier stages of the Industrial Revolution the master could be expected to be superior to the servant in the knowledge, skill and experience which had to be brought to bear upon the choice and handling of the tools. The control test was well suited to govern relationships like those between a farmer and an agricultural labourer (prior to agricultural mechanization), a craftsman and a journeyman, a householder and a domestic servant, and even a factory owner and an unskilled 'hand'. It reflects a state of society in which the ownership of the means of production coincided with the possession of technical knowledge and skill, and in which that knowledge and skill was largely acquired by being handed down from one generation to the next by oral tradition and not by being systematically imparted in institutions of learning from universities to technical schools. The control test postulates a combination of managerial and technical functions in the person of the employer, *i.e.*, what to modern eyes appears as an imperfect division of labour. The technical and economic developments of all industrial societies have nullified these assumptions. . . . What is, however, clear is that the control test is vanishing. This means that, in this respect, English law is coming much closer to some of the Continental systems. In France the test is whether the person doing the work is *'dans une situation de subordination'*, and this criterion which has been accepted by the Cour de Cassation does not mean *'une notion . . . de technicité'*. It means the submission of the employee to the employer's power *'de coordonner'*, *i.e.*, to organize. Otherwise, it is pointed out, there could be no contract of service, no *locatio conductio operarum* unless the employer possessed all the divergent technical capacities of the members of his staff. Similarly in Germany, where the test is that of 'dependence', which is very similar to the French idea of submission to the employer's co-ordinating power. This is another example of the similarity of developments in common law and 'civil law' systems which are simply enforced by the irresistible power of economic necessities.

On the other hand, even an 'organization' or 'integration' test, whilst it avoids the notion of subordination, still leaves open the problem of defining the nature of the relationship between the employee and the enterprise which employs him.

C. Drake, 'Wage Slave or Entrepreneur?' (1968) 31 MLR
at p. 417

If integration were to be used as the main test, there would remain the question of the type of integration to be used. In this country, it has been pointed out that 'the fact that the workers form an integral part of the company is ignored by the law' in contrast to the relationship between management and shareholders, although the latter may be less real in practice. In Germany, of the four streams of thinking about the corporation in a social market economy (entrepreneurial, neo-liberal, socializing and co-determinative), the latter, worker participation, has played a major part. Professor Michael P. Fogarty refers to the two views held in Germany concerning the corporation-worker relationship, namely, (a) the contract view, and (b) the incorporation view (*Eingliederung*), in which relationships are governed by participation in a community (*Gemeinschaft*). As we have seen, co-determination has, with certain exceptions, failed to make a major impact in the United Kingdom. If it did it would be another nail in the coffin of the control test.

Under the stress of these inherent difficulties, the attempt to draw a legal distinction between employment and self-employment has indeed 'collapsed in a maze of casuistry' (Kahn-Freund, op. cit., p. 502). The judges faced with this issue tend to proceed by starting with the 'right to control' test, but drawing attention to its shortcomings. They then invoke the notion of a 'multiplicity of factors' such as power of selection and dismissal which are said to point to the existence of an employment relationship. They then set up the contrasting model of a worker who is also an entrepreneur. They finally invoke a notion of 'consistency with a contract of service', which is entirely meaningless in the absence of a clear notion of the identifying attributes of a contract of service. Thus ill-equipped, the court proceeds to classify by an intuitive process the particular case before it. Through this mist, we can see the courts struggling to give effect to a sharp distinction in relation to employments which are truly equivocal as between the integrated and the independent working relationship. The classification for social security purposes of a part-time market research interviewer provides a good illustration.

Market Investigations Ltd v. *Minister of Social Security* [1969]
2 QB 173 (QBD)

COOKE J.: The observations of Lord Wright, of Denning L.J. and of the judges of the Supreme Court suggest that the fundamental test to be applied is this: 'Is the person who has engaged himself to perform these services performing them as a person in business on his own account?' If the answer to that question is 'yes', then the contract is a contract for services. If the answer is 'no', then the contract is a contract of service.

. . . The application of the general test may be easier in a case where the person who engages himself to perform the services does so in the course of an already established business of his own; but this factor is not decisive, and a person who engages himself to perform services for another may well be an independent contractor even though he has not entered into the contract in the course of an existing business carried on by him.

In the present case it is clear that on each occasion on which Mrs Irving engaged herself to act as an interviewer for a particular survey she agreed with the company, in consideration of a fixed remuneration, to provide her own work and skill in the performance of a service for the company. I therefore proceed to ask myself two questions: First, whether the extent and degree of the control exercised by the company, if no other factors were taken into account, be consistent with her being employed under a contract of service. Second, whether when the contract is looked at as a whole, its nature and provisions are consistent or inconsistent with its being a contract of service, bearing in mind the general test I have adumbrated.

As to the first question: The facts found by the Minister show that the control of the company is exercised at two stages. Before the interviewer engages herself for the particular survey, she will probably have seen the company's 'Interviewer's Guide'. This document contains detailed instructions on the technique of interviewing, and much of it is couched in imperative language.

. . . On the Minister's findings, I have no doubt that the instructions in the 'Interviewer's Guide', after having been seen by the interviewer, are incorporated into the terms of any contract which the interviewer may thereafter make with the company to participate in a particular survey.

The second stage of control comes after the interviewer has agreed to take part in a particular survey, that is to say, after the contract has been made. The interviewer is then sent instructions which according to the Interviewer's Guide give details of whom to interview, what to say to informants, how to handle the questionnaire and other forms, and also deal with contact with the office. In addition to that, the interviewer might in particular cases be required to attend the office of the company for instructions, or might receive instructions from a supervisor.

The control which the company had the right to exercise was, however, limited in various ways. They had no right to instruct Mrs Irving as to when she should do the work. The only requirement imposed on her was that the work should be completed within a specified period. During that period Mrs Irving was free to do similar work for other organizations, so that the company had no right to prohibit her from doing that. No doubt it would be agreed before Mrs Irving accepted the assignment that her work would be in a given area; if so, the company would have no right to send her to another area. In addition to those limitations on the right of the company to give instructions to her, there was a practical limitation on the possibility of giving instructions to her while actually working in the field, because, as found by the Minister, the supervisor would then have no means of getting into touch with her.

It is apparent that the control which the company had the right to exercise in this case was very extensive indeed. It was in my view so extensive as to be entirely consistent with Mrs Irving's being employed under a contract of service. The fact that Mrs Irving had a limited discretion as to when she should do the work was not in my view inconsistent with the existence of a contract of service. . . . Nor is there anything inconsistent with the existence of a contract of service in the fact that Mrs Irving was free to work for others during the relevant period. It is by no means a necessary incident of a contract of service that the servant is prohibited from serving any other employer. Again, there is nothing inconsistent with the existence of a contract of service in the master having no right to alter the place or area within which the servant has agreed to work. So far as concerns practical limitations on a master's power to give instructions to his servant, there must be many cases when such practical limitations exist. For example, a chauffeur in the service of a car hire company may, in the absence of radio communication, be out of reach of instructions for long periods.

I therefore turn to the second question, which is whether, when the contract is looked at as a whole, its nature and provisions are consistent or inconsistent with its being a contract of service.

Mr Pain, for the company, points first to the fact that Mrs Irving was appointed on each occasion to do a specific task at a fixed fee. He points to the fact that the company's officers were of the opinion that they could not have dismissed Mrs Irving in the middle of an assignment. He says that these factors are more consistent with the conception of a contract for services than a contract of service.

As to the first factor, appointment to do a specific task at a fixed fee, I do not think that this is inconsistent with the contract being a contract of service. See, for example, *Sadler* v. *Henlock* (1855) 4 E. & B. 570.

. . . Then Mr Pain says that the fact that the contract makes no provision for time off, sick pay and holidays, suggests that it is not a contract of service. I cannot accept that this is a test which is of great assistance in the present case. The fact that the contract makes no provision for time off is merely a reflection of the fact that there are no specified hours of work. I have already dealt with this. The fact that there is no provision for sick pay and holidays is merely a reflection of the fact that the contract is of very short duration. If a man engages himself as an extra kitchen hand at a hotel for a week in the holiday season, there will be no provision for sick pay and holidays, but the contract will almost certainly be a contract of service.

The company then refer to the fact that Mrs Irving's work was performed under a series of contracts, each for a specific survey. They say that the relationship of master and servant is normally conceived of as a continuous relationship, and that the fact that there is a series of contracts is more consistent with those contracts being contracts for services than contracts of service. For my part, I doubt whether this factor can usefully be considered in isolation. It must I think be considered in connection with the more general question whether Mrs Irving could be said to be in business on her own account as an interviewer. In considering this more general question I take into account the fact that Mrs Irving was free to work as an interviewer for others, though I think it is right to say that in this case there is no finding that she did so. I also take into account the fact that in her work as an interviewer Mrs Irving would, within the limits imposed by her instructions, deploy a skill and personality which would be entirely her own. I can only say that in the circumstances of this case these factors are not in my view sufficient to lead to the conclusion that Mrs Irving was in business on her own account. The opportunity to deploy individual skill and personality is frequently present in what is undoubtedly a contract of service. I have already said that the right to work for others is not inconsistent with the existence of a contract of service. Mrs Irving did not provide her own tools or risk her own capital, nor did her opportunity of profit depend in any significant degree on the way she managed her work.

Taking all the factors into account and giving full weight, I hope, to Mr Pain's persuasive arguments, I am clearly of opinion that on the facts of this case the Minister was right in concluding that Mrs Irving was employed by the company under a series of contracts of service, and the appeal accordingly must fail.

What, then, is the present state of the art of distinguishing between the contract of service and the ´contract for services? Is there any rational alternative to the tautology to which the attempt to establish a principled distinction between the two relationships so readily descends? It is a kind of tautology which can easily become tendentious; for instance, Hepple and O'Higgins have pointed out that the rather tautologous question, are the arrangements in a given case consistent with a contract of service or a contract for services, can easily suggest its own answer depending on which way round that question is put (*Employment Law*, 4th edn 1981, p. 67). In other words, the consistency test creates a slight presumption against a contract of service if it is put as the question, is the arrangement in question consistent with there being a contract of service? Yet there is no good reason why the test should be put one way round rather than the other, so any such presumption is quite unwarranted. There may, however, be some way out of the impasse. The courts have latterly made considerable use of the 'in business on own account' test which Cooke J. proposed, as we have just seen, in the *Market Investigations* case. In *Young & Woods Ltd* v. *West* [1980] IRLR 201, it was used in the Court of Appeal in a case in which a skilled sheet-metal worker was held to be an employee despite arrangements which purported to establish him as self-employed; in *Warner Holidays Ltd* v. *Sec. of State for Social Services* [1983] ICR

440, it was used as the overriding test in demonstrating that entertainers for a holiday season at a holiday camp were employees, and in *Nethermere (St Neots) Ltd* v. *Gardner* [1983] ICR 319 the EAT used the test as the predominant consideration in holding that a homeworker in the clothing manufacturing industry was an employee. On the other hand, a number of recent cases also indicate that a control or organization type of test still has some popularity. In a group of cases concerning musicians in orchestras, considerations of that kind pointed in the directions of self-employment – *Winfield* v. *London Philharmonic Orchestra Ltd* [1979] ICR 726 (EAT), *Addison* v. *London Philharmonic Orchestra Ltd* [1981] ICR 261 (EAT), *Midland Sinfonia Concert Society Ltd* v. *Sec. of State for Social Services* [1981] ICR 454 (QBD). In *WHPT Housing Association Ltd* v. *Sec. of State for Social Services* [1981] ICR 737 (QBD), similar considerations (disguised under a new near-tautology consisting in asking whether the principal obligation of the contract was that the employee provided himself to serve or that he provided his services) produced the conclusion that a freelance architect, accepting work as allocated, should be regarded as self-employed. The different use of these two types of test suggests an analytical path to be followed.

The point is that, whatever the difficulties in applying them, neither the control or organization tests on the one hand, nor the 'in business on own account' test on the other, are wholly tautologous; they suggest some way of drawing the distinction to which they are directed. In fact they suggest two distinct frames of reference for the discussion. The control or organization tests suggest a primarily social frame of reference in terms of the social power of the employing enterprise. The question is whether the worker is effectively subordinated to that social power or, in a looser sense, integrated into the social organization represented by the employing enterprise. The 'in business on own account' test on the other hand, creates a primarily economic frame of reference, in which the question is approached from the perspective of the worker rather than that of the employing enterprise, and the issue is whether the worker constitutes an independent economic unit. Given that the former sort of test seems to point in the direction of self-employment, while the latter sort of test lends itself to findings in favour of contracts of employment, it is important to consider whether there is any basis for regarding one sort of test as more accurate or informative than the other. In her research study, *Contractual Arrangements in Selected Industries* (Department of Employment Research Paper No. 39 (February 1983) at p. 24), Patricia Leighton seems to favour the control or organization tests, at least to the extent of thinking that the fashionable view that they are inflexible and narrow may be ripe for re-evaluation. In her view, these tests at least avoid the confusing multiplicity of factors that tend to be introduced under the 'in business on own account' test, and they are relatively meaningful tests in relation to the empirical data she assembled about employment patterns in industries using outwork. On the other hand, we would suggest that the increasingly technical and specialized nature of most employments genuinely breaks down any real hope of maintaining a distinction between self-employment and employment in terms of subordination, control or social organization. We would suggest that the use of an economic frame of reference provides the better chance of leading to a scientific rather than intuitive and impressionistic method of classification. There is considerable scope for the deployment of more sophisticated economics than has hitherto been used. Thus it would be possible and useful, without resorting to complex mathematical argumentation, to take account of economists' explanations of the various ways in which risks are distributed and incentives created as between employers and workers both inside and outside the employment relationship in its ordinary sense. In this way one could hope further to substantiate the impression from recent case-law that an economic test is a relatively objective, meaningful and informative way of distinguishing between the two sorts of employment relationship under consideration. That the result of using this kind of test seems to be to push decisions in favour of employed status rather than self-employed status raises questions of social policy to which we should now turn our attention.

We have seen that the distinction between employment and self-employment has become genuinely fluid and difficult to draw at the margin, whatever pet theories one may have about the best way out of that kind of difficulty. Yet not only does the functional need for such a distinction remain embodied firmly in legislation and case-law, but it is also seen as necessary to maintain the distinction as a matter of social policy; for instance, in the construction industry.

Report of the Committee of Inquiry under Professor
Phelps Brown into certain matters concerning Labour in
Building and Civil Engineering (Cmnd. 3714, 1968)

RECOMMENDATIONS ON SELF-EMPLOYMENT

422. We come now to the question of policy, and begin by reviewing the evidence to see what if anything in the part played by self-employment in construction calls for remedy.

423. We note first that the industry has long contained a large element of self-employment whose *bona fides* are not in dispute. These are men genuinely in business on their own account. Most of them are engaged in repair and maintenance and minor alterations, and work direct to clients not themselves engaged in construction; but sometimes also they may take work under sub-contract in new construction. There are also some processes in new construction, notably roofing, which in some places at least have long been carried out by self-employed workers under sub-contract.

424. We note also that access to the status of self-employment can provide a sense of independence which some men value. Some who have gone on to build substantial businesses have got their first start in this way. The small gang of self-employed men,

used to working together, constitutes an informal partnership that can work very efficiently, and this arrangement has been said to result in higher productivity than is commonly attained under a group bonus paid to normally employed labour, because the sense of independence contributes an added incentive.

425. On the other hand, self-employment in construction is associated with a number of shortcomings. There is first the risk to the self-employed man himself of sustaining an injury for which he or his dependants can obtain no compensation from an employer, or receive benefit under the Industrial Injuries Scheme. A man who elects to be self-employed may be expected to realize that he will not be able to draw injury benefit during a period of incapacity for work just as he will not be able to draw unemployment benefit; but he may not realize how much he or his family may lose through his ineligibility for disablement benefit and for the benefits payable to his family should he be permanently disabled or killed – even though he would normally be covered for flat rate national insurance, sickness and widow's benefits.

426. There is further the risk to third parties of suffering an injury at the hands of a self-employed man for which they are unable to obtain compensation. Another workman on the site or a member of the public who is injured by the fault of a self-employed man can recover no damages from him unless he can identify him and prove that he personally was at fault. . . .

427. Besides this gap in fault liability there is a gap in organization. The growth of self-employment in construction is disruptive of the industry's own arrangements and of the provisions made by Parliament for taxation and national insurance.

428. The industry's own arrangements include collective agreements on the terms and conditions of employment: the self-employed stand apart from these. One purpose of such agreements is to put a floor under competition by precluding wage-cutting, and many sectors of construction are highly competitive. But we have seen how the firm whose labour force becomes self-employed gains a substantial relief from imposts, and this it can draw on to undercut its competitors. Any reduction in the sum of work available to the industry will increase the temptation to do this. If a number of firms required their labour to become self-employed, as some have done or tried to do already, others would be under some pressure to follow suit. The apprehension and resentment that these potentialities of self-employment in construction have aroused in trade unions and employers' associations seem to us warranted.

429. The industry's arrangements also include those for training. By tradition, but equally today under the aegis of the CITB [Construction Industry Training Board], the responsibility for getting training done rests on the employer. But where there is self-employment there is no employer.

430. Training, moreover, is only one instance of the positive employment policies on which we have already touched and which we believe can make a special contribution to the improvement of construction as an industry to work in. But these are essentially policies to be adopted and applied by the employer for a labour force of which a substantial part remains with him for the long term. The fragmentation of the labour force by self-employment precludes the application of these policies, and preserves the present image of the industry as one of casual employment.

431. The growth of self-employment also thwarts what we believe to be the purposes of Parliament in the regulations it has made for taxation and national insurance in relation to wages. It is a feature of construction as of sections of some other industries that many of its processes happen to allow the worker to perform them as a self-

employed man, whom the courts will accept as such, even though he works in a way hardly distinguishable from that of a normally employed worker on the same site. Opinion in the industry distinguishes such self-employment sharply from that of the tradesmen whom it has long recognized as being genuinely in business on their own account. Yet those whose self-employment is thus felt to be only nominal avoid substantial charges that must be borne by normal employment.

Hence our system of legislation uses the employment relationship as the focus of provisions for the security and welfare rights of the worker, tending to leave the independent contracting relationship outside the scope of both those kinds of legislation. Although that tendency has recently been offset by the extension of much protective legislation to all contracts for the personal performance of services, and by the extension of social security contribution requirements to self-employment, a considerable incentive still remains to try to constitute employment relationships in terms of independent contracting while yet securing some of the mutual advantages of integration into the employing organization. This really brings us face to face with the difficulties of the traditional process of classification between employees and independent contractors. Parliament and the courts still feel that they are expressing an important and viable social policy by drawing this broad distinction between the two different bases for the supply of labour. But by so doing, and by leaving the parties the choice of form in which to constitute their relationship, the courts and Parliament seem to invite the avoidance of the obligations which they have seen fit to attach to the employment relationship. In order to explore the question of whether there is any way out of this dilemma, we shall look in the first instance at judicial activity in this area. We shall also seek to concentrate attention upon the relatively neglected question of how much legislative activity there has been or might be in this direction.

We begin then by looking at judicial activity in relation to this problem. If employers and workers constitute their labour relationships in the form of self-employment in order to avoid unwanted legal consequences attached to contracts of employment, a theoretically possible solution to the problems thus created is for the courts to thwart the aim of avoiding the obligations in question by looking behind the label the parties have attached to their relationship and holding that there in fact exists a contract of employment between them. Many decisions in this area could be analysed in those terms. Several important decisions in recent years display a conscious willingness to override the parties' attempts to impose a self-employed classification upon their relationship where the courts feel that such a classification would be artificial, misleading or downright inaccurate. The leading case of recent years in this direction was that of *Ferguson* v. *John Dawson Ltd* [1976] 1 WLR 346 (CA), where it was held that a labour-only sub-contractor in the building industry (see below, p. 94) could not escape liability for breach of a statutory safety duty owed to a building worker by pleading the fact that the worker had agreed to be taken on as a self-employed worker. This has been followed in a series of cases in which it has been held that workers were not prevented from claiming remedies for unfair dismissal by their own election to be treated as self-employed for tax and social security purposes, where the relationship was on a true view one of employment; it was so held in *Davis* v. *New England College of Arundel Ltd* [1977] I C R 6 (E A T), in *Tyne & Clyde Warehouses Ltd* v. *Hamerton* [1978] I C R 661 (E A T), and in the key Court of Appeal decision in *Young & Woods Ltd* v. *West* [1980] I R L R 201, where it was commented that the worker concerned would not be able to combine the benefit of employment protection rights as an employee with the fiscal advantages of self-employment, because the decision that he was an employee gave the Inland Revenue the right and duty to reclaim the tax deductions that he had been granted as a self-employed worker.

The approach typified in the *Young & Woods* case, however much one may welcome it, is not free from difficulties and has not gone unchallenged. It can be argued that the approach is not logically reconcilable with the line of cases in which in recent years it has been held that employees may be unable to claim employment protection rights where their contracts of employment are rendered illegal by an element of fraud on the Revenue (as where, for instance, remuneration is falsely characterized as expenses); recent decisions to that effect are those in *Tomlinson* v. *Dick Evans 'U' Drive Ltd* [1978] I C R 639; *Corby* v. *Morrison* [1980] I C R 564; *Newland* v. *Simons & Willer Ltd* [1981] I C R 521. But the courts have been at some pains to restrict the circumstances in which the employer can invoke such fraud against the employee – see for instance *Davidson* v. *Pillay* [1979] I R L R 275, and *Coral Leisure Group Ltd* v. *Barnett* [1981] I C R 503 – and it would generally be accepted that the element of deceit is more unequivocal in the cases concerning false expenses than in the cases concerning dubious self-employment, even if the amounts of tax evaded by the former means are no greater than those avoided or evaded by the latter means. (See generally C. Mogridge, 'Illegal employment contracts – loss of statutory protection' (1981) 10 *ILJ* 23.) There is also a wider sort of judicial objection to the reasoning in the *Young & Woods* case, which is expressed in the dissent of Lawton L.J. in the case of *Ferguson* v. *John Dawson Ltd* (above) and also in the decision of the Court of Appeal in *Massey* v. *Crown Life Insurance Ltd* [1978] I C R 590, where the manager of a branch office of an insurance company was successfully prevented from claiming unfair dismissal remedies by reference to his earlier agreement to change to self-employed status for tax purposes. This decision is shaped by a sort of contractualism which stresses the freedom of the parties to contract in the form of self-employment, but correspondingly asserts that the worker is bound by his election to be self-employed. Thus Lord Denning M.R. said ([1978] I C R 590 at p. 596):

In the present case there is a perfectly genuine agreement entered into at the instance of Mr Massey on the footing that he is self-employed. He gets the benefit of it by avoiding tax deductions and getting his pension contributions returned. I do not see that he can come along afterwards and say it is something else in order to claim that he has been unfairly dismissed. Having made his bed as being self-employed he must lie on it. He is not under a contract of service.

One might expect that the courts would not be at their most protective in relation to the sort of worker represented in that case, i.e. the well-informed worker clearly capable of balancing the advantages of the different forms of contracting; but it would be a mistake to view this as an isolated decision or to expect too much in the way of judicial overriding of the freely chosen label of self-employment. The judges would be too conscious of the dangers involved, in terms of the threat to the claims of objectivity and consistency by which the whole classification process is sought to be legitimated, to engage extensively in this particular kind of social engineering. It is sometimes suggested that the distinction between employment and self-employment should be differently drawn according to the purpose for which it is being made, so that for instance one might lean more heavily in favour of employment status in unfair dismissal cases or industrial safety cases than in tax or social security cases; these arguments are canvassed by Leighton in her research study – see her article, 'Employment and Self-employment – Some Problems of Law and Practice' (1983) *Employment Gazette* 197. It would, however, be quite untypical of the judiciary for them to engage in that kind of differentiation to the point where the definition of the contract of employment became fragmented according to the nature of the proceedings in which it was being applied, because that again would discredit the claim of the process of definition to be an objective one, and such a claim is necessary to give the internal strength with which alone the rather shaky edifice can be supported.

There is a marked tendency, which is consistent with the way that we are taught to approach many legal problems, to view the possible solutions to this kind of problem as consisting exclusively in judicial rather than legislative intervention. This is too narrow a perspective; there are increasing reasons for considering the possibilities of fresh legislative approaches to the problems raised by the distinction between employment and self-employment. There have indeed been important legislative interventions before now; it should be remembered that the extension of certain employment legislation to the contract personally to execute any work or labour is part of a tradition reaching back to the Truck Acts 1831–1940 via the definition of 'workmen', a tradition which has recently been resuscitated in individual employment law in the employment provisions of the sex and race discrimination legislation (see SDA 1976, s.82(1); RRA 1976, s.78(1)). The EAT in *Tanna* v. *Post Office* [1981] ICR 374 set its face against the inclusion of the small entrepreneur in this category, ruling that it did not cover the sub-postmaster who was free to delegate the performance of the work of the post office to staff employed by him. Nevertheless, the potential area of application of this kind of legislative provision is large, and such provisions simply cut the Gordian knot which judges and commentators have to untie at the cost of so much effort in terms of case-law. Michael Forde has described the general trend of European social security systems to assimilate the position of the self-employed to that of the employed, and the proposals at EEC level to carry this process further by way of ensuring portability of entitlements in respect of social security benefits for workers moving from one EEC member state to another ('The Self-Employed and the EEC Social Security Rules' (1979) 8 *ILJ* 1). There are some indications on the part of policy-makers of a growing awareness of the importance of self-employment as a section of the general labour market, and we saw in an earlier section of this chapter how the growth in self-employment is to some extent encouraged because of the alleviation of the problem of unemployment that it can produce (see above, p. 33). This process of change is usefully described by George Clark in his recent article, 'Recent Developments in Working Patterns' (1982) *Employment Gazette* 284, and the simple lack of awareness of the self-employed workforce as part of the general workforce is gradually being overcome by research of the kind already described (see above, p. 93) and by exercises in enumeration of the size of the self-employed sector of the kind described in a recent *Employment Gazette* article (1983 *Employment Gazette* 55) where the numbers were estimated at 2,057,000 in 1981, almost nine per cent of the employed labour force. Yet this consciousness is still a curiously patchy one; thus it is still possible for legislation to deal with the contract for services as an aspect of commercial law or consumer law without its impinging on the consciousness of labour lawyers. This is what seems to have occurred in the case of the Supply of Goods and Services Act 1982, Part II of which imposes implied obligations on the supplier of services which deserve comparison with the implied obligations of the employee under the contract of employment, but which has received little or no attention from this point of view. The tendency has been for labour lawyers to view the issue of whether greater regulation is needed of the terms on which self-employed work is done rather as a series of smaller issues relating to particular patterns of work such as labour-only sub-contracting, temporary work, part-time work or homeworking. It is to the extent of, and potential for, that kind of legal intervention that we now turn our attention.

(c) **Labour-only sub-contractors**
A situation which has been seen more than most as raising the question of whether it would be desirable for the law to control the choice of form of the employment relationship is that of labour-only sub-contracting. That is the process whereby skilled or semi-skilled manual workers, in the construction industry in particular, constitute themselves as independent suppliers of labour on a contract basis, sometimes by direct supply and sometimes through the intermediary of a sub-contracting employer. This form of provision of labour, which became popular precisely because it permitted the avoidance of various kinds of statutory regulation applying to employees, has caused concern both to the government because of the avoidance of social security legislation applying to employees, health, safety and welfare legislation

applying to employees and income-tax provisions applying to employees, and also to trade unions in the construction industry, where the pattern of union representation and membership was considerably disrupted by the growth of a labour force of labour-only sub-contractors who did not belong to unions or engage in collective bargaining (see above, p. 90).

From a legal point of view, the linked problems of the apparently independent status of the worker, and the indirectness of his relationship with the main employer where there was an intermediate employer, could be overcome, to a certain extent, by taking a deliberately wide view of the scope of the category of 'employer and employee'. The former Industrial Court engaged in that kind of wide interpretation in relation to tilers in their decision in *W. Creighton & Co. Ltd and Amalgamated Slaters, Tilers and Roofing Operatives Society* (IC Award No. 3107, 1966). But this kind of interpretation was sustained neither in the Industrial Arbitration Board (into which the former Industrial Court was transformed): see *Am. Soc. Woodworkers, Painters and Builders and A. & D. C. Barden & Sons Ltd* (IAB Award No. 3256, 1972); nor in the courts: see *Construction Industry Training Board* v. *Labour Force Ltd*. In that decision (which dealt with the relationship between contract workers and the agency that supplied them) the court showed itself strongly disposed to engage in objective classification of the relationship the parties had set up rather than to engage in the social engineering implicit in deeming the relationship to be a contract of employment. Were they not thereby providing employers and workers with an unnecessary incentive to dispense with the obligations of the employment relationship in pursuit of short-term pecuniary advantage?

Construction Industry Training Board v. *Labour Force Ltd*
[1970] 3 All ER 220 (DC)

COOKE J.: In approaching the question whether the workmen were employees of the respondents under contracts of service, the tribunal sought to apply the familiar tests which have been used to distinguish contracts of service from contracts for services. In that connection it is, I think, important to bear in mind that the sole question which the tribunal had to determine in this case was whether the contracts in question were contracts of service. If they were not, then it followed that the board must fail on a crucial point, and it mattered not whether the contracts in question were contracts for services or some third variety of contract which was neither a contract for services nor a contract of service. I will return to that hereafter.

Nevertheless, the tests which have been formulated for the purposes of distinguishing a contract for services from a contract of service are obviously of value in determining whether a particular contract is a contract of service, and I do not think that the approach adopted by the tribunal can be said to have been wrong. The tests which have been so formulated have been referred to in a number of recent cases, including *Ready Mixed Concrete (South East) Ltd* v. *Minister of Pensions and National Insurance* [[1968] 2 QB 497]. These tests are now so familiar that in my judgment it is unnecessary to set them out in detail. I merely observe this. First, that no lists of tests which has been formulated is exhaustive, and that the weight to be attached to particular criteria varies from case to case. Secondly, although the extent of the control which the alleged employer is entitled to exercise over the work is by no means a decisive criterion of universal application, it is likely in many cases to be a factor of importance. On the one hand, the tribunal pointed out that an hourly paid workman has no opportunity to deploy managing skills or make money by so doing. On the other hand, the tribunal took account of the undeniable fact that in the building industry there are many self-employed persons. I think that in the circumstances of this case, the tribunal was entitled to take account of that. The tribunal was asked to consider the nature of the contracts entered into by a large and indeterminate group of workmen in the industry. It was entitled, as it seems to me, to use its own knowledge of the undoubted fact that many of the workmen in the industry are self-employed. The tribunal referred to the declaration signed by the workman in which he purports to certify that he is employed on a sub-contract basis. Quite rightly, in my judgment, the tribunal held that this did not preclude it from inquiring into the true nature of the contractual relationship. On the other hand, it pointed out that the declaration contains terms which are undoubtedly terms of the contract, eg, those in regard to times and amounts of payments. It was, in my judgment, entitled to have regard to that, and it was also entitled to have regard to the workman's promise, because that is what it amounted to, to be responsible for his own income tax returns, national insurance contributions and holiday with pay payments. I agree with the tribunal when it said:

> It may be that if the contract in law is one of service, the term will not protect the employer who by statute is liable as employer, but that the parties did contract to bring about the position that employers' obligations of this type did not lie on [the respondents] cannot be ignored.

In my view, the fact that the parties have in express terms sought to make a contract of a particular kind, while it does not bind the courts to hold that they have succeeded, is a factor which can be considered in determining the true nature of the contract. The tribunal expressed their conclusions in these terms:

> Considering all the facts set out, and mainly because there was no control lying with [the respondents] at all, no continuity of contract, no ordinary responsibility of an employer at all such as for sick pay or holidays, no bar on the workman working for others when he liked, we think that the proper decision is that the contracts entered into between [the respondents] and the workman, from time to time as he worked, were contracts to provide services to agreed persons in return for an hourly payment for hours worked paid by [the respondents]. We do not consider that [the respondents] were the employer of these men. That means that in so far as [the respondents were] assessed on moneys paid to the workmen who worked for contractors, the assessment was not justified.

In my judgment, in reaching that conclusion the tribunal applied proper tests in a proper way. I can see no ground on which we could hold that the conclusion was wrong in law. In particular, in the circumstances of this case I think that the tribunal was right in attaching considerable weight to the fact that the respondents had no control at all over the work. In this case I think that that particular feature was a strong indication that the contracts were not contracts of service. I think, however, that it is at any rate possible that the tribunal might have reached the same result in a simpler way. The sole question before the tribunal on this part of the case was, as I have said, whether the contracts were contracts of service. These contracts were contracts whereby the workman contracted with the respondents to do work for a third party, the contractor. It was not a question of the respondents' lending the services of one of their own employees to the contractor, because the workman never contracted to render services to the respondents at all. I think that there is much to be said for the view that where A contracts with B to render services exclusively to C, the contract is not a contract for services, but a contract *sui generis*, a different type of contract from either of the familiar two. Had it been necessary, I should have been prepared to uphold the decision of the tribunal on that ground.

In 1967 a committee of inquiry under the chairmanship of Professor Phelps Brown (see above, p. 89) was appointed to inquire into the engagement and use of labour in building and civil engineering with particular reference to labour-only sub-contracting. Their starting-point was the concern that had long been felt with the discontinuity of employment in the building industry; but their attention ultimately became concentrated upon the social and legal inadequacies of the labour-only sub-contracting form of employment relationship as we have described them above. The committee was in effect being asked whether the law should seek to eliminate this form of provision of labour in the construction industries. The committee did not recommend such basic intervention, if only because they were convinced that there was a real need for a supply of labour, particularly skilled labour, by independent contracting in that industry. They therefore recommended that the short-comings of the system of employment in construction should be remedied by a system of registration and control of the intermediate employers of sub-contracted labour.

Their recommendations have not been implemented, but the Finance Act 1971, ss.29–31, Finance Act 1974, s.25, and Finance (No. 2) Act 1975, ss.39, 68–71 and Sch. 12, made provision for the purpose of controlling the evasion of income tax and social security liabilities in the construction industry. The scheme, as tightened up in 1975, is that payments made by contractors to sub-contractors are subject to the deduction of tax at source unless the sub-contractor has obtained an Inland Revenue certificate. In order to obtain such a certificate, the sub-contractor must in effect show that he is running a bona fide business covered by adequate insurance and that he has a satisfactory history of tax compliance over a three-year period. (*Kirvell (Inspector of Taxes)* v. *Guy* [1979] Simon's Tax Cases 312.) The deduction scheme originally did not extend to sub-contracting companies as distinct from individual sub-contractors but it now covers both types.. The question is whether these provisions are limited in their objectives to controlling evasions of liability, or whether they seek in reality to discourage the practice of labour-only sub-contracting. It would seem that although these provisions certainly place difficulties in the path of the labour-only sub-contracting employer, they do not destroy the viability of his position.

Although the practice of labour-only sub-contracting in the construction industry has probably been contained it has certainly not been eliminated. The law has stopped short of controlling the choice of form in which the employment relationship may be constituted in this area. The Court of Appeal in *Ferguson* v. *John Dawson Ltd* [1976] 1 WLR 346 took, as we have seen, an important decision in favour of treating the worker employed under this kind of arrangement as an employee of the labour-only sub-contractor where it was necessary to do so in order to safeguard his rights as a worker – in that case rights connected with safety at work. The sex and race discrimination legislation allow for the *sui generis* nature of the labour-only sub-contracting arrangement to the extent of making special provision requiring the head contractor not to engage in discrimination *vis-à-vis* the contract worker or applicant to be a contract worker (SDA 1975, s.9; RRA 1976, s.7), though the EAT in *Rice* v. *Fon-A-Car Ltd* [1980] ICR 133 held this provision inapplicable to the case where the person in the role of labour-only sub-contractor was not obliged by his contract with the head contractor to employ contract labour. These measures, while imposing some limited regulation, endorse the basic freedom to arrange for employment by means of labour-only sub-contracting, and the various suggestions that have recently been and are currently being advanced for saving public-sector labour costs by sub-contracting for the performance of particular functions such as cleaning, refuse collection, laundering and so forth would seem to depend for their capacity to reduce costs upon the possibility of procuring labour by means of labour-only sub-contracting. We shall also see in a later chapter that recent trade-dispute legislation has dealt with certain collective aspects of the sub-contracting of work in provisions which seem at least partly concerned with labour-only sub-contracting and certainly endorse the continuation of this method of constituting the employment relationship (see below, pp. 860 *et seq.*).

(d) Temporary and casual workers

It is a striking fact that British employment law leaves to employers and employees a considerable, indeed almost untrammelled, freedom to determine the duration of the employment relationship. It is true that under the CEA 1972 [EPCA 1978, s.49] certain minimum lengths are attached to periods of notice. (See below, pp. 433–4.) It is true also that under the law of unfair dismissal the distinction between fixed-term contracting and contracting for an indeterminate period of time, with provision for termination by notice, is greatly reduced by the treatment of the expiry of the fixed-term contract without renewal as dismissal (see below, pp. 446–8). But despite these admittedly important statutory modifications, the basic freedom to determine the length of the employment relationship remains vested intact in the parties themselves.

In an important article, Hepple and Napier have shown how this voluntaristic approach to the form of the employment relationship leads to the neglect of the interests of temporary workers ((1978) 7 *ILJ* 84). They identify two sets of problems concerning temporary workers. The first is the problem of casualism associated with short-term hirings. The second set of problems arises from the fact that temporary workers are frequently supplied by intermediary agencies. These agencies may easily constitute a form of financial exploitation. (Private employment agencies concentrate on supplying workers for short periods of time, and hence the problems of temporary employment and agency employment overlap to a considerable extent.)

As far as short-term directly employed workers are concerned (as distinct from agency-supplied workers), Hepple and Napier show that these workers may fail to qualify for the whole series of statutory entitlements or protections. This may occur because the short-term nature of his employment identifies the worker as an independent contractor rather than an employee (compare the decision in *Market Investigations Ltd* v. *Minister of Social Security* [1969] 2 Q B 173 quoted earlier in this chapter (at p. 85)). Or it may be that the short-term worker, even though classified as an employee, fails to qualify for statutory protections by reason of the lack of the necessary qualifying period of continuous service. They show how the same is true for unemployment benefit, where in particular the seasonal worker is subject to specially restrictive rules before he can claim unemployment benefit. As far as agency-supplied labour is concerned, Hepple and Napier show how the British legislation, contained in the Employment Agencies Act 1973, limits itself to the licensing of agencies and the controlling of some aspects of their activities without placing limits on the duration of the supply of labour by these agencies, in contrast to the position in various EEC countries where control of duration of agency hiring is a central part of the system of control of agency supply of labour. They show also how the 1973 legislation fails to resolve the underlying difficulties about the legal status of the worker *vis-à-vis* both the agency and the user of the labour (see p. 95). They argue that the agency worker should be unequivocally deemed an employee of the agency so that the responsibilities of an ordinary employer would be placed squarely upon the employment agency. They say, however, that this solution requires further measures to prevent undercutting of patterns established by collective bargaining in industries which rely primarily on directly employed labour but draw to some extent on agency-supplied labour. On this system, special provision is also necessary to ensure that the temporary agency worker enjoys rights to freedom of association while working at the establishment of the user of his labour who will not actually be his own employer.

In a conclusion which is extremely interesting from the point of view of the present discussion, Hepple and Napier argue that the temporary worker needs to be separately identified as a category within British labour law and that valid reasons for employing temporary workers need to be identified, for instance, to meet seasonal changes in demand, to provide short-term replacement for permanent staff or to perform specific tasks. Outside these categories, Hepple and Napier suggest that a Temporary Work Act, having made a special provision for the groups of workers legitimately engaged on a temporary basis, should 'prevent the illegitimate use of short-term workers in order to evade statutory duties'.

The courts have recently shown some sensitivity to the risk that temporary, seasonal or casual workers may too lightly be denied the benefits of employment protection legislation. In *O'Kelly* v. *Trusthouse Forte plc* [1983] ICR 728, the EAT took the major step forward of holding that a casual worker might be (and, in this case, was) an employee even though he had to be regarded as employed under a series of short-term contracts rather than a single continuing contract, if each of the short-term contracts constituted a contract of employment in itself. The EAT decision challenged the assumption that the casual worker cannot be an employee if he has no continuing contract linking spells of casual work. Perhaps regrettably, the Court of Appeal overruled the EAT in this case ([1983] ICR 728), appearing to revert to the traditional view that engagement under a succession of intermittent short-term contracts rather than a single continuous contract points overwhelmingly towards self-employment. However, in *Ford* v. *Warwickshire County Council* [1983] ICR 273, the House of Lords construed the statutory continuity of employment provisions (see below, p. 571 *et seq.*) in favour of a seasonal employee (in this case a teacher employed each year for the academic session only). Important though these decisions are, they cannot, however, amount to a systematic address to the problem of the employment protection rights of the temporary, casual or seasonal worker, which we shall encounter again later in this book in our discussion of the duration of employment (see below, p. 432 *et seq.*)

At the time of writing, an EEC Draft Directive on Temporary Work which deals with the supply of temporary workers by employment businesses and the employment of workers on fixed-duration contracts, and has the aim of ensuring that temporary work is supervised by the state and that temporary workers receive social protection, is making its way through the legislative process of the EEC. So we see how a pattern begins to emerge which suggests that certain forms of employment relationship should be permitted to take place only in a certain limited range of situations and subjected to a certain amount of mandatory regulation as to its shape and content within those situations. We have seen how this is so in relation to labour-only sub-contracting and in relation to temporary employment; we now turn to consider the case of part-time employment with a view to seeing whether similar considerations might prevail there.

(e) Part-time workers and homeworkers

In the previous section we were concerned with those employment relationships which existed for intermittent periods of weeks or months – the temporary and casual employments. In the present section we are mainly concerned with those employments which provide work for part only of each week. (Part-time work is different from short-time working in that it represents a permanent arrangement from the outset and for the duration of the employment, unlike short-time working which is an abnormal situation arising by way of response to adverse circumstances which are conceived of as temporary.) In particular we are concerned with part-time *employees*, as independent contractors could not normally be categorized as full-time or part-time – the very terminology of part-time work implies an association with full-time employment.

An important article in *Industrial Relations Review and Report* (1978, No. 172, p. 2) suggests that part-time workers may constitute a 'second class' of workers by comparison with full-timers as far as their terms and conditions of employment are concerned. Hence this is another way in which the choice of form of employment determines or expresses the social and economic standing of the worker. But let us examine the findings of the article in slightly greater detail.

The definition of part-time work is interesting because it reveals a disparity between the social and the (more generous) legal definition. The *IRRR* survey shows how the DE for statistical purposes, and some negotiating groups, take thirty hours as the cut-off point. Employment protection legislation which has aimed at conferring the statutory floor of rights upon full-time rather than part-time workers, originally required a minimum of twenty-one hours weekly. Then in 1975 a new pattern was adopted which had a norm of sixteen hours weekly, but with a further drop to eight hours after five years' service. This link between the length of the working week and the period of continuous employment is important, for it places at a particular disadvantage the worker who is both temporary and part-time.[1] Why should such a worker be twice removed from the scope of protection, for instance, against unfair dismissal? Compare *Mailway (Southern) Ltd* v. *Willsher* [1978] ICR 511 (EAT).

The same survey reveals that if part-time work is defined on a thirty-hour basis, it included nearly forty per cent of the female labour force in 1976 (about six per cent of the male labour force) and that the number of female part-time workers had increased by nearly twenty-five per cent compared with 1972. Part-time work obviously commends itself to women with children for domestic reasons, and the disadvantages at which part-time workers are placed form an indirect aspect of discrimination against women as regards terms and conditions of employment. (Compare now *Handley* v. *H. Mono Ltd* [1979] ICR 147 (EAT); *Jenkins* v. *Kingsgate Ltd* [1981] ICR 715 (EAT), see below, p. 398; *Clarke* v. *Eley (IMI) Kynoch Ltd* [1983] ICR 165 (EAT) see above, p. 50 and below, p. 523.)

Outside the area of the statutory floor of employment rights, to what extent are part-time workers at a disadvantage compared with full-time workers?

[1] This qualification applies to: time off to look for work or make arrangements for training (ECPA 1978, s.31(2)); maternity pay and the right to return to work (s.33(3)(*b*)); minimum periods of notice (s.49(1)), written statements of reasons for dismissal (s.53(2)), unfair dismissal (s.64(1)(*a*)); redundancy payments (s.81(1), (4)). In each case the rights depend upon continuity of employment as statutorily defined (s.151(1) and Sch. 13). The definition links part-time and temporary workers by means of the five years/eight hours combination in Sch. 13, para. 6).

The same *IRRR* survey shows how there is a tendency for part-time workers to receive very low hourly or basic rates, and how they rarely qualify for overtime premia where these are paid on a weekly rather than a daily basis. They also sometimes fare badly in terms of other benefits, for example often enjoying no sick pay provisions. As far as pensions are concerned, the *IRRR* survey draws attention to the fact that the employer can contract out of the state scheme in respect only of his full-time workers, leaving his part-time workers to state pension benefits only, if he wishes to do so. Again, as far as maternity leave is concerned, collective bargaining will apparently sometimes improve on the statutory rights so far as full-time workers are concerned whilst leaving part-time workers no better provided for than the legislation requires. As for holidays, said the survey, the Civil Service makes no provision for annual leave for part-timers who work less than eight hours per week, and for those working for more than eighteen hours, holiday leave is proportional to the number of hours or days worked in each week.

To what extent then is there any tendency to control the choice of part-time work? There does not really seem to be any such trend, this form of employment being too well established. Employers, the *IRRR* survey argued, need part-time employees either because they cannot recruit enough full-timers or to extend plant utilization or opening hours, or to provide flexibility in manning levels necessary to meet periods of peak demand, or simply because they are cheaper to employ. Employees, as we have said, often have domestic reasons for seeking part-time work. The trade unions seem to be concentrating on recruiting part-time workers and striving to gain for them a status equivalent to that of full-time workers rather than on discouraging this form of employment. So the realistic question is not so much whether we can expect legal intervention to discourage part-time working as whether there is likely to be some correction of the imbalance that has developed between the statutory rights of part-time workers and full-time workers. For such correction there seemed to be some real need, on the evidence of the 1978 survey.

In the 1980s, there has seemed to be a heightened consciousness of the problems arising in relation to the legal régime of part-time employment. The problems have visibly assumed large social dimensions in the sense that conditions of recession have tended to accelerate a growth in the proportion of part-time employment to full-time employment (see above, pp. 5–6, and see George Clark, 'Recent Developments in Working Patterns' (1983) *Employment Gazette* 284). Indeed, as we saw in an earlier section (above, pp. 30–31), governmental measures such as the job-splitting have positively promoted that transformation because it is seen as a way of alleviating the problem of unemployment. At the same time, the important decisions of recent years, in which the disadvantages of part-time workers as compared with the advantages of full-time workers have been challenged as an aspect of discrimination against women (see above, p. 101), have tended to promote a consciousness of the need for measures to address directly the inequalities between part-time and full-time workers. At the time of writing, proposals for an EEC Directive on Voluntary Part-time Work are making their way through the EEC legislative process, a Draft Directive having been submitted by the EEC Commission to the EEC Council early in 1982 (reported [1982] 2 CMLR 133). This legislation if passed as proposed will do much to require part-time workers to be accorded parity of treatment with full-time workers, and indeed to require it to be ensured that workers enter into this form of work as the result of voluntary choice. This would necessitate extensive amendment to the details of employment protection legislation, and would indeed effect as substantial a revolution in individual employment law as that constituted by the various major measures of the 1970s in relation to the employment protection rights of full-time employees.

Alongside our discussion of part-time workers we may briefly consider the position of homeworkers. It is gradually being realized that this may well still be an area of exploitation, especially in terms of rates of pay. Here, again, is a situation where a choice of form of employment probably tends to operate to the particular disadvantage of women workers, who will of course predominate in the category of homeworkers. In December 1976 the Department of Employment referred to ACAS questions relating to the operation of the Button Manufacturing Wages Council and the Toy Manufacturing Wages Council, particularly in order to establish the extent to which homeworkers are needed in those industries and the importance of the wages councils in determining their terms and conditions of employment. The resulting report on the *Toy Manufacturing Wages Council* (ACAS Report No. 13, 1978, see below, pp. 104–5) addressed itself particularly to the position of homeworkers in view of the importance of homework as a major part of that industry. The conclusions from the inquiries made were that the extent of homeworking in the industry was unlikely to decline in the immediate future and that there was a continuing need for statutory protection in the absence of effective collective representation of their interests (paras. 7.43–4). It was recommended that in order to make minimum wages more effective for homeworkers than they were at present, the statutory body (whether a Wages Council or a Statutory Joint Industrial Council, see below, p. 150) should consider setting a special piecework-basis time-rate for homeworkers, so that a homeworker on piecework would earn a minimum hourly rate. This special hourly rate would, in recognition of the homeworkers' circumstances, be lower than the minimum rate for factory workers if it was linked to a lower rate of production, hence setting a more realistic hourly standard while allowing the minority of homeworkers who can work at the same rate as factory workers to earn the same reward as the factory worker (paras. 7.51–7.53). The special piecework-basis time-rate for homeworkers is already used by other wages councils. It will be seen that it represents a compromise with the special low-pay problems of homeworkers.

The further recommendations of the Report with regard to homeworkers are of particular relevance to the theme of this chapter because they concern the employment status of homeworkers. The questions are whether they are or should be treated as employed (as was done in *Airfix Footwear Ltd* v. *Cope* [1978] ICR 1210 (EAT) and in *Nethermere (St Neots) Ltd* v. *Gardner* [1983] ICR 319) or self-employed, and whether employment rights are or should be extended to them. In the extract which follows, the Report sets out its findings and two alternative suggestions for improvement of the present position. Which of the two would be preferable?

ACAS, *Toy Manufacturing Wages Council*
(Report No. 13, 1978)

7.20 Our inquiries suggested that there is currently considerable confusion about the status of homeworkers as between being self-employed and being employees of the firm for which they work. In our discussions with employers we found that it is customary to regard homeworkers as being self-employed. Indeed we encountered no employers who regarded their homeworkers as employees, neither did we find any evidence of employers making national insurance contributions in respect of their homeworkers.

7.21 When we spoke to homeworkers themselves, however, we encountered a different view. One hundred homeworkers (56 per cent of those interviewed) regarded themselves as employees of the firm which provided them with work. Forty-nine homeworkers (28 per cent) regarded themselves as being self-employed, while the remaing 29 (16 per cent) held no clear view about their status. We asked homeworkers whether national insurance contributions were made for them, either by themselves or by their firm. Only one homeworker claimed to be making contributions; none were aware of payments being made by their firm. Arrangements for payment of income tax are dealt with in paragraph 7.36.

7.22 We asked homeworkers about their views on employment status, security and protection under the law. These questions elicited very little response. This reaction may have been caused by uncertainty about the issues involved, although a number of homeworkers said that the advantages of being able to get work at home outweighed the uncertain legal status. Only on wage standards did a significant number – 53 (30 per cent) – say that they saw this as an area which should be improved. . . .

7.45 Minimum terms and conditions fixed by the Wages Council apply to all workers within the Council's scope, irrespective of whether they are employees or self-employed. The same situation applies with the Health and Safety Commission's proposals for homework which we discuss later in this section. Employers invariably regard homeworkers as self-employed while the great majority of homeworkers see themselves as employees of the firm which provides them with work. One way out of this confusion would be to follow the TUC suggestion for homeworkers to automatically become employees of the firm which provides them with work. The underlying desire to bring the benefits and protection of recent employment legislation to this particularly vulnerable section of the workforce is worthy of support and accordingly we propose that this reform should be considered. The nature of homework could make interpretation of employee entitlement provisions a difficult exercise. This would apply particularly where entitlement was based on number of hours worked or recompense determined by past earnings. These problems are particularly relevant for terms of notice provisions, payment in lieu of notice, unfair dismissal, redundancy payments, and maternity provisions. One example of the difficulties which could arise in this area is the situation posed by the 'above average' homeworker who completes a given amount of work in fewer hours than a 'below average' homeworker. Employee status would also carry the need for national insurance contributions on the part of both employers and homeworkers. This would have the effect of reducing the economic advantages of homework and could well be a factor leading to less work being made available to homeworkers.

7.46 One positive course which falls short of proposing employee status but which would help to reduce the confusion and uncertainty in this area would be to make it clear to homeworkers what their present status entails. This could be achieved by requiring employers to provide their homeworkers with a standard notice which sets out in simple terms what the difference is between a person who is an employee and a person who is self-employed, and which makes clear to their homeworkers which category the latter fall into. It would then be for the Wages Inspectors to ensure that this was done.

The discussion of the need for a reformed legal régime for homeworking has continued since the time of that ACAS report, and was brought together in a valuable article by Keith Ewing ('Homeworking: A Framework for Reform' (1982) 11 *ILJ* 94), in which the Report of the House of Commons Select Committee on Employment on the subject of Homeworking (HC 39, 1981–2) is examined and evaluated. The Select Committee report pointed to the growth in homeworking and to the relative weakness of the position of such workers and the corresponding need for improved legal protection. Ewing suggests some areas in which reform is needed. He points first to the need for a procedure for identifying or registering homeworkers. The Health and Safety Commission published for consultation in 1979 a set of draft Homeworkers Regulations to provide a registration procedure, but the draft regulations were heavily criticized by the Select Committee, and there seems little prospect of regulations being made before 1985. Ewing also suggests the need for a Homeworking Wages Council to help to secure minimum terms and conditions of employment for homeworkers, though as we shall see in a later chapter (see below, p. 144) the existing Wages Council system is sufficiently under threat to make reform in this direction an unlikely prospect for the time being. Ewing finally suggests the need for ensuring the application of employment protection legislation to homeworkers, and shows how the situation of homeworkers provides an urgent example of the various problems of differential application of employment protection legislation that we have been addressing in one form or another throughout this section of the present chapter. He concludes, however, with the warning that too much regulation would be ineffective because it would result either in the diminution of employment or in the evasion of the code of protection so established. That is indeed the ultimate problem for a system of labour law in which there is a freedom of choice about the form in which to constitute the work relationship, coupled with widely divergent legal régimes and therefore economic and social consequences according to the choice made. This brings us to the question of whether the employment relationship should be regarded in terms of status or of contract, to which we now turn by way of conclusion to this section.

(f) Conclusion – status or contract?

We should like to advance the suggestion that the foregoing discussion of choice of form of the employment relationship may have a bearing on the 'status or contract' debate. That debate arises as follows.

Lawyers and sociologists have from time to time faced the problem of whether it is appropriate to regard the individual employment relationship as a contractual one, or, to put it another way, have sought to identify the results of regarding the relationship as a contractual one. One form of response to this problem consists in the assertion that the employment relationship is so closely regulated by statutory provisions that it should be regarded as a matter of status rather than contract. Kahn-Freund has showed that this is really little more than a slogan used to voice a *laissez-faire* objection to the encroachment of welfare legislation.

> Kahn-Freund, 'A Note on Status and Contract in British
> Labour Law' (1967) 30 *MLR* at pp. 635–6, 640–1
> (*Selected Writings* (1978), pp. 78ff, 83ff)

THE labour law of Great Britain shares with that of the other nations in our orbit of civilization two essential jurisprudential features: it is based on the contractual foundation of the obligation to work and of the obligation to pay wages, and it is at the same time permeated by a tendency to formulate and to enforce an ever-growing number of imperative norms for the protection of the worker, norms which the parties to the contract cannot validly set aside to the detriment of the economically weaker party. This dual insistence on agreement as the legal basis of at least some of the essential rights and obligations and on mandatory regulation as the source of the content of the relationship has given rise to a jurisprudential dilemma which has so far not been clearly faced in the literature on the subject.

The dilemma arises from the ambiguity of the term 'status' in general jurisprudence. Contemporary writers are fond of reiterating that, under the impact of modern developments, Western society is moving from 'contract' to 'status'. This observation which has been repeated almost mechanically on countless occasions is intended to signify that our society and our law have taken a course in a direction opposite to that traced more than a century ago by Sir Henry Sumner Maine, whose celebrated dictum about the displacement of 'status' by 'contract' is often quoted, but seldom in full. Not infrequently one can sense in the statement that the tendency diagnosed by Maine has been reversed, a conscious or unconscious condemnation of a retrograde evolution. Did not Maine link his famous remark with the analysis of what he called 'progressive societies'? Does not the movement, or rather the alleged movement, from 'contract' to 'status' constitute a 'regression', a regression from the 'liberal', 'progressive' environment of the nineteenth century to more primitive forms of social organization such as those described by Maine in his work? . . .

How can we explain the conceptual confusion between two legal phenomena as different as the imposition of rights and duties irrespective of the volition of the person concerned, and the shaping of a contractual relation into which he has freely entered? Let us admit that in terms of legal policy there may but need not be a common factor. This is the desire to protect persons who, not only, as Maine thought, owing to lack of 'faculty of forming a judgment in their own interests', but also owing to inferior bargaining power, are liable to be exploited by others. This policy underlies some of the legal provisions or principles which, in Maine's sense, belong to the area of 'status'. They do underlie the law of infants, but certainly not that of aliens. But they also underlie those rules which shape the content of contracts. Yet the legal techniques employed by the two types of legal norms are so fundamentally different that their confusion needs to be explained. Why, then, do English lawyers see a reversion to 'status' in rules which leave the parties free to contract or not to contract, but restrict their freedom to contract except on certain minimum terms?

The reason must be found in a gap in the conceptual equipment of English law which itself reflects the social and jurisprudential principles of its growth. The distinction between *jus cogens* and *jus dispositivum*, between 'imperative' and 'optional' norms of the law of contract, is familiar to every practising lawyer in any Continental legal system. It fits naturally into the thinking of lawyers brought up and working in a world of legal thought in which the systematic regulation of the law of contract through general norms applicable to all contracts and special norms applicable to defined types has for almost two centuries been a commonplace. The distinction is not commonly used in English legal practice, although it is beginning to become more and more familiar to academic writers. The reason appears to be that the positive regulation of the substance of contractual relations has only within fairly recent times become one of the recognized functions of the legislature.

The view that employment is normally a matter of contract rather than of status depends upon the freedom of the parties to decide whether to enter into an employment relationship or not. Kahn-Freund's position is that even if that freedom is in practice curtailed by economic and social constraints, it remains as a formal legal freedom and as such has great significance. It is worth contrasting that view with the view that there is no meaningful freedom of choice whether to contract or not. From that initial premise, a rather different conclusion results.

Karl Renner, *The Institutions of Private Law and their Social Functions* (1949), pp. 121–2

Even more striking is the development which has taken place at the other pole of society, that of labour. It was not in vain that the workers, thrown together by the capitalists into compulsory associations, were in revolt for fifty years. According to Marx, and in fact during his lifetime, the capitalist hired the individual worker on the labour market for a wage that was individually agreed and took him into the workshop. The labour relation in its entirety was based upon individual regulation. But today the position is different, thanks to a century of struggle.

The prospective employee registers with a labour exchange, which is either a private establishment or run by the state, a municipality or a trade union. He is assigned to a job by rote. This state of affairs is unintelligible in an economy based upon freedom of contract, which can explain it no more than pure science can explain the working of a typewriter, which is a technical product. If the worker is accepted, at terms which are fixed beforehand and scarcely mentioned, he goes on the job. Formerly based upon contract, the labour relationship has now developed into a 'position', just as property has developed into public utility. If a person occupies a 'position', this means that his rights and duties are closely circumscribed, the 'position' has become a legal institution in character much like the fee of feudal times. The 'position' comprises the claim to adequate remuneration (settled by collective agreement or works rule), the obligation to pay certain contributions (for trade unions and insurance), the right to special benefits (sickness, accident, old age, death) and finally certain safeguards against loss of the position or in case of its loss.

What is the meaning of this development from the contract of employment to the position of work and service? The private contract, by means of the complementary institutions of collective agreement, labour exchanges, social insurance and the like, has become an institution of public law. It is still largely determined by the private will of the individuals concerned, yet this influence is continually decreasing, and the state element is almost of greater importance than the private element, the collective element more important than the individual element. It predominates today, when the job is becoming the 'established position'. The development of the law gradually works out what is socially reasonable. Labour, in fact, never is and never was a merely private affair, it has always been public service. Only an economic science unrelated to the state has transformed and disfigured the social necessity of labour into the private pleasure of individual capitalists and workers whose relations are established by acts of exchange.

In the form so far considered, the debate about 'status or contract' is ultimately one of terminology. Alan Fox has opened up the way to a more penetrating evaluation of the results of adopting a contractual model for the employment relationship. He suggests that the law of the contract of employment conceals, in the outward form of conventional contractual patterns, a reality in which a particular status is imposed upon the employee by the very nature of the law of the contract of employment.

> Alan Fox, *Beyond Contract: Trust, Power and Work Relations*
> (1976), pp. 181–4

The Employment Contract: Was it a Contract?
Before we pursue more fully the implications of collective bargaining for our analysis, other questions must be answered if we are to assimilate into that analysis what has been noted so far about the employment relation under industrialization. One of the master symbols of the emergent social order has been seen to be contract. Voluntary agreement forged through bargaining over specific terms, the essence of economic exchange, was seen as the mechanism which articulated atomistic, self-regarding individuals into the collaborative aggregates and linked processes necessary for civil society. How did the employment relation fit into this contractual society and into the ideologies prevalent within it? Can the contract of employment be seen as simply another manifestation of this increasingly pervasive form of exchange?

Certainly one would expect to find a strong ideological drive asserting it to be so. If mediaeval ideology, nourished and sustained by powerful interests, idealized the personalized bonds and commitments of feudal social structure as an equal balance of reciprocal diffuseness, the dominant ideology of newly emergent industrial society might be expected to idealize the employment contract, like all other contracts, in terms of an equal balance of reciprocal specificity. And evidence does indeed suggest a strain in this direction. Laski points to 'a growing sense, both in parliament and in the courts of law, that the nexus between master and man is purely economic, a relation, not a partnership implying reciprocal social duties'. And did not the evolving law of employment come increasingly during the nineteenth century to emphasize 'the personal and voluntary exchange of freely-bargained promises between two parties equally protected by the civil law alone'? . . . Capitalism indeed 'provides a legiti-mation of domination which is no longer called down from the lofty heights of cultural tradition but instead summoned up from the base of social labor. The institution of the market, in which private property owners exchange commodities – including the market in which propertyless private individuals exchange their labour power as their only commodity – promises that exchange relations will be and are just owing to equivalence'.

But the impersonal, calculating, low-trust attitudes of economic exchange were never universally accepted by employers, either in practice or in theory. Undoubtedly the general trend throughout the century was towards an 'impersonal management of labor which depended upon the formulation of the conditions of employment and upon elaborate controls which verified the workers' compliance with these conditions'. But persistently in some industries 'management depended upon a personal relationship between an employer and his workers, and hence upon the accidents of personal knowledge as well as upon the well-understood but unformulated relationship of trust which existed traditionally between a master and his men'. This persistence might have its roots not only in cultural isolation or inertia but also in a social philosophy which stressed the coincidence of business success with high moral practice and with the principle of the master conducting himself as trustee of his men's 'true best interests'. This philosophy recommending *social* exchange in master–man relations, so far from becoming extinct, was to enjoy a minor revival in circumstances to be examined later.

We must also note the coexistence of ideology celebrating the employment contract as 'the personal and voluntary exchange of freely-bargained promises' with practical attitudes expressing a clear determination that it should be nothing of the kind. Such was the inequality of power between the employer and the individual employee that to describe 'agreements' between them as 'freely-bargained promises' obscured the high probability that for much of the time the latter felt virtually coerced by the former into settling for whatever he could get – a picture hardly consonant with the glories of contract as celebrated by, for example, Spencer. Few of those who lauded the new industrial order were prepared explicitly to emphasize, as did Adam Smith a century before Spencer was writing, that 'It is not . . . difficult to foresee which of the two parties must, upon all ordinary occasions, have the advantage in the dispute, and force the other into a compliance with their terms. . . . In all such disputes the masters can hold out much longer. A landlord, a farmer, a master manufacturer, or merchant, though they did not employ a single workman, could generally live a year or two upon the stocks which they have already acquired. Many workmen could not subsist a week, few could subsist a month, and scarce any a year without employment. In the long-run the workman may be as necessary to his master as his master is to him; but the necessity is not so immediate.'

But it was not only that the brute facts of power made the employment contract something a good deal less than contract. Had this been the case we should simply be confronting the commonplace situation of a definition diverging from reality. There was, however, a further ambivalence relating to *definition*. The legal construction which was put upon the contract of employment left it virtually unrecognizable as contract. To appreciate the reason for this the starting point must be that, for employers and their sympathizers, the application of pure contract doctrine to the employment relation, had this ever happened, would have borne a damaging double edge. Certainly there seemed to be a strong legitimizing principle available to hand in the idea, betrayed in practice though it might usually be, of free and equal agents negotiating contractual arrangements on the basis of each seeking to maximize his utilities in competitive markets. The legitimizing strength of this idea could surely be brought to include within its persuasiveness those who contracted to participate as employees in collaborative associations for the production of goods and service, and thereby help to integrate and stabilize the productive system?

But application of the contract system proper to the employment relation would have suggested implications alarming to property owners. Since no employment contract could anticipate all relevant contingencies arising in work relations, many issues had to be settled during the everyday conduct of business. How hard was the employee to work? Under what material, social, and psychological conditions? With what tools, machines, and materials? Within what framework of rules, discipline, and sanctions? With what rights to demur against specific instructions, managerial policies, and proposals for change? These constituted the reality of life under an employment contract. But who was to settle them? How were the empty boxes of the contract clauses to be given the necessary content? The damaging implication of pure contract doctrine for the employer would have been that it could not allow him to be the sole judge of whether his rules were arbitrary or exceeded the scope of his authority. Certainly even under contract doctrine he might be granted – by the contract – the right to make rules, but he would not have the unrestricted right to decide whether the rules he had made or proposed to make were consistent with the contract. For, as noted earlier, contract theory included the notion of appeal by either party to some outside adjudicating body in the event of behaviour claimed to be inconsistent with the contract. This incipient threat to so integral a part of everyday control as their wide discretionary powers over the labour force would have been intolerable. It followed that contract as the pure doctrine defined it could not be seen by the property-owning classes as an adequate foundation for governing the employment relation. Their needs were met by infusing the employment contract with the traditional law of master and servant, thereby granting them a legal basis for the prerogative they demanded. What resulted was a form of contract almost as far removed from the pure doctrinal form as the status relationship which had preceded it.

Alan Fox in the above passages throws new light upon the 'contract or status' argument by identifying some underlying characteristics of the common law of the contract of employment. He shows how the common law moulded the contract of employment into a certain stereotype.

We have sought to show in the course of our discussion of the choice of form of the employment relationship that the present-day combination of common law and statutory regulation has created a more complex picture. Instead of a single stereotype of the contract of employment and another stereotype of the independent contracting relationship, there is a series of different types of employment relationship each characterized by a different outcome of the combination of common law, statutory regulation and market forces including collective bargaining; thus we may cite the categories of labour-only sub-contractor, temporary worker, part-time worker or homeworker. At the present day the 'status or contract' debate should therefore perhaps be re-stated by asking the questions, first, how far does there exist not one but a series of different kinds of status or contract relationship and, secondly, how far does and ought the law to control the status differentiations which can be created by the choice of the contractual form in which the employment relationship can be constituted?

It is hoped that the discussion in this chapter will have demonstrated the extent to which legal control of the size of the labour market, legal control of selection for employment, and legal control relating to the form in which the employment relationship is constituted, are interlinked issues. It will also have become clear in the course of the present chapter how closely inter-related are the areas of the formation, content, and termination of the employment relationship. In that sense, the discussion of the formation of the employment relationship would form a good starting point for a general study of employment even if one defined that subject as solely concerned with the individual employment relationship and therefore as a sort of branch of the law of persons. It will easily be inferred that we are in fact working to a more ambitious definition of the scope of labour law, and we have in fact begun with this topic because we think that it provides a useful background to the collective aspects of labour law to which we now turn our attention. We suggest that a sense of the working of labour market, and some understanding of the scope and possibilities of legal regulation of the individual employment relationship, are useful equipment with which to approach the discussion of the role of the law in relation to the process and phenomenon of collective bargaining which is the subject of the next chapter.

2
Collective bargaining and the law

In the previous chapter, we examined the economic and social considerations which are relevant to the constituting of employment relationships. We suggested that the law on that topic can only properly be evaluated against the background of those economic and social factors. That discussion showed the great significance of the processes which establish the terms of employment relationships. The study of industrial relations suggests that collective bargaining is the most important of those processes. A certain tradition within the study of labour law – which can probably claim to be the mainstream tradition – takes its starting point from that basic proposition, and concerns itself closely with the legal approach towards, and the legal regime governing, the process of collective bargaining. In this chapter we shall provide, first, a brief account of the development of collective bargaining in Britain, which is followed by a more extended discussion of the development of government policy towards collective bargaining and of the role of the law in the implementation of that policy. We shall then consider in some detail the nature of the current legal provision that exists to implement government policy in relation to collective bargaining.

1 Collective bargaining structures

By collective bargaining we mean those social structures whereby employers (either alone or in coalition with other employers) bargain with the representatives of their employees about terms and conditions of employment, about rules governing the working environment (e.g. the ratio of apprentices to skilled men) and about the procedures that should govern the relations between union and employer. Such bargaining is called 'collective' bargaining because on the workers' side the representative acts on behalf of a group of workers. That group may be a small group, as where a shop steward deals with a junior manager over the grievances of some workers in operating a particular machine in a factory which contains many machines, or it may be a large group, as where the national officials of a trade union bargain with the officials of an employers' association for an increase in the wage rates which will affect a whole industry. Thus, bargaining may be collective no matter at what 'level' it is conducted (at workshop, establishment or enterprise level with a single employer, or with a coalition of employers at district or national level). Indeed, collective bargaining may occur in respect of a particular group of workers at more than one level, and, as we shall see below (p. 294), the inter-relationship between the agreements concluded at the different levels is a frequent source of legal problems.

It is also clear from the examples given in the previous paragraph that collective bargaining need not, however, be collective on the employer's side. The sole proprietor of a small business who bargains with a union over the terms and conditions of his, say, twenty employees is said to engage in 'collective' bargaining, just as is a large company, in law also a single person, which bargains on its own with a trade union. Indeed, it is perhaps unfortunate that the same word 'employer' is used to refer equally to a sole proprietor and to a large, perhaps multinational, company, between which such an enormous social and economic gulf exists, especially as the word employer seems naturally to go with the pronoun 'he' rather than the pronoun 'it'. Thus, attention is implicitly drawn to the former rather than to the latter situation, even though collective bargaining is more widespread among large enterprises (invariably taking the legal form of companies) than among small ones. It might be thought, in fact, that a large enterprise, organized in the legal form of a single company, is indeed a collectivity, but a collectivity of capital and entrepreneurial skill, rather than of workers, as a trade union is. But for present purposes this does not matter, since the collective aspect of collective bargaining is seen as referring to organization on the employees' side alone. In short, the implicit contrast in the phrase collective bargaining is with individual bargaining whereby each employee makes his own deal with his employer (whatever legal form that employer may take). All this is reflected in the definition of a collective agreement contained in section 30 of TULRA 1974, as being an agreement or arrangement made by or on behalf of one or more trade unions (i.e. by organizations of employees and not by individual employees) and one or more employers or employers' associations (i.e. on the other side there need be only a single employer, though the employers also may be organized, if they so wish).

(a) **Trade-union membership**
If collective bargaining presupposes organization on the employees' side into trade unions, then it becomes of great interest to know how far trade-union

membership extends among the workforce in the UK. Table 1 shows that at the end of 1978 about half the workforce were members of trade unions and that this position had been reached from a situation where at the beginning of the century only about 10 per cent of the workforce was unionized. A high point was reached in 1979 when membership of unions affiliated to the TUC reached 52 per cent of the working population (some 12,200,000 members). Since then the dramatic rise in levels of unemployment has caused a sharp fall in union membership – to some 10,500,000 by the end of 1982, or only just on 50 per cent of the working population. Although union membership amongst those in work remains high, the overall drop in membership has caused serious concern to the TUC and its affiliated unions. In the case of some unions, the fall has been particularly sharp. For instance, between 1979 and 1982 the TGWU lost over a quarter of its 2 million members.

Table 1 Trade-union membership
1900–1978, United Kingdom

Year	Trade-union membership as a percentage of civil workforce
1900	11.7
1910	13.4
1920	34.9
1930	26.4
1940	31.6
1950	44.3
1960	40.5
1970	44.9
1971	45.0
1972	45.8
1973	45.5
1974	46.6
1975	47.2
1976	48.1
1977	49.4
1978	50.3

Source: ACAS, *Industrial Relations Handbook*
(1980), Appendix 4

The above figure of 50 per cent for 1978 is an overall figure and, of course, conceals wide variations among different groups of worker. Thus, there are variations as between manual and white-collar workers, as between men and women workers, as between the public and private sectors of the economy, as between manufacturing and non-manufacturing industry, as between large enterprises and small ones. The overall figure fortuitously coincides more or less with that for the percentage of manual workers in the private sector of the economy who are unionized, but probably only a little more than a quarter of the white-collar workers in this sector are unionized. On the other hand, if one focuses attention on manufacturing industry alone and excludes the smallest establishments (those employing fewer than 50 workers), the percentages rise to 82 per cent and 48 per cent respectively. But whether one is looking at private industry as a whole or just at manufacturing, the discrepancy between the densities of unionization of manual and white-collar workers is striking, and, as we shall see, it was a discrepancy that motivated the Donovan Commission in 1968 to propose the introduction of legal machinery to encourage employers to bargain with trade unions. In public employment, on the other hand, the proportion of workers unionized (manual and white-collar combined) is over four-fifths, and again we shall see that there are reasons of both public policy and law why this figure is higher than that for the private sector.

An alternative way of evaluating the position of the UK with regard to union density is to look at the position in other comparable industrialized countries. After making due allowances for the difficulties of comparing statistics relating to different countries which have not perhaps been compiled on an identical basis, it would seem that unionization in the UK is rather similar to that in Australia, but much higher than that in France or the USA. In those two countries the overall density is about one-quarter, although in the USA density in private manual employment is similar to that in the UK, and in France density in public employment is about 75 per cent. Overall density in West Germany is about three-quarters of the UK level, although again in public employment it is very high (over 90 per cent). In Sweden, however, union density is very much higher than in the UK at an overall figure of nearly 90 per cent.

These figures are no doubt interesting in themselves, but what accounts for the wide variations in the figures as between rather similar countries? Professor Clegg, from whose book *Trade Unionism under Collective Bargaining* (1976) the comparative figures are taken, explains the discrepancies by reference to features of the collective bargaining systems of the countries in question. He argues that high trade-union membership is associated with collective bargaining which is widespread in terms of the proportion of employees covered by the bargaining, with bargaining which involves local trade-union officials and shop stewards in the administration of the agreements concluded, and with employer support for the recruitment of members by trade unions. Thus, and this is hardly surprising, a crucial factor in encouraging high union membership turns out to be the extent of collective bargaining. Only where a union can represent its members in effective bargaining with the employer is a worker likely to obtain full value from his union membership. Accordingly, it is to the development of collective bargaining arrangements in the UK that we now turn.

(b) **The development of collective bargaining arrangements**[1]
The existence of collective bargaining in Britain of a type not unfamiliar to

[1]. In this section we draw heavily on E. H. Phelps Brown, *The Growth of British Industrial Relations* (1965); Allan Flanders, 'Collective Bargaining' in A. Flanders and H. Clegg (eds.), *The System of Industrial Relations in Great Britain* (1954); *Report of the Royal Commission on Trade Unions and Employers' Associations*, Cmnd. 3623, 1968; W. Brown (ed.), *The Changing Contours of British Industrial Relations* (1981).

modern eyes can be traced back at least as far as the middle of the nineteenth century. Like many British social institutions, modern collective bargaining is the result of a process of organic growth, adaptation and change which has gone on for a period of more than a century. It is difficult to understand the present-day system, its weaknesses and strengths, its potentialities and its limitations, without some understanding of its history. There is not, however, space here for a full history of the development of collective bargaining arrangements. What follows is a brief account which concentrates on three matters which are of paramount importance in any discussion of the relationship between the law and collective bargaining: the extent of collective bargaining (i.e. the range of workers covered by the arrangements), the scope of collective bargaining (i.e. the subject matter of the bargaining), and the level of the bargaining arrangements.

One can conveniently begin this brief history with the development of collective bargaining among craftsmen and skilled operatives in the 1850s and 1860s and its slow extension among these groups during the remainder of the century. At this stage collective bargaining did not bring within its scope unskilled workers, who did not have the industrial strength to maintain unions against employer opposition, unlike craftsmen, who had a bargaining strength derived from their control of entry to the trade, or the skilled operatives, who had the skill learned from doing the job even if they had no entry control. Nor did collective bargaining embrace white-collar workers, who often no doubt saw no need for it. Nevertheless, by the end of the century bargaining was widespread among skilled workers in most manufacturing and extractive industries, although that position had not been reached without many a bitter struggle.

Two further points need to be made about this early period which are crucial for an understanding of later developments, one relating to the organizational basis of the trade unions that were formed at this time and the other to the nature of the bargaining arrangements established. Given that the basis of the bargaining strength of those workers was their skill, it is perhaps not surprising that the unions which they succeeded in establishing were organized on an occupational basis, i.e. the principle of selection for membership was possession of the skill in question. Thus, the first modern unions were occupational unions, not industrial ones (attempting to organize all workers, whatever their actual tasks, working in a particular industry) nor geographical ones (attempting to organize all workers in a particular area, no matter in which industry they were employed) nor enterprise-based ones (aiming to organize all the employees of a particular employer). Second, the bargaining which these new unions succeeded in establishing was what was known as district bargaining, i.e. bargaining aiming at negotiations with all the employers in a particular industry in a particular area who employed members of the union. It was, thus, multi-employer bargaining and not bargaining with single employers on an enterprise or establishment basis.

District bargaining was, as Professor Phelps Brown has pointed out,[1] from the unions' point of view the path of least resistance. Employers might be persuaded to bargain with the union outside the plant, but they were not prepared to grant the union the recognition within the plant that single-employer bargaining would have implied. Multi-employer bargaining was necessarily confined to a relatively short list of matters, mainly wage rates, that was common to all the employers. Detailed conditions within particular factories, such as the organization of work, work loads, the exercise of disciplinary powers by foremen, are matters not easily reached by multi-employer bargaining. Nor, of course, did the majority of employers wish them to be. Whereas district bargaining over wage rates might offer an employer protection from wage-cutting competition from other employers in the district, and so confer some benefit upon him as well as upon the union, the employer would generally view union influence over the conduct of his business within the plant as an unmitigated restriction of his rights with no offsetting benefits.

The second stage of development began with the 'new unionism' of the 1890s and later years. Here for the first time unskilled workers managed to form and maintain unions, and to secure bargaining arrangements from employers. Because of the exclusive basis of organization of the existing unions, it was inevitable that this new wave of unionization should occur in general through the formation of new unions rather than through expansion of the existing ones. The bargaining strength of these new unions lay not in the possession of a skill in their members, but in their ability to prevent the employer recruiting an alternative labour force if his employees went on strike. Their principle of organization was thus necessarily inclusive rather than exclusive, and since an alternative, unskilled labour force might be drawn from anywhere, the new unions often crossed industrial boundaries. Thus, farm workers and labourers in steel mills joined the same union as dockers, and the gasworkers' union recruited unskilled labour in a variety of other industries: the 'general union' had been created. However, it would be wrong to identify the new unionism solely with the general union. A second, and lesser, form of its expression, especially in industries which had previously been largely non-union, was the creation of industrial-type unions, i.e. unions confining their recruitment to a particular industry but, within it, aiming to recruit all or a wide variety of grades. The Railways Servants' Union is a good example from this period. The 'new unionism' meant not merely that unskilled workers who had not previously been unionized were so now, but also that some industries where there had previously been little bargaining now acquired it – for example, public utilities and transport.

The progress made by the new unions was, however, neither quick nor easy. Strikes called by them were often met by stiff employer resistance and the use of blacklegs, whilst the workers responded with extensive and often violent picketing. A number of the leading decisions on the law of picketing today stem

[1]. Op. cit., p. 125.

from this period. Although 'new unionism' emerged in the 1890s, it made rapid progress only in the turbulent years immediately prior to the First World War, and even so by the outbreak of war collective bargaining arrangements covered perhaps only a quarter of industrial workers. More important from our point of view is that the bargaining arrangements secured by the new unions were largely still of the multi-employer, district variety. Only slowly in the years before the First World War did the district pattern of bargaining (whether in the skilled trades or the new unions) begin to change. Change, however, was not in the direction of single-employer bargaining, but towards multi-employer bargaining on a national scale in each industry. In the pre-war period the national bargaining machinery that did develop was procedural rather than substantive, i.e. it was not machinery for bargaining over wages and hours but for the handling of grievances which had arisen at plant level but which had not been settled there. However, the tendencies towards national bargaining, and now over substantive terms and conditions, were much encouraged during the First World War with its rapid price rises and greater government control of the economy.

At the end of the First World War the machinery of government control of the economy was rapidly dismantled, much more rapidly than at the end of the Second World War, and it might have been anticipated that the trend towards national bargaining would be reversed. In fact, it was confirmed and, for the first time, government took action to encourage the growth of collective bargaining arrangements. The war-time coalition government had been much disturbed by the growth of an unofficial and militant, even revolutionary, shop stewards' movement in certain industries, notably on the Clyde, operating at plant level, i.e. in the gap in the coverage of bargaining arrangements that multi-employer bargaining necessarily created. One of the purposes of the Whitley Committee, appointed in 1917 to consider 'suggestions for securing a permanent improvement in the relations between employers and workmen', was to re-establish official union control over employer/employee negotiations.[1] Its chosen solution was to encourage the pre-war developments towards national-level bargaining in all industries where organization of employers and employees was sufficient to admit of this. Its preferred model of national-level machinery was the National Joint Industrial Council, a permanent negotiating body with a written constitution and defined functions. However, there was to be no direct legal compulsion upon employers' associations and unions to establish NJICs, although in the four years after the war the newly formed Ministry of Labour actively encouraged them. By the end of 1921 some 73 NJICs had been established and in a number of other industries national machinery was established which did not follow the NJIC pattern. Where the levels of organization were not such as to support voluntary collective bargaining, the Whitley Committee recommended that

[1]. The Committee on Relations between Employers and Employed (Chairman: J. H. Whitley) issued five reports in 1917 and 1918.

government should establish a wages council to set a minimum wage.

With the onset of economic slump in the early 1920s government enthusiasm for the establishment of bargaining machinery was replaced by government enthusiasm for permitting employers to reduce wages in order to maintain international competitiveness. Perhaps a third of the newly founded NJICs collapsed and the others, especially those in industries exposed to foreign competition, struggled on with their nationally established rates often in danger of failing to secure observance in practice. For the same reasons, no doubt, the shop stewards' movement disintegrated, whilst the Whitley Committee's recommendations for the consultative works committees to supplement the NJICs seem never to have been implemented on any scale. Nevertheless, the Whitley Committee's recommendations had confirmed the trend towards multi-employer, national-level bargaining, which remained the predominant form of bargaining in Britain until well after the Second World War. Moreover, because collective bargaining was, at least for a brief period, actively encouraged by government, government employment itself became for the first time covered by bargaining arrangements on a large scale, so that a substantial segment of white-collar and female workers came under collective bargaining.

With re-armament in the late 1930s, and especially during the Second World War, conditions were created in which the area of collective bargaining could again be expanded. Some 56 NJICs were created or re-established between 1939 and 1946. However, the Second World War was perhaps much more significant for laying the foundations, together with the post-war economic boom (the very opposite of the slump that had followed the First World War), for the development, at least in manufacturing industry, of a permanent shop-steward system, which would at last fill the gap at plant level and which would ultimately ensure that in many industries multi-employer bargaining would cease to be the major determinant of terms and conditions of employment and be replaced in this role by single-employer bargaining.

Shop stewards (in some unions other titles are used) are employees selected by their fellow union members to represent them in negotiations with management and accredited by the union as its representatives in the workplace. Very often, shop stewards have thus a dual source of authority, deriving both from their selection by their fellow workers and from their endorsement by the union as an organization, although, as we shall see, the correct *legal* analysis of the authority of shop stewards has proved to be more complex than this simple model would suggest. In establishments where single-employer bargaining developed on an extensive basis in the 1950s and 1960s, a hierarchical structure of shop-steward organization appeared. In a typical case there would be at its base the ordinary stewards, elected by the various work groups in the plant, some of whom would be elected by their fellow stewards to a plant-wide shop stewards committee, the chairman of which (sometimes called a convenor) would be at the apex of the structure.

Where, as would be common, more than one union was represented in the plant, the joint shop stewards' committee would be an inter-union body. Indeed, in some cases there might be in a particular work group members of more than one union, so that the elected shop steward had representational functions *vis-à-vis* workers not in his own union. Whereas the ordinary stewards would probably spend rather little time on their representational duties, the convenor might be virtually full-time (though still paid by his employer) and be provided by the employer with rudimentary office facilities. In some cases the shop-steward organization spread beyond a particular establishment to embrace all the establishments of a multi-plant company or even group of companies.

One associated result of the development of collective bargaining at establishment level was that an opportunity was afforded to overcome the limitations as to subject matter that multi-employer bargaining necessarily involved. Although the scope of multi-employer bargaining had increased since its emergence in the second half of the nineteenth century, it could nevertheless be stated in 1954 that 'collective agreements are mainly concerned with settling the terms of employment, that is, with wages or salaries and working hours. . . .'[1] In contrast, Table 2, based on the results of a survey of shop-steward bargaining published in 1968, shows a much wider range of issues being discussed and settled by shop stewards.

Table 2 also shows that shop stewards bargain over wages and hours, i.e. the predominant subjects of national-level bargaining. Since multi-employer bargaining continued in those industries where it had already been established, the system of shop-steward bargaining that grew up was a supplement to, not a substitute for, multi-employer bargaining. This led, in the wages field, to a phenomenon that much concerned economists in the 1960s, namely 'wage-drift'. Increasingly, the wage rates set at national level were seen to constitute only minima, and effective rates were set only after supplementary bargaining by shop stewards at plant level. The 'drift' was the difference between the rates set at national level and the rates actually operating in practice. At first sight, there might seem to be a lot to be said for a bargaining system in which minimum wage rates and a limited number of common subjects are settled for all employers in an industry at national level, whilst effective wage rates and those subjects appropriately regulated at plant level are settled there in accordance with the potentialities and exigencies of particular enterprises and establishments. Yet it was the main concern of the Royal Commission on Trade Unions and Employers' Associations, which was appointed under the chairmanship of Lord Donovan in 1965 and which reported in 1968, to demonstrate that the systems of bargaining at national and at plant level operated not in co-operation with each other but in conflict.

The Commission pointed out, correctly, that the system of workplace bargaining had not developed under the control of the parties to national bargaining (usually national trade-union officials and officials of employers'

[1]. A. Flanders, op. cit., p. 299.

Table 2 Issues discussed and settled by shop stewards

	Ever	As standard practice	Rarely	Ever (grouped)	As standard practice (grouped)
	%	%	%	%	%
(a) *Wage issues:*					
piece-work prices	28	20	8		
other forms of bonus payments	43	25	18		
plus payments for dirty work, etc.	39	19	20		
job evaluation	33	20	13	83	56
allowances of any other kind	36	20	16		
merit money	33	17	16		
up-grading	45	24	21		
(b) *Working conditions:*					
distribution of work	43	25	18		
pace of work	38	22	16		
quality of work	39	27	12		
safety questions	72	54	18		
health questions	60	40	20	89	73
manning of machines	33	21	12		
transfer from one job to another	56	33	23		
general conditions in the workplace	74	56	18		
introduction of new machinery/jobs	39	23	16		
(c) *Hours of work:*					
level of overtime	47	34	13		
distribution of overtime	48	34	14	75	49
breaks in working hours	39	23	16		
stopping and starting times	44	24	20		
(d) *Discipline:*					
reprimands by the foreman	54	26	28		
suspensions	42	22	20	67	34
dismissals	49	23	26		
(d) *Employment issues:*					
taking on new labour	40	24	16		
number of apprentices	18	10	8		
acceptance of up-grading	35	21	14	67	43
short time	24	15	9		
redundancy questions	36	20	16		

Note: A small number of stewards said they also discussed and settled holidays or annual leave and a few other issues, but since these points were not put to all stewards no figures are shown.
Source: Government Social Survey, *Workplace Industrial Relations* (1968), p. 30.

associations) but as a result of the autonomous actions of workers and junior managers at plant level, of which the national-level parties might be in ignorance. Indeed, although usually powerless to prohibit these develop- ments, full-time union officials might be opposed to shop stewards' commit- tees, which brought together stewards from all the unions represented in the plant. The shop stewards' committee might, then, be an inter-union organization, with no parallel in the official union organizations existing outside the plant and to which the official structures had difficulty in relating. In any case, the development of shop-steward bargaining represented a shift in power to the shop floor which might not be welcome to full-time officials.

But it was not just the autonomy of workplace bargaining to which the Commission pointed. Looking at the style of bargaining that occurred at the workplace and adopting the analysis of Allan Flanders,[1] the Commission concluded that such bargaining was usually also informal and fragmented, informal in the sense of rarely leading to written agreements but only to the development of custom and practice, and fragmented in the sense of not being plant-wide bargaining but ad hoc bargaining on behalf of small groups of workers within the plant. These features, which were especially associated with piecework systems of wage payment, were thought to lead quite rapidly to anomalous and inequitable payments systems and to be a frequent cause of grievance among, and industrial action (often unofficial) by, the work groups. We set out below the Commission's statement of this view.

> *Report of the Royal Commission on Trade Unions*
> *and Employers' Associations,*
> Cmnd. 3623, 1968, paras. 143–50

143.   We can now compare the two systems of industrial relations. The formal system assumes industry-wide organisations capable of imposing their decisions on their members. The informal system rests on the wide autonomy of managers in individual companies and factories, and the power of industrial work groups.

144.   The formal system assumes that most if not all matters appropriate to collective bargaining can be covered in industry-wide agreements. In the informal system bargaining in the factory is of equal or greater importance.

145.   The formal system restricts collective bargaining to a narrow range of issues. The range in the informal system is far wider, including discipline, recruitment, redundancy and work practices.

146.   The formal system assumes that pay is determined by industry-wide agreements. In the informal system many important decisions governing pay are taken within the factory.

147.   The formal system assumes that collective bargaining is a matter of reaching written agreements. The informal system consists largely in tacit arrangements and understandings, and in custom and practice.

148.   For the formal system the business of industrial relations in the factory is joint consultation and the interpretation of collective agreements. In the informal system the difference between joint consultation and collective bargaining is blurred, as is the distinction between disputes over interpretation and disputes over new concessions; and the business of industrial relations in the factory is as much a matter of collective bargaining as it is at industry level.

149.   The formal and informal systems are in conflict. The informal system undermines the regulative effect of industry-wide agreements. The gap between industry-wide agreed rates and actual earnings continues to grow. Procedure agreements fail to cope adequately with disputes arising within factories. Nevertheless, the assumptions of the formal system still exert a powerful influence over men's minds

---

[1]. See especially A. Flanders, *Industrial Relations: What is Wrong with the System?* (1965) and *Collective Bargaining: Prescription for Change* (1967).

and prevent the informal system from developing into an effective and orderly method of regulation. The assumption that industry-wide agreements control industrial relations leads many companies to neglect their responsibility for their own personnel policies. Factory bargaining remains informal and fragmented, with many issues left to custom and practice. The unreality of industry-wide pay agreements leads to the use of incentive schemes and overtime payments for purposes quite different from those they were designed to serve.

150.   Any suggestion that conflict between the two systems can be resolved by forcing the informal system to comply with the assumptions of the formal system should be set aside. Reality cannot be forced to comply with pretences.

There was considerable debate at the time the Commission's report was published whether its analysis was generally applicable to British industrial relations or whether it was essentially an accurate description only of private manufacturing industry. Certainly, in industries, notably the nationalized industries and the public services, where a single company or organization dominated the field, the distinction between multi-employer bargaining at national level and single-employer bargaining at establishment level could not be so easily drawn. It was a case of bargaining at different levels within a single organization. Even in the private sector of manufacturing industry, as the Commission recognized, there were exceptions to the pattern of two-tier bargaining. Some large employers, often subsidiaries of US companies, found multi-employer bargaining restrictive, even in respect of their manual workers, and preferred to bargain on their own. In such cases domestic bargaining would not supplement industry-level bargaining; it would be the only bargaining covering the employees. More important, employers who had taken a conscious decision not to enter or to withdraw from an employers' federation in order to establish independent bargaining arrangements tended to opt for more centralized domestic bargaining, so that one might well find in these companies bargaining at enterprise as well as at establishment level. Some matters might be thought appropriate for company-wide arrangements, for example pensions and, increasingly today, even basic wage rates, whilst other matters would be left for plant-by-plant negotiation (large employers almost inevitably having multi-plant operations). These companies would tend, however, to discourage workshop-level bargaining and, certainly in the 1960s, often stood in strong contrast as far as their bargaining arrangements were concerned with federated employers where, as the Donovan Commission found, workshop bargaining had often grown up in a haphazard way, as a safety-valve for the pressures of the increased bargaining strength of the workgroups but without any overall guidance from either senior management or the trade unions as such. The greater centralization of bargaining arrangements in non-federated companies also meant that such bargaining was not completely in the hands of shop stewards. The company-level agreements of large employers, like Ford, Pilkingtons and ICI, were often negotiated by national union officials and today are perhaps more often negotiated on the unions' side by a combined team of full-time union officials and senior shop stewards from the various plants.

Indeed, it was the model of the non-federated company with a conscious policy of industrial relations that lay behind the Commission's main recommendations as to how workplace bargaining should be reformed. The aim should be to replace autonomous, informal and fragmented bargaining by comprehensive, written, plant or company-wide agreements, in the negotiation of which full-time union officials would play a part as well as shop stewards. The Commission did not see the legal system as having a major role in bringing about this change in bargaining practice and procedure, but did wish to see the establishment of a governmental agency to encourage voluntary reform. This was to be the Commission on Industrial Relations, set up by Royal Warrant in 1968 and placed on a statutory footing by the Industrial Relations Act 1971. In 1974 the CIR was replaced by the Advisory, Conciliation and Arbitration Service, and it is probably fair to say that bargaining reform has enjoyed a lower priority for ACAS than it did for the CIR.

However that may be, changes of the type envisaged by the Commission do in fact seem to have occurred over the decade since it reported. The Commission wished to encourage single-employer bargaining, albeit of a reformed type, rather than to try and suppress it in order to re-establish the primacy of multi-employer bargaining, as the Whitley Committee in different circumstances had recommended 50 years before. By 1978 it could be said that, for two-thirds of manual workers in manufacturing industry, single-employer bargaining had become the most important means of pay-determination. In many cases the nationally negotiated rates had become, in the words of Brown and Terry, not a floor but a safety net.[1] That is to say that an increase in the national rate by, say, ten per cent would not cause all pay rates in the industry to be increased by that percentage amount, but rather that only those workers being paid at within ten per cent above the old national rate would receive any benefit from the national increase. A survey carried out in 1978 found that, within the group of manual employees for whom single-employer bargaining was the most important, it was establishment-level bargaining that was indicated as the most important level for two-thirds of them, as against enterprise or corporate-level bargaining for the other third, although corporate bargaining tended to become more important the larger the size of the establishment.[2] As a not surprising concomitant of the growth of single-employer bargaining, the survey also found a four-fold increase in the number of full-time stewards over the decade. But the survey's single most important conclusion from one point of view was:

Shop stewards are no longer divorced from formal negotiating arrangements in the

[1]. W. A. Brown and M. Terry, 'The Changing Nature of National Wage Agreements', *Scottish Journal of Political Economy*, XXV, 119; but cf. R. F. Elliott, Note (1981) 19 *BJIR 370*.

[2]. W. Brown (ed.), op. cit.

way that the Donovan Commission had criticised. The formal arrangements have in the main been adapted to include them and the concomitant rise of single-employer bargaining has increasingly made stewards into the principal negotiators and guarantors of clear-cut factory agreements and procedures.[1]

Although the Donovan Commission did not recommend that general reliance should be placed on legal machinery to secure the reform of single-employer bargaining, there was one area where the Commission thought legal machinery could play an important role. That was in the establishment of bargaining arrangements in the first place or, as it is usually put, in the recognition by employers of trade unions as representative of their employees. The Commission was particularly struck by the low level of unionization among white-collar employees in the private sector of the economy (both manufacturing and services), and this they attributed to the reluctance of private-sector employers to bargain with representatives of their white-collar employees. We have already noted (above, p. 119) that government had accepted the principle of collective bargaining for its employees (who included many white-collar workers) in the aftermath of the First World War, and the extensive programme of nationalization effected by the Labour government after the Second World War brought a further group of white-collar employees under this policy. Indeed, as we shall see below (p. 198), the nationalized industries were placed under a legal obligation of recognition, though legal enforcement has been less important in practice than the declaration of public policy embodied in the statutes. But outside the public sector the picture was very different at the time of the Commission's report: 31 per cent membership among white-collar workers in insurance, banking and finance; 13 per cent in distribution, and 12 per cent in manufacturing industry.

Voluntary machinery for the securing of recognition was established under the auspices of the CIR in 1968. In 1971 the Industrial Relations Act established machinery to this end backed by legally enforceable sanctions. In 1975 the Employment Protection Act substituted a reformed version of the legally enforceable machinery, which operated mainly through ACAS and the Central Arbitration Committee. After an unsatisfactory history the 1975 machinery was abolished by the Employment Act 1980, leaving (outside the nationalized industries) only voluntary mechanisms to encourage recognition. It is debatable whether either of the two sets of legal machinery that were operative during the 1970s was ultimately very effective (albeit for different reasons in each case), though they no doubt operated to some extent to create a climate of public opinion favourable to recognition. However that may be, the fact is that union membership among and collective bargaining arrangements for white-collar workers in the private sector of the economy increased rapidly in the last decade. The survey quoted above found that in manufacturing industry, excluding the smallest establishments, nearly half of white-collar workers were unionized and that in nearly three-quarters of establishments

[1]. Ibid., p. 79.

collective bargaining arrangements for white-collar workers were reported to exist. Overwhelmingly, these arrangements were for single-employer bargaining; perhaps because, white-collar arrangements having developed predominantly since the Second World War, they have tended to take at once the single-employer form and to miss out the stage of multi-employer bargaining.[1] There have probably been similar developments in the financial services sector, but it is unlikely that the pace of development has been as rapid in distribution which is, as one shall see, a main area of operation for wages councils.

Thus, by the end of the 1960s collective bargaining arrangements were very widespread in British industry, for both manual and white-collar workers, for both manufacturing and non-manufacturing establishments, and for both men and women, as Table 3 suggests.

Table 3 Percentages of various classes of employees affected by collective bargaining arrangements (1978)

Full-time manual men	
(i) manufacturing industry	79.9
(ii) non-manufacturing industry	77.5
Full-time non-manual men	
(i) manufacturing industry	45.3
(ii) non-manufacturing industry	64.8
Full-time manual women	
(i) manufacturing industry	72.4
(ii) non-manufacturing industry	68.6
Full-time non-manual women	
(i) manufacturing industry	48
(ii) non-manufacturing industry	70

Source: Adapted from ACAS, *Industrial Relations Handbook,* Appendix I.
Notes
1. This table does not distinguish between the public and private sectors. No doubt, the figures for non-manual, non-manufacturing industry would break down rather differently as between the public and private sectors.
2. The figures for non-manual manufacturing industry (45.3 per cent for men and 48 per cent for women) are perhaps lower than the survey mentioned on p. 114 might suggest, but the figures from that survey relate to establishments, not employees, and exclude the smallest establishments, which are most likely not to have bargaining arrangements.

Thus, we can see that in this century there has been in the U K a remarkable growth in both the level of trade-union membership and in the scope of collective bargaining arrangements. Our main concern in this chapter is to examine the legal régime which governs the processes of collective bargaining

[1]. Ibid., pp. 13–16, 51–4.

and to see how far the developments in union membership and collective bargaining described above have been encouraged by the law. To that task we turn in the next section. However, a preliminary word of introduction is in order. For much of this century the law relating to collective bargaining has presented something of a paradox. On the one hand, governments have relied upon collective bargaining (rather than, say, legislation) to settle terms and conditions of employment and settle disputes between employers and employees. On the other hand, the state has done little to provide legislative encouragement of the institutions of collective bargaining. Consequently, we suggest that the salient features of the law relating to collective bargaining can best be displayed by asking what legal measures a government seeking to encourage collective bargaining might have adopted and then seeing how far the law falls short of this ideal. Finally, we shall seek to explain why this shortfall should have come about.

2 Collective bargaining and public policy

(a) Collective *laissez-faire* and the use of the law to support collective bargaining

What might be expected to be the basic elements in a legal policy designed to encourage the growth of collective bargaining? Although the list of measures such a policy could embrace would be a lengthy one, three fundamental provisions emerge clearly enough as the core of the policy. First, the law might be expected to protect actual or potential trade unionists from discriminatory acts by their employers designed to discourage them from joining, or taking part in the activities of, a trade union. This is the classical issue of how far the law protects employees' freedom of organization into workers' associations. In recent debate the 'right to associate' has been linked with the 'right to dissociate' or the legal protection of the freedom not to be a member of a trade union. However, as the Donovan Commission pointed out, the social function of these two 'rights' is very different: the 'right to dissociate' is 'designed to frustrate the development of collective bargaining, which it is public policy to promote, whereas no such objection applies to the ["right to associate"]' (para. 599). For this reason we shall consider in Chapter 5 the right not to belong and in this chapter the right to belong. However, no general legal protection against acts of anti-union discrimination by employers existed in this country until the passing of the Industrial Relations Act 1971. The protection has been continued after the repeal of that Act in 1974 and is now contained in the Employment Protection (Consolidation) Act 1978. As we shall see, however, the protection exists under the 1978 Act very much as an adjunct to the general protection in respect of unfair dismissals, and thus fails to reach discriminatory hiring policies.

Second, as we have already noted, trade-union membership is not usually regarded as an end in itself. Recruitment is valued for the force it gives to the union's claim to representativeness in its dealing with the employer. What role, then, has the law played in this country in requiring employers to bargain with representative trade unions? We have already seen that until the Donovan Commission's recommendations were (partly) enacted in 1971, there was (outside the nationalized industries) no general legal duty upon an employer to bargain with the organization representative of his workforce, and comparison unfavourable to UK law is sometimes made with that of the USA, where since the National Labor Relations Act of 1935 machinery has existed to this end. To expect such legislation in the UK before the realization, largely achieved by the Donovan Commission itself, of the importance of single-employer bargaining is perhaps anachronistic. Before the Second World War the only question that would have appeared to contemporaries to be worth asking would have been as to what legal machinery existed to encourage multi-employer bargaining on a district or national basis. Given the formidable difficulties surrounding the design of legal machinery that would compel effectively an employers' association to bargain with the trade unions operating in an industry, it is not surprising that the answer to our question is that no such direct legal compulsion existed. There did exist an indirect form of legal encouragement to multi-employer bargaining in the shape of wages councils, first established by statute in 1909 to deal with the problem of low wages in the 'sweated trades'. However, as we shall see later in this chapter, except in the years immediately after the First World War the record of wages councils in encouraging the establishment of voluntary and autonomous bargaining arrangements has not been a good one.

Thus, in respect of both freedom of association and recognition, no general legal provisions were to be found on these matters in British labour law before the legislation of the 1970s, implementing the principles recommended by the Donovan Commission (though not necessarily in the precise way envisaged by the Commission). With regard to the third of the basic provisions a legal system favourable to collective bargaining might be expected to contain – namely, provisions designed to ensure that collective agreements are observed – not even the last decade has seen the general introduction of such mechanisms. There are, of course, many arguments that might be put forward as to why collective agreements should be legally enforceable. To the lawyer the simple maxim *pacta sunt servanda* might seem a sufficient justification. However, in the present context the central argument is that if the terms of the bargain are not adhered to on either side to a sufficient degree, the incentive to engage in collective bargaining may be lacking for one side or the other. In practice the problem tends to be, not whether the parties to the collective agreement itself will abide by the agreement, but whether, where the parties on either side are oganizations, the members of the organization will accept the agreement. In the case of the parties to the bargain itself, their commitment, no doubt for different reasons on either side, to the bargaining process is usually sufficient to ensure their substantial compliance with the agreement struck, and if they have no such commitment, the law probably cannot supply it. Rather, on the union side the question may be whether the members of the union or the relevant workforce (union and non-union members) will abide by the collective agreement; on the employer's side, whether the members of an employers' association will abide by the agreement negotiated by the association. Thus, as against employers, the need for legal enforcement of the collective agreement tends to arise out of multi-employer rather than out of single-employer bargaining.

However, as the following passages demonstrate, because the interests of employers and unions tend to relate to the legal enforcement of different parts of the collective agreement, the question of legal enforceability must itself be broken down into two separate, but linked, issues.

O. Kahn-Freund, *Labour and the Law*, 2nd edn (1977),
pp. 122–3

A collective agreement is an industrial peace treaty and at the same time a source of rules for terms and conditions of employment, for the distribution of work and for the stability of jobs. Its two functions express the principal expectations of the two sides, and it is through reconciling their expectations that a system of industrial relations is able to achieve that balance of power which is one of its main objectives. What can the law do to protect these expectations?

To the two social functions of a collective agreement there correspond two actual or potential legal characteristics. The agreement may be, and in many countries is, a contract between those who made it, *i.e.* between an employer or employers or their association or associations on the one side and a trade union or unions on the other. At the same time the agreement is also potentially, and in many countries actually, a legal code. In this country it is generally neither a legally enforceable contract, nor (exceptions apart) a legally enforceable code.

The contractual function is mainly, but not exclusively, subservient to the maintenance of industrial peace. The 'peace obligation' has received different interpretations at different times and places. Does it mean that a union party to the agreement undertakes during its currency not to strike at all or only that it will not strike in order to change the terms of the agreement, *i.e.* is the 'peace obligation' absolute or relative? Does it bind the members of the union as well as the union itself? Does it impose on the organizations an obligation to press their members to apply the terms of the agreement, or only an obligation to make an effort in this direction? Or does it go so far as to impose on them a guarantee that their members will act in accordance with these terms? Do the parties make themselves legally liable to maintain common institutions, such as joint committees, or pensions funds, or a holiday scheme such as that which exists in some (including this) countries in the building industry? These are some of the very difficult legal problems attaching to the 'contractual function' of collective agreements.

The normative, *i.e.* the codifying and rule-making function, of a collective agreement serves to ensure that the agreed conditions are applied in the plant, enterprise or industry to which the agreement refers, *i.e.* applied by individual employers and workers. Many of them prescribe the terms of the individual employment relation, others the conditions under which that relation may or may not be created. A clause on wages or holidays or overtime belongs to the first, a clause on the reservation of jobs for skilled workers or on the employment of non-union members belongs to the second category. Still others prescribe the mutual rights and duties between union representatives, such as shop stewards, and employers. The comprehensiveness of the code varies from industry to industry, sometimes from enterprise to enterprise.

Report of the Royal Commission on Trade Unions and Employers'
Associations, Cmnd. 3623, 1968

467. The 'peace' obligation is imposed upon both sides, but it is more important in practice as a remedy to assist the employers than as a remedy to assist the unions; strikes are everywhere a more significant feature of industrial relations than lock-outs. This aspect of the legal enforcement of collective agreements is therefore of special importance to protect the interest of management in the continuous flow of production. Where this interest is thus legally protected, a corresponding legal protection usually exists for the interest of the unions in the maintenance of the standards laid down in the agreement. Under such a system employers who are themselves parties to collective agreements, or members of associations which are parties, are by operation of statute prevented from contracting out of the terms of the agreement to the detriment of their employees. This means that any contract of employment within the scope of the collective agreement which is concluded by an employer bound by its terms is automatically void insofar as it purports to be less favourable to the employee than the terms of the agreement; and that the corresponding terms of the agreement compulsorily become terms of the contract of employment in the place of those which, by operation of the statute, are void. The terms of the agreement thus become a compulsory code for all employers parties to the agreement or members of associations which are parties, and the agreement may by special administrative acts be extended to non-federated employers as well. These two matters, the agreement as a compulsory contract and the agreement as a compulsory code, are closely connected: the legal restriction of the freedom to strike is so to speak the consideration for the legal guarantee of the agreed minimum. The obligation to refrain from strike or other 'hostile' action is generally understood to be co-extensive with the scope of the substantive agreement: strikes are prohibited only in so far as they are intended to compel employers to consent to a change of the matters regulated in the agreement itself while that agreement is in operation, and industrial sanctions are permitted if their application is unrelated to matters dealt with in the collective agreement.

In view of the late and hesitant steps taken by the law in this country to guarantee the freedom to associate or to encourage recognition of trade unions by employers, it is no surprise to find a similar story in relation to the legal enforcement of collective agreements. The question of enforcing collective agreements as codes was raised in the 1920s and 1930s, as multi-employer bargaining at national level was placed in danger of collapsing, and did in some cases collapse, as a result of the unwillingness of individual employers in a recession to abide by national rates if the local labour market conditions suggested they could be undercut. Governments committed to maintaining the competitiveness of British goods in foreign markets rather than to maintaining real wages were generally unreceptive to arguments for enforcement, and their only substantial result was the Cotton Manufacturing Industry (Temporary Provisions) Act 1934, enforcing collective agreements as a code in a particular industry. However, during the Second World War, when, significantly, industrial action was placed under severe legal restriction, the principle of enforcement as a code was more widely adopted in Order 1305 (SR & O 1940, No. 1305) made under the Defence Regulations. The Order survived the War, but was amended and replaced by Order 1376 in 1951 (SI 1951, No. 1376), itself amended and replaced by the Terms and Conditions of Employment Act 1959, s.8, itself amended and replaced by Schedule 11 to the Employment Protection Act 1975, which was repealed and not replaced by the Employment Act 1980. In its peace-time role the above legislation operated, as we shall see below (pp. 159–63), so as to provide machinery for giving ad hoc (as opposed to general) legal enforceability to collective agreements as codes. It is somewhat ironic that only in the period when multi-employer bargaining was giving way to single-employer bargaining as the more significant determinant of terms and conditions of employment, did the principle of legal enforceability as a code become accepted in British law. As we shall also see, it was in many ways the attempt in 1975 to adapt a piece of legal machinery designed with multi-employer bargaining in mind to encompass also single-employer bargaining that led to the ultimate abolition of the machinery in 1980. War-time developments also led to a re-formulation in 1946 of the Fair Wages Resolution, which applied to government contractors and which could also operate to give ad hoc enforcement to collective agreements as codes. This Resolution is also discussed below (at p. 156).

The enforcement of the collective agreement as a contract was a major issue during the 1960s and one to which the Donovan Commission devoted much attention. We have seen that some of the forms of domestic bargaining that developed after the Second World War were accompanied by high levels of short, but also unofficial and unconstitutional, industrial action. The fact that these forms of action were unconstitutional, i.e. in breach of the procedures agreed betweeen employers and unions for the settlement of grievances, was seized upon by some as an argument for declaring them illegal. The Donovan Commission itself preferred to recommend voluntary reform of bargaining procedures (whose inadequacy was seen as contributing to unconstitutional action) rather than legal enforcement of the peace obligation in the un-reformed agreements. Such enforcement was contained, however, in ss.34–6 of the Industrial Relations Act 1971, which imposed an obligation upon the union not only to observe the agreement itself but also 'to take such steps as are reasonably practicable' to secure observance of the agreement by union members and, indeed, others (s.36(2)). For reasons which we shall examine below, this legislation had little effect in practice. It was repealed in 1974 and the present law (even after the 1980 and 1982 Acts) is not favourable to the legal enforcement of collective agreements as contracts. More to the point for present purposes, perhaps, is the fact that the argument for legal enforceability of the peace obligation in the 1960s was not so much that unconstitutional industrial action was in danger of leading to the collapse of collective bargaining – the unconstitutional action was on the contrary an expression of the development of domestic bargaining – as that this form of industrial action was undesirable in terms of the productivity of British industry. In other words it was the levels of industrial conflict associated with domestic bargaining that were the real cause for concern rather than simply their often unconstitutional nature. Consequently, we shall look further at the enforcement of collective agreements as contracts in the chapter which deals with the general problem of the legality of industrial action and confine our attention in this chapter to the enforcement of the collective agreement as a code.

Thus, in respect of none of the three fundamental provisions which a legal system aiming to be supportive of collective bargaining might contain does British labour law show a high degree of development. This was especially so up to the passage of the Industrial Relations Act 1971, which introduced for the first time general legal rules aimed to protect the freedom to associate and to require employers to bargain with trade unions (albeit under the 1971 Act in both cases in respect only of unions registered under that Act). Writing in 1959 Otto Kahn-Freund sought to explain the absence or relatively weak presence of such legal mechanisms at that time by resort to the notion of 'collective *laissez-faire*'. Kahn-Freund's theory of collective *laissez-faire*, which we shall have cause to discuss at various points in this book, had as its essence the notion that the state should in principle rely upon 'the regulatory function of collective forces in society' rather than itself determine terms and conditions of employment or, more broadly, the nature of the relations between employers and employees. As a theory of the role of the state, collective *laissez-faire*, like individual *laissez-faire*, led to the conclusion that that role, and in particular the role of the law, should in the field of industrial relations be a limited one. However, whereas individual *laissez-faire* meant reliance by the state upon 'the free play of the laws of a market between individuals assumed to be equal, and the use of the law to prevent the interference of collective entities such as trade unions with the operation of supply and demand', collective *laissez-faire* involved, not the restriction of the collective bodies, but positive reliance upon them by the state to discharge regulatory functions in a particular area of social life (see O. Kahn-Freund, 'Labour Law' in *Selected Writings of Otto Kahn-Freund* (1978), p. 8). For Kahn-Freund, individual *laissez-faire* could not be an alternative to state regulation of labour relations, because, as he always emphasized, whatever the assumptions of the law, the relationship between individual employee and employer was in fact one of subordination, not equality. See Kahn-Freund, *Labour and the Law* (2nd edn, 1977), pp. 22ff.

A number of interesting conclusions about the proper role of labour law in its various functions flowed from this theory. It meant most obviously that the determination of terms and conditions of employment was predominantly a matter for collective bargaining rather than for the law. In the 1950s the corpus of individual employment law in this country was indeed very small. We have already examined to some extent in Chapter 1 and we shall consider further below in Chapters 3 and 4 why from the early 1960s onwards this situation began to change, so that today for many people the vast bulk of individual employment law is synonymous with labour law. A second conclusion that Kahn-Freund drew from his theory was that the free functioning of collective bargaining required that the law take a liberal attitude towards the peaceful resort to economic sanctions by the parties to the bargaining if their negotiations did not produce agreement. Again, as we shall see in Chapters 6 and 7, this liberal or 'abstentionist' stance did characterize the law of industrial conflict in the 1950s, but a central legal and political issue since the Donovan Commission was set up in 1965 has been the question of whether this policy of abstention should not be abandoned, at least in part; and in 1971 and again in 1980 and 1982 the law of industrial conflict did cast aside its former restrained role.

But what of the implications of the theory of collective *laissez-faire* for our present topic, the role of the law in encouraging collective bargaining? Here, it might be thought, the theory of collective *laissez-faire* was not inconsistent with an active role for the law. If the state was to rely upon collective bargaining to regulate labour relations, should it not take steps to ensure that such bargaining machinery existed? Indeed, Kahn-Freund himself coined the phrase 'auxiliary legislation' to describe 'those branches of labour law which are designed to promote collective bargaining' (*Labour and the Law*, p. 48), and he recognized even in the 1950s that certain examples of this type of legislation could be found. In particular there were wages councils, the Fair Wages Resolution and the legislation concerning the 'extension' of collective agreements, all of which are discussed below. However, these were seen as somewhat anomalous provisions: the first two had their origins in the desire of government at the turn of the century to combat low pay in the sweated trades rather than a desire to extend collective bargaining, and the third originated during the Second World War, when strikes had been all but prohibited and the principles of collective *laissez-faire* substantially modified.

However, for Kahn-Freund collective *laissez-faire* was not merely an argument as to the stance the law ought to take towards labour relations, but also a description of the attitudes in fact held by the government, unions and employers on that matter. In this context the crucial fact explaining the absence of legislation on freedom of association and recognition was no doubt that by the 1950s there existed in the UK a stable and mature system of collective bargaining, at least for manual workers, which had been brought into existence without the help of such laws. In such circumstances neither the large unions nor the TUC, still essentially dominated by the interests of the manual workers, nor the government gave a high priority to legislation. No doubt, in union quarters there was some feeling that a non-interventionist system of law should be viewed as a seamless web: intervention by the law to support collective bargaining might bring less welcome intervention by the law in, say, the area of industrial conflict. The more sophisticated debates about the desirability of different types of interventionist law was something that developed only in the 1970s. However, to Kahn-Freund the fact that unions had not pressed for legislation indicated something more fundamental. Thus, the failure of trade unions to ask for legal recognition machinery, 'although, in the light of the political history of the last 20 years, we may surmise that if the unions had wanted such legislation they would have got it', demonstrated 'how much in particular union preference for industrial rather than political or legislative action dominates the impact of public opinion on the development of labour law in our time' (ibid., p. 12).

Why did this picture change, beginning with the Report of the Donovan Commission and the passage of the Industrial Relations Act 1971?[1] Why did collective *laissez-faire* cease to be the dominant ideology, thus opening the way to legal changes which rendered it also an inaccurate description of the law? The general cause lies in the relatively poor economic performance of Britain during the 1960s. During the boom of the 1950s the British collective bargaining system benefited from the general approbation accorded to the economy. In the 1960s, although the economy continued to grow, the much more rapid economic growth of other comparable countries became more noticeable, as did the problems of balance of payments deficits, persistent inflation and poor investment associated with the British economy. Government, saddled at least since the Second World War with general political responsibility for the performance of the economy, was no longer content to see collective bargaining as a largely autonomous, self-regulating system, for many of the deficiencies in British economic performance were linked in government's view to failures in the industrial relations system. This view was largely shared by employers.

These general developments do not, of course, explain the particular shape of the legal provisions in the 1971 Act, but they do explain the extensive discussion in the Donovan Commission's Report of whether it was feasible to use the law to reform collective bargaining practices and the attempt in the 1971 Act, introduced by the Conservative government of Edward Heath, to do so. Thus, the recognition procedure introduced in 1971 was designed as much to enable employers to deal with problems of overlapping unionism amongst the workforce as to compel reluctant employers to bargain with trade unions, although in fact few attempts were made by employers to use the recognition machinery in this way. The benefits of both the recognition machinery and the freedom of association provisions were confined, as far as unions were concerned, to unions which registered under the Act and so adopted the state-approved model of internal organization. In fact, all but a few unions affiliated

---

[1]. Of course, the 1971 Act was not a simple implementation of the Donovan proposals. In many ways the Act went contrary to the principles of the Commission, but the architects of both were prepared to embark upon legal changes difficult to reconcile with the notion of collective *laissez-faire*.

to the TUC refused to register (registration was optional), so that the impact of these new provisions was limited, but this does not affect the analysis of the reforming intent of the Act. And we have already noted the attempt in the Act (also unsuccessful) to enforce collective agreements as contracts.

Thus, a paradox of the 1971 Act was that, at the instance largely of government and employers, it introduced two basic legal protections for collective bargaining (recognition and freedom of association) in the face of strenuous opposition from the trade-union movement. The paradox disappears when it is appreciated that trade-union opposition was engendered mainly (but not wholly) by the restrictions on industrial action also contained in the Act, which we shall discuss in Chapters 6 and 7 and which were a main cause of the Act's repeal in 1974, whilst the measures supportive of collective bargaining were included by government because of the latter's view of their potential for the reform of bargaining. That the potential of these devices for reform of bargaining practices turned out to be rather limited is perhaps not surprising. Quite apart from the trade-union opposition to the Act (in legal terms expressed mainly in the TUC's campaign of non-registration), the fact is that government thought fit to use the law to shape the institutions and procedures of collective bargaining at a very late stage – more than a century after the first modern collective bargains were being struck between craftsmen and their employers. The greatest role that the law could perhaps be expected to play was in helping to fill and mould the gaps in a structure the main features of which were already fixed. Indeed, as we have seen, the Donovan Commission saw the role of the recognition law largely in this light. It was a mechanism whose main justification was the need to deal with the particular problems of white-collar workers in the private sector of the economy, although the Commission pointed out that the problem was not a trivial one given the growing proportion of the workforce represented by white-collar workers. The notion of using the recognition procedure to rationalize existing bargaining arrangements was an addition of the draftsmen of the 1971 Act and was perhaps doomed to failure.

More fundamentally, the late arrival of the law meant that trade unions as functioning social institutions owed very little in any positive way to the law for the achievement of their extensive bargaining machineries. The contrast here with unions in the USA is very instructive. There the legal procedures ushered in by the National Labor Relations Act of 1935 were instrumental in achieving a level of recognition by employers of trade unions which trade unions previously by their own unaided efforts had been unable to secure. The trade-union movement in that country has thus for a long time been prepared to accept, has even welcomed, a degree of legal regulation of collective labour relations that is foreign to the experience of trade unionists in this country. This means that there was little opportunity for the government in this country to do a political deal with the trade-union movement whereby, in exchange for recognition laws, the unions accepted restrictions upon, say, their freedom to engage in industrial action (which is, in a way, the settlement that was arrived at in the USA over a period of years with the National Labor Relations Act of 1935 and the Taft-Hartley Act of 1947).

The Industrial Relations Act was repealed by the Labour government elected in 1974. The provisions governing the legal enforcement of collective agreements as contracts were reversed. The guarantee of freedom of association was continued, now more firmly as part of the law of unfair dismissal than before. After a brief hiatus, a new recognition procedure was enacted in the Employment Protection Act 1975, ss.11–16. This new procedure lacked the reforming zeal of its predecessor and was more attuned to the aims of the Donovan Commission, viz. the extension of collective bargaining, albeit on a rational basis, into areas it had previously not penetrated. The new procedure was, in short, more unambiguously aimed at extending bargaining as opposed to reforming its procedures. The new procedure was available to trade unions (provided they were independent – the concept of registration had gone) but could not be initiated by employers. The 1975 Act also added a number of further supports for collective bargaining, all no doubt of lesser significance than the freedom of association and recognition provisions but all equally of some potential value to trade unions in the bargaining process. Thus an employer must disclose certain information to independent trade unions recognized by him where the information is needed for the purposes of collective bargaining (provisions in fact first introduced by the Industrial Relations Act 1971 but never brought into force and now contained in the Employment Protection Act 1975, ss.17–21). An employer must grant his employees a certain amount of paid time off to enable them to carry out trade-union duties and a certain amount of unpaid time off to engage in trade-union activities (provisions first introduced in 1975 and now contained in the Employment Protection (Consolidation) Act 1978, ss.27–8, 30 and 32). An employer proposing to dismiss any of his employees on grounds of redundancy must consult in advance with any relevant recognized union (provisions contained in the Employment Protection Act 1975, ss.99–107). More recently it has been provided that, where a transfer of a business from one employer to another is contemplated, both transferor and transferee employers may have to give information to or consult with recognized trade unions in certain circumstances (provisions contained in the Transfer of Undertakings (Protection of Employment) Regulations 1981 (SI 1981 No. 1794). Both the consultative duties owe their presence in British law in part – in the case of the transfer regulations, almost entirely – to Directives issued by the Council of the European Economic Community, which is playing a minor, but increasing, role in the development of British labour law.

The Employment Protection Act had the full support of the trade-union movement. This support represented, in terms of Kahn-Freund's analysis (above, p. 134), a willingness of the union movement, at least at the level of the TUC, to use the method of political or legislative action, if not instead of, then at least as a supplement to, industrial action, and it stood in some contrast to the TUC's attitudes towards the law in the 1960s. Indeed, the Act was a prime constituent of the 'Social Contract'[1] between the Labour government and the TUC, whereby, in exchange for considerable restraint in wage claims, the union movement achieved favourable legislative and administrative measures from the government. Whether the legislation turned out in practice to be as effective as the TUC had expected is debatable. However that may be, the Conservative government elected in 1979 dealt the structure of collective bargaining law created by the 1975 Act two severe blows in the Employment Act 1980. This Act repealed the recognition procedure of the 1975 Act and also Schedule 11 to the 1975 Act, which was the modern version of the war-time provisions on the enforcement of collective agreements as codes. Subsequently, in 1982, the government also rescinded the Fair Wages Resolution. That a Conservative government which was ideologically opposed to the corporatist implications of government by way of Social Contract and ideologically committed to greater regulation of labour relations by market forces would do something to dismantle the structure of the 1975 Act was to be expected. In some ways the surprising thing is that the repeal did not go further. The freedom of association provisions and all the lesser supports for collective bargaining introduced by the 1975 Act continue in force (no doubt in some cases because such provisions are required by international agreement to which the UK is party). These provisions will be discussed in detail below. What is interesting is that the Conservative government in 1980 saw its policies as best served by repealing rather than by reforming the recognition procedure (even though it was a Conservative government in 1971 that had first placed such a procedure on the statute book) and by repealing rather than reforming Sch. 11 to the 1975 Act (even though similar provisions, albeit in a less expansive form, had been part of British labour law since the Second World War).

What this suggests is that, after two different attempts in the 1970s, represented broadly by the 1971 and 1975 Acts, to reorient the relationship of labour law and collective bargaining, a third attempt is under way, but this history also suggests that none of the three exercises in reformulation has produced as coherent and acceptable a rationalization as was provided by the doctrine of collective *laissez-faire* in the 1950s. On the contrary, the law of collective bargaining has increasingly come to consist of the debris left behind by earlier failed efforts at reformulation and of the half-completed constructions of the current toilers in the sands of labour law reform.

(b) Collective bargaining, industrial conflict and the control of inflation

It is easier to describe, as we have just done, the erosion of collective *laissez-faire* as a theory explanatory of public policy towards industrial relations and

[1]. See J. Elliott, *Conflict or Cooperation?* (1978); Clark, Hartmann, Lau and Winchester, *Trade Unions, National Politics and Economic Management* (1980).

labour law, than to be sure of the reasons for such an important change. Nevertheless, more than a decade after the Donovan Commission's Report it is at least possible to identify the main factors that have brought about a rejection of the previously dominant theory of collective *laissez-faire*. There seem to be two main areas of concern, one as old as the institution of collective bargaining itself and the other a product of the post-Second World War period, and a third lesser theme, also one of ancient lineage but one of which relatively little had been heard until very recent times.

The main area of concern that has always been a concomitant of collective bargaining is the association between collective bargaining and industrial action. The legal controls upon the use of industrial action will be the topic for chapters 6 and 7 and, as we shall there see, it is necessary to an understanding of the present law to trace its development back at least as far as the legislation of the 1870s. Any autonomous system of collective bargaining presupposes that the parties to the bargaining will have access to autonomous social sanctions in order to secure and enforce agreements. On the workers' side this means the legal freedom to strike and to engage in other forms of industrial action; on the employer's side the legal freedom to lock out and generally to exercise managerial prerogatives in the face of industrial action by workers. Of course, the need for autonomous social sanctions does not rule out certain restrictions upon resort to industrial action, but in fact government after 1875, except during the two World Wars, seemed to accept a policy of preserving a broad area of autonomy for the parties' own sanctions, provided, of course, that what was at issue was the peaceful deployment of economic pressure. As we shall see, this was not a policy that always commended itself to the judiciary and the history of the law of industrial action until the last decade was in many ways a simple counterpoint between parliament and judiciary. Nevertheless, at the level of government policy the approach seemed well enough established, especially after the rejection of schemes of compulsory arbitration by the Royal Commission on Labour in 1894, the passage of the Trade Disputes Act in 1906 and the dismantling of the war-time controls in 1919. To Otto Kahn-Freund writing in the 1950s, government policy towards the law of industrial conflict was the second, and perhaps the more important, aspect of the doctrine of collective *laissez-faire*.[1]

In the context of the economic prosperity and historically low levels of industrial conflict of the 1950s, a doctrine of collective *laissez-faire* as applied to the law of industrial conflict seemed no doubt to have much to commend it. However, just as, in the past, rising levels of industrial conflict had led to challenges to the prevailing wisdom (e.g. the proposals for compulsory arbitration considered by the Royal Commission on Labour in response to the wave of strike activity associated with the 'new unionism'), so also we have seen that the rising levels of short, unofficial and unconstitutional action associated with the growth of domestic bargaining in the 1960s both provided

[1]. O. Kahn-Freund, op. cit., pp. 21–4.

a reason for setting up the Donovan Commission and influenced many of the proposals made to it. Like the Royal Commission on Labour before it, the Donovan Commission in fact largely rejected the proposals for greater legal controls over industrial action and opted instead for a solution more directly aimed at the causes of the problem, which were perceived to lie in the nature of the domestic bargaining system.[1] Unlike the Royal Commission on Labour, the Donovan Commission was less successful in carrying its views with government, and in the field of industrial conflict law the Industrial Relations Act 1971, as we shall see in Chapter 6, in fact contained certain restrictions which the Commission had rejected.

The Industrial Relations Act was repealed in 1974, and the Trade Union and Labour Relations Acts 1974–6 re-enacted in relation to the law of industrial conflict a modernized version of the doctrine of collective *laissez-faire*. Meanwhile, however, government perceptions of the nature of the underlying problems had changed. During the course of the 1970s the reforms in domestic bargaining advocated by the Donovan Commission were implemented over a fairly broad area of the economy and for this and other reasons the short, unconstitutional and unofficial strike ceased to be the main object of government concern. The centre of the stage was now occupied by a form of industrial action that was in many ways the direct opposite of that which had occupied the Donovan Commission's attentions. This was the large-scale, often industry-wide, strike, embarked upon only after the full exhaustion of negotiating procedures and completely official, concerning a national pay claim and more often arising in the public sector of the economy than in the private sector. It was a desire to limit the disruptive effects of such strikes that led to the enactment of restrictions upon picketing other than at one's own place of work and upon other forms of secondary industrial action in the Employment Act 1980.

However, it is when one looks at the cause of the conflict in many of these industry-wide strikes of the 1970s that the second main theme of the relations between the state and the collective bargaining system emerges, for in many cases the strike was an attempt, sometimes successful sometimes not, to achieve a higher rate of settlement than the government's incomes policy then in force would allow. Since the middle of the 1960s different forms of incomes policy have followed one another with bewildering speed, with occasional pauses for 'free' collective bargaining. Governments of both political parties have pursued incomes policies, but assessment of their success has not proved an easy task. Certainly none has achieved an institutional form that has shown any degree of permanence.[2] What does lie behind the policies is, however, an acceptance by government, although the issue is still controversial among economists, that a main factor in the rate of inflation is the ability of certain

[1]. *Report of the Royal Commission on Trade Unions and Employers' Associations.* Cmnd. 3623, 1968, Chaps. IV, VII, VIII, XIV.

[2]. H. A. Clegg, *The Changing System of Industrial Relations in Britain* (1979), Chapter 9.

groups of workers in a strong bargaining position to achieve levels of wage settlement in excess of increases in productivity. Incomes policies represent an attempt by government to reduce the rate of wage increases by applying governmental pressures (sometimes involving the use of the law, sometimes not)· to supplement what is seen as the inadequate powers of employers in collective bargaining to resist demands for wage increases.

It might seem that a government persuaded of the view that a main cause of inflation lies in the power of collectively organized workers to obtain excessive wage increases would not be at all in favour of legislation supportive of collective bargaining and would favour legislation restricting the legal freedom of workers to engage in industrial action. To some extent such legal restrictions might be seen as a substitute for a more formal incomes policy with its pay norms and list of permitted exceptions to the norm, and there is evidence that in some quarters the provisions of the Industrial Relations Act 1971 restricting industrial action were viewed in that light.[1] But, as we have seen, that Act also contained a recognition procedure because the government at that time was pursuing as an additional goal of the legislation a policy of encouraging the reform of bargaining procedures. Moreover, the view that government concern with inflation and levels of pay settlement ought simply to reinforce the collective *laissez-faire* doctrine so far as it applies to the absence of legal encouragement of collective bargaining ignores the difficulties governments have in securing compliance with their pay norms. One aim of government must be to secure the consent of employees and employers for the policy being pursued. One way of doing this may be to draw a distinction between the general system of collective bargaining (whose growth is to be encouraged) and the level of pay settlements resulting from the system (which is to be constrained). Indeed, government may couple a restraint of the general level of pay settlements with specific measures to help the low paid. Further, trade-union consent to the pay norm may be conditional upon the absence of legal measures restricting the freedom to engage in industrial action, even if it is anticipated that during the period of the consensual pay policy there will be less cause to engage in industrial action, at least over pay rates. This was the essence of the agreement between the TUC and the Labour government during the 'Social Contract'[2] period of 1974 to 1979. The repeal of the Industrial Relations Act 1971, a new recognition procedure in the Employment Protection Act 1975 and a re-vamping of the provisions extending collective agreements in Sch. 11 to the 1975 Act to help the low paid were three major provisions offered and accepted in exchange for agreement upon rates of pay increase below the level of inflation.

That the 'Social Contract' incomes policy collapsed during the winter of 1978–9 only partly explains why the Conservative government elected in 1979 decided to pursue a different sort of policy. That government was also opposed on constitutional grounds to so much of the nation's economic and social

[1]. D. Barnes and E. Reid, *Governments and Trade Unions* (1980), Part III.   [2]. See footnote to p. 137 above.

policies being decided by concordat between government and TUC and was convinced of the economic arguments for achieving prosperity through the interplay of market forces. Consequently, it did not seek the TUC's agreement to a new incomes policy and did not even seek to rely heavily on restrictions on the legality of industrial action to achieve anti-inflation goals, although, as we have noted, there is an element of that policy in the 1980 Act. Instead, the government allowed levels of unemployment to rise to the point where the labour market position of all but the strongest groups of workers was eroded, whilst pursuing in relation to its own employees and the employees in the public sector generally an incomes policy of the conventional sort. This policy represented the abandonment of the goal all post-war governments have had of combining high levels of employment with low levels of inflation, for it gave priority to the latter over the former.[1] Moreover, the emphasis upon market forces led to the resuscitation of an argument not much heard in the post-war period – and this is the third theme – that collective bargaining, by distorting labour markets, produces inefficiency. In particular, it was suggested that collective bargaining, by replacing individual bargaining, allowed the achievement of wage levels that reduce the overall levels of employment. This is in many ways the most fundamental criticism of collective bargaining because it goes to a basic purpose of the institution, which is to overcome the weakness and lack of bargaining strength that individuals in the labour market generally experience.

In the light of the above it is not surprising that governments' attitudes towards collective bargaining have become more ambiguous since the Second World War and especially since the middle of the 1960s. The simple commitment to a public policy (not necessarily to legislation) supportive of collective bargaining, enunciated by the Whitley Committee at the end of the First World War and adopted by governments since that time, came under question. However, different governments reacted to the problem in different ways. Some sought to continue to encourage the practice of collective bargaining whilst restraining its consequences, whether inflationary or in terms of working time lost. This was the case (in very different ways) with both the Conservative government that passed the IRA 1971 and the Labour government that passed the EPA 1975. The Conservative government elected in 1979, however, made a much more radical break with the past. As we shall see in this chapter, it dismantled a number of the legislative props for collective bargaining and, as we shall see later (below, pp.862–8), it even put obstacles in the way of industrial action aimed at extending recognition of or consultation with trade unions on the part of employers. In 1982 the government had to define its attitude towards collective bargaining in the context of the question of whether it would ratify the new ILO Convention concerning the Promotion of Collective Bargaining (No. 154 of 1981). The UK had ratified the pre-

---

[1]. See P. Davies and M. Freedland, 'Editors' Introduction' to Kahn-Freund, *Labour and the Law* (3rd edn, 1983).

decessors of the new Convention (Nos. 87 and 98 (1948 and 1949), concerning freedom of association and the right to organize). (See below, p. 178.) Article 5 of Convention 154 requires ratifying states to take steps (not necessarily legislation) to promote collective bargaining in various ways. The UK government commented in giving its reasons for not ratifying the new Convention:

The Government considers that while United Kingdom law should permit and facilitate the extension of collective bargaining by freely made agreements between employers and trade unions, which it currently does, it would not be appropriate to accept the obligation contained in Article 5 of the Convention to promote the extension of collective bargaining by direct Government intervention. [Cmnd. 8773, 1982, p. 1.]

We have sketched out the continuing problems that beset governments in reconciling the system of collective bargaining with acceptable levels of industrial conflict and acceptable rates of wage increase. It is perhaps worthwhile at this point to ask what are the advantages of collective bargaining, other than that it is the existing system of determining terms and conditions of employment. In the following passage Allan Flanders, addressing himself to the question 'What are trade unions for?', gives a threefold answer and directs our attention to the internal advantages of the system which must be weighed in any balance with the external costs discussed above.

Allan Flanders, *Management and Unions* (1970), pp. 41–2

Here one thing is at once certain, and it applies to all trade unions, and has applied throughout the greater part of their history. The activity to which they devote most of their resources and appear to rate most highly is collective bargaining. So the question we have to ask is what purposes do unions pursue in collective bargaining? The conventional answer is that they defend and, if possible, improve their members' terms and conditions of employment. They are out to raise wages, to shorten hours, and to make working conditions safer, healthier and better in many other respects.

This answer is right as far as it goes, but it does not go far enough. Collective bargaining may be what the words imply – that depends on how we define bargaining – but it is also a rule-making process. The rules it makes can be seen in the contents of collective agreements. In other words, one of the principal purposes of trade unions in collective bargaining is regulation or control. They are interested in regulating wages as well as in raising them; and, of course, in regulating a wide range of other issues appertaining to their members' jobs and working life.

Why do they have this interest in regulating employment relationships, and what social purpose does such regulation serve? It is certainly not a bureaucratic interest in rules for their own sake. Unions and their members are interested in the effect of the rules made by collective bargaining, which is to limit the power and authority of employers and to lessen the dependence of employees on market fluctuations and the arbitrary will of management. Stated in the simplest possible terms these rules provide protection, a shield, for their members. And they protect not only their material standards of living, but equally their security, status and self-respect; in short their dignity as human beings.

One can put the same point in another way. The effect of rules is to establish rights, with their corresponding obligations. The rules in collective agreements secure for employees the right to a certain rate of wages; the right not to have to work longer than a certain number of hours; the right not to be dismissed without consultation or compensation and so on. This surely is the most enduring social achievement of trade unionism; its creation of a social order in industry embodied in a code of industrial rights. This too is the constant service that unions offer their members: daily protection of their industrial rights.

Such rights could be, and to some extent are, established by law. But collective bargaining serves yet another great social purpose. Apart from providing protection, it also permits participation. A worker through his union has more direct influence on what rules are made and how they are applied than he can ever exercise by his vote over the laws made by Parliament. We hear a lot these days about participation, including workers' participation in management. I have yet to be convinced that there is a better method than collective bargaining for making industry more democratic, providing its subjects and procedures are suitably extended. Putting a few workers or union officials on boards of directors only divorces them from the rank-and-file. In collective bargaining trade unions must continually respond to and service their members' interests.

The constant underlying social purpose of trade unionism is, then, participation in job regulation. But participation is not an end in itself, it is the means of enabling workers to gain more control over their working lives. Nothing has happened over the post-war years to change that basic purpose or to lessen its importance.

3 Legal support for multi-employer collective bargaining

We now turn to look at the current legal provisions relating to the encouragement of collective bargaining. We have divided these provisions into two broad groups: those older provisions which have their origins in the period of multi-employer bargaining but which have endured, not always comfortably, into the modern period; and the more recent provisions which post-date the Donovan Commission's Report and which have as their focus a system of single-employer bargaining. The first group consists of the wages councils legislation (currently consolidated in the Wages Councils Act 1979), the Fair Wages Resolution 1946 and the provisions on the extension of collective agreements. We have seen that during much of this century governmental policy towards collective bargaining could be characterized as being a policy of collective *laissez-faire*, and it is thus perhaps surprising to find any legal mechanisms designed to encourage collective bargaining which pre-date the Donovan Commission's Report. It is certainly significant that in origin neither the wages councils legislation nor the fair wages resolution had the primary objective of encouraging collective bargaining, although at a later date this objective was superimposed upon the original one, whilst the extension provisions had their origins in the abnormal situation that obtained during the Second World War. The wages councils legislation and the Fair Wages Resolution were in fact two sets of minimum-wage measures and the extension provisions were an aspect of measures for dispute resolution and the control of industrial conflict. We therefore have to chart the interplay between these objectives and the policy of collective *laissez-faire* which has been associated with them. Moreover, the adaptation of the mechanisms for use in a period of predominantly single-employer bargaining had, as we shall see, a traumatic, in some cases even an extirpatory, effect upon them. The extension provisions and the principle of fair wages were conflated and much developed by the EPA 1975, Sch. 11, and that schedule and the Resolution then saw a period of very heavy use in the late 1970s. The government elected in 1979, however, repealed Sch. 11 by s.19(c) of EA 1980 and, later, secured the rescission of the FWR as from September 1983. The wages council system survives, but is under threat.

(a) Wages councils[1]

Wages councils are tripartite bodies consisting of an equal number of representatives of employers and of employees and not more than three independent persons, whose function is to lay down for a particular industry the minimum remuneration and other terms and conditions of employment to which employees in that industry shall be entitled. Wages councils do not exist in all industries but only in those industries which satisfy the criteria laid down in the Act (s.1) for their establishment and where the Secretary of State for Employment has established a wages council after following the requisite statutory procedures. In 1980 33 wages councils were in existence, covering some three million workers. In addition there is separate legislation for agriculture (and indeed for agriculture in England and Wales and agriculture in Scotland) which covers a further 400,000 workers. The system for agriculture is in its essentials similar to the general system and we do not propose to elaborate upon the differences. An order made by a wages council setting terms and conditions of employment has the effect of displacing any less favourable terms in the contracts of employment of the employees to whom the order relates (s.15), so that, in sharp contrast to the provisions of a voluntary collective agreement, as we shall see, the terms of the wages council order are automatically and compulsorily incorporated into the relevant individual contracts of employment. Further, failure by an employer to pay the minimum remuneration (including holiday pay) or to permit the employee to take the holidays fixed in the order is a criminal offence, although non-compliance with the other terms of an order is not a criminal offence. A Wages Inspectorate, employed by the Department of Employment, exists to enforce the orders, although an individual employee is, of course, free to initiate an action for breach of contract, if he wishes.

[1]. See F. J. Bayliss, *British Wages Councils* (1962); O. Kahn-Freund, 'Minimum Wage Legislation in Great Britain' (1948/9), 97 *U. Pa. LR* 778; *Report of Royal Commission on Trade Unions and Employers' Associations* (Cmnd. 3623, 1968), paras. 225–34, 257–66, 277–80; H. A. Clegg, *The Changing System of Industrial Relations in Great Britain* (1979), pp. 425–34; Craig, Rubery, Tarling and Wilkinson, *Labour Market Structure, Industrial Organisation and Low Pay* (1982).

The history of the wages councils legislation falls into four distinct phases. The first Trade Boards Act – the nomenclature 'wages council' was not introduced generally until 1945 – was passed in 1909 in order to deal with the evils of 'sweating', which had been defined by a House of Lords Select Committee in 1890 as work done in those industries characterized by 'a rate of wages inadequate to the necessities of the workers or disproportionate to the work done, excessive hours of labour, and the insanitary state of the houses in which the work is carried on'. The wages council was thus seen as a response to a problem of low pay and worse, and the solution was to be the establishment of a body that would directly decree a minimum wage in each of those industries where 'the rate of wages prevailing in any branch of the trade is exceptionally low, as compared with that in other employments, and [where] the other circumstances of the trade are such as to render the application of this Act to the trade expedient' (1909 Act, s.1(2)). From the very beginning wages councils had affinities with the then dominant form of voluntary bargaining, as demonstrated by the establishment of separate councils for separate industries, the presence on the council of representatives of employers and employees in the industry together with a small number of independents to ensure that a decision was reached, and the limited powers, since further reduced, of Ministers to control the content of wages councils orders. Nevertheless, the predominant aim at this stage seems not to have been to use wages councils to encourage the growth of voluntary collective bargaining in the sweated trades (these trades were probably thought to be beyond organization) but to provide an alternative to either doing nothing or setting minimum wages by direct, ministerial *fiat*.

However, it was precisely the close relationship between wages councils and collective bargaining upon which the Whitley Committee (1916–18) insisted and which constituted the major contribution of that Committee in this sphere. It will be recalled that the Whitley Committee was concerned to re-establish the control of union officials over collective bargaining (at the expense of bargaining by shop stewards which had developed in certain industries during the First World War) and to that end it supported the nascent developments towards national-level bargaining in each industry. Where employers and employees were well organized, bargaining at national level should proceed on a voluntary basis through Joint Industrial Councils; in the unorganized trades, wages councils should be established. This implied that a lack of organization coupled with low pay rather than just 'exceptionally low' wages should be the criterion for the establishment of a wages council, and in the Trade Boards Act 1918 the criteria for the establishment of a wages council became that 'no adequate machinery exists for the effective regulation of wages throughout the trade, and that accordingly, having regard to the rate of wages prevailing in the trade, or any part of the trade, it is expedient that the Act should apply' (s.1(2)). However, an even more important step taken by the Committee was its identification of wages councils as 'a temporary expedient facilitating organization within the industry, so that, in course of time, the workers or the employers will not have need of the statutory regulations' (Second Report, Cd. 9002, p. 5). Thus, wages councils became in the Committee's view, not a mere substitute for voluntary collective bargaining, but a positive encouragement along the road to the establishment of such voluntary machinery. In Bayliss's phrase, wages councils 'were to be the expression of the community's desire to foster the practice of collective bargaining in trades that could not support it unaided'. In many ways it was the failure of the wages councils to achieve this high objective that, much later, led to such disillusion with them, as expressed, for example, in the Report of the Donovan Commission.

After an initial hesitation the government of the day accepted the recommendations of the Whitley Committee concerning wages councils and implemented them with a will. Twelve new councils were established in 1919 and 23 in 1920. In some other industries the threat of the establishment of a wages council led employers and employees to form voluntary machinery for the industry. However, after a very short period of government promotion, wages councils began to be criticized for maintaining wages rates at 'unrealistically high' levels, and this type of criticism has been a continuing, if intermittent, feature of the history of the councils ever since, although the immediate cause of the criticism has varied from time to time. In 1921 the criticism was triggered by the deep recession that began to affect Britain and the other industrialized countries in the autumn of that year. Wage rates negotiated in the voluntary machineries began to fall; so also did the wages councils rates, but more slowly. The institutional mechanism for setting rates which the wages council contained proved to operate as a brake on the downward movement of wages (just as no doubt it would so operate in a period of upward movement) and the system of legal enforcement of wages councils' orders made it less easy for individual employers to take matters into their own hands and to ignore the established rate, as they often could with rates set in the voluntary machineries. In the face of mounting criticism from employers, the government established the Cave Committee[1] to inquire into the system of wages councils. That Committee in effect recommended in 1922 a return to the principles of the 1909 Act by confining the Minister's power to establish wages councils to the sweated trades and indeed went further by recommending that a wages council's powers should be limited to setting a subsistence (as opposed to a minimum) rate of wages. The view that wages councils were part of a national system of collective bargaining was expressly rejected. Because of the accident of a change of government the Committee's recommendations did not lead to legislation, so that the 1918 Act apparently survived intact. But in fact by administrative measures the governments of the day did what the Committee had suggested. They declined to set up any further wages councils

---

[1]. Report of the Committee appointed to inquire into the Working and Effects of the Trade Boards Acts, Cmd. 1645, 1922.

unless the stringent criteria of the Cave Committee could be satisfied, and in fact no new council was established until 1933. Thus, the second phase of the history of wages councils came to an end with the triumph of the policy of protecting the international competitiveness of British goods over a policy of promoting an entitlement to a minimum wage for British workers.

The strongly negative approach of government to the establishment of wages councils changed in the 1930s, when systems of guaranteeing minimum wages fitted in relatively well with the generally protectionist economic policy of that decade. But the policy of using wages councils at government initiative to encourage the development of collective bargaining in the unorganized industries was not resuscitated. Now government willingness to act was predicated upon a joint request from employers and unions in the industry to have a wages council established – a policy, of course, very much in line with a doctrine of collective *laissez-faire*. Some six new councils were established during this decade, but probably the most significant development was the passage of the Road Haulage Wages Act 1938, a complicated measure to govern remuneration in the road haulage industry, which contained a mechanism very like a wages council but which was in fact called a Central Wages Board.

The third phase of wages council history centres, however, around the passing of the Wages Councils Act 1945, a measure much influenced by the views of Ernest Bevin. With this Act the relationship between wages councils and collective bargaining was reasserted, but in a form rather different from that envisaged by the Whitley Committee. The Committee had been concerned with industries in which collective bargaining machinery was absent. Bevin was more preoccupied with industries in which bargaining machinery existed. His fear, however, was that in many industries voluntary bargaining machinery would not survive the economic slump which many anticipated would follow the end of the Second World War, as it had the end of the First. He anticipated that, as had happened in the 1920s, in many cases the rates set in the negotiations at industry level would simply be ignored by individual employers who found that they could obtain labour in the labour market at much less than the collectively agreed rates. This would be a particular problem if, as in the grocery trade, the collective bargaining machinery was in effect confined on the employers' side to a relatively small number of large multiple grocers, whilst there existed a large number of small shopkeepers, organized into a different employers' association and opposed to collective bargaining, who would always be prepared and able to undercut the collectively agreed rates. If this happened on a wide scale, the machinery at national level might collapse. Hence the notion came about of using wages councils with their legally enforceable orders as a prop for tottering bargaining machinery. Consequently, in the 1945 Act a change was made in the criteria for establishing a wages council so that the Minister could act not only where no adequate machinery existed for the effective regulation of remuneration but also where 'the existing machinery for the settlement of remuneration and conditions of employment . . . is likely to cease to exist or to be adequate for that purpose' (1945 Act, s.1(2)(b)). Further, the definition of adequacy was amended to make it clear that among the factors to be looked at was the extent to which in practice the voluntary agreements were being observed. These amendments have been carried through into the current law: WCA 1979, s.1(2)(c) and 3(5).

Since the Second World War, unlike the First, was in fact succeeded by a sustained period of economic boom, it might be thought that, the circumstances for which the 1945 Act was designed not having materialized, little implementation of the legislation would have followed. In fact, this was not so. Between 1945 and 1954 15 new wages councils were created. In particular, there was a great development of wages councils in the retail trades. Bayliss has explained much of this growth as being due to changes in the procedure for setting up wages councils and, in particular, to changes introduced as a result of the policy of voluntarism or collective *laissez-faire* that had emerged in the 1930s as the guiding principle in this area. Previously the Minister alone decided whether to establish a wages council (assuming the statutory criteria were satisfied), though in the thirties he had come to exercise his discretion only at the joint request of the parties in industry. The 1945 Act, whilst retaining the Minister's power to act unilaterally and indeed his ultimate decision on joint requests, put him under some pressure to accept the joint request, the aim of the framers of the legislation being to avoid a repetition of the situation in 1922 when the Minister managed to implement much of the Cave Committee's recommendations by administrative action – or, rather, inaction. Consequently, under the 1945 Act a joint request for the establishment of a wages council had to be referred by the Minister (unless it was clearly inadequately based) to a Commission of Inquiry (today the reference would be to ACAS) and, although the Minister might refuse to implement a Commission recommendation in favour of establishing a wages council, he would clearly be under some pressure not to refuse (see now WCA 1979, ss.1–3). Moreover, the Commissions of the 1940s, in Bayliss's analysis, tended to accept the need for a wages council if the parties wanted one, partly no doubt because they too were affected by the spirit of voluntarism that seemed to be embodied in the Act and partly because of the difficulty of being able to say categorically that existing bargaining machinery would remain adequate in the future. On the other hand, the parties themselves in asking for a wages council were under no statutory duty to satisfy themselves that the criteria for establishment were met and so, in Bayliss's analysis, the 1945 Act tended to operate so as to lead too easily to the establishment of wages councils.

However that may be, in the early 1950s the system reached its peak with well over sixty councils in operation, but at this time there began the transition into the fourth phase of the history of wages councils, a phase that has been dominated by a questioning of the role of wages councils and a shift in emphasis to proposals to abolish or merge existing councils rather than to create new ones. The Donovan Commission in its Report made two main criticisms of the wages councils. The first was that they seemed not in fact to have operated so as to encourage the growth of collective bargaining. Certainly, very few of the councils had been abolished: at the time of the Commission's Report only 11 had ever been abolished and none since 1963. In some cases it was thought that voluntary bargaining had in fact developed in a wages council industry, so that the council in effect rubber-stamped the voluntary agreement and the independent members had no real role to play, but that the employers' association was opposed to abolition because it saw the legal enforcement of wages councils' orders as a useful protection against undercutting by non-federated employers. In other cases, it was thought, and trade unions often took this view, that the existence of a wages council was a positive hindrance to the development of collective bargaining. Employers might use the existence of the council as a reason for not entering into voluntary bargaining, and employees in the industry might not see much point in membership of a union if their wages were thought to depend upon a legal order rather than their union's strength. The other criticism of the Donovan Commission was that wages councils seemed to have done little to raise levels of pay in wages council industries relative to industries covered by voluntary collective bargaining, or to raise the levels of pay of the low-paid in a wages council industry relative to those of the better-off in that industry. When this fact was coupled with the argument that in many cases labour market pressures in times of full employment would sustain the minimum rates fixed by the Council even in the absence of legal enforceability, the conclusion of this analysis also tended to be in favour of more freely abolishing wages councils.

Although the Donovan Commission's conclusions were somewhat tentative, their general thrust was in favour of abolition and merger in appropriate cases. Since the Commission's Report some 23 councils have been abolished or merged. The Report also led to legislative changes which would ease the path to abolition. Under the legislation existing in 1968 (WCA 1959, ss.5(2) and 6(2)) the criteria for abolition mirrored those for the creation of a council, i.e. that adequate voluntary machinery existed and was likely to continue to exist for the effective regulation of terms of employment. By a change introduced by the IRA 1971 this criterion was altered. In the case of applications by the relevant organizations of employers and workers, the question became whether 'the existence of a wages council was any longer necessary for the purpose of maintaining a reasonable standard of remuneration.' Where the Minister was acting on his own initiative and referred the matter to a commission of inquiry (as he normally would), the commission was freed of the need to take any particular criteria into account in judging the expedience of the abolition proposal. (See now WCA 1979, ss.5(2) and 6(2).) These changes represented in effect the abandonment of the encouragement of collective bargaining as a general goal of the system: if a reasonable standard of remuneration would continue to obtain after abolition, the absence of voluntary machinery was not to be an overriding objection to the proposal to abolish. In order to side-step employers' objections to abolition, the rules as to who could initiate proposals for abolition were also relaxed. Previously, such proposals could be made by the Secretary of State or by representative employers and unions jointly. Now, in addition, a union representing a substantial proportion of the employees covered by the wages council could initiate the abolition procedure (now WCA 1979, s.5(1)(c)).

However, in 1975 a slight modification of policy, in the direction of using wages councils to encourage collective bargaining, occurred. This reassertion of the Whitley Committee's view fitted in well, of course, with other elements in the EPA 1975, notably the statutory recognition procedure (discussed below, p. 201), but it did not amount to a wholesale rejection of the approach of Donovan and the IRA 1971. The criteria and procedures for the abolition of wages councils remained in their recently reformed state, but instead, by EPA 1975, ss.90–94 and Sch.8, the Minister acquired a new alternative to abolition or merger, namely, conversion into a Statutory Joint Industrial Council (SJIC). The SJIC was a halfway house between a full wages council and entirely voluntary machinery. An SJIC would contain no independent members, and so responsibility for the order would be thrown upon the employers' and workers' representatives, but legal enforcement of the order would be retained, thus allaying employers' fears about undercutting. In the case of deadlock the parties on the SJIC would have access to binding arbitration via ACAS. However, no SJIC has yet been established, although ACAS has twice made recommendations in that direction (see ACAS Reports Nos. 13, *Toy Manufacturing Wages Council* (1978), and 20, *The Contract Cleaning Industry* (1980)). Although the point has not proved significant in view of the failure to establish any SJICs, the contrast between the policies of the 1975 and 1971 Acts can best be seen in relation to the criteria for abolition. We have seen that references to the adequacy of bargaining machinery have been deleted in relation to the abolition of wages councils. The criteria for the abolition of an SJIC, however, require the Minister to be satisfied that upon abolition 'adequate machinery would be established for the effective regu-lation of the remuneration and other terms and conditions of employment . . . and is likely thereafter to be maintained' (WCA 1979, s.12(1)). Conse-quently, if the Minister decides not to abolish a wages council but to set up an SJIC, he has to be satisfied about more stringent criteria should he subsequently wish to move to abolition of the SJIC.

Most commentators were prepared to accept the Donovan Commission's conclusions that wages councils had done little to foster voluntary collective bargaining or to improve the relative position of the low paid. Although this was a severe indictment of the system of wages councils, in many ways the failure of the councils should not have caused surprise. The Whitley Committee never made completely clear its view of the mechanism whereby experience of the operation of a wages council could be expected to lead employers and unions to establish machinery for voluntary bargaining. True, a wages council would give both employers and unions experience of a form of joint regulation and thus perhaps break down their reluctance to engage in the activity, but effective collective bargaining would also require a high degree of organization on both sides of industry and, if the structure of the industry made organization difficult, the wages council would not by itself alter this fact. For example, in an industry consisting of a large number of small employers and subject to strong competitive pressures, an employers' association in the absence of legal enforceability might find it difficult to secure voluntary compliance by individual employers with the collectively agreed rates, and trade unions might find it difficult to recruit a sufficiently large number of employees to be able to bring pressure upon individual employers to comply. As to the second of the Commission's criticisms, one would scan the legislation on wages councils in vain to discover a statutory directive as to the level at which the minimum should be set. In such circumstances it is not surprising that the British wages councils have followed international experience with such mechanisms that in the absence of clearly established criteria 'it generally can be expected that those responsible for statutory minimum wage fixing will follow a rather conservative path, not going beyond the correction of manifest anomalies in industry wage relativities or the achievement of a marginally better alignment between the wages in the industry concerned and those paid elsewhere.' (G. Starr, 'Minimum Wage Fixing: International Experience with Alternative Roles' (1981) 120 *Int. Lab. Rev.* 545, 548.)

However, the above arguments would not necessarily lead to abolition of a wages council. It might still be argued that the council was necessary to prevent a fall in the standards of remuneration of the worst off in the industry which would result from removal of the legally enforceable wages council's order. It is here that the crucial, and much more debatable, argument was made that a wages council in many cases was not a necessary protection for these vulnerable groups because after abolition voluntary collective bargaining would develop to fill the vacuum left by the council. This is the argument that turns the relationship between wages councils and collective bargaining on its head: the wages council does not encourage voluntary collective bargaining; it hinders it. Alternatively, it might be argued that, in a period of full employment, labour market pressure alone would be sufficient to protect the vulnerable groups. It is fortunate that the abolition of wages councils is an area in which empirical research has been done to follow up the consequences of some of the abolition decisions that have been taken,[1] and the results of the research enable one to consider in the context of particular industries the

[1]. Department of Employment, *Abolition and After: the Paper Box Wages Council*, Research Paper No. 12, 1980; *Abolition and After: the Jute Wages Council*, Research Paper No. 15, 1980; *Abolition and After: the Cutlery Wages Council*, Research Paper No. 18, 1980.

arguments advanced in this and the previous paragraphs. The research into six abolition decisions was conducted by a group at the Department of Applied Economics at Cambridge University. Their general conclusion was that abolition had not led to the growth of effective collective bargaining. The main obstacles to effective regulation of terms and conditions of employment through collective bargaining were the structural ones noted above, especially small establishment size, intense competition and a traditionally non-union workforce, rather than the existence of a wages council. On the other hand, abolition had exposed the more vulnerable groups in these industries to a greater extent than when they could have claimed the protection of a wages order and the inspection system. Thus, there was evidence of a greater degree of payment below the collectively agreed rates than had previously existed in relation to the wages orders (which had themselves been by no means uniformly observed). See Craig, Rubery, Tarling and Wilkinson, *Labour Market Structure, Industrial Organisation and Low Pay* (1982), Chapters 3 and 4.

Although, as we have noted, public debate about wages councils has centred very much over the last decade on the question of the appropriate criteria for their abolition, some three million workers continue today to have their minimum terms and conditions of employment fixed by wages councils. Wages councils are particularly important in two service industries – catering and retailing – which together contain some 80 per cent of the employees within the scope of wages councils. It is therefore important to look, if only briefly, at some of the criticisms made about the day-to-day operation of the wages councils system.

We have already seen that an important feature of the system of enforcement of wages council awards is the use of the criminal law and the existence of a wages inspectorate to secure compliance with the obligation upon employers to observe the minimum rates set by the councils. Thus, this area of the law relating to collective bargaining has some affinities with the law relating to health and safety at work, whose enforcement also depends heavily upon the criminal law and a system of inspectors provided by the state. Of course, the wages council award also becomes an implied term in the contracts of employment of the relevant employees, but the unreality of expecting employees to be willing on any significant scale to sue their employers in the county court is perhaps reflected in the provisions now contained in the WCA 1979, s.15, that in certain circumstances the criminal court may order an employer upon conviction to pay statutory remuneration due (but not paid) to any of his employees over the previous two years. As with the health and safety inspectorates so with the wages inspectorate two main criticisms have been levelled at it: the inadequate resources made available to the inspection process, and the low number of prosecutions brought by the inspectors. The first, which is really a criticism of government, points to the fact that there are only some 150 inspectors to police some half a million establishments,[1] so that

[1]. For the statistics in this paragraph, see Low Pay Unit/Equal Opportunities Commission, *Minimum Wages for Women* (1980).

at present an average rate of inspection for any one establishment is probably only once a decade, though in fact the inspectorate's policy is flexible enough to include concentration at times on particular industries in particular areas where widespread underpayment is suspected. It is worrying that levels of underpayment discovered by inspectors have increased dramatically over the decade (from 14.8 per cent of employers underpaying in 1971 to 35.1 per cent in 1980) and this has led to the second criticism, for the number of prosecutions is usually fewer than 20 per year. In this respect also the wages inspectors appear to follow the policy of their colleagues in other inspectorates and resort to prosecution only where there is clear evidence of intentional disregard of the statutory levels.

The second area of controversy has concerned the level at which wages councils set minimum rates of pay, but in this area the councils have come under contradictory criticisms. We have already noted the Donovan Commission's finding that wages councils awards seemed to have improved neither the relative position of the low paid within industries covered by wages councils nor the relative position of those industries *vis-à-vis* other industries, and evidence gathered since then has tended to reinforce this conclusion. Given that the legislation contains no standard at which wages councils are to aim – an omission explicable in the early years of the century by the extreme reluctance of the legislature to interfere at all in setting wage levels – it is perhaps not surprising that wages councils have followed rather than exceeded trends elsewhere in industry. But it is precisely the following of trends set elsewhere in industry that has brought the wages councils under government criticism for being too generous, at least in one respect. In most industry-wide agreements the full adult rate is now paid at age 18, and wages councils have followed the trend of paying the adult rate at this age rather than, as was previously common, at age 21 (though in 1980 13 wages councils still paid the adult rate at a higher age). This policy has been criticized by government as 'pricing young workers out of jobs' and in the Young Workers Scheme,[1] introduced in 1981, one of a number of schemes for creating or subsidizing jobs now in operation, the government set the maximum wage level at which the full subsidy of £15 was paid to employers who engage employees aged 18 or under at £40 per week. This was in spite of the fact that the minimum adult wage set by all but two wages councils at the time the scheme was introduced exceeded £50. Although the Young Workers Scheme can in no way relieve an employer from paying the minimum legal entitlement, the formulation of the scheme does reveal an acute conflict in government policy and a downgrading of the value of wages councils in the government's eyes.

Thus, the system of wages councils is in a state of flux. Doubts about its efficacy have been voiced (for example in the Donovan Report) among people who might be regarded as natural supporters of it, and these doubts have led to legislative changes in the IRA 1971. On the other hand, the 1975

[1]. See Freedland (1982) 11 *ILJ* 41.

Act demonstrates that the policy of using wages councils to encourage the growth of collective bargaining has not lost all appeal. More significant is that the government elected in 1979 has begun to question the role of wages councils in a more fundamental way than at any time since the Cave Committee was set up in the early 1920s. The future may bring a drastic reduction in the scope of the system or even its abolition (subject to the UK's obligations to the International Labour Organization, which are discussed below, p. 162). But the mood of fundamental reappraisal could also express itself in a very different direction. British governments have always eschewed systems of national minimum wages (as found, for example, in the *Salaire Minimum National Interprofessionel de Croissance* (SMIC) in France), arguing that in the UK low pay is dealt with by other means, notably the wages councils. But if that system is thought to be ineffective, and the incidence of low pay is not thought to have decreased, the attractions of a national minimum wage may reappear. The Cambridge group, whose research was mentioned above, argue strongly in favour of a national minimum wage, because they see low pay not as a problem of specific industries, which is what the wages council system assumes, but as something found in pockets across a wide range of industries, whose average level of remuneration may be acceptable. Since they also see the labour market as firmly segmented into primary and secondary sectors, they see little chance of economic forces operating to eliminate the pockets of low pay – indeed they reinforce them – so that the attractiveness of a legal solution to the problem is increased. (See Craig *et al.*, op. cit., Chapters 5–8.) If these arguments are ever taken up by the government of the day, a new relationship between minimum-wage provisions and collective bargaining will be created. However, it should not be thought that that relationship would be particularly easier or its appropriate form more obvious than the relationship has been between collective bargaining and the industry-based minimum-wage measures represented by wages councils.

(b) The fair wages principle[1]

The second and third examples of legal support for collective bargaining which were developed in the period when multi-employer bargaining was the dominant form of the institution, can be considered more briefly. These examples are the legal enforcement of 'fair' wages and the enforcement of 'recognized' terms and conditions of employment, two policies which were, at least in recent times, closely related to each other. However, in pursuit of policies of regulation of economic activities by market forces, government has latterly dealt both of these supportive mechanisms heavy blows. The main embodiment of the fair wages principle was the Fair Wages Resolution of 1946, the last of three such Resolutions of which the earlier versions dated from 1891 and 1909, but the 1946 Resolution was rescinded by the House of Commons in

[1]. O. Kahn-Freund, 'Legislation through Adjudication' (1948) 11 *MLR* 269, 429, reprinted in *Selected Writings of Otto Kahn-Freund*, Chapter 4; B. Bercusson, *Fair Wages Resolutions* (1978).

1982 (the rescission to take effect in September 1983). The principle of the enforcement of recognized terms and conditions of employment dated from the period of the Second World War. It was enshrined in a series of legal measures, the most recent of which, Sch. 11 to the Employment Protection Act 1975, was repealed by the Employment Act 1980. Nevertheless, these measures of support deserve some mention, partly for their continuing residual presence in the law, partly for their historical significance, and partly for their embodiment of issues of policy which will continue to be the concern of governments even if the particular methods of resolving them, which these legal instruments represented, may have been abandoned.

The Fair Wages Resolution was not a statute, but a resolution of the House of Commons alone, in effect instructing the executive branch of government to insert a clause into the contracts it concluded for the supply of goods and services requiring the supplier to pay a certain minimum rate of pay to his employees. As a matter of strict law the binding force of the supplier's obligation derived from the contract between him and the relevant government department, rather than from the Resolution itself. However, since the Resolution caused government to develop standard fair wages clauses to insert into all its contracts, the looser practice developed of referring to the Resolution as the source of the obligation.

The first Fair Wages Resolution, adopted by the House of Commons in 1891, was the result of the same public agitation about the evils of 'sweating' as led to the first legislation about wages councils, the Trade Boards Act 1909. Indeed, the Resolution preceded the Act by some 18 years, because it proved easier to convince government that it ought not, in its private capacity as contractor for goods and services, to take advantage of the exploitation of the workers engaged in the sweated trades, than it did to convince government that it ought to impose this principle as a general rule upon all contractors. The Resolution thus has its origins as a measure to combat low pay. It required government to ensure its suppliers paid 'such wages as are generally accepted as current in each trade for competent workmen'. There was at this stage no express link between fair pay and collectively agreed rates, but no doubt in practice the accepted current rate was often the collectively agreed rate, so that the Resolution operated indirectly so as to enforce the substantive terms of the collective agreement so far as government contractors were concerned.

In 1909 the Resolution was amended so as to bring within its scope hours of work and conditions of employment as well as rates of pay, and in the new formulation of the standard to be observed the equivalence of the minimum rate and the collectively agreed rate was made explicit. The contractor must observe hours and rates 'not less favourable than those commonly recognised by employers and trade societies (or in the absence of such recognised wages and hours, those which in practice prevail amongst good employers) in the trade and district where the work is carried out'. However, this formulation was subsequently interpreted by government, and indeed was probably intended by the House, to mean that the collectively agreed rate as applied in practice was to be the standard of fairness; a collectively agreed rate that never secured compliance by employers in practice could not be used as the standard. This distinction between agreed and implemented rates became of crucial importance in the 1920s and 1930s when, as we have seen, the recession had the result that in some industries the agreements made between the trade unions and the employers' associations were ignored by individual employers who could, in practice, secure labour at rates below the collectively agreed ones. The 'fair' rate was what was implemented in practice, not what the industry agreement formally required.

The result was a campaign by the trade-union movement, which eventually bore fruit in the resolution of 1946, to have the fair rate identified with the collectively agreed rate, irrespective of the question of implementation. The 1946 resolution provided:

1.–(a) The contractor shall pay rates of wages and observe hours and conditions of labour not less favourable than those established for the trade or industry in the district where the work is carried out by machinery of negotiation or arbitration to which the parties are organisations of employers and trade unions representative respectively of substantial proportions of the employers and workers engaged in the trade or industry in the district.

(b) In the absence of any rates of wages, hours or conditions of labour so established the contractor shall pay rates of wages and observe hours and conditions of labour, which are not less favourable than the general level of wages, hours and conditions observed by other employers whose general circumstances in the trade or industry in which the contractor is engaged are similar.

The 1946 Resolution thus set out two standards of fairness, the collectively agreed rate and the rate actually prevailing, and made the former standard the primary test of fairness, because the latter could be appealed to only in the absence of a collectively agreed rate. The shift in terminology from 'recognized' rates in the 1909 Resolution to 'established' rates in the 1946 Resolution signified this change, and indeed the whole structure of clauses 1(a) and (b) of the Resolution depended upon clause 1(a) being taken as referring to agreed rates, whether implemented or not.

It is one of the supreme ironies of the history of our labour law that, at the precise moment this victory was achieved, developments were under way in the nature and, in particular, the levels of collective bargaining as a social institution which threatened to deprive the trade unions of the fruits of their political achievement. Clause 1(a) of the Resolution was framed, as was natural at the time, in terms of collective agreements resulting from multi-employer bargaining: the party to the agreement on the employers' side had to be an organization of employers. In those industries, especially private manufacturing industry, where plant-level collective bargaining developed strongly after the Second World War, national-level bargaining became decreasingly important, more and more confined to setting minimum rates of pay. However, plant-level agreements, being concluded with single employers, could not count under clause 1(a) of the Resolution. Their impact could only be felt under clause 1(b) in so far as plant agreements affected the general level of terms and conditions actually observed by employers, but appeal to the general level as the standard of fairness seemed to be blocked if there existed for a particular group of employees an applicable multi-employer agreement setting minimum rates.

Among a number of other important changes made by the 1946 Resolution was one relating to the forum for the resolution of disputes as to whether the employer was applying fair terms and conditions of employment. Again, strictly one might expect the forum to be the ordinary civil courts since the argument would be whether the supplier was in breach of contract. In practice no one wanted this forum. Indeed, issues about compliance were regarded by government as essentially disputes between trade unions (as guardians of the collectively agreed rates) and employers, and government relied heavily on complaints by trade unions or workers about non-compliance to set the machinery of enforcement in motion. Consequently, it was provided in the 1946 Resolution that the Ministry of Labour should attempt conciliation in cases of complaint of non-compliance by a supplier and that, if conciliation failed, the dispute should be referred 'to an independent tribunal for decision'. In practice this meant the Industrial Court, not a court but a standing arbitration tribunal, which was later renamed the Industrial Arbitration Board and was eventually replaced by the Central Arbitration Committee in 1976. There the issue would typically appear as one between union and employer. See, e.g., CAC Award No. 79/103, headed 'Question raised under the Fair Wages Resolution. Ailsa Shipbuilding Co. Ltd and Amalgamated Union of Engineering Workers', although the company's legal obligation in fact derived from a contract between it and the Ministry of Defence.

In large part because of the developments in collective bargaining referred to above, the case-load of the Industrial Court in the fair wages area was not a heavy one, at least initially. Before 1977 the number of cases decided each year rarely exceeded ten, but in the middle seventies two disparate developments occurred which breathed new life into the Resolution. First, the Industrial Arbitration Board in Award No. 3290, *Crittall Hope Ltd and Pay Board* (1974), sought to rescue the Resolution from irrelevance by drawing a distinction between minimum rates, which the parties expect to be supplemented by further collective bargaining at another level, and effective rates, which would be the collectively agreed rates that the bargaining parties would actually expect to prevail in practice as a result of this further process of bargaining. Where the complaint was that the employer was not paying fair, effective rates, the Board would be free to have recourse to the general level in setting the fair standard even if there existed a multi-employer collective agreement setting minimum rates. It was an irony that the Resolution became effective by a shift in the emphasis away from the rate agreed in multi-employer bargaining and back to the rate actually prevailing (where the results of plant bargaining would display themselves). It was also a bold piece of construction which the High Court in *Racal Communications Ltd* v. *Pay Board* [1974] I C R 590 felt unable to follow, the High Court feeling more constrained to vindicate the meaning of the drafters of the Resolution of 1946 and the Industrial Arbitration Board more constrained to adapt the Resolution to a system in which single-employer bargaining predominated. Nevertheless, the Board and later the Central Arbitration Committee adhered to their view, and the conflict between Board and court was never finally resolved.[1]

The second development was that in the incomes policies operated by the government in the late seventies a wage increase needed for compliance with the Fair Wages Resolution was not caught by the otherwise applicable restrictions on wage increases, and so unions, and even employers in some cases, had an incentive to bring themselves within the terms of the Resolution. The C A C made 115 fair wages awards in 1977; 286 in 1978; and 254 in 1979. With the demise of these policies at the end of the decade the numbers fell to 34 in 1980 and 16 in 1981.

The rescission of the resolution from 1983 has not effected, however, the complete extirpation of fair wages clauses from British labour law. Government is not the only public body to have adopted the practice of inserting fair wages clauses into its contracts. Indeed, the first bodies to use these clauses were the London local authorities, including the London County Council, from 1889 onwards. Not all local authorities are likely to follow the government's lead and abandon the use of these clauses. Nationalized industries have also used such clauses in the past; their position in future may be more equivocal.

Finally, there is a small number of cases in which the fair wages principle has achieved statutory force. Beginning with the British Sugar (Subsidy) Act 1925, Parliament has on occasion incorporated a fair wages obligation as a condition for receipt from government of some form of subsidy, grant or licence. The most elaborate example of this process, the Road Haulage Wages Act 1938, was repealed by the Employment Act 1980. The extant examples of the statutory fair wages principle are the Films Act 1960, s.42, the Public Passenger Vehicles Act 1981, s.28, and the Broadcasting Act 1981, s.25. However, since these statutes require employers to observe the terms and conditions of employment which would have to be observed under a contract which complied with 'the requirements of any resolution of the House of Commons for the time being in force applicable to contracts with government departments', the rescission of the Resolution renders these statutory obligations devoid of content.

---

[1]. Partly because of doubts about the extent of judicial review of the committee when acting on a fair wages reference. See *Imperial Metal Industries (Kynoch) Ltd* v. *Amalgamated Union of Engineering Workers* [1979] I C R 23 (CA).

(c) **The enforcement of recognized terms and conditions**[1]

We have already had cause to note that in the economic slump of the 1920s and 1930s proposals were made for the legal enforcement of the substantive aspects of multi-employer collective agreements as codes of terms and conditions of employment. This was a natural response to the frequent failure of such collective agreements to secure compliance in practice by employers who found that the rates in the labour market were lower than the collectively agreed rates. In other European countries, where the legal enforcement of collective agreements as codes is a long-standing practice, it is usual to make a clear distinction between enforcement of the code as against members of the employers' association and as against other, non-federated, employers engaged in the same industry (the latter type of enforcement being referred to as the 'extension' of the collective agreement). In British practice the distinction has not been important. Before the Second World War proposals for neither type of enforcement secured general acceptance; in the legal revolution brought about by the Conditions of Employment and National Arbitration Order (SR & O 1940 No. 1305) a mechanism was established which could lead indifferently to enforcement against either category of employer.

The reasons for this change of heart by government on the issue of enforcement of the collective agreement are to be found in the criminal prohibition (albeit a conditional prohibition) of strikes and other forms of industrial action by the Order as part of the process of putting the economy on a war footing. The Order contained a system of compulsory arbitration before the National Arbitration Tribunal for the settlement of trade disputes, but it also contained, and this was to be the historically more enduring part of the Order, a procedure for the enforcement of 'recognised terms and conditions of employment'. If the Order had deprived trade unions of the strike weapon in their efforts to secure compliance by employers, federated or non-federated, with the terms of the industry's collective agreement, then, it was argued, the Order must also provide a legal substitute for the lost social sanction.

Consequently, Article 5 of the Order provided:

5.–(1) Where in any trade or industry in any district there are in force terms and conditions of employment which have been settled by machinery of negotiation or arbitration to which the parties are organisations of employers and trade unions representative respectively of substantial proportions of the employers and workers engaged in that trade or industry in that district (hereinafter referred to as 'recognised terms and conditions') all employers in that trade or industry in that district shall observe the recognised terms and conditions or such terms and conditions of employment as are not less favourable than the recognised terms and conditions.

[1]. F. Tillyard and W. A. Robson, 'The Enforcement of the Collective Bargain in the United Kingdom' (1938) *Economic Journal* 15; O. Kahn-Freund, 'Collective Agreements under War Legislation' (1943) 6 *MLR* 112; O. Kahn-Freund, 'Legal Framework' in *The System of Industrial Relations in Great Britain* (eds. Flanders and Clegg, 1954), pp. 52–87; K. W. Wedderburn and P. L. Davies, *Employment Grievances and Disputes Procedures in Britain* (1969), pp. 192–213; B. Bercusson, 'The New Fair Wages Policy' (1976) 5 *ILJ* 129.

Perhaps surprisingly, non-compliance by the employer with this obligation was made a criminal offence, but it was also possible for the relevant trade union or employers' organization (as guardians of the collective agreement) to make a complaint via the Ministry of Labour to the NAT that an employer was not observing the recognized terms and conditions. If the NAT upheld the complaint, it would make an award as to the terms and conditions the employer should observe and that award would become implied by law into the contracts of employment of the employees to whom the award related, thus giving rise to civil enforcement of the recognized terms. The individual employee had no standing to make a complaint to the NAT, which emphasized the way in which the mechanism was a substitute for the loss of the collective right to strike, nor would the recognized terms be implied into the individual's contract of employment in the absence of an NAT award (*Hulland* v. *Saunders* [1945] 1 KB 78).

In 1951 the Order was replaced by the Industrial Disputes Order (SI 1951 No. 1376) and the NAT by the Industrial Disputes Tribunal, a very similar body. The criminal prohibition on strikes and lock-outs was removed, but the provisions concerning compulsory arbitration and the enforcement of recognized terms continued, albeit now also without the backing of the criminal law. In 1959 the Order was revoked, but the enforcement of recognized terms continued as s.8 of the Terms and Conditions of Employment Act 1959, with complaints now being referred to the Industrial Court (as for complaints under the Fair Wages Resolution). However, as with the Fair Wages Resolution, the case-load of the IDT and, later, the Industrial Court was not large: about 25 cases per year for the IDT between 1951 and 1959; perhaps on average half that number for the Industrial Court between 1960 and 1975. The explanation was, at least in part, the same: all the above enactments followed the precedent of the 1940 Order in enforcing recognized terms derived from collective agreements concluded between trade unions and 'organisations of employers'. These mechanisms could not be used to enforce agreements with single employers – indeed the whole problem to which they were addressed depended upon a context of multi-employer bargaining – but in the post-war period industry-level agreements came increasingly to be seen as setting only minimum terms rather than going rates.

As we have seen in the previous section, this development in collective bargaining led, in the case of the Fair Wages Resolution, to arguments, accepted by the Industrial Arbitration Board and the Central Arbitration Committee, that, where the industry agreement set only minimum levels, complainants should be able to have access to clause 1(b) of the Resolution, with its prescription of a 'general level' of terms and conditions, in which the results of plant bargaining would be reflected. But s.8 of the 1959 Act (like its predecessors) contained no alternative standard. By the early seventies s.8, in consequence, seemed set to fall into desuetude, from which it was rescued by its replacement by Sch. 11 to the Employment Protection Act 1975. That Act added an alternative standard, indeed the precise alternative standard of the 'general level' of terms and conditions of employment derived from clause 1(b) of the Resolution. With this development Sch. 11 ceased to be simply an instrument for the enforcement of collective agreements and was better seen as a generalization of the policy of requiring the payment of 'fair' wages and other terms of employment beyond government contractors to the whole economy. It acquired, in short, a distinct, additional policy justification expressed in terms of the prevention of low pay.

However, in some parts of the government that enacted the 1975 Act the consequences of Sch. 11 were thought to be likely to be highly inflationary. Accordingly, a compromise was reached whereby it was sought to draft the Schedule so as to make it clear that the general level was the subsidiary standard, to be appealed to only in the absence of recognized terms and conditions. This was, of course, the opposite to the view that had prevailed with regard to the Resolution, but in respect of the Schedule both the CAC and the courts came to accept that the wording of the Schedule had brought about the intended result (*R.* v. *CAC ex parte Deltaflow Ltd* [1978] ICR 534). In industrial relations terms the result was decidedly odd: whether or not a group of workers could use the mechanism of Sch. 11 to extend to themselves the benefits of bargaining at plant level in other establishments in the district depended upon whether there also existed for their industry at national level a collective agreement setting minimum terms. In general, this was less likely to be the case for white-collar workers than for manual workers. Nevertheless, in spite of this restriction, when the Schedule was incorporated alongside the Resolution as an exception to incomes policy, its use increased dramatically. The CAC handed down 149 Schedule 11 awards in 1977; 519 in 1978; 307 in 1979; and 139 in 1980, the year in which Schedule 11 was repealed by the Employment Act 1980.

Thus in its last five years the principle of the enforcement of recognized terms and the principle of enforcement of fair wages became inextricably entwined, and the removal of these two mechanisms in 1980 and 1982 was done also for similar reasons. Indeed the survival for two additional years of the Resolution seems to have been due to the fact that the UK had ratified the International Labour Organization Convention No. 94 concerning Labour Clauses in Public Contracts, which came into force in September 1952. In order to comply with the Convention, the UK needed to maintain the Resolution in force. However, like many ILO conventions, this Convention permitted ratifying states the periodic opportunity, in this case every ten years, to denounce the Convention and thus to be free of its obligations, the denunciation to come into effect one year after its registration with the ILO. This opportunity arose in the year beginning September 1982 and the government decided to avail itself of the opportunity. It is ironic that the Convention, whose substantive obligations are clearly modelled upon the British Resolution of 1946, should in the end have been the cause of a brief respite from extinction for its progenitor. (It is an irony that can also be detected to some extent in respect of Convention No. 26 concerning the creation of Minimum Wage-Fixing Machinery, which came into force in June 1930 and which was also influenced by British practice. This requires ratifying states to 'maintain machinery whereby minimum rates of wages can be fixed . . . in trades . . . in which no arrangements exist for the effective regulation of wages by collective agreement or otherwise and wages are exceptionally low'. Under this Convention the U K will have the opportunity to consider whether to denounce it in the year beginning June 1985.)

The reasons advanced by government for the removal of these mechanisms demonstrate the changes that have recently occurred in public policy towards collective bargaining, especially multi-employer bargaining. One of the advantages of the enforcement of such agreements as codes against both federated and non-federated employers has been the creation of a uniform, minimum standard of terms of employment, to the benefit both of employees in the industry and of the majority of employers, who are thus protected from what they might regard as unfair competition from employers paying below the minimum. This is one reason why employers, before the Second World War, were willing to participate in multi-employer bargaining but not in plant bargaining (which could not give rise to a common standard), and why Schedule 11, like its predecessors, allowed complaints to be made by the employers' associations as well as by trade unions. The attitude of the government proposing removal of these mechanisms[1] was that pay and conditions are best settled by reference to the particular circumstances of individual firms and not, even in part, by reference to a common standard. This view represents a logical, if extreme, development of the movement of change from support of multi-employer bargaining to support for single-employer bargaining, which it was the intention of the Donovan Commission to bring about.

It would be wrong to represent the above as the sole, or even perhaps as the principal, motivation on government's part for the removal of these mechanisms. Somewhat connected with the above argument about particular circumstances of individual firms was an additional objection to any form of unilateral access to binding arbitration, which both the Resolution and Schedule 11 represented. A rather separate objection on government's part to the policy of combating low pay reveals a classic difference of opinion over the definition of low pay. Parliament in 1975 probably saw low pay as a relative concept: people were low paid who earned appreciably below what was common in the industry in the relevant district. Hence the justification for extending the fair wages policy, in particular the general level requirement, to all employers. In 1980 government saw low pay in absolute terms. It was thus an objection to these mechanisms that they could be used by people in relatively high-paying industries to bring themselves up to the general level in

[1]. HL Deb., vol. 410, col. 807, 13 June 1980.

that industry. These mechanisms should be available only to those who were low paid on absolute criteria. This was, of course, the argument which we saw that the Cave Committee (above, p. 146) put forward for the repeal of the Trade Boards Act 1918 and a return to the criteria of the 1909 Act. One problem with this argument, even on its own terms, is that the removal of Schedule 11 and the Resolution deprives even the absolutely low paid of a mechanism of which they might have made use. Whatever the future may bring, it is difficult to believe that the linked issues of protection of the low paid and enforcement of the trade-union rate will disappear from the arena of public debate.

4 Legal support for single-employer collective bargaining

(a) Introduction

(1) *Recognized unions*
The Donovan Commission's prescription for the reform of industrial relations was the introduction of a more formal and comprehensive system of factory-wide bargaining, which would in the case of multi-plant companies perhaps take place within the framework of a company-wide agreement. That point of view is eloquently argued in the following passage in which the emphasis is wholly upon the advantages of collective bargaining with a single employer.

Report of the Royal Commission on Trade Unions and Employers'
Associations, 1968

162.   These recent changes offer some guidance as to the direction which a reform of our system of industrial relations might take. Its central defect is the disorder in factory and workshop relations and pay structures promoted by the conflict between the formal and the informal systems. Consequently the remedy must seek to introduce greater order into factory and workshop relations. This cannot be accomplished by employers' associations and trade unions working at industry level, or by means of industry-wide agreements. What is required is effective and orderly collective bargaining over such issues as the control of incentive schemes, the regulation of hours actually worked, the use of job evaluation, work practices and the linking of changes in pay to changes in performance, facilities for shop stewards and disciplinary rules and appeals. In most industries industry-wide agreements cannot deal effectively with these issues because individual companies have not delegated authority to settle them to their associations, and they have no intention of doing so now. Even if they were willing it would make no difference, for variations between firms in size, management structure, management policies, technology and market situations would defeat any attempt to exercise detailed control over most of these issues from outside the firm even before it had begun.
163.   A factory-wide agreement, however, can cover matters which industry-wide agreements must omit. It can, for example, deal with methods of production in the factory, and with the distribution of overtime. A factory agreement can regulate where an industry-wide agreement can only specify minimum conditions. It can, for instance,

specify in detail the method of timing jobs for systems of payment by results and determine a realistic conversion factor from time to money. A factory agreement, moreover, can settle differential rates of pay which apply to jobs as they are actually performed in that factory, and lay down rates of merit pay together with the means of deciding merit. For all these reasons a factory agreement can regulate actual pay where many industry-wide agreements can deal only with minimum payments, and can therefore be the means of settling an effective and coherent pay structure.

164. A factory agreement can set out a procedure for dealing with grievances within the factory which suits the organisation and managerial structure of the factory, and one that it is therefore reasonable to expect managers, shop stewards and workers to follow. It can also include the constitution for a factory negotiating committee. If this committee covers all the unions in the factory then it can help to put an end to fragmented bargaining. It can be empowered to deal with work practices within the factory, so that it can negotiate changes in work practices to suit existing or proposed production methods.

165. A factory agreement can deal with subjects commonly excluded from industry-wide negotiations, such as redundancy and discipline. The steps to be taken when a redundancy is proposed can be set out in the agreement, along with the method of selecting those to go. The agreement can include a disciplinary code, and prescribe a method of appeal for workers who feel aggrieved by disciplinary decisions.

166. A factory agreement can cover the rights and obligations of shop stewards within the factory. Within the limits of union rules it can set out the stewards' constituencies and the method of their election. The facilities for stewards to meet with each other and their chief steward can be covered, along with arrangements for meeting their constituents, access to a telephone and an office, and entitlement to pay while performing their jobs as stewards.

The Commission did not see the law as having a major role in bringing about bargaining reform, but, in so far as it did contemplate legal measures, it naturally envisaged them also within a framework of single-employer bargaining. In legislating subsequently Parliament has followed this view, even when departing from Donovan in other respects. Thus, the statutory recognition procedure in the Industrial Relations Act 1971 was designed to deal with 'questions relating to the employees of an employer or to the employees of two or more associated employers' (s.45(1)), where 'associated' was defined, not in terms of membership of an employers' association, but in terms of one company having control of another (s.167(8)). Equally, in the recognition procedure in the EPA 1975 'recognition' was defined as recognition 'by an employer or two or more associated employers' (s.11(2)) and 'associated' was defined as under the 1971 Act.

Further, most of the lesser supports for collective bargaining were confined to situations where an employer recognized a trade union. (It did not matter whether the recognition resulted from the statutory procedure or, as was more likely, was de facto recognition.) This was, and is, true of the employer's duty to disclose information for the purposes of collective bargaining (EPA 1975, s.17(2)); to consult over proposed redundancies (ibid., s.99(1)) or over proposed transfers of a business (Transfer Regulations 1981, Regs. 10 and 11) or over health and safety issues (HSWA 1974, s.2(4)); and to provide time off for trade-union duties and activities (EPCA 1978, ss.27(1) and 28(1)). The only exception in this list of legal props for collective bargaining, which will be discussed in more detail below, is the right not to be dismissed or to be subject to action short of dismissal because of membership of a trade union or participation in its activities (EPCA 1978, ss.23–26A and 58). This right could not be confined to unions recognized by an employer, since it is an essential protection for the organizing process, which will normally precede the claim for recognition (although the usefulness of the right is not spent once recognition is achieved). Nevertheless, it is perhaps not insignificant that the first, general legal recognition of the right to associate in 1971 coincided with the new emphasis in public policy of encouraging single-employer bargaining.

In spite of the statutory requirement for recognition by an employer (rather than an employers' association) it was, no doubt, inevitable that sooner or later a union would seek to argue that recognition by an association involved recognition also by the individual members of the association through the agency of the association. In the first case set out below the Court of Appeal rejected this argument as a general proposition, but the case also demonstrates the difficulty of knowing when an individual employer can be said to have done enough to be held to have recognized the union. This issue arises because recognition in the statute means recognition 'for the purpose of collective bargaining' (EPA 1975, s.126(1)). A relationship between employer and union falling short of a collective bargaining relationship does not count for statutory purposes as recognition. As the second case shows, the practical issue that has most frequently arisen has concerned the distinction between collective bargaining and the right of the union to represent individuals over grievances they may have against their employer.

National Union of Gold, Silver and Allied Trades v. *Albury Bros. Ltd*
[1979] ICR 84 (CA)

The respondent company dismissed four employees on grounds of redundancy without consulting the appellant union. The company, run by Mr Albury, was a member of the British Jewellers' Association, which, as a member in turn of a larger employers' federation, negotiated at industry level with the union. Three weeks before the dismissals, 8 of the company's 55 employees joined the union. The union's district secretary then arranged a meeting with Mr Albury at which the wages of one employee were discussed, but no agreement was reached.

SIR DAVID CAIRNS: Mr Sedley's first contention on behalf of the trade union was that the section of the British Jewellers' Association (which is a member of the British Jewellery and Giftware Federation Ltd) when it entered into a collective agreement with the union acted as agent for its members, of whom Albury Brothers Ltd was one; and that that agreement therefore constituted recognition of the union by Albury Brothers Ltd within the meaning of the Employment Protection Act 1975. Mr Sedley made it clear that it was not his argument that a trade association or a trade union in making a collective agreement was always acting as agent for its members, but he submitted that there was such agency here because the memorandum of association of the federation contains as one of the federation's objects:

> To negotiate terms and conditions and to enter into binding agreements with any trade union on behalf of any member of the association for or concerning the employment of any such members' employees.

This argument is obviously unsustainable. Even if the agreement can be regarded as an agreement made by the federation, the fact that a company is empowered by its memorandum to act as an agent is no ground for saying that on any particular occasion it did act as an agent. Furthermore, the collective agreement was expressed to be binding in honour only, and in my view is not within the scope of that part of the objects clause at all.

Admittedly the existence of the collective agreement is a factor to be taken into account in deciding whether there has been recognition; but the cases before the Employment Appeal Tribunal all proceed on the basis that some words or acts on the part of the particular employer concerned are needed to constitute recognition. I have no doubt that this is a correct view. I further agree with what was said by Phillips J. in delivering the decision of the Employment Appeal Tribunal in this case echoing what had been said by Lord MacDermott in *Transport and General Workers' Union* v. *Dyer* [1977] IRLR 93, 95 and in *National Union of Tailors and Garment Workers* v. *Charles Ingram & Co. Ltd* [1977] ICR 530, 533, that the acts relied on must be clear and unequivocal and usually involve a course of conduct over a period of time.

Mr Sedley contends that because of the definition of 'recognition' in section 126 (1) of the Act of 1975 and because of the provisions of section 11 (2) of that Act in these words:

> In this Act 'recognition,' in relation to a trade union, means the recognition of the union by an employer, or two or more associated employers, to any extent, for the purpose of collective bargaining.

one can then go to the definition of 'collective bargaining' in section 126 where 'collective bargaining' is defined to mean 'negotiations relating to or connected with one or more of the matters specified in section 29 (1) of the 1974 Act.' It follows, says counsel, that any discussion between a trade union representative and the employers about any of the matters referred to in section 29 (1) of the Act of 1974 must constitute recognition. I do not accept that reasoning. The definition in section 126 (1) merely defines the matters in relation to which recognition is applicable but does not define what is meant by the very word 'recognition.' 'Recognition' must I think mean recognition that the union is to be consulted about some of the matters referred to in section 29 (1); and the fact that such matters have been discussed on a particular occasion does not in itself necessarily mean that any such implication is to be made, particularly if the attitude of the employer is, as it appears to have been in this case, 'I hear what you say, but we have our own scales of payment which we intend to continue to operate.' That, I think, is the effect of Mr Shakeshaft's evidence where he said: 'On May 20 Albury said they had their own system. I said it must be in accordance with the minimum rate,' with which proposition it is clear that Mr Albury did not agree.

In my view the matters relied on here to establish recognition are too limited in scope, too inconclusive in character, and of too brief a duration to have any such effect as would constitute recognition. I am glad to be able to join in dismissing the appeal because the decision of the Employment Appeal Tribunal seems to me good law and good sense.

Union of Shop, Distributive and Allied Workers v. *Sketchley Ltd*
[1981] ICR 644 (EAT)

On a complaint about the failure of the employer to consult the union over proposed redundancies, the question arose as to whether the employer had recognized the union.

BROWNE-WILKINSON J.: ... On May 8, 1978, there was a meeting between representatives of the employers and the union; this led to an agreement being signed, from which we must quote at length. It is headed:

> Recognition for representation agreement between Sketchley Cleaners Ltd (the company) and the Union of Shop Distributive and Allied Workers ('USDAW').

The body of the agreement then provides:

> This procedure is additional to the general company grievance procedure in that it allows an individual to be represented beyond a certain level by the trade union.
>
> (i) The purpose of this agreement is to award recognition by the company to USDAW for representation purposes in respect of those staff in the company's branches who are members of USDAW.
>
> (ii) The company recommends all employees below the level of branch manager who may wish to join a union to become members of USDAW. The company also recommends all branch managers who may wish to join a union to become members of the Supervisory, Administrative and Technical Association, the USDAW white collar section.
>
> (iii) The company agrees to refrain from lock-out and USDAW agrees to refrain from stoppage of work or other unreasonable action until the procedure for resolving grievances set out in appendix A has been exhausted.
>
> (iv) The company will recognise the appointment of a properly elected shop steward within each of the Sketchley districts listed in appendix B. The arrangement will apply in each district upon USDAW obtaining 50 per cent of employees in membership.
>
> (v) The company agrees to deduct union contributions direct from wages upon receipt of a signed authorisation from each member concerned and USDAW agrees to the payment of 2½ per cent commission for the service.
>
> (vi) A member of USDAW covered by this agreement who has an individual grievance shall follow the procedures set out in Appendix A.
>
> (vii) If both parties agree to a matter of dispute being referred to arbitration, both parties will abide by the arbitration ruling. Unless the parties agree to the contrary any matters for arbitration will be referred to the Advisory, Conciliation and Arbitration Service.
>
> (viii) This agreement does not confer recognition by the company to USDAW for negotiation of terms and conditions.
>
> (ix) The agreement shall operate until such time as it is modified by written agreement between the parties or until it has been terminated by either party giving three months notice in writing to the other.

The first question for decision is whether by entering into this agreement, the employers 'recognised' the union within the meaning of those words, as we have sought to define them above. . . .

Shortly thereafter the employers started to select candidates for redundancy at their shops. On February 28, 1980, there was a meeting of the shop employees; both union and non-union. This meeting resolved to take strike action if the employers would not inform the union of the impending redundancies. Under this threat a further meeting was called between the employers and the union, which took place on February 29, and a memorandum was approved by all parties in the following terms:

1. Mr Roberts will inform Mr Clarke of the branches in N4 district where there is USDAW membership.

2. In respect of those branches, Mr Clarke will inform Mr Roberts of the intended hours reduction.

3. Mr Clarke will inform Mr Roberts with approximately two hours notice before he goes into a particular branch to discuss the de-manning with the branch manager and the staff.

4. Mr Clarke will inform the staff in each relevant branch that Mr Roberts has been informed, and that he will be available for them to speak to him by telephone and subsequently in person, if necessary, if they require his advice and help, over the exercise.

5. Union members will be reminded of the details of their grievance procedure under the union agreement.

6. The company will observe clause (vi) of the grievance procedure, where it applies.

7. We have already confirmed that it is company policy to retire employees who are already above retiring age. We have also confirmed that although we do not accept voluntary redundancies as such, where other factors are equal and a choice can logically be made, we will accept volunteers for redundancy. It is also already part of the company policy that reductions in hours, or transfers of labour, will be used where possible to avoid redundancies. Also payment for redundant staff, is as follows: . . .

Here the memorandum sets out certain payments to be made, some of which are in excess of the statutory rights.

8. Mr Fitzpatrick and Mr Roberts have agreed to recommend to their members that they do not take the proposed strike action from closing time on Monday night, pending today's discussions. . . .

(a) *The agreement of May 8, 1978*

We agree with the industrial tribunal that this agreement did not afford statutory recognition to the union. We will assume in favour of the union that matters of representation in grievance procedures and the appointment of shop stewards are matters of a kind referred to in section 29(1) of the Act of 1974. The crucial question in our view is whether the employers were recognising the union 'for the purposes of negotiation relating to or connected with' such matters. The statutory definition requires the recognition to be for that purpose and none other. In our view, the employers were affording to the union limited rights to represent their members in grievance procedures, together with facilities for appointing shop stewards and collecting union dues. As the heading to the agreement states, it is an agreement to provide 'recognition for representation,' not recognition for negotiation purposes. This distinction is again emphasised by clause (viii) of the agreement which expressly states that the agreement does not confer 'recognition . . . for negotiation of terms and conditions.'

Mr Hand, for the union, submitted that the distinction between recognition for representational purposes on the one hand and recognition for negotiation purposes on the other is artificial and unworkable. We cannot agree. First, to our minds, there is a clear distinction between the role of a person who, under existing grievance procedures, is entitled to make representations on behalf of an individual on the one hand and the role of a person who is entitled to negotiate over what the procedures themselves should be, on the other hand. Secondly, those of us who have experience in industrial relations well know that the progress towards full recognition of a union by an employer is often a slow and careful one. The first stage is often to concede to the union the right to represent its own members. Thereafter, matters may proceed further but normally only in carefully negotiated steps. To treat the first step (a representation agreement) as tantamount to recognition for negotiation purposes would be contrary to sound industrial relations practice. Thirdly, the dangers of so doing are great. Some employers are faced with a multiplicity of unions, each claiming to represent sections of the work force. All have representation rights for their individual members under grievance procedures, a practice which is obviously fair. However, only certain of the unions will be accorded full recognition and have negotiating rights. The employer's decision to recognise a union for negotiating purposes is carefully made and, once given, is equally carefully guarded by both sides. Quite often the recognised unions in an undertaking come together to engage in joint negotiations with the employer. What would be the cost to orderly industrial relations if every union which has obtained the right to represent its own members thereby became recognised for the purposes of section 99 and other purposes? For these reasons we do not consider that the agreement of May 8, 1978, conferred statutory recognition to negotiate on the union.

Mr Hand, in his reply, took a further point. He submitted that in the negotiations leading up to the agreement of May 8, 1978, the employers must have been treating the union as the body with whom they would negotiate as to grievance procedures. By so doing, says Mr Hand, the employers must have recognised the union as having negotiating rights, at least to that extent. We do not accept this argument. On this argument the union is asking the tribunal to draw an *inference* of an agreement by the employers to recognise the union for negotiating purposes. As we have said, it is clear that such inference is not to be drawn lightly but should only be drawn in clear cases. Such an inference is, in our view, impossible in a case such as this where clause (viii) of the agreement, as subsequently negotiated, specifically states that there was no intention by the employers to recognise the union for negotiating purposes. . . .

(c) *Did the events of February 29 give rise to statutory recognition?*
As we have said, the industrial tribunal have unfortunately not considered this question. We would not remit the matter to the industrial tribunal for further consideration if we were satisfied that, on the facts before us, no finding of statutory recognition was possible. But we think that it is.

It will be remembered that the events of February 29, 1979, took place in the face of a threat of imminent strike action. The memorandum states that the union has agreed to recommend withdrawal of such action and sets out certain redundancy procedures and rates of redundancy payment in excess of the statutory rates. It gives the union the right to prior information of a limited kind relating to redundancies. Nowhere does the agreement state expressly that the union is not being recognised for purposes of the negotiation.

In these circumstances, if the events of February 29, culminating in the memorandum, in fact represent a bargain struck between the union on the one hand and the employers on the other, giving the union certain rights relating to redundancy in consideration of a recommendation to withdraw industrial action, in our view the industrial tribunal could properly draw the inference that the employers were indeed recognising the union for negotiating purposes. In our view, an employer who enters into an agreement with a union relating to the terms and conditions of employment of members of the union runs a severe risk that the inference will be drawn that such an employer has recognised the union as having negotiating rights in that field.

We do not feel able to decide this matter for ourselves. The memorandum itself, although in some respects it is suggesting a bargain between the union and the employers, in other parts suggests that the employers are merely stating their position without entering into any commitment. We must, therefore, remit the matter to the industrial tribunal to determine whether or not the events of February 29, 1980, amounted to a bargain between the employers and the union and, if so, whether in all the circumstances it is right to infer a statutory recognition by the employers of the union.

A similar line of argument was developed by the High Court in *R*. v. *Central Arbitration Committee ex parte B TP Tioxide Ltd* [1981] ICR 843, which arose out of a claim by a union that the employer had not disclosed information in accordance with the provisions of EPA 1975. The union was entitled to make representations on behalf of members seeking re-evaluation under a newly completed job-evaluation scheme. It was held that this did not amount to recognition of the union so as to entitle it to require information from the employer about the scheme, even though it was accepted that the employer had recognized the union for the purposes of negotiations about salary levels. It is important to note that, whereas an employer is obliged to consult about proposed redundancies with all relevant unions recognized by him, no matter how limited the subject matter of the recognition may be, with regard to disclosure of information not only does the fact of recognition determine whether there is an obligation to disclose at all, but also the extent of the recognition (in terms of subject matter) controls the extent of the required disclosure (see further below, p. 207).

Thus, the statutory definition of recognition excludes both recognition through an employers' association unaccompanied by any relevant acts by the particular employer in question (thus emphasizing the policy of supporting single-employer bargaining), and recognition falling short of recognition for the purposes of collective bargaining (perhaps thus emphasizing a legislative policy that the normal relationship between employer and union should be centred on collective negotiations). The recognition requirement can, however, be seen as performing a third function, namely, as expressing the policy that the trade unions should be the 'single channel' of representation of the employees. In other words, the policy is that the law should be used to strengthen the representational role of the trade unions and not to establish a rival system of representation. Indeed, this policy is implicit in any categorization of the legal mechanisms discussed below as instruments of legal support for collective bargaining. However, it is possible to see how the measures requiring consultation (over proposed redundancies or transfers of businesses, or over health and safety matters) could with a small, but significant, change of emphasis come to express the policy of requiring consultation with bodies independent of the trade unions.

Indeed, this difference of view has already been displayed at a legislative level in respect of the HSWA 1974. As is discussed further below in section 4(f), the employer's duty is to consult over health and safety matters with safety representatives chosen from amongst his employees. In the original version of the Act passed by a Conservative government, the Secretary of State was empowered to make regulations both for the appointment of safety representatives by recognized trade unions (s.2(4)) and for the election of safety representatives by the employees (s.2(5)), but in EPA 1975, s.116 (passed by a Labour government), s.2(5) was deleted before any regulations were made. A comparable issue has arisen in relation to the implementation of EEC obligations. The duties to consult over proposed redundancies and transfers of businesses are derived, at least in part, from the UK's obligation to implement two EEC Directives (nos. 75/129 and 77/187). In other European countries it is common for legislation to require consultation by employers with works councils, which may exist, at least formally, independently of the trade unions. To date, the Directives have required consultation with 'workers' representatives' and have defined these as meaning 'workers' representatives provided for by the laws or practices of the Member States' (Directives 75/129, Art. 1(b); 77/187, Art. 2(c)). The UK government has then treated the Directives as meaning in a UK context representatives of recognized trade unions, but there is clearly scope for a different point of view, either at EEC or UK level, which would dramatically change the significance of these consultative mechanisms.

(2) *Listing and independence*
In those cases where the legislation confers rights on or in respect of recognized trade unions in order to support their activities as bargainers, it requires that the recognized trade union be also an independent one. Equally, the protection conferred against victimization on grounds of trade-union membership or activities, which is not confined to recognized trade unions, does nevertheless require that the trade union be independent. In this context 'independence' refers to independence from the employer. The notion is that to encourage collective bargaining is worthwhile only if it is conducted on an arms' length basis and so is capable of producing a genuine resolution of the issues in dispute between the parties. There is, however, a certain irony in the incorporation of a criterion of independence into the granting of rights which

are to be used against the employer, rights which a non-independent trade union might well be thought to be unlikely to wish to exercise. To establish, as the EPA 1975 did, an elaborate machinery for the granting or refusal of certificates of independence might be thought to result in the holding of the certificate becoming the crucial matter as indicating government approval of the union in question rather than the exercise of the rights to which the certificate grants access.

The policy of restricting legal benefits to independent unions can be found originally in the IRA 1971. In s.167(1) of IRA 1971 an independent trade union was defined as one 'not under the domination or control of an employer . . .' and s.30(1) of TULRA 1974 repeats this requirement but also adds that the union must not be 'liable to interference by an employer . . . (arising out of the provision of financial or material support or by any other means whatsoever) tending towards such control'.

Under the IRA 1971, however, the benefits of the legislation (if they can be so described without invidiousness) were available in the main only to registered trade unions. Independence was a pre-requisite for registration, but registration entailed also scrutiny of the union's rule-book by the Registrar of Trade Unions for compliance with Sch. 4 of the Act. All but one or two of the unions affiliated to the TUC refused to register (which was optional), not because they were not independent, but because they rejected 'state control' of the rule-book. Non-registration made sections of the IRA 1971 largely inoperable and the campaign for non-registration was the crucial expression of the TUC's political opposition to the Act. Under TULRA/EPA, registration is replaced by 'listing' (TULRA 1974, s.8) with the Certification Officer instead of the Registrar of Trade Unions. The change in nomenclature reflects a change of substance. Listing gives the CO no general control over the union's rule-book. An organization that satisfies the statutory definition of a trade union (TULRA 1974, s.28(1)) has a right to be listed upon payment of a small fee and the provision of some basic information about itself. Indeed, by s.8(2) most bona fide trade unions existing at the commencement date of the legislation were automatically listed without need for an application by them. There is still, however, a link between listing and independence. But whereas under the IRA 1971 independence was a prerequisite for registration, under TULRA/EPA listing is a prerequisite for an application by a union to the CO for a certificate of independence. The reversal of the sequence neatly illustrates the primacy of registration in the conceptual structure of the IRA 1971 and of independence in the current structure.

Thus an employees' organization[1] that wishes to take full advantage of the legislative provisions must first become listed and then claim a certificate of independence. On listing the main point of substance that is likely to arise is whether the organization is in fact a trade union. S.28(1) of TULRA 1974 defines a trade union as a permanent or temporary organization that consists wholly or mainly of workers and whose principal purposes include (but are not necessarily confined to) the regulation of relations between workers of the type in membership and employers or employers' associations.[2] As the CO said in his Annual Report for 1976, 'entry in the list is a simple process in the great majority of cases'. There is, however, at least one point of policy that could be raised at this stage, viz. the status of unofficial and only intermittently active shop-steward groups. See *Midland Cold Storage* v. *Turner* [1972] ICR 230.

A listed trade union obtains two significant advantages over an unlisted one: it receives tax relief on its provident income and it may (but need not) apply to the CO for a certificate that it is independent. The CO has exclusive jurisdiction over the question of whether a union satisfies the statutory definition of independence. The EAT, the CAC and ACAS and any court or industrial tribunal must treat the CO's grant of, or refusal to grant, a certificate as conclusive of the issue, and if the question of independence arises in proceedings before these bodies about a union upon which the CO has not made a decision, then the proceedings must be stayed and the question referred to the CO. (EPA 1975, s.8(1) and (2).) A union which has been refused a certificate by the CO may, however, appeal, curiously on grounds of both fact and law, to the EAT.

A union applicant for a certificate must supply the CO with a copy of its rules and latest accounts. If the CO has doubts about the union's independence or objections are received, for example, from another union – the CO must maintain a public register of the applications made to him and of his decisions on them – then members of his staff will carry out an investigation, typically interviewing officials of the union and perhaps employers and reading minutes of the union's executive committee meetings or of negotiating meetings between the union and managements. See the *First Annual Report of the Certification Officer* (1976), paras. 2.8–2.13. Although objections from other unions often cause the CO to investigate, if he does in fact decide after investigation to grant the certificate, the objecting union, strangely, has no right of appeal to the EAT (EPCA 1978, s.136(3); *GMWU* v. *CO* [1977] ICR 183). After a similar procedure the CO may withdraw a certificate from a union which in his view has ceased to be independent.

The CO's activities in granting or refusing certificates have proved controversial in two areas. First, unions affiliated to the TUC have sometimes objected to the granting of certificates to non-affiliated 'professional associ-

---

[1] An employers' association may also seek to enter itself on the list, but it is not clear why it should do so. The certificate of independence is by definition available only to trade unions and a listed employers' association obtains no tax advantages.

[2] The definition also extends to embrace organizations whose constituent bodies are trade unions provided that the 'umbrella' organization also seeks to regulate relations between employers and employees or among its constituents, e.g. the TUC or the Confederation of Shipbuilding and Engineering Unions. Since, however, it is the constituent unions that will want to exercise the new statutory rights, the umbrella organizations may well not seek to become listed. However, some unions, e.g. the NUM, consist of constituent areas, and such unions will wish to be listed.

ations', i.e. associations which recruit higher-level white-collar employees on the basis of their professional qualifications, and which are a feature of certain industries such as engineering, where the UK Association of Professional Engineers (UKAPE) has been attempting for some time to gain a foothold. Such associations tend to disrupt existing bargaining arrangements, the contours of which usually do not follow the professional qualifications of the employees, and they also tend to limit the possibilities of expansion of the (TUC-affiliated) unions organizing the lower-level white-collar employees. The independence (as distinguished from the militancy) of these associations is not, however, usually in doubt, and although it may be argued that the recognition of such associations would not be conducive to good industrial relations, that is not a question for the CO.

The second area of controversy concerns staff associations, where the question of independence is squarely in issue. The distinguishing marks of staff associations are that they are typically organizations of recent origin, not affiliated to the TUC, which recruit the white-collar employees of one employer only and which stand apart from mainstream trade unionism. They are notable features of the banking, insurance and building society industries. (See *Staff Associations: Supplement to the Annual Report of the Certification Officer 1979*.) None of this means they are necessarily not independent. However, it is a well-known strategy for an employer, faced with an approach to its employees from an 'outside' union, to encourage the formation of a 'house' union as an alternative, whose policies the employer is, in one way or another, able to control. The CO's task will often be to distinguish such a situation from one where the staff association is a genuine expression of the employees' desire to be represented by an organization which recruits only amongst themselves and which can bargain with the employer on an arm's length basis.

We set out below the criteria the CO has developed, largely on the basis of the experience of the CIR, to test the independence of applicants. These criteria were approved by the EAT in *Blue Circle Staff Association* v. *CO* [1977] ICR 224, where the Tribunal agreed with the CO that a staff association that had originally been formed by the employer had not subsequently done enough to establish its independence from the latter, and were approved again by the EAT in *Association of HSD Employees* v. *CO* [1978] ICR 21, where, however, the EAT disagreed with the CO's application of the criteria to the facts and concluded that the staff association, by the date of the hearing in the EAT, had established its independence from an originally dominant employer. (See also *A. Monk & Co. Staff Association* v. *CO* [1980] IRLR 431 (EAT)). Fundamental disagreement between the CO and the Appeal Tribunal was revealed in *Squibb UK Staff Association* v. *CO* [1978] ICR 115, where the EAT expressed its dissatisfaction with its own conclusion that it was prevented by the statutory definition of independence from considering the question of effectiveness, but the CO was upheld by the Court of Appeal.

First Annual Report of the Certification Officer 1976,
paras. 2.16–2.25

2.16   The following paragraphs set out the principal criteria which the Office has used in applying the statutory definition to individual cases.

2.17   *History*   Sometimes evidence is found that the union began with employer support and encouragement, or even as a creature of management. If that evidence relates to the recent past it is a powerful argument against the grant of a certificate. But experience indicates that over time some unions can and do evolve from a dependent to an independent state; and the decision must, of course, be based on the facts as they are at the time of the investigation and not as they were several years ago.

2.18   *Membership base*   From the outset the Office has taken the view that a union whose membership is confined to the employees of one employer is, on the face of it, more vulnerable to employer interference than a broadly-based union. This is less likely to be a critical factor for a large, well-established union backed up by strong resources than for a small, weak, newly-founded organization. In fact certificates have been issued to a number of single company unions which appear on all the available evidence to be capable of withstanding any pressure which might be brought to bear on them by the employer. Experience has confirmed that a narrow membership base may make the union's task of proving its independence more difficult but that it does not make it impossible.

2.19   *Organization and structure*   It is necessary to examine these both as they are set out in the union's rule book and as they work in practice. The main requirement is that the union should be organized in a way which enables the members to play a full part in the decision-making process and excludes any form of employer involvement or influence in the union's internal affairs. Particular attention is paid to whether employers or senior employees, especially those at or immediately below board level, are eligible to belong to the union and, if so, whether there are suitable restrictions on the part which they can play in its affairs.

2.20   *Finance*   While it is exceptional to find evidence of a direct monetary subsidy from employer sources, a union with weak finances and inadequate reserves is obviously more likely to be vulnerable to employer interference than one whose financial position is strong. Particular attention is therefore paid to such questions as the main sources of the union's income, whether this matches its expenditure, the level of its subscription rate and the state of its reserves.

2.21   *Employer-provided facilities*   These may take the form of premises, time off and office or other services which the union receives from employer sources. In the case of single company unions the normal practice is to cost these items in order to get a rough idea of the extent of the union's reliance on them in financial terms. But it is not just a question of finance. It is necessary to look too at the administrative convenience of having facilities provided by the employer, even if they are paid for, and how easy or difficult the union would find it to cope on its own if they were withdrawn. The greater the union's reliance on such facilities the more vulnerable it must be to employer interference.

2.22   The provision of facilities is, of course, common practice among good employers, but in the context of independence its significance may vary according to circumstances. A distinction can properly be drawn between a broadly-based union, which could continue to function even if an employer withdrew facilities from one or more of its branches, and a single company union which might well find it difficult or even impossible to carry on at all if such action were taken by the firm which employs its entire membership.

2.23   *Collective bargaining record*   This is almost always an important consideration. While a weak record does not itself indicate dependence, a strong record and the display of a robust attitude in negotiation are items on the credit side which may outweigh other factors unfavourable to the union's case. In assessing the record account must be taken of such factors as the limitations on the scope for collective bargaining imposed by incomes policy and the particular environment in which the union operates – for example, the kind of employer with whom it negotiates and the traditions and attitudes of the employees whom it represents.

2.24   This is the point at which independence and effectiveness overlap. The two concepts are not of course identical. A union is not necessarily dependent just because it cannot supply its members with the full range of services which major unions normally provide. But it is equally clear that an effective union is more likely to be independent than an ineffective one.

2.25   None of the factors listed above can be decisive by itself. It is necessary to look at the whole nature and circumstances of the union and then make a judgment about whether or not it satisfies the statutory definition. Because there is no convenient yardstick which can supply a ready-made answer there must often be a subjective element in the decisions, especially where the arguments for and against independence are finely balanced.

Squibb UK Staff Association v. *CO* [1979] ICR 235 (CA)

The staff association, formed in 1973, recruited solely amongst the supervisory, chemical and laboratory staff of E. R. Squibb & Sons Ltd, a manufacturer of specialized pharmaceutical products. The association was recognized by the company as the sole representative of these grades of workers of whom 231 out of a possible total of some 290 were in membership. The CO refused the association a certificate of independence. The EAT upheld the Association's appeal.

LORD DENNING M.R.: . . . . Such being the information before the Certification Officer, it became his duty under section 8(5) of the Act of 1967 [sic] to 'determine whether the applicant trade union is independent; . . . and (c) . . . if he determines that it is not, give reasons for his decision.' On the very next day, July 23, 1976, the Certification Officer gave his determination and reasons in this letter:

I am writing to inform you that in pursuance of the powers conferred on me by section 8(5) of the Employment Protection Act 1975, I have determined that the Squibb UK Staff Association is not an independent trade union within the meaning of part (b) of the definition of 'independent trade union' in section 30(1) of the Trade Union and Labour Relations Act 1974.

The reason for my decision is as follows. The association receives extensive facilities from the company which includes the following:
i   Time off with pay for its officials for the performance of duties on behalf of the association (in addition to time off for negotiations with management). ii   The free use of office accommodation and of rooms for meetings of the executive committee and for general meetings. iii   The provision of free stationery and the free use of the

employer's telephone, photocopying and internal mailing facilities. iv Free 'check-off' facilities.

The association relies on these facilities to a substantial extent and it is considered that, having regard to its narrow membership base, small size and limited resources, it would find it extremely difficult to operate effectively if they were withdrawn by the employer. . . .

From this digression I turn to the decision of the Employment Appeal Tribunal. They allowed the appeal and granted the certificate of independence. . . . In the present case the Certification Officer did appeal. He appealed on a question of law as to the true interpretation of the word 'liable' in section 30 of the Act of 1974. It arose whilst the Certification Officer was being cross-examined. The material words are 'liable to interference'. To be independent the trade union must be one which 'is not liable to interference by an employer . . . tending towards such control'.

The Certification Officer interpreted the words 'liable to interference' as meaning 'vulnerable to interference' or 'exposed to the risk of interference' by the employer. Whereas Mr Irvine for the association suggested that it meant 'likely' or 'not unlikely' to be subjected to interference by the employer. The Employment Appeal Tribunal preferred Mr Irvine's interpretation. They said [1978] I C R 115, 120:

> We feel that Mr Irvine's approach . . . is the better one and that the words must be construed as meaning that, in the circumstances and on the facts of each case, it is not unlikely that interference will take place and, that when it does, it is not unlikely to have the effect of some degree of control by the employer.

Applying that test, which I may call 'the likelihood of interference' test, the appeal tribunal held that there should be a certificate of independence. They said, at pp. 122–123:

> . . . on the evidence we have heard and the documents we have read, there is no real likelihood either of the facilities being withdrawn, or, if they were, of this in any way affecting the independence of the union from employer interference, and that therefore the union has successfully rebutted the presumption.

So there it is. They decided because there was no real 'likelihood of interference by the employer.'

I agree that there are two possible meanings of the word 'liable'. It is a very vague and indefinite word. Having heard very good arguments on both sides, it seems to me that the Certification Officer's interpretation of 'liable' is correct and the staff association's interpretation is not correct. One has to envisage the possibility that there may be a difference of opinion in the future between the employers and the staff association. It does not matter whether it is likely or not – it may be completely unlikely – but one has to envisage the possibility of a difference of opinion. It may be on the amount of pay; it may be on the question of a pension; it may be on the safeguards; and the like. Whatever it may be, there may be a difference of opinion. It may be a mere possibility. But when it arises, the questions have to be asked. What is the strength of the employers? What pressures could they bring to bear against the staff association? What facilities could they withdraw? Section 30(1) of the Act of 1974 contemplates that the association may be liable to interference arising out of 'the provision of financial or material support or by any other means whatsoever.'

The employers could take away the four facilities which the Certification Officer mentioned in his reasons. They could take away the facility of time off for meetings. They could take away the facility of free use of office accommodation, and so forth. Those are pressures which the employers could bring to bear on their side. On the other side, this association is rather weak. It has a narrow membership base. It has small financial resources. Weighing the two sides, one against the other, the Certification Officer came to the conclusion that the association was liable to interference in this way: the association was so weak that it was vulnerable, in that it was exposed to the risk of interference tending towards control by the employers.

The Employment Appeal Tribunal reversed the Certification Officer. It seems to me that it misdirected itself. It concentrated too much on the 'likelihood of interference' whereas it should have had regard to the 'vulnerability to interference.' I would therefore allow the appeal and restore the decision of the Certification Officer.

It is, of course, the case that the repeal of the statutory recognition provisions of the EPA 1975 by the EA 1980 greatly reduced the importance of certificates of independence. The certification procedure had, after all, been devised not least to reassure TUC unions that the statutory recognition procedure would not be available as a weapon against them in the hands of staff associations. But even after 1980 certification is much more than the grin left behind after the Cheshire cat of recognition has disappeared. In particular rights of unions to disclosure of information, or to be consulted over impending changes, or of individuals to time off for various purposes, or to protection of their freedom to associate, are given legislative shape only in relation to independent trade unions. It is to a consideration of these rights that we now turn.

(b) Freedom of association

(1) *The structure of the law*
The UK has ratified International Labour Organization Conventions Nos. 87 of 1950 (concerning Freedom of Association and Protection of the Right to Organize) and 98 of 1951 (concerning the Application of the Principles of the Rights to Organize and to Bargain Collectively). Article 1(2) of the latter requires ratifying states to protect workers against 'acts calculated to . . . cause the dismissal of or otherwise prejudice a worker by reason of union membership or because of participation in union activities outside working hours or, with the consent of the employer, within working hours'. It was not until 1971 that the government thought it necessary to introduce legislation to secure observance of this principle in the UK. Since then, the form of the legislation has changed a number of times, mainly because of changing views on the question of how far the law should seek to secure not only the freedom to join a trade union (as the Conventions require) but also the freedom not to join (which the ILO Conventions do not require, although some version of a right not to join may be required by the European Convention on Human Rights – see below, p. 657).

Section 5 of the IRA 1971 introduced the basic right to join a trade union and to take part in its activities 'at any appropriate time', but that section also created a right not to join trade unions or a particular trade union. Indeed, the right not to join was broader than the right to join because the latter applied only to registered trade unions, whilst the former was not so restricted. The legislation passed by the Labour government in 1974 and 1975 confined the right not to join to non-independent trade unions, in line with the policy, discussed in section 4(a)(2), of encouragement of collective bargaining only by unions not under employer domination. The effect was virtually to eliminate the right not to join. As a result of the changes made by the Conservative government in the EA 1980 and 1982, a right not to join equivalent to the right to join has been re-introduced (see EPCA 1978, ss.23 and 58, as amended). However, although the latest set of changes have re-introduced a formal equivalence between the right to join and the right not to join, in functional terms, as the Donovan Commission pointed out, the two rights are not equivalent. Discussing the right not to join and the right to join, its Report states: 'However, the two are not truly comparable. The former condition is designed to frustrate the development of collective bargaining, which it is public policy to promote, whereas no such objection applies to the latter' (para. 599). For this reason, we shall discuss in this chapter only the right to join and leave until Chapter 5 the right not to join.

The twofold nature of the right to associate, i.e. a right to join as such and a right to participate in trade-union activities, as identified in ILO Convention No. 98 and s.5 of IRA 1971, continues to be the basis of the present law. However, the nature of the right in the current law is somewhat different from that in the 1971 Act. In the latter the right to associate was an independent right; in the current law the right is very much a part of the general law on unfair dismissal, which is discussed below in Chapter 4. Thus, EPCA 1978, s.58, makes it unfair for an employer to dismiss an employee for exercising his freedom to associate and s.59(a) adds that selection of an employee for dismissal on grounds of redundancy (see below, p. 555) will constitute unfair dismissal if the reason for the selection was the exercise of the right to associate. Nevertheless, there are four ways in which the general law relating to unfair dismissal is especially adapted when the right to associate is involved.

First, and most important, the law of unfair dismissal is supplemented by protection covering action short of dismissal. By EPCA 1978, s.23(1)(a) and (b), 'every employee shall have the right not to have action (short of dismissal) taken against him as an individual by his employer for the purpose of (a) preventing or deterring him from being or seeking to become a member of an independent trade union or penalising him for so doing; or (b) preventing or deterring him from taking part in the activities of an independent union at any appropriate time or penalising him for so doing . . .' Without this additional protection, British law would not come near to fulfilling the requirement of ILO Convention No. 98 that the employee be protected against 'acts calculated to . . . cause the dismissal of *or otherwise prejudice*' him. The exact scope of s.23 will be examined below, but it is clear that, unlike s.5 of IRA 1971, neither s.23 nor s.58 of EPCA 1978 embraces refusals to engage an employee on grounds of union membership or activity. This is a remarkable lacuna given that the principle of regulating the employer's decisions about engagement has already been established in SDA 1975 and RRA 1976, although it does, nevertheless, remain generally true that managerial prerogatives are more closely regulated at the point of termination of the employment relationship than at its creation (see Chapter 1 above). Indeed, in *City of Birmingham DC* v. *Beyer* [1978] 1 All ER 910 (EAT, Kilner Brown J. presiding) it was suggested that s.58 applied only to dismissals on the grounds of trade-union activities carried on after the employment in question had commenced. The correctness of this interpretation of s.58 is open to doubt (see (1977) 6 *ILJ* 248), but, even if it is wrong, ss.23 and 58 give no protection against an employer who operates a blacklist of union activists provided the employer's recruitment procedures are effective to identify those on the list before they are hired.

Second, and almost as important, the protections of ss.23 and 58 are acquired by the employee immediately he is employed, whereas in the normal case of unfair dismissal the employee is not protected until he has been employed for 52 weeks or, in some cases, for two years (see below, p. 508). Thus, in the first year of employment proof that the dismissal was on grounds of union membership or activities means not only that the industrial tribunal must regard the dismissal as automatically unfair (instead of being required to assess the reasonableness of the employer's conduct as in the usual case – see below, p. 461), but also that, in the absence of such proof, the employee will not usually be able to require the tribunal to scrutinize the employer's reasons at all. Nevertheless, the courts have interpreted ss.64(3) and 64A(2) of EPCA 1978 as requiring the employee to show that the reason for his dismissal was union membership or activities if he wishes to escape from the normal length-of-service requirements, and this puts upon him an onus of proof that usually rests upon the employer, for s.57(1) states that it is for the employer to show the reason for the dismissal when the tribunal is determining the question of fairness or unfairness (see below, p. 472). In cases of short service, however, the reason for the dismissal, besides going to the fairness of the dismissal, also goes to the tribunal's jurisdiction, and the courts have held that it is for the complainant to show jurisdiction. See *Smith* v. *Hayle Town Council* [1978] ICR 996 (CA, Lord Denning dissenting on this issue) and *Marley Tile Co. Ltd* v. *Shaw* [1980] ICR 72 (CA) but cf. *Maund* v. *Penwith DC* [1984] IRLR 24 (CA). This may not be an easy task for the complainant to undertake and it is unclear how much help he will obtain from interlocutory procedures such as discovery (see *Science Research Council* v. *Nasse* [1979] ICR 921 (HL), noted (1980) 9 *ILJ* 52). Fortunately, but curiously, the same burden does not fall on the complainant under s.23, perhaps because there is no general protection against action short of dismissal. Here EPCA 1978, s.25(1) simply provides that 'it shall be for the employer to show the purpose for which the action was taken against the complainant'. It seems likely that Parliament thought it was laying down the same rule for dismissals on grounds of union membership or activities.

Third, where the employee has been dismissed on grounds of trade-union membership or activity, reinstatement or re-engagement will best vindicate trade-union rights. 'From the union's point of view the dismissal involves far more than unfairness to the employee. It is a blow aimed at the union itself, particularly in the case of dismissal of a union official. As the union sees the situation the whole prestige and credibility of the union is at stake. Monetary compensation for the employee . . . is an inadequate remedy' (*per* Sir John Donaldson in *Shipside (Ruthin) Ltd* v. *TGWU* [1973] ICR 503, 506). The importance of reinstatement in such cases is recognized in two ways in the legislation. Although, as we shall see below, p. 494, industrial tribunals are reluctant to order reinstatement, if they do so, the 'quasi-fine' of additional compensation payable by the employer to the employee on non-compliance with the order has always been higher in the case of dismissal on grounds of union membership than in other cases, and EA 1982 has increased the differential (EPCA 1978, ss.71 and 75A(2)). Further, a dismissed employee who under financial pressure has found another job in the period before the full tribunal hearing is much less likely to want his old job back. Accordingly, an employee alleging dismissal on grounds of trade-union membership or activities can seek a speedy award of 'interim relief' (EPCA 1978, ss.77–9) from a tribunal, provided he acts quickly (within seven days of the effective date of termination) and is supported by a certificate from the relevant trade union. See *Barley* v. *Amey Roadstone Corp. Ltd* [1977] ICR 546 and *Bradley* v. *Edward Ryde & Sons* [1979] ICR 488 (EAT). If at the speedy hearing the tribunal thinks that at the full hearing the applicant is likely to succeed, the tribunal may make an order for the continuation of the employee's contract until the full hearing, at least as far as the employee's entitlement to pay and other benefits is concerned, thus protecting him financially in the interim. 'Likely' has been interpreted to mean the relatively high standard of the complainant having a 'pretty good' chance of succeeding at the full hearing rather than the lower standard of a reasonable prospect of success. See *Taplin* v. *C. Shippam Ltd* [1978] ICR 1068 (EAT). How effective the procedure is in practice is unclear. The published statistics do not reveal whether, for instance, requests for and grants of reinstatement orders are more frequently made in cases of dismissal on grounds of trade-union membership and activity than in other classes of dismissal cases.

Fourth, the above modifications of the unfair dismissal laws were intro-duced, or continued, in the legislation of 1974 and 1975 in order to protect the position of those dismissed on grounds of trade-union membership and activity. With the introduction by EA 1980 and 1982 of a broad right not to join a trade union, these special protections have been extended also to those claiming the freedom to dissociate (see below, Chapter 5). In the case of the fourth modification, however, the process has operated in the opposite direction. By virtue of changes made in EA 1982 to the provisions of EPCA 1978, enhanced levels of monetary compensation are introduced. This was done in order to discourage employers from dismissing employees on grounds of their non-membership of a trade union but, by virtue of the formal equality that now exists between the freedom to associate and the freedom to dissociate, these provisions were applied also to dismissal on grounds of trade-union membership and activities. Because of the purpose behind these provisions we discuss them in detail in Chapter 5. Suffice it to note here that in cases of dismissal on grounds of union membership and non-membership the minimum basic award becomes £2000 (EPCA 1978, s.73 (4A)) and a new special award is created which will normally lead to a payment of at least £10,000 to a dismissed employee who seeks reinstatement (EPCA 1978, s.75A(1)), in addition to whatever is assessed by way of compensatory award. Although both the basic award and the special award are reducible by the tribunal where it thinks it just and equitable to do so on the grounds of any conduct of the complainant before the dismissal (subject to the new EPCA 1978, s.72A), these provisions are likely to lead to much higher monetary awards than in the usual case of unfair dismissal, where the levels of compensation are, on average, low (see below, p. 503).

The introduction of these new levels of compensation for unfair dismissal has created an odd contrast with the principles governing assessment of compensation in respect of acts short of dismissal. In particular, the notion of a penal element in compensation, which is now so clearly present in the sections governing compensation for dismissal, has been rejected by the EAT where action short of dismissal is concerned. Where a claim that s.23 of EPCA 1978 has been broken is made out, the Act provides that the tribunal shall make a declaration to that effect and may award such compensation 'as the tribunal considers just and equitable in all the circumstances having regard to the infringement of the complainant's rights under s.23 . . . by the employer's act complained of and to any loss sustained by the complainant which is attributable to that action' (s.26(1)). In *Brassington* v. *Cauldon Wholesale Ltd* [1978] ICR 405, the Appeal Tribunal said:

The object of Parliament in conferring upon employees the section [23] right was clearly to discourage employers from unfairly trying to prevent union activity in their undertaking. To effect that object it is necessary that there should be some sanction. Parliament could have chosen an expressly penal sanction, made infringement of the right an offence, and provided for penalties to be imposed by the ordinary criminal courts. But to bring the criminal law into the industrial field is widely thought to be unwise, and here Parliament has not done so. Parliament could have provided what would in truth have been a fine, but wrapped it up in a non-penal formula and imposed it not by the criminal courts but the industrial tribunal. A clear example is to be found in the Act of 1975 itself. By section 70 [now EPCA 1978, s.53], for an infringement of an employee's right to a proper statement in writing of the reasons of his dismissal, the industrial tribunal must award that the employer pay to the employee a sum equal to two weeks' pay. They have a discretion, in addition, to make a declaration as to what they find the employer's reasons really were.

But the sanction provided for an infringement of the section [23] right is different again. By section [24(3)], where the industrial tribunal find the right has been infringed they must make a declaration to that effect. They have a discretion, in addition, to make an award of compensation to be paid by the employer to the employee in respect of the action complained of, calculated in accordance with section [26]. Note the contrast to the mandatory quasi-fine and discretionary declaration provided for by section [53]. So, for infringement of the section [23] right, compensation for the employee, not a fine on the employer however tactfully wrapped up, is the basis of the discretionary monetary award.

Governed by this approach the Appeal Tribunal then held that the applicants could recover their expenses in going to the tribunal to vindicate their rights (including any pay lost through attendance), and also non-pecuniary losses such as the 'stress engendered by such a situation' leading to injury to health or if 'your deep and sincere wish to join a union . . . had been frustrated', but that the industrial tribunal could not award anything 'as compensation *ipso facto* by reason of the infringement itself'.

(2)   *The operation of the law*
The typical situation of discrimination against which the above provisions are intended to protect employees is one where an employer who is hostile to trade unions dismisses or takes action short of dismissal against an employee because he has joined a union and, perhaps, is also encouraging other employees to join it. In *Cotter* v. *Lynch Bros.* [1972] ICR 263, the National Industrial Relations Court interpreted s.5 of the IRA 1971 so as to protect an employee who had allegedly been dismissed for announcing an intention to join a union, even though he had not decided which one he intended to join. This reasoning would seem equally applicable to EPCA 1978, s.58(1)(a), which refers to discrimination on the grounds that the employee 'proposed to become a member of an independent trade union'. In the two cases set out below, the Employment Appeal Tribunal also took a broad approach but in the first case its decision was reversed by a more cautious Court of Appeal. The hesitation on the Tribunal's part which is to some extent noticeable in the second case is perhaps due to the Tribunal's desire to enable the industrial tribunals to weigh on a case-by-case basis the conduct of employer and employee (their function in an ordinary unfair dismissal case), whereas in cases of dismissal on grounds of trade-union membership or activity Parliament has taken the decision that the dismissal is unfair.

Carrington v. *Therm-A-Stor Ltd* [1983] ICR 208 (CA)
A trade union recruited 60 to 65 of the 70 manual workers employed by the employers at a new factory. On 28 April the union's district secretary wrote to

the employers asking for recognition. On 30 April the employers, who were biased against trade unions, decided immediately to make 20 employees redundant. Chargehands were given responsibility for selecting the employees to be made redundant and their selection was not made on the basis of trade-union involvement.

LORD DONALDSON M.R.: . . . As I see it, the first question for consideration is whether the fact that the chargehands undertook the selection for dismissal means that the chargehands' reason – probably last in first out – was the reason for the men's dismissal. Mr Tabachnik submits that so to conclude is to confuse the reason for dismissal with the basis for selection. As he rightly points out they are two quite different things and are so treated in section 59 of the Act in relation to redundancy. Where redundancy is the reason for the dismissal, the dismissal is not necessarily unfair. However, the method of selection for dismissal can make the dismissal unfair. For my part I think this is right and that the intervention of the chargehands can be disregarded as being concerned solely with selection and not with the reason for dismissal.

So far so good, but the four employees still have obstacles in their way. The industrial tribunal did not find that the employers or Mr Morris decided to dismiss the group of 20 men because any or all of them had joined the union or proposed to do so or had taken part in union activities or proposed to do so. He decided to dismiss them by way of reaction to the union's letter seeking recognition. The reason for the dismissals was the union's plea for recognition.

Mr Tabachnik seeks to overcome this obstacle by submitting that section 58 should be construed in such a way as to recognise what he called its 'collective dimension.' In his submission membership of a trade union is not a solo activity – it assumes other members. Similarly it is difficult, if not impossible, to take part in the activities of a trade union unless others do so. The whole concept of union activities has an essentially plural basis. Accordingly if the four employees were members of a wider group – they were all in fact members of the Transport and General Workers' Union – and the reason for the dismissals was the activities of that group, it follows, as he submits, that the reason for their dismissal was their union membership or activities, albeit with others.

I regard this as a valiant attempt at purposive construction of the statute, but in my judgment it goes beyond permissible limits. As I read the section it is concerned solely with the dismissal of *an* employee and provides that it shall be regarded as unfair if the reason was that the (i.e. *that*) employee had done or proposed to do one or more specified things. The reason why each of the four employees was dismissed had nothing to do with anything which the employee concerned had personally done or proposed to do. The section therefore has no application.

The appeal tribunal described this as a narrow construction and said that the section, so construed, would be rendered wholly inoperative in many instances where it must have been intended to apply. If by this they meant that some protection should be given to new employees if their jobs may be put at risk merely because a trade union has applied for recognition, I would not dissent. Indeed I would go further and agree that in such circumstances the union has a justifiable grievance. It is at risk of suffering considerable damage. If an employer can act in this way with impunity, employees in other factories might well hesitate before joining a union. I also agree with the appeal tribunal that it is the duty of the courts to give effect to the intentions of Parliament. However, the concept that Parliament 'must have intended' a particular result is not without its dangers. If regard is had solely to the apparent mischief and the need for a remedy, it is only too easy for a judge to persuade himself that Parliament must have intended to provide the remedy which he would himself have decreed if he had had legislative power. In fact Parliament may not have taken the same view of what is a mischief, may have decided as a matter of policy not to legislate for a legal remedy or may simply have failed to realise that the situation could ever arise. This is not to say that statutes are to be construed in blinkers or with narrow and legalistic literalness, but only that effect should be given to the intentions of Parliament as expressed in the statute, applying the normal canons of construction for resolving ambiguities or any lack of clarity.

Tempted as I am to provide the four employees with a remedy for what was an indefensible reaction to a simple request for union recognition, which could have been granted or politely refused, I cannot construe section 58 as being intended to deal with such a situation. The section is not concerned with an employer's reactions to a trade union's activities, but with his reactions to an individual employee's activities in a trade union context.

Lyon v. *St James Press* [1976] ICR 413 (EAT)

The applicants were employed by a small company whose workforce consisted of a manager and thirteen employees. The applicants wished to form a chapel (i.e. a branch) of the National Union of Journalists and approached all but two of the employees. They kept their plans secret from the manager because they thought he would oppose the idea and from two long-service employees. The manager and these two employees were 'extremely upset' and felt 'grossly insulted' at the formation of the chapel in secret. The applicants were dismissed shortly afterwards. The industrial tribunal found that a reason for the dismissal was the way the applicants had acted in forming the chapel and that this was not protected conduct. On appeal to the EAT:

PHILLIPS J.: Where an applicant who is alleging unfair dismissal has been engaged in trade union activities at the time of the events leading up to the dismissal and there is a connection between those activities and the conduct alleged by the employer to have justified dismissal in the terms of paragraph 6(8), [EPCA 1978, s.57(3)] the industrial tribunal hearing the case has a difficult task. The marks within which the decision must be made are clear: the special protection afforded by paragraph 6(4) [EPCA 1978, s.58] to trade union activities must not be allowed to operate as a cloak or an excuse for conduct which ordinarily would justify dismissal; equally, the right to take part in the affairs of a trade union must not be obstructed by too easily finding acts done for that purpose to be a justification for dismissal. The marks are easy to describe, but the channel between them is difficult to navigate.

With great respect to the very experienced industrial tribunal which decided this case, we think that it came to a wrong conclusion. The tribunal pointed out that it was not unknown for union spokesmen to enrol members, or even to form a chapel or branch, without telling the management. We agree. Indeed, it is our experience that the practice is very common. The reason is obvious. If the early steps are confined to like-minded enthusiasts, progress is likely to be more satisfactory than if the plans are announced before any steps have been taken. Mr Gray, for the employers, contended that such an approach was out of joint with the times. He pointed to the current call for consultation, for openness, for communication, for democracy and for mutual discussion. He prayed in aid the golden thread running through the fabric of industrial relations, *i.e.* consultation at all times and at all levels. Just as employees may be injured if it is lacking, so, he submitted, may employers. We see the force of this argument, but the two matters are not entirely on all fours. It does not require a majority to establish a chapel or some degree of union recognition. The fact that, had they been consulted, a majority of the employees might have been in the first instance against establishing a chapel would not necessarily be a good argument against a chapel being established if there was the sufficient minimum number of members ready and willing to form one – *i.e.* four.

The industrial tribunal went some way along this path of thought and their decision is based on the view that this was a special case. The specialty lay in the fact that this was a small firm, run on co-operative lines, where secrecy was *bound* to cause a rift. It is instructive to consider what would have happened had the employees followed the course proposed by Mr Gray, and endorsed by the industrial tribunal, *i.e.* openly declared their purpose from the start. There seems little doubt that it would have made more difficult their task of setting up a chapel and obtaining union recognition. So, from their point of view, they were proceeding in the more sensible way. The industrial tribunal say:

> They decided that they must keep this a secret from Mr Walsh because they considered, probably with a good deal of justification, that he would not welcome the idea and that, if he heard what was going on, he would discourage employees from joining the union.

So, even had they followed the course endorsed by the tribunal there would still have been disharmony, their plans would have encountered greater obstacles and there is no telling whether or when the same result would have been achieved, or, if so, what the relationships between the different members of the employers would then have been. Looked at in this way it seems clear to us that the acts in respect of which the employees were dismissed were done in the course of taking part in the activities of a trade union and that their dismissal for that reason was, in accordance with paragraph 6(4), unfair. We do not say that every such act is protected. For example, wholly unreasonable, extraneous or malicious acts done in support of trade union activities might be a ground for a dismissal which would not be unfair.

There is one afterthought which we wish to add, though not strictly necessary for the purpose of our decision. We would not wish it to be thought that we were recommending the method adopted by the employees in this case to secure union recognition as being the best one. We are only concerned with the question whether the employees were unfairly dismissed. For the reasons given we are of opinion that they were. But we are sure that, without following either of the extreme courses which we have discussed, a more tactful approach would have been possible. Difficult problems arise when it is sought to introduce union recognition into a small firm which is not used to it, and great care is needed. In particular, it is helpful if professional advice is sought at an early stage. We mention the matter in case it may be supposed that we consider what happened in the present case provides a model. We do not.
Appeals allowed.

In one respect the facts of *Lyon* v. *St James Press* can be said to present a copybook example of the organizing process, viz. secret recruitment of the majority of the employees into a trade union and then the presentation to the employer of a *fait accompli*. Very often, however, the organizing process is much less clear-cut. A grievance arises in the workplace, some of the employees form a loose grouping to secure redress, the question of union membership arises and someone may suggest contacting a local union office, the official may see an opportunity for recruitment and approach the company, and perhaps at the end of the day a fully-fledged recognition agreement between company and union emerges. But at what stage of the above process do the employees' activities attract protection?

To date, the decisions of the EAT do not speak with a clear voice. In *Chant* v. *Aquaboats Ltd* [1978] 3 All ER 102 the applicant, who was rightly of the opinion that the machinery the employees were required to use was not safe, acted as the spokesman of a group of employees in raising the grievance with the management, in organizing a 'round robin' petition and in contacting the local official of his union, which was not recognized by the company. His dismissal for these activities was held not to be an unfair one by the EAT which, by a majority, approved of the industrial tribunal's reasons:

> The next point the tribunal had to consider was whether the organization of the petition could be held to have been an activity of the trade union. We find that it was not an activity of the trade union. It is perfectly true that [the appellant] had drafted the petition and had taken it to be vetted by the union office before presenting it. But this vetting did not in any way make it a communication from the union to the employers. [The appellant] was not a shop steward. It is in fact signed by a number of men most of whom were not union members. It is of course open to employees in any firm to make representations by petition or otherwise to their employers about machinery which is unsafe. The mere fact that one or two of the employees making representations happen to be trade unionists, and the mere fact that the spokesman of the men happens to be a trade unionist does not make such representations a trade union activity.

In *Dixon* v. *West Ella Developments Ltd* [1978] ICR 856, however, the Appeal Tribunal took a broad view of the sections. On the hypothesis (which was not established on the facts) that the applicant had been dismissed because he had complained to his (unrecognized) trade union about the safety of his working conditions and the union had called in a factory inspector, the Appeal Tribunal would have held the applicant dismissed for an unfair reason, even though the two lay members of the industrial tribunal would have confined the protection to membership meetings and activities involving employees as trade unionists. The Appeal Tribunal said, in a dictum of importance to union-appointed safety representatives (below, p. 230), that the current law 'must have been intended to discourage employers from penalizing partici-pation in activities of a fairly varied kind and [ss.23 and 58 of EPCA 1978] should be reasonably, and not too restrictively, interpreted'.

Clearly, the prohibition on dismissals on grounds of trade-union membership restricts, like the law of unfair dismissal generally, the freedom of employers to dismiss employees for any reason that seems good to them. In the case of union membership Parliament has taken the view, in declaring such dismissals to be automatically unfair, that it is impermissible for an employer to make a link between a requirement that union membership be forgone and continued holding of a job. In the case of trade-union activities, however, the employer's claim to managerial prerogatives is not so easily ignored, because trade-union activities may interfere with the day-to-day running of the business. The ILO Convention No. 98, s.5 of IRA 1971 and s.58 of EPCA 1978 all attempt a reconciliation of these competing interests by confining the protection of trade-union activities to those carried on either outside working hours or within working hours but 'in accordance with arrangements agreed with or consent given by' the employer (EPCA 1978, s.58(2) – definition of 'appropriate time'). The meaning of 'working hours' was considered by the House of Lords under the IRA 1971 in *Post Office* v. *Crouch* [1974] ICR 378, in which Lord Reid made the following points which are equally applicable to the definition of 'working hours' in EPCA 1978, s.58(2). (See also *Zucker* v. *Astrid Jewels Ltd* [1978] IRLR 385 (EAT).)

. . . Section 5(1)(a) gives to every worker, as between himself and his employer, the right 'to be a member of such trade union as he may choose' and section 5(1)(c) gives to every member of a trade union the right 'at any appropriate time, to take part in the activities of the trade union'. It appears to me that the definition of 'appropriate time' in subsection (5) makes it quite clear that as well as including time when the worker is not on his employer's premises 'appropriate time' also includes periods when the worker is and is entitled to be on his employer's premises. The definition includes all time outside the worker's working hours and 'working hours' is defined as meaning time when in accordance with his contract with his employer he is required to be at work. I do not think that it was or can be disputed that 'at work' means actually at work and does not include periods when in accordance with his contract of employment the worker is on his employer's premises but not actually working. It is common knowledge, and Parliament was very well aware, that every day there are periods when a worker is on his employer's premises but is not expected or required to be actually working. He arrives at his employer's premises some time before he starts work. He leaves some time after his day's work is done. And I should think that in almost all cases he is not expected to work non-stop. There are recognized breaks for meals and perhaps other purposes during which he does and is expected to remain on his employer's premises. 'In accordance with his contract' does not, I think, mean in accordance with some formal condition, but rather in accordance with what the employer recognizes to be customary. It cannot matter whether provision for dinner and other breaks in working time is written into his contract or is merely a recognized concession. So, in my judgment, the Act entitles a worker who is a member of a trade union to take part in the activities of his union while he is on his employer's premises but is not actually working.

In relation to activities during working hours, where the employer's agreement or consent must be found if the activities are to be protected, the

Court of Appeal has taken a more cautious line.

Marley Tile Co. Ltd. v. *Shaw* [1980] I C R 72 (C A)

The employee, an electrician, had recently been nominated shop steward by the A U E W to represent the maintenance section of the employer's factory, although management had not accepted him as a shop steward and had reservations about his acting as such because of his short service with them. Nevertheless, the employers arranged a meeting at the employee's request to discuss the wage differentials of the maintenance employees, but at that meeting they refused to accept him as a shop steward. The employee left the meeting announcing his intention to telephone the union's district secretary (Mr Garwell) and to call a meeting of the maintenance employees. The employers' representative (Mr Wright) made no response to this declaration of intention. The meeting of the maintenance employees then took place during working hours and was attended also by shop-floor workers, so that a one-hour stoppage of production occurred. The industrial tribunal found that the reason for the employee's dismissal was the calling of the maintenance men to the canteen in working hours.

GOFF L.J.: . . . The matter then rests on the question of consent. It is not necessary to decide whether arrangements can only be express because this was not something done pursuant to any general arrangement. The question turns on the word 'consent.' In my judgment, in a proper case, consent may be implied but this is not such a case. I accept the view of the majority of the appeal tribunal, at p. 835. '. . . that the consent of the employers can[not] be deduced from their silence,' I add of Mr Wright, 'when Mr Shaw announced that he was going to call a meeting of his members and telephone Mr Garwell.' I accept the minority view of Mr Clement-Jones, at pp. 835–836:

> . . . unless there is a general agreement or arrangement which covers it, the shop steward unaccredited by the management at the relevant time cannot be taken to have implied permission to call such a meeting in working hours; particularly one which ends in an hour's stoppage of the shop floor workers, even if that was not intended by the shop steward. Furthermore, Mr Clement-Jones does not agree that an arrangement for the conduct of shop steward's duties can be reasonably assumed to exist either by extension from other factories in the Marley Group, or by having regard to custom and practice at their Dewsbury plant, inasmuch as it was found by the industrial tribunal that neither had the A U E W hitherto nominated a shop steward nor had the T G W U done so for their membership on production in the factory.

Mr Rose submitted that the calling out of the maintenance men to discuss the unexpected situation which had arisen was incidental to the original approach to the management to discuss the fitters' differential, which the employers had agreed should be in working time by giving the employee an appointment for that purpose and should, therefore, be treated as covered by that consent. I do not think that is right because it was not necessary to do this in working time and because it involved a much more significant interference with the work of the factory in which all five men were involved and not the employee only.

Alternatively, he relied on the speech of Lord Reid in *Post Office* v. *Crouch* [1974] I C R 378, 400, where, dealing with the precisely similar wording of section 5 of the Industrial Relations Act 1971, his Lordship said:

> But again this must be applied reasonably. It is one thing to ask an employer to incur expense or submit to substantial inconvenience. That the worker may not do. But it is a different matter to use facilities which are normally available to the employer's workers or to ask him to submit to some trifling inconvenience. Men carrying on activities of their union on their employer's premises must do so in a manner which does not cause substantial inconvenience either to their employer or to fellow workers who are not members of their trade union – and employers must tolerate minor infringements of their strict legal rights which do them no real harm. In my view the industrial tribunals are well fitted to deal with disputes about matters of that kind.

He argued that this applied to the present case and the employee's conduct was no more than that little inconvenience which employers must accept. In my judgment, however, it was much more than that, and I think the industrial tribunal thought so too, when they said, in paragraph 17:

> Such a meeting must mean that the men are not as readily available for work as they would otherwise be, even if in this particular case these men were maintenance workers and would still be on call when in the canteen.

In my view there is no ground for inferring an implied consent to all the maintenance men being suddenly called from their place of work to a meeting, particularly one such as in the present case where the problem which had arisen did not call for a desperately urgent solution. In my judgment, therefore, even if the conduct for which the employee was dismissed was taking part in trade union activities, which I have assumed, it was not at an appropriate time because it was carried out in working hours and was not in accordance with the arrangements agreed with or consent given by the company.

The definition of appropriate time would also seem to provide an answer to the question sometimes raised as to whether industrial action can count as a protected activity. In principle the answer might seem to be that it can, but it would have to take place at an appropriate time in order to be protected. Industrial action is likely to be effective only if it takes place during working hours and for activity at that time to be protected the employer must give his consent. But this approach would at least leave the employee protected if, say, during his lunch hour he joined a picket line outside another place of work as a gesture of solidarity, even though, as we shall see below, p. 850, his activities as a picket might leave him exposed to tortious liability at the suit of those whose business was interfered with. In *Drew* v. *St Edmundsbury B C* [1980] I C R 513, however, the E A T (Slynn J. presiding) took a different approach. By virtue of E P C A 1978, s.62, an industrial tribunal has no jurisdiction to hear a claim for unfair dismissal if the dismissed employee was taking part in a strike or other industrial action at the date of his dismissal and all the employees who were taking part in the action at that date were also dismissed. (These provisions are discussed below at pp. 901–31.) In this case the employee was alone amongst the workforce in taking part in a 'go slow' as a result of a directive from his union and was dismissed because of it. The Tribunal said:

... Under section 58, if an employer dismisses because a man has taken part in the activities of an independent trade union, then the dismissal is unfair. Under section 62, if an employee takes part in a strike or other industrial action, the position is entirely different. There, a man is not entitled to bring a claim that he has been unfairly dismissed when at the date of his dismissal he was taking part in a strike or other industrial action, unless he can show that other employees who, to put it broadly, were taking part in industrial action were not dismissed at the same time, or, if some were offered re-engagement, that he was one who was not. It is quite impossible, it seems to us and as Mr Tabachnik submits, for the same person to fall under both of those sections. Accordingly, it seems to us quite clear that there is intended by Parliament to be a distinction for the purposes of a claim for unfair dismissal between what is an activity of an independent trade union and taking part in industrial action. . . .

Accordingly, here, it appears that the industrial tribunal took the view that if what had been done by the employee was done pursuant to the national directive then that really was taking part in industrial action, particularly if regard is had to the purport of the directive contained in the phrase to which we have referred and which Mr Bradin used before us. This is not a matter on which there is really a very clear finding or evidence in the case, but it seems to us that if the tribunal were finding that what happened did amount to industrial action, they were right in saying that it could not at the same time constitute the activity of an independent trade union for the purposes of deciding whether the reason was an inadmissible one within the meaning of section 58(1) of the Act of 1978.

Do you agree with this line of reasoning? Suppose the tribunal did have jurisdiction because only some of those taking part in the industrial action were dismissed. Would it then be absurd for Parliament to have regarded industrial action as capable of being a protected union activity?

In all the above cases the situation that has presented itself to the court has been one of a conflict between employer, on the one hand, and employee, or employee and union, on the other. But the situation may be more complex than that. In *British Airways Engine Overhaul Ltd* v. *Francis* [1981] I C R 178 (Slynn J. presiding), the complainant was reprimanded by her employer for making a statement to the press which was critical of her union for not being consistent with its declared policy of seeking equal pay for women. The statement was made in the context of a claim by the women that they should be paid by their employer at the same rate as supervisory workers, who were all male, and the reprimand was for an alleged breach of an employer's rule about statements to the press about the company's business. The issue was whether the complainant could be said to have been taking part in the activities of an independent trade union when making the statement to the press. (It was assumed that the complainant had not in fact broken the company's rule concerning press statements.) The Appeal Tribunal said:

All the material seems to point to the fact that the employee was acting as the shop steward and she called her colleagues together as members of the union. They might, it is true, be criticising the several organs of the union for failing to carry out what the employee and her colleagues felt ought to be done. But discussion of matters with which an independent trade union is concerned, it seems to us, is quite capable of being an activity of an independent trade union within the meaning of the section. It seems here that these women were getting together, as union members, to discuss matters with which the independent trade union was concerned. It does not seem to us to be conclusive against the employee's claim that they did not do so at a meeting of some committee or at a formal meeting of the branch. They were a well-defined group of the union, meeting with their shop steward, and even though the criticism which they might be making might not be acceptable to higher branches, or higher officials in the union, it seems to us that they were still engaged in their discussion, their criticism, and in their resolution, in the activities of an independent trade union. It seems to us that it really would be ignoring the reality of the issue, and the immediacy of the issue to the women at this time, to say that it was all too remote from the activities of the union, and that it ought therefore not to be treated as being incidental to the activities of a union.

A second and more interesting category of the more complex cases contains situations where the employer has to deal with more than one union. Typically, the employer, who is not at all opposed to the principle of unionization, has recognized one union as representing a particular grade of worker, but finds that a second union has also begun to recruit members in that grade. The situation is likely to give rise to considerable inter-union rivalry, especially if, as is often the case, the recognized union is affiliated to the TUC and the non-recognized one is not. (Where both unions are affiliated, the TUC has its own machinery in the shape of the Bridlington Principles for the regulation of organizing activities. See below, pp. 611–17.) The question that arises is how far the employer can go in preferring the recognized union or encouraging membership of it without infringing the freedom of association of the employees who wish to join the non-recognized union. The situation often becomes one of employer plus recognized union against the unrecognized union, and it is a good example of the change in character that can be imparted to a legal rule designed primarily with anti-union employers in mind when it has to be applied to the issue of how far the employer can go in preserving established bargaining arrangements against encroachment.

Of course, the most extreme solution would be for the employer to sign a closed-shop agreement with the recognized union, though this course of action has become increasingly hedged about with legal restrictions, as we shall see in Chapter 5. Assuming the employer does not wish to do this, and assuming that he is also not willing to dismiss employees simply on grounds of their membership of the unrecognized union (which would clearly infringe EPCA 1978, s.58), the first question that arises is how far the employer may attach benefits for his employees to their membership of the recognized union.

Carlson v. *Post Office* [1981] ICR 343 (EAT)

The employee was a member of a union, EOTA, which was not recognized by the Post Office. He applied for but did not obtain a parking permit for his place of work. He was told by the employers that there was a local agreement between the Post Office and the Council of Post Office Unions, consisting of unions recognized by the Post Office, which in effect excluded members of unrecognized unions from consideration for permits. The employee complained that the Post Office had infringed EPCA 1978, s.23.

SLYNN J.: . . . It is important in these cases to bear in mind, before a breach is established, that what is done must (a) amount to action taken by an employer; (b) be against an employee as an individual; (c) be for the purpose of penalising the employee for being a member of an independent trade union. Moreover by virtue of section 25 of the Act of 1978 it is for the employer to show the purpose for which action is taken against a complainant and that it is not such a purpose as is referred to in section 23(1)(a), (b) or (c) of the Act.

In our judgment, the refusing of a parking permit is capable of being 'action taken.' Whether it is capable of amounting to 'penalising' is not entirely easy because of the history of this provision. Section 5(2) of the Industrial Relations Act 1971 provided that it was an unfair industrial practice: '(b) to dismiss, penalise or otherwise discriminate against a worker by reason of his exercising any such right' to belong to such union as he chose or to no trade union. In *Post Office* v. *Crouch* [1974] ICR 378, 401, Lord Reid, with whom three of their Lordships agreed, thought that discrimination

> could be either that by reason of the discrimination the worker is worse off in some way than he would have been if there had been no discrimination against him, or that by reason of the discrimination he is worse off than someone else in a comparable position against whom there has been no discrimination.

He thought the latter, Lord Simon of Glaisdale thought the former, was the more appropriate reading of the words. Nothing was said about the meaning of 'penalise.' In the present Act 'discriminate' does not appear. To penalise cannot be limited, in our view, to the imposition of what might be called a positive punishment or to a financial penalty. In our judgment, despite the absence of 'discriminate' from the current provision, to 'penalise' in this section is 'to subject to a disadvantage' and, unlike the industrial tribunal, we consider that the refusal of a parking licence is, as a matter of law, capable of amounting to 'penalising.'

The fact that some other members of the union who had parking licences before they joined EOTA were allowed to keep them does not in our judgment conclude the question as to whether the refusal of such a licence to the employee was for the purpose of penalising him (and others who did not previously have licences) for being a member of EOTA. In this we think the industrial tribunal were wrong. What has to be looked at is the purpose of the refusal to the individual.

Mr Carr submits that the fact that what was done was to carry out an agreement with the other unions is a sufficient purpose outside section 23 of the Act. We do not agree. It must depend on what are the terms of the agreement and what was its purpose. Here, as Mr Burke submits, there was no evidence as to the terms of the agreement or as to its purpose. Nor, contrary to Mr Carr's argument, can we say here that because non-union members were refused parking permits, that must establish that the refusal to the employee was not to penalise him for being a member of a union. We do not know anything about non-union members or how the agreement operated. Nor can we accept Mr Carr's proposition that the fact that parking licences are distributed through the union precludes automatically the possibility of a breach of the section.

Mr Carr further submits that there was here merely an arrangement between the Post Office and the recognised unions. At most there was action in favour of a recognised union either in the interests of industrial relations or of good administration. At most there was a disadvantage to the non-recognised union or to its members but nothing was done for the purpose of penalising any individual for belonging to a particular union. This may well be so. Many agreements between an employer and recognised unions must confer benefits on those unions and their members which may lead in fact to disadvantages being suffered by those who are members of other, non-recognised unions. That of itself is not a breach of the Act. What has to be found for there to be a breach is that the purpose of the action taken is to penalise an individual for membership of a particular union. Taking account of the onus in section 25, that will normally require that the employer establishes the purpose and that the industrial tribunal finds it as a fact so that it can be shown that it is not a purpose within section 23.

This case presented difficulties for the industrial tribunal because (a) the Post Office were not present (albeit for reasons which have been explained to us and which we accept) and (b) in their submission the Post Office covered points which did not arise and which were based on a misunderstanding of the claim being made.

It seems to us that if the majority of the industrial tribunal had not misdirected themselves as to whether the refusal of parking licences could have been penalising and as to the relevance of the fact that others were allowed to keep their parking licences although members of EOTA, they would have found it necessary to investigate the terms and the purpose of the agreement which was relied on and which was, apparently, a local agreement.

The second issue that may arise is how far the employer may restrict the recruitment and organizational activities of the unrecognized union on the employer's premises. This was the main point at issue in the House of Lords' decision in *Post Office* v. *Crouch* [1974] ICR 378 under the IRA 1971. Their Lordships' interpretation of s.5 of IRA 1971 was such as materially to restrict the employer's freedom to limit the activities of the unrecognized union. There were two strands in the decision. First, and more important, by granting organizing facilities to the recognized union, UPW, which were denied to the unrecognized union, TSA, the Post Office was held to have discriminated against the TSA and, by extension, against the members of the TSA. These facilities might well have gone beyond what the Post Office was obliged to grant to the UPW, so as to embrace, for example, activities during working hours, but the essence of the illegality was the discriminatory treatment of the UPW and the TSA. It seems that Parliament, when enacting EPCA 1978, s.23, intended to exclude this line of argument. As the EAT noted in the *Carlson* case, the word 'discriminate' was omitted from s.23 and the action taken which is prohibited by that section is action taken against an employee as an individual. The second, and more limited, argument was the one that was quoted in the *Marley Tile* case (above, p. 189). This was that it was inherent in the right to take part in the activities of an independent trade union that members of it could make use of the employer's facilities, normally available to the employees, for organizational activities, provided no sub-stantial inconvenience to employer or fellow workers was thereby caused. This was not a right that depended upon any comparison with the greater rights accorded to the recognized union, but one that stood on its own. It is a right the effective exercise of which during working hours the employer can prohibit by not giving his consent (see above, p. 188) but the employer cannot prohibit its exercise outside working hours and working hours were, as we have seen above, p. 188, broadly interpreted in the *Crouch* case. This second and more limited restriction upon the employer seems to have survived the reformu-lation of the legislation in 1975, and it was applied by an industrial tribunal in the following case.

Carter v. *Wiltshire CC* [1979] IRLR 331 (IT)

The complainant was a member of the British Fire Service Federation, an independent union but one not recognized by the employers, who recognized only the Fire Brigades Union for employees of the complainant's rank. The members of the Federation wished to hold a meeting in the social club at the complainant's fire station immediately after work ended. The chief fire officer refused permission on the grounds that to grant permission would set a precedent for other unrecognized unions in local government. He threatened disciplinary action against any employees who attended the meeting. The applicant complained that the employers had infringed EPA 1975, s.53, which is now EPCA 1978, s.23. The Tribunal said:

... The first question which we have to decide is whether the action taken on the respondents' behalf on 30 August was action short of dismissal within the meaning of s.53. Mr Vernalls has referred us to a recent case, *Bell* v. *Cornwall County Council*, which was heard by an Industrial Tribunal at Truro on 23.5.78. The applicant in that case was a member of the federation. He had requested permission from the chief fire officer to take part in certain activities of the federation on fire brigade premises. The chief officer wrote refusing permission. There was no other action by the respondents. The Tribunal decided that the chief fire officer's letter did not constitute action under the section. The Tribunal said, however, that its decision would have been different if the letter had contained a threat of disciplinary action. It considered two recent decisions of the Employment Appeal Tribunal, *Brassington* v. *Cauldon Wholesale Ltd* [1977] IRLR 479 and *Grogan* v. *British Railways Board* (unreported, 17.1.78). In the first of these two cases the Appeal Tribunal expressed doubt whether a threat could constitute action under the section. The point did not have to be decided because there was no appeal from that part of the Industrial Tribunal's decision. In *Grogan's* case it was held by a differently constituted Appeal Tribunal that a threat of disciplinary action did constitute action under the section. This decision is binding on us. In the present case there was a threat of disciplinary action and we must hold that Mr Carter succeeds on the question of whether action short of dismissal was taken.

The second question is whether the trade union activities referred to in s.53(1)(b) include activities on the respondents' premises. Mr Thomas submits that the Act imposes no obligation on an employer to provide facilities of this kind. Mr Vernalls relies on the decision of the House of Lords in *Post Office* v. *Crouch* [1974] IRLR 22. That case concerned the rights given to workers by s.5 of the Industrial Relations Act 1971. S.5 was very differently worded from s.53 of the Employment Protection Act, but for the purpose of the present case we think that its effect is the same. S.5(1) gave a right to every worker to (*inter alia*) take part at any appropriate time in the activities of a trade union of which he was a member. S.5(2) made it an unfair industrial practice (for which under s.106(3) an Industrial Tribunal could make an order determining the rights of the parties and could award compensation) to (*inter alia*) prevent or deter a worker from exercising any of his rights under s.5(1). There was no difference of any substance between the definition of 'appropriate time' in s.5(5) of the Industrial Relations Act and the definition in s.53(2) of the Employment Protection Act. In *Post Office* v. *Crouch* Lord Reid said that the definition in s.5(5) made it clear that 'appropriate time' included not only time when the worker was not on the employer's premises but also time when he was and was entitled to be on the employer's premises. Later in his speech (at page 25 paragraph 19) Lord Reid said this:

> But again this must be applied reasonably. It is one thing to ask an employer to incur expense or submit to substantial inconvenience. That the worker may not do. But it is a different matter to use facilities which are normally available to the employer's workers or to ask him to submit to some trifling inconvenience. Men carrying on activities of their union on their employer's premises must do so in a manner which does not cause substantial inconvenience either to their employer or to fellow workers who are not members of their trade union – and employers must tolerate minor infringements of their strict legal rights which do them no real harm.

We will deal in a moment with this aspect of the present case. At this stage we say only that we consider we are obliged by the decision in *Post Office* v. *Crouch* to hold that an employer cannot claim exemption from s.53(1) solely on the ground that the trade union activities took place on his premises.

Mr Thomas has referred to the words 'against him as an individual' in s.53(1). It is true that these words did not appear in s.5 of the Industrial Relations Act. The submission, as we understand it, is that the action taken against Mr Carter was in his capacity as a national officer calling a meeting on behalf of the federation. But, in our view, it was also action taken against him as a member to prevent him from attending a meeting. This would certainly have been the case if any other person who came to the meeting on 30 August had instituted a complaint under s.54(1), as he would have had a right to do. We cannot agree that our decision should be affected by the fact that it is Mr Carter who has brought the complaint and not one of his colleagues.

Reference has also been made to s.57(1) of the Employment Protection Act which deals with time off work for carrying out trade union duties. We do not see that this section is helpful in the present case, except that it is perhaps significant that s.57 applies only where the trade union is recognised by the employer, whereas s.53 must, by its wording, apply whether the trade union referred to in subsection (1)(b) is recognized or unrecognized.

We deal now with the question of reasonableness referred to in Lord Reid's speech in *Post Office* v. *Crouch*. On this question we are divided. One member considers that the request to hold the meeting was an unreasonable one because, having regard to Mr Vincent's evidence, it would not have been helpful to the respondents' industrial relations to have allowed the request. The majority view is as follows: It is clear that Mr

Carter was entitled to be in the social club after 9.00 pm on 30 August. Little or no extra expense was caused to the respondents, since the social club was in any event normally used by employees at that time. Nor is there any suggestion that there was inconvenience to fellow workers at a station where all but one were members of the federation. The majority cannot find that the request to hold a meeting was unreasonable.

The majority think that this point also meets Mr Vincent's fear that to have allowed the meeting would have opened the floodgates to other applications by members of unrecognized unions. The respondents are bound under the section to tolerate only activities which are not an unreasonable infringement of their rights. It does not follow from this case that all such applications by members of unrecognized unions must be acceded to.

Finally, in regard to Mr Vincent's point that this application is a roundabout way of seeking recognition, we are of course concerned in this case only with Mr Carter's rights as an individual. The section confers no right on a union. It is true that in *National Union of Tailors and Garment Workers* v. *Charles Ingram & Co Ltd* [1977] I R L R 147 (which was a case concerning an employer's duty under s.99 of the Employment Protection Act to consult representatives of a recognized trade union about proposed redundancies) it was held by the Employment Appeal Tribunal that an agreement to recognize could be implied from the employer's conduct over a period of time. But if the respondents have any fears on this score, it is open to them, when granting facilities, to make it clear that this does not imply recognition.

Among the papers submitted on behalf of the applicant there is an example of this being done in a letter dated 13.9.78 from the chief fire officer to a member of the federation in the Isle of Wight.

For these reasons we have decided that the complaint is well-founded. We do not make any award of compensation because we have no evidence of anything suffered by Mr Carter which would justify such an award.

This, then, represents the extent to which the law supports collective bargaining by means of protecting the freedom to associate in trade unions. In the 1970s (but much less so today) that kind of support for collective bargaining was envisaged by successive governments as a part only of a legal regime for collective bargaining which should include further measures to encourage collective bargaining in an acceptable form. The most important of such measures were statutory recognition provisions, which we now turn to consider.

(c) **Statutory duties to recognize trade unions**

In a British context it seems correct to say that the primary objective of individual trade unions has been to secure recognition from employers in order to be able to bargain on behalf of their members employed by those employers for the improvement of their terms and conditions of employment. The trade-union movement as a whole (through the T U C) has been at times an important political pressure upon government to secure legislative or administrative measures for the improvement of the position of working people in general. Nevertheless, the collective bargaining role for trade unions has usually been the predominant one, and hence the central concern of trade unions with recognition problems. These problems, as we saw at the beginning of this chapter, the trade unions overcame in large part through their own efforts, aided by the absence of virulent anti-union feeling on the part of employers (which characterized American employers in the earlier part of this century, and to some extent still does). Consequently, by the 1920s recognition was widespread at least amongst manual workers and in the public service, even though there was no general statutory procedure which unions could invoke to secure that recognition. Such a procedure was placed on the statute book only in the IRA 1971 after the Donovan Commission had recommended it in order to secure the extension of trade unionism amongst white-collar workers in private industry. The 1971 procedure was replaced by a rather different one in the EPA 1975, but that procedure was repealed by EA 1980 and nothing was put in its place.

Before looking briefly at the period of experimentation with general statutory recognition procedures, it is worth noting that for some decades publicly owned industries have routinely been put under an obligation in their constitutive statutes to recognize trade unions. Examples of such provisions can be found in statutes passed in the 1930s, but they became a notable feature of our law with the extensive programme of nationalization carried out by the immediate post-war Labour government. (See Sir N. Chester, *The Nationalisation of British Industry 1945–51* (1975), pp. 782–96.) Interestingly, the government was initially disinclined to include such provisions in the nationalization statutes on the grounds that it was inconceivable that the nationalized corporations, as good employers, would not deal with the representatives of their employees. However, the government changed its mind in the course of the passing of the Coal Industry Nationalization Act 1946, s.46 of which contained the relevant provisions, partly as a way of emphasizing that it was the nationalized corporation as employer and not the government that was responsible for negotiating terms and conditions of employment. Ironically, in recent times that policy has been frequently ignored by governments themselves desirous of reducing the rate of wage inflation, but the notion that the nationalized corporations did not really require the spur of legal obligation to recognize trade unions had a large impact upon the way the provisions were drafted. The exact wording of the sections has developed somewhat over time, but the following is a good example of the modern formula, taken from the statute whereby the Post Office ceased to be a government department and became instead a public corporation.

Post Office Act 1969, Sch. 1

11.–(1) Except so far as the Post Office is satisfied that adequate machinery exists for achieving the purposes of this paragraph, being machinery for operation at national level or local level or a level falling between those levels and appearing to the Post Office to be appropriate, it shall be the duty of the Post Office to seek consultation with any organization appearing to it to be appropriate with a view to the conclusion between it and that organization of such agreements as appear to the parties to be desirable with respect to the establishment and maintenance, for operation at any such level as aforesaid, of machinery for –

(*a*) the settlement by negotiation of terms and conditions of employment of persons employed by the Post Office, with provision for reference to arbitration in default of such settlement in such cases as may be determined by or under the agreements;

(*b*) the promotion and encouragement of measures affecting efficiency, in any respect, in the carrying on by the Post Office of its activities, including in particular, the promotion and encouragement of the training of persons employed by the Post Office; and

(*c*) the promotion and encouragement of measures affecting the safety, health and welfare of persons so employed.

(2) The Post Office shall send to the Minister and the Secretary of State copies of any such agreement as aforesaid and of any instrument varying the terms of any such agreement.

It will be observed that the difficult questions of which union to recognize, in what circumstances, in relation to which employees, and in respect of what matters, are dealt with by conferring the broadest of discretions upon the Post Office in its choice of unions with which to deal and then by confining the substantive obligation to 'seeking consultation ... with a view to' the establishment of collective bargaining machinery, without in any way attempting to determine the outcome of the consultation. It might be better to see these formulae not so much as legal obligations but rather as statements of public policy, for, as the following case suggests, the legally enforceable content of the obligation is small. The case is one of the now numerous pieces of litigation arising out of the attempt by the Post Office to reduce the number of unions it recognized.

R. v. Post Office ex parte Association of Scientific, Technical and Managerial Staffs [1981] ICR 76 (CA)

The Post Office recognized a small trade union (TCOA), which had about 1,000 members, as representing its sales representatives. There were plans afoot for the union to amalgamate with another small union which was recognized by the Post Office and which was thus a member of the Council of Post Office Unions. In 1979 the plans fell through and TCOA amalgamated instead with ASTMS, a large union which, however, had not previously been active in the Post Office and was not recognized by the Post Office. Although TCOA became an independent section of ASTMS, the Post Office with the support of the Council of Post Office Unions refused to recognize ASTMS on the grounds that this step was likely to lead to a fragmentation of bargaining arrangements. ASTMS claimed the Post Office was in breach of para. 11 of Sch. 1 to the Post Office Act 1969 (quoted above).

LORD DENNING M.R.: . . . On behalf of the section of the ASTMS Mr Harvey before us has said that it is certainly an 'appropriate' organisation within that paragraph, and it ought to have been recognised: because it is virtually the self-same organisation as the one which has existed for the last six years. He said that the same 1,000 men are members: it is the same organisation: it has the same officers: and it makes the same independent decisions, and the like, as it always has done. The difference is that it has become a section of the ASTMS. He submitted that that should not disqualify it from being an appropriate organisation. He said that the effect of the Post Office's decision now is that these 1,000 men are left unrepresented by any organisation: and that cannot be right. He said that in those circumstances it must be right for the Post Office to recognise the organisation as appropriate even though it is now a section of the ASTMS.

That argument sounded attractive in the first instance. But one has to consider the size of the Post Office and the problems facing it. I would stress that the organisation has to appear to the Post Office to be 'appropriate' in respect of a lot of other things. Such as: '. . . the settlement by negotiation of terms and conditions of employment of persons employed by the Post Office.' That may involve restructuring of the grading system. There is also 'the promotion and encouragement of measures affecting efficiency.' The Post Office say that far more efficiency can be obtained when there are only a few unions within the Post Office, which are members of the Council of Post Office Unions. That council can negotiate on one level with the Post Office without the intrusion of an outside body like the ASTMS. The Post Office pointed out that, if they were to recognise this section of the ASTMS, in future they would have to negotiate with two sets of people. On the one hand the Council of Post Office Unions; and on the other hand with this section of ASTMS separately: because this section is not a member of the council. If they had to have separate negotiations, there would be a danger of disagreement, and a danger of 'leap-frogging.' As soon as one grade arrived at a settlement, another grade would say: 'We ought to go higher,' and the like. The Post Office, in these circumstances, say: 'If we are to reach pay settlements sensibly; if we are to achieve the restructuring of grading sensibly; and if we are to carry out the objectives of recognition, we should consult with the Council of Post Office Unions and not have the intrusion of an outside body. This section – although nominally independent – will be under the umbrella of the ASTMS; and they will bring undesirable pressures to bear on our negotiations with our own people.'

That seems to me an approach which cannot be faulted. The Post Office are doing their duty. They have to seek consultation with organisations which appear to be appropriate with those objectives in view. They take the view – honestly and in good faith and, it seems to me, on reasonable grounds – that this section of the ASTMS is not appropriate for the purpose. I cannot see any fault in their reasoning in coming to their decision, either by taking into account things they ought not to have taken into account or failing to take into account things that they should.

There has only been one previous case on this section. It is *Gallagher* v. *Post Office* [1970] 3 All ER 712. In a way that was a stronger case than this one: because the Post Office did not consult with the men who were in their own guild. They only consulted with the Union of Post Office Workers. That decision was upheld by Brightman J. I need not go into the details of it, except to say that it is agreed on all hands that the judge put it too high when he said the Post Office had an absolute discretion in these matters. He put it too high when he said that the duty was no more than a duty to seek consultation with such appropriate organisations as it shall think fit to consult. That is not quite the right test. The requirement is that the Post Office must consider the appropriateness of the organisation. It did consider it fairly and reasonably and found it was not appropriate.

As for the general statutory procedures which existed during the 1970s, we have seen (above, p. 125) that the Donovan Commission were convinced of the need for greater government action if the existing degree of unionization was to be maintained and increased amongst a workforce containing an increasing percentage of white-collar workers; and their chosen method for encouraging recognition of trade unions by the employers was based on Allan Flanders' proposal for a body empowered to make inquiries into recognition disputes and produce recommendations which would not, however, be legally binding on the parties involved. The Commission on Industrial Relations was established in March 1969 as a result of the Donovan Commission's recommendations. Its task was the general one of developing and improving collective bargaining and the general conduct of industrial relations, but a major part of its work was concerned with recognition questions. The Commission received its references from the Secretary of State and operated much as Mr Flanders, who was one of the first Commissioners, had recommended. Inquiries were carried out by the Commission's trained industrial relations staff and the recommendations produced were implemented only in so far as the good sense of the recommendations commended them to the parties involved.

With the passage of the IRA 1971 much changed. Although the system of 'voluntary' references was maintained and used somewhat, there were added a number of 'compulsory' statutory machineries in which the CIR was to play a part, among them a new system for making recognition references. Under this machinery (IRA 1971, ss. 44–55) application could be made by the Secretary of State, employers or registered trade unions to the National Industrial Relations Court for a recognition issue to be referred to the CIR. The CIR would carry out its investigation very much as before, but the NIRC now had power, on the application of the employer or registered union involved, to make an order rendering compulsory the CIR's recommendations, if the majority of the workers covered by the recommendations voted in a secret ballot in favour of them. The NIRC naturally also had jurisdiction to determine whether its order was being complied with, and a system of unilateral arbitration through the Industrial Arbitration Board was provided as a sanction if the order was found to have been broken by the employer (ss.105(5), 125 and 127). Finally, there was an elaborate system of restrictions on industrial action to prevent pressure being applied whilst the statutory procedure was operating and to prohibit action which was designed to undermine the recommendations of the CIR or an order of the NIRC.

The IRA was repealed by TULRA 1974. The EPA 1975, however, contained a recognition procedure which was, in effect, half way between the purely voluntary approach of the CIR in its early days and the highly regulated procedure of the IRA 1971. The Employment Appeal Tribunal, in some ways the successor to the NIRC, played no role in the procedure. Applications for investigation were made directly to the Advisory, Conciliation and Arbitration Service, which inherited, *inter alia*, the functions of the CIR. Applications could be made only by unions, which must also be independent. The recommendations of the ACAS were not submitted to the EAT, nor to the employees affected for their approval in a secret ballot. Where the recommendation was in favour of recognition it was, however, in effect binding on the employer, for the Central Arbitration Committee (the successor to the Industrial Arbitration Board) had power to adjudicate upon complaints that the employer was not complying with the recommendation of the ACAS and, if the complaint was upheld, to award on a claim (which must accompany the complaint) that the relevant employees' terms and conditions should be improved. This was in effect a process of unilateral arbitration. (EPA 1975, ss.11–16.)

By the time the procedure came to be repealed in 1980 considerable dissatisfaction was being expressed with it by both trade unions and employers, although for different reasons. More surprisingly, dissatisfaction was being expressed also by the Council of ACAS, whose chairman was moved to write in June 1979 on its behalf a formal letter to the then Secretary of State for Employment. The letter (reproduced in the ACAS Annual Report for 1980) read in part as follows:

> In seeking to promote the settlement by agreement of recognition issues referred under the statutory provisions the Service has acted in the belief that ACAS was invested by Parliament with considerable discretion as to how it conducted its affairs. The Council understood that its constitution reflected Parliament's intention to bring together the collective wisdom of both sides of industry with a view to enabling the Service to carry out its general duties under section 1(2) of the Act. This belief is reinforced by the provisions in the Act relating to the Service's functions of conciliation, arbitration, advice and inquiry and the preparation of codes of practice, all of which allow the Service to exercise discretion in carrying out its duties.
>
> The statutory provisions on trade union recognition also allow for the Service to exercise an element of discretion in carrying out its duties. Under these provisions the Service has to consult all parties who it considers will be affected by the outcome of a reference and to 'make such inquiries as it thinks fit'. The Service has also to ascertain the opinions of workers to whom an issue relates 'by any means it thinks fit'. The Service was therefore intended to have a considerable degree of discretion in carrying out not only its general duties under section 1(2) but also its specific duties under sections 11 to 14 of the Act.
>
> A body such as the Council of ACAS requires this discretion in order to function properly. To reconcile the conflicting approaches of the two sides of industry to a matter like trade union recognition the Service has to find ways in which compromises can be reached. This essential discretion is now seen, as a result of judicial decisions, to be much narrower than the Service originally understood was Parliament's intention.

The Council has become increasingly conscious of the growing incompatibility between some of its statutory duties and the actions it would have preferred to take on the grounds of good industrial relations practice. Finally, the continued operation of the Council has been brought into question as a result of judicial comment on the role of Council members, requiring it to adopt a much more constrained legal procedure.

The Council, it should be clear, is not here commenting on the substance of the judicial decisions but on their effect on the practical operation of the Council and the Service. The Council is, however, concerned that its effectiveness in developing the voluntary approach to industrial relations problems is being undermined by the impression which is created by the number of cases under section 11 in which we are involved in the Courts.

The Council believes that some of the duties imposed on the Service by the provisions of sections 11–14 are not necessarily compatible with its duty to promote the improvement of industrial relations. For example, the Service has a duty to pursue and complete any reference made to it in respect of any group of workers that a trade union cares to define. In some instances, for the Service to proceed with these duties will be injurious to good industrial relations. The Service, however, has no discretion not to proceed however much it believes that its intervention would be harmful. This is particularly so in cases of competitive claims by unions which the Act appears to have encouraged. Examples have been seen in the water industry and amongst polytechnic teachers where the Act has been used as a vehicle for outside unions to challenge those already recognised by the employer through existing collective bargaining machinery.

The Grunwick[1] case established that the Service has a mandatory duty to ascertain the opinions of workers to whom a recognition issue relates. The statute provides for no discretion, so that even where an employer or a union refuses co-operation, the Service is left with a duty it cannot perform. The procedures are therefore statutorily binding on ACAS whilst leaving employers and unions free to co-operate with the Service on a voluntary basis. In some cases this has resulted in ACAS being unable to report under section 12 of the Act (as with the Michelin and Grunwick cases).

The Court of Appeal in the UKAPE/W.H. Allen case,[2] in addition to the matters discussed below, has said that the Service is obliged to make findings on a whole series of matters which it may consider irrelevant or unnecessary and in some cases harmful to industrial relations. For example, the Service could be required to pronounce on the appropriateness of a trade union for a particular group of workers. This would be quite contrary to the normal traditions of British industrial relations where trade unions organise on the basis of spheres of influence rather than on imposed structural criteria. Similarly, the Service could be required to pronounce on the appropriateness of a particular bargaining group even in cases where it does not intend to make a recommendation. This could prejudice the emergence of a more appropriate grouping in future.

On the other hand, the Act gives ACAS no guidance as to the criteria to be adopted in determining a bargaining group or the level of support which it should consider appropriate in deciding a recognition issue beyond the general formulations in section 1. Nor has it been possible for the Council to agree on any such criteria which would be generally applicable. The absence of criteria has made the decision-making duty of the Council increasingly difficult, and one which can only be carried out at all by the exercise of a wide discretion. As time passes without criteria, the risk increases of the

[1] *Grunwick Processing Laboratories* v. *ACAS* [1978] ICR 231.   [2] *UKAPE* v. *ACAS* [1979] ICR 303.

Council making apparently conflicting decisions on similar facts which may lead to the Council appearing to outsiders to be inequitable or partisan to the detriment of the impartial traditions of the Service in other areas such as conciliation and advisory work. There is also the risk of the Council being unable to reach, in some cases, agreed conclusions. . . .

The experiences of three years of operation of the statutory procedures have shown the difficulties of operating without criteria and the damaging effect on industrial relations which can result from the Courts' interpretation of the statute. The Services's ability to exercise its own judgments in recognition matters has always been circumscribed by the legislation. The discretion of the Council has been further limited by the decisions of the Courts which have made it progressively more difficult for the Council to exercise its industrial relations judgment in reaching decisions on recognition issues. Even the functioning of the Council is likely to become impracticable as a result of its being deemed to be acting in a judicial capacity. The Council therefore wishes me to advise you that in the light of the increasing difficulties which it is encountering it cannot satisfactorily operate the statutory recognition procedures as they stand.

There was, of course, an element of contradiction between the two complaints in the chairman's letter. As against the courts it was said that they had restricted the Service's discretion; as against Parliament that it had not done enough to provide criteria by which the Service should decide a recognition issue, but the specification of criteria would necessarily have restricted the Service's discretion. Ironically, by the time the government had committed itself to abolition, rather than reform, of the recognition procedure the House of Lords had considerably relaxed the degree of judicial scrutiny to which ACAS was subject in recognition cases. The approach of the Court of Appeal in the W.H. Allen case was overthrown by the House of Lords (see *UKAPE* v. *ACAS* [1980] ICR 201 (HL) and *EMA* v. *ACAS* [1980] ICR 215 (HL)) and the primacy of the Service's discretion was restored. Nevertheless, few people seem to have regretted the passing of the 1975 Act's recognition procedure.

It is also difficult to know how effective the procedures were. The density of unionization amongst white-collar workers certainly increased rapidly in the decade after Donovan reported, but the CIR in neither its voluntary nor its compulsory role handled very many recognition issues, and by ACAS's own estimation the 1975 Act's procedure, although heavily used, directly secured recognition for only some 65,000 people. It may be, however, that the existence of these procedures contributed to a climate of opinion which was favourable to recognition for white-collar employees.

With the disappearance of the statutory recognition procedure, the remainder of the statutory structure for the encouragement of collective bargaining (by means of ensuring the effectiveness of trade-union participation therein) was left rather as Hamlet without the Prince of Denmark, not least because employers would largely stultify the remaining provisions if they withheld recognition. On the other hand, since recognition voluntarily achieved was and remains far more extensive than statutorily imposed recognition ever was, so the rest of the statutory structure, which depends upon the fact of recognition, retains its importance in that context. One of its main pillars is the disclosure provisions, which we now turn to consider.

(d) Disclosure of information

Under ss.17–21 of the EPA 1975 an employer is obliged to disclose to any independent trade union recognized by him information without which the union representatives would be impeded to a material extent in carrying on collective bargaining with him, and which it would be in accordance with good industrial relations practice for the employer to disclose. A similar obligation was placed upon employers by IRA 1971, s.56 (although, after the manner of that Act, the obligation was owed only to registered trade unions), but that section was not brought into force during the lifetime of that Act.[1] The provisions of EPA 1975 have survived the repeals effected in the legislation supportive of collective bargaining by EA 1980 and 1982, so that the provisions can perhaps be said to have achieved a degree of general political support, or at least acquiescence. But what is the purpose of these provisions? As the authors of the following passage suggest, the apparent consensus over the desirability of provisions requiring disclosure of information may hide rather different views held by different groups as to why such provisions are required.

Marsh and Rosewell, 'A Question of Disclosure' (1976),
7 *IRJ* No. 2, pp. 8 and 10

The general arguments in favour of disclosure are difficult to resist. It is scarcely possible to deny the virtues and likely advantages of being well-informed; such a denial may all too easily appear to signify approval of ignorance and who, in a democracy, can credibly do that? Is it not better where collective bargaining is concerned that negotiations should be about facts rather than emotions? Is it not true that for any worker to give of his best he ought to understand his role and function in the productive process? For what other purpose has the last hundred years of public education been devoted?

It is thus hardly surprising that parliamentary debates on disclosure have been characterized by a remarkable consensus embracing all elements of the political spectrum. Unfortunately this general agreement is, in some respects, an illusion, for those who argue about the importance of disclosure frequently do so for very different reasons. This is hardly surprising, for they often approach the subject with widely differing assumptions and expectations, some of which may be false or at all events open to challenge.

Generally speaking, employers favour disclosure because they believe that it will

---

[1] Section 57 of IRA 1971 required large employers to make an annual statement to individual employees about the state of the enterprise, but that section was not brought in force either and the present law contains no equivalent provision. Under HSWA 1974 employees are entitled to information relevant to health and safety matters, both from their employers and others (see ss.2(2)(c) and 6(1)(c) and (4)(c)) and safety representatives (see below, p. 233) are entitled to further information (Safety Regulations, Reg. 7).

improve industrial relations to their advantage. So too do trade unions. Between them there is often a considerable difference as to what this implies. Company spokesmen tend to believe that disclosure and improved communications will produce rational and objective bargaining, prevent rumours, encourage approaches favourable to productivity improvements and job evaluation, enable workers to understand the affairs of the company and improve morale, workmanship and cost consciousness as well as creating a greater sense of involvement and identification with the firm. They argue that it will influence the behaviour of trade unions by stimulating professionalism and moderating some of their demands and attitudes.

Some employers are far more enthusiastic about disclosure than others. Some believe that the provision of more information can radically improve industrial relations and assist the development of forms of worker participation; others are sceptical about its advantages, voice a number of fears and believe that it will be of little value except as a public relations aid during strikes.

Although trade unions share some of these views, i.e. that information assists job evaluation exercises etc., overall they tend to support disclosure for substantially different ends. They and their supporters believe that it will redress an imbalance in collective bargaining and enable them to negotiate as equals and bargain in good faith, arm them with valuable information about when an employer can least afford a strike, provide ideological and agitational re-enforcement for claims, compel companies to justify their decisions and, hence, be less autocratic and generally aid the process of improving the status of workpeople in industry.

Industrial relations practitioners and politicians of both left and right also have different motives in supporting disclosure. Some believe that it will reduce the number of strikes, others the opposite. The Institute of Workers' Control see it as a means of exposing how capitalism works, of revealing its anti-social practices and of extending the frontiers of traditional collective bargaining and workers' control over such issues as investment, the company and the community. In contrast, others regard it as a means of overcoming the credibility gap about profits and persuading workers of the company's positive contribution to society. Some observers believe that disclosure will promote acceptance of redundancy and the need for co-operation and change to avoid it; others view it in terms of advance warning and the need to prepare for factory occupations and other forms of resistance.

. . . General
 (i) There is no firm evidence that disclosure of information will, in itself, improve industrial relations. There are many facts, for example those concerning job changes or planned redundancies, profit ratios or directorial salaries and contracts, which could stimulate conflict rather than reduce it.
(ii) Disclosure often assumes a rational, almost scientific, concept of industrial relations and supposes that 'facts' can overcome differences and opposing interests. Implicit in such a view is that information is accurate, objective and absolute. Not only can this be questioned; it is also unlikely that information, however accurate, will always be accepted or given its due weight. There are, moreover, a number of ways in which financial information can be presented, a fact not unnoticed by trade unions. The disclosure of 'facts', absolute and incontrovertible, is partially incompatible with collective bargaining. If Mark Twain could write, 'It is difference of opinion that makes horse races', the same is certainly true

of industrial relations. Trade union objectives, the bargaining strength of the parties etc. are all factors as important as 'facts'; and, whilst all factors are relevant, it is rarely the case that any are absolutely crucial, or likely to become so. In some situations, of course, where trade union organization is weak, information may serve as a partial substitute for bargaining power and thus project a misleading impression.

Overall, both parties in industrial relations, whilst discussing information, are unlikely to be constrained by it if they do not wish to be so. Freedom for manœuvre is often essential. Trade unions which urge disclosure tend to expect that it will uncover hidden profits or provide the proof as to why a proposed redundancy should not proceed. Facts which reveal the opposite might well be dismissed as unacceptable. Trade union reactions may vary as facts please or displease them.

Is it possible to say that any of the above views of the purpose of disclosure was *not* adopted by the legislature?

To some small extent Parliament has made a choice amongst these various possibilities by setting the outer bounds of the employer's obligation to disclose by reference to the extent of the employer's recognition of the union for the purposes of collective bargaining (s.17(2)). The right to information is, thus, an incident of recognition rather than an independent right which a union might use, for example, in order to decide whether or not to attempt to increase the range of matters bargained over. Moreover, as we have already noted above, p. 170, recognition is not merely a prerequisite of disclosure, but also the extent of the recognition determines the extent of the matters in relation to which disclosures of information can be called for.

R. v. *Central Arbitration Committee ex parte*
BTP Tioxide Ltd [1981] ICR 843

The union, ASTMS, wished the employer to disclose information about a job-evaluation scheme it had introduced. The union was recognized for the purposes of collective bargaining over salaries, but in respect of job-evaluation appeals it had the right only to make representations on behalf of individual members. The Central Arbitration Committee had required the employer to disclose the required information; the company applied to the High Court for an order of *certiorari* to quash the Committee's decision.

FORBES J.: . . . The committee's reason for concluding that the complaint was well founded is really to be found in paragraph 21 of their decision. Paraphrased it is that it would be contrary to a reasonable interpretation of the legislation to find that a union which holds a recognition agreement, under which it has two distinct roles, could demand information needed for one role but not that needed for the others. Mr Melville Williams's second argument is that such an approach is right. Let us then look at the Act.

If Parliament had intended that all collective bargaining by trades unions was to attract the benefits of section 17 they could have said so. They did not. It is clear that Parliament restricted, and intended to restrict, the benefits of the compulsory disclosure of information only to such collective bargaining as is set out in section 17(2). That restriction, so far as is relevant, is to 'matters . . . in respect of which the trade union is recognised.' This expression itself envisages that there may be matters, which might appropriately form the subject matter of collective bargaining but which are nevertheless matters in respect of which the trade union is not recognised. The committee say that it is dealing with an agreement which recognises the union for two different roles – a right to negotiate and a right to represent individual members. It is the fact of recognition which, the committee suggests, makes it contrary to the spirit of the Act to differentiate between the two roles. It is here that one must look at the definition of 'recognition.'

The definition section is section 126(1). Under it ' "recognition" has the meaning assigned to it by section 11 above and cognate expressions shall be construed accordingly.' Turning to section 11(2) – the relevant provision – it says:

> In this Act 'recognition,' in relation to a trade union, means the recognition of a union by an employer, or two or more associated employers, to any extent, for the purpose of collective bargaining.

One must then turn back to section 126(1) for the definition of 'collective bargaining,' which reads:

> 'collective bargaining' means negotiations relating to or connected with one or more of the matters specified in section 29(1) of the Act of 1974.

The matters specified in section 29(1) of the Trade Union and Labour Relations Act 1974 are:

> (a) terms and conditions of employment, or the physical conditions in which any workers are required to work; (b) engagement or non-engagement, or termination or suspension of employment or the duties of employment, of one or more workers; (c) allocation of work or the duties of employment . . .

I do not think I need read all of them. They are all particular matters set out in that section.

Thus not all matters about which negotiations may take place between unions and employers are properly called 'collective bargaining' but only those matters which fall within section 29 of the Act of 1974. Further, in relation to giving information, such matters must be those in respect of which the union is recognised (section 17). But 'recognised' means (section 11) recognised for the purpose of collective bargaining, and the synonym of collective bargaining is 'negotiations relating to section 29 matters.'

From these provisions I think one can deduce that the Act contemplates that there may be, in addition to collective bargaining which entitles a union to information, (1) bargaining between employers and unions which does not amount to collective bargaining because it does not relate to matters referred to in section 29 of the Act of 1974; (2) dealings, to use a neutral term, between employers and unions which do not amount to collective bargaining because they cannot be properly called negotiations; and (3) collective bargaining which does not attract the right to information because it is not about matters in respect of which the union is recognised for collective bargaining.

I can see no obstacle under the Act to an agreement which recognises the union's right to collective bargaining, i.e. negotiation, about one aspect of employees' terms and conditions of employment and also recognises a right to some form of dealings with the employers, which does not answer to the description of collective bargaining, perhaps because it cannot be called negotiation, about another aspect. Indeed, it seems to me that the definition of 'recognition' inevitably accepts this possibility as I have already indicated. The result of such an agreement would, of course, be that the union was entitled to information in respect of its collective bargaining role but not in respect of its other role under the recognition agreement. This seems to me to be a matter which the language of the Act plainly contemplates.

However, although the scope of the recognition determines the scope of the matters in relation to which disclosure can be required, the required disclosure is not limited to items of information which are directly about the recognized subject matters. Thus, an item of information about topic A, over which the union does not negotiate with the employer, may have to be disclosed if it is relevant to bargaining about topic B, in relation to which the union is recognized. Indeed, ACAS in its Code of Practice No. 2 (Disclosure of information to trade unions for collective bargaining purposes) clearly takes the view that information about matters which are probably not capable of being the subject of collective bargaining (because they do not fall within the list contained in TULRA 1974, s.29(1)) can be relevant to bargaining about other matters which are proper subjects for bargaining. Thus, para. 11 of the Code contains, as examples of potentially relevant information, information about, *inter alia*, return on capital invested, sales and the state of the order book, investment plans, profits and inter-group loans.

Of course, the fact that such information is potentially relevant does not mean that in a particular case it has to be disclosed. The statutory tests are that the information must be information without which the trade-union representatives would be to a material extent impeded in carrying on collective bargaining and information which it would be in accordance with good industrial relations practice for the employer to disclose. The latter is a rather open-ended control which allows the Central Arbitration Committee to moderate potentially broad claims for disclosure of information, as we can see in the following case where the Committee was faced with a claim from a union representing one group of workers for information about the terms and conditions of another group represented by a different union.

Daily Telegraph Ltd and Institute of Journalists, Award
No. 78/353, June 1978, paras. 17–40

General considerations
17. It is worthwhile in this exceptionally difficult case setting out the terms of the complaint made by the trade union and the reasons put forward. The information required is described as:

Earnings of certain other categories of employees in the company (the list is set out in Appendix A of this Report) and the formulae in the relevant agreements used to calculate those earnings.

This information is required so that consideration can be given as to whether, in the union's words:

(a) journalists' earnings have maintained their former level relative to those of other employees or have declined;
(b) that apart, journalists' earnings relative to those of other employees fairly and adequately reward the skill, training and responsibility called for;
(c) under successive stages of pay restraint, the employer has found ways of providing earnings for other employees in excess of the approved maxima, and, if so, whether these methods could be applied to journalists' earnings – we accept the employer's assurance that pay policy had not been breached at any time.

18. There is obviously, behind this request, a feeling of considerable heat that has been caused because the trade union feels sure that relativities amongst the work force have in recent times been changed so as adversely to affect their members. In the context of the impending round of bargaining they are looking for more systematic and reliable evidence to confirm, or perhaps refute, their opinion on the matter – to give, it might be said, a righteousness to their indignation. It is clear, and we made careful enquiries on this point, that the matter cannot be resolved by further conciliation. Certain basic principles are involved and we must consider the matter under s.19(4) of the Employment Protection Act 1975.

19. Under that Act we have to apply two tests, set out in s.17(1)(a) and s.17(1)(b), both of which must be satisfied. In addition, in respect of the second test, we must have regard to the Code of Practice (No. 2): Disclosure of information to trade unions for collective bargaining purposes, prepared by the Advisory, Conciliation and Arbitration Service, effective since 22 August 1977. It may also be noted at the outset that there are also to be considered a series of restrictions on the duty to disclose set out in s.18. None of these was raised by the parties but we checked them and confirm that they do not appear applicable in this case.

20. The tests with which we are concerned are formulated in deceptively simple terms. For information to be disclosed it has to be: s.17(1)(a) information without which the trade union representative would be to a material extent impeded in carrying out with the employer such collective bargaining. It is our belief that the purpose of this section is to encourage the flow of information. We certainly feel that we should interpret the law in this way. It might be argued, along these lines, that this test is then merely a question of relevance. All relevant information prima facie makes for more open, and by definition, better bargaining. But we note the negatively expressed rule. It speaks of evidence 'without which' the trade union would be impeded. This narrows considerably the test from one of relevance to one of importance. This we accept and we ask the question is the information sought in this case relevant and important in general terms?

21. Our answer must be yes. There is hardly a countervailing argument and we noted that the employer did not seek to resist the request on these grounds. At its most general level it can be argued that all information about the amount of money paid out by way of wages and salaries is essential information for those bargaining with an employer. Where, as is almost invariably the case, the employer conducts several wages bargains within differing 'bargaining units' there must obviously be an element of competition between the trade union bargainers. It is not necessarily true that the amount

'available' for wages and salaries is fixed yet it is reasonable to feel that settlements in one unit must have some effect on the settlements elsewhere.

22. At a more detailed level the matter is not quite so obvious yet the arguments are strong. It appears reasonable that the structure of wages and salaries throughout the company should be known to the bargainers. Here perhaps the point is clearer where there are established or recognized links or where the units are adjacent. It is possible to argue that units with little contact in the company structure are not so obviously in need of information about each other. This is a point that was not argued before us in this case nor is it necessarily correct and it is one to which we must return in discussing the second test.

23. In short, and tentatively at this stage, we feel that the information requested – certainly as to structure of rates – should be made available. Individual earnings or even spread of earnings are perhaps too detailed. Certainly the annual increase in the 'wage bill' in each unit is the type of information we would regard as important to a bargainer.

24. Before turning to the second test attention must be given to s.17(2). Neither party sought to argue the law before us. It nonetheless appears to be our duty to determine whether s.17(2) is restrictive in a way that debars this claim. The sub-section defines collective bargaining as used in s.17(1) where the basic duty to disclose is set out. It is '. . . about matters, and in relation to descriptions of workers (a) in respect of which the trade union is recognized by that employer': Paragraph (b) is not applicable here. It might be argued that this provision debars access to matters relating to separate bargains. The point is a difficult one.

25. The sub-section limits the trade union to the parameters of its own bargaining table. Collective bargaining is limited to workers and matters for which the trade union is recognized. Thus the trade union could not purport to bargain outside its prescribed area of recognition either in terms of worker or of subject matter. For example if a union were recognized to bargain for clerical staff it could not bargain for recently recruited computing staff without agreement that the scope of recognition be widened. The key to this is without doubt the terms of the agreed recognition for bargaining. As far as scope is concerned a claim to bargain upon pensions, where this topic had never previously been an accepted subject of the bargaining process, would fall foul of this provision unless and until the scope of bargaining was extended by agreement to that subject.

26. Thus we feel that these limitations are about the area of the bargaining and *not* about the type of information. Once the trade union, as in this case, has established that it is within the limits of its recognized bargaining powers – expressed in terms of worker and subject – then the information requested has to be tested in the light of the provisions of s.17(1)(a) and (b). Were s.17(2) to be read as a limitation not upon the scope of collective bargaining but upon the type of information that may be requested it would be seriously restrictive. Much of the information properly required will be of a general nature relating to the business as a whole and not restricted to the trade union's members or the unit in question. This confirms our view that s.17(2) defines the area of collective bargaining concerned; s.17(1) lays down the tests to be applied to the type of information requested.

27. The second test provides that the matter should be: s.17(1)(b) information which it would be in accordance with good industrial relations practice that he should disclose to them for the purposes of collective bargaining. It will be recalled that it is in respect of this test that we must have recourse to the guidance set out in the ACAS Code. Indeed it

was to this that we turned at the outset. The problem upon which we sought help was whether there was some limitation of the principles of disclosure based upon there being separate bargaining units. Much of the information listed in the Code is obviously company wide and would apply equally to all units, e.g. much of the information listed in paragraph 11(v) Financial. But some information is more restrictive in scope and relates to the position within a particular bargaining unit. Is it appropriate to order that others should be allowed to have access to it? The Code appears to give no clear guidance on this point which is crucial to this case.

28. We considered what the general practice is. In most public employment, and some private, salary scales are published or are readily available, being for example disclosed in advertisements of job vacancies. In general scales of this type are now associated with sophisticated collective bargaining but need not be so. In other areas, particularly where there is no collective bargaining, information is much less available. Indeed being based upon individual salaries it often could hardly be presented in tabulated form. It seemed to us necessary to assess the structure in the area we are considering.

29. Bargaining in a very large part of the *Daily Telegraph* is well established collective bargaining with the appropriate union. The position is however complicated and fragmented. Management appears to negotiate with a trade union chapel. Each distinct area appears to have its own chapel and the total number is about 50 we were told. The number in each chapel varies between 430 and 3. There is thus excessive fragmentation. Although there is a unified Federated House Chapel composed of all the trade unions (except the Institute of Journalists) we gather that this body concerns itself with general matters, such as health and safety, and does not form a bargaining unit in the usual sense. There appears to be no real co-ordination between the various units.

30. We have no doubt that at an informal level the trade unions will exchange a lot of information. The Federated House Chapel does not formally serve this function. No doubt the efficiency of exchange of information will depend upon the personal relationships between trade union officials.

31. There is here, we must acknowledge, an additional problem. Two trade unions organize journalists. This action was brought by one of them – the Institute of Journalists – which is not federated with the TUC. The other trade union – the National Union of Journalists – is a member of the TUC. Although these two trade unions form together a chapel to negotiate for journalists and to some extent appear to work in harmony (there is indeed some dual membership) it would be wrong to pretend that the relationship is always an easy one. Certainly in the wide company context we would not imagine that the Institute is fully informed by means of the informal network to which we have already referred.

32. If this description is reasonably accurate it appears to lead to two questions. Is the state of the bargaining structure such that there should be a wide distribution of information? Would such dissemination lead to inter-union strife and difficult industrial relations?

33. The first question leads towards a circuitous point. If the bargaining structure is fragmented and complicated it might be inappropriate to order disclosure yet unless there is further disclosure the position is unlikely to improve. Indeed one of the points the trade union made to us strongly was that to accept their approach would be to improve the industrial relations pattern – in the long run at any rate. Obviously we must be prepared to break this circle. Within what limits we will consider shortly.

34. Before doing so it is necessary to pay careful attention to the second question. The employers laid great stress upon this fear, and we have real sympathy with their concern. It was supported by letters indicating that other trade unions did not support the claim. They even indicated a positive hostile reaction. The Institute is not a TUC-affiliated trade union and this might sharpen the hostility. As far as this was the only ground for refusal we would regard it as improper and unwise. The rights under the Act are given to independent trade unions and we can see no reason to modify our approach which should be the same whether it was the NUJ or the Institute of Journalists seeking help. We do not expect a serious adverse reaction provided that our decision is soundly based in principle.

35. Our principle is this:– although in general terms we feel that all information that satisfied the first test laid down in s.17(1)(a) should be disclosed we accept that the state of bargaining in the *Daily Telegraph* precludes a blanket decision at this stage of development. We believe that in this case there should be an additional test of close relevance. Within that test we would without doubt include all information about salary rates of journalists. This would not extend to individual salaries but would indicate the various ranges paid. It was somewhat remarkable that although we gathered that much of this information is not readily available it was not specifically asked for.

36. As far as the information specifically requested – and set out in Appendix A – our view is that the detailed information sought of earnings in the specified departments is not at this stage appropriate for the statutory process of disclosure. Nonetheless we feel that information of the basic outline of pay settlements and their nature should be disclosed in appropriate instances which we shall attempt to define.

37. We were somewhat disturbed by the tone of the case put to us. As we see it the purpose of disclosure is to enable collective bargaining to be conducted more effectively and more scientifically. Many would argue that the greater the area of accepted fact the less likely are there to be aggravating mis-apprehensions. Yet the tone of the oral submission put to us at the hearing had an angry edge to it. For example, there were allegations that there had been increases obtained in some departments by logging of hours worked – and therefore money due – by certain unions and not by the management. Again we were told 'If we fail to get that information across the table, and learn by underhand methods that other groups have done better than us, we'll be urged to adopt methods that will secure a favourable settlement *by force*'. This statement is about the settlement rather than the information.

38. The principle to be applied, as we have already said, is that the basic outline of all pay groups should ideally be made available. In the light of the current position in the *Daily Telegraph* a start should be made on those areas where the work, or the general level of remuneration, bear a reasonably close relationship. As we have already pointed out the information about those groups we would regard as closest was not, for some reason, requested. In applying our principle to the groups listed we meet difficulty in that we lack the necessary detailed information. We could ask for it but at this stage – despite all the obvious industrial relations difficulties apparent in the relationships of which we heard – we intend only to set out our principle, carefully formulated. We hope that this will enable the parties to reach a satisfactory accord prior to their impending bargaining. If they fail to do so we would, of course, proceed to make a declaration under s.19(6).

39. The newspaper industry is notoriously complicated and difficult to comprehend. In

the context of the position as we understand it we consider that the bargaining groups whose remuneration structures are relevant are:—

(a) Journalists, management and other groups of similar level.

(b) Groups of high skill in the production department – it would be impossible for us to particularize without a lengthy inquiry which we wish to avoid. We believe that the parties themselves can, given good will on both sides, determine the appropriate groups. As guidance we would say that we would expect the groups chosen to be of more than average skill and the pay range would be at least roughly commensurate with that of journalists, but might be somewhat higher.

40. Once the groups are determined we would consider the following information about each group to be the subject of disclosure:

(i) Number employed in that group
(ii) Structure by which pay is determined, e.g. basic pay – hours worked, productivity schemes, bonus schemes, etc.
(iii) Total wages bill for that group for the year ending at the last annual review date
(iv) Outline of principal changes at last review, that is to say
    (a) increase in basic rates expressed as a percentage
    (b) changes to pay structure.

JOHN C. WOOD, *Chairman*
PATRICIA TURNER
JAMES WALWYN

It is typical of the Central Arbitration Committee's method of approach that it should seek first to resolve the issue by agreement between the parties. In this case agreement was not forthcoming and the Committee had to proceed to a declaration (see Award 78/353A) under EPA 1975, s.19(6), as to the information which the employer should disclose. Significantly, in the absence of agreement, the Committee was willing to be less bold in its view about what should be disclosed. It commented: 'Against a difficult industrial relations background, a liberal and optimistic approach cannot be justified. We will, therefore, be found to have revised the detailed approach to the specified information. We have done so in a genuine attempt to fulfil our view of the steps required by law but in a manner that will cause no sound excuse for a hostile reaction by others' (para. 20).

This sensitive approach to industrial relations considerations on the part of the CAC can be contrasted with the rather legalistic approach of the High Court to the other statutory precondition for disclosure, that of 'material impediment', in the following case. Although the case had been argued mainly on the defence of confidentiality (see below), the court went out of its way to consider the issue of material impediment.

Civil Service Union v. *Central Arbitration Committee*
[1980] IRLR 274

The Ministry of Defence proposed to change from using its own employees to clean certain of its establishments in Bath to using outside contractors for the purpose. The union representing the directly employed cleaners sought from the Ministry information about the tenders it had received from outside contractors, including information in respect of each tenderer about the number of cleaners who would be employed and the number of hours each cleaner would work. The Committee refused a declaration that the information be disclosed because they regarded it as confidential. The union applied to the High Court to have the award quashed and the matter remitted for re-hearing.

FORBES J.: . . . So those are the only two matters left outstanding; the number of cleaners and the hours worked; and the case made by the department was that they were not required to disclose that information because it was given in confidence; governed therefore by s.18(1)(c); and they produced a blank form of tender document which is headed 'Contracts in Confidence', a specimen of which is supplied and is before me. A great deal of this form was filled in by the department, but two paragraphs were left to be filled in by the tenderers. The numbers of cleaners and the hours of work worked would be entered in paragraph 8, and in paragraph 9 the actual tender prices. Now it is conceded by the union that the information in paragraph 9 was confidential and therefore, under s.18, protected from disclosure. The union wanted, they said, the numbers of cleaners and the hours of work worked in order to be able to calculate the cost of contract cleaning. In other words, while acknowledging that the actual prices were confidential, they wanted sufficient information to allow them to calculate those prices. Put in that way, and that is the only way in which, to be practical, it was put, the argument seems to me to go a long way towards establishing that the information required by the union was equally confidential with the contract prices.

But Mr Weitzman [counsel for the union] says that there is here an error on the face of the award. . . .

Now the error of which Mr Weitzman speaks arises, he says, in paragraph 22. He says that what was required of the Committee was an interpretation of s.18(1)(c). There are, he suggests, three factors in relation to that. Three matters: (a) confidence has to be reposed in the employer by someone other than the employer; (b) the information must be of a kind which is capable of attracting confidence; and (c) the confidence did in fact exist and operate on the mind of that person other than the employer. On the true construction of paragraph 22 he suggests, the Committee decided that the mere fact that the tender form was headed 'in confidence' was conclusive of the question whether confidence did in fact exist and operate on the mind of the contractor. In other words, they misdirected themselves by holding that the label 'in confidence' was conclusive of the nature of the transaction. This, says Mr Weitzman, is similar to a decision that the label 'licence' at the head of a document was conclusive of the question whether it was a licence or a lease.

Mr Brown concedes that if this is in fact the true construction of this paragraph then there is an error of law disclosed on the face of the award. It appears therefore that the sole issue on this aspect is what is the true construction of paragraph 22. . . .

Although the Central Arbitration Committee did not spell out as I have attempted to do, the relevant circumstances (a) to (e), these circumstances are only a combination of the information on the tender form and the matters set out in paragraphs 19, 20 and 21. Faced with the task of drawing inferences, what was the Committee to do except to conclude that it was a reasonable inference that tenderers who submitted information to the Ministry on a form headed 'in confidence' were relying on the preservation of the confidentiality of that information. They correctly point out that the confidentiality serves to protect the interests not of the Ministry, but of the contractor, and it might be added the last sentence of the preceding paragraph, paragraph 21, shows that the tenderers were asserting their reliance on the confidential nature of the information and that the Committee appreciated the significance of this. I apprehend that all the Committee intended to say in paragraph 22 was that, having regard to the facts they set out in paragraphs 19, 20 and 21, the inescapable conclusion is that tenderers who submit information to the Ministry on a tender form headed 'in confidence' do so because they are relying on that label to preserve the confidentiality of the information that they give. I cannot see that this is a misdirection of law and the application should fail on that ground. . . .

There is another aspect of this case. The Committee found (see paragraph 18 to which I have referred) that this information fell within s.17 of the Act. Mr Weitzman argues that I am precluded from considering this question as there is only before me his notice of motion referable solely to s.18. But if the Committee's decision about s.17 is wrong, this must be open to challenge by the Ministry of Defence, either in this Court, or on remission to the Committee by this Court. If I had found that the Central Advisory Committee had committed an error about s.18 and remitted the case to them, it seems to me that the Ministry of Defence could then have argued before a differently constituted Committee that the view about s.17, recorded in paragraph 18 of this decision, was wrong. It would be much more convenient that, in remitting the matter, the Court should give its views on the law affecting both s.17 and s.18 decisions together, and further, if the court considered that no reasonable Committee, properly directing itself, could come to the conclusion that the union's request fell within s.17, the Court could, in its discretion, refuse to quash the decision under s.18 because the result would still be that the information was not disclosable. It is not unimportant to remember that, before the Committee, the only case made by the union was that they required this information to enable them to calculate the cost of contract cleaning arrangements. Their contention was set out in paragraph 8 of the decision. I do not need to read it. Now on 11.2.80 the secretary of the Staff Side of the Whitley Council had been informed in these terms:

> We have now received the tenders for cleaning those offices at Bath at present cleaned by DEL (directly employed labour). In general we have rejected the cheapest firms because their work schemes call for production rates by their employees which we are not certain could be maintained over a long period. However, other firms offer acceptable work programmes which are less expensive than the current DEL service; around 18% on average. After including the 15% VAT rate, the selected contractors offer cost savings varying from 1½% to 10%, with an overall saving of some 5%.

The only purpose of any collective bargaining by the union on this aspect was to show that contract labour would not be cheaper than direct labour and thus avert redundancy notices for 68 of their members. This involves of course, a comparison of the costs of the two rival methods. If you wish to show that the employer is mistaken in suggesting that contract labour is cheaper than direct labour then you will seek to prove that the suggested figure for direct labour is too high or that its figure for contract labour is too low. Where both figures are estimates there is obviously room for considerable argument about the assumptions made in respect of the calculations. Where however the figure for the cost of contract labour is not an estimate but an actual tender or contract price there is no room for agument about it, unless you are going to maintain that the employer either cannot read the contract figure or is deliberately misleading you. The cost to the employer will be the contractor's price. However much you may calculate that the contractor's price ought to be 'x', if it happens to be 'y' the cost to the employer is 'y' and not 'x'. So long as the union's case rests solely, as it did in this case, on the necessity of having this information so that they may show that the price ought to be 'x', I cannot see how the process of collective bargaining can be impeded by the refusal to give them information to enable this calculation to be made. It is clearly an irrelevant, and therefore unnecessary, calculation and the information on which it is based is equally unnecessary for the process of collective bargaining. Now the only case made to the Committee was that they required the information to enable them to calculate the contractors' prices. On the basis of that argument I cannot see how any tribunal, properly directing itself, could come to the conclusion that the information was necessary to facilitate collective bargaining, or to put it more accurately, that the lack of such information would, to a material extent, impede the union in carrying out collective bargaining.

During the course of the argument in this case various other reasons were suggested why this information was required; in particular that it was required to enable the union to show that the contractors would be unable to do the job properly on the prices calculated on the basis of the information requested. Another possibility which occurs to me is that it might be possible to show that some of the lower tenders were suspect and that the only acceptable ones were higher than the cost of direct labour. If those had been the arguments before the Committee I can well imagine that that body might have accepted that, for that purpose, this was necessary information. But none of these matters was in fact put before the Committee. If therefore I had come to the conclusion that the Committee had erred in relation to s.18 I would either refuse to quash that decision on the discretionary ground that no tribunal could have found that the question fell within s.17 or, if I remitted the case on s.18, I would have remitted it on s.17 also, with the above indication of the findings of the court on that topic. I should add also that in view of the fact that the avowed object of obtaining the information was to enable the union to calculate the figure which they acknowledged to be confidential, it seems to me inescapable that the same confidentiality applies to the ingredients as applies to the finished cake. For this reason too, I would, in the exercise of the court's discretion, have refused the relief claimed. As however I find that there was no demonstrable error on the face of the award, it is only necessary for me to dismiss the application.

Thus, the employer's obligation to disclose relates only to information which is relevant to matters in respect of which the union is recognized for the purposes of collective bargaining (s.17(2)); it must be information without which the union would be under a material impediment in carrying on that bargaining (s.17(1)(a)); and it must be in accordance with good industrial relations for the employer to disclose the information (s.17(1)(b)). At the request of the trade-union representatives the disclosure must be in writing or confirmed in writing (s.17(5)), but the employer's duty does not extend to require him to produce or allow inspection of any document (except the one in which the information is conveyed) or to copy or make extracts from documents (s.18(2)(*a*)). Nor is he obliged to compile information where that would involve a level of work or expenditure 'out of reasonable proportion to the value of the information in the conduct of collective bargaining' (s.18(2)(*b*)). In addition EPA 1975, s.18(1) lists six types of information to which the duty to disclose does not apply. These include information disclosure of which would be against the interests of national security, confidential information, information that would cause substantial injury to an employer's undertaking if disclosed, information relating specifically to individuals (unless they consent), information obtained for the purpose of bringing or defending legal proceedings, and information disclosure of which would involve contravention of an enactment.

In the light of the generally qualified nature of the right to information contained in EPA 1975, it is not perhaps surprising that unions' use of the right seems not to have been extensive, judging by the number and nature of the Awards made by the CAC. In 1977 the Committee made 4 awards under the provisions; in 1978, 18; in 1979, 12; in 1980, 15; in 1981, 2. Others were withdrawn or settled before award, but even taking these into account the level of usage of the provisions is low. As to the nature of the requests for information, Howard Gospel and Paul Willman have concluded on the basis of an analysis of the awards up to the middle of 1980 (see (1981) 10 *ILJ* 10) that the main type of information sought was the rather unadventurous one of 'information concerning terms and conditions of the represented groups . . . with emphasis on job evaluation schemes, grading, pay scales, and wage systems. . . . The union success rate was relatively high in these areas. Information on profits, performance, non-labour costs and also information on closure and redundancy was much less frequently requested. The success rate in these areas to date has been negligible.'

The procedure that statute lays down for the CAC in handling disclosure claims is a fairly complex one. At no stage is an appeal to any other body from a CAC Award formally provided for, but, as we have seen, the normal processes of judicial review are available.

It is an interesting question what sort of award the Committee will feel it appropriate to make at the final stage of compulsory arbitration on a claim for improved terms and conditions of employment. Few cases have reached the end of the disclosure procedure, but the Committee had some experience with the equivalent unilateral arbitration provisions of the recognition procedure before it was abolished in 1980. This experience has been analysed by Brian Doyle (see (1980) 9 *ILJ* 154). He found that the Committee had been unwilling to award as a term of the contract of employment that the employer recognize the union (though it did sometimes award as a term that the employees should have the right to be represented by a union over individual grievances); that in making awards on claims for more standard improvements in terms and conditions (e.g. wages and hours) the Committee had refused to make generous awards in order to punish the employer for his failure to recognize; but that the Committee would try in its awards to compensate the union for the employer's failure to recognize it. The same basic approaches may be adopted in the disclosure area, though it should be noted that in *Holokrome Limited and ASTMS* (Award No. 79/451) the Committee did in fact award a term requiring the employer to disclose certain information as part of the contract of employment, a bolder approach than that adopted in the recognition area.

Finally, it is worth noting that the nationalized industries are often placed in their constitutive statutes under a particular duty to disclose information as well as under the general duty laid down by EPA 1975. We set out below a typical provision taken from s.7(5) of the Iron and Steel Act 1982. As with the recognition provisions for nationalized industries (above, p. 198) the draftsman of this section seems to have taken the view that many of the potential legal problems which are dealt with explicitly in EPA 1975 could be solved by the simple expedient of placing in the hands of the Corporation, after consultation with the unions, the decision as to what information it is necessary to disclose for the purposes of effective bargaining.

Iron and Steel Act 1982 s.7(5)

(5) Where it falls to the Corporation or a publicly-owned company to participate in the operation of machinery established under this section, and the operation involves discussion of a subject by other persons participating therein, the Corporation or the publicly-owned company, as the case may be, shall make available to those persons, at a reasonable time before the discussion is to take place, such information in their possession relating to the subject as, after consultation with those persons, appears to the Corporation or the publicly-owned company, as the case may be, to be necessary to enable those persons to participate effectively in the discussion.

(e) **Time off for trade-union duties and activities**
Statutory entitlements to time off, either with or without pay, are now an entrenched feature of our labour law (see below, p. 347). By EPCA 1978, s.29, employees have a right to time off without pay for the discharge of certain public duties, for example as a magistrate or member of a local authority. By EPCA 1978, s.31, an employee given notice of dismissal on grounds of redundancy is entitled to reasonable time off with pay (up to two days' pay) for the purposes of seeking new employment or making arrangements for training for future employment. Third, by EPCA 1978, s.31A (added by EA 1980), a pregnant employee is entitled to reasonable time off with pay for the purpose of receiving antenatal care (see below, p. 356). However, our present concern is with three further entitlements to time off which are linked, broadly, to collective bargaining between employer and recognized trade union. These three rights were enacted in the middle seventies and their enactment coincided with a general growth in the practice of employers to permit employees time off for collective bargaining or activities related thereto, a practice which was itself related to the growing formalization of plant- and

company-level bargaining arrangements in the wake of the Donovan Commission's Report (see above, p. 122).

The most spectacular example of the practice was the growth of 'full-time' stewards, i.e. of shop stewards employed by the employer nominally to perform some function in the employer's business but who in fact spend all their time in representational and bargaining activities. A survey found that in 1978 in 12 per cent of establishments with manual stewards at least one was full-time (2 per cent of establishments with non-manual stewards), giving rise to an estimate that there were 3,500 full-time manual stewards and some 300 full-time non-manual stewards in British manufacturing industry (see W. Brown (ed.), *The Changing Contours of British Industrial Relations* (1981), pp. 63–7). With the onset of recession the number may have dropped slightly since, but the most significant finding of the survey was the rapid growth in the number of full-time stewards that had taken place over the previous decade. It was estimated that during that time the number had quadrupled. The legislation stops far short of giving trade-union officials an entitlement to time off on a full-time basis. Rather, the legislation operates to provide a lesser entitlement, but one that is made available across the board, irrespective of the industry in question or the size of the establishment, factors which, the survey found, had a great impact upon the incidence of full-time stewards. The generalization of practice at a level below that to be found in the most advanced sectors is a typical function of labour legislation. See O. Kahn-Freund, 'Collective Bargaining and Legislation – Complementary and Alternative Sources of Rights and Obligations', *Festschrift für Max Rheinstein* (1969), pp. 1023–42.

The three rights to time off that are our present concern are as follows. First, under s.27 of the EPCA 1978 officials of independent trade unions recognized by an employer have a right to time off from work with pay, to a reasonable extent and subject to reasonable conditions, for the purpose of carrying out their duties which are concerned with industrial relations between the employer (or an associated employer) and the employees, or for the purpose of undergoing training relevant to the duties which has been approved by the TUC or the trade union. 'Official' is defined in s.30(1) of TULRA 1974 so as to include shop stewards. Second, there is an analogous right to time off with pay for safety representatives under the Safety Representatives and Safety Committee Regulations (see below, p. 227). Third, under s.28 members of recognized independent trade unions have a right to time off (without pay) subject to the same test of reasonableness for the purpose of taking part in the activities of the trade union and activities in relation to which the employee is acting as a representative of the union, though employer and union are of course free to agree that this time off shall also be paid. The ACAS Code of Practice 3 (Time off for trade union duties and activities) gives as examples of officials' duties:

(a) collective bargaining with the appropriate level of management;
(b) informing constituents about negotiations or consultations with management;

(c) meetings with other lay officials or with full-time union officers on matters which are concerned with industrial relations between his or her employer and any associated employer and their employees;
(d) interviews with and on behalf of constituents on grievance and discipline matters concerning them and their employer;
(e) appearing on behalf of constituents before an outside official body, such as an industrial tribunal, which is dealing with an industrial relations matter concerning the employer; and
(f) explanations to new employees whom he or she will represent of the role of the union in the work place industrial relations structure. [para. 13.]

With regard to s.28, the Code suggests that employees should have time off

for union activities such as taking part as a representative, in meetings of official policy-making bodies of the union such as the executive committee or annual conference, or representing the union on external bodies such as the committees of industrial training boards.

Members should be permitted to take reasonable time off during working hours for such purposes as voting at the workplace in union elections. Also there may be occasions when it is reasonable for unions to hold meetings of members during working hours because of the urgency of the matter to be discussed or where to do so would not adversely affect production or services. Employers may also have an interest in ensuring that meetings are representative. [paras. 21-2.]

ACAS is required to draw up the Code of Practice by s.6(2)(*b*) of the EPA 1975 and is required in particular to give advice on the thorny question of whether industrial action can count as an official's duty or as a trade union activity. On this the Code suggests:

A distinction should be made between situations where an official is engaged in industrial action along with his or her constituents and those where the official is not – for example, where only some of the constituents are taking unofficial action. Where an official is not taking part in industrial action but represents members involved, normal arrangements for time off with pay for the official should apply.

There is no obligation on employers to permit time off for union activities which themselves consist of industrial action, but where a group of members not taking part in such action is directly affected by other people's industrial action these members and their officials may need to seek the agreement of management to time off for an emergency meeting. [paras. 32 and 33.]

Disputes as to whether reasonable time off for trade-union duties or activities has been refused and whether it has been properly paid for, are determined by industrial tribunals with such assistance from the Code of Practice as they may derive. This task may take the tribunals into the heartland of collective relations, for settlement of disputes about time off cannot be divorced from a consideration of what are appropriate functions for union officials, especially shop stewards. As the CIR put it in its Report No. 17 (Facilities Afforded to Shop Stewards, Cmnd. 4668, 1971): '*If* functions and their extent have been agreed they can provide a basis upon which the principle of leave from the job and payment can be applied . . .' (para. 217 – our emphasis). Neither the Act nor the Code, however, gives the tribunals much guidance on this sensitive issue of what the tasks of shop stewards ought to be.

If the tribunal upholds the applicant's complaint it must make a declaration to that effect, and may award compensation to the employee 'of such amount as the tribunal considers just and equitable in all the circumstances having regard to the employer's default in failing to permit time off to be taken by the employee and any loss sustained by the employee which is attributable to the matters complained of' (s.30(2)) (cf. *Brassington* v. *Cauldon Wholesale*, above, p. 182, and the discussion thereof).

Time off with pay is the basic facility that a shop steward needs to perform his functions, but it is not the only one. The Code of Practice 3, here apparently going beyond the statute, suggests that employers make available generally the facilities stewards need, giving as examples accommodation for meetings, access to a telephone, notice boards and perhaps office facilities (para. 24).

Where the claim is for time off for safety representatives, disputes are also settled by industrial tribunals (see the Safety Regulations, Reg. 11 and *White* v. *Pressed Steel Fisher* [1980] IRLR 176, 178), and the tribunals have the same powers under the Regulations to make a declaration and award of compensation (Reg. 11(3)). In the case of claims for time off for training, the tribunal is required by Reg. 4(2)(*b*) to have regard to the Code of Practice on Time off for Training of Safety Representatives issued by the Health and Safety Commission. In general in relation to claims for time off for safety representatives the tribunal may, but apparently need not, have regard to the Code of Practice on Safety Representatives and Safety Committees and the Guidance Notes, both issued by the Health and Safety Commission (see further below, p. 233), which deal with the functions of safety representatives.

The main issue that has arisen in litigation has concerned claims for paid time off for trade-union duties or for training for them, and has been the question of how close a link must exist between the alleged duties and collective bargaining with the employer. The ACAS Code of Practice (above) clearly contemplates that collective bargaining is but one example of a trade-union duty and the courts have accepted that trade-union duties are not confined to collective bargaining. In the following case the issue was how far a trade union meeting preparatory to collective bargaining attracted paid time off.

Beal v. *Beecham Group Ltd* [1982] ICR 460 (CA)

The respondent company was divided into two sub-groups ('Pharmaceuticals' and 'Products') for the purposes of production and collective bargaining, with few matters being decided at the level of the entire company. Within each sub-group the employees were divided by occupation into various 'Common Interest Groups' or 'CIGs' for the purposes of collective bargaining. The division of employees by occupation alone meant that some CIGs contained employees from more than one of the company's many locations in the UK. The union, ASTMS, had formed a committee of its own, a National Advisory

Committee (NAC), for the purpose of bringing together officials of the union employed throughout the company. The NAC had no bargaining function with the employer. In December 1978 the union proposed to hold a meeting of the NAC to discuss, *inter alia*, the 1979 salary negotiations. The company was prepared to grant unpaid, but not paid, time off for its employees to attend the meeting of the NAC.

o'connor l.j.: ... In the present case there is no dispute that the union had members working in separate establishments of the employer who was a large industrial organization. It follows that the NAC was a properly constituted body under rule 19 (23) [of the union]. Its purpose was to provide a forum for an adequate exchange of information between the separate establishments and to determine policies affecting the members nationally; that is, in the separate establishments nationwide. I am clear that attendance at a meeting of the NAC called solely for the purpose of exchanging information would not qualify for time off with pay under section 27 (1) but would qualify for time off without pay under section 28 of the Act of 1978 as a trade union activity. The question is whether attendance at a meeting called to determine policies nationally qualifies under section 27(1).

The agenda for the meeting of December 14, 1978, as set out in Mr Sheppard's letters, together with the minutes of the meeting, show that it was called for both purposes. Any questions of 'prime purpose' or 'real purpose' or 'predominant purpose' are irrelevant to a decision as to whether the second purpose qualifies under section 27(1). Those questions may be relevant in deciding what is reasonable under section 27(2). . . .

It will be seen that it was the CIG that was the negotiating body and it is accepted that when negotiating the representatives were carrying out a duty 'concerned with industrial relations.' Further, the employer also accepts that a meeting of representatives to prepare themselves for the negotiations and formulate a claim is part of that duty and it has allowed time off with pay for such meetings.

It follows that there can be no doubt that the representatives had duties 'concerned with industrial relations,' and the only question is whether attendance at the NAC meeting was 'for the purpose of enabling them to carry out those duties.'

Mr Field, on behalf of the employer, submitted (i) that the duties within section 27(1) of the Act of 1978 must involve the actual transaction of industrial relations business or have a sufficiently close and proximate relationship to actual negotiations for them to be properly considered part of the collective bargaining process; (ii) that at the heart of section 27(1)(a) is collective bargaining – that is, one party making a claim on another; the employer has an interest in orderly and efficient organisation of collective bargaining, and that is the function for which an employer must pay. . . .

Mr Field submitted further that the duties carried out must be consistent with the recognition afforded to the union. He recognised that for these submissions to succeed would involve over-ruling the decision of the appeal tribunal in *Sood* v. *GEC Elliott Process Automation Ltd* [1980] ICR 1. That was a case which bore some similarity to this case. The same union had members employed in GEC Ltd and its subsidiary companies, of which Automation was one. The union had set up an NAC, but in addition they had set up a products advisory committee, whose function was to enable representatives from various subsidiaries and sites producing similar products to meet, exchange information and experience, and supply information to the NAC. The question was whether an official attending a meeting of the products advisory committee came within section $27(1)(a)$. The case was decided under the Employment Protection Act 1975, but the wording of the relevant sections, section 57 in particular, is the same. The industrial tribunal decided by a majority that attendance at the products advisory committee was not within the section. On appeal by the employee, counsel for the employer made the same submissions as those Mr Field has made to us. The appeal tribunal rejected the submissions. Slynn J., giving the judgment of the tribunal, said, at pp. 7–8:

> We share the view of the whole of the industrial tribunal that the provision permitting time off for the purpose of enabling a trade union official to carry out his duties does not of itself mean that he is to be allowed paid time off in order to prepare himself or to make himself a better trade union representative. That in our view is covered by section $57(1)(b)$. We also agree with the industrial tribunal that the phrase 'industrial relations' is not to be narrowly construed. It is capable of covering many matters which arise in connection with the relationship of employer and employee. We do not accept Mr Pardoe's argument that the test of an official's duties is to be limited by the recognition. It seems to us that recognition identifies the trade union whose officials are entitled to claim time off under the section. It does not limit those duties to collective bargaining or to the precise terms of the recognition. We think that it is not the intention of Parliament that a trade union official should only have time off for the purpose of meetings with representatives of management. It seems to us that when questions involving industrial relations arise, a union official may well be entitled, as part of his duties, to take part in the planning of strategy and in discussing with other workers who are at the time negotiating with their employers, so long as the latter employers are associated with a particular trade union official's own employers. Nor do we accept the argument that a trade union official is only entitled to take time off for the purpose of negotiating where the employers have laid down the particular industrial relations structure as Mr Pardoe suggests. It seems to us that the carrying out of the trade union official's duties for the purpose of the section can go wider than that. We do not accept the view of the second member of the industrial tribunal that the fact that these committees are set up purely by the trade unions, and for trade union functions, necessarily means that the duty of an official in connection with them prevents them from being duties concerned with industrial relations.
>
> The intention of section 57 of the Employment Protection Act 1975 is that trade union officials should have time off to enable them to perform certain duties. We do not think that Parliament intended we should approach the section on the basis that the words should be narrowly construed. On the other hand it is clear from the words themselves that the duties must concern industrial relations between the official's employer and its employees, and an associated employer and the associated employer's employees, in a case where both employers and both sets of employees are concerned with the particular industrial relations problem. So, if two associated companies are negotiating with the trade union, or are involved in an industrial relations problem which will or may need to be negotiated, then it seems to us that the official's duties in connection with such negotiations may fall within the section.
>
> There must however be some limit to the activities which fall within the section. In our view, the test is whether the time off is required to enable the official to carry out his duties in relation to a matter which arises in relations between employees and management. We do not consider that the mere exchange of information between the

trade union officials themselves necessarily qualifies, even if those officials represent workers in a particular group of companies.

The appeal tribunal held that the purpose of the products advisory committee meeting was to exchange information and experience, and so dismissed the appeal. Like the appeal tribunal I do not think it correct to limit 'industrial relations' in section 27 of the Act of 1978 to mean collective bargaining as defined in section 32. If that had been the intention of Parliament, section 27 would have read 'concerned with collective bargaining.' I agree with Slynn J. that 'industrial relations' in the section are not limited by the terms of the recognition agreement and I am content to adopt the passages from *Sood* v. *GEC Elliott Process Automation Ltd* [1980] ICR 1, which I have quoted as correct. The recognition agreement may well be of very great importance when considering what is reasonable under section 27(2): see *Depledge* v. *Pye Telecommunications Ltd* [1981] ICR 82, to which I shall refer later. . . .

Finally, Mr Field submitted that as the NAC had no negotiating function with the employer – indeed no function at all with the employer – attending its meeting could not be for the purpose of enabling the official to carry out his duties concerned with industrial relations. Once it is recognized that preparatory work falls within the discharge of duties concerned with industrial relations, then one looks to see if the preparatory work had some direct relevance to an industrial relations matter, and if so, it qualifies under section 27 (1) (*a*). As I have said, attending the NAC to exchange information would not have that direct relevance but to determine policies nationally may well be directly relevant, depending upon what the policies are. The agenda and minutes of the meeting show that some at least of the policies were concerned with industrial relations matters that were to go into the 1979 wage claim.

It follows that in my judgment when the employees attended the NAC meeting it was for the purpose of enabling them to carry out their duties concerned with industrial relations.

It must be remembered that time off under section 27(1) of the Act of 1978 is subject to, and in accordance with, subsection (2). This is the safeguard for employers against any attempt by a union to dress up what is an activity to make it look like a duty concerned with industrial relations. So too it is under subsection (2) that the question has to be decided whether it was reasonable for the employees to seek time off with pay for the NAC meeting in addition to their accepted CIG meeting.

Having reached the conclusion that I have reached on the true function of the NAC there is no difficulty in this case. . . .

The decision in *Beal* was followed by the Court of Appeal when it next considered the issue in *Thomas Scott & Sons (Bakers) Ltd* v. *Allen* [1983] IRLR 329. Here the union called a meeting of officials, including shop stewards, to discuss problems that had arisen over the operation of the final stage of the disputes procedure in the baking industry and, in particular, to consider the question of renegotiating its terms with the employers' association, the Federation of Bakers. The employing company was a member of the employers' association and part of a group of companies in the baking industry, called Allied Bakeries Group. Eleven shop stewards employed by the company sought paid time off in order to attend the union's meeting, but, on the instructions of the group's holding company, the employer permitted the employees to take only unpaid time off. On the question of whether attendance at the meeting by the stewards was a trade-union duty within EPCA 1978, s.27(1)(a), the employers sought to distinguish *Beal* on the grounds that any subsequent renegotiation of the disputes procedure would be a matter for the national officials of the union in discussions with the employers' federation and not a matter for the shop stewards in negotiations with their own employer. The Court of Appeal held, however, that the shop stewards' duties included the duty to give the national officials of the union the benefit of their experience and in consequence to suggest how the disputes procedure might be reformulated.

Young v. *Carr Fasteners Co. Ltd* [1979] ICR 844 shows the application of similar reasoning to a claim for paid time off for training, in this case to attend a course on pensions. The employer operated a pension scheme, but did not negotiate over pensions and the three trustees of the pension scheme were currently directors of the company. Nevertheless, the appeal tribunal held that the employee was entitled to paid time off. The employees might need advice as to their participation in the pension scheme. They might wish to make representations to the employers as to changes in the structure or administration of the scheme. These were matters which trade-union officials might expect to consider and discuss on behalf of their members, and so they fell within the scope of trade-union duties.

However, what the Court of Appeal in the *Allen* case gave with one hand with its broad interpretation of the scope of s.27(1)(a), it took away with the other in its approach to reasonableness under s.27(2). Or, to take the analogy with unfair dismissal (see below, p. 486), having taken a broad view of the threshold question of what a trade-union duty can consist of, the Court of Appeal was content to leave the issue of reasonableness as essentially one for the industrial tribunal and to discourage the Appeal Tribunal from interfering with the tribunal's exercise of its discretion, the Court of Appeal significantly here citing the unfair dismissal case of *Retarded Children's Aid Society Ltd* v. *Day* [1978] ICR 437 as a model to be followed. In particular, the Court of Appeal was not prepared to interfere with the tribunal's decision that the employer's refusal to pay for the time off was reasonable, even though the employer had been prepared to grant the employees unpaid time off on the view that the attendance at the meeting was a trade-union activity rather than a duty. This seems effectively to have overruled the decision of the EAT in *Beecham Group Ltd* v. *Beal (No. 2)* [1983] IRLR 317, decided a week previously, where, on similar facts, the Appeal Tribunal had taken the perhaps more logical view that, 'once it had been decided that attendance at the meeting was a duty and that it was reasonable in the circumstances to allow the [employees] to attend, their right to payment followed automatically. . . .'

A notable feature of the entitlement to time off with pay for training in relation to trade union activities is that the training must be approved by the TUC or the independent union to which the official belongs (EPCA 1978, s.27(1)(*b*)(ii)). The Safety Regulations do not impose this requirement in relation to the training of safety representatives, though the Health and Safety Commission's Code on Time Off for Training is written on the assumption that such approval is required. Thus, under EPCA 1978 an employee has no entitlement as against his employer for time off with pay in respect of non-approved courses, though, of course, the employer may allow it if he wishes. The really important issue, given the mutual suspicion of the value of each other's training that employers and unions sometimes manifest, is how far the provision by an employer of non-approved training reduces the employer's obligation to provide paid time off for approved training. The issue arose in relation to the training of safety representatives. Should the answer be different under EPCA 1978, s.27?

White v. *Pressed Steel Fisher* [1980] IRLR 176 (EAT)

The appellant was a TGWU safety representative at the respondents' Swindon plant. The union wished the appellant to attend a training course at a local technical college, but the respondents provided their own training course for safety representatives. The respondents' course was approved by neither the TUC nor the TGWU and these bodies also refused to participate in it. Consequently, the respondents' course lacked 'the trade-union aspect'. The respondents refused the appellant time off to attend the technical college course because they considered their own course satisfactory.

SLYNN J.: . . . Mr Tabachnik, who has appeared on behalf of Mr White, has attacked this decision. He says primarily that the Industrial Tribunal has not given any – or, if it has given some, has not given adequate – weight to the provisions of the Code of Practice relating to time off for safety representatives. In particular, they have wholly left out of account the requirement imposed by the Code of Practice that any course which is to be attended should be approved either by the TUC or by the union. Moreover, he says that they have paid too much weight to the indication in the Code that problems should be sorted out by agreement between the union and management. The basis of Mr Tabachnik's contention is that the intention is that it is the unions which should have responsibility for, and control over, the training of their own safety representatives. They have an absolute discretion, he submits, as to whether they will approve the course or not; there is no obligation on them in the statute to co-operate in any courses which are run or arranged by the employers. He says that any course, if it is to be in compliance with the requirements of the Code, must be one which is approved by the TUC or by the appropriate independent union(s). Further, the union can insist that a man should go to such a course for the purposes of training. The Industrial Tribunal cannot validly take into account, in considering the reasonableness of the training which is sought to be undertaken, that the particular man has had, or will have, or could have, a perfectly suitable course, unless the TUC or his union says that it is approved by them. This, Mr Tabachnik submits, flows inexorably from the fact that the safety representative is appointed and removable by the trade union as its watchdog; that, however good an employer's course might be, it does not comply with the Code if the union has not approved it. He says that it is not for the Industrial

Tribunal to decide whether the union should approve or not. Here, the criticism which is made of the union, implicitly in the decision of the Tribunal, for not cooperating, he says is thoroughly unjustified; moreover, there was no evidence to show that the TGWU, the man's own union, or any official of that union had refused to discuss the contents of the employer's course with management. The only evidence, he said, was that the TUC education officer in Bristol was not willing to take part because there was no trade union aspect. Mr Tabachnik says that it is quite wrong to draw from that a criticism of both the TUC and the TGWU in broad terms.

On the other hand, Mr Gibson on behalf of the company submits that Mr Tabachnik's approach is itself quite wrong. An Industrial Tribunal, he says, can have regard to the fact that in-plant training on the aspects of the safety representative's functions is available; that what the Tribunal has to decide is whether the time off is justified in all the circumstances. He submits that it is quite wrong to say that an Industrial Tribunal is to limit itself to considering courses approved by the TUC or by a union.

We are of the view that Mr Tabachnik is right in saying that, in the Code, the emphasis is clearly on the fact that such courses are to be provided or approved by the union. In many cases it may well be that this is the only way in which a course covering the necessary aspects of the functions can adequately be provided. But, in our judgment, the starting point is not the Code of Practice; the starting point is the statute, and the Regulations made under it. One must go to Regulation 4(2) to see what is the duty of the employer; it is Regulation 4(2) that the Industrial Tribunal has to consider, if a complaint is made that a man has wrongly been refused time off. That Regulation makes it clear that a safety representative is to be given 'such time off with pay during working hours as shall be necessary for the purpose of undergoing such training in aspects of those functions as may be reasonable in all the circumstances having regard to any relevant provisions of a Code of Practice approved by the Commission'. It is to be remembered, looking at those words, that by s.16 of the 1974 Health and Safety Act the Codes are to be issued by way of guidance. Here, the Tribunal and the employers must have regard to the provisions of any relevant Code. But, in our judgment, the question whether time off is necessary to undergo such training as is reasonable in all the circumstances is to be decided not merely by looking at the Code but by looking at all the circumstances, having regard to the provisions of the Code of Practice. Accordingly it seems to us that Mr Tabachnik's argument that the course cannot be adequate unless the TUC or the union has approved it – or, put another way, that it is always necessary to let a man go to a union approved course whether other training is available or not, or whatever experience a man may have – goes too far. In our judgment the right approach is to look at the needs of the man in the light of the Code to have training to enable him to carry out his functions. The Code is of weight – great weight – but is not decisive of the issue. The approval of the unions which the Code contemplates is a factor to be taken into account, but, unlike the provisions of s.27 of the Employment Protection (Consolidation) Act 1978 dealing with a different aspect of training, there is no statutory provision that the course has to be approved by the Trades Union Congress.

Accordingly we consider, in this case, that the Industrial Tribunal was entitled to have regard to the course available to the man at the plant where he worked. We do not accept the submission that the Industrial Tribunal gave no weight to the Code. They refer to it, they say they took into account, but they find on the facts that it was not necessary for Mr White to go to the course at Swindon. To that extent, it seems to us that their general approach to this matter was justified.

However, when one looks at paragraph 7 of the Reasons for the decision of the Industrial Tribunal, it seems to us that they considered that the course arranged by the company was adequate save that it did not contain a trade union aspect to it. That paragraph seems to us to be saying that on the technical aspect of training concerned with safety at the workplace the course was adequate and that it was not necessary for the man to take time off, because it was not reasonable in all the circumstances for him to go to Swindon to deal with this particular aspect of the matter. This, it seems to us, the Tribunal was entitled to decide. It is not suggested that there was no material on which they could reach that conclusion other than in connection with the prior approval of the TUC for the employer's own course.

But, the Tribunal seem to be saying equally that the trade union aspect was not covered, or not adequately covered, in the course provided by the company. It seems to us that this side of the training – the trade union or representational side – is clearly of importance, as s.2(4) and Regulation 4 of the 1977 Regulations make clear. It seems to us that the Industrial Tribunal rejected the application here because the union will not co-operate. Even if that were right – and Mr Tabachnik says there was no evidence for the broad way in which it was put – this is not, in our view, an answer to the claim. The important thing is that the safety representative should be given the necessary time off for such training as is reasonable in all the circumstances in regard to his functions. In our view, if the union thinks it right, the union is entitled to take the line that it prefers aspects of trade union or representational training to be taught on courses other than those under the aegis of the employers, and not to take part in those courses. Under the legislation they are entitled to take that line, but it is to be hoped – despite Mr Tabachnik's argument that there is no duty of co-operation – that there will in most cases be a proper degree of discussion and co-operation between the union and management, as the Code of Practice itself in its final sentence indicates. The fact that the union does not take part in the training of the representational side may not mean automatically that the course is necessarily defective; what it does mean, in our view, is that the failure of the union to participate, or the man to invoke the agreed procedures to deal with the matter, is not automatically an answer to his claim.

So, at the end of the day, we read the Industrial Tribunal's decision as saying that there was this gap in the course provided by the respondents. It is a gap in respect of a very important part of the functions defined by the section and by Regulation 4. We do not have enough information to know whether the employer's course is adequate in this respect; whether in the circumstances it is necessary to allow time off; whether it would be reasonable for Mr White to undergo training in this aspect of the matter. Accordingly we propose to allow the appeal and remit the case to the Industrial Tribunal for them to consider whether, under Regulation 11(5), it was here necessary for Mr White to have had time off to undergo training in the representational side of his functions as was reasonable in the circumstances, having regard to the relevant provisions of the Code.

If the Tribunal consider that it was necessary, and would have been reasonable, for him to go to Swindon for this aspect of the training, and if the course could have been severed so that this aspect of the training could be dealt with separately, then no doubt they will so declare. If, on the other hand, they come to the view that, in the light of the content of the employer's course, it was not necessary for him to go, and not reasonable in all the circumstances; or if the Swindon course could not have been divided up so as to allow him to go only for this trade union or representational side of his functions, then they will so declare and the application will fail.

(f) Consultation over health and safety matters

So far in this chapter we have adopted the view that the purpose of the legal mechanisms under review has been the encouragement in one way or another of the processes of collective bargaining. In some cases, as with the duty to disclose information, the law is explicitly related to this goal, but more generally trade unions see collective bargaining as the main purpose of union representation, so that legal rules designed to facilitate a union presence in the plant or office will in all probability be helping to facilitate the growth of collective bargaining. There are, however, three situations in which the employer is placed under a duty to consult with the representatives of his workforce: in relation to health and safety issues (HSWA 1974, s.2(6)); over proposed redundancies (EPA 1975, ss.99ff.); and over proposed transfers of a business (Transfer Regulations, Regs. 10 and 11). Indeed, with the repeal of the general statutory recognition procedure (above, p. 202) it is arguable that there is a greater, direct, legal pressure upon the employer to consult with representatives of his workforce than there is to bargain with them. The essence of the distinction between consultation and negotiation (or bargaining) is that in the former case the employer is committed only to receiving representations from those he consults and making reasoned replies to them, whilst in the latter he is committed to dealing with the representatives with the aim of reaching an agreement with them (though such agreement may not in fact be reached). In consultation the right to decide always remains formally with the employer; in negotiation the aim is a joint decision and the employer recovers the right to decide unilaterally only when negotiations have failed. Consequently, negotiation is a greater restriction upon managerial prerogative than consultation and hence has always been the objective of trade-union activity.

How, then, does it happen that legal obligations to consult are now a significant feature of our collective labour law? There seem to be two streams of social development which have contributed to this result, one indigenous and the other stemming from Britain's membership of the EEC. There has always been in the UK during this century a commitment amongst some employers and trade unions to the notion of consultation, even if it has been overshadowed by the development of collective bargaining.[1] In the inter-war period certain progressive employers, such as Cadbury, Rowntree and ICI, developed systems of consultation with their employees, generally through structures in which trade unions were accorded no role, the employee representatives being elected by and from the whole body of workers. Such forms of consultation can act as much to keep trade unions at bay as to involve

---

[1] See Clegg, *The Changing System of British Industrial Relations*, pp. 151–6.

employees in determining matters affecting their working lives. In the Second World War and the immediate post-war period there was a great development of Joint Production Committees, a tangible expression of the commitment of both unions and employers to the war effort, which committees the trade unions backed and were involved in. That joint commitment was dissipated in the 1950s and, with the growth of plant-level structures for bargaining with employers through shop stewards, the machinery for consultation, the lesser form of participation, naturally underwent a demise. In McCarthy's well-known words, the effect of workplace bargaining upon consultative committees was as follows: 'Either they must change their character and become essentially negotiating committees carrying out functions which are indistinguishable from . . . shop-floor bargaining, or they are boycotted by shop stewards and, as the influence of the latter grows, fall into disuse' (*The Role of Shop Stewards in British Industrial Relations* (1967), p. 33). However, in the seventies consultative committees have enjoyed something of a revival, for reasons that are complex but include the fact that they may provide a way of dealing with the pressures (discussed below, p. 252) to extend employee involvement even beyond the range of subject matters dealt with in plant bargaining. Faced with pressures for employee involvement in sensitive areas such as investment or the global policy of multinational companies, both employers and trade unions may see consultation as at least a practical first step.

Thus, enthusiasm for and the subject matters of consultation have varied from time to time, but one subject that has always had a reputation as being particularly suitable for consultation and unsuitable for bargaining is health and safety. Legal obligations to consult on this matter were imposed on the nationalized industries in the period immediately after the Second World War and these provisions continue in force. As the Post Office Act 1969 (quoted above, p. 198) indicates, the nationalized corporations are put under an obligation to take steps to set up negotiating machinery for the settlement of terms and conditions of employment (para. 11(1)(a)), but for health, safety and welfare the aim is simply to establish machinery for its 'promotion and encouragement' (para. 11(1)(c)). (The notion underlying the war-time Joint Production Committees can be seen in its modern form in para. 11(1)(b).) The view that health and safety is a matter particularly appropriate for consultation can be found in the *Report of the Committee on Safety and Health at Work* (Chairman: Lord Robens), Cmnd. 5034, 1972, which preceded the enactment of the HSWA 1974. Although this view commands by no means universal acceptance, it is a widely held one. The Committee said: 'Indeed, there is a greater natural identity of interest between "the two sides" in relation to safety and health problems than in most other matters. There is no legitimate scope for "bargaining" on safety and health issues, but much scope for constructive discussion, joint inspection, and participation in working out solutions' (para. 66). Thus negotiation is seen as the appropriate way to deal with conflicts of interest; consultation, on the other hand, is an exercise in problem-solving where the participants share the same goals. This has always been the most powerful, though by no means the only, argument in favour of consultation machinery, and this view of the purposes of consultation goes a long way to explain the opposition of shop stewards to it.

The Robens Committee thought that the greater involvement of the workforce was a necessary condition for raising standards of occupational safety and health, and also thought a statutory obligation upon the employer to consult his employees would be helpful in producing this involvement. The Committee's proposal was to generalize the rather vague obligation cast upon the nationalized employers, rather than to impose a specific requirement to appoint safety representatives or safety committees. On this latter point the Act differed from the Committee, at least to the extent of giving recognized trade unions the right to appoint safety representatives from amongst the employees, with whom the employer must then consult, and of giving the safety representatives the right to call for the creation of a safety committee. As we have noted above (p. 171), after some struggle the sole method of establishing safety representatives became their appointment by a recognized trade union. Thus, the HSWA 1974 does not merely create a general duty to consult, but it also provides for the creation of the bodies – safety represent-atives and safety committees – with whom the consultation is to take place. This is a novel departure for UK labour law, because the law is creating and shaping plant-level institutions for the handling of a particular industrial relations problem in a much more specific way than would have resulted from implementation of the Robens proposal that the employer be under a general duty to consult on health and safety matters but not through any specific machinery. In the latter case neither the institutional form of the bargaining nor its methods are in principle prescribed by law. The HSWA 1974 does, however, at least in broad outline, prescribe the nature of employee participation in safety matters.

Such intervention by the law in a particular area consorts oddly with the general reluctance of the legislature in the UK to regulate the institutions and procedures of collective relations. It is therefore perhaps not surprising that, having taken the step in principle, the legislature seems to draw back as far as possible from the consequences of its decision. In France, which has a very heavily legally-regulated system of labour relations, the rules governing the *Comités d'hygiène et de sécurité* provide that the committees must be set up in certain types of establishments and prescribe the membership of the committee and its chairman, the method of selecting the employee represent-atives, the frequency of its meetings, the circulation of the agenda and the registration of the minutes, the business to be transacted at meetings, the reports to be made to the government, its inquiry, supervisory and training functions, and its right to be consulted about internal works rules relating to health and safety. The rules are enforceable by the labour inspectorate.

It is hardly possible, given the nature of the decision in principle, that nothing should be said about these matters in respect of UK safety representatives and committees, but it is equally clear that the legislature wished to fit the new bodies around the existing, and very various, general systems of in-plant collective relations rather than to impose them rigidly and awkwardly upon the established social institutions. The Health and Safety Commission has attempted to find part of a solution in reliance upon norms which are not directly legally enforceable and thus are more flexible. Thus, besides the statute, which is exiguous, and delegated legislation,[1] the Commission has placed heavy reliance upon a Code of Practice issued under s.16 of the HSWA 1974, breach of which does not in itself render any person liable to civil or criminal proceedings (although breach creates a presumption of failure to comply with the statute or regulations in criminal proceedings in appropriate cases), and, to an even greater extent, upon Guidance Notes of a purely advisory character. Regulations, Code and Guidance Notes are published together by the Commission in its pamphlet *Safety Representatives and Safety Committees*.

As far as safety representatives are concerned, the Act merely provides in s.2(6) that:

> It shall be the duty of every employer to consult any such representatives with a view to the making and maintenance of arrangements which will enable him and his employees to co-operate effectively in promoting and developing measures to ensure the health and safety at work of the employees, and in checking the effectiveness of such measures.

The Regulations, however, provide much more detail about the functions of the safety representatives: they are to investigate complaints by employees or, on their own initiative, potential hazards, dangerous occurrences and the causes of any accident at the work-place, and to make representations to the employer in consequence of these investigations or on general matters affecting health and safety; they are to carry out inspections of the workplace, after giving notice to the employer, normally at three-monthly intervals but in any case where there has been a notifiable accident or dangerous occurrence or a substantial change in the conditions of work, and the employer must provide them with such facilities and assistance as they may reasonably require to carry out these inspections; they are entitled to copies of certain documents relating to health and safety which the employer is required by the Act to keep and to other information (subject to some broad exceptions) which the employer may have and which is necessary to enable the representatives to fulfil their functions; and, finally, as we have seen above (p. 222), they are entitled to such time off with pay from work as is necessary for them to perform their functions or to undergo reasonable training to perform them.

---

[1] The Safety Representatives and Safety Committees Regulations 1977, SI 1977 No. 500, which came into force on 1 October 1978.

The functions of safety representatives are, thus, fairly fully spelt out in the Regulations. The same cannot be said of safety committees. Under the Act (s.2(7)) and Regulations such committees must be established by the employer after consultation with the relevant trade unions if two or more safety representatives request it. The committee is to have 'the function of keeping under review the measures taken to ensure the health and safety at work of [the] employees and such other functions as may be prescribed'. Only in the Guidance Notes is anything said about the functions of the committee in any detailed way. Examples of appropriate functions are given,[1] but within the overall guidance that committees 'ought to consider the drawing up of agreed objectives or terms of reference' (GN 6).

The impression of the Regulations on the matter of function is paralleled in respect of appointment and composition in relation to both safety represent-atives and safety committees. Although the Regulations stipulate that safety representatives should be employees who, in the usual case, have been employed by the employer throughout the preceding two years or have two years' experience in similar employment (cl. 3(4)), provisions as to the number of representatives and the size and nature of their 'constituencies' are to be found only in the Guidance Notes. Under the Act and the Regulations the union seems free to appoint as many representatives as it wishes and to distribute their constituencies as it thinks fit. The composition of safety committees is also dealt with in the Guidance Notes, where the main guidance is that 'the membership and structure of safety committees should be settled in consultation between management and the trade union representatives concerned through the use of the normal machinery' (GN 9), but the number of management representatives should not exceed the number of employee representatives. The relationship between the safety committee and the safety representatives is not indicated in detail: the relationship 'should be a flexible but intimate one'; safety representatives might or might not be members of the committee.

The indefiniteness of the normative structure is reflected in the enforcement mechanisms. Suppose an employer does not consult, denies a representative the facilities due to him or otherwise hinders the work of representatives or committees. Except in relation to time off, where the Regulations confer

---

[1] Guidance Note 7 on Safety Committees gives the following examples:

(a) The study of accident and notifiable diseases statistics and trends, so that reports can be made to management on unsafe and unhealthy conditions and practices, together with recommendations for corrective action.

(b) Examination of safety audit reports on a similar basis.

(c) Consideration of reports and factual information provided by inspectors of the enforcing authority appointed under the Health and Safety at Work Act.

(d) Consideration of reports which safety representatives may wish to submit.

(e) Assistance in the development of works safety rules and safe systems of work.

(f) A watch on the effectiveness of the safety content of employee training.

(g) A watch on the adequacy of safety and health communication and publicity in the workplace.

(h) The provision of a link with the appropriate inspectorates of the enforcing authority.

jurisdiction upon the industrial tribunals, no doubt because of their similar jurisdiction under the EPCA 1978, the 'Commission have not suggested any new machinery for the resolution of disagreements which might arise between employers and trade unions over the operation of these Regulations or Code of Practice. The Commission believe that disagreements must be settled through the normal machinery for the resolution of industrial relations problems' (HSC, *Safety Representatives and Safety Committees*, 1976, p. 2). Thus, even when the norms in question have full legal force (as being laid down in the statute or the Regulations), the preference is for voluntary, rather than legal, dispute-settlement machineries.

However, to give primacy to the voluntary procedures will also require an act of self-abnegation on the part of the enforcement authorities, since in principle the standard mechanisms for enforcing the health and safety legislation are also available in respect of the Safety Representatives and Safety Committees Regulations. The mechanisms include, of course, criminal prosecutions, the historically typical method of enforcing safety legislation, although one which, as we have seen (above, p. 182), the EAT has regarded as out of place in the conduct of collective relations between employers and employees. The HSWA 1974 adds to the criminal prosecution the additional remedy of the improvement notice (HSWA 1974, ss.21–4), by which a factory inspector can require any person contravening the legislation (subject to the latter's appeal to an industrial tribunal) to take steps to comply with the relevant provisions, including the Safety Representatives and Safety Committees Regulations. The HSC has issued guidance, however, to the enforcement authorities not to institute criminal proceedings against safety representatives for any act or omission by them in the performance of their functions. In October 1978 the HSC issued guidance about the enforcement of the Regulations against employers. The primacy of the voluntary procedures emerges from the advice that the enforcement authorities should not normally concern themselves with the question of whether the employer is complying with his legal obligations unless asked to intervene by a trade union or safety representative; that enforcement action should not be used until all voluntary means of resolving the dispute have been tried; that in many cases the advisory arm of ACAS may be better able to produce a voluntary settlement than the enforcement authorities; and that where, as a last resort, the enforcement authorities take action, the improvement notice will normally be the appropriate first step. The Commission does not, however, have control over any civil action, whether for damages or an injunction, based upon the provision in s.47(2) that breaches of health and safety regulations are actionable on proof of damage unless the regulations provide otherwise, which the Safety Representatives and Safety Committee Regulations appear not to do, although a civil action is perhaps an unlikely prospect in this particular area.

The indefinite nature of the substantive legal norms and the stress placed by the Health and Safety Commission upon the use of voluntary procedures to resolve disputes both point to the importance of collective bargaining in the application of the rules to particular establishments. As yet the number of collective agreements dealing with safety representatives is not thought to be large, but one major union, ASTMS, has issued to its members guidance which lists no fewer than twenty areas arising out of the new structures that it regards as suitable matters for bargaining (see *Health and Safety Information Bulletin*, No. 33, 1978, p. 6). They are:

Numbers of safety representatives to be appointed; areas of representation of safety representatives; senior safety representative, where necessary and agreed function; joint union arrangements where necessary and desirable; procedure for dealing with health and safety issues (normally the existing procedure agreement); frequency of formal inspections; how much notice of formal inspections; will such inspections be carried out jointly with the employer; what will be done with formal inspection reports; time off work – agreed notification procedure; agreement on settlement of disputes about time off work; facilities for safety representatives; procedures for accident investigations; agreed regular information from employer; procedure for getting information from factory inspector; procedure for calling in independent advisers; agreement on setting up of safety committee; terms of reference of safety committee; frequency of meetings and conduct of meetings; representation on safety committee and relationship, if any, with safety representatives.

Thus both at the level of the substantive duty and at the level of enforcement the normative structure is a curious *mélange* of directly enforceable legal norms, indirectly enforceable (if enforceable at all) authoritative guidance, and social norms derived from collective bargaining. The attractions of intervention by the law in health and safety matters have been put by the Chairman of the HSC as follows: 'We are quite deliberately in this legislation setting up an additional force in the workplace at the point where accidents take place, and the employer has got to organize in order to face up to this new situation which is being created' (W.J. Simpson, 'Safety Representatives' (1977) 27 *Federation News* at p. 121). The fact that in the context of UK labour relations the resulting structure is untidy is not necessarily an argument against intervention. The French model of precise legal regulation of safety committees is clearly inappropriate for the UK. Whether, however, legal intervention will be successful in harnessing the power of the social institutions to the promotion of health and safety and whether the legal institutions will be able to live in harmony with the social institutions remains to be seen. The Chairman of the Commission has said on the one hand that it is 'absolutely essential to keep the functions of the safety representatives separate from those of the other overall functions that shop stewards have' – the Regulations leave it to the union to decide whether the safety representatives ought to be shop stewards or not – and on the other that 'we have been sensible in keying all this into the consultation procedures or the collective bargaining procedures which are already in existence' (ibid., p. 123). The tension between these two statements reflects a tension deliberately introduced into the normative structure.

(g) **Consultation over proposed redundancies**

Whether or not it is right to regard health and safety as an appropriate subject for consultation rather than bargaining, because it is said to be a topic over which the interests of employers and employees conflict to a lesser degree than over terms and conditions of employment, this view cannot possibly explain the presence in the law of a duty upon employers to consult with trade unions over proposed redundancies (and to notify the Department of Employment of the proposals). Where an employer is proposing to reduce his workforce by compulsory redundancy, he is clearly in a situation of acute conflict of interest with his employees. Since, as we have seen above (pp. 164ff.), the employer's duty is to consult only with representatives of a recognized, independent trade union, it might at first sight be thought odd that the employer is not required to bargain with the recognized union over the proposed redundancies. From the late sixties onwards a number of official bodies in the UK recommended that employers should deal with the relevant trade unions over proposed redundancies, but often only by way of consultation. It seems likely that a major consideration in favour of an obligation to consult rather than to bargain was that consultation does not commit the trade union to responsibility for approving the redundancy or selecting the employees to be made redundant to the degree that a joint agreement over these matters does.

In any event there operated upon the legislation that eventually became Part IV of the Employment Protection Act 1975, a second influence in favour of consultation, derived from the need of the UK to implement the European Communities' Directive on the Approximation of the Laws of the Member States Relating to Redundancies (Directive 75/129). The basis of the Directive, as far as the employees were concerned, was a duty upon the employer to consult representatives of the employees, and this reinforced domestic pressures in favour of a consultation mechanism. As we have already noted (above, p. 171), in many European countries in-plant collective relations are handled through a works council, which is often formally separate from the trade-union machinery. In many countries the ideology of the works council is that it should be an instrument of co-operation, not conflict, with the employer, and this tends to make consultation a natural model for relations between employer and works council. Thus, consultation becomes also a natural model for the European Communities to follow when seeking to further measures of approximation of national legal systems in the labour law area.

We have already noted (above, p. 171) the significance of the fact that the term 'workers' representatives' contained in the Directive has been translated into UK law as an official or other person authorized to carry on collective bargaining by the relevant, recognized, independent trade union (EPA 1975, s.99(1) and (2)). In spite of some imprecision as to who that authorized person may be (e.g. shop steward or full-time official, cf. *GMWU* v. *Wailes Dove Bitumastic* [1977] IRLR 45) in a particular situation, this approach does not seem to have given rise to major problems in practice. The scope of the duty upon the employer to consult is set out in some detail in s.99. The employer must give to the unions in advance of the dismissals the information specified in s.99(5) – notably information about the reasons for the proposed dismissals, the numbers and types of workers involved, and the proposed procedures for selecting the employees and carrying out the dismissals – and make reasoned replies to any representations the authorized person may make on the basis of the information (s.99(7)). The consultation with the union representative is required to begin 'at the earliest opportunity', and in any event at least 90 days before the first dismissal takes effect in the case of proposals to dismiss 100 or more employees at one establishment within a period of 90 days, or at least 30 days before the first dismissal in the case of proposals to dismiss 10 or more employees within a period of 30 days (s.99(3)). The second, specified, minimum period of 30 days was originally set at 60 days, but it was reduced by Order (see s.106(4)) in 1979 in spite of the increasing number of redundancies being declared at that time and in subsequent years. However, the employer's obligations to provide information, to consider and reply to representations, and to begin consultation at the appropriate time are modified where there are 'special circumstances which render it not reasonably practicable for the employer to comply with' the statutory requirements. In these circumstances he must take 'all such steps towards compliance' as are reasonably practicable (s.99(8)). The courts' interpretation of s.99(8), coupled with the fact that the employer comes under an obligation to consult only when he has formed a proposal to make employees redundant, has meant that in many cases of insolvency of the employing enterprise the employer's obligation to consult arises only in a very truncated way, as the following case shows.

Union of Shop Distributive and Allied Workers v. *Leancut Bacon Ltd*
[1981] IRLR 295 (EAT)

During the first half of 1979 the directors of the company were negotiating for a third party to take over the company. In September when the company's half-year accounts became available the prospective purchaser withdrew. The bank then withdrew the company's credit facilities and appointed a receiver, who immediately took over management of the company on a Friday evening. On Monday morning the union official was informed that the company would be closed that day and its workforce dismissed. The union claimed the company had not complied with the provisions of EPA 1975, s.99.

MAY . . . In considering the question of special circumstances the Industrial Tribunal said they had considered the case of *Clarks of Hove Ltd* v. *Bakers' Union* [1978] IRLR 366 to which we also have been referred in detail. That was a case in which Clarks of Hove Ltd, without warning, dismissed some 368 of 380 employees and on the same day the company ceased to trade. It ceased to trade because it was insolvent. Summarising the facts of that case substantially, there had been a gradually increasing insolvency; there was no sudden occurrence which made matters immediately worse for the company; the redundancy was the result of that misfortune which on occasions does overcome trading concerns. As there had been no consultation between Clarks of Hove Ltd and the Bakers' Union prior to the dismissals, the trade union made a complaint to an Industrial Tribunal, which the latter upheld and made a protective award. This is the relief which an Industrial Tribunal is to grant under subsection (3) of s.101 where it finds the trade union's complaint under subsection (1) to be well founded. On appeal to the Employment Appeal Tribunal, the latter remitted the case to the Industrial Tribunal for reconsideration. Before that took place, however, the employers appealed to the Court of Appeal. The only substantial point for that Court was to consider what was a special circumstance within subsection (8) of s.99 of the 1975 Act. In the judgment of Geoffrey Lane L.J. (as he then was) at p. 369 the learned Lord Justice said this:

> Where, as here, the employers have admittedly failed to give the requisite 90 days' notice the burden is clearly imposed upon them, by the statute, to show that there were special circumstances which made it not reasonably practicable for them to comply with the provisions of the Act, and also that they took steps towards compliance with the requirements, such steps as were reasonably practicable in the circumstances. There are, it is clear, these three stages: (1) were there special circumstances? If so, (2) did they render compliance with s.99 not reasonably practicable? And, if so, (3) did the employers take all such steps towards compliance with s.99 as were reasonably practicable in the circumstances?

The learned Lord Justice went on to consider the legal effect of the employer's successfully discharging the onus upon him on those three matters, and then returned to the crucial question in the case at p. 369 where he said:

> What then is meant by 'special circumstances'? Here we come to the crux of the case . . . it seems to me that the way in which the phrase was interpreted by the Industrial Tribunal is correct. What they said, in effect, was this, that insolvency is, on its own, neither here nor there. It may be a special circumstance, it may not be a special circumstance. It will depend entirely on the cause of the insolvency whether the circumstances can be described as special or not. If, for example, sudden disaster strikes a company, making it necessary to close the concern, then plainly that would be a matter which was capable of being a special circumstance; and that is so whether the disaster is physical or financial. If the insolvency, however, were merely due to a gradual run-down of the company, as it was in this case, then those are facts on which the Industrial Tribunal can come to the conclusion that the circumstances were not special. In other words, to be special the event must be something out of the ordinary, something uncommon; and that is the meaning of the word 'special' in the context of this Act.

> Accordingly it seems to me that the Industrial Tribunal approached the matter in precisely the correct way. They distilled the problem which they had to decide down to its essence, and they asked themselves this question: do these circumstances, which undoubtedly caused the summary dismissal and the failure to consult the union as required by s.99, amount to special circumstances; and they went on, again correctly, as it seems to me, to point out that insolvency simpliciter is neutral, it is not

on its own a special circumstance. Whether it is or is not will depend upon the causes of the insolvency. They define 'special' as being something out of the ordinary run of events, such as, for example, a general trading boycott – that is the passage which I have already read. Here again, I think they were right.

There was ample evidence upon which, on these correct bases, they could come to the conclusion which they did. But whether one would have reached the same conclusion oneself is another matter and is an irrelevant consideration.

The decision of the Court of Appeal in that case was considered by the Employment Appeal Tribunal shortly afterwards, in *Hamish Armour* v. *Association of Scientific Technical and Managerial Staffs* [1979] IRLR 24. . . .

On the first question which arises for decision upon this instant appeal – namely, was the finding by the Industrial Tribunal of a special circumstance justified? – we confess that but for the decision of the Scottish Employment Appeal Tribunal in the *Hamish Armour* case we might have reached a different conclusion. It can be said that it is not an infrequent occurrence, where a company is in financial difficulties, for its bank to refuse further facilities under any security which that bank may hold and, if necessary, to appoint a receiver and manager. On the basis that such a state of affairs is not unusual it is arguable that this is not sufficiently 'special,' in the physical or financial sense in a commercial context, to be a special circumstance within s.99(8) of the 1975 Act having regard to the ratio of the judgments in the *Clarks of Hove* case. However, in the *Hamish Armour* decision an application for a Government loan was considered to be sufficiently special to render it not reasonably practicable for the employer there at least to comply with the requirements of s.99(5) of the Act. In many respects the facts of the instant case are similar to those in the *Hamish Armour* case; where in the latter it was a Government loan that was being awaited, in the instant case it was a take-over by a third party that was being negotiated. And if and in so far as the passage from the judgment of Geoffrey Lane L.J. in the *Clarks of Hove* case indicates that at least a test of whether or not a circumstance is special is whether it is a sudden, as distinct from a gradual financial deterioration, in one case it is arguable that the sudden action of Barclays Bank Ltd in stopping further credit and appointing a receiver was itself a special circumstance.

That there was the element of suddenness about the failure of the respondent company in the instant case was borne out by substantial parts of the evidence which Mr Cockle gave to the Industrial Tribunal and which, as we have said, was the only evidence before them. To some parts of this evidence we have already referred. He said that his members had never told him of the decline of work within their employer's business, and, indeed, sometimes the work force were asked to work night shift, particularly in June, July and August of 1979. 'Barclays Bank Ltd called in the receiver,' said Mr Cockle in answer to a question, 'who moved very quickly.' He also made it clear in a number of places that this company had a good understanding with the trade union and with himself, and in the previous year, when they had considered making some 29 redundancies, there had been discussion, pursuant to the statutory provisions, between himself and the company. In fact the redundancies were ultimately not necessary because the company received a substantial order from Messrs Walls which changed the situation radically. That was in only September of 1978. Further, in the chairman's notes of evidence, which is all that we can go on and which must be taken to represent the material available to the Industrial Tribunal, Mr Cockle is also recorded as saying: 'In 1979 however, the prospective purchasers pulled out and the bank withdrew its support. The company had no control of the position. The company did not know the true state of affairs until 13.9.79. It affected Barclays Bank Ltd who stopped the supply of money and there was no money to pay the bills.'

On the two authorities to which we have referred, we think, first, that there was generally sufficient evidence before the Industrial Tribunal to justify it in coming to the conclusion that there had been special circumstances preceding the relevant redundancies which rendered it not reasonably practicable for the employer to comply with, indeed, any of the requirements of subsections (3), (5) or (7) of s.99. Further, if the suddenness of the event which produces an insolvency is a relevant consideration in deciding whether or not special circumstances had occurred, then we think that the Industrial Tribunal were entitled to find that the sudden action of Barclays Bank Ltd in stopping further credit and appointing a receiver was a special circumstance within subsection (8) of s.99. Whether we would have reached a similar conclusion ourselves is, in the words of Geoffrey Lane L.J. in the *Clarks of Hove* case, 'perhaps another matter but is in any event an irrelevant consideration'.

For these reasons, therefore, we do not think that we would be justified in disturbing the finding of the Industrial Tribunal in paragraph 12 of their reasons that there were in the instant case special circumstances under s.99(8) of the Act.

In so far as the second point taken by Mr Clarke on this appeal is concerned, we do not think that in paragraph 11 of its judgment in the *Hamish Armour* case the Employment Appeal Tribunal in Scotland was seeking to lay down any general requirement of consultation between those responsible for an ailing company and a recognized trade union prior to any proposal for dismissals on the basis of redundancy. Mr Clarke suggested that if the passage in the judgment to which we have referred were not given that wide meaning there would, in effect, be nothing for the second half of s.99(8) to operate upon. With respect, we do not agree. To take merely one example, in certain circumstances although there may have been a special circumstance rendering it not reasonably practicable for an employer to comply with subsection (5) of s.99, possibly because the full details and information were not then available to him or been decided upon, nevertheless an employer is bound to do what he can to consult a recognized trade union in relation to those matters once any proposals for redundancy are made. Subsection (8) refers back to subsections (3), (5) and (7); they each of them refer to 'consultation required by this section', which by subsection (1) is required only when an employer proposes to dismiss as redundant an employee of a description in respect of which the independent trade union is recognized by him. We cannot read s.99(8) as requiring an employer to do anything about consulting a trade union in respect of its employees unless and until a proposal to dismiss one or more of them on the ground of redundancy is at least in the mind of the employer. When that occurs, the obligation under the statutory provisions arises. If and to the extent that that passage from the *Hamish Armour* judgment is to be read as opening the obligation to consult wider than that, which we do not think it is, then respectfully we would disagree. In any event it is accepted in the present case that no proposal for redundancy was ever made before a relatively late hour on 14 September, and on Saturday 15 September the receiver made an appointment to discuss the matter with Mr Cockle very early on the following Monday 17 September. We agree with the Industrial Tribunal that, in the unfortunate circumstances which occurred, neither the company nor he could have done more than they did to comply with the requirements of s.99 of the 1975 Act; and, again, for those reasons we do not feel that we would be justified in disturbing the finding of the Industrial Tribunal in paragraph 14 of their reasons.

No doubt, in the standard case the employer works out the date by which he must begin consultation by reckoning backwards the relevant number of days (90 or 30) from the date proposed for the first dismissal, and the union works out whether the employer has in fact complied with the statutory obligation by reckoning backwards for the relevant period after the first dismissal has been effected. But the overriding statutory obligation is to begin consultation 'at the earliest opportunity', and where the union can show a delay between the formation of a proposal to dismiss and the beginning of consultation, it will have shown a breach of the statutory requirement, even if the consultation began 90 or 30 days before the first dismissal (cf. *GKN Sankey Ltd* v. *National Society of Metal Mechanics* [1980] I C R 148). Indeed, where the proposal is to dismiss fewer than 10 employees within a period of 30 days, there is no statutory minimum period for consultation, but the obligation to consult nevertheless arises. That obligation arises even in respect of a proposal to dismiss a single employee, and it arises whether or not that employee is a member of the trade union which has to be consulted (s.99(1)).

In addition to satisfying the statutory obligation as to consultation in advance of the first dismissal, the employer will have to comply with the periods of notice individual employees may be entitled to by statute or by contract for the lawful termination of their contracts of employment. (This is discussed in more detail below at pp. 432–5.) Indeed, there is a complex interrelationship among the employer's substantive duty to consult, his duty to start consultations a certain minimum time before the first of the proposed dismissals takes effect (i.e. in the case of dismissal by notice the date the notice expires), and the individual's right under his contract or the E P C A 1978, s.49 to notice of a certain length for lawful termination of his contract by the employer. It is possible that an employer may have to give notice to his employees of dismissal of such a length that consultation could begin the required minimum period before expiry of the notices, even though consult-ation does not begin until after the notices of dismissal have been issued. There is much to be said, however, for the view that in such a case the employer has not discharged his duty to consult about 'proposed redundancies' because he has in fact already decided on them. This was the view adopted by the E A T in *NUT* v *Avon C C* [1978] I C R 626, where the Appeal Tribunal also expressed the view that for the employer to issue notices of dismissal immediately after beginning consultation would be a failure by him to consult. Indeed, since the employer must consult about *inter alia* the proposed method of selection of the employees and the proposed method of carrying out the dismissals, there is much to be said for the view that notices of dismissal should not be issued until the process of consultation is complete. It might well be, therefore, that the notices of dismissal would not expire until after the end of the minimum period at the beginning of which the consultation process must begin. Such a situation appears to be contemplated by the Appeal Tribunal in *Talke Fashions Ltd* v. *Amalgamated Society of Textile Workers* [1977] I C R 833.

In the event of the employer's failure to discharge his duty to consult, the right of complaint under Part I V lies in the hands of the union and it is a right of complaint to an industrial tribunal. Unusually, therefore, the tribunal has to consider a complaint by the collective body on the employees' side rather than a complaint vested in the individual employee and, more important, the substance of the complaint raises collective issues about dealings between employer and union rather than the typical industrial tribunal issue of the dealings between employer and individual employee. The sanction that arises is a 'protective award' in favour of and enforceable by the individual employee, i.e. an entitlement 'to be paid remuneration by his employer for the protected period' (s.102(1)) conditional upon, in the usual case, the employee's being available for work should the employer wish to employ his services. The length of the protected period is to be such 'as the tribunal shall determine to be just and equitable in all the circumstances having regard to the employer's default in complying with any requirement of section 99' (s.101(5)), but subject to maximum periods of ninety days in the case of proposals to dismiss 100 or more employees at one establishment over a period not exceeding ninety days, of thirty (formerly sixty) days in the case of proposals to dismiss 10 or more employees at one establishment within a period of thirty days, and of twenty-eight days in any other case. The first two periods correspond to the *minimum* periods required by s.99(3), in the absence of special circumstances, to elapse between the commencement of consultation and the taking effect of the first of the proposed dismissals.

The question of what principles should be used by tribunals to fix within the maxima the actual length of the protective award in particular cases has proved a difficult one to answer. In the following case the Appeal Tribunal contrasts the differing statutory wording of the compensation provisions in relation to unfair dismissal (see below, p. 497), action short of dismissal on grounds of trade-union activities (see above, p. 182), failure to provide a statement of the reasons for dismissal (see below, p. 511) and failure to consult. How helpful is the guidance that the Appeal Tribunal gives to the industrial tribunals?

Spillers-French (Holdings) Ltd v. *Union of Shop, Distributive and Allied Workers* [1980] I C R 31 (EAT)

On 7 April 1978 the employers announced that they would close a number of bakeries in two weeks' time. At that date all but a few of the employees who had previously worked for the employers ceased employment with the employers. However, about a third of the bakeries were sold as going concerns to other companies, which took over nearly all the relevant employees without any break of continuity of employment. In a claim for a protective award by the union in respect of all the employees who had been made redundant, the question arose as a preliminary issue as to whether the industrial tribunal was empowered to make a protective award in respect of those redundant employees who had been immediately re-employed without suffering any financial loss. (The Transfer Regulations (see below, p. 250) were not at the time in operation.)

SLYNN J.: . . . In this case Mr Irvine [counsel for the employers] has submitted that the object of this section is to provide compensation for loss of remuneration resulting from failure to consult. He does not accept that there is any power in a tribunal to make an award at all, if it is shown that there was no loss of remuneration. He specifically challenges the assumption in one of the cases that what had been called 'concomitant sad features' justify the making of an award by way of solatium. Accordingly he would say that the fact that there is some form of hardship or disruption in the life of the employees, when they seek to obtain other work or find their domestic arrangements disturbed, is wholly irrelevant. His contention is that this legislation, properly construed, relates only to the payment of compensation for wages which have been lost and nothing else. In support of that contention he has referred us to a number of authorities. For example, he has referred to *Clarkson International Tools Ltd* v. *Short* [1973] ICR 191. That was a case in which the court said that the assessment of compensation was not to express disapproval of industrial relations policies; it was to compensate for financial loss. It is, however, right to bear in mind that that was a claim in respect of unfair dismissal – a situation where an industrial tribunal has to decide whether in all the circumstances an employer has behaved reasonably in determining employment. The court was satisfied that the object of compensation provided by section 161 of the Industrial Relations Act 1971 was limited to the assessment of financial loss; but there one must bear in mind that the section provided that compensation was to be such amount as the tribunal considered just and equitable in all the circumstances having regard to the loss sustained by the aggrieved party as a consequence of the matters to which the complaint related. We do not think that we get direct assistance from the provisions of that particular Act, in the context of the present inquiry where the wording is very different.

Then Mr Irvine has referred us to sections 53 to 56 of the Act of 1975 [now EPCA 1978, ss.23–26A]. Where a complaint is made to an industrial tribunal, under section 54, that action has been taken against an employee in relation to union or proposed union activities, the tribunal may assess compensation. The compensation is specifically said to be such amount as is considered just and equitable in all the circumstances having regard to the infringement of the complainant's right under section 53 by his employer's action complained of and to any loss sustained by the complainant which is attributable to the action. Once again there is a specific reference to the loss suffered by the complainant in the case. Therefore, it is perhaps not surprising that in *Brassington* v. *Cauldon Wholesale Ltd* [1978] ICR 405, this appeal tribunal should have come to the conclusion that what had to be assessed was the compensation for loss, and that Parliament was not in this section laying down simply a penalty. Again, we do not think that the words of those sections or that case really assist us in the present dispute.

In this body of legislation there are provisions where sums are to be paid without any assessment of actual loss being made. Thus, for example, in section 70 of the Act of 1975 [now EPCA 1978, s.53], it is provided that an employee is entitled to be given a statement on the termination of his employment, which contains particulars of the reason for his dismissal. If complaint is made that that has been unreasonably refused, a tribunal may make a declaration as to the reasons and, more important for our purposes, shall make an award that the employer pay to the employee the equivalent of two weeks' pay. Also it is clear that there is, in section 100 of the Act, in the group of sections with which we are concerned, a specific financial penalty if a notice is not given to the Secretary of State.

So it seems to us that despite the background of the desire to encourage consultation in order to avoid liability for unfair dismissal, and also despite the fact that in some areas the object of Parliament is clearly seen to be purely one of compensation, we have to look at the particular sections with which we are concerned and decide what precisely they lay down.

It seems to us that here it is important to bear in mind that the obligation which is imposed upon an employer is one in respect of descriptions of employees. As we read it, there is no necessary obligation upon an employer, when launching the necessary consultation, to identify the particular employees concerned. He may be able to do so; he may not. Indeed the object of this legislation quite clearly is to give an opportunity for consultation between employer, trade unions and the Secretary of State. The consultation may result in new ideas being ventilated which avoid the redundancy situation altogether. Equally it may lead to a lesser number of persons being made redundant than was originally thought necessary. Or it may be that alternative work can be found during the period of consultation. So one has to bear in mind that at this first stage the duty is to give the 'numbers and descriptions' of employees concerned. When the award is made, it is an award in respect of descriptions of employees who are specified in the award, being employees who have been dismissed or whom it is proposed to dismiss as redundant. There it may be that the terms of the award can be general. When a particular individual seeks to bring a claim, if the remuneration has not been paid to him, he is not required under section 103 of the Act to show that he was a person named in the protective award. What he has to show is that he is an employee of a description to which the protective award relates. Those matters, it seems to us, are of relevance when one comes to consider the kinds of matter with which the protective award is concerned.

Section 101(5) does not provide that the protected period is to be in respect of the date when each particular employee is dismissed; it is to be when the first of the dismissals to which the complaint relates takes effect, or, in a case where it is still proposed to dismiss employees, the date of the award (whichever is the earlier). So, clearly there is power in an industrial tribunal to make a protective award which may take effect earlier than the date when particular employees are in fact dismissed. When the tribunal comes to exercise its power, it is required to consider the relevant period. The relevant period is such period beginning with the appropriate date as the tribunal shall determine to be just and equitable in all the circumstances having regard to the seriousness of the employer's default in complying with any requirement of section 99 of the Act. It is striking that that provision does not refer, as did the definition of compensation under the Industrial Relations Act 1971, or the definition in relation to trade union activities in section 56 of the Act of 1975, to the loss suffered by the employee.

So it would seem that basically the question is, how serious was the employer's default in complying with the requirements of section 99? Obviously there can be defaults of different gravity. For example, one requirement of the Act is that necessary information shall be disclosed in writing. It might be that if all the information had been given orally to a trade union representative, a tribunal would not take a very serious view of that as a failure to comply with a requirement. On the other hand, failure to give reasons at all, or failure to include one of the matters specified in section 99(5), might be more serious. A failure to consult at all, or consultation only at the last minute, might be taken to be even more serious.

One of the main questions which arises in this case is whether the words 'just and equitable in all the circumstances' require or entitle the tribunal to go further. Mr Irvine submits that what they are required to do is to look at the effect upon the employee of the particular breach. He says in effect that the real question is, what are the consequences that flow from the breach? – consequences which really only are to be seen in terms of loss of wages. He says that that is to some extent supported by previous decisions of this appeal tribunal. He has referred us to a number of those decisions. Most important, we think it is agreed by both sides, is *Talke Fashions Ltd* v. *Amalgamated Society of Textile Workers and Kindred Trades* [1977] I C R 833. There, in giving the decision of the appeal tribunal, Kilner Brown J. considered the meaning and effect of some of these provisions. In that case the appeal tribunal said that they considered that in the linking of the period of an award with a period of notice to a trade union for purposes of consultation the primary consideration is to assess the consequences to the employees. They added, at p. 836:

> Plainly the seriousness of the employer's default has also to be considered. However, neither should be considered in isolation. Whether or not the employer's conduct should be penalised seems to us to beg the question. In other words the seriousness of the default ought to be considered in its relationship to the employees and not in its relationship to the trade union representative who has not been consulted.

The majority of the appeal tribunal took the view that the degree of the employer's default was a factor for increasing the period from short to long. That is some support for Mr Irvine's submission here that it is the consequences to the employees which are to be taken into account. It is however to be noticed, as we see it, that in that case the appeal tribunal was concerned in assessing the consequences by the number of days of consultation denied to the employees through their union representative. We do not see that in that case this appeal tribunal was concerned with the extent to which, if any, the employees had obtained alternative remuneration. We do not see that that case is really decisive of the issue which we have to consider. . . .

So it can be said here that there is, particularly in *Talke Fashions Ltd* and in *Transport and General Workers' Union* v. *Gainsborough Distributors (UK) Ltd* [1978] I R L R 460 (which followed the *Talke* decision) support for the view that what is to be done is to compensate.

But that does not seem to us to be the end of the question. The question is, to compensate for what? It seems to us that it is to compensate for the failure to consult. It seems to us that here Parliament is providing that employers should, in this kind of potential or actual redundancy situation, discuss the matter with the union and the Secretary of State in the hope of achieving one or other of the alternative courses to which we have referred. True it is that the tribunal has power to make a declaration. It seems to us that there is a duty, in the appropriate case, to make a declaration. In addition it seems to us that Parliament has given to the industrial tribunals the power, if they so decide, also to make a protective award which involves the payment of money. It seems to us that when that decision is taken, the question which has to be looked at is not the loss or potential loss of actual remuneration during the relevant period by the particular employee. It is to consider the loss of days of consultation which have occurred. The tribunal will have to consider, how serious was the breach on the part of the employer? It may be that the employer has done everything that he can possibly do to ensure that his employees are found other employment. If that happens, a tribunal may well take the view that either there should be no award or, if there is an award, it should be nominal. It does not seem to us that the tribunal has to be satisfied, before it can make an award, that the employees have been paid during the relevant period. Indeed, if the application is made before the dismissals take place, these facts may not be known. It might be quite impossible to know, until the end of the period, what is the position so far as earnings from the same employer or from other sources are concerned.

Mr Irvine (to whom we are indebted for a very careful and, if we may say so, able argument in this case which has put all the points and authorities before us) has relied upon section 102(3) of the Act. That is clearly an important section in considering what is the entitlement of an employee. It does not go so much to the making of the award itself as to the entitlement of an employee to an award. It provides:

> (3) Any payment made to an employee by an employer under his contract of employment, or by way of damages for breach of that contract, in respect of a period falling within a protected period shall go towards discharging the employer's liability to pay remuneration under the protective award in respect of that first mentioned period, . . .

What is said here by Mr Irvine, and said with force, is that the reference to 'any payment made to an employee by an employer under his contract of employment during the relevant period' is to any payment made to the employee by any employer under any contract of employment which exists during the relevant period. So Mr Irvine would say that if, after dismissal, an employee finds another job and is paid a wage during the protected period, then that amount is to be taken as discharging the employer's liability to pay remuneration under the protective award. He contends that 'an employer,' when first used in the subsection, would otherwise have been 'the employer.' 'An employer' he says in effect must be interpreted as any employer. We do not find it possible to accept that submission. It seems to us that this section is dealing with the position of the employer who has actually failed in his obligations and who has been made liable to pay remuneration under the protective award. In other words, where the words 'the employer' occurs the second time, it is really that defaulting employer's liability which is referred to. It seems to us that it is quite clearly only payments which are made under the contract of employment, or by way of damages for breach, by the particular employer who dismisses without consultation, which can go to satisfy that employer's obligation to pay money under the protective award. In the same way it seems to us plain that the second part of the subsection, which is providing for the discharge of a liability under the contract, or in respect of breach of contract, to be discharged pro tanto by any payment made under the protective award, is talking in both places of the same employer. It is payments under the protective award which go only to discharge the obligations of the particular employer who is concerned.

Accordingly it seems to us here that Parliament has declared that the payments by way of wages, or for damages for breach of contract, which are relevant to reduce the amount of the protective award are only those made by the employer in default. Parliament has so provided, but has left out of the statutory provision reference to any other payments by any other employers. It seems to us clear that those other payments are not to be taken into account so as to eliminate the possibility of a protective award being made at all, if it can be shown that during the relevant period there is no loss of wages, or, as was conceded here, any other kind of hardship suffered. . . .

Therefore this case will now go back to the industrial tribunal for them to decide, on the material before them, whether there should be a protective award and, if so, what should be the length of the period which they find to be just and equitable in all the circumstances having regard to the seriousness of the employer's default in complying with the requirements of the section. That, as the cases to which we have referred show quite clearly, will involve a consideration of the length of the period, the nature of the default, and the 'just and equitable' provision. It will also involve a consideration of the steps which were taken by the employers to deal with the situation which arose and to obtain other employment for their employees, even though they were in breach of the obligation to consult. Accordingly, despite the argument put forward by Mr Irvine, this appeal is dismissed.

The protective award, the nature of which is delineated by s. 102 of the EPA 1975, is essentially not an enforced continuance of employment (such as is provided for by way of interim relief in freedom of association cases under s. 77 to 79 of the EPCA 1978) but an award of remuneration for the protected period which is awarded (s. 102(1)). The remuneration is not the employee's ordinary remuneration but is assessed according to the statutory concept of a week's pay (i.e. the pay for normal working hours excluding voluntary overtime or average remuneration where there are no normal working hours – see below, p. 336 (s. 102(2)).

This right to remuneration is qualified by a series of provisions designed to ensure that if the employee is actually employed during the protected period, the employer will face no greater liabilities for remuneration than he ordinarily would were the period not a protected one, given that he would not be treating the employee unreasonably. Thus, contractual payments and protective award remuneration can be mutually set off against each other (s. 102(3)). In effect, the employer need not pay the employee for periods for which he would not ordinarily be paid under his contract of employment (s. 102(4)). If the employee is fairly dismissed during the protected period (other than for redundancy) or unreasonably terminates his contract, he need not be remunerated for the remainder of the protected period (s. 102(5)) and, if the employer makes the employee an offer of renewal of his contract or of re-engagement during the protected period, the right to remuneration under the protective award is forfeited if the employee unreasonably refuses the offer or accepts the offer for a trial period and later unreasonably terminates his contract (s. 102(6)–(11)).

The upshot is that the protective award can operate as a simple lump-sum award of remuneration for a specified period or it can operate as a guarantee of a continuance of remuneration during a period in which employment is prolonged. The statute seeks to encourage employers to prefer the latter alternative by preserving their normal safeguards if they do choose that alternative; but this may (like the procedure under the EPCA 1978, ss.87–8, for dealing with lay-off and short-time) prove over-elaborate and non-functional. For by the time the issue comes to an industrial tribunal the employer will in most cases either have decided to continue the employments in question by means of a reorganization of some kind, or will have decided to discontinue the employments altogether, in which case the award will be viewed purely as a pecuniary award for a lump sum. As a statutory model of protection of employment the protective award is therefore an interesting but over-sophisticated one. It was presumably devised in order to avoid the appearance of a purely pecuniary penalty at the individual level to sanction what is an essentially collective and procedural obligation. In practice, however, industrial tribunals markedly prefer pecuniary remedies to remedies savouring of specific performance of contracts of employment, as we shall see in the context of the law of unfair dismissal (below, p. 494).

The recognition in part IV of the EPA of a public interest in redundancies is much more muted. The EEC Directive, largely at the insistence of the UK, no longer requires, as had initially been proposed, that the consent of the public authorities be obtained before large redundancies can be effected. The employer's obligation under s.100 is simply to inform the Department of Employment, when he proposes to dismiss ten or more employees, of his intentions within the same minimum periods as those specified in s.99(3). The information which must be supplied to the DE will do something to enable it to organize effectively to meet demands from the dismissed workers for new jobs or for training places on government courses. Failure by the employer to discharge this obligation, which, of course, arises whether he recognizes an independent trade union or not, renders him liable either to have his redundancy rebate reduced by up to ten per cent by the DE (subject to appeal to an industrial tribunal) or to be convicted of a summary offence upon a prosecution authorized by the Secretary of State, leading to a maximum fine of £400 (but not to both). The taboo on criminal penalties in respect of relations between employers and employees thus does not apply in respect of relations between employers and the state.

A final issue that bears consideration is the interrelationship between an employer's failure to consult a recognized trade union over proposed redundancies and the individual's entitlement not to be unfairly dismissed (EPCA 1978, s.54), which we discuss at greater length in Chapter 4. How far can the employee rely upon the employer's failure to comply with the statutory procedure for consultation with the union in order to show that his individual dismissal was unfair? Opinion on the issue has varied. In *North East Midlands Co-op* v. *Allen* [1977] IRLR 212 and *Kelly* v. *Upholstery and Cabinet Works (Amesbury) Ltd* [1977] IRLR 91, the EAT for England and Wales, in two cases decided shortly after the introduction of the statutory provisions on redundancy consultation, came close to holding that a failure to consult fully would necessarily render the dismissals unfair at an individual level. However, in Scotland the EAT in *Forman Construction* v. *Kelly* [1977] IRLR 468 seemed to take the opposite view that non-compliance with s.99 was virtually irrelevant to the fairness of the individual dismissal, because of the provision in s.99(9) that 'this section shall not be construed as conferring any rights on a trade union or an employee except as provided by sections 101 to 103 below'. The approach of the EAT for England and Wales was in any case called into question by the subsequent general downgrading of the importance of employers' complying with correct procedure (see *Hollister* v. *NFU* [1979] ICR 542 (CA) and *British Shoe Machinery Co. Ltd* v. *Clarke* [1978] ICR 70 and see below, p. 478). However, the most recent trend has been for the EAT to try to reassert the importance of procedure in dismissals on grounds of redundancy. In *Williams* v. *Compair Maxam Ltd* [1982] ICR 156 and in *Grundy (Teddington) Ltd* v. *Plummer* [1983] ICR 367, consultation with the recognized union was listed as one of five 'principles of industrial relations practice' which reasonable employers will seek to follow in redundancy dismissals (see below, p. 490). Whether the English Court of Appeal will find this approach acceptable has yet to be seen, but the Northern Ireland Court of Appeal in *Robinson* v. *Carrickfergus BC* [1983] IRLR 122 has found an individual dismissal unfair because of absence of consultation with either the employee or his union, and Lord Lowry C.J., cautioned against too easy an acceptance of the view that compliance with correct procedure would not in fact have produced a different result and to this extent he modified the approach to be found in, for example, the *British United Shoe Machinery* case. There is no reason why this development should give rise to double compensation, for the length of the protective award or the amount of the compensatory award for unfair dismissal (see below, p. 497) could be appropriately adjusted. However, it would mean, in effect, that the union was no longer the sole channel of complaint about the employer's failure to consult it.

(h) Consultation over proposed transfers of business
The employer's duty to consult over a proposed transfer of a business shows several parallels with his duty to consult over proposed redundancies. Although there has been domestic pressure for legal regulation in this area, the proximate cause of the government's decision to act was the need to comply with an EEC Directive (No. 77/187). Indeed, the government chose to implement the Directive by issuing regulations (The Transfer of Undertakings (Protection of Employment) Regulations 1981, SI 1981 No. 1794) under the European Communities Act 1972, s.2(2) of which allows the relevant Minister to issue regulations 'for the purpose of implementing any Community obligation of the United Kingdom.' Further, the duty imposed upon the employer is owed to the relevant, independent, recognized trade union, and the nature of the duty and the method of its implementation are modelled upon, but not identical to, those found in EPA 1975, Part IV.

The Transfer Regulations have the effect, even more clearly than the redundancy handling provisions, of extending employee influence into an area often not covered by collective bargaining, even if it is also the case that the Regulations are concerned with employee influence over the consequences of the transfer rather than over the transfer itself. However, the Regulations are more important in establishing the principle of employee influence in this area than in conferring wide-ranging and effectively enforced rights upon the employee representatives. Thus, the employer's duty arises only where what is contemplated is 'a transfer from one person to another of an undertaking' (Reg. 3(1)). Consequently, the duty does not arise when what are transferred from one person to another are the shares in the company that owns the undertaking, so that the take-over bid, a very common way of transferring control of an undertaking, is not caught by these Regulations. Since what matters from the point of view of the employees is that control of the undertaking has passed to new hands, it seems odd that the employer's duty to deal with the trade union should depend upon whether, for example, a company which owns an undertaking transfers it to another company (where the Regulations would apply) or whether the shareholders of the company owning the enterprise decide to sell their shares to the second company (where the Regulations would not apply). At the other end of the scale the Regulations probably do not apply where what is being transferred is not a going concern but merely the assets previously used in the business (cf. *Melon* v. *Hector Powe Ltd* [1981] ICR 43 (HL) and see below, p. 577), and, more seriously, the Regulations expressly exclude an undertaking 'which is not in the nature of a commercial venture' (Reg. 2(1)), so that probably a proposal by a local authority to transfer its refuse-collecting activities to a private contractor would not be within the Regulations.

In terms of the content of the employer's duty, the duty under the Transfer Regulations (Reg. 10) is divided explicitly into a duty to inform and a duty to consult, the latter arising only in more restricted circumstances than the duty to inform. This is in contrast to the duty in relation to proposed redundancies, which is always a duty to consult, although part of that consultation duty is a duty to give information (see above, p. 238). Whenever an employee may be 'affected' by the proposed transfer, a duty arises upon his employer to give certain information to the relevant official of the recognized trade union. The employee in question may be employed by either transferor or transferee employer (the Regulations cover them both) and he may be an affected employee even though he is not employed in the part of the business that is to be transferred (but the Regulations do not otherwise seek to define the term 'affected'). The information to be given must embrace the approximate date of the transfer, the reasons for it, the legal, economic and social implications of the transfer for the affected employees, and the 'measures', if any, which transferor or transferee propose to take in relation to the employees. Where the employer does envisage such 'measures' (not defined), a more extensive duty to disclose information may arise, viz. in respect of those employees who may be affected by the measures but who would not have been affected by the transfer itself, and, more important, the employer comes under a duty to consult with the relevant trade union (defined in terms of considering and replying to representations, as in Part IV of EPA 1975). There is no minimum time period laid down for the commencement of the provision of information, nor an obligation to commence at the earliest opportunity. Instead, there is the general principle that the information shall be provided 'long enough before a relevant transfer to enable consultations to take place' (Reg. 10(2)). There is a 'special circumstances' defence for the employer in Reg. 10(7), identical to that in s.99(7) of EPA 1975.

As with the redundancy handling provisions, the right of complaint about the employer's failure to comply with the statutory obligation is confined to the recognized trade union (Reg. 11), and the complaint lies to an industrial tribunal. If the complaint is upheld, the order made by the tribunal, as under the 1975 Act, will normally be for a pecuniary payment in favour of individual employees, but instead of the elaboration of a protective award we find under the Regulations a simple payment of compensation (Reg. 11(4)(a)). The amount of the payment is such as the tribunal 'considers just and equitable having regard to the seriousness of the failure of the employer to comply with his duty', but, in a rider that does much to reduce the significance of the employer's duty, a maximum is set on the compensation of two weeks' pay (Reg. 11(11)). Of course, where as part of the transfer any employee is proposed to be made redundant, the employer will have to comply with the redundancy handling procedure as well, but the amount of any protective award can be set off against compensation under the Regulations (and vice versa) as can contractual remuneration and damages for breach of contract (Reg. 11(7)). The general impression one is given by the consultation provisions of the Transfer Regulations is of a complex substantive structure which is likely to have only a moderate impact on practice.

5 Future directions

It will be clear from what has been said above that the extent to which government currently sees it as an appropriate part of public policy to support the growth of collective bargaining is very much in question. The government elected in 1979 repealed the general statutory recognition procedure (above, p. 198) and Sch. 11 to the EPA 1975 (above, p. 161), rescinded the Fair Wages Resolution (above, p. 154) and has questioned the utility of the system of wages councils. Whether this policy will be taken further or whether, on the other hand, a reversion to the policy (expressed particularly in the EPA 1975) of providing legal supports for collective bargaining will occur depends upon future political developments which the authors of this book have no particular claim to be able to predict. In this concluding section, however, we wish to draw attention to two potential areas for employee involvement –

perhaps through collective bargaining and perhaps not – which seem likely to be of concern to policy makers in the future and which may result in legislation. These are the areas of corporate policy and the control of multinational companies, which are perhaps better seen as the national and international dimensions of a single problem.

The form of single-employer bargaining that the Donovan Commission was primarily concerned with was establishment-level bargaining. Where, however, a company operates two or more separate establishments – as medium-sized and large companies tend to do – it is possible for collective bargaining to operate at corporate level, either as well as or instead of at establishment level. It is clear that in Britain establishment-level bargaining is the predominant form of single-employer bargaining, but also that corporate-level bargaining is an accepted, if minority, practice. Thus, a recent survey of manufacturing companies found that for 11 per cent of the establishments surveyed the corporate level was the most important one for the determination of the wages of manual workers, compared to 42 per cent of establishments where the establishment level was the most important. (The figures for the wages of non-manual workers were 15 per cent and 40 per cent.) In the vast majority of the other establishments either there was no bargaining (10 per cent of establishments for manual workers, 25 per cent for non-manual workers) or some form of multi-employer bargaining was the more important level (36 per cent for manual workers, 18 per cent for non-manual workers). See W. Brown (ed.), *The Changing Contours of British Industrial Relations* (1981), pp. 7–16.

The legislation which we have discussed above in part 4 of this chapter under the heading of single-employer bargaining makes no explicit choice as between establishment- and corporate-level bargaining. Duties are placed upon the 'employer', and this terminology neatly avoids the issue. Indeed, in many companies the determination of the appropriate level for bargaining is an uncontroversial matter. In others, however, either unions have resisted management initiatives to move towards deciding more issues at corporate level on the grounds that this is likely to reduce the power and influence of the shop stewards at plant level, or management has resisted union challenges to a decentralized bargaining structure on grounds, for example, of the diversity of the products made or the technologies used in different parts of the company's business. The legal rules discussed in part 4 clearly do not allow either party to insist upon bargaining at one or other of these levels, but they may have an indirect influence upon the outcome of conflict between management and unions over this issue. Thus, it is difficult to believe that one day's pay for a few people justified the extensive litigation in *Beal* v. *Beecham Group* (above, p. 222) except in the context of a wider dispute over whether some forms of corporate bargaining (or, at least in that case, co-ordinated divisional bargaining) should be introduced. A decision that time off with pay was or was not to be permitted would not be determinative of the question of the level of bargaining, but might be thought to add legitimacy to the claims of one side or the other.

However, bargaining over corporate policy is not simply a question of the level at which bargaining is conducted, it is also, even predominantly, a question of the subject matter of bargaining. It may sometimes be controversial whether wages and other terms and conditions of employment should be settled at plant or corporate level, but even more controversial is the question of whether the employees should be recognized as having any role in the determination of corporate policy on matters beyond terms and conditions of employment. Here one comes up against the limits of the legal definition of collective bargaining. As defined in EPA 1975, s.126(1) and TULRA 1974, s.29(1), collective bargaining is limited to terms and conditions of employment (broadly defined) and machinery for the settlement of disputes. The negotiations must relate to or be connected with one or more of the following matters:

(a) terms and conditions of employment, or the physical conditions in which any workers are required to work;

(b) engagement or non-engagement, or termination or suspension of employment or the duties of employment, of one or more workers;

(c) allocation of work or the duties of employment as between workers or groups of workers;

(d) matters of discipline;

(e) the membership or non-membership of a trade union on the part of a worker;

(f) facilities for officials of trade unions; and

(g) machinery for negotiation or consultation, and other procedures, relating to any of the foregoing matters, including the recognition by employers or employers' associations of the right of a trade union to represent workers in any such negotiation or consultation or in the carrying out of such procedures.

However, employees may have an interest in negotiating about matters, such as investment policy, product development, the location of new plant, which may not be capable of being brought within the definition of collective bargaining – that would depend upon how far the phrase 'connected with' could be stretched – but which may be of crucial significance in determining the scope for bargaining over terms and conditions as such, if not immediately then certainly in the medium term. Indeed, decisions on these broader issues may well determine whether there will be any jobs over the terms and conditions of which bargaining can take place. Whether or not bargaining over such matters is collective bargaining (as legally defined), it is clear that very little such bargaining takes place. It was the bold proposal of the Committee of Inquiry on Industrial Democracy (Chairman: Lord Bullock; Report, Cmnd. 6706, 1977) that such bargaining should be encouraged by legislative action. The majority of the Committee took the view that collective bargaining, as normally conceived, would not operate effectively over issues of corporate planning and so they proposed, as an alternative, a scheme for employee representation on the boards of large companies. The collective bargaining model, however, very largely influenced the particular scheme of board representation the Committee put forward. There was to be an equal number of employee and shareholder representatives on the board (with a smaller group of co-opted independent members); the employee representatives were to be elected through the trade-union machinery (thus emphasizing the 'single channel' of representation (above, p. 171)); and the system of employee representation was to be capable of being instituted only in companies where trade unions were recognized for collective bargaining over terms and conditions of employment (thus emphasizing the supplementary or extensory nature of board-level representation). These proposals were strongly resisted by employers and some sections of the union movement.[1] The government produced a White Paper (*Industrial Democracy*, Cmnd. 7231, 1978) which proposed a watered-down version of the Bullock proposals, but political circumstances changed before even these could be enacted.

At present the only legislative encouragement in this general direction is contained in EA 1982, s.1, introduced by Liberal and SDP peers during that Act's consideration in the House of Lords. This section amends s.16 of the Companies Act 1967 so as to require directors of companies employing more than 250 employees in their report to shareholders to describe what action, if any, they have taken during the year, *inter alia*, to 'maintain or develop arrangements aimed at (i) providing employees systematically with information on matters of concern to them as employees, (ii) consulting employees or their representatives on a regular basis so that the views of employees can be taken into account in making decisions which are likely to affect their interests.' This section does not require management to take any particular steps; envisages forms of dealing with the employees that fall short of bargaining; does not require the dealing to take place via trade unions; and contemplates the shareholders' meeting as the appropriate body to which report on arrangements with the employees should be made.

If the development of machinery, whether collective bargaining machinery or forms of institutional representation such as employee representation on the board, has proved difficult where the goal has been to obtain for employees some influence over the corporate strategy of large companies located in a single state, the problem has seemed insuperable in the case of the corporate policy of multinational companies. Very little genuinely multinational, collective-bargaining machinery has been established.[2] Countries that have

---

[1] For a discussion of the proposals see O. Kahn-Freund, 'Industrial Democracy' (1977) 6 *ILJ* 65; Davies and Wedderburn, 'The Land of Industrial Democracy' (1977) 6 *ILJ* 197; Davies, 'The Bullock Report and Employee Participation in Corporate Planning in the UK' (1978) 1 *Journal of Comparative Corporate Law and Securities Regulation* 245; Benedictus, Bourn and Neal (eds.), *Industrial Democracy: The Implications of the Bullock Report* (1977).

[2] For a, perhaps slightly pessimistic, survey see H.R. Northrup and R.L. Rowan, *Multinational Collective Bargaining Attempts* (1979).

established legislative schemes for institutional forms of employee representation have naturally not generally felt able to give them extra-territorial effect
so that, for example, the German subsidiary of a US multinational company
will certainly have to comply with the German laws on employee representation on the board (see especially the *Mitbestimmungsgesetz* 1976), but the
American parent company, where the crucial policy decisions may be taken,
will not be subject to these laws. The Bullock Committee did not suggest its
proposals should have extra-territorial effect, and indeed it was prepared
somewhat to modify its proposals in favour of multinational groups whose
parent company was located abroad in order to allow the preservation of a
coherent group structure (see Chapter 11 of the Report).

It is in this context that the draft Directive of the European Community on
procedures for informing and consulting the employees of undertakings with
complex structures becomes of interest, for the European Community
provides a better, if not an ideal, framework for regulating the activities of
multinational companies than does a single nation state. An even better
framework might be the Organization of Economic Co-operation and
Development (OECD), which embraces western European countries beyond
the members of the European Community, North America and Japan and
which has produced a Code of Conduct for multinational companies,[1] but the
OECD, unlike the European Community, cannot legislate for its member
states. The draft Directive (usually referred to as the Vredeling Directive, after
the Dutch commissioner who originated the proposals) has a relatively weak
substantive content, for it is confined, as its title suggests, to imposing
obligations upon employers to inform or consult with the representatives of the
employees and does not require the employer to bargain with the representatives (cf. the discussion above at p. 230). The information to be disclosed,
however, according to the most recent draft of the Directive,[2] would embrace
the general business situation of the group as a whole and management's
future plans, and, since there is no specific limitation to information needed for
collective bargaining, the draft Directive's requirements would exceed those of
the existing UK law (EPA 1975, ss.17–21; see above, pp. 205–19). Consultation would be required where management 'of a parent undertaking proposes
to take a decision concerning the whole or a major part of the parent
undertaking or of a subsidiary in the Community which is liable to have
serious consequences for the interests of the employees of its subsidiaries in the
Community' (Art. 4). Again, the consultation obligation goes beyond what is
required under existing UK law (see above, pp. 237–52), which is itself very
much the product of earlier European initiatives.

The most interesting aspect of the draft Directive, however, relates to the

---

[1] OECD, Declaration on International Investment and Multinational Enterprises (1976, revised 1979),
noted by Lewis (1977) 6 *ILJ* 52.

[2] Reference is to the amended proposal of the Commission. See OJ No. C. 217, 12 August 1983. For a valuable
discussion of an earlier draft, see the 37th Report of the House of Lords Select Committee on the European
Communities, *Employee Consultation* (HL 250, 1980/81).

definition of the employers who are covered by it. The Directive applies only to multi-plant companies and to groups of companies, but applies to them whether the group is located wholly within a single member state or whether it is spread across more than one member state, and it also applies to some degree where the parent company is located outside the European Community but there are one or more subsidiaries within the Community. The obligation to inform and consult lies to some degree upon the managements of both parent and subsidiary companies. See Arts. 3(1)(4) and (5), and 4(1), (3) and (4). These provisions cause no great problem if the parent company is located in the same or another member state (provided all member states implement the Directive faithfully), but, of course, the provision would give rise to a major issue of extra-territorial effect where the parent company is located outside the European Community. In fact, the draft Directive seeks to avoid the problem by imposing the obligation either upon an agent within the Community designated by the parent or, in the absence of such designation, upon one or more of the subsidiary companies (Art. 1(2)). Nevertheless, the suggestion of extra-territorial impact coupled with an obligation to make group-wide disclosure of information has raised strong opposition amongst multinational companies, especially, but not only, American multinational companies, and the draft Directive may be considerably modified before it is finally adopted by the Council of Ministers.

Whatever may be the future directions for the development of collective bargaining and the law that regulates it, enough has been said in this chapter to show why collective bargaining should, according to a certain tradition, provide the focal point of labour law. There is, however, a different tradition of exposition of labour law which treats the individual employment relationship as the main focus of attention and which used indeed to insist upon viewing the common-law contract of employment as almost the central phenomenon of labour law. Although this approach has its shortcomings, it would be misleading to deny that a great part of our labour law is centred upon the content and termination of the individual employment relationship. To these we now turn our attention, but not before having sought in this chapter to establish a background in terms of collective bargaining and the law relating thereto, which, it is hoped, will provide a context for what follows.

3
The content of the individual employment relationship

I Introduction

(a) Individual employment law, legal regulation and collective bargaining

Textbooks on labour law have traditionally tended to divorce individual employment law from collective labour law. The growing importance and technicality of the law relating to individual dismissals in particular has also contributed to the tendency to dissociate individual employment law from collective labour law, and to regard it as an autonomous subject of study. In order to challenge that pattern we aim to show the continuity of the ultimately significant issues as between the law relating to collective bargaining and individual employment law.

So bold a claim requires substantiation. We suggest that the underlying search pursued by those concerned with the theory of industrial relations and its interconnection with the legal process is for the causes and the effects of legal intervention into the process of the regulation of the employment relationship. On the one hand, the most important source of regulation, alternative to legal intervention, is *collective* bargaining. On the other hand, the traditional and most popular form of legal regulation of this relationship in Britain is at the level of the *individual* employment relationship. For this reason a crucial relationship exists between the institutions of collective bargaining and the norms of individual employment law.

This may provide an insight into the long-pursued discussion of how far our labour law on the one hand is, or alternatively should be, abstentionist as opposed to interventionist in character. The assertion widely made and widely accepted that our labour law is abstentionist in character was based upon the premise that it refrained and sought to refrain from impinging upon the processes of voluntary collective bargaining of all kinds. Much has occurred to alter the ground rules upon which this characterization was based; but that is not so much our concern at this point, for we now seek to advance a different point, namely that the general characterization of our labour law as either interventionist or abstentionist has to be seen as a function not just of the extent of its regulation of the processes and institutions of collective bargaining, but also as a function of the extent of its regulation of the individual employment relationship. It is now clear with hindsight, and with a greater exposure to international comparisons with various European systems of labour law, that in the days when our system of labour law could be characterized as abstentionist, that abstentionism related as much to individual employment law as to the institutions of collective bargaining and industrial conflict.

This important fact was, however, masked by the prevailing tendency to conduct the voluntarist debate (i.e. the discussion about whether labour law should be interventionist or not) entirely in relation to the law about collective bargaining, trade unions, and industrial conflict. So marked was this tendency that governments of both political colours, from the mid-1960s onwards, felt that they could pass individual employment legislation without any major consequences in terms of the voluntarist debate. The Contracts of Employment Act 1963, the Redundancy Payments Act 1965, the unfair dismissal provisions of the Industrial Relations Act 1971, the individual employment law provisions of the Employment Protection Act 1975 were all enacted on that set of assumptions. So in a different way were the individual employment law provisions of the Equal Pay Act 1970, the Sex Discrimination Act 1975 and the Race Relations Act 1976. In that way by the later 1970s we came to find ourselves – almost unawares – endowed with a predominantly interventionist system of labour law which had become so primarily by development of individual employment law. After that time, indeed, the government had a programme of partial retrenchment upon individual employment legislation and justified this partly in voluntarist terms, asserting in effect that individual employment law, by unduly burdening employers, particularly small employers, was impeding the beneficial operation of the voluntary labour market (a claim considered above, see p. 39). So the scope and nature of individual employment legislation, which has in reality always been central to an analysis of our labour law in voluntarist/abstentionist terms, is now increasingly being viewed in that light by the policy-makers. We should approach the study of it accordingly.

It follows from this that we will wish to approach the large and elaborate corpus of individual employment law with the following issues primarily in mind. Firstly, what have been the reasons for the decisions of Parliament and of the courts to assume a regulatory role with regard to particular aspects of the individual employment relationship? Secondly, what impact has the introduction of legal regulation of various aspects of the individual employment relationship had; how has the legal process affected the pre-existing processes of regulation? There seem to be two forms of such impact which may usefully be identified. Firstly, the legal regulation of terms and conditions of employment may produce a direct reaction in the collective bargaining process either by altering the goals of the bargaining or by ousting it. For example, the legislation about guarantee payments in the event of short-time or lay-off (see below, p. 357) might replace collective bargaining about guarantee payments; or the goals of the collective bargaining might shift to the goals of supplementing statutory guarantee payments or demanding a shorter working week to reduce the incidence of short-time working as an *ad hoc* measure. Secondly, and more indirectly, the legal regulation of the terms and conditions of employment might affect the behaviour of the labour market, with a consequential impact on pre-existing patterns of regulation. For instance, equal pay legislation might reduce the attractiveness to employers of employing a part-time labour force composed predominantly of women workers (see below, p. 398). This might in turn thoroughly alter patterns of collective bargaining which assume the legitimacy of furthering the interests of full-time workers at the expense of part-time workers. These will frequently be difficult matters to assess; but they do provide the basis of a type of inquiry which is of real importance in relation to individual employment law. There is a third issue which we shall need to bear in mind when approaching individual employment law and in particular the law relating to the content of employment; but that issue is best explained in terms of the sources of legal control of the content of employment.

(b) The sources of legal control of the content of employment

The third and final issue which will form a theme for our discussion of the content of the employment relationship is the question of how far individual employment law takes account of the realities of industrial relations practice, and of what social model of the employment relationship is relied upon when doing so. These are questions that have certainly been posed, and sometimes to very good effect, in relation to the common law of the contract of employment; that, for instance, is the inquiry which Alan Fox's book, *Beyond Contract: Trust, Power and Work Relations* (1974), pursues. They have also, as we shall later see, been asked in relation to the new laws concerning the termination of employment, in particular the law of unfair dismissal. But these questions have not been addressed as fully as they should by now have been to that complex of statute law and case-law which the law governing the content of the individual employment relationship has now become. This is not untypical of the discourse by which the study of our law is developed; we tend all too readily to compartmentalize our consideration of, on the one hand, judges as developers of the common law, and, on the other hand, as interpreters of statute law. It is impossible to give an adequate account of the law concerning the content of the individual employment relationship without appreciating that those two judicial roles have in this context become inextricably conflated and merged. We tend to view the common law of the contract of employment as having the function of preserving in an unchanging form an archaic model of the employment relationship – like a mammoth in an iceberg – and to see statute law as gradually ousting that body of law. The reality is much less starkly defined; in fact, the common law of the contract of employment is continuing to develop, now mainly by way of response to the demands made by the new system of statutory individual employment law. It would be rash to assert that a wholly modernized social model of the employment relationship has developed accordingly. But equally it would be unwise to overlook the real adaptations that have taken place. That attempt to perpetuate the old common law of master and servant which seemed normal enough twenty years ago is now apt to appear as a relatively isolated judicial nostalgia for the past. The reason for this is to be found not least in the new necessity to develop the common law in the interstices of statute law rather than as a mystery of its own.

The starting point in identifying the different types of legal intervention into the content of employment is thus the conceptual device of the contract of employment. Having characterized the individual relationship as a contractual one (and Kahn-Freund reminds us how relatively recent and controversial that characterization is ((1977) 93 *LQR* 508)), the law then proceeds to operate upon the basis of the existence of this conceptual artefact in a variety of different ways, some of them inadequately marked off from each other. A number of different kinds of legal intervention are subsumed, for example, within the single heading of implying terms into the contract of employment. At one extreme, this is a process of identifying what the employer and employee agreed as to the content of their employment relationship. At the other extreme there is the imposition of specific norms which the courts presume, or Parliament insists, that individual contracts of employment will follow. Between the two extremes lies an undifferentiated middle ground in which the processes of recognition and imposition vie with each other, with one side – imposition – disguised in the uniform of the other. Because of these intricacies, we shall consider the topic of implied terms in some detail. But not every kind of legal intervention into the content of the employment relationship takes the form of an implied term in the contract of employment. In this respect we can, over a period of time, discern the swing of a pendulum. We can perhaps point to a first phase of development in which Parliament, in an attitude typified in the nineteenth-century truck legislation, simply forbade certain types of contract (see, for instance, Truck Act 1831, ss. 1–3). There then succeeded a phase in which Parliament, at once more attached to the contractual model of employment and yet more constructive in its aims, took to a mandatory fashioning of the contract of employment. The legislation and administrative measures concerned with the reduction of the problem of low pay can usefully be viewed in these terms (see above, pp. 143ff.).

It should not, however, be thought that the interesting aspect of the legal control of the content of employment is confined to or even primarily attaches to the method or technique of legal intervention. The other type of inquiry one should seek to pursue throughout is into the relationship between norms created by law and norms created by practice (especially perhaps by the practice of joint regulation). This inquiry permeates our discussion of implied terms; but it also takes us into regions not hitherto identified as distinct areas of study in expositions of individual employment law. We shall suggest that it is useful to consider further aspects of the control of remuneration under the heads of control of payment systems, control of security of earnings and control of payment structures. These are areas hitherto not clearly identified as distinct topics in legal treatises because the intensity of legal intervention varies so greatly within them.

Thus far our account of legal control of the content of employment will have concentrated somewhat upon legal sources and techniques of reasoning (implied terms) and upon various dimensions of control of remuneration (payment systems, security of earnings, payment structures). In a concluding section we shall turn our attention more to the control of the content of employment viewed as a social relationship and viewed also in terms of the control of reactions of employer and employee to changes in their mutual behaviour or normative demands upon each other. For these purposes we shall consider the topic of discipline, which will provide a link with the ensuing topic of control of termination of employment.

(c) Exemption from statutory regulation on the basis of collectively bargained arrangements

Earlier in this introduction we stated that one of our principal concerns when discussing individual employment law would be the interrelationship between statutory regulation and the processes of collective bargaining. In other words, we shall be concerned with the extent to which the law assumes a regulatory or on the other hand an auxiliary role in relation to collective bargaining, so far as the control of the employment relationship is concerned.[1] By way of introduction to the larger discussion which follows it will be useful to draw together in one place the different examples of one particular aspect of the contrast between regulatory and auxiliary legal intervention. This aspect consists in the practice which has grown up of qualifying regulatory statutes by provisions enabling the Secretary of State for Employment to confer exemption from statutory regulation in favour of collectively bargained arrangements. It is worth examining in relation to the different examples of this practice the particular auxiliary aim with which each provision was made, and the effect that each provision has had upon collective bargaining practice

---

[1] The contrast between regulatory and auxiliary legislation is explained by Kahn-Freund in *Labour and the Law*, 2nd edn (1977), pp. 46–8.

in the area concerned, so far as this can be known.

The first major instance of a legislative provision of the kind under consideration occurred in section 11 of the RPA 1965, now EPCA 1978, s.96, which enabled the Secretary of State for Employment (as he now is) to make orders conferring exemption from the Act where he is satisfied that the statutory redundancy payments provisions should not apply to employees who have a right to severance payments under a collective agreement. There has to be an application for this purpose by all the parties to the agreement concerned, and the agreement has to indicate the willingness of the parties to it to submit questions concerning individual rights to redundancy payment to an industrial tribunal. It would seem that this provision for exemption orders was made not so much because it was felt that there were many existing collectively-bargained schemes in respect of which exemption would be sought, but rather because it was expected that the particular conditions prevailing in certain industries would render the pattern of the RPA 1965 an unsuitable one, and would lead to the formulation of collectively-bargained alternatives as being more suitable to the requirements of the particular industry. It was thought for instance that the RPA 1965 would be ill-adapted to the needs of the construction industry, with its pattern of employments lasting in very many cases for much less than two years, the statutory qualifying period. In fact, relatively little use has been made of the facility of seeking exemption orders, and this probably reflects the general fact that the Act was for some years at least seized upon by all concerned as a convenient alternative to collective bargaining about redundancy payments, rather than as a stimulus to the making of different collectively-bargained arrangements. Although there is a good deal of ad hoc bargaining about the size of redundancy payments when redundancy situations actually arise, there is much less bargaining in advance about protection in the event of redundancy. Even when such bargaining does occur it is likely to operate by way of *supplementation* of the statutory scheme, and the collective bargaining parties would be unlikely to feel any very great incentive to seek exemption from the statutory scheme. In a sense the main demand for exemption from statutory regulation was tacitly embodied in the 1965 Act itself by the omission of civil service employees from the ambit of its provisions (see now EPCA 1978, s.138). The use of the formal statutory exemption mechanism has been, in effect, confined to certain isolated situations where employers and unions have made agreements for continuity of employment upon transfers within a group of employers outside the scope of the statutory provision for continuity – see SI 1980 No. 1052 (a group of voluntary aided schools); SI 1969 No. 207 (Centrax Group); SI 1970 No. 354 (Electricity Board). Those have been instances where the statutory scheme has been varied by collective bargaining rather than replaced by collective bargaining.

The second set of provisions for exclusions was made in respect of the unfair dismissal legislation. It was orginally contained in s.31 of the Industrial

Relations Act 1971 and re-enacted in TULRA 1974. It enabled the Secretary of State, on the application of all parties to the agreement, to designate a dismissal procedure agreement as operating in substitution for the Act's provisions concerning unfair dismissal, if the following rather elaborate conditions are satisfied:

EPCA 1978, s.65(2)

(2) On any such application the Secretary of State may make such an order if he is satisfied –
(a) that every trade union which is a party to the dismissal procedures agreement is an independent trade union;
(b) that the agreement provides for procedures to be followed in cases where an employee claims that he has been, or is in the course of being, unfairly dismissed;
(c) that those procedures are available without discrimination to all employees falling within any description to which the agreement applies;
(d) that the remedies provided by the agreement in respect of unfair dismissal are on the whole as beneficial as (but not necessarily identical with) those provided in respect of unfair dismissal by this Part;
(e) that the procedures provided by the agreement include a right to arbitration or adjudication by an independent referee, or by a tribunal or other independent body, in cases where (by reason of an equality of votes or for any other reason) a decision cannot otherwise be reached; and
(f) that the provisions of the agreement are such that it can be determined with reasonable certainty whether a particular employee is one to whom the agreement applies or not.

This was a provision enabling private *machinery* of dispute settlement to be the basis of exemption from the statutory provisions. It thus went further than the RPA 1965 which had said that there could be a private set of norms governing redundancy pay, but that the statutory machinery must still be used for adjudication. In this case there was certainly no supposition on the part of the legislators that dismissal procedures already existed on a large scale which would qualify for designation under this provision. But there was the hope of stimulating the making of dismissal procedure agreements, or at least the prediction that many employers would wish to make such agreements in order to ensure that dismissal disputes would come before jointly constituted domestic tribunals rather than before the less specialized and more public industrial tribunals. In the event, however, there has been little impetus towards substituting collectively agreed dismissal procedures for those of the legislation. There has been a good deal of revision of dismissal procedures and some development of jointly agreed procedures by employers anxious to ensure that dismissals will not be found to be unfair, but this has not led to applications for exemption from the statute. Perhaps the prospect of an appeal to an industrial tribunal or to other independent arbitration, where the voluntary procedure results in deadlock (see EPCA 1978, s.65(2)(e)), is seen as a threat to the integrity of the procedure and hence as an unacceptable price to pay for exclusion of the statute. There is one important exception. In 1979 an exemption order (dated 14 September 1979 but not embodied in a statutory instrument and therefore unpublished) was made in respect of the electrical contracting industry on the basis of a dismissal procedure provided by the Joint Industrial Board for that industry, which is a body jointly established, between the main employers' association and the main union for that industry. The procedure differs from the statutory procedure in that there are neither qualifying periods of service under it nor limitation periods for invoking it, and it seems to realize the objectives which underlie the provision for exemption from the statute in that reinstatement is much more freely awarded as the appropriate remedy under this procedure than under the statutory process, presumably because the domestic nature of the procedure makes reinstatement a more acceptable remedy in the view of all concerned (cf. below, p. 493).

Finally, the EPA 1975 made two more provisions for statutory exemption in favour of collectively bargained arrangements. The first of these was s.107, which enables the Secretary of State for Employment to adapt, modify or exclude any of the provisions of Part IV of the Act concerning procedure for handling redundancies. Such adaptation, modification or exclusion may take place where the Secretary of State is satisfied that arrangements which are on the whole at least as favourable to the employees concerned as the provisions of Part IV are made by a collective agreement, establishing arrangements for providing alternative employment for employees dismissed as redundant or arrangements for the handling of redundancies. This provision was inserted into Part IV during the passage of the Employment Protection Bill through Parliament; its insertion was perhaps to reflect an anxiety lest our obligation to comply with the relevant EEC Directive (No. 75/129 – see (1976) 5 *ILJ* 24) should be allowed to override existing collectively bargained arrangements by statutory mechanisms. In the event, use has not to our knowledge so far been made of these exemption provisions. The making of arrangements for providing alternative employment for redundant employees, or the making of arrangements for the handling of redundancies, tends to be an ad hoc reaction to particular redundancy situations, save perhaps so far as very large companies, groups of companies and public authorities are concerned. In a sense exemption provisions of this kind may be said to provide insufficient incentive to bring about the formulation of new collectively bargained procedures, for employers will tend, perhaps, to direct those organizational resources, which would be required to bring about new collectively bargained procedures, towards complying with the new forms of statutory regulation and the avoidance of liabilities under the statute, rather than towards the achievement of exemption from the statute.

This state of affairs in relation to redundancy payments, unfair dismissal provisions and procedures for handling redundancies may be sharply contrasted with the situation arising under the other of the two provisions of this kind originally contained in the EPA 1975. EPCA 1978, s.18 enables the

Secretary of State for Employment to confer exemption from the guarantee payments provisions, where there is in force a collective agreement or wages order providing employees with a right to guaranteed remuneration. The conditions upon which the Secretary of State may make such an order corresponded very closely with the conditions imposed by the equivalent provision under the RPA as described above, except that the right of complaint to an industrial tribunal in respect of the employer's failure to pay the whole or part of any guaranteed remuneration to which the employee is entitled under the collective agreement may be either to an internal procedure containing a final arbitration stage or to an industrial tribunal (EPCA 1978, s.18(4)). There clearly already exist many collectively bargained guaranteed pay arrangements making it possible to apply for exemption from the statute by merely inserting a new clause into the existing arrangements, enabling individual employees to make claims in respect of non-payment to internal procedures or to industrial tribunals. Twenty-one exemption orders had been made by 1982.

In some cases the employee is simply given the right to apply to an industrial tribunal as an addition to the possibility of his union raising the matter in the parties' own disputes procedure. Thus in Guarantee Payments (Exemption) (No. 13) Order 1977 (SI 1977 No. 1601) an agreement between the Multiwall Sack Manufacturers Employers' Association and various unions provides: 'Any dispute arising from this Agreement shall be dealt with under the Recognition and Procedure Agreements between the parties to this Agreement. Any employee may refer a complaint concerning guaranteed remuneration to which the employee is entitled under this Agreement to an industrial tribunal.' In other cases the employee is confined to the voluntary procedure, but with the possibility of arbitration, as in the agreement between the Refractory Users Federation and various unions (Guarantee Payments (Exemption) (No. 12) Order 1977 (SI 1977 No. 1583)):

6. *Handling of Disputes*

A dispute concerning entitlement to guaranteed minimum weekly earnings may in the event of a failure to agree at Stage 3 of Procedure (Clause 22.4) be referred for the arbitration of one or more independent persons appointed by the Advisory, Conciliation and Arbitration Service for the purpose.

Section 22 – *Recognition and Conciliation*

22.2 *Stage 1*

Procedure for negotiating any complaint must in the first place be through and by the Card Steward with his immediate supervisor or such other representative as may be or have been appointed by the Employer. In the event of there being a failure to agree the complaint is to be referred to the General Foreman or Site Agent of the Employer. Facilities will be provided for the Card Steward to carry out these duties.

22.3 *Stage 2*

In the event of failure to agree between the parties to the dispute on site the dispute is to be referred for negotiation between the Regional Representative of the Trade Union and a Representative of the Employer concerned.

22.4 *Stage 3*

In the event of failure to agree locally, the matter in dispute is to be referred to a Disputes Panel comprising an equal number of representatives nominated by the Federation and by the Head Offices of the Trade Unions. The decision of such a Panel shall be binding on both parties.

What is the position of an individual who disagrees with a conclusion of the Disputes Panel under Stage 3 of the Procedure that he is not entitled to a guarantee payment?

Hence in general the success of statutory provisions designed to bring about an auxiliary rather than a regulatory role for the legislation in question seems to depend very largely upon the extent to which existing collectively bargained arrangements already provide the basis for seeking exemption with little or no modification of their terms. Where this is not the case the strong tendency seems to be to adopt the statutory provisions as an alternative to new types of collective bargaining arrangements rather than as a stimulus towards them.

2 **Implied terms**

This section deals with the various sources of terms of contracts of employment apart from the source of express agreement between the parties as individuals. It is by the importation of terms from other, extraneous, sources that the law gives shape and substance to the contract of employment. Legislation and case-law combine to mould an ostensibly individual contracting process into a well-defined pattern or series of patterns. Hence political, social, and economic assumptions and value-judgments of very great importance are embodied in the legal rules whereby terms are implied into contracts of employment. The implying of terms into contracts of employment is a process of standardization. The standards are of various kinds – customary, collective, legislative or judge-made, but there is always a displacement of individual negotiation by externally fashioned and universalized norms (though it must be borne in mind that individual negotiation may be no more than a formal notion, and that inequality of bargaining power would in many situations prevent any meaningful negotiation from occurring). We are thus talking about the formulation and imposition of the standards governing the terms on which employment takes place, and so we are speaking of matters of high significance for social policy.

Nevertheless, Parliament, although it has over the years imposed many mandatory terms of contracts of employment, has on the whole left it to the common-law courts to decide by what rules, and on what principles indeed, terms are to be implied into contracts of employment. The chief exception is section 18(4) of TULRA 1974, which lays down the rules for determining whether 'no-strike' obligations derived from collective agreements can form part of individual contracts of employment; and this, as we shall see below

(p. 777), was a special case because of its peculiar significance to the law governing industrial conflict, and so quite outside the considerations governing implied terms generally. The lack of parliamentary intervention into the process of construing the terms of contracts of employment may seem unsurprising and natural enough to the lawyer or law student accustomed to viewing the common law and the common-law courts as the obvious and natural principles and forum for the resolution of this kind of question. But this is a much less obvious or axiomatic régime from the standpoint of a concern with industrial relations and with the resolution of disputes arising out of employment by the most straightforward and expeditious means. Activated by concerns of the latter kind, Parliament did indeed intervene, in the shape of the Contracts of Employment Act 1963, to require employers to issue employees with particulars of the main terms of their contracts of employment and to entrust to industrial tribunals the job of deciding whether the particulars as issued were complete and correct. But although, as we shall see in the course of the present section, this legislation had a very great impact upon the way contracts of employment were subsequently construed, it stopped short of transferring to industrial tribunals the primary process of construction itself and it stopped short also of laying down rules as to how that construction was to be carried out. Moreover, the enormous growth from that time onwards of individual employment legislation, much of it built upon the foundation of the common-law contract of employment, has necessitated even more reliance on the rather loosely textured principles of construction of that contract to resolve disputes essentially about statutory rights. We shall for that reason have to conduct a rather careful survey of a not uncomplicated landscape in order to understand how terms are currently implied into contracts of employment.

(a) Rule-books issued by employers
Employers, particularly larger employers, frequently issue to their employees handbooks known as 'Works Rules' which contain a mixture of rules of work, descriptions of the employer's enterprise and guidance as to the facilities which the employer makes available to the employee or requires him to use. The contractual status of such works rules is a matter of some controversy. The difficulties have been, if anything, increased since the CEA 1963 brought the statutory particulars of terms into being (see p. 277). Sometimes the works rules are treated by employers as a way of providing the required particulars of employment; at other times, particulars of terms are issued without reference to works rule-books, yet the latter are apparently regarded as retaining their original force. The leading judicial authority on the contractual status of works rules suggests that they operate not as terms of contracts of employment but rather as instructions representing the employer's statement for the time being as to how the employee's obligation of obedience (see below, p. 311) is to be fulfilled. However, as the following extract shows, the real concern of the court

in that case was to establish that the rule-book did not contain an *exhaustive* statement of the employee's contractual duties – because in the court's view the employees were subject to an overriding contractual duty of co-operation (see below, p. 309) – and it is not obvious why the rules in question should have been denied contractual status altogether. The issue was whether a 'work-to-rule' was in breach of individual contracts of employment.

Secretary of State for Employment v. *ASLEF*
(No. 2) [1972] ICR 19 (CA)

LORD DENNING M.R.: For this purpose, of course, we must consider what their contracts of employment are and see whether this conduct is in breach of those contracts. So we have been referred to the contracts of employment. They are contained in a series of collective agreements made by the Railways Board with the trade unions. The terms are set out in some books which have been put before us. They contain detailed provisions on all sorts of matters, such as hours of duty, meal times, rates of pay, rest days and so forth.

The rule book is entirely different. It has 280 pages and 239 rules with many sub-rules. Each man signs a form saying that he will abide by the rules. But these rules are in no way terms of the contract of employment. They are only instructions to a man as to how he is to do his work. Some of them are quite out of date, such as that the coal on the engine must not be stacked too high. Others contain trivial details, such as that the employees must on duty be neat in appearance. A few are important in this case, particularly rule 2(1), which says that employees must see that the safety of the public is their chief care under all circumstances, a rule to which all would subscribe. Rule 126(1), which was specially emphasized in the instructions to the men, says: 'The driver and fireman MUST . . . satisfy themselves that the engine is in proper order.' Rule 176 is a compendious rule which is worth noting: 'Inspectors, shunters, guards, drivers, signalmen and all others concerned, must make every effort to facilitate the working of trains and prevent any avoidable delay.'

Those rules are to be construed reasonably. They must be fitted in sensibly the one with the other. They must be construed according to the usual course of dealing and to the way they have been applied in practice. When the rules are so construed the railway system, as we all know, works efficiently and safely. But if some of those rules are construed unreasonably, as, for instance, the driver takes too long examining his engine or seeing that all is in order, the system may be in danger of being disrupted. It is only when they are construed unreasonably that the railway system grinds to a halt. It is, I should think, clearly a breach of contract first to construe the rules unreasonably, and then to put that unreasonable construction into practice.

If one examines employee handbooks in use one finds that they are frequently ambiguous as to their contractual status. They often contain an historical accretion of different views about the terms in which an employer can appropriately issue working guidelines to his employees. There is often a set of 'company rules' reminiscent of times when employers were free to post their own rules of conduct on the walls of the factory and to regard them as having almost the force of bye-laws. There are then to be found 'conditions of contract' which seek to impose specifically contractual obligations upon employees in respect of matters such as membership of the company's pension scheme. There are, finally, often statements of enlightened policies of personnel management and appeals to goodwill and a shared sense of purpose as between the company and its workforce. Examples of the different modes of norm-making in relation to employees are to be found in the following extracts from a set of works rules. To what extent is each of them capable of giving rise to contractual obligations?

PERSONNEL AND TRAINING POLICY

The Company's success and progress involves a constant improvement to methods and the design of new and better products, but above all progress is dependent upon its investment in personnel. We must have fresh people coming forward, either from within the Company by developing the talents of existing employees, or from outside by the recruitment of qualified people. Those with ability are scarce, so generally we must depend on our own resources for success.

The Company's personnel policy is therefore –

  (a) By education, training, selection and opportunity to encourage everyone to make their fullest contribution;
  (b) To make manpower an important determining factor in our forward planning, thus avoiding extensive recruitment and redundancy;
  (c) To retain our good overall standard in earnings and conditions and to ensure fair discipline without favouritism;
  (d) To give all employees an opportunity for promotion based on their ability, judging every employee by the value of the service they give to the Company;
  (e) The communication with employees by providing an opportunity for joint consultation and negotiation by way of Staff and Works Councils.

TRAINING

The Company believes that job training is an essential part of its operation. Laid down training programmes are in use for most factory operators. Additional training programmes are written and implemented for specialists' jobs as required.

The Company runs in-Company training courses on various subjects to which employees may be seconded. In addition, to assist in the personal development of any employee and to further technical knowledge, employees may be nominated to attend external courses. . . .

DISCIPLINARY POLICY

This disciplinary policy is a statement of the general disciplines which apply to employees who have completed the probationary period, i.e. 6 months of continuous service. It is published in connection with provisions under the Employment Protection Act and is to be read in conjunction with the Statement of Employment.

In normal circumstances any employee joining the Company will anticipate continued employment provided that the conditions are satisfactory and the required performance maintained. There will inevitably be occasional situations when the application of discipline arrangements, including dismissal, are necessary, therefore, rules and procedures are essential for promoting fairness and order in the treatment of individuals and the maintenance of good industrial relations. It follows that employees should understand that misconduct or lack of ability to carry out expected job requirements could result in disciplinary action being taken. The action will depend on circumstances of the individual case and could include warnings, transfer to other work, suspension or dismissal. . . .

WAGE STRUCTURE

Job grading
All jobs have been graded under the Company's Job Evaluation Scheme (Appendix 1), which was adopted as a fair method of assessing your job and fixing the appropriate basic rate, which may vary according to the job in which you are employed. Whilst it is to the advantage of yourself and the Company that you should become established in your particular job, it may be essential on occasions, at the discretion of the Company, for a transfer without notice, either temporarily or permanently, to take place. The wide experience thus obtained makes you more valuable to the Company and creates greater job interest.

Incentive bonus
The bonus can be earned by all operatives who are employed on jobs that have been measured and to which the Company's Work Measurement Based Incentive Scheme has been applied. The amount of bonus is determined by applying a bonus percentage to the basic rate of pay for the hours worked on incentive. This percentage, for example, at a standard performance is 22.3%.

New employees and anybody transferred to incentive based jobs receive a merit payment until they are fully trained and able to participate in incentive earnings.

Merit payment
Employees whose jobs are not included in the Company's Work Measurement Based Incentive Scheme are eligible for merit payment. . . .

TIME RECORDING
With the exception of full time hourly staff, all employees are required to record their working hours on a clock card. This enables the Wages Department to calculate pay entitlement correctly. The Company considers it a serious offence justifying instant dismissal to clock the card of another employee.

Employees leaving early or arriving 3 minutes after normal starting times have pay deducted to the nearest quarter hour. Later comers must report to their Foreman before commencing work and staff employees are also required to give their names to the Security Officer at the gate house. Late starts over one hour have to be specially authorized.

An employee leaving the Company's premises during working hours must obtain a pass out slip from the Foreman to give to the Security Officer. Non-staff and part time employees should give their names to Security when leaving and returning to the premises. Shift employees are permitted to leave Company premises during their paid meal break providing non-staff employees clock out and in and staff employees advise Security.

HOURS OF WORK
You normally work a forty hour week, spread over five days or shifts. In the case of continuous shift workers a shift rota gives an average working week of 42 hours over a four week cycle. The starting and finishing times vary and are dependent on the job

being performed. . . .

Your individual hours are as set out in the last page of this statement. All employees are required to work reasonable overtime as the need arises. Overtime must be authorized in advance by your Supervisor and payment will be made for the authorized time at the appropriate overtime rate. Employees working on a continuous shift system are required to cover, by overtime working, absence of their colleagues due to holidays, sickness or other unforeseen circumstances. Every effort will be made to provide cover for sustained absence. . . .

STAFF STATUS AND SPECIAL AWARDS

On the recommendation of your Supervisor, after completing five years' continuous full time service you will be considered for appointment to hourly staff status. The advantages of Staff Status are as follows:–

(a) Increased benefits if absent due to sickness;
(b) Full time employees will no longer be required to record working hours on a clock card;
(c) An extra hourly sum is included in your wage calculation.

In recognition of continuous service (whether full time or part time) with the Company you will be presented with a gold service pin every five years. Twenty-five years' service is additionally recognized by the presentation of a gold watch and an invitation to join the Quarter Century Club, which holds an annual dinner. . . .

GENERAL CONDITIONS
WORKS COUNCIL

As the Works Council provides a direct channel of communication between employees and Management, it is a most important part of the Company's procedure for negotiation and consultation with its employees.

All departments are represented on the Council and the employee committee members are elected annually in January by a properly constituted election. The Factory Manager acts as Chairman and the Personnel Manager together with other Management representatives are nominated by the Company. The Council generally meets once a month and any matters affecting the general terms and conditions of employment can be discussed.

An employee wishing to raise any matter associated with the work of the department should first discuss it with his Foreman. If the Foreman cannot assist, the matter may then be referred to the Works Council representative for discussion with the Superintendent following which it can be raised at the next meeting of the Council.

The existence of the Works Council in no way affects an employee's right to belong to or not to belong to any particular union or organization.

Works rules in general are based upon a strong assumption of unilateral regulation-making powers on the part of employers; hence, perhaps, the tendency towards emphasis on community of objective between employers and their workforce as some palliative against the coercive nature of the works rules. The survey conducted by E.O. Evans of works rule-books in the engineering industry brought to light the equivocality of the aims of many such sets of works rules, as the following extract demonstrates. It reveals the same

confusion between the employer's norm-making function and his infor-
mation-giving or administrative function as we shall see exists in relation to
statutory statements of contractual terms (see below, p. 279).

> E.O. Evans, 'Works Rule Books in the Engineering
> Industry' (1971) 2 *IRJ* 54 at p. 58

When asked why they had rule books, managers tended to reply in terms of the book
providing information, and further questioning usually revealed that the information
they had in mind was of an administrative kind: pension rights, the firm's welfare
benefits, entitlements to special leave and procedures in connexion with these seemed
to be uppermost in their thoughts, and it was not uncommon for managers to say that it
was the constant need to deal with such queries which had led to the production of a
rule book in the first place.

In contrast to this verbal testimony, examination of the texts shows them to be full of
wide ranging claims of managerial 'rights' and strongly worded clauses referring to the
'obligations' of employees, which read as if they are designed to support the employer's
position should the terms of the contract ever come to the judgment of a court of law.

The simplest explanation for this apparent conflict between how managers see their
rules and what the rules actually say would be that though employers do not take the
legal aspect of rule books very seriously and think it only a remote possibility that they
may ever be involved with the courts over them, they do nevertheless take the
precaution to cover themselves. Or, since the doctrine of 'managerial functions' is still
an explicit part of Federation Procedure, the rule books may simply reflect this, without
reflecting the way in which such claims are significantly moderated in practice by the
power situation on the shop floor.

While these explanations have an attractive simplicity about them they do not seem
entirely adequate. Since engineering books are not peculiar in this respect – those of
other industries reading much the same – it might be that managers tend to take for
granted, as part of their perception of the situation, that the law supports an
employment relationship in which managerial prerogative is legitimate and proper,
and that though they recognize that in practice the courts are rarely appealed to, they
may think that if they *were* they would support the employer. The fact that both
employers and trade unions are traditionally reluctant to seek clarification of these
matters in the courts means that such views as managers may hold are rarely tested
against reality.

(b) **Custom, practice and statutory statements of contractual terms**

Tillyard, writing in 1923, illustrated the contract of service formed by conduct
by describing the case where a labourer is picked out by the foreman from
among a group of men waiting at the factory gate for work, who asks no
questions about his terms because he has been out of work for some time, and
discovers what his hours and wages are either by asking his mates or by finding
out by experience on pay-day (see Tillyard, *The Worker and the State*, 1st edn
(1923), p. 4). We can see from Tillyard's model of the formation of the contract
of employment how strong the tendency has been to rationalize the informally
created contract of employment as a process whereby the employee accepts

employment according to the custom and practice prevailing in the employment he enters.

Although this approach to the informally created contract of employment has been somewhat overtaken by the effects of the CEA 1963 (see below, p. 277), it retains residual importance in relation to terms and conditions not covered by the statutory provisions for written particulars of terms (as was recently illustrated, in relation to an employer's contractual right of lay-off, by the judgment of the EAT delivered by Arnold J, in *Waine* v. *Oliver (Plant Hire) Ltd* [1977] IRLR 434). It also helps to explain the approach to implied terms derived from collective bargaining (see below, pp. 281ff.).

The approach which treats workplace custom as a source of contractual terms appears on the face of it to represent a sympathy towards workgroup autonomy and workgroup regulation of patterns of working. Certainly writers on industrial relations and labour history have attached importance to customs and practice as a form of worker regulation. They have observed a continuity between the protective trade customs of nineteenth-century craftsmen and the 'custom and practice' in industry at the present day. For example, Clegg described how building workers in the nineteenth century sought to protect the customs of their trades against the growth of 'general contracting' because the general contractor would be unlikely to observe the traditional rules and customs of the various specialized building trades. Clegg shows how trade customs gave way to direct trade-union decisions about minimum conditions for the acceptance of work and how these decisions in turn gave way to collective bargaining, but in such a way as to leave some matters still controlled by 'custom and practice', for instance, rules governing apprenticeship or rules governing promotion to skilled jobs on the basis of seniority (Clegg, *The System of Industrial Relations in Britain*, 3rd edn (1976), pp. 4–6).

However, the Webbs sought to show how custom and practice, as a determinant of wages and conditions on a wide scale, amounted to little more than a perception of minimum levels for subsistence within different trades and social groups, and how even as such it was so dubious and imprecise as to be an ineffective method of regulation of terms. They described how, as a matter of more or less instinctive custom, 'the young engineer or plumber, unencumbered by wife or child, indignantly refuses to work for a wage upon which millions of his fellow-citizens not only exist, but marry and bring up families' (see Sidney and Beatrice Webb, *Industrial Democracy* (1897), pp. 693–7).

In the form in which it is encountered in more recent industrial relations history, custom and practice appears as a more specific institution than the generalized instinctive standards the Webbs have in mind; but its relationship to the contract of employment is none the clearer for that. For custom and practice is a rule-making process only in a very unusual sense. It consists of an area of departures from the formal rules of work by the workforce, which is more or less tacitly acquiesced in by management and vice versa. This state of affairs amounts to an assertion within groups of workers of a degree of self-regulation which countervails managerial prerogative – but only in a very informal sense does it result in rules or norms of work. The peculiarly intangible relationship between workers and management which results from custom and practice is well illustrated by the following passage.

William Brown, *Piecework Bargaining* (1973), p. 103

The Acceptance of C&P

Although C&P rules become widely accepted as a solid basis for working relationships between junior management and men, the attitude of senior management to them may be one of studied avoidance and disapproval. Although C&P may be pragmatically accepted as 'the way things are done' at shopfloor level, senior management may deny the legitimacy of the rules.

An example of this is given by a factory where it had been tradition for many years for pieceworkers in the machine shop to 'black' jobs on which they failed to gain an acceptable job value. Management then customarily took the jobs 'off the clock' onto time rates although they recognized that this was 'contrary to all national agreements'. In the mid-1960s management decided that 'to minimize repercussions, while not sanctioning blacking' they would not ask workers on subsequent shifts to touch blacked jobs. Consequently this became established as a C&P rule. When a new works manager arrived he tried to reverse the practice, so precipitating a series of strikes. The particular interest of the case for this discussion is that there was a difference of opinion among senior management on this. The personnel department argued that he should 'respect C&P' and that if he wanted to change the rule he should take it through procedure. The works manager refused to credit any legitimacy to what he considered a scandalous practice.

Hence it follows that if the practice of the workplace is to be taken as a guide to the terms of the contract of employment, certain questions must be answered, i.e.

1. Is the practice the outcome of (a) managerial prerogative, (b) joint regulation or (c) 'custom and practice' in its technical industrial relations sense?
2. Which of these is the relevant criterion of contractual terms?
3. Is the practice concerned intended to be the subject of a contractual term?

If we turn to consider the judicial authorities on custom as a source of contractual terms, we do not find that these issues have been considered, nor do we find the sympathy for workgroup self-regulation which might be thought to follow from the notion of custom as a source of implied terms. Instead, the courts seem to have identified the practices of employers, in the exercise of managerial prerogative, as giving rise to terms implied by conduct merely because the employees have acquiesced in the practices concerned. This view of the judicial approach was exemplified in the following passage from *Sagar* v. *Ridehalgh*. The passage cited should also be contrasted with the judgment at first instance in the same case ([1930] 2 Ch. 117), where Farwell J. stood out against the recognition of 'customs' which amounted to the conferment of unlimited managerial discretion upon the employer (see ibid., pp. 132–4).

Sagar v. *Ridehalgh & Son Ltd* [1931] 1 Ch. 310 (CA)

LAWRENCE L.J.:

The employers based their contention [that the practice of making deductions for bad work formed part of the plaintiff's contract of service] on two alternative grounds; either that the established practice of making reasonable deductions for bad work in the defendants' mill was incorporated into the plaintiff's contract of service by reason of his having agreed to be employed upon the same terms as the other weavers in that mill, or else that the general usage of making reasonable deductions for bad work prevailing in the cotton weaving trade of Lancashire was so well known and understood that every weaver engaging in that trade must be taken to have entered upon his employment on the footing of that usage.

As regards the first of these grounds, it is clearly established by the evidence of Mr George Ridehalgh that the practice of making reasonable deductions for bad work has continuously prevailed at the defendants' mill for upwards of thirty years, and that during the whole of that time all weavers employed by the defendants have been treated alike in that respect. The practice was therefore firmly established at the defendants' mill when the plaintiff entered upon his employment there. Further, I think that it is clear that the plaintiff accepted employment in the defendants' mill on the same terms as the other weavers employed at the mill. I draw this inference not only from the statement of claim (as explained by the particulars) and from the plaintiff's own evidence, but also from the fact that this action is avowedly brought to test the legality of the practice prevailing at the defendants' mill, and not to determine whether this particular plaintiff was employed upon some special terms which would make that practice inapplicable to his contract of service. Although I entirely agree with the learned judge in finding it difficult to believe that the plaintiff did not know of the existence of the practice at the mill, I think that it is immaterial whether he knew of it or not, as I am satisfied that he accepted his employment on the same terms as to deductions for bad work as the other weavers at the mill.

In the result, I have come to the conclusion that the practice of making reasonable deductions for bad work prevailing at the defendants' mill was incorporated in the plaintiff's contract of service.

Further, I am of opinion that the second ground is also established by the evidence – namely, that the practice in the defendants' mill is in accordance with the general usage of making reasonable deductions for bad work prevailing in the weaving trade of Lancashire, which usage, in the absence of any stipulation to the contrary, would be incorporated into every contract of service as a weaver in a Lancashire cotton mill without special mention. This usage seems to me to receive recognition in the Joint Rules for the Settlement of Trade Disputes appended to the Uniform List of Prices (to which Rules both the plaintiff and the defendants were subject: see p. 3 of the plaintiff's particulars delivered on 8 May 1929) inasmuch as r. 4 expressly provides that in the case of an underpayment by the employer of the Uniform List of Prices where the employer either admits the underpayment or refuses to consent to an inspection of the work, the workman is to be at liberty to take whatever action he thinks fit without the necessity of bringing the matter before either the Local or Central Employers' Committee.

In a much more recent decision, the requirements of reasonableness, certainty and notoriety were applied much more rigorously than by the Court of Appeal in the *Sagar* case, with the result that the court rejected a customary term alleged on behalf of the employers. This was the case of *Bond* v. *CAV Ltd* [1983] IRLR 360, where one of the issues in relation to one of the plaintiffs was whether there was a customary term of employment entitling the employer to lay the employee off without pay in the event of dislocation of production due to an industrial dispute. Peter Pain J. held that any such custom of the trade had been subsumed into the engineering national collective agreement concerning guaranteed pay of 1964 and that, outside the operation of that agreement, there was no custom affecting the particular employment in question which supported the term alleged by the employers and passed the tests of reasonableness, certainty and notoriety. This seems much more in accordance with current thinking about the implication of terms of employment than does the approach of the Court of Appeal in *Sagar*. For, as we shall see, the courts have in recent years assumed such extensive powers to imply terms on the basis of reasonableness alone that it is unlikely that they would regard it as necessary or advantageous to engage in elaborate evaluation of alleged trade custom, for which the incorporation tests remain relatively severe.

As we indicated above, the sphere of operation of terms derived from custom and practice has been curtailed by the provisions for statutory statements of the principal terms and conditions of employment as originally contained in s.4 of the Contracts of Employment Act 1963 and as now contained in the EPCA 1978, s.1. A study of the effects of the legislation was recently published by Leighton and Dunville, engagingly titled 'From Statement to Contract' ((1977) 6 *ILJ* 133). They show how in the eyes of the courts the written statements of terms, although clearly intended, as they put it, to confirm what was already in existence and not to create anything at all, have inexorably assumed the character of contractual documents whose terms are binding upon the parties. We shall see later what difficulties this has caused in relation to the incorporation of the results of collective bargaining into individual contracts of employment (below, pp. 281ff.).

Leighton and Dunville go on to show, by reference to a survey of the practice of employers in the Lea Valley which they conducted, how dangerous it would be to assume that employees generally were being kept reliably informed in writing of their principal terms of employment. This is first because of the weakness and impracticability of the enforcement machinery, which consists essentially of the supply of particulars or amendment of defective particulars by industrial tribunals. It looked at one stage, following the decision in *Construction Industry Training Board* v. *Leighton* [1978] IRLR 60, as if the industrial tribunals would be denied jurisdiction to construe contractual terms or rectify statutory particulars where there was no evidence of positive agreement between the parties as to the terms in question. The Court of Appeal has since asserted a more creative view of this jurisdiction in *Mears* v. *Safecar Securities Ltd* [1982] ICR 626, but the fact remains that there is no provision for penalizing employers or compensating employees for non-compliance with these statutory obligations. Leighton and Dunville also noted that long-serving employees were in practice at a disadvantage, either because employers failed to issue statutory statements to employees already in service when the legislation first came into effect in 1963, or because they have tended to lose their contractual statements within such substantial periods of time. The authors accordingly advocate the mandatory issuing of a fresh statement every five or ten years.

Despite these weaknesses Leighton and Dunville conclude that section 4 (EPCA 1978, s.1) nevertheless created a much greater tendency than ever existed before to issue employees with written contracts of employment and has also resulted in the issue of many documents which are ambiguous as to whether they are written contracts or written statements of terms. This last development is one of very great importance for labour lawyers, for it amounts in effect to a mixing up of the employer's role as the proposer or imposer of terms of employment with his role as the provider of information as to what the terms of employment are. This confusion is a natural one in the sense that the employer is typically in a better position than the employee both to propose or impose the norms of employment and to carry out the bureaucratic function of keeping the records as to what the employee's rights and duties are.

At the same time the legislators have some of the responsibility for intensifying this confusion, for they have chosen to use the mandatory provision of information as a form of norm-making. This first occurred when the IRA imposed upon the employer a duty to include, in the statutory statement of terms, particulars of the employee's rights in relation to trade-union membership and activity (a provision since repealed) and also details of a grievance procedure which the employee might invoke (Industrial Relations Act 1971, s.20(2)). The former of these two provisions was in practice complied with by means of a recital, paraphrase, or summary of the statutory provisions concerning trade-union membership and activity, but its intention seems to have been to go further and to require the employer to declare how those provisions applied in the particular circumstances of the employment concerned. The provision concerning notification of a grievance procedure in practice required many employers to devise a grievance procedure in order to have something to notify (now EPCA 1978, s.1(4)(*b*)).

The same result may be attributed to the further requirements which were added by the EPA 1975 that the employer should notify the employee, in the statutory statement, of any service reckonable for continuity purposes before he entered his present employment, of his job title and of any disciplinary rules applicable to him (EPCA 1978, s.1(2)(*c*), (3)(*f*), 4(*a*)). It is not surprising that a substantial number of employers first became aware of what is now EPCA 1978, s.1, when it was amended in 1971, and that some other employers first became aware of it when it was further amended in 1975, for these amendments have tended to appear to the layman to have effected substantive changes in the employee's contractual rights. This ambiguity between statement and contract serves to extend the employee's articulated rights but can, on the other hand, appear to extend the employer's normative powers. Section 1 has to that extent had an effect diametrically opposed to that of custom and practice as a source of contractual terms.

On the other hand, there has seemed recently to be a reaction on the part of the courts against the according of a normative effect to statutory particulars of terms. This is a welcome development but brings certain problems with it. The first example of this development occurred in 1981 in *System Floors (UK) Ltd* v. *Daniel* [1982] ICR 54, where the EAT allowed the employer to lead evidence proving that the employment had begun later than the statutory particulars showed, firmly taking the point that an employee's signed acknowledgement of receipt of the statement need not be an indication that it was itself the contract of employment. The second example is provided by *Jones* v. *Associated Tunnelling Co. Ltd* [1981] IRLR 477, where the EAT admitted evidence derived from the practice of the employment to show that the employee's obligation as to mobility was not as extensive as his statutory particulars suggested. The same trend may be seen as being at work in *Mears* v. *Safecar Securities Ltd* [1982] ICR 626, where the Court of Appeal held, as we saw above, that where statutory particulars were silent on the question of entitlement to sick-pay, the industrial tribunal jurisdiction to supply and correct the deficiencies of the particulars permitted the most wide-ranging inquiry into the appropriate term to be implied in the light of the practice of the particular employment relationship. This, as we shall see later (p. 308), has important consequences for the theory by which terms are implied by law into the contract of employment. It certainly swings the balance back from statutory statements of particulars towards the custom and practice of the parties as a source of terms of the contract of employment.

We indicated that we can see problems arising from this generally welcome trend. The problems consist in the fact that the courts, when they turn their gaze from statutory statements of particulars to the actual practice of the parties, do so on a very individuated basis. There is a danger that this doctrine will leave employees exposed to the weaknesses that they suffer when a model of individual bargaining is employed in matters where collective interests may be at stake or where a collective bargaining model would tend to protect their interests. Thus in the *System Floors* case, the individuated issue was how much the employee personally knew about when he was transferred from an employment agency to working for the employer directly. This perhaps masked the collective consideration that the employer was in control of the administrative process whereby that transfer occurred and the employees were not. Again, in *Jones* v. *Associated Tunnelling* what may well have been a collective issue of the extent of the mobility obligation for specialist construction workers at collieries was resolved in terms of what this individual had done or acquiesced in during his employment. Then in *Mears* v. *Safecar Securities* the Court of Appeal addressed the question of whether this employee had an entitlement to sick-pay in such individuated terms as entirely to omit any collective dimension to the issue at all:

Mears v. *Safecar Securities Ltd* [1982] ICR 626 (CA)

STEPHENSON L.J.: It was the practice of the company not to pay wages to employees absent sick, and the practice was well known to the company's employees. The company would not have made an exception in the employee's favour. He did not ask about sick pay before taking on the job, though the practice varies with different employers. If he had asked and been told what the practice was, he would most probably have taken the job. He took leave without sick pay for nearly seven months out of the 14 months his employment lasted, and never asked for sick pay but accepted what his colleagues told him was the practice, and he probably – though he disputed this – submitted no sick certificate. Even after the end of his employment he asked for holiday pay, for which the terms of reference expressly provided, and it was some time before he thought of asking for sick pay. He plainly never expected to get sick pay and he never got it. It may well be that, as Sir Stanley Rees suggested in argument, the nature of the job, guarding property, explains both the company's practice and his acquiescence in it.

A useful corrective to this severely individuated approach was provided by the EAT in the case of *Howman & Son* v. *Blyth* [1983] ICR 416, where the issue was the duration of the employer's liability to continue to pay the employee during absence due to sickness. It was held that where there was a contractual obligation to pay sick-pay but no agreed term as to its duration, an industrial tribunal should imply a reasonable term having regard to the normal practice in the industry, and that a reasonable term as to duration of sick-pay was in this case prima facie to be derived from the national working rule agreement (i.e. the national-level collective agreement) for the industry. As Browne-Wilkinson J., the President of the EAT, put it, 'In an industry where the normal practice is to provide sick pay for a limited period only, the reasonable term to imply is the term normally applicable in that industry' (ibid. at p. 420). This, as we shall shortly see, is a statement and an approach of great significance for the incorporation of collective agreements into individual contracts of employment. It also does much to reassert the importance of industry-wide custom in construing contracts of employment. But it is important not to over-estimate the availability of solutions of that kind, both in terms of their feasibility in fact situations and in terms of the willingness of the courts to approach problems of construction in that way.

Let us resume, then, with an assessment of the current standing of statutory particulars as a *de facto* (though not *de jure*) source of terms of contracts of employment. Leighton and Doyle rightly point out that 'the judgments of *System Floors* and *Jones* effectively remind employers of the immense residual power of the courts to construe employment contracts in the light of all the evidence' ((1982) 11 *ILJ* 118, 119). Those cases provided a corrective to the tendency to treat statutory particulars as conclusive of the terms of the contract of employment which as we shall see (below, p. 286) reached its high point in relation to the incorporation of collective agreements, in *Gascol Conversions Ltd* v. *Mercer* [1974] ICR 420. The corrective development of the *System Floors, Jones*, and *Mears* cases has since been taken further in *Robertson* v. *British Gas Corporation* [1983] ICR 351, which we consider below (p. 288) in the context of the incorporation of collective agreements. Between them these cases have substantially limited the power of statutory statements to override other evidence of the terms of contracts of employment. This must accord with the intentions of the legislators, whose aim was that statutory particulars should resolve disputes about contractual rights by accurately recording the contract, rather than that they should provide a pre-emptive legal determination of the content of the contract simply by adopting as binding the version of the contract preferred by the employer.

(c) **Collective bargaining**
The incorporation of norms derived from collective agreements into individual contracts of employment has been, and rightly, the focus of considerable interest on the part of labour lawyers. With the decision to accept the non-enforceability of collective agreements as contracts between the collective parties (see above, pp. 129–32) the individual contract of employment provides one of the main points of contact between the legal process and the collective bargaining process (though not the sole point of contact, another being the statutory disclosure provisions (see above, pp. 205–19)). The existence of those other dimensions to the relationship between law and collective bargaining should be kept in mind in the course of the ensuing discussion.

Accounts of the modern law of incorporation of collective agreements into individual contracts tend to distinguish between three methods of incorporation:

(1) incorporation by conduct,
(2) incorporation by agency, and
(3) incorporation by express reference in written contract or particulars.

We shall consider these three methods in turn and then discuss

(4) certain problems common to all three forms of incorporation.

We shall then on that basis attempt to arrive at

(5) a general theory of incorporation of the results of collective bargaining.

(1) *Incorporation by conduct*

The basic problems of incorporation can best be examined in relation to incorporation by conduct, sometimes known as implied incorporation. The recent development of the law on this topic finds its starting-point in Kahn-Freund's description of collective bargaining as 'crystallized custom', to be imported into contracts of employment on the same basis as trade customs. Do you think the following passage provides a satisfactory rationale for the incorporation of collectively-bargained terms into individual contracts?

> O. Kahn-Freund in *System of Industrial Relations in Great Britain*, ed. Flanders and Clegg (1954), pp. 58–9
>
> In the majority of cases, as we have seen, the parties to the contract of employment do not expressly lay down its terms, and the gap is filled by 'custom'. Here we can see the legal significance of the collective agreement. We can normally assume that its terms are the 'customary' terms and that employers and employees within its scope contract on this basis. It does not, in the writer's opinion, matter whether the worker is a member of a union party to the agreement or whether the employer is or has at any time been a member of a 'contracting' association. What does matter is whether the terms of the agreement are in fact applied in the industry and district. The wage scales and other 'codes' it contains can easily become 'crystallized custom'. If they do, they will be considered as tacitly embodied in the relevant contracts of employment. The labourer in Sir F. Tillyard's example [p. 273] will presumably be understood to have the contractual right to the 'trade union rate' of wages. Anyone desiring to find out what holidays he can claim, what hours he must work, what notice he and the employer must give, etc., will have to consult the relevant collective argeements, arbitration awards, decision of J I Cs, etc. This is not because these agreements, awards, or decisions have any legally binding force as such, but because their terms must be presumed to be implied terms of the contract of employment. What a court enforces is that contract and nothing else, but the substance of the contract is determined through the set of rules laid down in the collective agreements, etc., rules which the individual employer and employee have, by their silence, chosen to make their own and to embody in their contract. In the overwhelming majority of all cases in practice this is the way collective bargaining is translated into law, and, in so far as it is, the parties to the collective agreement act, in fact, as legislators for the trade. They act as legislators in the same sense as Parliament when it makes a law out of which the parties can contract.

The notion of 'crystallized custom' may well provide the most convincing basis for incorporation of terms from collective agreements, but it raises some of the problems of incorporating 'custom' which were discussed in section (b) above, and it also involves further problems which follow from the nature of the collective bargaining process. One such problem concerns the choice which often has to be made about which levels of bargaining are to be treated as creating individual contractual obligations. To that problem we shall revert shortly (below, pp. 294–5). The more immediate question is that of what conduct, if any, on the part of the individual worker is required to establish the link between the crystallized custom and his particular contract.

Industrial tribunals and courts in their search for a link between collective bargaining and the individual contract of employment have from time to time considered the extent of the particular worker's knowledge of and participation in the bargaining process as a basis for decision whether a particular collectively-bargained term or arrangement should be regarded as included in that worker's contract of employment. For example, in the case of *Joel* v. *Cammell Laird Ship-repairers Ltd* (1969) 4 I T R 206, the issue before an industrial tribunal was whether a collective agreement relating to transfers of employees between repair work and shipbuilding work had been incorporated into individual contracts of employment. It was held that it was incorporated into the contracts of both the applicants because they were found to be 'very conscious of trade-union affairs', and because their conduct when discussing their proposed transfer with the personnel officer demonstrated that they were aware of the relevant provision in the collective agreement. There is some artificiality in this process, since this kind of knowledge and participation differs greatly between workers who would be regarded as sharing the same terms of employment. The extreme instance of that problem is the issue of how far collective bargaining is to determine the terms and conditions of workers within the workgroup covered by the collective bargaining but who are not members of any of the recognized unions. The fact that even such workers would often derive their terms and conditions from collective bargaining demonstrates the limits of the appeal to knowledge and participation.

The courts and tribunals will tend to feel that they are on firmer ground when they can rely on some other basis than conduct for incorporating the results of collective bargaining. In *Joel* v. *Cammell Laird* the tribunal did not have to rely on conduct alone; they were also able to rely on the fact that the employees' statutory written particulars of their terms of employment referred to the collective agreement in question for the purpose of describing the employees' rates of pay. Without that, they might have hesitated to incorporate the mobility requirement on the basis of conduct alone.

There is another difficulty about the incorporation of collectively-bargained terms by reference to the conduct of the parties. Even where there is a long-standing custom of treating collective agreements as determining terms and conditions of employment, the concluding of a collective agreement may not result in an *automatic* incorporation of its results into individual contracts. This was demonstrated in *Dudfield* v. *Ministry of Works, The Times*, 24 January 1964,[1] where an increase in wages for certain government manual workers was agreed by a Joint Council (which was a joint negotiating body) for part of the industrial civil service. The Ministry refused to pay the increase because a governmental pay pause had intervened. It was held that the individual employee had no contractual claim to the increase until the Ministry had put the collective agreement into effect, or at least until Treasury authorization for

---

[1] Contrast *Brand* v. *L C C, The Times*, 28 October 1967 (Cty Ct.), where a National Joint Council award was held to be automatically incorporated in individual contracts as soon as made. But the risk of an application of *Dudfield* in future cannot be ruled out.

so doing had been received.

In one recent case, the EAT cut neatly through these difficulties of linking the collective agreement to the individual contract of employment, in a way which comes right back to Kahn-Freund's notion of crystallized custom. This was *Howman & Son* v. *Blyth* [1983] ICR 416 where, as we have seen, the issue was the duration of the employer's obligation to pay sick-pay. While it was accepted that the national working-rule agreement for the industry concerned (the building industry) did not in a formal sense form part of this employee's contract of employment, it was on the other hand adopted as the prima facie (and, in this case, decisive) guide to what would be a reasonable term to imply. As Browne-Wilkinson J. said, 'we consider that we are entitled to come to the conclusion which industrial relations common sense demands' (ibid., p. 421). But it is no coincidence that this kind of approach should have been taken in the very kind of case that Kahn-Freund most probably had in mind, namely the case where a multi-employer, indeed a national-level, collective agreement provided a widely accepted labour standard throughout an industry. As we saw in the previous chapter, that has in recent years become a less and less typical state of affairs in industry at large, with the growing predominance of single-employer collective bargaining. It is in this context that the old assumptions become hard to maintain, and give way to the necessity for a more technical approach to the incorporation of collective agreements into individual contracts.

(2) *Incorporation by agency*

At the level of the technicalities of incorporation of the results of collective bargaining into individual contracts, one of the legal doctrines which tend to be invoked is that of agency. The suggestion is that individual contracts are affected by the collective bargaining process because the union bargains as agent for the employees concerned. Whilst this concept eliminates any difficulty as to the mechanics of incorporation, the courts and tribunals have tended to be wary of the idea of the union as agent for individual workers in the bargaining process. Perhaps agency is regarded as too specific and exact a legal relationship to be capable of being effectively applied to the relationship between the union and the individual worker (see Hepple and O'Higgins, *Encyclopedia*, para. 1–104). The judicial statement most favourable to the view of the union as agent for its members occurred in the House of Lords in *Heatons Transport Ltd* v. *TGWU* [1972] ICR 308 where Lord Wilberforce, delivering the single joint opinion, said at p. 393 that by the agreement which each member entered into by joining the TGWU he 'joins with all other members in authorizing specified persons or classes of persons to do particular kinds of acts on behalf of all the members who are referred to collectively as the union'. But it must be remembered that this statement was made as a preliminary to holding that the *union* was bound by the agency of its shop stewards in the matter of industrial action, rather than that the individual was bound by the agency of the union in the matter of terms and conditions of employment. In the latter context, so far as the agency concept is deployed at all it tends to be invoked in a restrictive sense, i.e. as a reason for taking a *narrow* view of the impact of the collective agreement upon the individual contract. Thus in *Singh v. British Steel Corporation* [1974] IRLR 131 (see Hepple (1974) 3 *ILJ* 166) the issue was whether twenty Indian workers who had been members of the union BISAKTA were bound by the terms of a new shift system negotiated between that union and their employers after those workers had shown that they no longer wanted to belong to that union or it to negotiate for them. The industrial tribunal looked for evidence, either that BISAKTA had been appointed the sole negotiating agent for the workers concerned, or that their contracts of employment could be varied without their consent by agreement reached between the employers and the union. In other words, they required evidence of implied authority strong enough to override the evidence suggesting that the workers had cancelled any mandate the union might have had. Although this is not a decision of a higher court, it does show how agency is the most difficult of the three methods of incorporating the results of collective bargaining into individual contracts.

Examples are occasionally to be found of collective agreements where the union is expressly identified as the agent of the workgroup in negotiating terms, e.g. in an agreement between Henry Wiggins Ltd and the AUEW reached in 1974. But this seems to represent the isolated importation of a North American formal style of collective agreement, and cannot be said to constitute a typical approach to the collective bargaining relationship in Britain.

(3) Incorporation via statutory statements of terms
Again at the level of legal techniques for the incorporation of collective agreements into individual contracts, enormous changes have been wrought by the Contracts of Employment Acts 1963 and 1972. By requiring employers to give particulars of the major terms of employment (EPCA 1978, s.1) and by, on the other hand, enabling employers to discharge that obligation by referring to any documents containing terms and conditions of employment (EPCA 1978, s.2(3)), the legislation created a habit among employers of referring to collective agreements, especially national-level collective agreements, as sources of contractual terms, with little regard for the problem of the relationship between the collective agreement and the individual contract. Although employees are entitled to object to their particulars of terms as not representing the true terms of their contracts (EPCA 1978, s.11(2)), they can normally be relied upon not to object until a specific issue, such as a redundancy payments issue, has actually arisen, and by that time an industrial tribunal or court may well be prepared to take the view that the contract of employment incorporates the collective agreement virtually at large. If the statutory particulars happen to be headed 'Contract of

Employment' and happen to be signed by the employee, such a presumption can become virtually irrefutable,[1] as the case of *Gascol Conversions Ltd* v. *Mercer* shows. The issue in that case was whether the normal weekly working hours of a gas conversion inspector consisted of the 40 hours specified as the normal working week in the relevant national collective agreement, or of the 54-hour working week which the employee actually worked in pursuance of a local agreement for the district where the employee worked. The further relevant facts appear in Lord Denning's judgment. Was the court in your view grasping at an easy way out of the problem of incorporation of collective agreements, and ignoring real difficulties of which they should have taken account?

Gascol Conversions Ltd v. *Mercer* [1974] ICR 420 (CA)

LORD DENNING M.R.: . . . Now in this case I will assume that when Mr Mercer was first employed in 1969 there was a fixed time of 54¼ hours, which was binding on both sides. The employer was bound to provide it and the man to do it. The tribunal seem to have accepted that view. So have the Industrial Court.

But the agreement seems to have been varied later. In 1970 the men's union came to an agreement with the employers' association. The men belonged to the General and Municipal Workers Union. The employers belonged to the Gas Conversion Association. They came to an agreement in 1970, which was repeated in substance in 1971 and 1972. It was made nationally to cover all men employed in the industry:

Normal Working Week

1.1 The working week shall consist of 40 hours hereafter referred to as the normal working week. The 40 hours shall be worked Monday to Friday, 5 days of 8 hours . . .

Overtime

3.1 Employees will be expected to work overtime where necessary for completion of the conversion work. Overtime rates shall be payable for time worked in excess of 40 hours in any pay-week where so authorized by the employer.

As I read the agreement, the only fixed hours were 40 hours a week. The employers were not bound to provide any more. The men were not bound to do more. They were only 'expected' to work overtime when necessary, but were not bound to do it. Applying the *Tarmac* [[1973] ICR 273] case, the 'normal working hours' were 40 hours.

In addition to that national agreement, there was a local agreement for the district where Mr Mercer worked. We have notes of an agreement between management and union on 26 August 1971. It says:

The working hours whilst in Berwick will revert to 54 per week, and that the starting time on the Monday morning will be revised to 0800 hours (previously 0745 hours).

This was relied upon by Mr Mercer to show that there was a local agreement for 54 hours working week. But at the end of the notes there are these words:

[1] See Leighton and Dunville (1977) 6 *ILJ* 133 at pp. 134–9. The document may of course be intended from the outset to be a contract rather than particulars of a contract, in which case one is dealing with *express* incorporation of the results of collective bargaining, as in, for example, *National Coal Board* v. *Galley* [1958] 1 WLR 16; *Callison* v *Ford Motor Company Ltd* (1969) 4 ITR 74.

The parties intend that any agreements contained in these notes shall be binding in honour only, and that they should not give rise to any legal obligation.

I do not think the local agreement should be regarded as varying the national agreement: see *Loman and Henderson* v. *Merseyside Transport Services Ltd* (1968) 3 ITR 108. In any case the national agreement contains an express provision that 'where the agreement is at variance with other national and local working agreements, it is to take precedence'.

But it is unnecessary to go into those matters, because there is a supervening event of much importance. In February 1972 the Industrial Relations Act 1971 came into operation. By Schedule 2, Part II [see now EPCA 1978, s.1(3)(c)], the employer was bound to give to the employee a written statement specifying among other things '(c) any terms and conditions relating to hours of work (including any terms and conditions relating to normal working hours)'. In pursuance of that statutory obligation, the employers, Gascol Conversions Ltd, on 25 February 1972, sent a new contract of employment to each of their men. One was given a copy of it for himself to keep. He agreed to it by a document in these terms which he signed himself:

> I confirm receipt of a new contract of employment dated 25 February 1972, which sets out, as required under the Industrial Relations Act 1971, the terms and conditions of my employment.
> Signed J.W. Mercer . . . Date 21.3.72.

That was clearly a binding contract. Being reduced into writing, it is the sole evidence that is permissible of the contract and its terms. Turning to the terms themselves, the opening words are clear. They follow the very words of the national agreement:

> The normal working week consists of 40 hours which shall be worked Monday to Friday, 5 days of 8 hours, at times specified by the department concerned.
> *Overtime.* Employees will be expected to work overtime where necessary for completion of the conversion work. You will be paid at the rate of 1 ½ times the basic hourly rate on week days, and at double time on Sundays.

That agreement seems to me to be conclusive. There is no possible ground for setting it aside. There was no mistake, misrepresentation or misunderstanding of any kind. It shows that the normal working week was 40 hours and the employers were not bound to provide any more. Even the employees were not bound to work more. They were only 'expected' to work extra hours when necessary.

Faced with that agreement, Mr Mitchell had to admit it was conclusive unless he could show that subsequently to it there had been a variation of it or a waiver of some of its terms. I asked him: what evidence is there of any subsequent variation or waiver? He said that the men had gone on working the 54 hours and were being paid. That is no evidence of variation or waiver. It is quite consistent with the written agreement. The 54 hours consist of 40 hours, the normal working week, and 14 hours overtime for which they were paid 'overtime rates'. In my opinion, therefore, the redundancy payments should be calculated on normal working hours of 40 hours a week.

It has already been suggested in this chapter (p. 281) that the decision in the *Gascol* case gave a more conclusive effect to statutory particulars than the legislators seem to have intended. We have shown how in a number of cases the courts have found ways of circumventing the doctrine in the *Gascol* case;

we refer in particular to the cases of *System Floors (UK) Ltd* v. *Daniel* [1982] ICR 54, *Jones* v. *Associated Tunnelling* [1981] IRLR 477 and *Mears* v. *Safecar Securities Ltd* ICR 626 (see above, pp. 280–1). We shall show later (pp. 301–6) how, in the latter two cases in particular, ways were developed of giving effect to the actual operation of the contract in practice where that conflicted with the statutory particulars. Of special interest, however, in relation to the incorporation of collective agreements via statutory particulars, is the decision of the Court of Appeal in *Robertson* v. *British Gas Corporation* [1983] ICR 351. That was a test case to ascertain whether the Gas Corporation could effectively terminate its contractual obligation to pay incentive bonuses to meter readers/collectors by giving six months' notice to terminate the collective agreement embodying the incentive bonus scheme. The Gas Corporation relied for this purpose on the statutory statements issued to the employees, of which the relevant particulars were in these terms:

The provisions of the Agreement of the National Joint Council for Gas Staffs and Senior Officers relating to remuneration and increments will apply to you. Any payment which may, from time to time, become due in respect of incentive bonuses will be calculated in accordance with the rules of the scheme in force at the time.

The Corporation's contention was that this statement made it clear that if no bonus scheme was in force under the NJC Agreement, there was no individual contractual right to a bonus payment. The Court of Appeal held unanimously to the contrary that the termination of the bonus scheme at the collective level had not terminated the individual rights. The two principal judgments, of Ackner and Kerr L.JJ., reach this conclusion by different routes. The third judge, Sir David Cairns, simply agreed with both judgments. Of the two principal judgments, Ackner L.J.'s is the more directly concerned with the effect of the statutory particulars. He held that the *Gascol* case was to be distinguished here, as it had been in the *System Floors* case, as turning on the fact that the statutory statement was expressed to be a contract of employment and not just particulars thereof. He endorsed the view in the *System Floors* case that statutory particulars were not conclusive of the terms of the contract, and he indicated that the burden of negating the evidence of the statutory particulars might not be as heavy upon the employee as upon the employer ([1983] ICR 351, 354–5). He rejected any suggestion that the statutory particulars might have constituted a variation of the original contract, or that the employees might be estopped from denying the accuracy of the particulars, for such an estoppel would be an estoppel in support of the employer's breach of his statutory duty to supply correct particulars; so the estoppel would be an unconscionable one. He went on to hold that the true term of the contract of employment here was to be found in the letter of appointment, which said: 'Incentive bonus scheme conditions will apply to meter reading and collection work.' He held that this gave an individual right to bonus payments of some kind; the collective agreement provided the tariff for this bonus, and changes in the collective scheme would effectively change the level of payments to which the individual was entitled. But the unilateral termination of the collective agreement would simply leave the last agreed tariff still in force at the individual level.

The judgment of Kerr L.J. proceeds on the rather different footing that the difference in wording between the letter of appointment and the statutory particulars was not significant; so his judgment is equally applicable to the kind of express incorporation of terms from collective agreement that occurred, for instance, in *National Coal Board* v. *Galley* [1958] 1 WLR 16; or, for that matter, in the *Gascol* case as viewed by the Court of Appeal that decided it. The view of Kerr L.J. focused on the unilateral character of the abrogation of the collective agreement and made the point that where an individual contract of employment submitted a particular term to variation by a subsequent collective agreement, it did not thereby submit that term to being abrogated by unilateral withdrawal from the collective agreement. The employer could not rely on the reference to the collective bargaining process to give himself a freedom unilaterally to resile from individual obligations merely by exercising his undoubted freedom to withdraw from the non-legally binding collective agreement. The result is not dissimilar from that in another case about incorporation of collective agreements that we shall shortly examine, that of *Burroughs Machines Ltd* v. *Timmoney* [1977] IRLR 404 (see below, p. 296). In both cases, the link between the collective agreement and the individual contract was held to be flexible rather than rigid. The individual contract could be modified by changes at the collective level, but it could not be stultified by them. In this case, Kerr L.J. held that the incentive bonus scheme was so integral to the individual contract of employment as a whole that it could not be right to construe it as defeasible by this kind of indirect unilateral abrogation. In this respect his judgment, and indeed the decision of the Court of Appeal as a whole, exemplify a trend which we remark elsewhere in this section (p. 307), namely a tendency to take a more creative and progressive view of what is necessary for the 'business efficacy' of the contract of employment than earlier generations of judges seemed prepared to do.

(4) *Problems common to all three forms of incorporation: procedural terms and normative terms*

The process of incorporation of collective agreements into individual contracts by any of the three methods considered above requires the courts to distinguish between the procedural and the normative elements in the agreements reached. Whereas the normative parts of collective agreements are usually capable of incorporation into individual contracts, the procedural parts are in principle collective in nature and incapable of incorporation into individual contracts, unless the court undertakes deliberately to devise an individual version of the collective obligation. The point becomes all the more important in view of the preference for procedural over substantive rules in

industrial-level collective bargaining. The kind of error that can be per-
petrated when this distinction is overlooked is well illustrated by the *Camden
Exhibition* case. The relevant issue there was whether an overtime ban
amounted to a breach of individual contracts of employment.

Camden Exhibition & Display Ltd v. *Lynott*
[1966] 1 QB 555 (CA)

LORD DENNING M.R.: This is a dispute between the plaintiffs, who are the employers,
and two of their men, the defendants. It is about working overtime. It arises out of an
agreement between the employers and trade unions in the exhibition industry. This
industry is concerned with making arrangements for exhibitions, putting up stands and
so forth. It employs men of various trades, carpenters, signwriters and technicians of all
kinds. There is a National Joint Council for the industry which regulates the working of
the men. The council has an 'operatives panel' to represent the workmen's side. It has
nine men on it, three from the Woodworkers' Society, three from the Painters' Society
and three from the Building Trades' Federation. The employers' panel has nine
representatives. The National Joint Council has laid down working rules for the
industry. These rules set out rates of wages and the hours of working, namely, 40 hours
a week. There is also a rule about overtime. It is working rule 6(a): 'Overtime required
to ensure the due and proper performance of contracts shall not be subject to
restriction, but may be worked by mutual agreement and direct arrangement between
the employer and the operatives concerned.' The rates of pay for overtime are specified:
the first two hours at the rate of time-and-a-half; and thereafter until starting time next
morning, double time; and so forth. . . .

First of all, we must look at the working rules. In an ordinary contract of employment
a man is bound to work his proper hours during his working week. But he is not bound
to do overtime. Overtime is a matter for agreement between him and his employers. Do
these working rules alter the position? It seems to me that, since the Contracts of
Employment Act, 1963, these working rules are incorporated into the terms of
employment of all men in the industry. A notice was issued under that Act saying to
every man: 'Your rate of wages, hours of work, holidays and holiday pay are in
accordance with the provisions of the constitution and working rule agreement issued
by and under the authority of the National Joint Council.' In view of that notice these
working rules are not only a collective agreement between the union and the employers.
They are incorporated into the contract of employment of each man, in so far as they
are applicable to his situation.

What is the true interpretation of this working rule 6(a)? I think it is clear that the
unions agreed that when overtime was necessary to ensure the proper performance of
contracts, the unions would not impose a restriction on overtime, and would not
authorize their stewards, or anyone on their behalf, to impose a restriction on overtime.
Overtime was to be arranged by mutual agreement and direct arrangement between
the employers and the men.

Suppose that no authority is given by the unions for a ban on overtime, but some of
the men seek together to restrict overtime, without any official sanction. Does this rule
prevent it? Can the men put a collective unofficial embargo on overtime? This is a
difficult point. On the whole I think this working rule means that the men will not,
officially or unofficially, impose a collective embargo on overtime when it is required to

ensure the due and proper performance of contracts. It follows that, if the defendants did induce the men to put a collective embargo on overtime, they were inducing them to break the working rules and hence their contracts of employment.

Thus, a majority of the Court of Appeal adjudged the overtime ban to be in breach of contract, on the grounds that it violated a provision in a national-level collective agreement which they regarded as having a substantive effect both at collective and individual levels. Russell L.J., who dissented on this point, was alone in the Court of Appeal in realizing that this provision in the national-level collective agreement was intended as a *procedural* stipulation, to the effect that no maximum level would be set for overtime working at the national level of collective bargaining, and not as a normative provision whereby each employee would abjure the opportunity to limit the level of his overtime working.

RUSSELL L.J.: First of all, my present view of the construction of working rule 6(a) is that it merely states that on the National Joint Council no ceiling is imposed by the working rules upon hours of overtime, the extent of overtime working being left to agreement between employers and operatives. As I see it, in my mind's eye, the parties of the joint council round the table said: 'Are we in these rules going to fix a ceiling on the hours of overtime worked by any man?' Answer: 'No.' Hence the first part of rule 6(a). They then proceeded to say, by way of addition: 'It is to be left to agreement between operative and employer.' If that be so, it certainly cannot import into the contract of any particular operative an agreement not to limit or refuse to work overtime save for a reason special to himself. Therefore, in my view no breach of contract has been induced or procured.

As we shall see, the view can be taken that the majority of the Court of Appeal fashioned an individual contractual obligation out of a collectively bargained procedure which was normative but may have had no individual connotation. This leads to the second problem, namely that of the appropriateness of collective terms for incorporation into individual contracts.

Appropriateness for incorporation A general problem in the relationship between collective bargaining and the individual contract of employment consists in the notion of appropriateness whereby some of the matters with which collective bargaining is concerned and some of the arrangements or heads of agreement which emerge from the collective-bargaining process are deemed to have no impact upon individual contracts of employment because they are said to be inappropriate for inclusion into those individual contracts. This concept of inappropriateness addresses itself to the problems of how far collective norms can meaningfully be individuated and of how far this can properly be done where the collective parties intend their agreement not to give rise to legal obligations between them. This, incidentally, is the exact reverse of the problem of deciding when collective parties should be regarded as being in breach of collective agreements by virtue of the actions of individuals. Anyway, the problem of how far collective obligations can and should be individuated is one of great interest and relevance to many aspects of labour law. The current examples of the problem are found in the discussions as to the circumstances in which closed-shop agreements become part of individual contracts of employment, and as to the kind of procedural obligations which the CAC might be able to impose upon individual contracts of employment by way of sanctions against employers for refusal to comply with obligations of disclosure of information (see above, Chapter 2). In linguistic terms any collective obligation is capable of individuation. Do you think that the following passage helps to establish a legal category of inappropriateness for individuation, given that such individuation is verbally feasible?

Wedderburn, *The Worker and the Law*, 2nd edn (1971), p. 193

Two other problems add to the area of uncertainty. First, not every collective term is appropriate for incorporation into the individual contract of employment. Some of them will be only a code agreed between the collective parties. For example, it is not easy to incorporate into any individual worker's contract the clauses: 'Each Trade Union party to this agreement may have Shop Stewards' (Vehicle Building 1961) or 'the proportion borne by the aggregate number of boys to the aggregate number of men [in certain departments] shall not exceed one boy to every four (or fractional part of four) men' (Boot and Shoe 1962). These are matters between the unions and the employers. Other clauses could be incorporated only with some semantic juggling: e.g. 'No female shall be allowed to use nails longer than 1¾ inches' (Packing-case Agreement 1942). Many other clauses (quite apart from wages, hours, and the like) are capable of being incorporated, e.g. 'Secretaries of Line Committees shall be allowed free rail travel on the Region concerned when engaged in the execution of their secretarial duties' (Railways 1960). With minimum ingenuity this could be expressed as an implied term of the individual contract of employment of each secretary if the lawyers so desired. Presumably, too, a '100 per cent membership' agreement can become an individual obligation to join a union if incorporated into the employment contract.

Some writers, for instance Wedderburn, take the view that the notion of inappropriateness for individuation provides the best guide to what was wrong with the decision in *Camden Exhibition* v. *Lynott*. Wedderburn says of that case (ibid., at p. 194) that while Russell L.J. identified the issue as one of inappropriateness for individuation, Lord Denning had seen the Working Rule quite differently, deeming it to restrict each worker's right to impose a *collective* embargo on overtime while not restricting his freedom to impose a purely personal ceiling on his overtime working.

How do you think the difficulty encountered in that case can best be analysed? Is the problem common to *all* procedural obligations in collective agreements or only to those which relate to the *level* at which the bargaining decision is to be taken? Does the dissenting view of Russell L.J. in the *Camden* case make it more difficult to incorporate clauses about unconstitutional strike action (see above, pp. 138–9) into individual contracts of employment?

Ultimately the idea of appropriateness for individuation offers a check upon incorporation of collective agreements which is rather abstract in nature, and one should expect it to have only a limited importance in the face of judicial pragmatism. This prediction is reinforced by developments in the actual processes of collective bargaining and of formulating contracts of employment. The survey of collective bargaining carried out by the Industrial Relations Research Unit at Warwick University whose results are set out in Brown (ed.), *The Changing Contours of British Industrial Relations* (1980), shows how there has been a considerable growth since the late 1960s in formalized collective bargaining at plant and company level (see op. cit., pp. 7–13) and how in particular there has been a great growth of formal closed shop agreements at that level of bargaining. Equally it would seem that there has been a parallel formalization of the collective dimension of the process of formulating contracts of employment in that there has been a strong tendency expressly to incorporate the terms of plant- and company-level collective bargaining into individual contracts of employment. That the courts will give effect to these two parallel developments without over-scrupulousness about appropriateness for individuation, is powerfully indicated by the decision of the Court of Session in *Partington* v. *NALGO* [1981] IRLR 537 (Outer House). There, the individual contracts of employment of engineers employed by Scottish Gas expressly incorporated the terms of a union membership agreement between Scottish Gas and a number of unions including NALGO. The issue in the case turned on this term of the union membership agreement:

10. The trade unions party to this agreement recognise that British Gas have a special duty and statutory obligation to protect the safety of the public and to maintain a safe system of gas supplies; and that therefore, at all times, it is the responsibility of British Gas to determine the necessary cover and arrangements to ensure safety or to deal with emergencies. Nevertheless, it is agreed that in the event of industrial action being taken, the trade unions and employers will have prior discussions about the necessary cover and arrangements to ensure safety or to deal with emergencies and will reach agreement, whenever possible, on the identity of those employees who are required to provide such cover. It is therefore agreed that the trade unions will grant special dispensation to any members so identified. The trade unions will also grant special dispensation to members who exercise their professional judgment in unforeseen emergency situations for which cover has not been provided.

The Court of Session saw no difficulty in treating that term of the collective agreement as incorporated into individual contracts of employment with the result that Scottish Gas could, having held the necessary discussions with the unions, instruct the employee to remain at work during a strike called by his union. Perhaps this should have been seen as a no-strike clause falling within TULRA 1974, s.18(4) (see below, p. 777); more important for our present purpose is that it was seen as presenting no problem with regard to individuation. The court was indeed prepared to view the union membership agreement as a tripartite one between employer, employee and union. One could not be confident that this view of the relationship as a tripartite one would extend to other sorts of collective agreement, but it is an approach which may signify a way of avoiding the whole issue of appropriateness for incorporation into the individual contract of employment.

In slight contrast, perhaps, with the approach to incorporation taken in the *Partington* case, was that taken in the recent case of *Tadd* v. *Daily Telegraph Ltd* [1983] IRLR 320. This was an action for defamation brought by a former employee in respect of a document submitted by the managing editor of the *Daily Telegraph* to a joint committee in the course of a disputes procedure relating to the dismissal of the employee. The general issue was whether the employee had contracted to accord absolute privilege to the proceedings in question, and one particular issue was whether the clause in the collective agreement between the Newspaper Publishers Association and the Institute of Journalists, which contained the Conciliation Procedure in question, formed part of the contract of employment of the individual employee. Hirst J. accepted the argument advanced by counsel for the employee that this clause was inappropriate for incorporation into individual contracts of employment because it dealt with the relationship between the union and the *Daily Telegraph* in a way which was outside the ambit of the individual employment relationship. This was not of great consequence to the decision as a whole, because Hirst J. went on to hold that the Conciliation Procedure had been placed on a contractual footing between the individual employer and employee by the plaintiff's *ad hoc* submission to the procedure; but it does serve to indicate that the appropriateness argument still has some vitality in practice, especially where the procedural provisions of collective agreements are concerned.

Voluntary arrangements and obligatory arrangements The last of the general problems common to all three forms of incorporation which we have to consider is that of the distinction between voluntary and obligatory arrangements. This distinction has been developed by the courts in relation to collective arrangements and particularly to agreements for overtime work (see also below, pp. 335ff.). Here the courts tend to treat only centralized and formal bargaining as creating such obligations. They tend to rationalize more localized and informal bargaining as a mere exchange of assurances of goodwill between employers and employees.

For example, in *Loman and Henderson* v. *Merseyside Transport Services Ltd* (1968) 3 ITR 108, the issue was the length of the contractual working week of two lorry drivers. A national agreement regulating hours and terms of employment in the road haulage business (which was set out in a statutory wages regulation order) provided that road haulage workers would get guaranteed weekly remuneration on the basis of a 41-hour week. This was varied in relation to the particular employees concerned by an agreement between employers and trade-union officials in regard to the working of shunters at the Barking Depot of the Liverpool Warehousing Company, which provided for a guaranteed 68-hour working week. Evidence was given for the employers that the local agreement was 'in the nature of a gentleman's agreement for ironing out local difficulties and for providing an incentive for co-operation with the mechanics of operation the employer wished to adopt'. The Divisional Court accepted that this description of the local agreement provided a valid basis for regarding it as not being intended to have contractual effect, despite the fact that the evidence showed that an employee who refused to accept the local agreement would have been moved to another job. See Wedderburn (1969) 32 *MLR* 99 and compare the similar result obtained by different reasoning in *Gascol Conversions Ltd* v. *Mercer* [1974] ICR 420 (above, p. 286).

Judgments of that kind are open to the objection that they assume a unitary framework of relations between employers and employees where in fact a pluralistic analysis would be more correct. That is to say, they assume an identity of interests where interests in fact conflict and are perceived to conflict. We shall return to that aspect later on. There is also the objection that they treat the collective bargaining process as if it were stabilized around the formal-level bargaining. In fact there is a considerable tension between the formal and the informal levels of bargaining as we saw in an earlier chapter of this book (see above, pp. 119–27). The contrary result was reached in *Barrett* v. *National Coal Board* [1978] ICR 1101 in relation to a local agreement for shift working by surface workers to ensure the safety of the mine, but this result was attributable to the fact that the employee's contract of employment incorporated the terms of a national collective agreement which expressly contemplated local agreements for additional shift working to ensure the safety of the pit concerned. In general, the potential still remains for discounting local variations upon collective agreements as non-obligatory in character, though this tends to become less of a practical issue as the growth of formalized plant or company-level bargaining serves to eliminate the gap between formal agreements at, say, national level and informal localized variants thereon.

(5) *A general theory of incorporation of the results of collective bargaining?*

It may be possible to suggest a general theory about the incorporation of the results of collective bargaining into individual contracts of employment in the following terms. There exists a loose parallel between the law on this issue and the law concerning intention to create legal relations as spelled out in *Edwards* v. *Skyways Ltd* ([1964] 1 WLR 349). That case set forth the rule that an agreement or arrangement capable of taking effect as a contractual agreement or undertaking should be rebuttably presumed to be intended to create legal relations when it occurs in the context of an existing contractual or commercial relationship, but should be rebuttably presumed not to be so intended where it occurs outside such a relationship. As far as the incorporation of the results of collective bargaining into the individual contract of employment is concerned, the courts have in effect created a presumption of more or less systematic translation of the results of collective bargaining into individual contracts where those results are in practice operative and effective in controlling the terms on which employment takes place. There is probably a contrary presumption where the results of collective bargaining are not manifestly operative in practice. This produces the result that where collective bargaining deals with procedures not normally or frequently invoked – for example redundancy procedures – or where it deals with long-term issues of policy or matters of corporate planning, so that its operativeness is not manifestly obvious, the inclusion of its results in individual contracts of employment will be relatively difficult to establish. For instance in *British Leyland (UK) Ltd* v. *McQuilken* [1978] IRLR 245, the EAT in Scotland refused to treat as implied into individual contracts of employment a collective agreement concerning a planned reorganization which would involve redundancies, on the grounds that the collective agreement was a long-term plan dealing with policy rather than with the rights of individual employees. It is quite hard to explain the contrast between this case and that of *Joel* v. *Cammell Laird Ltd* (see above, p. 283), except on the basis that the collective agreement in this case had not hitherto been operative in practice.[1] If that is indeed the distinction which has been applied, might it not give rise to a presumption against the inclusion into individual contracts of employment of *strategic* as opposed to *tactical* collective bargaining?

A general theory about incorporation of the results of collective bargaining into individual contracts has to deal with the effects of statutory statements of contractual terms. Where the statutory statements incorporate collective agreements by reference, the courts have tended to override their normal presumptions about the inclusion of terms from collective agreements. This is particularly true where the documents under consideration are ambiguous as to whether they are contracts or mere statements of terms (see above, p. 285). This is not to say that the courts systematically incorporate collective agreements referred to in statutory statements where they would not otherwise incorporate them, but rather that the presence of the statutory statement causes them to use a different set of criteria. That set of criteria tends to be dominated by the preference for written evidence over parol or extrinsic evidence. There are, however, signs that this preference may be giving way to a willingness to consider conduct and practice. If so, the general theory proposed above may assert itself even in the presence of statutory statements which refer to collective agreements. For instance, in *Burroughs Machines Ltd* v. *Timmoney* [1977] IRLR 404 the statutory statement of terms referred to the engineering national agreement on guaranteed pay, which provided for suspension of the guarantee when production in a federated establishment was dislocated as a result of an industrial dispute in 'that or any other federated

---

[1] Compare *Dudfeld* v. *Ministry of Works*, The Times, 24 January 1964 (above, p. 283), where the agreement was not yet operative in practice.

establishment'. The employers resigned from the Engineering Employers' Federation in 1973. A continued literal application of the national agreement would thereafter have disentitled the employers from suspending the guaranteed-week provisions in the event of an industrial dispute in their own establishment (because it had ceased to be a federated establishment). The EAT, sitting in Scotland, upheld this literal approach. The Inner House of the Court of Session reversed them, however, and held that, just as the employees had acquired a vested right to the continuance of the guaranteed-week arrangements despite the employer's withdrawal from the EEF, so the employer had acquired a corresponding vested right to the protection of the proviso allowing suspension of the guarantee when production was dislocated as a result of an industrial dispute in the establishment itself. The Court of Session was clearly influenced by the fact that the guaranteed-week arrangements had in practice survived the employers' resignation from the EEF and that all concerned had assumed that those arrangements remained in substance unchanged. The statutory statement of terms was thus allowed to operate as a flexible rather than a rigid link between the individual contract of employment and the collective bargaining process.

(d) Conduct, job-definition and variation of terms

We have so far touched upon conduct as a source of terms of employment under the headings of 'custom and practice' (see above, pp. 273ff.) and of 'incorporation of collective agreements' (see above, pp. 281ff.). So far we have mainly considered collective or group conduct as a source of contractual terms. Certain problems come into focus more sharply when we turn to consider individual conduct also as a source of contractual norms. The issue can in almost all cases be identified as a problem of job definition (whether in an occupational or geographical sense) which, as we shall see, is not necessarily or invariably synonymous with the definition of the terms of the contract of employment. The employment protection legislation has been a fruitful source of disputes and decisions about job definition. Such decisions have frequently been required in relation to issues concerning redundancy payments (see below, pp. 531ff.) and latterly in relation to unfair dismissals, especially where constructive dismissals are concerned (see below, pp. 448ff.). They are also required for the purpose of comparing men's work with women's work in applying the concept of 'like work' under Section 1 of the Equal Pay Act 1970 (see below, pp. 372ff.). For all these purposes the essential issue is whether the job as a legal abstraction (primarily expressed by the contract of employment) is defined by the practice of the employment concerned, or whether one party, typically the employer, has a right to maintain that the legal job-definition differs from the practice under which the employer and the employee have been operating; whether, in other words, the legal job-definition is different from the *de facto* job-definition.

When the issue is stated in these terms, it becomes apparent how closely it is linked with the law concerning variation of terms of employment. The two topics are indeed linked, to the point where they can usefully be considered as a single issue which centres upon the extent of the employer's prerogative to impose changes in the arrangements under which the employment takes place. Where the employer seeks to bring about a change of working arrangements and the employee asserts a vested right to the continuance of the status quo the issue can be expressed in one of a number of legal forms.[1] For our present purposes there are two significant forms the issue may take. The first situation is that in which, in the absence of written evidence, conduct is relied upon to establish the extent of managerial prerogative. This can be regarded as a question of formation of terms of employment by conduct. The second situation is that in which the employer asserts that he has a prerogative to insist upon a change of arrangements, and where the employee asserts a countervailing right to the status quo, saying that the employer's original right has been varied so that a new status quo has been created by conduct. This can be regarded as an issue of variation of terms by conduct. But the similarities between the two situations are clearly more significant than the differences between them. Indeed, the whole idea of distinguishing between the two situations is the product of the lawyer's commitment to the idea of the original formation of contractual terms as an instantaneous and static process, complete as soon as the contract is made. The process is, on the contrary, a continuing and dynamic one.

Once this discrepancy is grasped, between the lawyer's static model of the formation of the terms of employment and the dynamic or evolutionary character of the actual practice of employment, it becomes easy to understand why the courts have not been very successful in evolving clear or convincing principles concerning the formation and variation of terms of employment by conduct. For example, an area of extreme difficulty in relation to redundancy payments in particular has been the question of whether an employee has the right not to be transferred away from the place at which he has worked for a substantial period of time. Because the law of contract does not lend itself to an analysis whereby the employee gradually acquires such a right the courts are forced to postulate an original contract which either unequivocally requires the employee to be mobile or unequivocally entitles him not to be mobile. Depending upon which of these analyses is adopted it then either falls to the employer to argue that a mobility obligation has to be engrafted upon the original contract, or it falls upon the employee to establish a new agreement, by conduct, entitling him to refuse a transfer. In *O'Brien* v. *Associated Fire Alarms Ltd* [1968] 1 W L R 1916, of which the facts and judgment are extracted below, p. 532, the Court of Appeal opted for the former alternative, but in *Managers (Holborn) Ltd* v. *Hohne* [1977] I R L R 230, the E A T approached the matter in the latter way, with the contrary result because the weight of the law

---

[1] There is an obvious comparison here with the 'status quo' issue in relation to collective bargaining – see S. Anderman (1975) 4 *ILJ* 131, especially at pp. 140–1. See also above, pp. 890–1.

is thrown against the engrafting of extra terms upon contracts. Hence the lawyer's process of reasoning results in the making of an arbitrary choice between two diametrically opposed alternatives, neither of which may correspond to the practice of the employment in question.

Furthermore, this contrast between the lawyer's static model of the formation of terms and the evolutionary character of actual practice enables us to understand why the legal requirement for consideration for each variation of contract (see *Stilk* v. *Myrick* (1809) 2 Camp. 317), and the distinction between variation of an existing contract (requiring fresh consideration) and the replacement of the existing contract by a new one (for which the consideration is supplied by the mutual abandonment of the former contract) (see *Strange Ltd* v. *Mann* [1965] 1 WLR 629) are obscure and would be rather incongruous if widely applied in practice. In a couple of recent cases the courts have side-stepped this kind of problem by holding that a contract of employment may be divisible[1] into a basic part and one or more supplementary parts, and that the supplementary parts may be determined separately from the basic part by express or implied reasonable notice without breach of the contract of employment as a whole. Thus in *Land* v. *West Yorkshire County Council* [1981] ICR 334, the Court of Appeal held that a local authority could validly abolish the part-time duties of a fireman without breaking his basic contract of employment, because there was a separable supplementary contract for those part-time duties which was distinct from his basic contract relating to his full-time duties. Thus again in *Bond* v. *CAV Ltd* [1983] IRLR 360, it was held by Peter Pain J. in the Queen's Bench Division that plant-level or even more localized collective agreements for resolving disputes about the operation of a piece-work bonus system could validly be incorporated on a temporary basis into individual contracts of employment as supplemental agreements, and could equally validly be terminated and severed again from those contracts of employment upon reasonable notice without breach of the contracts of employment concerned. However, this approach in terms of supplemental contracts lends itself more obviously to those cases where the alleged supplementary contract deals with a subject matter not covered by the basic contract, as was true in these two instances. One can envisage that the approach in terms of supplementary agreements could cause severe difficulties when applied to the evolution of contractual terms relating to something that was expressly or impliedly dealt with by the original, basic contract of employment.

In this situation it is not surprising that the courts are, perhaps unconsciously, seeking new and different techniques for dealing with the problem of the impact of conduct and practice upon the mutual legal rights of employer

---

[1] This kind of divisibility of contractual terms from the basic contract is to be distinguished from the kind of divisibility which is involved in the traditional discussion, in general contract law, of 'entire and divisible contracts'. The latter doctrine deals with the divisibility of performance and obligations to pay for performance; our present discussion is concerned with the severability of *terms* from the principal contract.

and employee. It was for this reason that we asserted above that the law concerning job-definition is not entirely limited to the contractual approach. First there is an increasing tendency to evade the purely contractual issue by asking whether one or other party has by his conduct estopped himself from denying a certain view of the mutual rights of the obligations of employer and employee. For instance in *Waine* v. *Oliver (Plant Hire) Ltd* [1977] IRLR 434, the issue was whether the employee, by accepting lay-off on an earlier occasion, had estopped himself from denying that there was an implied power to lay him off when the employer found it necessary. The EAT concluded that the employee's behaviour in accepting lay-off on the previous occasion was not to be viewed as giving rise to an estoppel because it would not be fair to view him as having made a concession relating to his legal rights. By contrast, in *West Yorkshire District Council* v. *Platts* [1978] ICR 33, where the issue was whether it was part of the employee's duties to paint lamp-posts when asked to do so, there had been an inconclusive dispute between the employers and the employee's union about this matter, and the employee had thereafter continued for about a year to do a certain amount of painting work. The EAT thought that it would be possible to hold that, where an employee does work in accordance with an agreement, even though the agreement has been a source of dispute, he has accepted the interpretation put upon the agreement by the employer, or ought, by his conduct, to be subject to the terms of the formal agreement, and they remitted the case back to another industrial tribunal for re-hearing accordingly.

In both these cases the EAT found the doctrine of estoppel a more convenient and flexible method of doing justice according to the facts than was offered by purely contractual reasoning. The continuing popularity of this technique is reflected in two subsequent decisions of some importance. In *Hawker Siddeley Power Engineering Ltd* v. *Rump* [1982] IRLR 425, the issue was whether a heavy goods vehicle driver was subject to an obligation of country-wide mobility. He was employed in 1973 with a pro forma contract requiring country-wide mobility but with an oral promise from a manager that he would only work in Southern England. In 1976 he was issued with statutory particulars requiring full mobility in accordance with a Working Rule Agreement, to which he did not object. The EAT held that there had been no valid or effective variation of the oral term in 1976; but they went on to indicate, obiter, that they would if necessary have been prepared to hold that that the employer was obliged to give reasonable notice to withdraw this concession of some years' standing. There is an analogous point, though one less strictly within the realm of variation of terms, in the case of *Bond* v. *CAV Ltd* [1983] IRLR 360. Here a group of engineering workers had refused to operate a particular machine because of a dispute about their piece-work bonus, and the issue was whether they were entitled to be paid for the days during which they had so refused. It was held that although their refusal was in breach of their contracts of employment, the plaintiff was nevertheless entitled to be paid for the days in question because the employers had waived his breach of contract by allowing and facilitating his working on other machines during the days concerned. Having so approbated the plaintiff's contract of employment, the employers could not subsequently reprobate it by refusing to pay for what he did. Peter Pain J. added that 'It seems to me that every successful employment relationship is marked by numerous occasions when employer and employee do not stand strictly upon their contracts' (ibid., p. 365). So the growing recourse to extra-contractual considerations is quite significant.

There is yet a further sense in which the courts are gradually moving away from traditional contractual reasoning when assessing the impact of conduct as a factor in the formation of the mutual rights and duties of employer and employee. The traditional approach to the contract of employment involves the assumption that there are certain natural terms, if we may so style them, of the contract of employment which apply in the absence of a contrary indication. Sometimes, as we shall see in the next subsection, these 'natural terms' are viewed as terms implied by law. Sometimes they are viewed as presumptions about the intentions of the contracting parties, as with the presumption about sick-pay which has been thought to derive from *Orman* v. *Savile Sportswear Ltd* [1960] 1 WLR 1055. On either view, they do not depend for their existence upon supporting evidence derived from the conduct of the parties after the employment relationship was embarked upon; indeed, they tend to override or to exclude such evidence. There are recent indications, however, that the courts are becoming more willing to admit evidence of that kind to determine implied terms. For instance, in *Jones* v. *Associated Tunnelling Co. Ltd* [1981] IRLR 477, the EAT had to consider the extent of the geographical mobility obligation of a tunneller working for a specialist tunnelling firm to which the National Coal Board sub-contracted work. The view was urged upon them that as the original contract of employment said nothing expressly about mobility, this must mean there was no obligation of mobility. The EAT successfully circumvented that argument, and so enabled account to be taken of what had actually happened during the performance of the contract as tending to show what its original terms must have been. Note how in the following passage this result is achieved, and how the business efficacy test is subtly transformed so that it dictates not the absence of a mobility obligation (the traditional view) but merely that the contract must be viewed as saying *something* about mobility, whether that something is yes, no or up to a point.

Jones v. *Associated Tunnelling Co. Ltd*
[1981] IRLR 477 (EAT)

BROWNE-WILKINSON J.: The starting point must be that a contract of employment cannot simply be silent on the place of work: if there is no express term, there must be either some rule of law that in *all* contracts of employment the employer is (or alternatively is not) entitled to transfer the employee from his original place of work or some term regulating the matter must be implied into each contract. We know of no rule of law laying down the position in relation to all contracts of employment, nor do we think it either desirable or possible to lay down a single rule. It is impossible to conceive of any fixed rule which will be equally appropriate to the case of, say, an employee of a touring repertory theatre and the librarian of the British Museum. Therefore, the position must be regulated by the express or implied agreement of the parties in each case. In order to give the contract business efficacy, it is necessary to imply *some* term into each contract of employment.

The term to be implied must depend on the circumstances of each case. The authorities show that it may be relevant to consider the nature of the employer's business, whether or not the employee has in fact been moved during the employment, what the employee was told when he was employed, and whether there is any provision made to cover the employee's expenses when working away from daily reach of his home. These are only examples; all the circumstances of each case have to be considered: see *O'Brien* v. *Associated Fire Alarms* (1969) 1 AER 93; *Stevenson* v. *Teesside Bridge and Engineering Ltd* (1971) 1 AER 296; *Times Newspapers* v. *Bartlett* (1976) 11 ITR 106.

Looking at the circumstances of this case, what would the parties have said had an officious bystander asked them 'At what sites can Mr Jones be asked to work?'. The employers might have replied 'Anywhere in the United Kingdom'. But the Industrial Tribunal's findings indicate that Mr Jones, as one would expect, would have objected to being transferred anywhere outside daily reach of his home. The employers were in business as contractors working at different sites; so the parties must have envisaged a degree of mobility. In 1969, Mr Jones himself was moved from his original place of work to Hem Heath Colliery without objection. All the statements of terms and conditions subsequently issued contain mobility clauses, albeit in varying terms. From these factors we think that the plain inference is that the employers were to have *some* power to move Mr Jones's place of work and that the reasonable term to imply (as the lowest common denominator of what the parties would have agreed if asked) is a power to direct Mr Jones to work at any place within reasonable daily reach of Mr Jones's home. Such a term would permit Mr Jones to be required to work at Florence Colliery.

This approach, however, is challenged by Mr Hughes on behalf of Mr Jones. He submits that in order to imply a term, it is not enough to say that some term has to be implied and for the court then to imply a reasonable term. He submits that before any term can be implied it is necessary to show precisely what term the parties (if asked) would have said was obvious. In this case, as in all contracts of employment, it is impossible to state with certainty what the term as to mobility would have been. It might have been the term that the Industrial Tribunal suggested: but it might also have been mobility within a defined area or within a given radius of Mr Jones's home. Therefore, says Mr Hughes, it is not possible to imply any term since one cannot be certain what that term should be.

The foundation for this submission is the decision of the House of Lords in *Trollope and Colls Ltd* v. *North Western Metropolitan Regional Hospital Board* (1973) 2 AER 260. In that case, a building contract provided for the work to be done in three phases. There was a fixed date for completion of Phase 1 but the architect was given power to extend that date and in fact did so. Phase 3 was to commence six months after practical completion of Phase 1. The contract provided that Phase 3 was to be completed by a date specified in the contract, there being no express power to extend the date for completion of Phase 3. It was argued that there ought to be implied into the contract a term extending the date for completion of Phase 3 if, as happened, the date for completion of Phase 1 was extended by the architect. The House of Lords held that no term could be implied, reversing the Court of Appeal decision that a reasonable term could be implied. The majority of the House of Lords gave two reasons for their decision: the first, that as the contract dealt unambiguously with the date for completion there was no room for any implication; the second (being the one directly in point in this case) that as any one of a number of possible terms might have been agreed by the parties to cover the position if they had directed their minds to the problem, it was not possible to imply any term: see Lord Pearson at pages 268–9; Lord Cross at page 272.

In our judgement, that decision is distinguishable from the present case. In that case, there was no need to imply any term: the express terms of the contract were unambiguous and covered the event which had happened, albeit in a way which was surprising in its result. Therefore any term which was to be implied would be varying the unambiguous express terms of the contract. In the case of contracts of employment containing no mobility clause, the position is quite different. As we have sought to show, it is essential to imply *some* term into the contract in order to give the contract business efficacy: there must be some term laying down the place of work. In such a case, it seems to us that there is no alternative but for the Tribunal or court to imply a term which the parties, if reasonable, would probably have agreed if they had directed their minds to the problem. Such a term will not vary the express contractual terms. This view is supported by the very many cases in which the courts have decided what terms as to mobility ought to be included in a contract of employment: see for example the cases cited above. If Mr Hughes's submission were correct, all those cases would have been wrongly decided since it is never possible to state with certainty exactly what the parties would have agreed as to mobility if they had directed their minds to the question.

We therefore reach the conclusion that we are entitled to hold, and do hold, that the right term to imply into Mr Jones's contract from the outset was that he could be required to work at any place within reasonable daily commuting distance from his home. If we are right on this, none of the later documents (with the possible exception of A2/A6) can have affected the position, since A3 is silent on the point and A4 and A5 both contain terms as to mobility wider than that implied term. It was submitted that if A2/A6 was the last contractual document, the mobility clause in A2/A6 is void for uncertainty and therefore the employers would not be able to show that they had any power to move Mr Jones's place of work. There are many possible answers to this submission, but in our view the decisive one is that adopted by the Industrial Tribunal, namely that it was unable to find that A2/A6 had been issued to Mr Jones at all. Unless and until it is proved that A2/A6 had been issued, its terms cannot affect the position between the parties.

The same sort of reasoning was used by the Court of Appeal in *Mears* v. *Safecar Security Ltd* [1982] ICR 626 in order to provide a new approach to the old problem of whether payment continues during sickness where the contract of employment is silent about sick-pay (see below, pp. 348–51). Note how impossibly thin the dividing line between contractual formation and contractual variation becomes when this approach is taken.

Mears v. *Safecar Security Ltd* [1982] ICR 626 (CA)

STEPHENSON L.J.: Mr Clark made a more important submission, that the tribunals were not entitled to look at the subsequent actings of the parties in interpreting this written contract; to do so would be to disregard the law laid down by the House of Lords in *Whitworth Street Estates (Manchester) Ltd* v. *James Miller and Partners Ltd* [1970] AC 583 and *Wickman Machine Tool Sales Ltd* v. *L. Schuler AG* [1974] AC 235. I have already expressed my view that this agreement was oral, but even if it was partly in writing, we are concerned with the search for a term that was not written down, and there is nothing in those authorities which prevents the court from looking at the way the parties acted for the purpose of ascertaining what that term was. Common sense suggests that their subsequent conduct is the best evidence of what they had agreed orally but not reduced to writing, though it is not evidence of what any written terms mean; and Mr Tabachnik has put before us binding authority for that common sense view.

I have no doubt that the manner in which this contract of employment was in fact carried out or interpreted by both parties was properly considered to see whether it led to the implication of the term to be determined.

Mr Tabachnik, whose helpful submissions are to a large extent adopted in this judgment, submitted that the decision of the appeal tribunal could be supported on the ground that the parties had agreed to the employee's employment on a 'no work, no pay' basis by a subsequent variation of their original agreement. But he has given no respondent's notice of this point, nor was it argued before either tribunal, and we thought it right to exclude this alternative way of looking at the subsequent actings of the parties from our consideration.

Mr Tabachnik legitimately sought support for consideration of the subsequent conduct of the parties in *Liverpool City Council* v. *Irwin* [1977] AC 239; *Ferguson* v. *John Dawson & Partners (Contractors) Ltd* [1976] 1 WLR 1213 and *Wilson* v. *Maynard Shipbuilding Consultants AB* [1978] ICR 376. What was there said and decided is, I think, helpful to a court approaching the task of determining from all the circumstances what the parties to an incompletely expressed contract must have agreed in fact or be taken to have agreed.

In *Wilson* v. *Maynard Shipbuilding Consultants AB* [1978] ICR 376 this court held that where one cannot ascertain from the terms of the contract itself what was agreed about a relevant term – in that case, the place where under his contract an employee ordinarily works – one may look at what has happened and what the parties have done under the contract during the whole contemplated period of the contract for the limited purpose of ascertaining what that term is: see *per* Megaw L.J., at pp. 675 and 677, applied in *Todd* v. *British Midland Airways Ltd* [1978] ICR 959, 964, where Lord Denning M.R. said that in considering the particular question where the parties have agreed that an employee should ordinarily work, the court gets less help from the terms of the contract than from the conduct of the parties and the way they have been operating the contract: see also what Sir David Cairns said in *Todd* v. *British Midland Airways Ltd* at p. 967.

But in *Wilson* v. *Maynard Shipbuilding Consultants AB* [1978] ICR 376 the court was applying a more general principle stated by Lord Wilberforce in *Liverpool City Council* v. *Irwin* [1977] AC 239, 253D, that in order to complete a contract which is partly but not wholly stated in writing, 'it is necessary to take account of the actions of the parties and the circumstances'. That case was cited not only to the Court of Appeal in *Wilson's* case and in *Ferguson* v. *John Dawson & Partners (Contractors) Ltd* [1976] 1 WLR 1213, but to the appeal tribunal in the instant case: see [1981] ICR 409. As was pointed out in *Ferguson* v. *John Dawson & Partners (Contractors) Ltd* [1976] 1 WLR 1213 by Megaw L.J., at p. 1221, and Browne L.J., at p. 1229, in deciding whether an oral and only partially expressed agreement was a contract of service or a contract for services, the court was not merely entitled but bound to take into account what was done under the contract, not to construe the contract but to infer what its terms were, either originally or by subsequent variation. As I have said, we are not considering subsequent variation in this case.

In a very valuable note on this case ((1982) 11 *ILJ* 185), Leighton and Doyle draw attention to the significance of this new flexible approach to implied terms, referring to the 'demise of the officious bystander'. They attribute to the present authors the suggestion that this broader approach has hitherto been more or less limited to the essentially flexible or evolving aspects of the contract, the 'job definition' aspects. The *Mears* case, they say, applies this approach to what might be termed a 'static' term of the contract, that is a term which is usually only subject to minor modifications during the continuance of the relationship, and to a term which is being considered in an original, as opposed to varied, form. We would take issue with this argument to the extent that it suggests that terms of the contract of employment can be classified by their subject matter as static or evolving terms. This is liable to prove as ultimately misleading as the idea that terms can be classified by their subject matter as conditions or warranties. A very real point which none-theless emerges is that the courts have long struggled with the difficulties of implying terms by the use of a static model of contractual formation. They are now adapting to the fact that they are liable to need an evolving model of contractual formation in order to do justice to the fact-situations which may arise in relation to more or less any proposed implied term in the contract of employment.

The development of a new and more flexible approach to the implying of terms into contracts of employment was confirmed by the EAT in *Howman & Son* v. *Blyth* [1983] ICR 416. There, as we have seen, the issue was the duration of the employer's obligation to pay sick-pay. It was argued on behalf of the employee that in the absence of an express term on this point, the industrial tribunal should have applied a common-law presumption, relied upon in *Marrison* v. *Bell* [1939] 2 KB 187, that wages continue throughout absence due to sickness so long as the contract has not been terminated. We shall return later to the particular issue of sick-pay – our present concern is with the theory put forward by the EAT for deciding what term should be implied. It was expressed as follows:

Howman & Son v. *Blyth* [1983] ICR 416 (EAT) at p. 420

BROWNE-WILKINSON J.: It seems to us that the burden of the Court of Appeal decision in the *Mears* case is that, before applying 'what is left' of *Marrison* v. *Bell*, the industrial tribunal must first seek to discover what are the implied terms of the contract. Those implied terms may be of two types. The first, which goes back to *The Moorcock* (1889) 14 P.D. 64 and which we will call 'the *Moorcock* type' are terms which the parties, if they had been asked at the time of contract whether the term was part of the contract, would have immediately agreed that it was. The second type, described in *Lister* v. *Romford Ice and Cold Storage Co. Ltd* [1957] AC 555, and which we will call 'the *Lister* type,' applies to cases, such as contracts of employment, where the relationship between the parties requires that there should be some agreed term which has not in fact been agreed but both parties would not have agreed what that term would be if they had been asked. In the *Lister* type of case, the court implies a reasonable term.

In the present case we start from the position that there is undoubtedly a contractual obligation to pay sick pay but there is no agreed term as to the duration of the sick pay. There must be some contractual term regulating the duration. The question is whether we are free to imply a reasonable term or are bound by *Marrison* v. *Bell* [1939] 2 KB 187 to hold that sick pay lasts until the employment is terminated. In our judgment, before applying the *Marrison* v. *Bell* presumption it is legitimate to imply a term as to the duration of the *Lister* type. In an industry where the normal practice is to provide sick pay for a limited period only, the reasonable term to imply is the term normally applicable in that industry.

Let us try to sum up in the light of this latest in a series of innovative cases. Where a term of a contract of employment is not expressed or not fully expressed or at least can be regarded as not fully expressed, the courts have now asserted a considerable latitude to imply the term that will best do justice in the circumstances. This, as we have already seen, can permit a freer use of norms derived from collective bargaining than would otherwise be possible. It also cuts through the difficulties of implying terms on the basis of custom and practice and conduct; and it tends to eliminate artificial distinctions between contractual formation and contractual variation. It also, as we shall see in the next subsection, tends to erode the distinction between terms implied in fact (which we have been discussing hitherto) and terms implied in law (which we now come to discuss). But before doing so, we should observe that the latitude which is asserted in these cases is a latitude to engage in judicial legislation about the terms of the contract of employment. We are in an era when judicial confidence is high in relation to exercises of this kind, but the restraints which the courts imposed upon themselves in a more formalistic era may still be re-asserted if the courts should find themselves in a less creative mood.

(e) Common-law implied terms

Even in these days when employers are required to issue particulars of individual contracts of employment, the contract of employment remains a very largely standardized and conventional contract as far as a large part of its content is concerned. By entering into a contract of employment the parties normally subscribe to an extensive body of common law and statute law which imposes the legal character of employment upon their relationship. Although an increasing role is being played by statutory obligations which cannot be contracted out of by the employer, the common-law presumed terms of employment are still of considerable importance in establishing the contract, and still serve to express important social assumptions about the appropriate nature of the employment relationship.

In recent years the implied terms of the contract of employment have been crucial to deciding upon the legality of certain kinds of industrial action (see below, pp. 720–1) and in determining the scope of constructive dismissal (see below, pp. 448ff.). For these reasons it is important to consider what the approach of the courts is towards implied terms; do they stress managerial prerogative and disciplinary control, or do they stress the rights of employees? Do they take a wide or a narrow view of the matters which can be expressed as implied terms? Are they willing or reluctant to formulate new implied terms as social conditions and employment practices change?

This degree of standardization of the contract of employment by means of common-law implied terms is quite striking, not least because the common-law judges so strongly disclaim any norm-making function as far as implying terms is concerned. A typical such disclaimer of legislative responsibility was given by Lord Wright in *Luxor (Eastbourne) Ltd* v. *Cooper* [1914] AC 108 at p. 137:

> The general presumption is that the parties have expressed every material term which they intended could govern their agreement, whether oral or in writing, but it is well recognized that there may be cases where obviously some term must be implied if the intention of the parties is not to be defeated, some term of which it can be predicated that 'it goes without saying', some term not expressed but necessary to give to the transaction such business efficacy as the parties must have intended. This does not mean that the court can embark on reconstruction of the agreement on equitable principles. . . .

Does not this notion of 'business efficacy' take it for granted that the shape and purpose of the contract are agreed on all hands? In other words, is the 'business efficacy' test meaningful only when the courts have given a particular type of contract an outline shape, so that only relatively minor details remain to be supplied? Otherwise, who is to say what business efficacy means?

The extent to which the 'business efficacy' test enables the courts to impose their own views as to what would constitute fair terms and conditions is shown in the case of *Horrigan* v. *Lewisham London Borough Council* [1978] ICR 15. This was an unfair dismissal case where the main issue was whether overtime, which the employee refused to work, was contractually obligatory upon him. The EAT, following a fairly consistent policy in the courts of treating overtime as being voluntary, held that although overtime had been habitually and regularly worked over a period of years it had not been shown to be necessary, as a matter of business efficacy, for that degree of overtime to be contractually obligatory upon the employee.

The business efficacy and officious bystander tests, even though they in fact give courts quite wide discretion in deciding whether to imply terms or not, tend to present themselves psychologically as fairly unyielding obstacles to the process of implication. It is not surprising, therefore, in an era where the courts assert a relatively wide overt control over contractual terms, that they should recently have adopted a new technique for the implication of terms, which we may call the 'legal incidents' test, and which somewhat bridges the gap between terms implied in fact and terms implied in law. The technique was used in *Mears* v. *Safecar Security Ltd* [1982] ICR 626 to decide whether to imply an obligation to pay sick-pay, where in the following passage Stephenson L.J. carries on from the proposition, considered at p. 304, that *Liverpool City Council* v. *Irwin* authorized the court to approach this kind of problem by looking at the actual conduct of the parties during the employment relationship.

Mears v. *Safecar Security Ltd*
[1982] ICR 626 (CA)

On examination *Liverpool City Council* v. *Irwin* [1977] AC 239 is not, in any opinion, as helpful to the employee's case as was *Lister* v. *Romford Ice and Cold Storage Co. Ltd* [1957] AC 555 to the tenants Mr and Mrs Irwin. As I read the speeches of their Lordships in *Lister's* case, particularly those of Viscount Simonds at pp. 576–579, and Lord Tucker at p. 594, and in *Liverpool City Council* v. *Irwin* [1977] AC 239, particularly those of Lord Wilberforce at pp. 254 and 255, Lord Cross of Chelsea at pp. 257 and 258, Lord Edmund-Davies at pp. 265 and 266 and Lord Fraser of Tullybelton at p. 270, the House of Lords has laid down that there are contracts which establish a relationship, e.g. of master and servant, landlord and tenant, which demand by their nature and subject matter certain obligations, and those obligations the general law will impose and imply, not as satisfying the business efficacy or officious bystander tests applicable to commercial contracts where there is no such relationship, but as legal incidents of those other kinds of contractual relationship. In considering what obligations to imply into contracts of these kinds which are not complete, the actions of the parties may properly be considered. But the obligation must be a *necessary* term; that is, required by their relationship. It is not enough that it would be a reasonable term.

In *Irwin's* case the House implied an obligation on the landlords, Liverpool City Council, to repair the means of access to the tenants' flat, although the obligation would not have been agreed to by the landlords and although the contract would have worked, though unsatisfactorily for the tenants, without it.

Now it cannot be said that as a general rule a legal incident of a contract of employment is that there should be no sick pay; indeed if there is a legal incident, it is that there should be sick pay. But it can be said that if an employee is off work sick he must either be paid or not be paid. There must be some term as to his remuneration when off sick and the best indication of what that term is is the fact that he was paid or not paid. When the facts of the employee's absences for sick are considered, the right term to imply is obvious, even if the majority view of the industrial tribunal is preferred to the minority view and the strict common law test is therefore not satisfied: see *In re An Arbitration between Comptoir Commercial Anversois and Power, Son & Co.* [1920] 1 KB 868, 899, per Scrutton L.J.

Accordingly we are, in my judgment, entitled to rely on *Liverpool City Council* v. *Irwin* [1977] AC 239, applied in *Ferguson* v. *John Dawson & Partners (Contractors) Ltd* [1976] 1

WLR 1213, where the parties must have worked either under a contract of service or under a contract for services, as supporting the decision of the appeal tribunal, although Slynn J. did not refer to it. We can treat as an agreed term a term which would not have been at once assented to by both parties at the time when they made the contract, e.g., where one party would at once have assented to it and the other would have done so after it had been made clear to him that unless he did so there would be no contract – which is, I think, this case.

So we see here how the 'legal incidents' test can be used *together with* the doctrine in the *Liverpool City Council* case to enable the courts to combine the maximum of flexibility with the maximum of capacity for judicial legislation. As we have seen (above, p. 305), this large scope for judicial creativity was reasserted in *Howman & Son* v. *Blyth* [1983] ICR 416 where, moreover, the distinction between terms implied in law and terms implied in fact was stated in minimal terms as a mere difference between terms of 'the Moorcock type' and terms of 'the Lister type', the latter being those reasonable terms which 'the court will imply where the relationship between the parties requires that there should be some agreed term which has not in fact been agreed but both parties would not have agreed what that term would be if they had been asked' (ibid., p. 420). The question then is what implied content have the courts given to the contract of employment in the exercise of these fairly extensive powers. We may usefully embark on the answer to that question by looking at the development of one of the most general and socially significant of the suggested implied terms, namely that dealing with the implied contractual duty of co-operation. In the following extract the Court of Appeal envisages such a duty of co-operation as being placed upon the employee in relation to both individual and collective conduct. What assumptions about the nature of the employment relationship are embodied in an implied term of this kind? Is there an analogy here with those cases concerning the doctrine of frustration, in which the judges envisage a community of purpose between the two parties to a contract? The issue was whether a 'work-to-rule' was in breach of individual contracts of employment.

Secretary of State for Employment v. *ASLEF (No. 2)*
[1972] ICR 19 (CA)

LORD DENNING M.R.: Thus far, I have spoken only of particular breaches such as the one I have mentioned of that extra hour's overtime; but the principal discussion before us (and it is the most important discussion for the purposes of the case) was as to the general instruction to the men to 'work to rule', or, as it is put more fully in the instructions, 'Strictly observe all BRB rules.' The meaning of that instruction is not in doubt. It is well known to everyone in the land. The instruction was intended to mean, and it was understood to mean, 'Keep the rules of your employment to the very letter, but, whilst doing so, do your very utmost to disrupt the undertaking.' Is that a breach of contract?

Now I quite agree that a man is not bound positively to do more for his employer than his contract requires. He can withdraw his goodwill if he pleases. But what he must not do is wilfully to obstruct the employer as he goes about his business. That is plainly the case where a man is employed singly by a single employer. Take a homely instance, which I put in the course of argument. Suppose I employ a man to drive me to the station. I know there is sufficient time, so that I do not tell him to hurry. He drives me at a slower speed than he need, with the deliberate object of making me lose the train, and I do lose it. He may say that he has performed the letter of the contract; he has driven me to the station; but he has wilfully made me lose the train, and that is a breach of contract beyond all doubt. And what is more, he is not entitled to be paid for the journey. He has broken the contract in a way that goes to the very root of the consideration; so he can recover nothing. Such a case is akin (it has been said we have had no authorities on the subject) to the many cases where there is an implied term not wilfully to prevent the carrying out of the contract.

So much for the case when a man is employed singly. It is equally the case when he is employed, as one of many, to work in an undertaking which needs the service of all. If he, with the others, takes steps wilfully to disrupt the undertaking, to produce chaos so that it will not run as it should, then each one who is a party to those steps is guilty of a breach of his contract. It is no answer for any one of them to say 'I am only obeying the rule book,' or 'I am not bound to do more than a 40-hour week.' That would be all very well if done in good faith without any wilful disruption of services; but what makes it wrong is the object with which it is done. There are many branches of our law when an act which would otherwise be lawful is rendered unlawful by the motive or object with which it is done. So here it is the wilful disruption which is the breach. It means that the work of each man goes for naught. It is made of no effect.

So I hold that the concerted course of conduct was in breach of the contracts of employment.

By assuming a community of purpose between employer and employee and by construing the obligations of the contract of employment in those terms, the courts are perhaps preferring a unitary to a pluralistic concept of the employment relationship. In *Industrial Sociology and Industrial Relations* (1966), Alan Fox asserts that the employment relationship can only be satisfactorily understood in pluralistic terms (a position which he has admittedly since somewhat modified). Would a pluralistic view of the employment relationship lead to a different approach to the problem under discussion in the previous extract?

Brian Napier, in a survey of developments in judicial attitudes towards the employment relationship ((1977) 6 *ILJ* 1 at pp. 8–10), concludes that the *ASLEF* case was indeed one where the court chose the 'unitary' frame of reference for industrial relations, and that there are in general indications of a movement towards such a view of industrial relations in which common interest and partnership 'and not conflict and subordination' are emphasized as features of the employment relationship. He observes that although in the *ASLEF* case it happened to be the employers who benefited from the court's emphasis on co-operation and common purpose, it can happen that this approach places restrictions on how an employer may lawfully behave towards his employees. We shall consider later how far the recent judicial treatment of implied terms of the contract of employment for the purposes of the law of constructive dismissal bears out Napier's view in this respect (below, pp. 316–17).

The foregoing discussions of business efficacy and contractual cooperation suggest the existence of a common-law contract of employment with a well-determined profile, by the use of which some substance can be given to the idea of contractual co-operation. That profile has traditionally been provided by specialized kinds of implied terms, namely those implied terms which laid down a code of conduct for employees by stating the conditions upon which an employer might summarily dismiss his employee. The most important of these was that which stipulated obedience by the employee to all reasonable and lawful orders (see Freedland, *The Contract of Employment* (1976), pp. 197–200). This implied term had the effect of lodging managerial prerogative firmly in the centre of the structure of the contract of employment. However, in cases such as *London Borough of Redbridge* v. *Fishman* [1978] IRLR 69 the EAT has recently favoured the notion of a critical review, in unfair dismissal cases, of the reasonableness of instructions given by employers, thus virtually equating the common-law view of reasonableness with the statutory issue of fairness.

Another very important common-law implied term of the contract of employment is that whereby the employee is regarded as undertaking that he has the skill and will exercise the care necessary for the proper performance of his work (on pain of summary dismissal and/or compensation to the employer). This implied term began life as a dubious analogy between the position of an employee and that of an independent contractor, drawn by Willes J. in *Harmer* v. *Cornelius* (1858) 5 CBNS 236 at p. 246: 'When a skilled labourer, artisan or artist is employed, there is on his part an implied warranty that he is of skill reasonably competent to the task he undertakes – *spondes peritiam artis*. Thus if an apothecary, a watchmaker, or an attorney be employed for reward, they each impliedly undertake to possess and exercise reasonable skill in their several arts.' In *Lister* v. *Romford Ice and Cold Storage Co. Ltd* [1957] AC 555, this proposition was widened to include an implied undertaking to use care as well as skill, and was extended to include a duty to indemnify the employer from liability caused by the employee's negligent driving when engaged to drive a lorry. In *Harvey* v. *R.G. O'Dell Ltd* [1958] 2 QB 78, there was something of a retreat to the position that there must be some general holding out by the employee of his ability or skill for the task in question, so that there was no implied agreement to indemnify the employer where a storekeeper as a concession to his employers from time to time used his motorcycle combination to travel to outside jobs with a fellow employee as a passenger.

Even when thus limited, the doctrine of implied indemnity tends to place upon the employee a responsibility which the employer should at least share, namely the responsibility for ensuring that the employee is recruited for and allocated only to tasks which are within his range of ability. That this is coming to be perceived as an expectation that the employee has of his employer is indicated by the recent decision, admittedly of only minor authority, in *McNally* v. *Welltrade International Ltd* [1978] I R L R 497, where an employee who was recruited on the basis of inadequate or misleading information about the nature of the job offer, who turned out to be unacceptable to a foreign client of the employer, and who suffered loss of employment as a result, was able to recover damages for misrepresentation in the job offer made to him. How in your view should the risks arising out of recruitment and job allocation be distributed between employers and employees? Compare here *City of Birmingham* v. *Beyer* [1977] I R L R 211 (above, p. 180) and *Taylor* v. *Furness Withy Ltd* [1969] 1 Lloyd's Rep. 324.

By means of the obligations which the common law imposes upon employees concerning fidelity towards their employers, the contract of employment is shaped in various different ways. By their decisions on these matters the judges imply views as to the nature of the moral responsibilities owed by employees to their employers in relation to trade competition, work for other employers or on one's own behalf, and disclosure of information concerning the employment. The most recent reaffirmation of these ethical duties occurred in *Thomas Marshall (Exports) Ltd* v. *Guinle* [1978] I C R 905, where the Vice-Chancellor approved the view that these duties applied to acts done by the servant outside his hours of work as in *Hivac Ltd* v. *Park Royal Scientific Instruments Ltd* [1946] Ch. 169, where a company was injuncted from employing its rival's skilled workers in their spare time which exposed their employer to damaging competition. In *Marshall*, the duty of fidelity as it relates to confidential information was formulated as follows: protected items of information or trade secrets are those where (1) the release of the information is believed by its owner to be potentially injurious to him; (2) the owner believes that the information is not or not yet in the public domain; (3) the owner's beliefs as to (1) and (2) are reasonable and (4) the information can be judged confidential in the light of the usage and practices of the particular industry or trade. One off-shoot of the judicial formulation of implied obligations of confidentiality is that the employee has no automatic liberty to disclose to his trade union information about his employer's enterprise which may be essential to effective collective bargaining – *Bent's Brewery Co. Ltd* v. *Hogan* [1945] 2 All E R 570. Hepple and O'Higgins suggest that this aspect of the duty of fidelity may sometimes in practice be overridden by clauses in collective agreements designed to oust the duty of fidelity, in relation to legitimate protection by trade unions of the interests of their members, these clauses being then incorporated into individual contracts of employment (*Encyclopedia*, para. 1–190.) This issue may have become of somewhat less concern in so far as the employer is himself now placed under duties of disclosure of information to trade unions for collective bargaining purposes; but those duties arise only where a trade union has been recognized by the employer (see above, pp. 205ff.).

The working out of the implied obligation of fidelity on the part of the employee is, in fact, emerging as one of the critical areas of judicial creativity *vis-à-vis* the individual employment relationship. In this area, the courts have to try to resolve a tension between two conflicting sets of considerations. On the one hand, the interests of the enterprise and the dictates of commercial morality are seen to require high standards of fidelity on the part of the employee. On the other hand, there is a countervailing tradition which asserts that the employment relationship does not give rise to a contract *uberrimae fidei* (of the utmost good faith), no doubt in order to stress the narrowly contractual nature of the mutual expectations that employer and employee may have of each other – to stress, in other words, that employment confers only a contract and not a status. The recent decision of the Court of Appeal in *Sybron Corporation* v. *Rochem Ltd* [1983] 2 All ER 707, gives some clear pointers as to the way the courts may be expected to resolve that tension in future. In that case, the Court of Appeal held that the manager of the European affairs of an American financial conglomerate had been under an implied contractual duty to report to his employers the complicity of some of his fellow employees in a massive commercial fraud upon his employers of which the evidence showed he had been aware. There are two interesting features of this part of the decision. One is that it seems to be felt by the courts to be more straightforward to imply obligations to disclose the misconduct of fellow employees than to imply obligations to disclose one's own misconduct. This takes up a trend from *Swain* v. *West (Butchers) Ltd* [1936] 3 All ER 261 and side-steps the limits on this kind of duty of fidelity apparently posed by *Bell* v. *Lever Bros. Ltd* [1932] AC 161.

The other interesting feature – and this is crucial – is that the Court of Appeal saw the implication of a duty of disclosure of the misconduct of fellow employees as being especially appropriate because of the elevated position of the employee in the hierarchy within the enterprise. This indicates a trend towards treating the senior manager in the same way as the company director has traditionally been treated. A parallel trend towards hierarchical treatment of employees was displayed in the recent controversy concerning maintenance workers sleeping during night-shifts at a Plessey factory, where an industrial tribunal held that foremen were fairly dismissed for failing to report the misconduct of workers under their supervision (*Cooper* v. *Plessey Semi- conductors Ltd, The Times*, 11 August 1983). The chairman of the Industrial Tribunal commented:

When a man is made a foreman he becomes part of management, and to hear a man say this happened because of the incompetence of management is very wrong. These three men were in a position of trust. They should have come to management at the earliest time to say this sort of thing was going on and sought guidance how to deal with it.

These developments answer very well indeed to the analysis of current approaches to the employment relationship advanced by Alan Fox in *Beyond*

Contract: Trust, Power and Work Relations (1974), in which he suggests that there tends to be an increasing allocation of discretion and placing of trust in employees, and a correspondingly greater attribution of obligations of loyalty, as one progresses up the hierarchy of an employing enterprise. It is tentatively suggested that this high-trust/low-trust analysis may be at least as useful an aid to the understanding of the development of implied terms of the contract of employment as the unitary/pluralistic analysis which has found favour in recent years.

The process of judicial legislation inherent in the formulation of common-law implied terms becomes obvious when it is sought to imply rights for employees, because the common law has rather taken for granted its own capacity to impose a set of obligations and code of conduct upon employees, but has been relatively little concerned with performing a similar function against employers. Hence the attempt to construe a right to strike out of the implied terms of the individual contract of employment has proved somewhat beyond the capacity of the common law and has been seen to require Parliamentary intervention. The difficulties in implying such a term as a matter of common law perhaps arise from the fact that the idea of doing so is such a recent one, the common law hence being viewed as presenting a pattern into which a contractual right to strike cannot easily be fitted. Thus, in *Simmons* v. *Hoover Ltd* [1977] ICR 61 (see below, p. 903), the EAT held that there was no implied term restricting the employer's right to dismiss the striking employee for refusal to work. As we shall see in more detail later on, the EAT in reaching this conclusion simply treated as nugatory a whole sequence of judicial and legislative development, basically on the ground that this was too complicated a matter for satisfactory judicial innovation, although the common-law contract of employment thereby admittedly failed to keep step with much of current employment practice.

Just as the courts seem to find some sense of incongruity in the attempt to draft a common-law implied right to strike, so they find it hard to give a specific content as a matter of common-law implied terms to the notion of the employee's right to work. The following extracts show how the notion of the right to work was ultimately reduced to the standing of a right to have the opportunity to earn remuneration. The suggestion that the employee has a further right to carry out his work for the sake of the experience and self-fulfilment which it may provide has so far proved difficult to secure acceptance by the courts. Does this represent a judicial view of what can and cannot be contained within the scope of common-law implied terms? If so, is this another aspect of the discussion of appropriateness of terms for inclusion in individual contracts which was encountered in relation to collective bargaining, or does it represent some other parameter of the implied-term doctrine?

Langston v. *AUEW (No. 2)* [1974] ICR 510 (NIRC)

In *Langston (No. 2)* a central issue was whether the employers, by suspending

Langston on full pay, had broken his contract of employment. Only if this was the case could Langston show that the AUEW had committed an unfair industrial practice under the Industrial Relations Act 1971 by persuading Chrysler UK to suspend the plaintiff.

SIR JOHN DONALDSON: In fact the complainant has throughout asserted that he has a 'right to work' and that his exclusion from the factory breached that right. No one seriously suggests that this alleged right is statutory. If it exists, it is contractual and the union must be taken to have intended to induce the employers to breach it.

Does it exist? The Court of Appeal [1974] ICR 180 did not decide this point. Lord Denning M.R. clearly thought that in the 1970s it ought to exist. Cairns and Stephenson L.JJ. thought that the point was arguable but that there were obstacles in the complainant's way. Mr Webster and Mr Alexander have greatly assisted us by a detailed survey of the route. The complainant has contributed a sublime faith that we shall get there, but he makes no claim to be a legal navigator. There is no doubt that over the years there has been an increasing acceptance of the proposition that everyone has a right to work, in same sense that he has a right to eat and a right to be housed. Thus article 23(i) of the Universal Declaration of Human Rights adopted in 1948 by the United Nations provides:

> Everyone has the right to work, to free choice of employment, to just and favourable conditions of work and to protection against unemployment.

Nagle v. *Feilden* [1966] 2 QB 633 and the authorities there cited illustrate this trend. But it is a general right, not a right to work for any particular employer or in any particular place. The right is based upon public policy rather than contract (see *per* Danckwerts L.J. in *Nagle's* case, p. 650) and for present purposes we are concerned only with contractual rights.

Paragraph 9 of the Code of Practice provides:

> ... management should recognize the employee's need to achieve a sense of satisfaction in his job and should provide for it so far as practicable.

This is more specific in that it is concerned with particular employment. However it is not contractual. Rather it is a guide to good industrial practice. It does not, therefore, assist the complainant.

In our judgment, the crucial question to be asked is, 'What is the consideration moving from the employers under the contract of employment?' In the case of theatrical performers it is a salary plus the opportunity of becoming better known. Thus a failure to pay the salary produces a partial failure of the consideration, and thus a breach of contract. But so does the cancellation of the performance even if the salary is paid: see *Herbert Clayton and Jack Waller Ltd* v. *Oliver* [1930] AC 209. Similarly the consideration in a commission or piece-work contract of employment is the express obligation to pay an agreed rate for work done plus the implied obligation to provide a reasonable amount of work: see *Devonald* v. *Rosser & Son* [1906] 2 KB 728. In a contract for the employment of one who needs practice to maintain or develop his skills, the consideration will include an obligation to pay the salary or wage, but it may also extend to an obligation to provide a reasonable amount of work. The complainant's work as a spot welder may have been the 'skilled' category, but we do not think that he needs practice in order to maintain his skills. There are, however, other cases in which the sole consideration moving from the employer is the obligation to pay a wage. An example is provided by *Turner* v. *Sawdon & Co.* [1901] 2 K B 653.

[Where a salesman employed for four years was refused work by his employers although they were willing to continue his wages. Held there was no action for damages for breach of contract in those circumstances; the employer was under no obligation to enable the salesman to become or remain *au fait* with his work.]

In relation to the employee's right to be given work to do, it would seem that the effect of *Turner* v. *Sawdon & Co.* has been reduced by the E A T in *Breach* v. *Epsylon Industries* [1976] I C R 316, where it was held that it might constitute constructive dismissal to keep a chief engineer idle on full pay. This constitutes in Brian Napier's view, expressed in a survey on traditional attitudes towards the employment relationship ((1977) 6 *ILJ* 1 at pp. 10–11), an open invitation to courts on subsequent occasions to give the narrowest of interpretations to the rule that there is generally no obligation on an employer to give his employee work to do. For Napier this represents a situation in which it is the employee who benefits from the application of a unitary approach to the employment relationship, which he considers to be a general recent trend in the courts.

However, as we have already suggested, it is questionable whether this is the best explanation of recent judicial approaches to implied terms of the contract of employment. We shall see later (pp. 448–53) that the law of constructive dismissal has created an important new stimulus to fresh judicial rule-making in the form of terms implied by law into contracts of employment. In this context, as we shall later show in detail, the judges have started to develop a new profile of the fair and reasonable contract of employment as they view it. On the whole this has taken the form of a willingness to formulate new implied rights for employees. For instance, in *British Aircraft Corporation Ltd* v. *Austin* [1978] I R L R 332 the E A T held that the employer's general duty to take reasonable care for the safety of his employees gave rise to a particular implied contractual obligation to act reasonably in investigating promptly complaints of lack of safety raised by employees. This entitled the employee to resign and claim constructive dismissal in the instant case where her complaint, that safety goggles suitable to her as a wearer of spectacles had not been supplied to her, was not investigated or remedied over a period of many months.

There are a number of other such examples of formulations of new implied terms in favour of employees. Are the courts really manifesting a unitary approach when formulating such implied terms? Surely not, for a unitary approach would suggest none of these implied terms in favour of employees but rather that the adverse interests of the employees are subordinate in importance to the larger interests of the enterprise as a whole. To suggest that the unitary approach does not involve this subordination of adverse interests is to refine one's view of the unitary approach to the point where it is indistinguishable from pluralism. Surely the point is that the EAT in developing these implied terms has been promoting an approach of enlightened pluralism. The stage has indeed been reached where even so staunch a unitarian as Lord Denning M.R. saw fit, in his last judgment in the area of individual employment law, to recognize, however tentatively, the progress made by enlightened pluralism. This occurred in the constructive dismissal case of *Woods* v. *WM Car Services Ltd* [1982] ICR 693, where the question was whether various changes in terms and conditions imposed on the employee after a take-over had constituted constructive dismissal. Having introduced an account of the modern law of constructive dismissal by a description of the old law of wrongful dismissal, Lord Denning went on to say the following:

> *Woods* v. *WM Car Services Ltd*
> [1982] ICR 693 (CA)

Now under modern legislation we have the converse case. It is the duty of the employer to be good and considerate to his servants. Sometimes it is formulated as an implied term not to do anything likely to destroy the relationship of confidence between them: see *Courtaulds Northern Textiles Ltd* v. *Andrew* [1979] IRLR 84. But I prefer to look at it in this way: the employer must be good and considerate to his servants. Just as a servant must be good and faithful, so an employer must be good and considerate. Just as in the old days an employee could be guilty of misconduct justifying his dismissal, so in modern times an employer can be guilty of misconduct justifying the employee in leaving at once without notice. In each case it depends on whether the misconduct amounted to a repudiatory breach as defined in *Western Excavating (ECC) Ltd* v. *Sharp* [1978] ICR 221.

The circumstances are so infinitely various that there can be, and is, no rule of law saying what circumstances justify and what do not. It is a question of fact for the tribunal of fact – in this case the industrial tribunal. Once they come to their decision, the appeal tribunal should not interfere with it. Thus when the manager told a man: 'You can't do the bloody job anyway,' that would ordinarily not be sufficient to justify the man in leaving at once. It would be on a par with the trenchant criticism which goes on every day. But if the manager used those words dishonestly and maliciously – with no belief in their truth – in order to get rid of him, then it might be sufficient: because it would evince an intention no longer to be bound by the contract. At any rate an industrial tribunal so held in *Courtaulds Northern Textiles Ltd* v. *Andrew* [1979] IRLR 84 and the appeal tribunal did not interfere with it.

The language of this passage is no doubt unitary in its overtones with its talk of considerate employers and faithful servants. But the substance of the passage is that the dictates of enlightened pluralism have come to prevail, at least in the industrial tribunals, and the Employment Appeal Tribunal. Having thus surveyed the state of judicial approaches to implied terms of the contract of employment, we may now turn to some examination of the actual content of the employment relationship. Let us begin by looking at the wage–work bargain and such law as relates specifically thereto.

3 The wage–work bargain

At the centre of the contract of employment, behind the intricate mesh of implied terms and ancillary obligations, stands the wage–work bargain. Although it constitutes the very core of the contract, the wage–work bargain has escaped the attention of lawyers to an extent which is really quite surprising. The existing literature on the contract of employment, concerned as it is with the pursuit of general principles, devotes surprisingly little space to considerations of the different forms which the wage–work bargain may take, that is to say to the different payment systems which are to be encountered in practice, or to the extent to which these different payment systems reflect different expectations among various kinds of workers as to the extent of the security of their earnings in the various events affecting their availability for work, or the availability of work for them to do. In this section we attempt to differentiate between payment systems and to suggest the implications of these differences. The questions to be asked are how far does employment law respond to the differences between payment systems, and how far should it do so?

In the course of this section, it will be seen how the form of the wage–work bargain can be both a source and an expression of social differentiation between certain types of workers. This applies particularly to the contrast between workers who are paid fixed salaries (see below, p. 319) and those who are paid hourly-rated wages (see below, p. 322) or whose pay varies according to output or results (see below, p. 325). This is a *source* of social differentiation in the sense that it represents the conferring of a higher security of earnings upon the fixed-salary workers – a group traditionally known as staff or salaried employees, and performing non-manual tasks. This poses a problem for the labour law and social-security law system, which has to decide how far it will permit the employer by means of a low-security payment system to transfer economic risks from himself to the employee and via the employee to the social-security function of the state itself.

The contrast between fixed-salary and variable-wage payment systems is also an *expression* of social differentiation in the sense that it demonstrates what Alan Fox describes as the 'high trust' characteristic of the relationship between staff workers and the enterprise that employs them (see Fox, *Beyond Contract: Trust, Power and Work Relations* (1974), at pp. 54–7). That is to say, the loyalty and commitment of the staff worker to the enterprise is counted upon to the point where it is thought to be unnecessary to tie his salary to his output or to his hours worked. By contrast payment by results systems rely upon the worker's economic motivation rather than his commitment to the goals of the enterprise, while the measured day-work system (see below, p. 329) relies upon highly surpervised progress towards predetermined targets. There is, incidentally, an interesting paradox here. For the 'low-trust' worker in Fox's calculus is the (manual) worker whose job-specification and remuneration are closely tied to specific tasks and to whom a relatively slight range of discretion is accorded. But where such a worker is paid on a piece-work or other payments by results system, he may acquire from that system a greater control over the relationship between his work and his wages than the fixed-salary worker enjoys.

This brings us to the point of identifying another effect of different payment systems; they may reflect different distributions of control over the wage–work bargain as between employers and workers or unions. The fixed-salary system entirely separates bargaining about remuneration from bargaining about the employee's workload, although the one will obviously affect the other. In payment by results systems, on the other hand, bargaining about pay is integrally linked with bargaining about workload via the process of rate-fixing for work performed. Indeed this process of rate-fixing for particular tasks tends to individuate and fragment the bargaining process so that the bargaining can and does occur at all sorts of different levels down to the individual on the shop-floor. This, as we shall see, poses problems from the point of view of the public interest in stable and effective collective bargaining (see below, pp. 328–9).

This brings us in turn to a problem which relates especially to the hourly-rated wages system, namely that of voluntary overtime (pp. 335ff.). There is often perceived to be a public interest in limiting voluntary overtime working, on the ground that it represents a loosely controlled variable in wage-rates which generates inflation. Employment protection legislation seeks to exclude voluntary overtime from the statutory calculation of the week's pay (see below, pp. 335ff.). This could represent an aim of reforming plant bargaining by reducing voluntary overtime and getting employers to exert a more ordered control over the wage–work bargain. In fact this measure is probably less reformist in its aims, and is simply an attempt to prevent employees from benefiting twice over from what is viewed as an incidental and temporary accretion to their basic pay. The question arises of whether it is fair to hourly-rated employees to discount even regularly worked voluntary overtime in this way. We proceed to pursue these themes in detail.

(a) **Fixed-salary contracts**

In the lawyer's concept of the contract of employment there tends to be a stereotyped pattern whereby remuneration is given for specified periods of work such as the week or the month. In this stereotype, the employee's remuneration does not normally vary according to the number of hours worked, or according to output. For this reason he is sometimes said to be paid for availability for work rather than for actual work done. He contracts to make himself available to the employer, and the employer contracts to pay him a fixed remuneration in return for that availability, and the amount is hence not sensitive to the length of time actually spent at work. That this is the lawyer's stereotype is demonstrated by the following passage which constitutes part of an attempt to define the employee in contradistinction to the independent contractor.

Chitty on Contracts, 25th edn (1983), para. 3382

In the normal case of employment the employee is selected by his employer, works 'full-time' as part of the employer's organization, with regular working hours, at a fixed place of work, with equipment provided by the employer, and under some degree of supervision (arranged by the employer) over his method of working; he enjoys a fixed wage or salary paid at regular intervals, fixed holidays on full pay, and has some security of employment in that he cannot be dismissed without notice (except for misconduct), and until the expiration of his notice of dismissal he is entitled to receive his full wages or salary, whether or not his employer can actually provide him with work to do. The instances which come before courts are those where some, but not all, of these normal features of employment are present, and it must be decided whether the departure from the normal pattern of employment is sufficiently important to justify the conclusion that the relationship is not employment for the purpose of the legal rule in question.

To the observer of employment practice this stereotype corresponds to one major type of employment arrangement rather than to employment arrangements at large. The fixed remuneration system is associated with 'staff' employees as opposed to manual workers in industry. It tends to go with professional, managerial or clerical employment, and to signify a relatively high status within an employment hierarchy, in which a high degree of trust between employer and employee is reflected in the security of earnings implicit in a fixed remuneration system. The following extract shows the extent to which fixed remuneration, identified as 'salary' as opposed to wages, forms part of a process of class differentiation between staff and non-staff workers.

T. Lupton and Angela Bowey, *Wages and Salaries* (1974), p. 106

Differences between wages and salaries

To determine how a salary differs from a wage we must first examine the difference between a wage earner and a salary earner. A wage earner is usually a manual worker, and also one of many workers with the same job title performing much the same tasks for the same employer. A basic rate of pay (hourly or weekly) is usually set for that job either by negotiation between the employer or employer's national representatives, and the representatives of the workers, or unilaterally by the employer (bearing in mind legal or nationally agreed minimum rates). Any additional items in the pay packet, such as local supplements to the basic rate, overtime pay or incentive bonus pay are probably also negotiated for him, or at least the rules and procedures for regulating them are. He is paid directly for the work he does and the way that he does it, and there is no suggestion that he might be paid for what he 'is' rather than what he 'does'. By contrast, the salary earner's weekly, monthly, or even quarterly salary, is more frequently negotiated by him personally, and will depend in part on his senior's *personal* appraisal of him in the job. He is most unlikely, except in some exceptional cases discussed below, to be a manual worker. The salary earner is typically a routine clerical worker, a technical man (e.g. a draughtsman or work-study engineer), a professional man (e.g. an accountant or lawyer or chartered engineer), or a manager. Leaving aside for the moment routine clerical workers, who are closer to manual workers in this respect, the other groups of salary earners have expectations of advancement, based upon age, seniority, qualifications, experience, performance, to higher levels of monetary reward. The wage earner's expectations are much more limited.

Traditionally in the British industrial culture the salary earner was seen as having greater job security than the manual worker. In return it was expected that he would exhibit a greater commitment to the organization than the wage earner, who was regarded as being easier to part with on short notice than the 'staff' (as salary earners were and still are usually called). This tradition dies hard, but, as we shall be discussing below, it is under pressure from such things as technical change, legal prescriptions and trade union power. But the status distinctions are still strong; the words 'staff' and 'hourly paid' or 'payroll' are still the standard industrial vocabulary and although the pattern is changing the manual worker's job is still at greater risk than that of the salary earner.

Whatever may be one's views as to the equations

$$\text{manual worker} = \text{wages}$$
$$\text{others} = \text{salary}$$

there was a good reason for the distinction. The pattern of basic wage plus factory additions offered in many instances the flexibility required to respond to fluctuating workloads on production facilities, by relating these additions to output, productivity or working overtime. The workload of the professionals and the managers is not so directly affected, partly because they are working on longer time scales, partly because they are not so close to the process of production. The distinction between wage and salary arose when employers perceived a need to vary the levels of manning of production processes in line with fluctuations in the level of orders for their products, so as to keep labour costs low. This implied, particularly for those directly engaged on production tasks, a short period of notice – say a day, even an hour. This need would obviously be urgent where direct labour costs were a high proportion of total product costs and competition was severe in the product market (that is, in highly labour-intensive firms operating in an uncertain product market environment). Wages were therefore probably seen as the appropriate reward to the variable short-contract part of the labour force. That part of the labour force might also for the same reason have its earnings related to its level of output.

The distinction between staff and non-staff workers is, in some sectors of industry, being deliberately removed by the introduction of single status arrangements, as the following extract shows. The process is, in effect, one of bringing all employees up to staff-status terms.

IDS Study No. 130 (1976), 'Staff Status in 1976', at p. 1
The 15 companies – both private and public – interviewed for the purposes of this Study have achieved more or less equal conditions for their employees. The ones with

the 'most equal' conditions are single status companies. Those who are approaching equality however are the most significant, for IDS has found that the equalization of conditions can be pursued and attained not through a staff status agreement as such, but through collective bargaining at company level and at industry level. The use of the staff status agreement is becoming more and more limited and is generally applicable to a company who want to give a specific group of employees a specific incentive for staying on. The sense in which 'staff status' is often understood – that of gradually reducing differentials in conditions between manual and non-manual workers (however they are defined) at management initiative – is becoming a thing of the past.

A 'policy of harmonization' is the more frequently used term – implying not a paternalistic move from above but a gradual, negotiated, process of removing some differentials for some employees, while retaining enough incentives and perks to maintain dignity without deprivation for the rest.

A further IDS study on the same subject in 1982 (No. 273) showed that the process of harmonization was continuing apace and was being widely used as an inducement to manual workers to accept changes in working methods for the improvement of labour productivity. It has also been seen as conducive to the centralizing of collective bargaining to company level and the elimination of fragmented local bargaining.

The fixed-salary staff-status contract of employment represents the kind of employment relationship in which the employee enjoys a relatively stabilized and advantageous framework of terms and conditions. Ought the law to seek to place all full-time employees in that situation? Is our employment protection legislation tending to that end by means of its provisions concerning guarantee payments, rights to time off, maternity rights and minimum periods of notice? It is interesting in this connection that the first of a new series of ACAS Discussion Papers was devoted to the topic of harmonization ('Developments in Harmonization' (1982)). The aim of this new series is to describe the factual situation in the particular area of industrial relations concerned, rather than to prescribe policies, which is in accordance with their auxiliary role *vis-à-vis* collective bargaining. Nevertheless, such discussion documents often appear in retrospect to have been developing a case for or against legislative intervention. This discussion paper indicates the virtues of harmonization as tending to improve the prospects for efficient and flexible use of labour, and indeed as helping to secure co-operative attitudes and some degree of common purpose and commitment from employees.

Harmonization measures tend to these ends chiefly by dint of giving manual employees various kinds of protection of their security of earnings – in matters such as sick-pay and guaranteed pay – which before had been conceded only to staff workers. So we shall encounter the harmonization issue and the debate we have just described at various points in the next section of this chapter.

(b) Hourly or daily pay

Under hourly or daily payment systems remuneration is still, as in fixed-salary systems, assessed according to periods of time rather than according to output, but because the pay is assessed by reference to small units of time it can thus be said to be sensitive to the amount of time actually spent at work and hence depends upon actual work done rather than 'availability for work'. Hence these payment systems make no inbuilt provision for security of earnings in the event, for instance, of absence due to sickness, and these payment systems tend, in general, to be associated with manual industrial employment in which security of earnings is significantly less well protected than under fixed-salary systems. In the following extract Lord Denning sketches out a scheme of analysis of different types of employment which reveals this kind of social differentiation between employments according to the payment system used.

A.T. Denning (1939) 55 LQR 343 at 354

(i) Where a man is paid by piece work, the actual performance of the work is the consideration for his wages. Indeed, the amount of his wages can only be calculated by the amount of work he has done. If he is prevented by sickness from doing his work, he is entitled to nothing, even though the relationship of master and servant has not been determined.

(ii) Where the man is paid by the day, the actual performance of each day's work is usually the consideration for that day's wages. . . .

(iii) Where the man is paid by the week, much depends on the nature of the employment. In some occupations actual performance of each week's work is the consideration for that week's wages. Thus in *Browning* v. *Crumlin Valley Collieries* [1926] 1 KB 522 where miners were prevented from working for a time by the physical condition of the mine, which was not due to any default of them or their employers, it was held that during the stoppage the men were not entitled to wages. Greer J. said (at p. 528): 'The consideration for work is wages, and the consideration for wages is work. Is it to be implied in the engagement that the wages are to be paid when through no fault of the employer the work cannot be done?'

(iv) Where the man is paid by the month or at longer intervals, it would seem that usually the consideration is not actual performance of the work but faithful service.

Overtime payments and shift-work premiums are normally associated with hourly payment systems. In the following passage, the move towards overtime payments by junior hospital doctors, and in the public sector generally, is described. Does this involve hourly payment systems for white-collar workers?

IDS Study No. 133 (1976), 'Premium Pay: Public Sector
Staff', at p. 1

Overtime and shift rates used to be for manual workers. Staff, managers and professional people had salaries, not rates to which vulgar premia could be addended. But more and more over the last few years wearers of white collars have been less jealous of their senior and separate status and more interested in their differentials. Doctors used to accept an individual responsibility for providing 24-hour patient care. Junior doctors in hospitals lived in and were on call permanently and only since 1967 has there been official discussion about how much time off they should be allowed. Not, as in other employment, how many hours extra they should work, but how many afternoons and evenings they should be permitted to take off. Since then, in increasingly bureaucratic hospitals, they have shed some of their personal responsibility and status. They have claimed against the system for compensation for their 'unacceptable working conditions'; they have taken industrial action in support of their claims just like the dockers; they have threatened national strikes, wobbled the pay policy and won. To a lesser extent many other staff groups have done the same.

The details [contained in this survey] show clearly the extent to which, in the public sector, salaried workers have negotiated additional payment for work outside the basic working week. Some get an hourly overtime rate linked to their annual salary, but more receive a premium, sometimes described as an unsocial hours allowance or a long hours gratuity. The higher up the scale the less likelihood there is of getting separate payment for overtime, but ceilings on payments have increased more than salaries and there are fewer clauses stating that overtime is 'expected' if 'reasonable' and is covered by an 'element in salary'.

This suggests a rather different view of the relationship between fixed salary and hourly pay from that which we have so far considered. It suggests that staff and professional employees may be open to exploitation precisely because their remuneration does not reflect the number of hours they actually work, and that the incidental advantages associated with staff status may be an inadequate compensation for that disadvantage. Is that a problem with which employment protection legislation should be concerned, or is it a matter to be left to the workings of the collective-bargaining process? Compare the facts under consideration in *Evans* v. *Elementa Holdings Ltd* (below, p. 343).

There is a further aspect of hourly pay which it is important to understand, and which is not allowed for in the traditional account of the difference between manual workers' hourly payment system and the staff workers' fixed-salary system. One might envisage the wage–work bargain for the hourly paid worker simply as giving rise to a basic hourly rate for a certain number of hours per week and enhanced or overtime rates for further hours worked in each week. We shall indeed have to consider the hourly wage–work bargain from that point of view in a separate discussion of overtime – see below, p. 335. But even in relation to the basic working hours, the hourly wage–work bargain does not remain in that simple form. It becomes a composite bargain not for a series of unit hours but for a basic working week envisaged as itself a unit, albeit a unit defined by reference to a number of hours (for instance, 'the 40-hour week'). This observation might seem a mere abstraction, but it is in fact of very great practical importance. It forms the background to demands from the trade-union movement for a shorter working week without loss of earnings which has been a specific aim of the TUC since 1972. Indeed, sections of opinion within the TUC now favour legal intervention to this effect. Although the move to a shorter working week increases the employer's hourly labour costs, it may be acceptable to employers as a way of reducing their labour provision without effecting redundancies. An IDS study in 1982 (No. 264) showed how the national engineering agreement of 1979 (which reduced the basic working week to 39 hours) initiated an extensive series of reductions of the basic working week in many sectors of industry. Although it has not yet been the subject of legislative intervention, the length of the basic working week could easily be seen as a matter for state intervention whether by way of employment protection tending to require reduction or by way of incomes policy tending to discourage it – it is to be noted, for instance, that the Labour government's White Paper, *Winning the Battle Against Inflation* (Cmnd. 7293, 1978), argued that the consequential inflationary effects would actually tend to increase unemployment. At the time of writing, the current preference seems to be in the direction of encouraging the reduction of working hours. There have been initiatives in this direction in certain EEC member states, especially Holland, which we may come under pressure to follow in the UK.

(c) **Payment by results**

The general heading of 'payment by results' comprises a number of different payment systems having the common characteristic that the amount of payment is sensitive to output or profits in some way. This heading therefore comprises systems of commission and bonus payments, and also piece-rate working. An enormous amount of energy has over the years been devoted to the devising of different kinds of 'payment by results' systems designed to maximize the profitability of various kinds of employment from the point of view of the enterprise. The following extract gives some indication of the scope of the variety between different kinds of 'payment by results' systems encountered in practice.

T. Lupton and Angela Bowey, *Wages and Salaries*
(1974), p. 72

The contract of employment between an employer and an employee hardly ever specifies exactly what the employee undertakes to do during each hour or day of his employment. It is neither possible nor desirable to define every action and sequence of actions precisely, because the employer usually seeks a degree of freedom to direct the work-force to perform tasks which are appropriate to the changing demands of customers, the availability of materials, breakdown of machinery or equipment and so on. And the employee seeks a degree of freedom to respond as he thinks fit. The limits within which these freedoms may be exercised are sometimes written into a contract and sometimes 'understood', but in either case custom and practice will further elaborate what it is reasonable for the employer to demand of the employee and vice versa.

Another aspect of the contract which cannot be written into a document is the amount of enthusiasm and commitment the employee brings to his job. Although many employers think they have a right to expect their employees to work as hard as they can in the way that they are asked, the employee does not necessarily see the situation this way. He has not sold himself body and soul for his earnings; he has sold an amount of effort which is more or less acceptable to the employer, and which he himself is prepared to put in, in return for the rewards offered. The pay packet or salary forms a large part of this reward.

Employers long ago realized that it was possible to tie the rate of earnings to the rate of working and/or the quality of the work done. Piecework and bonus-payment systems of all kinds have been devised, some with high basic pay, some with low basic pay, some with a one-to-one relationship between work and money, some with an increasing ratio the more work is done, some with a decreasing ratio and so on. These schemes are aimed at offering the worker an incentive to do his job to the best of his ability or to achieve some set standard of performance. As such they are based implicitly or explicitly on theories about human motivation, as indeed are all systems of payment.

Under the provisions of employment protection legislation, the statutory calculation of the week's pay includes the variable element involved in the payment by results system. The rule is that where remuneration varies with the amount of work done (including cases of commission or similar payment), the statutory week's pay is the employee's average pay for the twelve weeks ending with the calculation date. Where the employee has a pattern of normal working hours, the average is taken of the pay for those hours (EPCA 1978, Sch. 14, Pt II, paras. 3(3), (4), 6). Since the statutory calculation excludes payment for voluntary overtime working (see below, pp. 335ff.), the tribunals and courts have to distinguish between payment by results and payment for voluntary overtime. This distinction may become obscure in practice, as the following extract shows.

Ogden v. *Ardphalt Asphalt Ltd* [1977] ICR 604 (EAT)

On an application for a redundancy payment the question arose as to how the amount of the payment should be calculated under what is now Sch. 14 of the Employment Protection (Consolidation) Act 1978.

KILNER BROWN J.: Before the industrial tribunal the employees were represented by their trade union adviser who was in fact the organizer and secretary of the Amalgamated Union of Asphalt Workers. When the case was put to the tribunal it was put on this basis. The summary can conveniently be found in the notes of evidence taken by the tribunal when the first of the employees was called to give evidence. This is what Mr Ogden said:

> My hourly rate of pay was 94p for a basic 40 hour week. I received a redundancy payment of two weeks' wages of £37.60. I produce the working rules and refer the tribunal especially to rr 1 and 2.

Then when he was cross-examined it emerged quite clearly that the way the employees were putting their case was in this form: 'We are guaranteed eight hours' work a day. In the previous 12 weeks although the basic was 40 hours I was averaging between 70 and 80 hours a week for payment purposes.' As the lay members of the tribunal know, and have expressed their knowledge, this form of approach and this form of calculation is very well known throughout industry as a whole. In other words, if there is a 40 hour week and the basic pay is £1 per hour, that means that the basic pay at the end of the week is £40. But if in fact, through various means, the take-home pay of a worker is £80, instead of working out under the various heads whether it is overtime, whether it is an incentive or productivity bonus, or whatever allowance it might be, it has become common practice to say, 'Well, if it is a 40 hour week and I took home £80, that means I worked 80 hours that week for payment purposes', because the basic pay is £1 per hour. It seems to us that this unfortunately put everybody on the wrong track.

Counsel for the employers, who appeared before the industrial tribunal and has appeared before us (and to whom we are very much indebted for his help in this matter), said that they were at least made aware that one of the basic points on behalf of the employees was linked to the working rules and conditions of the National Joint Council for the laying side of the Mastic Asphalt Industry. The first rule dealt simply with the hours of labour, wage rates and overtime. Rule 2 (the schedule) had under (viii) these significant words: 'The stated quantities of work will be required for a normal eight-hour period. Extra work done over and above the quantities stated will be paid for proportionately.' If it had been apparent to the industrial tribunal that they were not simply looking at the working rules in terms of hours of labour, wage rates and overtime, and a schedule of minimum output under r. 2, perhaps the matter would not have achieved the unsatisfactory state that in our judgment it ultimately reached. The clue to the whole problem is in those words: 'Extra work done over and above the quantities stated will be paid for proportionately.' This never was a case in which overtime was under consideration. This never was a case in which one could look at it on the basis that the man did the equivalent of 70 hours' work in terms of pay.

It is said that this is an important case in the whole field of industry because it is desired that certain statements of principle might be considered in view of the fact that a number of industrial tribunals have already interpreted the Redundancy Payments Act 1965 in one way, whereas certainly one, if not two, perhaps three, industrial tribunals seem to have interpreted it differently, much along the lines urged on us by counsel for the employers in this case.

The term 'piecework' has crept into this argument, and again the lay members of the tribunal are most anxious that that term might be allowed to die the death, because the working arrangements for the last 20 or 25 years in industry have long since passed from the old notion of piecework when people were paid so much money for so many pieces. It is of great importance to recognize that the statutory definition of what used to be called 'piecework', or the sort of situation where piecework might have applied, is quite clear that it relates no longer to the actual pieces of work but it is in terms related to the amount of work done. The statutory definition now is 'where the amount of pay varies according to the amount of work done'. . . .

The argument which was put before the industrial tribunal, and which was put before us by counsel for the employers, is this: that the average hourly rate of remuneration should be the basic, in this case something of the order of 95p. Counsel for the employers in support of his general argument (which was the one which appealed to the industrial tribunal) says that where you have an incentive or productivity bonus built into the wage structure that is really analogous to overtime; it is something which is additional; it is not within the hourly rate, and it is not within the ordinary weekly number of hours. This is a case, said counsel for the employers before the industrial tribunal and here, which turned simply on the normal working hours. And that is what the tribunal in fact did. What they did was, they multiplied the figure 40, which was the number of normal working hours, by the basic hourly rate of remuneration, something in the order of 95p. The point of law here which has been urged on us, and which we accept as being correct, is that that is the wrong way of going about it, and that what the industrial tribunal should have done, in accordance with those two schedules, parts of which I have read, was to have proceeded as follows: they should have determined the average hourly rate of remuneration which was in fact paid to the employees in respect of the four [now twelve] weeks ending with the last complete week.

Then when one looks back again at the person who is in effect treated as the old-fashioned former pieceworker might have been treated, and asks the question, 'Is this a case where the amount of pay varies according to the amount of work done?' the answer is plain: it does. And that was part of the agreement here: that extra work done over and above the quantity stated would be paid for proportionately. In the view of this tribunal, once one bears that definition in mind, once one looks to see that there is this plain distinction made in [EPCA 1978, Sch. 14, para. 3(2)] between the time worker, set against the person who earns something more, then it is quite plain in our judgment that in effect what the industrial tribunal should have said was: 'Let us find out what is the average pay that these men had in each week of each of the last four [now twelve] weeks, and let us average it out.'

The 'payment by results' system contains no inherent provision for the security of earnings in the event of the unavailability of work or the unavailability of the employee to perform his work. In order for such systems to form part of viable contracts of employment they have in practice to be supplemented by arrangements concerned with the guaranteeing of minimum rates of earnings, such as the guaranteed-week provisions made by collective bargaining in, for example, the engineering and construction industries. Guaranteed-week arrangements are also often imposed by the terms of a wages council order setting minimum terms of employment in the industry concerned. We consider guaranteed-week arrangements in more detail under the heading of 'Security of Earnings' – see below, pp. 357ff.

'Payment by results' systems operate, essentially, by giving the employee a greater control over his output of work than he would otherwise be allowed, coupled, ideally from the employer's point of view, with a corresponding incentive to maximize output. Such systems therefore represent some degree of participation by employees in the making of decisions concerning the administration of their work. The social effects of this kind of participative mechanism have been the subject of considerable examination by industrial relations writers, for whom this dimension of 'payment by results' schemes has appeared as one of their principal characteristics, as the following extract suggests.

William Brown, *Piecework Bargaining* (1973), pp. 53–4

In factories with high Topsy factors [the 'Topsy factor' is the tendency towards complex fragmented and ad hoc payment structures – the kind which 'just growed'], the individual pieceworker is in a position of considerable power. If he fails to agree a job value with the ratefixer he will be paid at or close to his past average earnings. Thus such a failure to agree will cost the worker little while the low effort he puts into the job in question (if he works at it at all) will frustrate management's production plans. Put against this there is an obligation on the worker, that will probably be brought to his notice by his shop steward if he fails to observe it himself, not to 'push things too far'. An undue strain on the day-to-day working relationships that the pieceworker has with junior management could lose him many personal favours that he values. In the long run it could bring more drastic intervention from senior management.

Bargaining is carried out over two distinct aspects of the job. The first is the time within which the man might be expected to carry out the job when working at a 'reasonable' effort – that is, the 'floor-to-floor time'. The rate-fixer requires skill and experience to estimate this in the face of likely attempts by the worker to mislead him. The second aspect of the job which is bargained over is the level of earnings which the worker 'ought' to receive on the new job value. Both sides are likely to argue over this in terms of fair comparisons.

Thus the level of earnings which the pieceworker finally gets depends upon several factors. It will depend upon the level of effort which he is willing to maintain and, with supervisors exerting little or no pressure on effort levels, they vary considerably between men. It will depend upon the pieceworker's success in fooling the ratefixer on floor-to-floor times and the extent to which the technical features of the job help in this. Another factor is the aggressiveness of the worker and the extent to which he is willing to strain his relationship with junior management and his fellow workers by exploiting the system. The degree of fatalism that pieceworkers exhibit in accepting tight times without appeal and reobservation varies. So also does the latitude left by the pieceworker's success in fooling the ratefixer on floor-to-flooring slack job values. Finally, it depends upon the comparisons that he uses and upon the ratefixer's sense of what would be 'fair'.

It would require an extreme enthusiasm for this form of joint regulation to regard these manœuvrings as being particularly productive or beneficial. Their absence, however, in non-unionized plants might leave open the possibility of manipulation of employees against their interest by skilfully contrived 'payment by results' systems. This could raise a theoretical case for the intervention of employment protection legislation; in practice, though, the problems of piecework systems are problems of industrial and collective relations.

It is not suggested, however, that payment by results systems consist entirely in the sort of piecework bargaining so far described. In *The Changing Contours of British Industrial Relations* it was noted that by 1977/8, while 64 per cent of establishments surveyed had payment by results for some of their workers (which was thought to represent no great overall change from a decade earlier), almost two-thirds of the establishments reporting payment by results also reported having work study (i.e. some sort of measurement of labour input as a control on payment by results) and there was evidence that the forms of payment by results which tended to give rise to fragmented bargaining were on the decline. Not only has there been a growth of work study methods tending to control the operation of payment by results, but there have also been important experiments with systematic alternatives to piecework bargaining.

For some years, from the late 1960s, a preferable system was thought to be that of 'measured day-work'. This system sought to combine the incentives of piecework with the structural regularity of fixed payment systems. The idea was to establish precise output targets as in a piecework system but to reflect deviations not by adjusting the pay but rather by industrial disciplinary or dispute resolution mechanisms. So measured day-work was really a fixed payment system with a particular emphasis on precisely calculated production targets. In 1973 Allan Flanders pointed out in a major article ('Measured Daywork and Collective Bargaining' (1973) XI *BJIR* 368) that if measured day-work was to function better than the decayed payment by results systems that it was designed to replace, nothing less was required than a thorough-going overhaul of attitudes towards and structures for collective bargaining. Above all, it would be necessary to achieve joint regulation of production standards and work regulation. In fact this probably identified the underlying difficulty about measured day-work because it is ultimately a way of asserting managerial control over those very matters.

By the later 1970s it was fairly clear that measured day-work had not provided an easy way of avoiding the disadvantages of payment by results systems. On the other hand, there was little reason to return to the sort of payment by results systems which measured day-work had replaced. In broad terms this dilemma gave rise to a new wave of productivity bargaining. This was greatly encouraged by the White Paper, *The Attack on Inflation after 31st July 1977* (Cmnd. 6882, 1977), which ushered in Stage Three of the Labour government's incomes policy and recognized self-financing productivity deals as an exception to general pay norms. The huge numbers of productivity schemes that sought to exploit this opportunity are described in IDS Studies 162 (1978) and 186 (1979). The schemes were of many sorts – the process of contracting for greater efficiency and flexibility may take many forms – but a very significant trend to have emerged was the tendency towards bonus schemes assessed on a plant-by-plant basis. Perhaps the most important and best-known such schemes were those introduced by the National Coal Board in 1977 and BL in 1979; there have been many others too. Experience of these schemes would suggest that the making of incentive payments on a plant-wide rather than an individual level is fraught with consequences for collective bargaining and industrial relations generally. It may constitute an effective way of fragmenting the collective bargaining strength of trade unions by giving workers in plants (or pits) where bonuses are higher an interest in conflict with that of the workers in low-bonus plants. It is interesting in light of this to be reminded by IDS Study 143 (1977) how much plant-wide incentive schemes owe to United States exponents of scientific management, in particular the eponymous authors of the Rucker and Scanlon plans.

The use of incentive schemes as part of the wage–work bargain has not really been the subject of much interest for labour law. We should not conclude from this that the topic has no potential interest to labour lawyers. It has as much potential interest as many topics that have been identified as meat for labour law because there is some labour law relating to them. At stake here is the freedom to adopt forms of wage–work bargain which may in extreme cases be deemed oppressive of employees but which, more practically, have a very great significance for the structure and vitality of collective bargaining. Consideration of this should figure largely in any deliberations which may in future occur about how the Government is to encourage the development and maintenance of an effective collective bargaining system.

(d) **Profit sharing**

Thus far, in considering incentive payment schemes, we have been considering forms of the wage–work bargain in which pay is related to labour output in some sense. We have seen how labour output may be measured for this purpose not just at the level of the individual worker but at more generalized levels, such as that of the workshop, plant or even the enterprise as a whole. It seems in one sense only a short step from such generalized incentive schemes to schemes in which pay is related to the output or profit of the enterprise as a whole rather than just its labour output. Indeed, one of the many sub-cultures which flourish within the realm of scientific management devotes itself precisely to accomplishing that transition in the form of so-called 'added value' payment schemes (see I D S Study No. 189 (1979)) whereby some sort of direct relationship is created between pay and gross output minus the cost of purchased materials and purchased services (that is, to look at it in another way, net output plus wages and salaries and interest).

In another sense, however, these minutiae of pay calculation conceal a shift of profound significance from hiring the worker for reward to sharing the risk of the venture with him – therefore to a fundamentally different form of wage–work bargain. Incentive payments create an interest among employees in maximizing productivity; profit sharing creates a further interest in minimizing pay (a point clearly brought out in the judgment in the *Lotus Cars* case, see below, p. 337). Traditionally in British industry profit sharing has been accordingly associated with particular experiments in unitary forms of management, i.e. those which stress the association of the employees' interests with those of the enterprise as a whole. These experiments have for the most part taken the form of rewarding employees with shares in the employing enterprise – a form of reward which further seeks to stress and express their participation in the risks of the venture upon which the enterprise is engaged. The political fortunes of the movement towards this form of the wage–work bargain are usefully surveyed by John Elliott in a book about industrial democracy written in 1977:

Elliott, *Conflict or Co-operation?* (1977), pp. 184–7

Employee share ownership
Until relatively recently the financial participation method of involving individual workers in the fortunes of their companies has held little appeal for most British industrialists, who have rarely been interested in sharing the ownership of their companies with employees. This attitude, which is hardly surprising in the British

political and industrial system, has been matched on the other side of industry by scant trade union interest either in individual workers holding shares or, indeed, in the more socialist solution adopted by Labour movements abroad of advocating centrally collectively held employee share funds. The primary trade union objections to workers holding shares in their own companies are first that they are doubling their insecurity when the company fails, (an argument that is refuted by companies which say that profit-sharing means workers are receiving *extra* cash), and second that companies rarely if ever allow the shareholders to carry any corresponding influence over management decisions. In any case, the TUC pointed out in its 1974 Industrial Democracy document, 'they do little or nothing to reduce the inequality of wealth and they do not include the public sector.' Further union objections to all such types of schemes are that they use employees' money as cheap investment and that the shares saved can in effect amount to a backdoor approach to incomes policies and wage restraint because some money that otherwise might have been added to the pay packet is taken out of the economy.

Abroad however there has tended to be more interest, and schemes have been introduced by people as disparate as the Shah in Iran and De Gaulle in France; the main enthusiasm is to be found in the United States, where they are sometimes linked with pension arrangements. The British Wider Share Ownership Council has estimated that at least 197,000 American companies have set up such share schemes (Wider Share Ownership Council, 1977). This growth has mainly been during the past ten years and has recently been encouraged by legislation which boosts them as cheap ways of raising capital. Compared with this figure, there were early in 1977 barely 100 schemes in the UK (although there were 1000 for top executives alone) and most of them only involved about 10 per cent of the employees.

'Sharing wealth' at ICI
The best known of these schemes is one run since 1953 by ICI. Its 95,000 monthly and weekly paid staff receive a profit-related annual share allocation – worth in 1975 for example an average of £112 each after tax – which they can either keep or sell. Over the years a lot of the stock has been sold (about 60 per cent at the last count in 1971), but ICI still feels that the amount retained is significant. The company does not overplay the employee participation importance of the scheme, however, and would not suggest that it has a major motivational role among its work force, although some of its managers would like to see it play a larger role in factory-level incentives. The official ICI view however is that, within its overall policies (see Chapter 11), it helps to build a company-wide identity and corporate image quite separate from the company-trade union pay and productivity bargains. A report prepared by an ICI working party late in 1976, which approved its continuation subject to some reforms, put this view clearly:

> The effects on employees of a broadly based profit sharing scheme, no matter how well designed and implemented, in such a large company as ICI, are necessarily limited. It is very doubtful if it can by its own nature have a direct effect on their motivation. Its contribution is more likely to be to the background of the feelings of employees about, and their interests in, the company. There is no doubt that the existing scheme is valued by a large majority of employees. It is something distinctive about the company which helps to give many employees a sense that ICI is a good company to work for. It helps as one of the background factors to give employees a feeling of cohesion with others in the company and to encourage co-operation.

This statement of interest is specially significant because the report was produced by a joint management-employee committee that included twenty-three elected shop steward and other worker representatives. The shop stewards were therefore backing a form of direct employer-employee participation that their unions usually dismiss – sometimes dubbing them 'grace and favour' handouts. Indeed, revisions proposed for the ICI scheme in its report were aimed at removing some of the paternalistic overtones, especially by replacing the ICI board's right unilaterally to fix the annual bonus rate with a permanent formula (based on the company's results on an added value or wealth created concept). But ICI is not interested in raising the proportion of its employees' income provided by the scheme. This is partly because it feels the pay-out should not be large enough either to cause hardship when it is cut back in bad years (for those who cash it in immediately) or to attract the attention of trade union negotiators as a significant item.

Industrialists become interested

The general lack of enthusiasm among industrialists in the past was expounded, with overtones of the proprietorial preoccupations of top management, in the CBI's 1973 report, *The Responsibilities of the British Public Company*, prepared under the chairmanship of Lord Watkinson (see also Chapter 9). The report said the CBI approved of voluntary schemes in certain circumstances but opposed their mandatory imposition and added: 'We dislike a situation in which an individual other than a director has the bulk of his savings in the company that employs him.'

By 1977 however the CBI was changing its stance and had set up a working party which was moving towards a position just adopted in a Conservative Party 'green paper' that such schemes should be encouraged by the Government. The Conservatives' idea was that workers selling their shares should be taxed for the profits made only on a sliding scale with the amount of tax being reduced the longer the shares had been owned. The renewed CBI interest stemmed not only from this Conservative Party initiative (which itself had been encouraged by the Wider Share Ownership Council) but from results of a survey it had commissioned in 1976 on employee attitudes. Industrialists interpreted the survey as showing that employees were far more interested in profits than was often assumed (only 8 per cent said they thought profit a 'dirty word') and that more than half those questioned (58 per cent) thought that less profit ought to be distributed to directors and shareholders and more distributed to themselves.

By the middle of 1977 several major companies were introducing share ownership schemes for the first time. It seemed indeed that the changes that were beginning to emerge in the attitude of industrialists towards participation in management affairs were also being reflected in a cautious new approach to employee financial participation through share ownership. Up to this time ICI had been almost the only large company to have such a scheme, and its early experiences with workers selling off their first shares allocations in 1953 at its factory gates had helped to build up a mythology in the City and elsewhere that workers did not want to own shares.

There are however still very few companies at the heavy manufacturing (often militant) end of British industry with schemes and some of the new companies in 1977 reflected the underlying attitudes involved. Among some of the largest for example, one (Marks and Spencer) is non-union while another (British Home Stores) has only a tiny minority of unionised employees. A third (Barclays Bank) is white-collar and largely non-militant and in any case does not give shares to its most junior staff who receive profit-related cash handouts instead. Another company – Joseph Lucas – was partly motivated by the fall-off in managers' living standards when it introduced its scheme for white-collar staff, not for its heavily unionised shopfloor workers.

So while it may seem attractive to industrialists to try with company shares to lure their employees away from joining or reflecting the views of their unions, and towards involving themselves in the fortunes of their companies, not many heavily unionised companies have decided to run the risk of clashing on the subject with their unions, who would probably want the money spent in other ways. There is also great scepticism among many industrialists and personnel experts about whether share schemes really help employee–employer relationships. On the other hand, in a more liberal and ideological vein, a few companies may be deciding that it is illogical of them to perpetuate the class divisions of company ownership when they are allowing employees increasing democracy in management affairs. But the more down-to-earth reason for the increased interest in such schemes has been the growing employer concern to make employees understand the realities of company affairs through increased communication. There has also been a realisation that, since the growth of industrial democracy might well lead to worker director systems, there is likely to be an advantage in encouraging financial awareness among shop stewards. Some optimists even hope that such financial awareness and employee share ownership might reduce boardroom disputes about the size of shareholders' dividends in the days of worker directors.

Meanwhile, on a more political level, Conservative interests (partly looking early in 1977 for employee participation policies that a future Conservative government could implement) and organisations like the Wider Share Ownership Council (anxious to bolster up the credibility of the City) have been lobbying industrialists about the value that an injection of worker-shareholders could be to the survival of the mixed economy. Then, in the late summer of 1977, the Liberals persuaded the Labour Government to draw up its own proposals for profit-sharing including tax concessions to encourage it.

Since Elliott wrote in those terms, the Labour government, in pursuance of its political pact with the Liberal Party (for whom 'industrial co-partnership' has been a long-cherished goal), included in the Finance Act 1978 provisions creating a favourable tax régime for profit-sharing schemes (ss.53–61) and the Conservative government took further measures to improve the tax attractions of such schemes (Finance Act 1980, s.46). Although the 1978 Act encouraged the creation of many new schemes, an IDS Study in 1979 (No. 204) suggested that the overall number of such schemes was still small compared for instance with the overall number of productivity schemes. Since that time there has been a decline in the profits generally available for sharing, and less has been heard of this kind of initiative. Indeed – and this is surely a reflection of more general changes in attitudes – the ideas underlying profit-sharing schemes now tend to issue forth in schemes for transforming workforces, or at least the managerial grades of workforces, into proprietor managers by selling or distributing the equity in the enterprise to them. In the private sector, one hears of many such schemes in the form of 'management buy-outs'. There seem also to be important parallels in the public sector, for example in the recent sale of the National Freight Corporation to its workforce.

(e) **Overtime**

The payment systems which have been considered in the foregoing sections tend, normally with the exception of fixed salaried employees, to become overlaid with systems of overtime payment. These systems reflect the fact that the basic contract of employment is regarded as committing the employee only to a stated number of working hours within each week. Beyond that basic working week any hours worked by the employee tend to be regarded as, to some extent, the result of a voluntary decision on his part to undertake further working hours, and in any event meriting payment at enhanced rates. The relation between overtime working and the basic working week has been a matter of some social concern in so far as overtime working has been viewed as inflationary in its implications, and destructive of the rationality of payment structures (see also p. 369).

> E.G. Whybrew, 'Overtime Working in Great Britain'
> (1967) (Royal Commission on Trade Unions and
> Employers' Associations, Research Paper No. 9)

A. Generalisations

273. The paper has pulled together evidence that confirms the C B I's conclusion that 'a good deal of overtime is worked for non-productive reasons' and the Electricity Council's contention that heavy overtime has led to uneconomical uses of manpower and the development of unsatisfactory work practices. It has shown that this inefficient practice is more extensive in Britain than in most other countries and that it has increased rather than diminished in the period since advanced managements and academics have stressed its shortcomings and costliness.

274. This situation has not resulted entirely from the reductions in normal working hours. It has come from pressures operating at the workplace. These pressures have been given free play by the scarcity of statutory controls and the fact that collective agreements all leave the decisions on overtime to be made at the workplace. At this level there are numerous circumstances in which management feel that overtime is justified and moreover there are always some people only too willing to work the extra hours. Seeing some apparently improving their living standards by working overtime, others develop a desire for it, so that pressures to spread the overtime build up in the workplace. Local union representatives see the short-term direct interests of their members and do little to discourage overtime. The result is that all semblance of control is lost and actual overtime ceases to be worked for the reasons management desire when authorizing it in general terms. Moreover the association of high overtime with low average earnings suggests that the workers' long-term interests are not served by high overtime.

The concern about the unchecked growth of overtime has been reflected in legislative attempts to link rights based on the 'week's pay' (see Chapter 4) with the basic working week alone. The present legislation shows the difficulty of distinguishing between the non-obligatory character of overtime and the premium rate character of overtime as the crucial identifying feature of the overtime phenomenon.

EPCA 1978, Sch. 14, Pt I

NORMAL WORKING HOURS

1. For the purpose of this Schedule the cases where there are normal working hours include cases where the employee is entitled to overtime pay when employed for more than a fixed number of hours in a week or other period, and, subject to paragraph 2 below, in those cases that fixed number of hours shall be the normal working hours.

2. If in such a case –

(a) the contract of employment fixes the number, or the minimum number, of hours of employment in the said week or other period (whether or not it also provides for the reduction of that number or minimum in certain circumstances), and

(b) that number or minimum number of hours exceeds the number of hours without overtime,

that number or minimum number of hours (and not the number of hours without overtime) shall be the normal working hours.

In so far as statute law has taken non-obligatoriness as the identifying feature of overtime working, it has tended to assume that the contract of employment forms a ready way of testing for obligatoriness, but in the absence of litigation about the contractual results of refusals to work overtime the law of the contract of employment in fact provides very little guidance in this respect (see above, pp. 326ff.; see also *ITT Components Group (Europe)* v. *Kolah* [1977] ICR 740). The following extract shows how difficult it is for the courts to offer any kind of guiding principle in relation to this problem.

Tarmac Roadstone Holdings v. *Peacock* [1973] ICR 273 (CA)

STAMP L.J.: The respondents' contracts of employment were subject to the relevant national agreement, which provided that the normal week should be 40 hours actual work, for which 40 hours should be paid. Under it all workers were bound to work overtime in accordance with the demands of the industry during the normal week and/or at weekends. At the outset the respondents were told or given to understand in effect that they were expected to do more than that, and unless prepared to do so, could not have the job. Throughout their employment they were called on to do and did do many more than 40 hours a week. In fact, they regularly did at least 57 hours a week and on occasion more. It may be that their services would have been dispensed with had they not done so. There are, however, in my judgment, no findings of fact in the tribunal's findings which could lead to the conclusion that the employers ever bound themselves to provide the men with 57 hours per week. The 57 hours they worked were regular but were not fixed in the sense that it ever became a term of the employment that the employers should employ them for that time. Does the case then fall within subparagraph (1) of paragraph 1 of Schedule 2 to the CEA 1963 [EPCA 1978, Sch. 14, para. 1] to which one is referred by the RPA 1965, in which case the redundancy payments should be calculated by reference to a 40-hour week? Or does it fall within subparagraph (2) [ibid., para. 2]? Unless the case is taken out of subparagraph (1) by the effect of subparagraph (2), the former subparagraph will, so far as regards this case, apply. Subparagraph (2) provides, in effect, that if a minimum number of hours for which the employee is bound to work is fixed by the contract of employment, and the minimum number of hours includes overtime, that minimum becomes the yardstick. That, as I understand it, is the effect of all the cases cited to this court and to which Lord Denning M.R. has referred. The present case does not in my judgment fall within subparagraph (2). As I have said, it was never a term of the contract that the men should work and be paid for 57 hours, for the employers were not bound to provide them with that number of hours' work. I cannot accept the view indicated by Sir John Donaldson that, in order to come within subparagraph (2), the obligation to work overtime does not have to be mutual or that the employer does not have to be under an obligation to provide overtime. For if he is under no such obligation, it cannot, in my judgment, be truly said, within the meaning of subparagraph (2)(*a*), that '*the contract of employment fixes* the number, or the minimum number, of hours of employment'. I underline those words 'the contract of employment fixes,' because it is upon those words, with particular emphasis upon the word 'fixes', that in my judgment, the case turns.

Thus in the case of overtime we find that there has been indirect legal intervention in the form of an attempt to exclude overtime hours from the reckoning of employment protection rights so far as those depend on hours worked. The questions arise of whether any purpose is served by this kind of indirect intervention, and, if so, whether the right criterion has been adopted for the overtime hours which are to be excluded from the statutory calculations. Is there not a danger here of merely penalizing the hourly paid worker by comparison with the fixed-salary-staff status employee? The danger that the doctrine in the *Tarmac* case may have a penal operation is apparent from the decision of the Court of Appeal in *Lotus Cars Ltd* v. *Sutcliffe* [1982] I R L R 381, where it was held that the week's pay should be based on a 40-hour week on the following facts (to quote from the headnote):

According to the company's staff handbook, the basic working week was 40 hours. But 'because of our facility utilisation, it is necessary that works staff work a "standard week" of 45 hours, the additional five hours over the "basic week" of 40 hours being regarded as "normal extra time" and carrying a supplementary pay increment'. The five extra hours were paid at normal basic hourly rate plus ⅓. Basic salary was defined in the handbook as 'the weekly rate of salary exclusive of any extra time'. The handbook also set out the guaranteed week provisions under which all permanent weekly staff were guaranteed their salary based on a 40-hour week subject to a number of conditions. One of these was that the staff were prepared to work a 45 productive hour standard week. There was also a profit sharing scheme based on the achievement of production levels in a maximum of 45 hours a week. A condition of the scheme was that employees were ready and willing to work the standard 45 hour week should that be necessary to achieve the production targets. Other benefits such as holiday pay and sick pay were calculated on the basis of the 40-hour basic week.

The leading judgment is that of Cumming-Bruce L.J., once a judicial member of the E A T who nevertheless began by saying that 'The terms and conditions of the contracts were all in writing to be collected from the notice of terms of employment and the staff handbook. It is not therefore a case in which the particular industrial expertise of the lay members of the Employment Appeal

Tribunal is significant . . .' (p. 382). It was on this basis, and by resort to legalism of a high order, that the Court of Appeal saw fit to overturn the finding of the industrial tribunal and the EAT that the 45-hour week, referred to in the conditions of employment as the 'standard week' and expressly described as the normal working week, should constitute the working week for statutory purposes. Thus the *Tarmac* rule was treated in the *Lotus* case as meaning that a given level of hours must be obligatory upon the employer (as well as the employee) not just in an industrial relations sense as it was here, but also in the narrowest contractual sense. This is surely to deal harshly with an employee who in fact worked a 45-hour week as a matter of course, according to a set timetable in his conditions of employment. There was no question of including the fruits of uncontrolled overtime working.

(f) Pensions and other benefits after retirement as part of the wage–work bargain

Traditionally pensions and other benefits conferred after the retirement of the employee have not been regarded as part of the wage–work bargain. It is not hard to explain this within a pluralist frame of reference. On the part of employees it would be felt that employers should not be relieved of any part of their obligations in respect of current wages on the basis of the pension benefits they would provide after the retirement of their employees. On the part of employers it would be felt that pensions and other post-retirement benefits should not be payable as of right but as a distinct act of benevolence on the part of employers. It is worth pointing out that some important cases in the law of trusts in the last twenty years have concerned pension or other post-retirement provisions made by the heads of companies, and that the approach to such provisions is very much conditioned by the characterization as acts of benevolence that attaches to dispositions made by way of discretionary trusts – compare, for instance, *In re Flavel's Will Trusts* [1969] 1 WLR 444 (Ch. D); *McPhail* v. *Doulton* [1971] AC 424.

As social conditions have changed and the general social expectations of maintenance or replacement of income after retirement for the whole of the workforce have increased, the traditional view of pensions has become a more myopic one. It has proved difficult to create a consciousness of the importance that trade unions should accord to pensions in the collective bargaining process, despite some effort in that direction on the part of the TUC. Even in the EqPA it is accepted that the cost of applying the equal-pay principle to pensions would be too great, so they are specifically excluded: s.6(1A).

These indications of reluctance to regard pensions as part of the wage–work bargain – as 'deferred pay' – are at variance with what we shall see (below, p. 364) was a major political decision in the mid-1970s expressed in the Social Security Pensions Act 1975 to accord to occupational pension schemes a major and central role in the state plan for retirement provision.

Some progress away from that reluctance has been made both in British case law and by the use of E E C provisions on equal pay, though it is fair to say that labour lawyers, who share the widespread lack of interest in pensions, have not generally perceived their importance in this respect. The first such development occurred in the context of the law of accident compensation in *Parry* v. *Cleaver* [1970] AC 1 (HL), where the question was whether disability benefit payable under an occupational pension scheme was deductible from the damages payable by the tortfeasor who caused the disability. It was held that the disability pension was not deductible, and one of the arguments that Lord Reid in particular accepted as conducing to this result was that the pension was to be regarded as deferred earnings (and therefore as a benefit to which the plaintiff had entitled himself independently of the accident). Lord Reid puts it thus, making the further important point that the distinction between 'employer's contributions' and 'employee's contributions' is a purely nominal and notional one:

Parry v. *Cleaver* [1970] AC 1 (HL)

LORD REID: What, then, is the nature of a contributory pension? Is it in reality a form of insurance or is it something quite different? Take a simple case where a man and his employer agree that he shall have a wage of £20 per week to take home (leaving out of account PAYE, insurance stamps and other modern forms of taxation) and that between them they will put aside £4 per week. It cannot matter whether an insurance policy is taken out for the man and the £4 per week is paid in premiums, or whether the £4 is paid into the employer's pension fund. And it cannot matter whether the man's nominal wage is £21 per week so that, of the £4, £1 comes from his 'wage' and £3 comes from the employer, or the man's nominal wage is £23 per week so that, of the £4, £3 comes from his 'wage' and £1 comes from the employer. It is generally recognised that pensionable employment is more valuable to a man than the mere amount of his weekly wage. It is more valuable because by reason of the terms of his employment money is being regularly set aside to swell his ultimate pension rights whether on retirement or on disablement. His earnings are greater than his weekly wage. His employer is willing to pay £24 per week to obtain his services, and it seems to me that he ought to be regarded as having earned that sum per week. The products of the sums paid into the pension fund are in fact delayed remuneration for his current work. That is why pensions are regarded as earned income.

This acceptance of pensions as earned income was followed in *The Halcyon Skies* [1977] QB 14 (QBD) where Brandon J. held that the employer's contribution to the pension fund as well as the employee's counted as 'wages' for the purposes of bringing them within the scope of the Admiralty jurisdiction to enforce claims for seamen's wages *in rem* against ships.

Some progress has also been made in a similar direction in cases brought under Art. 119 of the Treaty of Rome, though it is important to appreciate the limited nature of its provisions. Up to a point, the comprehensive equal pay principle of Art. 119 has provided a way of circumventing the exclusion of provisions relating to retirement or death from the Eq PA and the SDA (see below, pp. 382, 409). Thus in *Garland* v. *British Rail Engineering Ltd* [1982]

IRLR 111 (ECJ), the ECJ held that travel facilities accorded to employees after retirement are 'pay' within Art. 119 so that provision by an employer of special travel facilities for former male employees and their families which were not also provided for former female employees and their families constituted discrimination within the meaning of the article. But the decision of the ECJ in *Worringham* v. *Lloyds Bank Ltd* [1981] ICR 558 reminds one of the restrictions on this principle in relation to pensions as such. The complaint was that the Lloyds Bank terms of employment and pension scheme favoured men by providing for them to contribute to the pension scheme below the age of 25, while the women contributed only from age 25, and by making an addition to the salary of men under 25 to compensate for their contributions. It was held that the complaint related to 'pay' within the meaning of Art. 119; but on no wider ground than that the men's contributions affected calculations based on gross pay such as redundancy payments, unemployment benefits and family allowances as well as mortgage and credit facilities. It was held that the complaint gave rise to a directly applicable right under Art. 119; but on no wider ground than that these other benefits were affected by the inequality in gross salary and that on leaving the scheme before retirement, men would receive a premium equivalent to their contributions made under the age of 25 where women would not. This leaves substantially untouched the question of whether pensions count as 'pay' on the basis that they are deferred pay, and whether inequality of pension benefits falls within the ambit of sex discrimination, at least as covered by the directly applicable aspect of Art. 119. The omens are inauspicious for that wider application of Art. 119 to pensions, for Advocate-General Warner's opinion in this case reminds us of the apparent applicability to occupational pension schemes in the UK of the doctrine developed by the ECR in the first *Defrenne* case (*Defrenne* v. *Belgian State* [1971] ECR 445) that pensions fall outside Art. 119 where they operate in substitution for the whole or part of a state social security pensions scheme (rather than as a supplement thereto). It is by means of that doctrine that the ECJ expresses an underlying reluctance to permit, in the absence of specific legislation for the purpose, a direct onslaught on inequality of pension benefits as between men and women. So, because no doubt of the considerable cost and upheaval of so doing, the process of recognizing pensions as an integral part of the wage–work bargain is as yet only just embarked upon.

Indeed, the decision of the ECJ in *Burton* v. *British Railways Board* [1982] ICR 329 shows that the question whether or not a person is entitled to benefit under a retirement scheme (as distinct from issues of quantum of entitlement) is not a question of 'pay', but rather of access to benefits, and hence is outside the scope of Article 119 of the Treaty. The decision is confirmed and followed in that sense by the EAT in *Roberts* v. *Tate & Lyle Food Ltd* [1983] ICR 521. As we shall see below (p. 409), the differentiation between men and women in the rules of pension schemes, which was under attack in those cases, will be controlled by EEC provisions as and when a currently proposed Directive on equal treatment in occupational social security schemes becomes law. That development would impinge indirectly upon the question of pensions as part of the wage–work bargain, to the extent that a concern with equality in occupational social benefit schemes reflects a general recognition of such schemes as relevant to the wage–work bargain. The proposal would not confer a recognition upon pensions as 'pay' in a formal sense. But the present discussion of the scope of the wage–work bargain is not intended to be confined to formal issues of definition; the underlying trend of extending equal treatment measures to all social benefits constituting a consideration for employment is an important one.

(g) Itemized pay statements and the Truck Acts

The foregoing discussion of payment systems has demonstrated their complexity and the obscurity which often surrounds the calculations by which the amount of an employee's remuneration is arrived at. The employee has since the time of the Contracts of Employment Act 1963 been entitled to written particulars of his terms and conditions of employment relating to remuneration; he must be informed of the scale or rate of his remuneration or the method by which it is calculated (EPCA 1978, s.1(3)(a)). Since the time of the EPA 1975 this right to an initial statement of terms and conditions has been supplemented by the right to an itemized pay statement on each occasion on which remuneration is paid (EPCA 1978, s.8). Those who drafted this provision clearly had in mind the problems posed by complex payment systems, for they require that, where different parts of the net amount of remuneration are paid in different ways, particulars should be provided of the amount and method of payment of each part payment (EPCA 1978, s.8(d)).

It should, however, be added that the purpose of itemized pay statements is not solely that of ensuring that payment systems are made clear. The other or perhaps even the primary purpose is that of making sure that any deductions from pay are clearly itemized and explained. We shall in a later section examine the substantive and procedural controls imposed by the Truck Act 1896 upon disciplinary deductions and deductions for bad work (see below, p. 422). The legislation concerning itemized pay statements backs up these controls by enabling employees to recover substantial financial remedies in relation to unnotified deductions (EPCA 1978, s.11(8)). These sanctions apply as well to failure to notify deductions for income tax or social security contributions as to deductions for bad work.

By describing later in this chapter the controls which the Truck Acts place upon disciplinary deductions from wages (p. 422) we shall have indicated the main current effects of the truck legislation. It is worth recalling that the truck legislation was originally concerned not with these matters but rather with various special kinds of payment system whereby the employee was compelled to accept goods and services in kind from his employer or his employer's agents in lieu of remuneration. Now that payment systems which amounted to enforced trading between employer and employee on the employer's terms have ceased as far as we know to be a method of unfair exploitation of employees, the basic Truck Act requirement of payment to artificers in full in current coin of the realm and not otherwise (Truck Act 1831, s.3) has remained in being as an archaic safeguard which has had to be modified in employees' own interests in order to enable them to be paid by cheque or credit transfer (Payment of Wages Act 1960).

In March 1983 the Department of Employment issued a consultative document which canvassed proposals for updating the law relating to the payment of wages. These proposals included the suggestion of the complete repeal of the Truck Acts, to which the denunciation by the United Kingdom of ILO Convention 95 on the Protection of Wages would be a necessary preliminary. The government's intention to proceed with the proposals in the consultative document was confirmed in July 1983. The purpose of the proposed repeal is as part of a programme for facilitating the payment of wages other than in cash. But it is recognized that it would not be appropriate simply to dispense with all legal control over deductions from wages; the proposal includes the creation of a new right to complain to an industrial tribunal of arbitrary deductions from wages. The intention is to define arbitrariness by reference to statutory, contractual or customary rights. We consider later, in the context of legal control of discipline at work, the adequacy of this proposed substitute for existing Truck Act protection (see below, p. 423). It is, however, worth drawing attention in the present context to the risk that employees may jeopardize the security of their earnings and affect the balance of the wage–work bargain as much by accepting disadvantageous contractual provisions for disciplinary deductions as by accepting adverse terms relating, for instance, to lay-off due to unavailability of work. The reality of this risk in relation to disciplinary deductions has been documented by Tamara Goriely in a recent article on this proposed repeal of the Truck Acts ((1983) 12 *ILJ* 236).

(h) **Legal control over change in the wage–work bargain**
In recent years employers have tended to respond to difficult economic conditions by altering terms and conditions of employment in ways that employees often regard as adverse to their interests; sometimes the changes concerned are changes to the structure of the wage–work bargain. Such changes may be viewed by the employers imposing them as absolutely necessary for the efficient conduct of the business of the enterprise; but they may on the other hand be viewed by the employees affected as destroying the whole acceptability of their job. Such cases may provide vivid illustrations of the potential for conflict between static expectations based upon the contract of employment and evolving expectations asserted as an inherent feature of managerial prerogative. Where such a conflict leads to termination of

employment, the law of unfair dismissal may provide a more extensive and discriminating legal control than the common law can. An excellent example is the case of *Evans* v. *Elementa Holdings Ltd* [1982] I C R 323, the judgment in which deserves quotation at length. Note how closely the legitimacy of the managerial action is analysed. The case was in effect that of a change from hourly paid work to a fixed-salary contract. The further facts appear from the judgment.

Evans v. *Elementa Holdings Ltd* [1982] I C R 323 (EAT)

BROWNE-WILKINSON J.: . . . Mr Evans, the employee, was employed by Elementa Holdings Ltd, the employers, for two and a half years until he was dismissed on July 10, 1981. The employers were engaged in manufacturing metal work for the building industry and specialised in shopfitting. The employee's job was as a 'setter-out,' which is a job connected with design in the nature of a draughtsman. When he was dismissed, he applied to the industrial tribunal complaining of unfair dismissal. That application was unanimously dismissed by an industrial tribunal. He appeals to this appeal tribunal.

When the employee started his employment he was sent a letter setting out his terms of employment. That provided, amongst other things, for holidays of four weeks after one year's service. It provided '*Overtime* – Payable after the first five hours worked. *Sick Pay* – At Management's discretion. *Hours* – 8.30 a.m.–5.00 p.m. Monday–Friday.' He worked under those conditions of employment. By the time he was dismissed he was the only person employed as a setter-out. The number of employees of the firm was approximately 70 in all. The employee's evidence (which appears to have been accepted by the industrial tribunal) was that he never did any overtime work either on weekdays or on Saturdays although he was often involved in travelling outside normal hours. He gave evidence (though this is not referred to in the industrial tribunal's reasons) that on one or two occasions he had been asked to work overtime and had declined.

A new general manager, Mr Goossens, was appointed. He was disturbed to find that there were no proper contracts of employment issued to each of the employees but merely ad hoc letters of appointment. Over a period of some two months Mr Goossens, the departmental managers and the managing director worked out a standard form of contract. They did not consult the workforce about it. That new form of contract was presented to the members of the employee's department at a meeting on July 1, 1981, which was addressed by the contracts manager, Mr Johnson. The new form of contract was a substantial document dealing with a large number of different matters: it was certainly not a mere confirmation of the employees' previous contract. In a number of respects it was more beneficial: he was given an extra week's holiday; sick pay was no longer discretionary and, most important, there was a salary increase of some 12·4 per cent. Of that, 6·2 per cent. represented the nationally agreed annual increase in salary; the remaining 6·2 per cent. was offered on the basis of compensation for the new provisions as to overtime which were included in that contract. The new proposed provisions as to overtime read:

3. Your normal hours of work are: 8.30 a.m.–5.00 p.m.
However, due to the responsible nature of your position and fluctuations in the work

load, you will be expected to work past your normal hours as required by your manager during the evening and up to four hours on a Saturday. Your salary has been calculated taking this into account.

You are allowed one hour for lunch.

If you are requested to work more than four hours on any Saturday or at any time on a Sunday you will be paid on an hourly basis at a rate equivalent to the hourly rate for your normal hours.

When the employee learnt of that contract on July 1, he indicated that he could not accept it on the ground that it contained an open-ended obligation as to the amount of overtime he could be required to work. He had an interview with Mr Goossens on the following day when again he said he could not accept the contract. He then wrote saying that he could not do so. He then had an interview with the managing director, but the managing director was obdurate that he would not make any exception in the employee's case. When the employee asked Mr Goossens if a rider could be put in limiting the amount of the overtime, Mr Goossens was not prepared to consider that and asked the employee to take the employers on trust. The employee was still not prepared to work under the new contract. He was given a week's paid leave to think the matter over. He did do so but, having thought the matter over, he reached the conclusion that he was not prepared to accept the unlimited compulsory overtime which, in his view, the new proposed contract would have involved. As a result, he was dismissed. All the other employees accepted the new proposed terms of contract.

Before the industrial tribunal the employers argued that the reason for the dismissal was his refusal to accept the new form of contract. That, it was submitted, was a 'substantial reason of a kind such as to justify the dismissal of an employee holding the position which that employee held' within section 57(1)(b) of the Employment Protection (Consolidation) Act 1978. The employers also submitted that, for the purposes of section 57(3), the dismissal was fair. The industrial tribunal found in favour of the employers' contention on both those points. They held that it was confusing to management to find employees working under different agreements regarding their terms of employment; they said: 'We find that there was a commercial need of discernible advantage to rationalise the contracts of employment for harmony of relationships in the work-force . . .' and they therefore found a substantial reason within section 57(1)(b). They then considered section 57(3), said that the question was whether the employee was right or wrong in refusing to accept the change in his contract, and went on:

> We find that [the employee] was given ample opportunity to consider his position, and had no reason to suppose that his actual working conditions were about to change for the worse. We find that it was desirable for all employees to be issued with formal contracts of employment. We find that the terms of the contracts were not objectionable or oppressive, and contained reference to grievance procedure. The [employee] was given an opportunity by the [employers] to state his case. In all the circumstances we find the dismissal of the [employee] was within a range of responses open to a reasonable employer and was not unfair.

On this appeal, the employee's case has been presented with conspicuous ability by Miss Laing. She submits, first of all, that the industrial tribunal, in considering whether there was a substantial reason for dismissal, misdirected itself by concentrating on the question whether there was a commercial need for the standardisation of the contracts of employment. She says that the relevant question here was whether there was a substantial commercial need to alter the provisions as to overtime and that the tribunal did not really direct their minds to that matter. Secondly, she submits that there was inadequate evidence to enable the employers to have discharged the burden of proof that the standardisation of contractual terms was necessary in order to harmonise, or to produce harmony, in the relationships between members of the work-force. She points out with considerable force that there was little, if any, evidence of lack of harmony flowing from the non-standardisation of the contracts that had hitherto existed. Finally, she submits that the decision that the dismissal was fair under section 57(3) is vitiated by omissions and misdirections made by the tribunal in reaching its conclusion.

We do not find it necessary to reach any concluded view on Miss Laing's first two submissions. We think there may well be substantial force in her submission that what was shown here did not amount to a substantial reason within section 57(1)(b), but it is unnecessary for us to express any concluded view on that point. We will simply direct ourselves to section 57(3).

Before so doing, we must analyse what was the position as to overtime under the original contract and under the proposed new contract. It appears to have been accepted both by the employers and by the employee that under his original terms of employment he was not obliged to work overtime at all: the overtime was optional. Under his original contract he was only paid for overtime, or would only have been paid for overtime, after he had worked five hours. That is to be contrasted with the position which would have existed under the revised contract if he had accepted it. The wording of the overtime clause in the new contract is in some respects obscure: Mr Haw, who appeared on behalf of the employers, accepts that its true construction is not altogether clear. However, it was and is the employers' view that it imposed a mandatory obligation to work overtime if requested so to do. Once one gets to that position, which was the position adopted by the employers, there is no limit on the number of hours of overtime which an employee can be required to work. Moreover, overtime can be required during any evening and up to four hours on a Saturday and the increase in salary was to cover all such overtime worked. Therefore, however many hours of overtime are required between Monday and Friday there will be no additional payment for it. Only if overtime is required to be worked for more than four hours on a Saturday or at any time on a Sunday would there be any additional payment made. Even then, the payment would not be at time and a half or double time but at the basic hourly rate. As it seems to us, that contractual term, if accepted, would have produced a fundamental change in the employee's contractual obligations in relation to overtime: it became mandatory and unlimited.

It is against that background that one has to look at the industrial tribunal's decision that the dismissal was fair. We accept that the question whether or not a dismissal is fair, for the purposes of section 57(3), is a question of fact for the industrial tribunal and one which can very seldom be interfered with on an appeal. However, there is a factor in this decision which satisfies us that there was here a material misdirection by the industrial tribunal in reaching their conclusion. We quote again the passage: 'We find that the terms of the contracts were not objectionable or oppressive, and contained reference to grievance procedure.' The question under section 57(3) is whether the employers' conduct in dismissing was reasonable. But, as the industrial tribunal recognised, that question necessarily required the industrial tribunal to find whether it was reasonable for the employee to decline the new terms of the contract. If it was reasonable for him to decline those terms, then obviously it would have been unreasonable for the employers to dismiss him for such refusal. It was therefore a necessary part of the industrial tribunal's decision on this point that the terms of the contract were not objectionable or oppressive. So far as we can see, at no stage do they analyse what is, or would have been, the effect of this alteration in the contractual position. In our view, it is simply not a possible view to have reached, after analysis, to say that the employee was unreasonable in refusing to accept a contract which imposed upon him an unlimited obligation to work overtime, he being a man who under his existing contract did not have to work on Saturdays or do any overtime. That is particularly so in the light of certain evidence which was given which might suggest that the employers were envisaging that for the future he would, like his colleagues, be expected to work overtime three Saturdays out of four. If it had been shown in this case that there was some immediate need for the employers to increase the overtime worked or to require mandatory overtime as opposed to voluntary overtime, that might have fundamentally altered the position. But there was no evidence of any kind directed towards a need to change the provisions as to overtime for the current working needs of the company. On the contrary, there was evidence that the workload had not increased and there was evidence that the number of setters-out had fallen from three to one. That is inconsistent with a view that overall there was a need for more work to be done though flexibility might have been required.

We find, therefore, that in reaching their conclusion under section 57(3) the industrial tribunal have proceeded on the untenable view that it was not reasonable for the employee to refuse the new contract. We think that is a wholly unsustainable view. He was not objecting to the contract as a whole: he was only objecting to the provisions as to overtime. The tribunal seem to have attached importance to the fact, as they said, that he had no reason to suppose that his actual working conditions were about to change for the worse. In the light of the evidence given as to possible Saturday working, we find that a surprising conclusion. In any event it is not the relevant matter. This case turns on the imposition of a new contract of employment, not new working practices. If he had accepted the new contract, he would have bound himself for the future to perform the contract in its revised form. Managements change and if, in the future, a new management were to require substantial overtime, he would have had no answer. Even Mr Goossens appears to have had doubts about the wisdom of the new overtime provisions. The chairman's note records him as saying:

> If the employee asked for a limitation on overtime, it would be reasonable if everyone else made the same request. It is conceivable that management got it wrong and there should be some limit to compulsory overtime. I have no answer to it. I might consider a limit to compulsory overtime.

This decision is, it must be admitted, unusual in the readiness it displays on the part of the court to enter into the merits of the employer's decision to change the structure of the wage–work bargain. It may not accurately represent the trend of unfair dismissal decisions. As we shall see in the next chapter, the approach has already been rejected by another EAT, in a rather different factual context, in the case of *Chubb Fire Security Ltd* v. *Harper* [1983] IRLR 311 (see below, p. 470). But the *Evans* decision does indicate the possible scope for constructive use of the unfair dismissal jurisdiction for the better protection of this crucial aspect of the employee's interest in the content of his employment.

4 Security of earnings

(a) Introduction
In the previous section, we saw how the form taken by the wage–work bargain has extensive implications for the employee's security of earnings. In other words, the nature of the payment system under which the employee works determines the social content of the employment relationship, and determines in particular the extent to which the employee may look to the employing enterprise as his insurer against the vicissitudes of working and domestic life in so far as these affect availability for work and availability of remunerative opportunities. Control of security of earnings is thus a crucial aspect of the control of the content of the employment relationship generally. This is therefore an extremely important area of activity for collective bargaining and also an important area for possible statutory regulation. We shall therefore seek in this section to show how and why the borderline between collective bargaining and statutory regulation is drawn in this area. On the whole there has been surprisingly little statutory control of the content of employment so far as security of earnings is concerned. This has perhaps hitherto been viewed as an area where legal intervention should be in the form of social security provisions rather than in the form of the regulation of the terms of employment. As we saw in an earlier section (p. 144), the wages councils system provided something of an exception to this generalization with its gradually broadening provisions for the control of minimum terms of employment as well as minimum remuneration in the industries concerned. These wider powers were precisely developed in relation to the control of security of earnings – for example in relation to paid holidays and guaranteed weekly remuneration. Moreover the EPA 1975 represented a substantial move towards legislative regulation of the security of earnings, by reason of its provisions concerning guarantee payments (EPCA 1978, ss.12–18), remuneration during suspension on medical grounds (EPCA 1978, ss.19–22), maternity pay (EPCA 1978, ss.34–44) and paid time off for trade-union duties (EPCA 1978, s. 27) and for the purpose of looking for work and/or making arrangements for training (EPCA 1978, s.31). Indeed, it is chiefly by this new movement towards legislative protection of security of earnings that the EPA 1975 accomplished the crucial transition from a statutory floor of rights concerned primarily with the termination of employment to a statutory floor of rights concerned with the content of the employment relationship as with its termination.

Although the EPA 1975 thus started to make security of earnings a major area of statutory intervention, it would be misleading to view this topic in terms of a simple interplay between collective bargaining and legislative control. It is in fact necessary to envisage a three-way interaction between collective bargaining, legislative control, and social security provision. The developments of recent years can only really be understood in those terms. We shall proceed to examine that interaction in a number of specific areas.

(b) Sick-pay

In the area of sick-pay, the interaction between (1) employment practice and common law, (2) collective bargaining and (3) social security legislation has been particularly significant. Employment practice has changed a good deal since the Second World War. At that time, staff workers would tend to continue to receive their salary during sickness, at least for a limited period; hourly or manual workers in industry would tend not to do so. It was one of the key distinguishing features between staff and non-staff terms and conditions of employment (see above, p. 320). The common-law courts were either ignorant of this distinction or unwilling to give effect to it. They tended to lean in favour of sick-pay not so much because they thought an employer ought to pay sick-pay as because their model of the contract of employment was the fixed-payment model which applied to some salaried staff workers. This led to incongruous results when hourly-paid workers successfully invoked the common law to claim sick-pay – compare *Petrie* v. *MacFisheries Ltd* [1940] 1 K B 265. Nevertheless, for many years the common law was regarded as operating a presumption in favour of sick-pay on the rather slight authority of *Orman* v. *Savile Sportswear Ltd* [1960] 1 W L R 1055, though this always seemed simplistic and remote from actual employment practice, even in relation to staff workers. When the issue came before the courts again in *Mears* v. *Safecar Security Ltd* [1981] I C R 409 (E A T), [1982] I C R 626 (C A), both the E A T and the Court of Appeal denied the existence of a common law presumption of sick-pay, and stressed the importance of looking at the circumstances of the particular employment (including, as we have seen, evidence of relevant practice after the formation of the contract, see above, p. 304) to the exclusion of all else. They could offer no more in the way of a rationale for distinguishing between types of contract of employment than the rather theoretical contrast between cases where consideration for wages was actual work and where it was readiness and willingness to work if of ability to do so. This was the rather scholastic form in which Lord Denning had conceptualized the distinction between, broadly speaking, fixed payment contracts of employment and hourly or piece-rate contracts of employment, in a case-note he wrote in 1940 (above, p. 323). It was a reflection of the impoverishment of the common law of the contract of employment in both prescriptive and descriptive terms that no more cogent or socially accurate analysis could be advanced in the 1980s.

For if the common law had, at least until very recently, taken on the whole a socially static approach to sick-pay, there had on the other hand been considerable progress made by collective bargaining and by parallel developments as a matter of unilateral regulation by employers. The decision of the EAT in *Howman & Son* v. *Blyth* [1983] ICR 420 managed to build on the decision in the *Mears* case while at the same time relating the implied content of the contract of employment to the results of collective bargaining so far as sick-pay was concerned. This was achieved by first applying the *Mears* doctrine that there was effectively no longer any presumption of automatic continuance of pay during sickness such as had apparently been envisaged in *Marrison* v. *Bell* [1939] 2 KB 183. But the *Howman* decision, as we saw earlier in this chapter (above, at p. 305), rather than attempting to fill this vacuum by an *a priori* theoretical analysis, has regard to normal practice in the industry. On this basis it was held that the right term to imply in the present case was for the full rate of pay for a 40-hour week less state sickness benefit received, for a duration that was reasonable; and that, prima facie, a reasonable duration was that provided by the national working-rule agreement for the industry. This was rightly regarded by the EAT as an approach more responsive to modern industrial realities than one which offered only the choices between no sick-pay and indefinite continuation of pay during sickness. This makes it important to consider what the profile had actually become of sick-pay provision in practice.

The National Joint Advisory Council Report on Sick-Pay Schemes in 1964 recorded that schemes negotiated by collective bargaining at industry level seemed to be spreading. Their report, as was not untypical of the NJAC, implicitly made out a case for voluntarism in this area and against legislative regulation of occupational sick-pay (hereafter OSP). It appeared from the New Earnings Survey of 1970 that about 73 per cent of all male workers and 67 per cent of all women workers were covered by sick-pay schemes. A survey carried out by the Department of Health and Social Security in 1974 (*Survey of Occupational Sick-Pay Schemes*, DHSS, 1977) shows that by then 80 per cent or more of full-time employees received some sort of OSP, though there were wide variations between groups of workers: white-collar workers 95 per cent, male manual workers 74 per cent, female manual workers 55–58 per cent covered (see Lewis (1982) 11 *ILJ* 249, for discussion of those and further statistics). It is also important to realize that OSP has very often been given subject to detailed conditions; it is not simply a question of the continuation or non-continuation of ordinary remuneration during sickness.

An account of recent developments in the practice of sick-pay schemes (Incomes Data Services Study No. 138 (January 1977), pp. 9–22) suggests that the important variants around which development has been taking place are as follows:

(1) *the duration of entitlement to sick-pay*. Entitlement to full pay ranges very widely from two to fifty-two weeks. The entitlement is frequently related to the employee's period of continuous service with the employer.

(2) *the rate of sick-pay*. Full sick-pay is sometimes limited to normal basic pay and is frequently net of social security benefits and, apparently, income tax

refunds. Periods of entitlement to full sick-pay are frequently succeeded by further periods of entitlement to various reducing fractions of full pay (typically starting with half-pay).

(3) *waiting days.* There are frequently provisions in sick-pay schemes that there is to be no payment for the first three days of absence due to sickness unless they are succeeded by a further period of sickness covered by a medical certificate.

(4) *conditions.* There are frequently conditions disentitling employees from sick-pay, concerned with the recovery of any damages the employee may receive, visits to check up on the employee if he is absent for a long time, and misconduct or negligence by the employee.

The existence of these variants in collective bargaining and employer's practice is as we shall see an important matter in relation to the impact of the new statutory sick-pay provisions of the Social Security and Housing Benefits Act 1982, to the consideration of which we now turn. But first a prefatory word is necessary about the role of social security legislation in the development of OSP. For this account of the development of occupational sick-pay would be quite incomplete, and indeed the recent introduction of statutory sick-pay would be quite incomprehensible without some reference to the relationship with social security sickness benefit (hereafter SSSB). There is a long history of income replacement during sickness being regarded as a social security matter rather than as the responsibility primarily of employers. This dates in some sense from the assumption by the state of supervisory responsibility for the work done by the Friendly Societies, which was accomplished by the National Insurance Act 1911. Since the National Insurance Act 1946, comprehensive cover against the loss of earnings through sickness became available to employed and self-employed people as part of the general national insurance scheme. Indeed, SSSB has until the 1982 legislation been tenable in addition to OSP, and the primary responsibility emphasized by the fact that OSP schemes can and very often do provide for deduction from OSP in respect of entitlement to SSSB. The common-law cases on OSP have considered (and in general rejected) the proposition that OSP is impliedly subject to deduction of SSSB; but it has been a clear assumption in any such discussion that if there is any off-setting as between the OSP and SSSB, it is in the direction of reduction of OSP – compare *Marrison* v. *Bell* [1939] 2 KB 187.

All this makes it the more significant that the Department of Health and Social Security should have mounted a major policy initiative in the direction of transferring the responsibility for income replacement during short-term sickness from the social security system to the employer. This was proposed in the DHSS Green Paper, 'Income During Initial Sickness: A New Strategy' (Cmnd. 7864, 1980) and implemented in the Social Security and Housing Benefits Act 1982 with effect from April 1983. The aims of this measure were to relieve the DHSS of the administrative burden of short-term sickness benefit and to bring sickness benefit into taxation and liability to social security contributions as income. To this end, Part I of the 1982 Act replaces sickness benefit previously payable under existing social security legislation by statutory sick-pay (hereafter SSP) payable by employers during the first eight weeks of any period of incapacity for work. It is important to note that the obligation to pay SSP is framed in such a way as closely to reflect, with some modifications on policy grounds, the SSSB it replaces; it does not follow the contours of the contract of employment. This is evident from the sections setting out the conditions in which SSP is due. It is payable in respect of any day of incapacity for work (s.1, which deploys social security concepts of 'specific disease or bodily or mental disablement' to develop the notion of incapacity) forming part of a period of incapacity for work (s.2, which brings in the social security notions of minimum periods of incapacity – four days – and the 'linking rule'). Periods of incapacity can thus be aggregated to meet the four-day rule if, but only if, they are not more than five weeks apart. The equivalent linking rule for SSSB was eight weeks so this is a stiffer policy. Furthermore, the day concerned must fall within a period of entitlement (s.3). This provision adapts the social security notion of insurance-based periods of entitlement to a notion of entitlement within the duration of the contract of employment subject to controls upon termination of the contract by the employer for the purpose of avoiding liability to SSP (s.3(7)). The day concerned must also be a qualifying day (s.4), which brings into play the social security 'normal idle day' rule, interestingly adapted so that the employer and employee may make an agreement to determine which days of the week shall be those on which the employee is required by his contract of service to be available for work. The day concerned must also fall within the limitations on entitlement (s.5) which brings in the social security notion of three waiting days before SSP becomes payable and the eight weeks per tax year limit on SSP (after which SSSB takes over again). The social security origins of SSP are also evident in the provisions about the rate of payment (s.7), which (as annually up-rated for inflation, in the manner of social security benefits, to 1984) set rates of £42.25 p.w. where weekly earnings are not less than £68, £35.45 p.w. where weekly earnings are not less than £50.50, and £28.55 p.w. in any other case. These stepped fixed rates originate in the policy of equating SSP as far as possible with SSSB, which ceased to be earnings-related by virtue of the Social Security (No. 2) Act 1980, s.4. The stepping of the rates is to prevent low-paid workers receiving more while absent sick than they earn at work. Finally, the social security origins of SSP are most prominent in the provisions for adjudication of liability to SSP (ss.11–16), which is simply entrusted to the social security authorities rather than to industrial tribunals. This must reflect the fact that SSP is really disguised SSSB administered by employers, which it is in the sense that employers may recoup themselves for the SSP they pay out, either by deduction from their social security contributions or if necessary by direct claim from the DHSS (s.9).

To what extent has SSP affected employment practice? It is early days to hazard an answer, but there are one or two indications. The transfer of liability for initial sickness absence is primarily an administrative transfer rather than an economic transfer in the sense that, as we have just seen, employers are able to recoup the cost of SSP from their national insurance contributions. Generally employers with OSP schemes will already be making provision at least as generous as is involved in SSP. But there is evidence that employers are under effective pressure to adjust their OSP to compensate employees for the liability to tax on SSP where SSSB was free of tax (and liability to national insurance contributions) – see (1982) 286 *IRRR* 11–13. Probably as significant in collective bargaining terms is the contemporaneous move to self-certification instead of sick notes from doctors for short-term sickness absence (Social Security (Medical Evidence, Claims and Payment) Amendment Regulations 1982 (SI 1982 No. 699)). This locates the problem of control of absence more directly between employer and employee than before. The overall effect is of a marked rolling back of the limits of welfare state activity in relation to sick-pay, the operation having been carried out in a manner which maximizes the onerousness of sick-pay for the employer while doing nothing to encourage collective bargaining or to improve employees' security of earnings. It is hard to see what gains there are to balance the costs of this operation.

(c) Paid holidays

A crucial area of security of earnings where there has been surprisingly little statutory intervention is that of holidays with pay. The position is very comparable to that which obtained until recently in relation to sick-pay. The EPCA 1978 requires the employer to particularize to the employee what arrangements if any there are for paid holidays (section 1(3)(*d*)(i)) and requires pay to be given for holidays properly taken during statutory periods of notice (Sch. 3, para. 2(1)(*c*)). The Factories Act 1961 makes provision concerning the allowance of paid public holidays to women and young persons. The wages council legislation enables wages orders to provide for paid holidays and they frequently do so. The Holidays with Pay Act 1938 which first enabled wage-regulating authorities to make provision for holidays and holiday remuneration survives only to the extent of enabling the Department of Employment to assist voluntary schemes for securing holidays with pay for workers in any industries. The preference for voluntary determination of holidays with pay over statutory regulation has resulted in the non-implementation of the European Social Charter so far as it requires states to ensure a minimum of two weeks' annual holiday with pay for all workers, and has resulted also in the non-ratification of the ILO Convention No. 132 which requires a minimum of three weeks' annual paid holiday for all workers. It is very difficult to determine why the topic of paid holidays was not affected by the shift of emphasis from voluntary regulation to statutory regulation of the content of the employment relationship which is embodied in the EPA 1975. What can have brought about this particular omission? The position in practice as brought about by company schemes and collective bargaining was described in an Incomes Data Study in 1978.

IDS Study No. 168 (1978) 'Holidays 1978', at pp. 1–3

LEVELS OF ENTITLEMENT

According to figures covering manual workers published by the Department of Employment, 99 per cent now receive three weeks' holiday or more, 34 per cent of whom are entitled to four weeks and over. Our own sample is not typical, judging from the DE returns, because out of the 56 companies in the Record Section for which we have manual entitlements, 50 allow four weeks, and two others not included in this total give additional 'company' days, bringing the entitlement, effectively, to 20 days; this discrepancy probably arises because the DE looks at industry agreements with minimum entitlements, whereas we are concerned with the level within individual companies. . . .

National figures for staff employees are now out of date. The last DE survey was published in December 1974 and a full commentary may be found in Study 134 (p. 2) and IDS Report 202 (p. 28), but from our Record Section we note that four weeks is also the normal entitlement for staff, although a differential occasionally exists over manual employees. . . .

RECENT MOVES

In the last three years, high inflation and the need to maintain living standards have meant that collective bargaining has been concerned almost entirely with wages and earnings levels. Couple this with a pay policy requirement that increased costs arising from improved terms and conditions must be offset against the pay limits – and it is no surprise that holidays and the other fringe areas have taken a back seat in wage claims in recent years.

At industry level the impact is obvious. Between May 1973 and August 1975, 110 industries' leave arrangements changed. Between September 1975 and August 1976, a period roughly coinciding with the £6 limit, the number fell to 24; to the year ended August 1977, when the five per cent rule existed, there were no changes. Since then entitlement has improved in seven industries, and a few more are promised for 1978–9. . . .

The figures published by the Department of Employment showing the amount of holidays received by manual workers indicate how small the change has been since January 1976, soon after the beginning of the Attack on Inflation policies:

Entitlement	Jan. 1976	Sept. 1977
	%	%
2 weeks	1	–
2–3 weeks	1	1
3 weeks	17	18
3–4 weeks	51	47
4 weeks or more	30	34

The effect of the incomes policy has been to freeze the holiday structure for the last two years.

The evidence is that negotiators have been unable to improve on basic holidays, but change has occurred in the more peripheral holiday connected arrangements, in particular leave related to service and the levels of holiday pay. We consider changes to these areas later on in the Study.

CHANGES UNDER INCOMES POLICY

A peculiarity of the changes in holiday entitlement during the past few years is that far more improvements were negotiated under the Conservatives' statutory incomes policy than under the 'voluntary' policies in force since 1975. For example, nine years ago, in our first holiday Study, we reported that only a minority of manual workers received three or more weeks' holiday, yet, by the end of 1972, practically all industries had negotiated a basic entitlement of three weeks; similarly in January 1974 only four per cent of manuals received four week's holiday, in January 1975 the fruits of collective bargaining had increased this to 28 per cent.

Looking at the Department of Employment figures covering the period from when the Conservatives took power in 1970, to about the end of their pay policy in July 1974 (the final stages of which were perpetuated by Labour), we can see these changes in percentage terms:

Entitlement	Sept. 1970	Jan. 1975
	%	%
2 weeks	45	1
2–3 weeks	9	1
3 weeks	44	30
3–4 weeks	2	40
4 weeks	–	28

Only two per cent of manual workers received less than three weeks' holiday in 1975, compared with 54 per cent in 1970, furthermore 68 per cent had more than three weeks in 1975 against two per cent in 1970.

Loopholes and profits

We offer two explanations for these changes. Firstly, negotiators do not operate in a vacuum, but react to such bargaining criteria as the retail price index, or changes in average earnings and so on. Under an incomes policy, these traditional points of reference are held in abeyance and attention focuses more on 'what is allowed'. The Conservatives, in both phases two and three of their pay policy, allowed a degree of flexibility to increase holidays. Under phase two, they allowed increases to three weeks outside the pay limits: phase three had a similar arrangement allowing bargainers room to negotiate four weeks.

If incomes policies have a fault (or advantage, depending on your level of pay), it is that the 'ceiling' becomes the 'norm'. Unable to bargain about pay (£1 plus four per cent, or seven per cent on earnings was taken for granted), the negotiators turned their attention to whatever else was allowed: holidays, unsocial hours or 'flexibility'. The same thing has happened under the Labour Government's policies, improvements in sick pay schemes, for instance, are allowed outside the pay limits and, in our recent Study on sick pay (no. 165), we note the proliferation of improved schemes since 1975.

A second factor leading to increased holidays according to one trade union research officer, is that the inflation of 1974–5 showed up in vastly increased cash profits. The unions used these figures to embarrass companies into giving more benefits, and some employers sought to 'head off trouble'. Unable to give more cash because of the limits on pay, they looked at the other benefits allowed by incomes policy. It was as much in employers' interest as the unions' to agree the maximum allowed.

We have noted elsewhere that few improvements in holiday entitlement have been agreed under the pay policies since 1975. The reason lies in the rigidity of the Attack on Inflation guidelines, which offer no scope for cost-inducing changes outside the pay limits. From the point of view of negotiating better holidays, incomes policies have successively been the hero and the villain of the piece.

SERVICE-RELATED EXTRAS

Manual workers
Service-related leave for manual workers, which went into decline during the early 1970s, is enjoying a resurgence. The DE figures for 1970 reveal that 25 per cent of manual employees had some element of service-related leave but by 1974 this proportion had fallen to 13 per cent. Today it has risen to around a third.

It seems to be one way in which negotiators are bending incomes policy to improve holidays, for example both the Ford workers and the petroleum tanker drivers introduced better holidays for longer serving employees as part of their last settlements; at Ford, the arrangement is 22 days after ten years and 23 after 25; while the tanker drivers get an extra (fifth) week's holiday after, in the case of Mobil Oil, 25 years.

Staff
Service holidays are much more the perk of the white-collar worker. Of the 71 companies in the Record Section, 38 have improved provisions for long service staff compared to 16 which give service holidays to their manual workers. The service sector gives a lower basic entitlement to their bottom grades and uses a lengthy service requirement to bring them up to four weeks. . . .

Public Sector
White-collar workers in the public sector often enjoy a service-related holiday scale. Some of those scales are quite long: the GLC gives one day for every five years up to thirty years, i.e. in six steps; in Gas Supply grades usually have at least five steps to the maximum, and Electricity Supply staff employees have eight separate improvements before the maximum is reached. Employees, therefore, receive a steady increase in holidays rather than having to wait, say, 25 years and receive a fifth week all in one go. The maximum amount of service entitlement varies. Police officers above superintendent get eight weeks after ten years' service and although no other arrangement is that generous, a maximum of six weeks exists in the British Airports Authority, Civil Service and the GLC with the rest giving some improvement up to five weeks.

Service leave for public sector manual workers is uncommon and where it does exist adds only a couple of days to basic entitlement after five or ten years' service. The basic entitlement for manual workers is low anyway, around 15 to 16 days in most cases, and even including 'privilege' days the service improvement only brings the maximum entitlement to four weeks.

A further IDS Study in 1982 (No. 275) reported that the trend was still towards improvement in provision for paid holidays. The 1979 National Engineering Agreement had set the pace for a basic entitlement to 25 days of paid holiday per year (i.e. normally five weeks). They further reported that service-related holiday entitlements were falling from favour because of their adverse implications for job mobility. Statistics published in the *D E Gazette* for April 1982 showed that by the end of 1981, 87 per cent of manual workers subject to national-level collective agreements had a minimum entitlement to four weeks or more of paid holiday, and that by that time, of the five million workers covered by national-level collective agreements or wages orders, two million had a total entitlement to five weeks of paid holiday. It would seem that recession conditions have if anything tended to produce an increase in paid holiday entitlement because the granting of such increases provides a form of work-sharing, like the reduction of the length of the working week (see above, p. 325). In these circumstances it seems unsurprising that there is no particular new pressure towards legislative provision for paid holidays. It is however to be noted that if the wages councils legislation should be repealed (see above, p. 154), a major source of legal protection of the right to paid holidays would disappear in the sector of the labour market where paid holidays are least effectively ensured by voluntary processes.

(d) Maternity pay and time off for ante-natal care

The position concerning maternity pay can be briefly described. Outside the area of public employment, it was not very extensively treated by company schemes or by collective bargaining. The introduction of a statutory right to maternity pay was one of the major initiatives contained in the EPA 1975. This initiative was probably stimulated by the fact that legislative provision for maternity pay has existed for some time in EEC countries. Our own system now provides essentially for six weeks' maternity pay at the rate of nine-tenths of the normal week's pay for employees of not less than two years' standing who remain at work until the eleventh week before their expected date of confinement (EPCA 1978, ss. 34–5). The statutory scheme (minus flat-rate maternity allowance) is funded by a Maternity Pay Fund to which employers are required to contribute and from which they may claim a *full* rebate in respect of statutory maternity payments (EPCA 1978, ss.37, 39). So this aspect of security of earnings has moved from an unregulated state to a state of regulation by compulsory statutory social insurance, financed by contributions levied from employers.

Ogus and Barendt have remarked that the statutory right to maternity pay from the employer has, to a large extent, superseded in importance the social security maternity allowance as an instrument of income maintenance (*The Law of Social Security*, 2nd edn (1982), p. 249). On the other hand, Upex and Morris have pointed out that the scope of the statutory right is greatly circumscribed in practice by its being limited to full-time workers (i.e. those working for 16 hours a week or more), and that DHSS calculations indicated that, of all the women bearing children in a year, less than 16 per cent qualify for maternity pay ((1981) 10 *ILJ* 218, 221).

The Employment Act 1980, s.13 (new EPCA 1978, s.31A), added a further right to paid time off for ante-natal care. The provision is that an employee who has made an appointment for ante-natal care on the advice of a doctor or midwife shall have the right not unreasonably to be refused paid time off during working hours to keep the appointment. The employee may complain of default to an industrial tribunal which may award compensation (s.31A(6)–(8)). It is interesting that it was seen as appropriate to confer the right to paid time off for ante-natal care without any kind of social insurance, but rather as a direct liability upon the employer. The likelihood is that the liability was sufficiently limited to make social fund insurance unnecessary.

(e) Guaranteed pay, lay-offs and short-time working

Another crucial and sensitive area within the topic of control of security of earnings is that of the allocation of risk of unavailability of work. Part of the allocation of risk takes place in the formation of the employment relationship. It has to be decided at that stage whether employment is to be full-time or part-time, and short-term or long-term. But an important part of the allocation of that risk can be considered as a problem of security of earnings; it is the question of how far the employee is liable to suffer loss of earnings by being laid off or placed on short-time. The transfer of this risk away from the employer need not be a transfer to the employee; it may be a transfer to the social security system or directly to the tax-payer by way of governmental subsidy. We have in fact to consider, in relation to guaranteed pay, a complex interaction between common law, collective bargaining, social security law, employment protection legislation and governmental subsidies.

We begin by picking up a theme from our discussion of the wage–work bargain. The hourly-rated or piece-rated contract of employment lends itself to allowing the employer a power of laying workers off for a period or putting them on short-time. The question is how far the common law will imply a term limiting this power. The decision in *Devonald* v. *Rosser & Son Ltd* [1906] 2 KB 728 constituted an important piece of judicial construction of the contract of employment in favour of the worker; it is interesting that it occurs in the years shortly preceding the introduction of limited national insurance against unemployment by the National Insurance Act 1911. In that case, the Court of Appeal found an implied obligation on the part of the employer to provide a piece-rate manual industrial worker with sufficient work to enable him to earn a reasonable rate of remuneration, that is to say a rate of remuneration bearing a reasonable relationship to his earnings when work is fully available. This progressive decision was offset by that in *Browning* v. *Crumlin Valley Collieries Ltd* [1926] 1 KB 522, where a wide power of lay-off was implied in the event of unavailability of work 'due to causes beyond the employer's control', which was held wide enough to cover the facts under consideration which were that the plaintiffs were coal-miners who had refused to work until the mineshaft had been put in a safe condition by the carrying out of necessary repairs. Greene J. said that he was satisfied that no employer would have consented to agree that the workmen should be free to withhold their work if the mine became dangerous through no fault on his (*sic*) part and yet should be entitled to their wages. That he saw no objection to the endorsement of this position by the common law must be a reflection of the hardening of positions towards labour generally and miners in particular around the time of the General Strike, and also of the resistance to anything amounting to a claim to take industrial action without loss of pay, no matter how compelling the cause for doing so. That the doctrine in that case long retained its nominal authority must indicate the extent to which employment practice left the common law behind in its development.

The recent trend, however, seems to be in favour of limiting the scope of the *Crumlin Valley* case. In *Johnson* v. *Cross* [1977] ICR 872, the EAT asserted the primacy of the principle which they considered was to be derived from the *Devonald* case, namely that the employer had no power to lay off in the absence of a specific or implied agreement but, on the contrary, was under an obligation to provide reasonable work or pay in lieu during the notice period. This principle was envisaged as being applicable to lay-offs caused by shortage of cash and lack of liquidity as well as to those caused by inclement weather, shortage of work or lack of supplies. This theme was taken up and re-asserted in *Neads* v. *CAV Ltd* [1983] IRLR 361, where Peter Pain J. adopted what the EAT had said in the *Johnson* case, and added that the *Crumlin Valley* case rested upon the terms which were implied in the circumstances of the case and did not throw any doubt on the principle established in the earlier authorities (ibid. p. 366). The courts in these two cases seem minded to ensure that no generally implied right of lay-off is available to employers to undermine the substance of the statutory rights to notice that employees now have.

The introduction of the law of unfair dismissal, and particularly the development, within that, of the law of constructive dismissal (see below, pp. 448 *et seq.*), have meant that the employee may have a new sort of challenge to the employer's assertion of a power to lay him off or put him on short-time – as was successfully done, for instance, in *Waine* v. *Oliver (Plant Hire) Ltd* [1977] IRLR 434 (EAT). But this challenge can be made only on dismissal or by the employee's resigning and claiming constructive dismissal, and so it is unsurprising that there has been no radical redevelopment of the common law by that route. (The same practical considerations rendered almost inoperative the elaborate provisions originally made by the Redundancy Payments Act 1965, s.6, and now contained in EPCA 1978, ss.87–89, to enable a worker who is laid off or put on short-time to claim to have been dismissed for redundancy payments purposes upon pursuing an excessively complicated procedure.)

Let us turn then to the developments produced by collective bargaining, which have been very important in this area. From the Second World War onwards there have been many collectively bargained provisions for guaranteed minimum weekly wages in the event of lay-off or short-time working. This pattern of collective bargaining was greatly stimulated by the example and impact of the war-time Essential Work Orders, where guaranteed-week provisions were thought to be a just protection for workers who were tied by the orders to particular workplaces in essential industries (see Kahn-Freud, *Labour and the Law*, 2nd edn (1977), p. 20). These provisions were an important aspect of national-level collective bargaining in the engineering industry; and in *Burroughs Machines Ltd* v. *Timmoney* [1977] IRLR 404 (see above, p. 296) one can see the Court of Session faced with the problems of how to give effect to the guarantee provisions of the national engineering agreement in the face of disintegration of national-level collective bargaining in that industry. An indication of the significance of collectively bargained guaranteed pay provisions is that it is the one area in which extensive use has been made of the possibility of seeking exemption from employment protection legislation on the basis of equally favourable collectively bargained arrangements. Obviously, however, guaranteed pay provisions come under pressure in conditions of deep and sustained recession. A recent IDS Study (No. 235, 1981) indicated that clauses suspending guaranteed pay in various circumstances such as lay-off in consequence of industrial action (the provision in the *Burroughs* v. *Timmoney* case, above, is an example) had become paramount in guaranteed week provisions and are often used by employers to create a significant collective sanction. So, for instance, in the 1982 two-year settlement for manual employees at BL Cars, while the guaranteed pay provisions are improved to cover up to 117 hours per quarter-year, this change is stated to be conditional on the support and co-operation of the workforce in minimizing the need for lay-offs 'including suitable re-deployment or retraining as may be required' ((1982) 76 PBB 3). The IDS Study also points out that many guaranteed pay provisions in practice become inoperative if short-time working is introduced.

One recent decision in the Queen's Bench Division helps to strengthen the position of employees in relation to clauses suspending guaranteed pay agreements. In *Neads* v. *CAV Ltd* [1983] IRLR 361, Peter Pain J. had to interpret the suspension clause in the 1964 engineering national agreement on guarantee of employment – the clause which had been under consideration in the *Burroughs* v. *Timmoney* case. The question was whether, in order to suspend the agreement in the event of dislocation of production in a federated establishment as a result of an industrial dispute, the employer had to show that the dislocation of production had resulted in an unavailability of work for the employees in question. In holding that there had to be an unavailability of work, Peter Pain J. was vindicating a broad principle that there is no general right of lay-off either at common law or as a matter of construction of express agreements. Indeed, he expressly left open (ibid., p. 367) the question whether the employer could rely on the 1964 agreement where it would derogate from the employee's common-law rights. In other words, he was suggesting that contracts of employment might be construed as incorporating the 1964 agreement only in so far as it fulfilled its historical role of improving upon the common-law rights of industrial workers. One cannot, however, feel confident that the courts generally would pursue this approach.

So what, one then asks, is provided by way of social security to cover lay-off or short-time? As Ogus and Barendt point out (*The Law of Social Security*, 2nd edn (1982), p. 90), the task of compensating for loss of earnings during suspension, lay-off and short-time working has traditionally been undertaken by the conventional unemployment insurance scheme where other countries have generally developed special schemes for 'partial unemployment'. But, as those writers go on to point out, there have long been felt to be powerful objections to this use of the social security scheme, which tends to subsidize particular industries which regularly lay off workers. In 1966 the Labour government adopted a strategy of seeking to get employers to assume the burden of making guaranteed pay provisions universally. This they did by providing that the first six days of suspension from work would not count as qualifying days for the payment of the newly introduced earnings-related supplement to unemployment benefit (National Insurance Act 1966, s.2). The intention was in due course to extend this rule to basic flat-rate unemployment benefit. But the expected response from employers never materialized to the extent necessary to make this further step possible without serious detriment to employees. The 1966 measure itself was later to be submerged in the general abolition of earnings-related supplement by the Social Security (No. 2) Act 1980. The trade-dispute suspension of unemployment benefit in the event of lay-off in consequence of industrial action is considered later in this book (see below, p. 937).

By the time the Labour Party returned to government in 1974, it was clear that further progress in the direction of getting employers generally to make guaranteed pay provisions would require statutory regulation of the contract of employment and this was introduced by the guaranteed pay provisions of ss.22 *et seq.* of the EPA 1975, now EPCA 1978, ss.12–18. But these provisions were modest in their scope, and did little more than usher in the principle of statutory regulation. They provide for guarantee payment for up to five working days lost per quarter-year up to a maximum rate of, originally, £6.60 per day and £10 per day by February 1984 (SI 1983 No. 1962). The quarters concerned were originally fixed as those beginning on 1 February, 1 May, 1 August and 1 November of each year. But the government became concerned at the fact that in the major national industrial disputes of 1978–9 and 1979–80, the fixed-quarter system enabled many workers laid off in consequence of the disputes to claim two lots of guaranteed payment in quick succession. The system was accordingly altered by the Employment Act 1980 so that the five days maximum was applied to rolling quarters, i.e. to any three-month period since the maximum amount was last paid. Paradoxically, this is in most circumstances a more favourable system from the employee's point of view; but in general the statutory provisions are so cautious as to have done little to improve the overall position for employees; indeed, Hepple, Partington and Simpson showed how some employees could be rendered worse off than before by the interaction between guaranteed pay provisions and the rules concerning unemployment benefit ((1977) 6 *ILJ* 54).

By the later 1970s, the government was conscious of the inadequacy of the provisions of various sorts thus far described to provide a socially acceptable response to the growing problem of lay-offs and short-time working brought about by increasingly adverse economic conditions. They had become involved in various Temporary Employment Subsidy schemes for subsidizing employers to enable them to guarantee the pay of employees who it could be shown would have been made redundant but for the subsidy. These schemes were coming under heavy pressure from the EEC Commission as amounting to an improper distortion of competition, notably for their effects on the textile, footwear and clothing manufacturing industries where the subsidies were especially widely used because of the particularly adverse situation in these industries. The immediate response to that particular pressure was to shift the emphasis from subsidizing employment generally to subsidizing short-time working, which apparently was more acceptable to the EEC Commission; this was the special feature of the Temporary Employment Subsidy for the Textiles, Clothing and Footwear Industries from May 1978 onwards. (It should be explained at this point that these various employment subsidy schemes are constituted under legislation – currently the Employment Subsidies Act 1978 – which gives the Department of Employment the most sweeping powers of departmental legislation without even the necessity of laying their proposals before Parliament in the form of statutory instruments – a fact which has led one writer to characterize these subsidy schemes as 'Leaflet Law' ((1980) 9 *ILJ* 254) (see also above, p. 29). For these various reasons, the government made proposals for a new scheme of compensation for short-time working. (Consultative Document on Short-time Working, Department of Employment, 1978.) These arrangements were to consist of a permanent structure whereby employers would have been required to provide guaranteed pay representing 75 per cent of normal gross pay with a rebate of perhaps 50 per cent from a short-time Working Fund to which all employers would contribute. There would also be a temporary structure to replace the existing Temporary Employment Subsidy, whereby the government would reimburse the costs of short-time working compensation to employers who could show that short-time working was being used as an alternative to redundancy. The aim of these proposals was to transfer most of the risk of short-time working from the social security system to the Exchequer in temporary emergencies and, in the normal way, to that sort of special contingencies fund built up from employers' compulsory contributions which was used to finance redundancy payments (see below, p. 529) and maternity pay (see above, p. 356). The first, permanent, tier of these proposals was embodied in the Short-time Working Compensation Bill 1979, but this fell with the Labour government and the Conservative government which succeeded them gave no indication of intending to legislate along those lines.

It had been perceptively argued in a note by Partington on the 1978 proposals ((1978) 7 *ILJ* 187) that the intended distinction between the normal and the emergency situations might well be an unreal and an over-optimistic one. The 'emergency' part of the 1978 proposals were implemented, more or less, in the Temporary Short-time Working Compensation Scheme, made under the Employment Subsidies Act 1978; it remained in effect till March 1984. The Scheme originally provided for subsidies of up to 75 per cent of the workers' full pay for up to 12 months. The Conservative government continued the Scheme but progressively whittled it down, first reducing it to 75 per cent of pay for 6 months (July 1979) then to 50 per cent of pay for 9 months (November 1980), then to 50 per cent of pay for 6 months (December 1981 with effect from July 1982), and announced at the latter stage that it would be closed down for further applications from March 1984. Whether or not the Scheme is revived or replaced, it remains the case that the law about guaranteed pay in the event of lay-off or short-time is a curiously ramshackle structure of common law, social security law and employment protection law, precariously roofed over by the flimsy tiles of 'Leaflet Law'.

(f) Pensions

There is some disinclination among labour lawyers to discuss the subject of pensions. It is not the most inviting of subjects. But it deserves a central place in any study of labour law which aims to foresee areas of future importance and not just to perpetuate the discussion of areas of present or past importance. We have already considered the case for regarding pensions as an integral part of the wage–work bargain and seen how the courts are moving towards recognition that this is the appropriate frame of reference for occupational pensions (see above, p. 338). Having thus located the topic within labour law we may recognize it as raising issues concerned with security of earnings – issues both general and particular. The general issue, as with many other aspects of security of earnings, is how the responsibility of providing financial support for employees after their retirement is distributed between employers and the social security system, and what role collective bargaining has played in that distribution. The particular issues are, given that distribution of responsibility, what provision is made by the state to ensure the security of pension rights provided by employers.

Taking first the general issue, we find that there has been a long tradition of regarding pensions as primarily a social security matter rather than a matter for collective bargaining or legislation imposing duties upon employers to pay pensions (except in the civil service and the public sector, where there is an equally long and important tradition of legislation providing pensions for public servants as a consequence of their public employment).

In their treatise on *The Law of Social Security* (2nd edn, 1982), Anthony Ogus and Eric Barendt describe how the social security system has very greatly predominated over occupational schemes as the major source of retirement pensions. They show how it has not been possible for governments to rely on occupational pensions even to remedy the deficiencies of state provision, let alone to act as the principal source of retirement pensions. The state has borne the responsibility of general contributory flat-rate pension provision since the time of the Widows, Orphans and Old Age Contributory Pensions Act 1925. The creation of a system of full subsistence retirement pensions was one of the major items in the programme for the creation of the welfare state as envisaged by the Beveridge Report in 1942 and was realized by the National Insurance Act 1946. The role of state pensions as income replacement during retirement (rather than simple subsistence provision) was enhanced when earnings-related, or graduated, contributions and benefits were introduced by the National Insurance Act 1959.

From the early 1970s onwards the presence of continuous high inflation created the necessity for major new measures to provide for income replacement in retirement. It would hardly be over-dramatic to say that fifty years hence, the Pensions (Increase) Act 1971 by which public service pensions were indexated and the Social Security Pensions Act 1975 by which a new pensions régime was created for the private sector will appear in retrospect to have been as significant to labour law as the Industrial Relations Act 1971 and the Employment Protection Act 1975. The Pensions (Increase) Act 1971 was the product of a political will to use pensions as a means of effective income replacement in retirement in the public service. The Conservative government of the day intended, as their White Paper *Strategy for Pensions* (Cmnd. 4755, 1971) shows, to foster the development of occupational pension schemes in the private sector also. The White Paper envisaged a scheme in which flat-rate benefits would be provided by a state scheme and earnings-related benefit primarily by occupational pensions schemes, or failing that by a state reserve scheme. These intentions were embodied in the Social Security Act 1973 which among other things set up the Occupational Pensions Board to monitor and control the operation of occupational pensions schemes, these being a central feature of the new pensions scheme. Upon coming into power in 1974, the Labour government put this legislation into abeyance (except for the provisions setting up the Occupational Pensions Board and regulating occupational pensions) because their overall pension strategy was a different one. In their plan, for the political implementation of which bi-partisan support was ultimately procured, the state scheme was to have a major role in providing both flat-rate and earnings-related pensions. But there was still to be a role for occupational pensions schemes in that there was to be a freedom partly to contract out of the earnings-related part of the state scheme where an occupational scheme provided a better alternative.

This scheme was implemented in the Social Security Pensions Act 1975 and came into effect in 1978, although it is important to realize that the earnings-related scheme is based only on years of service from 1978 onwards, so that it builds up only gradually and is not fully effective until 1998. Labour lawyers will one day come to realize how important the debate about pensions that took place during the 1970s was. A valuable analysis of it is offered by Creedy in his recent book *State Pensions in Britain* (1982), as the following extract will serve to suggest:

Earnings-related benefits

It has been seen that in the development of the present system there has been some conflict between the objectives of income replacement and of preventing poverty in old age. Although initially there was greater emphasis on preventing poverty, while also attempting to avoid some of the difficulties associated with the operation of the Poor Law and the means-test, in recent years there has been greater emphasis on income replacement. There has also been considerable growth in the means-tested sector. The recent emphasis which has led to earnings-related benefits has to some extent been associated with what has been referred to as the insurance myth, but the specific official arguments have not usually been made explicit. But as one study recently argued, poverty prevention, 'may indeed suffer to some extent if attention is mainly concentrated on the replacement of unequal incomes by unequal pensions after retirement'.

It is of course most important to stress that the final decision will depend on political judgement about the desirability of redistribution, as well as on considerations of administrative efficiency, and on possible incentive effects. One main objective of this study has been to attempt to make explicit the nature of the trade-offs involved in moving from one type of scheme to another. The extent to which different policies represent consistent aims can therefore also be seen.

Now it may be felt by the policy maker that the main purpose of a pension scheme is to provide suitable income replacement in old age, and that individuals will not make the appropriate decisions relating to savings over their working life. This may be either because of a lack of foresight, or because they do not have access to the kind of information necessary to make useful decisions – including information about future government policy – or because it is extremely expensive to collect the information and a great deal of skill is required to make appropriate judgements. The same policy maker may feel that poverty prevention is best dealt with by other methods of income transfer, and that the aged poor should be helped in just the same kind of way as other groups of deserving poor. Such arguments will lead to the suggestion that there should be a compulsory system of earnings-related state insurance, financed from a special hypothecated tax (such as National Insurance contributions); the fact that such a system cannot easily pay a high basic pension – as shown in chapter 3 – will be of little concern. But to propose that individuals should then be able partially to contract out of the state scheme, to join a private scheme, requires further argument for its support. To further suggest that contracted out individuals should receive special tax advantages requires even more specific detailed support. If, for example, it is thought to be more efficient for the state to administer an earnings-related scheme (efficiency in information collection, in decision making and record keeping), then the support of partial contracting out must appeal to a different kind of argument. The arguments for the very strong support for the private pension industry which is provided by the present state scheme have not been made explicit, however.

Having thus looked at the general issue of distribution of responsibility for providing pensions, we can now turn to look at some particular issues concerning the security of pensions. In this discussion, we shall aim to point out, where appropriate (which it often is), the similarity of the issue and its outcome to issues and outcomes within the traditionally accepted confines of labour law. The first issue is that of legal measures to ensure the solvency of the fund; note the parallel with the discussion of the solvency of the employer later on in this book (see below, pp. 568 *et seq.*). There is no general legal requirement that pensions must be provided from a fund distinct from the employer's general resources. In that sense, pensions could simply be a contractual claim on the employer's current assets. However, it is generally viewed as preferable for occupational pension schemes to be separately funded; this is seen as a way in which the pension expectations of employees may be protected, and as a way for employers to obtain certain tax advantages. But funded pension schemes have to be approved by the Inland Revenue if they are to enjoy tax relief. The concern of the Revenue is not the protection of employees or pensioners but rather the restriction of pensions as a method of tax avoidance. They carry out this task on the terms of a code they have drawn up under the Finance Act 1970 as amended in 1971. The interest of the Revenue includes ensuring that pension contributions are not disposable by the employer, so for that reason the pension has to be provided through the mechanism of an irrevocable trust for Revenue approval. But this merely requires a separate fund and not *per se* a fund whose adequacy or solvency is ensured. The provisions of the Social Security Act 1973 were, by contrast, concerned with protecting the interests of employees and pensioners. Section 51(7) of that Act enabled regulations to be made to ensure that employees could not be required to contribute to any pension fund in whose case the OPB was satisfied that benefits were not adequately secured or that it is otherwise unsound in respect of management or financing. But this particular enabling power has not been exercised. Moreover, under section 59(2) of that Act, the OPB, before it can recognize a scheme for contracting out of the state scheme, must be satisfied that the reserves of the scheme are sufficient to secure guaranteed minimum pensions. But this refers only to protection of the minor component in private schemes which is needed to match the benefits of the state scheme, and so provides no substantial protection.

The Labour government which came into power in 1974 was concerned to ensure that the interests of employees and ex-employees were adequately protected in pension schemes and charged the OPB with the task of considering solvency, disclosure of information and member participation in occupational pension schemes. This could in theory have led to legislation for pension schemes on the lines of the Employment Protection Act 1975. But the political impulse was not strong enough to produce such parallel developments for pension schemes. The OPB reported in 1975 (Cmnd. 5904) that so far as solvency was concerned, the type of controls contained in the 1973 Act were broadly adequate; they went on to make proposals for the disclosure of scheme information to members, but concluded that membership participation legislation would be premature. The government, unpersuaded of this view, issued in 1976 a White Paper on the role of members in the running of occupational pension schemes (Cmnd. 6514), which distinguished between terms and conditions of employment and pension scheme administration and recommended that the former should be matters for collective bargaining and the latter a matter for participative management of the schemes themselves. The White Paper recommendations that recognized independent trade unions should have the right to 50 per cent representation on management bodies of pension schemes caused immense controversy and were not implemented (see (1977) 6 *ILJ* 188). The only governmental activity in that direction has been the introduction of a requirement of consultation with the relevant recognized independent trade unions over employers' decisions to contract out of the state pension scheme (Occupational Pension Schemes (Certification of Employments) Regulations 1975 (SI 1975 No. 1927)).

It may be questioned whether the positive recommendations of the 1975 OPB Report and the 1976 White Paper would, even if fully implemented, have approached the fundamental problems in this area. Controls over funding and solvency are not very significant if they relate only to guaranteed minimum pensions, because it is not at that level that solvency becomes a problem. Disclosure of information to scheme members is insignificant because they are on the whole unlikely to find that information meaningful or be able to assess its potential importance to them. Even membership participation in scheme management is not very significant if it excludes the determination of the terms in which pensions are promised to employees, because the important decisions lie precisely in that area. Outside that area, scheme management consists really in managing the investments, and distributing the benefits largely according to predetermined rules. Membership participation in managing the investments is not very meaningful unless some kind of guidance or policy formulation exists on questions such as whether the pension fund is free to invest back in the enterprise of the employer concerned. As yet that question has not been approached either in statute law or case-law or any governmental code of conduct. Nor, it must be said, is collective bargaining about pensions anything like sufficiently well developed or sophisticated to address such issues in any general kind of way.

It is, then, in the terms of the pension contract with the individual worker that the crucial features of occupational pension schemes are embodied, and it is just starting to be realized what vital issues about security of earnings are involved here. The first such issue to attract major attention (apart from the question of equal treatment of men and women in pension schemes, which we consider separately, see below, pp. 407ff.) has been the nature of provision made for early leavers, i.e. those leaving their employment before the normal retirement age contemplated by their pension scheme. In the 1970s that was perceived of as a problem mainly for those transferring from one job to another. In the 1980s it presents itself also as a problem for those being made redundant from their jobs. Before the Social Security Act 1973, there were no legal controls upon an employer contracting with an employee that the employee should forfeit his pension rights (even those representing his own contributions) upon leaving his employment before retirement. In practice, the rights of many early leavers were indeed confined to the simple return of their own contributions. The Conservative government of 1970 to 1974, anxious as it was to accord a central role to occupational pension schemes, and perceiving what a formidable restraint upon the employee's job mobility such provisions in pension schemes might constitute, legislated by section 63 of the Social Security Act 1973 for the compulsory vesting of occupational pensions upon the leaving of employment before retirement and gave the OPB a continuing responsibility in this regard. Schedule 16 of that Act, which contains the detailed provisions amplifying the deferment principle contained in section 63, has an interesting anti-discrimination provision, whereby it is required not to discriminate against short-service benefits by comparison with ordinary full-service benefits. But all this fails to attack a fundamental inbuilt disadvantage which deferred pensions are liable to have. A pension based on final salary at retirement age contains an inbuilt protection against inflation down to retirement (to the extent that wages and salaries keep pace with inflation). An early leaver who gets a deferred pension loses that inbuilt protection unless there is some provision to indexate his pension rights down to his retirement date. This kind of protection is known as revaluation; it is required by the 1975 Act only so far as the guaranteed minimum pension element is concerned. By the end of the 1970s it was becoming clear that this left early leavers unduly vulnerable to inflation and the OPB was asked to consider this problem. Their report, *Improved Protection for the Occupational Pension Rights and Expectations of Early Leavers* (Cmnd. 8271, 1981), identified the crucial issue as being that of whether it is a reasonable expectation that a pension for a given period of service at a given salary should be comparable for all members of a pension scheme whether or not they all went on to serve in the employment until pensionable age. They concluded that there was sufficient basis for this expectation to justify and indeed necessitate more legislation – which should in their view both extend the pension preservation requirements and require revaluation of preserved benefits in accordance with inflation up to a ceiling of 5 per cent compounded per annum. Even so cautious an approach to mandatory revaluation would be immensely costly for pension schemes; the Report caused a storm of protest and has not been implemented by legislation.

This public discussion of the protection of early leavers suggested the need for a still more fundamental examination of the relationship between pension rights and pension expectations. For at the end of the road which had been taken by the inquiries we have looked at so far lay an inquiry into how far occupational pensions should be protected against inflation once they were in the course of payment – a protection conferred upon public service pensions, as we have seen, by the Pensions Increase Act 1971. For occupational pension schemes, increases of pensions while in payment was required by s.57 of the 1973 Act at a rate of not less than 3 per cent compounded per annum, but only in relation to the guaranteed minimum pension; this provision was repealed in 1975 without having been implemented, and was not replaced. The common law of the contract of employment has not hitherto been envisaged as conferring any implied rights in this respect; and indeed the recognized legal régime for occupational pension schemes, i.e. the discretionary trust fund, maximizes the discretionary character of benefits and probably effectively insulates the employer from direct obligations because of the doctrine of privity of contract. A recent IDS Study (No. 277, 1982) shows how widely pension scheme practice varies in this crucial matter.

The OPB was finally asked to consider this kind of issue and reported late in 1982. Their report, entitled *Greater Security for the Rights and Expectations of Occupational Pension Scheme Members* (Cmnd. 8649, 1982), recommended a thorough and early review of the legal basis of occupational pension schemes in trust law and called for voluntary action by schemes to maintain the real value of pensions in the course of payment, with scheme rules making specific provision for pension increase, and consequent change in contribution rates. But progress in the direction of thorough statutory reform is likely to be slow and refuge is likely to be taken in much less significant legislation about disclosure of information to pension scheme members. Recent public discussion suggests, moreover, that the pursuit of the goal of statutory reform may be delayed by diversionary activity concerned with promoting the idea of 'portable' pensions; that is to say, personal pension schemes arranged directly between the employee and the financial institution of his choosing. Whatever the virtues of proposals of this kind, they are unlikely to conduce towards a clarification or rationalisation of the relationship between pension expectations and pension rights. In fact the idea of legislating for the protection of pension *expectations* places an immense potential weight upon existing assumptions about pension fund solvency, investment policy and funding generally. It also suggests the need for a new kind of collective bargaining in which the traditional trade-union role of maximizing the earnings of those currently in employment to the exclusion of all others may have to be succeeded by a more sophisticated balancing of the interests of those in work and those in retirement – for only in this way can there ultimately be any full protection of the security of earnings.

5 Payment structures and the inequality of pay

(a) Introduction

Earlier in our present discussion of the impact of the law upon the formation of the terms and conditions of employment we were concerned with the impact of the law upon payment systems, that is to say with the different kinds of relationship between work and remuneration. We now turn our attention from payment systems to payment structures, that is to say to the structures by which one person's pay is related to that of other persons within the enterprise concerned. Let us illustrate this distinction between payment systems and payment structures. Measured day-work is a payment system in that it is directed towards achieving a particular relationship between output and remuneration, namely one where remuneration does not vary according to the particular output achieved in a particular payment period, the failure to achieve the measured day-work targets being reflected in other ways than in the diminution of pay. A grading system, on the other hand, is concerned with the structure of payment in the sense that it establishes a relationship between the remuneration of different workers by assigning particular workers to grades which attract a certain remuneration. Clearly a given set of rules about the calculation of pay may operate both as a payment system and as a payment structure; for example, a measured day-work system will establish pay relativity between workers in so far as it assigns values to particular functions within the enterprise and expresses these as the remuneration associated with measured day-work targets. But despite the overlap it is nevertheless useful to think of payment systems and payment structures as two distinct aspects of the process of determination of pay.

With the repeal of Schedule 11 of the Employment Protection Act 1975 and the rescission of the Fair Wages Resolution (see above, pp. 144, 154), there remains only one important form of legal intervention into payment structures, namely that concerned with securing equal pay as between men and women. However, these legal provisions concerned with equal pay serve as a good example of the whole problem of legal regulation of payment structures. For they raise the issues of how the law can set about making fair comparisons between the rates of payment given to particular workers for doing particular jobs, and of how that process of fair comparison can be reconciled with the need to preserve fair differentials with other workers placed elsewhere in the payment structure concerned. Those issues have arisen in the past (and may well arise again in the future) in situations where it is sought to make fair comparisons, that is to say to consider parity claims, between workers as a means of tackling problems of low pay, or as an exception to general norms of an incomes policy. In order to discuss this particular exercise in establishing fair comparisons and fair differentials it will be necessary to consider a complex combination of UK legislation and EEC provisions concerning equal pay. Before embarking upon that exercise, one disclaimer is called for.

The operation of the relevant EEC provisions raises great and interesting problems about their direct applicability in the UK. These problems are of great constitutional significance. We do not for the present purpose lay claim to giving either a full or still less an authoritative treatment of the direct applicability problem. With that disclaimer one may embark upon a consideration of the relevant provisions, which it will be useful to sub-divide in order to address separately what we perceive of as a number of distinct aspects of the process of equalization.

(b) Equal Pay – the extent of equalization

By 'extent of equalization' we mean the terms that can be compared and the persons or jobs whose terms can be compared to establish equal pay, and also the searchingness with which the equalization is carried out. Less need be said about the terms that can be compared than about the persons or jobs that can be compared. It should be noted that the EqPA applies to terms and conditions of employment generally rather than just pay (s.1(2), 'terms (whether concerned with pay or not)', s.3(1) 'any provision') so that, as we shall see later, the overlap with the Sex Discrimination Act 1975 is more extensive and complex than might at first appear (see below, p. 405). On the other hand, as we have seen, there is a crucially important exclusion of pension provisions from the EqPA (s.6(1A)) and an underlying question in relation to Article 119 of the Treaty of Rome whether 'pay' includes pension provisions. But, although the pension and retirement benefits question is a 'hot potato', the acutely sensitive political question facing the legislature and the courts is that of which jobs or persons may be compared, and it is to the development of the law on that point that we must address ourselves at greater length.

A very useful account of the origins of the EqPA is given by Snell, Glucklich and Povall ('Equal Pay and Opportunities', DE Research Paper No. 20, 1981). They show how during the late 1960s and early 1970s the argument that legislative intervention was required if women were to obtain equal pay and opportunities of work gained momentum. It came to be widely felt that traditional voluntary methods of collective bargaining had failed to improve women's pay and opportunities or to promote policies of equalization, despite the growth in women's participation in the labour force and the increase in particular of older married women in the workforce. The demand for equal pay developed as a distinct force at the forefront of this whole movement. It had a long history as a distinct demand made by the TUC which was endorsed by international instruments. In particular there was pressure from the TUC from the sixties for the UK to ratify ILO Convention No. 100 of 1951 which declared the principle of equal remuneration for men and women workers for work of equal value. (The UK ratified in 1971.) The demand for legislation was generally seen as challenging the traditionally voluntarist approach to employment relations less directly, less fundamentally, and less controversially than equal opportunities legislation would do, though as we shall see that voluntarism dictated a cautious, even a minimalist, approach to the equal pay legislation itself. Moreover by the end of the sixties there was starting to be some reluctance to legislate in a way that could be seen to stoke the fires of wage inflation by enforcing parity claims. However, the equalization of the pay and conditions of women workers came to be seen by the Labour government as a way of dealing with certain industrial relations problems following the celebrated women machinists' strike for more pay at Ford's Dagenham plant in 1968, and the EqPA was passed in 1970 to come into effect in 1975 by which time it was made part, though still a distinct part, of the Sex Discrimination Act of that year.

The EqPA made provision for three specific kinds of equalization exercise. We shall first specify these, and then consider the extent of equalization that they involve.

(i) It implied into contracts of employment an equality clause which modifies other terms and conditions of employment so as to eliminate inequalities between men and women employed in the same employment on like work (section 1(2)(a)).

(ii) An equality clause was similarly implied and given an overriding effect where men and women are employed in the same employment on work rated as equivalent (s.1(2)(b)). This situation will arise where a job evaluation exercise has been carried out within an enterprise and where two jobs are or would be accorded an equal value by the application of those criteria within the job evaluation scheme which are themselves non-discriminatory (i.e. those criteria which look directly to the nature and extent of the demands made by the job) as distinct from criteria which set different values for men and women on the same demand (s.1(5)).

(iii) The Act provides a procedure for the elimination of provisions in collective agreements and formal pay structures which apply specifically to men only or to women only (s.3). The Act establishes rules for the amendments which are to be made for this purpose to collective agreements or formal pay structures (s.3(4)). The task of deciding what amendments need to be made has been delegated to the Central Arbitration Committee on reference by any party to the collective agreement or by the Secretary of State for Employment (s.3(1)).

As we shall see later in this section, the Equal Pay Act was later to be amended by the Equal Pay (Amendment) Regulations 1983 to include a fourth and potentially more far-reaching kind of equalization measure consisting in a claim to equal pay for work of equal value. The additional provision is set out below at p. 384. Even before this occurred, there had been superimposed upon the Equal Pay Act the equal pay provisions of Article 119 of the Treaty of Rome and EEC Council Directive 75/117 of 1975, which as we shall see have been accorded some measure of direct applicability in the UK, and so give rise to a further set of equalization requirements. We shall first deal with the basic provisions of the Equal Pay Act as it came into force in 1975.

(c) The like work concept under the Equal Pay Act

The flagship of the little fleet of provisions contained in the Equal Pay Act was undoubtedly the like work concept of s.1(2)(a). It is to be noted that s.1(2) confines 'like work' comparisons to employees 'in the same employment' which is defined by s.1(6) in such a way as to restrict comparison to employees with a single common employer or associated employers, and moreover to employees at the same establishment or another establishment where common terms and conditions are observed. The idea here was that the Act should not set out to prevent the payment of regional differentials and still less to create inter-employer comparisons; but that there should at the same time be a provision to prevent employers from avoiding their obligations under the Act by employing men and women in separate establishments. The 'like work' concept is defined and elaborated by s.1(4) as follows:

(4) A woman is to be regarded as employed on like work with men if, but only if, her work and theirs is of the same or a broadly similar nature, and the differences (if any) between the things she does and the things they do are not of practical importance in relation to terms and conditions of employment; and accordingly in comparing her work with theirs regard shall be had to the frequency or otherwise with which any such differences occur in practice as well as to the nature and extent of the differences.

The application of this concept has been treated as involving a process of comparing terms and conditions of employment in order to discover whether they, taken together with the employee's task specification, suggest that the jobs are the same for pay purposes. Not only is this combination of job-package definition and task-function definition important elsewhere in labour law – for instance in relation to the concept of redundancy (see below, p. 530) but it is the very stuff of which much of plant- and company-wide collective bargaining about pay consists. The following case illustrates the process at work. The facts appear from the judgment of the EAT. Note also how it was held the equality clause would operate once it had been concluded that the man and the woman were doing like work.

Dugdale v. *Kraft Foods Ltd* [1977] ICR 48 (EAT)

PHILLIPS J.: ... Each of the appellants was employed in the quality control department of Kraft Foods Ltd, the employers, and the work which each of them did (which was not identical) was typical of that done by a number of other employees. Mrs Dugdale was a quality control inspector grade II, Miss Gray was a senior line-up inspector grade I, Mrs Wellens was a weight control assistant grade III, Mrs Roache was a finished produce laboratory assistant (or analyst) grade I, and Mrs Owen was a junior analyst grade III. For the purposes of their applications the appellants

compared the work done by each of them with the work done by the male quality
control inspectors, of whom there were six. The industrial tribunal has set out the
reasons for their decision fully and clearly.

Amongst the exhibits put in at the hearing were various job descriptions, including
A. 1 job description – quality control inspector (female), A. 2 job description – quality
control inspector (male) and A. 3 job description – quality control inspector (male) –
night shift. From these job descriptions, the other exhibits, and the evidence given, it
was easy to see what work each of the appellants and the six male quality control
inspectors did. It is obvious from the reference in the heading to certain of these job
descriptions, which refer to 'male' or 'female,' that they came into existence at a time
when it was permissible to discriminate in that way. It might be thought that they thus
tend to support the view that the work (and remuneration) was deliberately arranged
in a manner to discriminate between men and women. That fact, of course, is not
enough to enable the appellants to succeed; in order to do that they must show that they
come within the provisions of the Act of 1970.

Exhibit R. 1 sets out certain wage scales which were in operation at the material time.
In some respects the details were difficult to follow, and for this reason we made an
exception to our normal practice and received evidence to explain them. Item 4 of the
exhibit, headed 'Laboratory,' sets out the basic wage rate for male staff and shows that
a man aged over 19, employed for two years, received a basic wage of £42·45. Included
in this scale were the six male quality control inspectors. The male quality control
inspectors were employed on a three-shift system, changing weekly so that each would
work a night shift once every three weeks. Item 6 sets out under the heading 'Shift
Allowances' the remuneration payable in respect of the shift worked. For either the
morning or afternoon shift £5·80 would be paid, and for the night shift £11·60. Thus a
male quality control inspector working the morning or afternoon shift would receive
£42·45 plus £5·80. The female staff, including the appellants, employed in the quality
control department were employed on a two-shift system, and the details of their
remuneration is set out at item 4 under the heading 'Laboratory – Shifts (37½ p.w.).' It
will be seen that, unlike the male quality control inspectors, the female workers in this
department were graded into three grades, I, II and III. Thus a grade II female
worker would be paid £30·80 after one year. She would receive similar shift allowances –
i.e. £5·80 per shift worked. The female workers in the quality control department did not
work on the night shift. Thus, at this time, the difference in remuneration between a
male quality control inspector and a grade I female worker in the quality control
department was £42·45 minus £32·80, equals £9·65. The male quality control inspectors,
unlike the female workers, in the quality control department also worked a Sunday
morning shift once every three weeks. Work by the male quality control inspectors on
the night shift was compulsory, but work by them on the Sunday morning shift was
voluntary, though they all in fact did work on Sundays. It would have been unlawful for
the female workers in the quality control department to have worked on the night shift
or upon the Sunday morning shift: see section 93 of the Factories Act 1961. The
employers had not applied for an exemption from this prohibition.

In accordance with the provisions of section 1(1) of the Equal Pay Act 1970 (as
amended) the appellants' contracts of employment are deemed to include an equality
clause. The question is whether the equality clause in the circumstances of the case has
effect as provided in section 1(2). It was not suggested that this case fell within
paragraph (*b*) of that subsection, for there had been no evaluation study. Accordingly,

the question was whether the appellants were employed on 'like work' with the male quality control inspectors, being men in the same employment, as defined in subsection (6). The answer turns upon the application of section 1(4) to the facts of the case.

The first step is to determine whether the work done by the appellants and that done by the male quality control inspectors was of the same or a broadly similar nature. The industrial tribunal did not answer this question in terms, but it seems to us to be clear that the answer, certainly in the case of Mrs Dugdale, and very probably in the case of the other appellants, is that her work and the men's work was of at least a broadly similar nature. The question then is whether the difference between the things which she did and the things which they did are of practical importance in relation to terms and conditions of employment. The industrial tribunal found that they were. It is necessary to look a little carefully at the way in which they reached this conclusion.

The industrial tribunal, in considering the application of section 1(4), first considered in detail the case of Mrs Dugdale, being inclined to the view that if she could not succeed nor could the other appellants. In the view of the industrial tribunal the fact that the appellants and the male quality control inspectors worked in different departments was not of much significance, nor did they accept the argument that the work done by the male quality control inspectors required significantly greater versatility. They further regarded as unimportant the fact that the male quality control inspectors did more and heavier lifting than the appellants, and that on the morning shift the male quality control inspectors took the place of the raw material technician and in his absence were responsible for drawing off and testing samples. However, they took a different view of the fact that on the Sunday morning shift the male quality control inspectors did pre-production overtime, carrying out laboratory analysis tests.

It appears, however, from the subsequent paragraphs of the decision that the industrial tribunal were doubtful whether this difference between the work done by the male quality control inspectors and that done by the appellants was by itself alone sufficient to defeat the appellants' claim. But they did say in paragraph 12:

We take the view that if there is a difference between the man's job and the woman's job which, even if it occurs relatively infrequently, nevertheless arises from statutory prohibitions, and is in respect of work which is vital to the employer, then it cannot be said to be 'not of practical importance,' and therefore it would negative the alleged broad similarity between their jobs.

Nonetheless it appears that the industrial tribunal would not have found against the appellants – or, at least, might not have done – but for the importance which they attached to the night shift working. They point out in paragraph 13 that the appellants could not do night work. They say that there is only one relatively small production line operating at that time, but add that the night time is used for the absolutely essential cleaning operations. They continue in paragraphs 13 and 14:

the fact that the female applicants do not, and as things stand, cannot do night work represents a substantial dissimilarity between their respective work and that of the male quality control inspectors whom they put forward as doing broadly similar work. . . . This night working every third week is, in our view a substantial element of difference which is of practical importance and which negatives any argument that the work of the female and the male quality control inspectors is broadly similar. . . . We find therefore against all the appellants, irrespective of other matters, on the basis that the work of the male quality control inspectors includes, as a normal part of their job, Sunday overtime and night working which are essential to the employers and which the appellants, in the absence of any exemption from statutory prohibitions, cannot do. This of itself is a difference of such practical importance in relation to terms and conditions of employment as to negative any alleged broad similarity between the appellants' work and that of the male quality control inspectors.

To summarise: it seems to us on the admitted facts to be clear that the appellants' work (or certainly Mrs Dugdale's) and that of the male quality control inspectors was of the same or a broadly similar nature, and that the question, then, was whether the differences between the things which the appellants did and the things which they did were of practical importance in relation to terms and conditions of employment. This involves a consideration of two separate matters: (1) the fact that the male quality control inspectors unlike the appellants worked at night and on Sunday morning, and (2) the nature of the work which they did on those occasions. It is not clear to us that the industrial tribunal in reaching its decision distinguished between these two matters.

It appears to us to be necessary to decide, as a matter of the construction of section 1(4), whether the first of these matters, i.e. the fact of doing work at a different time, falls within the words 'the things she does and the things they do.' To simplify the question by an example: take a factory in which a simple repetitive process of assembly takes place, employing men and women engaged upon identical work. Suppose that the men did, but the women did not, work at night and on a Sunday morning doing the same work. Undoubtedly, the women's work and the men's work would be of the same or a broadly similar nature. Prima facie, therefore, they would be employed on 'like work.' Does the fact that the men work at night and on Sunday morning, and the women do not, constitute a difference between the things which the women do and the things which the men do? It may be that either view is possible. A man, if asked what he does, might reply, 'I assemble radio components,' or he might reply, 'I assemble radio components on the night shift.' We have come to the conclusion that, in the context of the Equal Pay Act 1970 (as amended), the mere time at which the work is performed should be disregarded when considering the differences between the things which the woman does and the things which the man does. Were it not so, the Act could never apply in cases where it must obviously have been intended to apply, where the men doing the same work are engaged on a night shift.

Some support for this view is to be obtained from the judgments of the Court of Appeal in *Johnson* v. *Nottinghamshire Combined Police Authority* [1974] ICR 170. That was the case of a claim for a redundancy payment. Women clerks were dismissed because they were, for good reason, unwilling to change from ordinary day work to an alternating shift system. The work which they had done was substantially the same as the work which was done by their replacements. The only difference was in the hours worked. In order to succeed it had to be established that the requirement of the employers for employees to carry out work of a particular kind had diminished. The Court of Appeal held that the change in the hours of working, without any change in the tasks performed, did not effect a change in the particular kind of work. Certainly, that case is not directly applicable, and it is true that it depends in part on the reference in section 1 of the Redundancy Payments Act 1965 to the place of employment. But it seems to us to be generally in line with our thinking on the subject. In short, in our judgment, in applying section 1(4) no attention should be paid to the fact that the men work at some different time of the day, if that is the only difference between what the women do and they do.

It does not seem to us that this interpretation of section 1(4) would lead to any unfairness; rather the reverse. Where the work done is the same, and the only difference is the time at which it is done, the men will be compensated for the extra burden of working at night or on Sundays by the shift payment or premium. There seems to be no reason why the women should not have equality of treatment in respect of the basic wage, or in respect of the day shift payment, if any. In a case in which the men are not paid a shift payment or premium for night working or Sunday working, but are paid at an enhanced basic wage to reflect their readiness to work at nights or on Sundays, there seems to us to be no reason why, in giving effect to the equality clause in accordance with section 1(2)(a)(i), the terms in the women's contracts as to remuneration should not be so modified as to take account of the fact that the men do, and they do not, work at nights or on Sunday. It should be emphasised that the equality clause is to have effect so as to modify any less favourable term of the women's contracts so as to be not less favourable, i.e. it need not produce equality if, though they are engaged on 'like work,' the payment to the men includes remuneration for something affecting the men but not the women, such as working at night.

Turning to the facts of this case, it is thus necessary, in deciding whether the differences between the things which the appellants do and the things which the male quality control inspectors do are of practical importance in relation to terms and conditions of employment, to disregard the fact that the men do, and the appellants do not, work at nights and on Sunday mornings. In answering the question attention must be confined to the work which they do. It is not clear to us from an examination of the industrial tribunal's reasons what conclusion they would have reached if they had approached the matter in this way, because they have considered the two matters simultaneously; that is, the fact of the men working at a different time from the women and the nature of the work done by the men on those occasions. Accordingly, in our judgment it is necessary that the case be remitted to the industrial tribunal, or, in the event of difficulty over the availability of the members, to such other industrial tribunal as the regional chairman may determine. We think it desirable that there should be a rehearing.

This decision helped to establish an inclusive approach to the notion of 'like work' which treats jobs as like work where the task function is similar, and is not deterred by differences in the terms and conditions, i.e. in the 'job package'. We shall see that this method of definition of an employee's 'work' was adopted in relation to the redundancy concept with momentous consequences (see below, p. 540). It has also been unconsciously adopted in this context in that the EAT treated it as uncontroversial in two cases (*Handley* v. *Mono Ltd* [1979] ICR 147, *Jenkins* v. *Kingsgate Ltd* [1981] ICR 715) that a man and a woman carrying out the same task specification were engaged upon 'like work' although they were doing so on, respectively, a full-time and a part-time basis. As we shall see, the comparison of full-time and part-time workers is seen as raising other difficulties (see below, p. 398), but it is significant that they have been regarded as doing 'like work.'[1]

(d) The concept of work rated as equivalent under the Equal Pay Act

It will be clear from our discussion of the 'like work' concept that even if interpreted on the broader 'task function' basis it sets up a relatively narrow basis of comparison between workers. It is very much at one end of the spectrum of possible approaches to the concept of equal pay. It typifies and expresses the cautious approach of the 1970 Act. On the one hand it must be admitted that similarity of jobs is the most specific, concrete, and convincingly objective basis on which to recognize the social claim to equal pay. On the other hand it was clear to the legislators that to recognize only that basis would not do enough to meet the demand for equal pay; it was necessary to recognize some wider form of the demand. The parallel with the development of collective bargaining is interesting. A claim that there is a legitimate expectation of parity of pay in situations outside that of 'like work' must be appealing to some notion of equality of worth; in other words, to some implicit notion of fairness or distributive justice. The same demand occurs in the collective pay bargaining process, and it has been sought to meet it by developing supposedly scientific and objective methods of job evaluation, whereby the intrinsic relative worth of jobs can be established.

The Eq PA accepted parity established by properly conducted job evaluation as a basis for an equal pay claim (s. 1(2)(b)). But, as examination of the defining provision will show, the preference for voluntarism dictated that the standard of equivalence of rating was available only when a job evaluation study had actually taken place in relation to the employment concerned.

Equal Pay Act 1970, s.1(5)

A woman is to be regarded as employed on work rated as equivalent with that of any men if, but only if, her job and their job have been given an equal value, in terms of the demand made on a worker under various headings (for instance effort, skill, decision), on a study undertaken with a view to evaluating in those terms the jobs to be done by all or any of the employees in an undertaking or group of undertakings, or would have been given an equal value but for the evaluation being made on a system setting different values for men and women on the same demand under any heading.

It is vitally important to realize that the process of job evaluation is ultimately itself a method of collective bargaining or dispute resolution; it is not free from the normal characteristics and problems of collective bargaining or dispute resolution processes. This manifests itself in three specific ways. Job

---

[1] The very same point is made in relation to Article 119 of the Rome Treaty (see below, p. 381). Paras. 3(a) and 3(b) use the terminologies 'same work' and 'same job'. Advocate-General Warner makes the point in *Jenkins* v. *Kingsgate Ltd* that these are contrasting terminologies and that a part-time worker and a full-time worker might be regarded as doing 'the same work' although not doing 'the same job' for the purposes of Article 119 ([1981] ICR 592 at p. 598E-G). Indeed, he shows that the same contrast of terminology arises in all the other community languages.

evaluation methods, although laying claim to establishing objective ways of comparing jobs, may themselves be a vehicle for sex discrimination; for they may reproduce discriminatory assumptions underlying the collective bargaining process. A simple example would be one where a job evaluation process attributed such a high relative value to physical strength as compared with, say, dexterity, as to favour men over women. Section 1(5) itself deals only with overt sex discrimination in job evaluation studies. EEC Directive 75/117 Art. 1 goes further and requires that a job classification system must be so drawn up as to exclude any discrimination on grounds of sex. The EOC regards this as a major problem and has published guidance on how to eliminate discrimination from job evaluation schemes.

Secondly, as job evaluation is likely to be part of a collective bargaining process or else will be a substitute for collective bargaining, it may be challenged as being unfair or unacceptable just as any other bargaining position may be. This has meant that the EAT has had to guide ITs as to how far they should admit such challenges to job evaluation studies where the latter are advanced as the basis of equal pay claims. Initially the EAT seemed willing to countenance such challenges. In *Eaton Ltd* v. *Nuttall* [1977] ICR 272, the EAT with Phillips J. presiding commented that s.1(5) could apply only to a valid evaluation study, meaning one that was thorough in analysis and capable of impartial application (p. 277H). To like effect was *Greene* v. *Broxtowe District Council* [1977] ICR 241. But by the time of *England* v. *Bromley London Borough Council* [1978] ICR 1, it was clear that if challenges to validity of job evaluation were made by employee claimants – who were therefore necessarily asking to have their equal pay claims upheld on the basis of the job evaluation exercise *with the defect eliminated* – the IT could accept those challenges only at the price of in effect engaging in its own job evaluation exercise, which the EAT was not willing to require or contemplate. This effectively relegated employees to the 'like work' basis of claim where they disagreed with the findings of a job evaluation exercise, while still leaving open, however, the validity of the job evaluation study. In *Arnold* v. *Beecham Group* [1982] ICR 744 the EAT with Browne-Wilkinson J. presiding expressed doubt as to the extent of such a right of challenge (p. 753G).

Thirdly, job evaluation exercises share the characteristic of collective bargaining processes generally in that a particular line of bargaining may be embarked upon but may founder on disagreement between the collective parties preventing its effective implementation. This has left the EAT with the need to give guidance to ITs on what degree of completeness or implementation of job evaluation studies is necessary to their availability as a basis for equal pay claims. In *England* v. *Bromley LBC* (above) the EAT said that it must be reasonable to regard the job evaluation study as governing the situation of the employees in question at the material times ([1978] ICR 1 at p. 4F). In *O'Brien* v. *Sim-Chem. Ltd* [1980] ICR 573 the House of Lords managed to stretch this to include the case where the collective bargaining process was complete but the results of the job evaluation study were not implemented because the employers feared that implementation might infringe the government's pay policy. In *Arnold* v. *Beecham Group* [1980] ICR 744, a job evaluation study for supervisory staff was completed by a joint committee of management and the union, but its implementation encountered great problems when the engineering supervisory staff rejected it and sought to be treated as a separate negotiating group, which ultimately caused the employers to abandon the scheme. The EAT with Browne-Wilkinson J. presiding accepted that it would create a disincentive to entering upon job evaluation exercises if the *O'Brien* decision was applied to give effect to such exercises before they had been accepted as a valid study (p. 751F–H), though they went on to hold that such acceptance might be complete even though remuneration was never governed by it. They held that these conditions were satisfied here in relation to the supervisors other than the engineers, in relation to whom the individual gradings had been agreed and appeals heard and disposed of. But the EAT recognized (pp. 751H–752B) that women seeking equal treatment by reference to job evaluation were ultimately at the mercy of the employers and the unions; there was the need for some other basis of comparison if employers were not to be free effectively to minimize the impact of the legislation. We now turn to the question of how far any such basis of equalization existed within the original framework of the 1970 Act as it came into force in 1975.

(e) Elimination of unequal differentials under s.3 of the Equal Pay Act

So far we have looked at positive equalization measures – that is, at conditions in which the claim to equality is established by showing conformity to a positive model, be that one of similarity or established equivalence of worth of the work being compared. The question whether there are any other methods of equalization is of considerable general significance to labour law, because the answer will indicate the parameters of legal control of relative and selective decisions, and therefore to an important extent the frontiers of labour law. An examination of the working of equal pay legislation does seem to suggest a third possibility. So far, the process has concentrated on the work side of the equation. The third possibility arises from concentrating on the pay side of the equation. In this analysis the theoretical model consists of a pay structure which can be said to fulfil the condition of 'equal pay for men and women'. This is a composite concept which amounts to 'sex equality in relation to pay'. The process of equalization on this model is a negative one. The model is seen as requiring the absence of sex discrimination and the actual pay structure is tested against the model negatively for freedom from the taint of discrimination. This may in truth be no more than the obverse face of the coin of comparison by reference to the 'work' side of the equation; but it creates a different emphasis, a different process of reasoning and therefore possibly different results. This is of great importance to understanding how this kind of labour law works.

Section 3 of the Eq PA represents a modest incursion into this kind of control process. Because it is rightly perceived to be a potentially extensive mode of testing for fair differentials, *locus standi* is confined to parties to collective agreements or the Department of Employment (s.3(1)). Moreover the control exercisable under section 3 is confined so that it applies only against provisions in collective agreements or pay structures 'applying *specifically* to men only or to women only' (s.5(3), emphasis added). Because this control process culminates, in an award of an essentially arbitrational character, it was entrusted to the Industrial Court (later renamed the Industrial Arbitration Board) and passed by inheritance to the Central Arbitration Committee (s.3(1) as amended). As a recent study has shown (Davies [1980] *CLP* 165), the CAC treated s.3 as enabling them to test for anything amounting in substance to sex discrimination in pay structures or provisions in collective agreements dealing with terms and conditions of employment. The study goes on to show that the Divisional Court in *R.* v. *CAC ex parte Hy-Mac Ltd* [1979] IRLR 461 was probably historically correct in restricting the CAC to the control of *explicitly* sex-based differentials – in other words that this was what was intended to be the effect of s.3; but that this intention was the product of a voluntarism or abstentionism which was outmoded by the time the Eq PA came into effect, so that the maintaining of this voluntarism against the preferred style of the CAC was socially counter-productive albeit formally justifiable.

Similarly, when it came to the point of remedies, the Divisional Court was probably closer than the CAC to the intentions of the legislators when they insisted that the curiously intricate provisions of s.3(4) (which conferred powers to amend collective agreements so as to eliminate the discrimination with which s.3 deals) did not authorize the sort of general wage review that the CAC had embarked upon; but that sort of wider wage review had by 1979 become more accepted as the proper function of the CAC so that the Court was restricting the effective realization of the goals of the legislation as they appeared in the current context. This is, of course, not an unfamiliar relationship between the courts and one of the administrative agencies of our labour law. It did mean that s.3 would rapidly become to all intents and purposes defunct, and this perhaps helped to shift the focus of attention, in the search for further grounds of equal pay comparison, to Article 119 of the Treaty of Rome, to which we must now turn our attention.

(f) Article 119 of the Treaty of Rome

The pursuit of the principle of equal pay for men and women has always been a prominent objective of the EEC. The principle lies within an area of consensus in which the member states can convince themselves that economic liberalism can be combined with social progress. For this reason, the Treaty of Rome of 1957 embodied an adapted version of ILO Convention No. 100

under the title of Social Policy in the following terms (as translated):

Treaty of Rome 1957, Article 119

Each Member State shall during the first stage ensure and subsequently maintain the application of the principle that men and women should receive equal pay for equal work.

For the purpose of this Article, 'pay' means the ordinary basic or minimum wage or salary and any other consideration, whether in cash or in kind, which the worker receives, directly or indirectly, in respect of his employment from his employer.

Equal pay without discrimination based on sex means:

(a) that pay for the same work at piece rates shall be calculated on the basis of the same unit of measurement;

(b) that pay for work at time rates shall be the same for the same job.

The first and greatest problem is what is meant by 'equal pay for equal work'. The ILO Convention declared the principle in terms of 'equal pay for work of equal value'. It seems reasonable to think that the EEC was by this differentiation of words adopting a narrower principle more akin to the 'like work' principle of the EqPA. This view is reinforced by the fact that in all the other language versions of the Treaty, a single terminology is used for what in the English version appears as 'equal work' in para. 1 of Article 119 and 'same work' in para. 3. Moreover in the definitive French text of the Treaty the common terminology is *'même travail'* which has few connotations of equal value. Indeed in *Jenkins* v. *Kingsgate Ltd*, Advocate-General Warner makes the point in terms that 'No significance attaches in my opinion to the change from "equal work" in the first paragraph of article 119 to "the same work" in sub-para. (a) of the third para., for that change occurs only in the English text of the Treaty' ([1981] ICR 592, 598E–F).

However, the positive development of the equal pay principle remained a continuing objective of the EEC Commission, and the member states were reminded of their obligations in this respect by EEC Council Directive 75/117 of 1975 which mainly consists of articles instructing member states to take various steps to implement Article 119, but which begins with an article expounding the meaning of Article 119 in the following terms:

EEC Council Directive 75/117 of 1975, Article 1

The principle of equal pay for men and women outlined in Article 119 of the Treaty, hereinafter called 'principle of equal pay,' means, for the same work or for work to which equal value is attributed, the elimination of all discrimination on grounds of sex with regard to all aspects and conditions of remuneration.

In particular, where a job classification system is used for determining pay, it must be based on the same criteria for both men and women and so drawn up as to exclude any discrimination on grounds of sex.

It is arguable that in its reference to 'work to which equal value is attributed' the Directive so far exaggerates the meaning of Article 119 as to put itself *ultra vires* the Treaty. But the European Court of Justice does not feel this to be a difficulty, and has on the contrary declared Article 1 of the Directive to say nothing that is not implicit in Article 119, so that Article 1 of the Directive can be in effect read back into Article 119 and Article 119 can be applied in that extended form – see *Jenkins* v. *Kingsgate Ltd* [1982] ICR 592 (ECJ). There have been various attempts to use the provisions of Article 119 and 117/1 to establish a wider basis of equal pay comparison than the EqPA affords. The arguments for doing so have been very complex and very much bound up with the constitutional problem of the direct applicability of EEC provisions in UK courts. It will be useful to evaluate the use that has been made of the EEC provisions by referring back to the three modes of equalization we encountered under the EqPA, i.e.

(a) comparison on the 'like work' basis
(b) comparison on the basis of 'work rated as equivalent'
(c) measures designed to detect and eliminate discrimination in pay structures.

So far as the comparison on the 'like work' basis is concerned, Article 119 has served as a way of circumventing the exclusion of retirement provisions from the scope of EqPA provided that the complaint can be shown to relate to 'pay', which was successfully done in *Worringham* v. *Lloyds Bank Ltd* [1981] ICR 558 (ECJ); [1982] ICR 299 (CA); and in *Garland* v. *British Rail Engineering Ltd* [1982] ICR 420 (ECJ & HL) (see above, p. 341). More significantly from our present point of view, the 'same work' concept of Article 119 has been held to include comparison between workers doing the same work non-contemporaneously, whereas the EqPA is confined to contemporaneous comparison. In this respect Article 119 is directly applicable in the UK courts, though it is not clear whether Article 119 operates as a source of law in itself or by way of overriding re-formulation of the EqPA: *McCarthys Ltd* v. *Smith* [1980] ICR 672 (ECJ & CA); *Albion Shipping Agency* v. *Arnold* [1982] ICR 22. This extension of comparison is important, but as we shall see, the facility by which a worker can invoke a comparison with his predecessor in the job of the opposite sex depends for its significance entirely on how that comparison is conducted – which we shall consider shortly under the heading of 'equal pay and the labour market'.

So far as the question of 'work rated as equivalent' is concerned, the EEC provisions have turned out to represent a crucial extension of comparison beyond the scope of the EqPA. As we have seen, the 'work rated as equivalent' criterion of the UK legislation is critically restricted by the fact that it becomes available only where a job evaluation study is carried out – so the employer could frustrate the application of this criterion. It has not been clearly established whether or how far Article 119 can be viewed as overriding this restriction by means of a *directly applicable* standard of equal pay for work of equal value or a directly applicable principle of elimination of sex discrimination with regard to pay. Lord Denning M.R. supported a positive view of Article 119 in *Shields* v. *Coomes (Holdings) Ltd* [1978] ICR 1159 at pp. 1164-7. But the European Court of Justice took a less creative approach in *McCarthys Ltd* v. *Smith* [1980] ICR 672, treating comparison between the woman applicant and a hypothetical man doing her work as lying outside the directly applicable scope of Article 119. (Their finding in favour of the employee was on the narrower basis that non-contemporaneous work could be regarded as 'same work'.) A similar restrictiveness is again displayed in the decision of the ECJ in *Jenkins* v. *Kingsgate Ltd* [1981] ICR 592. Here the court seems to have seen the presence of sex discrimination, so far from being a *sufficient* condition for the application of Article 119, as an additional and *necessary* condition over and above the basic issue of equal pay for the same work. However, the question whether there is any way round these restrictions on the direct applicability of Article 119 has been somewhat overtaken by events, because Article 119 has had an indirect impact on the position in the UK by reason of other developments of great importance to which we now turn our attention.

(g) Equal value under the Equal Pay (Amendment) Regulations 1983

The further developments, just referred to, began with enforcement proceedings brought by the EEC Commission against the United Kingdom Government in 1981 alleging a failure on the part of the UK to comply with Article 1 of the 1975 Directive No. 75/117, which, as we have seen, requires the abolition of sex discrimination with regard to payment for work to which equal value is attributed. In enforcement proceedings of this kind against a member state of the EEC, there is, of course, no need to show direct applicability: it is clear that a Directive can impose mandatory requirements upon a member state to legislate in a certain way. The sole issue in these proceedings was whether the United Kingdom could rely on the provisions of the Equal Pay Act 1970 concerning work rated as equivalent (i.e. s.1(2)(b), s.1(5)) as a sufficient compliance with the obligation to legislate to give effect to the principle of equal pay for work of equal value. In *EEC Commission* v. *United Kingdom (Case 61/81)* [1982] ICR 578, the European Court of Justice held that the UK was in derogation from its obligations under the Directive, because the Equal Pay Act made it a requirement that a right to equal pay for work of equal value should only be available where a job-evaluation study had been carried out with the consent of the employer; this amounted to a denial of the right where no job classification had been made. The court rejected the argument of the UK that 'work to which equal value is attributed' meant less, for this purpose, than 'work of equal value'. This meant that the Equal Pay Act had to be amended to give more general effect than it did to the principle of equal pay for work of equal value.

The result was the making, by the Secretary of State for Employment, under the powers conferred by the European Communities Act 1972, of the Equal Pay (Amendment) Regulations 1983, to come into operation from the beginning of 1984. These amend the Equal Pay Act 1970 and fundamentally alter the whole law of equal pay. The central provision of the Regulations is one which provides a right to equal pay for work of equal value in the following terms:

Equal Pay Act 1970, s.1(2)(c), as added by Reg. 2(1) of the Equal Pay (Amendment) Regulations 1983

Where a woman is employed on work which, not being work in relation to which paragraph (a) or (b) above applies, is, in terms of the demands made on her (for instance under such headings as effort, skill and decision), of equal value to that of a man in the same employment—

(i) if (apart from the equality clause) any term of the woman's contract is or becomes less favourable to the woman than a term of a similar kind in the contract under which that man is employed, that term of the woman's contract shall be treated as so modified as not to be less favourable, and

(ii) if (apart from the equality clause) at any time the woman's contract does not include a term corresponding to a term benefiting that man included in the contract under which he is employed, the woman's contract shall be treated as including such a term.

We shall return shortly to the question of how effectively, and in what sense, this implements the principle of equal pay for work of equal value. Suffice it at this point to note that the new section 1(2)(c) is qualified by a new defence which renders the equality clause inoperable in relation to an inequality of pay or contractual terms which is genuinely due to a material *factor* which is not the difference of sex; where equal-value claims are concerned, this factor does not have to amount to a material *difference* between the woman's case and the man's (as it does in relation to 'like work' or 'work rated as equivalent' claims). This new defence, which is crucial, is contained in section 1(3) of the 1970 Act as amended by Reg. 2(2) of the 1983 Regulations, which is set out below at p. 388. We shall consider its scope in the next subsection of this chapter.

By way of implementation of the equal-value principle as thus enacted, the Equal Pay (Amendment) Regulations go on to deal with procedure before industrial tribunals in cases where the new equal-value principle may be involved (Regulation 3, of which Reg. 3(1) adds a new s.2A to the 1970 Act). These provisions, as to procedure before industrial tribunals in such cases, are to be amplified and supplemented by a further set of regulations,[1] which will make consequential alterations to the Rules of Procedure for Industrial Tribunals. It is necessary to descend to this degree of detail in expounding the new equal-value provisions, because these ostensibly procedural provisions in fact contain the substantive rules which give practical shape to the equal-value principle, and express the limits on the application of that principle. Thus, the new s.2A(1)(b) of the Equal Pay Act which is introduced by the Amendment Regulations requires industrial tribunals to commission and receive a report

[1] Now implemented by the Industrial Tribunals (Rules of Procedure) (Equal Value Amendment) Regulations 1983, SI No. 1807.

from a member of a panel of independent experts designated by ACAS before deciding an equal-value issue; unless, that is, they are satisfied that there are no reasonable grounds to support a finding of equal value, in which case the new s.2A(1)(a) enables the tribunal to give a peremptory decision against the claim. Administrative lawyers will be quick to perceive a slight risk here: industrial tribunals disposed towards a narrow view of the equal-value principle might, in effect, decide the substantive equal-value issue negatively against the employee, without the intervention of an independent expert, under the guise of deciding the purely preliminary point of whether there is a case to answer. This is of some potential importance, because certain procedural guarantees to be provided in favour of employee claimants only come into play if the issue gets as far as the independent expert. Thus, it is proposed that the procedural regulations will place the independent expert under a duty to prepare a reasoned written report and to take account of any representations which the parties wish to make, and that they will give the parties the right to challenge the report before it is accepted as evidence by the tribunal.

The further development, by both the Equal Pay (Amendment) Regulations and the proposed procedure amendment regulations, of these purportedly procedural aspects of the new equal-value claim, serves to multiply the limits on the reference to independent experts; and, in some cases, to introduce substantive restrictions upon the whole response to the ruling of the European Court in the enforcement proceedings which gave rise to this legislation. Thus, it is proposed that the industrial tribunal will be required, before hearing the parties on an equal-value claim, to engage in a sort of conciliation process in which it invites the parties to seek an adjournment for the purpose of attempting to settle the claim, and that the industrial tribunal will have to grant the adjournment if requested to do so. Moreover, it is also proposed to provide that if the hearing does proceed, the industrial tribunal shall, unless it considers that it is inappropriate so to proceed, consider first whether a material factor which is not a difference of sex exists, such as would result in no award of equal pay even if the jobs were found to be of equal value; if so, there is no reference to an independent expert. So the defence of genuine material factor may, according to that proposal, be treated by the tribunal as a prior issue, and a finding by the tribunal that there is no such defence may be treated as a pre-condition for a reference to the independent expert. Yet, as we shall see in the next subsection, the defence is not really conceptually separable from the equal-value issue; it is integral to it. So this is a significant fragmentation of the process of applying the equal-value principle. Moreover, the Equal Pay (Amendment) Regulations go on to develop the rule that the tribunal may determine an equal-value claim without reference to an independent expert if they are satisfied that there is no equal-value case to answer. This rule is so developed as to embody the important substantive point that a finding of unequal value by a job-evaluation exercise already carried out decides the equal-value issue against the claimant without reference to an independent expert, unless the claimant can show a case to answer to the effect that the job-evaluation study involved unjustifiable sex discrimination (see Reg. 3(1), enacting new s.2A(2), (3) of the Equal Pay Act 1970). So where a claimant wishes to develop an equal-value claim which contradicts the results of an equal-value study actually carried out, she has to proceed by way of challenge to the job study, and make out a prima facie case for such a challenge, before the equal-value issue goes for independent report. This may bring back into play the obstacles to challenging an existing equal-value study which we considered under the head of 'work rated as equivalent' (see above, p. 378).

Let us assume, however, that, despite these various considerations, the normal course for an equal-value claim to take is that an industrial tribunal addresses the equal-value issue directly, on the basis of an independent expert's report which has also addressed the issue directly. What, in those circumstances is the nature and extent of the new equal-value claim? The first point, and it is a crucial one, concerns the meaning of the word 'equal'. It is suggested that the 1983 Regulations have in effect attached to the equal-value principle the meaning, 'the same pay for work of the same value'. This they have done by using, as we have seen, the mechanism of the equalization clause to implement the equal-value principle, just as it was used to implement the principles of equal pay for like work or work rated as equivalent. The equalization clause in effect requires exact parity of pay and equivalence of other terms of employment. That is because the equalization clause expressly requires not less favourable treatment; but if the claimant were accorded more favourable treatment than the comparator in discharge of that obligation, the effect would merely be to give the comparator a new claim in reverse. So the equal-value claim is confined to the case where the claimant can find an exact target comparator and demand the same treatment as that comparator. It is not, as implemented in this legislation, a claim to comparable pay for any work of comparable value. It does not enable the claimant to invoke directly the question of what the notional or hypothetical person of the opposite sex doing the same work would have been paid for doing it. It does not enable the claimant directly to challenge differentials on the ground that they embody sex discrimination, in the absence of an exact equal-value comparator somewhere in the differential structure. Hence it does not, as McCrudden has pointed out in a study of the new regulations ((1983) 12 *ILJ* 197 at p. 209), realize that possibility of a shift of focus from the work side to the pay side of the equation, to which we referred earlier in this section (see above, p. 379).

Given, then, that we are concerned with claims based on parity of value, how is that parity to be ascertained? McCrudden in his article (op. cit. at p. 201) suggests that there are four methods of ascertainment which could possibly be regarded as appropriate. These are (1) by measuring market value, (2) by measuring marginal productivity, (3) by formal job-evaluation-study methods, and (4) by informal evaluation of job content on a points method. The difference between (3) and (4) is that (3) involves some kind of formal industrial relations procedure, whereas (4) need not. McCrudden concludes that the wording of the legislation coupled with contemporary statements from the Department of Employment about its intended effect point clearly towards basis (4) as the one envisaged as appropriate by the legislators. As he points out, this involves two sorts of problems of implementation. One is how to provide an adjudicative substitute for the input of bargaining and negotiation which, as we sought to show above at p. 377, is generally integral to the formal job-evaluation process. The other problem is that of ensuring the elimination of sex discrimination from the application of a points method. This turns in practice on the scope that is given to the defence of justifiability. It is ultimately a problem of the depth at which pay comparisons are pursued. As such, it is a facet of a problem about the relationship between pay equalization and the labour market which underlies the whole of the equal-pay legislation in varying degrees, and which we turn to consider in the next subsection.

(h) Equal pay and the labour market

Equal pay is a fruitful topic for labour lawyers to consider because it requires them to address an aspect of employment they are generally unfamiliar with – the working of the labour market. (The current wisdom is that there is not just one labour market but several of them because people compartmentalize the market by restricting their availability within it.) The equal pay principle challenges the working of the labour market by reference to some notion of equity to which, it is asserted, overriding effect should be given. The labour market is an abstraction used to characterize the phenomena which determine patterns of employment and pay. If payment structures are seen to offend a principle of equal pay, that principle must therefore represent an asserted restriction upon the legitimate scope of operation of the labour market. So far we have been examining under the heading of 'extent of equalization' the nature of the restriction that is asserted under the banner of equal pay. But against any such principle, there is always in practice advanced a series of arguments to the effect that some features of the labour market have a countervailing legitimacy of their own. (The *laissez-faire* argument in its pure form asserts that the working of the labour market has a composite legitimacy *per se* – but we are concerned with more specific forms of the *laissez-faire* argument.) To the extent that these arguments of countervailing legitimacy are accepted, they limit the depth to which equal pay comparisons can be pursued. Both the EqPA (as it stood before the 1983 amendments) and the EEC provisions as construed by the ECJ made some allowance for this kind of argument. The Equal Pay Act as it stood before the 1983 amendments simply provided that an equality should not operate in relation to a variation between contracts if the employer proved that the variation was genuinely due to a material difference (other than the difference of sex) between the two cases in question (s.1(3)). The Equal Pay (Amendment) Regulations 1983 introduced, as we shall see, a wider defence in relation to the new equal-value claim, and they enacted the wider and the narrower defences in the following composite provisions:

> Equal Pay Act 1970, s.1(3), as substituted by Reg.2(2) of the
> Equal Pay (Amendment) Regulations 1983

An equality clause shall not operate in relation to a variation between the woman's contract and the man's contract if the employer proves that the variation is genuinely due to a material factor which is not the difference of sex and that factor–

(a) in the case of an equality clause falling within subsection (2)(a) or (b) above, must be a material difference between the woman's case and the man's; and

(b) in the case of an equality clause falling within subsection (2)(c) above, may be such a material difference.

This in substance reiterates the genuine material difference rule for claims of like work and work rated as equivalent; it does not seem that any significance attaches to the change from 'material difference' to 'material factor which must be a material difference'. The wider defence to the equal value claim reflects interpretation by the ECJ of Article 119, which the British legislation has thus now adopted. This interpretation makes allowance for differences produced by factors which are objectively justified and not related to sex discrimination.

These notions constitute the very pivot upon which the whole law of equal pay turns. It is easier to postulate these concepts than to give them meaning. In order to distinguish between the legitimate and the non-legitimate features of the working of the labour market, some sort of critique of the working of the labour market based on an internal analysis of it is needed. That is what Sir Henry Phelps Brown offers in his book, *The Inequality of Pay* (1978), where he inquires into the way in which sex discrimination comes about in the labour market. He seeks to measure the extent of discrimination within the market by assessing how far the process of economic valuation of women's work is distorted by reference to a conventional status differentiation between men and women workers. He begins from the starting-point of the popular explanation of pay differentiation between men and women being attributable to conventional *status* differentiations between them. In the following extract he questions the value of that popular explanation and so concludes that the problem of discrimination within the market is slight compared with that of discrimination before the market in this area.

Sir Henry Phelps Brown, *The Inequality of Pay* (1978),
pp. 155–8

The explanation of women's lower pay developed in this way thus rests on the assumption that employers are unable to estimate the value of women's work, so that they do not bid against one another for it until they have raised the wage to as much as the work is worth; while the women themselves do not push, singly or in combination, to raise it. Employers then apply a conventional valuation of women's work, that is based on the three-sided notion of status, station in life, and the minimal expenditure required to maintain that station. Alternatively, whether or not employers are able to estimate the value of women's work, they are held to agree spontaneously in applying the conventional valuation, so that they enter tacitly into monopsonistic discrimination against women. An employer who did judge that women's work was 'cheap at the price' would still be restrained from bidding in more women, by the resistance of the men.

If the view that employers simply follow a conventional valuation of women's work were called in question because they evidently are willing to pay more for some kinds of women's work than others, the answer might be that the conventional valuation is based on status: the status accorded to the ability to do more skilled work being higher, correspondingly higher must be the station in life of the skilled woman, and what she needs to earn to be able to maintain that station. For all grades of labour above the unskilled, the conventional valuation based on the lower status of women would thus be applied in practice as a discount on what is paid to men doing similar work.

But when the explanation is set out in this way, much that seemed illuminating at particular points fails to carry conviction as a general theory, for there is much other evidence in conflict with it. This evidence shows that there are objective reasons for the value of women's work in certain jobs being less than that of men's; that employers are in fact able to estimate that value; and that some measure of 'unequal pay' is therefore economically appropriate, as being 'equal pay for work of equal value'; though it does not show that the actual extent of inequality does not exceed that.

In some manual work, to begin with, women are handicapped by lack of physical strength. An inquiry into British farmers' estimates of women's work outputs as a percentage of men's in 49 tasks on the farm found that though in one or two tasks, such as attending poultry and picking fruit, women's output was higher than men's, in the others it was lower. At the lowest, in heavy tasks, it was less than half; in the middle third of the tasks the percentage lay between 70 and 90; the median percentage was 79. The average minimum hourly rate for women in British agriculture was 72 per cent of the men's in 1938, rising to 82 per cent in 1941. The source already cited for wages in Mao's China quotes a scale that gave women in agriculture seven-tenths of the man's day rate, this being justified on the ground that women's output was lower in the same proportion.

It is significant that the differential between the pay of men and women for similar work has not been the same at all levels of qualification and earnings, but has varied inversely with that level. In the United Kingdom, down to the end of the Second World War, 'the spread of the differential [was] from some 50 per cent of the men's rate in the lower ranks of industry to 10 per cent or nothing at all in the higher ranks of some of the professions'. If the differential depended throughout simply on status, this would be hard to account for, but it is intelligible if we suppose that the differential was based on differences in the value of men and women as employees. For if we consider the relative importance of two factors on which that value depends, physical strength and intelligence, we see that physical strength, in which women are generally inferior to men, becomes of less importance as we rise in the scale of qualifications and earnings, while intelligence, in which women are equal to men, becomes of progressively greater importance. So far as the capability of the workers depends on these two factors, therefore, the difference between the capabilities of women and men, and their values in similar employment, will be less, the higher the qualifications that the employment requires.

To the differences in the value of work that make themselves felt at any one time must be added one, already touched on, that in the past at least has appeared in the value of employees reckoned over their whole period of service. It has arisen especially in the white-collar occupations in which physical strength is not required, but the usefulness of the employee does depend very much on his training and experience on the job. In such employments the value of a type of labour depends on the length of service to be expected from it; or, inversely, on its rate of turnover. Most women get married, and most of these again leave paid employment at least for a time in order to raise a family. Employers given a choice between engaging men and women for a given type of work must expect that on the average they will receive a smaller return on investment in the training of women than of men, and that fewer of the women will be available for advancement on the basis of the experience they have gained with the firm. The effect has been to make employers prefer men to women as entrants where the rate of pay is the same for both, or to regard a lower rate for the women as a necessary offset to the lower value of their work as reckoned over their expected period of service; in particular, it has made them reluctant to admit women on equal pay with men, or admit them at all, to jobs requiring any considerable period of on-the-job training. The women who will in fact give long service suffer because they cannot be distinguished initially from the others. . . .

From this discussion we can draw two conclusions. First, in more than one way judgments of status have made people regard it as only right and proper that women should be paid less than men in similar employment. But, second, in many employments there are objective reasons for the work of women being of lower net value than that of men; and employers do estimate such net value and take it into account. If then (a) competition between employers for labour, and (b) the pressure of labour itself for higher pay, were effective in keeping women's rates up to the limit set by the net value of women's work; and if (c) the employers' estimate of that limit were unbiased by masculine prejudice: then there would be no discrimination against women. But we do not know how far any of these three conditions is satisfied. We have reason to think that none of them is satisfied fully in all cases, but the outcome will differ in different places, employments, and periods. In particular, it seems probable that the upheavals of the two World Wars, both of which in the United Kingdom brought a rise in the general level of women's rates relatively to men's, will have given market forces freer play as against the conventional. We remain uncertain how far, if at all, existing differentials exceed differences in net value. But it seems highly probable that the disabilities of women workers spring far more from our first two forms of discrimination, in upbringing and in opportunity, rather than in the two with which we have dealt here, discrimination by monopsony and according to status.

The foregoing discussion perhaps gives us a basis for evaluation of the case-law applying the concepts of genuine material difference other than a difference of sex. The question is, are the courts alive to the possibility that a conclusion that material differences exist may be reached because of a conventional status differentiation between men's work and women's work?

The clearest and most direct kind of status differentiation occurs where it is assumed and accepted without specific justification that a man's work is actually worth more than that of a woman. The E A T and the Court of Appeal took this point in *Coomes (Holdings) Ltd* v. *Shields* where the issue was whether it was in order to pay male counter-hands in betting shops more than female counter-hands where the men were regarded as having a protective role. To *assume* that men had this quality and women did not was conventional status differentiation. Lord Denning put it thus:

> *Coomes (Holdings) Ltd* v. *Shields*
> [1978] I C R 1159 (C A)
>
> It would be otherwise [i.e. the rate for the job need not be the same] if the difference was based on any special personal qualification that he had; as, for instance, if he was a fierce and formidable figure, trained to tackle intruders, then there might be a variation such as to warrant a 'wage differential' under s.1(3). But no such special personal qualification is suggested. The only difference between the two jobs is on the ground of sex. He may have been a small nervous man, who could not say 'boo to a goose'. She may have been as fierce and formidable as a 'battle-axe'. Such differences, whatever they were, did not have any relation to the terms and conditions of employment. They did not affect the 'rate for the job'.

In that form of differential rate-setting we see a straightforward version of the conflict between the equal pay principle and labour market functioning which it is sought to justify as objective and not sex based. A more sophisticated version occurs where an employer seeks to reconcile the demands of the equal pay principle with the demands of the labour market by creating special *ad hominem* (or *ad feminam* – see *MoD* v. *Farthing*, below, p. 393) categories for pay purposes. This is the red circling problem, which arises where an employer reorganizes his pay structure but places existing employees, whose pay would be adversely affected by the restructuring, in a protected pay category. The question then arises whether there is a claim for equal pay as between men within the protected category and women outside it but carrying out work which is like that of the men in the protected category. A consideration of the Phelps Brown concept of conventional status differentiation will reveal at once that there is a great danger that red circling may be nothing more nor less than the perpetuation of conventional status differentiation between men and women workers. On the whole the courts have proved astute to this danger by insisting that a red circle differentiation will be acceptable only where the original pay category which is protected by red circling was itself open to men and women workers alike. In other words the courts are alert to the possibility that red circling may itself be a form of conventional status differentiation between men and women, as the following extract from the judgment in the *Charles Early Ltd* and *Snoxell* cases may be thought to show.

Charles Early & Marriott (Witney) Ltd v. *Smith; Snoxell* v.
Vauxhall Motors Ltd [1977] ICR 700 (EAT)

In the first case a male warehouseman, Mr Steptoe, who had worked for the
employers for a number of years was transferred in 1966 to a lower-paid job as
a ticket writer, but his wages were not reduced. Instead, he was placed in a
protected pay category ('red circled') by the employers. In 1976 female ticket
writers claimed equality of pay with him, but the employer was held to have a
good defence under s.1(3) of the Act, because the higher pay, which was
protected, was not originally based on any discrimination and the reason for
the 'red circling' was not a sex-based one. In the second case the employers
originally maintained separate wage scales for their male and female
inspectors, the former being more highly paid. The employers regraded the
male inspectors as a result of which they were downgraded, but the inspectors
already employed were 'red circled' and maintained at the higher rate. All new
male employees were paid at the lower rate. Later the scales for male and
female inspectors were unified and the females were all subsumed to the new
lower male rate. The female inspectors who had been employed at the time of
the regrading of the male inspectors claimed to be entitled to be paid at the
higher rate. The employers were held not to have a defence under s.1(3) of the
Act, because the variation in pay was due to past sex discrimination. In
explaining its decisions the EAT took the following hypothetical cases:

PHILLIPS J.: On the evidence at present available there is no reason to suppose that
the red circling of Mr Steptoe was directly or indirectly attributable to an act of sex
discrimination. Accordingly, the case throws up for consideration the situation where
wages are protected by being red circled for good reasons, and the differential is
maintained. In our judgment the correct approach for an industrial tribunal,
confronted with a claim by an employer under section 1(3) that a variation is genuinely
due to such a material difference, is to elicit and analyse *all* the circumstances of the
particular case; and it is unwise and likely to lead to error merely to say that a particular
case is a red circle case. In practice, most cases involve several features, and it is
probably only rarely that a red circle situation arises in its purist form. But, supposing
that it does, and that there is a case where it can be demonstrated that there is a group of
employees who have had their wages protected for causes neither directly nor indirectly
due to a difference of sex, and assuming that the male and female employees doing the
same work who are outside the red circle are treated alike, we see no reason why the
employers should not succeed in their answer. In such circumstances it would seem to
us that the variation in pay is genuinely due to a material difference (other than the
difference of sex) between the woman's case and the man's case. Thus in *Snoxell and
Davies* v. *Vauxhall Motors Ltd*, on the information at present available to us, we would not
expect a claim by a male inspector outside the red circle, based on a comparison of his
case with that of Miss Snoxell and Mrs Davies who will be within it, to succeed. We
should expect Vauxhall Motors Ltd to be able to say that the variation between Miss
Snoxell's and Mrs Davies's contracts and his contract was genuinely due to a material
difference (other than the difference of sex) between his case and theirs: for their
presence within the red circle, and his absence from it, would be neither directly nor

indirectly attributable to a difference of sex.

Returning to the appeal of *Charles Early & Marriott (Witney) Ltd* v. *Smith and Ball*, it can be seen that it raises the additional question of the effect of the prolonged continuation of a red circle. If Mr Steptoe had been transferred from warehouse duties to ticket writing in 1972, at a time when ticket writing was in a lower grade and attracted a lower rate of remuneration, and had then been red circled, it is difficult to see why the employers should not have had a good answer to his claim. The case would have been a simple uncomplicated one of a man having his wages protected, and therefore of the employers being able to say that the variation was due to a difference between the women's case and his, other than a difference of sex. Does it make any difference that the red circling is continued, even continued indefinitely? In principle, we do not see why it should. Assuming that there are no additional factors, and that in other respects affairs are operated on a unisex, non-discriminatory basis, the situation will continue to be that the variation is genuinely due to a material difference other than the difference of sex. The red circle will persist, ageing and wasting until eventually it vanishes. In the case of Vauxhall Motors Ltd we do not see why they should not continue to have available a good answer under section 1(3) to any claim by male or female inspectors based on a comparison with the inspectors within the red circle; provided, of course, there are not other circumstances of which we are ignorant, and no new factor appears. At the same time, it seems to us to be desirable where possible for red circles to be phased out and eliminated, for they are bound to give rise to confusion and misunderstanding. One of the difficulties seems to be that although understood and accepted as fair when first introduced, with the passage of time memory dims, the reason for their institution is forgotten, and they are seen as examples of discrimination.

These difficulties in explaining why red circling should be regarded as non-sex-based are even more graphically illustrated in *Ministry of Defence* v. *Farthing* [1980] ICR 705, which tells us a good deal about how collective bargaining within the enterprise can set up its own particular versions – or distortions – of labour market forces. Before the EqPA was passed, the MoD, which paid drivers in groups or 'bands' of pay rates, had men's bands of rates and less favourable women's bands of rates for given driving jobs. Between 1970 and 1975 they dealt with the equal pay problem *ad hoc* by transferring women in women's band 4 (for drivers of light vehicles) to women's band 6 (for drivers of heavy vehicles), which gave them equal rates to those of men's band 4. After 1975 they established common bands for men and women, but recognized the claim of the particular women who had been in women's band 6 to go on to common band 6 because they had attained 'band 6 status'. When the men in common band 4 complained of unequal pay as compared with them, it was held that the women in band 6 had been validly red circled, for that purely historical reason which was personal to them. Otherwise everybody, both the men and in consequence the subsequently recruited women in band 4, would have had to get band 6 rates and the pay structure would have been in ruins.

A similar kind of artificial version of labour market forces, produced by a pay structure within an enterprise, occurs where the pay structure consists of a grading scheme which differentiates pay not according to job evaluation but by a rating of the performance of the individual person. Here again, the problem in accepting different grade ratings as attributable to genuine material non-sex-based differences between a man and a woman is that the grading scheme may conceal sex-based differences rationalized according to conventional status differentiation; so here we have another example of the problem of depth of comparison, which was under consideration in the *National Vulcan Engineering* case. There the Court of Appeal in effect declared that there were limits to the scepticism which an industrial tribunal ought to display in relation to a grading scheme which happened to result in the less favourable treatment of a particular woman as compared with a particular man. Do you think that the test of genuineness of operation of the grading scheme goes far enough? Should the burden of proof on the employer be higher if the grading is a unilateral matter within management's discretion?

National Vulcan Engineering Insurance Group Ltd v. *Wade*
[1978] I C R 800 (C A)

LORD DENNING M.R.: . . . Now I come to the claim of Mrs Wade. She is aged 50. She was employed as a policy clerk with the company. She had to prepare new policies of insurance, amend existing ones, calculate charges and rebates and so forth. She was assessed by the management early in January 1975 as category 6D. Her assessment was as follows: 'Mrs E. M. Wade (grade 6D: no change). Mrs Wade has a fair knowledge of the procedures and works quite well when concentrating, but unfortunately is easily distracted.'

There was a man also in the same grade as Mrs Wade, that is 6D. He was Mr I. He was getting the same salary. The assessment said of him: 'Has a fair knowledge of the procedures, is willing and can be a good worker when he concentrates on the job. However, he is easily distracted which results in careless mistakes.' So there it was. Mrs Wade and Mr I were placed on an equal footing. Both were easily distracted: both were put in the same grade and received the same salary of £2,028.

Mrs Wade was working in a department where there were 18 policy clerks all told, all doing the same work, 14 men and 4 women. The work of all 18 was the same. Each of them was handed a bundle of papers estimated to take two hours to process, and they were expected to process them in that time. But the quality and accuracy of the work done by those 18 varied according to each individual. Some needed more supervision than others. The management made a difference in grading and rating according to the quality of each individual's performance.

We have a table of the grading of each of those 18. I am afraid that Mrs Wade and Mr I were the lowest graded of all. One man was graded above them at 6C: he received £2,202. One man was graded at 6B, and he received £2,301. There was one man at 7E who received £2,223. I will speak of him later: he is a Mr McCann. Then in grade 7D there were five men and one woman all getting the same, £2,334. In grade 7C there were five men and two women, all getting £2,535.

That is the table which was put before the court by the employers, showing how their grading scheme operates. It applies equally, as far as can be observed, for men and women. Indeed they put two cases before the tribunal of a man, Mr F, and a woman, Mrs L, who were both in grade 7C. The assessment of Mr F was 'has a good overall knowledge of the procedures gained through his experience, but he tends to lack confidence in his own abilities,' and that Mrs L

> is one of the more experienced members of the S A L section who has been useful this year in teaching other members of the staff the finer points of the various periodics done in the section.

So there it is. According to that evidence before the tribunal (which I am afraid they did not analyse as we have had it analysed before us) the employers were operating their scheme fairly and evenly according to the skills and experience of the individuals and not according to their sex.

I now come back to the Equal Pay Act 1970. It came into operation on 29 December 1975. I need not read all the clauses, but an equality clause is written into contracts by that Act. Section 1(2)(a) of the Act, as amended by section 8 of the Sex Discrimination Act 1975, reads:

> . . . (a) where the woman is employed on like work with a man in the same employment – (i) if (apart from the equality clause) any term of the woman's contract is or becomes less favourable to the woman than a term of a similar kind in the contract under which that man is employed, that term of the woman's contract shall be treated as so modified as not to be less favourable . . .

That is when it is like work.

Mrs Wade claims that she was employed on like work with a man because all 18 employees were doing the same work. On 10 March 1976 she applied to the industrial tribunal and made this claim in her own handwriting:

> I claim that the work I am doing is the same as that being done by my male colleagues who are graded higher and paid more than myself. I therefore claim equal pay for equal work.

At the hearing before the tribunal on 3 June 1976, on behalf of Mrs Wade there was called a young man, Mr McCann, who was graded higher than her and was doing like work. He was graded 7E, because he had been assessed by the management 'as a young man going places'. He had not been employed by them as long as Mrs Wade, but they evidently rated his skill and ability as more than hers. Mrs Wade called that young man as a witness and said that she ought to be graded as high as he was and that she ought to be receiving the same pay.

. . . [The employers] say that this variation is genuinely due to the difference in the skill, capacity and experience of the individual. It has nothing to do with the sex. A better person, whether he be man or woman, is given a higher grading and more pay than a worse man or a worse woman. They say that the difference is due to the employees' skill, capacity and experience and is not due to their sex at all.

I will read what the manager of the policy department said in evidence:

> If two-hour bundles are given to a 7C clerk I would expect them to be done better than if they were done by a 6D clerk and a 6D clerk's work would be positively checked by the supervisor. I look for quality and accuracy, quantity is not the prime consideration. We try to reflect these matters in the grading a person received. . . . Nothing in the assessments contains a built in bias against the female sex, the applicant's assessment of 6D in April 1975 was a genuine judgment by me as to her value. . . .

In their findings the Employment Appeal Tribunal seems to have accepted that the grading was a personal assessment dependent upon the qualities of the individual: but they took it as a point against the employers. I must say that I can see nothing against the employers' case on that. There was ample evidence that the grading had nothing to do with the sex of the individual. That is borne out by the evidence I have read out about the 18 persons in the department. All of them were doing like work. Some were better workers than others, and therefore were given a better grading and a bigger salary. No distinction was drawn between the men and the women: all in the same grade were paid the same salary.

All this makes me wonder why, on those facts, the industrial tribunal and the Employment Appeal Tribunal found against the employers. I am afraid that it must rest on a misconception as to the burden of proof on the employers.

. . . In these cases, under section 1(3), it seems to me that this court must say that the burden of proof upon the employer is not a very heavy burden of proof. It is the ordinary burden of proof in a civil case. It is on the balance of probabilities. If that test is applied in this case, it seems to me that there can be no doubt on the evidence whatsoever that the employers discharged the burden upon them. They proved that the difference between Mrs Wade and Mr McCann was due to a material difference in their skill and capacity and was not due to any difference in sex at all.

I must say that the consequences of any other decision would be most serious for any business. . . .

If it were to go forth that these grading systems are inoperative and operate against the Equal Pay Act 1970, it would, I think, be disastrous for the ordinary running of efficient business. It seems to me that a grading system according to ability, skill and experience is an integral part of good business management: and, as long as it is fairly and genuinely applied irrespective of sex, there is nothing wrong with it at all. It ought not to be challenged and made inoperative by reason of the Equal Pay Act 1970. The contrary view would leave grading systems open to challenge.

As time went on, the stakes in the game of equal pay comparison were raised. The protagonists of the equal pay principle pushed the attack against conventional status differentiation further and further. It was sought to counter by a more and more direct appeal to the legitimacy of labour market forces. In *Clay Cross Ltd* v. *Fletcher* (1978) there came the direct confrontation, stripped of the complexities of red circling or grading schemes. A woman sales clerk complained that she was being paid less than a man who was being paid the higher rate he had earned in his previous job. The employer countered that the man had been the only suitable applicant and would not have accepted the post for less pay. The Court of Appeal rejected this direct appeal to labour market forces. They insisted that these were irrelevant extrinsic forces. This is how Lord Denning put the matter. Note the course he predicts the discussion will take in relation to Article 119. If anything Lord Denning was too generous to the ECJ in predicting how they would approach the problem. Events were to show that they would certainly have protected the equal pay principle no more vigorously than the Court of Appeal did in *Clay Cross*.

Clay Cross Ltd v. *Fletcher* [1979] ICR 1 (CA)

LORD DENNING M.R.:

Material difference

The issue depends on whether there is a material difference (other than sex) between her case and his. Take heed to the words 'between her case and his.' They show that the tribunal is to have regard to *her* and to *him* – to the personal equation of the woman as compared to that of the man – irrespective of any extrinsic forces which led to the variation in pay. As I said in *Shields* v. *E. Coomes (Holdings) Ltd* [1978] ICR 1159, 1170E, section 1(3) applies when 'the personal equation of the man is such that he deserves to be paid at a higher rate than the woman.' Thus the personal equation of the man may warrant a wage differential if he has much longer length of service, or has superior skill or qualifications; or gives bigger output or productivity; or has been placed, owing to down-grading, in a protected pay category, vividly described as 'red-circled'; or to other circumstances personal to him in doing his job.

But the tribunal is not to have regard to any extrinsic forces which have led to the man being paid more. An employer cannot avoid his obligations under the Act by saying: 'I paid him more because he asked for more,' or 'I paid her less because she was willing to come for less.' If any such excuse were permitted, the Act would be a dead letter. Those are the very reasons why there was unequal pay before the statute. They are the very circumstances in which the statute was intended to operate.

Nor can the employer avoid his obligations by giving the reasons why he submitted to the extrinsic forces. As for instance by saying: 'He asked for that sum because it was what he was getting in his previous job,' or, 'He was the only applicant for the job, so I had no option.' In such cases the employer may beat his breast, and say: 'I did not pay him more because he was a man. I paid it because he was the only suitable person who applied for the job. Man or woman made no difference to me.' Those are reasons personal to the employer. If any such reasons were permitted as an excuse, the door would be wide open. Every employer who wished to avoid the statute would walk straight through it.

In saying this, I find support from the words of Phillips J. in *National Coal Board* v. *Sherwin* [1978] ICR 700, 710:

. . . the general principle [is] that it is no justification for a refusal to pay the same wages to women doing the same work as a man to say that the man could not have been recruited for less . . .

and he applied it to the man in that case, saying, at p. 711:

. . . what was being paid was the rate necessary to secure his services. For ourselves, we do not see why this is a material difference between his case and that of the complainants.

Other cases

During the argument Mr Lester drew our attention to Community law and to United States' law. I found them helpful.

(i) *Community law*

In *Shields* v. *E. Coomes (Holdings) Ltd* [1978] ICR 1159, 1165, I pointed out that article 119 of the EEC Treaty is part of our law. It provides for equal pay for equal work. It contains no exception, such as is in section 1(3) of the Equal Pay Act 1970. But

I have no doubt that the European Court of Justice, with its liberal approach, would introduce an exception on the same lines. I do not suggest that we should refer the matter to them. Suffice it that I feel confident that it would have regard to the personal equation of the man and the woman, and not to any extrinsic forces.

In fact the subsequent cases are in effect devoted to testing out Lord Denning's view of how the European Court would approach Article 119. The next battleground was that of unequal pay as between full-time men and part-time women doing the same work. This is the point at which the equal pay principle confronts a status differentiation which permeates the labour market – that is, the differentiation between full-time workers and part-time workers. It is undoubtedly the case that women form a much larger proportion of the part-time labour force than of the full-time labour force. So the key question is whether the equal pay principle will be applied so as to penetrate the full-time/part-time differential. In *Handley* v. *Mono Ltd* [1979] ICR 147, the EAT accepted the employer's arguments that there was a genuine material non-sex-based difference between the men's full-time work and the women's part-time work, in that the part-time worker's machine would be idle for a greater part of the time than if it had been operated by a full-time worker; and they also held that this fell within the implicit exception to Article 119. In *Jenkins* v. *Kingsgate Ltd*, a part-time woman worker went to the ECJ in the hope of using Article 119 as a way of attacking full-time/part-time differentiation directly as sex discrimination. She came back with an interpretation which not only rejected the view that so broad a comparison could be made under Article 119 but which also recognized an implicit limitation as to the *depth* of comparison possible under Article 119 which was a greater limitation than that of the genuine material non-sex-based difference of s.1(3) of the EqPA. When the case came back to the EAT, they applied the ECJ decision in such a way as to save as much as possible of the *Clay Cross* approach of excluding extrinsic factors. This they could do by holding that it was not inconsistent with Article 119 to take the case on the EqPA and give the employee the benefit of the fact that s.1(3) posed less of an obstacle than the implicit limit on Article 119. On this basis they gave the industrial tribunal the following guidance:

Jenkins v. *Kingsgate Ltd* [1981] ICR 715 (EAT)
(on reference back from ECJ [1981] ICR 592)

BROWNE-WILKINSON J.:

(4) *Is it sufficient for the purposes of section 1(3) of the Act of 1970 and Article 119 for the employer to show only that he had no intention of discriminating or must he also show that the differential in pay is objectively justified for some other reason?*

This is the question which has caused us the greatest difficulty. It is highlighted in this case because of the findings of fact of the industrial tribunal and the facts agreed by the parties. No one has yet apparently considered whether the payment of a lower rate of pay to part-time workers in this case is in fact an effective or necessary way to reduce absenteeism and increase utilisation of the employers' machinery. All that has been found is that the pay differential was introduced with that intention thereby negating an intention to discriminate against women. Therefore, in order to decide this appeal, we have to answer this question: unfortunately it is not one on which the judgment of the European Court of Justice gives us clear guidance.

It is desirable first to state the sense in which we are using certain terminology. We use the phrase 'direct discrimination' to mean cases where a distinction is drawn between the rights of men and the rights of women overtly on the ground of their sex. 'Indirect discrimination' covers cases where, because a class of persons consist wholly or mainly of women, a difference drawn between that class and other persons operates in fact in a manner which is discriminatory against women, e.g. the present case. Indirect discrimination may itself be either intentional or unintentional. It is intentional if the employer (although not overtly discriminating) treats the class differently because he intends to differentiate on grounds of sex, i.e. he is dissimulating his real intentions. Indirect discrimination is unintentional where the employer has no intention of discriminating against women on the ground of sex but intends to achieve some different purpose, such as the greater utilization of his machinery.

The fact that indirect discrimination is unintentional does not necessarily mean that it is lawful. Thus, under the Sex Discrimination Act 1975, indirect discrimination is rendered unlawful by section 1(1)(b) even if it is unintentional. To escape acting unlawfully, the alleged discriminator has to show that the requirement which operates in a discriminatory fashion is justifiable because, viewed objectively, the requirement is reasonably necessary to achieve some other purpose. The same is true in relation to racial discrimination under the Race Relations Act 1976, and under the law of the United States of America: see *Griggs* v. *Duke Power Co.* (1971) 401 U.S. 424. The question we have to decide is whether the same principle applies to section 1(3) of the Act of 1970, or whether for the purposes of section 1(3) it is enough to show that the employer had no actual covert intention of discriminating against women.

Were it not for the judgment of the European Court of Justice, we would have held that section 1(3) requires an employer to do more than disprove an intention to discriminate. The equality clause implied by section 1(2) of the Act of 1970 operates to counteract all discrimination whether direct or indirect and whether intentional or unintentional: it looks at the effect of the contractual terms, not at whether they are expressed in overtly discriminatory words or with any particular intention. Section 1(3) then operates by taking out of subsection (2) those cases where the variation in the terms between men and women is 'genuinely due to a material difference (other than the difference of sex) between her case and his.' The words 'genuinely' and 'other than the difference of sex' plainly prevent an employer who is intentionally discriminating (whether directly or indirectly) from escaping the effect of the equality clause. In our view, for the variation in pay to be 'due to' a material difference it would have to be shown that there was some other matter which in fact justified the variation. It would not be enough simply to show that the employer had an intention to achieve some other legitimate objective (although this might disprove any intention to discriminate): the employer would have to show that the pay differential actually achieved that different objective.

This view is supported by authority. In *Shields* v. *E. Coomes (Holdings) Ltd.* [1978] ICR 1159, the Court of Appeal held that so far as possible the Sex Discrimination Act 1975 and the Equal Pay Act 1970 should be construed together so as to produce a harmonious result. Bridge LJ said, at p. 1178:

In the sphere of employment the provisions of the Sex Discrimination Act 1975 and the Equal Pay Act 1970 aimed at eliminating discrimination on the ground of sex are closely interlocking and provide in effect a single comprehensive code. The particular provisions designed to prevent overlapping between the two statutes are complex, and it may often be difficult to determine whether a particular matter of complaint falls to be redressed under one Act or the other. But what is abundantly clear is that both Acts should be construed and applied as a harmonious whole and in such a way that the broad principles which underlie the whole scheme of legislation are not frustrated by a narrow interpretation or restrictive application of particular provisions.

To make section 1(3) of the Act of 1970 accord harmoniously with section 1(1)(b) of the Sex Discrimination Act 1975 requires that it should be construed as imposing on the employer the onus of proving that the variation in pay is in fact reasonably required to achieve some other objective.

Moreover, in the *Clay Cross* case [1979] ICR 1, Lord Denning MR treated the principles laid down in the *Griggs* case as applicable to section 1(3) of the Act of 1970. The principle of the *Griggs* case is that requirements which operate in an indirectly discriminatory fashion have to be objectively justified as being required for some purpose other than a purpose linked to the sex of the person on whom the requirement is imposed. This again indicates that section 1(3) is not satisfied merely by the employer showing that he had no intention to discriminate.

However, when one turns to the judgment of the European Court of Justice one is left in considerable doubt as to the effect of Article 119 in relation to unintentional indirect discrimination. There are passages in the judgment which support the view that it is not enough for the employer simply to show that he had no intention of discriminating. Thus in paragraph 11 [1981] ICR 592, 613, the judgment states that in cases where both male and female part-time workers are paid less than full-time workers:

the fact that work paid at time rates is remunerated at an hourly rate which varies according to the number of hours worked per week does not offend against the principle of equal pay laid down in Article 119 of the Treaty in so far as the difference in pay between part-time work and full-time work is attributable to factors which are objectively justified and are in no way related to any discrimination based on sex.

This approach is again reflected in paragraph 12 of the judgment and echoes the opinion of the Advocate-General. He adopted the approach of the United States Supreme Court in the *Griggs* case and plainly required that indirect discrimination must be objectively justified irrespective of the employer's intention.

On the other hand the formal ruling of the full court seems to approach the matter on the basis that if, by showing some other intention, the employer negates any covert intention to discriminate there will be no infringement of Article 119; this same approach is reflected in paragraphs 14 and 15 of the judgment.

We will assume, without deciding, that Article 119 as construed by the European Court of Justice does not apply to cases of unintentional indirect discrimination. How then are we to construe the United Kingdom statute? Although we must construe the United Kingdom legislation so as not to conflict with Article 119 and so far as possible to make it accord with Article 119, it does not necessarily follow that the United Kingdom legislation must in all respects have the same effect as Article 119. It would not contravene section 2 of the European Communities Act 1972 if the United

Kingdom statutes conferred on employees greater rights than they enjoy under Article 119. Since the Act of 1970 is an integral part of one code against sex discrimination and the rest of the code plainly renders unlawful indirect discrimination even if unintentional, it seems to us right that we should construe the Equal Pay Act 1970 as requiring any difference in pay to be objectively justified even if this confers on employees greater rights than they would enjoy under Article 119 of the EEC Treaty. We therefore hold that in order to show a 'material difference' within section 1(3) of the Act of 1970 an employer must show that the lower pay for part-time workers is in fact reasonably necessary in order to achieve some objective other than an objective related to the sex of the part-time worker.

To sum up, an industrial tribunal in considering cases of part-time workers under the Act of 1970 will have to consider the following points. (1) Do the part-time workers consist mainly of women? (2) Do the part-time workers do 'like work' to full-time male employees of the same employer? (3) If the answers to (1) and (2) are 'yes', the equality clause will apply unless the employer can justify the differential in pay by showing a material difference for the purposes of section 1(3). (4) If the industrial tribunal finds that the employer intended to discriminate against women by paying part-time workers less, the employer cannot succeed under section 1(3). (5) Even if the employers had no such intention, for section 1(3) to apply the employer must show that the difference in pay between full-time and part-time workers is reasonably necessary in order to obtain some result (other than cheap female labour) which the employer desires for economic or other reasons.

Applying these principles to the present case, the industrial tribunal decided in favour of the employers on the short ground that the fact that the applicant was a part-time worker whereas the comparable man was a full-time worker was, by itself, a material difference for the purposes of section 1(3). That is not a correct approach in law. We must therefore allow the appeal. We will remit the case to the industrial tribunal to find whether the lower rate of pay for part-time workers paid by the employers in this case was in fact reasonably necessary in order to enable the employers to reduce absenteeism and to obtain the maximum utilisation of their plant.

We are conscious that our decision may have far-reaching consequences. In particular it is likely to involve many industrial and other employers in increased labour costs at a time when they and the country can ill afford it. This in turn may lead to a decrease in the total number of women employed. But it is not our function to weigh these factors, even if we were capable of assessing them, against the merits of the social policy reflected in the Acts of 1970 and 1975. Our function is simply to seek to apply the law as it now is. It is unfortunate that in a case of such importance we have not had the advantage of legal argument on behalf of the employers and we would welcome an early consideration of the matter by a higher court.

This progressive approach depended, however, on the possibility of being able to take the case under the EqPA. What would happen when the facts lay outside the area of comparison permitted by the EqPA?

That issue next arose in relation to the question of comparison between non-contemporaneous workers. As we have seen (p. 382), the ECJ had been prepared in *McCarthys Ltd* v. *Smith*, albeit on the narrow basis of 'same work', to admit non-contemporaneous comparison. But they had given clear notice in their decision [1980] ICR 672, para. 12 of the decision) that they did so subject to an implicit exception for non-sex-based differences in pay at least as wide as the 'genuine material non-sex-based difference' doctrine of Eq PA, s. 1(3).

The non-contemporaneous comparison problem arose again in *Albion Shipping Agency* v. *Arnold* [1982] I C R 22 (E A T). Here the employers came armed with their argument in terms of economic forces. They had made their office manager redundant following a reduction in the volume of business and in profits. The complainant had taken over the job at a substantially lower salary. The E A T took the case under Article 119 and not under the Eq PA because of non-contemporaneity. This meant they had to consider how far Article 119 admitted economic forces as a justification for unequal pay. They felt that in light of *McCarthy's Ltd* v. *Smith* and *Jenkins* v. *Kingsgate Ltd* (see above, pp. 381–3 and 398–401), the ECJ was committed to a fully-fledged 'implied economic circumstances' exception to Article 119 – so wide as to be inconsistent with the *Clay Cross* approach to the corresponding provision of s. 1(3). As Browne-Wilkinson J. put it, Lord Denning and Lawton L.J. had thought that by excluding economic forces in *Clay Cross,* they were producing harmony between Eq PA and Article 119 – 'in fact subsequent decisions of the E C J far from creating harmony have created a marked dissonance' ([1982] I C R 22). The result was that the E A T, which clearly favoured the *Clay Cross* approach, felt bound to conclude that the I T had been wrong in law in finding for the employee on a simple *Clay Cross* basis, because Article 119 (whether applied as a source in itself or by way of amendment of the Eq PA) gave a wider allowance to economic circumstances. So the industrial tribunal were given fresh instructions by the E A T in terms which express the current state of affairs with regard to depth of comparison.

Albion Shipping Agency v. *Arnold*
[1982] I C R 22

BROWNE-WILKINSON J.: When the industrial tribunal reconsiders the matter, they will first have to decide whether the engagement of the applicant at a lower wage in the place of Mr Larsen was in fact due to a change in the trading position of the employers leading to a drop in profitability. If so, the employers will have shown a 'material difference.' If this had been the only question, we would have felt able to answer it ourselves on the material before us. But the industrial tribunal will have to go on to consider whether the difference is 'other than the difference of sex' (see section 1(3) of the Act of 1970) or 'unconnected with any discrimination on grounds of sex' (see paragraph 12 of the judgment of the European Court of Justice in *Macarthy*'s case). As it seems to us, in order to satisfy this requirement the employers will have to satisfy the industrial tribunal that they did not give the job to the applicant at her existing wage just because they could get a woman but not a man to work at that wage. Only if the industrial tribunal are satisfied that the employers were not taking advantage of the applicant's position as a woman to get the work done at a rate less than a man would have asked will the employers have shown a good defence.

So the law on this vital question was left very much in a state of flux, the subject of an unhappy and vulnerable compromise. Most recently, indeed from the beginning of 1984, the introduction of the new claim to equal pay for work of equal value by the Equal Pay (Amendment) Regulations 1983 altered the nature of the relationship between the equalization process and the labour market. This is partly intrinsic in the move to an equal-value principle, which obviously in a broad sense challenges the working of the labour market at a more fundamental level than the previously existing legislation did. But it is also partly due to the fact that the equal-value claim was subjected by the legislators to a wider defence of justifiability than the defence of material difference which we have hitherto been discussing in relation to the Equal Pay Act 1970. That is to say, whereas the claims to equal pay for like work and work rated as equivalent by a job evaluation exercise were and remain subject to a defence of genuine material non-sex-based *difference* between the woman's case and the man's, the new claim to equal pay for work of equal value is subject to a defence of genuine attributability to a non-sex-based *factor*, whether or not such a factor amounts also to a *difference* (Reg. 2(2), substituting new Equal Pay Act 1970, s.1(3), set out above, at p. 388). In the remainder of this section, we consider the effect and significance of this new defence.

To what extent, then, and for what reasons, did the 1983 legislation introduce a wider defence to the equal-value claim than to the previously existing types of equal pay claim? McCrudden's study of the new legislation ((1983) 12 *ILJ* 197) is helpful on this point. He suggests that there may be four types of 'material factor', of which the last two fall outside the narrower concept of 'material difference'. The four types are:

(1) Considerations personal to the particular employee, such as seniority;
(2) Difference in average profitability between work done by men and by women in a given fact situation;
(3) Diversities in collective bargaining strength affecting internal relativities within the payment structure of an enterprise;
(4) The pressures of wage structures external to the enterprise – that is to say, the pressures of labour market forces.

This analysis therefore suggests that the restriction of the material *difference* defence to type (1) and possibly type (2) which was established in the *Clay Cross* case ([1978] ICR 1) does not apply to the material *factor* defence. McCrudden maintains that the legislators made this differentiation because they regarded labour market forces arguments as having greater legitimacy as an answer to equal-value claims than to like-work, or equivalent-rated-work, claims. Presumably this was seen as an appropriate way of limiting the disruptive and inflationary consequences of introducing the equal-value claim.

The acceptance of this position without any qualification would, however, create a major difficulty. That is because an unrestricted 'material factor' defence, if envisaged as including reference to labour market forces, could entirely negate and cancel out the equal-value claim. It is for that reason that we asserted earlier (see above, p. 387) that the defence cannot be isolated from the equal-value claim; it is integral to it. The extent of the equal-value claim is very largely a product of whatever restrictions are placed on the material factor defence. The terms of the new section 1(3) of the Equal Pay Act 1970 introduce the following requirements for the material factor defence:

(1) There is a requirement of *genuine attributability*; the variation in pay or terms in question must be genuinely due to the factor relied on.
(2) There is a requirement that the factor *must not be the difference of sex*.
(3) There is a requirement that the factor must be *material*.

How might these verbal restrictions be deployed in practice? The answer will dictate the depth to which equal-value comparisons are pursued under the new legislation. Again McCrudden's study (loc. cit.) is helpful on this point. His analysis suggests that the verbal restrictions on the defence, when fully implemented, give rise to the following limits upon material factor defence:

(1) One may argue that attributability, materiality or freedom from reference to sex difference should be *objectively* rather than subjectively judged, so that supporting facts have to be advanced to sustain the perceptions or intentions that the employer advances by way of defence. McCrudden argues that the judgment of the EAT on reference back from the ECJ in the *Jenkins* case ([1981] ICR 715, see the extract set out above at p. 398) supports this argument in relation to the material difference defence and is equally applicable, in so doing, to the material factor defence.
(2) One may argue that, in order for a variation to be genuinely attributable to a factor which is not the difference in sex, and in order for that factor to be material, there must be an absence both of direct and indirect discrimination. This may be seen as a more ambitious version of the first argument.
(3) One may argue that attributability and materiality require some degree of *necessity*, in the sense of absence of choice on the employer's part, so that an alleged submission to internal collective bargaining strengths or external labour market forces must be shown to be necessary rather than merely convenient or the product of like inclination. This may be seen as a more specific version of either of the first two arguments, at least in certain situations.

The courts, and hence the industrial tribunals, are more likely to frame their reasoning in terms of arguments (1) or (3) than in terms of argument (2), because arguments (1) and (3) may appear to follow more immediately from the words of section 1(3) than argument (2) does. In fact it is arguable, and the EAT in the *Jenkins* case effectively accepts, that if the equal pay comparisons, for which the Equal Pay legislation provides, are to be pursued at the proper depth then all three of these propositions should be recognized as inherent limits upon the material factor, and *a fortiori* the material difference, defence.

6 Sex and race discrimination in the content of employment

(a) The legal framework
In one sense, as we have just seen, it was in relation to the content of employment that the first major legal intervention to control sex discrimination occurred, in the shape of the equal pay legislation. The sequence in fact was that equal pay legislation acted as the flag-bearer for general sex discrimination legislation in relation to employment, and general sex discrimination legislation led the way for general race discrimination legislation. In the outcome, then, the sex and race discrimination legislation deal with the content of employment in the same way, except that the sex discrimination provisions are cumulative with the EqPA whereas the race discrimination provisions cover the ground as a single set of provisions. In fact most of the discrimination issues with regard to content of employment arise in relation to sex discrimination rather than race discrimination, and fall under the EqPA whose equalization provisions do, after all, cover all terms and conditions of employment where the nexus of like work or work rated as equivalent exists (s.1(2)). The remaining issues falling under the general discrimination legislation tend as we shall see to be issues concerned with *access* to benefits of one kind or another. Indeed the idea of equality of access or opportunity is the ideological starting point for general discrimination legislation, which is why, as we have seen, that legislation focuses primarily on *selection* for employment. However, although this means the SDA and the RRA have perhaps been less prominent in relation to the content of employment than in relation to hiring for employment, they have nevertheless provided the means of challenge to some very important sorts of managerial decisions arising in the course of the employment relationship especially with regard to promotion and other kinds of internal job allocation process. Indeed, the operation of the two Acts in those areas, limited though it may be, has some very interesting features for the labour lawyer, whose concern is the extent to which and ways in which the law can regulate the employment relationship. In a certain sense the legal control of the content of the employment relationship brings about an even more acute confrontation with the voluntarist objection to labour legislation than does legal control over its formation or termination. It will be useful to examine this part of the law in those terms, looking first at the scope and then at the manner of exercise of this kind of legal control rather as we did in relation to the equal pay legislation.

What, then, is the scope of the sex and race discrimination provisions in relation to content of employment? The relevant provision of the SDA approaches content in terms of access to benefits, but a catch-all reference to detriments is added at the end:

Sex Discrimination Act 1975, s.6(2)

It is unlawful for a person, in the case of a woman employed by him at an establishment in Great Britain, to discriminate against her –

(a) in the way he affords her access to opportunities for promotion, transfer or training, or to any other benefits, facilities or services, or by refusing or deliberately omitting to afford her access to them, or

(b) by dismissing her, or subjecting her to any other detriment.

The RRA makes exactly similar provisions (s.4(2)(b), (c)), but adds a reference to discrimination in the terms of employment that are afforded to the person employed (s.4(2)(a)), presumably to complete the parallel with the sex discrimination legislation, where the EqPA deals with terms of employment (see above, p. 370). These definitions of scope are broad enough to have remained mercifully free of complex problems of interpretation (we shall come to those when we look at the manner of exercise of these powers). The EAT in *Deson* v. *BL Cars Ltd* (CRE Annual Report for 1981, Case 10, p. 93) rejected an employer's argument that the transfer of a process worker to less attractive work (in response to shop-floor pressure) was not a detriment within the meaning of the RRA on the ground, as the employer argued, that it involved no loss in job status or pay. To like effect was the decision of the EAT in relation to a clerk at a job centre who was transferred from interviewing job applicants to working as a filing clerk without contact with the public – *Kirby* v. *Manpower Services Commission* [1980] ICR 420. (Comparison may be made with the interpretation of the concept of 'reasonable refusal of suitable alternative employment' as it arises in the law of redundancy payments; see below, p. 552.)

The matters that have been the main ones to be complained of within the categories covered by these provisions of the SDA and RRA are selection for promotion, allocation of jobs, work rules favouring one sex or group such as a rule letting women leave a shift before the men. We have looked in an earlier chapter at the way in which discrimination is defined. The difficulties in applying the concept of discrimination relate to the manner of application to problems of proof rather than to the scope of the matters that may be regarded as constituting discrimination, and we accordingly consider those issues in the next subsection. The SDA contains a provision to prevent overlap between its provisions and those of the EqPA so far as the content of employment is concerned; s.6(5) provides that s.6(2) does not apply to benefits consisting of the payment of money when the provision of those benefits is regulated by the contract of employment. This is important because it means that the more all-embracing sex discrimination concept of the SDA is not available to make good the shortcomings of the EqPA arising out of the limits on the concepts of like work and work rated as equivalent so far as pay matters are concerned.

Just as the EEC provisions on equal pay have constituted both a pressure on the UK Government to change the legislation and to some extent a way of circumventing the restrictions of that legislation by direct applicability, so the EEC provisions on equal treatment have been a pivotal point for the same kind of pressure on the SDA. The EEC provisions consist of Council Directive 76/207 of 1976, of which the crucial provisions are those of Articles 1 and 2.

EEC Council Directive 76/207, of 1976

Article 1

1. The purpose of this Directive is to put into effect in the Member States the principle of equal treatment for men and women as regards access to employment, including promotion, and to vocational training and as regards working conditions and, on the conditions referred to in paragraph 2, social security. This principle is hereinafter referred to as 'the principle of equal treatment.'

2. With a view to ensuring the progressive implementation of the principle of equal treatment in matters of social security, the Council, acting on a proposal from the Commission, will adopt provisions defining its substance, its scope and the arrangements for its application.

Article 2

1. For the purposes of the following provisions, the principle of equal treatment shall mean that there shall be no discrimination whatsoever on grounds of sex either directly or indirectly by reference in particular to marital or family status.

2. This Directive shall be without prejudice to the right of Member States to exclude from its field of application those occupational activities and, where appropriate, the training leading thereto, for which, by reason of their nature or the context in which they are carried out, the sex of the worker constitutes a determining factor.

3. This Directive shall be without prejudice to provisions concerning the protection of women, particularly as regards pregnancy and maternity.

4. This Directive shall be without prejudice to measures to promote equal opportunity for men and women, in particular by removing existing inequalities which affect women's opportunities in the areas referred to in Article 1(1)

The EOC has proposed to the government a number of amendments to the SDA in order both to make the Act achieve its broad objects more fully and to bring it into full compliance with 76/207, and EEC Commission proceedings were successfully brought in 1983 to require the UK government to take measures to remedy certain of these shortcomings.[1] The restrictions which the EOC suggested should be removed are those excluding the legislation in relation to employers of four employees or less (s.6(3)(*b*)) and in relation to small partnerships (s.11(1)). But the most important suggested repeal is that of the subsections which exclude provisions in relation to death or retirement (ss.6(4), 11(4) and 12(4)), and it is necessary to add a word or two more about the position in relation to pensions. The policy of excluding pension provisions

---

[1] *EEC Commission* v. *U.K.* (Case 165/82) [1984] ICR 192. The formal infringement proceedings were initiated on the grounds that the British legislation failed to give effect to the requirements of the Directive insofar as the SDA makes no provision for rendering null and void collective agreements which violate the equal treatment principle and allows exceptions not provided for in the Directive for firms with fewer than five workers and for midwives.

from the Eq PA and SDA is to be explained in terms of the enormous expense that would be involved in eliminating sex discrimination in relation to pensions, and in terms also of the fact that it would be unrealistic to attempt to do so while the state scheme involves the basic differentiation between men's and women's retiring ages. UK legislation has addressed the problem of sex discrimination in pension schemes only to the extent of making a narrow set of provisions about equality of access to pensions schemes in the Social Security Pensions Act 1975, of which the core provision is as follows:

Social Security Pensions Act 1975, s.53

s.53. (1) The provisions of sections 54 to 56 below shall have effect with a view to securing that the rules of occupational pension schemes conform with the equal access requirements.

(2) Subject to subsection (3) below, the equal access requirements in relation to a scheme are that membership of the scheme is open to both men and women on terms which are the same as to the age and length of service needed for becoming a member and as to whether membership is voluntary or obligatory.

(3) Regulations may –

    (a) provide for the equal access requirements to apply, whether to an occupational pension scheme, or to terms of employment relating to membership of it, or to both, with such modifications and exceptions as the Secretary of State considers necessary for particular cases or classes of case;

    (b) modify those requirements in any manner which he thinks appropriate with a view to securing the orderly implementation of the provisions of sections 54 to 56 below and to obtaining general compliance with those provisions.

(4) A rule does not contravene the equal access requirements only because it confers on the scheme's trustees or managers, or others, a discretion whose exercise may result in a person being more or less favourably treated than he otherwise would be, so long as the rule does not provide for the discretion to be exercised in any discriminatory manner as between men and women.

(5) This section and sections 54 to 56 below shall have effect in relation to any occupational pension scheme which is in force on, or comes into force after, the day on which this section comes into operation, being a scheme whose resources are derived as mentioned in section 40(1) above.

(6) Regulations may make provision –

    (a) for the Equal Pay Act 1970 to have effect, in relation to terms of employment relating to membership of an occupational pension scheme, with such modifications as may be prescribed;

    (b) for imposing requirements on employers as to the payment of contributions and otherwise in case of their failing or having failed to comply with any such terms;

    (c) for the consequential modification of a scheme's rules where there has been an alteration under the Equal Pay Act 1970 of any such terms.

(7) A reference in this section to terms of employment includes (where the context permits) –

    (a) any collective agreement or pay structure;

    (b) a wages regulation order within section 4 of the Equal Pay Act 1970; and (*c*) an agricultural wages order within section 5 of that Act.

The next three sections make the Occupational Pensions Board the arbiter of whether those equal access requirements are satisfied in relation to any particular pension scheme, and give them the power if necessary to modify or order the modification of the scheme to achieve compliance (ss. 54, 56). The OPB itself has reported on the narrow scope of these provisions and recommended further legislation in order to bring about greater equalization of women's conditions compared with men's conditions in relation to pension schemes; particularly in order to bring about equal benefits and not just equal expenditure (OPB Report on Equal Status for Men and Women in Occupational Pension Schemes, Cmnd. 6599, 1976).

There is now some prospect of EEC legislation along the lines that the OPB thought desirable. There already exists an EEC Council Directive issued in 1979 (79/7/EEC) which requires member states to legislate for equal treatment in *statutory* social security schemes by 1985. In April 1983 the EEC Commission submitted to the Council of Ministers a proposed Directive on equal treatment for men and women in *occupational* social security schemes which would apply to the same areas of social security protection as are covered by the Directive that applies to statutory schemes, and also to all other social benefits constituting a consideration for employment (see *European Industrial Relations Review* No. 113, June 1983, pp. 8, 31). The proposal would require equal treatment of men and women under occupational pension schemes both as to access, contributions and benefits. A debate will undoubtedly rage among economists about how to realize the principle of equal treatment in all these respects in view of the work patterns, mortality patterns and other demographic characteristics which differ as between men and women, and that debate is likely to have a counterpart among policy-makers which may mean that the enactment of this Directive will take a long time.

Meanwhile, some progress has been achieved by the direct application of existing EEC provisions (see Ellis and Morrell (1982) 11 *ILJ* 16). As we have seen (above, p. 339), certain differences in pension scheme contributions and benefits were classified as differences in pay by the ECJ in *Worringham* v. *Lloyds Bank Ltd* [1981] ICR 558 so as to render Article 119 directly applicable against them (see [1982] ICR 299, for the declaration made by the CA on the reference back from the ECJ). In *Burton* v. *British Railways Board* [1983] ICR 329, a male employee invoked EEC provisions against a voluntary redundancy scheme which operated during the five years before the national pension age of 65 for men, 60 for women; he complained, therefore, of the disadvantage at which men were placed by their higher retirement age. The ECJ, regarding this as a problem of access to benefits rather than of equality of pay, ruled that the principle of equal treatment contained in Article 5 of Directive 76/207 applied to the conditions of access to voluntary redundancy benefit. Article 5 is the article of the Directive in which the general principle of equal treatment, set out in Articles 1 and 2 thereof (see above, p. 407), is applied to working conditions including the conditions governing dismissal; we shall return to this discussion in the context of the termination of employment (see below, p. 438). The point to be made here is that the ECJ went on to find that there had been no discrimination within the meaning of Article 5 because, in effect, employers were entitled to align their voluntary redundancy scheme with the state pension retirement age, which as we have seen makes this sex differentiation. So that obstacle still lies at the end of all roads, both under UK legislation and existing EEC provisions, as will be realized from a consideration of this case, and the two others heard with it in the Court of Appeal, namely *Roberts* v. *Cleveland Area Health Authority* and *MacGregor Wall Coverings Ltd* v. *Turton* [1979] ICR 558, to which we return in a later chapter (see below, p. 438). The decision in the *Burton* case was confirmed and followed, as to the rulings we have just described, by the EAT in the case of *Roberts* v. *Tate & Lyle Food Ltd* [1983] ICR 521, so there the matter seems likely to remain until the enactment of the proposed Directive, which we described above, overtakes this discussion.

When we turn from considering the scope of control of discrimination in the content of employment to considering the manner of exercise of that control, we come to the central issue of how the legislators and the courts approach the task of instructing industrial tribunals how to scrutinize managerial decisions for unlawful discrimination. We have already considered the distinction between direct and indirect discrimination (see above, p. 44) and shown in what form both tests are applicable (SDA, s.1(1)(*a*), (*b*); RRA, s.1(1)(*a*), (*b*)). Both tests contain implicitly or explicitly a provision somewhat comparable to the 'genuine material non-sex-based difference' concept of s.1(3) of the EqPA. In the direct discrimination test, the exception is implicitly present in the sense that the less favourable treatment is required to be on the ground of sex or race (SDA, s.1(1)(*a*); RRA, s.1(1)(*a*)). In the indirect discrimination test, it is explicitly provided that the requirement or condition complained of be one that the employer cannot show to be justifiable irrespective of the sex (SDA, s.1(1)(*b*)(ii)) or race (RRA, s.1(1)(*b*)(ii)) of the person to whom it is applied. It is perhaps because the idea of justifiability is introduced in these diverse forms that the generality of the issue of justifiability is not clearly appreciated in judicial reasoning about testing for discrimination. Thus, although most of what we shall have to say in the ensuing paragraphs is about justifiability, the discussion, in so far as it defers to the way judges have proceeded, will not always or even for the most part be in that form. It would not be an unfair summary to say that the courts have tended to operate according to quite a broad notion of justifiability without overtly recognizing such a general defence to liability.

That is certainly a fair characterization of judicial reasoning in relation to the first area we have to consider, namely that of employers' provisions giving special protection to the health, safety and welfare of women. That can be complained of by men as sex discrimination against them, as was done in *Peake* v. *Automotive Products Ltd* [1977] ICR 968 in respect of a works rule permitting the women workers to leave work five minutes before the men at the end of the shift in order to prevent the women from being jostled in the rush for the gates. The EAT (reversing the IT) slightly reluctantly upheld the complaint, saying that the practice complained of was 'Harmless enough, no doubt, but no longer permitted' ([1977] ICR 480, 489H). The Court of Appeal sought more actively for a way to reconcile their perceptions of the dictates of common sense with the provisions of the SDA. Goff and Shaw L.JJ. purported to do so by concluding that there was no 'benefit' to the woman or 'detriment' to the man in such an inherently sensible rule. Lord Denning M.R., more instinctively alert to the danger that this route was a blind alley, based himself on the ruling that 'arrangements which are made in the interests of safety or in the interests of good administration are not infringements of the law even though they may be more favourable to women than to men . . .' ([1977] ICR 968, 974E–F). All three judges were seeking to define an implicit limit on the notion of discrimination; it was surely impossible to do so by denying that there was any discrimination at all as Goff and Shaw L.JJ. in effect did. Lord Denning's view, which would require a degree of unethicality on the part of the employer, was the more analytically sound approach, but challenged the goals of the SDA more directly.

By the time the point came before them again in *Ministry of Defence* v. *Jeremiah* [1980] ICR 13, the Court of Appeal had conceded defeat in this matter. In this case a male examiner in an ordnance factory complained that the dirty and dusty work in the colour bursting shop was allocated only to men. His complaint was upheld, Lord Denning M.R. disclaiming as wrong the exception for chivalry and administrative practice he had sought to create in *Peake* v. *Automotive Products*, a decision which he now said was defensible only on the basis of *de minimis non curat lex*. Brandon L.J. moreover denied the suggestion made by Shaw L.J. in the earlier case that a differentiation must in order to constitute an act of discrimination against men be in some way inherently adverse or hostile to their interests. These were both cases where a court could if it wished treat the acts complained of as infringing the SDA without thereby reflecting unfavourably upon the ethics of the employers. These lines tend to be less clearly drawn where a finding of sex or, even more, race discrimination would carry greater stigma.

There was, however, one more case which gave rise to the same sort of ethical issues as those at stake in *Peake* and *Jeremiah*; this was the case of *Page* v. *Freightline Tank Haulage Ltd* [1981] ICR 299, where a woman lorry-driver complained of the employer's refusal to let her drive a particular sort of cargo of chemicals on the ground that it was believed to be dangerous for women of child-bearing age to do so. This represents one of the key issues of sex discrimination, namely whether it enables women to complain of measures which restrict their access to work on protective grounds. The EAT felt that it was not possible in light of *Jeremiah* to carve out the sort of implicit exception to the requirements of the SDA that had been contemplated in *Peake*. But they rested their decision on the express statutory exception of SDA, s.51(1), which permitted compliance with other statutes; in this case the action could be regarded as compliance with the Health and Safety at Work Act 1974 on the basis that the refusal to allow the woman to do this work was the only reasonably practicable way to meet the requirements of that Act.

When we move on to the wider area of allocation of tasks, and of opportunities for training and of promotion, we find that the practices involved, although to a large extent comparable with those recruitment practices which may be challenged as discriminatory, are often even more deeply embedded in the framework of employment practice and industrial relations. This may be observed in relation to the facts of *Steel* v. *Union of Post Office Workers* [1978] ICR 181. A postwoman complained of the operation of a system for the allocation of postal rounds or 'walks' according to seniority in the employment of the Post Office. The seniority system operated against women in that seniority was counted only on the basis of time spent as a member of the permanent or established staff, and that permanent status had been unavailable to women before 1975. This seniority system was the result of an agreement with the Union of Post Office Workers. They indeed were the prime movers of this system; the complaint in this case was partly against them. So the Post Office preferred to let this historical discrimination work its way gradually through the system than to upset their agreement with the union. In the words of Phillips J., 'In effect the attitude of the Post Office is the not uncommon one of supporting sex equality – but not yet' ([1978] ICR 181 at p. 184G). Phillips J. as President of the EAT was a considerable champion of the aims of the EqPA and SDA. The EAT under his chairmanship held that the justifiability of the practice under consideration in this case should be assessed in much the same way as the red circling cases were approached under the EqPA (see above, p. 391). That this justification should not be lightly conceded was made clear in the following terms:

Steel v. *Union of Post Office Workers* [1978] ICR 181 (EAT)

PHILLIPS J.: It may be helpful if we add a word of detail about what we consider to be the right approach to this question. First, the onus of proof lies upon the party asserting this proposition, in this case the Post Office. Secondly, it is a heavy onus in the sense that at the end of the day the industrial tribunal must be satisfied that the case is a genuine one where it can be said that the requirement or condition is necessary. Thirdly, in deciding whether the employer has discharged the onus the industrial tribunal should take into account all the circumstances, including the discriminatory effect of the requirement or condition if it is permitted to continue. Fourthly, it is necessary to weigh the need for the requirement or condition against that effect. Fifthly, it is right to distinguish between a requirement or condition which is necessary and one which is merely convenient, and for this purpose it is relevant to consider whether the employer can find some other and non-discriminatory method of achieving his object.

Turning to the facts of this case, it will be right to inquire whether it is necessary to allot walks by seniority or whether some other method is feasible, to consider whether the seniority rule could not be revised so as to give the women some credit for their temporary service, and to consider the extent of the disadvantage which the women suffer under the present system in terms of numbers and likely duration. Assistance may be obtained from the judgments in the Supreme Court of the United States in *Griggs* v. *Duke Power Co.* (1971) 401 US 424. Although the terms of the Act there in question are different from those of the Sex Discrimination Act 1975, it seems to us that the approach adopted by the court is relevant. In particular, the passage at p. 431 is helpful where it is said:

> Congress has now provided that tests or criteria for employment or promotion may not provide equality of opportunity merely in the sense of the fabled offer of milk to the stork and the fox. On the contrary, Congress has now required that the posture and condition of the job-seeker be taken into account. It has – to resort again to the fable – provided that the vessel in which the milk is proffered be one all seekers can use. The Act proscribes not only overt discrimination but also practices that are fair in form, but discriminatory in operation. The touchstone is business necessity. If an employment practice which operates to exclude Negroes cannot be shown to be related to job performance, the practice is prohibited.

A similar approach seems to us to be proper when applying section 1(1)(b)(ii) of the Sex Discrimination Act 1975. In other words a practice which would otherwise be discriminatory, which is the case here, is not to be licensed unless it can be shown to be justifiable, and it cannot be justifiable unless its discriminatory effect is justified by the need – not the convenience – of the business or enterprise.

The Industrial Tribunal to whom the case was remitted to apply this test found for the claimant ([1978] IRLR 198). The case is something of a milestone for labour law; it marks in its way a significant challenge to the voluntarist stance towards industrial relations, a challenge nonetheless potent for its progressive rather than repressive origins. Indeed might one not fairly conclude that it was the move to individual employment protection and anti-discrimination legislation which really gave legal absentionism its quietus in the mid-1970s far more effectively than the collective restrictionism of the early seventies had done? It was, after all, in decisions like this one that the unacceptable consequences of collective bargaining were most effectively displayed; compare, in this respect, the interesting case of *British Airways Engine Overhaul Ltd* v. *Francis* [1981] ICR 278 (EAT).

The EAT has not always been quite as searching in its pursuit of discrimination. The cases on task allocation, in the absence of a seniority system, present interesting examples of the interplay between the real concern to give due effect to the legislation and on the other hand a habit of legitimating the ubiquitous managerial search for the path of least resistance. In *Deson* v. *BL Cars Ltd* (CRE Report for 1981, p. 93), the EAT with Slynn J. presiding was to overturn an industrial tribunal decision that no 'detriment' was involved in allocating a black worker to a different job to preserve industrial peace. On the other hand, when in *Pel Ltd* v. *Mogdill* [1980] IRLR 142 a challenge was mounted to a situation of *de facto* segregration of Asian workers in the paint-spraying shop at the company's furniture factory, the EAT held that the complaint must fall between various stools; the employer was to some extent sheltered behind the Furniture Trade Union against whom the complaint was also brought but whose conduct was held not to be specifically discriminatory; he was also sheltered by the fact that the segregation had gained a momentum of its own in that the workers of Asian origin in the paint shop preferred candidates of their own racial origins for any vacancy arising in their shop. This meant that the employer had not himself engaged in the act of segregating a person from other persons on racial grounds, which is expressly characterised as discriminatory by s.1(2) of the RRA 1976. The employers were in effect able to point to this situation as requiring a degree of affirmative action for its remedy which the RRA did not require of them. So the company's appeal against the industrial tribunal decision was allowed on the basis that the employer had no active policy of segregation. No doubt this was a hard case; but it would produce some curious results if employers' conduct of the employment relationship were judged solely or primarily by reference to their articulated policies in relation thereto, if only in view of the degree to which the handling of that relationship is permeated by empiricism.

Perhaps somewhat comparable, though no doubt another hard case, was the decision in *Kirby* v. *Manpower Services Commission* [1980] ICR 420. Here a clerk at a job centre complained that he had been victimized within the meaning of s.2 of the RRA, in that he had been moved from being a first-tier clerk conducting interviews to being a filing clerk out of contact with the clients. He alleged that this had been done because he had reported prospective employers to the local Council for Community Relations for discriminating against coloured applicants, and because he had used, when so reporting, information acquired in confidence in the course of his job. The EAT upheld the argument of the MSC that this was not victimization because they would have treated any other sort of breach of confidence in the same way. This approach immediately locates the action complained of within an ethically acceptable framework. But the essence of a provision against victimization is surely that it asks simply, would the employee concerned have been so treated if he had not engaged in the protected conduct, rather than if he had engaged in some comparable but unprotected conduct? It is yet another illustration of the extent to which labour law which proceeds by compulsory comparison is made or broken by the decision as to who the appropriate comparator is. An apparently quite objective and anodyne choice of comparator may represent a crucial policy decision, for example to endorse a set of assumptions made by management which the legislation in question had offered to challenge.

When we come to the question of discrimination in decisions about promotion, we again find questions arising about the manner of exercise of legal control which are really an expression of the difficulty of evaluating managerial decisions in a highly sensitive area. Decisions about promotion appear at first sight to raise problems very comparable with those that arise in relation to recruitment; but in fact the promotion issues tend to be more personalized and to that extent more sensitive. The employer will typically be making a selection based on an evaluation of the work and personality of a particular employee or several competing employees; the employee or employees for their part will be likely to have expectations of promotion, whether systematized or not derived from their past employment. These tensions expressed themselves in the issue of confidentiality and privilege of reports on individual employees used for decisions about promotion. In *Science Research Council* v. *Nassé* [1979] I C R 921, although the E A T (Phillips J. presiding) ordered discovery, the C A and H L leaned in favour of confidentiality, the H L requiring that the objective of disposing fairly of the case be balanced against the damage involved in overriding confidentiality, and that discovery should be ordered of confidential reports only as a last resort where absolutely necessary and subject if need be to protective measures.

Eventually the courts had to consider directly how complaints of, in particular, racially motivated denials of promotion were to be evaluated. In *Eke* v. *Customs & Excise* [1981] I R L R 334, the primary facts complained of had occurred before the R R A came into force, so the complaint had to be directed at the failure to investigate the primary complaint of discrimination after the Act came into force. The E A T, Slynn J. presiding, remitted the case to the I T to consider whether the failure to investigate was itself racially motivated. In *Jeffers* v. *Thorn Consumer Electronics Ltd* (see C R E Report for 1980 at p. 90), the need for positive direction to the industrial tribunals revealed itself when an external white candidate was promoted in preference to a suitable internal black candidate to the post of foreman mechanical inspector. The underlying difficulty in deciding how far to allow or require the inference of discrimination from the fact that an heir apparent is passed over is well brought out in the majority and minority views of the E A T as reported by the C R E:

Jeffers v. *Thorn Consumer Electronics Ltd* (E A T, unreported, 1980)
C R E Report for 1980, pp. 90–1

23. External white candidate promoted in preference to suitable internal black candidate
Mr Irving Jeffers, a black Trinidadian, was employed by Thorn Consumer Electronics Ltd, at their Enfield North London factory, as a leading hand in mechanical inspection and ranked immediately below the foreman mechanical inspector. He was an able and conscientious employee and carried out all aspects of his duties to the complete satisfaction of his employers. The job of foreman mechanical inspector was due to become vacant on 31 May and the vacancy was advertised internally. Mr Jeffers applied and was by far the best internal candidate. The employers then advertised the post externally in the local press and a white employee of one of the respondent's associate companies replied to the advertisement. Although he did not have the relevant experience, he was offered the post in preference to Mr Jeffers. Mr Jeffers

therefore complained of racial discrimination on his employer's part.

In March 1979 a London Industrial Tribunal, by a majority, decided 'with considerable hesitation' that, on the balance of probabilities, Mr Jeffers had not established that his employers had discriminated against him. The Industrial Tribunal found that the decision to advertise externally was only reached after the internal applications had been received and appraised. They found the employer's explanation for that inconclusive and unsatisfactory. The majority were very troubled about the point and concluded that the decision to advertise after the internal applications had produced an apparently suitable candidate (Mr Jeffers) was 'largely unexplained'. The minority member took a different view. He thought that, in the light of Mr Jeffers' suitability for the job, there was discrimination when the decision to advertise externally was taken and that the qualifications advertised were deliberately lowered to enable Mr Jeffers to be excluded by the appointment of some other candidate. Mr Jeffers appealed against the Industrial Tribunal.

The Employment Appeal Tribunal was also divided. By a majority they dismissed his appeal.

Mr Justice Slynn, the President of the Employment Appeal Tribunal, said: 'This Tribunal' – i.e., the Employment Appeal Tribunal – 'has said on a number of occasions that since direct evidence of, or an admission of, discrimination on the grounds of colour is unlikely to be available, Industrial Tribunals must investigate to see whether, on the facts, the right inference to draw is that there has been discrimination whatever the explanation put forward by the employer . . . The majority members of this Tribunal have been concerned as to whether the right inference on all the facts was drawn by the Industrial Tribunal. Having read the Industrial Tribunal's findings and the notes of evidence they are particularly concerned about the decision to advertise the post externally when an apparently well qualified, experienced, suitable man was available, who in the usual course of industrial practice might have had promotion. On the other hand, the Industrial Tribunal was well aware of the difficulties; they considered them at length and only after much doubt they decided against Mr Jeffers . . . The majority members find it impossible to say, whatever doubts they may have felt about the case, that this is a perverse decision.'

Mrs D Lancaster, the minority member of the appeal tribunal, stated: 'In employment discrimination cases, particularly those involving race, there is unlikely to be any direct evidence to support the facts which are themselves often unclear and usually disputed. Thus, in a hearing before an Industrial Tribunal, much more depends on nuances and the drawing of inferences from the facts than happens in other employment cases. This approach has been accepted by the Employment Appeal Tribunal in *Bains* v. *Avon County Council* (EAT/143/78) and in *Piperdy* v. *UBM Parker Glass* (EAT/459/78).'

In the minority member's view, if, in a race discrimination case, an Industrial Tribunal draws a number of inferences which the evidence only equivocally supports; does not apply, or sufficiently apply, the 'cumulative principle' set out in the *Bains* case; does not apply, or sufficiently apply, the probing techniques enunciated in the *Piperdy* case; does not pay attention, or sufficient attention, to section 65(2)(b) – i.e. inferences to be drawn from replies to, or failure to reply to, the statutory questionnaire – then in the member's opinion, the Appeal Tribunal should either reverse the Industrial Tribunal decision or send the case back to be reheard by a different tribunal. The key question was why did the employer – in view of the fact that Mr Jeffers had the requisite experience and qualifications for appointment to the foreman's vacancy – not appoint him but proceed to place an external advertisement *after* receiving his application? In view of the employer's unsatisfactory explanation on this point, and on other matters, the minority member would have allowed the appeal.

The following year a very comparable issue came before the EAT, Browne-Wilkinson J. presiding, in *Khanna* v. *Ministry of Defence* [1981] ICR 653. Here the EAT identified a central problem. On the one hand, the IT had avoided a real address to the merits of the promotion decision by invoking fairly complex notions about shifting burdens of proof. On the other hand, if they were required to proceed without any such technical rules to legitimate their decision, they might have even greater difficulty in penetrating the non-discriminatory explanation for the selection which will typically be advanced if only because discriminatory decisions are generally rationalized, by those taking them, as depending on objective or, at least, non-discriminatory grounds. The guidance given to industrial tribunals in the case is a model of the fulfilment of the purposes of a specialist appellate tribunal for employment law.

Khanna v. *Ministry of Defence* [1981] ICR 653 (EAT)

Mr Khanna, a senior photographer born in India, applied for promotion to the post of principal photographer which was vacant in his unit. The promotion board chose Mr Spooner, an external candidate, who was white. The IT concluded that the complainant had not discharged the onus which lay on him of proving on the balance of probabilities that there had been racial discrimination, the employers having discharged the evidential burden which shifted to them once it was shown that an obvious candidate who was coloured had been rejected.

BROWNE-WILKINSON J.: In the future, we think industrial tribunals may find it easier to forget about the rather nebulous concept of the 'shift in the evidential burden.' The phrase was not treated with any marked enthusiasm by the Privy Council in *Jayasena* v. *The Queen* [1970] AC 618. It has in the past been used by the Employment Appeal Tribunal in cases under the Race Relations Act and the Sex Discrimination Act. But in our view it is more likely to obscure than to illuminate the right answer. In this case the industrial tribunal would, we suspect, have found the case rather more straightforward if, looking at all the evidence as a whole, they had simply decided whether the complaint had been established. No useful purpose is served by stopping to reach a conclusion on half the evidence. The right course in this case was for the industrial tribunal to take into account the fact that direct evidence of discrimination is seldom going to be available and that, accordingly, in these cases the affirmative evidence of discrimination will normally consist of inferences to be drawn from the primary facts. If the primary facts indicate that there has been discrimination of some kind, the employer is called on to give an explanation and, failing clear and specific explanation being given by the employer to the satisfaction of the industrial tribunal, an inference of unlawful discrimination from the primary facts will mean the complaint succeeds: see *Moberly* v. *Commonwealth Hall (University of London)* [1977] ICR 791, 794 and *Wallace* v. *South Eastern Education and Library Board* [1980] IRLR 193. Those propositions are, we think, most easily understood if concepts of shifting evidential burdens are avoided.

So, in this case, the industrial tribunal has drawn the inference of possible discrimination from the fact that there was no obvious reason why the applicant should not have got the job: on the other side are the factors they summarised in paragraph 8 of the reasons. The function of the industrial tribunal was, on all the facts of the case, to reach a decision on balance of probabilities.

We turn now to consider Mr Menon's third submission, namely that the industrial tribunal had abdicated its function by leaving the matter to be decided on the burden of proof. We have great sympathy with the industrial tribunal in the difficult task they had to discharge. To decide that there has been discrimination in the face of sworn evidence that there was no such discrimination is unpalatable: equally, racial discrimination does undoubtedly exist, and it is highly improbable that a person who has discriminated is going to admit the fact, quite possibly even to himself. The judicial function, however unpalatable, is to resolve such conflicts by a decision if possible.

There may be cases in which the ultimate decision will turn on the burden of proof, e.g. if the case turns on the evidence of the complainant and the industrial tribunal is unable to decide whether that evidence is truthful. But we are satisfied that, on the facts as found by the industrial tribunal, this is not such a case. Here the industrial tribunal has found an 'unavoidable inference' of discrimination in the absence of satisfactory explanation from the employers. The employers have given an explanation (i.e. the evidence of the board members). Although the industrial tribunal in their reasons say that it is bound to accept the evidence of the board members as to the reason for not ruling out Mr Spooner on the grounds that he lacked the necessary skills, the industrial tribunal has at no stage found that it accepts the evidence of the board members generally and in particular their evidence that they were not motivated by racial discrimination. As we see it, on the facts as found by the industrial tribunal, either the tribunal accepts the evidence of the board members that they were not motivated by racial considerations (in which case the claim fails) or it does not (in which case the claim is established by reason of the unavoidable inference the industrial tribunal has found). The failure by the industrial tribunal to decide that issue does not leave the matter decided by the burden of proof: it leaves the whole case undecided.

This then is the state of development of judicial approaches to the problem of controlling discrimination in the content of employment; we should, however, attempt some assessment of the social operation of the legal provisions concerned, in order to avoid falling into the trap of assuming that appeals to the courts systematically display the real problems of operating the legislation concerned.

(b) The social operation of the discrimination legislation

The assembling of information about the social operation of legislation is often difficult and the results are often patchy. This should not be seen as depriving the attempt to do so of all its value, for the alternative is a view distorted by the accidents of litigation. We have spoken earlier of the usefulness of the work of the EOC and CRE, as committed administrative agencies, when it comes to assessing the social effects of the legislation (see above, p. 63). So far as the content of employment is concerned, the recent annual reports of the CRE are relatively uninformative. They show that a relatively high proportion of the employment problems coming to them arise in the area of content of employment. Thus in 1981, of a total of 547 formal applications for assistance received by the CRE from individual complainants concerning discrimination in employment, 17 allegations concerned discrimination in the terms of employment, 176 concerned discrimination in affording access to opportunities for promotion, transfer, training or other benefits, facilities or services, and 324 concerned dismissal or subjecting the complainants to any other detriment on racial grounds (though most of that 324 may have concerned dismissal as such) (CRE Annual Report for 1981, p. 14). But the recent reports of the CRE are mainly concerned with recruitment and training, so far as employment is concerned, and devote little or no specific attention to issues of internal task allocation or promotion. The same is true of the CRE's Code of Practice.

The EOC's recent reports are a good deal more informative on the corresponding issues for sex discrimination. The information they give about the distribution of complaints within the employment is derived from statistics about applications to industrial tribunals. Thus of 256 such applications in 1981, 91 related to access to opportunities for promotion, training, transfer and other benefits and 19 related to other unfavourable treatment apart from dismissal (6th Annual Report 1981, p. 30). Their report for 1980 admirably identifies the social consequences of the burden of proof issue which, as we have seen, the courts have considered in relation to promotion in race discrimination cases (above, p. 417). It is worth setting the passage out in full:

EOC Fifth Annual Report for 1980

Burden of Proof

3   There has been an increasing awareness of the difficulties facing many, if not the majority, of applicants in presenting individual complaints under the Sex Discrimination Act. A lack of direct evidence, which is the usual situation, requires that inferences of discrimination, where appropriate, should be drawn. The appellate courts have stated that unless appropriate inferences of discrimination can be drawn, anti-discrimination legislation will be largely defeated. The Commission is concerned that the problem identified by the appellate courts may have already sapped the resolve of many would-be complainants, which the Commission believes may have contributed substantially to the reduction of the number of individual cases under the Sex Discrimination Act (see the statistics of Industrial Tribunal Cases in Appendix 2 below). As the number reduces so the level of practical awareness of the scope of the legislation is also likely to reduce, resulting in a vicious circle of decline in confidence in the effectiveness of the legislation. The Commission has reached the conclusion therefore, that there should be a more equitable distribution of the burden of proof in sex discrimination cases, and has so recommended to the Secretary of State.

The recent annual reports have also identified some important specific problems in relation to promotion and transfer. Thus in their report for 1980 they say:

Promotion and Transfer

13   Complaints in this area indicate that sex discrimination in promotion is more likely to take place in instances where there is no formal procedure for selection and where internal vacancies fail to be advertised. It seems that women in these circumstances are particularly vulnerable to being overlooked completely or bypassed in favour of their male colleagues, irrespective of individual merit. In one successful case assisted by the Commission, *Crocker* v. *J C Bamford (Excavators) Ltd* (see para. 14, Chapter 2) the employer had chosen to promote a man with less experience allegedly because he had more long-term potential than the female candidate.

14   Another trend which gives cause for concern is the decision by employers, sometimes assisted or encouraged by trade unions, to recruit from a particular grade, which often means in practice that selection takes place from a single-sex pool of labour. In these circumstances, job segregation naturally reinforces the barriers to promotion encountered by many women.

and in the following report:

EOC Sixth Annual Report for 1981

Promotion and Transfer

29   Complaints concerning promotion continue to originate principally in organisations where selection and promotion procedures are confidential. Where managerial posts are involved women may not be considered because of the operation of the 'old boy network'. This has implications of both direct and indirect sex discrimination. The Commission has recently assisted a case to test this aspect of the law before an Industrial Tribunal and a decision is awaited. In another case a woman complained to the Commission that, unlike her male colleagues, she was excluded from the hospitality extended by her employers to her personal customers and that this lack of informal contact subsequently had a limiting effect on her performance in her job.

30   The Commission is concerned that part-time service is not always included in length-of-service calculations where seniority is the basis of transfer. This is particularly worrying in the current economic climate where transfer may be the only alternative to redundancy.

31   A number of collective agreements restrict the transfer of workers between certain job categories, and some of these are discriminatory in their effects. In one case men were not allowed to transfer to work in the sewing room and women were unable to transfer out of that section because of the restrictions imposed by protective legislation. In another case women were not allowed to work in the men's jobs and *vice versa*. The original agreement was made before the Sex Discrimination Act with a view to protecting women's jobs. This is a further illustration of the importance of reviewing past agreements to ensure that they comply with the provisions of the Sex Discrimination Act 1975.

The same specific concern with promotion, transfer, and training is evident from the EOC's Draft Code which contains the following recommendations in relation thereto:

EOC Code of Practice – Revised Consultative Draft, 1982

23. It is therefore recommended that:

(a) where an appraisal system is in operation records are monitored to examine how the scheme is working. The assessment criteria should be examined to ensure they are not unlawfully discriminatory.

(b) where a group of workers predominantly of one sex is excluded from an appraisal scheme, they should nevertheless have similar access to promotion, transfer and training and to other benefits, facilities or services.

(c) promotion and career development patterns are reviewed to ensure that the traditional qualifications for promotion are justifiable in relation to the job to be done. Promotion on the basis of length of service alone could amount to unlawful indirect sex discrimination as it could affect more women than men.

(d) where general aptitude is the main requisite, promotion criteria should be wide enough to allow the inclusion of candidates whose training and experience may be traditional to their sex.

(e) rules which restrict or preclude transfers between certain jobs should be questioned and changed if they are found to be discriminatory. Employees of one sex may be concentrated in sections from which transfers are traditionally restricted without real justification.

(f) policies and practices regarding selection for training, day release and personal development should be examined for direct and indirect discrimination. Where there is found to be an imbalance in training as between sexes, the cause should be identified to ensure that it is not discriminatory.

(g) age limits for access to training and promotion should be questioned.

(h) it should not be assumed that employees with young children are not available for residential training; when staff are selected for residential courses they should where possible be informed well in advance, so that child-care and other personal arrangements can be dealt with; employers with their own residential training facilities should consider whether child-care facilities could be provided.

Of course, the assessments made by a committed administrative agency are not conclusive of the policy discussion in this area. But they do serve to indicate a number of dimensions to the process of legal control of discrimination in the course of the employment relationship which would not emerge from a survey of the legislative provisions alone or from a study of the case-law interpreting those provisions.

7 **Legal control of discipline at work**

The employer's disciplinary powers over the employee represent a crucial feature of the content of the employment relationship, and, since discipline includes both dismissal and action short of it, the topic provides a link between legal control of the content of the employment relationship and legal control of the termination of it, especially the law of unfair dismissal. Alongside questions relating to remuneration they express the social character of the relationship and the nature and extent of the employee's subordination to the enterprise which employs him. At least until recently the state was content to endorse the authority which the enterprise (or single employer) acquired as a matter of economic and social ordering. Indeed until the legislation of 1875 the most active support was lent by the state to employer's disciplinary authority by the treatment of employee's breach of contract as a criminal offence and even after that date certain types of employee's breach of contract continued to be criminal and all types remained matters for remedy in the civil courts, as we shall see in relation to the law concerning industrial conflict (see below, pp. 777ff.).

Not only did the state buttress the employers' disciplinary authority from a remedial point of view but it also upheld the substantive distribution of power embodied in employers' disciplinary systems. Thus there were implied in favour of the employer in the contract of employment the widest powers of summary dismissal for misconduct, disobedience to lawful orders (what a meagre qualification!) and for incompetence (which included the employers' own errors of selection).[1] The law concerning the employers' disciplinary powers short of dismissal tended to be derived from the law relating to dismissal. For instance in *Marshall* v. *English Electric Ltd* [1945] 1 All ER 653 (see below, p. 433), the employer's power of disciplinary suspension was upheld[2] in relation to hourly-paid manual workers on the basis that they were dismissible at such short notice that they had no cause for complaint at merely being suspended without pay instead of being dismissed. On the other hand in *Hanley* v. *Pease & Partners Ltd* [1915] 1 KB 698, it was held that an express power of dismissal excluded an implied power to impose suspension without pay before dismissal.

The main exception to this picture of a non-interventionist legal system content to acquiesce in severe discipline by employers was provided by the Truck Act 1896. This placed real restrictions on the employer's powers, as far as manual workers and shop assistants were concerned, to link discipline with remuneration by means of fines and deductions for misconduct or poor or negligent work. We set out below section 1 of the Truck Act 1896, which deals with fines. Similar conditions are applied by section 2 to deductions in respect of damaged goods. In what ways do the conditions imposed actually control the disciplinary powers as distinct from merely requiring them to be formalized?

Truck Act 1896, s.1

1. (1) An employer shall not make any contract with any workman for any deduction from the sum contracted to be paid by the employer to the workman, or for any payment to the employer by the workman, for or in respect of any fine, unless

(a) the terms of the contract are contained in a notice kept constantly affixed at such place or places open to the workmen and in such a position that it may be easily seen,

---

[1] See Freedland, *The Contract of Employment* (1976), pp. 195–202.

[2] The issue in the case was whether disciplinary suspension contravened the war-time Essential Work Order which governed the employment in question. The EWO allowed for such suspension for up to three days if the employee's conditions of service permitted it. A majority of the Court of Appeal held that it was so permitted.

read, and copied by any person whom it affects; or the contract is in writing, signed by the workman; and

(*b*) the contract specifies the acts or omissions in respect of which the fine may be imposed, and the amount of the fine or the particulars from which that amount may be ascertained; and

(*c*) the fine imposed under the contract is in respect of some act or omission which causes or is likely to cause damage or loss to the employer, or interruption or hindrance to his business; and

(*d*) the amount of the fine is fair and reasonable having regard to all the circumstances of the case.

(2) An employer shall not make any such deduction or receive any such payment, unless

(*a*) the deduction or payment is made in pursuance of, or in accordance with, such a contract as aforesaid; and

(*b*) particulars in writing showing the acts or omissions in respect of which the fine is imposed and the amount thereof are supplied to the workman on each occasion when a deduction or payment is made.

(3) This section shall apply to the case of a shop assistant in like manner as it applies to the case of a workman.

We have described earlier in this chapter (at p. 342, above) the government's proposal to repeal the Truck Acts and to institute instead a right to complain to an industrial tribunal of arbitrary deductions from wages, arbitrariness being defined in terms of breach of statute, contract or custom. Tamara Goriely has argued in an article on these proposals ((1983) 12 *ILJ* 236) that this would be to dispense with a protection for employees which may still be of some importance. In particular, she argues for, and produces some empirical evidence in support of, the proposition that there is quite a widespread problem of employees whose wages are very greatly eroded by the operation of disciplinary rules, forming part of the contract of employment, authorizing deductions in respect of cash or stock shortages or faulty work. Intended as incentives to care and scrupulousness (and no doubt there is often a functional case for such incentives), it would seem, however, that some deduction rules transfer to employees the risks of error, or dishonesty on the part of customers, to an extent which is quite penal. The evidence suggests that this is a particular problem in the employment of cashiers at petrol filling stations. Thus the factual context in which it is proposed to repeal the Truck Acts may be less dissimilar than we are wont to assume to the context in which, for instance, the Truck Act of 1896 was enacted. The adequacy of the proposal to treat freedom of contract as a limit upon the control of 'arbitrary' deductions from wages has to be assessed in that context.

Has the creation of a new statutory floor of employment protection rights brought about any change in the law concerning discipline at work? From 1971 onwards the Industrial Relations Code of Practice made recommendations about disciplinary practice. These were chiefly concerned with the formalization of disciplinary rules and disciplinary procedure. The process of formalization normally brings about an increase in the safeguards afforded to the employee because one cannot in practice go through a process of formalization without becoming to some extent aware of the dictates of regularity and natural justice. In 1976, ACAS, which had inherited the code-making function of the Commission on Industrial Relations, issued a code on Disciplinary Practice and Procedures in Employment following a draft code issued in 1976 (see Freedland (1976) 5 *ILJ* 257 and (1977) 6 *ILJ* 121). This Code amplifies somewhat the notions of formalization of rules and procedure which were to be found in the 1971 Code. It is to be doubted whether ACAS had enough new initiatives in relation to discipline to make their code a significant one. Some thought was clearly being given to increasing the role of trade unions and trade-union representatives. The final version of the Code was stronger on this point than the draft (cf. paras. 10(g), 15(a)) but showed less enthusiasm than the draft had done for a trade-union role in the formulation of the disciplinary rules themselves (compare para. 20 with para. 21 of the Draft). Although the Code is not an especially innovatory document it will probably have had quite some impact in practice, because the Employment Protection Act amended the Contracts of Employment Act 1972 so as to require employers to specify or refer to a document specifying any disciplinary rules applicable to the employee and to specify a person to whom the employee can apply if he is dissatisfied with any disciplinary decision relating to him (EPCA 1978, s.1(4)). Many employers will doubtless look to the Code for guidance as to how to comply with that requirement, and will revise their disciplinary procedures somewhat in the course of so doing.

Perhaps more radical in its impact on discipline is the law of unfair dismissal. By controlling the employer's decisions about dismissal, the law of unfair dismissal addresses itself to the most drastic of all the disciplinary decisions which the employer may take. The use of the other sanctions available to employers (normally suspension with or without pay, demotion or transfer, fines and deductions, formal written warnings and verbal warnings) will tend to derive its pattern from the employer's practice over dismissal – the latter will as it were calibrate the scale of disciplinary penalties. There is also another way in which the law of unfair dismissal has affected the whole range of the employer's disciplinary practice. As we shall see in a later chapter (pp. 448ff.), the notion of constructive dismissal enables the employee in certain circumstances to leave his employment and complain of the termination of his employment as being attributable to some adverse action by the employer during the continuance of the employment. This links the law of unfair dismissal with the *content* as well as the termination of employment. One particular way in which this link-up may occur is that the employee may complain of, as an unfair dismissal, some disciplinary decision falling short of dismissal. In *Western Excavating Ltd* v. *Sharp* [1978] ICR 221 the Court of Appeal decided that the employee must be able to point specifically to the repudiation by the employer of some implied term of the contract of employment, as distinct from an action which an industrial tribunal might feel to be in a general sense unreasonable (see below, p. 449). That very decision – the leading case on constructive dismissal – concerned a disciplinary decision falling short of dismissal, namely the decision to impose five days' suspension without pay. The point at issue was whether the employer had constructively dismissed the employee by refusing to make him a loan to tide him over the period of suspension without pay. The employer had no practice of making loans in these circumstances, and the Court of Appeal was clearly concerned that he should not be liable to unfair dismissal proceedings for refusing to mitigate the disciplinary penalty that had been imposed. In a sense the wheel has come full circle, and we are again in a situation where the law about discipline at work will be to a large extent the by-product of the law about dismissal.

It is perhaps worth considering how these developments relate to the processes of collective bargaining. As we have said, the ACAS Code on Disciplinary Practice and Procedures makes some provision for the role of trade unions and trade-union representatives in the area of discipline at work, but this has no directly mandatory force. Mellish and Collis-Squires in 1976 advanced a fundamental critique of the law relating to discipline and dismissal, that it failed to allow for a collective dimension to the problem of the proper extent and nature of the employer's disciplinary powers ((1976) 5 *ILJ* 175). They show how the current approach, for instance, in industrial tribunals assumes a straightforward dichotomy between punitive discipline and corrective discipline. The progressive preference between these two is for corrective discipline and that preference is seen, by those who hold it, as a radical stance. But, argue Mellish and Collis-Squires, this is to neglect the extent to which disciplinary decisions constitute the formulation of norms which affect workgroups as a whole. Therefore this is to neglect the extent to which such decisions might be proper matter for some degree of joint regulation of discipline, and they conclude by advancing the view that discipline should be viewed as an aspect of collective industrial relations. Thus, for instance, status quo provisions comparable with those relating to overtly collective disputes might be appropriate (cf. Anderman, 'The "Status Quo" Issue and Industrial Disputes Procedures: Some Implications for Labour Law' (1975) 4 *ILJ* 131). Their ultimate conclusion amounts to an assessment of the actual and potential effectiveness of statutory regulations in the area of discipline at work, and is worth quoting as a starting-point for discussion. Does their thesis make sufficient allowance for a category of genuinely individual cases and problems within the area of disciplinary action?

Mellish and Collis-Squires, 'Legal and Social Norms in Discipline and Dismissal' (1976) 5 *ILJ* 175–6

Our studies convince us that discipline is not a special area of industrial relations because of the individual nature of the issues involved and the essentially integrative method of solving them. What makes a matter an individual disciplinary issue rather than a collective bargaining issue is firstly the extent to which management tries to control any given features of the behaviour of their employees (whether it be timekeeping, output, respect for supervisors, or whatever). It will also depend on the manner in which such a control is sought. For example, increased effort from workers can be sought either by enforcement of a given set of rules by management personnel or else by reliance on incentive payment schemes, in which management-initiated discipline will not be involved. The O M E [Office of Manpower Economics] reported that where 'measured daywork schemes replaced traditional piecework schemes, foremen were given new responsibilities for cracking down on individuals who failed to meet output targets'. As well as management initiatives, what determines the status of an issue is the collective response of employees. This will depend on their organization and also on the bargaining strength which they think they have and their history of using this strength. It will depend on whether they can identify with the individual concerned and whether they support or are indifferent to any action taken against him by management. These factors will be interrelated in any given situation and also will operate in an historical context in which the values of parties about what they *should* and their perception about what they *can* do will be formed.

The implications of this view of discipline for the operation of dismissal law are largely negative. It says that the factors which determine whether a dispute is an individual or a collective one are complex and it cannot be supposed that tribunals either could or would take all these into account in attempting to understand any case before them.

[The authors then show that tribunals are bound to individualize the issues before them and to treat the employer's disciplinary rules as in effect unquestionable.]

But there is in fact good reason to suppose that the effects of law are much less dramatic than this individualizing would suggest. The law clearly does provide an individual remedy, but one that is generally used by those who have no collective alternative. These will generally be the unorganized or those with little collective strength. Elsewhere employees will continue to define an issue as an individual or collective one for the reasons suggested above. It is extremely unlikely that where employees have a collective interest in a certain practice which contravenes employers' rules, they will let an employer enforce such rules – albeit with procedural and other safeguards insisted on by tribunals – simply because of the availability of tribunals in cases where procedures or good personnel management practices have not been followed. If this does not suggest positive improvements to be made in the law, it does suggest reasons why industrial disputes over discipline and dismissal have probably not declined since the introduction of unfair dismissal law and indeed there is no reason to suggest that the extension of this law by the Employment Protection Act will cause the number to diminish.

The variance between social and legal norms of discipline and dismissal that we have noted suggests that the general view that the law provides a statutory floor of rights for individual employees needs refining. Two corollaries of this view are that the law provides individual rights where collective bargaining is absent and that it provides a base upon which unions can build by collective bargaining. The 'holes' in the statutory floor of rights through which the unorganized and the unqualified can slip have been noted in other contexts. We would further suggest, from the example of unfair dismissal law, that the type of remedies the law gives individuals and the principles on which these are given may differ not only in *extent* but also in *kind* from those achieved by collective bargaining. This means, firstly, that individuals do not get – in the tribunal machinery – a sort of legal substitute for collective bargaining, and, secondly, that the legal principles enumerated in tribunals are not always seen as appropriate in collective bargaining situations. One implication of this may be that law which promotes collective bargaining directly may improve individual rights in employment more than law which gives employees individual rights against an employer.

Does this view of the relationship between collective bargaining and statutory regulation of employment accord with the views of that relationship which you have derived from reading the present chapter?

4
Termination of employment

1 Introduction – the rise and fall of job property?

It may well be that the twenty years from 1963 to 1983 will in retrospect be regarded as the two decades which saw the rise of the idea of job property in our labour law – and also, perhaps, its partial or complete fall. The point has certainly been reached where it seems useful to survey the state of the law about termination of employment by reference to the idea of job property. For this purpose it is necessary to attempt to define the concept. Job property is the interest, viewed as proprietary in nature, which a worker has in the continuation of his employment as the result of legal measures or social systems which protect the expectation and security of continued employment. We can illustrate this notion by taking the case of a fixed-term contract of employment with ten years to run. Let us suppose that a legal process existed which guaranteed that the employee could not be dismissed within that time and provided the remedy of reinstatement for the employee dismissed within that time. In that case the expectation of ten years' continued employment might well be regarded, in the discourse that has been current in recent years, as an example of job property. The same would be true where that degree of job security was guaranteed by a process of collective bargaining and grievance procedure covering dismissals. In these cases the employee is in that sense regarded as owning the right to his job; or, according to the terminology sometimes used, owning the job itself.

It should be emphasized from the outset that the notion of job property normally involves a loose, extended use of the idea of property. It would generally be accepted that a precise use of the word property implies some idea of a right to exclude third parties from possession of or access to the object of the property right in question. The use of the word property may also have connotations of the alienability of the object of the property right in question, though this is generally regarded as of lesser significance in the identification of proprietary rights. The idea of ownership of jobs does not necessarily or even normally fall within the scope of proprietary rights as precisely understood. The protection of job security, upon which the notion of job property is based, may well be a protection solely against a single employer which neither binds third parties nor is transferable to third parties. But to say this much is not to deprive the idea of job property of its interest or importance or to relegate it to the status of a merely irrational misnomer. On the contrary, it makes it the more challenging to discover why the habit of viewing job security as proprietary in nature has arisen and why that proprietary characterization has been a force in the recent development of labour law. An examination of these questions gives rise to a method of analysis and evaluation of recent trends in the law concerning the termination of employment.

In order to explain the growth of ideas of job property in our labour law we must digress briefly into the area of public office-holding. It is often maintained that our labour law makes no general distinction between public and private employment. Yet in one sense a fundamentally different treatment is accorded to public as opposed to private employment, for public employment is to a considerable extent viewed in terms of office-holding, to which very different assumptions are applied. So much is this the case that office-holding and the law relating to it are usually regarded as no part of the concerns of employment law. This is understandable in the sense that in the past public offices very often resembled franchises rather than ordinary employment relationships; but in this way it escapes notice that we do in fact have a well-developed distinct law of public employment. There is a long history of public office-holding being regarded as proprietary in character. From the seventeenth century onwards, tenures of office, for example, in the civil service, were styled as freeholds. They could be disposed of by sale or by inheritance. We shall examine the extent of tenure of public offices later on (p. 435). Our present point is that a consideration of this system of tenured public offices helps us to explain what is meant by job property. The nomenclatures applied to tenured offices – freeholds, reversions etc. – were not the source but a consequence of their being regarded as proprietary in nature. The same is true of their alienability.

The reason why, and the sense in which, these public offices were regarded as proprietary was that the holder's expectation of continuance in office was secure. The security was conferred by convention and by customary law. This observation enables us to suggest a general proposition. It is that the idea of job property is a concretization of the idea of job security. The idea of job security is in turn an abstract notion expressing the existence of social or legal mechanisms controlling and restricting the employer's freedom to terminate the employment relationship. The existence of such controls is necessary to the existence of job property as properly understood. This fact has a very important corollary. The corollary is that mechanisms for compensation for loss of employment, or mechanisms for entitling employed persons to compensation or remuneration after the termination of employment do not *ipso facto* tend to create job security or job property. This applies to severance payments and to pensions even if those payments and pensions reflect, as they often do, the length of service of the employed person in question. The fact that such rights to payment reflect accrued service leads to their being regarded as accrued rights and the expectation of those payments may well be regarded as proprietary in character. But, and this is crucial, these accrued rights are not job property, for they are not rights to future employment. The discourse about job security and job property is often confused by the failure to make that distinction. It is of course true that compensation mechanisms may have the purpose and effect of controlling decisions about termination of employment. For example, we shall see (p. 653) that the Employment Act 1982 made compensation provisions in relation to dismissal for membership or non-membership of trade unions which were deliberately set at prohibitively high levels with the aim of preventing employers from terminating employment on those grounds. But in such a case the measures are compensatory only in form; in substance they are measures of control, and so do not impinge upon the point we have made about the irrelevance of compensation measures to job property.

In the context of British labour law, developments tending towards the recognition of job property can usefully be contrasted with a certain kind of contractualism associated with the individual contract of employment. In the late eighteenth and nineteenth centuries particularly, the definition and exposition of the employment relationship in contractual terms (see Kahn-Freund, 'Blackstone's Neglected Child: The Contract of Employment' (1977) 93 *LQR* 508) represented an emphasis on the freedom to constitute the employment relationship on a short-term basis in which the employer assumed the minimum of responsibility for the employee's job security. This was in contrast with the pre-industrial view of the employment relationship which stressed the extent of mutual obligation on a much longer-term basis. The contrast was particularly marked in the common law of the USA which came in the nineteenth century to envisage the contract of employment as a contract at will (see Sanford Jacoby (1982) 5 *Comparative Labour Law* 85).

As we shall see below (p. 432) the common law of England did not go quite so far in the direction of purely economic as distinct from social contracts of employment. As Alan Fox shows in *Beyond Contract* (see above, p. 108), in English law it was thought preferable to preserve some of the elements of pre-nineteenth-century master and servant law in the nineteenth-century exposition of the contract of employment so that it would operate as a framework of discipline for employees. Moreover British employers, although free to make so-called 'minute contracts', i.e. contracts terminable by a minute's notice, were generally unwilling for quite so extensive a trade-off between their freedom to dismiss and the employees' freedom to strike. Even so, by the end of the nineteenth century the combination of common law and employers' contracting practice had created a legal régime for manual workers in industry which consisted generally of hourly or at best weekly contracts of employment, and this represented the low ebb of job property in British labour law.

In Britain the trade unions in the mid-nineteenth century had positively espoused this species of contractualism because of the freedom to strike which it conferred. They were not, perhaps until the Employment Protection Act of 1975, to seek to challenge by legislative means the wide managerial prerogative of dismissal conferred by this contractualism, and in so far as a countervailing collective power was brought to bear on dismissals, it took the form mainly of threatening or taking industrial action in the face of dismissals on an *ad hoc* basis rather than the form of joint regulation of dismissal decisions by means of collective bargaining. Frederic Meyers in his study *Ownership of Jobs* (UCLA Institute of Industrial Relations, 1964) shows on the other hand how in the United States the true development of ideas of job property occurred as a product of collective bargaining whereby unions won a degree of joint regulation of dismissal decisions and in particular achieved the recognition of employees' seniority rights as a constraint upon managerial prerogative.

The notice provisions of the Contracts of Employment Act 1963 (see below, p. 434), and the severance payment provisions of the Redundancy Payments Act 1965 (see below, p. 528) represented in our view fairly cautious attempts to embody the seniority bargaining model in a British 'floor of rights' programme of employment legislation; but this programme, as we shall see, stopped well short of an institutionalized take-over of employers' decisions about dismissal. The idea of job property was there, but the actuality was not.

The nearest approach to a general realization of job property yet achieved in Britain occurred in the form of the unfair dismissal legislation first introduced by the Industrial Relations Act 1971. In its conception this legislation made substantial steps in the direction of job property, a trend even more prominent in the reforms in the unfair dismissal legislation made by the Employment Protection Act 1975. But the application of the legislation by industrial tribunals and its interpretation by the courts, however even-handed as between employers and employed, have, as we shall see, served to demonstrate the residual strength of contractualist restrictions upon job property. Nevertheless, the unfair dismissal legislation, however much eviscerated in its application and construction, has demonstrated four very important propositions about job property. The first is that the protection of job security and hence job property is very powerfully served by a process which requires *reasons* for dismissal to be substantiated, for such a process exposes the merits of those reasons to scrutiny. The second is that job property is likewise vindicated by a process which exposes the *procedure* of dismissal to scrutiny, for such scrutiny tends to establish control over the substantive decisions. The third proposition is that adequate control over duration of employment requires control over the content of employment as well; for otherwise job property can be undermined by adverse action by employers falling short of dismissal. In other words, there has to be the capacity to control constructive dismissal as well as outright dismissal. The fourth proposition is that the protection of job property depends crucially upon the availability of remedies which place the employer under some real pressure to reinstate the worker whose job security it is sought to vindicate. That, as we shall see, has not generally been the case with the unfair dismissal legislation.

The law of unfair dismissal, then, may have failed to realize the protection of job property; but it has indicated the conditions on which a legal system might lay claim to achieving such a protection. It is beginning, as we shall see, to emerge that there may be the potentiality for such protection in our legal system by the interaction of statute law and public law (see below, p. 513). But this is to hint at possibilities which must as yet be regarded as strictly speculative. The immediate fact is that the notion of job property, as thus described, does at least provide a useful framework for the analysis and evaluation of the development and present state of the law about the termination of employment.

2 The duration of employment

One of the important factors in an assessment of job property is the position of the law concerning the duration of employment. That position has three aspects today. The first concerns the common law and statute law regarding the duration of the contract of employment. The second concerns tenure of office. The third concerns the statutory concept of normal retirement age.

(a) The contract of employment

The law of the contract of employment evolved in the eighteenth and nineteenth centuries out of the older law concerning the master and servant relationship. It acquired a framework based on the pre-industrial custom of annual hiring especially of agricultural and domestic servants. The employment was envisaged as a series of contracts each for the fixed term of a year. This conferred relatively high security of tenure. In the nineteenth century the preference developed for more limited contracts of employment, by which employers could minimize their economic risks and employees could maximize their freedom to strike (in face of the criminal penalties for employees' breaches of contracts which survived until virtually abolished by the Master and Servant Act 1867 and the Employers and Workmen Act 1875). This growing preference dictated the view that the primary form of the contract of employment was the contract of indefinite duration terminable by the notice which was reasonable for the particular type of employee concerned.

By implying 'reasonable' notice in the absence of express stipulation about notice, the courts could follow employment custom and in particular could reflect social differentiation between manual and non-manual workers in industry. For whereas white-collar workers were customarily entitled to substantial periods of notice such as one month, three months, six months or even a year, manual workers were typically regarded as entitled to a week's, an hour's or even a nominal minute's notice. This was an important aspect of the differentiation between 'staff' and manual workers or salaried workers and wage-earners which we have previously considered in relation to the content of employment (see above, p. 320). In its heyday it expressed the weakness of manual employees' legal protection against the exercise of managerial prerogative and managerial discipline, as the following case well shows. (By the same token, of course, it expressed the width of the contractual freedom to strike until the courts became unwilling to view strikes as terminating the contract of employment, a matter to which we return in a moment.)

Marshall v. *English Electric Ltd* [1945] 1 All ER 653 (CA)

An engineering worker was suspended for two days without pay as a disciplinary measure. He sought a declaration that this was contrary to the Essential Work Order, a piece of wartime delegated legislation regulating employment in essential industries. The EWO allowed disciplinary suspension provided that it was a practice incorporated in the worker's contract of service.

LORD GODDARD: We are here dealing with a man whose contract of service was liable to be determined by an hour's notice given by either side, as indeed are those of the great majority of manual workers in factories and kindred establishments throughout the country. *Sagar* v. *Ridehalgh* [above, p. 276] shows that an established practice at a particular factory may be incorporated into a workman's contract of service, and whether he knew of it or not, it must be presumed that he accepted employment on the same terms as applied to other workers in that factory. The findings of the judge show that there was this practice at the respondents' factory: the employers had always asserted a right to suspend, the workmen had acquiesced in it and moreover in one instance had insisted on this penalty being imposed on an inspector who had struck a youth. It seems, therefore, that in the days before the Essential Work Order men including the plaintiff who could have left at an hour's notice if they did not like this practice have continued in their employment with knowledge of it and have insisted on its enforcement when they thought it right to do so. In my opinion it follows that the practice ought to be regarded as incorporated in the contract of service. But it is said that when analysed this practice is not suspension but dismissal in the case of a man subject to an hour's notice. As to this the respondents say that the contract is continuous; it does not renew from hour to hour but exists until notice is given and may last, and very likely in many cases does, for 20 years or more. So they contend that if they merely suspend and do not give a man notice they do not dismiss him but merely tell him that he is not to work for a specified time and they are not going to pay him during that time. What then is left of the contract of service during that time? Everything, say the respondents, except the obligation to work on the one side and to pay on the other. But in the case of an hourly servant are there any rights or obligations left except possibly the obligation to pay for one hour? It was suggested there might be pension rights, but there was no evidence that the appellant had any right to a pension, nor would one expect that a pension was secured as of right to a man subject to dismissal at one hour's notice.

In my opinion what is called suspension is in truth dismissal with an intimation that at the end of so many days, or it may be hours, the man will be re-employed if he chooses to apply for reinstatement.

The customary differentiation between the relatively tenured contract of the staff worker and the relatively severable contract of the manual industrial worker was often seen in terms of an equation between the notice period and the period of assessment or payment of remuneration, so that the monthly-paid worker was entitled to a month's notice and the hourly-paid worker to an hour's notice. This rule systematically linked the distinction between wages and salaries to the tenure aspect of staff status. Another version of the same complex of customs was to be found in the view that the employment relationship was still, as with the old yearly hiring, constituted of a series of fixed-term contracts, with the length of the fixed term corresponding to the payment period (i.e. monthly, weekly or hourly fixed terms). This view of the ordinary contract of employment was reasserted as recently as 1977 in the judgments of the EAT, Phillips J. presiding, in the frustration cases of *Egg Stores (Stamford Hill) Ltd* v. *Leibovici* [1977] ICR 260 and *Hart* v. *Marshall & Sons (Bulwell) Ltd* [1977] ICR 539. But it is by now a rather archaic view of the legal nature of the employment, one which minimizes the element of job property and one which overlooks the impact of the statutory provisions concerning notice, to which we must now turn.

The Contracts of Employment Act 1963 took a modest step in the direction of greater tenure particularly for industrial manual workers. It introduced minimum periods of notice for employees depending on length of service and minimum remuneration during such periods of notice. They are minimum periods in the sense that the contract of employment may still validly provide for longer notice periods, whether by express provision or by the operation of the common law implied right to a reasonable period of notice. The original scale of these rights was one week's notice after two years rising to four weeks' after four years. Successive amendments have enlarged upon these rights, so that EPCA 1978 s.49(1) now provides for one week's notice after four weeks and up to two years' employment and thereafter one week per year of service, up to a maximum of twelve weeks. S.50 ensures the right to be paid during such notice at the rate of the statutory 'week's pay' (see above, pp. 326–8), which excludes non-contractual overtime. These provisions destroyed the symmetry which had hitherto prevailed between employer's notice and employee's notice, for s.49(2) merely requires employees employed for four weeks or more to give one week's notice regardless of length of service. They also destroy the interconnection between notice and payment periods. They thus generally impart a minimum tenure greater than that provided by the common law. One of the initial aims of the legislators was to control wildcat strike action by requiring a correspondingly greater notice to terminate from the employee. This intention was abandoned before the Bill became an Act, but the sense remained that there was now a statutory framework by which the contract of employment imposed more than transient mutual obligations. Surely therefore it was not entirely a coincidence that the courts should so soon after the passage of the 1963 Act, in *Rookes* v. *Barnard* [1964] AC 1129 and *Stratford* v. *Lindley* [1965] AC 269, develop a doctrine which virtually foreclosed the possibility of treating strike action as the exercise of the freedom to terminate the contract of employment, deeming it instead to be normally breach of contract even if preceded by notice (see below, p. 719). It was as if the courts were asserting the responsibilities which they saw as correlative to the new rights that employees now enjoyed. The modern approach to the duration of the contract of employment perhaps owes more to the 1963 legislation and its successors than is often acknowledged.

(b) Tenure of public office

In recent years attention has rightly been directed to the need to overcome artificial conceptual barriers placed between the law of employment and the law of office holding; see for instance Ganz, 'Public Law and Dismissal from Employment' (1967) 30 *MLR* 288. There has been valuable development towards an account of office-holding as part of our labour law; see Napier, 'Office and Office-Holder in British Labour Law' in *In Memoriam Sir Otto Kahn-Freund* (Munich, 1980), at pp. 593 *et seq.* These processes can perhaps be furthered by articulating the modern law of tenure of public office as part of the law of duration of employment. Of late, as we shall see below (p. 513) there has been much preoccupation with the extent of the applicability of public law principles, particularly those of natural justice, to dismissal from public employment. That has obscured the question, on what tenure is public office now held?

Although the history of public office-holding would no doubt furnish examples of tenure of office in perpetuity or for life, we can effectively confine our attention to two tenures of offices which have been applicable to public employment in recent times. These are office-holding at pleasure and office-holding during good behaviour. In the first of these the office-holder is subject to dismissal at will; in the second he is subject to dismissal for good cause. They represent the two alternatives to the contractual employment relationship in Lord Reid's famous tripartite analysis of the employment/office-holding relationship in *Ridge* v. *Baldwin* [1964] AC 40, 65. The difficulty about them is that although it is fairly universally perceived that they no longer represent a complete legal framework for the public employment relationship, there seems equally universal uncertainty as to what that legal framework now is. In order to find the explanation, we have to make a sharp distinction between Crown service and other public employment because Crown service is attended by its own particular conceptual legal problems such as that of whether it can ever, or does generally, take contractual form.

It would seem that in public service which is not Crown employment the office-holder during good behaviour typically also now has a contract of employment, which in the absence of express provision for termination by notice is viewed as a contract for permanent employment, i.e. until retirement unless the employee is dismissed for good cause. This is borne out by the rather under-estimated decision of the House of Lords in *McClelland* v. *Northern Ireland General Health Services Board* [1957] AC 594, which concerned what was apparently a gross case of discrimination against married women, where the Board purported to exercise an implicit power to give six months' notice to a senior clerical officer whose post had been advertised as 'permanent and pensionable' and whose conditions of service referred to dismissal only for gross misconduct, inefficiency or unfitness for continued employment. In holding, admittedly only by a narrow majority, that there was no power to dismiss except on these grounds, the House of Lords was marking the difference in approach between the private contract of employment and the contract of employment covering a public office-holding relationship. It would seem that this form of public office-holding relationship is widespread in the public service. One particular manifestation of it has become the subject of controversy in recent years, namely the relationship between the tenured university teacher and his university. There have been suggestions for legislation to prevent universities from conferring such tenures in future on the ground that their existence stands in the way of necessary economy measures which universities might otherwise wish to take. The argument is not in fact as narrowly confined to the question of academic tenure as it is generally perceived to be.

The generality of this kind of tenured relationship in the public service is also reflected by the nature of Crown service. It seems to be the case that for constitutional reasons the tenure of office which the Crown servant holds of the Crown will be a holding at the pleasure of the Crown rather than a holding during good behaviour except for certain traditionally accepted categories of the latter tenure, such as that of judges. And it is probably not correct to view Crown servants as having contracts of employment which confer a more secure tenure, for although the unfair dismissal legislation has been applied to Crown servants (see EPCA 1978, s.138), it has never been enacted by statute or clearly decided by the courts that the employment relationship with the Crown is or even can be contractual in its nature. But Crown servants are employed on terms and conditions which are drawn directly from or based on the model of the Civil Service Pay and Conditions of Service Code, which is promulgated under the authority of the Civil Service Order in Council 1982. That Code envisages 'permanent' employment for established civil servants. It makes the following provisions about the date of retirement:

Para. 10441. An officer may on age grounds retire at his own wish or be retired at the instigation of his department. In either case retirement may be effected when the officer has reached his minimum retirement age or at any time thereafter. The date of retirement of any officer who is being retired is a matter entirely within the discretion of the head of each department.

Para. 10442. Any officer who has not completed 20 years' reckonable service on reaching 60 should, provided he is fit, efficient and willing to remain in service, be allowed to continue until he has completed 20 years' reckonable service or has reached age 65, whichever is the earlier. Officers with short service generally have special claims to retention.

In a recent decision of the EAT, the following comment was made about the status of these provisions of the Code in relation to an employee of the Department of Trade and Industry in the coastguard service:

Secretary of State for Trade and Industry v. *Douglas* [1983] IRLR 63
(EAT) at p. 65, para. 12

LORD MCDONALD: The first matter to consider is whether the Civil Service Code applied to the terms and conditions of the respondent's service. In our opinion it did. Counsel for the respondent sought to argue that the code, and in particular para. 10441, did not apply to the respondent as it was never formally incorporated in his contract of employment. We cannot accept this. The code is statutory in origin and mandatory in its terms. It confers a discretion upon departments as to the circumstances in which they may extend an employee's service beyond the age of 60 but this does not affect the normal retiring age. We would not expect it necessarily to be incorporated, either directly or by reference in the letter of appointment of every civil servant. We certainly do not consider that the absence of any reference to it involves that the code does not apply.

It is suggested with respect that it is unclear whether the coastguard could have had a contract of employment as such. But the passage does serve to identify the position of civil servants today which, correctly viewed, is that they have a public employment relationship with the Crown on the terms and conditions of the Civil Service Code, or Staff Codes based on it, which provide for employment till retirement subject to earlier termination for good cause. It will have become apparent in the course of this discussion that the duration of the contract of employment and even more particularly the duration of the public service relationship are dependent on the notion of retirement age. We may usefully turn to some consideration of the concept of retirement age, which has in recent years been the subject of a number of decisions interpreting the statutory notion of 'normal retirement age'.

(c) Retirement age

It is notable how a certain tradition or habit of legal analysis can cause major social phenomena to remain entirely below the threshold of legal consciousness. No doubt labour law shares this characteristic with many other legal topics. A good example is the lack of attention accorded to retirement in the traditional account of the duration and termination of the individual employment relationship. Yet no doubt retirement is the mode of termination of a very high proportion of all employment relationships. But the scantness of the attention accorded to retirement should not be regarded merely as an instance of lawyers' exclusive preoccupation, which Otto Kahn-Freund always stressed, with the pathological as opposed to the normal social condition. There is rather more to it than that. The accepted analysis of the contract of employment envisages its termination either by the expiry of a term of years expressly agreed upon – say two or five or ten years – or by the giving of reasonable notice. Those are the bounds set on what is otherwise envisaged as a contract 'of indeterminate duration'. The social reality is that contracts of employment are usually, so far as the expectations of the parties are concerned, contracts until retirement age subject to earlier termination as prescribed, i.e. by non-renewal of a fixed term, by notice, or by dismissal for cause. The failure or refusal of the law of the contract of employment to reflect that social expectation has important presentational consequences; the insecurity of the contractual relationship is thereby stressed and job property is minimized. It may also have important legal consequences, as the following discussion will seek to show.

The question of retirement age has come into prominence in recent years because it has been one of the policies governing the unfair dismissal legislation to deny the protection of that legislation to employees employed after retirement age except so far as dismissal for trade-union membership, non-membership or activity is concerned. This policy seems to reflect an unstated assumption that people employed beyond retirement age should count themselves fortunate to be employed at all and should not therefore expect the benefit of protective legislation in relation to their employment. There is also an assumption that it is unobjectionable to discriminate against women by denying them that protection in many cases five years before they would, if men, be denied it; that assumption rests on the premise that the social security scheme makes that discrimination in the first place, by fixing the state pensionable age as 65 for men but 60 for women.

In *Roberts* v. *Cleveland Area Health Authority* [1979] ICR 558, it was held that s.6(4) of the SDA 1975 protected a contractual retirement age of 60 for women and 65 for men; and in *Southampton Health Authority* v. *Marshall* [1983] IRLR 237, it was held by the EAT that neither Article 119 of the Treaty of Rome nor Directive 76/207 of 1976 (the equal treatment directive) could be invoked to challenge that state of affairs until their paramountcy over s.6(4) was established by a decision of the House of Lords or the European Court. In *Burton* v. *British Railways Board* [1982] ICR 329, moreover, the European Court took the view that Directive 79/7 of 1979 (equal treatment in state social security schemes) should not prejudice the right of member states to determine their own pensionable ages. It seems possible, however, that there may shortly be a proposal to establish in the UK a common, flexible, state pensionable age of 63 for men and women alike. A recommendation to that effect has been made in the Third Report for 1981–2 of the House of Commons Social Services Committee – see *Industrial Relations Review & Report* No. 291 (March 1983), p. 2. Such a proposal would, if implemented, eliminate much of the present difficulty but will of course encounter the objection that it diminishes the state pension rights of women.

The retirement-age disqualification from unfair dismissal protection is expressed in the following terms:

EPCA 1978, s.64(1): Subject to [the saving for trade-union membership, non-membership or activity, the right not to be unfairly dismissed] does not apply to the dismissal of an employee from any employment if the employee . . . (b) on or before the effective date of termination attained the age which, in the undertaking in which he was employed, was the normal retiring age for an employee holding the position which he held or, if a man, attained the age of sixty-five or, if a woman, attained the age of sixty.

This provision is basically ambiguous in failing to specify what the relation is between the normal-retiring-age condition and the age 65–60 condition. The House of Lords in the case of *Nothman* v. *Barnet London Borough Council* [1979] ICR 111 decided that the normal-retiring-age condition had primacy, so that the age 65–60 condition applied only in the absence of a normal retiring age. This placed even more weight on the concept of normal retiring age. The NIRC, Sir John Donaldson its President presiding, had decided that this concept should be construed as a purely descriptive one – *Ord* v. *Maidstone Hospital Management Committee* [1974] IRLR 80; it should mean the age at which people usually retired at that position in that undertaking.

But a different view later prevailed in which the concept was normatively defined – it meant the age at which a person must retire unless his employment is extended by agreement with his employer – *Howard* v. *Department for National Savings* [1981] ICR 208 – and that requirement was to be derived primarily or, as some argued, solely from the contract of employment (compare with the *Howard* case, *Post Office* v. *Wallser* [1981] 1 All ER 668). The House of Lords affirmed this approach, while at the same time rejecting an exclusively contractual method of definition of it, in *Waite* v. *Government Communications Headquarters* (1983). Their approach is set out in the following extract from the speech of Lord Fraser with which the other four Law Lords agreed.

Waite v. *Government Communications Headquarters*
[1983] ICR 359

LORD FRASER: I therefore reject the view that the contractual retiring age conclusively fixes the normal retiring age. I accept that where there is a contractual retiring age, applicable to all, or nearly all, the employees holding the position which the appellant employee held, there is a presumption that the contractual retiring age is the normal retiring age for the group. But it is a presumption which, in my opinion, can be rebutted by evidence that there is in practice some higher age at which employees holding the position are regularly retired, and which they have reasonably come to regard as their normal retiring age. Having regard to the social policy which seems to underlie the Act, namely the policy of securing fair treatment, as regards compulsory retirement, as between different employees holding the same position, the expression 'normal retiring age' conveys the idea of an age at which employees in the group can reasonably expect to be compelled to retire, unless there is some special reason in a particular case for a different age to apply. 'Normal' in this context is not a mere synonym for 'usual'. The word 'usual' suggests a purely statistical approach by ascertaining the age at which the majority of employees actually retire, without regard to whether some of them may have been retained in office until a higher age for special reasons, such as a temporary shortage of employees with a particular skill, or a temporary glut of work, or personal consideration for an employee who has not sufficient reckonable service to qualify for a full pension. The proper test is, in my view, not merely statistical. It is to ascertain what would be the reasonable expectation or understanding of the employees holding that position at the relevant time. The contractual retiring age will prima facie be the normal retiring age, but it may be displaced by evidence that it is regularly departed from in practice. The evidence may show that the contractual retirement age has been superseded by some definite higher age, and, if so, that will have become the normal retiring age. Or the evidence may show merely that the contractual retiring age has been abandoned and that employees retire at a variety of higher ages. In that case there will be no normal retiring age and the statutory alternatives of 65 for a man and 60 for a woman will apply.

Although this passage stresses that contractual terms are not decisive, it also contains some indications that they will usually determine the issue in practice. This is borne out by the decision of the House of Lords in the case before them (the facts are set out below, at p. 443), where they held that the fact that one quarter of the relevant comparator group had been retained beyond the age of sixty 'fell far short of showing that the contractual retiring age had been abandoned or departed from' (ibid., p. 1018). So the primacy of contract is fairly clear.

The normative and primarily contractual approach to the concept of normal retirement age has required a consideration of how far employees are contractually promised employment until the age when, in purely descriptive terms, they normally retire. The notion of a mandatory contractual retirement age coupled with discretionary extension has encouraged a non-contractual construction of many undertakings, giving employees cause to hope they will be retained beyond their minimum retirement age. The outcome is one in which managerial discretion is maximized and job security minimized. The process is sufficiently important to warrant three citations by way of example.

The first of these is *BP Chemicals Ltd* v. *Joseph* [1980] IRLR 55 (EAT). Here the employee had originally been employed subject to written terms and conditions stating that the normal retirement age for men was 65. In 1970, following a series of take-overs, he was offered and accepted a transfer of pension rights into the BP pensions scheme, for which the normal retirement age was 60. As the result of anxiety felt by this employee and others, a letter was sent by BP Chemicals to its staff which gave reassurance about the prospect of working till 65 in the following terms:

BP Chemicals v. *Joseph* [1980] IRLR 55 (EAT)
at p. 57, para. 11

SLYNN J.: . . . It appears that apart from the anxiety which Mr Joseph felt about the change in the retiring age from 65 to 60 others too were troubled; and so the company put out a statement which was supplied to managers in local places of work ('The Noel Gee letter'). That document was intended to be used for the purpose of explanation to existing staff. It stated that 'the normal retirement age under the BP pension scheme is 60. Staff who joined the BP Chemicals when the normal retirement age was 65, that is, before 1.6.70, will want to know whether transfer into the BP scheme means that they will no longer be able to work on to 65 if they want to.' It then said that the company did not guarantee employment until a given age, any more than staff bound themselves not to leave. It referred to the view that it was in the interests of industry, the company and the staff that the age at which members actually retired should come down steadily. It went on:

> Nevertheless, older staff with short service have certain expectations of security of employment with the company and look forward to the prospect of earning reasonable retirement pensions.
>
> The company will, therefore, continue to employ staff beyond the new normal retirement age, though not beyond 65, irrespective of the option they have exercised, provided:
>
> i) They have expressed a desire to stay on, eg, because of a relatively unfavourable pension position;
> ii) It is practicable from the company point of view;
> iii) In the opinion of the company they are medically fit and doing a satisfactory job; and
> iv) They are not seriously blocking promotion or preventing reorganisation of work.
>
> Staff thus continuing to work beyond the new normal retirement age, whom the company subsequently no longer wishes to retain, will be given adequate notice of the company's intention to retire them.

The EAT held that the pension transfer had brought the contractual pension age down to 60, and that the letter of reassurance had not brought it up to 65 again; partly because it was issued after the pension transfer for this particular employee and partly for the following reason:

[1980] IRLR 55, para. 18

The only matter which appears to have troubled the Tribunal was the doubt about the meaning of the Noel Gee letter. One thing is important in this case: this is not a situation where it is contended, as it was contended in *Stepney*, that any option was conferred which was legally enforceable. Here it is accepted that the statement put out was not intended to be, and was not regarded as being, contractually binding. Accordingly the letter is not a document which creates a contractual right upon which any employee could rely. The Tribunal were satisifed of this and both sides have accepted it before us. It was a statement of the intention and policy which no doubt the company, in 1970, intended to follow. The mere fact that the Tribunal and the parties have had doubts about the precise ambit of this document indeed supports the view that it was not intended to be contractually binding. Had it been necessary to express an opinion about the matter, we ourselves would have been disposed to the view that Mr Joseph was someone who was of 'short service' within the meaning of the document, though there may be doubt as to whether the policy stated is in the result limited to such persons. Moreover we would not have agreed with the definition of 'practicable' given by the Industrial Tribunal, although in the result we think that they may well have been entitled to accept that the change in economic factors, and the need to reduce staff by not continuing to employ those who had reached age 60, rather than to make redundant younger persons, might well have justified the company in saying that it was not 'practicable' from the company's point of view to retain someone like Mr Joseph beyond the age of 60, so that in any event he was not someone who could claim, on the facts as they happened in 1979, the benefit of the company's intention in 1970.

This approach reveals a real reluctance to accord contractual effect to undertakings to the employee about retirement age, a reluctance further demonstrated in *Duke* v. *Reliance Systems Ltd* [1982] ICR 449 (EAT). Here a clerical worker was employed under a contract of employment which referred to a voluntary pension scheme 'available to all full-time employees aged 18 and under 65'. The pension scheme, to which this employee belonged, had a normal pensionable age of 65 for men and women alike. The employee was retired at the age of 60 in pursuance of a policy of retiring women at 60. The EAT held that this employee had no right to complain of being retired at 60, either because the practice of retiring women at 60 gave rise to an extra-contractual normal retiring age of 60, or on the basis of the age 60 for women rule in the statute. The important point was that the employee had no contractual right to stay till 65 for the following reasons:

Duke v. *Reliance Systems Ltd* [1982] ICR 449 (EAT)
at p. 453D–G

BROWNE-WILKINSON J.: In our view it is impossible to imply any contractual term that the normal retiring age for women was 65. Such implication could only be made either on the grounds that there was a custom and practice to that effect or that such implication was necessary to give business efficacy to the contract, due weight being given in any event to the reference in the contract to the pension scheme which had a normal pensionable age of 65 for women. As to implication by custom and practice, the finding of the industrial tribunal that the practice was for women to retire at the age of 60 is fatal. As to implication on the grounds of business efficacy, such implication can only be made if *both* parties would have regarded the term as an obvious and necessary term to adopt to make their contract effective. The first point to note is that there is no need for any contract of employment to specify a normal retiring age. Many, probably most, contracts of employment do not contain any provision as to age of retirement: age of retirement is normally a matter of policy adopted by the employer, not of contractual arrangement between employer and employee. Secondly, although the reference in the contract to the pension scheme was misleading to the employee and would plainly have made her think that there was an implied term allowing her to continue to work until her normal pensionable age of 65, in view of the employers' long-standing policy notwithstanding the pension scheme that women should retire at the age of 60, it is plain that if the employers had been asked at the date of contract whether there was a contractual term permitting women employees to work to the age of 65 they would certainly not have agreed that there was any such term. Therefore, in our view, the employee's claim fails if she has to show that under the contract of employment alone her normal age of retirement was fixed at the age of 65.

The third example of this counter-contractual approach to assurances of employment till 65 occurs in the decision in the Court of Appeal in *Waite* v. *Government Communications Headquarters* (1983), which was later affirmed by the House of Lords on a point different from the one with which we are now concerned. The facts are set out in the judgment of the Court of Appeal as follows:

Waite v. *Government Communications Headquarters*
[1983] ICR 359

ACKNER L.J.: The employee was born on October 30th, 1917. After a distinguished career in the Army he retired in December 1961, aged 44. He had been the commanding officer of a Royal Signals Regiment and on his retirement he took up an appointment as a higher executive officer in the London Communications Security Agency which was the predecessor of the Government Communications Headquarters, the respondent employers. He thus became a 'temporary' civil servant, a status which he enjoyed until the 13th March 1967 when he became an 'established' civil servant. On 30th April 1978 his employment ended. He was then re-employed in a lower rank without prejudice to his contention that there was no power for him to be so retired. . . .

The employers' case, quite simply, was that when the employee accepted the appointment to a permanent post in the Civil Service in March 1967, he became subject to the regulations which are now contained largely in the Civil Service Pay and Conditions of Service Code (the 'Estacode') which provided in essence for a minimum retiring age of 60 years, after which age it was entirely within the discretion of the Department whether or not to retain him up to the age of 65.

The employee's case was that in 1961, when he was considering the advertisement inviting experienced communications officers who were leaving the armed forces on premature retirement to apply to join the London Communications Security Agency, his main aim was to achieve a second career which would last until he was 65. He contended that the terms of the interview which he attended, and the letter of 11th October 1961 offering him the appointment, made it clear that he was to be employed up to the age of 65. It was argued on his behalf that to impose on him a retirement age of 60 was a variation of his contract which the respondents were not competent to make. They had failed to make it abundantly clear to him that his appointment as an established civil servant would have the effect of changing his retiring age.

The Court of Appeal found it clear beyond argument that these transactions gave the employee no possibility of arguing that his true retirement age was 65. It is quite striking that their counter-contractual perceptions of the expectation of employment till 65 are so strong as to make the result seem self-evident in the eyes of the court:

ACKNER L.J. [ibid. at p. 365]: . . . The position in our view was quite a simple one.

The letter of the 11th October 1961 offering him his initial employment, stated, *inter alia*: 'This offer is, of course, subject to satisfactory references and to confirmation after a probationary period of 6 months. Thereafter there will be the prospect of employment until 65, subject to continued satisfactory service.'

Miss Slade for the employee, submitted that this letter gave an assurance that, subject to satisfactory service, Colonel Waite would be employed until age 65. Yet she firmly disavowed any suggestion that he had been provided with a fixed-term contract. In our judgment, all the letter did was to inform Colonel Waite that there was the hope, or expectation, that he might be employed until 65. There was no question of his being given an assurance to this effect. Of course, as a temporary civil servant, there was no question of his employment being pensionable.

Miss Slade further submitted that the offer that he become an established civil servant, if it be interpreted as only providing a normal retirement age of 60, would have been less advantageous than the terms of employment which he was enjoying at the time when the offer was made. We are quite unable to accept this submission. The offer of established employment gave him the assurance of employment up to the age of 60, whereas no such assurance then existed. It provided the prospect of retention until 65 and under the departmental policy, to which we will refer in greater detail later, even a right of appeal against a decision not to retain him until that age. Added to all this was the right to a pension where none had previously existed.

The letter of November 23, 1966 informing the employee of his opportunity to become an established civil servant said in terms: 'that the Treasury have approved the establishment within the C E S D of a department executive class which will be linked to the general service executive class for all purposes.' There was enclosed a super-annuation example as part of the material to assist the employee in coming to a conclusion as to whether to accept the offer of establishment. This showed the financial situation of a hypothetical established civil servant retiring at 62 years and 3 months.

The Industrial Tribunal, having considered the documents and heard oral evidence from the employee, found that he understood the implications of his becoming an established civil servant and, in particular, that he would thereafter be subject to the Civil Service Pay and Conditions of Service Code. Like the Employment Appeal Tribunal, from whose decision on May 7, 1981 the employee now appeals, we have no doubt at all that the industrial tribunal was correct in making this decision.

The employee did not appeal to the House of Lords on this point; for the purposes of his appeal to the House of Lords he accepted that his employment was governed solely by the Estacode rather than by the letter which had governed his initial employment. But the House of Lords made a further counter-contractual point about the meaning of paragraph 10442 of Estacode (which is set out above, at p. 437). They held that the effect of its provision that the officer 'should' in the stated circumstances be retained, was not to give the officer a right to be retained, because it was addressed to the departmental officer who would take the decision whether to retain, purely as an instruction as to the policy to be applied. This indicates the narrowness in practice of the approach of the House of Lords to the 'rights and reasonable expectations' of the employee which, as we have seen, they regarded as the determinant of normal retiring age.

There are, as we have said, particular difficulties in advancing a contractual analysis of civil service employment. But neither the Court of Appeal nor the House of Lords sees that as the nature of the problem. Their counter-contractual analysis is of common application to Crown employment and to other public-sector and private-sector employment. It seems anachronistic to analyse terms of employment relating to retirement age as if they dealt with a matter of marginal significance in which employers' discretions rather than employees' expectations were the overriding factor. The anachronism is intensified when it operates to limit the unfair dismissal jurisdiction of industrial tribunals. That is an interaction between the common law of the contract of employment and the statute law of employment protection which we shall encounter at a number of points in the present chapter.

3 The concept of dismissal

(a) Introduction

The floor of statutory protection for employees has been built primarily upon the termination of employment. Although employment-protection legislation now also deals with hiring and with the content of the employment relationship, its heartland is still to be found in the area of termination of employment. Thus the existence of employment-protection legislation has resulted in a requirement for a working concept of termination of employment by the employer to which statutory consequences can be attached. The word 'dismissal' has been adopted for this purpose and turned into a term of art. Hence we have a statutory concept of dismissal which, similarly defined, does duty under the two crucial pieces of employment-protection legislation associated with the termination of employment, namely the redundancy payments legislation (EPCA 1978, Part VI) and the unfair dismissal provisions of EPCA 1978, Part V.

It is worth noting that the concept of dismissal is not the inevitable choice for doing the job in hand. The ILO in its instruments which set standards in this area – Recommendation No. 119 of 1963 and now the 1982 Convention and Recommendation – uses the terminology of 'termination of employment at the initiative of the employer'. Although Napier in his admirably useful account of the new ILO Standards ((1983) 12 *ILJ* 17) describes this as 'a convoluted way of describing what is, to all intents and purposes, dismissal', there may nevertheless be some advantages in this conscious avoidance of the term 'dismissal'; some limitations which we shall see are readily ascribed to the concept of dismissal may be avoided. But the British legislators have never hesitated to use the notion of 'dismissal' while on the other hand feeling it necessary to enact a statutory definition of it; we set out by way of introduction to our discussion the relevant provision in relation to the law of unfair dismissal:

EPCA 1978, s.55(2): Subject to subsection (3), an employee shall be treated as dismissed by his employer if, but only if,
(a) the contract under which he is employed by the employer is terminated by the employer, whether it is so terminated by notice or without notice, or
(b) where under that contract he is employed for a fixed term that term expires without being renewed under the same contract, or
(c) the employee terminates that contract, with or without notice, in circumstances such that he is entitled to terminate it without notice by reason of the employer's conduct.

The interesting question arises, in relation to this statutory concept, of whether it has been or ought to be defined and developed in a neutral or an instrumental fashion. The problem may be stated as follows. Let us assume that Parliament in framing the legislation, and the courts in interpreting it, are concerned to further the general aim of employment protection in favour of the employee. Should they seek to further that purpose by a deliberately positive approach to the definition of dismissal? Or should they on the other hand view the concept of dismissal as a cautiously but firmly defined concept upon which further statutory and case-law branches may be grafted where necessary? We shall proceed to consider various aspects of the definition of dismissal with this underlying problem in mind and we shall discover that the courts have generally tended towards a policy-oriented or instrumental approach to the concept (i.e. an approach which seeks to use the concept of dismissal in such a way as to be instrumental in achieving the purposes of the legislation). We shall find, however, that the courts have been pulled in various directions by a number of different policy considerations. The variety and indeed disparity of these policy considerations arises from the fact that the dismissal issue occurs as a preliminary point in relation to many different causes of action. We begin by considering the expiry of fixed-term contracts, which illustrates the point very clearly.

(b) Expiry of fixed-term contracts
From the time of the RPA 1965 onwards, employment-protection legislation has consistently extended the concept of dismissal beyond the cases covered by that term in everyday usage to include the case of expiry without renewal of a fixed-term contract (EPCA 1978, s.53(1)(c), 55(2)(b), 83(2)(b)). This fundamental step of preventing the placing of a fixed term upon employment obligations has been effective, in practice, in assimilating all contracts of employment into a single pattern of indefinite duration, though employers may still, for the purposes of unfair dismissal issues, characterize an employment as a temporary one for a predetermined period: *Terry* v. *East Sussex CC* [1976] ICR 536. The main challenge to the efficacy of the fixed-term provisions occurred by an oversight. Both the redundancy payments and the unfair dismissal legislation provide for the possibility of prior waiver of statutory rights by employees in relation to the expiry of fixed-term contracts

for two years or more in the case of redundancy payments, one year in the case of unfair dismissal (EPCA 1978, s.142 as amended by EA 1980, s.8). In *BBC* v. *Ioannu* [1975] ICR 267 the Court of Appeal denied the efficacy of such a waiver in the case of a contract of employment which was for a fixed period but which was also terminable by notice within the period. Such an arrangement has become known as an 'apparent fixed term'. It was not realized at the time that the obvious consequence of this decision was to exclude such cases from the ambit of the legislation itself, on the ground that there had been no 'expiry of a fixed-term contract' within the meaning of the statute and hence no dismissal. When this point was taken, the EAT met it by ruling that the expiry of an apparent fixed term should count as the 'expiry of a fixed-term contract' for the purpose of the dismissal provisions, though not for the purpose of the waiver provisions: *Dixon* v. *BBC* [1978] ICR 357. The Court of Appeal in the same case agreed with the EAT about the proper definition of dismissal, but finding the idea of two different meanings of fixed-term contract within the same statute unacceptable, stated *obiter* that the same rule should prevail in relation to the waiver provisions also, contrary to the view they had taken in the *Ioannu* case ([1979] IRLR 114). This egregious exercise in statutory interpretation shows how readily the statutory concept of dismissal will be used as the handmaiden to the policies of the legislation. The danger is always that the courts, once embarked upon such a process, may be reduced to ever more elaborate shifts and self-contradictions.

Since the gyrations of the *Ioannu* and *Dixon* cases, there has been one important policy decision about the application of the concept of dismissal by expiry of the fixed-term contract to the task or purpose contract. The task or purpose contract has always been of dubious acceptability as a species of contract of employment. In *Wiltshire County Council* v. *NATFHE* [1980] ICR 455, the trade union representing teachers in further education supported litigation to clarify the position of part-time teachers engaged on a session-by-session basis. It was held that a contract for a full academic session was a fixed-term contract; but it was commented by Lord Denning M.R. and Lawton L.J. that a contract which was terminable on the happening of a specified future event at some uncertain future time was not a fixed-term contract. Lord Denning specifically applied this idea to the task or purpose contract, giving the following grounds:

> *Wiltshire County Council* v. *NATFHE* [1980] ICR 455(CA) at
> p. 460B–C

If I may seek to draw the matter together, it seems to me that if there is a contract by which a man is to do a particular task or to carry out a particular purpose, then when that task or purpose comes to an end the contract is discharged by performance. Instances may be taken of a seaman who is employed for the duration of a voyage – and it is completely uncertain how long the voyage will last. His engagement comes to an end on its completion. Also of a man who is engaged to cut down trees, and, when all the trees have been cut down, his contract is discharged by performance. In neither of those instances is there a contract for a fixed term. It is a contract which is discharged by performance. There is no 'dismissal.' A contract for a particular purpose, which is fulfilled, is discharged by performance and does not amount to a dismissal.

This reasoning would apply to justify the driving of a complete coach and horses through the notion of the expiry of the fixed-term contract as dismissal. It tends therefore to negate Parliament's policy in so treating the expiry of fixed-term contracts as dismissal in the first place. It is surely rather late in the day to treat the task or purpose worker as being outside the scope of employment protection legislation.

(c) Constructive dismissal

The concept of dismissal is employed in legislation when it is desired to attach statutory consequences to cases where employment is terminated by the employer. This presupposes a contrasting and differently treated set of cases where it is the employee who terminates his own employment. The ends of justice are normally seen to demand some kind of provision to include in the category of dismissal those cases of termination of employment by the employee which are, when properly understood, cases for which the employer is responsible, and where he is the prime mover of the process of termination. It is this category of cases which comes to be grouped under the concept of 'constructive dismissal'. If there were no law of constructive dismissal, it would be necessary to invent one. The legislature having invented one, the courts had to decide what limits to place upon it.

In the present era of employment protection legislation, the concept of constructive dismissal was ushered in quietly and modestly by s.3(1)(c) of the RPA 1965. (See now EPCA 1978, s.83(2)(c).) In order to establish constructive dismissal the employee had to show that he had been entitled to terminate his employment by reason of the employer's conduct and that he had done so without notice or with less than the notice due for a termination lawful *per se*. The idea of this rather curious requirement that the employee must not give due notice in order to claim constructive dismissal was to limit claims based on constructive dismissal to those instances where the employee had identified his termination of his employment as an action responsive to something the employer had done. The idea was that in those circumstances, but only in those circumstances, the employee would terminate without due notice. Of course, this did not work. If employees failed to give due notice, it was hardly because they had s.3(1)(c) of the RPA 1965 in mind. If they thought about the matter at all their natural reaction was to give due notice in order, as they fondly thought, to put themselves in the right. This was the situation in the crucial case of *Marriott* v. *Oxford and District Co-operative Society Ltd* (No. 2) [1970] 1 QB 186 (see below, p. 458). Mr Marriott fell neatly and for the best of reasons into the 'no-notice trap'. The Court of Appeal rescued him by extending the notion of 'actual' (s.3(1)(a)) (see now EPCA 1978, s.83(2)(*a*)) as opposed to 'constructive' dismissal so as to include the case where the employer repudiates his obligations under a contract of employment by unilaterally worsening the employee's terms and conditions of employment.

Lord Denning, the author of this method of extending the scope of the concept of dismissal, was later (when an express statutory concept of constructive dismissal, whether with or without notice, had been introduced and the Court of Appeal wished to control its scope) to disavow this doctrine, saying, with a fine touch of cynicism, 'It was not really an (*a*) case: but we had to stretch it a bit' (*Western Excavating (ECC) Ltd* v. *Sharp* [1978] ICR 221, 227B). But at the time this rescue operation was so effective that it was thereafter possible to hold the view that there was no need for a distinct statutory concept of constructive dismissal. The unfair dismissal provisions of IRA 1971 indeed said nothing about constructive dismissal. Its critics said that this was because the legislators did not want cases of constructive dismissal to be included. Its defenders said that the legislators had wanted such cases to be included and had been confident that they would be included as a matter of common law by virtue of the *Marriott* doctrine. The TULRA 1974 removed this uncertainty by introducing for unfair dismissal an express constructive dismissal provision without the no-notice trap (see now EPCA 1978, s.55(2)(*c*)). The EPA 1975 removed the no-notice trap for the redundancy payments legislation also (see now EPCA 1978, s.83(2)(*c*)).

It thus follows from the legislative history that the introduction of an express constructive dismissal provision in TULRA 1974 effected little or no substantial change in the law. Nevertheless, it served to stimulate a complete re-examination of the concept of constructive dismissal. In particular, the idea gained currency that constructive dismissal was not limited, as had previously been thought, to cases of repudiation or fundamental breach of contract by the employer, but extended to any case where the employer's conduct could be said to be unreasonable by the application of the test for unfairness which was contained in para. 6(8) of the first schedule [EPCA 1978, s.57(3)]. This view, which seems to have originated with the case of *Gilbert* v. *Goldstone Ltd* [1977] ICR 36 (EAT), had the result that the two-stage inquiry as to whether the employee (i) was dismissed and (ii) was unfairly dismissed, was in effect replaced by a single criterion test, namely was the employment terminated by reason of the unreasonable action of the employer? The EAT and indeed the Court of Appeal wavered in uncertainty for some time as to whether to adopt this approach, but ultimately rejected it in favour of a test of constructive dismissal firmly based on the traditional ground of repudiation of contract: *Western Excavating (ECC) Ltd* v. *Sharp* [1978] ICR 221. The virtues claimed by the Court of Appeal for the repudiation of contract test are, rather ironically, its simplicity of application and its accessibility to the ordinary man of common sense. It is precisely on these grounds that the courts will in many other situations espouse a criterion of reasonableness and reject a criterion based on the technicalities of contract law. In this case the Court of Appeal had clearly become worried that the contrary decision would open the doors to fanciful claims. It seems to have been a hard case that finally made the law, for the industrial tribunal had treated as constructively terminatory the employer's action in refusing to make a loan or to advance holiday pay in circumstances where he was under absolutely no contractual obligation so to do. Usually a reasonableness test would not produce results significantly more lenient towards employees than a repudiation of contract test. It is true, however, that the repudiation of contract test places the industrial tribunal under the restraint of having to find an implied contractual obligation upon which to ground a constructive dismissal.

Patrick Elias argued ((1978) 7 *ILJ* 100, especially at pp. 105–6) that the adoption of the contractual test for constructive dismissal would stimulate the EAT into achieving by development of implied contractual terms that which could have resulted from applying a reasonableness test for constructive dismissal. Certainly he was able to point to a significant development in that direction in the decision in *Gardner Ltd* v. *Beresford* [1978] IRLR 63, where Phillips J. ruled that it was reasonable in most circumstances to infer a term along the lines that an employer will not treat his employee arbitrarily, capriciously or inequitably in matters of remuneration. Such reasoning opens the way, as Elias shows, to the importation of the sort of controls with which administrative lawyers are familiar and also to requirements of non-discrimination as between employees. A corresponding development outside the area of remuneration occurred in *Robinson* v. *Crompton Parkinson Ltd* [1978] IRLR 61, where Kilner Brown J. was prepared to envisage a wide obligation upon the employer to maintain for his part 'that mutual trust which ought to exist between master and servant'. In that case it was held that a fresh tribunal ought, on the basis of this obligation upon the employer, to consider whether an employee had been constructively dismissed where he had been falsely accused of dishonesty.

It is still too soon for a confident evaluation of the development in the *Western Excavating* v. *Sharp* case. It looked at first as if the choice of the contractual rather than the 'industrial' test (i.e. the 'reasonableness' test) for constructive dismissal might invite a new judicial formalism at the point of deciding whether there had been repudiation of the contract by the employer. Certainly there have been occasions when the sort of contractual argument normally associated with commercial cases has occurred. In *Walker* v. *Josiah Wedgwood Ltd* [1978] ICR 744, for instance, the EAT upheld an IT in the view that a manager could not claim to have been constructively dismissed where he had failed sufficiently to indicate his reliance on the employer's breach as repudiation. Again, in *Cox Toner Ltd* v. *Crook* [1981] ICR 823 the EAT, reversing an IT, held that a director could not claim to have been constructively dismissed where he had remained at work for seven months following the employer's breach of contract, because he had affirmed the contract. But it would not seem that these were decisions generated by the existence of the contractual framework. One suspects that some parallel rationale would have had to be devised for the same decisions even if the industrial test had been adopted instead of the contractual test.

Indeed in one sense at least the case-law development displays a more creative use of contractual techniques than one might have anticipated. The growth of implied terms in favour of the employee has proceeded apace. There has been further development, for instance, in the notion of the employees' right not to be treated arbitrarily in matters concerning pay. Thus in *Pepper & Hope* v. *Daish* [1980] IRLR 13, the EAT upheld an IT in the view that there had been a constructive dismissal where a silversmith maker-up was not paid a general increase, for the workforce as a whole, of 5 per cent on the hourly rate of pay. And in *Hill Ltd* v. *Moroney* [1981] IRLR 259, the EAT upheld an IT in treating it as a constructive dismissal where the formula for a salesman's entitlement to commission was changed from a percentage basis to a target basis. Again, the notion has developed effectively in recent years that changes in terms and conditions imposed by the employer should be evaluated to see whether they amount to a *de facto* demotion and hence to constructive dismissal. Important in this respect was the decision of the Court of Appeal in *Ford* v. *Milthorn Toleman Ltd* [1980] IRLR 30.

In these circumstances, the process of precise verbal definition of the implied terms which may give rise to findings of constructive dismissal has proved less important than it promised at one stage to become. The EAT in *Post Office* v. *Roberts* [1980] IRLR 347 effectively laid the verbal controversy to rest by confirming the general principle to be one of mutual trust and confidence rather than an all-embracing notion of reasonableness which would subvert the doctrine in *Western Excavating* v. *Sharp* by simply reading the industrial test into the contract of employment. The EAT has since engaged in the business of resisting supposedly fanciful implied terms in *White* v. *London Transport Executive* [1981] IRLR 261, where they clearly felt that the implied term contended for in favour of a probationary employee would have shifted the whole burden of making the probation a successful one from the employee to the employer. Lord Denning reduced the discussion about the verbal formulation of the general implied term to the level of bathos by identifying it as the counterpart to the obligations of the master under the old law of master and servant. He said in *Woods* v. *WM Car Services (Peterborough) Ltd* [1982] ICR 693, 698D–F:

It is the duty of the employer to be good and considerate to his servants. Sometimes it is formulated as an implied term not to do anything likely to destroy the relationship of confidence between them. . . . But I prefer to look at it in this way: the employer must be good and considerate to his servants. Just as a servant must be good and faithful, so an employer must be good and considerate. Just as in the old days an employee could be guilty of misconduct justifying his dismissal, so in modern times an employer can be guilty of misconduct justifying the employee in leaving at once without notice.

Howevever, Lord Denning's slightly nostalgic analysis projects, perhaps unsurprisingly, a rather over-simplified view of the working of the notion of constructive dismissal. The courts have introduced some new dimensions to the discussion in recent years. In *Frank Wright Holdings Ltd* v. *Punch* [1980] IRLR 217, the EAT (Waterhouse J. presiding) introduced a subjective exception based on some commercial contract cases to the effect that the employer's conduct was not repudiatory if he conscientiously believed it to be a proper exercise of his contractual rights. The Court of Appeal travelled some distance down that road in *Financial Techniques Ltd* v. *Hughes* [1981] IRLR 32, where they reversed the EAT in holding that there was no constructive dismissal where the employers insisted on their construction of a profit-sharing scheme. Templeman L.J. sounded a warning about the dangers of unlimited subjectivity which was heeded by the EAT in *Millbrook Furnishing Ltd* v. *McIntosh* [1981] IRLR 309, where the 'temporary' transfer of some machinists was held to be constructive dismissal despite an argument based on subjectivity to the contrary. On the other hand, the EAT has recently in *BBC* v. *Beckett* [1983] IRLR 43 (Neill J. presiding) swung right over to the acceptance of a view that the employer's conduct may be repudiatory even if it is both subjectively and objectively the exercise of the employer's contractual rights in a narrow sense – as here where the employer exercised a contractual power of disciplinary downgrading in a way that the IT and the EAT viewed as grossly disproportionate to the misconduct concerned. This amounts to another reassertion of the 'industrial' test in a new guise, and indicates that the contractual test is still under stresses and strains which are concealed in Lord Denning's bland formulation.

In this connection another recent trend becomes important. Perhaps in order to avoid the legalism which these tensions threaten to give rise to, the courts have latterly asserted that many of the issues in constructive dismissal cases, in particular the issue of whether there has been repudiation, are issues of fact alone or mixed fact and law so that the findings of industrial tribunals are reviewable only in extreme cases. Two IT decisions about constructive dismissal were upheld on this basis by the CA in *Pedersen* v. *Camden LBC* (1980) [1981] ICR 674 (Note) and *Woods* v. *WM Car Services (Peterborough Ltd)* [1982] ICR 693. Hugh Collins has welcomed this development in a learned note on these cases ((1981) 10 *ILJ* 256) on the basis that the lay justice provided by the ITs is a better determinant of these issues than the jurisprudence of the EAT and the CA. But the doctrine in these cases will not always have the effect of ensuring the primacy of the tribunal of first instance and past experience indicates the transience of attempts to refer fundamental problems in this area back into the arena of lay justice. Perhaps in the end, however, the most effective resolution of the tensions and uncertainties here described will be the ruling of the Court of Appeal in *Savoia* v. *Chiltern Herb Farms Ltd* [1982] IRLR 166, which laid to rest the rigidifying notion that a constructive dismissal was necessarily and automatically an unfair dismissal. This was a case where the enforced transfer of the supervisor of a packing department to the job of production foreman was held to be a constructive dismissal, but one which was fair by reason of the employee's refusal to substantiate the threat to his health which he adduced as the reason for refusing the transfer. That decision provides the context for a liberal approach to the jurisdictional question of whether there has been a constructive dismissal by rendering inclusive decisions on jurisdiction compatible with the sort of cautious options on the substantive question of unfair dismissal which the courts are always anxious to preserve.

(d) Dismissal, mere warning, and termination by agreement

There has, from time to time, been a danger that the courts will so analyse certain sequences of events associated with the termination of employment as to avoid the conclusion that there has been a dismissal, by allocating the employer's actions to other contractual categories such as mere warning or termination by agreement. On the whole, the NIRC tended to resist these incursions into the concept of dismissal. Thus, in *Maher* v. *Fram Gerrard Ltd* [1974] ICR 31 the NIRC effectively overturned the notion, which had been upheld by the Divisional Court in *Morton Sundour Fabrics Ltd* v. *Shaw* (1967) 2 ITR 84, that an undated notice of termination or fundamental change of terms given by the employer could constitute a 'mere warning' causally dissociated from the employee's termination of his employment in response to the warning.

The EAT may be taking a somewhat different line. They have ruled, following the *Morton Sundour Fabrics* case, that it is neither constructive nor actual dismissal (*Devon County Council* v. *Cook* (1977) 12 ITR 347; *British Leyland (UK) Ltd* v. *McQuilken* [1978] IRLR 245) for the employer to create such uncertainty about the future of his job that the employee resigns. Under Part IV of the EPA 1975, collective safeguards come into operation as soon as an employer 'proposes to carry out dismissals' (see above, pp. 237ff.). Should the definition of dismissal be such as to provide protection for the individual employee as soon as that point is reached?

Another form of the same problem occurs where the termination of employment, although instigated by the employer, is the subject of negotiation and agreement with the employee as to the terms of termination, on the basis of which the employer argues that there has been no dismissal but instead termination by agreement. The NIRC and its successors seemed on the whole to reject this kind of argument. They rightly perceived that the crucial question was whether the employer was the prime mover in the process of termination, and that it should not matter that the employer had secured the agreement of the employee as to the terms on which the termination of his employment would occur; see, for instance, *Lees* v. *Arthur Greaves Ltd* [1974] ICR 501 and *Burton, Allton & Johnson Ltd* v. *Peck* [1975] ICR 193. Somewhat to the contrary effect, however, was the decision of the EAT (Arnold J.

presiding) in *Sheffield* v. *Oxford Controls* [1979] ICR 396, where the director of a small family company was first threatened with dismissal and then agreed to resign on good terms which were offered to persuade him to do so. In holding that there was a termination by agreement, the EAT reasoned that the threat was no longer a causative factor. This rather left the way open to arguments that resignations procured by carrots were not dismissals even if resignations procured by sticks were dismissals. Upex in a note on the case ((1980) 9 *ILJ* 183) makes the important point that it should in such cases be considered whether the agreement in question is rendered void by EPCA 1978, s.140, in so far as it purports to limit the operation of the unfair dismissal legislation. It would certainly seem that the policy underlying section 140 points against an over-ready acceptance of the analysis which was applied, perhaps in the special situation of the director/employee, in the *Sheffield* case.

Another variant of this problem has occurred in a number of cases where employers have stipulated that employment will be terminated by the employee's being absent without leave for a stated period. This has arisen in a number of cases where immigrant workers have returned to their countries of origin and overstayed their leave from work. Employers have sought to get these cases classified as self-dismissal, as we shall see presently (p. 457) or as cases of termination by agreement – and so not dismissal. The latter argument succeeded in the EAT (Phillips J. presiding) in *British Leyland UK Ltd* v. *Ashraf* [1978] ICR 979. As in relation to the *Sheffield* case, it would seem arguable that the agreement in question should have been seen as an attempt to contract out of the unfair dismissal legislation and *pro tanto* void under EPCA 1978, s.140. But it has appeared to be unnecessary to develop that argument in that the EAT has subsequently been at pains to distinguish the *Ashraf* decision on comparable facts. Thus in *Midland Electric Manufacturing Co. Ltd* v. *Kanji* [1980] IRLR 185 (EAT, Talbot J. presiding), a stipulation substantially similar to that in *Ashraf* was treated as a unilateral statement of intention by the employer to dismiss the employee if she did not return by the due date; and in *Tracey* v. *Zest Equipment Co. Ltd* [1982] ICR 481, the EAT (Neill J. presiding) ruled that provisions of this kind were to be construed subject to a presumption that the employee would not normally intend to give up his statutory rights. These cases reflect the generally growing preference we have already observed for an inclusive approach to the concept of dismissal which brings cases within jurisdiction and leaves the merits to be assessed under the heading of fairness.

(e) Dismissal and frustration of contract

At one time the doctrine of 'frustration of contract' threatened to be the basis of an incursion into the scope of the concept of dismissal even more extensive than those threatened by the 'mere warning' and the 'termination by agreement' doctrines just considered. The doctrine of 'frustration of contract' appeared to afford the employer the possibility of arguing that there had been an automatic termination of employment, without any intervention on his part, by reason of the prolonged absence of the employee due to sickness or injury: see, for instance, *Jones* v. *Wagon Repairs Ltd* (1968) 3 I T R 361. However, although the application of the doctrine is still theoretically possible in employment cases: *Egg Stores Ltd* v. *Leibovici* [1977] I C R 260, it has been decisively limited by the reluctance of the courts to allow employers to claim that there has been a prior termination of employment where they have acquiesced in the apparent continuance of the employment: see *Marshall* v. *Harland & Wolff Ltd* [1972] I C R 101, *Hebden* v. *Forsey Ltd* [1973] I C R 607 and *Hart* v. *Marshall & Sons Ltd* [1977] I C R 539.

There in fact now seem to be only two main areas in which the issue of frustration arises in any significant sense. The first of these is that of ill-health and absence due to sickness. Here the E A T has virtually now ruled out frustration in all ordinary cases; compare for instance *Harman* v. *Flexible Lamps Ltd* [1980] I R L R 418, where the E A T (Bristow J. presiding) held that frustration is normally relevant only where the contract of employment is for a long term not terminable by notice, and *Converfoam (Darwen) Ltd* v. *Bell* [1981] I R L R 195, where, with Browne-Wilkinson J. presiding, it was held that frustration was not available in relation to the risk of recurrence of a works manager's heart condition (as it might have been, for instance, in relation to a sole wireless operator on a seagoing ship). The other main area within which case-law on frustration has arisen latterly is that of prison sentences passed on employees. The Court of Appeal in *Hare* v. *Murphy Brothers Ltd* [1974] I C R 603 clearly envisaged a substantial prison sentence on the employee as bringing about a termination of the contract of employment without there being a dismissal by the employer. But they seemed divided as to the nature of the legal mechanism of termination; Lord Denning M.R. alone regarded it as frustration of the contract while the others were unclear as between that and, in effect, self-dismissal on the part of the employee. A comparable combination of a reluctance to apply the doctrine of frustration with a desire to achieve the same results as frustration would have was visible in *Tarnesby* v. *Kensington Area Health Authority* [1981] I C R 615, where the issue was whether a consultant psychiatrist's hospital employment was terminated by his being struck off the medical register. The House of Lords treated this as termination by statutory impossibility rather than by frustration. There are in fact two objections which are felt to the application of the doctrine of frustration in this area, and they are ultimately inconsistent with each other. One objection is that frustration postulates an absence of fault, whereas the convicted employee is often perceived to be the author of his own misfortunes. The other objection is that frustration is automatic in its operation, which is seen as being at variance with the factual situations where the employer initiates the termination of employment. These objections were overridden in *Harrington* v. *Kent County Council* [1980] I R L R 353 (E A T), but have since tended to prevail in varying degrees in *Chakki* v. *United Yeast Ltd* [1982] I C R 140 (E A T), *Norris* v. *Southampton City Council* [1982] I C R 177 (E A T) and *Kingston* v. *British*

Railways Board [1982] ICR 392 (EAT). In the last case, the frustration issue did not have to be directly decided because the EAT was clear that even if a dismissal, the employer's action was not unfair. The clear leaning of the EAT towards the view that there was a dismissal albeit a fair one reflects the current preference for bringing cases within jurisdiction and then using the jurisdiction sparingly, a preference which has also manifested itself in the discussion of 'self-dismissal' to which we now turn.

(f) Self-dismissal and repudiation by the employee

A conceptual alternative to dismissal, which has met with some success from time to time, has been automatic termination of the contract upon repudiation or impossibility of performance induced by the employee. This is in a sense the counterpart of constructive dismissal by the employer; it is constructive resignation by the employee. The difference is that constructive dismissal is expressly recognized in the statutory definition of dismissal (see above, p. 448), whilst constructive resignation is a notion derived purely from common law which serves to exclude the operation of the legislation. However that may be, the notion of repudiation by the employee, or impossibility induced by the employee, terminating the contract, was accepted in the cases of *Hare* v. *Murphy Brothers Ltd* [1974] ICR 603 (employee's prison sentence) and *Gannon* v. *Firth Ltd* [1976] IRLR 415 (industrial action by employees) – although it was held in *Chappell* v. *Times Newspapers Ltd* [1975] ICR 145 (see below, p. 893) that the employer could not cast the employee in the role of repudiator merely by issuing him an ultimatum to dissociate himself from threats of industrial action issued by his union. The view that these cases are cases of repudiation by the employee rather than dismissal by the employer seems again to be the product of policy-oriented interpretation designed to protect the employer in these situations. This can perhaps be illustrated by reference to the decision in *Thomas Marshall (Exports) Ltd* v. *Guinle* [1978] ICR 905 where the boot was on the other foot, because the employee wished to rely upon his own wrongful repudiation as the means of avoiding the future obligations of his service agreement. The Vice-Chancellor had little difficulty in holding that the contract of employment continued in force so that repudiation did not bring about its automatic termination.

In this way irreconcilable inconsistencies may be brought about in the course of manipulating the common law of the termination of the contract of employment in order to do justice in a particular situation. One may, for instance, contrast that decision with the decision in *Sanders* v. *Ernest Neale Ltd* [1974] ICR 565 that the contract of employment was automatically terminated by the employer's wrongful repudiation where that repudiation consisted in an ultimatum to return to work addressed to workers who were taking industrial action. However, that decision too was policy-oriented in its own way for it enabled the dismissal to be identified as a sanction for industrial action for which the employer incurred no liability, rather than as the dismissal for redundancy which it would otherwise indubitably have been.

The intractability of the theoretical problem is further illustrated by *Gunton* v. *Richmond-upon-Thames LBC* [1980] ICR 755, where a college registrar claimed a declaration that his purported dismissal was contractually wrongful and therefore void so that he remained in office. This raised the question of the effect of unaccepted wrongful repudiation of the contract of employment. The Court of Appeal were unanimously of the view that the employee could not enforce a claim to be treated as if his contract of employment had remained in force until his retirement but only as if it had remained in force for a lawful notice period served when the proper disciplinary procedure, if followed, could have been concluded. In coming to this view, Buckley and Brightman L.JJ. held that an unaccepted wrongful repudiation did not determine the contract of employment because the law of the contract of employment follows the general principles of the law of contract. Shaw L.J., on the other hand, held that the contract was determined by wrongful repudiation because the preservation of the contractual relationship was necessarily co-terminous with the ability of the law to compel performance. So the theoretical debate remained as intellectually stimulating and as unsatisfactory in practice as it has ever been, as the meaninglessness of treating the contractual relationship as still in being in the absence of remedies to maintain it vied for priority with reluctance to allow the contractual wrongdoer to profit from his own wrong.

Within this ambit of uncertainty, the EAT continued to fluctuate as to whether there could be self-dismissal taking cases out of the unfair dismissal jurisdiction. The important decisions in favour of self-dismissal were *Smith* v. *Avana Bakeries Ltd* [1979] IRLR 423 (employee leaving work indefinitely after repeated warnings that he would be regarded as dismissing himself if he did) and *Kallinos* v. *London Electric Wire* [1980] IRLR 11 (employee sleeping on duty) (Talbot J. presiding in the EAT in both cases). Eventually the debate about self-dismissal appeared to be settled by a majority decision of the Court of Appeal against self-dismissal in *London Transport Executive* v. *Clarke* [1981] ICR 355. In that case the self-dismissal argument was adduced as the right approach to the problem we have already encountered of the (immigrant) worker failing to return from absence abroad. Templeman and Dunn L.JJ., while perfectly clear that no reasonable tribunal could have viewed dismissal in these circumstances as unfair, brought the case within the unfair dismissal jurisdiction on the basis that wrongful repudiation required acceptance by the employer, and this acceptance terminated the contract so that the employer had effected a dismissal.

Lord Denning's dissent merits special mention. His assertion that the case should be regarded as self-dismissal represented more than a mere contrary view in a doctrinal debate about the working of the law of contract. It amounted to a view that cases of this kind ought to be dealt with by the common law of the contract of employment alone and ought not to fall within the statutory unfair dismissal jurisdiction. In his own words ([1981] ICR

355, 366C): 'In the circumstances of this case, all members of this Court think that this man should not be awarded thousands of pounds compensation or any compensation. I think that the only legitimate way of achieving this result is to hold that the man dismissed himself.'

We have seen throughout this section that the trend in recent years has been against the mistrust of justice as provided by industrial tribunals that this statement implies. On the whole, the courts and in particular the EAT have ended up by preserving rather than curtailing the unfair dismissal jurisdiction in the face of contractually based threats to it such as the doctrines of termination by agreement, frustration and, latterly, self-dismissal.

(g) Trial periods under the redundancy payments legislation

Under the redundancy payments legislation (EPCA 1978, Part VI), the concept of dismissal is modified by provisions concerning trial periods (s.84(3)–(7)). The purpose of the trial period provisions is to protect an employee faced with the unilateral imposition upon him of new terms and conditions of employment by his employer. If the employee decided to experiment with the new set of terms and conditions for a short period instead of leaving immediately, he ran the risk of forfeiting the claim to a redundancy payment which he might otherwise have based upon the change.

This problem first presented itself as a problem engendered by doctrines of the common law of the contract of employment. It appeared that where the employee stayed on after a change of terms and conditions or a change in the nature of his work, there might be deemed to be either termination of his original contract by mutual agreement, variation by agreement or simply repudiation by the employer unaccepted by the employee, rather than dismissal within the meaning of the legislation. Fortunately these various notions were firmly scotched by the Court of Appeal in *Marriott* v. *Oxford & District Co-op Ltd (No. 2)* [1970] 1 QB 186 which established that unilateral change of terms by the employer was a termination of the existing contract of employment and hence amounted to dismissal (see *GKN (Cwmbran) Ltd* v. *Lloyd* [1972] ICR 214).

This was not, however, the end of the problem, because the RPA 1965 contained statutory provisions designed to negate dismissal where the employee accepted a new contract of employment beginning within four weeks of the ending of the old contract, provided that the change of terms was spelt out in writing to the employee (which had not been sufficiently done in *Marriott's* case) (RPA 1965, s.3(2), see now EPCA 1978, s.84(1)). The same rule extended to a re-engagement by the acquirer of the employer's business (s.13(2) – see now EPCA 1978, s.94(2)) or by an associated company (s.48(1); see now EPCA 1978, s.84(7)). These provisions were designed to prevent employees from claiming redundancy payments in cases where they did not need them or had no strong case for them because they were going straight into fresh employment. But they could operate to defeat the meritorious claims of employees who experimented unsuccessfully with the new terms, perhaps with the new employer also, for a short period. Parliament therefore intervened by introducing (in the EPA 1975) the notion of the trial period. The trial period provisions have the effect that the employee can accept the new terms (and the new employer) for up to four weeks from the beginning of his new work without forfeiting the claim to treat the termination of the original employment as a dismissal if the trial period is terminated by him for any reason, or by the employer for a reason 'connected with or arising out of the change . . . to the new employment' (whatever that means). (EPCA 1978, s.84(4)–(6) and s.94(1)–(2).) Because of this safeguard it is no longer thought necessary to require the offer leading to the trial period to be in writing (EPCA, s.84(1)). The trial period provisions seem to be working satisfactorily.[1]

4 Unfair dismissal

(a) Origins and purpose of the legislation

The law of unfair dismissal originated in the defects of the common law of wrongful dismissal. That is to say, the new law of unfair dismissal represented a reaction to the inadequate protection afforded to the employee by his contract of employment. The common law had developed in such a way that the law of wrongful dismissal left the worker exposed and unprotected in two main respects. First, it accorded to the employer so wide an implied right of summary dismissal that the employee's chances of successfully challenging a dismissal for cause were slight indeed. Secondly, the wrongfully dismissed worker was entitled to so extremely limited a set of remedies that it was hardly worth his while to sue in the courts, and he rarely did so unless he was, for instance, a director of a company who had been granted a fixed-term contract. In the generality of cases the wrongfully dismissed worker faced the prospect of obtaining at best an award of compensation more or less limited to his remuneration for the period of notice required to terminate his contract, and had no chance of obtaining an order of reinstatement because the doctrines concerning the equitable remedies of specific performance and injunction were rigorously opposed to the positive implementation of employment relationships. It was this unavailability of a remedy of reinstatement, and the contrast which could be drawn, for instance, with grievance arbitration in the USA in this respect, which provided the champions of reform with a crucial point of criticism of the existing law. (See, for instance, G. de N. Clarke (1969) 32 *MLR* 532.)

The report of the Donovan Commission espoused the cause of reform of the law of dismissal and gave it the status of a compulsory element in any future

---

[1] Except that there is a doubt whether a parallel *common law* trial period, not limited to four weeks, exists alongside the statutory trial period. See *Turvey* v. *Cheyney & Son Ltd* [1979] IRLR 105 (EAT).

programme of labour legislation. The Report shows very clearly why such legislation might be expected to commend itself to the government of the day, or their successors in office, and demonstrates how the common law was perceived to be obsolete, neglected, and, in consequence, unjust. A reformed law would have the advantages of compliance with international standards and would bring about a closer harmony with labour legislation in European countries and grievance arbitration practice in the USA. It would increase the impact of the legal process upon the employment relationship and hence tend to promote 'the rule of law' in what was increasingly seen to be an embattled field where the law had an inadequate presence. A new law of unfair dismissal could also be used to implement certain specific policies, for instance that of the protection of freedom of association (above, p. 178). However, we may see in the Donovan Report traces of the influence of the law of wrongful dismissal. The following passage, for instance, expresses the now famous equivocation of the authors of the Report in relation to compulsory re-instatement.

Report of the Royal Commission on Trade Unions and
Employers' Associations (1968), Cmnd. 3623

551. Ideally, the remedy available to an employee who is found to have been unfairly dismissed is reinstatement in his old job. However, there are strong arguments against laying down reinstatement as the only remedy. The courts have always refused to grant decrees for the specific performance of contracts of employment, whether sought by employer or employee. In foreign countries such obligations to reinstate as are laid upon the employer are generally, though not invariably, coupled with an option to pay compensation as an alternative; moreover in France, where the law prohibits the dismissal of a statutory works councillor without the consent of the works council or a Ministry of Labour representative, the courts have laid down that the only remedy available to an employee dismissed in defiance of this prohibition is an action for damages (see *Sortais* c. *Cie Industrielle des Téléphones*, Cass. Soc. 27.11.1952, D.1953, 239). An employee may have the most compelling reasons for not wishing to work any longer for an employer who has dismissed him unfairly. Difficult cases could also arise where an employee had obtained another job while his claim was pending. The experience of other countries indicates that reinstatement is more likely to be brought about under a voluntary procedure, and that the remedy usually preferred in practice under a statutory procedure is compensation.

552. It is therefore our view that reinstatement and compensation should both be envisaged as remedies. It would be possible to provide that an order for reinstatement should be the primary relief, but that at the option of either employer or employee compensation should be granted instead. However it would be more in accord with reality, and in our view therefore preferable, to lay down an order for compensation as the primary relief, with the order lapsing only in the event of both parties exercising the option of reinstatement within a brief time limit. (Where voluntary procedures are concerned reinstatement may appropriately be provided for as the primary remedy, with or without payment of wages for the period between the dismissal and the reinstatement.)

The legislation which resulted from those recommendations of the Donovan Report was the 'unfair dismissal' part of the Industrial Relations Act 1971. Those who were responsible for that legislation probably viewed that part of the Act as a fairly uncontroversial *quid pro quo* for the restraints placed upon and penalties exacted from trade unions and workers elsewhere in that Act. It is unlikely that they could have foreseen that the 'unfair dismissal' part of the Act would prove the only part to survive, or that it would have such far-reaching social consequences and jurisprudential significance. Hence it seems fair to say that the draftsmen of the legislation had the task of embodying in words an absolutely fundamental new principle of English law on the basis of fairly scanty guidance from the policy makers, since nobody had a very precise idea of how to elaborate the concept of unfair dismissal beyond a generally shared conviction that it should represent a radical departure from the common law of the contract of employment.

(b) **The general idea of fairness: concept or conception?**
The draftsmen of the legislation were thus committed to the necessity of devising a criterion of lawfulness of dismissal which would be at once more exacting and yet more flexible than the implied terms offered by the law of the contract of employment. They achieved this feat by the combination of requiring the employer to show good cause for the dismissal (see now EPCA 1978, s.57(1)), and of an overriding test of the reasonableness of the employer's decision to dismiss (ibid., s.57(3)). The requirement of reasonableness, although probably intended as no more than a stop-gap provision to deal with hard cases, has proved to be, psychologically at least, the central and defining point of the concept of unfairness. It is by that requirement of reasonableness that the legislators have been seen to appeal to a deliberately undefined notion of justice which would be worked out by industrial tribunals on a case by case basis. The great jurisprudential interest of this method of legislation consists in seeing how industrial tribunals and the courts to which appeal lies from them behave when entrusted with such a generalized duty of working out justice in individual cases. It is here that we may look to jurisprudential theorists to see how far they illuminate and explain the judgments of industrial tribunals and of the appeal courts from an appeal from them. We shall mainly be concerned to see whether jurisprudential speculation about the nature of justice is of assistance in this context, but before doing that we shall consider two jurisprudential insights into this method of framing legislation. The first concerns the desirability of the use in legislation of wide, vague, or open-ended concepts such as that of 'unfairness'. The second concerns the process whereby meaning is attached to so indeterminate a concept as unfairness.

As far as the desirability of wide, general clauses in legislation is concerned, we can usefully contrast the views of two American sociologists of law, Unger and Selznick. In the following passage Unger characterizes the use of wide, general clauses in legislation as part of a 'post-liberal' phase of legal and social development, in which the legal process becomes increasingly politicized, being thereby, in his view, deprived of much of its sanctity and moral force. How far do you think that Unger's critique has validity in relation to unfair dismissal legislation? It should be added that Unger writes from a standpoint of general suspicion of welfare legislation.

R. M. Unger, *Law in Modern Society* (1976), pp. 197, 199

Open-ended clauses and general standards force courts and administrative agencies to engage in ad hoc balancings of interest that resist reduction to general rules. One of the corollaries of generality in law is a severe limitation of the range of facts considered relevant to the making of official choices. If the number of pertinent factors of decision is too large, and each of them is constantly shifting, then categories of classification or criteria of analogy will be hard to draw and even harder to maintain. But the kinds of problems to which comprehensive standards characteristically apply tend to defy such limitations. They involve the conflict of numerous and inchoate interests against the background of a refusal to sacrifice any one of these interests completely to the others.

When attempts are made to codify standards, to reduce them to rules, their character is distorted. Either a large area of uncontrolled discretion and individualization subsists under the trappings of general norms, or the flexibility needed to make managerial decisions or to produce equitable results is lost. . . .

Overarching standards invite their appliers to make use of the technician's conception of efficiency or the layman's view of justice. If, for example, one seeks to give content to the conception of good faith in contract law, one must go outside the narrow confines of lawyers' learning to consult the practices and enter into the thought patterns of a certain social group.

As purposive legal reasoning and concerns with substantive justice begin to prevail, the style of legal discourse approaches that of commonplace political or economic argument.

An opposite view is presented by Selznick in his important work on *Law, Society and Industrial Justice* (1969). His view is that in a mixed economy the state has the right and duty to ensure the presence of industrial justice in individual employment relationships, and that this can best be achieved by the importation into the sphere of employment relationships in private industry of general notions and standards of public law. In his view this involves legislation, whether Parliamentary or judicial, of the generalized character appropriate to the central concepts of public law. In the following extract he develops the idea that law should 'affirm reason' and that it must do so if 'due process' (which is, of course, a concrete and well-developed notion in United States constitutional law) is to be upheld. What comparisons or contrasts might one draw between the concept of fairness and that of the affirmation of reason? Does either have any meaning? Do you share Selznick's faith in the strength and force of the ideal of legality as he identifies it?

Selznick, *Law, Society and Industrial Justice* (1969),
pp. 253–4

The making and the application of law should affirm reason. This ideal accounts for much in the positive law of due process. It restates the essential notion that whatever is arbitrary is offensive to legality. Rule-making that is based on evident caprice or prejudice, or that presumes the contrary of clearly established knowledge, violates due process. Procedure cannot be 'due' if it does not conform to the canons of rational discourse or if it is otherwise outside the pale of reasoned and dispassionate assessment. Thus legislative classification of persons or groups may be struck down as arbitrary and against reason if they have no defensible connection with, or inherently frustrate, the professed aims of the legislation. Similarly a host of administrative actions, though they may enjoy large grants of discretion, are subject to this ultimate appeal.

This injunction, that reason be affirmed, can easily lead to an abuse of judicial authority. Nevertheless, it is inescapable if legality is to be upheld. Applied with caution, as a guiding ideal, it demands only a gradual conformity with the rational consensus of the community. By its own logic, the process of affirming reason may well recognize the absence of secure knowledge, including the fact that relative ignorance is the normal state of human affairs. Given that ignorance, much must be left to commonsense problem-solving and to politics rather than to the judicial process.

If the foregoing discussion has left the reader with some belief in the utility of the 'unfairness' formula in legislation, he may be further reinforced in that view by the second of our two jurisprudential insights into this kind of legislation, which occurs in Dworkin's essays on *Taking Rights Seriously* (1977). Dworkin argues that there is an important distinction between 'concepts' and 'conceptions'. He identifies a 'concept' as a general idea or ideal and a 'conception' as a specific presentation of the generalized concept. He develops this distinction in the following extract and, usefully for our present purpose, takes fairness as his example.

Dworkin, *Taking Rights Seriously* (1977), pp. 134–5

But the theory of meaning on which this argument depends is far too crude; it ignores a distinction that philosophers have made but lawyers have not yet appreciated. [The argument referred to is the contention that a proper interpretation of vague clauses in constitutions would confine those clauses by reference to the rights recognized by the framers of the constitution at the time when they framed it.] Suppose I tell my children simply that I expect them not to treat others unfairly. I no doubt have in mind examples of the conduct I mean to discourage, but I would not accept that my 'meaning' was limited to these examples, for two reasons. First I would expect my children to apply my instructions to situations I had not and could not have thought about. Second, I stand ready to admit that some particular act I had thought was fair when I spoke was in fact unfair; or vice versa, if one of my children is able to convince me of that later; in that case I should want to say that my instructions covered the case he cited, not that I had changed my instructions. I might say that I meant the family to be guided by the *concept* of fairness, not by any specific *conceptions* of fairness I might have had in mind.

This is a crucial distinction which it is worth pausing to explore. Suppose a group believes in common that acts may suffer from a special moral defect which they call unfairness, and which consists in a wrongful division of benefits and burdens, or a wrongful attribution of praise or blame. Suppose also that they agree on a great number of standard cases of unfairness and use these as benchmarks against which to test other, more controversial cases. In that case, the group has a concept of unfairness, and its members may appeal to that concept in moral instruction or argument. But members of that group may nevertheless differ over a large number of these controversial cases, in a way that suggests that each either has or acts on a different theory of *why* the standard cases are acts of unfairness. They may differ, that is, on which more fundamental principles must be relied upon to show that a particular division or attribution is unfair. In that case, the members have different conceptions of fairness.

If so, then members of this community who give instructions or set standards in the name of fairness may be doing two different things. First they may be appealing to the concept of fairness, simply by instructing others to act fairly; in this case they charge those whom they instruct with the responsibility of developing and applying their own conception of fairness as controversial cases arise. That is not the same thing, of course, as granting them a discretion to act as they like; it sets a standard which they must try – and may fail – to meet, because it assumes that one conception is superior to another. The man who appeals to the concept in this way may have his own conception, as I did when I told my children to act fairly; but he holds this conception only as his own theory of how the standard he set must be met, so that when he changes his theory he has not changed that standard.

On the other hand, the members may be laying down a particular conception of fairness; I would have done this, for example, if I had listed my wishes with respect to controversial examples or if, even less likely, I had specified some controversial and explicit theory of fairness, as if I had said to decide hard cases by applying the utilitarian ethics of Jeremy Bentham. The difference is a difference not just in the *detail* of the instructions given but in the *kind* of instructions given. When I appeal to the concept of fairness I appeal to what fairness means, and I give my views on that issue no special standing. When I lay down a conception of fairness, I lay down what I mean by fairness, and my view is therefore the heart of the matter. When I appeal to fairness I pose a moral issue; when I lay down my conception of fairness I try to answer it.

Once this distinction is made it seems obvious that we must take what I have been calling 'vague' constitutional clauses as representing appeals to the concepts they employ, like legality, equality, and cruelty.

In *Devis & Sons Ltd* v. *Atkins*, the first unfair dismissal case to reach the House of Lords, the judges faced what they regarded as a conflict between the terms of the unfair dismissal legislation and their own conception of fairness. The conflict arose from the fact that the legislation could require remedies to be given to a fraudulent employee whose fraud was not known to the employer at the time of his dismissal. It will be argued later on that this conflict between the legislation and an appropriate notion of justice was apparent rather than real (see below, p. 480); the case is cited at this point because of the varying reaction of the judges to the nature of the legislation as they saw it. In the EAT, for instance, Phillips, J. argued that the legislators had had a very specific conception of unfair dismissal in mind, which by no means coincided with the generally held conception of unfairness.

Devis & Sons Ltd v. *Atkins* [1976] ICR 196 (QBD);
[1977] ICR 377 (CA); [1977] ICR 662 (HL)

The manager of an abattoir was dismissed on the ground that he refused to implement his employers' purchasing policy. He was offered an *ex gratia* severance payment of £6,000 by his employers, but before he accepted it the employers discovered matters which convinced them of earlier dishonest conduct on his part. They withdrew the offer of £6,000 and sought to re-classify the dismissal as a summary dismissal for gross misconduct. They had not known of any misconduct on his part when they dismissed him. The industrial tribunal, EAT and Court of Appeal held that the employers could not justify the dismissal by reference to matters unknown to them when they dismissed. The House of Lords agreed on the law as it then stood, but took the view that a nominal or nil amount of compensation would be proper.

PHILLIPS J.: Naturally, in developing his submissions, Mr Bresler has pressed me strongly with the cases of *Boston Deep Sea Fishing and Ice Co.* v. *Ansell* (1888) 39 Ch. D. 339 and *Cyril Leonard & Co.* v. *Simo Securities Trust Ltd* [1972] 1 WLR 80. But, quite apart from the two cases under the Industrial Relations Act 1971, which I cited, it has to be borne in mind, I think, that there is a considerable difference between the position at common law and the position under the Industrial Relations Act 1971 and, now, under the Trade Union and Labour Relations Act 1974. The common law is concerned merely with the contractual relationship between the parties, whereas a complaint of unfair dismissal under the Act of 1974 is concerned with the statutory right of an employee not to be unfairly dismissed. It is important to note, I think, that the expression 'unfair dismissal' is in no sense a common sense expression capable of being understood by the man in the street, which at first sight one would think it is. In fact, under the Act, it is narrowly and, to some extent, arbitrarily defined. And so the concept of unfair dismissal is not really a common sense concept; it is a form of words which could be translated as being equivalent to dismissal 'contrary to the statute' and to which the label 'unfair dismissal' has been given.

The truth of the matter was that the unfair dismissal legislation broke away from the conceptual framework through which the judges were accustomed to view dismissals, namely that of the law of *wrongful* dismissal. By comparison with that body of law, the new law of unfair dismissal was an employee's charter; it could therefore give rise to hard cases in which it might appear as a rogue's charter. That was not because Parliament had sought to restrict the concept of unfair dismissal according to some obscure purposes of their own, but rather because in general they aimed to leave it as broad as possible.

By using the idea of 'fairness' as the criterion of legality for dismissals, Parliament gave the industrial tribunals the task of applying a concept of no legal precision and loose, often misleading, moral connotations. This meant that the appellate courts were called upon to regulate the way in which industrial tribunals were to perform that task. Moreover, their job of regulation was as substantial and as difficult as the statutory definition was imprecise and charged with ethical overtones. In this situation, a discussion has developed among labour lawyers partly about what Parliament intended in enacting the idea of fairness, partly about what the industrial tribunals have made of that idea, but most of all about the way in which the appellate courts have regulated the application of the idea of fairness by industrial tribunals.

We have already considered in the context of the content of employment (above, p. 425) a preliminary contribution to this discussion by Mellish and Collis-Squires ('Legal and Social Norms in Discipline and Dismissal' (1976) 5 *ILJ* 164). They accepted that the law of unfair dismissal encouraged what Anderman had identified as a 'corrective' approach to industrial discipline which was more enlightened than the punitive approach embodied, for example, in the common law about summary dismissal under contracts of employment. They criticized the corrective approach because they argued that it understated the collective interests which were in truth at stake in many dismissal issues. Subsequent writings have concentrated more closely upon the case-law of the appellate courts and widened the area of discussion to include non-disciplinary dismissals. Patrick Elias ('Fairness in Unfair Dismissal: Trends and Tensions' (1981) 10 *ILJ* 201) argued that the development of the concept of fairness by the appellate courts consisted in the interplay of a number of competing considerations, of which the most prominent were (1) the idea that industrial tribunals exceed their function if they substitute their views for those of employers; (2) the often countervailing idea that employers must be required to implement enlightened ideas about management of the employment relationship particularly in a procedural sense; and (3) the notion, countervailing to that, that employees should not be able to invoke enlightened procedural standards where notions of substantive fairness which favoured the employer on the merits of the case would be offended by so doing. Elias concluded that although the appellate courts had on the whole taken an active rather than a passive approach to the insistence on enlightened standards of management, they had been disappointingly willing to allow procedural considerations favouring employees to be outweighed by substantive considerations favouring employers.

Hugh Collins in a major contribution to the radical evaluation of individual employment law ('Capitalist Discipline and Corporatist Law' (1982) 11 *ILJ* 78, 170) engaged in a more fundamental criticism of the concept and operation of the law of unfair dismissal. He argued that the law of unfair dismissal had been unsuccessful as a major control upon managerial prerogative in relation to dismissals. He suggested that the reasons for this were to be found in the attitudes of the appellate court judges towards the legislation. In particular, his argument runs, these judicial attitudes tend to undermine the corporatist tendencies of the legislation (though he finds neither the corporatism, nor the undermining of it, very admirable). He suggests that the unfair dismissal legislation was corporatist in its conception and aims to the extent that it sought to substitute a judicialized, state-imposed standard of behaviour for the voluntary operation of collective forces in relation to dismissals. He goes on to argue that the appellate court judges preferred a looser, less exacting control of managerial actions because they are both institutionally and ideologically committed to the pursuit of an ideal of neutrality towards the employment relationship. That ideal of neutrality gives rise in his view to abstentionism in relation to managerial decisions to dismiss employees and an endorsement of the generality of managerial practice as sufficiently protective of employees' interests.

To what extent can we satisfactorily base an exposition of the law about unfairness upon what these writers have said? There can be no doubt that they have contributed enormous insights to the discussion about unfairness, the use of which is now indispensable to a proper understanding of the subject. Their contributions are in fact complementary of each other in a way that the authors might not fully have allowed for. Elias was primarily concerned with the control of industrial tribunals by appellate courts. Collins was primarily concerned with the industrial consequences and implications of the working of the legislation. The law about unfairness can only satisfactorily be understood by combining both those aspects. In an immediate sense, the law about unfairness is the product of the attempts by the appellate courts to work out a viable framework of operation for the industrial tribunals. The principles the appellate courts lay down in this area are far more directly addressed to the institutional working of industrial tribunals and to their own relation to the tribunals than to the realization of fairness as an abstract ideal or as an ideological perspective upon the employment relationship. The principles they lay down in this way do of course have the wider significance that the writers have in their different ways attributed to them. It would be naïve to suggest otherwise. But that wider perspective can best be developed from the recognition that the appellate courts have for the most part defined fairness institutionally as the criterion which industrial tribunals implicitly follow if they do the right job in the right way. To try and identify what is emerging as the right job and the right way of doing it, we have to look initially at the statutory formulation of fairness and then at the fashioning by the appellate courts of the role of industrial tribunals in judging fairness. In due course we shall refer to the social operation of the law so produced.

(c) **Reasons and reasonableness**

So far we have emphasized the breadth and open-endedness of the statutory concept of unfairness, and referred to the reasons why the legislators positively sought so broad an approach. It would nevertheless be misleading to neglect what the legislation does say by way of definition and refinement of the notion of unfairness or to overlook the reasons for such statutory exposition as does exist. The general provisions about fairness are as follows:

EPCA 1978, s.57, as amended by EA 1982, s.6

57.–(1) In determining for the purposes of this Part whether the dismissal of an employee was fair or unfair, it shall be for the employer to show –

(a) what was the reason (or, if there was more than one, the principal reason) for the dismissal, and

(b) that it was a reason falling within subsection (2) or some other substantial reason of a kind such as to justify the dismissal of an employee holding the position which that employee held.

(2) In subsection (1)(b) the reference to a reason falling within this subsection is a reference to a reason which –

(a) related to the capability or qualifications of the employee for performing work of the kind which he was employed by the employer to do, or

(b) related to the conduct of the employee, or

(c) was that the employee was redundant, or

(d) was that the employee could not continue to work in the position which he held without contravention (either on his part or on that of his employer) of a duty or restriction imposed by or under an enactment.

(3) Where the employer has fulfilled the requirements of subsection (1), then, subject to sections 58 to 62, the determination of the question whether the dismissal was fair or unfair, having regard to the reason shown by the employer, shall depend on whether in the circumstances (including the size and administrative resources of the employer's undertaking) the employer acted reasonably or unreasonably in treating it as a sufficient reason for dismissing the employee; and that question shall be determined in accordance with equity and the substantial merits of the case.

(4) In this section, in relation to an employee, –

(a) 'capability' means capability assessed by reference to skill, aptitude, health or any other physical or mental quality;

(b) 'qualifications' means any degree, diploma or other academic, technical or professional qualification relevant to the position which the employee held.

There are then a number of specific provisions. The area of trade-union membership, non-membership and activity is separately treated by EPCA, s.58 (see pp. 178ff., 637 ff.). Dismissals in connection with lock-outs, strikes or other industrial action are, as we shall see (pp. 896ff., 901ff.) largely excluded from jurisdiction by section 62. Dismissal on the ground of pregnancy is specially dealt with by s.60, and the dismissal or the replacement of a woman exercising her maternity rights is regulated by s.61. Dismissal in connection with the transfer of an undertaking is the subject of special modifications to the law of unfair dismissal under Reg. 8 of the Transfer of Undertakings (Protection of Employment) Regulations 1981, which we consider later (see below, p. 586). The following special provision was made about fairness in relation to dismissals on the ground of redundancy:

EPCA 1978, s.59, as amended by the EA 1982

59. Where the reason or principal reason for the dismissal of an employee was that he was redundant, but it is shown that the circumstances constituting the redundancy applied equally to one or more other employees in the same undertaking who held positions similar to that held by him and who have not been dismissed by the employer, and either –

(*a*) that the reason (or, if more than one, the principal reason) for which he was selected for dismissal was one of those specified in s.58(1); or

(*b*) that he was selected for dismissal in contravention of a customary arrangement or agreed procedure relating to redundancy and there were no special reasons justifying a departure from that arrangement or procedure in his case,

then, for the purposes of this Part, the dismissal shall be regarded as unfair.

It seems quite likely that the legislators intended this to constitute a complete special treatment of redundancy dismissals just as there was a complete special treatment of unfairness in relation to trade-union membership or industrial action. On this view, unfairness in redundancy situations would have been limited to the special cases of violation of rights to freedom of association or expectations derived from agreed redundancy procedures. But the NIRC decided that s.59 did not constitute an exhaustive definition of unfairness in relation to redundancy dismissals, with the result that a redundancy dismissal could be found unfair under the general provisions of s.57 although not unfair within the meaning of s.59. This was decided in *Bessenden Properties Ltd* v. *Corness* [1973] IRLR 365 (upheld by the Court of Appeal in 1974); [1977] ICR 821 (Note). The decision that the general test of s.57 was cumulatively applicable with the special test of s.59 was a landmark in the judicial development of the concept of unfairness. It was perhaps the product of the commitment of the NIRC under the presidency of Sir John Donaldson to what Hugh Collins has styled as the corporatist aim of the unfair dismissal legislation as embodied in the Industrial Relations Act 1971 to achieve as extensive as possible a reduction of dismissal disputes (except where trade-union membership and industrial action were concerned) to the ordered and ordering scrutiny of industrial tribunals. It is to the implications of that generality of the notion of unfairness, confirmed by this judicial interpretation, that we now turn.

There are two aspects of the general provisions relating to fairness which deserve comment at this stage. The first relates to the reasons which the employer has to show and the second relates to the criterion of whether the employer acted reasonably. So far as reasons are concerned, the notable point is how widely, openly and inclusively the category of reasons capable of constituting fair reasons is defined. It would have been possible to define the concept of fairness by reference to a set of reasons identified as unfair reasons. The special provisions relating to trade-union membership, redundancy and pregnancy go some way towards this, and the dismissal provisions of the sex and race discrimination legislation (see below, pp. 521ff.) perform the same sort of role. But the basic trend of the legislation is to define fairness by reference to a category of positively acceptable reasons for dismissal. That category is, however, such a wide one that most dismissals which are rationally motivated and not merely arbitrary will fall within it. As a result, section 57(1) operates primarily as a procedural rather than a substantive requirement – a procedural requirement that it is the employer who must establish the grounds for dismissal rather than a substantive requirement that he justify the dismissal in any exacting sense.

This is all the more true because of the approach that the courts have taken to the catch-all concept in s.57(1)(b) of 'some other substantial reason of a kind such as to justify the dismissal of an employee holding the position which that employee held.' The courts have held that the concept includes the imposition by employers of changes in terms and conditions of employment which they judge advisable in the interests of the enterprise. Thus in *Hollister* v. *National Farmers Union* [1979] ICR 542, the Court of Appeal effectively added the category of 'reorganization for business reasons' to the category of redundancy as a reason capable of justifying dismissal. And in a series of decisions, of which the first was *RS Components Ltd* v. *Irwin* [1973] ICR 535 (NIRC) and the most recent significant one was *Evans* v. *Elementa Holdings Ltd* [1982] ICR 323 (EAT), the courts have insisted that a dismissal for refusal to accept change in the terms and conditions of work cannot be challenged as unfair on the ground solely that the employer had no contractual right to insist on the change concerned. Hugh Collins rightly points out ((1982) 11 *ILJ* 170, 175–6) that this represents a sense in which the law of unfair dismissal is actually less protective of job security than the common law of the contract of employment which it was on the whole designed to improve upon.

This trend has continued to develop in very recent cases. The notion of reorganization as coming within the category of 'other substantial reason' was reaffirmed by the EAT in *Chubb Fire Security Ltd* v. *Harper* [1983] IRLR 311 and in *Gilham* v. *Kent County Council* [1983] IRLR 353. To it was added, in *Dobie* v. *Burns International Security Ltd* [1983] ICR 478, the notion of insistence on dismissal by a third party having effective control of the dismissal decision (such as a major customer). Moreover, the view that breach of the contract of employment, in the imposition of new terms, does not necessarily render the dismissal unfair was reaffirmed in the *Chubb* case, and to it was added the further proposition, in the *Kent County Council* case, that breach of a collective agreement does not per se render the dismissal unfair either. This virtual abandonment of any evaluative control at the stage of deciding whether there is 'some other substantial reason' throws great weight on the issue of reasonableness in cases within that category. There are various conflicting impulses at that stage. In the *Dobie* case, for instance, the EAT insisted that the question of injustice to the employee resulting from dismissal at the insistence of a third party must be considered, as part of the reasonableness issue. In the *Kent County Council* case it was held that industrial tribunals were entitled to take a very serious view of breaches of national collective agreements at the stage where reasonableness was considered. In the *Chubb* case, on the other hand, the EAT rejected the view expressed, also by the EAT, in the *Elementa Holdings* case that if it was reasonable for an employee to decline new contractual terms, it would be unreasonable for the employers to dismiss him for such refusal. In the *Chubb* case, the EAT insisted that the only relevant issue was the reasonableness of the employer's conduct, to which the employee's reaction was not seen as directly relevant. This is to adopt a managerial perspective with a vengeance, and one may doubt whether this approach will find general favour, at least as so expressed. In any case, this is to anticipate our general discussion of the reasonableness issue, which we must now directly address.

In the context of this very wide and inclusive approach to the definition of acceptable reasons for dismissal, most of the weight of the whole question of fairness falls upon the second-stage question posed by s.57(3), namely whether the employer acted reasonably or unreasonably in treating his reason for dismissal as a sufficient reason for dismissing the employee. By going on to require that this question shall be determined in accordance with equity and the substantial merits of the case, the statute uses up almost the whole stock of emotive concepts with which the law disguises the idea of 'the right answer', that is to say 'fairness', 'reasonableness' and 'equity'. The one major omission is the notion of 'common-sense', and this is an omission that the courts have not hesitated to make good in their discourse on the subject. These strictures may be thought unwarranted; but the invoking of the notion of reasonableness has had a very great significance in the development of the law about fairness. Its presence does much to explain what both Elias and Collins point to as the standard-reflecting rather than standard-setting approach to the unfair dismissal jurisdiction. For Elias, the tendency to be norm-reflecting rather than norm-setting was the exception rather than the rule (see (1981) 10 *ILJ* 201 at 212–13). For Collins, the same tendency represents the essential and typical outcome of the approach of the appellate courts to the unfair dismissal jurisdiction ((1982) 11 *ILJ* 78 at 92–3).

Both writers focus on the decision in *Saunders* v. *Scottish National Camps Association* [1980] IRLR 174 (EAT), affirmed [1981] IRLR 277 (Ct of Sess.), as a key example of the tendency. That was a case where the dismissal of a teacher because he was a homosexual was upheld as fair largely on the basis that employers in general would take the view that homosexuals should not work with children. This case is prominent in that a view which offends some liberal values as an unduly stereotyped assessment of the behaviour of homosexual people is rationalized by attributing it to the generality of employers. In this respect the *Saunders* case is fairly isolated. But there is a far more general sense in which the presence of the reasonableness test has resulted in a standard-reflecting use of the unfair dismissal jurisdiction. This is emphasized by the change in the expressed basis of assessing reasonableness which was made by the 1980 Act. Section 6 of the 1980 Act modified s.57(3) of the 1978 Act by specifying that the circumstances relevant to the reasonableness of the employer's action should include the size and administrative resources of the employer's undertaking. The purpose of this modification was to reduce the burden of the legislation upon small employers. In particular it was to make sure that small employers were judged by standards of small employers rather than being held to the standards of large employers which might be expected to be higher in so far as large employers would devote more resources to professionalizing their management of the employment relationship. It is significant that in taking this step towards standard-reflecting rather than standard-setting, s.6 of the 1980 Act was confirming the very same doctrine which had been articulated by the EAT as part of the case-law (*Royal Naval School* v. *Hughes* [1979] IRLR 384). To the extent that s.6 of the 1980 Act promotes the tendency to standard-reflecting, we may see standard-reflecting as expressing a conscious policy of limiting the impact of unfair dismissal law. To the extent that it emerges from the case-law, Hugh Collins explains it as the product of judicial abstentionism (see above, p. 467). It is perhaps useful, however, to try to understand standard-reflecting as something that the appellate courts have felt to be necessary if industrial tribunals are to have a coherent and rational method of exercising their jurisdiction. In order to elaborate this view, it will be helpful to divide the further discussion of the treatment of the concept of fairness into the areas of (1) burden and quantum of proof, (2) substance and procedure, and (3) errors of fact and law.

(d) **Proving unfairness – burden and quantum**

It was suggested in the foregoing discussion of the statutory definition of unfairness that the problem of defining unfairness could usefully be seen as the problem of setting industrial tribunals a coherent way of carrying out their task of adjudication. It follows from this that the statutory provisions and appellate court decisions can usefully be assessed in terms of the burden and quantum of proof that they establish in relation to unfairness, for this is the primary function involved in specifying the function of an inferior court or tribunal (a fact which, as we shall see later, can easily be obscured by an excessive preoccupation with the *review* function of appellate courts, which is rather different). The legislators have been much concerned with getting the *burden* of proof right. The original formulation of the burden in the Industrial Relations Act 1971, s.24, was as it is now; that is to say the employer had to prove his reason for dismissing and that it was a reason capable of justifying dismissal, as is now required by s.57(1), while there was no express burden of proof in relation to the issue of whether the employer acted reasonably under what is now s.57(3). The decision of the legislators in 1971 to throw no express burden of proof on either party in relation to this issue (which as we have seen is the crucial issue) seems to have been in furtherance of an aim of making the unfair dismissal legislation as overtly neutral as possible between employer and employee.

The attempts to explain the practical consequences of the failure to cast a burden of proof were not very convincing or helpful – see *Merseyside Electricity Board* v. *Taylor* [1975] ICR 185 at 187C–E – and the Trade Union and Labour Relations Act 1974 placed the onus of proof of reasonableness on the employer in what was no doubt an effort to make the unfair dismissal legislation seem a more efficacious means whereby employees could secure justice at the hands of industrial tribunals. But the change of onus did not seem to make a great deal of obvious practical difference and, although section 6 of the Employment Act 1980 put the law back into its original 1971 form, this reversion was not, it seems, envisaged as having major practical effects. That is perhaps because it is effectively inherent in the unfair dismissal process that the employer has to justify his action in dismissing, so the real onus of proof has always lain with the employer. In return – and it is a significant return in practice – the employer has opportunity to state his case first, which means that the managerial perspective upon the whole issue is in a procedural sense primary however critically the management decision is evaluated.

Thus enactments and decisions about *burden* of proof are not of central importance. But appellate courts are crucially concerned with the adequacy of the proof of unfairness before industrial tribunals, and therefore the defining of the *quantum* of proof of unfairness should be seen as a central issue. The simple statement as to quantum of proof is that the bearer of the onus of proving a particular assertion must prove it on the balance of probabilities rather than beyond reasonable doubt, these being civil proceedings (though note here the possible impact of the doctrine newly propounded in *R.* v. *Milk Marketing Board, ex parte Austin* (QBD, *The Times*, 21 March 1983) that the criminal standard of proof is appropriate to a decision directly affecting a person's livelihood). But that simple statement disguises the fact that the issue to be tested is a complex one, if only because of the two-stage process by which fairness is ascertained. It is useful to see quite a lot of the case-law as trying to carry out a necessary clarification of the quantum of proof as to the two questions:

(a) has the employer shown what his reasons for dismissal were and that they were justificatory reasons?
(b) did the employer act reasonably in treating the reason as sufficient reason for dismissing?

We shall therefore address the question of quantum of proof in relation to these two questions in turn.

So far as the quantum of proof of the employer's reasons for dismissal is concerned, the key issue is how far an objective basis for the reasons has to be proved. On the whole the approach of the appellate courts has been to view the question as a subjective one treating 'the reason for dismissal' as meaning 'the ground upon which the employer acted' rather than 'the factual basis for the employer's action'. If the employer believed that the employee had stolen money, that belief was the reason for the dismissal even though ill-founded. This is not to say that there is no element of objectivity involved in the proof of fairness; but the objectivity comes into play effectively only at the second stage of the inquiry. This is certainly true in relation, for example, to dismissals for redundancy where the EAT has maintained an abstentionist objection to inquiries as to whether the employer's belief that the need for work had diminished were grounded in fact or not – see, for instance, *Moon* v. *Homeworthy Furniture Ltd* [1977] ICR 117 (see below, p. 556). It is even true in relation to dismissals for misconduct such as dishonesty, where one might expect the 'reason for dismissal' to have a high objective factual content. The issues to be proved in such cases were defined by the EAT in *British Home Stores Ltd* v. *Burchell* [1980] ICR 303 in a way that has received much subsequent judicial approbation, presumably because it provides a relatively clear specification of the job the industrial tribunal has to do. There the test to be applied was explained as follows.

British Home Stores Ltd v. *Burchell* [1980] ICR 303 (Note) at
p. 304B–F

ARNOLD J.: . . . The case is one of an increasingly familiar sort in this tribunal, in which there has been a suspicion or belief of the employee's misconduct entertained by the employers; it is on that ground that dismissal has taken place; and the tribunal then goes over that to review the situation as it was at the date of dismissal. The central point of appeal is what is the nature and proper extent of that review. We have had cited to us, we believe, really all the cases which deal with this particular aspect in the recent history of this tribunal over the past three or four years; and the conclusions to be drawn from the cases we think are quite plain. What the tribunal have to decide every time is, broadly expressed, whether the employer who discharged the employee on the ground of the misconduct in question (usually, though not necessarily, dishonest conduct) entertained a reasonable suspicion amounting to a belief in the guilt of the employee of that misconduct at that time. That is really stating shortly and compendiously what is in fact more than one element. First of all, there must be established by the employer the fact of that belief; that the employer did believe it. Secondly, that the employer had in his mind reasonable grounds upon which to sustain that belief. And thirdly, we think, that the employer, at the stage at which he formed that belief on those grounds, at any rate at the final stage at which he formed that belief on those grounds, had carried out as much investigation into the matter as was reasonable in all the circumstances of the case. It is the employer who manages to discharge the onus of demonstrating those three matters, we think, who must not be examined further. It is not relevant, as we think, that the tribunal would themselves have shared that view in those circumstances. It is not relevant, as we think, for the tribunal to examine the quality of the material which the employers had before them, for instance to see whether it was the sort of material, objectively considered, which would lead to a certain conclusion on the balance of probabilities, or whether it was the sort of material which would lead to the same conclusion only upon the basis of being 'sure,' as it is now said more normally in a criminal context, or, to use the more old-fashioned term, such as to put the matter 'beyond reasonable doubt.' The test, and the test all the way through, is reasonableness; and certainly, as it seems to us, a conclusion on the balance of probabilities will in any surmisable circumstance be a reasonable conclusion.

The important point for our present purpose is that the second and third elements of the *Burchell* test, i.e. the elements of reasonable grounds to sustain the belief and a reasonable amount of investigation are viewed as going

entirely to the second-stage question of whether the employer acted reasonably rather than to the first-stage question of whether the employer had an
acceptable reason for dismissing. In 1978 when the *Burchell* case was decided
and in 1979 when it was endorsed by the Court of Appeal in *Weddel & Co. Ltd* v.
Tepper [1980] ICR 286, the employer bore the formal onus of proof at both
stages; but this allocation of the objective aspects to the second stage has been
reconfirmed, in decisions taken since s.6 of the EA 1980 relieved employers of
the formal burden of proof at the second stage. The point is made absolutely
clear in the following judgment of the EAT where, having cited the passage in
the *Burchell* case that we have set out above, the court applies it in the following
way. The employee, a coach-driver, had been dismissed because his employers
believed a complaint from a customer that he had driven dangerously.

Henderson v. *Granville Tours Ltd* [1982] IRLR 494 (EAT) at
pp. 495–6, para. 9

WATERHOUSE J.: It is, of course, clear here that the ground of dismissal was the belief
of the employers that the appellant had driven dangerously and erratically on 28.9.80.
If one looks at the wording of s.57(3) of the Employment Protection (Consolidation)
Act 1978, as amended by s.6 of the Employment Act 1980, the question that the
Tribunal had to determine ultimately was whether or not the employers had acted
reasonably or unreasonably in treating that reason as a sufficient reason for dismissing
the employee; that question being determined in the light of the circumstances,
including the size and administrative resources of the employers' undertaking, and in
accordance with equity and the substantial merits of the case. We quote the subsection
because it is always salutary to go back to the words of the statute to see how the tests
formulated in the *Burchell* case fit in with that definition. At the heart of this case,
therefore, lay the reasonableness or otherwise of the belief of the employers at the
moment when the decision was taken to dismiss on 3.10.80. That issue could only be
decided by looking at the evidence about the investigation carried out by the employers
and the reasonableness of their belief in the light of that investigation. Thus, in many
cases, including the instant case, it is more convenient to consider the third question
formulated by Arnold J., before reaching a decisive conclusion about the second
question.

So the upshot is that the quantum of proof on the issue of employer's reasons is
relatively small, and the weight of the issue is on the second stage at which
reasonableness is ascertained. This brings us to a further aspect of the
quantum of proof because there are several different possible approaches to
the proving of reasonableness.

The formulation of the test which industrial tribunals should be directed by
in assessing reasonableness has proved as difficult as the formulation of the
right way to direct juries in criminal trials and perhaps for comparable
reasons. The NIRC under the presidency of Sir John Donaldson likened the
role of the industrial tribunal in assessing reasonableness to that of a jury, and
adopted the metaphor of the 'industrial jury', as for instance in *Bessenden
Properties Ltd* v. *Corness* [1973] IRLR 365 at p. 366, para. 13 (upheld on
appeal, see above, p. 469). This view, which as we shall see later was developed

in order to stress the autonomy of industrial tribunals as against the appellate courts (see p. 487), stresses the ability of industrial tribunals to test the issue of reasonableness by reference to their own common sense and experience of industrial matters. So the first test for reasonableness emerges; the question is, do you the industrial tribunal as reasonable men think that the employer's action was reasonable?

There was, however, a subsequent reaction against this approach, particularly in redundancy selection cases. The reaction tended to stress the view that industrial tribunals exceeded their functions if they simply substituted their own view for that of the employer by holding that an employer had acted unreasonably in that the tribunal would not have dismissed the employee in the circumstances involved. This led to a very much narrower test for unreasonableness in *Vickers Ltd* v. *Smith* [1977] IRLR 11 (EAT, Cumming-Bruce J. presiding), where it was ruled that

not only was it necessary to arrive at the conclusion that the decision of the management was wrong but . . . it was necessary to go a stage further if [the industrial tribunal] thought that the management's decision was wrong and to ask themselves the question whether it was so wrong that no sensible or reasonable management could have arrived at the decision at which the management arrived in deciding who should be selected for redundancy. [[1978] *IRLR* 11 at p. 12, para. 2.]

The doctrine thus expounded in *Vickers Ltd* v. *Smith* was felt by the EAT subsequently to have caused problems by suggesting an inordinately strict test for unreasonableness. In *Watling & Co. Ltd* v. *Richardson* [1978] ICR 1049, the EAT (Phillips J. presiding) set out to explain *Vickers Ltd* v. *Smith* in such a way as to suggest a less severe test for unreasonableness.

> *Watling & Co. Ltd* v. *Richardson* [1978] ICR 1049 (EAT) at
> pp. 1056D–1057A

PHILLIPS J.: . . . One view – now rejected in the authorities, and to be regarded as heretical – is that all the industrial tribunal has to do is say to itself, reciting the words of paragraph 6(8), 'Was the dismissal fair or unfair?'; that having done that it has arrived at an unappealable decision; and that in answering that question it is not required to apply any standard other than its own collective wisdom. What the authorities, including *Vickers Ltd* v. *Smith*, have decided is that in answering that question the industrial tribunal, while using its own collective wisdom, is to apply the standard of the reasonable employer; that is to say, the fairness or unfairness of the dismissal is to be judged not by the hunch of the particular industrial tribunal, which (though rarely) may be whimsical or eccentric, but by the objective standard of the way in which a reasonable employer in those circumstances, in that line of business, would have behaved. It has to be recognised that there are circumstances where more than one course of action may be reasonable. In the case of redundancy, for example, and where selection of one or two employees to be dismissed for redundancy from a larger number is in issue, there may well be and often are cases where equally reasonable, fair, sensible and prudent employers would take different courses, one choosing A, another B and another C. In those circumstances for an industrial tribunal to say that it was unfair to select A for dismissal, rather than B or C, merely because had they been the employers that is what they would have done, is to apply the test of what the particular industrial tribunal itself would have done and not the test of what a reasonable employer would have done. It is in this sense that it is said that the test is whether what has been done is something which 'no reasonable management would have done.' In such cases, where more than one course of action can be considered reasonable, if an industrial tribunal equates its view of what itself would have done with what a reasonable employer would have done, it may mean that an employer will be found to have dismissed an employee unfairly although in the circumstances many perfectly good and fair employers would have done as that employer did. (Consider, *Trust Houses Forte Leisure Ltd* v. *Aquilar* [1976] IRLR 251 and *Trust Houses Forte Hotels Ltd* v. *Murphy* [1977] IRLR 186.)

The moral is that none of the phrases used in the authorities, such as 'did the employer act in a way in which no reasonable employer would have acted?,' is to be substituted as the test to be applied. The test is, and always is, that provided by paragraph 6(8) [now EPCA 1978, s.57(3)]. The authorities do no more than try, according to the circumstances, to indicate the *standard* to be used by the industrial tribunal in applying the paragraph. But every time the starting point for the industrial tribunal is the language of the paragraph.

This really amounts to the third formulation of how to test for reasonableness, which is by asking whether the employer's action falls within the range of responses to the factual situation which the generality of employers would have regarded as reasonable. It stresses the existence of an area within which reasonable employers may differ as to whether dismissal is appropriate while all recognizing that dismissal would be reasonable. It has become part of the orthodoxy of the EAT and was put thus by the President of that court:

Iceland Frozen Foods Ltd v. *Jones* [1983] ICR 17 (EAT) at
pp. 24b–25a

BROWNE-WILKINSON J.: Since the present state of the law can only be found by going through a number of different authorities, it may be convenient if we should seek to summarise the present law. We consider that the authorities establish that in law the correct approach for the industrial tribunal to adopt in answering the question posed by section 57(3) of the Act of 1978 is as follows: (1) the starting point should always be the words of section 57(3) themselves; (2) in applying the section an industrial tribunal must consider the reasonableness of the employer's conduct, not simply whether they (the members of the industrial tribunal) consider the dismissal to be fair; (3) in judging the reasonableness of the employer's conduct an industrial tribunal must not substitute its decision as to what was the right course to adopt for that of the employer; (4) in many, though not all, cases there is a band of reasonable responses to the employee's conduct within which one employer might reasonably take one view, another quite reasonably take another; (5) the function of the industrial tribunal, as an industrial jury, is to determine whether in the particular circumstances of each case the decision to dismiss the employee fell within the band of reasonable responses which a reasonable employer might have adopted. If the dismissal falls within the band the dismissal is fair: if the dismissal falls outside the band it is unfair.

It is to be considered whether this test is really a restatement of the *Vickers Ltd*

v. *Smith* test in a different form, and how far the difference in form may be expected to affect the outcome of applying the test. To the extent that the 'range of responses' test is really a restatement of the *Vickers Ltd* v. *Smith* test, it tends to make the legislation work in a standard-reflecting rather than a standard-setting way. If so, perhaps that demonstrates that the courts have found this necessary if they are to formulate a test which gives tribunals a clear task that they can carry out satisfactorily. But the answer to the question whether that is so is intimately bound up with two further aspects of the adjudication of fairness to which we shall now successively turn, namely (a) the balance between substance and procedure and (b) the extent of appellate court control of industrial tribunals, defined in terms of the distinction between errors of fact and errors of law.

(e) Substance and procedure

The central problem in defining the meaning of reasonableness for the purposes of the law of unfair dismissal has been to resolve the question of how far the employer can be said to have acted unreasonably in failing to go through a fair procedure for dismissal when the substantive merits of the case as it is presented to the industrial tribunal suggest that there were good grounds for dismissal. The same underlying problem often presents itself in the form of the problem of how far account can be taken of matters upon which the employer did not act in deciding to dismiss, perhaps because they came to light only after the dismissal. But that is not the only form in which the problem arises; it is, however, the form in which the problem seems most intractable. As we shall see, it has complicated the whole discussion and made the law about reasonableness very uncertain.

In the early years of the unfair dismissal legislation, after 1971, when the National Industrial Relations Court was the appellate court for the industrial tribunals, the primacy of procedural considerations was firmly asserted, as for instance in the following passage in one of the first leading cases on unfairness.

Earl v. *Slater & Wheeler (Airlyne) Ltd* [1972] ICR 508
(EAT) at p. 510

SIR JOHN DONALDSON: Mr Burke submits that the tribunal should have found that the employee was unfairly dismissed because (i) no dismissal is fair unless the employee has an opportunity to state his case before or at the time of his dismissal; (ii) as is admitted, no such opportunity was given to the employee; (iii) no tribunal could reasonably hold that the employer had satisfied the onus of proving that he had acted reasonably in dismissing the employee, unless the employee had had an opportunity of stating his case. His arguments in support of these submissions fall into two categories, namely, those based upon the concept of natural justice and those based upon public policy as summarised in section 1 of the Act of 1971, and upon the code of practice and the construction of section 24 of the Act of 1971.

Mr Burke conceded that prior to the Act of 1971 the principle of audi alteram partem had no general application to the case of master and servant, but he relied upon *Ridge* v.

Baldwin [1964] AC 40, where Lord Reid, after stating the position in relation to 'a pure case of master and servant,' said, at p. 65:

> But this kind of case can resemble dismissal from an office where the body employing the man is under some statutory or other restriction as to . . . the grounds on which it can dismiss them.

Mr Burke went on to submit that section 22 of the Act of 1971 imposed such a restriction upon dismissal as to import this principle. The difficulty about this submission, as Mr Burke very fairly admitted, is that it logically leads to the conclusion that the employee was not effectively dismissed, although dismissal is of the essence of his claim. Suffice it to say that we have to deal with this appeal on the basis of an effective dismissal. However, Mr Burke can and does rely upon the speech of Lord Morris of Borth-y-Gest in *Ridge* v. *Baldwin*, at p. 113, for the proposition that natural justice is only fair play in action.

This brings us to his arguments based upon section 1 of the Act of 1971, the code of practice and section 24.

Section 1 of the Industrial Relations Act 1971 contains the guiding principles which both the industrial tribunals and this court are required to apply. Mr Burke relied in particular on the principle of developing and maintaining orderly procedures in industry and submitted that this was fundamentally inconsistent with summary dismissal. We do not agree. The principle requires orderly procedures, but does not exclude procedures which, in exceptional cases, provide for or permit of summary dismissal.

The code of practice is much more relevant. Paragraphs 130–133 are concerned with disciplinary procedure. Paragraph 130 provides:

> there should be a formal procedure except in very small establishments where there is close personal contact between the employer and his employees.

The employers' establishment is certainly not large. We were told that there were between 40 and 50 shop floor and between 15 and 27 management employees – but it hardly ranks as 'very small.' However, whether or not it is 'very small,' the principles of conduct should be the same, size being only relevant to the need for formality. Accordingly, the employee is fully entitled to rely upon paragraph 132, which provides that the disciplinary procedure should 'give the employee the opportunity to state his case and the right to be accompanied by his employee representative.' So far as representation is concerned, the employers neither knew nor had any reason to know that the employee had recently become a member of a trade union, but the procedure which they operated contravened the code of practice in that, in the circumstances of the employee's case, it did not give him the opportunity to state his case.

But quite apart from the code of practice, good industrial relations depend upon management not only acting fairly but being manifestly seen to act fairly. This did not happen in the case of the employee. Granted that his work had been unsatisfactory over a long period and that he had been told that it must improve, the fact remains that the decisive matters leading to his dismissal were all discovered whilst he was absent due to sickness. He was unable to satisfy the tribunal that he had any answer to these complaints, but the employers did not know this when they dismissed him and they took no steps to find out. Whilst we do not say that in all circumstances the employee must be given an opportunity of stating his case, the only exception can be the case where there can be no explanation which could cause the employers to refrain from dismissing the employee. This must be a very rare situation. The employee's case was far removed from this. The manner of his dismissal cannot possibly be justified, notwithstanding the fact that if a proper procedure had been adopted, he would still have been dismissed and would then have been fairly dismissed.

But there was also in those years a recognition by the NIRC that a procedural defect did not inevitably require a finding of unfairness (*James* v. *Waltham Holy Cross UDC* [1973] ICR 398) and although, as we have seen (above, p. 464), the appellate courts in *Devis Ltd* v. *Atkins* [1976] ICR 662 upheld the rule that a dismissal could not be justified by reference to subsequently discovered misconduct on the part of the employee, they did so with patent reluctance and only on the basis that compensation could be reduced to nil because of the misconduct concerned. Indeed, the House of Lords indicated that to the extent that that possibility was to be foreclosed by the changes in the law of compensation made by the EPA 1975 (see below, p. 497), it would then be appropriate to abandon the rule that subsequently discovered misconduct could not be viewed as making good the fairness of an otherwise unfair dismissal.

Although the courts did not take up that suggestion, perhaps because of the havoc that might have been caused by instructing industrial tribunals to operate such an internally inconsistent set of rules, the years after *Devis Ltd* v. *Atkins* have on the whole seen an erosion of the procedural dimension of fairness. In the first edition of this book, we suggested that this reflected a preparedness on the part of the courts to give primacy to substantive over procedural considerations (pp. 361–71). Hugh Collins prefers a different explanation. He says that 'This tendency does not illustrate a willingness to impose substantive judgments, but rather a deliberate attempt to avoid them' ((1982) 11 *ILJ* 170, 174). In other words, he says, the appellate courts tend to downgrade procedural requirements because these conflict with their abstentionist approach to the legislation. He says that we do not give a reason for the increasing willingness of the EAT and the Court of Appeal to use intuitive substantive judgments of fairness, for in truth, he says, the pattern does not exist and therefore requires no explanation (loc. cit., p. 174). The dichotomy between abstentionism and willingness to give primacy to substantive considerations is, of course, a conceptual one rather than a practical one in so far as they point in the same direction where the substantive considerations offset a conclusion that a dismissal is unfair for procedural reasons. But we remain unrepentant to the extent of wishing to suggest that the appellate courts do see it as appropriate to steer industrial tribunals according to substantive conclusions which they do not shrink from putting into effect. Indeed, we suggest that they have often viewed the forming and implementing of primary substantive judgments as a necessary part of the task, properly understood, of adjudicating the issue of unfairness. But the case-law has been and remains conflicting on this point, and we must now briefly describe its recent development in this area.

In 1977 Lord Denning's Court of Appeal intervened in two leading cases to reverse EAT judgments in favour of employees, the Court of Appeal being of the view that the procedural considerations which favoured the employees were outweighed by substantive considerations which favoured the employers. These were the cases of *Retarded Children's Aid Society Ltd* v. *Day* [1978] ICR 437 and *Alidair Ltd* v. *Taylor* [1978] ICR 445. In the latter case, where an airline pilot had been dismissed following an inquiry into a flying incident and the industrial tribunal had taken the view that there were defects in the inquiry procedure, Lord Denning said that the real question was not whether the inquiry was at fault but whether the employers were at fault (ibid., at p. 450E). This perfectly encapsulates the robust approach which gives primacy to the perceived merits of the employer's substantive case over defects in the procedure by which the decision to dismiss was arrived at.

Meanwhile at the level of the Employment Appeal Tribunal a more measured but more insidious encroachment upon the procedural aspect of unfairness was taking place. In *Lowndes* v. *Specialist Heavy Engineering Ltd* [1977] ICR 1 an EAT, presided over by the then President of the Tribunal, Phillips J., indicated the possibility that a procedural defect might be disregarded if it was clear that the outcome would have been the same even if due procedure had been followed. In *British United Shoe Machinery Ltd* v. *Clarke* [1978] ICR 70, the EAT (Phillips J. presiding) declared that an industrial tribunal *must* consider in relation to a procedural defect whether the outcome was affected by the defect. Then, in what has come to be regarded as the decision identifying this doctrine, the EAT with its next President, Slynn J., presiding, held in *British Labour Pump Co. Ltd* v. *Byrne* [1979] ICR 347 that in order for the employer to show that he acted reasonably (the onus being at that time on him to do so, see above, p. 472) despite a defect in procedure, it was sufficient for him to show on the balance of probabilities that he would reasonably have decided to dismiss after due procedure, and that it was unnecessary for him to go further and show that he would inevitably have done so.

The Court of Appeal joined in this exercise with gusto and confirmed its capacity substantially to downgrade the employee's procedural safeguards. In *Bailey* v. *BP Oil (Kent Refinery) Ltd* [1980] ICR 642, the employers failed to inform the employee's trade-union official of the proposal for dismissal as their disciplinary procedure required them to do. The Court of Appeal held the employer's failure to show the outcome would have been the same if this had been done was not fatal to his claim to have acted reasonably; it was merely a factor in the employee's favour which was not enough to vitiate the industrial tribunal decision in favour of the employer. Moreover, in *W. & J. Wass Ltd* v. *Binns* [1982] ICR 486 the Court of Appeal by a majority used the doctrine of the *British Labour Pump Co.* case to uphold an industrial tribunal finding of fairness in a case of summary dismissal for misconduct in spite of a manifest failure to warn about earlier misconduct or give an opportunity to explain the present misconduct. In a powerful dissent, Sir George Baker demonstrated the objections to applying the *British Labour Pump Co.* test in favour of the employers in the circumstances of the present case. His dissent is a sufficiently powerful vindication of what were in the early years understood as the proper goals of the unfair dismissal legislation to justify setting it out extensively here.

W. & J. Wass Ltd v. *Binns* [1982] ICR 486 (CA)
at pp. 496A– 501A

SIR GEORGE BAKER: With reluctance and regret I have reached a different conclusion. The employee was a troublesome fellow, but in February 1980 he had been employed by the employers for almost 13 years continuously as a HGV Class 1 driver and, with a six-month break, for nine years before that. He was 60. There had been complaints about him since he ceased to be a shop steward about a year before he was dismissed. A composite description of him was 'He started arguing with his own shadow.'

He said that on Saturday February 16 he went into his employers' premises to see what he was to do on the Monday as the vehicle he usually drove was going in for an MOT test. He saw a fitter who told him he would more than likely be on local work on the Monday until about 2 p.m. Mr Anthony Wass, the traffic manager, said he did not know the employee had been in on the Saturday, but there was no contradiction of the assertion and no finding by the tribunal about it.

On the Monday morning the employee clocked in for work at 8 a.m. Mr Anthony Wass asked him to go and check a particular vehicle because he might have to take it to London as its driver had not turned up. Ironically that driver arrived half an hour later. The employee's reply was: 'There is no way I am taking that f-ing four wheeler to London,' or according to Mr Philip Wass: 'You must be f-ing joking there is no way you will get me to take that f-ing lorry outside. Get one of your men who drives f-ing four wheelers. I am off.' He normally drove an articulated vehicle but sometimes did drive four wheelers. Mr Anthony Wass replied: 'That's fair enough then.' What that meant was never explained. The employee stormed off giving what was described as a 'V' sign Harvey Smith style and left the premises. He did not return to work that day.

Mr Philip Wass reported to Mr William Wass, the managing director, who discussed it with Mr Jack Wass, a director. The letter of dismissal, which Waller L.J. has already quoted, was prepared and delivered by hand the same afternoon.

The employers' reply to the industrial tribunal resisting the claim of unfair dismissal states: 'Mr Binns refused to carry out instructions, became abusive and left the premises without any explanation.'

This seems to me to rest their case on, and solely on, the events of February 18 and the industrial tribunal clearly purported to reach their conclusions on that basis. They say, in paragraph 10: 'However, in our view, this case really has to be determined on the basis of what occurred on February 18.' But did they?

The employers were allowed to develop a case before the tribunal that, as their solicitor put it, 'enough is enough.' Mr Anthony Wass said: 'It had got to the stage when the company had to make a stand . . . I had had enough. It is true I would rather leave than have Binns back.'

To support this case evidence was given which seems to me irrelevant and open to objection as inadmissible on the employers' written case. The employee did object to one incident when he said: 'I was not told this would be brought up against me today or I would have been legally represented.'

The employers referred to: (1) Bad time-keeping. (2) A complaint from a customer, the Staffordshire Pottery Co. – which was described as a clash of personalities. (3) Drinking with his vehicle parked outside the pub. (4) Previous rudeness and bad language. (5) Previous refusals to take particular loads. (6) Objections to certain destinations. (7) Going off in a huff: sometimes coming back next day, sometimes not. (8) There had been this sort of outburst before.

The employers had complained but they had never given him a serious warning that repetition would lead to dismissal or that they were no longer going to tolerate his tantrums. As the employee said: 'Wass had lots of opportunities of sacking me before – drinking and driving, lateness.'

The industrial tribunal expressed itself thus in paragraph 11:

> We have come to the conclusion that the respondents did act reasonably in dismissing the applicant for his behaviour on February 18. It is, of course, quite clear that whereas it will not normally be reasonable to dismiss an employee, particularly a long-service employee, for a single refusal to carry out his duties, if he persists in doing so after a warning of the consequences, then dismissal will normally be fair. In the circumstances of this case the applicant simply walked off the job using, in our view, foul language in an abusive way to the traffic manager (and, incidentally, it is quite obvious to us from what occurred during the hearing that Mr Binns has no regard whatsoever for Mr Anthony Wass and an actual dislike for him) and in the view of the tribunal the respondents acted reasonably in deciding that enough was enough and that it was appropriate to dismiss the applicant for his behaviour on that day.

The tribunal had previously referred to the vulgarity as 'language which (as we are well aware) is far from uncommon in the haulage industry, and we do not attach much importance to it,' and Mr Anthony Wass had said: 'He did not abuse me.' However, I have throughout had in the forefront of my mind the words of Lord Denning M.R. in *Retarded Children's Aid Society Ltd* v. *Day* [1978] ICR 437, 443:

> The decision is entrusted in the ordinary way by Parliament to the tribunal. I do not think it would be right to upset them and have fresh hearings on points of meticulous criticism of their reasoning. Looking at it broadly and fairly, as long as they directed themselves properly and fairly on the facts and they have not gone wrong in law, it seems to me that the Employment Appeal Tribunal should not interfere with their decision even though they would themselves have come to a different decision.

So, should it be thought that this contradiction in the tribunal's reasons has been brought to light by the toothcomb operation, I concentrate on what with all respect to the industrial tribunal is the confusion in this finding.

Mr Mitting for the employers contends that the critical facts were those of February 18 *and nothing else*. I find this an impossible conclusion. The phrase 'in the view of the tribunal the respondents acted reasonably in deciding that enough was enough' cannot relate solely to the events of February 18 in isolation. They can only refer to the history given in evidence which led up to the February 18 incident, the last straw. So not only was the hearing open to procedural objection and the decision in my opinion contradictory, but most important of all this long serving cantankerous employee had been lulled into a sense of: 'They do not really mind what I have done. They grumble but they do not dismiss me.'

Of course there can be little sympathy for such an employee and if that had been the whole story I would have taken a practical view and agreed with Waller and O'Connor L.JJ. But the failure to give the employee any opportunity to explain why he should not be dismissed seems to me to be in the circumstances of this case a denial of natural justice which eliminated equity or fair play. There are cases where instant dismissal without an opportunity of explaining would be fair. See Lawton L.J. in *Bailey* v. *BP Oil (Kent Refinery) Ltd* [1980] ICR 642, 648C–E, where he gives the example of the employee seen to stab another on the shop floor. Then there must be many cases where it is clearly for the tribunal to decide whether, in the words of Stephenson L.J. in *W. Weddel & Co. Ltd* v. *Tepper* [1980] ICR 286, 297G, the employers have acted 'without making the appropriate inquiries or giving the employee a fair opportunity to explain himself . . .'

Viscount Dilhorne in his speech in *W. Devis & Sons Ltd* v. *Atkins* [1977] ICR 662 having referred to the decisions in *Earl* v. *Slater & Wheeler (Airlyne) Ltd* [1972] ICR 508 and *St Anne's Board Mill Co. Ltd* v. *Brien* [1973] ICR 444 said, at p. 677:

> If, however, the reasons shown appear to have been a sufficient reason, it cannot, in my opinion, be said that the employer acted reasonably in treating it as such if he only did so in consequence of ignoring matters which he ought reasonably to have known and which would have shown that the reason was insufficient.

Like Waller L.J. I do not think that this throws any doubt on the reasoning in the later decision of the Employment Appeal Tribunal (Slynn J.) in *British Labour Pump Co. Ltd* v. *Byrne* [1979] ICR 347 which the industrial tribunal in the present case purported to apply as the right test. They asked the question (in paragraph 15):

> What would have happened if the respondents [employers] had adopted the course which they ought, both as a matter of common sense and justice, and in accordance with the disciplinary rules they had themselves promulgated some six months before they dismissed Mr Binns, namely, before making their decision given the applicant an opportunity of defending himself and of representation by his trade union had he so desired?

Now what was the evidence? The disciplinary rules referred to provided for an oral warning for a first disciplinary offence and a written warning for a similar offence within six months, with a clear statement that a further offence would render him liable to dismissal. Then they state: 'In the case of serious offences either or both warnings may be dispensed with.' The offence of February 18, however serious, was no different in substance from what he had done before in respect of which the industrial tribunal concluded: '. . . he had not (in the view of all of us) ever received previously any formal warning about his conduct.'

The rules continue: 'Before a decision is taken, the employee . . . shall have an opportunity to explain his conduct and/or put forward mitigating circumstances.'

I am not, I hope, so unworldly as to reject the possibility that if the employee had been asked to explain or to mitigate he would simply have again given the 'V' sign with or without an inappropriate oral outburst. But that is not the point. The procedure adopted by the employers was prima facie unfair as recognised by the chairman in paragraph 3 of his decision of July 15, 1980, refusing an application for review.

The hearing was bedevilled not only by the introduction of evidence of previous misconduct, but more importantly by the employee's story which the tribunal rejected, and in my view rightly rejected, of having made a previous appointment to see his doctor. This seems to have obscured the undoubted fact that he did go to his doctor after he walked out and he produced that doctor's certificate that he was 'suffering from exhaustion, injury to ribs,' and unable to work.

The industrial tribunal accepted that he received sickness benefit for five weeks (paragraph 8). It seemed to me at first sight that the guarded terms in which this was expressed might be significant, but when emphasising their view that the employee had not made the appointment with the doctor prior to the incident, the chairman said (see the decision on application for review reason 2): '. . . the tribunal accepted that the probabilities were that the rib injury referred to had occurred prior to this incident.'

The solicitor for the employers said he was in no position to challenge the accuracy of the certificate. Mr Anthony Wass said in evidence: 'If the applicant had said he was going to doctors I would have accepted that.' So if the employee had said he had a rib injury and felt jaded and under the weather, as he said at the hearing, it is inconceivable that he would have been required to drive to London, if only because of the risks in driving, and to stay the night and drive back the next day. He was never given a further chance to explain his condition. Had he done so the employers who had never before dismissed a man and are obviously caring and very responsible would never have made their subsequent decision conveyed in the dismissal letter.

The first limb of the test in the *British Labour Pump* case, namely, that after he had given his explanation they would probably still have dismissed him, cannot in my opinion be satisfied. The dismissal was thus unfair. The chairman of the industrial tribunal expressed his very considerable doubt whether the dismissal was really fair but he did not feel sufficiently strongly to dissent from the view of the majority.

In many cases it will be difficult, even impossible, to draw the line between substituting an appellate court's opinion of what was fair for that of the industrial tribunal, and a case in which the industrial tribunal have clearly erred and come to a wrong decision. It has been argued that the tribunal's decision is as sacrosanct as that of a jury, and it is commonplace nowadays to refer to a tribunal as an 'industrial jury.' But great care is taken to ensure that irrelevant evidence and evidence of which the probative value is outweighed by its potential prejudice is not heard by a jury. So it was in the days when special and common juries gave the verdict in many civil cases. Juries must be properly directed and cases may even be withdrawn from their consideration. Also what would happen if the present decision had been by a judge exercising a discretion? Evidence was considered which he ought not to have considered. Evidence of the fact of illness was disregarded. In my judgment the final inference drawn was insupportable, and this conclusion was reached by a wrong exercise of discretion and would be reversed by an appellate court. The Act of 1978 requires equity – fair play, and that is fair play for all including the awkward, the rude and the troublesome Mr Binns. He did not have it.

The industrial tribunal reached a result which no properly directed jury, understanding such directions, could have reached, and under whatever label it is criticised, it was I think so plainly wrong that I regret I am compelled to say so. Thus, for different reasons, I have arrived at the same result as the Employment Appeal Tribunal, and I would dismiss this appeal.

The EAT, with its President, Browne-Wilkinson J., presiding, reviewed the status of the *British Labour Pump Co.* doctrine in *Sillifant* v. *Powell Duffryn Timber Ltd* [1983] IRLR 91. Their judgment was that although the *British Labour Pump Co.* doctrine was bad law, they were bound by the decision of the Court of Appeal in *Wass Ltd* v. *Binns* to give effect to it. They took the view that the doctrine was bad law because it conflicted with the principle established by *Devis Ltd* v. *Atkins* (above) that fairness and reasonableness must be judged with reference to what was known to the employer when he took the decision to dismiss. They further took the view that the doctrine was undesirable in its effect because, in relation to matters going to the whole substance of the fairness issue and not just to procedural considerations, it required industrial tribunals to engage in a second stage of evaluation based on hypothetical facts and requiring inferences to be drawn from those hypothetical facts which could be little more than mere guesswork. In effect, then, the EAT has declared its position to be that the majority in *Wass Ltd* v. *Binns*, by upholding the *British Labour Pump Co.* doctrine and envisaging its application as they did, were creating a highly convoluted and unsatisfactory process of decision for industrial tribunals, and that there were other and preferable techniques whereby industrial tribunals could decide what weight to accord to procedural considerations. In order to appreciate the significance of that approach, it is necessary to consider the last dimension of the fairness issue, which lies in the question, how far in judging fairness are industrial tribunals in principle susceptible to guidance from the appellate courts?

(f) Errors of fact and law

Many of the issues that we have been considering under the heads of quantum of proof and the balance between substance and procedure can alternatively be viewed in terms of the autonomy of industrial tribunals or the degree to which they are susceptible to guidance from the appellate courts. Appeals from the industrial tribunals are confined to issues of law, so the question of tribunal autonomy resolves itself into a consideration of the distinction between errors of fact and errors of law. It is on the whole accepted that this distinction operates so that the decision of an industrial tribunal may be set aside where but only where it is perverse in the sense that it can be said that no reasonable industrial tribunal properly directed could have arrived at that decision. A clear instance of this view of the appellate jurisdiction in operation is provided by the case of *London Transport Executive* v. *Clarke* [1981] ICR 355 which we have considered earlier in relation to self-dismissal (see above, p. 457). The majority of the Court of Appeal, while unwilling to hold that the employee had dismissed himself, held that the decision of the industrial tribunal that his dismissal was unfair was a perverse decision in the sense we have outlined. Lord Denning M.R., on the other hand, with a judicial reticence so uncharacteristic as to seem a little disingenuous, held that because he could not regard the decision as to fairness as a perverse one, he had to find self-dismissal in order to prevent the employee from being unjustly enriched. More generally, the issue of perversity comes to pivot upon the question of what is meant by a properly directed industrial tribunal, and this raises the whole issue of tribunal autonomy and appellate guidance.

Perhaps the crucial issue in this regard is how far appellate guidance is to be equated with an exacting notion of fairness, and how far tribunal autonomy is to be equated with a broad deference to managerial prerogative. There is, of course, no direct and necessary link between tight control of tribunals and tight control of employers. Thus in *Jowett* v. *Earl of Bradford (No. 2)* [1978] ICR 431, the EAT told the industrial tribunals to regard *Vickers Ltd* v. *Smith* (see above, p. 476) as not establishing a fixed rule for which they had to follow. This was because of a perceived risk that *Vickers Ltd* v. *Smith*, if applied by the industrial tribunals as a binding precedent, would lead to an excessively *loose* approach to fair dismissal whereby dismissal would be held fair unless it was egregiously unfair. But on the whole it seems that the main trend has been in the opposite direction; that is to say, tight control of tribunals has amounted to tight control of employers, and vice versa. This is predictable and under-standable in the sense that an appellate court such as the EAT, feeling itself charged with the duty of creating a viable task specification for industrial tribunals, will tend to formulate guidelines which suggest specific criteria to be applied in evaluating employers' action, which thus amount to specific controls upon employers.

The development of the case-law in this respect has been as follows. The National Industrial Relations Court tended to give fairly precise guidelines to industrial tribunals; indeed, as we have seen (above, p. 478), the NIRC was responsible for a positive development of the procedural dimension of unfairness. Although the NIRC emphasized the discretion which should be accorded to industrial tribunals as industrial juries, they were more concerned in doing so to stress the entitlement of industrial tribunals to decide reasonableness as against employers than to stress their autonomy of the appellate courts. The President of the NIRC, Sir John Donaldson, en-couraged the use of the Industrial Relations Code of Practice issued under the IRA 1971 as providing guidelines to industrial tribunals, and the EAT has continued to favour similar use of the surviving parts of that code and the ACAS Code of Practice No. 1 on Disciplinary Practice and Procedures in Employment, which superseded the corresponding paragraphs of the IR Code in 1977. But these Codes, unlike for instance the ACAS Codes of Practice on Disclosure of Information and on Time Off for Trade Union Duties and Activities, do not have the function of defining or elaborating a statutory concept, in this case the concepts of fairness and reasonableness in dismissing. So the existence and use of these codes do not resolve the issue of how far industrial tribunals may be subjected to guidelines by the appellate courts.

The Employment Appeal Tribunal tended to take up the NIRC tradition of setting out guidelines for industrial tribunals and developed that tradition in the direction of collective and individual consultation about redundancy and reorganization (where the N I RC had been primarily concerned with natural justice in cases of misconduct and want of capability) – compare for instance *Kelly* v. *Upholstery & Cabinet Works (Amesbury) Ltd* [1977] I R L R 913, where the EAT treated the duty created by Part IV of the EPA 1975 to consult with recognized trade unions about proposed redundancies as being relevant to the fairness of dismissals for redundancy. Then the Court of Appeal moved to correct what they saw as an excessive zeal on the part of the EAT to allow procedural defects in employers' dismissal processes to be raised as leading to errors of law in industrial tribunal decisions in favour of employers. In these cases anti-proceduralism in the Court of Appeal went hand in hand with the vindication of industrial tribunal autonomy as against the EAT. This pattern is already evident in Lord Denning's judgment in *Retarded Children's Aid Society* v. *Day* in 1977 as the following passage shows:

Retarded Children's Aid Society Ltd v. *Day* [1978] I C R 437 (C A) at
pp. 443C–444A

LORD DENNING M.R.: . . . Now there is an appeal to us. I would like to say at once, as I have said already, that an appeal from an industrial tribunal can only be on a point of law. Certainly no point of law was taken by counsel before the industrial tribunal. The argument was solely upon the facts, and the industrial tribunal considered it upon its own facts and circumstances. In those circumstances it is a strong thing to say that they have gone wrong in point of law. The only way in which it is suggested they went wrong is that they are said to have overlooked the provision in the Code of Practice about giving an oral warning or giving a second chance, and they overlooked the guidance which Sir John Donaldson gave in that case which I read. I cannot believe that they overlooked it. I should have thought that the industrial tribunal would have had the Code of Practice on the table before them all the time and they would have had the words of Sir John Donaldson in mind. It is true that the tribunal did not mention those matters specifically in their reasoning: but it does not mean that they did not have them in mind or that they went wrong in law. I go further. If you read their reasons in a broad sense, it seems to me exceedingly likely that they did have those points very much in mind. As Lord Russell of Killowen indicated in the course of the argument, the tribunal themselves took the point. In the course of the evidence they asked the person in charge about the final warning, and she said: 'I never gave a final warning to Peter. I did try to show how I felt.' So they themselves raised the question of the final warning. As to its being a first offence, in their reasons they said: 'Bearing in mind that this was a first offence,' so they had that very much in mind. They probably had the Code of Practice in mind because they treated this as an abnormal case. This tribunal in their reasons said: '. . . this is a very special case,' and not a normal one. So, reading between the lines, it seems to me that, although not stated explicit in the reasons, this tribunal very probably did have all the considerations in mind which it is suggested they may not have had.

I would add this. The decision is entrusted in the ordinary way by Parliament to the tribunal. I do not think it would be right to upset them and have fresh hearings on points of meticulous criticism of their reasoning. Looking at it broadly and fairly, as long as they directed themselves properly and fairly on the facts and they have not gone wrong in law, it seems to me that the Employment Appeal Tribunal should not interfere with their decision even though they would themselves have come to a different decision. After all, the Employment Appeal Tribunal did not see the witnesses. They did not see Mr Day and his reactions. They did not see the matron, and so forth. One gets a very different impression from reading the notes than one gets from hearing oral evidence. It seems to me that this is a case where the industrial tribunal's decision should be upheld. They did not go wrong in point of law, this appeal should be allowed accordingly.

The same pattern is repeated as an objection to requirements of consultation about reorganization in *Hollister* v. *National Farmers Union*, as the following passage demonstrates.

Hollister v. *National Farmers Union* [1979] ICR 542 (CA) at pp. 551–2

LORD DENNING M.R.: . . . Here we come to a point which was discussed in the appeal tribunal. It seems to have been said on several occasions that in order for a dismissal to be justified there nearly always ought to be consultation before a person is dismissed. A man should not be dismissed without proper consultation. That is said to be based on some phrases in the Industrial Relations Code of Practice (HMSO 1972), which of course has some statutory effect. Paragraph 65 says:

Consultation means jointly examining and discussing problems of concern to both management and employees. It involves seeking mutually acceptable solutions through a genuine exchange of views and information.

In the present case it was stressed several times in the course of the judgment of the appeal tribunal that there had been no negotiations. We were referred to several passages, one of which is at [1978] ICR 712, 720G: 'In particular, nothing was said about any future course of negotiation. The matter was left as it was.' In the absence of a finding that there had been any negotiation – and, in that sense, consultation – the appeal tribunal felt there had been a failure in this case by the employers to do all they ought to have done, and therefore the dismissal was unfair.

I must say that I think that is going too far and is putting a gloss on the statute. It does not say anything about 'consultation' or 'negotiation' in the statute. It seems to me that consultation is only one of the factors. Negotiation is only one of the factors which has to be taken into account when considering whether a dismissal is fair or unfair. *Lowndes* v. *Specialist Heavy Engineering Ltd* [1977] ICR 1, seems to go further, but the decision in that case seems to me to be erroneous. I will take one passage, at p. 4:

No doubt, as a general rule, a failure to follow a fair procedure, whether by warnings or by giving an opportunity to be heard before dismissal, will result in the ensuing dismissal being found to be unfair.

There is something similar to be found in *Kelly* v. *Upholstery & Cabinet Works (Amesbury) Ltd* [1977] IRLR 91 where somewhat similar words are used. It seems to me that that would be putting the case far too high. One has to look at all the circumstances of the case and at whether what the employer did was fair and reasonable in the circumstances prior to the dismissal.

The Court of Appeal decision in *Bailey* v. *BP Oil (Kent Refinery) Ltd* [1980]

ICR 643 was to like effect, and there Lawton L.J. stated the same case against both proceduralism and over-tight control of industrial tribunals by means of error of law (see pp. 648B–649A). It is perhaps significant that when Donaldson L.J. returned to the problem of appellate court control over industrial tribunals in *UCATT* v. *Brain* [1981] ICR 542, his insistence on the dangers of over-legalism was again designed to protect the capacity of the industrial tribunals to apply forthright judgments against employers (in this case a trade-union employer) who had failed to follow good procedure. This is a policy conflict which at the time of writing the Court of Appeal has yet to resolve. Meanwhile the EAT has sought to develop some fresh guidelines for industrial tribunals in a form which will be acceptable to the Court of Appeal. They did this in *Williams* v. *Compair Maxam Ltd* [1982] ICR 156, where they laid down what were, in all but name, guidelines for industrial tribunals (under the formal rubric of current standards of fair industrial practice to which regard should be had) about consultation with recognized trade unions over redundancies. The reconciliation of this position with that of the Court of Appeal which was attempted in this case is sufficiently subtle to be worth setting out in full.

Williams v. *Compair Maxam Ltd* [1982] ICR 156 (EAT) at pp. 160A–162B

The industrial tribunal had rejected the employees' complaint that they had been unfairly selected for redundancy; the industrial tribunal accepted the employer's argument that they were in a 'survival situation' where further warning of impending redundancies or consultation had not been possible.

BROWNE-WILKINSON J.: There remains the question whether the decision of the industrial tribunal was perverse. This appeal tribunal has jurisdiction to deal only with appeals on a point of law. Some appeals are concerned with obvious points of law, e.g. the construction of statutes. Many more are concerned with cases where the point of law is less obvious, e.g. the industrial tribunal can err in law by finding facts which there is no evidence to support, or by failing to find facts as to which there was undisputed evidence. Again many appeals allege that the industrial tribunal mis-directed itself in reaching their conclusion by overlooking some supposed principle of law (e.g. that there must always be consultation before dismissal). It is in relation to these types of appeal that the Court of Appeal has repeatedly said that the appellate courts should not be astute to interfere and lay down principles of law: the question whether a dismissal was fair for the purposes of section 57(3) is a question of fact for the industrial tribunal: see *Hollister* v. *National Farmers' Union; Bailey* v. *B P Oil (Kent Refinery) Ltd* [1980] ICR 642 and *Union of Construction, Allied Trades and Technicians* v. *Brain* [1981] ICR 542. We are bound by these decisions. Even if we were not, with respect we agree that it is not in the best interests of the system of industrial tribunals if this appeal tribunal seeks to lay down detailed principles of law as to what is fair or unfair, and then finds that an industrial tribunal has misdirected itself by failing to observe such legal principles.

However, there is one other ground on which an industrial tribunal can be said to have erred in law, namely, that their decision is perverse. In the legal sense, a decision is perverse only if no reasonable tribunal of the kind in question properly directing itself in law could have reached that decision. It is not enough that the appellate court would not have reached the same decision. Obviously the cases in which this appeal tribunal can intervene on the ground of perversity are few, and the approach enjoined by the Court of Appeal to the exercise by this appeal tribunal of its jurisdiction generally must apply with even greater force to appeals on the ground of perversity. But there is a limited number of cases where the conclusion reached by the industrial tribunal is so plainly wrong that the only possible conclusion is that it must have misdirected itself: see for example *London Transport Executive* v. *Clarke* [1981] I C R 355, 372 and *Edwards* v. *Bairstow* [1956] A C 14.

In considering whether the decision of an industrial tribunal is perverse in a legal sense, there is one feature which does not occur in other jurisdictions where there is a right of appeal only on a point of law. The industrial tribunal is an industrial jury which brings to its task a knowledge of industrial relations both from the view point of the employer and the employee. Matters of good industrial relations practice are not proved before an industrial tribunal as they would be proved before an ordinary court: the lay members are taken to know them. The lay members of the industrial tribunal bring to their task their expertise in a field where conventions and practices are of the greatest importance. Therefore in considering whether the decision of an industrial tribunal is perverse, it is not safe to rely solely on the common sense and knowledge of those who have no experience in the field of industrial relations. A course of conduct which to those who have no practical experience with industrial relations might appear unfair or unreasonable, to those with specialist knowledge and experience might appear both fair and reasonable: and vice versa.

For this reason, it seems to us that the correct approach is to consider whether an industrial tribunal, properly directed in law and properly appreciating what is currently regarded as fair industrial practice, could have reached the decision reached by the majority of this tribunal. We have reached the conclusion that it could not.

The first question is: how should the industrial tribunal have directed themselves in law? It being conceded in this case that the applicants had been dismissed on the grounds of redundancy (and there being no agreed or customary procedure as to redundancy), in law the only question is whether the requirements of section 57(3) of the Act of 1978, were satisfied. That subsection as amended by section 6 of the Employment Act 1980 provides:

Where the employer has fulfilled the requirements of subsection (1), then, subject to sections 58 to 62, the determination of the question whether the dismissal was fair or unfair, having regard to the reason shown by the employer, shall depend on whether in the circumstances (including the size and administrative resources of the employer's undertaking) the employer acted reasonably or unreasonably in treating it as a sufficient reason for dismissing the employee; and that question shall be determined in accordance with equity and the substantial merits of the case.

For the purposes of the present case there are only two relevant principles of law arising from that subsection. First, that it is not the function of the industrial tribunal to decide whether they would have thought it fairer to act in some other way: the question is whether the dismissal lay within the range of conduct which a reasonable employer could have adopted. The second point of law, particularly relevant in the field of dismissal for redundancy, is that the tribunal must be satisfied that it was reasonable to dismiss each of the applicants on the ground of redundancy. It is not enough to show simply that it was reasonable to dismiss *an* employee; it must be shown that the employer acted reasonably in treating redundancy 'as a sufficient reason for dismissing *the* employee,' i.e. the employee complaining of dismissal. Therefore, if the circumstances of the employer make it inevitable that some employee must be dismissed, it is still necessary to consider the means whereby the applicant was selected to be the employee to be dismissed and the reasonableness of the steps taken by the employer to choose the applicant, rather than some other employee, for dismissal.

In law, therefore, the question we have to decide is whether a reasonable tribunal could have reached the conclusion that the dismissal of the applicants in this case lay within the range of conduct which a reasonable employer could have adopted. It is accordingly necessary to try to set down in very general terms what a properly instructed industrial tribunal would know to be the principles which, in current industrial practice, a reasonable employer would be expected to adopt. This is not a matter on which the chairman of this appeal tribunal feels that he can contribute much, since it depends on what industrial practices are currently accepted as being normal and proper. The two lay members of this appeal tribunal hold the view that it would be impossible to lay down detailed procedures which *all* reasonable employers would follow in *all* circumstances: the fair conduct of dismissals for redundancy must depend on the circumstances of each case. But in their experience, there is a generally accepted view in industrial relations that, in cases where the employees are represented by an independent union recognised by the employer, reasonable employers will seek to act in accordance with the following principles:

1. The employer will seek to give as much warning as possible of impending redundancies so as to enable the union and employees who may be affected to take early steps to inform themselves of the relevant facts, consider possible alternative solutions and, if necessary, find alternative employment in the undertaking or elsewhere.

2. The employer will consult the union as to the best means by which the desired management result can be achieved fairly and with as little hardship to the employees as possible. In particular, the employer will seek to agree with the union the criteria to be applied in selecting the employees to be made redundant. When a selection has been made, the employer will consider with the union whether the selection has been made in accordance with those criteria.

3. Whether or not an agreement as to the criteria to be adopted has been agreed with the union, the employer will seek to establish criteria for selection which so far as possible do not depend solely upon the opinion of the person making the selection but can be objectively checked against such things as attendance record, efficiency at the job, experience, or length of service.

4. The employer will seek to ensure that the selection is made fairly in accordance with these criteria and will consider any representations the union may make as to such selection.

5. The employer will seek to see whether instead of dismissing an employee he could offer him alternative employment.

The lay members stress that not all these factors are present in every case since circumstances may prevent one or more of them being given effect to. But the lay members would expect these principles to be departed from only where some good reason is shown to justify such departure. The basic approach is that, in the unfortunate circumstances that necessarily attend redundancies, as much as is reasonably possible should be done to mitigate the impact on the work force and to satisfy them that the selection has been made fairly and not on the basis of personal whim.

Later in the similar case of *Grundy (Teddington) Ltd* v. *Plummer* the President of the EAT restated the case for guidelines more openly and boldly in the following terms:

> *Grundy (Teddington) Ltd* v. *Plummer* [1983] IRLR 98 (EAT) at
> p. 102, para. 15

Mr Howard, although relying on the remarks of Lord Justice Lawton, did not take them to their logical conclusion. He accepted that in certain cases (such as the *Burchell* case) guidelines were appropriate but said that those laid down in the *Compair Maxam* case were not appropriate. He distinguished the *Burchell* type of guidelines on two grounds: first that they were guidelines to Industrial Tribunals as to how to apply s.57(3) (and not guidelines as to what constituted fair industrial conduct); secondly he said that the codes were silent on the matters covered by the guidelines in *Burchell* (whereas the codes do deal with redundancy). We do not consider these to be valid distinctions. Guidance to Industrial Tribunals as to how they should approach the question whether an employer's conduct is reasonable necessarily involves (by implication) guidance as to how in general an employer should approach similar problems if his conduct is to be held reasonable by an Industrial Tribunal. Such guidance therefore indirectly establishes what is reasonable industrial conduct. The fact that the codes contain some guidance as to what is reasonable conduct does not necessarily mean that they give sufficient guidance in a developing field. Without further guidance, inconsistent decisions and consequent confusion would result. We agree that it would be better if these matters were dealt with more fully by the codes and the codes were subject to more frequent review. But unless and until that happens, in the absence of some additional guidance, employers and employees could form no proper view of their rights until, after the event, an Industrial Tribunal decides whether the employer's conduct was reasonable.

At that stage, then, the determination of the Court of Appeal was overtly awaited for what, after more than ten years of litigation on appeal from industrial tribunals, was the crucial unresolved question about the proper design of the task of industrial tribunals both in policy terms and practical terms.

(g) Reinstatement and re-engagement

The legislators of the unfair dismissal legislation clearly thought that reinstatement or re-engagement were the fairest remedies or those which most directly expressed the aims of the legislation. The best way of controlling unfair dismissal was to prevent such dismissals from taking place. Accordingly they placed a duty upon industrial tribunals, once unfair dismissal had been found, to recommend re-engagement where that would be practicable and in accordance with equity (Industrial Relations Act 1971, s.106(4)). That duty was later extended to include reinstatement or re-engagement (TULRA 1974, Sch. 1, para. 17(2)). However, the industrial tribunals never showed much enthusiasm for these remedies, usually preferring to award compensation. For instance, in 1973 there were ninety-one recommendations of re-engagement (one per cent of all unfair dismissal applications) compared with 969 awards of compensation (10.4 per cent of all applications) (*Department of Employment Gazette*, June 1974, p. 504). The NIRC had no great impulse to correct this tendency, hardly adverting to the desirability of reinstatement in the many appeals they heard which concerned the quantum of compensation. In the small number of appeals they heard from recommendations of reinstatement or re-engagement, they contributed little by way of general theory. In *Curtis* v. *Paterson Ltd* [1973] ICR 496, they rejected an appeal by an *employee* who had been employed as an 'approved electrician' from a recommendation that he be re-engaged as an ordinary electrician; but they took the sting out of this finding by allowing his appeal against a reduction of his compensation. The reduction (from £102 to £50) had been for his refusal to implement the recommendation. The NIRC held that he had been justified in refusing the offer of re-engagement because he knew that it would be in breach of a collective agreement for him to be employed other than as an 'approved electrician' (a skilled grade). If this rather confused result points to anything, it is to a trend we shall encounter many times in discussing remedies, namely a preference for giving effect to value-judgments by providing monetary compensation rather than by granting or withholding reinstatement or re-engagement. In *Shipside (Ruthin) Ltd* v. *TGWU* [1973] ICR 503 (NIRC), the Industrial Court assumed the role of arbitrator in a collective dispute which had arisen out of the dismissal of two workers for shooting with air rifles during their lunch break. In their arbitrators' frame of mind they recommended re-engagement as a basis for the re-establishment of harmony. This approach was not typical in unfair dismissal cases, and was probably a reaction to the fact that the litigation itself had been collective in origin, having been a complaint under s.96 of the IRA against the union in respect of picketing action.

Since that time, the case-law both in NIRC and in the EAT has returned to the normal trend of shifting the emphasis away from reinstatement or re-engagement towards compensation. This preference made the courts the more willing to see industrial relations difficulties as a reason for refusing reinstatement or re-engagement. Thus in *Coleman* v. *Magnet Joinery Ltd* [1975] ICR 46 (CA), two skilled craftsmen who had resigned from UCATT because of their view that it was pursuing an insufficiently aggressive policy on their behalf, and who were dismissed in response to pressure from their fellow workers (there being a closed shop), were refused recommendations of re-engagement at all levels up to and including the Court of Appeal on the grounds that re-engagement would not be 'practicable' where it was to be predicted that serious industrial strife would result from the attempt to implement it. (The alternative approach, which was rejected, was in effect to view the issue of practicability as turning solely upon the availability of a job which the applicant could do.) This line of thought seems to have been taken still further in *Meridian Ltd* v. *Gomersall* [1977] ICR 597 (EAT) where two women millworkers were held to have been unfairly dismissed for clocking two other employees in five minutes before they actually returned to work. In deciding that the industrial tribunal had been wrong in ordering reinstatement, the EAT treated it as a material argument against reinstatement that 'the atmosphere in the factory had been poisoned against these girls' and that 'the then union representative had lost any desire to support the two girls and in fact gave evidence against them'. It is to be doubted whether the courts would be so swayed by such considerations if they were enthusiastic about reinstatement in the first place.

It will be noted how the terminology changed in the course of the foregoing discussion from 'recommendations' to 'orders'. That is because there was a determined attempt in the EPA 1975 to shift the balance of remedies towards reinstatement and re-engagement. Various steps were taken for this purpose. The power became that of making orders rather than recommendations (EPCA 1978, s.68(1)). Disobedience to an order for reinstatement or re-engagement is the subject of specific statutory sanctions rather than the open-ended common-law sanctions for contempt of court; but those statutory sanctions have been increased in severity compared with the former sanctions for refusal to comply with a recommendation. In particular, there is now required to be an additional element of compensation specifically attributable to the employer's refusal to reinstate or re-engage, and that additional award must be of at least thirteen weeks' pay (ibid., s.71(2)(*b*)(ii)). Moreover, there is provision for certain special awards in relation to dismissals for trade-union membership, non-membership or activity, and for certain higher additional awards for dismissals which constitute unlawful sex discrimination or racial discrimination (ibid., s.71(3), s.75A as amended or added by EA 1982, s.5). Furthermore, Parliament attempted to force the availability of reinstatement or re-engagement upon the attention of industrial tribunals and of employees by requiring the tribunal to explain to successful complainants what orders for reinstatement or re-engagement can be made and to ask successful complainants whether they wish for such an order (ibid., s.68(1)). The tribunal's power to make an order for reinstatement or re-engagement depends upon the employee expressing the wish for such an order – ibid., s.68(1).

However, even this direct assault failed to dislodge the industrial tribunals from their position of preference for compensation over the specific remedies (see below, pp. 479ff.). The availability of the specific remedies tends to be discussed with complainants in a rather perfunctory way and with a lack of conviction or urgency. An industrial tribunal chairman who had read the judgment in *Meridian Ltd* v. *Gomersall* ([1977] ICR 597 above) could indeed be forgiven for supposing that he was not required officiously to strive to persuade the complainant to accept reinstatement or re-engagement. He is unlikely in practice to strive to that end, for he and his colleagues seem to share with the judges of the EAT a positive preference for the remedy of compensation as a means of achieving more exact and discriminating justice in dismissal cases. This was confirmed in an interesting way by the decision of the EAT in *Timex Corporation* v. *Thomson* [1981] IRLR 522, where the employer appealed against an order for re-engagement that had been made in a redundancy situation. The ground of appeal was that it had not been established that re-engagement was practicable. This ground of appeal was rejected, the EAT pointing out that practicability needed only to be considered and not positively established. But they also pointed out that, on the other hand, practicability was a necessary condition for the making of an additional award of compensation for failure to comply with the order for reinstatement or re-engagement. This means that the employer has the opportunity to convince the industrial tribunal that they would not, with the benefit of hindsight, have awarded reinstatement or re-engagement. If so persuaded, the tribunal may proceed as if compensation had been decided upon as the appropriate remedy in the first place.

Meanwhile, there has been some study of the practice of industrial tribunals to see why reinstatement and re-engagement are not more commonly awarded. Dickens, Hart, Jones and Weekes, writing in 1981 ('Re-employment of Unfairly Dismissed Workers: The Lost Remedy', 10 *ILJ* 160) on the basis of a survey and other research into the workings of the tribunal system in the later 1970s, concluded that it was the failure of the tribunals and the ACAS conciliators to promote these remedies which caused their low incidence, rather than the applicants' lack of enthusiasm for them or their non-viability. Paul Lewis, also writing in 1981 ('An analysis of why legislation has failed to provide employment protection for unfairly dismissed workers', 19 *BJIR* 316) on the basis of unpublished DE statistics and a survey and postal question-naire carried out by the author, argued that applicants' choice of com-pensation was a more important factor against reinstatement or re-engage-ment than Dickens *et al.* thought. In particular he argued that a very high proportion of applicants who had wanted reinstatement or re-engagement at the stage of making their initial application had ceased to want those remedies by the time of the tribunal hearing because the lapse of time had made them seem impracticable or at least unattractive. Dickens *et al.* wrote a rejoinder ((1982) 20 *BJIR* 257) in which they queried, on the basis of their own researches, Lewis's finding that 71 per cent of applicants who won their cases had requested re-employment at the time of their original application. They assert that there is nothing like so large a falling-off of applications for re-employment as between original application and hearing, and that the low rate of orders for re-employment is after all to be explained in terms of the way that ACAS conciliators and industrial tribunals approach that choice. (See, however, a subsequent rejoinder by Paul Lewis (1983) 21 *BJIR* at 232.) At all events this seems to be a matter in which the preferences of all those concerned – the parties, the ACAS conciliators, the industrial tribunals and the appellate courts – point in the same direction, even if it is difficult to disentangle the precise causative factors at work. The upshot is that there is a fairly profound disinclination to operate the unfair dismissal legislation as an instrument of positive job security.

(h) Compensation

In the original legislation of 1971, Parliament clearly intended to give the industrial tribunals as free a hand as possible in the awarding of compensation for unfair dismissal. They expressed this intention by a set of provisions whose main thrust was to confer upon industrial tribunals a power to award such sums as should seem just and equitable in all the circumstances having regard to the loss sustained by the complainant as a result of the dismissal. With this authorization the NIRC gradually shaped a system of principles relating to compensation which enabled compensation to assume its present role as the primary remedy for unfair dismissal. In order to achieve this effect the Industrial Court evolved two main lines of principle. First, they restricted compensation closely to pecuniary loss. Secondly, and on the other hand, they insisted that a wide and imaginative view should be taken of attributable pecuniary loss. After the system thus created had been working for several years, the legislature intervened and imposed a shift of direction by creating a new distinction between the basic award and the compensatory award of compensation for unfair dismissal (EPCA 1978, ss.72–4). The maximum basic award is £4,350 and the maximum compensatory award is £7,500 (as from 1 February 1984). The newly-created Employment Appeal Tribunal responded in turn to this imposed shift of direction by taking a narrower view of the loss attributable to unfair dismissal. Let us develop each of these rather large statements in turn.

It is probably fair to say that when they were first entrusted with the unfair dismissal jurisdiction, the industrial tribunals and the industrial court shared an anxiety that the industrial tribunals might be required to hear fanciful or unduly subjective claims that employees had suffered a loss of standing and reputation as the result of the fact of being unfairly dismissed or of the manner of such a dismissal. They perhaps feared, moreover, that the assessment of compensation for unfair dismissal might assume an impressionistic and erratic character. The NIRC made it its business quickly to set these fears at rest, in the case of *Norton Tool Co.* v. *Tewson* [1972] ICR 501, by insisting that the reference to the employee's loss in the statutory formula for the award of compensation was paramount and that hence the industrial tribunals had been entrusted with a purely pecuniary exercise in the assessment of compensation. In particular, a claim that the employee had suffered damage to his reputation could be entertained only so far as it issued forth in identifiable pecuniary loss consisting in specific damage to his employment prospects. This approach has been consistently accepted and welcomed both in the industrial tribunals and in the appellate courts from that time onwards, and was reasserted by the E A T in the case of *Brittains Arborfield* v. *Van Uden* [1977] I C R 211.

In return for this restriction of compensation to pecuniary loss the industrial court was determined to ensure that the pecuniary loss should be assessed as fully and imaginatively as possible. Not only did they take a more scientific approach to pecuniary loss flowing from dismissal than had been taken under the common law of wrongful dismissal, but they also harnessed science to the maximizing of damages rather than to the minimizing of them. Hence in particular they achieved a fuller recognition of the extent of loss of statutory and other seniority rights than had ever previously been shown.

This recognition of the value of seniority rights proved fairly straight-forward in relation, for instance, to the loss of protection against future unfair dismissal (there being at that time a two-year qualifying period); and it shortly proved possible to establish a modest quantum for rights of that kind. The tribunals and courts were, however, to become bedevilled by the problem of quantifying the loss of protection against future redundancy; and they found it particularly hard to find a logical basis for the avoidance of double compensation in the case of unfair dismissals for present redundancy: see, for example, *Yorkshire Engineering Co. Ltd* v. *Burnham* [1974] I C R 77; *Millington* v. *Goodwin & Sons Ltd* [1975] I C R 104.

In view of these latter difficulties associated with the quantification of loss of future redundancy protection it was not surprising that the draftsmen of the E P A 1975 should decide to systematize this aspect of compensation for unfair dismissal by requiring there to be a basic award in all cases of compensation for unfair dismissal, which would be equivalent to the redundancy payment to which the complainant would be entitled[1] but which was subject to a minimum value of two weeks' pay (E P C A 1978, s.73). By virtue of that provision, loss of redundancy protection could henceforth be confined to the amount by which a severance payment made by the particular employer would have exceeded the statutory entitlement to redundancy payment (this is the effect of E P C A 1978, s.74(3)), and in practice industrial tribunals have largely ceased to worry about this aspect of compensation.

No doubt the legislators of the E P A intended to engraft the basic award upon a system of assessment of compensation which would remain otherwise unchanged. Here, however, they counted without the perceptions of the industrial tribunals and of the courts as to what constituted fair compensation. The industrial tribunals, having been taught to regard compensation as being linked with pecuniary loss, cavilled slightly at the fact that the basic award has

---

[1] The basic award is assessed according to the statutory concept of the week's pay (E P C A 1978, Sch. 14) and therefore does not include payment for voluntary (even if habitual) overtime working (*Brownson* v. *Hire Service Shops* [1978] I C R 517 (E A T)). But net loss of overtime pay should be included in the award of compensation for loss of earnings (ibid. and *Mullet* v. *Brush Electrical Machines Ltd* [1977] I C R 829 (E A T)).

to be made quite irrespective of whether the complainant sustained any loss –
compare, for instance, *Cadbury Ltd* v. *Doddington* [1977] ICR 982, where an
appeal was necessary to vindicate the clear statutory rule to that effect. Hence
we find that the EAT, commencing its existence as it did in the basic award
era, has tended to deploy those energies which the NIRC used in maximizing
compensation, in minimizing the compensatory element. Thus they have
insisted that an award must readily be reviewed when indications appear that
subsequently arising facts have made it excessive (*Help the Aged Housing
Association* v. *Vidler* [1977] IRLR 104). Thus also they have been careful to
stress the restrictions which should be observed in quantifying the loss of
compensation rights (*Smith Kline & French* v. *Coates* [1977] IRLR 220), and
they have insisted on the deduction of unemployment benefit received (*Mullet*
v. *Brush Electrical Machines Ltd* [1977] ICR 829). Furthermore, they have
required that claims of loss should not be speculative – see *Lifeguard Assurance
Ltd* v. *Zadrozny* [1977] IRLR 56.

   In another direction the EAT has gone still further than this in restricting
the quantum of loss attributable to dismissal: and it is arguable that they have
gone to the lengths of undermining the substance of the unfair dismissal
finding. The Industrial Court recognized in one of the very early cases of
compensation for unfair dismissal the feasibility of arguing in certain cases
that the claimant had sustained no loss from his unfair dismissal, in that he
would shortly have been dismissed anyway had he not been unfairly dismissed
(*Earl* v. *Slater Wheeler (Airlyne) Ltd* [1972] ICR 508). The NIRC clearly
intended that this blockbuster should be reserved for cases where there was
overwhelming evidence that the claimant had by his misconduct or incapacity
merited dismissal and where the unfairness of his dismissal was therefore
merely procedural, or 'technical' as it has come to be known.

   The EAT has not merely embraced this method of limiting the quantum of
loss but has thrown aside the restraints which the NIRC placed or would
undoubtedly, if necessary, have placed upon the whole idea. Thus the EAT
has made it not merely permissible for, but actually mandatory upon,
industrial tribunals to consider the possibility that the claimant would shortly
have been dismissed without unfairness in any event, as the following extract
shows.

British United Shoe Machinery Co. Ltd v. *Clarke*
[1978] ICR 70 (EAT)

PHILLIPS J.: In some cases it will happen that the industrial tribunal reaches the
conclusion that had everything been done which ought to have been done it would not
have made the slightest difference so far as the claimant before them was concerned.
That is to say, that whatever had been done, he would still have been dismissed and no
other employment would have been found. What in those circumstances is the correct
order for the industrial tribunal to make? Should they say that the case is not one of
unfair dismissal, or should they say that although the dismissal was unfair the
compensation to be awarded is nil? In our judgment in those circumstances either

course is open to the industrial tribunal, and they may (we do not say that they are obliged to) say that the dismissal was not unfair: see *Lowndes* v. *Specialist Heavy Engineering Ltd* [1977] ICR 1 (not a case of redundancy, but the same principle applies; though in a case of lack of capacity, etc., great care ought to be taken before saying that a warning would have been of no value) and *Clarkson International Tools Ltd* v. *Short* [1973] ICR 191. Or, they may say that although the dismissal was unfair the case is one for nil compensation; in which case they should state their reasons. The answer depends on what view the industrial tribunal forms when applying their mind to paragraph 6(8) of Schedule 1 to the Trade Union and Labour Relations Act 1974 [EPCA 1978, s.57(3)]. The confusion which sometimes exists about this question is made worse by a tendency to isolate one factor (such as, for example, that consultation would have done no good) rather than to consider all the facts and all the circumstances at the same time when applying paragraph 6(8). In such a case where the industrial tribunal finds that the dismissal was unfair it will be necessary for them to proceed to assess compensation, and for that purpose to make some estimate of what would have been the likely outcome had that been done which ought to have been done. It is often a difficult question, but one which the industrial tribunal in their capacity as an industrial jury are well suited to answer, and in respect of which they will not go wrong if they remember that what they are trying to do is to assess the loss suffered by the claimant, and not to punish the employer for his failure in industrial relations.

Moreover, the conclusion that the employee would shortly have been dismissed in any event need not, apparently, be attributable to his culpability but can be the product of an impending redundancy situation: *Young's of Gosport Ltd* v. *Kendell* [1977] ICR 907. This wide-ranging possibility of reducing the compensatory award tends to undermine the expressive quality and effect of a finding of unfair dismissal and tends also, perhaps, to encourage in industrial tribunals a view which the judges of the EAT freely express, that many dismissals are unfair in a 'merely technical' sense. For the NIRC, the finding that a dismissal was unfair seemed to be more morally cogent than it is for the EAT.

This tendency in the case-law of the EAT was taken up and expanded upon by the legislators in the EA 1980. Those responsible for the framing of that legislation shared the view that had been voiced by the judges in *Devis Ltd* v. *Atkins* (see above, p. 464) that it was quite unacceptable that an applicant should be able to recover compensation for an admittedly unfair dismissal where the substantive merits were against him because, for instance, of concealed misconduct during his employment. The legislators shared the perception of the various judges at the different stages of that case that the basic award provisions of the EPA 1975 could bring about that unacceptable result because they were not susceptible to overriding considerations of justice and equity in the way that the pre-1975 compensation provisions had uniformly been and the post-1975 compensatory award provisions had remained. By way of implementation of this policy, the following changes were made to the basic award provisions by section 9 of the EA 1980. Firstly, the overriding minimum of two weeks' pay was abolished. Secondly, provision was made for the amount of the basic award to be reduced where the employee has unreasonably refused an offer of reinstatement (new EPCA 1978, s.73(7A)). This partially re-introduces the duty to mitigate loss to the basic award, to which it had not previously been applicable. Thirdly, by way of direct response to the problem identified in *Devis Ltd* v. *Atkins*, it was provided that the basic award should be reduced by reason of any pre-dismissal conduct on the part of the applicant making it just and equitable so to do (new EPCA 1978, s.73(7B)). The basic award had always been susceptible to consider-ations of contributory fault (EPCA 1978, s.73(7), see below, p. 503); the new provision enables account to be taken of pre-dismissal conduct which did not contribute to the dismissal because, for instance, the employer did not know of it when he took the decision to dismiss. The commitment is evident to a view of substantive justice which demands that the employee shall not receive more than his just deserts by reason of having been unfairly dismissed. It is a stance which has on the whole been maintained since then by the appellate courts. Thus even to the extent that the EAT has on occasions been critical of the doctrine in *British Labour Pump Co.* v. *Byrne* (see above, p. 481) as a doctrine about what constitutes unfairness, they have at the same time stressed that the same doctrine is a perfectly legitimate limit upon compensation; i.e. that an applicant should not be compensated for the unfairness of a dismissal beyond the extent to which the unfairness affected the outcome in the sense of producing a dismissal that would not otherwise have occurred. This is made quite clear, for instance, in the *Sillifant* v. *Powell Duffryn* case (see above, p. 486) in which the attack upon the *British Labour Pump Co.* approach to the question of fairness was most powerfully developed.

In a sense the recurring theme in this discussion is the confidence that Parliament and the courts seem to have in the remedy of compensation as a means of achieving exact and discriminating justice. There are many manifestations of this confidence. For instance, in *Abbotts* v. *Wesson-Glynwed Steels Ltd* [1982] IRLR 51, where it was held that the applicant's dismissal for redundancy had been procedurally unfair, the EAT felt confident enough of its ability to ensure that compensation exactly fitted the projected outcome if there had been no unfairness, to move from nil compensation on the footing that dismissal would have occurred in any event to compensation for two weeks' loss of pay on the footing that due consultation would have deferred the dismissal by that length of time. This confidence in compensation as a means of achieving fine-tuning (which incidentally in that case led to a re-invention at an individual level of the protective award provisions which are made at a collective level by Part IV of the EPA 1975 (see above, pp. 243ff.)) can sometimes lead to a presentation in almost scientific terms of what is ultimately surely an impressionistic assessment. Consider for example the following faintly comical passage in which the EAT assesses compensation in a case of dismissal by reason of the applicant's record of absences due to ill-health:

Townson v. *Northgate Group Ltd* [1981] IRLR 383 (EAT) at
p. 385, paras. 15–17

MAY J.: In the circumstances, we are quite satisfied that we can do what is just and
equitable between the parties in all the circumstances, having regard to the loss
sustained by the complainant in consequence of the dismissal, just as well as the
Industrial Tribunal were this matter to go back to it. We think that the just and
equitable compensatory award, having regard to the loss sustained by this particular
applicant as the result of his dismissal and all the circumstances in this case, is to give
the complainant his lost wages at the nett rate of £71 per week between 3 June and 6
August when he got the fresh employment in 1980. In addition to that, he must have the
£20 which is the nominal figure for the loss of statutory industrial rights. From the total
must be deducted the money which he received in lieu of notice and the tax rebate.

We add this, that we have borne in mind Mr Harris's submission that the fact that
this employee lost his fresh employment early in September 1980 was not his own fault
nor was it attributable to the ill-health which had dogged his path during his
employment with the employers in the present case. It is one of the circumstances
which we have taken into account. We have also taken into account the fact that that
job he did get in August 1980 happened to be at a substantially greater wage than the
one he was receiving from his previous employers. These are all matters which must go
into the melting pot and, in the end, the Industrial Tribunal, or ourselves on this
particular occasion, must come up with a figure which is not just plucked out of the air,
but is one arrived at in the exercise of discretion, bearing in mind the statutory
provisions to which we have referred, and one which is fair in all the circumstances of
the case.

Consequently, the cross-appeal will be dismissed and the appeal will be allowed to
the extent that the compensatory award will be increased from a nett figure of nil to
£265.

All this expenditure of adjudicative wisdom and energy on the determination of the precise quantum of compensation masks a real obscurity about the
underlying function of compensation for unfair dismissal. Sometimes, though
rather rarely, these issues are addressed in the case-law. For instance in *Daley*
v. *Dorsett (Almar Dolls) Ltd* [1982] ICR 1, one question was whether the
applicant might reasonably refuse to mitigate his loss of earnings where the
alternative employment in question was at a lower rate of pay than what he
was receiving in unemployment benefit. Having held that this refusal was in
the particular circumstances reasonable, the EAT went on to hold that it had
been wrong of the industrial tribunal to limit compensation on the ground that
it was the state and not the dismissing employer that should bear the cost of
loss of earnings up to the level of unemployment benefit. But these strategic
questions do not often figure in the assessment of compensation, and could not
indeed satisfactorily do so because it would be hard to relate the quantum of
compensation to any systematic goal connected with job security or attribution of liability for income support. This becomes very clear when one
considers the relatively low levels of most awards of compensation. Statistics
published by the Department of Employment show that the median level of

awards of compensation was £375 in 1978, £401 in 1979, £598 in 1980, £963 in 1981 and £1,201 in 1982. One may note how low the level was before 1980 and how sharp the rise was in 1981. There is no obvious explanation for the 1981 increase, certainly no visible change in policy to account for it. Perhaps the cause was an increase in the length of the period of unemployment for which compensation was being awarded, as is suggested in *IRLIB* 227 at p. 14. Perhaps also conditions of recession brought about a relative increase in the number of successful applicants of substantial seniority in their employment whose basic awards were therefore high. But even on the 1981 figures, it is clear that the unfair dismissal jurisdiction gives rise to income replacement for weeks rather than months or years. This is made all the more true by reason of the diminution of compensation on the ground of contributory fault, to the consideration of which we now turn.

(i) Contributory fault

The conscious or subconscious preference of the industrial tribunals and appellate courts for compensation rather than reinstatement or re-engagement may be attributable in part to the fact that compensation can be reduced to express the tribunals' view of the claimant's contributory fault, whereas orders for reinstatement cannot, once made, give effect to a view that the claimant was partly at fault, whilst orders for re-engagement can do so only theoretically in relation to the terms of re-engagement (EPCA 1978, s.69(5)(*c*), (6)(*c*) and proviso). By contrast, contributory fault has always been a central element in the assessment of compensation, and provision is now made for it to go in reduction of the basic award as well as of the compensatory award (EPCA 1978, ss.73(7), 74(6)). As in our discussion of the quantification of loss, we may again usefully contrast the approaches of the NIRC and of the EAT to these provisions. The former was indeed concerned to ensure that reduction of compensation by reason of the employee's contributory fault should, in principle, be widely available. The statutory provision relating to contributory fault which the NIRC had to interpret spoke of reduction of compensation where the complainant had contributed to 'the matters to which the complaint relates' (Industrial Relations Act 1971, s.116(3)). This formulation raised the argument that there could be no reduction of compensation where the complainant's fault went to the substance of the matter but the respondent's unfairness consisted in procedural defects. The NIRC dealt firmly with this argument in *Maris* v. *Rotherham Corporation* [1947] ICR 435, holding that in such a case the complainant had contributed to his dismissal, albeit not to its unfairness, and hence that compensation could properly be reduced. In so holding the NIRC was primarily concerned to vindicate the principle of contribution rather than to encourage its general use as a means of containing the size of awards of compensation. The EAT, on the other hand, has in general been concerned to maximize the use of the contribution provisions. Not all its judges are prepared to go to the lengths of their Lordships in Scotland in insisting that there is nothing wrong with a 100 per cent reduction in compensation by reason of contributory fault: *Courtney* v. *Babcock & Wilcox Ltd* [1977] IRLR 30. But even in its gentler lowlands the EAT has envisaged, for instance, a *duty* on the part of industrial tribunals to consider the question of contributory fault, as distinct from a capacity to do so: *Sutcliffe & Eaton Ltd* v. *Pinney* [1977] IRLR 319. The analogy here with their approach to the quantification of loss needs no elaboration. However, the EAT has come to realize that if it treads too far the path of maximizing contributory fault (compare *Patterson* v. *Bracketts Ltd* [1977] IRLR 137), it will enable employers to adduce twice over their grounds for dismissing the employee where those grounds have by definition been insufficient to stave off a finding that the dismissal was basically unfair. The EAT responds to this problem in the cases of *PO* v. *Mughal* [1977] ICR 763, *Garner* v. *Grange Furnishing Ltd* [1977] IRLR 266, *Hazell's Offset* v. *Lockett* [1977] IRLR 430 and *Kraft Foods Ltd* v. *Fox* (see extract below) by finding various ways of holding down the quantum of contributory fault.

Kraft Foods Ltd v. *Fox* [1978] ICR 311 (EAT)

KILNER BROWN J.: In this case the company, the well known Kraft Foods Ltd, appeal against the finding of an industrial tribunal held at Liverpool on 19 October 1976. On that occasion the tribunal came to the decision that the employee, Mr Fox, had been unfairly dismissed; they also came to the conclusion that he himself, by his conduct, had contributed to his dismissal to the extent of 50 per cent. They went on to adjourn the question of the amount of compensation; but it is not with that in view that this appeal is made. The company are of the opinion, in our view rightly, that there was an error of law in the finding of this industrial tribunal. It is an interesting point and is one which in our view requires clarification.

The facts need to be very shortly stated. The employee was appointed to an office as clerk manager at the company's factory at Kirkby, near Liverpool. He succeeded a Mr Norman Brand who was promoted. Mr Brand became production director at the head office of this very large and well known organization. It is quite plain from the evidence that he, Mr Brand, had set very high standards and was a highly efficient person. It may well be that the standards which were set by Mr Brand were so high that it would have been difficult to find someone adequately to succeed him. It is quite plain that the employee was not capable of carrying out this position in accordance with those high standards.

The application before the industrial tribunal was founded on accusations of personality differences. The company came to the industrial tribunal with a clear concession, very properly made, that there was a dismissal by them, and the justification for the dismissal was that the employee unhappily was inadequate for the position to which he had been appointed.

The critical paragraph in the reasons of the industrial tribunal is paragraph 12. Having dealt with the facts as we have stated them and with the efficiency and high standard set by Mr Brand, the tribunal said: 'We consider this to be a case of Mr Brand's successor accepting a position which was not as suitable to his training and capabilities . . .' Then as Mr Hammond [counsel for the appellant company] – who has conducted this case in the absence of the employee with propriety and fairness – indicates, the industrial tribunal seem to have found themselves in some difficulty and, perhaps quite understandably, have arrived at a decision which was really a compromise decision and one which did not logically and clearly reach a conclusion one way or the other upon the evidence.

[The appellant company's first point of law was then considered and rejected.]

Where, however, in our judgment there is a plain error of law arises [*sic*] with regard to the question of contribution. This is a point of importance and one which we consider does require some clarification. If an employee is incompetent or incapable and cannot, with the best will in the world, measure up to the job, it seems to us to be wrong to say that that condition of incapacity is a contributory factor to his dismissal. The whole point about contribution is that it is something by way of conduct on the part of the employee over which he has control. Thus a man may be guilty of misconduct, he may misbehave. He does not have to misbehave. He does not have to do something which can be categorized as misconduct. In the case of a man who falls short, he may not try. He may not be doing his best. That is something over which he has control. However, if he is doing his best and his best is not good enough, it does not seem to us to be proper to say that in those circumstances he has contributed and therefore a finding in his favour should be reduced by whatever proportion the industrial tribunal has decided. In this case, this is what this industrial tribunal did. Quite obviously they were doing their best to be fair and reasonable. There are grounds for hoping that we also, and the company, will be and are being reasonable. . . . Consequently we are unanimously of the opinion that the decision of this industrial tribunal must be set aside.

There are two courses open to us. One is to remit it. That is very inconvenient, is unfair and in the circumstances of this case would be unjust. Here is a man who has left the country. It is inconvenient and unnecessary for him to come back on this occasion; it would be even more so if he had to come back on a later occasion. In our view, on the evidence in this case it would be very difficult for an industrial tribunal to say that there had been an unfair dismissal. Certainly it is, in our view, on the facts of this case, quite wrong to say that the employee, if there was an unfair dismissal, contributed to the extent of 50 per cent. As Mr Hammond put it, this is either a case in which the employee should win altogether or should lose altogether. In our view the probabilities, and the overwhelming probabilities, are that, looked at broadly speaking, he would lose altogether.

Consequently it seems to us that the sensible way out of this case – with the assistance of the company who have been very generous, very helpful and have acted very properly – is to say that rather than have a remission we will set aside this award and allow the appeal. That is done upon the clear undertaking given to this court that the company intend to act generously by way of *ex gratia* payment to assist this employee in the costs of his removal to his new appointment elsewhere. That seems to us to be the sensible, fair and best way out of this case.

There is another aspect to the judicial approach to the question of contributory fault. In the case of *Devis & Sons Ltd* v. *Atkins* [1977] I C R 662, the various appellate courts confronted the limits of the doctrine of contributory fault in the situation where the employee was heavily at fault (in that he was thought to have defrauded his employer) but where that fault in no way contributed to his dismissal because it was unknown to the employer when he was dismissed. The House of Lords decided the case under the old provisions for compensation and therefore before the basic award provisions had come into effect, but they anticipated the day when the basic award provisions would be in effect and when they would be unable to give effect to the claimant's fault either as a matter of contributory fault or on the basis that he had sustained no loss (because the basic award would still be payable despite the absence of loss). Their Lordships took the view that it would in those circumstances be proper to hold that the claimant had never been unfairly dismissed in the first place. Would it be unfair to suggest that the courts feel the need to respond to fault on the part of the employee and that the contributory character of that fault is therefore ultimately a subordinate consideration in their minds? If that is so, the unfair dismissal process tends to become an arbitration as to whether and in what degree the employer or the employee is more blameworthy than the other. This may be thought to be one form of industrial justice but the expressive and educational purpose of the law of unfair dismissal tends to get lost in such a process.

The most recent years have on the whole seen a confirmation of the trend towards maximum use of the contribution provisions in order to give effect to perceptions of the merits pointing against the employee. Admittedly, the Court of Appeal seemed to take the opposite direction in *Nelson* v *BBC (No. 2)* [1980] ICR 110, where they ruled that in order to treat the applicant's conduct as contributory, the industrial tribunal had to be satisfied that it was culpable or blameworthy in the sense that, whether or not it amounted to a breach of contract or tort, it was foolish or perverse or unreasonable in the circumstances (see *per* Brandon L.J. at p. 121). But this was offset by the later decision of the Court of Appeal in *Hollier* v. *Plysu Ltd* [1983] IRLR 260, where it was stressed that the apportionment of contribution to the applicant turned on issues of fact rather than of law, so that only a clearly perverse apportionment would be appealable. This decision tends to maximize the capacity of the industrial tribunals to arrive at high reductions of compensation. An instance of the kind of approach to contribution that was so endorsed by the Court of Appeal is provided by the decision of the EAT in *Ladup Ltd* v. *Barnes* [1982] ICR 107. An employee at a casino had been dismissed following his being arrested and charged with the growing and possession of cannabis. The industrial tribunal held that his dismissal had been unfair for lack of proper investigation, and refused a review of compensation when the applicant was later convicted of these offences. The EAT held that the conviction showed that the applicant had been entirely to blame for his dismissal and ordered that he contribute to his compensation as to 100 per cent, remarking merely that 'that is a percentage which some might think illogical but has the blessing of authority' (at p. 110). So it would seem that such restraints as still exist upon the undermining of procedural considerations in relation to the question of unfairness disappear entirely at the stage of awarding compensation and reducing that compensation in order to express perceptions about the substantive merits.

(j) **The social operation of the unfair dismissal legislation**
One may usefully consider the social operation of the unfair dismissal legislation from three distinct points of view. First, one may consider the success of the industrial tribunals process as a method of dealing with disputes over dismissals. It may be useful to draw attention to some figures. During 1977 there were 32,497 (1976: 31,614) applications to industrial tribunals alleging unfair dismissal, and there were 12,800 (13,800) cases dealt with by tribunal hearings, 22,500 (18,000) cases being dealt with by the ACAS conciliators. Of the tribunal hearings, 26 per cent (28) resulted in awards of compensation and 1.4 per cent (2) resulted in reinstatement or re-engagement. Of the conciliated applications 52 per cent (58) resulted in the payments of compensation and 2.6 per cent (4) resulted in reinstatement or re-engagement. The median figure for compensation agreed in conciliation was £150, whilst the median compensation awarded by tribunals was £400. The average time from the making of a complaint to the industrial tribunal hearing (where one takes place) is nine weeks. The great increase in applications as between 1975 and 1976 was thought to have levelled off: see Dudley Jackson, 'Use of the Law of Unfair Dismissal' (University of Aston Management Centre Working Paper No. 95, 1978). That increase was thought to be mainly attributable to the two-stage reduction by the Trade Union and Labour Relations Act 1974 of the qualifying period of service from two years to six months. The picture given by these figures is that of a reasonably speedy process which was quite heavily used (one source suggests that in 1977 there was a complaint of unfair dismissal in one in every fourteen dismissals) and which was producing quite a high success rate from the point of view of employees using the process.

For the years 1979 to 1981, the corresponding figures are shown on p. 508 (*IRLIB* No. 227 (February 1983), based on figures published by the Department of Employment). The drop in applications in 1980 was presumably attributable to the extension of the qualifying period from 26 weeks to 52 weeks by the Unfair Dismissal (Variation of Qualifying Period) Order 1979, SI No. 959, and some further diminution in applications was presumably brought about by the further extension in the qualifying period to two years in the case of employers of no more than 20 employees, which was effected by section 8 of the EA 1980, both measures being designed to reduce the burden of employment protection legislation upon employers in general and small employers in particular. One would expect that these measures would tend to eliminate many complaints about dismissals for incompetence or want of capability on the part of new employees who have in effect failed to satisfy formal or informal periods of probation. One would then expect that the upsurge in applications in 1981 reflected a more than compensating increase in the number of applications from employees who had been made redundant because of the recession. This may in turn help to explain the decline in the

Unfair dismissal applications, 1979, 1980 and 1981

	1979		1980		1981		PHAs[1]	
	Number	Per cent	Number	Per cent	Number	Per cent	Number	Per cent
Cases disposed of	33,383	100	28,624	100	36,276	100	2188[2]	100
Withdrawals	10,256	30.7	9081	31.7	11,463	31.6	1243[3]	56.8
Agreed settlements	11,422	34.2	9506	33.2	11,377	31.4	304[4]	13.9
Tribunal hearings	11,705	35.1	10,037	35.1	13,436	37.0	641	29.3
Outcome of Tribunal hearings								
Cases dismissed	8518	72.8 (25.5 of all)	7259	72.3 (25.4 of all)	10,302	76.7 (28.4 of all)	532	83.0 (24.3 of all)
Cases upheld	3187	27.2 (9.6)	2778	27.7 (9.7)	3134	23.3 (8.6)	109	17.0 (5.0)
Remedies awarded by Tribunals								
Reinstatement	76	0.6 (0.2)	55	0.6 (0.2)	93	0.7 (0.3)		
Re-engagement	23	0.2 (0.1)	23	0.2 (0.1)	57	0.4 (0.2)		
Compensation	2388	20.4 (7.2)	1994	19.9 (7.0)	1945	14.5 (5.3)		
Redundancy payment	153	1.3 (0.5)	100	1.0 (0.3)	165	1.2 (0.4)		
Other remedy	547	4.7 (1.6)	606	6.0 (2.1)	874	6.5 (2.4)		

Note: 'PHA' = pre-hearing assessment.
[1] In period 1.10.80–31.12.81.
[2] Cases where PHA ordered and ultimate outcome is known.
[3] Includes cases withdrawn before PHA took place.
[4] Includes cases settled before PHA took place.

success rate of application between 1980 and 1981, since industrial tribunals tend to accord employers a rather freer hand in dismissing for redundancy than in dismissing for misconduct or incompetence. Provision was made by the Industrial Tribunals (Rules of Procedure) Regulations 1980, SI No. 884, for a pre-hearing assessment to be held on the application of either party in order to discourage the pursuit of arguments having no reasonable prospect of success, the sanction being that the tribunal may warn one of the parties at the pre-hearing assessment that he will proceed further at his peril in terms of costs (Rule 6). The indications are that the PHA or the threat of it operates as quite an effective way of reducing the number of claims that are pursued to a hearing. So there have been a number of measures which have tended to reduce the number of industrial tribunal hearings, and given the very large numbers of dismissals that have occurred in the most recent of the years for which figures are available because of the recession, one must conclude that there has been some degree of successful discouragement, producing at least stagnation if not underlying decline in the use of the industrial tribunal process as a way of processing dismissal disputes.

The second point of view from which one may consider the social effect of the unfair dismissal legislation is that of its effect upon employers' policies in relation to personnel management and manpower planning. A valuable study has been made in this area by W.W. Daniel and Elizabeth Stilgoe for the Policy Studies Institute ('The impact of employment protection laws', PSI Report No. 577, June 1978). They were partly concerned to establish the truth of the view widely held among employers that employment protection legislation was creating an active disincentive to the recruitment of labour; we considered in the first chapter their conclusions on that point (below, pp. 39ff.). They also examined the impact of the legislation on the practice of personnel management generally. They took a sample of the views of managers in 300 plants employing 50 to 5,000 people in manufacturing industry. They found that managers regarded the unfair dismissal legislation as having much the greatest impact upon them of all the employment protection legislation, the impact being more marked still in plants which had experienced falling or variable demand for products in the previous twelve months. The impact seemed to consist in a stimulus to changes in procedures relating to discipline, dismissals and selection. It had also produced a fall in rates of dismissal for reasons other than redundancy. The authors of the report had conducted a survey which showed the virtual disappearance by 1977, compared with 1969, of plants with very high levels of dismissal – in 1969 a survey conducted by Sandra Dawson had found a significant percentage of plants dismissing eleven per cent or more of their employees within a twelve-month period.

In terms of managerial opinion about the costs and benefits of the legislation, Daniel and Stilgoe found a fairly even division of opinion as to whether or not employment protection legislation, particularly unfair dismissal legislation, had been to their organization's advantage. Some managers welcomed the necessity that the legislation had imposed to establish formal procedures especially with regard to discipline (see above, p. 40), and felt that this tended to save them from the consequences of line managers or supervisors taking arbitrary and idiosyncratic action. It had also increased the care and attention devoted to personnel management, job specification and training, and 'the influence of the personnel function had increased'. Managers who viewed the impact of the legislation as adverse tended to concentrate their criticisms on the increase in work it had brought about – in particular the work of self-protective record keeping and the preparation of defences against claims. They said that the processes of recruitment and dismissal had been made more difficult, time consuming and therefore costly. It is interesting that Daniel and Stilgoe found that a balance of opinion existed about these matters. Their findings are usefully summarized in an article by Daniel (1978 *Department of Employment Gazette*, pp. 658–61).

The third point of view from which one may seek to evaluate the social effects of the legislation is that of its impact upon collective bargaining about dismissal or arrangements for representation of or by trade unions in relation to dismissal. We have already considered the impact (limited to the point of virtual non-existence) of the provision for exemption from the legislation where a voluntary joint procedure exists (EPCA 1978, s.65) (see above, p. 264). The fact that there is little or no impetus to apply for exemption from the legislation on the basis of voluntary joint procedures should not however disguise the importance of voluntary joint arrangements as an effective alternative to the use of industrial tribunals as a means of dealing with disputes about dismissals. Some of the data about the use of industrial tribunals point in that direction. We know that relatively highly-unionized industries are under-represented and vice versa so far as complaints to industrial tribunals of unfair dismissal are concerned. Three relatively poorly-organized industries in terms of trade-union membership – construction, distribution and miscellaneous services – account for half of the complaints of unfair dismissal, whereas mining, shipbuilding and public services are under-represented, presumably on the basis of the existence of effective voluntary machinery. In their survey of manufacturing industry, Daniel and Stilgoe found that managers' accounts of the effect of the unfair dismissal legislation tended to fall into a pattern whereby the higher the level of trade-union membership in plants the less likely managers were to report any effect. They concluded that in the very highly-organized plants dismissal procedures were more likely to have pre-dated the legislation, so that its introduction had had less impact there. Two of Dudley Jackson's main findings in his Working Paper (see above, p. 507) were that low-paid workers were over-represented in terms of complaints of unfair dismissal, and that very considerable use of the statutory machinery was being made by short-service employees (the two categories being somewhat coincident). It is possible that these findings further reflect the use of the unfair dismissal legislation as a substitute for voluntary joint procedures by those in poorly organized categories of workers.

This is not to say, however, that the legislation operates simply as an alternative to voluntary joint procedures without having any impact upon them. Daniel and Stilgoe found that managers who regarded the legislation as on balance advantageous sometimes attributed to it an improvement in the climate of industrial relations, because it had brought about a state of affairs in which employees and their representatives knew where they stood. Other managers, on the other hand, complained that managerial authority had been eroded. All this is as one might expect: by providing employees with procedural and substantive protection against dismissal, the legislation has presumably paved the way, in a range of situations, for more effective trade-union representation in disputes about dismissal. Is this after all a case where primarily regulatory legislation might have some auxiliary role in relation to processes of voluntary joint resolution of dismissal disputes? Might it conceivably have widened the extent to which dismissals are perceived as matters for joint regulation? It will be some time before any conclusions can be drawn, but possibilities of significance to the pattern of our labour law have clearly been opened up.

These possibilities may be seen as assuming an even greater importance in a climate which has, as we have seen earlier in this book (Chapter 2, *passim*), favoured the dismantling of direct legal supports to the collective bargaining process and the role of trade unions therein. But on the other hand the decline in efficacy of the unfair dismissal legislation which we have described earlier in this subsection may well have eroded the significance of that legislation in its auxiliary aspect as well as in its employment protection aspect. For instance the TUC in 1982 made the following comment on the unfair dismissal statistics for 1981: 'These figures reinforce the TUC's advice in previous years that trade union officials should use collective agreements at the workplace to deal with disciplinary questions and that applications to tribunals should only be used as a last resort when a satisfactory outcome cannot be reached by other methods' (*TUC Industrial Relations Bulletin* for November 1982). The danger inherent in the situation exposed by that comment is that as unfair dismissal proceedings are seen as less and less of a cogent alternative to collective action about dismissals, the existence of the legislation will exert less and less pressure towards the creation and maintenance of voluntary procedures for the orderly joint regulation of dismissal issues. In that sense the social operation of the unfair dismissal legislation in an auxiliary collective role is directly linked to the success or failure of its social operation as an individual employment protection measure.

(k) Written statements of reasons for dismissal

The first few years of operation of the unfair dismissals legislation drew attention to a gap in the rights of the dismissed employee, namely that the employer was under no obligation to supply a statement of the reasons for the dismissal. Employers were and are required to provide details of dismissals to the Department of Health and Social Security for the purpose of determining whether the dismissed employee should be temporarily disqualified from unemployment benefit by reason of his having left for misconduct or having left voluntarily without good cause; but the dismissed employee has no right to see or receive a copy of the employer's answers to such a questionnaire. This gap was at least partly filled by s.70 of the EPA 1975, which gave employees the right to a written statement of reasons for dismissal and empowered and required industrial tribunals to award two weeks' pay to an employee who establishes a violation of that right (EPCA 1978, s.53). The reasons for doubting whether this gap in the employee's protection has been wholly filled is that s.70 was narrowly drafted and contained some important qualifications.

The most important of these qualifications consisted in the fact that the obligation to supply a written statement arises only upon a request being made by the employee (EPCA 1978, s.53(1)). A complaint of failure to comply with such a request is subject to the same time limits as a complaint of unfair dismissal (ibid., s.53(5)), so an employee, although he had already filed a claim for unfair dismissal, might discover that he was too late to request such a statement. Moreover, this qualification tends to characterize the giving of written statements as an occasional obligation, to be carried out at the instance of an employee who knows his rights, rather than as a matter of course for all dismissals.

This qualification is itself further qualified, for an industrial tribunal can grant a remedy only where the employer refuses to comply with a statutory request and does so unreasonably (ibid., s.53(4)). Although the EAT has ruled that a reasonable employer cannot simply ignore the employee's statutory request where he is asked not to reply to any correspondence by police investigating alleged theft by the employee (*Daynecourt Insurance Brokers Ltd* v. *Iles* [1978] IRLR 335), there has been an indication from the EAT sitting in Scotland that EPCA 1978, s.53 should be strictly construed, and that full weight should be given to the distinction between unreasonable refusal to provide reasons and mere inaction in response to a request (*Charles Lang & Sons Ltd* v. *Aubrey* [1978] ICR 168). On the other hand the EAT in England has sought to give full effect to the requirement that the written statement must give 'adequate' particulars (EPCA 1978, s.53(4)), by holding that the written statement must at least contain a simple statement of the essential reasons for the dismissal, even if it went on to give further detail by means of reference to other documents (*Horsley Smith & Sherry Ltd* v. *Dutton* [1977] ICR 594). One is, however, left with the general impression that there is a great difference in practice between an unqualified obligation to give written reasons for dismissal and an obligation to do so only upon request from the employee.

Indeed, as the rather extraordinary discussion of the section 53 point in *Rowan* v. *Machinery Installations (South Wales) Ltd* [1981] IRLR 122 indicates, the obligation not unreasonably to refuse to give written reasons on request may amount to much less than an obligation to give written reasons on request. (The case is reported in [1981] ICR 386, but not on this point.) There the refusal was treated as not unreasonable because a manager representing the company had thought that it was a reference rather than written reasons that were being requested. It is quite curious how what would seem to be an elementary and fairly uncontroversial procedural protection for the dismissed employee has been rendered of slight worth by the combination of legislative caution and negative judicial interpretation.

(l) Unfair dismissal under public law

In our earlier discussion of tenure of public office (above, pp. 435ff.), we found that the law about the duration of employment in the public sector could be satisfactorily explained only by recognizing the existence, in however embryonic a form, of a public service employment relationship which overlaps with but operates differently from the private law contract of employment. We must similarly recognize that the law about dismissal from employment in the public sector has also developed to a point where the private law of wrongful dismissal no longer provides a complete explanation of the structure, and that there exists a distinct law of unfair dismissal under public law. The statute law of unfair dismissal applies to public employment as an automatic consequence of the fact that workers in the public sector outside the civil service have contracts of employment; and the unfair dismissal legislation is applied to civil servants, whether or not they have contracts of employment, by what is now section 138 of the EPCA 1978. But in speaking of a law of unfair dismissal under public law, we refer not to that body of statute law but to an emergent aspect of that part of the common law which is known as administrative or, increasingly, public law. As a body of doctrine, the public law of unfair dismissal is permeated with uncertainties both of a conceptual and of a practical nature; but to deny its very existence on that ground would be the equivalent of the denial of the existence of a general body of administrative law which for so long stood in the way of an orderly and rational development of that branch of the law.

It is possible to trace the growth of the public law of unfair dismissal through a small number of leading cases, though it must be acknowledged at the outset that these cases become more and more fraught with uncertainties as we come inevitably closer to the problems of defining this body of law in its distinct form. It is useful to take as the starting-point the case of *Ridge* v. *Baldwin* [1964] AC 40. There is admittedly a significant pre-history; there are some cases in the late 1950s where the courts can be seen to start to address the problems of the application of emergent administrative law principles to certain kinds of public service employment relationships, for example *Vine* v. *National Dock Labour Board* [1957] AC 488 (registered dock workers) and *Barber* v. *Manchester Regional Hospital Board* [1958] 1 WLR 181 (doctors in National Health Service hospitals). But it was not until the watershed case of *Ridge* v. *Baldwin* that there was anything like a systematic attempt to face up to the problems of how far the administrative law principles of natural justice had altered the common law of employment. In that case the House of Lords accepted and enforced a vigorous view of the application of the principles of natural justice to dismissal from public office, in this case the office of chief constable. But they were prepared to do so only on the basis of a rigid and mutually exclusive distinction between the public office-holding relationship and the private employment relationship. But even as that position was stated, it was coupled with a recognition that there were some employment relationships in the public service that could not be forced neatly into that pattern, as the following key passage from Lord Reid's judgment shows:

> *Ridge* v. *Baldwin* [1964] AC 40 (HL) at p. 65
> LORD REID: So I shall deal first with cases of dismissal. These appear to fall into three classes: dismissal of a servant by his master, dismissal from an office during pleasure, and dismissal from an office where there must be something against a man to warrant his dismissal. The law regarding master and servant is not in doubt. There cannot be specific performance of a contract of service, and the master can terminate the contract with his servant at any time and for any reason or for none. But if he does so in a manner not warranted by the contract he must pay damages for breach of contract. So the question in a pure case of master and servant does not at all depend on whether the master has heard the servant in his own defence: it depends on whether the facts emerging at the trial prove breach of contract. But this kind of case can resemble dismissal from an office where the body employing the man is under some statutory or other restriction as to the kind of contract which it can make with its servants, or the grounds on which it can dismiss them. The present case does not fall within this class because a chief constable is not the servant of the watch committee or indeed of anyone else.

It is within that area implicitly recognized by Lord Reid of the employment relationship which is not a 'pure case of master and servant' that the public law of unfair dismissal has falteringly developed.

It will, we think, be clear in retrospect that the real breakthrough in this direction was made by the case of *Malloch* v. *Aberdeen Corporation* [1971] 1 WLR 1578, a case in the House of Lords on appeal from the Court of Session in Scotland. The case was brought to test the legality of the dismissal by a Scottish education authority of a certificated teacher for not being a registered teacher under a new scheme for registration of teachers in Scotland that had been introduced in 1967. In holding by a bare 3:2 majority that teachers in Scotland had a general right to be heard before they were dismissed, and that a purported dismissal without a hearing was null and void, the House of Lords effectively broke down the simple distinction between servant and office-holder which seemed to have survived in *Ridge* v. *Baldwin* and gave flesh, admittedly in a fairly inchoate form, to an 'impure case of master and servant' which had been only distantly contemplated in the earlier case. The following extract, again from a judgment of Lord Reid, will demonstrate the point.

Malloch v. *Aberdeen Corporation* [1971] 1 WLR 1578 (HL) at pp. 1581–4

LORD REID: The case for the respondents is threefold. First, they say that because the appellant held his post at pleasure he was not entitled to be heard before he was dismissed. Secondly, they say that, even if in general a teacher has a right to be heard before an education authority dismisses him, to have afforded him a hearing in this case would have been a useless formality because, whatever he might say, they were legally bound to dismiss him. And, thirdly, they say that even if he was entitled to a hearing he is not entitled to have their decision to dismiss him reduced or annulled. I must consider each of these three contentions in turn.

The first depends on a submission that the status of teachers in Scotland is simply that of an ordinary servant. At common law a master is not bound to hear his servant before he dismisses him. He can act unreasonably or capriciously if he so chooses but the dismissal is valid. The servant has no remedy unless the dismissal is in breach of contract and then the servant's only remedy is damages for breach of contract.

In my opinion, that is not the present status of teachers employed by Scottish education authorities. There is no doubt that prior to 1872 parish schoolmasters appointed by the heritors held office ad vitam aut culpam. But the Education (Scotland) Act of that year enacted by section 55 that teachers should in future be appointed by the new school boards 'and every appointment shall be during the pleasure of the school board.' The result was that their status was reduced to that of an ordinary servant. That appears clearly from the opinions in *Morrison* v. *Abernethy School Board* (1876) 3 R. 945.

But soon Parliament began to have second thoughts. In the Public Schools (Scotland) Teachers Act 1882 certificated teachers are said by section 3 to 'hold office' under school boards and their dismissal without 'due deliberation' is forbidden. In particular it is enacted that no dismissal shall be valid unless three weeks' notice of a meeting to consider a motion for dismissal is given both to every member of the board and to the teacher. I can see no possible reason for requiring notice to the teacher other than to give him an opportunity to prepare his defence, and it appears to me to be implicit in this requirement that the teacher shall be entitled to submit his defence to the board. Moreover, a school board refusing to hear the teacher whom it proposed to dismiss could hardly be said to proceed with due deliberation. It was said that this three weeks' notice may have been intended to give the teacher extra time to find new employment. I cannot accept that because until the motion for dismissal is put to the vote he does not know whether it will be carried – that required an absolute majority – and it would be premature for him to look for other employment: indeed if the board knew he was already looking for other employment that might affect the voting.

Then it was said that there was no obligation to give notice of any reason why it was proposed to dismiss him – so how could he prepare his defence? That appears to me quite unrealistic. It is extremely unlikely that such a motion could be put to a body of elected members representing a small area without the teacher getting to know its cause. A private employer may act in secret but a responsible elected public body can hardly do so.

Then it was said that it is inconsistent that a body should be entitled to act at pleasure but nevertheless bound to hear the teacher before acting. I can see no inconsistency. Acting at pleasure means that there is no obligation to formulate reasons. Formal reasons might lead to legal difficulties. But it seems to me perfectly sensible for Parliament to say to a public body: you need not give formal reasons but you must hear the man before you dismiss him. In my view, that is what Parliament did say in the 1882 Act.

Then by the Education (Scotland) Act 1908, section 21, a teacher could petition the Education Department for an enquiry into the reasons for his dismissal. If the department were of opinion that the dismissal was not reasonably justifiable they could give the school board an opportunity of reconsidering the matter and on refusal could award to the teacher up to a year's salary to be paid by the board. So there was not thought to be any difficulty in practice in discovering why the board had dismissed the teacher.

An elected public body is in a very different position from a private employer. Many of its servants in the lower grades are in the same position as servants of a private employer. But many in higher grades or 'offices' are given special statutory status or protection. The right of a man to be heard in his own defence is the most elementary protection of all and, where a statutory form of protection would be less effective if it did not carry with it a right to be heard, I would not find it difficult to imply this right. Here it appears to me that there is a plain implication to that effect in the 1882 Act. The terms of that Act have been altered by later legislation, but I can find nothing in any later Act which can reasonably be interpreted as taking away that elementary right.

Then it was argued that to have afforded a hearing to the appellant before dismissing him would have been a useless formality because whatever he might have said could have made no difference. If that could be clearly demonstrated it might be a good answer. But I need not decide that because there was here, I think, a substantial possibility that a sufficient number of the committee might have been persuaded not to vote for the appellant's dismissal. The motion for dismissal had to be carried by a two-thirds majority of those present, and at the previous meeting of the committee there was not a sufficient majority to carry a similar motion. Between these meetings the committee had received a strong letter from the Secretary of State urging them to dismiss the teachers who refused to register. And it appears that they had received some advice which might have been taken by them to mean that those who failed to vote for dismissal might incur personal liability. The appellant might have been able to persuade them that they need not have any such fear.

Then the appellant might have argued that on their true construction the regulations did not require the committee to dismiss him and that, if they did require that, they were ultra vires. The question of ultra vires was not argued before us and on that I shall say no more than that it is not obvious that the Secretary of State had power under any statute to make regulations requiring the dismissal of teachers who failed to acquire and pay for a new qualification such as registration. But the question of the proper construction of the regulations was argued and there I think that the appellant had at least an arguable case. . . .

So, if in general Scottish teachers have a right to be heard before they are dismissed, then I think that the appellant had that right and that the respondents' committee were in breach of duty in not hearing him. I fully realise that it would have been highly inconvenient to hear 38 teachers in succession. But that arises from the very clumsy machinery which had to be used if the respondents' interpretation of the regulation is correct.

If, then, the respondents were in breach of duty in denying the appellant a hearing, what is his remedy? It was argued that it would not be right to reduce the resolution of dismissal because that would involve the reinstatement of the appellant – in effect granting specific implement of his contract of employment which the law does not permit. But that would not be the effect. There would be no reinstatement. The result would be to hold that the appellant's contract of employment had never been terminated and it would be open to the respondents at any time hereafter to dismiss him if they chose to do so and did so in a lawful manner. Unless they chose to do that the appellant's contract of employment would continue.

Then it was said that the proper remedy would be damages. But in my view if an employer fails to take the preliminary steps which the law regards as essential he has no power to dismiss and any purported dismissal is a nullity. We were not referred to any case where a dismissal after failure to afford a hearing which the law required to be afforded was held to be anything but null and void.

A further significant advance in the march of the principles of public law into the land of public employment was made in the case of *Stevenson* v. *United Road Transport Union* [1977] ICR 893, which concerned the dismissal of a regional officer employed by a trade union. In holding the purported dismissal of the regional officer by the executive committee to be null and void by reason of non-compliance with the requirements of natural justice, the Court of Appeal was no doubt more disposed to apply administrative law principles than they would have been in the case, for example, of employment by a public authority, given that the relevant terms of the regional officer's employment were derived from the union rule-book and that the courts were well used to applying administrative law principles in that context. In any event, the application of public law in this case was as positive as its limits were obscure, as the following extract from the judgment of the Court of Appeal will show.

Stevenson v. *United Transport Workers Union* [1977] ICR 893 (CA)
at p. 902 C–H

BUCKLEY L.J.: Mr Rose, for the union, has contended that the principles applicable here are those applicable to the dismissal of a servant by his master, where, as Lord Reid pointed out in *Ridge* v. *Baldwin* [1964] AC 40, 65, the master is under no obligation to hear the servant in his own defence (and see *Malloch* v. *Aberdeen Corporation* [1971] 1 WLR 1578, 1581, *per* Lord Reid). Mr Rose contends that there is no circumstance in this case which elevates the plaintiff's position to that of an officer whose tenure of his office or whose status as an officer cannot be terminated without his being given an opportunity to answer any charges made against him or any criticisms of him or of his conduct. In our opinion, it does not much help to solve the problem to try to place the plaintiff in the category of a servant, on the one hand, or of an officer, on the other. It is true that in *Ridge* v. *Baldwin* Lord Reid, at p. 65, divided cases of dismissal into three classes: (1) dismissal of a servant by his master, (2) dismissal from an office held during pleasure, and (3) dismissal from an office when there must be something against a man to warrant his dismissal; but he goes on in the next paragraph to point out that, although in 'a pure master and servant case' the master need not hear the servant in his own defence, dismissal of a servant by a master can resemble dismissal from an office where the body employing the man is under some statutory or other restriction as to the grounds on which it can dismiss its servants. Moreover, the problem is not confined to termination of contracts of employment. It may arise in relation to the termination or denial of a privilege, as in *Russell* v. *Duke of Norfolk* [1949] 1 All ER 109, or of an office which does not involve any contract of employment, as in *Breen* v. *Amalgamated Engineering Union* [1971] 2 QB 175. In our judgment, a useful test can be formulated in this way. Where one party has a discretionary power to terminate the tenure or enjoyment by another of an employment or an office or a post or a privilege, is that power conditional upon the party invested with the power being first satisfied upon a particular point which involves investigating some matter upon which the other party ought in fairness to be heard or to be allowed to give his explanation or put his case? If the answer to the question is 'Yes', then unless, before the power purports to have been exercised, the condition has been satisfied after the other party has been given a fair opportunity of being heard or of giving his explanation or putting his case, the power will not have been well exercised.

In the most recent years, the public law of unfair dismissal has continued to develop, but the uncertainties have if anything intensified. There was something of a setback in *Gunton* v. *Richmond-upon-Thames LBC* [1980] ICR 755. This concerned the dismissal of a college registrar employed by a local authority; it was a disciplinary dismissal and there was a failure to comply with regulations prescribing a procedure for disciplinary dismissals which formed part of the plaintiff's contract of employment. The plaintiff sought a declaration that the purported dismissal was null and void or at least ineffective to determine his contract with the result that he remained in post as registrar. The Court of Appeal decided the case in terms of the private law of the contract of employment, and we have referred earlier (above, p. 457) to their contribution to the discussion of whether a wrongful dismissal nevertheless effectively terminates the contract of employment. The interest that their decision on that knotty point has attracted has rather tended to obscure the other aspect of the case, which was that this was a straightforward attempt to invoke the public law of unfair dismissal. The Court of Appeal was unanimous in rejecting this general approach to the case. Shaw L.J. put it thus: 'There are situations in which the impact of some statutory provision on the status of an employee gives rise to special considerations and consequences. The relationship between the council and the plaintiff was free from such trammels' (at p. 764). Buckley L.J. said this: '[Counsel for the respondent plaintiff] referred us to a number of cases in which employers of persons in the public service, such as school teachers, were held to be disentitled to dismiss employees otherwise than in accordance with particular procedures or upon limited grounds. I do not find those authorities helpful in the present case, in which, as it seems to me, the plaintiff's rights were purely contractual' (at p. 774). Finally Brightman L.J. said, most dismissively of all, 'I accept that a statutory authority has to act reasonably and that it should exercise reasonably its statutory powers to hire and fire its servants. But I do not know of any principle of law which confers on a public employee a greater security of tenure than is enjoyed under a comparable contract of employment with a non-statutory authority' (at p. 777). It is important to note that in these statements each of the three members of the Court of Appeal acknowledges the potential application of public law principles to the public service employment relationship; and none of them offers any principled distinction between the present case and the cases where public law has been successfully invoked.

Moreover it is also significant that the Court of Appeal in the *Gunton* case, despite the declared positions we have just examined, fell into the discourse of public law when discussing the effect of the disciplinary regulations. In particular they tended to adopt the terminology of an *ultra vires* argument. Thus Buckley L.J. says, 'I am, however, myself of the opinion that the adoption of the disciplinary regulations and their consequent incorporation in the plaintiff's contract of service did *disenable* [emphasis added] the council from dismissing the plaintiff on disciplinary grounds until the procedure prescribed by these regulations had been carried out' (at p. 765). Although the then President of the EAT later rightly observed in *Young* v. *Gripperrods Ltd* (unreported) (EAT 302/82) that these words were intended to be used in an entirely contractual sense, the fact remains that the idea that public authorities' purported acts are null and void where they are in excess of their powers is one of the most important contributions that public law has to make in this area. At all events, it is clear that the decision in *Gunton* did not permanently check the growth of the public law of unfair dismissal, for significant further steps have since been taken in the case of *R.* v. *BBC ex parte Lavelle* [1983] ICR 99. In this case the applicant was employed as a tape examiner by the BBC who proposed to dismiss her for an alleged offence involving dishonesty, subject to her appeal under their internal disciplinary procedure. She took these proceedings in order to stay the hearing of her internal appeal until after the conclusion of criminal proceedings which were due to take place in respect of the same matter. Her application was rejected by Woolf J. in the Queen's Bench Division, and it might at first sight appear as if the case did not advance the public law of unfair dismissal at all. After all, Woolf J. did hold that the procedure of application for judicial review under Order 53 of the Rules of the Supreme Court was not appropriate in this case because of its private law rather than public law character, and he took a very cautious view as to the circumstances in which it would be appropriate to grant an injunction to restrain the hearing of an internal appeal pending criminal proceedings (see the annotation to the case in (1983) 12 *ILJ* at pp. 43–5). But despite his view that it was the procedures and remedies of private law that were appropriate, Woolf J. did make a vitally important recognition that the principles of the public law of unfair dismissal were applicable. By contrast with the approach of the Court of Appeal in the *Gunton* case, he took the view that a public authority employer which adopts a disciplinary procedure does thereby limit its powers in a public law sense. Furthermore, he thought that the statute law of unfair dismissal had eroded the whole distinction which existed at common law between the office-holder and the employee under a private law contract of employment. The crucial conclusions are set out in the following extracts.

R. v. BBC ex parte Lavelle [1983] ICR 99 (QBD) at pp. 111–13

WOOLF J.: . . . When one has regard to the framework of his employment, one finds that the BBC has engrafted on to the ordinary principles of master and servant an elaborate framework of appeals. This framework restricts the power of the BBC as an employer to terminate the employee's employment. It clearly presupposes that the employee should have more than one opportunity of being heard. It may be right, as was submitted, that the reason this is done is to avoid any question of the dismissal being regarded as being unfair. However, here I would adopt the argument advanced by Mr Evans, on behalf of the applicant, that the employment protection legislation has substantially changed the position at common law so far as dismissal is concerned. In appropriate circumstances the statute now provides that an industrial tribunal can order the reinstatement of an employee. It is true that the order cannot be specifically enforced. However, the existence of that power does indicate that even the ordinary contract of master and servant now has many of the attributes of an office, and the distinction which previously existed between pure cases of master and servant and cases where a person holds an office are no longer clear. . . .

In this case it seems clear to me that the applicant had a right to be heard and that there was a restriction as to the circumstances in which she could be dismissed. Although the restriction was largely procedural, as the respondent contends, it did alter her rights substantially from what they would have been at common law. In my view, this had the consequence of making her contract of employment different from those referred to by Lord Reid where in the past the sole remedy was one of damages. I have therefore come to the conclusion that in the appropriate circumstances, in the case of employment of the nature here being considered, the court can if necessary intervene by way of injunction, and certainly by way of declaration.

This judgment does leave some major questions unanswered. If it is the statute law of unfair dismissal that has caused a breaking of the narrow bounds of the public law of unfair dismissal, that might suggest that all employees are now entitled to the benefit of the public law of unfair dismissal who are entitled to invoke the statute law of unfair dismissal. Yet even the most ambitious of protagonists of the public law of unfair dismissal would be expected to accept that it was confined in some sense to employment in the public sector. These are questions that can now be answered only by means of an acceptance of the fact that there is now a distinct body of public law of unfair dismissals whose exact terms now have to be spelt out.

5 Discriminatory dismissal

We can deal with the law relating to discriminatory dismissals relatively briefly because with one or two exceptions the issues raised are the same as those already discussed in relation to discrimination in the formation of the employment relationship (see above, pp. 41ff.) and in the content of the employment relationship (see above, pp. 405ff.). The law of sex and race discrimination in employment are both specifically applied to dismissal from employment (SDA 1975, s.6(2)(*b*); RRA 1976, s.4(2)(*c*)). The law of unfair dismissal may also be invoked in respect of discriminatory dismissals; it was held in *Clarke* v. *Eley (IMI) Kynoch Ltd* [1983] ICR 165, that although it did not necessarily follow that an unlawfully discriminatory dismissal was unfair within the meaning of the unfair dismissal legislation, it would need very special circumstances to justify a holding that an unlawfully discriminatory dismissal was fair. There is in fact an increasingly important overlap between the unfair dismissal legislation and various sorts of discrimination legislation, which is not unnatural for, as we have seen earlier (above, p. 460) the elimination of discrimination provides one approach to the whole question of how the goal of fairness in dismissals should be achieved. Thus dismissal on the ground of pregnancy is singled out as one of the kinds of dismissal automatically treated as unfair. This provision was originally made by the EPA 1975 as part of the collection of maternity rights created by that Act; it is now contained in section 60 of the EPCA, 1978. Because the qualifying period requirements of the unfair dismissal legislation apply to section 60, the question has arisen whether dismissal on the ground of pregnancy falls within the SDA which makes no such qualifying period requirements. In *Turley* v. *Allders Department Stores Ltd* [1980] ICR 66, the EAT held by a majority that to dismiss someone because she was pregnant was not to dismiss her because she was a woman; that the underlying intention of the SDA was limited to eliminating the treatment of people unequally solely by reason of their sex; that a pregnant woman was not merely a woman but a woman with a child for which there was no masculine equivalent, and that accordingly dismissal on the ground of pregnancy was not covered by the SDA. This conceptual argument has provoked a good deal of debate, but the issue is perhaps better regarded as one of policy for Parliament, the sole remaining policy issue being really that of whether qualifying period requirements should apply. There are other, more fundamental, problems of overlap between the legislation about unfairness and the legislation specifically about discrimination which can usefully be brought together into a single discussion which has become increasingly important in conditions of recession. This discussion turns on the question of how far controls of unlawful discrimination against groups of people operate to protect members of those groups against being selected to be made redundant. In this situation the interests of the members of the groups protected from discrimination are in very direct competition with the interests of other individuals outside those groups. This has produced particular kinds of tension which the appellate courts are having to try to resolve. The discussion of this problem may serve as a bridge between the previous section of this chapter devoted to unfair dismissal and the following one devoted to redundancy.

The first issue of this kind to emerge as an important question from the case-law was that of selection for dismissal by reference to unlawfully discriminatory stereotypes. In *Noble* v. *David Gold & Son Ltd* [1980] I C R 543, employers who ran a print warehouse and distribution centre had selected women workers for redundancy on the ground that the women workers did the lighter work while the men did heavier work which the women were incapable of doing, and that it was the lighter work rather than the heavy work for which the need had diminished. The Court of Appeal held that the difference between the heavy and the light work was sufficient to defeat both a claim for equal pay and a claim that the selection for dismissal had been unlawfully discriminatory. Lord Denning M.R. held that it was as if there were two separate units or establishments within the warehouse, one doing heavy work staffed by men and one doing light work staffed by women. In order to provide a homely analogy, he said that it was like the Inns of Court, where the heavy work is done by male porters and the waiting and serving of meals by women (at p. 549). This idea of two notional separate establishments, however much it may have been justified by the evidence in this particular case, seems to lend itself to a particular kind of stereotyping, for it militates against a consideration of how far individual women could have been as it were transferred to the male establishment as an alternative to being made redundant. In other words it treats the initial allocation of work as between men and women as virtually decisive of how the selection for redundancy may lawfully be carried out. In a rather different context, one particular sort of stereotyping was successfully countered in *Skyrail Oceanic Ltd* v. *Coleman* [1981] I C R 864. The case concerned a clerk in a firm of travel agents who became engaged to a man working for a rival firm. The two firms agreed that one or other of the two employees had to be dismissed because of the danger of leakage of confidential information between the two firms which would in their view exist once the two employees got married; and they further agreed that it was the woman who should be dismissed because they assumed that of the two the husband would be regarded as the breadwinner. The Court of Appeal held by a majority that it was unlawfully discriminatory to select the woman on the basis of that assumption. This was not a case of redundancy, but it did raise the sort of question of discriminatory selection that arises in redundancy cases. The Court of Appeal, having taken a positive approach on the substantive issue, did take a rather restrictive approach to the question of compensation by reducing the award of £1,000 compensation for injury to feelings to the sum of £100 on the ground that injury to feelings was only compensable in so far as it resulted from the knowledge that it had been an act of sex discrimination that had brought about the dismissal and that this award had been disproportionate. This restriction would presumably be prominent in a redundancy situation where it would be easy to regard the redundancy situation itself as the primary cause of the dismissal for this purpose.

The courts have since had to address even more difficult problems in relation to discriminatory selection for redundancy. One of these arises from a certain kind of segregation of the labour market which we have seen in earlier chapters raises particularly acute problems about sex discrimination; this is the concentration of women workers into part-time working (see above, pp. 376–7 and 398ff.). In *Clarke* v. *Eley (IMI) Kynoch Ltd* [1983] ICR 165, the EAT held that certain dismissals had been both unlawfully discriminatory and in fact, though not as an automatic consequence, unfair where the selection for redundancy on a last-in, first-out basis had been varied by dismissing part-timers before full-timers and where that variation had favoured men and disfavoured women because in the department concerned the part-time workforce consisted entirely of women while the full-time workforce consisted partly of men and partly of women. The case for holding that there was unlawful sex discrimination rested on the ground of indirect discrimination i.e. the imposition of a condition or requirement that operated disproportionately against persons of the applicant's sex and which the applicant could not comply with (see above, pp. 44ff.). The EAT held that the existence of past opportunities to comply in the sense of past opportunities to become a full-time worker did not stand in the way of the complaint that it was indirectly discriminatory to make preference for retention as an employee conditional upon being a full-time worker when the selection was made. The EAT also had to confront the underlying problem of what constitutes justification for the imposition of indirectly discriminatory conditions in making selections for redundancy, since the definition of indirect discrimination enables the employer to negate such discrimination by showing the existence of non-sex-based justification (SDA, s.1(1)(*b*)(ii)). Despite the reduction in the standard of justification from one of necessity to one of rightness and propriety in the circumstances which the EAT acknowledged as having been brought about in the *Panesar* case and the *Ojutiku* case (see above, pp. 55ff.), the EAT had no great difficulty in upholding the conclusion of the industrial tribunal that the application of the 'part-timers first' rule in this case was not justified; but on the other hand they were at some pains to suggest that a straightforward last-in first-out rule should normally be regarded as justifying any indirectly discriminatory consequences that its operation might have. The following extract contains the court's views on this point.

Clarke v. *Eley (IMI) Kynoch Ltd* [1983] ICR 165 (EAT)
at pp. 174–5

BROWNE-WILKINSON J.: In case this or some other matter goes to the House of

Lords, we would express some apprehension as to the direction in which the decisions of the courts are going on this issue. To decide whether some action is 'justifiable' requires a value judgment to be made. On emotive matters such as racial or sex discrimination there is no generally accepted view as to the comparative importance of eliminating discriminatory practices on the one hand as against, for example, the profitability of a business on the other. In these circumstances, to leave the matter effectively within the unfettered decision of the many industrial tribunals throughout the country, each reflecting their own approach to the relative importance of these matters, seems to us likely to lead to widely differing decisions being reached. In our view, the law should lay down the degree of importance to be attached to eliminating indirect discrimination (which will very often be unintentional) so that industrial tribunals will know how to strike the balance between the discriminatory effect of a requirement on the one hand and the reasons urged as justification for imposing it on the other.

In the course of argument Mr George emphasised the difficulties with which the company and other employers were faced. He said that, following the industrial tribunal's decision, the employers had been considering whether they could for the future lawfully adopt even the time-hallowed formula of 'last in, first out' in making selection for redundancy. The fear is that it might be said that, by reason of child-bearing and other domestic commitments, fewer women than men might have long service and therefore the criterion 'last in, first out' might be unlawfully discriminatory.

It is most undesirable in present circumstances where redundancies are, unhappily, an everyday event that there should be a doubt as to the question whether or not the formula 'last in, first out' is lawful. Therefore, although we cannot ourselves decide the point, it is right that we should indicate our view so as to give as much reassurance as possible. In our view, bearing in mind that Parliament has encouraged the making of redundancy agreements between employers and unions and that 'last in, first out' has for very many years been far the most commonly agreed criterion for selection, it would be right for an industrial tribunal to hold that the adoption of 'last in, first out' was a necessary means (viewed in a reasonable and common sense way) of achieving a necessary objective, i.e. an agreed criterion for selection. Accordingly such need outweighs the limited discriminatory effect of adopting the criterion 'last in, first out,' if any. In our view, to select on the basis 'last in, first out' is quite different from selecting on the basis 'part-time workers first.' Although 'last in, first out' may have a limited discriminatory effect, taking part-time workers first is grossly discriminatory. In the present case, 100 per cent of part-time workers were women; nationally over 80 per cent of part-time workers are women. Therefore, in balancing the need for an agreed criterion for selection for redundancy against the discriminatory effect of the criterion adopted, the scales are quite differently loaded in the two cases.

The favourable approach to last-in, first-out systems (LIFO) on the part of the EAT in the *Eley Kynoch* case (an approach which some consider to be sanguine as to the possibilities of discrimination implicit in LIFO systems) makes it crucial to consider what controls the various sorts of discrimination legislation in fact place on seniority systems of selection for redundancy, and how far those controls are reinforced by the law of unfair dismissal. The decision of the EAT in *Timex Corporation* v. *Hodgson* [1982] ICR 63 is important in this respect as indicating one specialized form that the argument may take under the discrimination legislation. This was a case where in the process of selection between three supervisors for redundancy, the normally applicable LIFO rule was varied in favour of the one woman supervisor, on the ground that her retention would mean that a woman supervisor remained available to deal with the personal problems of the other women employees. The claim of unlawful sex discrimination brought by one of the redundant male supervisors was disallowed, and the important point is that the case was decided not as a case of dismissal from the existing employment but as a refusal to hire the applicant for or transfer him into the single supervisor's post that remained. This let in an argument under SDA, s.7(1) (see above, pp. 445), that being a woman was a genuine occupation qualification for the single supervisor's post, and the case was remitted to the industrial tribunal to consider whether that argument succeeded on the facts. So an important shift in the emphasis of the argument was brought about, and it may be that this kind of selection would be easier to justify under the specific head of genuine occupational qualification than under the general tests for discrimination. The possibility of specialized lines of argument of this kind in a sense makes it doubly important for the broad notions of justification under the discrimination legislation to be clarified, and for it to be ascertained how far the law of unfair dismissal will be aligned with the specific anti-discrimination laws in this kind of case. As we have seen (above, p. 523, the *Eley Kynoch* case indicates that the unfair dismissal outcome will normally though not automatically follow the discrimination outcome where the applicant can establish unlawfully discriminatory dismissal. This sense of a common alignment between the discrimination legislation and the unfair dismissal legislation is perhaps reinforced by the decision of the EAT in *Seymour* v. *British Airways Board* [1983] IRLR 55. This concerned a disabled loader driver who had been selected for redundancy in implementation of a policy of considering 'non-effective staff' as appropriate in certain circumstances to be the first to be selected for redundancy. The applicant claimed discontinuance of employment without reasonable cause contrary to section 9 of the Disabled Persons Registration Act 1944 and therefore that he had been unfairly dismissed. The EAT upheld the industrial tribunal in the view that it had been reasonable on the part of the employer, for the purposes both of the Disabled Persons legislation and the unfair dismissal legislation, to dismiss this particular disabled person following the review, prompted by financial considerations, of staff restricted in their work for medical reasons. It is of course the case that the nature of the argument in relation to this kind of discrimination is significantly different from the kind of arguments that arise where sex or racial discrimination are alleged. Nevertheless, the case serves to indicate the extent to which protection of particular groups from selection for redundancy is ultimately bound up with broad notions of fairness in selection for redundancy, and, having considered those broad notions to some extent in our earlier discussion of fairness and reasonableness under the unfair dismissal legislation (see above, pp. 461ff.), we shall return to those questions specifically in the context of redundancy in the next section (see below, pp. 555ff.).

6 Redundancy

(a) Introduction

It would scarcely be an exaggeration to say that redundancy has been a central preoccupation of labour law since the mid-1960s. In one sense that is scarcely surprising, since we can date the decline away from post-war full employment from about that time and we know that the rate of workforce reduction has continued to accelerate, with some fits and starts, since that time, reaching an enormous rate in the 1980s (giving rise, for instance, to a growth in the level of unemployment in the workforce in the UK from 3.3 per cent in 1971 to 12.5 per cent in 1982). We can also see that labour legislation has been visibly responding to the phenomenon of redundancy throughout this period, most obviously with the redundancy payments legislation originating in the Redundancy Payments Act 1965 which will be a central topic of this section, and the legislation about Procedure for Handling Redundancies contained in Part IV of the EPA 1975 which requires consultation with recognized trade unions about and notification to the Department of Employment of proposed redundancies and which was considered in Chapter 2 of this work (see above, pp. 237ff.). It is also clear that redundancy dismissals have loomed increasingly large in the operation of the unfair dismissal legislation (see above, pp. 467ff. and below, pp. 555ff.). But the main point that we wish to make in this introduction is that there are many other aspects of labour law which also, though rather less obviously, form part of the legal régime in relation to redundancies. John Gennard has contributed a valuable analysis of the extent of laws relating to or relevant to redundancy in his chapter on Great Britain in a recently published ILO survey (ed. E. Yemin), *Workforce Reduction in Undertakings* (1982), which examines the position in a range of countries belonging as members to the ILO.

Gennard suggests that 'The evaluation of the system of protection for workers in cases of reduction of the workforce in the undertaking can be made against a number of criteria: for example, to what extent is the need for redundancy avoided or reduced? to what extent has the system minimised conflict over redundancies? and to what extent is the redundant labour re-absorbed into employment instead of increasing the size of the unemployment register?' (at p. 133); and he deals with a large number of legal or administrative provisions which fail to be assessed by these criteria. We proceed to refer to these provisions in order to explain how far they receive discussion in the course of this book.

In addition to the items of legislation so far referred to, Gennard lists the following matters as relevant to workforce reductions. Firstly, the statutory right to minimum periods of notice (see above, pp. 434–5). It is easy to overlook the fact that this may often have a pecuniary value as great as that of the statutory redundancy payment. Secondly, the statutory right to time off from work with pay to look for work or make arrangements for training. This right was originally conferred by the EPA 1975 as part of a collection of rights to time off, and is now contained in EPCA 1978, s.31. Under that section, the right is to 'reasonable' time off for these purposes, and the employee may complain to an industrial tribunal of the employer's failure to grant reasonable time off, and may be awarded compensation subject to a limit of two-fifths of a week's pay (which also, under s.31(9), defines the extent of the employer's liability to grant *paid* time off as well as the maximum of compensation). The right is confined to workers under notice of dismissal by reason of redundancy (s.31(1)) and would therefore presumably not extend, for example, to workers dismissed by reason of a reorganization falling short of redundancy, which might be unsatisfactory in so far as the functional need for this time off might be just as great in those circumstances as in a redundancy situation in the strict sense. Gennard also lists as relevant to workforce reduction the provisions for guaranteed weekly payments in cases of lay-off or short-time which we discussed in the previous chapter (see above, pp. 357ff.), thus making the important point that there is a vital continuity between measures concerned with security of employment and measures concerned with the security of earnings during employment. He also refers to the measures for the protection of employees in the insolvency of the employer or employing company, which we consider later in the present chapter (see below, pp. 568ff.) and which must indeed be envisaged as an increasingly important aspect of protection in the event of redundancy. One may also mention in this connection the measures for the protection of employees in the event of transfers of undertakings, which we also consider in a later section of this chapter (see below, pp. 576ff.).

Gennard then turns to a number of legal or administrative measures which lie outside the scope of labour law as traditionally defined, but which he regards, as we do, as fully relevant to this aspect of labour law. In this class, he lists, firstly, unemployment and other state financial benefits available to redundant workers. The relevant social security provisions are discussed briefly in the course of the present section (see below, pp. 564 *et seq.*), and we would link with them measures controlling the provisions which occupational pension schemes may make for early retirement, and measures concerning the taxation of payments made upon the termination of employment. Secondly in this class Gennard lists state aids to find alternative employment, and includes under this head (i) the Employment Service, (ii) measures to aid geographical mobility, (iii) training to increase the probability of finding employment. We share the view that it is important to regard these as part of labour law and referred to them as such in Chapter 1 (above, pp. 27ff.). Finally in this class, Gennard lists the areas of economic management to protect employment, in which he includes measures to maintain existing industrial capacity, and subsidies to employers to avoid making workers redundant. Although Gennard is not concerned to argue the case for these being regarded as part of labour law, we share his implicit perception that they may appropriately be so regarded, and have mentioned them elsewhere in this book on that footing (see above, pp. 27ff., 357ff.). Gennard also considers the extent to which private arrangements made by employers either unilaterally or jointly with unions by way of collective bargaining have resulted in the minimizing of redundancies or in the evolution of alternatives to redundancy or protections for workers in the event of redundancy. We regard this as an increasingly important technique for the adequate exposition of any aspect of labour law and have sought to employ that technique in relation to redundancy later in this section (see below, pp. 562ff.). Having thus attempted to indicate the existence of a broad spectrum of different aspects of labour law which we see as relevant to the question of redundancy, we shall proceed in this section to develop the most prominent aspects of that topic which are not dealt with elsewhere in this book.

(b) **The redundancy payments legislation: aims and techniques**
With hindsight we can see that the enactment of the Redundancy Payments Act 1965 marked the crossing of the Rubicon so far as employment protection legislation was concerned. Up till that time the legislation had confined itself to adjustments to the common law of the contract of employment, for instance in the Payment of Wages Act 1960 and, most obviously, in the Contracts of Employment Act 1963. In 1965, however, employment protection took off on its own as a body of statute law conceptually distinct from the contractual system. Once this first decisive step had been taken and the industrial tribunals had thereby been established as labour courts for the arbitration of cases concerning individual employees, the natural and fairly inevitable consequence was the coming of unfair dismissal legislation.

This momentous piece of legislation has been the subject of a great deal of argument about its effectiveness and social utility. In order to evaluate its effectiveness it is necessary to agree on what its aims were. The question is one of some obscurity, and many alternatives contend for the field. One possibility is that the government had the aim of ushering in gently and unobtrusively a generalized system of compensation in the event of dismissal and a generalized system of adjudication by industrial tribunals. This generalized entitlement was to be a seniority right based upon length of service (half a week's pay for each year of service between the ages of 18 and 21, one week's pay for each year of service between the ages of 21 and 40 and one-and-a-half week's pay for each year of service between the ages of 40 and 60 for women or 65 for men (EPCA 1978, Sch. 4, para. 2) up to a maximum of 20 years at a maximum rate of £145 per week (with effect from 1 February 1984, see SI 1983 No. 1962)) and this fact in turn would achieve simplicity of adjudication and administration. But if this were so, why was the entitling even confined to the concept of redundancy, thus excluding the majority of dismissal cases? Another possibility, which would avoid this difficulty, is that the government was concerned to stimulate redeployment of labour in order to take advantage of technological advances in industry and that it was therefore specially concerned with technologically generated redundancies rather than with dismissals generally. This would explain why the legislation makes redundancy a more attractive proposition than it would otherwise be for employees and also more attractive in a sense for employers by providing them with rebates from the Redundancy Fund, though that would commend itself only to employers who would be forced by extra-legal pressures, such as those of collective bargaining, to make voluntary severance payments even in the absence of a statutory obligation. But this explanation leaves open the question of why so little was done to harness the redundancy payments system to any kind of constructive system of manpower planning. Why then, for instance, was the redundancy payment made payable irrespective of whether the employee in fact obtained new employment or not? And why also was the Department of Employment provided with so little by way of advance warning of, and control over, proposed redundancies? If the answer is given that the RPA 1965 was really a system for the making of lump sum severance payments based upon seniority then we are back in the earlier difficulty that it was a system which catered for so limited a category of termination of employment.

The answer to this dilemma may lie in a distinction between aims, effects and techniques. The legislation probably had the *narrow aim* of rendering redundancy due to technological change acceptable to the workers affected by it and hence to the country at large (rather than the aim of 'protecting job property' in a positive sense (see Meyers, *Ownership of Jobs* (1964), pp. 1–3)). Its *effects* were wider than its aims because for the first time it turned dismissal into a prima facie compensable event rather than a generally non-compensable event. Moreover, since the *raison d'être* of industrial tribunals was in truth the general adjudication upon dismissal issues it was not surprising that the RPA should be treated by all concerned as the peg upon which to hang a wide jurisdiction over dismissals generally. This approach was in a sense encouraged and fostered by certain of the *techniques* employed in the legislation, namely the introduction of a statutory seniority system and the establishment of a Redundancy Fund to act as an insurance mechanism for compensation. (After an initial phase in which the rate of rebate provided from the Fund was increased in the upper age groups the Fund now provides rebates at a rate which is uniform throughout the age scales and which is currently 41 per cent. See EPCA 1978, Sch. 6, Part 1.) The corresponding lack of commitment to positive manpower planning is explicable in terms of the government's desire to keep the work of the industrial tribunals as simple and automatic as possible and also to the reluctance of the Department of Employment to assume the responsibility for the deployment of labour in private industry.

In a sense the RPA 1965 carried the seeds, if not of its own destruction, then at least of its own diminution in importance. The perhaps unintended logic of the RPA led directly to a truly generalized system for adjudication upon dismissals which was, of course, realized in the unfair dismissal legislation. With the coming of that legislation the RPA was somewhat relegated to a back seat. The unfair dismissal legislation held out the prospect of far more substantial compensation for dismissal than that afforded under the 1965 Act, especially with the introduction of the dual basis – basic and compensatory – of awards of compensation for unfair dismissal in 1975. Employers who had hitherto sought every means to deny that they had made their employees redundant now grasped at redundancy as a means of establishing the fairness of a dismissal. By the same token employees who had hitherto asserted that they were redundant now sought to deny it. By the time this mutual *volte face* occurred the concept of redundancy had already acquired a jurisprudence of its own. Does this jurisprudence accurately and justly mirror the relevant process of decision-making by management? How does the case-law on redundancy now co-exist with that part of the law of unfair dismissal which is concerned with unfair selection for (justified) redundancy? It is to these questions that we turn in the next subsections.

(c) **The concept of redundancy**

(1) *Introduction – the concept of the job*
We may take it from the foregoing discussion that the 1965 Act had, in broad terms, the aim of compensating employees who lost their jobs through no fault of their own but rather as the result of a change in the employer's labour requirements. It follows from this that the precise concept of redundancy selected by the legislators is of crucial significance when one comes to assess the success of the legislation in achieving its aims. The definition which was chosen had two limbs: the first of these was

the fact that the employer has ceased or intends to cease to carry on the business for the purposes of which the employee was employed by him or has ceased or intends to cease to carry on that business in the place where the employee was so employed [EPCA 1978, s.81(2)(*a*)].

This limb of the definition relates to the straightforward case where a business is shut down. Such situations, of course, raise great practical problems for industrial relations and collective bargaining and may result in disputes about the amount and method of payment of compensation for employees or may even result in industrial action, such as a sit-in directed at contesting the necessity for the shut-down, but such cases have not so far raised problems of characterization as to whether there is a redundancy situation or not.

The problems of characterization have hitherto arisen where the content of jobs is reorganized within an enterprise that continues to function. The second limb of the definition deals with that kind of case by characterizing as redundancy the fact that the requirements of [the] business for employees to carry out work of a particular kind or for employees to carry out work of a particular kind in the place where [the employee was employed] have ceased or diminished or are expected to cease or diminish [EPCA 1978, s.81(2)(*b*)].

The significance of this method of definition is that the legislators avoided any express reference to the employee's lack of fault by constructing their definition around the concept of the job as distinct from the employee who happened to be doing that job for the time being. The idea clearly was that the question of whether the employer continued to require a particular function was an objective issue capable of assessment both by the employer and by the industrial tribunal, independently of the personal characteristics of the employee in question. We proceed to examine the use which the courts have made of this job-defined concept of redundancy, and we shall then attempt to assess how capable such a concept is of adequately covering the cases which might be described in non-technical terms as loss of employment through no fault of the employee's own. It will in general terms be suggested that the statutory concept of redundancy is rather a narrow one and that it omits significant groups of situations which might appropriately be included in the enjoyment of this form of employment protection. On the other hand it will be suggested that in another sense this is an over-simplified statement for the following reason. Since the introduction of the unfair dismissal legislation in 1971, the whole question of the definition of the concept of redundancy has become inherently more difficult than before both in theoretical terms and in policy terms. That is because, as we have seen (above, p. 468), the unfair dismissal legislation adopts the concept of redundancy as expressing one of the reasons for dismissal on the basis of which it may be found that a dismissal was fair. This has meant that the concept of redundancy has had to be applied for two essentially contradictory purposes; on the one hand it is the basis for establishing the employer's liability to pay statutory redundancy payments, while on the other hand it provides a basis for an employer's claim to negate his liability for unfair dismissal. With this irresoluble tension at the centre of the issue, it is not surprising that the waters of the case-law have become muddied to an extreme degree. Our present discussion, while recognizing this tension and referring to it when necessary, will nevertheless primarily refer to the definition of the concept of redundancy in its original function as the necessary condition for liability to make redundancy payments.

(2) *Contract versus expectation in the process of job-definition*
By choosing their particular concept of redundancy, the draftsmen of the 1965 Act relied on the existence of a method of job-definition, since such a process of job-definition was a necessary part of the process of applying the redundancy concept to concrete cases. As was the case with the statutory concept of dismissal, the law of the contract of employment offered the most readily available yardstick for this purpose; and it was accordingly used as the basic

criterion. In other words, the job was viewed as a package whose contents were defined by the employee's contract of employment, and the redundancy issue was whether the employer, by offering employment on changed terms, was withdrawing the job package as it had hitherto existed. As we shall see, there has been some departure from this approach to the concept of redundancy, in relation to some aspects of the job-specification; but the approach via the contractual package has remained in fairly constant use for the purpose of defining the geographical scope of the employment concerned – that is, the 'place at which the employee is employed' within the meaning of the statute.[1]

This reliance on the contractual package can lead to a distinction between legal rights as embodied in the contract and factual expectations entertained by the employee. The expectations in question are that the occupational and geographical scope of his employment would remain unchanged, or at least would attract and require some consideration for being changed. The application in practice of the RPA 1965 threw a new strain on the process of contractual job-definition and meant that these decisions had to be resolved by a new analysis of the process of implying terms into contracts of employment. For instance, as far as geographical mobility was concerned there was a real problem of how far a contract of employment which was silent about the employee's requirements to be geographically mobile should be deemed to protect the employee's negative expectations that he would not be asked to work elsewhere than at his existing normal place of employment. In the crucial decision of *O'Brien* v. *Associated Fire Alarms Ltd* (see extract below) the Court of Appeal protected this negative expectation by throwing the onus on the employer to establish an implied term to the effect that the employee could be required to be geographically mobile.

> *O'Brien* v. *Associated Fire Alarms Ltd* [1968]
> 1 WLR 1916 (CA)

LORD DENNING M.R.: This is the first case to come before the Court of Appeal about redundancy payments. A company called Associated Fire Alarms Ltd have an extensive business throughout the United Kingdom. They supply and install fire and burglar alarms. They have divided the country up into large areas, each of which is controlled from a branch office. In this case we are concerned with the North-Western area controlled from the Liverpool office. It is a very large area, extending from Aberdovey in Mid-Wales to Whitehaven in Cumberland. It must be 200 miles long at least.

The case concerns three men who were employed at Liverpool: Mr O'Brien and Mr Browning, who were electricians, and Mr Pritchard, who was an electrician's mate. They all had their homes at Liverpool. They joined the company at Liverpool. They had been employed at Liverpool for some years. In particular, Mr Browning for seven

---

[1] The contractual approach to the definition of the 'place at which the employee is employed' was adopted in *Stevenson* v. *Tees-side Bridge and Engineering Ltd* [1971] 1 All ER 296 (D.C.); *Sutcliffe* v. *Hawker Siddeley Aviation Ltd* [1973] ICR 560 (NIRC) and *UK Atomic Energy Authority* v. *Claydon* [1973] ICR 128 (NIRC). In each case the place where it was held the employee could be required to work extended beyond the place in which he had habitually worked.

years. They worked from their homes, going out each day to houses in the vicinity of Liverpool and back each night. They were engaged mainly on fire alarms. But it was quite open to them, as they were electricians, to be put on burglar alarms as an alternative.

Then a time arrived when the work in the vicinity of Liverpool fell off. The company had not enough work to employ these three men in that neighbourhood. A new young manager came to take charge of the North-Western area. He decided that these three men ought to go up to Barrow-in-Furness and work there. It is quite a journey to get from Liverpool to Barrow. The men would have to go by road up to Kendal and back down the peninsula. They could not possibly do it in the day. It must be 120 miles by road, and not an easy journey at that. If the men were to work at Barrow it would take them away from Liverpool where their wives and families were. It meant leaving their homes for some months. (The period is not specified in the facts before us.) Thereupon these men quite reasonably said: 'We are not willing to go to Barrow.' They refused to go. Thereupon the new young manager gave them dismissal notices. He dismissed them at a week's notice, although by their contract they were entitled to four weeks' notice. They claimed redundancy payments under the Redundancy Payments Act 1965. The tribunal rejected their claim. They appealed to the Divisional Court on a point of law. The Divisional Court refused their appeal. Now the matter comes, with our leave, to this court.

The scheme of the Act is this: If a man has served his employers for two years or more and is then dismissed because they have no work for him, he is entitled to be paid a redundancy payment: but if he is dismissed because of his own conduct, he is not entitled to a redundancy payment. Nor is he so entitled if the employer offers him suitable alternative employment which he unreasonably refuses.

In this case the employers said that the men were bound, under their contract of employment, to go to Barrow as directed: and that it was a breach of contract for them to refuse. Accordingly, the men were dismissed by reason of their own conduct and were not entitled to a redundancy payment: see [EPCA 1978, s.82(2)(b)]. But the men said that they were not bound to go to Barrow; and that they were not in breach of their contract. They were dismissed, they said, because there was no work for electricians at Liverpool – which was 'the place where they were employed' – and claimed, therefore, to be entitled to redundancy payments: see [EPCA 1978, s.81(2)(b)].

In considering this dispute, it is important to remember that 'an employee who has been dismissed by his employer shall, unless the contrary is proved, be presumed to have been so dismissed by reason of redundancy': see [EPCA 1978, s.91(2)]. The men start off, therefore, with an initial advantage. It is to be presumed that they were not in breach of their contracts of employment. But still it was open to the employers to prove that they were in breach. And that is what the employers set out to prove. They said it was a term of the contracts of these men that they could be required to go to any place within the north-western area which was directed from the Liverpool office, that is, anywhere from Aberdovey to Whitehaven. There was nothing in writing to that effect. The tribunal so found. They said:

> This requirement to move to another part of the area is not to be found in any written contract. We were not told that this particular company operates any national or local agreement which would require any employee to be mobile.

Nevertheless, although there was no express term to that effect, the tribunal found that there was an implied term. They said:

> It appears to us that it must be an essential term of the employment of any operative by a contract electricity firm doing work of this or any similar type that such operatives should be liable to be sent to any part of the company's area in order to carry out a particular job of installation or maintenance.

Accordingly, they found that the men were in breach of their contract and were not entitled to redundancy payments. The Divisional Court upheld the tribunal's decision. Lord Parker c.j. read the paragraph about the 'essential term' and said: 'That is a finding of fact and is binding on this court.'

I venture to differ. I have always understood that the question whether a term is to be implied in a contract is a question of law for the court and not a question of fact. The primary facts, of course, and the surrounding circumstances have to be found by the tribunal of fact. But, that being done, the implication of a term is an implication of law. That was clearly stated in this court by Scrutton L.J. in *In re Comptoir Commercial Anversois and Power Son & Co*. It is also apparent from the elaborate discussion as to the terms to be implied in a contract of employment in *Lister* v. *Romford Ice and Cold Storage Co. Ltd*.

In my opinion, therefore, the finding of an implied term could have been reviewed by the Divisional Court; and it can be reviewed by this court. On the facts found by the tribunal, I am quite clear that there was no such implied term. These three men were recruited from the Liverpool area. They had their houses in the Wirral. They worked from their homes for years, going each day to work and returning home each night. They could not reasonably be expected to go off for months to a far place like Barrow, leaving their wives and children behind and only getting home at weekends. The tribunal, in several places of their written decision, admitted as much. The tribunal recognized that the employers could not dismiss the men at a moment's notice for their refusal, but would have to give them their full four weeks' notice. When talking about suitable alternative employment, they said they had 'no difficulty at all or doubt in holding that the refusal to go to Barrow was reasonable, in view of the domestic difficulties and the distance of travel'. All this goes to show that there was no implied term that they could be sent anywhere in the north-western area. The only persons who suggested that the men could be sent anywhere were the young executives. One of them had been at the Liverpool office for four months. The other for 14 months. They said they 'considered' that the men could be sent anywhere in the area. That is quite insufficient to found the alleged implied term. I think that the only term to be implied in their contracts was that they should be employed within daily travelling distance of their homes or, if you please, within a reasonable distance of their homes. Barrow is far beyond a reasonable distance.

Thus the various rules and techniques of the law of contract designed to limit the implication into contracts of unexpressed terms operated to protect the employee against the employer. This position has been broadly speaking maintained since that time. This is borne out by our discussion in the previous chapter of recent cases about implied terms (see above, pp. 301ff.) and in particular by the approach of the EAT to this problem in *Jones* v. *Associated Tunnelling Co. Ltd* [1981] IRLR 477, where it was held that geographical mobility is one of the matters about which some term must necessarily be implied, whatever its content, in order to give business efficacy to the contract if the parties had been silent on the point; that in implying the appropriate term the court or tribunal was not limited to a term that would have appeared obvious to both parties but was free to look openly at the actual circumstances of the case; and that in this case where the plain inference from those circumstances was that the employers were to have some power to move the employee's place of work, the reasonable term to imply as the lowest common denominator of what the parties would have agreed if asked was a power to direct the employee to work at any place within reasonable daily reach of his home. Although this term was broader as to geographical mobility than the position that the applicant in this case was contending for, it was nevertheless the product of an approach which contains substantial inbuilt safeguards for employees against the sudden imposition of a mobility obligation quite out of keeping with the previous practice of their employment, which is in reality little more than a mask for a redundancy situation.

However, there have been indications that the courts will in effect distinguish between negative expectations of not having one's terms and conditions changed and positive expectations that one's present employment will be maintained indefinitely, and that they will be reluctant to protect the employee's positive expectations unless there is some strong reason for viewing those positive expectations in contractual terms. Thus, in the case of *North East Coast Shiprepairers* v. *Secretary of State for Employment* [1978] I C R 755, the problem was whether an apprentice to the shiprepairing trade could claim to be redundant within the meaning of the statute when his expectations of becoming a journeyman fitter at the conclusion of his apprenticeship were defeated by the unavailability of journeyman's work. It was held that his expectation was extra-contractual and that the concept of redundancy was concerned only with the discontinuance of existing employment and not with the refusal of new employment. This narrow adherence to contractual thinking overlooks the importance of the fact that the redundancy payments legislation requires effect to be given to some extra-contractual expectations by including the expiry of fixed-term contracts without renewal in its definition of dismissal. Renewal of the employment under a new contract is certainly a matter in the realm of expectations rather than contractual rights; yet the statute, by its very structure, gives weight and effect to that expectation. It is a distortion and misunderstanding of that structure to defeat such expectations by a narrowly contractual view of the concept of redundancy. The EAT seemed to perpetrate precisely that distortion in the case of *Nottinghamshire County Council* v. *Lee* [1979] I C R 818, which concerned a teacher employed by a local authority who entered into a one-year fixed-term contract with that local authority as a lecturer in a teacher training college. The EAT held that because the employee had known when he accepted the one-year appointment that the need for lecturers was diminishing, he could not claim a redundancy payment in respect of the non-renewal of his fixed-term contract because there was not the necessary further diminution in the employer's need for work of that kind as compared with the position known to the employee. However, the Court of Appeal allowed the employee's appeal, rightly recognizing that the argument which had prevailed in the EAT turned upon their view of the fixed-term contract as inherently temporary in nature and failed to give effect to the scheme of the legislation whereby when the necessary conditions are satisfied, the non-renewal of a fixed-term contract is fully equated with any other sort of dismissal despite the non-contractual character of the expectation that the contract will be renewed ([1980] ICR 635).

On the other hand, although the negative and restrictive features of the contractual approach to the definition of redundancy may have been controlled so far as they lie in the direction suggested by the *North East Shiprepairers* case and by *Nottinghamshire County Council* v. *Lee* in the EAT, the restrictiveness which may result, in another direction, from the contractual approach to job-definition has been made very clear by the case of *Cowen* v. *Haden Ltd* [1983] ICR 1. We have so far tended to look at the contractual approach to job-definition as a kind of protection for the employee in that it enables the employee to claim a redundancy payment if his existing contractual job-package is altered or withdrawn. The alteration or withdrawal of the job-package makes good the claim to a redundancy payment by in itself constituting the diminution in need for work of a particular kind on which this sort of claim to redundancy payment has to be based. But the contractual approach to job-definition operates to protect the employee's claim to a redundancy payment only where the contractual job-definition is as narrow as the job-specification which has actually operated in practice, both in a geographical and in an occupational sense. This protection falls away where the contract of employment validly ensures to the employer a continuing right to require occupational or geographical mobility of the employee greater than that which the employee has been called upon to display before the situation which he claims to be a redundancy situation arose. It is now clear in retrospect that this is the significance of the difficult case of *Nelson* v. *BBC* [1977] ICR 649. In that case the applicant was employed as a producer in the BBC Caribbean Service and was dismissed in consequence of the termination of the Caribbean Service, having been offered and having refused another post in the BBC. He claimed to have been unfairly dismissed, and by the time his case came to Court of Appeal the issue had resolved itself into the question of whether he had been dismissed for redundancy; if his dismissal was for redundancy, this would result in the dismissal being regarded as fair. The applicant's contract of employment entitled the Corporation to require an established employee to serve when, how and where they demanded. Having regard to this clause in the contract, the Court of Appeal decided that the applicant had to be regarded as a general producer rather than a producer in the Caribbean Service and that he was therefore not redundant and therefore had been dismissed unfairly in the particular circumstances of the case. The full potential damaging force of this kind of argument for redundancy payment claims was revealed in *Cowen* v. *Haden Ltd* (above) by the decision of the EAT. The case concerned a surveyor who had been employed as a regional surveyor and later promoted to divisional contracts surveyor, his contract of employment providing throughout that he would be required to undertake 'any and all duties which reasonably [fell] within the scope of his capabilities'. The applicant was dismissed in consequence of the employers' decision to abolish the position of regional contracts surveyor because of a reduction in the volume of their business. The applicant claimed to have been unfairly dismissed and as in the *Nelson* case, his success in this claim came to depend on his having been dismissed other than for redundancy. The EAT accepted that they were required by the authority of the *Nelson* case to accept that the employee had not been made redundant in the statutory sense unless there was no job for him not only as divisional contracts surveyor (where there clearly was no job for him) but also within the whole range of jobs as a surveyor that he could by the contract have been required to undertake as lying within the range of his capabilities. It had not been established that there was no job for the applicant within this wider range so his situation could not be characterized as one of redundancy. The Court of Appeal allowed the employer's appeal on the ground that the contractual requirement to undertake any duties within the scope of the employee's capabilities was to be construed as confined to the duties of his present post of divisional contracts superveyor. This brought the occupational mobility clause back into line with the job-package actually enjoyed by the employee, but it did not detract from the principle that a wider contractual obligation of mobility will militate against a claim of redundancy. We shall consider later on (see below, p. 548) the criticisms that have been advanced of the decision of the Court of Appeal and the relationship of the doctrine in this case to other aspects of the definition of the concept of redundancy; suffice it at this point to note the importance of the treating of contractual mobility obligations as restrictions on the scope for findings of redundancy.

(3) Technical or social change viewed as leaving the job intact
We have indicated that the statutory concept of redundancy proceeds by way of a theoretical separation between the job and the employee who occupies the job for the time being. This separation has lent itself to a narrowing of the concept of redundancy by the use of the idea that a job may remain in principle the same despite the impact of technical or social change upon the method of its performance. This can have, and has had, the result that there is held to be no redundancy even in certain cases where it is genuinely clear that an employee has become unable to do the job in question through no fault of his own. It was so held in the key case of *North Riding Garages* v. *Butterwick* [1967] 2 QB 56 (QB Div. Ct), where a garage worker engaged on the servicing of cars was made redundant because of his inability to operate the newer and more

mechanized car-servicing processes introduced by a combine that had acquired the garage for which he had worked for many years. An equivalent decision in quite a different context was that of *Vaux and Associated Breweries* v. *Ward* (see extract below), where there was held to be no redundancy where a brewery dismissed a cosy, middle-aged barmaid in order to replace her with a young girl who would be more in keeping with the youthful atmosphere they wanted to create in the pub. In both cases the crucial finding was that the job vacancy still remained, albeit that it required a different kind of person to fill it. This was to take to extreme lengths the dichotomy between the job and the worker which the statute creates. Was there any need to have gone so far; could not the job have been more closely identified with the characteristics of the employee who had been engaged and retained over the years to do it?

Vaux and Associated Breweries v. *Ward* (1969)
7 KIR 308(DC)

LORD PARKER C.J.: This appeal from a decision of the industrial tribunal dated 5 February 1968, by which the tribunal by a majority awarded the respondent a redundancy payment, first came before the court on 10 July 1968, when it was remitted to the tribunal to hear further evidence and to make a further decision. It now comes back to the court by way of appeal from the second decision of the tribunal made on 28 November 1968, whereby the tribunal again by a majority upheld their original decision to grant the respondent a redundancy payment.

Though the matter was fully dealt with in the judgment of this court on 10 July 1968, it is important, if only to ascertain what has happened subsequently, to recite a little of the facts, which I take from that judgment. It appears that the respondent, Mrs Ward, entered the employment of the appellants in October 1949, as a barmaid at premises known as the Star and Garter Hotel in Blyth. In May 1967, she was dismissed by the manager. His evidence, which was not accepted by the tribunal, was that he had dismissed Mrs Ward because she refused to serve a customer, or that she had been impertinent. The tribunal, having heard all that evidence, came to the clear conclusion that his evidence was not to be believed and that the real reason why he had dismissed her was because he wanted a younger and more glamorous barmaid. In paragraph 10 of the original reasons given by the tribunal, they said:

> We are satisfied that the manager did say, on more than one occasion, in the public house and in the presence of Mrs Ward, that they wanted younger staff. They wanted young blondes and 'bunny girls'. We do not think that, when he said he wanted bunny girls, he was necessarily serious, but we are quite satisfied that he did want younger staff who would attract the new customers who, they hoped, would come to the premises.

In paragraph 11 they said:

> We are of opinion that he dismissed her because he wanted younger staff.

Accordingly, they were in effect saying that that amounted to a dismissal by reason of redundancy, it being said that the case came under [section 81(2)(*b*) of EPCA 1978], in that the requirements for employees to carry out work of a particular kind had ceased or diminished. The chairman, on the other hand, took the quite definite view in the minority that that could not amount to a dismissal by reason of redundancy, and that accordingly the employers had discharged the burden which was upon them under [section 91(2) EPCA 1978].

When the matter came before the Divisional Court, the court took the view that the mere fact that an employee was dismissed because a younger employee was preferred was not of itself a dismissal by reason of redundancy, but that something more would be necessary; the further question had to be answered, namely, whether the particular kind of work on which the barmaid had been engaged had ceased or was likely to cease or diminish or, put more shortly, as I said in giving judgment, 'Was the work that the barmaid in the altered premises was going to do work of a different kind to what a barmaid in the unaltered premises had been doing?'

When the matter went back to the tribunal, further evidence was called, in particular the evidence of a Mr Embleton as to the exact nature of the work expected of the barmaid, both before and after certain alterations had been effected to the premises. In the latest decision, the tribunal unhesitatingly said that the work was in no way different. In paragraph 4 of their reasons it was stated:

> The tribunal were of opinion that the work to be carried out by a barmaid after Mrs Ward was dismissed was not different from that which she had carried out. She was engaged in serving behind the bar, either directly to customers or to waitresses to take to customers. Occasionally, if the waitress was not present, Mrs Ward would carry drinks to customers in the buffet. 70 per cent of the drinks dispensed were beer . . . The present barmaid serves behind the bar, only occasionally going in front of the bar to serve customers.

That finding was followed by this:

> The tribunal reaffirms the findings of fact contained in paragraphs 10 and 11 of the previous reasons. In particular, it reaffirms the opinion expressed in the last sentence of paragraph 11. Its opinion is (and was at the first hearing) that the manager wanted younger staff because they would be physically more attractive than the existing staff, and more likely to attract new customers. The reason was not that the work had changed and could be done more efficiently by younger staff.

I confess that having regard to the history of this matter, and in view of that finding, I should have thought there could only be one answer, namely that the present appellants had discharged the burden upon them, and it had been shown that the dismissal of Mrs Ward was not by reason of redundancy.

However, despite that finding, the majority of the tribunal, the chairman again dissenting, upheld their original decision. In paragraph 9 they said:

> Mr Boyd and Mr Hailes were of opinion that the requirements of the business for employees to carry out the work which the applicant carried out had declined. Mr Boyd stated his reasons thus: 'I am of opinion that, on the basis that the onus to prove that Mrs Ward was dismissed for some other reason than redundancy is on the employers, to my mind that has not been proved. Within the opinion of the court I believe the work of Mrs Ward had diminished and for that reason she was made redundant.' The particular facts on which he relied were: (a) the business of the respondents had been declining before she was dismissed; (b) the reasons given by the manager for dismissing her he rejected as false; (c) she was replaced by an employee who had been employed part-time, and that employee was not immedi-

ately replaced. It is true that the tribunal found that the manager had dismissed her because he wanted younger staff, but this should not be taken into account as against the weight of the other evidence. Mr Hailes agreed with Mr Boyd.

As it seems to me, this is a case in which it would have been the easiest thing in the world for the tribunal, in giving their first decision, to say that the employers had not discharged the onus upon them in that it may be that while alterations were being effected to the premises, there was a diminution, albeit temporary, in the requirement for work of the kind which Mrs Ward was doing. They did not do so, and presumably they did not do so because they were not impressed by that evidence. They decided the case on the ground that the real reason for dismissal was the desire to get a younger and a more attractive member of the staff, and that that of itself they wrongly found to be a dismissal by reason of redundancy.

As it seems to me on a remission to the tribunal, it would be perfectly proper for it to decide the case on a point which they could have decided it on originally, in other words, merely that the burden had not been discharged. But it does not seem to me that this is such a case. Mr Robson contends, and I am inclined to agree with him, that this finding, reiterated over and over again, that the real reason for dismissal was to get younger and more attractive staff, is really quite inconsistent with the reason being a diminution, albeit temporary, in the nature of the work which she had performed before. Accordingly, in my judgment I would allow this appeal, upholding the view of the chairman of the tribunal.

(4) The distinction between the job as a function and the job as a package of terms and conditions

We described earlier how the courts have adopted a contractual approach to the process of job-definition. In the early days of the application of the RPA 1965, indeed for the first few years of its existence, the courts seemed willing to hold, as the necessary corollary of this approach, that a substantial change in contractual terms and conditions necessarily amounted to a withdrawal by the employer of the existing job package and hence to a redundancy if that job package had no identifiable successor in the employer's disposition. This was held to be the case however strong and justifiable the employer's reason for introducing change in the job package. There was no stigma in the conclusion that the employer was creating a redundancy situation. Hence for instance in the case of *Dutton* v. *C.H. Bailey Ltd* (1968) 3 ITR 355 (DC), the court classified as redundancy the dismissal of certain shiprepair workers who refused to abandon restrictive practices, the continuance of which made their employment uneconomic but abandonment of which would have permitted the continuance of their employment on a profitable basis.

The fact that there has been a fairly fundamental change in this approach during the seventies can perhaps be explained as the product of a changed environment where redundancy could no longer be regarded as a sign of economic health but had to be conceded to represent the decline in job opportunities brought about by the underlying recession in productive activity. It was probably this, rather than any particular shift of sympathy towards employers, which brought about a narrowing of the concept of redundancy. The new idea, ushered in by *Chapman* v. *Goonvean & Rostowrack China Clay Co. Ltd* (see below) and perpetuated in *Johnson* v. *Nottinghamshire Combined Police Authority* (see below) and *Lesney Products Ltd* v. *Nolan* (see below), was that as long as the employer retained a need for the function in question there was no redundancy situation, even though he might withdraw existing job-packages in order to get the functional need in question met by other means involving lower labour costs. On this view, the fact that the employer ceases to offer a certain pattern of shift working, or ceases to offer a transport service to enable his workforce to live in one place and work in another, does not give rise to a redundancy situation as long as he can show that he continues to require the work of the employees in question.

Chapman v. *Goonvean and Rostowrack China Clay Co. Ltd*
[1973] ICR 310 (CA)

LORD DENNING M.R.: The china clay industry has been very active in Cornwall in recent years. So much so that a firm at St Stephen in the south has drawn men from Port Isaac in the north. That is 30 miles away along the narrow winding roads of those parts. There is no public transport. So the firm provided a bus to take the men to and from the works. This was imported as a term in their contract of employment. So they were entitled by contract to free transport to work. The tribunal so found.

In March 1972, there were ten men regularly travelling by the bus from Port Isaac to St Stephen and back. Then there was a trade recession in the china clay industry. The firm decided to dismiss 12 out of their 200 men. Nine were selected because they were over age and due for retirement. That left three to be made redundant. The firm selected the three with the shortest service. All three happened to be men from Port Isaac. Those three got redundancy payments. But the dismissal of those three had an unfortunate result on the bus service. It cost the firm £20 a week. That expense was justified when the bus carried ten men to and fro, but it was not economic for seven men. So the firm decided to cut off the bus service and leave the seven men to find their own way to work. The firm told these seven that work was still available for them if they were prepared to make their own arrangements to get to work. But none of them could make such arrangements. Only two had cars, and those were old and unsuitable and the insurers refused to give passenger cover. So those seven told the firm that they could not get to work and would have to give up. The firm were reluctant to lose them as they were good men, but they could not see their way to pay the expense of the bus. So the seven men left and the firm replaced them by seven other men who lived at or near St Stephen.

The seven Port Isaac men then claimed that they had been dismissed for redundancy. They claimed redundancy payments. The industrial tribunal rejected the claim. Their decision was affirmed by the National Industrial Relations Court. The men appeal to this court.

There is no doubt that the seven men were 'dismissed' by the employer. The employer's conduct (in withdrawing the bus in breach of the contract) amounted to a repudiation which entitled the men to terminate their contract: see section [83(2)(c) of EPCA 1978].

Although the seven men were 'dismissed', the question is whether they were dismissed 'by reason of redundancy'. This depends on section [81(2) of EPCA 1978] which, so far as material, says that:

> . . . an employee who is dismissed shall be taken to be dismissed by reason of redundancy if the dismissal is attributable wholly or mainly to . . . (b) the fact that the requirements of that business for employees to carry out work of a particular kind, or for employees to carry out work of a particular kind in the place where he was so employed, have ceased or diminished or are expected to cease or diminish.

Taking those words as they stand, this case is not one of dismissal for redundancy. The requirements of the business – for the work of these seven men – continued just the same as before. After they stopped work, the firm had to take on seven other men to replace them and to do the work that they had been doing. The requirements for work of that kind in that place had not ceased or diminished, nor were they expected to do so. So it would seem that the case does not come within the statute.

But the men say that the words of the section cannot be taken as they stand. They point out that the employers sought to alter the terms of the contract of employment to the disadvantage of the men. They took away the free transport and left the men to pay their own travelling expenses. This free transport cost the firm £2 a week for each man (£20 for 10 men, £2 for each man). It would cost the men much about the same. So it would mean that the men would take home £2 a week less. If the employers sought to reduce wages by that sum – and the men refused to accept the reduction – would not it be a dismissal for redundancy? So say the men.

Lord Denning went on to consider two cases which supported the employees' case and re-presented the then existing state of the law, namely *Dutton* v. *C.H. Bailey Ltd* (above) and *Line* v. *C.E. White & Co.* (1969) 4 ITR 336:

I come back, therefore, to section [81(2)(b)] and I am afraid that I cannot read into it the words 'on the existing terms and conditions of employment'. I think the two cases were wrongly decided. I have less hesitation in overruling them because I notice that Lord Parker C.J. himself decided as he did with reluctance: and I can see why. It is very desirable, in the interests of efficiency, that employers should be able to propose changes in the terms of a man's employment for such reasons as these: so as to get rid of restrictive practices: or to induce higher output by piecework: or to cease to provide free transport at an excessive cost. Take an instance very like the present case. The employers are able to obtain all the labour they need from places near their works without paying travelling expenses. So, as vacancies occur, they replace them locally and gradually reduce the number of men coming from a distance. The number falls so low that it is an unwarranted expense to provide a bus to bring them. Are employers then to keep on a bus so as to bring seven, six, five, or less men to work? Clearly not. The employers can properly say to the men:

> You have not lost your jobs because you are redundant. You have lost your jobs because you live so far away that it is not worth our while paying the cost of bringing you here – when we can get all the men we need nearby.

So, in *Dutton* v. *C.H. Bailey Ltd*, the men did not lose their jobs because they were redundant. They lost them because they were parties to restrictive practices and refused to alter them. Likewise in *Line* v. *C. E. White & Co.*, the men lost their jobs, now because they were redundant, but because they insisted on being paid on a time basis which was unproductive.

In *Johnson* v. *Nottinghamshire Combined Police Authority* the new idea was refined by reference to the concept of a 'redundancy situation'. Is there, in your view, a real distinction between the redundancy situation and the reorganization in the interests of efficiency as described in the following passage?

Johnson v. *Nottinghamshire Combined Police Authority*
[1974] ICR 170 (CA)

It was held that two women clerks were not redundant where they refused to change from normal hours and a five-day week to a shift system and a six-day week.

LORD DENNING M.R.: It is settled by [the cases of *Blakeley* v. *Chemetron Ltd* (1972) 7 ITR 224 and *Chapman* v. *Goonvean* (above)] that an employer is entitled to reorganize his business so as to improve its efficiency and, in so doing, to propose to his staff a change in the terms and conditions of their employment: and to dispense with their services if they do not agree. Such a change does not automatically give the staff a right to redundancy payments. It only does so if the change in the terms and conditions is due to a redundancy situation. The question in every case is: was the change due to a redundancy situation, or not? If the change is due to a redundancy situation, he is entitled to a redundancy payment. If it is not due to it, he is not.

Typical of redundancy situations are these. There may be a recession in trade so that not so many men are needed. There may be a change in the kind of work done, as from wood to fibre glass, so that woodworkers are no longer needed: *Hindle* v. *Percival Boats Ltd* [1969] 1 WLR 174. The business may be no longer profitable so that the employer has to cut down somewhere. Or he may be overstaffed. The employer may meet such a situation by dispensing with the services of some of the men: or alternatively he may lower the wages: or put men on part time. If he does it by making a change in the terms and conditions of employment, it is due to a redundancy situation. Those who lose or leave their work in consequence are entitled to redundancy payments.

It is often difficult to know whether the employer's proposals are due to a redundancy situation or not. But at this point the statute comes in to help the employee by providing that he is presumed to be dismissed by reason of redundancy: see [EPCA 1978, s.91(2)]. So in all the cases where there is a change in the terms and conditions of employment, it is for the employer to prove that it was done for efficiency, and not so as to meet a redundancy situation.

It remains to apply these principles to a change in hours of work. It is a change in the terms and conditions of employment. It does not automatically give rise to a right to redundancy payments. If the employer proves that it was due to a reorganization so as to achieve more efficient working, the man is not entitled to redundancy payments. The decision of the Industrial Court in Scotland of *Blakeley* v. *Chemetron Ltd*, was, I think, correct.

In *Lesney Products & Co. Ltd* v. *Nolan* [1977] ICR 235, the Court of Appeal reconfirmed the idea set out in *Chapman* and *Johnson* but resiled from the 'redundancy situation' test, perhaps because of its inherent circularity or perhaps because of its tendency in practice to defeat the new notion introduced by *Chapman*. This means that we must confront directly the problem of whether 'reorganization in the interests of efficiency' can properly be regarded as falling outside the statutory concept of redundancy. Does Lord Denning in the *Lesney* case make out a convincing case for that viewpoint?

Lesney Products & Co. Ltd v. *Nolan* [1977] ICR 235 (CA)

It was held that six machine setters were not redundant when they refused to change to double day-shift working from a single long day-shift plus overtime.

LORD DENNING M.R.: While I adhere to what I said [in *Johnson* [1974] ICR 170, 176] I think the phrase 'a redundancy situation' may be misleading. It is shorthand: and it is better always to check it by the statutory words. The dismissal must be attributable to 'the fact that the requirements of that business for employees to carry out work of a particular kind . . . have ceased or diminished', etc.

In applying that principle, it is important that nothing should be done to impair the ability of employers to reorganize their workforce and their terms and conditions of work so as to improve efficiency. They may reorganize it so as to reduce overtime and thus to save themselves money, but that does not give the man a right to redundancy payment. Overtime might be reduced, for instance, by taking on more men: but that would not give the existing staff a right to redundancy payments. Also when overtime is reduced by a reorganization of working hours, that does not give rise to a right to redundancy payment, so long as the work to be done is the same.

It seems to be that the problem in this case is whether this reorganization – whereby the one long day shift plus overtime was altered into two day shifts for the machine setters – was done in the interests of efficiency or whether it was due to a drop in the amount of work required for the men employed in the factory. The employers gave evidence (which was not contradicted) that the amount of work coming into the factory and being done on the day shifts by all the direct operatives was just the same as before. There was no reduction in it. The night shift was done away with for want of work – and on that accord the night shift people would get redundancy payments. But the day shifts turned out the same amount of work by the same number of women operatives. So far as the machine setters were concerned, they did the same work for the day shifts as they did before. They saw that the machines were properly set and maintained, and turned out the toys as before. In these cases the reorganization was not done because of less work but it was done in the interests of efficiency and to save the employers having to pay so much overtime.

It is shown by the evidence that the employers did not reduce the number of machine setters. They still wanted the whole of the 36. When some of them refused to come back, the employers needed others to replace the men. They put advertisements in the papers for them. So they wanted the same number of men.

No doubt the men at work would not get as much overtime as they had done under the previous system. But the employers had a scheme for alleviating the position. The men got compensation in that they received the basic wage plus 17½ per cent shift premium. It seems that on average a person who previously received £70 a week might now only be getting £54. So there was to that extent a saving in the money which the company spent on overtime.

The decisions of the industrial tribunals were very carefully considered; but they do seem to have been led into error by asking whether there was 'a redundancy situation' instead of looking at the words of the statute and asking whether the amount of work had ceased or diminished.

It seems to me on the evidence that it was sufficiently proved so as to satisfy the burden of proof given in [EPCA 1978, s.91(2)]. So, although it is a difficult case, it seems to me to be covered by the *Johnson* case and I think the appeal [from a finding of the industrial tribunal and of the EAT that a redundancy payment was payable] should be allowed.

If we take this trend in conjunction with the notion discussed immediately before it (namely that of the differentiation between the job and the personal characteristics of the employee) the combined result is somewhat startling. A concept ostensibly designed to protect the employee against the adverse consequences of managerial development and change, especially when it is of technological origin, has very substantially ceased to fulfil that function. On the one hand the employee is unprotected against technological change resulting in his no longer being employable, subject only to the proviso that his job is nominally prolonged into the future in the hands, typically, of a younger worker with different skills or attributes. If, on the other hand, the employer, unable to preserve the viability of the job by means of this kind of change in its content, seeks to preserve its viability by changes in the terms on which it is performed, he can apparently do so without risk of liability to redundancy payment on the basis that, in this alternative sense, the job remains intact. The original aim was to protect the employee by establishing an objective concept of his job, which would be independent of him as an individual, and hence would serve to identify cases where he was dismissed through no fault of his own. By successive stages that aim has been subverted to the point where the objective notion of his job lies as a stumbling block in the path of the employee who no longer conforms to the employer's operational requirements. This threatens to narrow the scope of the EPCA 1978, Pt VI, to the point where it deals primarily with the shutting down of enterprises rather than with the shedding of employees. It is indeed startling to compare this effect with the aims which we must attribute to the legislators of 1965.

Apart from the policy objections to the job-function approach to redundancy associated with the *Chapman* case, there are also some theoretical complexities and difficulties raised by it with which we must attempt to deal. Firstly, there are clearly difficulties in establishing the limits of the idea of non-redundancy reorganization as introduced by the cases of *Chapman, Johnson* and *Lesney*. The question really is whether at a certain point the reorganization of terms and conditions will be viewed as sufficiently destructive of the substance of the job as to amount to evidence of redundancy. In other words, does a change of terms when sufficiently fundamental and sufficiently indicative of a need on the part of the employer to shed or reduce the cost of labour amount to constructive redundancy, just as, when it is imposed in breach of the contract of employment, it may amount to constructive dismissal? In one sense this is a false question in so far as it simply repeats in a more complex form the simple question of whether the dismissal was for redundancy in the first place; but it is a falsity generated by the falsity of the whole idea of non-redundancy reorganization as a distinct concept, and therefore a question inherently posed by the *Chapman* line of cases. Indeed, courts in those cases have had to recognize the existence of that problem, for example in the case where the employer's reorganization takes the form of cutting pay. In *Chapman*, Lord Denning sought to deal with that problem in these terms:

[1973] ICR at pp. 315–16

LORD DENNING M.R.: I would, however, remark that if an employer sought to reduce the wages of his men on the plea that otherwise he could not keep the business going – or if he employed women in the place of men to save expenses – with the result that some men lost their jobs, then I think the employer would have difficulty in resisting a claim. There is a presumption that the men were dismissed by reason of redundancy: see [EPCA 1978, s.91(2)]. I expect that the tribunal would in those circumstances hold that the presumption was not rebutted. The reduction in wages would probably be because a redundancy situation had arisen or was expected to arise.

Buckley L.J. proposed the following escape from the difficulty:

[1973] ICR at pp. 318–19

We are concerned, however, with a case in which it is said that the requirement of the employer's business for employees to carry out work of a particular kind was expected to cease or diminish. Whether such an expectation can justifiably be said to have existed must depend upon the circumstances in which it was supposed that the business would be conducted in the future. The test cannot, I think, be a purely subjective one, depending only upon the apprehensions, justified or unjustified, of the employer. The employer must, I think, justify his expectation by reference to objective circumstances relating to the commercial situation of his business and those commercial and economic conditions which exist generally at the relevant time or which could then reasonably be anticipated in the future. There seems to me, however, to be nothing in the language of the section to suggest that the employer should be treated as bound or likely to carry on his business in all, or indeed in any, respects in precisely the way in which he was carrying it on at the time when the facts have to be considered.

Suppose, for instance, that the employment is of a kind for which there is a recognized rate for the job, and that an employer in a period of affluence and in the interests of good staff relations has been paying his employees more than that rate. If a time comes when he can no longer afford to pay his employees more than the recognized rate for the job but he is prepared to continue to employ them at that rate, there is nothing in [EPCA 1978, s.81] to suggest that for the purpose of considering whether his requirement for employees to do that particular job is likely to cease or diminish he must be treated as an employer who is going to continue to pay the higher rate. . . . The facts would not, it seems to me, establish that the employer's need for employees to carry out work of the particular kind was expected to cease or diminish, but only that the employer was no longer able to pay his employees on so generous a scale as before. The position would be quite different if an employer dismissed his employees because he was no longer able to pay them either the recognized rate for the job, where one existed, or a fair wage at which he could secure the services of other employees in the labour market.

These judicial remarks may be thought to demonstrate the ultimate difficulty about the idea of non-redundancy reorganization, namely that it forces industrial tribunals to consider, according to undefined principles, the *legitimacy* of the reorganization that the employers seek to introduce. Surely the draftsmen of the legislation had no intention of introducing considerations of legitimacy?

Another facet of the problem created by the idea of non-redundancy reorganization manifested itself in *Robinson* v. *British Island Airways Ltd* [1978] I C R 304. The facts were summarized in the headnotes to the report as follows:

The employee worked as flight operations manager of the employers. He was answerable to the general manager operations and traffic. The employers effected a reorganization of their staff to achieve efficiency and economy. The reorganization resulted in fundamental changes. The posts of flight operations manager and of general manager operations and traffic were abolished and a single job, that of operations manager, created. The new job was more important than the previous jobs, called for different qualities in the incumbent and involved different tasks, new responsibilities and enhanced status. Subsequently, both the employee and the general manager operations and traffic were dismissed and another person appointed as operations manager. The employee was awarded appropriate redundancy pay. He complained to an industrial tribunal that he had been unfairly dismissed in that he was not redundant. The tribunal dismissed the complaint.

It was sought to persuade the E A T (on behalf of the employee, this being an unfair dismissal case) that this was a case of non-redundancy reorganization on the basis that the total amount of operations management work to be done had not diminished. The E A T succeeded in rejecting this argument on the ground that the kind of work involved in the two separate posts was not the same as the kind of work involved in the single amalgamated post. Suppose, however, that such a conclusion had not been available upon the facts, in other words, that the amalgamated post manifestly did embody the same kind of work as the two separate posts. In that situation, would the concept of redundancy operate so narrowly as to make the employee bear the risks created by the inefficiency of the original job structure?

That very problem arose in *Carry All Motors Ltd* v. *Pennington* [1980] I C R 806, where a transport clerk was dismissed following the employers' decision that the depot was overstaffed and that the work of the transport manager and transport clerk could be carried out by the transport manager alone, apparently without any important change in the kind of work done by the transport manager. The E A T held (in favour of the employer, on the employee's claim of unfair dismissal) that this was a case falling within the statutory definition of redundancy, as was in their view made clear if due weight was given to the fact that the statutory definition speaks not just of diminution in requirements for work of the particular kind in question, but of diminution in requirements for employees to carry out that work. The EAT addressed the problem of reconciling this approach with the doctrine of non-redundancy reorganization in the *Chapman* line of cases. They concluded that they were free in terms of authority to follow the approach that they did despite the existence of the *Chapman* doctrine, but they failed really to suggest a theoretical reconciliation. This is not surprising, because the two approaches really are divergent to the point of inconsistency in this kind of case. It is suggested that *Carry All Motors* gives the more correct approach to the construction of the statutory definition, and that the *Chapman* doctrine is the extraneous and unwarranted gloss on the statute. Ultimately the idea of non-redundancy reorganization bedevils the concept of redundancy in very much the same way as the concept of self-induced frustration bedevils the concept of frustration.

Finally among the problems generated by the job-function approach to the definition of redundancy, we have to consider its relationship to the contractual job-package approach which we examined earlier (see above, p. 531). Hugh Collins has argued that the taking of the job-package approach in *Cowen* v. *Haden Ltd* [1983] ICR 1 was inconsistent with the job-function approach in the *Chapman* line of cases, and he criticizes the Court of Appeal in the *Cowen* case for the way they took and applied the job-package approach ((1982) 11 *ILJ* 255). We would argue for a different evaluation of the relationship between the two lines of cases. It is quite true that the *Chapman* doctrine was inconsistent with the contractual job-package approach to the definition of redundancy that had prevailed before those cases were decided. The inconsistency consisted in the fact that the job-function approach tended to erode the concept of redundancy where the job-package approach had tended to reinforce it. We have argued that the *Chapman* approach was unwarranted in this respect. But as we have seen in earlier pages, the use of the job-package approach by the EAT in *Cowen* v. *Haden Ltd* showed how that approach also could operate to restrict the concept of redundancy where the employee was subject to a wide contractual obligation of geographical or occupational mobility. So the job-package approach in that aspect is not inconsistent with the job-function approach in *Chapman*; rather, it operates cumulatively with it as a further restriction on the concept of redundancy. But Collins is not in fact criticizing this restrictiveness; rather, he criticizes the Court of Appeal for mitigating this restrictive consequence of the job-package approach by their narrow construction of the contractual obligation of occupational mobility in that case with the result that the employee could be regarded as dismissed for redundancy. If this seems paradoxical, it is because Collins sees the protection of employees as residing more in a narrow view of the concept of redundancy for unfair dismissal purposes than in a wide view of redundancy for the purposes of statutory entitlement to redundancy payment. So we come back to the tension between the two conflicting purposes to which this argument has nowadays to be put, which has produced what the EAT has described as the 'U-turn' in the cases about the definition of redundancy, and which they have suggested necessitates a re-examination of the law of redundancy (*O'Hare* v. *Rotaprint Ltd* [1980] ICR 94 at p. 98). We would argue, contrary to Collins's view, that it is more important and appropriate to maintain the concept of redundancy in its full effectiveness for its original purpose of defining entitlement to redundancy payments, because as we have asserted earlier (see above, pp. 473ff.) in a discussion that we shall recapitulate upon shortly, the law of unfair dismissal contains so many other techniques for limiting the employee's claims in respect of redundancy dismissals if the tribunals or courts are so minded that it is pointless to sacrifice the concept of redundancy to what is in the end a fruitless aim of protecting the claims of employees in the context of unfair dismissal legislation by means of this kind of argument.

(5) *The employer's honest belief in non-redundancy grounds*

A further slight narrowing of the redundancy concept is brought about by the fact that the courts have regarded it on the whole as a subjective concept, that is to say they have tended towards the result that there is a redundancy situation only where the employer thinks that there is a redundancy situation. If he thinks that he is dismissing for a non-redundancy reason the courts will accept that there is not a redundancy situation provided only that they are satisfied that his belief was genuine and held in good faith, that there was some factual basis upon which that belief could be based (*Hindle* v. *Percival Boats Ltd* [1969] 1 WLR 174) and that the employer had made a proper appraisal of the requirements of his business (*Delanair Ltd* v. *Mead* [1976] ICR 522).

This may not sound very startling in itself, but its impact will be appreciated if one adds that the 'non-redundancy' reason proffered by the employer is typically a claim that the employment concerned was no longer profitable to the employer. Because the courts accept this as a valid subjective non-redundancy reason, they place outside the area of statutory protection some cases which would come within a socially adequate definition of redundancy. In other words, by accepting the notion of subjectivity they focus attention on the narrowness of the statutory concept of redundancy.

Hindle v. *Percival Boats Ltd* [1969] 1 All ER 836 (CA)

The appellant was a highly skilled craftsman in wood-working who had been employed most of his life on boat-building. From 1960 onwards no boats were built but the employee was employed on repair work. During this time fibreglass boats appeared on the market. In 1966 the employers began building fibreglass boats and to use fibreglass in the repair of wooden boats. In 1966 the employers discovered that the amount of time put in by the appellant on jobs was out of proportion to the amount that could be recovered from the boat owners: he was 'too good and too slow'. The appellant was dismissed and his work taken over by the remaining employees.

SACHS L.J.: The present claim for a redundancy payment was made under s. 1(2)(b) of the Redundancy Payments Act 1965 [EPCA 1978, s.81(2)(b)]. Such a payment could only become due to the employee if it was found by the tribunal (having due regard to the onus of proof) first that the requirements of the employer's business for employees to carry out work of a particular kind had diminished or was expected to diminish, and secondly, that his dismissal was attributable wholly or mainly to such a diminution. It is convenient to refer to these findings as being the first and second conditions precedent to entitlement.

As regards the first of the conditions precedent the test is purely objective in the sense that the test to be applied concerns the actual requirements of the business and not the opinion of the employers or anyone else on that point. Unless the tribunal comes to a conclusion in favour of the employee on that first point the second does not arise.

As regards the second condition there was much discussion in this court whether a tribunal ought to apply an objective or subjective test in deciding whether or not the dismissal is attributable to some established diminution in the requirements of the business. For my part I found, as did Widgery, L.J., that the posing of such a question tended to confusion, at any rate when linked, as counsel for the appellant desired, with attempted distinctions between the motives of the employer and the reasons for the dismissal.

To my mind the position in law on this point clearly emerges when one considers the case of an employer who in truth dismisses his most efficient workman solely because of some genuine but mistaken belief and who but for that belief would have retained that employee in his employment – and indeed would have kept him above all others of his employees. Instances could include a belief that he had been guilty of some deplorable act outside his duties (e.g., an indecent assault on his employer's daughter). It would be impossible to hold that because the belief was mistaken the dismissal was attributable to some established diminution in the above-mentioned requirements – and I reject the submissions of counsel for the appellant to the contrary. Similarly when the requirements of the business remain constant over the relevant comparable periods (in a seasonal business the relevant comparison may well be as here between the periods each of a complete year) and an employee is dismissed because it is believed, whether rightly or wrongly matters not, that his work does not 'pay for his keep', then if in truth he is simply dismissed on that account the dismissal cannot be attributed to a non-existent diminution in the above requirements. . . .

If the facts so warrant or if they are bona fide believed by the employer so to warrant, an employer is entitled to come to a genuine conclusion that despite the requirements of his business he prefers to have a vacancy in his staff rather than to take on an unsuitable replacement. Again, the mere fact that the dismissed employee quickly gets another job may do no more than reflect the scarcity of labour or some other relevant factor. Thus the new employer may have some customers to whom money is no object, and the requirements of his business may for this or other reasons not be the same as those of the old employer.

I would add that, provided the requirements of the business referred to in [s.81(2)(b)] remain constant, it does not matter whether the slowness of the employee which leads to the failure to 'pay for his keep' stems from the onset of years, from some physical cause, or from over great addiction to what is sometimes termed perfectionism. Unfortunately for such addicts, perfectionism can produce a form of inefficiency in many walks of life – not merely in a workshop – however much one may praise the look of the product.

The onus placed on the employer [EPCA 1978, s.91(2)] is simply to show (using the standard test of balance of probabilities applicable where the facts are largely within the knowledge of a party against whom a claim is made) that the dismissal of the employee was not attributable to redundancy. There are cases, as where the tribunal find in favour of the employer on the first condition precedent, when it is not necessary to inquire further into the precise ground on which the employee was dismissed. But in any event once the tribunal is satisfied that the ground put forward by the employer is genuine and is the one to which the dismissal is mainly attributable the onus is discharged – and it ceases to be in point that the ground was unwise or based on a mistaken view of facts, though such matters may well be relevant for consideration by the tribunal when assessing the truth of the employer's evidence.

The above conclusions are all consistent with my view, differing unfortunately in some respects from those just stated by Lord Denning M.R., that compensation is provided by the Act for one, but one only, of life's changes of fortune as between employee and employer: that is dismissal on account of redundancy within the meaning of the Act. It thus neither purports to, nor does, provide for other changes of fortune, such as ill-health or a deterioration in the employer's views of the capabilities of the employee. Similarly, it does not provide for the case where an employer wishes to see if someone else can do the job better; it could indeed be industrially unfortunate if it puts a brake on employers seeking to get the best man for any given job. Nor does it provide for any case where an employer simply wishes not to continue to employ a particular employee, if the dismissal is not mainly attributable to redundancy. It has moreover been held that so long as the requirements of the business for employees of a particular kind remain the same the Act does not provide for changes consequential on a reorganization (see *North Riding Garages Ltd* v. *Butterwick*). In short it does not provide security of employment in the accepted sense of that phrase.

The issue of whether redundancy is a subjective or an objective concept has not often arisen since the *Hindle* case. This would seem to be because the kind of question that was raised in that case has since 1971 tended to be raised as wholly or partly an issue of fairness under the unfair dismissal legislation. The issue does nevertheless occasionally arise in a distinguishable form as part of the problem of defining the concept of redundancy. For instance, in *O'Hare* v. *Rotaprint Ltd* [1980] ICR 94 the employers, who manufactured printing machines, expanded their workforce in the expectation of increased sales which failed to materialize. They maintained a constant level of production but dismissed 10 per cent of their workforce to cut costs because of the lack of increased demand. This case concerned a claim of unfair dismissal arising from these facts, where it was argued on appeal on behalf of the employees that there was no redundancy and accordingly that the dismissals were unfair on the ground that the diminution in the need for employees to do work of the particular kind had no objective existence but existed purely by comparison with the employers' subjective and unfounded expectation that the need for work would have increased. The EAT decided the appeal in favour of the employers on the basis that the dismissals were fair and reasonable whether they were for redundancy or not. The EAT indicated that the case probably did fall within the definition of redundancy, though they were reluctant for that to be the case because they thought that result would discourage employers from taking on fresh labour to meet future predicted demand. The significant feature of the case for our present purpose is that it showed how even an issue identified as going to the problem of whether redundancy is a subjective or an objective concept can be effectively side-stepped when it arises in the context of an unfair dismissal application. The case is also an example in support of our argument that the achievement of a narrowing of the definition of redundancy is of little real help to applicants in unfair dismissal cases because of the other ways in which finding in favour of employers can be supported in this kind of case. So more and more of the weight of the issue in redundancy cases is coming to turn on questions of fairness rather than directly upon the application of the concept of redundancy, though that still, of course, controls the entitlement to statutory redundancy payments as such.

(d) **The unreasonable refusal of suitable employment**
An important part of the strategy of the RPA 1965 consists in its provision (in s.2(4); see now EPCA 1978, s.82(5)), that an employee disentitles himself from redundancy payment by unreasonably refusing an offer of employment from his existing employer which is a suitable offer in relation to him. That disqualifying provision is extended also to include an offer from a new employer to whom the business has been transferred[1] (EPCA 1978, s.94(3)) or an associated employer (s.82(7)). The practical importance of this provision in redundancy payments cases is very considerable. Its purpose is not wholly clear. The Act does not in general seek to deprive the employee of a redundancy payment on the grounds that he is immediately able to obtain fresh employment elsewhere. Why then should he be under particular pressure to accept employment from his existing employer? There does not seem any special reason why he should be under such pressure in terms of the public interest in his remaining in employment, since that interest would require him to be under equal pressure to accept employment elsewhere. The answer seems to be that the EPCA 1978, Pt VI, is viewed for this purpose in its role as the source of a new liability upon the employer. It is therefore seen as being appropriate to enable the employer to avoid this liability by making a suitable offer of fresh employment. It is also seen as appropriate to extend the same facility to the transferee employer or the associated employer, despite the element of involuntary transfer of the contractual relationship which is implicit in such a provision (see below, pp. 576ff.).

Although the provision thus operates as a self-protective facility for the

[1] See below, pp. 577ff., for a discussion of the scope of 'transfer of a business'.

employer, it closely resembles the protective rule which operates in relation to state liability for unemployment benefit, that an employee may be disqualified from benefit for refusing to accept suitable alternative employment offered to him whether by his original employer or not (and typically not by his original employer). Anyway, whatever the functional role of this provision in the Act, it is hard to see what policies the courts might be expected to achieve in their interpretation of this provision. Not surprisingly, therefore, they have omitted to pursue any particular policy and concentrated on the whole upon avoiding the imposition of sub-rules upon this provision, though there has been some feeling for allocating personal factors to the 'unreasonable refusal' and objective factors to the 'suitability of the job' (cf. *Carron Co.* v. *Robertson* (1967) 2 ITR 484). They have also rejected the notion that an equivalence of pay automatically ensures suitability (*Taylor* v. *Kent County Council* [1969] 2 QB 560).

Perhaps somewhat surprisingly, however, they at one stage insisted, in a curiously formalistic decision, that it was no concern of the employee's that the offered job might itself not offer the prospect of long-term security: *Morganite Crucible* v. *Street* [1972] ICR 110. There has, however, been some retrenchment on that position by the EAT in Scotland in their decision in *Thomas Wragg & Sons Ltd* v. *Wood* [1976] ICR 313. We set out here the reasoning in that decision. Can you think of ways in which the quality of the discussion of this kind of issue could be improved upon? (See also *Paton Calvert & Co. Ltd* v. *Westerside* [1979] IRLR 108 (EAT).)

> *Thomas Wragg & Sons* v. *Wood* [1976] ICR 313 (EAT)
> LORD MACDONALD: The short point for decision, therefore, is whether or not the employee acted unreasonably in refusing the employers' offer of alternative employment, which indeed was the course which he adopted.
> The tribunal have taken the view that the employee did not act unreasonably in refusing that offer. Their reasons for so concluding are summarized in their decision, in the following terms:
>
> > The tribunal feels that [the employee] having committed himself to the new job, and having all the fears of a man of 56 who faces unemployment, and having received the offer not too late but . . . as late in the day as within 24 hours of the expiration of his notice, was not unreasonable in refusing the offer and, consequently, he succeeds in his claim.
>
> Counsel for the employers argued before us that this reason involved three factors and that two of those factors, as matter of law, should not be considered. The three factors were: first, that the employee had committed himself to accept a new job; secondly, that one of his reasons for refusing the employers' offer was fear of unemployment in the future in a contracting industry; and thirdly, the lateness of the offer of alternative employment.
> So far as the second and third of those factors are concerned, counsel for the employers argued that those fell to be discounted completely as they were not factors which, in law, should be considered. In connection with the fears of the employee that

he would or might become redundant in the near future if he accepted the employers' offer of re-engagement, our attention was directed to *James & Jones* v. *National Coal Board* (1968) 4 ITR 70. That was a case in which it was certainly held that it was unreasonable on the part of employees to refuse an offer of re-engagement simply because they considered that the industry was a contracting one and that their futures were not assured. There does not appear to have been any other factor, such as the acceptance on their part of another job elsewhere, or any other consideration which fell to be taken into account; and in that situation an industrial tribunal took the view that the refusal was not reasonable. We do not, however, extract from that case the proposition that the situation in a particular industry may not be a factor which, together with others, could properly be taken into account in deciding whether or not the refusal was reasonable. . . . Accordingly, the two factors which have been criticized by counsel for the employers as being wholly irrelevant as matters of law are not, in our view, irrelevant to that extent. They are factors which we consider can be taken into account, provided other factors also exist.

There is one further point of importance in relation to the unreasonable refusal of suitable employment. Some of the issues which have recently been taken in relation to the definition of redundancy could have been presented as issues of suitable alternative employment. In particular, the whole issue in the *Chapman*, *Johnson* and *Lesney* cases (see above, pp. 541ff.) of whether a reorganization of terms and patterns of work gives rise to statutory redundancy could have been handled under the EPCA 1978, s.82(5). The fact that the EAT and the Court of Appeal preferred to relate the issue to the definition of redundancy is significant. It enabled what was really a policy issue, which would have appeared as such under s.82(5), to be presented as a formal problem of statutory interpretation (consider, for instance, the fair wages aspect of the issue, discussed above at p. 546). It therefore enabled the issue to be ruled upon by the courts as a matter of law rather than being left to the industrial tribunals as a matter of discretion, which is how the questions of the suitability of the offer and the unreasonableness of the refusal have always been regarded.

It is in fact now fairly clear that the issue of unreasonable refusal of suitable employment has been deprived of much of its former importance by the combination of the job-function approach to redundancy associated with the *Chapman* case which pre-empts many of the unreasonable refusal issues, and the tendency we have previously referred to for many issues of this kind to be taken as issues of unfairness rather than under the specific heads of the redundancy payments legislation. When the issues of unreasonable refusal and suitability of employment have nevertheless arisen before the appellate courts, they have on the whole construed those concepts in a manner protective of the interests of employees. Thus, as to the suitability of employment, it was held by the EAT in *Hindes* v. *Supersine Ltd* [1979] ICR 517 that the correct test of suitability remained that of substantial equivalence, so that a reduction in pay established a prima facie case of unsuitability which was not rebutted by the rest of the evidence. On the other hand in *Standard*

Telephones Ltd v. *Yates* [1981] IRLR 21, it was held that an offer of employment could validly be judged unsuitable even though the test of substantial equivalence had not been specifically applied; in other words, disequivalence is not a *sine qua non* of unsuitability. We find the same sort of thing in relation to the question of the reasonableness of the employee's refusal. Thus, in *Executors of Everest* v. *Cox* [1980] ICR 415 it was held by the EAT that the reasonableness of the employee's decision was to be judged subjectively in his or her terms, so that the refusal was not rendered *per se* unreasonable by virtue of the employee's erroneous belief that she was about to be offered other employment by the firm that had acquired the catering concession under which the employee had hitherto worked. And in *Tocher* v. *General Motors Scotland Ltd* [1981] IRLR 55, a refusal was held not unreasonable in the face of an offer involving a reduction in both pay and status, so that the notion of substantial equivalence was carried through from the suitability of the offer to the reasonableness of the refusal, thus reinforcing the protection of the employee's claim to redundancy payment. But it is a protection not very often figuring in the case-law; perhaps an additional reason for this is that the redundancy coupled with an offer of alternative employment is more likely to arise in the course of the sort of reorganization because of technical advance for which the redundancy payments legislation was originally envisaged than in the sort of conditions of severe recession in which the legislation has latterly had to operate, where the sort of issue more likely to arise is whether the employer acted unfairly in making no offer of alternative employment. We now turn briefly to consider that type of issue.

(e) Unfairness and redundancy – a résumé

It follows from what has been said in the preceding sections that the scope of the redundancy payments legislation has become fairly narrow. Part IV of the EPA 1975, whilst being concerned with redundancy, approaches the problem entirely from a collective standpoint and affords no locus standi to the individual applicant. In view of these things it is hardly surprising that there has been a shift of emphasis towards the unfair dismissal legislation as the chief source of remedy for the individual employee who is made redundant; and it was perhaps in response to the relative narrowness of the redundancy concept that the Industrial Court was prepared as we have seen (above, p. 469) to create a general category of unfair selection for redundancy.

How extensive has the category of unfair redundancy proved to be? On the one hand the courts have insisted that the process of selection for redundancy must be a reasoned one (*Bristol Channel Shiprepairers Ltd* v. *O'Keefe* [1978] ICR 691 (EAT)). On the other hand they have recognized that this decision lies squarely within the realm of managerial prerogative, and at one stage limited their intervention to those decisions which no reasonable management could in their view properly take: *Vickers Ltd* v. *Smith* [1977] IRLR 11 (EAT) (see above, pp. 476ff.). Specifically, they have insisted that it is not for them to question the employer's view that he no longer has a certain kind of work available. Is it not striking that the courts, who had hitherto treated the employer's assertion that he had a non-redundancy reason for dismissal as being his own subjective decision, should later treat as equally subjective the employer's assertion that he *did* have a redundancy reason, the assertion being made in order to avoid liability for unfair dismissal? Perhaps the courts regard employers' methods of evaluating the levels and types of manpower they need as benign and therefore tend to validate those decisions in whatever form the particular legislation requires. Perhaps they have been primarily concerned to restrict their own intervention in order to preserve their effectiveness. This approach is well illustrated by the following extract, which probably typified the approach to unfairness in redundancy cases at the time when it was decided.

Moon v. Homeworthy Furniture Ltd [1977] ICR 117 (EAT)

KILNER BROWN J.: This is an appeal by four employees (who were representatives of the total workforce) against the unanimous decision of an industrial tribunal sitting at Newcastle-upon-Tyne on 3 and 4 February 1976. At the end of the hearing the applications for compensation for unfair dismissal were rejected. The appeal raises a novel and important issue under the new legislation.

It was a case where a complete factory was closed down and the whole of the workforce made redundant. Mr Stephenson, counsel for the employees, made it plain at the outset that there was a challenge to the validity of the redundancy process and that there was not a genuine redundancy situation. There was no suggestion that it was a contrived redundancy in any sinister sense but that the employees did not accept that it was justifiable to say that the factory was not economically viable. Broadly put, they considered that it was unfair to the workforce to close down the factory, unfair to declare redundancy and therefore dismissals resulting therefrom must also be unfair.

With admirable perspicacity the chairman of the industrial tribunal recognized the inherent difficulties in this line of argument. He inquired how far the industrial tribunal could go into policy decisions of a board of directors on trading and economic matters. He had in mind, and kept in mind, that the definition of redundancy was to be found in section 81(2) of the [EPCA 1978]. Redundancy arises where in fact the employer has ceased or intends to cease to carry on business or where there is a reduced requirement of labour. However, in order to determine the scope of the inquiry and to delineate the area of the evidence it was agreed to call a director of the employers, Mr Bullard, to give evidence as to what had happened and why it had happened and he was cross-examined along the lines of the general views and beliefs of the workforce. One thing emerged with clarity and that was that there was a history of unhappy industrial relations, an involvement of trade union representatives on a local and national level, and an enlistment of the services of the local Member of Parliament. It is obvious, therefore, that when matters have reached this sort of pitch nothing that the employers did would be likely to be acceptable and a trading decision would be regarded as a cloak for an industrial relations decision. As a result of Mr Bullard's evidence it must have seemed plain to most people that there were genuine economic problems. It was still not accepted by the employees that they were sufficiently genuine to oust all political or industrial reasons. Nevertheless one common factor emerged and that was that, whatever the rights and wrongs of the original and persistent labour troubles, the economic difficulties both preceded and succeeded the labour difficulties. It was a classic instance of the age old problem as to whether or not the chicken or the egg came first. The irrelevance and futility of the question is matched only by the irrelevance and futility of the answer.

After this evidence was called, legal argument followed. Mr Perkoff, for the employers, has before us, as he did then, founded his argument on paragraph 6(2)(*c*) and (7) of Schedule 1 to the Trade Union and Labour Relations Act 1974 [EPCA 1978, ss.57(2)(*c*), 59]. In paragraph 6(2)(*c*) redundancy is stated to be a valid reason for dismissal and in paragraph 6(7) certain methods of operating redundancy are declared unfair. No power is given to investigate the reasons for creating redundancy. What may be done is to investigate the operating of a redundancy situation. Here, everybody was made redundant and there was nothing unfair about that. There was no complaint about unfair selection or lack of notice and matters of that kind. . . . After the evidence of Mr Bullard was given, the chairman of the industrial tribunal with acute cogency asked Mr Stephenson whether or not he accepted that there was a cessation of work and therefore a closure. With integrity and common sense Mr Stephenson conceded the point. Technically, therefore, a redundancy situation was proved up to the hilt. But Mr Stephenson hung on to his proposition that if the reason of redundancy was relied on it ought to be open to challenge the declaration of redundancy on its merits. In the view of this appeal tribunal the argument then began to go off the rails. There was a long discussion as to the meaning of paragraph 6(8) of Schedule 1 [EPCA 1978, s.57(3)] and whether or not in the circumstances a reasonable exercise of judgment or assessment of the situation required to make a dismissal fair extended also to the decision to close down the factory. In other words, did the guidelines as to fairness of dismissal entitle the employees to challenge the creation of a redundancy? This brought the industrial tribunal back to realities and Mr Stephenson was asked what evidence he had other than evidence which sought to challenge the validity of the decision to close down. As he had none the tribunal ruled that as this was evidence he could not call he was bereft of any ammunition and his case must go by default.

Notwithstanding the care and the ability with which Mr Stephenson put his case, we are unable to criticize the way in which the chairman handled the matter or to find fault with his reasoning. However we would prefer to put the matter on a much broader and, in our view, more important basis.

The employees were and are seeking to use the industrial tribunal and the Employment Appeal Tribunal as a platform for the ventilation of an industrial dispute. This appeal tribunal is unanimously of the opinion that if that is what this matter is all about then it must be stifled at birth, for it was this imaginary ogre which brought about the demise of the National Industrial Relations Court. The Act of 1974 has taken away all powers of the courts to investigate the rights and wrongs of industrial disputes and we cannot tolerate any attempt by anybody to go behind the limits imposed on industrial tribunals.

The result is therefore that whether this appeal is considered upon the basis on which it was argued or on the more fundamental basis of jurisdiction, the decision of the industrial tribunal was right and there could not and cannot be any investigation into the rights and wrongs of the declared redundancy. There are no grounds for finding any error of law and the appeals are dismissed.

How far has the position changed since 1976 when that case was decided? How, in fact, has the law about unfairness in selection for redundancy developed in response to conditions of severe recession? It would seem that in general, while the law in this area has tended to become more complex and technical with the growth in the volume of cases in the appellate courts (presumably reflecting a great increase in applications to industrial tribunals in respect of redundancy dismissals), there is still an underlying recognition of a managerial discretion to decide upon labour requirements and upon the criteria to be used when reductions in the workforce are seen as necessary. This is coupled with a concern to ensure that, within those parameters, the decisions are implemented with as much consultation at an individual and collective level as is reasonably practicable. One interesting product of the combination of these two lines of policy is that where a collectively agreed procedure is used in redundancy selection, or where a procedure is implemented with active consultation at a collective level, the existence and use of that procedure can often be successfully invoked by the employer against a challenge to the substantive merits of the decisions that have been taken in making selections for redundancy. But there are some substantial unresolved problems, in particular with reference to selection procedures which involve the practice known as 'bumping'. We proceed to illustrate these assertions by looking at some of the most important of the recent cases.

The first point to be made in this connection concerns the relationship between the general test of fairness under EPCA 1978, s.57(3) and the special test in redundancy cases under s.59, in particular the test under s.59(b) of selection in contravention of an agreed procedure or customary arrangement without special justification. Although the principle, established in cases such as *Bessenden Properties Ltd* v. *Corness* (see above, p. 469), that the general test of s.57 is applicable over and above the special test of s.59 in redundancy cases remains in full force and effect, nevertheless the existence of the special test of s.59 has rather tended, in cases where an agreed procedure exists, to confine the challenge that may be made to the employer's decisions to the scope of s.59 itself, i.e. to allegations of contravention of the procedure without justification. Thus in *Evans* v. *A B Electronic Components Ltd* [1981] IRLR 111, the EAT upheld the finding of an industrial tribunal that the employer had acted fairly in selecting the applicants for redundancy in implementation of an agreement reached at the time of the redundancy with the closed-shop union that non-union members would be dismissed first. Although the EAT was at pains to satisfy itself that s.57(3) had been properly applied, and although they ruled that s.59 was not strictly relevant, nevertheless this seems to have been a case where s.59 shaped the discussion in favour of the view that a selection which complied with the agreed procedure was prima facie valid – (despite the overt discrimination against non-members of the union, which would now be caught by the provisions of EPCA 1978, s.58 as amended by the EA 1982 – see below, pp. 637ff.).

The same tendency is visible in the case of *McDowell* v. *Eastern British Road Services Ltd* [1981] IRLR 482. In this case there was an agreed procedure for selection on a seniority or LIFO basis subject to consultation with the union, and certain other conditions. The applicants appealed from the decision of the industrial tribunal that dismissals carried out on a LIFO basis had been fair in this case. Their appeal alleged that the employers should have been regarded as contravening the agreed procedure within the meaning of s.59 by failing to consult the union at the appropriate level. The EAT rejected this appeal on the ground that the notion of contravention of agreed procedure referred to selection which violated the agreed criteria and did not extend to failure to engage in the required consultation. Of course, s.57(3) was still residually applicable; but the issue was effectively shaped in favour of the employer by the discussion in terms of s.59. This is even more obviously true of the decision of the EAT in *Valor Newhome Ltd* v. *Hampson* [1982] ICR 407, where the employee challenged under s.57(3) the fairness of a selection for redundancy carried out on a LIFO basis in accordance with an agreed procedure, the employee's contention being that her seniority had been assessed on an insufficiently generous basis. The industrial tribunal decided in favour of the applicant, but the EAT allowed the employer's appeal on the ground that the tribunal had not accorded enough weight to the fact that the employer had acted in compliance with the agreed procedure as s.59(*b*) required him to do. So s.59 was there viewed as producing a presumption that selection in accordance with an agreed procedure will normally be viewed as fair for the purposes of s.57(3). To similar effect is the decision of the EAT in *GEC Machines Ltd* v. *Gilford* [1982] ICR 725, where the industrial tribunal held that the dismissal was unfair in that, although the employers purported to be selecting for redundancy in accordance with an agreed LIFO procedure, they had not on the facts been justified in making an exception to the LIFO rule on the grounds of the employee's allegedly unco-operative attitude. The EAT allowed the employer's appeal and remitted the case for rehearing on the ground that the tribunal had not made it clear whether they were applying s.59 or s.57(3). So s.59 effectively fragmented the area within which a redundancy selection could be held to be unfair and again operated as a protection for a selection in so far as it could claim to fall within the ambit of s.59 as having been made in accordance with an agreed procedure.

Even apart from the effect of s.59, many of the cases seem in a general sense to suggest that the courts feel that a redundancy dismissal should not normally be held to be unfair. This is a perception not narrowly limited to redundancy in its technical statutory sense, as the decision in *Hollister* v. *National Farmers Union* (see above, p. 470) so significantly shows; but it does seem to apply with particular force when the employer is implementing a LIFO procedure. Thus in *Atkinson* v. *George Lindsay & Co.* [1980] IRLR 197, the Court of Session upheld the EAT in rejecting the claim that failure to consult with the trade union should on the facts have been regarded as making the dismissal unfair.

The employer had selected for redundancy on a LIFO basis, and the court expressed the view that where a dismissal was for redundancy and had survived the test of s.59, it would in most cases be extremely difficult to show unreasonableness within s.57(3). This, as we shall shortly see, goes further than the English courts have done in rejecting purely procedural considerations, but the EAT has taken a similar line about the propriety of LIFO selection in a substantive sense. Thus, we have seen earlier how in the *Eley Kynoch* case (see above, p. 523) the EAT made a point of stressing the defensibility of LIFO selection in terms particularly of the discrimination legislation [1983] ICR 165, 175. And in the case of *Cowen* v. *Haden Ltd*, the EAT expressly regretted the fact that the narrow approach to the definition of redundancy which they felt bound by authority to take, contrary to their inclinations, would make it more difficult for employers to justify dismissals on the ground of redundancy – [1983] ICR 1, 8. Again, in *BL Cars Ltd* v. *Lewis* [1983] IRLR 58 the EAT allowed an employer's appeal against a finding of unfairness and remitted for rehearing in a case where the employee had been selected for redundancy on the basis that he fell within an expressed exception to the LIFO procedure that the employers were following in that he rated badly compared with the other possible candidates for redundancy on an overall assessment of his length of service, job and skills. The appeal was allowed on the ground that the industrial tribunal in finding unfairness was thought to have substituted its view for that of the employer rather than confining themselves to the question of whether the employers could reasonably have acted as they did. The powerful tendency is to validate redundancy dismissals as long as the employer has rationally and conscientiously applied some not obviously unreasonable criteria of selection. The underlying need for the reduction in the workforce tends not to be susceptible to challenge at all.

All this is not to say that no control is exercised in terms of fairness in cases of selection for redundancy. We have seen in an earlier section how the EAT made out the case for ensuring that due regard was had for the need for consultation with recognized trade unions in *Williams* v. *Compair Maxam Ltd* [1982] ICR 156. And in *Grundy (Teddington) Ltd* v. *Plummer* [1983] IRLR the EAT stressed that all the apparently procedural considerations outlined in the *Compair Maxam* case (see above, p. 490) should be regarded as capable of going to the whole substance of the issue of fairness. But on the other hand this control is heavily qualified by the doctrine in the *British United Shoe Machinery* case (see above, pp. 481ff.). So, for instance, in *Abbotts* v. *Wesson-Glynwed Steels Ltd* [1982] IRLR 51, a finding in relation to one employee that a selection for redundancy was unfair for want of consultation led only to compensation for the two weeks by which it was thought that consultation would have postponed the inevitable decision, and a finding in relation to another employee that the selection was not unfair in the first place was upheld on the same ground of inevitability of the outcome of dismissal even if due procedure had been applied. Similarly in *Freud* v. *Bentalls Ltd* [1983] I C R 77, where the E A T allowed an employee's appeal against a finding that a redundancy selection had been fair despite the lack of prior discussion or consultation, the court nevertheless felt obliged to remit the issue back for rehearing to ascertain whether due consultation would have made any difference. It would seem that this 'same outcome' doctrine is likely to have a particularly restrictive effect in redundancy cases, for in those cases there is inherently unlikely to be a distinct 'employee's side of the story' to emerge and make a difference on the assumption that due procedure had been followed, as might more easily be envisaged in cases for example of dismissal for misconduct.

Finally we refer briefly to the problems arising from the practice known as 'bumping'. This is the practice whereby, instead of a simple selection for redundancy, one employee is transferred into the job of another employee who is accordingly dismissed; the first employee thus 'bumps' the second employee out of his job. This may occur because of some managerial consideration, such as that it will produce a better balanced or more skilled workforce than a simple dismissal of either the first or the second employee would. On the other hand, it may be wholly or partly a recognition of the priority that the first employee has over the second employee under a seniority system, which may be the subject of an agreement with a trade union. There are considerable difficulties in applying the law of redundancy payments and the law of unfair dismissal to 'bumping' practices. In *Thomas & Betts Manufacturing Ltd* v. *Harding* [1980] I R L R 255 the E A T and the Court of Appeal rather surprisingly upheld an employee's claim that she had been unfairly selected for redundancy in that adequate consideration had not been given by the employer to the possibility of dismissing somebody more junior whose job this employee might then fill. This seems to have been a rather artificial position created by the fact that the employer had simply stated his decision not to offer alternative employment without justifying it; it should not normally be difficult for an employer to convince a tribunal that 'bumping' was not a readily available option. This was subsequently made fairly clear by the decision of the E A T in *Huddersfield Parcels Ltd* v. *Sykes* [1981] I R L R 115, where the E A T, although upholding the industrial tribunal in the view that the selection for redundancy was unfair by reason of failure to consult with the employee, rejected an argument that this employee should have been allowed to 'bump' an employee of lesser seniority, the *Thomas & Betts* case being distinguished on the ground that in the present case there had been discussion and an agreement with the trade union about the selection for redundancy. The E A T indicated that the contrary view on the 'bumping' issue would place the employers in the difficulty that the employee displaced by the 'bumping' would have an unanswerable claim of unfair dismissal.

This has not proved the end of the difficulties arising out of 'bumping'. In *Tocher* v. *General Motors Scotland Ltd* [1981] I R L R 55, an employee who had been redeployed in pursuance of a 'bumping' agreement with the trade union into a job involving a reduction in pay and status, claimed that he had thereby been constructively dismissed for redundancy and unfairly dismissed. The EAT, while rejecting the claim of unfairness, held that the employee was entitled to a redundancy payment, and that the 'bumping' agreement was rendered void by EPCA 1978, s.140, in so far as it amounted to a purported contracting out of that right on the part of the applicant by purporting to limit his opportunity for a trial period and ultimate rejection of the job into which he was transferred. See the note by Schofield at (1981) 10 *ILJ* 176. If the redeployed employee can claim to be redundant if the redeployment is an unsuitable one that he could reasonably refuse, what is the position of the displaced employee? Can he be said to be redundant despite the fact that he has been replaced in his job; in other words, can the redundancy of the redeployed employee be related to the displaced employee? In *Elliott Turbomachinery Ltd* v. *Bates* [1981] ICR 218, the EAT allowed the employer's appeal against a finding of unfair dismissal in this situation, and remitted the case for rehearing so that the possibility of 'transferred redundancy' could be considered as a ground on which the dismissal might be treated as fair. On the other hand, in *Cowen* v. *Haden Ltd* [1983] ICR 1 the EAT indicated that the approach they felt obliged to take to the definition of redundancy (see above, p. 537) was going to make it very difficult for employers to show redundancy for unfair dismissal purposes in any cases involving 'bumping' (at p. 8). So this issue remains open and this whole area rather obscure.

(f) The effect of the redundancy payments legislation upon collective bargaining

There is no particular reason to think that Parliament in enacting the Redundancy Payments Act, whatever purposes they had in mind, aimed for any specific interaction with the processes of collective bargaining. We have examined, in the shape of EPCA 1978, s.96, the main exception to that generalization, where provision was made for the making of exemption orders where collective bargaining provided an equally favourable alternative. But apart from this the statute cannot be said to have been concerned with stimulating collective bargaining, nor, on the other hand, with replacing it as such, though there is reason to think that Parliament was consciously extending to industry at large the best results achieved by collective bargaining in particular industries so far as severance payments were concerned. This discussion is, of course, limited to the level and form of severance payments, as distinct from the level of and selection for the redundancies themselves; that latter aspect of redundancy was not really dealt with by the 1965 legislation (except so far as it facilitated small-scale redundancies in response to technological development). The level of, and selection for, redundancies were however dealt with by Part IV of the Employment Protection Act at a procedural level, and we have considered the impact of that legislation upon collective bargaining in Chapter 2.

What then has the effect of the 1965 legislation been on the size and form of severance payments? Initially and for some years the legislation seems to have acted as a substitute for collective bargaining in the sense that it established norms from which there was little impulse to depart. Agreements for larger severance payments tended to be ad hoc matters largely confined to small numbers of professional or executive employees – the kind of agreement under consideration in *Edwards* v. *Skyways Ltd* [1964] 1 WLR 349. The legislation coincided with current practice in so far as it provided for single lump sum payments and this statutory form of compensation was also little departed from by collective bargaining.

A report in the *Financial Times* of 15 March 1978 by Christian Tyler showed, however, that there had been two tendencies away from that state of affairs; first, the level of compensation for redundancy had tended to increase over the statutory level, and secondly the payments were tending to consist partly of a continuation of income for a period of time as well as a lump sum payment. Both of these characteristics had long been present in relation to compensation for loss of employment in the civil service or upon the nationalization of private industries, and much of the evidence which Tyler presented to support these trends turns out to relate to the public sector in the wider sense. Thus he cited recent steel industry closures in Hartlepool and Cardiff as providing examples of payments well above the statutory norm and paid in weekly instalments for up to two years or more, and he recorded that similar patterns were to be expected in relation to the British Leyland closure of the Speke Plant in Merseyside. Other schemes for payments substantially over the statutory norms turn out to be the product, direct or indirect, of government action – for instance, the continuing shedding of registered dock workers under the statutory Dock Work Scheme (65,000 men in the previous fifteen years, as Tyler reported) and the scheme contained in the Shipbuilding Redundancy Payments Act 1978, which also provided for periodical payments for up to two years.

It would seem, according to a British Institute of Management survey in 1974 to which Tyler referred, that in private industry this trend to improve on the statutory level of redundancy payments operated in 1974 in 80 per cent of companies. Moreover Tyler cited instances of schemes in private industry for periodical payments after redundancy, for instance the agreement reached early in 1978 covering Typhoo Tea workers in Birmingham and the joint union–management 'programme for action' for introducing new technology in newspaper printing – a plan which contained an element of maintenance of income over a period of time, but which was voted down on the shopfloor in 1977, perhaps partly because of the general preference for lump sum payments. It seemed possible at that time to draw the tentative conclusion that there was a linked movement both of legislation and governmental action on the one hand, and of collective bargaining on the other, towards severance payments larger than the general statutory level and concerned with the maintenance of income for a period of time as well as capital payments. A good example of continuing initiatives of this kind in a nationalized industry is provided by the special redundancy measures for the coal-mining industry. These measures, and the associated financing legislation culminating in the Coal Industry Act 1982, are described in an informative note by William Rees – (1982) 11 *ILJ* 178.

How, in general, has the position as it stood in 1978 been affected by the conditions of severe recession that supervened? The indications are that the changes may have been quite considerable. An *Incomes Data Study* published in December 1982 (No. 280) throws considerable light on this question. That study concluded that the extent of the recession had brought about a change in the climate of bargaining on the subject of extra-statutory redundancy payments. They found that some companies were renegotiating their redundancy agreements to eliminate clauses on the level of payments. Others when declaring redundancies were either paying strictly according to their agreements or attempting to negotiate their waiver. In contrast to the past, fewer companies were improving on the terms of their agreements when implementing redundancies. The study found that the changes had been primarily among companies which were declaring redundancies because of a lack of work and which were financially stretched. By contrast, the companies which had changed working practices or which remained financially sound or were able to call on the resources of a larger financially strong holding company were still able to implement their agreements and improve on them. But several employers' organizations were now advising their members that severance terms should not form part of any agreement. On the other hand severance terms in the public sector remained higher on average than those in the private sector. This really serves to support the proposition that the redundancy payments legislation is a measure which is on the whole confined in its effectiveness to the sort of relatively limited scale of redundancy associated with gradual technological change such as was still the norm in 1965. In conditions of severe recession and high unemployment the goal of financial self-sufficiency for the Redundancy Fund becomes unsustainable – the Fund had a deficit of £232 million by November 1982 – and the statutory redundancy payments system is no longer capable of exerting its former gentle upward pressure on the level of extra-statutory payments under collective bargaining. In this situation other measures such as social security provisions relevant to redundancy assume a greater significance, and it is to the consideration of such measures that we now briefly turn.

(g) Social security and other measures relevant to redundancy
The purpose of this subsection is briefly to draw attention to the range of measures which are relevant to redundancy but which are not generally recognized as having a place in our labour law alongside that of the

redundancy payments legislation, the redundancy procedure legislation and the unfair dismissal legislation as it applies to redundancies. These measures are relevant to redundancy in the sense of contributing to the definition of the social terms on which redundancies will take place, and therefore perhaps influencing employers, workers and trade unions about the circumstances in which and conditions on which redundancies will happen. It is not suggested to the student readers of this book that they attempt to assemble or assimilate the details of these various measures, but rather that they alert themselves to the relevance of these measures as part of the background to their general reading in and around the area of labour law. For it is only in this way that the strict compartmentalization of topics, which prevails in labour law as much as in more traditional legal disciplines, can ever be liberalized.

Firstly as to social security measures. Social security pension provisions have a great potential impact in this field because they in practice determine the age at which workers dependent on them retire. At the moment social security pension entitlement is conditional upon the attainment of the fixed pensionable age, which is 65 for men and 60 for women (Social Security Act 1975, ss.27–9). But there has been in recent years and continues to be discussion of proposals both to reduce the pensionable age, to apply a common standard to men and women and to make the pensionable age flexible. (See Ogus and Barendt, *The Law of Social Security* (2nd edn, 1982), pp. 194–6.) The conditions on which flexibility was introduced would have a major impact on decisions about selection for redundancy. Social security, unemployment benefit and supplementary benefit have a broad significance for redundancies in constituting the income support provision that will be available on a continuing basis for workers made redundant. So the sort of issues that we discussed in Chapter 1 in relation to these benefits such as the policies followed as to earnings-related supplement to unemployment benefit (see above, pp. 24ff.) will be important in the present context too. Some aspects of the rules relating to these benefits may have a more specific impact on decisions relating to redundancy, for example the disqualification from unemployment benefit for up to six weeks for voluntary leaving of employment without just cause under s.20 of the Social Security Act 1975. In *Crewe* v. *Anderson* [1982] I C R 706 the Court of Appeal decided that a teacher who had applied for early retirement under a local authority scheme approved by the Department of Education and Science which aimed to reduce the numbers of teachers employed and to replace older teachers with younger ones had left his employment without just cause within the meaning of the statute, the court taking the view that the policy of the legislation was that the insured person had a responsibility to all those who underwrote the national insurance fund not to become unemployed by his own voluntary act. The question is whether that policy should be an overriding one even when it conflicts with the policy of achieving necessary redundancies by means of voluntary early retirement of older workers.

Another immediately relevant set of social security rules is that by which claimants are disentitled to supplementary benefits if their capital resources exceed a given figure (£3,000 from November 1983). By virtue of the Supplementary Benefits (Resources) Regulations 1981 (SI 1981 No. 1527), this is a complete cut-off of entitlement once that figure is exceeded, and this may in certain circumstances place recipients of lump sum redundancy payments under a powerful incentive to spend those sums quickly.

Secondly, the law relating to early retirement provisions under occupational pension schemes is of importance in relation to redundancies. This is true both in a general and a specific sense. In a general sense it is significant that extensive use has been made of early retirement provisions in occupational pension schemes as a way of encouraging voluntary redundancies and ameliorating the consequences of redundancies generally. Some restraints are imposed upon this use of occupational pension schemes by the Inland Revenue conditions for the approval of pension schemes, these conditions having the aim of ensuring that pensions are not the means for an undue avoidance of income tax. In particular these conditions restrict the minimum ages at which early retirement pensions may be paid, currently to age 50 for men and 45 for women in the case of voluntary early retirement. The Inland Revenue rules are not, however, specific on the question of the minimum age at which pensions may be paid on early retirement at the instigation of the employer, and apparently the approval of the Superannuation Funds Office of the Inland Revenue has to be sought on an *ad hoc* basis for such measures. On the other hand, the question arises whether the interests of the employee who retires early are adequately protected so far as his rights under an occupational pension scheme are concerned. Provision was made by the Social Security Act 1973, s.63, to ensure minimum rights under occupational pension schemes upon early retirement by way of benefits preserved until retirement (or transfer payments into a new scheme) and the Occupational Pensions Board was given a continuing responsibility in this regard. But the preservation requirements, currently made by the Preservation of Benefit Regulations 1973 S I No. 1469, are minimal and cannot be regarded as adequate to deal with the problem of erosion by inflation. They fall short of the goal of ensuring that occupational pension schemes shall not discriminate between members who leave before normal retirement age and members who remain employed until that age. The problem was the subject of a report by the Occupational Pensions Board in 1981 ('Improved Protection for the Occupational Pension Rights and Expectations of Early Leavers', Cmnd. 8271, 1981) which concluded that there should be legislation to extend the preservation requirements and ensure the statutory revaluation of preserved benefits to keep pace up to a certain extent with inflation.

Thirdly, measures concerning compensation for loss of office are extremely important in relation to redundancies. It is of very great significance that there is a long tradition of providing statutory compensation for loss of office in relation to redundancy situations in the public sector. The practice of providing statutory compensation for loss of office in the public sector has represented and continues to represent an important difference between the legal régimes for employment in the private and public sectors. The redundancy payments legislation is really no more than a minor counterpart in the private sector for provisions long since current in the public sector, where the approach both to lump sum and to periodical payments has long been based upon relatively generous assumptions reflecting a better developed notion of job security in the public as compared with the private sector. An important current example is provided by the Local Government Compensation Regulations 1982, SI No. 1009. It is these measures, consisting in statutory regulation or special statutes for particular industries and occupations within the public sector which serve to maintain the higher expectations of severance payments which prevail in the public sector to which we have referred. Of comparable importance in establishing the real terms on which redundancies take place, are the measures for the taxation of compensation for loss of office and other payments upon termination of employment including severance payments. The legislation is contained in ss.187–8 of the Income and Corporation Taxes Act 1970 as amended by the Finance Acts of 1978 and 1981 which provide an important income tax exemption, currently limited to £25,000, for payments on the termination of employment subject to a number of specific conditions. The policy and the details of this legislation are centrally relevant to our present discussion as representing another concealed source of labour law.

Finally in this connection, we should refer to special governmental measures for the maintenance of employment, some of which have a direct impact on actual or potential redundancy situations. We have considered measures such as the Job Splitting Scheme to be relevant to the creation of employment rather than the termination of it (see above, p. 31) and we have discussed the Temporary Short-time Working Compensation Scheme under the heading of security of earnings (see above, pp. 361–2). But these are largely classifications of convenience which should not disguise the broad relevance of those measures to redundancies. Moreover there is one set of measures which is particularly relevant in this context, namely the Job Release Scheme. The Scheme provides for the payment of allowances to employees who retire in circumstances such that their jobs can be regarded as having been released to other workers who would otherwise be unemployed or come within some priority category. There is currently provision for the payment of such allowances in relation to early retirements by disabled men aged 60 or over, and on a further set of conditions men aged 64 and women aged 59. In 1983 the scheme was extended to cases where full-time jobs are released by employees' transferring to part-time work as well as by retiring outright (the Part-time Job Release Scheme). Measures of this kind are obviously very significant determinants of decisions about selection for redundancy, and further serve to indicate the range of measures which deserve to rank equally for consideration by labour lawyers with the redundancy payments and unfair dismissal legislation.

7 The guarantee function of the state in relation to employers' insolvency

In a set of provisions which has perhaps received insufficient academic notice, the Employment Protection Act achieved a fundamental re-allocation of responsibility in relation to employers' insolvencies. These obviously represent an important area of termination of employment and one where the employee is at grave risk that his pecuniary entitlements against the employer will not be realized. The traditional method of protecting the employee's interests was to give him priority in the employer's insolvency or liquidation in respect of four months' remuneration but subject to an overall limit of £800, as revised by the Insolvency Act 1976, s.1 and Sch. 1, and in respect of all accrued holiday remuneration (Bankruptcy Act 1914, s.33 and Companies Act 1948, s.319). This method of protection was extended by section 63 of the EPA 1975 (EPCA 1978, s.121) to include the main new pecuniary rights created by the Employment Protection Act, namely guarantee payments, remuneration on suspension on medical grounds, statutory payments for time off and remuneration under protective awards. This method of protection is however both limited in its scope, difficult for the employee to enforce and uncertain as to its effectiveness, as even priority over other creditors does not guarantee repayment in full, especially since that priority is shared by the Inland Revenue, and by the Department of Health and Social Security in respect of twelve months' unpaid social security contributions.

The legislators therefore embarked upon a further method of protection already in operation in relation to statutory redundancy payments. This consists in making the state the guarantor of some of the employee's rights, by enabling the employee to look to the Redundancy Fund in the event of the employer's insolvency (which includes the appointment of a receiver) for payment of up to eight weeks' arrears of pay,[1] any outstanding pay for the statutory minimum period of notice, any outstanding holiday pay relating to the previous twelve months (up to a maximum of six weeks) and any unpaid basic award of compensation for unfair dismissal (EPCA 1978, s.122). These amounts are to be calculated at the maximum rate of £145 per week (see s.122(5)–(6) and orders made thereunder). The employee may complain to an industrial tribunal of the failure of the Secretary of State for Employment to make the appropriate payment from the Redundancy Fund (s.124) which is an interesting instance of an industrial tribunal being given power to review the exercise by the Secretary of State of an administrative function conferred upon him by the statute. The Secretary of State is subrogated to all the rights of the

---

[1] Defined by s.122(4) so as to include the other rights referred to in the previous paragraph.

employee in respect of the payments for which the Redundancy Fund acts as guarantor (s.125). A similar set of provisions is made in respect of unpaid contributions to occupational pension schemes (s.123) and a parallel set of provisions is made for recourse to the Maternity Pay Fund in respect of maternity pay outstanding upon an employer's insolvency (ss.40–42).

How important is this guarantee role of the state in practice? On the face of it, it seems limited compared to the scope of the employee's priorities in insolvency. But although the guarantee is limited to eight weeks' pay, compared with the four months' pay to which priority is given, the latter is limited to £800 in all, whereas the former is subject to a flexible limit, at present fixed at £1,160 from February 1979 onwards.[1] The assumption of this liability by the state marks an increase in the use of the social security type of fund to protect rights accrued in private employment. In practical terms considerable use is being made of these provisions, but they are giving rise to protracted, elaborate and costly tripartite litigation between employees, liquidators and the DE.

The importance of the guarantee function has clearly been increased by the onset of conditions of severe recession, producing large numbers both of redundancies and employers' insolvencies. The number of direct payments from the Redundancy Fund more than quadrupled between 1978 and 1982, rising from over 12,000 in 1978 to nearly 54,000 for the first nine months of 1982. Government policy has apparently been to maintain the efficacy of the guarantee function; thus the EA 1982 made three amendments to s.122 of the EPCA 1978 designed to eliminate prejudicial features of the operation of s.122 from the employee's point of view. These amendments, to be found in paras. 3 and 4 of Schedule 3, Part 1 to the EA 1982, ensure *inter alia* that payments may be made expeditiously out of the Redundancy Fund and that sums such as protective award payments may be included within the guarantee although not accruing until after the employer's insolvency. The presence of measures tending to increase the protection of employees is a matter for some remark in relation to the EA 1982; it is of course the case that the strengthening of the guarantee function of the state is not inconsistent with the reduction of the burden of employment protection legislation upon employers, especially since the commitment to the Redundancy Fund's being fully financed by employers' contributions has had to be abandoned.

Proposals for change in the nature of the guarantee system have recently been made which would if implemented enhance the character of the guarantee system as a form of social security provision rather than as a charge on employers by way of employment protection. The Report of the Review Committee on Insolvency Law and Practice (known, from the name of its

[1] The state guarantee could of course exceed the level of employees' priority to a more substantial extent. If the state guarantee is held so that it does not exceed parity with employee's priority, the Redundancy Fund benefits from this parity, since its liability is covered in principle by priority claims upon the company. The loser is the unsecured creditor of the company, often a small trader.

chairman, as the Cork Committee (Cmnd. 8558, 1982)) made proposals designed to improve the position of unsecured creditors of companies and firms, but was concerned to do so without causing a deterioration in the protection accorded to employees in an employer's insolvency. They accordingly recommended that while the employee's preferential rights in an insolvency should be broadly unchanged, the Secretary of State's right of subrogation in respect of direct payments to employees from the Redundancy Fund should become non-preferential, on the ground that 'the priority accorded to employees in an insolvency is a social measure, intended to alleviate special financial hardship, and that in modern times the cost of meeting such social needs ought properly to be borne by the community' (para. 1435). (See the annotation to the Report by Upex at (1982) 11 *ILJ* 268.) So commercial policy and employment protection policy are thus envisaged as having a common alignment towards the guaranteeing of employees' rights in an employer's insolvency more and more directly by the state itself.

8 Continuity of employment and transfer of employment

Many of the employment rights of individual employees are governed by a time factor, in that they are rights for which the employee qualifies only by completing a certain period of employment, or they are rights whose extent depends upon the employee's length of time in employment. Very many of the new statutory individual employment rights are in one sense or another subject to this kind of time factor. The existence of this sort of time factor creates the problem of measurement of the employee's period of continuous service. The most obvious basis for such measurement should be the contract of employment. Using that basis of measurement, one would ask whether there was continuity of contract during, for example, periods of absence due to industrial action or sickness or during periods of temporary unavailability of work. However, the law of the contract of employment may not give clear answers to questions of this type, or it may be desired to provide a different concept of continuity of employment from that offered by the application of the law of the contract of employment. There has been in recent years some clarification of the law of the contract of employment in matters of this kind and also considerable legislative experimentation with other methods of approaching the problem of continuity of employment.

Where the rights of individual employees are subject to a time factor in this way, the protection of those rights raises problems, not only of continuity of employment, but also of continuity of employer. The employee's accumulated rights may be protected by their transfer from one employer to another when the employee himself transfers or is transferred between employers. In such a case, there is in effect continuity of employer. Once it is recognized that accumulated seniority ought where possible to be transferable from one employer to another with the employee; once, in other words, we have recognized a doctrine of continuity of employer, it should as a matter of equity follow that an employee whose rights are not transferable upon change of employer should at that point be compensated for the effects of the loss of his accumulated seniority. In one sense problems of this kind are inherent in any case where an employee transfers from one employer to another. However, the situations which are regarded as raising this kind of problem most specifically are those where the transfer is in practice outside the control of the employee, because it takes place by reason of a takeover of the employer's business or a merger of that business into a larger concern. As we shall see in the course of this section, the Transfer of Undertakings (Protection of Employment) Regulations 1981 have had some impact on that kind of situation.

(a) **Continuity of employment**
Situations where employees are laid off by reason of unavailability of work give rise to difficult problems concerning continuity of the contract of employment. In the following extract the Industrial Court took the view that a contract of employment could remain in force during such periods of lay-off as the employer chose, in his discretion, to impose. Is this decision compatible, in your view, with the basic obligations of the employer under the contract of employment? Can there be a continuing contract of employment when the employer has an almost unlimited right of lay-off?

Puttick v. *John Wright and Sons (Blackwall) Ltd* [1972]
ICR 457 (NIRC)

The employee was employed as a boiler scaler from 1948 doing specific jobs for the same employers, in the intervals between which he was laid off for short periods. In 1972 he claimed a redundancy payment, but the industrial tribunal held that he did not have the necessary continuous employment to create an entitlement.

LORD THOMSON: In support of their view the tribunal quoted a number of cases said to be authority for a general rule of law that in a contract of employment where the only terms are that the employee shall do such work as the employer requires and shall be entitled to payment only for work done, there is an implied obligation on the employer to provide work for the employee to do, and without such an implied obligation 'such a contract could not exist'. In our opinion, the cases cited do not warrant that extreme conclusion. We think it quite possible to envisage circumstances in which A may consider it in his best interests to undertake to do such work of a particular kind as B provides for him, A holding himself available to do such work as required and being paid only for the work he actually does, while B undertakes to make available to A such work of that particular kind as from time to time comes to hand. In such an arrangement between A and B, A in effect agrees to be 'temporarily suspended' or 'laid off' for such periods as no work is in fact available. It may well be that in the present case the parties never put their minds to the full legal implications of such an arrangement, but it does not seem to be disputed that such an arrangement was in fact what they contemplated and intended and believed they had entered into. This is in our view borne out by the history of the relationship between the parties, particularly the basic continuity of the employee's employment with the employers over some 23 years, the fact that at no time when he was laid off was he given notice of dismissal and the fact that he always held himself available for work from the employers and they always (until February 1971) gave him work to do with only very short periods of interruption between jobs. We are unable to find anything in any of the quoted cases to suggest that such an arrangement does not amount to a contract of employment binding in its terms. Indeed, as regards the Act of 1965, such an arrangement would seem to have been specifically contemplated as a category of contract of employment (see section 5(1) of the Act of 1965). [EPCA 1978, s.87(1).]

Statutes confirming individual employment rights have sought to avoid the problems of contractual continuity during lay-off by creating a concept of 'temporary cessation of employment', during which continuity of employment may be preserved even though there is no subsisting contract of employment. In the following passage, it is recognized that the relationship of 'temporary cessation of employment' can be recognized as having existed upon the evidence of hindsight alone, without evidence of prior mutual promises for the resumption of employment. Does this approach, in your view, deprive the concept of temporary cessation of employment of any serious meaning?

Fitzgerald v. *Hall Russell & Co. Ltd* [1969] 3 All ER
1140 (HL)

LORD MORRIS OF BORTH-Y-GEST: The facts concerning the eight weeks are set out in the decision of the tribunal. The respondents are shipbuilders. Because there was a shortage of work they reduced their labour force between June 1962 and December 1962. In June 1962, the force was 805, in December 1962, it was 440. So in all 365 men were dismissed. Of these 78 were welders. The appellant was only dismissed towards the end of the period. He was one of a group of 52 men who were dismissed on 28 November. He was one of 20 out of that number who were welders. A document then sent by the respondents to the Ministry of Labour stated that the dismissals were due to 'the present shortage of work'. The decision of the tribunal records that the appellant stated that the foreman who had given him notice had assured him and the other discharged men that they would 'soon be back'; the decision adds 'but there was no corroboration of this'. But if the tribunal accepted the appellant's evidence that the foreman had made some such remark then no corroboration of the appellant was necessary before treating the evidence as evidence which was relevant to the issue before the tribunal.

It is clear that the appellant was dismissed on 28 November 1962. He was then free to take up other employment. But the facts as found suggest that it was the hope of the appellant that he would soon be employed again and that it was the hope of the respondents that they would soon be able to employ him again. The mutual hopes were soon fulfilled. The appellant had been employed by the respondents as a welder from July 1958 to November 1962; after an interval of nearly eight weeks he was back again. Had he been 'absent from work on account of a temporary cessation of work'? Unfortunately the decision of the Tribunal hardly deals with the problem. Their decision was as follows:

We concluded that the [appellant] had been dismissed by reason of redundancy on 28 November 1962 and that his service with the Respondents had been broken on that date.

Undoubtedly he was dismissed; undoubtedly his service was broken. The whole question was whether, notwithstanding those circumstances, the eight weeks are to 'count as a period of employment'. A question of law is involved whether on the facts as found it could be held that in those weeks the appellant was absent from work 'on account of a temporary cessation of work'.

My Lords, it is important, in my view, to remember that the words being considered are the words used in their context in the Contracts of Employment Act 1963. Section 1(5) provides that Sch. 1 to the Act applies for ascertaining the length of an employee's period of employment and whether it has been continuous. The very purpose of para. 5 [EPCA 1978, Sch. 13, para. 9], as I have earlier indicated, is to make certain weeks count in the employee's favour although he was away from work and had no contract of employment. The build-up of the period of 'continuous employment' (on the length of which the length of notice to terminate will depend) is arranged in the interests of employees. The situation to be contemplated is that there will have been employment, then dismissal, and then (after an interval) re-employment. Then if at some later date it is desired to give a notice to terminate the contract of employment the question will have to be asked – Why in that period between the two contracts was the employee absent from work? If it was a period during which he would have been at work but for the fact that his employer could not find work for him but which period ended when the employer did find work for him, I consider that it could properly be said that he was absent from work on account of a cessation of work even though the employer's business or the particular department of it had not completely closed down. Then if in the light of all the facts and circumstances (on a backward look as from the date when it is being decided what notice must be given) it could be said that such cessation of work was only 'temporary', then by operation of law the period when in fact there was no working and no contract would 'count' as part of a period of continuous employment.

For the reasons which I have given I consider that the tribunal erred in law in holding that the appellant's qualifying period commenced on 21 January 1963. They should have held on the facts as found that between 28 November 1962 and 21 January 1963, the appellant was absent from work on account of a cessation of work. As their approach, leading to a wrong conclusion, was, in my view, erroneous they did not have to give consideration to the word 'temporary'. We were invited to take the view that had there been a correct approach on the part of the tribunal and had they considered the word 'temporary' they could only, on the facts as found by them, have come to the one conclusion viz., that the cessation of work was in this case a 'temporary cessation of work'. While there is much to commend this view, an appeal in this case must relate to questions of law. I think that the matter will have to be remitted to the tribunal. If they decide that the cessation of work was 'temporary' then they will have to determine the amount of the redundancy payment.

In determining whether a cessation of work has been temporary the guidance given by Lord Parker C.J. in *Hunter* v. *Smiths Dock Co. Ltd* [1968] 1 WLR at p. 1869 should, in my view, be followed. If in reference to the time when a cessation of work begins there is evidence showing that both the employer and the employee expected and anticipated that the cessation would only be for a relatively short time, that would be very relevant evidence in considering at a later time whether there had been a temporary cessation of work. But the absence of any such evidence would certainly not be decisive. It is to be remembered that there must be a looking back process and that it is at some time subsequent to re-engagement and in reference to a past period of absence from work that the question is raised whether the employee was absent from work on account of a temporary cessation of work. All relevant evidence and all relevant factors will have to be taken into account. Questions of fact arise. The duration of one period relative to or in relation to the antecedent and subsequent periods will be one relevant factor.

Behind the problem of continuity of employment during lay-offs due to temporary lack of demand for work lies an even more fundamental problem of how far employment protection rights will by means of recognition of their continuity of employment be extended to seasonal workers, sessional workers, and other workers regularly employed under intermittent fixed-term contracts. The outcome of decisions about continuity of employment for these workers can have an important effect on the way that employment is constituted, especially when employment is in general scarce. In *Ford* v. *Warwickshire County Council* [1983] ICR 273, the House of Lords, overruling the Court of Appeal, has in an important decision extended to workers of this kind the same liberal approach to continuity of employment that the House of Lords took towards laid-off workers in the *Fitzgerald* v. *Hall Russell* case. The case concerned the continuity of employment of a part-time temporary teacher who was not employed during successive summer holidays. While the House of Lords in the present case was careful to assert that they were not laying down a rule of universal application to all sessionally employed teachers and lecturers, the judgment of Lord Diplock in particular did make it clear that they had the wider range of such cases, such as those of seasonal work in agriculture or the hotel and catering trade, in mind, and could contemplate the finding of continuity in such cases provided that the length of the period between two successive seasonal contracts was short enough in comparison with the length of the season of employment to be properly regarded as no more than temporary, in the sense of transient, cessation of employment ([1983] ICR 273, 286).

There is a further provision, now contained in EPCA 1978, Sch. 13, para. 9(1)(c), for preserving continuity of employment during periods where (although no contract of employment is in force) the employee is 'absent from work in circumstances such that by arrangement or custom he is regarded as continuing in the employment of his employer for all or any purposes'. This provision was probably intended by the draftsmen to cover some of the situations which have in fact been treated as cases of 'temporary cessation of work'. The courts have tended to regard para. 9(1)(c) as obscure (see Lord Parker C.J. in *Hunter* v. *Smiths Dock Co. Ltd* [1968] 1 WLR 1865 (DC)) and interpreted it negatively in relation to a provision in a national collective agreement for preservation of seniority rights during secondment between Electricity Boards – *Southern Electricity Board* v. *Collins* [1970] 1 QB 83. It was, however, allowed to operate on arrangements made by the National Coal

Board for keeping a worker on as a member of their pension scheme after his transfer to a company carrying out development at various NCB mines – *Wishart* v. *National Coal Board* [1974] ICR 460; and its application, in *Lloyds Bank Ltd* v. *Secretary of State for Employment* [1979] IRLR 41 (EAT), to 'one week on, one week off' employment was a significant new departure.

Further problems of contractual continuity of employment may arise in respect of prolonged periods of absence due to sickness where the employee is not in receipt of any remuneration, because his absence exceeds the period covered by any sick-pay arrangements the employer may have or, now, the period during which statutory sick pay is payable. The difficulties in assessing contractual continuity are well exemplified by the following passage concerning the contractual status of the 'holding departments' into which many employers transfer employees when they are absent and no longer in receipt of sick pay. The employee placed in a 'holding department' is regarded as still 'on the books' of the firm; but does his contract of employment continue in force? In *Marshall* v. *Harland & Wolff Ltd* [1972] ICR 101 (NIRC), the court, having held that the employee's absence through illness had not led to a frustration of the contract, went on to say:

> We have been caused some concern by Mr Bingham's suggestion that our decision could lead to employers abandoning the admirable practice of keeping sick employees 'on the books', thus giving them assurance that, other things being equal, they will be able to get work as soon as they have recovered. We see no reason why this practice should be disturbed. If employers are worried that in the event of a redundancy situation arising a very long time after the employee has left the active list, they will thereby expose themselves to an unintended liability and so be tempted simply to dismiss, an alternative exists. They can (and it is a much better approach to the problem) transfer such an employee to a 'holding department' as was done in *O'Reilly* v. *Hotpoint Ltd* (1969) 7 KIR 374. The effect of such a transfer is that the employee ceases to be employed in any legal sense, but is on a list of men in respect of whom there is a voluntary arrangement between the employers and any relevant union, or the employees themselves, that all concerned will do their best to provide them with work as soon as they are again fit. In putting forward this suggestion we should like to stress that it is only made in relation to the long-term sick. Those who are absent for shorter periods should, in accordance with good industrial practice, be maintained in employment, whether or not in receipt of full wages or sick pay.

These difficulties about contractual continuity during absence due to sickness are to some extent avoided by the provision for statutory continuity during absence due to sickness now contained in EPCA 1978, Sch. 13, para. 9(1)(a); but as that provision preserves statutory continuity only for twenty-six weeks where no contract is in force, it is still necessary to consider contractual continuity in relation to periods of absence due to sickness exceeding six months' duration.

The subject of continuity of employment during strikes (and lock-outs) has received particular attention in so far as loss of continuity of employment can be regarded as a possible sanction against the taking of industrial action. We discuss this below in Chapter 7.

(b) Transfer of employment

The common law of the contract of employment makes no provision for continuity of employer, in the sense of automatic transfer of the employee's rights along with changes in ownership of the employing enterprise. Such changes in ownership may take place behind the veil of the corporate structure, but if there is a change of legal personality involved, the common law positively attaches importance to the avoidance of automatic transfer of contracts of employment, as the following passage shows. In this instance, the non-transferability of contracts of employment was asserted in order to protect the individual employee from a transfer of employer over which he had no say and of which he had no knowledge. Does the common law in general carry out a protective function by means of this approach to the assignment of contracts of employment?

Nokes v. *Doncaster Amalgamated Collieries Ltd*
[1940] AC 1014 (HL)

A colliery worker was sued by his apparent employer for breach of his contract of employment. The objection was taken on his behalf that there was no contract of employment in force, because the respondent had absorbed the company that had employed him without his having the opportunity to object to the new corporate employer. The Court of Appeal rejected this submission on the ground that the statutory procedure for amalgamations now contained in the Companies Act 1948, ss.206–8, resulted in the automatic transfer of contracts of employment.

LORD ATKIN: When one regards the remarkable legal consequences of the construction adopted by the courts below one is driven to ask what the reasons may be supposed to be that brought about this revolution in the law, and that led to one class of person, companies under the Companies Act, being able to shake off the restrictions which bind ordinary persons, though only when they are minded to transfer their business to another and probably a larger company. Before 1928 no such privilege existed. Amalgamations, a vague term, were possible: companies could dispose of their undertaking to other companies. But it was necessary to invoke the machinery of a winding up: assets would be transferred by conveyances to which the liquidator was party: assignments had to be negotiated: and dissolution of the company could not take place until after the winding up had been completed. But all such sales of undertaking were subject to the ordinary law, and had of course to respect the rights of third parties. Nothing was transferable by a company that was not transferable by an individual: and in particular no one suggested that contracts of service could be transferred. On the contrary, a winding-up order or resolution operated as a discharge of existing servants, resulting in the right to claim damages for wrongful dismissal. It is true that the transferee company would ordinarily offer to employ the former servants of the transferor company: and an unreasonable refusal to accept such offer would mitigate or perhaps get rid of any damages. But the servant was left with his inalienable right to choose whether he would serve a new master or not.

Now the new procedure operates to remove much of the complexity of the former system. . . . There has thus been provided a much more rapid mode of carrying out a reconstruction or amalgamation which avoids a winding up, an improved procedure akin to the various modern conveyancing provisions made in other statutes. But why this beneficent procedure should be tainted with the oppression and confiscation which in some cases would certainly be caused, or why in the interests of companies big or small for the mere purposes of an amalgamation it should violate all the rules as to transferability depending on some occasions on principles of our law and on other occasions on contract, I cannot imagine. It is said that one company does not differ from another: and why should not a benevolent judge of the Chancery Division transfer the services of a workman to another admirable employer just as good and perhaps better. The answer is two-fold. The first is that however excellent the new master may be it is hitherto the servant who has the choosing of him, and not a judge. The second is that it is a complete mistake in my experience to suppose that people, whether they are servants or landlords or authors do not attach importance to the identity of the particular company with which they deal. It would possibly hurt the feelings of financial gentlemen with large organizing powers and ambitions to know how strongly some people feel about big combinations, and especially amalgamations of small trading concerns. But it is said how unreasonable this is: for the big company can buy the majority of the shares in the old company: replace the directors and managers: change the policy and produce the same result. Be it so: but the result is not the same: the identity of the company is preserved: and in any case the individual concerned, while he must be prepared to run the one risk, is entitled to say that he is not obliged to run the other. The truth is that this argument was tried out and repelled over forty years ago by Stirling J. in *Griffith* v. *Tower Publishing Co.* [1897] 1 Ch. 21, where an author was held justified in refusing to allow his contract to be transferred to another company.

Hence legislation concerned with the protection of individual employment rights has had to devise its own extra-contractual formulae for continuity of employment as between an employer transferring the enterprise in which the employee works, and the employer who acquires the enterprise concerned. The legislation identifies the area within which it will impose continuity of employer by reference to the concept of transfer of a business. In the following passage the Court of Appeal considers whether there is the requisite continuity of employer in the case where the enterprise changes its function while the particular working environment of the employee remains the same. Do you consider their decision against continuity of employment in these circumstances to be a defensible one?

Woodhouse v. *Peter Brotherhood Ltd* [1972] ICR 186 (CA)

LORD DENNING M.R.: In this case two men claim redundancy payments. Each worked for many years at a factory at Sandiacre in Derbyshire. Mr Woodhouse worked there for 40 years as a machine tool setter. Mr Staton worked there for 24 years as a planer. But during their service the factory had been owned by two different firms in succession. Up to August 1965 the factory had been owned by Crossley-Premier

Engines Ltd and the men were employed by Crossleys; but in August 1965 the factory was bought from them by Peter Brotherhood Ltd. They took on the men and used the factory for their own products. In 1971 Peter Brotherhood Ltd dismissed the men for redundancy. Peter Brotherhood Ltd admitted that the men were entitled to redundancy payment, but they said it was to be calculated on their six years' service with them. But the men said it ought to be calculated on the maximum of 20 years, seeing that each of them had been working at the factory for more than 20 years, at first with Crossleys and then with Peter Brotherhood Ltd.

The industrial tribunal, by a majority of two to one, held that the redundancy payments were to be calculated only on the six years of Peter Brotherhood Ltd. But the National Industrial Relations Court held that it was to be calculated on the maximum of 20 years; and there is now an appeal to this court – the first appeal from the National Industrial Relations Court.

In order to determine the appeal it is necessary to state the facts relating to the sale of the factory in 1965. Crossleys, as engineers, were mainly engaged in the manufacture of diesel engines. In 1965 they decided to stop making those engines at their Sandiacre factory and to make them at their factory in Manchester. About the same time Peter Brotherhood Ltd, the big engineers of Peterborough, were anxious to expand. They wanted to find a factory in which to manufacture spinning machines, compressors and steam turbines. So a deal was arranged which suited both firms. Crossleys sold their factory at Sandiacre together with the plant and equipment to Peter Brotherhood Ltd for £500,000. Much of the plant and equipment could be used by Peter Brotherhood Ltd for their work, and the men could go on working at their particular jobs just as before. Only the finished articles were different. Instead of diesel engines, it was spinning machines, compressors and steam turbines.

The take-over, however, was not entirely clean cut. In August 1965 Crossleys were building four or five diesel engines at Sandiacre. It was arranged that Peter Brotherhood Ltd should complete these engines and charge Crossleys with the cost. This was done by January 1966 and thenceforward the factory made no diesel engines at all. There was some special plant and equipment needed for those diesel engines. That was not bought by Peter Brotherhood. It was taken off by Crossleys to Manchester.

Another thing was that, before August 1965 there was some work being done at the factory in making spinning machines and so forth for Peter Brotherhood. It was done by Crossleys on sub-contract for Peter Brotherhood. After August 1965 Peter Brotherhood did it themselves, of course, as part of their general output from the factory.

Although there was this broad change in the ultimate products of the factory, nevertheless so far as the men were concerned, there was little change. In July 1965 Peter Brotherhood called the men together and offered them work on the selfsame terms as they had with Crossleys. All the men but one accepted the offer and stayed with Peter Brotherhood, with the same cards, the same pay, the same pension rights and so forth. Virtually the whole labour force was transferred almost automatically to work for Peter Brotherhood. Their work was much the same as before, but the goods produced were different.

So far as the legal documents were concerned, Crossleys only transferred to Peter Brotherhood Ltd the physical assets. They transferred the land and buildings and the plant and equipment. They did not sell the goodwill, nor did they enter into any restrictive covenant. They did not assign their book debts or their work in progress. They simply went off to Manchester and carried on their activities there. . . .

Now what is the effect of the transfer from Crossleys to Peter Brotherhood Ltd? It all depends on whether the 'trade or business or an undertaking' of Crossleys was 'transferred from one person to another', within paragraph 10(2) of Schedule 1 to the Contracts of Employment Act 1963 [EPCA 1978, Sch. 13, para. 17(2)] which is to be read into and with the Redundancy Payments Act 1965, especially Schedule 1(1) and section 13 of it. I will not go into those provisions again because I went through them in *Lloyd* v. *Brassey* [1969] 2 QB 98. I there stated the effect of them and the previous cases in these words, at p. 103:

> If the new owner *takes over* the business as a going concern – so that the business remains the *same* business but in different hands – and the employee keeps the same job with the new owner, then he is not entitled to redundancy payment. His period of employment is deemed to continue without a break in the same job: so that, if he is afterwards dismissed by the new owner for redundancy, his payment is calculated on the whole period in that job.

To that passage I would now add this: if the new owner does *not* take over the business as a going concern, but only takes over the physical assets – using them in a *different* business – then the workman is entitled to redundancy payment from the outgoing owner. He may be taken on by the new owner straight away and thus loses no wages, but nevertheless he is entitled to redundancy payment from the outgoing owner. It is, in a real sense, compensation for long service with that owner. In due course, if he serves more than two years with the new owner, and is afterwards dismissed by the new owner for redundancy, he will be entitled to redundancy payment from the new owner, calculated on his length of service with him.

So, by and large, the Act works fairly. The employee either gets one redundancy payment in respect of his entire service, or he gets two redundancy payments in respect of the two parts of it. But the trouble in this case is that the transfer took place in August 1965 before the Act came into force. So the men may only be entitled to the second period.

So the question is this: was there a 'transfer' of the 'business' or only a transfer of the 'physical assets'. If there was a 'transfer' of the 'business', the men get redundancy payments for 20 years' service. If there was no transfer of the 'business' but only of the 'physical assets', they get it for six years' service only. . . .

This brings me to the present case. It seems to me that this factory is quite different from the farm in *Lloyd* v. *Brassey* [1969] 2 QB 98. In that case there was the same business being carried on both before and after the transfer. Here it was a different business. I would ask a similar question to that asked by Salmon L.J. in *Lloyd* v. *Brassey* [1969] 2 QB 98, 106: if anyone had been asked prior to August 1965: 'What business is being carried on in the factory at Sandiacre?', his answer would have been 'The manufacture of diesel engines.' And if he had been asked the same question in January 1966, his answer would have been 'The manufacture of spinning machines, compressors and steam turbines.' If he had been asked 'Is it the same business?', he would have said 'No. The manufacture of diesel engines has now gone to Manchester. All that is being done at Sandiacre is the manufacture of spinning machines etc.' True the same men are employed using the same tools: but the business is different.

That is how the majority of the tribunal looked at it. The Industrial Court looked at it differently. They seem to have asked themselves the question: was there a change in the working environment of the men? It seems to me that that was not the right question. The statute requires the tribunal to see whether there was a transfer of the 'business' of the employer. So you look at the nature of the business of the employer and not at the actual work being done by the men. Looking at it in that way, I am quite satisfied that in 1965 Crossleys did *not* transfer their business at Sandiacre to Peter Brotherhood Ltd. They took it off to Manchester. They only transferred the physical assets to Peter Brotherhood Ltd. The result is that, as from 1965, the men were employed in a different business, namely, that of Peter Brotherhood Ltd: and are only entitled from Peter Brotherhood to redundancy payment for the period of their service with Peter Brotherhood. So I think the majority of the tribunal were right. I would therefore allow the appeal and restore their decision.

The restrictive approach taken in the *Woodhouse* v. *Peter Brotherhood* case to the concept of transfer of a business or undertaking was maintained by the House of Lords in the case of *Melon* v. *Hector Powe Ltd* [1981] ICR 43, which concerned a similar situation of employees continuing to work on the same machines after the take-over of the factory in which they worked by a company who would use it for a rather different type of business. The House of Lords maintained the distinction between the assets of the business and the business itself, and rejected the argument that the transfer of assets could in a case such as this be regarded as the transfer of part of a business within the meaning of the continuity and transfer provisions. In this case they took that decision in favour of the affected employees, in that the employees were claiming against their original employer that the transfer had constituted their dismissal for redundancy, and the employers were relying on the transfer as the transfer of the business so as to negate their claim to redundancy payment under EPCA 1978 s.94. However, although this is another of the situations in which the same concept has come to be argued in opposite directions for different purposes, we nevertheless suggest that the interests of employees are ultimately better protected by a broad, employee-oriented approach to the notion of transfer of an undertaking than by a narrow commercially defined approach.

Thus we can see that common-law contractual principles concerning transfer of employment are open to manipulation against the interests of employees, and the statutory rights of employees are still often built upon common-law foundations. This was well illustrated in a decision concerning a practice known as the making of 'hiving-down agreements'.

Pambakian v. *Brentford Nylons Ltd* [1978]
ICR 665 (EAT)

The receivers of Brentford Nylons Ltd, in order to make an advantageous disposal of the business of the company, acquired for the company a wholly-owned subsidiary company called Kinwon Ltd. The business was sold to Kinwon Ltd by means of a hiving-down agreement, the essence of which was that Kinwon Ltd became the owner of the business while Brentford Nylons

Ltd continued to employ its employees for the time being and sub-contracted them to Kinwon Ltd. The latter company was renamed Brentford Nylons (1976) Ltd and sold as a going concern to Lonrho Ltd. Some of the original employees were shortly afterwards dismissed at the instance of Lonrho Ltd. Could the dismissed employees claim their statutory rights against Brentford Nylons (1976) Ltd, for Brentford Nylons Ltd had been turned into a man of straw by the sale of its assets? An industrial tribunal said that Brentford Nylons Ltd had remained the employers. The EAT remitted the question for rehearing with the following comments.

PHILLIPS J.: We were invited by counsel to make any observations which we thought might be of assistance to the industrial tribunal upon the remission. The situation which has arisen in the present case, though common enough when businesses fall into financial difficulties and a transfer is in prospect, presents difficult problems when it comes to determining whether the employees have left the employment of their original employer and have entered that of the new proprietors. Of course it is well recognized, as indeed the industrial tribunal has pointed out, that employees cannot be 'transferred' as though they were property, and it is necessary that in each individual case there should be a separate agreement between each employee and the new employers. Otherwise, as pointed out in *Nokes* v. *Doncaster Amalgamated Collieries Ltd* [1940] AC 1014, 1026, men would be serfs and not servants. Nonetheless, and without in any way condoning the unacceptable view that employees can be transferred like so much plant, it has to be recognized that in practice and in reality when a large business is transferred from one owner to another the way in which the matter is often handled lacks personal consideration of individual cases, and there is a tendency to deal with employees in categories and classes. Thus in practice it is often idle to look for the individual offer and acceptance that one would expect to find at the start of employment when considering an individual case, and wrong to conclude from the lack of such acts that there had been no 'transfer' of an employee. Furthermore, it often happens in practice on such occasions, even where it is obvious that employees must have been transferred from the employment of the old proprietors to that of the new proprietors, that a very long period elapses after the change of employment has plainly come about before the matter is regularized in the form of amended or new documents, or contracts of employment. Accordingly, it would be wrong to conclude from the lack of such documents that a 'transfer' of employment has not taken place. Furthermore, it has to be remembered that apart from those employees who may wish to be dismissed and to take a redundancy payment, the probability is that the majority of the employees would hope that they will be 'transferred' to the service of the new proprietor. It is thus often difficult to tell whether or when such a 'transfer' has taken place, and it is necessary to make inferences from all the relevant circumstances, many of which on some occasions may be of a trifling character. Looked at from the point of view of the new proprietors, it will usually be the case that they will not intend to employ all the old employees, and therefore will have it in mind to make some announcement. But in practice these affairs are often so sloppily conducted that it can sometimes be seen that by the time the new proprietor gets around to saying that he does not wish to retain the services of X or Y it is plainly to be seen that in fact X or Y must by then have entered his employment.

The correct test to be applied in these circumstances seems to us to be an objective one. What must be done is to look at all the facts and circumstances, including what was said, what was done, and all the documents, and then inquire whether bearing these matters in mind the circumstances are such that the only reasonable conclusion is that the new proprietors must be taken to have agreed to employ the claimant, and the claimant must be taken to have agreed to serve the new proprietors.

It was suggested in the course of the hearing that we might say something about the propriety or otherwise of hiving-down agreements. We do not think that we can accept this invitation, except in the most tentative form. As was pointed out by Mr Boswood [counsel for Brentford Nylons Ltd], our primary task is to decide the appeal as a matter of law, and in any event it would be unwise to make general pronouncements on the basis of a single case. Provided that the transactions are genuine, as they were in the present case, it is a question of the precise legal effect of what was done in each case. Nonetheless we have seen enough in this case, and in other cases, to know that such agreements add new complications to the problems which in any event arise in the field of redundancy payment and unfair dismissal when a company falls into financial difficulties. All we would say is that when amending legislation is under consideration attention ought to be directed by those responsible to the problems which arise in such cases. For example, if the decision of the industrial tribunal is right – and as there is to be a rehearing we should emphasize that we wish to express no opinion one way or the other – since Brentford Nylons Ltd is without assets the whole responsibility for the payment of the redundancy payments will fall upon the redundancy fund, and hence upon the taxpayer; and the employees will not be able to recover the compensation for unfair dismissal to which they have been found to be entitled. The gainers will be the secured creditors; and, if the hiving-down agreement has resulted in the sale of the business as a going concern on terms which otherwise might not have been possible, those employees who have been re-employed by Lonrho Textiles Ltd, and who, or some of whom, otherwise might also have been made redundant. But there are many conflicting interests involved, and it would not be right for us to express any general conclusions.

Finally there is the question of industrial relations in circumstances such as those which have arisen in the present case, and here we feel it is necessary to say something. In such situations the handling of redundancies is a matter of extreme difficulty, requiring a careful and sensitive approach on the part of the employers. Consultation is essential and the necessity for it has been asserted by the National Industrial Relations Court and by the Employment Appeal Tribunal, and to a certain extent it is now imposed by statute. In these cases timing is all-important, and it is difficult to combine the publicity which consultation entails with the secrecy which the negotiation of takeover deals requires. Nonetheless it is essential to try. Nothing that we have heard in the course of the argument satisfies us that the practice of 'hiving-down' can justly be used as an excuse for avoiding consultation. It is to be remembered that different employees will have different aspirations; and whereas many, perhaps most, will hope to be taken on by the new proprietors, there may well be some who would prefer to be dismissed and to receive a redundancy payment. On the information contained in the documents made available upon the hearing of the appeal it seems to us that there was a failure on all sides in the present case to have proper consultation. The letter of 28 May 1976, though beginning to explain the hiving-down operations to the extent of disclosing that the trading assets had been transferred to Brentford Nylons (1976) Ltd, made no attempt to explain what was further contemplated, or in general terms what progress had been made, or to inform the employees what options were open to them, or what were their prospects. And the last paragraph of the letter, whatever its intention, is certainly not so worded as to be likely to yield much enlightenment. We say no more about this, because we have been told by Mr Morison [counsel for Brentford Nylons (1976) Ltd] that in fact far more was done by way of consultation than appears in the papers, both by way of meetings, interviews and the distribution of documents. In these circumstances it would not be right for us to say any more, except to repeat that the use of the hiving-down practice in no way reduces the need for consultation; that it seems to us that it is desirable that receivers and managers should be aware of the requirements of good industrial relations in this respect as much as employers; and that from what we have heard in the present case we are not satisfied that at present they are. . . .

Finally we wish to say a word about conciliation. Under the Employment Appeal Tribunal Rules 1976 we have the task, where it seems appropriate, to promote conciliation. On the first day of the hearing of the appeal we asked for arrangements to be made if possible for a director of Lonrho Ltd to attend on the following day so that we could have an opportunity of discovering at a high level of responsibility the attitude of the company to the appeal. It was not found possible for this to be done, and the hearing of the appeal ended on the second day. We considered whether to adjourn the proceedings and to invite or order the attendance of a representative of Lonrho Ltd for the purpose of conciliation, but have decided that inasmuch as all the applications will have to be reheard such a course would be inappropriate. However, before further time and costs are consumed in what is likely to be a lengthy bout of litigation, we think that it is desirable that Lonrho Ltd should give some further consideration to their wider responsibilities in this matter. After all, they have taken over as a going concern the business and undertaking of Brentford Nylons Ltd, they have employed most of the employees of that company, the taxpayer is being left to shoulder the burden of the redundancy payments of the few who were made redundant, and, if the decision of the industrial tribunal turns out to be right, those employees who were unfairly dismissed will have to whistle for their compensation. Quite apart from what may turn out to be the legal position as eventually determined by the industrial tribunal which is to rehear the applications, it may well be that Lonrho Ltd will think it proper to consider their wider extra-legal responsibilities in the matter. Accordingly we direct in accordance with rule 23 of the Employment Appeal Tribunal Rules 1976, that a copy of this judgment be served upon Lonrho Ltd, and that within 42 days of the receipt thereof they lodge with the registrar of the appeal tribunal a statement of the steps (if any) they are prepared to take towards satisfying the employees' claims, and, in any event, the reason for their decision. Upon receipt of the statement we shall give such further directions as may seem fit. . . .

The present writers examined the implications of the *Pambakian* case and the workings of the practice of hiving down in an article written in 1980 ('The Effects of Receiverships upon Employees of Companies' (1980) 9 *ILJ* 95), and concluded that there were a number of major unresolved legal problems about the rights of employees in transfer situations of this kind which pointed up the general need for a positive implementation, at the very least, of the relevant EEC Directive, to the consideration of which we now turn.

The EEC Directive on Acquired Rights of Workers on Transfers of Undertakings (No. 187 of 1977; EEC *OJ* No. L61/26 (see above, pp. 250ff.) necessitated a more positive approach in British labour legislation to the question of continuity of employer in the event of transfer of an undertaking. The British government was under an obligation to give effect to the Directive by March 1979 though it was not until 1981 and only after the threat of enforcement proceedings by the EEC Commission that this was finally done. Bob Hepple in a valuable article ((1976) 5 *ILJ* 197) and a supplementary note ((1977) 6 *ILJ* 196) described the development from the Draft Directive to the Directive in its final form.

The Draft Directive would have applied the protection of workers' acquired rights to mergers, takeovers and concentrations of undertakings. The final version of the Directive is limited in its application to the transfer of an undertaking as a result of a legal transfer or merger (Art. 1(1)). This severely limits its impact upon the existing law, especially as it was implemented in such a way as to include only cases where there is a formal change of employer and not the more common case where the ownership or control of a company is changed by share purchases.

The Directive deploys various techniques for the protection of the workers' acquired rights. The first of these is the automatic transfer of contracts of employment to the transferee of the undertaking. The Draft Directive provided for the transfer of rights arising out of 'customary industrial practice', but the final version dropped this category. The transfer of contracts of employment is on the other hand a fundamental new development, reversing the policy underlying *Nokes* v. *Doncaster Amalgamated Collieries* (above).

The Directive requires that the transferee employer should observe terms and conditions collectively bargained with the transferor (Art. 3(2)). (It allows the period of such observance to be limited to one year.)

The Directive also requires that transfers shall not constitute in themselves good grounds for dismissal and that such dismissals must be 'for economic technical or organizational reasons' (Art. 4(1)) (originally 'for pressing business reasons' at the draft stage). This fundamental development would tend to create a new category of automatically unfair dismissal but would limit it according to a wide new concept of organizational necessity.

The Directive requires the preservation of the legal status and function of employee representatives upon a transfer 'if the business preserves its autonomy' (Art. 5). This is a concept new to British company law which has proved controversial in its application.

The Directive requires the disclosure to employee representatives of information about the transfer, and requires consultation with them about measures for the protection of employees 'where the transferor or transferee envisages [such measures]' (Art. 6(1), (2)). (The Draft Directive had provided for negotiation and arbitration, but those proposals were dropped.) The implementation of this requirement created, as we have seen above, p. 250, a complex interrelationship between consultation obligations upon the transfer of undertaking and consultation obligations in relation to proposed redundancies under EPA 1975, Part IV (see above, pp. 257ff.). It is in general quite striking how many significant new patterns of statutory intervention it seemed necessary to introduce for the purpose of compliance with these EEC obligations.

The legislation which was ultimately enacted by way of implementation of the EEC Directive was the Transfer of Undertakings (Protection of Employment) Regulations 1981, SI No. 1794, the first major piece of employment legislation to take the form of delegated legislation made under the authority of the European Communities Act 1972. (See Davies and Freedland, *Transfer of Employment* (1982), which sets out and annotates the regulations.) We have referred earlier to the rather slight impact of the Regulations on collective labour law (see above, p. 252). So far as individual employment law is concerned, their impact is also a great deal more limited than might at first appear. The key provision is that of Regulation 5, which appears on the face of it to change the law fundamentally by reversing the principle in *Nokes* v. *Doncaster Amalgamated Collieries*:

Transfer of Undertakings Regulations 1981, Regulation 5

Effect of relevant transfer on contracts of employment, etc.

5.–(1) A relevant transfer shall not operate so as to terminate the contract of employment of any person employed by the transferor in the undertaking or part transferred but any such contract which would otherwise have been terminated by the transfer shall have effect after the transfer as if originally made between the person so employed and the transferee.

(2) Without prejudice to paragraph (1) above, on the completion of a relevant transfer –

(a) all the transferor's rights, powers, duties and liabilities under or in connection with any such contract, shall be transferred by virtue of this Regulation to the transferee; and

(b) anything done before the transfer is completed by or in relation to the transferor in respect of that contract or a person employed in that undertaking or part shall be deemed to have been done by or in relation to the transferee.

(3) Any reference in paragraph (1) or (2) above to a person employed in an undertaking or part of one transferred by a relevant transfer is a reference to a person so employed immediately before the transfer, including, where the transfer is effected by a series of two or more transactions, a person so employed immediately before any of those transactions.

(4) Paragraph (2) above shall not transfer or otherwise affect the liability of any person to be prosecuted for, convicted of and sentenced for any offence.

(5) Paragraph (1) above is without prejudice to any right of an employee arising apart from these Regulations to terminate his contract of employment without notice if a substantial change is made in his working conditions to his detriment; but no such right shall arise by reason only that, under that paragraph, the identity of his employer changes unless the employee shows that, in all the circumstances, the change is a significant change and is to his detriment.

The impact of Regulation 5 is severely restricted by a number of factors. The definition of relevant transfer in Reg. 3 excludes take-overs by transfer of share control, where, however, the effect of Reg. 5 is in a sense automatically achieved in that there is no formal change of employer in the first place; but the definition of undertaking in Reg. 1 also excludes all non-commercial undertakings. It is arguable that the ambit of Reg. 5(1) is severely limited by the reference to contracts which would otherwise have been terminated by the transfer, since it is arguable that transfer does not, in many situations, in itself terminate the contract of employment; it is only the consequential cessation of employment that does that. The exclusion of occupational pension provisions by Reg. 7 deprives Reg. 5 of what might otherwise be its most important area of application, and even if Reg. 5 does operate to transfer statutory continuity of employment, which is far from certain, it is not clear that in doing so it goes beyond the existing statutory continuity provisions that we have examined. It would appear to do that only if the concept of transfer of an undertaking for the purposes of the Regulations transcends the restrictions of that concept as we have observed them to exist under the previous statute law.

In so far as Reg. 5 does nevertheless effect a transfer of contracts of employment on the transfer of an undertaking, its main impact would be to render the acquirer of the undertaking potentially liable under the unfair dismissal legislation for a dismissal associated with the transfer. That liability is qualified by Reg. 8 which makes the following amendment to the unfair dismissal legislation for this purpose:

Transfer of Undertakings Regulations 1981, Regulation 8

Dismissal of employee because of relevant transfer

8.–(1) Where either before or after a relevant transfer, any employee of the transferor or transferee is dismissed, that employee shall be treated for the purposes of Part V of the 1978 Act and Articles 20 to 41 of the 1976 Order (unfair dismissal) [Northern Ireland] as unfairly dismissed if the transfer or a reason connected with it is the reason or principal reason for his dismissal.

(2) Where an economic, technical or organisational reason entailing changes in the workforce of either the transferor or the transferee before or after a relevant transfer is the reason or principal reason for dismissing an employee –

(a) paragraph (1) above shall not apply to his dismissal; but

(b) without prejudice to the application of section 57(3) of the 1978 Act or Article 22(10) of the 1976 Order (test of fair dismissal), the dismissal shall for the purposes of section 57(1)(b) of that Act and Article 22(1)(b) of that Order (substantial reason for dismissal) be regarded as having been for a substantial reason of a kind such as to justify the dismissal of an employee holding the position which that employee held.

(3) The provisions of the Regulation apply whether or not the employee in question is employed in the undertaking or part of the undertaking transferred or to be transferred.

(4) Paragraph (1) above shall not apply in relation to the dismissal of any employee which was required by reason of the application of section 5 of the Aliens Restriction (Amendment) Act 1919 to his employment.

Although primarily intended to protect the employee under the law of unfair dismissal in the transfer situation, this Regulation creates so generous a basis for fair dismissal by way of exception to its general proposition as actually to amount in the event to a possible protection for the employer. To the extent that new liabilities upon the transferor or transferee employer result from the combination of Reg. 5 and Reg. 8, they would apply particularly in the situation of hiving down, possibly so as to destroy the utility of that practice as a method by which receivers can salvage viable parts of businesses in receivership. Because that was thought to be an undesirable outcome, the following special provision was made for that situation.

Transfer of Undertakings Regulations 1981, Regulation 4

Transfers by receivers and liquidators

4.–(1) Where the receiver of the property or part of the property of a company or, in the case of a creditors' voluntary winding up, the liquidator of a company transfers the company's undertaking, or part of the company's undertaking (the 'relevant undertaking') to a wholly owned subsidiary of the company, the transfer shall for the purposes of these Regulations be deemed not to have been effected until immediately before –

(a) the transferee company ceases (otherwise than by reason of its being wound up) to be a wholly owned subsidiary of the transferor company; or

(b) the relevant undertaking is transferred by the transferee company to another person;

whichever first occurs, and, for the purposes of these Regulations, the transfer of the relevant undertaking shall be taken to have been effected immediately before that date by one transaction only.

(2) In this Regulation –

'creditors' voluntary winding up' has the same meaning as in the Companies Act 1948 or, in Northern Ireland, the Companies Act (Northern Ireland) 1960; and

'wholly owned subsidiary' has the same meaning as it has for the purposes of section 150 of the Companies Act 1948 and section 144 of the Companies Act (Northern Ireland) 1960.

This regulation means that the automatic transfer consequence is postponed in a hiving-down situation until the ultimate transfer to the purchaser, so that the receiver can separate the viable part of the business off from the rest by making a hiving-down agreement, while effectively leaving the employees with the original employer unless and until a purchaser of the hived-off part of the business can be found. This brief résumé fails to do full justice to the complexities of the Regulations, but does perhaps serve to indicate the problems and imperfections that can result from the necessity of importing principles and norms derived from EEC Directives directly into a highly technical branch of British employment and commercial law. It remains to be seen what impact this will have on the structure of the underlying principles relating to continuity and transfer of employment.

5
Trade-union law and the closed shop

1 **Introduction**

In this chapter we aim to cover five broad areas of law. Historically, the first of these areas to achieve prominence was that of the freedom of employees to associate in trade unions and the legal status of unions as organizations. In this context freedom of association meant, not the protection of union members from acts of discrimination by their employers (which we discussed in Chapter 2), but the prior question of whether the state took action to prevent employees from forming, joining or taking part in the activities of a trade union. This question, and the linked question of the legal status of trade unions, were the central questions of trade-union law in the nineteenth century. Behind these legal questions was the fundamental social question of whether trade unions were to be, or could force themselves into being, accepted as part of the social and political fabric of the country. As the century wore on, and especially after 1870, the underlying social question came to be answered in the affirmative, and this led also to resolution of many of the legal issues. However, since the link between issues of social policy and of legal policy is not a crudely mechanical one, some of the legal issues, especially those relating to the legal status of trade unions, lived on into the twentieth century and even survive today. This tendency was accentuated by the fact that the legislators of the Trade Union Act 1871 (which was the central statute in this area until its repeal by the IRA 1971) were not whole-hearted in their acceptance of trade unions into the fold of respectability.

The second area of law which we shall deal with can also be seen as an aspect of freedom of association, but again it does not concern the protection of union members against discriminatory action by their employers. Rather it is the question of what legal remedies may be available to a person who wishes to become or remain a member of a trade union which wishes to exclude or expel him. As Professor Kahn-Freund has said: 'Freedom of organization needs to be protected against high-handed action by employers. It also needs to be protected against high-handed action by trade unions.'[1] Underlying these legal questions is also a social question as to the functions that trade unions perform, or are perceived as performing, in modern industrial society. In particular, are trade unions perceived as essentially voluntary organizations, like social clubs, in respect of which only exiguous legal controls would seem appropriate, or are they seen as compulsory bodies, not in the sense that the law has ever required membership of a trade union, but in the sense that membership is necessary if a person is to have effective control over his working life? The trade union is most obviously a compulsory association where it is a party to a closed-shop arrangement, i.e. where membership of the union is a condition for obtaining or retaining a particular job. Here the analogy with discriminatory acts by the employer is at its strongest. However, even where there is no closed shop the union may participate through collective bargaining in regulating conditions of employment and the employee can most effectively have his say in that process of regulation through membership of the union. To quote Professor Kahn-Freund again: 'His membership is the only way open to a worker in our kind of society of being an active participant in the shaping of his own occupational existence. It may – in a closed shop – also be his only access to the labour market.'[2]

The arguments for seeing trade unions as compulsory associations because of their participation in collective bargaining is, of course, of much more general application than the argument based on the closed shop. It suggests it would be appropriate generally to protect individual rights of admission to and retention of membership of trade unions. In the period after the Second World War the courts, with Lord Denning in the van, began to develop such protections at common law. Although the principles that were developed apply to all exclusions or expulsions, it seems clear that the motive power behind the case-law developments was the perception of trade unions as controlling the individual's access to a livelihood – his 'right to work', as Lord Denning was wont to call it.[3] Indeed, initially at least, the developments in the case-law did not concentrate exclusively upon trade unions but looked generally at associations controlling access to trade – the Jockey Club, the British Boxing Board of Control, the Pharmaceutical Society, the Showmen's Guild, this last being in effect an association of small businessmen. As time went on, trade unions began to figure more prominently in the cases and a considerable body of law developed.

Nevertheless, the conceptual basis of these developments remained rather confused. They depended upon an unstable mixture of private law ideas –

---

[1] O. Kahn-Freund, *Labour and the Law* (2nd edn, 1977), p. 180.   [2] Ibid., p. 181.

[3] For an analysis of this development, see Davies and Freedland, 'Labour Law' in Jowell and McAuslan (eds.) *Lord Denning, the Judge and the Law* (forthcoming).

based upon treating the union's rule-book as a contract between union and member – and notions derived from public law: subjecting domestic tribunals, in this case the union's disciplinary committee, to judicial review and even reviewing the union's rules themselves by seeing them as analogous to bye-laws. As we shall see below (p. 595), not all the suggested developments seem to have embedded themselves in the law, notably in relation to the courts' powers to strike out union rules. Moreover, the common law proved much more adept at controlling expulsions than exclusions, where the absence of a contractual relationship with the applicant proved a stumbling block to the establishment of a coherent basis for review. Perhaps because of doubts about the scope of the common-law controls, the government in both the IRA 1971 and the EA 1980 moved to supplement the common law with statutory provisions on admission and expulsion. Unlike the IRA 1971, ss.4 and 5 of EA 1980 apply only where there is a closed shop in operation. Where this is not the case, the claimant can rely only on his common-law remedies. Indeed, as we shall see, they may even be more attractive to him than the statutory remedies where there is a closed shop in operation. The aim of the Labour government in power between 1974 and 1979 was to exclude statutory controls over admission and expulsion, and it ultimately succeeded in doing so. Thus, one can see that the conflict between the policies of collective *laissez-faire* and restriction reveals itself in the area of trade-union law as well.

Sections 4 and 5 of EA 1980, and the common-law provisions mentioned above, deal only with the position of the 'willing unionist', i.e. the person who wishes to join or remain a member of a trade union, but whom the union will not accept. Much more controversy has revolved around the position of the person who does not wish to be, or does not any longer wish to be, a member of a trade union. This is the third area of law we shall consider. Since the law does not require people to participate in industrial government through member-ship of a trade union, that aspect of the compulsory nature of trade unions causes no problem in this regard. What does cause a problem is the closed shop: can the non-joiner (or lapsed member) insist that his employment position be not jeopardized by his non-membership of the union? This raises the question of whether the law should protect the right to dissociate as well as the right to associate, two rights which, as we have seen (above, p. 127), the Donovan Commission did not regard as equivalent because the effect of the latter was to promote collective bargaining whilst the effect of the former was to hinder it and because public policy should favour the extension of collective bargaining. Nevertheless, the thrust of both the IRA 1971 and of the EA 1980–2 has been towards the equal treatment of these two rights. In the case of the latter statutes this reflected a much reduced commitment to the promotion of collective bargaining in any event, so that the counterpoise to considerations of protecting individual freedom was seen by the legislators of EA 1980 and 1982 as carrying much less weight. In recent years the debate has occurred, not only in relation to domestic law, but also in relation to the European

Convention on Human Rights, to which the UK is a party.

We have noted that the right to associate may need to be exercisable against employer as well as trade union (and also against the state, though this is now of less importance). The same is true of the right to dissociate: it has dimensions that relate to employers as well as to trade unions. Indeed, it can be said that both rights need primarily to be exercisable against employers. Whether a person is a unionist or a non-unionist, his main concern is that his employer should not dismiss or otherwise penalize him on account of that fact. Consequently, our discussion of the non-joiner will take us beyond the bounds of trade-union law proper to embrace in addition a discussion of some aspects of the law of unfair dismissal. Indeed, so thorough has the legal regulation of the closed shop now become that we shall also have to look at the regulation of certain commercial contracting practices and at the law of industrial action. Again, we can note that the law as it stands after EA 1980 and 1982 is in sharp contrast to the law in operation before 1971 or between 1974, and more especially between 1976, and 1980. Not surprisingly, policies of collective *laissez-faire* and of restriction lead to very different views as to the desirability of giving legal protection to a right to dissociate.

The fourth area that we shall examine is that of democracy within trade unions. The 'industrial government' argument for viewing trade unions as compulsory associations (above, p. 589) tends to suggest that the law should protect the interests of individuals in access to trade unions. It might also be thought to suggest that the law should go further and ensure the democratic functioning of trade unions, in order that the individual member is in fact able to make his voice heard in the internal affairs of the trade union. In fact, the law has never gone to the lengths of imposing upon trade unions a model to which they must adapt their internal relations. It is not surprising that the common law should have eschewed this burden, but the remark applies also to the legislative provisions on trade unions. Unlike companies, which are creatures of statute and in respect of which the Companies Acts contain, explicitly or implicitly, a model of the appropriate relations between shareholders, board of directors and management (even if in practice that model is stood on its head), trade unions are the creations of their members and a wide variety of patterns of internal structure can be found among British trade unions. On the other hand, the law, whilst accepting the value of trade-union autonomy and variety in the matter of internal structure, might nevertheless seek to lay down certain basic criteria to which the internal functioning of trade unions must conform. Except in relation to the political fund, even this more limited objective, however, was thought to be incompatible with the policy of collective *laissez-faire* and it was not until the IRA 1971 that such a policy came to be enshrined in legislation. TULRA 1974 returned to the traditional stance of the law and the EA 1980–2 did not grasp this particular nettle, except to the extent of encouraging, but not requiring, secret ballots on certain issues. The Green Paper, *Democracy in Trade Unions*

(Cmnd. 8778, 1983) makes more radical proposals, but proposals which are still narrowly focused upon the matter of secret ballots, which it is now proposed to make compulsory in certain circumstances.

Finally, there is the matter of the political activities of trade unions. In part this is a genuine issue of trade-union law. Should a person be put in a position where he must choose between relinquishing membership of a trade union and contributing to political objectives he disagrees with? This was the problem the Trade Union Act 1913 sought to solve, by requiring unions which wished to support political objectives (as defined) to establish a separate political fund, to which the individual members of the union could contribute or not as they pleased. In part this is a problem of party politics. Trade unions expend money overwhelmingly in support of the Labour Party. Conservative government proposals in the Green Paper for requiring employees to contract in, if they wish to pay the political levy, rather than to contract out (the present system), if they do not, are put forward in the name of individual liberty, but they raise more general questions about the financing of political parties by interest groups (e.g. corporate donations to the Conservative Party) and about the possible role of public money in supporting political parties. These more general questions lie outside the scope of this book.

Of these five areas we can briefly dispose of the first at this stage. After the Combination Laws Repeal Act 1824, mere association in a trade union ceased to be a statutory conspiracy, although various other statutory prohibitions might be relevant, as the case of the Tolpuddle martyrs shows, but it was not until the 1870s that trade unions came to achieve at least limited acceptance within the broader society and trade unions were given protection against the common-law doctrine of restraint of trade.

For more than a century thereafter trade-union law was preoccupied above all with the linked questions of the illegality of trade unions as organizations and their capacity to sue and be sued. The Trade Union Act 1871 conferred legality upon trade unions but refrained from endowing them with corporate capacity and placed certain limits upon their capacity to sue and be sued. The conferment of legality upon trade unions involved the provision of an immunity from the effects of the restraint of trade doctrine which threatened trade unions with liability in criminal conspiracy and with a virtual incapacity to make contracts or to create trusts and hence to hold property. That immunity has remained necessary and is afforded today by section 2(5) of TULRA 1974.

The conferment upon trade unions of immunity from the restraint of trade doctrine did not however resolve the underlying question of whether to grant them the status of legal persons, corporate or not. The legislators of 1871 deliberately refrained from so doing, activated perhaps by a desire not to identify trade unions as institutions of the state further than was necessary. The legislation remained in that form, with case-law establishing an effective though theoretically contentious capacity of trade unions to sue and be sued in their own name (see below, pp. 763–5) until the IRA 1971 conferred corporate status upon registered trade unions. This conferment of corporate status had the taint, in the eyes of the trade unions, of the Act's general intention of bringing the constitutions of trade unions under state control. Accordingly, when the IRA 1971 was repealed, these provisions were replaced by provisions making it clear that trade unions do not have corporate status nor are they to be treated as if they did: TULRA 1974, s.2(1). But the same provision explicitly confers upon a trade union the power to make contracts, hold property through trustees, to sue and be sued in its own name, to be prosecuted and to have judgments enforced against its property.

It was part of the policy underlying the 1871 Act not only to deny corporate status to trade unions but also to subject them to certain specific incapacities to sue and to be sued. This emerged from an alliance of opposites between those who were reluctant to place trade unions in a position to sue their members, for example for refusing to obey instructions to go on strike, and the trade unions themselves which were anxious not to be exposed to litigation from individual members. Section 4 of the Act provided that certain contracts between members of trade unions should not be directly enforceable, including contracts for the payment of subscriptions or to provide benefits for members, and also any agreement between one trade union and another.

In the event the courts proved adept at establishing a basis for individual members to sue trade unions. The main effect of s.4 was to place an unintended restriction upon the enforcement of certain collective agreements as contracts because the definition of 'trade union' was broad enough to embrace employers' associations. That restriction was finally removed in 1971, and s.4 is now wholly a thing of the past (although of course s.18 of TULRA regulates the enforcement of collective agreements as contracts by reference to the parties' intentions; see below, p. 777).

2 Exclusion and expulsion from trade unions

(a) Common-law controls over expulsion

The controls developed by the common law over expulsions from trade unions have roots in notions of both private law and public law. As far as private law is concerned, the main source of regulation is the idea of the rule-book as a contract between union and member (or between the members *inter se*). Any expulsion from the union will be unlawful if it is not carried out in accordance with the provisions (procedural and substantive) of the union's rules. As much can be said about dismissal by an employer: it will be wrongful unless carried out in accordance with the terms of the contract of employment. However, compliance with the contract has a very different impact in relation to the contract of membership as compared with the contract of employment. With regard to the contract of employment, the common law implied a term (in the absence of express provision) that the contract could be terminated at any time and for any reason upon the giving of reasonable notice. It needed the introduction of a law of unfair dismissal to enable the employee in the ordinary case to challenge the employer's reasons for and methods of dismissal. In relation to the contract of membership, no such term was implied. On the contrary, the courts insisted that the grounds for any termination of membership by the union must be found in the rule-book itself. This gave the courts, as we shall see (below, p. 606), by virtue of their power to construe the contract, the possibility of reviewing at least to some degree the adequacy of the union's reasons for terminating the individual's membership. The courts have generally been astute to preserve the vigour of the rule. See, for example, the reluctance of Plowman J. in *Radford* v. *NATSOPA* (below, p. 599) to accept an argument that the member was in breach of an implied term in his contract of membership. The now extensive jurisprudence on implied terms in the contract of employment, imposing obligations upon employee and, more latterly, employer, has no counterpart in relation to the contract of membership.

Thus, at the level of the substantive law the common law proved able to develop more extensive, contractually based, controls over the union's decision to expel than over the employer's decision to dismiss. The same contrast appears at the level of remedies. We have seen that the common law set its face against specific performance of the contract of employment as being a contract for personal service, and the consequent disfavouring of reinstatement as the normal remedy for wrongful dismissal has even carried over into the law of unfair dismissal (above, p. 493). The contract of membership, not being viewed as a contract of personal service, did not encounter this obstacle to specific performance. An injunction restraining the union from acting upon the member's unlawful expulsion is the standard common-law remedy in such cases. Indeed, until first the House of Lords in *Bonsor* v. *Musicians' Union* [1956] AC 104 and then statute (now TULRA 1974, s.2(1)(c)) cleared up the matter, it was thought to be easier to obtain an injunction against a union than damages, because in the case of the latter remedy the unincorporated nature of the union gave rise to the possibility of arguing that the expelled member had authorized his own expulsion (or, rather, had authorized it as much as any other member of the union).

However, control by the common law is not confined to requiring compliance with the rule-book. The union is also required to comply with the essentially public-law rules of natural justice. This additional set of restrictions upon expulsion was developed initially, it seems, on the grounds that expulsion interfered with the member's proprietary rights (in the funds of the association), but that argument is less often heard today. In so far as any justification is thought today to be required – and the need to meet the rules of natural justice has become so deeply embedded in this area of the law that justification is not usually thought to be necessary, although no such equivalent development took place with regard to the contract of employment

– it is usually sought in the likely adverse impact upon the member's ability to earn his living that expulsion may have. The procedural requirements of natural justice, now usually regarded as imposed by the law *ab extra* rather than as implied terms in the contract of membership, complement whatever procedural provisions the rule-book itself may contain. Again in comparison with the contract of employment before the introduction of unfair dismissal legislation, the procedural provisions of union rule-books tend to be relatively well developed (if not always very clearly expressed).

These two common-law controls, compliance with the rule-book and the tenets of natural justice, are by now well established. In theory, at least, the degree of supervision that they allow the courts to exercise is not unlimited. The rules of natural justice are procedural controls. The provisions of the rule-book are under the control of the union itself. If the rule-book contains an unreasonable rule but it is applied after following due procedure, can the courts nevertheless hold the expulsion to be unlawful? Fear that they might not be able to do so led some judges to suggest ways in which the courts would be empowered to strike out rules regarded as unreasonable. Doctrines of restraint of trade, *ultra vires* and the control of arbitrary action have all been pressed into service to this end, especially in *Edwards* v. *SOGAT* (see below, p. 600). Three comments suggest themselves. First, the doctrinal basis of the common law's power to supervise the content of unions' rule-books has not yet been satisfactorily articulated. Second, the courts have proved remarkably adept at using the well-established controls of compliance with the contract and with natural justice to limit what they regard as unreasonable behaviour on the part of trade unions, without having to resort to the power to strike out rules. Third, now that s.4 of EA 1980 has given the courts an explicit power to control expulsions on grounds of reasonableness (at least where there is a closed shop), some of the pressure for further development at common law may have been released.

The law concerning trade-union discipline and expulsions is an apt topic for contrasting the legal approach with the industrial relations approach because the two approaches are particularly remote from each other in this area. In what sense are there two approaches? The legal approach, as we have seen, views expulsion from a trade union as a potential encroachment upon the contractual and proprietary rights of the individual who is expelled. The sole question asked by the courts is whether those rights have been strictly respected. As the disciplinary process is invariably carried out by laymen, as distinct from lawyers, it is normally fairly easy for lawyers to point to defects in the process. It is like asking a panel of doctors to evaluate a process of first aid carried out by a team of boy scouts. It may be necessary to do that if medical, and by analogy legal, standards are to be maintained in even a rudimentary sense. There is, however, likely to be a community of aims between the doctors and the first aid team. Can the same be said of the courts and the trade unions? It would seem on the whole that the same cannot be said of the relationship between the courts and the trade unions over expulsions. The trade unions are not merely or even primarily amateur courts when they consider expulsion questions, although the courts themselves often seem to view them solely in that light. The difference is, of course, that the union is pursuing collective aims and policies to which individual issues will frequently be subordinated.

There is an extensive literature which documents the legal approach and which shows how it deploys the notions of

(1) strict adherence to the rules and constitution of the union viewed as a contract;
(2) the obligation of a domestic tribunal to obey the rules of natural justice;
(3) the obligation of a body whose actions impinge upon people's livelihoods to refrain from arbitrary behaviour affecting those interests;
(4) the obligations of the union as a quasi-corporation to remain within its powers as defined by its express and implied constitution;
(5) the proprietary interest of the member in remaining part of the association (more influential in the late nineteenth century than today).

The significant feature of the legal approach is not simply that it draws variously upon all these different grounds for invalidating union disciplinary decisions, but that the courts are very willing to use these ideas cumulatively in conjunction with each other. For example, we often see contract and natural justice linked together (though the present trend is to insist on the independence of natural justice from contract in order to ensure the applicability of natural justice in non-contractual situations, e.g. as between the union and the applicant for admission). In the following case the decision of the union branch is comprehensively upset, but does the reasoning of Plowman J. pay any regard to the industrial relations merits of the dispute or to the lay composition of the decision-making body?

Radford v. *National Society of Operative Printers, Graphical and Media Personnel* [1972] ICR 484 (Ch. D)

The defendant union (NATSOPA) negotiated an agreement with the applicant's employers (IPL) whereby, upon the closure of the printing works where the applicant was employed, all employees were to have the choice of leaving the printing industry entirely, but with redundancy payments higher than those provided for in RPA 1965, or of accepting alternative employment with an associated employer without any redundancy payment but with continuity of employment. The applicant wished to have both a redundancy payment and an alternative job in the industry and put his case before the relevant branch of the union, which operated a labour supply shop in this area of the industry. The branch refused the request because there were more employees wanting jobs within the jurisdiction of the branch than there were jobs available, and ordered the applicant to accept the alternative employment.

The applicant, however, consulted solicitors, who claimed from I PL a redundancy payment on the applicant's behalf. Upon hearing this the branch secretary instructed the applicant to appear before the branch committee on 2 May 'for refusing to carry out a decision of the committee'. At the meeting of the branch committee the applicant appeared but the charge was not proceeded with. Instead the committee decided to hold an investigation into the applicant's conduct in seeking legal advice and to require him to produce the correspondence with his solicitors. He was subsequently written to in these terms. On 23 May the applicant appeared before a branch committee chaired by a Mr O'Brien and refused to discuss or disclose the correspondence with the solicitors. The committee then decided that the applicant had 'voided' his membership under rule 20(13) of the rules, which provides: 'An action taken against the [union] by individual members . . . except where redress under rule has been sought, as provided in these rules, shall be declared a wilful breach of rules, and shall void the membership of the member or members so acting.' The applicant's card was withdrawn and he was unable to obtain work in the printing industry. He claimed that his expulsion from the union was unlawful and void.

PLOWMAN J.: . . . I turn now to the legal position. The first question which arises is the construction of rule 20(13) which appears at first sight to result in the automatic voidance of membership in the events specified in the clause. Unlike rule 20(9) there is no express reference to the opinion of the branch committee, or to any other subjective test. If, indeed, the clause were one for automatic forfeiture of membership without the necessity for any charge or hearing by the union, it would, in my judgment, be ultra vires and void. As Lord Denning M.R. said in *Edwards* v. *Society of Graphical and Allied Trades* [1971] Ch. 354, 377: 'No union can stipulate for automatic exclusion of a man without giving him the opportunity of being heard.'

It is no answer to that objection to say that in the present case the applicant was given an opportunity of being heard because the question is not how the rule was operated but what, on its true construction, it requires. But it is, I think, possible to construe the clause in such a way as to uphold its validity. It provides that certain conduct 'shall be declared', not 'is hereby declared', 'a wilful breach of the rules'. And the words 'shall be declared' in my opinion point to a declaration by the appropriate organ of the union, which I take to be the branch committee. If that is so, there would be read into the clause the requirement that the member whose conduct was being called into question should be given notice to appear before the branch committee, informed in advance of the charge against him and given an opportunity of stating his case. This requirement would result either from applying clause 10 [which provided for disciplinary hearings by branch committees] to the case by analogy or from applying the rules of natural justice. In the present case the applicant was held to have voided his membership without having been given any advance notice that his membership was at stake. What he was told was that the committee proposed to investigate his action of seeking legal advice. He was never charged with anything at all. That, in my judgment, is sufficient to render the branch committee's determination void.

In *Abbott* v. *Sullivan* [1952] 1 K B 189, the Court of Appeal said that a letter which was merely an invitation to a meeting to discuss a particular incident was not a charge or notice of a charge, and whatever the plaintiff may have thought or guessed it was essential that he should have been given reasonable warning that he was to be charged: *per* Denning L.J.., at p. 199, and Morris L.J., at p. 211.

Those considerations are, in my judgment, applicable to the letter of 11 May 1967, which I have read. But there is another fatal objection to the branch committee's decision; namely, that, in my judgment, there was no evidence on which they could properly reach it. The legal principle involved is stated as follows by Denning L.J. in *Lee* v. *Showmen's Guild of Great Britain* [1952] 2 QB 329, 345:

> In most of the cases which come before such a domestic tribunal the task of the committee can be divided into two parts: firstly, they must construe the rules; secondly, they must apply the rules to the facts. The first is a question of law which they must answer correctly if they are to keep within their jurisdiction; the second is a question of fact which is essentially a matter for them. The whole point of giving jurisdiction to a committee is so that they can determine the facts and decide what is to be done about them. The two parts of the task are, however, often inextricably mixed together. The construction of the rules is so bound up with the application of the rules to the facts that no one can tell one from the other. When that happens, the question whether the committee has acted within its jurisdiction depends, in my opinion, on whether the facts adduced before them were reasonably capable of being held to be a breach of the rules. If they were, then the proper inference is that the committee correctly construed the rules and have acted within their jurisdiction. If, however, the facts were not reasonably capable of being held to be a breach, and yet the committee held them to be a breach, then the only inference is that the committee have misconstrued the rules and exceeded their jurisdiction. The proposition is sometimes stated in the form that the court can interfere if there was no evidence to support the finding of the committee; but that only means that the facts were not reasonably capable of supporting the finding.

I return, therefore, to rule 20(13) and will first consider what the branch committee has to find before it can decide that a member has voided his membership. Let me read part of the rule again:

> Any action against the [union] by individual members, or members acting collectively, except where redress under rule has been sought, as provided in these rules.

The words 'except where redress under rule has been sought, as provided in these rules' refer, I think, to rule 20(11). That says: 'Any member having a complaint against the [union] or another member shall bring the matter before the branch committee.' It follows, therefore, that the relevant questions were, first, whether the applicant had a complaint against the union and, secondly, whether, not having brought it before the branch committee, he had taken any action against the union.

The committee did not regard the mere fact that the plaintiff had approached a solicitor to seek legal advice as falling within clause 13, but their view was it would do so if his action in going to a solicitor was directed, however obliquely, against the union and not just IPL, and the object of their investigation was to find out whether it was so directed. It may well be that the matter about which the applicant went to see his solicitor was not a complaint against the union or action against the union at all, and was therefore incapable of falling within clause 13, but leaving that aside, it is clear on the evidence of Mr O'Brien that the branch committee's view was that the applicant's refusal to discuss the matter meant that he had something to hide, or else he would have given the information they were seeking. And it is equally clear, both from Mr O'Brien's evidence and the letter of 26 May 1967, that it was that which led them to their decision.

The question then arises whether that was an inference which they could properly draw. In my judgment, it was not. If there is evidence against a man, the fact that he refuses to answer questions may be a reason for accepting that evidence, however slight, but where there is no evidence at all his silence is no substitute for evidence. In the present case, in my judgment, there was no evidence, on which the branch committee could conclude that the applicant's conduct fell within clause 13, even assuming that the committee's own view of its meaning was right.

It remains for me to consider certain additional arguments submitted by Mr Hawser, for the union, as to why the applicant's claim should fail. Mr Hawser submitted that the rules of the union provided for an appeal from the decisions of the branch committee to the executive council and ultimately to the general council of the union, and that the applicant ought to have exhausted the appeal procedure before coming to this court. Mr Turner-Samuels, for the applicant, submitted that on a true construction of the relevant rules no right of appeal existed in the present case. Let me assume, however, that Mr Turner-Samuels is wrong about this. Even so the rules are not in what I may call a *Scott* v. *Avery* [(1856) 5 H L Cas. 811] form, that is to say that they do not require recourse to the domestic tribunal to be exhausted before recourse is taken to the courts; and, accordingly, there can be no doubt that I have jurisdiction to deal with the matter, subject to a discretion to withhold it until the domestic remedies have been exhausted: see *Lawlor* v. *Union of Post Office Workers* [1965] Ch. 712; *Leigh* v. *National Union of Railwaymen* [1970] Ch. 326. In the present case the dispute is, in my opinion, one which is peculiarly appropriate for the court, depending as it does partly on construction and partly on the question of the sufficiency of evidence. I, therefore, reject Mr Hawser's submission on this point.

Mr Hawser then submitted a proposition of an entirely novel character in this field; namely that the applicant was in breach of an implied term of his contract with the union, that this breach amounted to a repudiation of that contract and that on 23 May 1967, the union through the branch committee elected to accept the applicant's repudiation, thus putting an end to the contract with the consequence that he ceased to be a member. . . . It is not altogether clear what is the conduct of the applicant which is said to amount to a breach. In so far as it is conduct before 23 May it was in my opinion too late on 23 May to accept it as a repudiation because by treating the applicant as a member up to 23 May the branch committee must be taken to have already elected not to treat it as such. In so far as it is the applicant's conduct on 23 May, in the first place that conduct is not, in my judgment, a breach of the alleged implied term. Secondly, it was not treated by the branch committee as a breach of any term of the contract except rule 20(13); and, thirdly, the branch committee was treating the contract as still alive for the purposes of applying clause 13. All this of course assumes that the contract contained an implied term such as is pleaded. In my judgment, however, no such term can be implied. In view of the very specific enumeration in rule 20 of the circumstances in which a member can be deprived of his membership by the union there is no scope or necessity for the implication of any additional obligation, for breach of which the applicant was liable to lose his membership.

Mr Hawser then submitted that the applicant was not entitled to an injunction or damages for the reason that the union had grounds on which they could have expelled the applicant if they had gone about it properly and would inevitably have done so; a mere irregularity in procedure should not, it was suggested, be allowed to make any difference to the result. This too is a novel submission and I reject it. I am certainly not prepared to assume that the applicant would have been found guilty before he had been properly tried, and there is no knowing what might have happened at his trial. Moreover, if there was any substance in the submission the courts would have been wasting their time in those expulsion cases in which the whole question has turned on the observance of the proper formalities.

The above case illustrates the ground rules of this area of the law, now so well established as to be unremarkable. In recent years the question has been whether the courts will develop the principles noted above so as to acquire control over the substantive content of the rule-book. The boldest attempt so far is that of the Court of Appeal in *Edwards* v. *SOGAT*, where the notions of non-arbitrariness, the right to work and natural justice are all deployed in harness with each other.

Edwards v. *Society of Graphical and Allied Trades*
[1971] Ch. 354 (CA)

The plaintiff was employed in a closed shop where the employer operated a 'check-off' i.e. deduction, of union dues from the employees' wages.[1] Because of an oversight by a union official, the plaintiff's dues were not deducted over a period of time, but the plaintiff was not aware of this until a local union official told him he had ceased to be a member under a rule providing for automatic termination of membership (see below, p. 617) of temporary members who were six weeks in arrears. Two applications for readmission were rejected by the branch committee and under threat of a strike the employers dismissed the plaintiff. Because the branch operated a labour supply shop he could not obtain other work in the industry in the district. The plaintiff was eventually readmitted and the union conceded that the plaintiff had been expelled in breach of the rules. The only question at issue was damages. On the question of the assessment of damages the union argued that the damages should be nominal because under Rule 18(4) of the rule-book a temporary member such as the plaintiff had to relinquish his card 'immediately upon application by the Branch Committee' and was granted no right of appeal to the executive council.

SACHS L.J.: ... The courts have always protected a man against any unreasonable restraint on his right to work even if he has bargained that right away: and it matters not whether the bargain is with an employer or with a society (see *Dickson* v. *Pharmaceutical Society of Great Britain* [1970] AC 403, and the cases there cited). A rule that in these days of closed shops entitles a trade union to withdraw the card of a capable craftsman of good character who for years has been a member, even if styled 'temporary' member, for any capricious reason such as (to mix conventional and practical examples) having incurred the personal enmity, for non-union reasons, of a

[1] See *Hewlett* v. *Allen* [1894] AC 383 and *Williams* v. *Butlers Ltd* [1975] ICR 208.

single fellow member, the colour of his hair, the colour of his skin, the accent of his speech, or the holding of a job desired by someone not yet a member, is plainly in restraint of trade. At common law it is equally clearly unreasonable so far as the public interest is concerned. Is it then protected by either section 3 or section 4 of the Trade Union Act 1871? It cannot be said that a rule that enabled such capricious and despotic action is proper to the 'purposes' of this or indeed of any trade union. It is thus not protected by section 3 and is moreover ultra vires. Nor can I find any protection for it in section 4. It is thus void as in restraint of trade [see now T U L R A 1974, s.2(5)].

Mr Hooson sought to controvert that conclusion by aid of certain observations in the speeches in *Faramus* v. *Film Artistes' Association* [1964] AC 925. That case, however, concerned a specific rule as to the *eligibility* of those who had suffered convictions for admission to a trade union shown by evidence to be operating in special conditions. Those observations cannot, however, have been intended to be applied generally to rules giving a right of *expulsion* (see the speech of Lord Pearce at p. 947) on completely capricious grounds.

In addition, if Mr Hooson's claim that the rule is one which permits the union to act without regard to the rules of natural justice (or 'fair play in action', as it is often styled nowadays) is correct, it is clearly void also on that ground: it would indeed be lamentable if members of 12 years' standing, albeit labelled 'temporary', could be thus expelled. With regret I am inclined to think that a rule so intended and likely to be so regarded by those most concerned must be interpreted as claimed.

If, however, adherence to rules of natural justice is to be implied in that rule, that seems to me also to destroy the 'nominal damages' submission, as similarly does the last-minute suggestion of Mr Hooson that alternatively the rule gave the union a discretion to terminate the plaintiff's membership which it must be presumed they would exercise reasonably, for there was no evidence of any material enabling such a discretion to be properly exercised. (It is thus unnecessary to comment on the alleged presumption.)

It follows that, whatever be the true construction of the rules, other than any that are void, a temporary member is given upon admission a right not to have his membership ended for completely arbitrary reasons nor in a way which does not accord with natural justice. Once admitted, he is entitled *to retain* that membership unless there exists some proper ground upon which the union can terminate it. No evidence whatsoever was before the court of the existence or likely existence of any such ground as regards the plaintiff. The submissions based on *Lavarack* v. *Woods of Colchester Ltd* [1967] 1 QB 278 are rejected.

In the light of that conclusion it is not necessary to determine whether a rule that allows completely arbitrary refusal *to admit or to readmit* to the union a duly qualified craftsman of good character and thus in effect permits the union to preclude him from full opportunity to exercise his skills is valid, or whether it is something that, in these days when so many big firms operate on a 100 per cent union basis, is so destructive of the 'right to work', in the sense of 'right of equal opportunity to obtain work', that it is invalid as being contrary to public policy for the reasons discussed in *Nagle* v. *Feilden* [1966] 2 QB 633.

The dangers of such unappealable powers to exclude a citizen from his right to work is a matter which has been discussed in the Donovan Report and again in the more recent 1969 White Paper [*In Place of Strife*, Cmnd. 3623]. So has the arbitrary power to enforce automatic forfeiture of membership for non-payment of dues and the parallel power to refuse readmission after such forfeiture. It is thus not necessary to say anything further on the subject save to note one feature in the present case. When on 13

November 1967, the branch committee for the second time refused the plaintiff's application for readmission (the first occasion was 23 May), it has been conceded that he was not invited to attend: yet, according to paragraph 7 of the defence, the 'branch committee fairly and properly considered the plaintiff's application', and rejected it on grounds which included matters arising since 23 May, of which, it was common ground before this court, no notice had been given him. There is thus provided a striking instance of how 'completely arbitrary' power can be used. One assumes that such cases are rare in the trade union world, but the fact is that they can occur.

Before turning to the facts affecting the assessment that has to be made, it is necessary to refer to one further submission made in this court on behalf of the trade union. It was urged that they, who wrongfully put such obstacles in the way of the plaintiff regaining his position in the printing trade, were entitled in effect to demand that in mitigation of damages he should have done or should now do one of two things. Either he should, despite having spent a quarter of a century in acquiring the skills of his craft, have himself retrained in some quite different occupation and forgo those skills. Alternatively, it was suggested, he should remove himself and his family from the Manchester area and go to some quite different part of this country with a view to taking his chance as to whether some other branch of the union might be more disposed to admit him to membership and permit him the normal opportunities of exercising those skills. Coming from a defendant whose wrongful act caused the situation, who could and should have taken all possible steps to end it, and who took the opposite course, I confess this submission was viewed by me with repugnance and I reject it. It lies particularly ill in the mouth of this trade union defendant to say it can in effect dictate the whole way of life to be pursued by the plaintiff.

The legislature responded to the Court of Appeal's use of the doctrine of restraint of trade in the *Edwards* case when in TULRA 1974, s.2(5), it extended the statutory protection against this doctrine to embrace not only the union's purposes (as the Trade Union Act 1871 had provided) but also its rules, although Lord Pearce had argued in *Faramus* v. *Film Artistes' Association* [1964] AC 925 that the protection of a union's purposes must extend at least to the protection of rules designed to achieve one of the protected purposes. However, it is doubtful whether this provision by itself would be sufficient to prevent further development of the various other bases of control suggested by Sachs L.J. For example, in *Greig* v. *Insole* (see below, p. 623) Slade J. thought that the right to work was a concept distinct from that of restraint of trade.

Lack of judicial sympathy with the collective aims of the unions whose conduct they are called upon to evaluate is exemplified by the courts' approach to the issue of whether a member must first exhaust his rights of appeal within the union (his internal remedies) before having resort to the courts. A recent study[1] of trade-union rule-books showed that 75 out of 79 rule-books examined provided for a right of appeal against disciplinary action to a higher body than that which made the original decision. Sometimes there might be several stages of internal appeal. A variety of bodies in different unions constitute the final stage of appeal. Sometimes it is the executive

[1] J. Gennard, M. Gregory and S. Dunn, 'Throwing the book' (1980) 88 *Employment Gazette* 591.

council or general council, sometimes the union's annual conference, some-times a permanent appeals tribunal. The choice of final stage of appeal has some influence upon the speed of the appeal procedure: executive councils, meeting on a regular basis, usually dispose of appeals relatively quickly; annual conferences clearly often cannot act quickly.

The judicial stance seems to be that if the rules of the union expressly require the exhaustion of internal appeals before judicial remedies are pursued, that constitutes an attempt to curtail the authority of the courts by which the courts are not effectively restrained. The mere provision *per se* of internal appeals is not seen as a challenge to the authority of the courts, but constitutes no more than a discretionary check upon the power of the courts to intervene before the internal remedies have been sought. The following case indicates how the court regards itself as the natural arbiter of a wide range of disciplinary issues. Does not this view leave out of account a legitimate trade-union interest in autonomy of decision? Could the courts not devise a framework which would enable them to control abuse of power by trade unions without thus overriding or disregarding the organizational needs of the union?

Lawlor v. Union of Post Office Workers [1965] Ch. 712 (Ch. D)

The plaintiffs, who constituted a majority on the committee of a sectional council in London, sought to impose an overtime ban in response to the Post Office's decision to introduce part-time labour in accordance with an agreement negotiated with the defendant union. The general secretary of the union required the committee to withdraw their proposals but they refused. The executive council of the union then decided to expel the plaintiffs for breach of the rules, but did not give the plaintiffs notice of the charge against them or an opportunity to defend themselves. Rule 3(e) of the union's rules provided for an appeal from the executive's decision to the union's annual conference, consisting of delegates from branches from all over the country.

UNGOED-THOMAS J.: . . . Trade union rules clearly cannot oust the jurisdiction of the courts. Contracts, including a contract constituted by trade union rules, may provide that recourse to domestic tribunals shall be exhausted before there is recourse to the courts, and the courts may recognize and give effect to that contract; but that does not oust its jurisdiction. So in this case, the court has jurisdiction, and here there is no contractual provision requiring domestic remedies to be exhausted before resort to the courts. Should that jurisdiction be exercised now, or should it be withheld, in the circumstances, pending appeal to annual conference?

This case involves the construction of the rules of the trade union, and it is for the courts, and not a domestic body, to decide questions of construction, as matters of law. It involves questions of natural justice, which are matters for the courts to decide. And pending the hearing of any appeal to the annual conference, which I am told will not be held until May 1965, the appellant would be excluded from membership and office in the union as, unlike the trade union constitution in *White* v. *Kuzych* [[1951] AC 585], the constitution of the union does not, as I have said, provide for any stay at all of expulsion pending the appeal. So the domestic appeal could not, in any event, provide all the relief which the court might provide; and if the court were to refuse relief until all domestic remedy had been exhausted, the remedy might be quite inadequate and substantial injustice might be suffered. Further, it is debatable whether improper failure to observe the rules of natural justice makes a decision void or voidable (see *White* v. *Kuzych*). If it is void, it has been said to be not subject to appeal at all. But only the courts can decide whether it is void or voidable and whether, in this case, the executive council decision is a complete nullity and, therefore, not subject to appeal at all to the annual conference.

So, in my judgment, this is not a case in which the court's jurisdiction is ousted or in which the court should decline to intervene on the ground that an appeal should first be made to and be heard by the annual conference of the union.

Then it is said that even though the rules of natural justice be applicable here and have been disregarded, and even though it is a case in which the court should not decline to intervene unless an appeal to the union annual conference has been heard, yet no sufficient case has been made for the interlocutory relief now claimed.

It is rightly pointed out that loss of membership of the union does not mean loss of job, so that the disadvantage to the plaintiffs is not of a financial character. But the disadvantage is more than merely social. The expulsion does affect the expelled member in his work. It affects his standing with and relation to other members. The trade union is concerned with members in their capacity as workers in their jobs, and expulsion excludes from the advantages which such membership confers. Trade unions, to their honour, also develop strong ties of loyalty amongst their members, and loss of membership, particularly amongst members of standing like some of the plaintiffs, strikes deep, and not the less so because it may not strike at the pocket. Failes, who is not himself a plaintiff, expresses that attachment when he says in his affidavit: 'My union card was my most treasured possession.' The plaintiffs have been elected to office by an electorate of 28,000 members to represent their interests, and such a position not only carries status and honour, but also responsibility to the members who have elected them. Although so elected, and although an appeal to annual conference were successful, they would not, without the court's intervention, be able to stand for election next time, as I am told that that election occurs before the appeal to annual conference could be heard. And of course, if they were not to stand next time their position in the union might be prejudiced, perhaps permanently. These considerations favour the granting of interlocutory relief.

But the general secretary has gone so far as to express the view that, if the relief now sought is granted, and I quote his words, 'it will be quite impossible to conduct reasonable meaningful negotiations' (that is, with the postal authorities) 'and there will be a very real risk of postal chaos and hardship to the general public'. I fully appreciate the difficulty of his responsible task, and the importance of the postal services. But for the plaintiffs it was submitted that failure to grant relief would exacerbate the dispute within the union to the public detriment. And I have the evidence of members of the executive council itself that a less drastic course than expulsion was sought; and that there was at any rate substantial support for a less drastic course had that not been ruled out of order as impossible under the rules. There have been put in evidence letters from the London District Postmaster to some of the plaintiffs, speaking well of their reasonable and helpful attitude in negotiation. To one of them he wrote: 'You are well known to us as an awkward talkative old "so and so", but in the last analysis you were always genuine, reasonable and helpful. We will miss you very much.' I am in no position to decide on these differences of view, and it is most undesirable that I should attempt to do so. My duty here is to the best of my ability to administer justice according to law. I am not concerned with the political or economic consequences of doing so. To do that would be to dabble in politics, and that is not my function here. I am only concerned with matters of public policy so far as they are expressed in legal principles of general application; and there is no legal principle that relief against ignoring natural justice must be denied if it is feared that it might prejudice industrial negotiations. Such fears are for others to deal with; and it may well be that there would be no great difficulty in dealing with them in this case. Nor am I trying the plaintiffs for being, in the parliamentary language of a civil servant, 'awkward so and sos'. I have merely to decide whether, prima facie, natural justice has wrongly been denied to the plaintiffs, and if so whether, within the well-established principles of the law, relief should be granted.

In my judgment, for the reasons which I have given, the plaintiffs should have the relief claimed.

There are two particular situations where the case-law on expulsions from trade unions demonstrates a clear conflict between the self-interest of individual members and the collective goals of the majority of the union's membership. These situations are expulsion for refusing to take part in industrial action called by the union, and expulsion in order that the union can comply with the Bridlington Principles governing the relations between T U C unions or, more particularly, with an award of the Disputes Committee of the T U C applying the Bridlington Principles (see below, pp. 611ff). The Bridlington Principles, drawn up and implemented wholly by the T U C, have traditionally been treated with suspicion by the courts, because they have appeared as a process of resolving institutional conflicts of interest between trade unions in which individual members can appear as mere ciphers, to be allocated to one union or another as the institutional interests dictate. On the other hand, no one can gainsay the proposition that the principles operate to resolve inter-union conflicts, to which the British trade-union movement is particularly prone, given the historical evolution of various different bases of trade-union organization and recruitment (see above, pp. 116 ff.). It is perhaps in recognition of this that, after three forensic defeats for the Principles (see *Spring* v. *NASD* [1956] 1 WLR 585; *Walsh* v. *AUEW*, *The Times*, 15 July 1977; and *Rothwell* v. *APEX* [1976] ICR 211), in the latest detailed consideration by the courts of the Principles the expulsion was upheld (see *Cheall* v. *APEX* [1983] ICR 398), though admittedly at a time when Parliament had provided some basis for an alternative challenge under s.4 of EA 1980.

We turn first, however, to a discussion of the cases of disciplinary expulsion for refusal to participate in industrial action, a matter which has been the centre of some political controversy in recent years and upon which, as we shall see below (p. 627), the Code of Practice on Closed Shop Agreements and Arrangements makes some observations. The study of trade-union rule-books noted above found that 63 out of 79 rule-books studied contained a general clause giving the union broad powers to expel, e.g. for 'action contrary or detrimental to the aims and interests of the trade union or its members'. Such clauses are often invoked in cases of refusal to participate in industrial action. In addition, many rule-books contain specific disciplinary rules covering breaking the rules of the union, disobeying the instructions of an authorized official or committee of the union or working during disputes. As far as the courts are concerned, they have tended to see the individual as particularly at risk where he falls to be considered by a committee of people who in all likelihood took part in the industrial action and suffered the consequences of so doing, indeed who probably took a leading part in organizing it, especially if the action was not wholly successful and the acts of those who refused to join in seem likely to have contributed to the lack of success. Formally, of course, at common law the courts have no power to assess the reasonableness of the disciplinary committee's views on the merits of the case, but the court can insist upon the observance of natural justice and can, which has proved more important in practice in these cases, assert its ultimate power of interpretation of the rule-book. The courts have adopted a strict contractual construction of the rule-book, even in cases of blanket clauses and even where the blanket clause has contained some such phrase as conduct which is detrimental 'in the opinion of the branch or the executive committee'. In other words, the courts have refused to accept that the broad clauses seek to express the collective aspirations of the union as a body and to enable the various organs of the union to work out these objectives according to their own discretion. On the other hand, the process of strict construction as applied to such deliberately broad clauses is often a rather artificial one.

The process of construction has tended to fasten upon the union's rules governing the calling of industrial action. If a member has refused to participate in industrial action which has not been called for in accordance with the union's rule-book, then it is extremely unlikely that the court will uphold any disciplinary action taken against him, even under the broadest of blanket rules. The question then becomes one of how much deference the courts are prepared to show towards the disciplinary tribunal's interpretation of the union's rules. Whilst it is commonplace for the courts to assert that 'it is well established that this court will not interfere with the decision of a domestic tribunal which is bona fide arrived at . . .' (*Esterman* v. *NALGO*, below), the courts have in fact developed principles of intervention which are quite extensive. *Esterman* v. *NALGO* demonstrates two of these principles. First, although formally the test applied by the court was whether no reasonable tribunal could have come to the conclusion that the plaintiff was unfit to be a member of the union (which apparently gives the domestic tribunal some scope in its interpretation of the union's rules), in practice the test applied seemed to be more like whether a reasonable member might consider the call for industrial action a breach of the union's rules or even simply unwise (a very different test). Second, we have noted that the courts do not require the exhaustion of internal remedies before they intervene. In *Esterman*, however, the court intervened even in advance of the domestic tribunal's initial hearing of the case. Such intervention places no value upon the settlement of membership disputes domestically.

Esterman v. *National and Local Government Officers Association*
[1974] ICR 625 (Ch. D)

The rules of the defendant union provided for a ballot to be held before the members of the union could be instructed to strike, though the national executive could request members to strike in emergencies 'such as to preclude the taking of a ballot'. In 1974 the union was in dispute with the employers about London weighting allowances and also with the government, which would not authorize the employers under the then operative incomes policy to increase the allowance. A ballot was held by the union on the question of selective strike action and 49 per cent of those voting were in favour. The union then instructed members of certain branches, including the plaintiff's, not to volunteer to assist returning officers in the London borough elections in May 1974. The plaintiff refused to obey the instruction and duly acted. The branch secretary then wrote to the plaintiff requiring her to attend a special disciplinary meeting to be held on 20 May to consider whether her conduct merited her expulsion from the union. Rule 13 of the branch rules provided that: 'Any member who disregards any regulation of the branch or is guilty of conduct which, in the opinion of the executive committee, renders him unfit for membership, shall be liable to expulsion. . . .' The rule also provided for an appeal to the national executive council. Before the special disciplinary meeting could be held the plaintiff sought an interlocutory injunction against NALGO and representatives of the branch committee restraining them from taking disciplinary action against her for assisting in the borough elections.

TEMPLEMAN J.: . . . On this application, I have listened to very long and very learned argument on the interesting question of whether, on the true construction of the rules and also on the construction of the procedure for strike action, the national executive council had power to issue the order dated 8 April 1974. It is sufficient for present purposes that not only am I in some doubt now as to the answer to that question, but also that every member of NALGO who received the order could not have been clear as to whether there was power to issue that particular order. It is not clear, for example, whether NALGO had power to take industrial action against a returning officer with whom the association had no quarrel. It is not clear whether the association had power to interfere with a right of a member to employ his spare time by assisting the returning officers in an election, the holding of which had no direct relevance to the claim for London weighting allowance. Whatever the powers of the association, it is not clear whether the national executive council had power to issue the orders which they did issue in the absence of a ballot. But even if, after great deliberation, it would appear that NALGO and the national executive council in fact had the power which they claim to exercise, the special circumstances in this case are such, in my judgment, that a member could very well come to the conclusion that this was an order to which the national executive council had no right to demand his obedience and it was an order which, as a person – a loyal member of NALGO – acting in its best interests, he felt bound to disobey.

We have this background: although there was only 49 per cent support in the only ballot for selective strike action, the national executive council had already ordered the whole of the Islington branch to strike. A member could take the view that this 49 per cent might be a sufficient number to justify the national executive council in making a recommendation for a strike; it was no warrant for an order to strike with the threat in the background of expulsion for any member who had voted against the strike and thought that a strike was not in the interests of NALGO.

A member could take the view that action against the returning officers had never been submitted to a ballot and that whether or not a ballot was strictly necessary the national executive council, following the spirit as well as the letter of the instructions with regard to strikes, ought not to order, but rather – if they wished – to recommend, action against the returning officer. A member may have thought that such an order did not reasonably command obedience and that there was a possibility that it gave the appearance of coercing those who thought that action against the returning officers was not in the best interests of NALGO. He might take the view that, in all the extraordinary background of this case, he could not conscientiously accept an order given by the national executive council without a ballot or a fresh ballot against the wishes of the Minister and the secretary of the Trades Union Congress and in the existing national conditions, particularly since 100 per cent obedience to the order of the national executive council would seem to imply that 100 per cent of the members were firmly in support of the action which was being taken. A member might take the view that the national executive council order was an abuse of their powers, because, without any mandate by way of a ballot, it had the appearance, some might think, of seeking to wreck the local elections for the purpose of bringing pressure to bear on the Minister. A member might think that if the public thought that, then the reputation of NALGO might be irreparably damaged. In brief, in my judgment, a member was entitled to take the view that this was an order which he might be under a positive duty to disobey. Of course, the suspicions or fears of a member that the national executive council had no power to issue the order aimed against the returning officers, or that the national executive council, even if they had the power, were misusing it and exercising it in a way objectionable to numbers of members and injurious to the reputation of NALGO, all those fears could be ill-founded. But, in my judgment, a member, faced with the order, was entitled to doubt. On the face of the order and the constitution and the rules and against all the background, there was a very large question mark hanging over the validity of the order and whether it was a proper order to issue even if there was power to do so.

Those doubts were due entirely to the insistence, as I have said no doubt bona fide and thought to be in the best interests of NALGO, but nevertheless the insistence, of the national executive council on taking a step which not only had never been put to a ballot but really was an extraordinary step to take, peremptorily ordering every member of NALGO to withdraw assistance from the local election, when what they were after dealt with London weighting allowance and they had no quarrel with the returning officers.

As at present advised, I emphatically reject the submission that it was the duty of every member blindly to obey the orders of the national executive council in the prevailing circumstances and that he could only disobey the order if he were prepared to take the risk of being expelled from NALGO. I also reject the submissions that a member who disobeyed the particular order given by the national executive not to assist returning officers showed prima facie that he was unfit to be a member of NALGO. An Act of Parliament carries penalties for its breach, but it is a fallacy to assume that every democratically elected body is entitled to obedience to every order on pain of being found guilty of being unfit to be a member of an association. It must depend on the order and it must depend on the circumstances and, in my judgment, if implicit obedience is to be exacted, those who issue the order must make quite sure that they have power, that no reasonable man could be in doubt they they have power and that they are making a proper exercise of the power, and that no reasonable man could conscientiously say to himself that 'this is an order which I have no duty to obey'. In the present case, it was not so clear.

I return to the plaintiff. She deposes that before receiving the instruction not to assist the returning officer she had volunteered to do so as she had for 26 years past. When she received the instruction she decided to ignore it for three reasons. First, she did not think it right or honourable to withdraw the offer of assistance she had already made. Secondly, she thought that the object of the instruction and NALGO's campaign was to compel the employers to pay or persuade the Minister to approve an allowance beyond the permitted increases under the Counter-Inflation Act 1973 and the Pay Code. Thirdly, she thought the object of the instruction was to sabotage the election and this, she thought, was insupportable and objectionable. She read, she said, the constitution and rules of NALGO and the rules of the Islington branch and could not find power for NALGO or the branch executive to issue the instruction to her not to volunteer to assist the returning officer.

The plaintiff, as the evidence now runs, therefore questioned whether the national executive council had the requisite power and, if so, whether they were abusing that power. I am not prepared to say that her fears were fanciful. Holding the views which she did, she could not be expected blindly to obey the order and her disobedience forms no ground for the allegation that her act of disobedience demonstrated her unfitness to be a member of NALGO.

In the circumstances, I conclude that no reasonable tribunal could bona fide come to the conclusion that disobedience of this order demonstrated any unfitness to be a member of NALGO and I propose to protect the plaintiff pending trial against having to appear before the executive committee.

In subsequent reported cases, notably *Porter* v. *NUJ* [1980] IRLR 404 (HL) and *Partington* v. *NALGO* [1981] IRLR 537 (Ct Sess.), the courts have tended to construe the union's power in its rules to take industrial action narrowly and in such a way as to render the subsequent disciplinary action unlawful, although the broader dicta from *Esterman*'s case, referring to the unwisdom of the industrial action as a basis for the illegality of the disciplinary measures, have not been expressly disavowed. In *Partington* the union had entered in an agreement with the employers, British Gas, which, it was agreed between the parties, had also been incorporated into the plaintiff's contract of employment, whereby, in the court's view, in the case of a strike the employer ultimately had the right to require certain employees to remain at work in the interests of safety. The plaintiff initially joined in a strike called by the union, but later returned to work when his employers invoked the safety provisions in the agreement. He was later expelled by his branch for breach of a rule which permitted expulsion for disregarding a regulation of the branch or for conduct which in the opinion of the branch committee rendered him unfit for membership. The Outer House held that on neither ground could the expulsion be upheld, because the union's powers under the rule had to be read in the light of the agreement entered into with the employers. This amounted to holding that the disciplinary action was unlawful because requiring the safety workers to remain on strike was a breach, not of the union's rules, but of an agreement existing outside the rule-book, albeit one to which both union and member were parties, in the sense that the relevant terms were contained in the separate agreements that each had entered into with the employers.

The decision in *Partington* was an unsatisfactory one because the precise basis for the holding that the disciplinary action was unlawful was not made clear and the relevance of certain statutory provisions was not discussed. For example, a possible basis for the unlawfulness of the disciplinary action was that the union's instructions caused the employee to break his contract of employment. However, the court did not consider whether the provisions of s.18(4) of TULRA 1974 (see below p. 777) stood in the way of the incorporation of the safety provisions into the contracts of employment, and in any case the Court of Appeal in *Porter* v. *NUJ* [1979] IRLR 404 had held that the union in that case did have the power to order industrial action in breach of the contracts of employment. The view of that court was that to require employees to terminate their contracts before striking would, in the light of the differing periods of notice required of different employees, be to render strike action impossible. (See further below, pp. 718–20.) On the other hand, it must be admitted that the generally restrictive tenor of the judgment in *Partington* v. *NALGO* is very much in line with recent pronouncements by other courts. Thus, an alternative basis for the decision, mentioned in some remarks of Lord Allanbridge, was that the employee's continued participation in the industrial action was in breach of the collective agreement betweeen union and employer. On this point the dicta of Lord Allanbridge chime in with similar remarks by Lord Denning in *Porter* v. *NUJ*. The acceptance of such a view would have a highly restrictive effect upon the legality of union's disciplinary action, especially if it were coupled with acceptance of a parallel suggestion, made in *Sherard* v. *AUEW* [1973] ICR 421, that the union in that case had no power to call industrial action that was not 'in contemplation or furtherance of a trade dispute' (see below, pp. 792–817). It is not clear at present whether these suggestions will be further developed nor, indeed, whether they are merely principles of construction of union rules or, rather, mandatory restrictions upon the autonomy of the rule-book. However, it is significant, as we shall see below (p. 627), that the Code of Practice on Closed Shop Agreements and Arrangements recommends that disciplinary action should not be taken by a union against a member where the latter has refused to engage in industrial action which is, *inter alia*, outside the golden formula or in breach of a procedure agreement.

It can be argued that too much weight should not be attached to the judgments in *Esterman* and *Partington* because they were decisions on inter-locutory applications and thus delivered without benefit of full argument on points of law. Although this may formally be true, as examples of practice on interlocutory applications the case may be of the greatest significance, for as the House of Lords made clear in *Porter* v. *NUJ* the interlocutory injunction will normally be readily available to the disciplined member or member threatened with discipline. As we shall see below (pp. 765–77), the granting of interlocutory injunctions in trade dispute cases has been made the subject of certain controls, because of a perception that in such cases the granting or refusal of the interlocutory injunction in fact disposes of the case, for a full trial rarely takes place. In trade-union membership cases the courts' perception of the matter is very different. In *Porter* (at p. 406), Lord Diplock said:

If the actions raised any serious question of fact or law to be tried the balance of convenience would appear clearly to lie in favour of maintaining the *status quo* until the trial. To lose their union cards upon expulsion from the NUJ could not fail to be a serious handicap to the plaintiffs. . . . On the other side of the balance there would appear to be no more than the understandable desire on the part of those members of the NUJ who suffered financial hardship by participating loyally in the strike for speedy vengeance on those who went on working and earning. But if the strike order was issued contrary to the rules, the plaintiffs were entitled to disregard it, while if at the trial it is held to have been lawful, vengeance will only have been postponed.

The ready availability of the interlocutory injunction is likely to increase the incidence of legal intervention in advance even of the domestic tribunal's initial hearing of the charge against the member.

When we turn to the Bridlington Principles – more accurately the TUC Principles Governing Relations between Unions – we find that here also the TUC and its affiliated unions have over the last three decades had an uphill struggle to preserve the efficacy of their procedures for handling inter-union disputes against legal challenges brought by individuals (sometimes acting as surrogates for institutional interests). The Bridlington Principles deal with a number of inter-union issues, but two of them are of central importance. Principles 2, 3, 4 and 6 deal with the issue of 'poaching', i.e. the circumstances in which a person who is or has been a member of an affiliated union can be accepted into membership of another affiliated union. In brief these principles provide that the membership forms of all unions should include questions about the applicant's membership of other unions; that no applicant who is or has recently been a member of another union should be accepted into membership without inquiry being made by the union of the other union; that if the other union objects, the applicant should not be accepted into membership and that if discussion between the unions cannot solve the matter, it should be referred to the TUC for adjudication. It is specifically provided that the applicant should not be accepted into membership if he is under discipline from the other union, engaged in a trade dispute or in arrears with his contributions to the other union. Principle 5 deals with the second main issue, viz. the circumstances in which a union may start organizing activities amongst a group of workers in relation to whom another union has an interest. The problem here is not necessarily poaching – the union may be attempting to recruit people who are not members of any union – but the undesirability of having more than one union representing a particular grade of workers. On the other hand, it is also undesirable to enable an ineffective union to exclude other unions from organizing activities by virtue of its having established a weak presence amongst a grade of workers. These competing considerations are reflected in the present formulation of Principle 5 and, more particularly, of the Notes to the Principle.

TUC Disputes Principles and Procedures (1979)

PRINCIPLE 5

No union shall commence organising activities at any establishment or undertaking in respect of any grade or grades of workers in which another union has the majority of workers employed and negotiates wages and conditions, unless by arrangement with that union.

Note on Principle 5

Where a union has membership but does not have a majority in respect of any grade or grades of workers and/or does not negotiate terms and conditions of employment for such grade or grades, another union wishing to organise should engage in consultation as soon as it is aware (or has drawn to its attention by the existing union) that another union has membership in the grade or grades concerned before it commences organising activities. If there is no agreement, and the matter is referred by either union to the TUC and a Disputes Committee adjudicates, the Disputes Committee will have regard to the following factors:

> (i) the efforts which the union opposing the entry of another union or unions has itself made in trying to secure or retain a majority membership, the period over which any such efforts have been made, the extent and causes of any difficulties encountered by that union, and the likely prospect of that union securing or regaining a majority membership and/or negotiating rights;
> (ii) any existing collective bargaining or other representation arrangements in the establishment, company or industry.

The Disputes Committee of the TUC, which settles matters between affiliated unions arising out of the Bridlington Principles if the unions themselves cannot settle them, is composed of senior officials of affiliated unions and is serviced by a small TUC staff.[1] Its procedure is governed by a set of Regulations. The TUC and its affiliated unions do not regard the Principles as legally binding but as constituting 'a code of conduct accepted as

---

[1] For a consideration of this area see Kalis, 'The Adjudication of Inter-union Membership Disputes' (1977) 6 *ILJ* 19, and Ball, 'The Resolution of Inter-union Conflict' (1980) 9 *ILJ* 13.

morally binding by affiliated organizations'.[1] Although the Principles are not a collective agreement within the meaning of s.30(1) of TULRA 1974 and so not subject to the presumption of no intention to create legal relations in s.18 of that Act, Stone v.c. in *Spring* v. *NASD* [1956] 1 WLR 585 thought the view that the Principles were not legally binding was 'one which . . . it would be difficult to challenge as being otherwise than an accurate definition. . . .' Legal actions by one union against another for enforcement of the principles as such have thus not arisen, but various other possibilities of legal challenge are available. It is common for the Disputes Committee to award that workers who have been accepted into membership of an affiliated union in breach of the Bridlington Principles (whether those relating to poaching or Principle 5 covering organizing activities) should be expelled from membership by that union and advised to join (or re-join) the appropriate union. A common form of legal challenge to the Principles then arises by way of a claim by the expelled member that this expulsion was unlawful. The union movement has been engaged in a long, and now at least partially successful, battle, to create for itself the power to comply with the Bridlington Principles whilst not infringing the rules of the common law governing expulsions.

In *Spring*'s case the union, which had expelled the plaintiff from membership in order to comply with an award of a Disputes Committee, fell foul of the requirement that the grounds for expulsion must be found in the rule-book. The union had no clause permitting expulsions in order to comply with an award of the Disputes Committee and the court refused to imply such a term into the rule-book. It was argued for the union that the Bridlington Principles were part of the context in which all affiliated unions operated, but that argument met the full weight of judicial reluctance to imply terms into contracts from mere context alone (though this is not a reluctance which has been displayed in relation to the contract of employment), and the individual's interests were protected by a traditional application of the 'officious by-stander' test. In response to this case and a similar holding in the previous year in *Andrews* v. *NUPE* (*The Times*, 9 July 1955), the TUC advised affiliated unions to include in their rule-books a model rule expressly permitting expulsions in order to comply with awards of the Disputes Committee. That model rule permits the executive committee of the union to give six weeks' notice to terminate a person's membership 'if necessary in order to comply with a decision of the Disputes Committee of the Trades Union Congress'.

In *Walsh* v. *AUEW* (*The Times*, 15 July 1977),[2] however, the limitations of this model rule were exposed. Here the union, having encouraged the plaintiff to join in breach of the poaching rules, subsequently changed its mind upon a complaint from the former union and expelled the plaintiff without waiting for the matter to be taken to a Disputes Committee. This belatedly meritorious conduct by the union, however, was held not to fall within the provisions of the

---

[1] *TUC Disputes Principles and Procedures* (1979), p. 7.

[2] Printed in full in the first edition of this book at p. 121.

model rule, which the union along with the overwhelming majority of affiliated unions had incorporated into its rule-book, because there had been no award by the committee. Further, the court refused to construe a general power under a different rule for the executive council 'to do such things as are in their opinion necessary and expedient for the welfare or good government of the union' so as to permit an expulsion in order to comply with the Bridlington Principles. The specific rules relating to expulsions should be seen as a comprehensive code on this matter: 'rules must not . . . be stretched to facilitate the termination of a person's membership and so throw him out of work'.

A fundamental challenge to the model rule was mounted in *Cheall* v. *APEX* [1983] ICR 398, where the union's rule-book did contain the rule and the union had expelled in accordance with an award of the Disputes Committee. The challenge was mounted on grounds of natural justice, public policy and the rule of contractual construction that a person is presumed not to be entitled to rely upon his own breach of contract as bringing the contract to an end. The House of Lords held that Cheall was not entitled to make representations to the Disputes Committee because the only parties to the dispute that was before the committee were the unions concerned, nor was he entitled to make representations to the executive committee of APEX before they expelled him because in the circumstances the only way in which the executive committee could act in the best interests of the union as a whole was by complying with the award. The alleged public policy was the right of every person to join and remain a member of the trade union of his choice, which it was sought to derive from Article 11 of the European Convention on Human Rights (see below, pp. 657ff.), but their lordships interpreted this Article as creating a freedom of association in the sense of protecting individuals from adverse consequences as a result of their associating with others in trade unions and not as creating an obligation upon the others to accept the individual into the association: 'freedom of association can only be mutual; there can be no right of an individual to associate with other individuals who are not willing to associate with him' (at p. 405). The point of construction was dealt with, perhaps a little simplistically, by holding that the wrong, which consisted of admitting Cheall to the union in breach of the Bridlington Principles, might have been a wrong *vis-à-vis* other affiliated unions, but it constituted no breach of any contract between Cheall and the union.

Although the model rule has survived its first major legal challenge, it cannot be assumed that the possibility of invalidation, especially on grounds of public policy, has been totally excluded. In *Cheall* itself Lord Diplock said that 'different considerations might apply if the effect of Cheall's expulsion from APEX were to have put his job in jeopardy, either because of the existence of a closed shop or for some other reason' (at p. 405), and it seems that the TUC has not proposed a broadening of the scope of the model rule to deal with the problem revealed in the case of *Walsh* because of fear of inviting challenges on grounds of public policy. Moreover, as both the *Cheall* case and the following case demonstrate, there is a variety of other grounds upon which a decision of the Disputes Committee can be challenged in a complaint by an individual of wrongful expulsion from the affiliated union or, indeed, as was threatened in the dispute between the TUC, EMA and TASS in 1977–8, upon a direct complaint brought by the dissatisfied union against the TUC seeking a declaration that the Committee's award is void and an injunction against the TUC restraining it from taking disciplinary action against the dissatisfied union for non-compliance with the award. In the latter form of legal action, the clash of institutional interests is made explicit. In complaints by individuals that conflict is somewhat disguised, even distorted, but one can be sure that it was no accident that in *Rothwell* v. *APEX* the individual complainant was the former general secretary of SAGA (the General Accident staff association).

Rothwell v. *APEX* [1976] ICR 211 (Ch. D)

A TUC union, ASTMS, had for some years been attempting to organize the employees of the General Accident Fire and Life Insurance Corporation Ltd, against opposition from both the company and a staff association (SAGA). At the relevant date ASTMS had about one quarter of the employees in membership and SAGA forty per cent. APEX, another TUC union and a long-standing rival of ASTMS, then appeared on the scene and effected a transfer of engagements with SAGA. ASTMS raised the matter in the Bridlington Procedure and a Disputes Committee awarded that APEX was in breach of Principle 5 and should expel its recently acquired members. Mr Rothwell, the former general secretary of SAGA, challenged the APEX decision to expel him in the High Court.

FOSTER J: . . . *The model rule (rule 14)*
Counsel for the plaintiff submitted that the rule is void as being contrary to public policy. Public policy is always dangerous ground for a court to use to decide a case and I do not think that I need decide this question on the view which I take. But if the rule is a valid rule, each counsel admitted that it could not be every or any award which comes within it. Counsel for APEX submitted that the rule did not apply to a decision which was contrary to a statute or is itself criminal. Counsel for the TUC submitted that an award which was made in bad faith or was perverse or made in breach of natural justice would not come within rule 14. For the plaintiff it was submitted that it did not apply to an award which was void as being ultra vires the disputes committee, or of the general council. Counsel for the TUC submitted that there was an implied obligation upon APEX to do nothing which would put it outside APEX's power to carry out an award. For my part I cannot see that there can be an implied obligation to carry out any decision of an award, and particularly not to do anything before the decision is made. There may be an obligation after the general council's decision to implement the award is made, but not before. I have come to the conclusion that rule 14 does not apply to an award which is ultra vires the disputes committee or the general council.

In considering the other issues in the case I think it is of importance to separate them into three stages as different considerations apply at each stage. The three are: the hearing of the case by the disputes committee, the award of that committee and the general council's decision to implement the award.

The hearing. As I have said, no point was taken by counsel for the plaintiff on the way in which the disputes committee was set up nor on the fact that the matter never came before the general council at all before the award. No doubt those advising the TUC will consider whether the procedure adopted was or was not in accordance with the rules; but it was submitted that the award was a nullity as being in breach of the rules of natural justice or of its duty to act fairly between APEX, the plaintiff and the other SAGA members. It was submitted that the memoranda by ASTMS and APEX were only available at the hearing itself and that the plaintiff was not allowed to be present and to speak. I do not think that those two facts make the hearing so unfair as to bedevil the award. But it is to be noticed that ASTMS claimed a membership of 4,000 persons in 1968, a figure which was never substantiated, and the committee was never told that APEX had on or about 28 May 1974, entered into a binding contract with SAGA for the transfer of engagements.

The first part of the award. For the TUC it was submitted that Bridlington 5 has no legal effect but that, as described by Mr Lionel Murray in his affidavit, those principles constitute, and I quote: 'a morally binding code of conduct made between persons of similar views'. It may well be that the disputes committee may not be bound by the principles but its decision was that APEX had acted in breach of that principle. It is obvious that the transfer of engagements in no way contravened that principle as ASTMS never had anything like a membership of over fifty per cent of the General Accident employees. Further, I do not think that APEX ever commenced organizing activities at General Accident by offering to SAGA a transfer of engagements under the Act of 1964. It follows that in my judgment the first part of the award is ultra vires and void.

The second part of the award. It is clear that ASTMS never asked the committee to decide whether ASTMS or APEX was the appropriate union but merely to ask APEX to desist from taking a transfer of engagements from SAGA so that ASTMS and SAGA could continue trying to get recognition and bargaining rights. I can find no power in the committee to decide a question not before it and this would seem to be the corollary to regulation J of the regulations governing procedure in regard to disputes between unions which reads:

> No charges or countercharges beyond those included in the written complaint may be raised at the hearing without the consent of the disputes committee.

It appears that once there is a decision that trade union A is the appropriate trade union for some particular industry or company, the other trade union must withdraw entirely from it and expel all employees from its own membership. It is therefore a decision of some magnitude and to come to such a decision without being asked and with no submissions before it makes in my judgment the second part of the award also ultra vires and void. It is I think idle to suggest that, once the award is made, APEX should have acted on it and not proceeded with the registration of the transfer of engagements under the Act of 1964, since the award itself has no effect unless and until the general council, or the TUC if it is referred to it, decides to put it into effect; and in any event by the time the award was made APEX was legally bound and could have been forced by SAGA to complete the transaction.

The general council's decision. By the time that the general council decided to enforce the award by requiring APEX to expel its members who were former members of SAGA, which I think must have occurred at its meeting on 18 December 1974, the transfer of engagements had lawfully taken place in accordance with the Act of 1964. Just as in my judgment the disputes committee's award required APEX to break a legal obligation already entered into, so the decision of the general council had the effect of trying to undo that which had been lawfully done by statute. Such a decision cannot in my judgment be intra vires the general council and cannot therefore come within the ambit of the model rule 14.

Conclusion

In my judgment not only was the disputes committee award made ultra vires and void, but the general council's decision to enforce it was also ultra vires and void and APEX cannot therefore use rule 14 to expel the former members of SAGA.

Since the events that gave rise to the *Rothwell* case the Bridlington Principles and the associated Regulations have been revised twice, in 1976 and 1979, partly in response to the case. It is now made clear that the Principles and the notes to them 'are to be read together as having equal status and validity',[1] so that the mere fact that the complaining union does not have a majority of the workers in membership would not render Principle 5 inapplicable. It did not prove possible to achieve consensus among affiliated unions on the question of whether mergers between unions should be subject to Principle 5. Instead, that matter is now dealt with as a note to Principle 1 (which concerns joint working arrangements between unions) and it is provided that affiliated unions should consult other interested affiliated unions when contemplating a merger with a non-affiliated organization and that in the event of disagreement any affiliated union can refer the matter to the TUC for advice and conciliation, but not for adjudication except with the agreement of all the affiliated unions involved. In 1979 the Regulations were also revised so as to take more explicit notice of the requirements of natural justice and take account of some of the other points made by Foster J. Revising the Principles, although a process of some tactical utility, is, however, ultimately unlikely systematically to prevent judicial intervention because the whole procedure is one in which the interests of the individual are disposed of by reference to collective interests; and this will always arouse the sensibilities of the courts, however fair the adjudication between the unions can be made.

Before leaving the matter of common-law controls over union expulsions, we ought to glance briefly at automatic forfeiture clauses. Union rule-books frequently provide for the automatic forfeiture of membership where the member falls into arrears with his contributions to a specified extent. The IRA 1971 prohibited automatic forfeiture of membership by providing that a person's membership of a union should not be terminated unless reasonable notice of the proposal to terminate his membership and the reason for it had been given to him (s.65(9)). This prohibition was repealed without replacement in TULRA 1974 so that there is now no direct prohibition upon

[1] *TUC Disputes Principles and Procedures* (1979), p. 7.

automatic forfeiture clauses. But, as we have seen, there is an inherent problem of the acceptability in legal terms of automatic forfeiture clauses, and the courts have from time to time indicated that they would be prepared to strike down automatic forfeiture rules. (See *Edwards* v. *SOGAT*, above, p. 600 and *Radford* v. *NATSOPA*, above, p. 596.) The basis for striking down automatic forfeiture rules would be that they circumvent the legal controls placed upon union decisions to expel a member. But the problem of automatic forfeiture rules goes deeper than that. They are more than a mere device to circumvent controls upon decisions to expel. It is not unnatural that lawyers should tend to view them as if they were a stratagem devised by lawyers. But their place in the custom of the relationship between unions and individuals in the workgroup is a far more central one than that would suggest. Being up to date with the payment of contributions tends to be regarded by all concerned as the chief indication of the individual's continuing allegiance to the union. That is not to say that it is the sole basis of allegiance, nor to say that it does not reflect the union's dependency upon the flow of contributions. It is because of the fallaciousness of those limited views of the significance of being 'fully paid up' that the statutory agency shop created by the IRA 1971 so dismally failed to reflect the aspirations of trade unions (see below, p. 639). It is rather that the collection and payment of contributions represents, or at least used to represent before the spread of the check-off,[1] the chief means of systematic contact between the individual and the officers or lay officials of the union. Moreover custom has identified the decision to go into arrears with contributions as an often mutually convenient method whereby the individual may express his loss of identification with a union – a kind of 'voting with his feet'.

But the ascription of this central function to rules providing for automatic forfeiture of membership in the event of non-payment of contributions has the following unexpected consequence. It means that there will, from time to time, be within the workgroup individuals who are apparently members of the trade union, who have in fact forfeited their membership by non-payment of contributions, but whose non-membership has not yet been identified, confirmed, or relied upon by the union. The problem is akin to that of the ultra vires and void act of an administrative authority with which administrative lawyers have had to grapple at such length. The question is, can membership be said to be void until it has been identified as such? In other words, is the member automatically transformed into a non-member without further action on anybody's part? We know from the cases of *Faramus* v. *Film Artistes' Association* (below, p. 620) and that of *Martin* v. *Scottish TGWU* [1952] 1 All ER 691 that the courts will not treat the fact of apparent membership as a reason for refusing to hold that an individual never validly became a member of a trade union. Would they apply this rather surprising logic to the automatic forfeiture of membership where the trade union allowed the individual to continue as an apparent member? On the other hand, can the union identify

[1] See W. Brown (ed.), *The Changing Contours of British Industrial Relations* (1981), pp. 71–3.

and rely upon automatic forfeiture of membership in relation to a particular individual, without also identifying and relying upon automatic forfeiture by any other individuals in arrears of contributions within the workgroup? In other words, could the automatic forfeiture rule be operated in practice so as to give rise to selective and discriminatory enforcement of the closed shop? Is it, for example, proper for a union to tolerate non-membership consisting of arrears of contributions as long as the individual concerned does not actively oppose or injure the collective interest of the trade union, but to invoke his forfeiture of membership if and when he does? See also below, pp. 641ff. These are problems to which the answers are speculative, but they serve to demonstrate the central importance of automatic forfeiture rules and the complexity of the relationship between the union and the non-member.

So far we have been concerned with the situation where it is the union which asserts an individual's non-membership and attaches consequence to it. Another important situation is that where an individual who has been a member of a union seeks to assert his non-membership of it and where the union refuses to accept that assertion. The individual may make that assertion in order to express his withdrawal of allegiance from the union or in order to enable him to join another union. The union may wish to deny his assertion of non-membership in order to maintain their disciplinary authority over him, or because it enables them, under the Bridlington Principles (above, p. 611), to resist his admission into a rival TUC union. Rules providing for automatic forfeiture of membership are often viewed by all concerned as providing the member with a right to resign. The IRA 1971 provided in terms for a right to resign, and this was perpetuated in TULRA 1974, s.7, in the following terms:

7. Every member of a trade union, or branch or section thereof, shall have the right, on giving reasonable notice and complying with any reasonable conditions, to terminate his membership at any time of the trade union or branch or section thereof.

This was amended to the following formulation by TULRA 1976, s.3(1):

7. In every contract of membership of a trade union, whether made before or after the passing of this Act, there shall be implied a term conferring a right on the member, on giving reasonable notice and complying with any reasonable conditions, to terminate his membership of the union.

The purpose of this amendment was to make it clear that the statutory right to resign existed solely at a contractual level and did not provide a new cause of action in respect of detriment caused to the individual by or in consequence of the union's refusal to accept his resignation.

(b) Common-law controls over exclusion

We have seen how a very considerable body of common-law rules has developed to control expulsions from trade unions. With regard to exclusions the common-law controls have always been rather stunted, partly for doctrinal reasons, partly because the common law has traditionally accepted it as legitimate in principle for a union to attempt to match the supply of and demand for labour by controlling entry into the union. Both these factors can be seen to be operating in the following case, where the House of Lords specifically endorsed a non-interventionist stance in relation to the pre-entry closed shop.

Faramus v. *Film Artistes' Association* [1964]
AC 925 (HL)

The appellant had been a member of the union since 1950. When joining he had made a written statement that he had never been convicted of any offence. In fact he had been sentenced to three months' imprisonment in 1938 and six months in 1940, on both occasions in Jersey. Rule 4(2) of the union said that no person convicted in a court of law of a criminal offence (other than certain motoring offences) should be eligible for or retain membership of the union. In 1958 the union discovered the previous offences and claimed that the appellant had never been a member. The appellant unsuccessfully sought a declaration that he was a member. On the argument that the rule was void at common law as an unreasonable restraint of trade, Lord Evershed said:

My Lords, the normal case in which the principles of unreasonable restraint of trade come under the review of the courts is that of a contract made between two persons whereby something in unreasonable restraint of the trade of one of them is imposed by the contract upon the happening of some event. True it is that the whole of the rules of the respondents' association here constitute a contract between the members. On this ground, therefore, it might no doubt be contended that the second part of the relevant sub-rule (that which provides that membership shall automatically cease upon the member being convicted of any criminal offences, however trivial, with one trifling exception) could be regarded as being unreasonably in restraint of the member's trade, particularly since, as your Lordships were told, the union has in fact achieved what is commonly called a 'closed shop' so that no film artiste within a radius of 50 miles of Charing Cross can obtain employment as such unless he is a member of the union. Upon this matter, however, I would for myself prefer to express no final view since it does not, in the event, matter to the result of this appeal. And I prefer also not to express a concluded opinion that the operation of the sub-rule as regards the appellant in the circumstances of his case should be said to amount to an unreasonable restraint of trade – that is, to an unreasonable restraint upon his right and power to earn his living as a film artiste. I do not forget that, as I have earlier observed, it is one of the objects of this association which has been at the present time achieved, that only members of the association can in fact obtain employment in the neighbourhood of London as film artistes. It is, however, no less clear from the facts stated to your Lordships that there is work available for only about one-fourth of the total number of persons who each year apply for membership as film artistes within the area defined. It follows, therefore, that the rules as to admission of membership must inevitably be in some degree arbitrary – for example, if they provided that the successful candidates were to be drawn by lot. I am unaware of any case in which the principles of unreasonable restraint of trade have been held to be applicable to the rules made by any institution or association laying down the qualifications of persons to become members of the institution or association.

In this respect I apprehend that I share the view of Diplock L.J. in the Court of Appeal.

(His Lordship went on to hold that the rule was in any event covered by s.3 of the Trade Union Act 1871. See now TULRA 1974, s.2(5).)

The law was maintained in this non-interventionist position until 1966, when it was decided in the case of *Nagle* v. *Feilden* that the common-law concept of the right to work established a fount of jurisdiction which would suffice as the basis for an injunction to restrain a trade union from a refusal of admission which would have the result of denying access to an employment where the labour market was regulated by the union. What criteria of *acceptability* are suggested by the following extracts from the judgments in *Nagle* v. *Feilden*? What changes do they represent from the position taken up in *Faramus* v. *Film Artistes' Association*?

Nagle v. *Feilden* [1966] 2 QB 633 (CA)

LORD DENNING M.R.: . . . We cannot, of course, decide the matter today. All I can say is that there is sufficient foundation for the principle for the case to go to trial. We live in days when many trading or professional associations operate 'closed shops'. No person can work at his trade or profession except by their permission. They can deprive him of his livelihood. When a man is wrongly rejected or ousted by one of these associations, has he no remedy? I think he may well have, even though he can show no contract. The courts have power to grant him a declaration that his rejection and ouster was invalid and an injunction requiring the association to rectify their error. He may not be able to get damages unless he can show a contract or a tort. But he may get a declaration and injunction. Thus in *Abbot* v. *Sullivan* [[1952] 1 KB 189] the cornporter (although he had no contract with the committee) obtained a declaration that he was entitled to be reinstated on the register: and this court would, I think, have granted an injunction but for the fact that he had already been reinstated before the judgment. In *Davis* v. *Carew-Pole* [[1956] 1 WLR 833] the livery-stablekeeper (although he was not a member) obtained a declaration that the decision of the stewards disqualifying him was void, and an injunction restraining them from treating him as a disqualified person. I know that in the later case of *Byrne* v. *Kinematograph Rentals Society Ltd* [[1958] 1 WLR 762], Harman J. thought that those two cases could be based on contract. But I think that could only be done by inventing a fictitious contract. All through the centuries courts have given themselves jurisdiction by means of fictions; but we are mature enough, I hope, to do away with them. The true ground of jurisdiction in all these cases is a man's right to work. I have said before, and I repeat it now, that a man's right to work at his trade or profession is just as important to him as, perhaps more important than, his rights of property. Just as the courts will intervene to protect his rights of property, they will also intervene to protect his right to work.

In the present case the plaintiff does not seek admission as a member of the Jockey Club. She only applies for a trainer's licence. But this makes no difference. If she is to carry on her trade without stooping to subterfuge, she has to have a licence. When an association, who have the governance of a trade, take it upon themselves to license persons to take part in it, then it is at least arguable that they are not at liberty to withdraw a man's licence – and thus put him out of business – without hearing him. Nor can they refuse a man a licence – and thus prevent him from carrying on his business – in their uncontrolled discretion. If they reject him arbitrarily or capriciously, there is ground for thinking that the courts can intervene. I know that there are statements to the contrary in some of the cases. We were referred to one by myself in *Russell* v. *Duke of Norfolk* [[1949] 1 All E R 109]. But that was 17 years ago. The right to work has become far better recognized since that time. So has the jurisdiction of the courts to control licensing authorities. When those authorities exercise a predominant power over the exercise of a trade or profession, the courts may have jurisdiction to see that this power is not abused.

In this case the plaintiff alleges that the stewards of the Jockey Club make a practice of refusing any woman trainer who applies for a licence. She is refused because she is a woman, and for no other reason. The practice is so uniform that it amounts to an unwritten rule. The only way she can get round it is to get her head lad to apply. The licence is granted to him, not to her.

It seems to me that this unwritten rule may well be said to be arbitrary and capricious. It is not as if the training of horses could be regarded as an unsuitable occupation for a woman, like that of a jockey or speedway-rider. It is an occupation which women can and do engage in most successfully. It may not be a 'vocation' within the Sex Disqualification (Removal) Act, 1919, but still it is an occupation which women can do as well as men: and there would seem to be no reason why they should be excluded from it.

DANCKWERTS L.J.: . . . In the same way, in my opinion, the courts have the right to protect the right of a person to work when it is being prevented by the dictatorial exercise of powers by a body which holds a monopoly. This principle is not novel. The courts have supported the right of a person to earn a living, even though it involved a breach of contract.

For instance, in *Whitwood Chemical Co.* v. *Hardiman* [[1891] 2 Ch. 416], a manager had agreed to give the whole of his time to a company's business. An injunction was refused because its inevitable result would be to compel him to work for the plaintiff company or starve. Lindley L.J. said:

It appears to me the difficulty of the plaintiffs is this, that they cannot suggest anything which, when examined, does not amount to this, that the man must either be idle, or specifically perform the agreement into which he has entered.

Reference has been made to *R.* v. *The Benchers of Lincoln's Inn* [(1825) 4 B & C 855], which was the case of an application for a mandamus where the applicant wished to become a member of the Bar and had been refused. In this case the judges who, exercising visitorial jurisdiction, control the exercise of the discretion of the benchers of an Inn, had declined jurisdiction because the applicant was not a member. But that course has not been consistently followed. A few years ago a student of Lincoln's Inn was expelled by the benchers because he was convicted of a crime for which he served a term in prison, and the decision was upheld by the judges on his appeal. He twice petitioned the benchers for reinstatement and on the second occasion the judges required him to be reinstated as a student, so that he was called to the Bar, with the unfortunate result that after a few years the benchers were compelled to disbar him for improper behaviour as a barrister and his appeal was dismissed by the judges. Before his reinstatement as a student after expulsion he was, of course, not a member of the Inn. But in the Inns of Court there is this check on the exercise of the discretion of the benchers by the supervision of the judges.

In the case of the stewards of the Jockey Club there does not appear to be any check upon the exercise of their discretion, and unless some protection is provided for persons whose livelihood is involved, such persons are at the mercy of decisions which may be made capriciously and without any proper consideration of the merits of the case.

There is no question of membership of the Jockey Club in the present case. But the possession of a trainer's licence is essential to the plaintiff if she is to be a trainer of racehorses. Her application is not considered simply because she is a woman.

That is arbitrary and entirely out of touch with the present state of society in Great Britain. The subterfuge which is adopted of granting a licence to her male employee does not improve the situation. It underlines the absurdity of it. The Sex Disqualification (Removal) Act, 1919, whether it applies to the present case or not, shows the position of present-day thought. The practice of the stewards is out of date and no longer justified by present conditions.

The Master of the Rolls has gone through the cases and I need not repeat the process. In my view the plaintiff has shown a prima facie case and the action should be allowed to proceed.

The legislators of the IRA 1971 had the aim of placing *Nagle* v. *Feilden* on a statutory footing. This they did in one of their actionable guiding principles for the conduct of trade unions. The guiding principles were eventually done away with completely by TULRA 1976 (see below, p. 625), and TULRA 1974 had already extended to the *rules* of trade unions the protection from the restraint of trade doctrine which had hitherto been conferred upon the *purposes* of trade unions (TULRA 1974, s.2(5)). However, Slade J. in *Greig* v. *Insole* [1978] 3 All ER 449, 509 suggested that the right to work was a concept distinct from that of restraint of trade.

That the courts still contemplate the possibility of judicial activity in this area is indicated by the Vice-Chancellor's judgment in *McInnes* v. *Onslow-Fane* ([1978] 3 All ER 211). The plaintiff had been refused a boxing manager's licence by the British Boxing Board of Control, which is a private unincorporated association exercising *de facto* control over professional boxing. He was refused an injunction to compel the board to give him reasons for their refusal or an oral hearing. Sir Robert Megarry said in effect that this situation was one of a class of situations where non-statutory bodies exercised control on a national scale over activities important to many people, either by granting or refusing licences, or by accepting or rejecting applications for membership. He specifically instanced trade unions, making it clear that he had the model of the closed shop in mind. He indicated that the requirement of fairness would always attach to such a decision. The further duty to apply the principles of natural justice (in particular the requirement of a hearing) would attach only where there was the forfeiture of a licence or of membership or where the applicant had a 'legitimate expectation' of success arising from past circumstances such as to make his case akin to one of forfeiture rather than one of simple application for a voluntary concession. Where the duty of fairness alone applied, it required the body to reach an honest conclusion without bias and not in pursuance of any capricious policy. It was held that an adverse decision could be fair in that sense even where the plaintiff's suitability for that for which he applied was not in doubt, provided that the context was one in which there might be good reasons for an adverse decision which were wholly unconnected with the applicant. The example was given of the situation where 'there were already too many licences for the good of boxing under existing conditions'. One wonders whether the Vice-Chancellor had in mind the analogy of a pre-entry closed shop in a vocation which too many people wanted to enter. If so, would the application of the rule complained of in *Faramus* v. *Film Artistes' Association* be judged to be fair? The Vice-Chancellor went on to hold that the requirement of mere fairness could not, at a procedural level, be held to create a duty to give reasons or to hold a hearing, for otherwise academic bodies refusing places, charities refusing grants and publishers refusing manuscripts might all have to change their procedures. Would a similar distinction between substance and procedure be applied in favour of trade unions? In what circumstances might an application for membership of a trade union be treated as a case of legitimate expectation arising from past circumstances? Might a former member who had unwittingly forfeited his membership by failing to pay his dues come into this category? Could the decision in *Edwards* v. *SOGAT* (above, p. 600) have been explained in these terms?

(c) Statutory controls over expulsion and exclusion

The burden of the materials in the previous two sections has been to suggest that in matters of trade-union discipline and, especially, expulsion, a considerable degree of protection is afforded to individuals by the ordinary courts, albeit sometimes through judicial adoption of principles (such as construction of the rule-book) that are not expressly designed for this end and at the cost of devaluing the claims of the collective goals of trade unions. It might be thought that a better balance between individual and collective interests could be obtained through parliamentary development of principles which address themselves directly to this conflict and which might in consequence foster a more rational and explicit case-law. It might also be argued that the settlement of disputes arising out of such principles should be given to more specialized tribunals. We have also suggested that the common-law controls over exclusion are much less highly developed than those over expulsion and it might be thought that, if protection is needed at the point of entry, it would need to be provided by statute.

The Donovan Commission recommended in favour of the creation of an independent statutory body to which, ultimately, individuals should be able to appeal against unfair disciplinary action by a trade union and also to which they could appeal in respect of their exclusion from a trade union where there was a closed shop in operation (see paras. 609–17 and 625–31). The statutory body envisaged by the Commission was not the industrial tribunals but a review body consisting of a lawyer as chairman and two other members chosen from a panel of trade unionists appointed by the Secretary of State for Employment. The review body would have the power to award compensation but not to order the admission or reinstatement of the complainant. Under the IRA 1971, 'guiding principles' were established for the conduct of all trade unions (registered or not), complaints by members of breaches of which could be brought before industrial tribunals. Section 65(7) provided that no member should be subjected to 'unfair or unreasonable disciplinary action' and in particular no disciplinary action could be taken against a member for failing to take part in industrial action which was illegal under the Act. This latter provision shows perhaps that the draftsmen of the guiding principles saw them not only as a way of protecting individuals but also as a way of buttressing the restrictions on industrial action found elsewhere in the Act, and this no doubt accounts for much of the unpopularity of the guiding principles with trade unions. For registered unions the guiding principle against unfair disciplinary action was supplemented by a requirement that the rules of the union specify 'the descriptions of conduct in respect of which disciplinary action' could be taken by the union, the nature of the disciplinary action available for each description of conduct, and the procedure to be followed. It is impossible to say what sort of jurisprudence the tribunals and the appeal courts might have generated on the basis of this guiding principle; in the event s.65(7) was little relied upon in litigation. This was true also of s.5 of TULRA 1974 which, at the insistence of the Conservative opposition, carried over the essence of s.65(7) into the new law. Section 5 of TULRA 1974 was, however, repealed by TULRA 1976, although only as part of a political compromise that led to the establishment of the Independent Review Committee (below, p. 630). The IRA 1971 also established guiding principles in relation to admission (s.65(2)). No worker of the relevant description who was appropriately qualified for the employment was 'by way of any arbitrary or unreasonable discrimination' to be excluded from membership of the union, and the rules of registered unions had to specify the descriptions of persons eligible for membership and a procedure for dealing with applications. This guiding principle was also carried over by TULRA 1974 and eventually repealed in 1976.

Given this concern on the part of Conservative governments to provide statutory remedies against unfair expulsion or exclusion from trade unions, it was not surprising that this was one of the matters dealt with in EA 1980. By ss.4 and 5 of that Act a remedy is given against 'unreasonable' exclusions or expulsions, a remedy that is to some extent modelled upon the statutory protections against unfair dismissal by an employer (although there is, of course, no general protection against an unfair refusal to employ). However, the statutory remedies against trade unions apply only where a person is in, or is seeking, employment in respect of which a closed-shop (union membership) agreement or arrangement operates (s.4(1)). It is where trade-union membership is compulsory, in the sense that obtaining or retaining a job is dependent upon it, that the statutory provisions operate. Complaint lies, again, to the industrial tribunals (rather than to the more specialized body recommended by the Donovan Commission, on the one hand, or the ordinary courts, as originally proposed by the government, on the other). The tribunals' jurisdiction is squarely based upon a power to review the merits of the union's decision: the question of whether the union acted reasonably 'shall be determined in accordance with equity and the substantial merits of the case' (s.4(5), cf. EPCA 1978, s.57(3)). The fact that the union has or has not complied with its rule-book (often the crucial question at common law) is expressly stated not to be determinative of the issue of whether the union has acted reasonably or unreasonably (s.4(5)). One may guess also that the question of whether the union has acted in accordance with natural justice will be only one element in the assessment of the merits of the union's actions. Indeed, on this issue the tribunals and the appeal courts may face something of a conflict of analogies. The analogy with unfair dismissal would suggest that a procedural error on the part of the union should be forgivable if it can be shown that following the correct procedure would have made no difference to the ultimate decision (see above, pp. 478–86). On the other hand, the common law courts, no doubt because of the narrowness of their jurisdictional base, were unwilling to accept this type of argument in expulsion cases (cf. *Radford* v. *NATSOPA*, above, p. 600).

Indeed, a whole range of problems that have had to be solved in relation to the unfair dismissal laws will also arise in relation to this jurisdiction, in particular problems as to how closely the tribunals will be encouraged to supervise unions' decisions (will the concept of a range of reasonable responses (above, p. 477) be adopted here also?) and as to how closely the EAT will be encouraged to supervise the tribunals. On this latter point there is a significant contrast with the unfair dismissal provisions, in that appeals to the EAT under s.4 of the 1980 Act lie on points of fact as well as of law (s.4(8)), though the re-hearing is not such as to allow the parties to introduce fresh evidence on appeal (*NATSOPA* v. *Kirkham* [1983] ICR 241 and *NGA* v. *Howard* [1983] IRLR 442 (EAT)). However, to date there has been very little litigation under s.4 of EA 1980, a fact which perhaps helps to support the Donovan Commission's view (para. 622) that 'it is unlikely that abuse of power by trade unions is widespread' (which is not to say that it does not exist). Consequently, there is little evidence as to how the industrial tribunals (and, more important, the EAT and the appeal courts) will approach these matters. Nevertheless, it is worth glancing briefly at the two issues that we have seen to be controversial at common law and, to some extent, under the provisions of the IRA 1971, namely, the relationship between the new statutory provisions and union discipline arising out of industrial action, on the one hand, and the Bridlington Principles, on the other.

On the first issue of industrial action, important provisions are to be found in the Code of Practice on Closed Shop Agreements and Arrangements, issued by the Secretary of State under s.3 of EA 1980, originally in 1980, but revised in 1983. Under s.4 the tribunals have an apparently unfettered discretion to regard an expulsion or exclusion for non-participation in industrial action as reasonable or unreasonable, according to the circumstances of the case. However, the Code of Practice contains some very specific provisions on the matter, laying down five situations in which disciplinary action 'should not be taken or threatened'. In paras. 61 and 62 of the Code it states:

61. Disciplinary action should not be taken or threatened by a union against a member on the grounds of his refusal to take part in industrial action called for by the union:

(a) where there were reasonable grounds for believing that the industrial action was unlawful[1] or that it involved a breach of statutory duty or the criminal law; or that it constituted a serious risk to public safety, health or property; or

(b) where the member believed that the industrial action contravened his professional or other code of ethics;

(c) where the industrial action was in breach of a procedure agreement; or

(d) where the industrial action had not been affirmed in a secret ballot.

62. Furthermore, disciplinary action should not be taken or threatened by a union against a member on the ground that he has crossed a picket line which it had not authorised or which was not at the member's place of work.

[1] i.e. industrial action which does not have immunity under the Trade Union and Labour Relations Act 1974 as amended by the 1976, 1980 and 1982 Acts.

The effect of this 'guidance' is to put industrial tribunals in a rather difficult position. On the one hand, failure to observe the Code 'shall not of itself render a person liable to any proceedings' (s.3(8)), so that the tribunals' discretion is preserved, but, on the other, the tribunal must take account of the Code when it is relevant to any question before it (ibid.), and, in the light of the wording of these paragraphs, it will be difficult for a tribunal to have regard to them and yet still find the expulsion to be reasonable (disciplinary action short of expulsion does not, of course, fall within s.4). The tribunals will not be able to find a way out of the problem through the hope that the Code will be relevant only in marginal situations. There will be few examples of industrial action that do not fall within one of the five categories, especially given the relative infrequency with which unions hold secret ballots before industrial action. To this extent, even in advance of implementation of the proposals in the Green Paper, *Democracy in Trade Unions* (below, p. 682), the Code already exerts pressure on unions to hold secret ballots before industrial action.

Patrick Elias has commented upon the propriety of including such provisions in the Code as follows (see (1980) 9 *ILJ* 211, referring to the first version of the Code):

Leaving aside the highly contentious ideological assumptions lying behind the code – is it, for example, obviously unreasonable for a union to discipline a member who will not participate in a strike because no ballot has been called? – it is constitutionally unacceptable that provisions of this kind should be in a code rather than the body of the law. It comes close to the Government directing the tribunal to reach a particular decision and then disowning responsibility for it. It is seeking in advance to indicate unambiguously that in many contentious situations where individual and collective interests are in conflict – and often where collective security is absolutely vital to the union – the resolution should be in favour of the individual. It will be extremely difficult to make industrial action obligatory as opposed to voluntary. The danger is that confidence in the tribunals will be undermined, and also that codes of practice, which have until now provided valuable and relatively uncontroversial guidance, will be viewed with hostility and cynicism.

Nevertheless, this aspect of the Code was strengthened upon its revision in 1983. The original version of the Code in para. 54 suggested that disciplinary action should not be taken where it was the fact that the action fell within one of the relevant categories that had led the member to refuse to participate in it. In the 1983 Code this restriction is removed, and at a press conference called on the publication of a consultative draft of the revised Code the Secretary of State for Employment showed no hesitation at the idea of giving guidance of this type to industrial tribunals. He said:

In particular we have strengthened the Code so as to safeguard those who find themselves intimidated by their trade union into taking part in industrial action against their will. For instance, paragraph 61 says that a union should not discipline a member who refuses *for whatever reason* to take part in industrial action if that industrial action has not been affirmed in a secret ballot or if it is in breach of a procedure agreement or if there are reasonable grounds for believing it to be unlawful.

Industrial tribunals will have to take this guidance into account wherever they consider it relevant. Once the new Code is in force any employee who complains to a tribunal under the 1980 Act that he has been unreasonably expelled from his union as a result of refusing to take industrial action is much more likely to win his case, especially if the strike is unlawful or if there has been no secret ballot.[1]

The Bridlington Principles, by contrast, do not receive the same degree of specific consideration in the Code. They are mentioned as one of the matters to which unions should have regard in deciding whether to admit a person into membership (para. 56), but no mention of them is made in the paragraphs dealing with expulsion, perhaps because they are drafted primarily in terms of disciplinary expulsions, perhaps because the authors of the Code did not want to approve the Principles as a potentially good reason for expelling a member from a union. Thus, in this area the tribunals' discretion is much less encroached upon by the Code. One can only speculate as to how it may be exercised. The limited evidence provided by practice under the IRA 1971 suggests that industrial tribunals, at least, did regard the Bridlington Principles as legitimate grounds for excluding workers from membership, but were more cautious in accepting them in all cases as legitimate grounds for expulsion.[2] This was in line with the general approach of the tribunals and the

---

[1] Department of Employment, Press Notice, 8 December 1982, p. 2.
[2] See Weekes, etc., *Industrial Relations and the Limits of the Law* (1975), p. 87.

NIRC which was, following the common law, to be more easy to convince that an exclusion was reasonable (e.g. because there were too many workers seeking the jobs available) than that an expulsion was reasonable, where individual factors tended to be predominant. To some extent this approach is sanctioned by the Code of Practice, which (in para. 56) enjoins unions when considering admissions to have regard to the fact that 'the number of applicants or potential applicants has long been and is likely to continue to be so great as to pose a serious threat of undermining negotiated terms and conditions of employment'. However, the standard of undermining negotiated terms and conditions is a higher one than the tribunals in fact seemed to apply under the 1971 Act, where a demonstrable imbalance between jobs and job-seekers was enough to justify exclusion, without any particular evidence being required of the likely further impact of unrestricted admissions upon collectively agreed rates.

We have already noted the paucity of litigation under s.4 of EA 1980 and a possible reason for this situation. However, even where the complainant has a claim under s.4, there may be more attractive avenues open to him in the guise of a claim at common law. The statutory claim does not replace, but is cumulative with, the common-law claim (s.4(3)), and although the statutory remedy probably has the advantage of the more attractive forum of the industrial tribunal (likely to be cheaper, speedier and more informal than the High Court), the common law has the advantage of the more attractive remedy in the shape of the injunction (in addition, of course, to damages). One consequence of the decision to give the statutory claim to the industrial tribunal was that compensation became the primary remedy, sometimes compensation with a penal element, but nevertheless a money remedy. Thus, under s.5 of EA 1980, if the tribunal upholds the complaint, it shall make a declaration to that effect and, if the union admits or re-admits the complainant, his remedy is confined to a claim for compensation (to be brought no less than four weeks and no more than six months after the declaration was made) to be assessed by the industrial tribunal. The amount of the compensation is assessed in this case by reference to what the complainant has lost by reason of his initial exclusion or expulsion but may not exceed the sum of the maximum compensatory award for unfair dismissal and 30 times a week's pay, i.e. the maximum basic award for unfair dismissal (see above, pp. 497–503).

Where, however, the union does not admit or re-admit the complainant, his remedy is still compensation. In this case the claim is made for an assessment to be carried out by the EAT and the amount is assessed on the principle of what is just and equitable in all the circumstances (not necessarily restricted to the complainant's loss). In this case also the maximum compensation awardable is increased beyond the maximum before an industrial tribunal by the addition of a further 52 weeks' pay (i.e. the maximum additional award for unfair dismissal (above, p. 495)). Thus, as with unfair dismissal, the pressure to admit or re-admit is only financial; indeed, in the trade-union cases the tribunal is not even given the rather empty power that it has in respect of unfair dismissal to make an order for admission. Whether compensation is awarded by industrial or appeal tribunal, it may be reduced on grounds of the complainant's failure to mitigate his loss or of his having caused or contributed to any extent to his exclusion or expulsion. Because of the relative weakness of the statutory remedies the complainant may choose to pursue his claim at common law, where both courses of action are open to him, which is particularly likely with an expulsion. It may even be that the common-law claim in some circumstances will be more attractive on substantive grounds. If in dealing with procedural defects the industrial tribunals are influenced predominantly by their practice in the area of unfair dismissal, whilst the High Court adheres to its strict view as to the consequences of a failure to observe natural justice, then a purely procedural objection to an expulsion would stand a better chance of success before the common-law courts than before the tribunals. The interaction between common-law and statutory jurisdictions is likely to be one of the fascinating aspects of this area of the law.

Finally, we have noted that one possible criticism of the common law is its capability for intervention before the union's internal remedies have been exhausted and even in advance of the initial disciplinary hearing. The latter criticism cannot be advanced of the statutory procedures because the applicant can complain only of an existing decision to expel or exclude him. However, no more than the common law does the statutory procedure require exhaustion of internal appeals before resort is had to the tribunal. The only indirect encouragement of the complainant to exhaust internal remedies consists in the fact that he has in principle six months from the date of the exclusion or expulsion to present a complaint to the tribunal, instead of the usual three months (s.4(6)).

(d) The Independent Review Committee of the TUC

In previous sections we have seen how the functioning of the judicial process in disputes between individuals and trade unions leaves open an argument that such disputes could with advantage be handled by a body whose scrutiny of the actions of trade unions in relation to individuals would be at once more searching in its terms of reference and yet more responsive to the collective goals of trade unions than are the courts. We also saw how the repeal of the provisions in IRA 1971 and TULRA 1974 enabling individuals to bring proceedings before industrial tribunals in respect of the actions of trade unions raised acute and fierce political controversy. Out of that controversy there emerged an undertaking by the TUC to establish an Independent Review Committee.[1] This was put forward as a basis for reconciling the general insistence that individuals aggrieved by the conduct of trade unions have some recourse to an independent body outside the union, particularly where there

[1] Information about the work of the Committee is contained in appendices to the *Annual Reports* of the TUC from 1976 onwards.

was a closed shop, with the reluctance of trade unions to be submitted to the scrutiny of any body remotely resembling the courts or staffed by people drawn from sectors of society unsympathetic to their aims. The IRC was established in 1976.

How successfully does the Independent Review Committee of the TUC accomplish this reconciliation? Its terms of reference are limited to cases where individuals are expelled or excluded from trade unions and, because membership is a condition of employment, a job is accordingly lost. These terms of reference could in theory extend to the case of refusal to admit an individual where there is a pre-entry closed shop. But since the applicant to the Independent Review Committee has to establish the loss of a specific job opportunity, and since where there is a pre-entry closed shop the applicant for employment who lacks union membership will not normally be offered a particular job, the terms of reference do not in the result normally apply in the case of refusal to admit where there is a pre-entry closed shop. So the terms of reference do not extend to non-unionists generally but rather to the specific situations of (i) members who are expelled from trade unions, for instance for conduct prejudicial to the union, and lose their job in consequence, (ii) members who leave or are expelled from a union and whom the union refuses to re-admit when their jobs are in jeopardy, and (iii) cases where a hitherto open shop becomes a closed shop with consequential loss of jobs by those who are not members of a trade union. Moreover, the process in its nature operates only against trade unions affiliated to the TUC and the sanction against the union is limited to the perhaps unreal ultimate threat of expulsion from the TUC.

There is one final point about jurisdiction. A type of situation with which the IRC is commonly faced is that where the applicant has sought to transfer from one union to another and ends up out of employment because the transfer violates the Bridlington Principles and Procedures governing transfers between TUC unions (see above, pp. 611–17). These cases are the most complex of those the IRC deals with. It is to be expected from its nature and its terms of reference that the IRC will be resorted to more readily in these cases than in cases where the individual is unwilling to belong to any union at all. But neither by its terms of reference nor in practice is the work of the IRC limited to cases where there is more than one union involved, or to cases raising the Bridlington type of problem.

As far as the conduct and criteria of its proceedings are concerned, in what ways is the Independent Review Committee to be contrasted with the courts? At the commencement of its first hearing, its chairman, Lord Wedderburn, declared the independence of the Committee from the individual complainants and from the particular trade unions appearing before them (*1976 Report*, p. 397). He said that the Committee would try to reach conclusions which would strike a just balance between the interests of individual complainants and the interests of trade unions seen in the context of the whole trade-union movement. The IRC must nevertheless have been exposed to the criticism that it is disposed to find in favour of the union as against the individual complainant (see (1978) 173 *IRRR* at p. 12), and in their report for 1978 they found it necessary to point out that the Committee was not satisfied merely by the fact that a union had complied with its rule-book, but went on to consider whether in addition it, and for that matter the complainant, had behaved reasonably in the circumstances. To fail to do this would be regarded by the Committee as a dereliction of its duty (*1978 Report*, p. 391). The 1978 Report provides two examples of criticism of a union's conduct without its being suggested that the union was in breach of its rules (*Wilson and National Union of Dyers* (*1978 Report*, 396 at p. 397); *Thompson and Boilermakers, GMWU* (*1978 Report*, 403 at p. 406, para. 2)).

It is possible to discern some ways in which the Committee is more sympathetic towards the interests of the whole trade-union movement than perhaps the courts have been or would be. Thus the Committee will insist under its terms of reference on the exhaustion of internal procedures (see *Morgan and AUEW (E)* (*1978 Report*, 402 at p. 403, para. 1)), whilst the courts on the whole will not impose that pre-condition or indeed allow it to be imposed (see above, p. 602). The Independent Review Committee has on several occasions urged the party whom it has identified as having right on his side to be conciliatory towards the party in the wrong. (See, for instance, *Dennis and EETPU, NUGMW* (*1976 Report*, 396 at paras. 3, 5); *Walmsley and SOGAT* (*1977 Report*, 340 at p. 341); *Collins and EETPU, TGWU present* (*1978 Report*, 398 at pp. 400–1, paras. 4–5.) This the courts cannot do and would not wish to do, particularly where they found in favour of an individual against a trade union.

The IRC is, of course, both able to, and bound to, engage in conciliation to a far greater extent than the courts do. The Committee declared from the outset its aim of bringing about, wherever possible, an agreed solution by means of conciliation between the parties (*1976 Report*, p. 397). Latterly the Committee has placed great emphasis upon post-hearing conciliation, directed particularly at ensuring that the complainant does not remain unemployed if he is at the time of the hearing (*1978 Report*, p. 391). By the time of the 1978 Report, post-hearing conciliation had occurred in six cases. The Committee also seems increasingly to pave the way for post-hearing concili-ation by desisting wherever possible from concluding its findings in terms of fault on either side; it prefers more and more to go as directly as possible to the point of considering what moves towards a settlement might be forthcoming; see *1978 Report, Docherty and APEX, TGWU* at p. 394; *Thompson and Boilermakers, GMWU* at p. 405; *Curry and NUPE, TGWU* at p. 412.

The main criticism that is levelled at the IRC is the ineffectiveness of its remedies[1] not so much in securing admission or re-admission to the union, but

---

[1] For a general assessment of the IRC, see Ewing and Rees, 'The TUC Independent Review Committee and the Closed Shop' (1981) 10 *ILJ* 84.

in securing the re-engagement by employers of members who have now obtained or recovered their union membership. The fact that the employer is not before the Committee, which has no jurisdiction over him, has often proved an insuperable barrier. However, the matter today is perhaps of less importance: since the introduction of the statutory remedies under EA 1980, the use of the IRC's jurisdiction has very much declined: in 1980/81 it made only two awards and in 1981/2 none. The total of complaints received since it was set up in 1976 was about 50.

3 The closed shop

(a) The closed shop as a social institution

We have already noted in this chapter the influence that the institution of the closed shop has had upon the development of the common law relating to exclusion and expulsion from a trade union and, indeed, that the statutory protections in this area under ss.4 and 5 of EA 1980 are confined to employment in a closed shop. However, the closed shop is important not only in relation to exclusion or expulsion from a union, but also in various other areas of law, notably the law of unfair dismissal, and these further areas we examine in this section. Before doing so, however, it seems sensible to draw together the available research that has been carried out on the closed shop as a social institution. This will provide a background for an assessment of the now extremely complex legal provisions in this area.

There have been two major studies from an industrial relations point of view of the closed shop, one carried out by W. E. J. McCarthy in the early 1960s and published as *The Closed Shop in Britain* (1964), and the other carried out by J. Gennard and S. Dunn in 1978–9, supported by finance from the Department of Employment. The full results of the latter study have been slow to be published, but the main lines of its conclusion have been made clear,[1] and it is very much in the light that the second study throws upon developments since the first that the interest of the two studies consists. Although there is now for the purposes of the legislation a statutory definition of a closed shop in the shape of the definition of a 'union membership agreement' (TULRA 1974, s.30(1)), which we shall examine below, for the purposes of the industrial relations studies the researchers were prepared to adopt the simple definition first put forward by McCarthy of the closed shop as 'a situation in which employees come to realise that a particular job is only to be obtained or retained if they become and remain members of one of a specified number of trade unions'. This definition stresses the fact which is at the centre of public

[1] See Gennard, Gregory and Dunn, op. cit., n. to p. 602; Gennard, Dunn and Wright, 'The content of British closed shop agreements', (1979) 87 *Employment Gazette* 1088 and 'The extent of closed shop arrangements in British industry' (1980) 88 *Employment Gazette* 16; 'New findings on the closed shop' (1983) 289 *IRRR* 2; and S. Dunn, 'The Growth of the Post-Entry Closed Shop in Britain since the 1960s: Some Theoretical Considerations' (1981) 19 *BJIR* 275.

debate on the legitimacy of the closed shop, namely, the dependence of the employee's access to or continuance in the job upon his acquisition and maintenance of membership of the appropriate union.

Within the definition of the closed shop it is conventional to make a distinction (which we shall follow) between pre-entry and post-entry closed shops. In the former the employee must obtain membership of the union before being offered the job by the employer; in the latter he must take up membership within a short time of commencing employment. However, it must be said that the crucial distinction is probably the slightly different one, namely, that between a closed shop operated by a closed union and one operated by an open union. In the latter case the union is in principle prepared to admit any appropriately qualified person who wishes to join it (though, of course, particular individuals may be excluded, for example, because their previous conduct has been hostile to the union). In the former case the union, as was the case in *Faramus* v. *Film Artistes' Association* (above, p. 620), may deliberately seek to limit the total number of persons admitted to the union or some particular section of it. Closed unions usually aim for pre-entry closed shops; open unions are usually content with post-entry shops, so that the two distinctions generally amount to the same thing. We shall follow that convention but it must be admitted that in case of divergence the more important question is whether the union is likely to admit the applicant at all and not the point in time by which the membership must be obtained.

What are the functions of the closed shop? In McCarthy's analysis[1] there are three potential roles for the closed shop and in all three cases the roles are expressive of a notion of the closed shop as being an instrument of trade-union power, to be used against the employer or employers in general. The first function he calls the 'membership function', i.e. the use of the threat of not obtaining or of losing a job to recruit or retain members. The second is the 'discipline function', i.e. the use of this threat to secure obedience to the union's rules, customs and leadership. Both pre-entry and post-entry closed shops can be used for these purposes. The third function, however, is capable of being discharged only by a pre-entry closed shop. The 'entry control' function is designed to bring the number of job-seekers into a rough balance with the number of jobs available. Clearly, all unions need to recruit and retain members, to exercise a degree of internal discipline and to take steps to secure jobs for their members, and yet the closed shop is not a feature of all industries nor even could one say, at least at the time that McCarthy carried out his researches, that in all situations where the union seemed strong enough to obtain a closed shop it had in fact sought to do so. Most unions in most cases sought to deal with the problems of membership, discipline and jobs through mechanisms other than the closed shop. McCarthy thus had to explain why in some cases these problems had led the union to seek and obtain a closed shop, whilst in other cases they had not. He found the answer to this problem in the

[1] Op. cit., pp. 95–106.

concept of 'an additional readiness'[1] in some cases for members and unions to take collective action against non-members, which additional readiness he sought to explain by reference to specific events in the history of the union in a particular industry or firm. Thus, for example, the union might seek a closed shop on membership grounds if it operated in an industry with a high degree of labour turnover, scattered membership and inter-union competition for membership. It might seek a pre-entry closed shop if the industry in question was characterized by a chronic over-supply of labour, casual working and fragmented employing organizations. A closed shop for disciplinary reasons might be sought where the leadership had experienced particular problems in the past in conducting effective strikes. Two general points emerge from this analysis. First, mere objection to 'free riders' (i.e. non-members obtaining the benefits of union activity) was not found by McCarthy to have been a major pressure for creating a closed shop, although it is the most frequently articulated public defence of the practice. Had the 'free rider' argument had more operational impact, the closed shop would have been more widespread, because the argument could be generally applied to situations of collective organization. Second, in this analysis the closed shop appeared predominantly as a way of remedying defects in collective organization on the employees' side.

The later study by Gennard and Dunn showed a considerable growth in the practice of the closed shop. McCarthy had found that one-sixth of all employees were in closed shops; by 1978 (the date of the Gennard and Dunn study) it had increased to nearly one-quarter of all employees (5.2 million workers), though that number has probably fallen with the recession, which has hit especially hard some industries with extensive closed-shop arrangements. McCarthy had found the closed shop to be concentrated in relatively few industries. The growth between the time of his study and 1978 was not to be explained by its further development in those industries – indeed during this period levels of employment in some of the traditional closed-shop industries, such as mining and shipbuilding, fell heavily – but by its spreading into industries not traditionally noted for its existence. In the private sector of the economy the closed shop spread particularly into the food, drink and tobacco industry, clothing, footwear, chemicals, petroleum products and distribution. There was also rapid growth in the public sector, especially nationalized industries (where three-quarters of manual employees are now covered by the closed shop) and Labour-controlled local authorities. Finally, where McCarthy had found the closed shop to be predominantly a feature of the employment of manual workers, by 1978 one-fifth of those in closed shops were white-collar workers and closed shops covered about one-tenth of all white-collar employment.

Even more interesting than the global figures relating to the extent of the practice are the findings of Gennard and Dunn as to nature of the new closed-shop practices and the reasons for their development. McCarthy had found

[1] Ibid., p. 82.

the typical closed-shop arrangement to be informal, based on custom and practice and sustained essentially by the unilateral efforts of the employees. During the later 1960s and 1970s, however, there was a marked trend towards formal, written agreements with management on the closed-shop issue, to the point where about half those in closed shops are covered by such agreements. Gennard and Dunn explain this growth of formal closed-shop agreements by reference to two factors. The major one, they suggest, was the general growth of more formalized, plant-level relations in the wake of the Donovan Commission's Report. They trace the recent growth of the closed shop back to the late 1960s and suggest that the well-documented boom in the spread of the closed shop in 1975 to 1977 was merely the result of the release of a pent-up demand which had been restrained by the IRA 1971 (see below, p. 638). Second, they point to the need since 1974 for the closed-shop agreement or arrangement to meet the statutory definition of a union membership agreement if the employer is to be protected against claims for unfair dismissal (see below, pp. 640–47), and this gave management an interest in coming to an explicit and formal arrangement with the union on the matter. Gennard and Dunn also found that the growth of closed shops had been almost entirely growth of the post-entry closed shop. Coupled with the fact that a number of traditional pre-entry closed-shop industries had seen a decline in employment in this period, this meant that the proportion of the closed-shop population in pre-entry closed shops had fallen from one-fifth to sixteen per cent, and it has probably fallen further since 1978 as the recession has reduced employment in the traditional closed-shop industries even further.

The fundamental question raised by these changes is whether the changes in the form of the closed shop, in particular the increase in formal agreements with management on the matter, reflect also a change in its function. Is the closed shop still a simple expression of unilateral trade-union power, or is the formal closed-shop agreement, at least, a joint management and union institution, which serves the interests of both? It seems likely that this has become increasingly the case over the last fifteen years, but even in the context of this analysis different views can be held as to which interests of management and unions are served by the closed shop. A strong view, put forward by Moira Hart,[1] is that the advantages of the closed shop to management often outweigh its disadvantages. The closed shop helps to stabilize relations between employer and union, protects those relations from challenge by other unions, ensures the union represents all the workforce and perhaps even makes the union more willing to come to agreements with the employer that will be unpopular with some elements of its membership. This rather chilling prospect of the closed shop as an instrument of joint management and union discipline over member-employees should not be over-emphasized, but it seems likely that it represents reality in some situations. The weaker view, put forward by Stephen Dunn,[2] is that the closed shop has no particular

[1] 'Why bosses love the closed shop', *New Society*, 15 February 1979. [2] Op. cit., n. to p. 633.

advantages for management, but equally it is increasingly seen by management as having few disadvantages where union organization is already strong. In other words, the closed shop is now seen as a formal and natural way of marking the existence of a strongly collectivized pattern of industrial relations, which does not in itself add anything much to the power the union and the employees already exercise. Whether Dunn or Hart is nearer the mark is not a question we can answer, but on either view the closed shop appears in a very different light from that in which it appeared in McCarthy's study. It can lay claim to a place in the mainstream of collective organization and perhaps expect to be to some extent protected by both unions and employers against legislative attack. However, it should not be supposed that no employers will be influenced by the new climate to move to end existing closed-shop arrangements. Such moves can perhaps be expected especially in the public sector and especially after periods of acute conflict with the trade unions, as with the partial suspension by British Rail of its closed shop after the strikes of 1982 and with the decision by the water authorities in late 1983 to end their closed shop.

(b) The closed shop and the law of unfair dismissal

Since it is the consequence of non-membership for the employee's retaining his job that has been the centre of public debate in recent years, it is not surprising that the legal debate has come to centre upon the employee's remedies at the point of dismissal for non-membership of the relevant union and, in particular, his potential remedies on grounds of unfair dismissal against the employer. The employee might also have a remedy at common law on grounds of wrongful dismissal. However, this will not usually be so because the employer in the typical case of employment of indefinite duration may terminate the contract on reasonable notice without having to justify his reasons for so doing, although the occasional employer has been tripped up by the common-law requirements (see *Hill* v *C. A. Parsons & Co. Ltd* [1972] Ch. 305 (CA) – inadequate notice given to a senior and long-serving employee). Consequently, the legal relationship between the closed shop and the employer's freedom to dismiss has been a matter of relatively recent concern, flowing from the introduction of protection against unfair dismissal in 1971. Nevertheless, because dismissal is the nerve-point in the system of enforcing the closed shop, it has seemed at times since 1971 that the law relating to the closed shop consisted entirely of the relevant provisions of the unfair dismissal legislation, so intense has the public debate on this point been and so complex have the unfair dismissal provisions become.

Before turning to the details of this legislation some general points need to be made. First, from an individual's point of view protection against dismissal on grounds of non-membership of the relevant union may not be an adequate protection of his interests. Clearly, it is an inadequate protection in a pre-entry closed shop where the employee is refused a job because he is not in membership of a union, and the burgeoning legal controls upon dismissal may cause employers even in post-entry shops to screen out applicants for jobs who, they think, will not be likely to join or remain in the union once employment has commenced. The IRA 1971 recognized the force of this point and s.5 of that Act gave protection against refusals to hire on grounds of non-membership as well as against dismissals on these grounds (except where the closed shop conformed to the statutory models of an agency or approved closed shop). However, as we noted in Chapter 1, controls upon refusals to hire (except on grounds of race or sex) are largely absent from the current law. Whether there should be such protection is a question of general importance for employment protection law, but, because of the extensive development of the law of unfair dismissal in relation to the closed shop, the contrast between remedies at the point of dismissal and at the point of refusal to hire is particularly acute in this area.

Second, protection against dismissal does not give protection against discriminatory action short of dismissal by an employer on grounds of non-membership, except in so far as the employer's conduct amounts to constructive dismissal (above, p. 448) and the employee chooses to treat it as such, resign and lodge a claim for unfair dismissal. Developments in the area of constructive dismissal, especially in relation to an employer's duty not to act capriciously, no doubt give such claims a good chance of success in many cases, but they do require that the employee abandon his job. A more direct remedy would be to enable the employee to complain of the employer's treatment of him whilst retaining his job (though it might be a brave employee who would exercise this right). Such a right was provided by the IRA 1971 and is now contained in s.23 of EPCA 1978 (as amended). There is in the 1978 Act no general protection for employees against unfair action short of dismissal taken by the employer, but s.23 does confer such protection in respect of action taken on grounds of union membership or activities or non-membership of a union. In general, the law relating to action short of dismissal for non-membership in a closed shop has proceeded in parallel to that relating to dismissal, and in what follows such equivalence may be assumed unless we state otherwise.

Third, it is sometimes said that it is inappropriate that an employee's primary remedy for dismissal for non-membership in a closed shop should be against the employer rather than the union. To the extent that the closed shop has become a joint institution of management and union, the force of this argument is reduced. Even where the closed shop is mainly an expression of union power, the majority of the Donovan Commission thought the employer should be the party at risk, because 'the decision to dismiss is the employer's, taken ultimately because he considers it to the advantage of his business' (para. 564). However, both in the IRA 1971 and since 1980 some concession has been made to the opposite point of view by provisions enabling third parties (unions, officials or workers) to be joined in the unfair dismissal claim.

Between 1974 and 1980 the Commission's view prevailed in the law (see below, p. 654).

However, the above discussion assumes that it is desirable to grant employees protection against dismissal on grounds of non-membership in a closed shop. This was certainly the stance of the government that introduced the general protection against unfair dismissal in the IRA 1971. Section 5(1)(*b*) of that Act enacted a general right (not confined to the closed shop) for an employee (as against his employer) not to be a member of a trade union. By itself, this would have rendered every dismissal for non-membership in a closed shop unlawful, but s.5(1)(*b*) was modified, within narrow confines, to take some account of the post-entry closed shop.

In relation to the post-entry closed shop, the 1971 Act delineated the area within which the employer was protected in the event of dismissal by reference to two statutory institutions which the legislators were content to regard as containing an acceptable set of conditions upon which employees could be subjected to detriments in relation to their unwillingness to belong to a union. The first of these two institutions, and that which embodied the primary policy aims of the legislators, was the 'agency shop': IRA 1971, s.11.

The distinguishing features of the agency shop were that it gave the employee the option of paying contributions to a (registered) trade union without belonging to it, and also that it enabled employees to pay equivalent contributions to a charity if they could establish themselves as conscientious objectors to belonging to any trade union or paying contributions thereto. A statutory agency shop could be established either by agreement between registered trade unions and employers or, where an employer was unwilling so to agree, by application to the NIRC for a ballot of the workers affected. In the event trade unions were not attracted towards the making of agency shop agreements, not only because of their general unwillingness to employ the statutory machinery of the IRA, with the corresponding submission to the requirements which the Act placed upon registered trade unions, but also because the agency shop in its very nature seemed inadequate to effect all the purposes for which trade unions would seek a closed shop, namely for the assurance of solidarity within the work-group concerned.

This inability of the statutory agency shop to satisfy the aspirations of trade unions became sufficiently clear to the government of the day during the passage of the Industrial Relations Bill through Parliament for them to decide to avoid chaos in those industries where the whole pattern of industrial relations was traditionally dependent upon the existence of a closed shop. This they did by providing for approved closed-shop agreements (s.17). Such agreements were to be approved by the NIRC upon application by employers and trade unions jointly. It was necessary for a report to be received from the CIR declaring that a closed shop was necessary for the purposes of enabling the workforce to be organized, of maintaining reasonable terms and conditions of employment and reasonable prospects of continued employment for the workers concerned, and for promoting or maintaining stable arrangements for collective bargaining relating to the workers concerned, and for preventing collective agreements from being frustrated (Sch. 1, para. 5). There was also a requirement that the agreement must include provisions enabling conscientious objectors to contribute to a charity instead of belonging to a trade union (Sch. 1, Pt. IV). The vital difference between the approved closed shop and the agency shop was, of course, the absence in the approved closed shop of the category of non-member contributors to the union. The National Union of Seamen and the actors' union Equity joined with the employers in seeking an approved closed shop in their respective industries. Since this required their remaining as registered unions, this involved their temporary expulsion from the TUC.

The 1971 Act duly authorized an employer to dismiss, penalize or otherwise discriminate against an employee for not belonging to a trade union or paying appropriate contributions to it in the case of an agency shop or not belonging to a trade union in the case of an approved closed shop, unless in either case the employee concerned had established a valid conscientious objection (s.6(2), (5), s.17(5), (6)). These provisions, however, hardly fell to be applied or interpreted, because the provisions concerning agency shops and approved closed shops were little used. All the evidence suggests that the actual practice of the closed shop continued substantially unaffected despite the attempt to force it within the confines of the statutory institutions and to ban it in so far as it did not fall within those confines. Hence the legal and the factual positions continued at acute variance with each other throughout the period during which the IRA 1971 remained in force.

With the repeal of the Act the Labour Government set about legalizing the closed shop as it existed in practice, in both pre-entry and post-entry versions, rather than according to preconceived desiderata. Yet paradoxically, because of their own commitment to certain preconceptions as to how best to identify the closed shop and also because of a temporarily successful rearguard action by the Conservative opposition, they succeeded in rendering the closed shop far more vulnerable to litigation than it had in practice been under the IRA 1971. It would in theory be possible to legalize the closed shop simply by allowing the employer to plead pressure from fellow employees as a ground for fairly dismissing a worker who refused to belong to a union. In fact the present legislation in general specifically disallows the employer from relying upon pressure from other employees as a ground for dismissing a worker (EPCA 1978, s.63). Consequently in TULRA 1974 a narrower method of legalization of the closed closed was chosen.

> Trade Union and Labour Relations Act 1974, Sch. 1,
> para. 6(5) and s.30, definition of union membership
> agreement (as originally enacted)

6(5) Dismissal of an employee by an employer shall be regarded as fair for the purposes of this Schedule if –

(*a*) it is the practice, in accordance with a union membership agreement, for all the employees of that employer or all employees of the same class as the dismissed employee to belong to a specified independent trade union, or one of a number of specified independent trade unions; and

(*b*) the reason for the dismissal was that the employee was not a member of the specified union or one of the specified unions, or had refused or proposed to refuse to become or remain a member of that union or one of those unions:

unless the employee genuinely objects on grounds of religious belief to being a member of any trade union whatsoever or on any reasonable grounds to being a member of a particular trade union, in which case the dismissal shall be regarded as unfair.

30(1) 'Union membership agreement' means an agreement or arrangement which –

(*a*) is made by or on behalf of, or otherwise exists between, one or more independent trade unions and one or more employers or employers' associations; and

(*b*) relates to employees of an identifiable class; and

(*c*) has the effect of requiring the terms and conditions of employment of every employee of that class to include a condition that he must be or become a member of the union or one of the unions which is or are parties to the agreement or arrangement or of another appropriate independent trade union; . . .

The following features of this set of provisions should be noted. The provisions made it necessary to consider, firstly, whether there is a qualifying agreement in force, and, secondly, whether the practice is such as to qualify for the application of the exemption from unfair dismissal liability. As to the qualifying agreement, s.30 as originally enacted required that the agreement related to each and every one of the workers concerned, i.e. that it aspired to universality of application. The agreement also had to relate to the terms and conditions of employment of the employees concerned and, as the result of a Conservative amendment, it appeared to have to give every employee the option of belonging to any appropriate independent trade union. Moreover, not only was it necessary for the agreement to aspire to universality of coverage but it was also necessary for the practice of the closed shop to apply to all the employees of the class concerned. In the celebrated case concerning power workers at the Ferrybridge 'C' Power Station, *Sarvent* v. *CEGB* [1976] IRLR 66, an industrial tribunal held that a closed-shop agreement failed to attract the statutory immunity because it was not universally applied in practice. The dismissal concerned therefore fell to be judged according to the ordinary principles of unfair dismissal, and was held to be unfair because it could not be shown that the employees concerned had not been singled out for discriminatory application of the closed shop against them. In this way the dismissed employees were enabled to benefit twice from the non-universal application of the closed shop. First, it enabled them to show that the statutory immunity did not apply, and, secondly, it enabled them to show that the application of the *de facto* closed shop to them was unfair.

Thus, the legislators had ended up by restricting the legitimate closed shop according to a value-judgment that it must be a universally applied closed shop. Brian Weekes, in an article published in December 1976, contended that the requirement of total application was at variance with the actual practice of the closed shop.

Weekes, 'Law and Practice of the Closed Shop' (1976) 4
ILJ, p. 214

At any time . . . where a closed shop covers large numbers of workers (particularly if it is industry-wide) it is likely that a number of employees will be out of compliance with their appropriate trade union. This non-membership arises from a number of causes: defective trade union organization, a less than 100 per cent check-off, non-acceptance at the place of work of non-specified union cards, and those who out of grievance take the decision not to remain in the union or lapse because of apathy. In addition, there may be other non-members who fall into a recognized category for exclusion under the closed shop agreement. More commonly individuals with strong religious or moral objections are allowed to blend in with the general run of non-members or are tolerated although there is no formal agreement permitting them to remain outside the union.

Further case-law decided under the 1974 Act somewhat widened the area of application of the closed-shop immunity. In *Home Counties Dairies Ltd* v. *Woods* [1977] ICR 463, it was decided that a closed-shop agreement could comply with the terms of the Act even though it did not provide the employee with the option of belonging to any appropriate trade union. That was held to be an option exercised by the union in making the agreement rather than an option required to be present as a choice for the employee within the formulation of the agreement. In *Gayle* v. *John Wilkinson & Sons (Saltley) Ltd* [1978] ICR 154, it was further decided that fairly slight evidence sufficed to show that a closed-shop agreement operated upon individual contracts of employment. But the requirement of universality of application remained as a major restriction.

After long and bitter political controversy the law relating to the closed shop was reformed by TULRA 1976. This swept away, first, the requirement that the agreement must aim for universality of application; secondly, the requirement that the agreement must operate on individual contracts of employment; and, thirdly, the reference to the option of belonging to an appropriate union. It also removed the requirement that the agreement must be universally effective in practice, and it narrowed the scope of conscientious objection so that only religious objection would suffice, it being no longer sufficient to object on reasonable grounds to membership of any particular trade union.

TULRA 1976, ss.1(e) and 3(3)–(6)

1. The following provisions and passages of the Trade Union and Labour Relations Act 1974 (hereafter in this Act referred to as 'the principal Act') are hereby repealed, that is to say –

... (*e*) in paragraph 6(5) of Schedule 1 (cases where dismissal is to be regarded as fair), the words 'or on any reasonable grounds to being a member of a particular trade union'.

... 3(3) In section 30(1) of the principal Act (interpretation), in paragraph (*c*) of the definition of 'union membership agreement', –

(*a*) for the words 'of requiring the terms and conditions of employment of every employee of that class to include a condition that he must' there shall be substituted the words 'in practice of requiring the employees for the time being of the class to which it relates (whether or not there is a condition to that effect in their contract of employment) to'; and

(*b*) for the word 'appropriate' there shall be substituted the word 'specified',

and at the end of that definition there shall be inserted the words 'and references in this definition to a trade union include references to a branch or section of a trade union; and a trade union is specified for the purposes of, or in relation to, a union membership agreement if it is specified in the agreement or is accepted by the parties to the agreement as being the equivalent of a union so specified'.

(4) After section 30(5) of the principal Act there shall be inserted the following subsection:–

'(5A) For the purposes of this Act employees are to be treated, in relation to a union membership agreement, as belonging to the same class if they have been identified as such by the parties to the agreement, and employees may be so identified by reference to any characteristics or circumstances whatsoever.'

(5) In paragraph 6(5) of Schedule 1 to the principal Act (cases where dismissal is to be regarded as fair) for the words 'all the employees of that employer or all employees' there shall be substituted the words 'employees for the time being'.

(6) In paragraph 6(9) of Schedule 1 to the principal Act (definitions), after the word 'paragraph' there shall be inserted the words 'unless the context otherwise requires, references to a trade union include references to a branch or section of a trade union, and'.

TULRA 1974, Sch. 1, para. 6(5), as amended, was consolidated in EPCA 1978, s.58(3). The definition of union membership agreement is still contained in TULRA 1974, s.30 (as amended).

After a somewhat uncertain start in *Himpfen* v *Allied Records Ltd* [1978] ICR 684 (EAT), the courts came to recognize and to give effect to the fact that TULRA 1976 had removed both the requirement in the definition of union membership agreement that the agreement itself should aspire to universality of application and the corresponding requirement in EPCA, s.58(3) (formerly TULRA 1974, Sch. 1, para. 6(5)), that the practice actually prevailing should amount to universal membership. This process can be seen at work in the following case.

Taylor v. *Cooperative Retail Services Ltd* [1982] ICR 600 (CA).
The employee was a milk-roundsman at a dairy where the employees were traditionally members of USDAW. A number of employees first left

USDAW, but, in 1976, after the employer had entered into a closed-shop agreement, they joined the TGWU. After an award of the Disputes Committee of the TUC, the employees were expelled from the TGWU and most rejoined USDAW. The employee and nine others refused to rejoin USDAW and were dismissed. The industrial tribunal found the dismissals to be fair by virtue of the closed-shop provisions in TULRA 1974, as amended by TULRA 1976.

FOX L.J.: . . . I turn to condition (ii). This requires the establishment of a practice for employees of the relevant class to belong to USDAW. It is contended on behalf of Mr Taylor that no such practice is established because (*a*) the number of consenting employees was insufficient to justify the description 'practice' at all, (*b*) at the date of the dismissal of Mr Taylor the situation under which most of the employees were members of USDAW was of insufficient duration, and (*c*) there can be no practice without consensuality and that those employees who joined USDAW did not do so voluntarily but under threat of losing their jobs.

As to the argument based upon numbers, the factual position is as follows. I will assume in Mr Taylor's favour that the relevant employees are the milk-roundsmen only. Of those there were 96 at the beginning of March 1976; 46 of the 96 were members of TGWU, and the remaining 50 were members of the USDAW. On April 19, 1977, the TGWU membership of the 46 came to an end. Late in April the 46 were pressed by the employers to join USDAW. Most of them did so. Mr Taylor did not. The result was that thereafter there were 10 persons who were not members of USDAW. Of the 10, one was a member of AUEW. Mr Taylor was not a member of any union and the remaining eight were probably not members of a union either.

There may be some doubt as to the accuracy of the total figure of 96. Again in Mr Taylor's favour I will treat it as 90. It is said that if 10 out of 90 are not members of USDAW, the employers fail to establish a practice.

That would no doubt have been right on the language of paragraph 6(5) in its original form which read:

(*a*) it is the practice, in accordance with a union membership agreement, for *all* the employees . . . to belong to a specified independent trade union, or to one of a number of specified independent trade unions. . . .

But paragraph 6(5) as amended by the Act of 1976 is in a different form. The word 'all' is omitted and it reads:

it is the practice, in accordance with a union membership agreement, for employees for the time being of the same class . . . to belong to a specified independent trade union. . . .

It seems to me that Parliament must have regarded the word 'all' as too restrictive and, by its omission in the Act of 1976, deliberately loosened the requirements of the section. We were referred to the decision of the appeal tribunal in *Himpfen* v. *Allied Records Ltd* [1978] ICR 684. I do not think that case, as reported, gives any authoritative guidance on the present point since it appears to proceed upon the basis that the word 'all' remains in paragraph 6(5) as amended by the Act of 1976.

I agree with the appeal tribunal that the amended paragraph 6(5) does not require that a tribunal be satisfied that any particular percentage of employees belong to an independent trade union. The question is one of fact for the tribunal and I find it impossible to say that a tribunal could not reasonably conclude (looking at the matter in terms of numbers) that a practice exists if over 90 per cent of the employees are involved.

I deal next with the argument as to the consensual element. The submission, in effect, is that paragraph 6(5) of Schedule 1 should be read as if it stipulated that the practice must be voluntary on the part of the employees whose membership of the union is relied upon as establishing the practice.

In my judgment there is no justification as a matter of construction for the introduction into paragraph 6(5) of such a stipulation. The paragraph contains nothing which points to it. All that the paragraph requires is the establishment of the practice. A practice, in my view, is a matter of fact. It may be the consequence of whole-hearted consent, indifference, laziness or some form of pressure.

If employees agree under pressure from employers to join a union, the position may be that left to themselves they would not join but will do so in order to get the benefits of continued employment. In one sense they join the union voluntarily and in another they do not. But I see no reason to suppose that Parliament contemplated that industrial tribunals should have to embark upon inquiries as to employees' motives for agreeing to join a union. The inquiry, in some instances, might involve many thousands of people. The position is made more difficult by the absence of any statutory guidance as to what precisely is meant by 'voluntary'. In fact the language of the statute seems to me to point against rather than towards the incorporation of any such principle. Thus paragraph 6(5) refers to 'the practice, in accordance with a union membership agreement. . . .' Employees however are not parties to a union membership agreement (which is made between the unions and the employers) and such an agreement is by definition (section 30 (1)(c) of the Act of 1974 as amended) one which has the effect in practice of '*requiring*' the relevant employees to become members of a union. That is not a structure which suggests wholly consensual arrangements at the will of employees. In my view the argument is without substance and I reject it.

The next of the three questions is that of the duration of the state of affairs relied upon as constituting a practice. Paragraph 6(5) provides:

> Dismissal of an employee by an employer shall be treated as fair . . . if–(*a*) it is the practice . . . for employees for the time being of the same class as the dismissed employee to belong to a specified independent trade union. . . .

The paragraph is concerned with the question whether dismissal was fair. In view of the use of the present tense ('it *is* the practice') and the reference to employees 'for the time being', I think that the point of time with which the paragraph is dealing is the date of dismissal. The question is whether it was the practice at that time for employees to belong to USDAW. In my judgment there is no ground for importing into paragraph 6(5) any requirement that the practice must be of long standing or must be something in the nature of a custom in the legal sense. The Act of 1974 had repealed the provisions of section 5 of the Act of 1971 relating to the right of a worker to be a member of such trade union as he chose or of no trade union. The purpose of paragraph 6(5) in the Act of 1974 was to enable union membership agreements to be enforced. They were of course, only to be enforced within the framework of the statutory provisions but I see no reason to suppose that the operation of the provisions was to be deferred during some lengthy period while 'practices' could be established. Suppose that, immediately after the statute came into force, a union membership agreement is entered into and, in response to the employers' requirements, all the members of a substantial workforce join a union in accordance with the union membership agreement. And suppose that a week or two later one of them leaves the union, refuses to rejoin and is dismissed. As a matter of policy, I can see no reason to suppose that the statute intended to prohibit such a dismissal. And, as a matter of language, it seems to me quite accurate to say that, at the time of dismissal, it was the practice for the relevant employees for the time being to belong to the union. It was not the practice for long, but it was what the great majority actually did as a practical matter.

In the present case, from the end of April 1977, over 90 per cent of the milk-roundsmen were, in response to the employers' request, members of USDAW. That was still the position on June 27 when Mr Taylor was dismissed. The question whether it was, at that date, the practice for employees for the time being to belong to USDAW is one of fact for the industrial tribunal. In my opinion, looking at the matter thus far, the appeal tribunal were correct in their view that the industrial tribunal were, on the evidence, entitled to conclude that the practice was established. I see no ground for saying that the industrial tribunal misdirected themselves. Accordingly, we are not entitled to interfere with their decision.

However, the most controversial of the changes made in 1976 was probably the confining of the exception to the rule that dismissals for non-membership in a closed shop are fair to situations of objection on grounds of religious belief to being a member of any trade union. Even after the courts had held that the reference was to the religious beliefs of the employee and not to the 'official' views of the sect to which he belonged (*Saggers* v. *British Railways Board (No. 2)* [1978] IRLR 435 (EAT)), this was, and was intended to be, a very narrow exception to the rule of non-liability on the part of the employer. Some limits were set to the new statutory structure by the courts, but by and large it survived legal challenges to it by employees (of which, in any case, there was not a large number). After some vacillation the EAT eventually decided in *Leyland Vehicles Ltd* v. *Jones* [1981] IRLR 269 not to apply what is probably the general rule of unfair dismissal law that a dismissal may be justified by the employer's reasonable belief that a certain fact exists. Where that fact is that the employee is not a member of the union the employer must prove it to the satisfaction of the tribunal, i.e. on the balance of probabilities. Further, in *Curry* v. *Harlow DC* [1979] ICR 769, following *Jeffrey* v. *Laurence Scott & Electromotors Ltd* [1977] IRLR 466, the EAT held that, where the union membership agreement contains a procedure which the employer must follow before dismissing an employee for non-membership, failure to follow the essentials of the procedure disentitles the employer from relying upon the non-liability rule. This approach was reconciled with the wording of s.58(3), which seemed to require simply that the reason for the dismissal be non-membership of the union and which did not mention procedure, on the following basis: '. . . a tribunal is entitled to say that a reason for dismissal is not made out unless the employer is able to demonstrate that it really was the reason for dismissal, and that an employer is not able to demonstrate that it really was the reason for the dismissal unless he shows that he gave proper consideration to what his reason was' (at p. 776). This expresses a strong view of the effect of a failure to follow correct procedure and of the impact of such failure upon the employer's substantive reasons which is not, as we have seen (above pp. 478–86), generally reflected in the law of unfair dismissal.

Given the long-standing hostility to the closed shop by the Conservative Party on grounds of its infringement of personal liberty and given the image, perhaps exaggerated, of the closed shop as the strongest embodiment of union power, it is not surprising that in both EA 1980 and 1982 the government elected in 1979 turned its attention to the relationship between the law of unfair dismissal and the closed shop. In view of the difficulties experienced between 1974 and 1976 in drafting a satisfactory definition of a union membership agreement, it is some relief that this definition in s.30(1) of TULRA 1974 has not been further amended, nor has the reference to the practice of the union membership agreement in EPCA 1978, s.58(3), been amended so as to re-insert a requirement of universal effectiveness. Thus *Taylor* v. *CRS* (above) remains good law on these issues. The EA 1980 to 1982 operated instead on three other aspects of the law of unfair dismissal. First, the range of situations in which dismissal for non-membership in a closed shop will be automatically unfair has been dramatically increased beyond the simple situation of religious objection envisaged by TULRA 1976. Second, there has been an equally dramatic increase in the levels of compensation available to people unfairly dismissed in such situations. Third, there has been a considerable elaboration of the notion of joinder of unions, workers and officials to unfair dismissal proceedings. We will look at each of these three areas in turn. We have omitted any consideration of the constitutionally interesting but essentially transitory provisions of Sch. 1 to the EA 1982 which enable the Secretary of State to pay retrospective compensation to those who were dismissed for non-membership of a union between 1974 and 1980 and who, had the provisions of EA 1980 been in force, would have been able to bring a successful complaint of unfair dismissal. For a discussion of these provisions, see Ewing and Rees, (1983) 12 *ILJ* 148.

(1) *The categories of unfair dismissal*
In the first area the effect of the changes made has been such that the exceptions have virtually swallowed up the rule derived from TULRA 1974–6 that dismissal of an employee for non-membership of the appropriate union in a closed shop is fair. This development is underlined by the fact that EA 1982, s.3 has substituted new sections 58 and 58A for old s.58 of EPCA 1978 – references henceforward will be to these sections as substituted – and by the fact that s.58(1)(*c*) of EPCA 1978 now adopts the same approach as IRA 1971, s.5(1)(*b*) and states generally that dismissal of an employee for non-membership of any union or of a particular union shall be unfair. Between

1974 and 1982 this was stated to be the case only in respect of dismissal for non-membership of a non-independent trade union (see above, p. 179). Similar provisions also operate in respect of action short of dismissal (see the amendment made to s.23(1)(c) of EPCA 1978 by EA 1980, s.15(1)). As with the IRA 1971, if s.58 of EPCA 1978 made no further qualification to the statement in s.58(1)(c), then all dismissals for non-membership in a closed shop would be unfair. However, s.58(3) provides that the dismissal shall be fair if it is dismissal for non-membership where 'it is the practice, in accordance with a union membership agreement, for employees of the employer who are of the same class as the dismissed employee to belong to a specified independent trade union, or to one of a number of specified independent trade unions.' (See EPCA 1978, s.23(2A), for action short of dismissal.) If this qualification to the principle stated in s.58(1)(c) were not itself qualified, all dismissals for non-membership in a closed shop would be fair. It is on the large number of qualifications introduced by EA 1980 and 1982 to the non-liability rule stated in s.58(3) that the claim that the exceptions have swallowed up the rule rests, and it is to these qualifications and exceptions that we must now turn.

Of the five qualifications to the non-liability rule which EA 1980 and 82 have introduced potentially the most important is the one requiring that the union membership agreement be approved by the relevant percentage of the employees to whom it applies in a secret ballot. This qualification, which is stated in principle in s.58(3)(c) itself and is developed at greater length in s.58A, falls into two parts. The first part, which is derived from the provisions of EA 1980, applies only to union membership agreements coming into force after 14 August 1980 (the date of the coming into force of EA 1980). The requirement is that employees of the class to whom the union membership agreement relates shall have approved the agreement in a secret ballot in which 80 per cent of those entitled to vote voted in favour of the agreement (s.58A(1) and (2)). If no ballot is held or if the relevant level of approval is not obtained, the continued operation of the closed shop is not, as such, unlawful, but any dismissal of an employee for non-membership will be unfair. The level of approval required is extraordinarily high – an abstention in effect counts as a vote against – and it is clear that the provision was intended to discourage the further spread of the closed shop. In this it may have come too late. The Gennard and Dunn study suggested that by the late 1970s the closed shop had already spread to all areas where it was feasible to introduce it – elsewhere unions were too weak or employer opposition too strong – so that further large-scale expansion of the closed shop was not in any case to be expected.

Under the provisions on balloting as introduced in 1980 no further ballot was required of a post-1980 agreement after the first successful ballot, no matter how long had elapsed since the first ballot or how much circumstances had changed, nor was any ballot required of a pre-1980 agreement. The first

Code of Practice on Closed Shop Agreements and Arrangements (1980) recommended periodic review of closed-shop agreements, of which ballots would form a part, but these recommendations had no direct legal force. The 1982 Act deals with both these matters. In order that the dismissal for non-membership be automatically fair it is provided in s.58(3)(c) that the closed-shop agreement, whenever it came into force, must have received the requisite level of approval in a secret ballot within five years before the date of dismissal. The relevant level of approval in the first ballot of a post-1980 agreement is as stated above. In all other cases the level is either 80 per cent of those entitled to vote or 85 per cent of those voting (s.58A(1) and (2)). The alternative standard of 85 per cent of those actually voting is still a very high one, but probably it represents a marginal relaxation of the standard set in 1980 because abstentions do not count as votes against. Eighty-five per cent of those voting on a very low turn-out will do.

The impact of these new provisions on secret ballots is potentially very great. In any case where an agreement has not been successfully balloted within the previous five years, no matter how long-standing the agreement, the dismissal will be automatically unfair from the date of the coming into force of the relevant parts of E A 1982. However, whereas the rest of E A 1982 was brought into force by the beginning of 1983, the second limb of the balloting provisions is not due to be implemented before November 1984 (although that date could be advanced). Until that time only post-1980 agreements need to be balloted. The ostensible reason for this delay is to enable ballots to be held, for it is not by any means customary for employers and unions to hold ballots on the closed shop, so that the immediate implementation of the legislation would simply sweep away the no-liability rule in most cases. However, there is an element of political conflict in the decision. The T U C's policy is that affiliated unions should not participate in ballots held on this issue, and the government may wish to see whether that policy stands the test of time, whilst in the meantime holding the threat of advancing the date for implementation as a sword of Damocles over the closed shop. There is nothing in the legislation which requires union participation in the ballot to make it valid – indeed the legislation does not say who is to conduct the ballot – but an employer may calculate that a ballot is not likely to be successful without at least tacit union support. Once a successful ballot has been held the timing of the next ballot becomes of crucial importance. This is because an unsuccessful second ballot renders any subsequent dismissal unfair even if it falls within the unexpired portion of the five-year period commencing with the previous successful ballot (s.58A(7)). The ballot must be conducted in such a way as to secure, as far as reasonably practicable, that all those entitled to vote have the opportunity of voting and of voting in secret, but within those requirements a workplace ballot is as effective as a postal ballot (s.58A(5)). Those entitled to vote are the members of the class of employees to whom the union membership agreement applies. We have already noted (above, p. 643) that T U L R A 1976 added a clause to the definition of union membership agreement in TULRA 1974 (s.30(5A)) entitling the parties to the agreement to treat employees as belonging to the same class 'by reference to any characteristics or circumstances whatever.' This created the possibility of concluding a closed-shop agreement which applied only to employees who were members of the union at the time it was introduced, but s.58A(6) of EPCA 1978 prohibits the definition of those entitled to vote by reference to their membership (or objection to membership) of a union.

The second exception to the no-liability rule is that the dismissal will be unfair 'if the employee genuinely objects on grounds of conscience or other deeply-held personal conviction to being a member of any trade union or of a particular trade union' (s.58(4)). This subsumes the religious objection provisions of TULRA 1976 and considerably expands this ground of objection, both by covering deeply held personal convictions, whether religious or not, and by allowing the objection to operate in respect of a particular trade union as well as trade unions as a whole. It seems likely that some kinds of disagreement between a member and his union over union policy could develop into objection to membership of the union because of deeply held personal conviction, but the question of the scope of this imprecise concept has not yet had to be faced by the courts, even though this exception was introduced in 1980. This exception, like all the others to be discussed, operates independently. The fact that an agreement has secured the requisite level of approval in a ballot will not prevent a person dismissed for non-membership succeeding in a claim for unfair dismissal, if he does have conscientious grounds for objection to membership of the union.

The third exception – and probably the last of the main exceptions – concerns employees who were not members of the union at the time the union membership agreement came into force, who have not subsequently joined the union and who have been dismissed for non-membership. In this case the dismissal is unfair (s.58(5)). A slight variant of this protection applies to an employee covered by post-1980 agreements who was not a member of the union at the date of the ballot (s.58(6)). Since the ballot might be held after the agreement came into effect and since the employee might have been a member at the earlier date, he could not rely on s.58(5). If between the date of the coming into force of the agreement and the holding of the ballot the employee ceased to be a member of the union, he could nevertheless rely on s.58(6). The argument put forward by the government to explain the provisions of s.58(6) was that until a post-1980 agreement was successfully balloted, the dismissal of the employee for non-membership would be unfair for that reason and that he should be given the opportunity to preserve that legal position by ceasing to be a member of the union before the ballot was taken. This argument, which might be thought more appropriate to tax legislation than labour legislation, did not, however, receive any further statutory elaboration when the balloting provisions were extended, in principle, to all union membership agreements in 1982. In respect of pre-1980 agreements, then, a member dissatisfied with the closed shop may voice his disagreement by voting against it on a ballot, but he does not improve his legal position by ceasing to be a member in advance of the ballot. The extent of the protection that should be afforded to 'existing non-members' was at the heart of the controversy over the closed shop operated by British Rail and the railway unions, which went to the European Court of Human Rights (see below, p. 658). However, it is in fact fairly common for union membership agreements specifically to exempt non-members at the time the closed shop is introduced from the obligation to join. Thus Gennard and Dunn found in their study (which, of course, was carried out at a time when there was no legislative protection for existing non-members) that some two-thirds of the agreements they studied placed no obligation upon existing non-members to join the union. To the extent that this figure is correct – and later research has cast some doubt on it – the legislation in EA 1980–2 is merely generalizing a protection already fairly widely found in practice.

The fourth exception renders it unfair for an employer to dismiss an employee for non-membership where a tribunal has found that employee to have been unreasonably excluded or expelled from the union contrary to s.4 of EA 1980 (s.58(7); see above, pp. 624–30), and the same protection applies when the member has merely complained to a tribunal of unreasonable exclusion or expulsion and his complaint has not yet been dealt with. In this case, however, the unreasonably expelled or excluded member will not be protected against dismissal if he has subsequently failed to accept the union's offer of membership or if the union has made it clear that he will be admitted (or re-admitted) if he applies for membership (s.58(11)).

The fifth exception indicates the legislators' concern to undermine the link between membership of a union and the obligation to participate in industrial action, which we have already seen to be present in the Code of Practice on the closed shop (above, p. 627). S.58(8) deals with such a situation and it is significant that the government thought fit to make explicit provision for it, even though the majority of the cases likely to fall within s.58(8) are probably already covered either by the provisions relating to deeply held personal convictions (s.58(4)) or those relating to unreasonable expulsion or exclusion from the union (s.58(7)). Where an employee 'holds qualifications which are relevant to the employment in question' and is subject to a written code of conduct for the holders of these qualifications and he has either been expelled from a union for refusing to take part in industrial action which would be a breach on his part of the code of conduct or has refused to join a union because membership would require him to take part in industrial action that would be a breach of the code, then his dismissal for non-membership of the union will be unfair. The introduction of this provision was in part a response to the industrial action that took place in the National Health Service in 1982.

Finally, it should be noted that s.58(13) treats dismissal of an employee because he objects to having to make a payment or suffer a deduction from wages in the event of his ceasing to be a member of the union as equivalent to dismissal for non-membership of the union, so that the protections of s.58 apply. Thus, the agency shop (above, p. 639), which was the main approved model of the closed shop under the IRA 1971, is subject to the same restrictions as other forms of the closed shop under EA 1982.

The law relating to action short of dismissal proceeds in parallel to the law relating to dismissal for non-membership (see EPCA 1978, s.23 (as amended)). However, under the provisions of EPCA 1978, s.23, as originally enacted, there was one feature of that section which was not shared by the provisions on dismissal. This related to the right of employees not to have action short of dismissal taken against them for the purpose of deterring them from taking part in the activities of an independent union at an appropriate time. This provision is discussed above at pp. 178–97. However, where there was a union membership agreement in operation, s.23, as originally enacted, removed that right from employees of the same class as those to whom the union membership agreement applied and from employees in the same grade or category (but not in the same class) where these activities took place on the employer's premises, unless the union in question was one specified in the union membership agreement. The purpose of this rather complex qualification to the general right stated in s.23(1)(b) was to protect the closed-shop arrangement from challenge by non-specified unions by enabling the employer to control the activities on his premises of such unions. As amended, the qualification to s.23(1)(b) applies only to employees of the class covered by the union membership agreement (s.23(2A)(a)) and only if the agreement has received the requisite level of approval in a ballot, if the agreement is one to which the ballot provisions apply (s.23(2B)). Thus, non-approved agreements may be undermined by the activities of competing unions on the employer's premises, subject, of course, to the general restraints on the s.23(1)(b) right (see above, pp. 188–97).

Thus, the value-judgments which it is sought to embody in the unfair dismissal provisions relating to the closed shop have become so elaborate that, although in formulation they fall short of a direct rule that closed-shop dismissals are unfair, they come close to producing that result simply because the institution itself is not capable of adjusting to such precise regulation in the way that, for example, financial institutions are capable of responding to fiscal legislation. This is a delusion which makes quite a lot of exercises in labour legislation otiose, though of course it enables the legislation to be presented to Parliament and the public as an exercise in fine-tuning in which all views are given weight.

(2) *The remedies for unfair dismissal*
From the point of view of the degree of protection conferred upon individuals, merely to create a range of situations in which dismissal will be unfair is not

enough, unless the remedies available to dismissed employees are adequate. As we have seen above (pp. 496ff.), there is considerable reason to suppose that the remedies generally available for unfair dismissal are in fact inadequate. We have noted the extreme infrequency with which orders of reinstatement or re-engagement are made, and this pattern seems to apply to dismissal for non-membership of a union as well. Indeed, in *Coleman* v. *Magnet Joinery* [1975] ICR 46 the Court of Appeal held in a case arising under the IRA 1971 that it was legitimate for a tribunal, when considering whether it was practicable to recommend reinstatement, to take into account the likelihood of industrial action by the unionists if the non-unionists were reinstated. If this general approach continues to prevail, then compensation will be the primary remedy for the employee dismissed for non-membership, as it is for other unfairly dismissed employees.

The EA 1980–2 have done nothing to alter the principles upon which consideration is given to reinstatement or re-engagement in cases of dismissal for non-membership, but EA 1982, ss.4–6, have dramatically improved the monetary remedies available. The new provisions on remedies apply to all dismissals which are regarded as unfair by virtue of new s.58 (and indeed s.59(*a*)). This means they apply to all unfair dismissals for non-membership of a union (whether or not the dismissal arises out of a closed shop) and to all unfair dismissals for membership of a union or participation in its activities. Thus, the enhanced remedies apply to protect freedom of association (above, p. 178) as well as the freedom to dissociate. On the other hand, the new provisions do not apply to action short of dismissal, with the remedies for which (see above, p. 182) there is now a rather strong contrast. This situation may give some employees an incentive to treat action short of dismissal by an employer as a constructive dismissal.

The three elements in the compensation awardable in the standard case of unfair dismissal are the basic, compensatory and additional awards of compensation, the latter being relevant only where the employer has failed to implement an order of reinstatement or re-engagement. The compensatory award, which is compensation for loss suffered as a result of the dismissal, is not affected by the new provisions. The new provisions relate to the basic award and also create a new 'special' award, which replaces the additional award in this context, but which is not confined to situations of failure to implement an order of re-employment. As far as the basic award is concerned, the EA 1980 abolished the old minimum basic award of two weeks' pay, but EA 1982, s.4 (inserting new EPCA 1978, s.73 (4A)), has re-introduced it for dismissals in breach of EPCA 1978, ss.58 and 59(*a*) and set it at the very high level of £2,000, equivalent to about 15 weeks' pay. More dramatic still are the details of the new special award. Where the tribunal has ordered reinstatement or re-engagement but the employee has not been re-employed, the tribunal shall award the claimant 156 weeks' pay (the normal limit on a week's pay (see above, p. 528) not applying in this case) or £15,000, whichever is the greater (new EPCA 1978, 75A(2), inserted by EA 1982, s.5). This is considerably more than the maximum additional award (52 weeks' pay calculated subject to the usual limits on a week's pay), but it might be thought to be a relatively marginal change unless tribunals become more willing to order re-employment. More significant, then, may turn out to be the provisions of new s.75A(1) that the tribunal shall make the claimant a special award of 104 weeks' pay (without limit) or £10,000, whichever is the greater, but not more than £20,000, provided that the claimant asks to be re-employed, even if the tribunal decides to make no such order (new s.72, proviso).

Consequently, an employee unfairly dismissed contrary to the provisions of EPCA 1978, s.58 or 59(a), can have a firm expectation of compensation of at least some £12,000, plus compensation for whatever loss the dismissal has caused him, provided only that he asks the tribunal to order him to be reinstated or re-engaged. However, the tribunal may in certain circumstances reduce the amount of the basic or special awards, the most general situation being where the tribunal considers that any conduct of the complainant before the dismissal was such that it would be just and equitable to do so (EPCA 1978, s.73(7B), subject to s.73(7C) for the basic award and s.75A(4) for the special award). This reduction provision is itself qualified, however, by new EPCA 1978, s.72A (inserted by EA 1982, s.6), which requires the tribunal, when considering a reduction, to disregard the employee's behaviour in so far as it consists in his refusal to comply with a requirement that he should join a union, make a contribution in lieu of membership, not join a union or not take part in its activities. Thus, to take a relevant example, a tribunal which has found an employee to be unfairly dismissed for non-membership of a union would not be able to reduce his compensation on the grounds that it was just and equitable to do so because his refusal to join the union had caused the dismissal. This merely prevents the policy of the legislators being undermined at the remedies stage. Nevertheless, s.72A would not seem to be applicable where the employee's behaviour consists of something more than just a refusal to join, e.g. where he flaunts his non-membership before fellow workers and goads them into taking action against him, as in *Cory Lighterage Ltd* v. *TGWU* [1973] ICR 339 (CA). Here reduction would seem to be permitted and ought to be made.

(3) *Joinder*

We have already noted in an earlier chapter (above, p. 181) the extension of the provisions concerning interim relief to dismissal for non-membership of a union (EA 1982, s.8), which will be significant if it leads tribunals more readily to make orders for re-employment in such cases. This leaves for consideration the provisions on joinder (EA 1982, s.7 (dismissal) and s.11 (action short of dismissal)). There were provisions in the IRA 1971, s.33(3)(a), which made it unlawful to take industrial action in order to cause an employer to dismiss an employee unfairly, but such action could be complained of only by the employer (s.105(1)). In the structure of s.33 the provisions of s.33(3)(*a*) were the counterpart to the provisions in s.33(1) that any industrial action taken against the employer in order to persuade him to dismiss an employee should be disregarded in assessing the fairness of the dismissal. This latter provision survived the repeal of IRA 1971 and now appears as EPCA 1978, s.63. However, no equivalent to s.33(3)(*a*) continued after 1974, but in the EA 1980 the legislators introduced a complex set of joinder provisions, whereby persons organizing industrial action could be joined to the unfair dismissal proceedings. The joinder, however, was still at the option of the employer and the result of joinder might be that the third party was ordered by the tribunal to make a contribution (up to a complete indemnity) to the employer. In the EA 1982 these provisions were completely recast. As far as dismissal is concerned, EA 1982, s.7 inserts a new EPCA 1978, s.76A, which operates wherever the employer is induced to dismiss an employee through pressure consisting of industrial action brought against him because of the dismissed employee's non-membership of a union. The persons (including trade unions) calling, organizing, procuring or financing the industrial action may be joined in the unfair dismissal proceedings. The novel factor in the 1982 Act is that either the employer or the complainant may join the third party – the tribunal has no power to refuse the joinder if the request for it is made before the hearing of the complaint – and the compensation payable may be made wholly or partly payable by the third party directly to the complainant. The employer can thus no longer protect his industrial relations against disruptive joinders by complainants, even where the complainant has no financial interest in joinder because the employer is solvent, but no doubt it would be permissible for the employer to reimburse the third party in respect of the award made against him. Moreover, the new joinder provisions in all but name confer a new cause of action upon the complainant against the third party, whom the complainant may regard as the prime mover in the events giving rise to the litigation.

(c) **The closed shop and human rights**
The previous section will have demonstrated the complexity of the present law of unfair dismissal in its relation to the closed shop. However, two underlying features of that law stand out clearly enough. First, the law now contains the assertion of a general right not to belong to a trade union and not merely, as previously, a right not to belong to a non-independent trade union. Second, the exception made to this rule in order to cater for the closed shop has itself become increasingly hedged about with qualifications and restrictions, to the point where the employers' and, indeed, trade unions' and workers', protection against unfair dismissal claims arising out of the operation of closed-shop agreements or arrangements has become quite uncertain and with the full implementation of the EA 1982 may even become illusory. How should one evaluate this shift in the stance of the law of unfair dismissal? We

have already quoted the view of the Donovan Commission (para. 599) that the right to join a trade union, which, of course, both the Labour government's legislation and the present law assert, does not in policy terms lead to the equal assertion of a right not to join a trade union. This was because the effect of a right to join was to encourage trade-union organization and collective bargaining whilst the tendency of a right not to join was to undermine these collective activities. Hence the Labour government's legislation confined the right not to join to non-independent trade unions, whose activities the legislators of that time did indeed wish not to encourage. The perspective of the Donovan Commission also provides a standpoint from which to criticize the EA 1980–2. The creation by those Acts of a general right not to be a member of a union takes its place alongside the repeal of Sch. 11 to EPA 1975 (above, p. 161), the rescission of the Fair Wages Resolution (above, p. 154) and the repeal of the statutory recognition procedure (above, p. 198) as part of a policy whose general effect is to reduce the ability of workers to organize themselves collectively in trade unions, to secure recognition from employers and to extend the impact of collective agreements. The legislation on the closed shop has been powerfully criticized from this point of view by Roy Lewis and Bob Simpson,[1] and from a broader perspective by Lord Wedderburn and Jon Clark[2] as contributing to the general 'restrictive' tendency of the EA 1980–2.

However, there is another mode of discourse about the right to join a union which we should consider. The arguments of the Donovan Commission were for a classic use of the law for the purposes of social engineering and this is the stance that seems to have underpinned the legislation of 1974–6. The right to join is created primarily for the purposes of supporting the social institution of collective bargaining and the right not to join is confined to non-independent unions because to do otherwise would be to contradict this goal. The right to join is conferred upon individuals, but because they are technically the best enforcers of this right and not out of any belief that the collective interest in the development of the social institution is not the predominant one. The alternative mode of discourse sees the right to join a trade union or the freedom of association as a fundamental human right, along with rights such as freedom of expression, freedom of thought or freedom of assembly. Indeed, to the human rights lawyer freedom of association is by no means confined to association in trade unions, which tends to be the primary, even the exclusive, connotation given to the phrase by the labour lawyer. More important, although the effective guarantee of the freedoms listed above (and others) is seen in the context of discussions on human rights as an indispensable underpinning of a democratic society, the freedoms are not usually seen as designed to foster any particular democratic institution. In the human rights

---

[1] 'Disorganising Industrial Relations' (1982) 11 *ILJ* 227.

[2] Wedderburn and Clark, 'Modern Labour Law: Problems, Functions and Policies' in Wedderburn, Lewis and Clark, *Labour Law and Industrial Relations* (1983).

context freedom of association serves much more general ends than the encouragement of collective bargaining. This is not to say that the enactment of a right to freedom of association for reasons such as those espoused by the Donovan Commission is inconsistent with a right to associate viewed from the standpoint of fundamental human rights, but it is to say that the approaches of the labour lawyer and the human rights lawyer tend to be based upon different types of reasoning.

However, there is one issue that may bring these approaches into collision. We have explained how from the Donovan perspective the right not to join is very definitely not viewed as a logical or policy corollary of the right to join. From the perspective of the human rights lawyer, however, the equivalence of the two rights seems to arise naturally. The fundamental rights conferred are envisaged as intended to enhance the potentiality and responsibility of the individual. From the standpoint of individual liberty and self-determination the position of the individual seems only to be strengthened by the addition of a freedom to dissociate to the better-known freedom to associate. Thus, the concurring minority in *Young, James and Webster* v. *UK* (below) described the right not to join or 'the negative aspect of freedom of association' as 'necessarily complementary to, a correlative of and inseparable from its positive aspect', whilst Professor Kahn-Freund has described such arguments as 'shallow legalism'.[1]

The English legal system, lacking both (or being inflicted with neither) a written constitution and a constitutional court, normally provides no forum in which the grand themes of human rights can be debated. However, the United Kingdom, along with some 18 other European countries, is a signatory to the European Convention for the Protection of Human Rights and Fundamental Freedoms (1950). Like the majority but not all of the signatories, it has adopted the article that allows the individual the right to petition the European Commission of Human Rights and, ultimately, the European Court of Human Rights. Article 11 of the Convention provides:

1. Everyone has the right to freedom of peaceful assembly and to freedom of association with others, including the right to form and to join trade unions for the protection of his interests.
2. No restrictions shall be placed upon the exercise of these rights other than such as are prescribed by law and are necessary in a democratic society in the interests of national security or public safety, for the prevention of disorder or crime, for the protection of health or morals or for the protection of the rights and freedoms of others. This Article shall not prevent the imposition of lawful restrictions on the exercise of these rights by members of the armed forces, of the police or of the administration of the State.

In *Young, James and Webster* v. *UK*[2] (below) the Court was given the opportunity to consider the implications of Article 11 for the closed shop. The majority

---

[1] *Proceedings of the Colloquy on the Freedom of the Worker to Organise* (1980), Vol. 2.
[2] Noted by Forde (1982) 11 *ILJ* 1 and Von Prondzynski [1982] *CLJ* 256.

judgment cannot be said to have been a fine example of the judicial art, lacking as it did both logical exposition of legal rules and bold appeal to basic principles. Its weaknesses were exposed by both a concurring minority opinion and a dissenting minority opinion.

Young, James and Webster v. *United Kingdom* [1981] IRLR 408
(European Court of Human Rights)

The three applicants were all former employees of British Rail, of varying seniority. At the time they commenced their employment with British Rail there was no obligation upon them to join a specified trade union. In 1975 British Rail concluded a closed-shop agreement with the NUR, TSSA and ASLEF, whereby membership of the appropriate one of these unions became a condition of employment for BR employees in the grades in question. The applicants refused to join any of these unions and were dismissed in 1976 (i.e. when TULRA 1974-76 were in force). Mr Young objected to the unions' political policies and affiliations; Mr James refused to join the NUR (the relevant union for him) because he did not believe it acted efficiently in taking up and pursuing members' grievances; and Mr Webster objected to the whole system of collective bargaining.

Judgment of the Court: . . .
1 *The existence of an interference with an Article 11 right*
A substantial part of the pleadings before the Court was devoted to the question whether Article 11 guarantees not only freedom of association, including the right to form and to join trade unions, in the positive sense, but also, by implication, a 'negative right' not to be compelled to join an association or a union.

Whilst the majority of the Commission stated that it was not necessary to determine this issue, the applicants maintained that a 'negative right' was clearly implied in the text. The Government, which saw the Commission's conclusion also as in fact recognising at least a limited negative right, submitted that Article 11 did not confer or guarantee any rights not to be compelled to join an association. They contended that this right had been deliberately excluded from the Convention and that this was demonstrated by the following passage in the *travaux préparatoires:*

> On account of the difficulties raised by the 'closed-shop system' in certain countries, the Conference in this connection considered that it was undesirable to introduce into the Convention a rule under which 'no one may be compelled to belong to an association' which features in [Article 20 s.2 of] the United Nations Universal Declaration (Report of 19.6.50 of the Conference of Senior Officials, Collected Edition of the *'Travaux Préparatoires'*, vol. IV, p. 262).

The Court does not consider it necessary to answer this question on this occasion.

The Court recalls, however, that the right to form and to join trade unions is a special aspect of freedom of association (see the *National Union of Belgian Police* judgment of 27.10.75, Series A no.19, p.17, section 38); it adds that the notion of a freedom implies some measure of freedom of choice as to its exercise.

Assuming for the sake of argument that, for the reasons given in the above-cited passage from the *travaux préparatoires*, a general rule such as that in Article 20 s.2 of the

Universal Declaration of Human Rights was deliberately omitted from, and so cannot be regarded as itself enshrined in, the Convention, it does not follow that the negative aspect of a person's freedom of association falls completely outside the ambit of Article 11 and that each and every compulsion to join a particular trade union is compatible with the intention of that provision. To construe Article 11 as permitting every kind of compulsion in the field of trade union membership would strike at the very substance of the freedom it is designed to guarantee (see, *mutatis mutandis*, the judgment of 23.7.68 on the merits of the '*Belgian Linguistic*' case, Series A no. 6, p. 32, section 5, the *Golder* judgment of 21.2.75, Series A no. 18, p. 19, section 38, and the *Winterwerp* judgment of 24.10.79, Series A no. 33, p.24, section 60).

The Court emphasises once again that, in proceedings originating in an individual application, it has, without losing sight of the general context, to confine its attention as far as possible to the issues raised by the concrete case before it (see, *inter alia*, the *Guzzardi* judgment of 6.11.80, Series A no.19, pp. 31–32, section 88). Accordingly, in the present case, it is not called upon to review the closed shop system as such in relation to the Convention or to express an opinion on every consequence or form of compulsion which it may engender; it will limit its examination to the effects of that system on the applicants.

As a consequence of the agreement concluded in 1975 (see paragraph 39 above), the applicants were faced with the dilemma either of joining NUR (in the case of Mr James) or TSSA or NUR (in the cases of Mr Young and Mr Webster) or losing jobs for which union membership had not been a requirement when they were first engaged and which two of them had held for several years. Each applicant regarded the membership condition introduced by that agreement as an interference with the freedom of association to which he considered that he was entitled; in addition, Mr Young and Mr Webster had objections to trade union policies and activities coupled, in the case of Mr Young, with objections to the political affiliations of the specified unions (see paragraphs 53, 57 and 64 above). As a result of their refusal to yield to what they considered to be unjustified pressure, they received notices terminating their employment. Under the legislation in force at the time (see paragraphs 24 and 27–30 above), their dismissal was 'fair' and, hence, could not found a claim for compensation, let alone reinstatement or re-engagement.

The situation facing the applicants clearly runs counter to the concept of freedom of association in its negative sense.

Assuming that Article 11 does not guarantee the negative aspect of that freedom on the same footing as the positive aspect, compulsion to join a particular trade union may not always be contrary to the Convention.

However, a threat of dismissal involving loss of livelihood is a most serious form of compulsion and, in the present instance, it was directed against persons engaged by British Rail before the introduction of any obligation to join a particular trade union.

In the Court's opinion, such a form of compulsion, in the circumstances of the case, strikes at the very substance of the freedom guaranteed by Article 11. For this reason alone, there has been an interference with that freedom as regards each of three applicants.

Another facet of this case concerns the restriction of the applicants' choice as regards the trade unions which they could join of their own volition. An individual does not enjoy the right to freedom of association if in reality the freedom of action or choice which remains available to him is either non-existent or so reduced as to be of no practical value (see, *mutatis mutandis*, the *Airey* judgment of 9.10.79, Series A no. 32, p.12, section 24).

The Government submitted that the relevant legislation (see paragraph 35 above) not only did not restrict but also expressly protected freedom of action or choice in this area; in particular, it would have been open to the applicants to form or to join a trade union in addition to one of the specified unions. The applicants, on the other hand, claimed that this was not the case in practice, since such a step would have been precluded by British Rail's agreement with the railway unions and by the Bridlington Principles (see paragraph 36 above); in their view, joining and taking part in' the activities of a competing union would, if attempted, have led to expulsion from one of the specified unions. These submissions were, however, contested by the Government.

Be that as it may, such freedom of action or choice as might have been left to the applicants in this respect would not in any way have altered the compulsion to which they were subjected since they would in any event have been dismissed if they had not become members of one of the specified unions.

Moreover, notwithstanding its autonomous role and particular sphere of application, Article 11 must, in the present case, also be considered in the light of Articles 9 and 10 (see, *mutatis mutandis*, the *Kjeldsen, Busk Madsen and Pedersen* judgment of 7.12.76, Series A No.23, p. 26, section 52).

Mr Young and Mr Webster had objections to trade union policies and activities, coupled, in the case of Mr Young, with objections to the political affiliations of TSSA and NUR (see paragraphs 53 and 64 above). Mr James' objections were of a different nature, but he too attached importance to freedom of choice and he had reached the conclusion that membership of NUR would be of no advantage to him (see paragraph 57 above).

The protection of personal opinion afforded by Articles 9 and 10 in the shape of freedom of thought, conscience and religion and of freedom of expression is also one of the purposes of freedom of association as guaranteed by Article 11. Accordingly, it strikes at the very substance of this Article to exert pressure, of the kind applied to the applicants, in order to compel someone to join an association contrary to his convictions.

In this further respect, the treatment complained of – in any event as regards Mr Young and Mr Webster – constituted an interference with their Article 11 rights.

2. The existence of a justification for the interference found by the Court
The Government expressly stated that, should the Court find an interference with a right guaranteed by para. 1 of Articles 9, 10 or 11, they would not seek to argue that such interference was justified under para. 2.

The Court has nevertheless decided that it should examine this issue of its own motion, certain considerations of relevance in this area being contained in the documents and information with which it has been furnished.

An interference with the exercise of an Article 11 right will not be compatible with para. 2 unless it was 'prescribed by law', had an aim or aims that is or are legitimate under that paragraph and was 'necessary in a democratic society' for the aforesaid aim or aims (see, *mutatis mutandis*, the *Sunday Times* judgment of 26.4.79, Series A no.30, p.29, section 45).

The applicants argued that the restrictions of which they complained met none of these three conditions.

The Court does not find it indispensable to determine whether the first two conditions were satisfied, these being issues which were not fully argued before it. It will assume that the interference was 'prescribed by law', within the meaning of the Convention (see the above-mentioned *Sunday Times* judgment, pp.30-31, sections 46-49), and had the aim, amongst other things, of protecting the 'rights and freedoms of others', this being the only one of the aims listed in para. 2 that might be relevant.

In connection with the last point, the Court's attention has been drawn to a number of advantages said to flow from the closed shop system in general, such as the fostering of orderly collective bargaining, leading to greater stability in industrial relations; the avoidance of a proliferation of unions and the resultant trade union anarchy; the counteracting of inequality of bargaining power; meeting the need of some employers to negotiate with a body fully representative of the workforce; satisfying the wish of some trade unionists not to work alongside non-union employees; ensuring that trade union activities do not enure to the benefit of those who make no financial contribution thereto.

Any comment on these arguments would be out of place in the present case since the closed shop system as such is not under review (see paragraph 82 above).

On the other hand, what has to be determined is the 'necessity' for the interference complained of: in order to achieve the aims of the unions party to the 1975 agreement with British Rail, was it 'necessary in a democratic society' to make lawful the dismissal of the applicants, who were engaged at a time when union membership was not a condition of employment?

A number of principles relevant to the assessment of the 'necessity' of a given measure have been stated by the Court in its *Handyside* judgment of 7.12.76 (Series A no.24).

Firstly, 'necessary' in this context does not have the flexibility of such expressions as 'useful' or 'desirable' (p.22, section 48). The fact that British Rail's closed shop agreement may in a general way have produced certain advantages is therefore not of itself conclusive as to the necessity of the interference complained of.

Secondly, pluralism, tolerance and broadmindedness are hallmarks of a 'democratic society' (p.23, section 49). Although individual interests must on occasion be subordinated to those of a group, democracy does not simply mean that the views of a majority must always prevail: a balance must be achieved which ensures the fair and proper treatment of minorities and avoids any abuse of a dominant position. Accordingly, the mere fact that the applicants' standpoint was adopted by very few of their colleagues is again not conclusive of the issue now before the Court.

Thirdly, any restriction imposed on a Convention right must be proportionate to the legitimate aim pursued (p. 23, section 49).

The Court has noted in this connection that a majority of the Royal Commission on Trade Unions and Employers' Associations, which reported in 1968, considered that the position of existing employees in a newly-introduced closed shop was one area in which special safeguards were desirable (see paragraph 21 above). Again, recent surveys suggest that, even prior to the entry into force of the Employment Act 1980 (see paragraph 32 above), many closed shop arrangements did not require existing non-union employees to join a specified union (see paragraph 18 above); the Court has not been informed of any special reasons justifying the imposition of such a requirement in the case of British Rail. Besides, according to statistics furnished by the applicants, which were not contested, a substantial majority even of union members themselves disagreed with the proposition that persons refusing to join a union for strong reasons should be dismissed from employment. Finally, in 1975 more than 95% of British Rail employees were already members of NUR, TSSA or ASLEF (see paragraph 46 above).

All these factors suggest that the railway unions would in no way have been prevented from striving for the protection of their members' interests (see the above-mentioned *National Union of Belgian Police* judgment, p. 18 section 39) through the operation of the agreement with British Rail even if the legislation in force had not made it permissible to compel non-union employees having objections like the applicants to join a specified union.

Having regard to all the circumstances of the case, the detriment suffered by Mr Young, Mr James and Mr Webster went further than was required to achieve a proper balance between the conflicting interest of those involved and cannot be regarded as proportionate to the aims being pursued. Even making due allowance for a State's 'margin of appreciation' (see, *inter alia*, the above-mentioned *Sunday Times* judgment, p.36, section 59), the Court thus finds that the restrictions complained of were not 'necessary in a democratic society', as required by para. 2 of Article 11.

There has accordingly been a violation of Article 11.

III. The alleged violation of Articles 9 and 10

The applicants alleged that the treatment of which they complained also gave rise to breaches of Articles 9 and 10. This was contested by the Government.

Having taken account of these Articles in the context of Article 11 (see paragraph 90 above), the Court, like the Commission, does not consider it necessary to determine whether they have been violated in themselves. . . .

Concurring opinion of Judges Ganshof van der Meersch, Bindschedler-Robert, Liesch, Matscher, Pinheiro Farinha and Pettiti
(Provisional translation)

We voted in favour of the operative provisions of the judgment, but the reasons which it contains do not appear to us to reflect properly the scope of freedom of association as guaranteed by Article 11 of the Convention.

By confining itself strictly to what it calls the 'substance' of the right, the Court's judgment leaves outside the protection of the Convention numerous situations entailed by legislation permitting the closed shop.

In fact, as we understand Article 11, the negative aspect of freedom of association is necessarily complementary to, a correlative of and inseparable from its positive aspect. Protection of freedom of association would be incomplete if it extended to no more than the positive aspect. It is one and the same right that is involved.

The '*travaux préparatoires*' of the Convention – which anyway are not conclusive – speak only of 'undesirability' and so do not enable one to conclude that the negative aspect of trade union freedom was intended to be excluded from the ambit of Article 11.

In its judgment, the Court rightly states that, in the present case, Article 11 has implications in the area covered by Articles 9 and 10 of the Convention. We should like to point out that it is not necessary, for there to be a violation of Article 11, that the refusal to join an association was justified by considerations connected with freedom of thought, of conscience or of religion, or with freedom of expression. In our view, the mere fact of being obliged to give the reasons for one's refusal constitutes a violation of freedom of association.

Trade union freedom, a form of freedom of association, involves freedom of choice: it implies that a person has a choice as to whether he will belong to an association or not and that, in the former case, he is able to choose the association. However, the possibility of choice, an indispensable component of freedom of association, is in reality non-existent where there is a trade union monopoly of the kind encountered in the present case.

Here, the sanction – be it the giving of notice or dismissal – which was a consequence of the system instituted by the law, did not give rise to but simply aggravated the violation. The violation, already constituted by compulsion in the shape of obligatory membership, is irreconcilable with the freedom of choice that is inherent in freedom of association. . . .

Dissenting opinion of Judge Sørensen, joined by Judges Thor Vilhjalmsson and Lagergren
To my regret I am unable to agree that Article 11 of the Convention has been violated in the present case, and I wish to state the reasons of dissent as follows.

The issue under Article 11 is whether or not freedom of association as protected by that Article implies a right for the individual not to be constrained to join or belong to any particular association, or in other words whether or not the so-called negative freedom of association or – in the terminology adopted by the Court – the negative aspect of the freedom of association is covered by Article 11.

The answer to this question must take account of the statement made by the Conference of Senior Officials in its report of 19.6.50 (see paragraph 78 of the judgment). It clearly emerges from this element of the drafting history that the States Parties to the Convention could not agree to assume any international obligation in the matter, but found that it should be subject to national regulation only.

The attitude thus adopted was entirely consistent with the attitude previously adopted within the framework of the International Labour Organisation. In dealing with questions of trade union rights and freedom to organise, the competent bodies of that organisation had traditionally held that union security arrangements were matters for regulation in accordance with national law and practice and could not be considered as either authorised or prohibited by the texts adopted in the ILO (see C. Wilfred Jenks, *The International Protection of Trade Union Freedom*, London 1957, pp. 29–30; Nicolas Valticos, *Droit international du travail*, Paris 1970, pp. 268–69; Geraldo von Potobsky, *The Freedom of the Worker to Organise according to the Principles and Standards of the International Labour Organisation*, in *Die Koalitionsfreiheit des Arbeitnehmers*, Heidelberg 1980, vol. II, at pp. 1132–36). This understanding has been maintained ever since and also been expressed by the States Parties to the European Social Charter of 1961 with respect to the obligations undertaken in virtue of that instrument (see Appendix, Part II, Article 1, para. 2).

During the proceedings in the present case it was argued on behalf of the respondent Government by the Solicitor-General that 'the scale of the closed shop system within Britain and the state of the common law was such that the inclusion within Article 11 of the right not to be compelled to join a union would inevitably have required the United Kingdom to make a reservation in respect of any such right' (verbatim record of the hearing on the morning of 4.3.81, doc. Cour (81) 19, p. 75).

Reference to the 'substance' of freedom of association is not relevant in the present context. Although the Court has often relied on the notion of the substance of the rights guaranteed by the Convention, it has done so only when the question was what regulation or limitation of a right was justified. It has held that even in cases where regulation or limitations were allowed explicitly or by necessary implication, they could not go so far as to affect the very substance of the right concerned. In the present case, however, the problem is whether the negative aspect of the freedom of association is part of the substance of the right guaranteed by Article 11. For the reasons stated above the States Parties to the Convention must be considered to have agreed not to include the negative aspect, and no canon of interpretation can be adduced in support of extending the scope of the Article to a matter which deliberately has been left out and reserved for regulation according to national law and traditions of each State Party to the Convention.

This conclusion is perfectly compatible with the nature and function of the rights in question. The so-called positive and negative freedom of association are not simply two sides of the same coin or, as the Court puts it, two aspects of the same freedom. There is no logical link between the two.

The positive freedom of association safeguards the possibility of individuals, if they so wish, to associate with each other for the purpose of protecting common interests and pursuing common goals, whether of an economic, professional, political, cultural, recreational or other character, and the protection consists in preventing public authorities from intervening to frustrate such common action. It concerns the individual as an active participant in social activities, and it is in a sense a collective right in so far as it can only be exercised jointly by a plurality of individuals. The negative freedom of association, by contrast, aims at protecting the individual against being grouped together with other individuals with whom he does not agree or for purposes which he does not approve. It tends to protect him from being identified with convictions, endeavours or attitudes which he does not share and thus to defend the intimate sphere of the personality. In addition, it may serve the purpose of protecting the individual against misuse of power by an association and against being manipulated by its leaders. However strongly such protection of the individual may sometimes be needed, it is neither in logic nor by necessary implication part of the positive freedom of association.

It follows that union security arrangements and the practice of the 'closed shop' are neither prohibited nor authorised by Article 11 of the Convention. Objectionable as the treatment suffered by the applicants may be on grounds of reason and equity, the adequate solution lies, not in any extensive interpretation of that Article but in safeguards against dismissal because of refusal to join a union, that is in safeguarding the right to security of employment in such circumstances. But this right is not among those recognised by the Convention which – as stated in the Preamble – is only a first step for the collective enforcement of human rights. At present, it is therefore a matter for regulation by the national law of each State.

The central difficulty in the court's (majority) judgment was its attempt to find a basis for deciding against the United Kingdom without, however, committing itself to the proposition that Art. 11 enshrined the 'negative right' not to be compelled to join a trade union. One can only guess why the court attempted this difficult task, but it seems likely that the reasons that led the Scandinavian judges to dissent from the court's judgment were influential in the matter. As the dissentients point out, the *travaux préparatoires* (a permissible and indeed mandatory guide to construction) seem to indicate clearly enough that the negative right was not intended to be guaranteed by the Convention – the concurring minority are unconvincing on this point – and to hold the opposite would be to depart from the practice of the International Labour Organization, the primary international body in the field of labour law. However, the court, being unwilling to join the concurring minority in finding the negative right to exist but being also unwilling to join the dissentient minority in finding the UK not in breach of the Convention, is driven into maintaining a number of unsatisfactory propositions, whose lack of conviction is only enhanced by the court's unclarity about the relationship between the different strands of argument.

The court's main argument was that the positive right to join a trade union, which Art. 11 clearly did guarantee, also implied 'some measure of freedom of choice as to its exercise'. It is no doubt possible to draw a line between protecting the 'willing unionist', who is being penalized for not being a member of a particular trade union, and protecting the right not to join a trade union at all, although, as both the Irish and the German experience shows,[1] courts that begin by protecting freedom of choice among unions usually end up by including within that freedom the choice not to belong to any union. More important, however, the distinction does not really help with the difficulty caused by the *travaux préparatoires*, since in the context of the UK a general right to choose among trade unions would be almost as destructive of the closed shop as the right not to belong at all, given the overlapping and competing nature of British trade unions, so that it is difficult to imagine that the UK in 1950 was prepared to accept the right to choose if it was not prepared to accept the right not to belong at all. Most important, the argument appeared irrelevant to the facts of the case before the court, since the applicants were asserting a right not to belong at all rather than a right to choose a union other than NUR, TSSA or ASLEF. Possibly each of the applicants would, if asked, have been able to describe an ideal union which he would have been prepared to join, but to extend freedom of choice to such fictitious unions is to reduce the distinction between this freedom and the right not to join a union at all virtually to the level of semantics.

To the common-law mind, seeking the narrowest ratio that will fit the facts of the case, the argument that the applicants' Art. 11 rights were being infringed because at the time they began their employment they were not contractually obliged to join a union, is an attractive one. It also has the merit of being a rule which is now embodied in British law (see above, p. 650). The argument here might be that, by accepting employment which is known in advance to require membership of a specified union, the employee waives his freedom to choose the union he will join. However, it would probably be wrong to place too much weight upon the hope that a subsequent court might interpret the decision under discussion in this way, simply because of its

[1] Von Prondzynski, op. cit., pp. 257–9.

attractiveness to British lawyers and practitioners, for it is only one of a number of rationales thrown out by the court. The court appears, for example, also to attach weight to the fact that the penalty the applicants suffered for non-membership of the specified union was loss of a job, thus suggesting that a lesser penalty might have been found not to infringe Art. 11, and to the fact that they were compelled to join a union 'contrary to their convictions'. There are obvious objections to both these lines of argument: if what the applicants were being compelled to do was contrary to Art. 11, surely any significant degree of pressure upon them (say, denial of promotion) would be as objectionable as dismissal, whilst, if the applicants' convictions were at the centre of the judgment, it is odd that the court did not elaborate further upon Arts. 9 (freedom of conscience) and 10 (freedom of expression).

The search for a satisfactory basis for the court's decision among the competing rationales of freedom of choice, existing non-membership, loss of a job and protection of personal convictions (or any permutation of these) is by no means merely an intellectual game. As a signatory to the Convention the UK is under an obligation in international law to bring its domestic law into line with the standards laid down in the Convention. However, even the law as enacted after EA 1982 is not consistent with a clear right not to join or even with some of the more extreme forms of the right-to-choose thesis. A right to choose would also cast doubt upon the validity of the Bridlington Principles (above, p. 611) and indeed this lesson was drawn by Lord Denning M.R. in *Cheall* v. *APEX* [1982] ICR 543. That case concerned the applicant's claim to be a member of a particular trade union and the House of Lords (above, p. 614) rejected it, *inter alia*, on the grounds that there was a distinction between being penalized (for example, by an employer) for exercising one's freedom of choice of trade union and asserting the right to require others to associate with you. The latter, the House thought, was not embraced by Art. 11, although they specifically reserved their position should a case, contrary to the facts of *Cheall*, arise subsequently out of a closed shop. On the other hand, if the rationale of the *Young* case is to be found in the existing non-unionist point or even the point about the applicants' convictions, the present law stands a better chance of surviving a challenge before the European Court of Human Rights. The main significance of the judgment in that case would lie in the restrictions it placed upon a future government that wished to return to a legal régime more like that established by TULRA 1976.

However, perhaps the most unsatisfactory feature of the court's judgment, and one which cannot be laid at the door of the court, was the decision of the Conservative government, reversing its Labour predecessor, not to rely on Art. 11(2) if the UK was found to be in breach of Art. 11(1). The argument available under Art. 11(2) was that the closed shop was necessary for the development and maintenance of collective bargaining and thus for the protection of the rights and freedoms of workers. It is understandable that a Conservative government should be unwilling to argue a proposition so obviously contrary to the domestic legislation it was enacting, but the result was that the European Commission on Human Rights refused to consider Art. 11(2) at all and the court did so only in terms of the question of whether the dismissal of the applicants was necessary in a democratic society to protect the freedoms of others. Not surprisingly, the court gave a negative answer, but, as von Prondzynski has pointed out,[1] this was surely not the correct question. The way in which the UK had breached Art. 11(1) was not by dismissing the applicants but by enacting the legislation permitting the closed shop. Had the necessity of the closed shop as an institution been canvassed, perhaps a clearer judgment with a more articulated balance between collective and individual interests would have emerged.

(d) Union labour and commercial contracts

So far we have viewed the closed shop as a matter concerning the employer and his employees. However, a requirement of union membership may in effect be imposed by a group of workers upon the employees of other employers, most commonly where employees refuse to handle goods which have come into their hands from an outside supplier who employs non-union labour or where they refuse to work alongside the non-union employees of an outside employer who have come on to the premises to install or repair equipment or, simply, to deliver goods. The refusal to handle non-union goods or to work alongside non-union labour is, of course, a form of industrial action on the part of the trade unionists, and the main issues to be discussed are the circumstances in which such action will involve the commission of a tort on the part of the unionists and the extent to which statutory immunity is provided against the tortious liability. These issues we shall mention briefly in the next section and discuss at greater length in Chapter 7. However, it may well be that the employer of the trade unionists is prepared to fall in with their wishes and in consequence refuses to contract with suppliers who cannot or will not use union labour in fulfilment of the contract. It is the legality of this action of the employer that we discuss here. Normally, the employer in question will have a closed-shop agreement or arrangement covering his own employees before he uses his contracting power to require outside suppliers to use union labour, but the relevant legal rules do not in fact depend upon such an arrangement being in existence.

The IRA 1971 did not directly concern itself with this matter. It was first dealt with by EA 1980, s.10 (introducing new EPCA 1978, ss.76B and 76C). The provisions were added to the Bill at a late stage and sought to address the situation via a complicated double-joinder procedure for unfair dismissal claims. By s.76B, where an employer ('the contractor') entered into a contract with an outside supplier and the contract required the work under the contract be done by union labour and, to put the matter briefly, an employee of the supplier was in consequence dismissed, then in any unfair

[1] Ibid., p. 265.

dismissal proceedings brought by the dismissed employee against his employer the outside supplier could join the contractor as a third party. Subject to certain conditions being proved, the contractor would then be obliged to indemnify the outside supplier in respect of any compensation payable to the employee. The contractor could in turn join any persons who had, by organizing industrial action or threatening to do so, put pressure upon him not to release the outside supplier from his contractual commitment (s.76C). Such persons might be ordered to indemnify the contractor or only to make a contribution to the compensation payable by him.

Thus, the EA 1980 sought to deal with this area as part of the re-formulation of the relationship between the closed shop and the law of unfair dismissal. Between 1980 and 1982 this approach came to be seen as containing the disadvantage that dismissal was the only possible detriment flowing from 'union-only' requirements that was compensable, whilst a broader range of losses was thought in fact to flow from such requirements. Moreover, ss.76B and C operated only where the contract required the use of union labour, whilst again it was possible in practice to impose a union-only requirement without resort to inserting such into the contract. Consequently, EA 1982 repealed s.10 of EA 1980, and ss.12 to 14 of EA 1982 set up a new scheme of a broader nature, ss.12 and 13 in effect replacing s.76B and s.14 dealing with industrial action arising out of union-only requirements.

Sections 12 and 13 have broken away entirely from the law of unfair dismissal, and their main impact has been to create a new statutory tort. S.12(1), however, first declares any term or condition of a contract for the supply of goods or services void in so far as it purports to require any of the work done for the purposes of the contract to be done by persons who are members of a trade union or a particular trade union or, indeed, persons who are not members of a trade union or a particular trade union. Like the new compensation provisions, s.12 thus applies as much to the right to associate as to the right to dissociate. Making such terms void protects the outside supplier against claims for damages for breach of such terms by the other party to the contract and, rather more important, prevents the employer imposing the requirement from terminating the contract for non-compliance where compliance with the requirement has been made a condition of the contract. S.12 is not, however, confined to contractual terms. It also deals with failure to include a person on a list of approved suppliers, excluding a person from a group of persons invited to tender for a contract, refusing to allow a person to submit a tender, refusing to contract with a person and terminating a contract for the supply of goods or services (s.12(2) and (3)). In each case the act is unlawful if it is done 'on the ground of union membership', i.e. on the ground that the work done or to be done involved or is likely to involve the use of non-union members or members of unions (or non-members or members of a particular trade union) (s.12(4)–(6)). It is here that the concept of a statutory tort is employed. The specified acts, done on ground of trade-union membership, do not amount to an offence, but the obligation not to do the specified acts on the specified grounds is a duty owed to the other actual or potential contracting party and to 'any person who may be adversely affected by its contravention' (s.12(7)). The government had in mind in particular when it included this latter catch-all phrase sub-contractors adversely affected when an employer failed to obtain a contract for the supply of goods or services and an employee made redundant as a consequence of such a failure, although one can foresee such cases giving rise to difficult issues of causation and remoteness.

The scope of s.12 is very broad in terms of the contracts it covers. The phrase 'a contract for the supply of goods or services' may exclude a contract of employment (as being a contract of service), but otherwise it seems all-embracing, certainly broad enough to include contracts for services and other *sui generis* contracts under which many workers are today employed (see above, pp. 86–106). Lewis and Simpson[1] have given the example of the union membership clauses in contracts for services concluded between actors, members of Equity, and members of the Society of West End Theatre Managers. Such clauses are rendered void by s.12. More important, the refusal of a manager to contract with an actor on grounds of his non-membership of Equity would seem to involve the commission of the statutory tort. On the other hand, s.12 renders the acts in question unlawful only when they are done on grounds of union membership. A refusal to contract on the grounds, say, that the potential contractor does not pay union wage rates or provide adequate safety training and equipment for his employees would not, provided it is the genuine ground for not contracting, seem to be caught by s.12. This may prove to be important to local councils that refuse to place on approved lists of tenderers employers who do not pay 'fair wages' (see above, p. 158). If the reasons for doing the prohibited acts are mixed, partly union membership grounds and partly other grounds, then s.12 makes it clear that the act is unlawful, even if union membership is only the subordinate reason for the act. However, imposition by certain local councils of a union recognition requirement upon their contractors, a practice which came to light after the Bill was published, did lead to the amendment of the Bill on the grounds that the union recognition requirement was too close a substitute for a union membership requirement. Accordingly, s.13 extends the provisions of s.12 to cover 'union exclusion', i.e. a contractual term requiring a person to recognize a trade union or to consult with a union or its officials is rendered void, and the doing of the acts specified in s.12 on grounds of non-recognition of or consultation with a union or its officials is brought within the statutory tort. S.13 does not cover the converse case of, say, a refusal to contract on the grounds that the potential contracting party *does* recognize a trade union. Although s.13 was probably envisaged by the government as merely blocking a potential loophole in the provisions of s.12, it has also achieved a certain

[1] Op. cit., p. 228.

symbolic status. Not only has the government ceased to give its support to the growth of union recognition after the repeal of the statutory recognition procedure by EA 1980, but it has now also rendered unlawful the use of private contracting power to that end. S.13 thus very clearly marks the change in government policy towards collective bargaining.

(e) Union labour and the law of industrial conflict

We ought finally to mention briefly at this point the relationship between the closed shop and the law of industrial conflict. One way of restricting the legality of the closed shop would be to declare that industrial action taken to secure the setting up or maintenance of a closed-shop agreement or arrangement is unlawful, i.e. no longer protected in respect of liability arising from the law of tort (see Chapter 6). Indeed, in so far as the closed shop is viewed as a unilateral instrument of trade-union power this might seem to be a very effective way of restricting it. There were certain provisions to this end in the IRA 1971, but as far as the closed shop as such is concerned the present law limits the special liabilities that can arise to joinder in unfair dismissal cases (above, p. 654). There are no special rules relating to immunity from tort liabilities so far as industrial action is concerned which is aimed at closed-shop arrangements between an employer and his employee, although, as we shall see in Chapter 7, the extent of the immunity against tort liability has been much curtailed in recent years, no matter what the purpose of the industrial action. However, when it comes to the imposition of union-only requirements upon other employers, there are special disabilities for such industrial action. S.14(1) of EA 1982 removes the immunities against tort liability from industrial action aimed to secure the inclusion in a contract of a term rendered void by ss.12(1) or 13(1) or the contravention of the duty imposed by ss.12(2) and 13(2) not to engage in certain contractual practices on grounds of union membership or union exclusion. We shall examine s.14(1) and indeed s.14(2)–(4) in more detail below (pp. 862–8), after we have looked at the basic structure of the law of industrial conflict.

It will have become clear that ss.12–14 of EA 1982 rival in complexity anything that can be found in the recent Employment Acts. However, it must not be thought that these sections deal only with problems that might exist in the minds of examiners. Large private-sector companies, at least in certain industries, traditionally employ large numbers of sub-contractors and, with the pressures for 'privatization' in the public sector, a greater use of contractors to provide services may be expected there also.

4 The law and democracy in trade unions

(a) Introduction

There is an extensive and long-standing literature on the question of how far trade unions are, or can be expected to be, democratic. The most persuasive argument that trade unions should be democratic in their internal affairs is a variation upon the general argument that the holders of power should be accountable to those on whose behalf they claim to exercise the power. Trade-union officials are, to varying degrees, holders of power to be exercised on behalf of the members of the union and should be accountable to the members for its exercise. This general argument should not, however, be taken to entail more than it does. The argument does not tell us very much about what degree of accountability should exist, about whether, for example, some degree of accountability should be sacrificed to other goals, such as speedy decision-making. Nor does the argument tell us very much about what mechanisms of accountability are most appropriate to trade unions. At a time when government proposals on trade-union democracy have come to centre upon secret ballots, it is important to remember that the underlying question is as to how far trade-union officials are responsive to the wishes of the membership, and secret ballots constitute only one way, and possibly not the best way, of achieving the underlying goal of accountability.

The government announced its intentions to develop legislative proposals in the area of trade-union democracy in its Green Paper, *Democracy in Trade Unions* (Cmnd. 8778, January 1983). After a period of consultation the Secretary of State for Employment announced in the House of Commons on 12 July 1983 that the government had three specific proposals that it would be bringing forward in a Bill in the autumn of 1983.[1] Each of these proposals had at its core the requirement of a secret ballot. It was envisaged that secret ballots would be required for elections to the governing bodies of trade unions, for industrial action called or endorsed by a trade union, and for the maintenance of political funds by trade unions. In this section of this chapter we shall deal with some of the issues raised by the first of these proposals, which is, of the three, the one that most clearly raises the issue of trade-union democracy. We shall deal with the third of these proposals in the next section of this chapter, where, as we shall see, the issue of union democracy is intertwined with rather different considerations relating to the financing of political parties. Finally, we shall deal with the second issue in Chapter 7. In this case there is a high degree of overlap between issues of internal democracy and the government's policy of restricting the legality of industrial action, for, as we shall see, the proposed sanction in respect of a failure by a union to hold a required ballot is that it should lose its normal immunities against liabilities in tort arising out of industrial action.

We now turn to issues of trade-union democracy as such. The Green Paper was based upon the view that trade unions are at present undemocratic or, at least, insufficiently democratic. As the Green Paper put it, 'at present few trade unionists can be confident that their unions' electoral arrangements are such that ... those who take decisions at the highest levels are properly representative of, and accountable to, the membership as a whole' (para. 5). Does the existing literature, which is well summarized in Jackson, *Industrial*

[1] Subsequently the Trade Union Bill (see Appendix).

Relations (2nd edn), pp. 75–82, suggest that a general worry about democracy in trade unions is in order? A good deal has been written about this issue and it may perhaps be useful to group the writings into four schools, or at least trends, of thought.

First, there is a point of view that democracy is an unreal ideal in a trade-union context. This is the view associated with Michels (*Political Parties* (1915)) and it is to the effect that once direct democracy becomes impracticable and is replaced by any less democratic form of organization, an inexorable tendency towards organizational oligarchy is set up. Upon this negative view one would presumably see legal intervention designed to secure union democracy as being essentially futile and unproductive.

Secondly, there are writers who view democracy as a feasible aim for trade unions but who insist that some special or even esoteric structure has to exist before that ideal can be realized. The best-known example of such thinking is the insistence by Lipset, Trow and Colman (*Union Democracy* (1956)) that the presence of an organized opposition within the union was necessary to the existence of internal democracy. In a similar though less esoteric vein Roderick Martin ('Union Democracy: An Explanatory Framework', *Sociology*, 1968) suggests that the existence of democracy within a trade union can be measured by reference to the survival of factions limiting executive ability to disregard rank and file opinion. Martin goes on to use his notion of the survival of factions to identify a series of factors which will tend to conduce to effective internal democracy.

Thirdly, there is a school of thought which seems to say that one should view British trade unions as being, on the whole, internally democratic, even if the reasons for so regarding them are not immediately obvious, that is to say, one should accept their democratic character even if that is not revealed by any simple litmus paper test for the existence of democracy. This seems, for instance, to be the conclusion reached by Clegg, who thinks that of all the various checks that can exist on union leadership, enough will normally exist in any given case to refute the suggestion of autocracy.

H. A. Clegg, *The System of Industrial Relations in Great Britain*[1] (3rd edn, 1976), pp. 112–13

To sum up, it is clear that British trade unions are not autocracies, and that trade union members have available to them a number of channels, varying from union to union, through which they can exert influence over their leaders. As in other large organizations, there is a tendency in trade unions for power to concentrate at the top, but there are also a number of checks upon leaders. Elections are held in all unions, and frequent elections in some. There are instances of rigged elections, but they seem to be relatively rare; and the low polls of most unions do not prove that votes are unrepresentative of the views of the members. Factions exist openly in almost all major unions, and in some unions they have wide liberty of action. Division of power between

[1] This thesis is developed at greater length in Clegg, *The Changing System of Industrial Relations* (1979), pp. 200–13.

two or more central decision-making bodies can act as a check especially where it is strengthened by decentralization to regions, districts, trade groups or branches. Workplace organization often has considerable autonomy in practice, and work groups can use this both to settle their affairs for themselves, and also to protest against decisions which national union leaders have taken or propose to take. The body of full-time officers may also exercise some restraint over the national leaders of a major trade union. To determine the extent to which any one union is democratically governed would require an examination of the working of all these formal and informal arrangements, and probably others, in its decision-making processes. Consequently there can be no simple test of whether a union is democratic.

Another more specific example of this third type of approach is perhaps provided by V.L. Allen (*Power in Trade Unions* (1954)) who argues that trade-union democracy will be secure as long as the association is a voluntary one (though he presumably would doubt the safety of internal democracy where there is a closed shop). A variant upon this theme is Fox's notion (*Sociology of Work in Industry*, 1971, pp. 123–4) that the authority of the leaders will inevitably come into question unless they pay a certain minimum of regard to the aspirations and views of their membership. The difficulty perhaps of accepting with Allen and Fox that we may take comfort in the nemesis which awaits trade-union leaders who overreach themselves is that substantial periods of time may have to elapse, during which internal democracy is at a very low ebb, before the structure gives way under the strain which the leadership has placed upon it.

The fourth school of thought (though it would be rash to insist on too rigid a distinction between these schools) is that which maintains that internal democracy does exist to a reasonable extent in some British trade unions but not in others, and that the drawing of this distinction depends upon a whole range of empirical factors. The most developed exposition of this line of analysis seems to occur in the research paper prepared by J. Hughes for the Donovan Commission ('Trade Union Structure and Government', Research Paper 5 (Part 2), 1968). His chief contribution was to emphasize above all the importance of the level of participation by the membership, and to develop an account of factors militating for or against high membership participation in the government of trade unions.

Perhaps one may suggest that the majority view is that democracy exists within trade unions to a sufficient degree and that for those who have doubts these do not particularly focus upon the issue of secret ballots for trade-union office. (The argument of Michels is clearly somewhat apart, since he denies the proposition that representative democracy can exist in the long run: either the members take all the decisions themselves or the decisions not so taken will be taken by oligarchies.) From our point of view, however, perhaps the outstanding feature of the literature we have summarized is that it consists of sociological writings: the legal literature on democracy within trade unions is exiguous. To a large extent this can no doubt be explained by the fact that at present there is little statutory regulation of internal trade-union affairs in the name of democracy and that this is not a new situation but rather reflects the history of our trade-union law. However, such an explanation merely pushes the inquiry one stage further back: why should our trade-union law be marked by the absence of such legislation? No doubt, regulation of trade-union government initially benefited (or suffered) from the reluctance of the legislators of the Trade Union Act 1871 (see above, p. 592) to do more than relieve trade unions from the restraint of trade doctrine, whilst, later, non-interference in internal trade-union affairs was accepted as an aspect of the doctrine of collective *laissez-faire*, an approach buttressed by the view that trade-union officials, as the Donovan Commission found, rarely abused their power. However, Professor Kahn-Freund suggested a more principled reason for abstention of the law in this area:

O. Kahn-Freund, *Labour and the Law* (2nd edn, 1977), pp. 211–12

But why should there be no parties inside the unions if there are parties in central and even local government? Though one (it seems not unsuccessful) attempt at party government has been made in one big American union, this has remained an isolated example even in the United States. As far as I know, no such experiment has ever been made in this country or elsewhere in Europe. I suggest that it cannot be made. Why not? Apart from the type of behaviour known as treason, the Government, the State, does not have to reckon with secession, split, breakaway, and neither does a municipal corporation. They can afford to have political parties as long as they are not threatened with a civil war. However violently a member of the opposition may disagree with those in office, the government remains his government; he cannot quit. His party cannot 'secede' and form a fresh Kingdom or urban district council. But a union opposition can secede. The formation of organised groups with different programmes is a mortal threat to a voluntary association such as a political party or a trade union. There cannot in a union or other voluntary association be 'parties' – there can only be 'factions' or 'coteries' who do not operate at the hustings or in the market place but in a backroom or an antechamber.

This, I suggest, is vital. It explains why, for example, electioneering, the most normal and legitimate form of political agitation, is frowned upon by many union constitutions; why participation in union elections is so poor (there is no fight between groups with which the voter can identify himself); why it is so easy for minorities representing outside interests or creeds to dominate elections. There is a formidable case against an overdose of elective democracy in a voluntary body, and especially in a body always and inevitably threatened by disruption because it is a fighting body which may be attacked by outside hostile interests working from inside.

Is not all this fairly obvious? Why mention it here? Because it teaches a very important lesson on the role the law can or cannot play in these matters. It is impracticable, or at least inadvisable, for the law to lay down minimum rules of 'democracy' to be followed by all unions, irrespective of the constitutions they themselves have adopted. To this extent, then, the *pouvoir constituant* of each union should remain inviolate and not be transferred to the State and its law. I am saying this not only because of the obvious need for protecting the autonomy of the unions, but also because I do not believe that union democracy is so clearly desirable that it should to any extent be imposed by the State. In fact the comparison of any given set of union constitutions in this country – take the two largest, the TGWU and the AUEW – shows the wide differences in the dose of 'democracy' injected into these constitutions. Here – and I do not believe this is at all controversial – autonomy is better than uniformity.

Before examining the way in which our statute law between 1871 and 1971 reflected the view that it was 'impracticable, or at least inadvisable' for the law to prescribe internal structures for trade unions, the changes made by the IRA 1971, the reversion to the policy of abstention in TULRA 1974–6, and the present proposals, it is worth saying something by way of description about the component parts of the machinery of trade-union government. Precisely because statute has not prescribed a model for trade-union government but rather has left trade unions to develop in the way that seemed best to the members and officials of each trade union, this is a subject upon which it is very difficult to generalize. Many accounts of trade-union government take as a basic unit the branch, which is sometimes based on a workplace but more usually consists of all the members of the union, no matter by whom employed, who work in a particular geographical area. The branch may elect representatives to an annual conference, which decides the general policy of the union. An elected executive council may be responsible for running the union's affairs on a day-to-day basis within the policy declared by conference, and a general secretary (a full-time employee of the union) executes the decisions of the council and supervises the union's other full-time officials. Such might be a simplified account of trade-union government. It must be emphasized that many unions depart from this simple model and in any case such an organizational chart may give one a misleading picture of actual relations between its constituent parts. The general secretary may, for example, dominate the executive council rather than act as its servant, and the executive may guide conference as much as conference guides the executive. Nevertheless, as the Green Paper points out, 'common to all trade unions . . . is a governing body and some form of national lay conference' (para. 24), and the organizational chart at least indicates the main features of unions' constitutions. Its main defect, in fact, is that it gives no place to union organization below the level of the branch in terms of workshop representation through stewards and convenors. Indeed, many union rule-books do not refer to workplace representation in any systematic form because its growth is relatively recent, but to many workers the union *is* the shop steward and the integration of workplace organization into union structure is as important for union democracy as the integration of workplace bargaining into the 'formal' system of collective bargaining is for the determination of terms and conditions of employment (above, p. 122).

(b) Legal control of trade-union rules

The modern law of trade-union government dates from the Trade Union Act

1871, which was the basic statute in this area for a century, before it was repealed by IRA 1971. As we have already noted (above, p. 592) for a variety of reasons the legislators in 1871 were unwilling to provide legal remedies on a broad basis in relation to matters arising out of internal trade-union affairs. There was perhaps a greater feeling at that time than today that the law should not interfere in the internal affairs of private associations, and the policy was applied particularly strongly to the newly legalized trade unions. The best-known expression of this policy was s.4 of the 1871 Act, but the policy also informed the provisions of the Act concerning trade-union government. The essence of the policy was that the form and structure of the internal government of the trade union was for the union itself to decide upon. All the Act did, in s.14 and Sch. 1, was to require the union to have rules on a limited range of matters. The nature of the rules was for the union to decide; the aim of the Act was simply to ensure that the rules 'provided the main essentials of a legal constitution'.[1] Some fourteen matters were listed in Sch. 1, of which the most important (from our point of view) were the union's objects, the appointment and removal of a committee of management, trustees and a treasurer, and the periodical audit of accounts.

Thus, the Act did not require the union's rules to take any particular form (any method of appointment or election, for example, of the committee of management was permissible) nor was any such power conferred upon the Registrar of Friendly Societies, the state official charged with supervision of the law relating to trade unions. This policy was not significantly entrenched upon in the succeeding century. Only in relation to the rules concerning the political fund did the legislature in the Trade Union Act 1913 (still the governing legislation on this matter) require union rules to contain specific provisions, the most important being that union members should be entitled to claim exemption from the obligation to contribute to the political fund. We shall discuss the law relating to the political fund in greater detail in the next section. To a large extent the provisions of the IRA 1971, in so far as they related to union rules, followed the policy of the 1871 Act. Sch. 4 of IRA 1971 regulated the rule-books of registered trade unions and in large part required unions to have rules on certain matters rather than to have particular rules. There were some important departures from this principle. For example, it was required that 'the rules must make provision . . . for the election of a governing body and for its re-election at reasonable intervals' (para 4). The choice of method of appointment of the governing body was thus removed from the hands of registered unions. The schedule also required unions to have rules on matters not covered by the 1871 Act, for example, as to the bodies or officials of the union who were authorized to call industrial action on behalf of the union. Although the union could choose the form of rules it wished to have, so that this requirement did not seem to depart from the policy of the 1871 Act, the clear link between this provision as to unions' rules and the removal

[1] *Citrine's Trade Union Law* (3rd edn, 1967), p. 232.

elsewhere in the Act of unions' immunity from suit arising out of industrial action (see below, pp. 819–26), caused Sch. 4 of the IRA 1971 to be treated as a whole with great suspicion by trade unions.

The policy of the Labour government elected in 1974 was to exorcize the spectre of state control of unions' rule-books and, after some delay caused by Conservative opposition to TULRA 1974, this result was achieved with TULRA 1976, and the current law is as contained in these two Acts. The policy of exorcism was seen to require even the abandonment of the policy of the TUA 1871. There are currently no statutory provisions relating to the content of the unions' rules, except those in the TUA 1913 concerning the political fund.[1] TULRA 1974, s.6, which had carried over the provisions of Sch. 4 of IRA 1971, was repealed by TULRA 1976, s.1(*b*) and there was no revival of the requirements of Sch. 1 to TUA 1871. In practice this may be thought to matter little, since unions do in fact have rule-books that cover the matters listed in the 1871 Act. On the other hand, it is worth mentioning at this point that the disclosure provisions of TULRA 1974, ss.10–12 and Sch. 2 represent a considerable advance upon the provisions contained in the TUA 1871. The Act requires all trade unions to keep proper accounting records, to have the accounts audited and to submit an annual return to the Certification Officer (who is now the statutory supervisory official). The annual return and the union's rules which must accompany it are open to public inspection. The Act also requires unions that operate a members' superannuation scheme to have it periodically examined by a qualified actuary.

Given, however, the exiguous statutory controls over unions' rule-books, how have the courts decided cases raising issues of internal democracy? The first point to be made about the case-law is that one should not expect to find in it any overt commitment on the part of the judges to any particular theory about internal trade-union democracy. Indeed, the very notion of internal democracy does not figure at all prominently in the judgments, and when it does it tends to be seen far more in terms of the individual right of access to the democratic process than in terms of an aim of representativeness for the organization seen as a whole. Instead of the arguments about the dictates of trade-union democracy that one finds in treatises on industrial relations, one finds in the judgments the same concern with natural justice, with the strict enforcement of the rule-book as a contract, with the restraining of *ultra vires* or arbitrary action, as is found throughout the reasoning in cases on trade-union discipline and expulsion (and, for that matter, refusal of admission). This is not to say, however, that the judges are not concerned with internal democracy. They are astute enough to discover instances of autocratic behaviour by the ruling majority in a trade union, however constituted. Perhaps the most developed use of these techniques is to be found in the judgment of Lord Denning M.R. in *Breen* v. *AEU* (below). Although his was a

---

[1] Under the Trade Union (Amalgamations etc.) Act 1964 the Certification Officer must approve the instrument of amalgamation or transfer (s.1).

dissenting judgment, the other judges based their judgments upon a point of fact and would not, it is thought, have taken a very different view of the law had they shared Lord Denning's view of the facts.

Breen v. *Amalgamated Engineering Union* [1971] 1 QB 175 (CA)

In 1965 the plaintiff was elected shop steward by his fellow workers, but under the union's rules his appointment needed also the approval of the union's district committee. On 9 December 1965 the committee decided not to approve the plaintiff's election and re-confirmed its decision on 30 December, after a protest from the plaintiff. The plaintiff was not invited to attend either meeting. After the second meeting Mr Townsend, a full-time official of the union and the committee's secretary, was instructed to write to the plaintiff giving the committee's reasons for the refusal. One of the reasons given, that the plaintiff had in 1958 resigned as shop steward in the aftermath of an allegation about misappropriation of union funds, was false. The committee had the falsity of the reason pointed out to it at its meeting on 6 January, but nevertheless decided to stand by the letter. The plaintiff sought a declaration that the committee's decision was invalid and damages. The trial judge found that the false reason had not been mentioned at the meeting of 9 December and that Mr Townsend had written his letter in the honest, but mistaken, view that what he said was correct.

LORD DENNING M.R.: . . . So here we have Mr Breen. He was elected by his fellow workers to be their shop steward. He was their chosen representative. He was the man whom they wished to have to put forward their views to the management, and to negotiate for them. He was the one whom they wished to tell the union about their needs. As such he was a key figure. The Royal Commission on Trade Union and Employers' Associations ((1968) Cmnd. 3623) under Lord Donovan paid tribute to men such as he, p. 29, para. 110:

> shop stewards are rarely agitators pushing workers towards unconstitutional action . . . quite commonly they are supporters of order exercising a restraining influence on their members in conditions which promote disorder.

Seeing that he had been elected to this office by a democratic process, he had, I think, a legitimate expectation that he would be approved by the district committee, unless there were good reasons against him. If they had something against him, they ought to tell him and to give him a chance of answering it before turning him down. It seems to be intolerable that they should be able to veto his appointment in their unfettered discretion. This district committee sit in Southampton some miles away from Fawley. None of them, so far as I know, worked in the oil refinery. Who are they to say nay to him and his fellow workers without good reasons and without hearing what he has to say?

To be fair to them, the district committee did not claim that they could act without good reasons. They said that they had good reasons. They were set out by their secretary with their authority in the letter of 31 December 1965. And, when examined, the very first reason they gave was a bad reason. It was that he had misappropriated union funds seven years ago; whereas in truth he had done nothing of the sort and had been acquitted of the charge. So long as that letter stands as the vehicle of their reasons, their disapproval must be utterly invalid; for, on the face of it, they were actuated by a highly prejudicial consideration which was entirely erroneous and which they ought not to have taken into account at all. Call it prejudice, bias, or what you will. It is enough to vitiate the discretion of any body, statutory, domestic, or other. To make it worse, they did not give him a chance of answering it or correcting it. They condemned him unheard.

At a very late stage, however, the district committee threw over the letter, or, at any rate, this reason which it contained. They said that it was never discussed at their meeting and was a mistake made by their secretary. They called some of those present to give evidence of what they remembered of the meeting four years before. The judge summarized the result in these words:

> Some members may have had a lurking and quite undefined impression in their minds about some trouble in 1958 about money. At least two of them indeed have given evidence saying that they had such an impression in their minds. What I am quite sure about, however, and so hold, is that there was no mention at the committee of the 1958 episode and no discussion about it: it played no part in the committee's decision.

In so finding, the judge made no reference to Mr Townsend. Mr Townsend certainly was influenced by the bad reason. He wrote it down in the letter. He repeated it later, saying to Mr Breen 'You had the money, brother.' I expect the judge thought that Mr Townsend's state of mind did not matter because he had no vote. But I think it mattered a lot. He was the district secretary, a paid official there permanently. The others were elected annually. They came and went. He stayed on. He knew all about the episode in 1958. It was his job to know it. It is true that he had no vote, but he had a voice and he had a pen. The judge finds that there was little discussion at the meeting, but I would venture to ask: were there not private discussions beforehand? We know that does happen in the most sophisticated committees. Things are often decided beforehand so as to save discussion and dissension at the meeting itself. And when this committee were asked for their reasons, they told their secretary, Mr Townsend, to write them down for them. What better evidence could there be that he participated, at some stage or other, in the decision-making? And that the reason given by him in his letter was a reason which influenced some of the members, at any rate? I would, therefore, for myself reject the judge's finding that the reason 'played no part in the committee's decision'. It obviously played an important part.

In any case, however, I think it was not open to the district committee to throw over the reason stated in the letter. A week later, after the truth was out, they deliberately decided to stand by the reason. They stood by it in their pleading for a long time. They only renounced it years later. It was then too late. On principle it seems to me that, when a committee or body of persons, who are entrusted with a decision, give reasons for it in writing which are clear and unambiguous, then it is not open to the individual members of that body, be they one or many, to give evidence to add to, vary or contradict the reasons which have been given authoritatively on behalf of all. If that were permitted, one of them might say one thing; another another: and no one would know which was correct especially when the evidence comes years after the meeting, as happened here. More important, the party affected by the decision is entitled to go by the stated reasons. It is on the basis of them that he determines whether to accept the decision or to challenge it. It would be unfair to him to allow individual members of the committee to go back on the stated reasons. Lord Goddard c.j. put a similar point clearly in *R.* v. *Licensing Authority for Goods Vehicles for the Metropolitan Traffic Area, Ex parte B. E. Barratt Ltd* [1949] KB 17, 22:

> where the language of a tribunal . . . is clear and there is no ambiguity, it would be quite wrong for this court to entertain affidavit evidence or other matter to try to

explain that the tribunal, whether it is justices or any other tribunal, meant something different from what it said.

I hold, therefore, that the committee are bound by the reason stated in the letter. It was a reason which showed that they were activated by extreme prejudice against Mr Breen, which was quite unjustified. Their decision, therefore, cannot stand.

The general thrust of Lord Denning's judgment was to vindicate the individual's interest – or, in Lord Denning's words, his 'legitimate expectation' – in being approved as shop steward by the committee after his election by his fellow workers. This individualist approach is a direct application of the kind of rhetoric found in the expulsion and exclusion cases rather than a manifestation of any particular theory of internal democracy, but it does tend, of course, to reduce the importance attached by the courts to issues of collective effectiveness. A similar approach, although one much more firmly grounded in this case in the traditional basis of the contract embodied in the trade union rule-book, can be found in *Leigh* v. *National Union of Railwaymen* [1970] Ch. 326 (concerning the right to be a candidate for president of the union); and in *Stevenson* v. *URTU* [1977] I C R 893 (concerning the dismissal of a trade-union official – above, p. 517) notions derived from administrative law were, as in *Breen*, deployed to the benefit of the plaintiff.

(c) Secret ballots and other methods of control of trade-union government
In the previous section we looked at the limited extent to which the law controls the content of trade-union rule-books. Control of trade-union government need not, of course, take the form of control of the rule-book. As with control of the employment relationship, control may take the form of a mandatory shaping of the contract (as with the Equal Pay Act) or of stipulations that operate from outside the contract but nevertheless override contrary provisions in the contract (as with the right not to be unfairly dismissed). What is the extent of the legislation of the latter type that exists on matters of trade-union government? Given the policy of the legislators of the TUA 1871 it is not surprising that that legislation yields no examples of the type we are looking for. The IRA 1971, however, did contain 'guiding principles' for the conduct of internal trade-union affairs, as we have already noted (above, p. 625), and some of these concerned trade-union government, as distinct from questions of admission or expulsion. The guiding principles applied to all trade unions, registered or not, and so in practice were more important than the Sch. 4 provisions on the content of the rule-book, which applied only to the few registered unions. Contravention of the guiding principles amounted to the commission of a statutory tort by the union. The relevant provisions of IRA 1971, s.65, were as follows:

(4) No member of the organization, or of any branch or section of the organization, shall, by way of any arbitrary or unreasonable discrimination, be excluded from –

(a) being a candidate for or holding any office in the organization or in a branch or section of it;

(b) nominating candidates for any such office;
(c) voting in any election for any such office or in any ballot of members of the organization or of a branch or section of it; or
(d) attending and taking part in meetings of the organization or of any branch or section of the organization.

(5) The voting in any ballot of members of the organization, or of a branch or section of the organization, shall be kept secret.

(6) In any ballot, and on any motion, in respect of which he is entitled to vote, every member of the organization shall have a fair and reasonable opportunity of voting without interference or constraint.

S.65(4) in particular seemed to reflect the individualist bias of the common law rather than any underlying theory of trade-union government. However, it led to little litigation before the repeal of the IRA 1971 in 1974 and there was little evidence that it brought about in this period any significant changes in the practice of trade unions. The present law contains no provisions comparable to the guiding principles of s.65(4)–(6), but as part of the enactment of anti-discrimination legislation the law does now impose upon trade unions in their internal affairs the requirement not to discriminate on grounds of sex, marital status, race, colour, nationality, or ethnic or national origins. By the SDA 1975, s.12(3)(*a*) and RRA 1976, s.11(3)(*a*), the principle of non-discrimination is applied to 'access to any benefits facilities or services' provided by the union and by ibid., s.12(3)(*c*) and 11(3)(*c*), the union is required not to discriminate by subjecting the member to 'any other detriment', which would include, presumably, the denial of the freedom to do the things mentioned in s.65(4) of IRA 1971 on the forbidden grounds. It will be interesting to see whether these provisions of the SDA and RRA trigger off any more general common-law developments, perhaps by extension of the notions of administrative law utilized in *Breen* and *Stevenson*, perhaps by borrowing from company law notions of fiduciary duty, so as to impose upon trade unions a general duty of non-discrimination, both in the internal affairs of the union proper and in the union's representational activities *vis-à-vis* outsiders, especially employers. In this way might English law begin to create its own duty of fair representation along the lines of American law.

However things may turn out at common law, the most recent legislative changes and, more important, proposals for change in this area, by concentrating upon the question of secret ballots, have marked a decisive change of emphasis. The individualist concerns of the guiding principles seem to have been abandoned, or at least regarded as having been sufficiently satisfied by the provisions on admission and expulsion contained in EA 1980 (above, pp. 624–30), for, whatever one may think of the theory, it does seem clear that the ballot proposals are based upon *a* theory of trade-union government. It should be made clear at the outset that the principle of mandatory, statutory ballots is not a new one for trade-union law, since both the TUA 1913 (for the political fund) and the Trade Union (Amalgamations etc.) Act 1964 (for mergers between unions) contain examples of such provisions. In both these cases, however, the purpose of the statutes containing the ballots was such as to win trade-union support for them, whereas the proposals put forward in the Green Paper, *Democracy in Trade Unions* (1983), were perceived by trade unions as hostile to their interests. The TUA 1913 provided a statutory procedure, of which a ballot is, as we shall see, an integral part, whereby to avoid the common-law decision of the House of Lords that the unions could not spend any of their funds on political purposes (see *Amalgamated Society of Railway Servants* v. *Osborne* [1910] AC 87). The 1964 Act, passed without debate in Parliament following pressure for legislative reform by the TUC, is, as Patrick Elias makes clear,[1] the latest of a series of statutes, beginning with the Trade Union (Amendment) Act 1876, whose purpose has been to facilitate mergers between trade unions. To this end the requirements to be met before a merger can take place have been progressively eased, so that, today, as far as voting is concerned, an amalgamation requires the consent of a majority of those voting in each amalgamating union and a transfer of engagements the consent of the majority of those voting in the transferor union only. Not surprisingly the transfer of engagements is the more popular method of amalgamation. Without these statutory provisions any single member of the amalgamating unions might well be able to block the merger. The proposals in the 1983 Green Paper, on the other hand, were based upon the view that the internal procedures of trade unions needed reform, as being insufficiently democratic, rather than upon a policy of facilitating the unions' own objectives.

Thus, it was not so much the proposed statutory requirements for ballots that aroused controversy, as the reasons put forward in the Green Paper for extending the ballot requirements. The Green Paper in fact put forward a number of suggested rationales for a much extended balloting requirement as part of the machinery of trade-union government, but it was perhaps not sufficiently careful to distinguish among the different implications of the rationales. One argument was that trade-union rule-books are often 'confused, self-contradictory and obscure' about the method of appointment of the governing body and sometimes other bodies and officials (para. 10). This is not an argument for any particular method of appointing the governing body, let alone for the use of secret ballots, but only for compelling unions to have clear rules on the matter. It is, in fact, very much the sort of argument that animated the legislators of the TUA 1871 and it does not provide a justification for going much beyond the provisions of that Act. A second argument or set of arguments was that present union election arrangements produce only a low turn-out and are open to manipulation through various forms of malpractice (paras. 9 and 12). It is unclear how far the latter allegation is correct, but even so these are arguments only in favour of requiring unions to use effective, secret ballots where the union decides that an

---

[1] 'Trade Union Amalgamations: Patterns and Procedures' (1973) 2 *ILJ* 125.

election or a ballot is the appropriate way of deciding a particular matter. They are not arguments for requiring a union to use secret ballots when it would otherwise have not employed a ballot at all to decide the matter. It might, for example, simply appoint an official rather than elect him.

However, since the general thrust of the Green Paper, although it was formally only a consultative document, was that trade unions should be required not only to have clear rules, not only to use secret ballots when they decide to ballot at all, but also to use secret ballots on occasions when they might at present not think a ballot appropriate, it was the third rationale which was clearly at the heart of the Green Paper. This was variously expressed as being that 'in the case of many unions the role and influence of the rank and file seems to be minimal and all too often it is evident that the policies which are being pursued do not reflect the views and interests of the members' (para. 1) and that 'time and again union leaders are seen to be out of touch with their rank and file and often appear to be neither representative of the majority of their members nor directly responsible to them' (para. 7).

Three comments may be briefly offered on these central propositions. First, no empirical evidence is set out or referred to in support of them nor is any of the literature summarized at the beginning of this section referred to. It might be thought that that literature does not support the strong statements contained in the Green Paper (except the writings of Michels, the corollary of whose views is, presumably, that any legislation that does not insist upon direct democracy will be ineffective), and, more important, that the literature suggests that the question of union officials' responsiveness to the members involves much more than merely issues of election versus appointment and the choice among various electoral systems. Second, there is implicit in the Green Paper, and especially in its discussion of strike ballots (paras. 56–70, discussed in greater detail below (pp. 830, 883)), the view that making union officials more accountable to their members will cause them to pursue more moderate policies. It must be said that it is doubtful whether there is any long-term tendency for union leaderships generally to be more militant than their membership, and some evidence that instincts for institutional preservation, which may be expected to be found more strongly among leaders than led, are likely to make union national officials, at least, more conservative than their members. Finally, there was no discussion in the Green Paper of the arguments against enforced democracy in trade unions or of the need to balance the arguments pro and con. There was no reference, for example, to the arguments of Kahn-Freund, quoted at the beginning of the section, about the dangers of too much democracy to the cohesiveness of the union as a fighting body or to the well-known debate about the need to give leaders, whether union officials or not, the freedom to take initiatives and about the unwisdom of treating them as mere delegates of those they represent. The authors of the Green Paper seemed to feel themselves able to ignore these issues because their view seemed to be that unions are so undemocratic that corrective action is unlikely to run the risk of conflict with these other organizational goals.

Perhaps because the government itself felt the force of some of these arguments, the government's conclusions, announced in the document *Proposals for Legislation on Democracy in Trade Unions*, published in July 1983 after the period of consultation initiated by the Green Paper, were confined to a proposal to legislate so as to require secret (but not necessarily postal) ballots as the method of selecting the members of the governing bodies of trade unions. This proposal would embrace also the presidents or general secretaries of trade unions if they had a vote or a casting vote on the governing body of their union. The ballot, which would be required at least once every five years, would in addition have to be based on the principles of marking a ballot paper, equal and unrestricted opportunities for each member of the union to vote, and direct election of the members of the governing body (as against, say, election by a national delegate conference of the union). These obligations, it was proposed, should constitute a statutory duty owed by the union to each of its members and be enforceable by any member of the union, ultimately by the penalties of contempt of court.[1] Legislation confined to governing bodies might in the end go little beyond the provisions of Sch. 4 to IRA 1971 (above, p. 676), although it would no doubt have a greater impact in practice because not confined to registered unions.

Whatever may be the legislative outcome of these proposals, the EA 1980 already contains two minor provisions concerning secret ballots. By EA 1980, s.1 the Secretary of State may by regulations set up a scheme to reimburse trade unions for certain costs incurred in holding secret ballots (s.1(5)) for the purposes of obtaining the views of the membership on the calling or ending of industrial action or on the acceptability of an employer's offer, of carrying out an election provided for by the rules of the union, of electing a trade unionist to represent his fellow employees (i.e. a shop steward), of amending the rules of the union or of obtaining a decision in a proposed merger (s.1(3) and SI 1982 No. 953). A scheme for payment was subsequently established by statutory instrument, which confined the reimbursement to secret *postal* ballots and also did not provide for reimbursement in respect of ballots held for all the purposes specified in the Act. Elections of workplace union representatives were wholly excluded and only certain elections provided for by the rules of the union were included, notably elections to the national executive committee of the union, to the presidency or chairmanship of the union, and to any position as an employee of the union. The scheme has had little impact in practice because the unions affiliated to the TUC decided not to make claims for reimbursement. A similar fate has befallen s.2 of EA 1980. This enables recognized unions to require all but the smallest employers to permit their premises to be used for the holding of a secret ballot for one or more of the purposes covered by s.1. The employer must comply with the request if it is reasonably practicable for him to do so. Non-compliance may lead a tribunal to award the

[1] See now Appendix.

union such compensation as is just and equitable in the circumstances, having regard to the employer's default in failing to comply with the request and any expenses incurred by the union as a result. This seems to be the only situation in which a tribunal may award compensation to the union for itself and not, as with, say, the protective award, in favour of its members.

5 Trade-union political funds[1]

In contrast to the general picture of non-intervention by the law in matters of trade-union government which emerges from the previous section, the particular area of the collection and expenditure by trade unions of funds for political purposes is one that has been closely regulated by statute since the passing of the Trade Union Act 1913. In some ways the existence of the TUA 1913 is the result of an accident. One may guess with some confidence that, but for the decision of the House of Lords in *Amalgamated Society of Railway Servants v. Osborne* [1910] AC 87, this aspect of trade-union activity would have continued to benefit from the legislative policy of abstention evidenced by the TUA 1871 and the Trade Union (Amendment) Act 1876, subject, of course, to any general legislation on the matter of financing political campaigns such as is contained at present in the rather inadequate Representation of the People Act 1949, s.63. However, in that case the House of Lords, in a decision remarkable even in a period of fundamental judicial decisions on labour law matters, held that for a union to impose upon its members a compulsory levy for the purposes of creating a parliamentary fund to promote Labour Members of Parliament was unlawful as being *ultra vires* the union, i.e. beyond its legal capacity. The decision involved three legal steps. First, the House had to treat the union as a corporate or, at least, a quasi-corporate entity, for the doctrine of *ultra vires* has no application to unincorporated bodies; second, the House had to treat the definition of a trade union in the TUA 1876 as an exhaustive statement of the proper objects of a trade union; and, third, these objects had to be construed as not permitting political activity, at least of the type contemplated by the union in this case.

All three steps in this argument were controversial. We have already noted (above, p. 592) that it seems highly unlikely that the legislators of the TUA 1871, in relieving trade unions from the restraint of trade doctrine, intended to confer corporate or quasi-corporate status upon them. It also seems unlikely that the statutory definition of a trade union in s.16 of TUA 1876 was intended to be a statement of trade-union capacity: if an organization was to count as a trade union it clearly had to meet the requirement of s.16 that it be a 'combination . . . for regulating relations between workmen and masters, or between workmen and workmen . . . or for imposing restrictive conditions on the conduct of any trade or business', but it did not necessarily follow that any purpose additional to the statutory ones was *ultra vires*. Given the *laissez-faire*

[1] See generally Keith Ewing, *Trade Unions, the Labour Party and the Law* (1982), to which we are much indebted.

approach of the legislators of the TUA 1871–6 it seems more likely that the definition was intended to identify the purposes that were to be relieved from the restraint of trade doctrine rather than to prohibit a trade union from having broader purposes. Finally, the rejection of the argument that it was reasonably incidental to the pursuit of the statutory objects to engage in the promotion of Labour MPs amounted to a strict application of the *ultra vires* doctrine. Indeed, if it is right that the *ultra vires* doctrine should be so strictly applied to the issue of 'implied powers', then that must place in doubt the legality of political donations by companies when, as is often the case, the company has no express power in its constitution permitting political donations. Yet such donations are usually assumed to be *intra vires*.[1]

It seems clear that the House in the *Osborne* case, or at least the majority of their lordships, were determined to clear these three hurdles because of an underlying constitutional objection to what the union was proposing to do. That objection stemmed from the view that the individual MP is a representative of his constituents but not a delegate and must act on the dictates of his reason and not vote in a particular way because he is beholden to any outside group. In particular, there was objection to the fact that the union was prepared to promote only Labour MPs. The acceptance of the Labour whip would oblige the MP to vote in the way the Parliamentary Labour Party wished, even if this contradicted the Member's view as to what was in the best interests of his constituents. However, as Keith Ewing has argued,[2] the modern party system, with the executive being the dominant factor, was already well established in Parliament by the early twentieth century. Consequently, the judges, in striking at the promotion of Labour candidates by trade unions, were not attacking a unique departure from the philosophy of Edmund Burke on the part of the trade unions, but were simply making it more difficult for the nascent Labour Party to compete on equal terms with the established Conservative and Liberal Parties. However wrong-headed the constitutional argument of the judges in the *Osborne* case may have been, it does serve to remind us of the dual nature of the question of whether a union should be permitted to impose a compulsory levy on its members to finance party political activity. The one aspect is the issue of how political parties should be financed; the other is whether the individual should be obliged to contribute to a particular political party as part of the price of joining a union. Our concern is primarily with the latter issue, although the two are not always clearly separable. A Conservative Minister, in a Cabinet memorandum of 1924, quoted by Dr Ewing,[3] put the matter as follows in a passage which, while striking, perhaps does not capture all the possible reasons behind such legislation:

The real point which we have to decide is this. Do we wish to attack trade unions as

---

[1] See, for example, *Gower's Principles of Modern Company Law* (4th edn, 1979), pp. 170–1, relying especially upon *Evans* v. *Brunner Mond & Co.* [1921] 1 Ch. 359, which concerned, however, a charitable donation.

[2] Op. cit., pp. 30–2.   [3] Ibid., pp. 50–1.

such or do we not? . . . . the major part of the outcry against the political levy is not motivated by a burning indignation for the trade unionist, who is forced to subscribe to the furtherance of political principles which he abhors. It is based upon a desire to hit the Socialist party through their pocket. . . . What I submit is that at least we should not delude ourselves as to our intentions.

The policy of the Liberal government that passed the TUA 1913 was clear enough. It was that trade unions should be free to support the Labour Party or to engage in other party political activities, but that the individual who did not wish to contribute funds to this end should be free not to do so. Consequently, s.1(1) of TUA 1913 provided that the fact that an organization had objects or powers in addition to the statutory objects did not prevent it being a trade union as defined by the TUA 1871–6. This provision was later repealed because it was rendered otiose by the insertion by TULRA 1974 of a new definition of 'trade union' in s.2 of TUA 1913. This definition, identical to that found in s.28(1) of TULRA 1974 (above, p. 173), makes it clear that to be a trade union an organization's principal purposes must include, but need not be confined to, the regulation of relations between workers and employers. Had the legislators of the TUA 1913 stopped at this point, they would in effect have reversed the *Osborne* judgment *tout court*, which was, indeed, what the Labour Party of the time argued for. The principle that the *ultra vires* doctrine was applicable to trade unions would have been accepted – that aspect of the *Osborne* case has never been reversed – but trade unions, like limited companies, would have been able to give themselves power to engage in political activities and to levy their members compulsorily to that end provided only that there was an appropriate set of provisions in the union's rule-book. In fact, however, the whole thrust of the remaining provisions of the TUA 1913 was to impose a set of restrictive conditions which the rules of a union governing its party political activities would have to meet and, in particular, to deprive the union of the power compulsorily to levy its members in this regard. In the course of these provisions the legislature made a number of novel interventions into matters of trade-union government.

The restrictive conditions imposed by the 1913 Act were threefold in nature: the requirement for a ballot of union members to approve the adoption of political objects, the mandatory provisions to enable individual members to contract out of contribution to the political fund, and a safeguard against discrimination on grounds of non-contribution to the political fund. Each of these three sets of provisions involved notable departures from the spirit of *laissez-faire*. We have already remarked upon, in our discussion of current proposals for a greater use of mandatory ballots, the existence of the requirement in the TUA 1913 that, before a union adopts rules to enable it to pursue political objects, it must put to its members in a ballot the question of whether the union should adopt such objects (s.3(1)). Moreover, the ballot must be conducted in accordance with rules which are adopted by the union but which must also be approved by the Certification Officer, who must satisfy himself that 'every member has an equal right, and, if reasonably possible, a fair opportunity of voting, and that the secrecy of the ballot is properly secured' (s.4(1)). Thus, this first set of conditions involves not only a mandatory ballot but also control by a state official of a part of the union's rules. The Certification Officer has in fact drawn up a set of Model Rules to govern the holding of ballots, which rules assume a system of postal voting. A union would seem to be free not to use postal voting, provided its rules meet the standards established by s.4(1), but, if it does use postal voting, it may be able, if it wishes, to claim reimbursement of expenses incurred under s.1 of the EA 1980.[1] The requirement for a ballot contained in the 1913 Act is, however, perhaps the least well known of its provisions and, in a sense, rightly so. It is an initial, once-and-for-all requirement. A positive vote by a simple majority of those voting, even on a small turn-out, will be effective to approve the adoption of political objects and, once adopted, the vote will bind future generations of union members, unless the resolution approving political objects is rescinded. However, for this purpose no ballot is required; instead the union's own procedure for altering its rules is adopted (s.3(4)). The government proposes (see *Proposals for Legislation on Democracy in Trade Unions* (July 1983)) to alter this situation by requiring an affirmative ballot of the membership of the union every ten years to approve the continued operation of the political fund.[2]

It is appropriate to mention at this point what is meant by 'political objects'. These are defined, in a slightly archaic way, by s.3(3) and amount in practice to the expenditure of money on the selection or election of candidates for public office; the maintenance of Members of Parliament or holders of other public offices; and the holding of political meetings and the distribution of political literature. In fact, the subsection does not specifically mention the way in which unions spend the bulk of their political funds, namely, upon the payment of affiliation fees to the Labour Party, but affiliation fees are caught by the prohibition in s.3(1) that a union must not apply funds in furtherance of political objects 'either directly or in conjunction with any other ... association or body or otherwise indirectly' unless the stipulations of the Act are met. What is important to note is that, because of the change originally made by s.1(1) of the TUA 1913, a union is now free, provided its rules permit, to collect and spend money as it wishes on political objects not covered by the 1913 Act. These range from the election of candidates to the European Parliament (being neither Parliament nor a 'public office' as defined by s.3(3)) to donations to pressure groups which are not engaged in the political activities defined in s.3(3)) (e.g. Amnesty International or the Anti-Nazi League). It seems unions may legitimately make such payments out of the general funds; indeed, the question is rather whether such payments can legitimately be made from the union's political fund.[3] Again, the government's proposals of July 1983 include the modernization of the definition of 'political objects.'

[1] The point is not entirely clear. See Ewing, op. cit., pp. 99–100.

[2] See now Appendix

[3] Ewing, op. cit., pp. 93–6.

This last question brings us on to the second and third sets of restrictive provisions contained in the TUA 1913. Once the resolution to adopt political objects has been passed, the union must adopt rules to give effect to the resolution and these rules must contain the provisions laid down in s.3(1)(*a*) and (*b*) of the 1913 Act. S.3(1)(*a*) requires payments in furtherance of political objects to be made from a separate (political) fund from contribution to which any member of the union must be exempted if he has given notice in accordance with the simple procedure laid down in s.5. S.3(1)(*b*) requires the union's rules to provide that an exempted member 'shall not be excluded from any benefits of the union, or placed in any respect either directly or indirectly under any disability or at any disadvantage as compared with other members of the union (except in relation to the control of management of the political fund) by reason of his being so exempt and that contribution to the political fund of the union shall not be made a condition for admission to the union'. In so far as the political fund rules deal with these two matters they need the approval of the Certification Officer, but the CO and his predecessors have in fact produced a set of Model Rules dealing with the political fund generally which many unions have adopted. As we shall see, the question of whether the principle behind s.3(1)(*a*) is the correct one has been highly controversial, but its operation in practice has given rise to difficult litigation only in respect of the check-off. Because employers are often unwilling to deduct different amounts from employees' wages, according to whether they are exempt or not exempt from contributing to the political fund, unions have adopted the practice of periodically refunding exempt members such amount deducted by their employer as represents the political levy. In *Reeves* v. *Transport and General Workers Union* [1980] ICR 728, the EAT held that a refund paid by union to member in advance of the deductions by the employer was lawful and also that a refund paid as soon as reasonably possible after deduction would be lawful if a rebate paid in advance was not practicable and provided that the refund was paid automatically, i.e. without the need for the exempt member to claim it. This was a liberal interpretation of the statutory requirement that the rules governing the political fund should 'provide that the relief shall be given as far as possible to all members who are exempt on the occasion of the same periodical payment' (s.6) where a single contribution is levied on all union members, containing contributions both to general and political funds.

By contrast the anti-discrimination provision of s.3(1)(*b*) has been more difficult to interpret. It should be noted that it operates, not *ab extra* like the SDA 1975 and RRA 1976, but by requiring the union to introduce a rule relating to discrimination on grounds of non-contribution to the political fund. If the union introduces such a rule but then breaks it, the member's cause of action is for breach of the rules. This is significant because s.3(2) provides that complaints relating to breaches to the rules required to be introduced by s.3(1)(*a*) or (*b*) lie to the Certification Officer (previously the Registrar of Friendly Societies). This provision was introduced in 1913 because of fears that s.4 of the TUA 1871 (see above, p. 593) would prevent a member from complaining to the ordinary courts about breaches of rule. It is doubtful whether this was so, but in any case s.4 is now a thing of the past. Section 3(2) continues, however, and indeed probably confers an exclusive jurisdiction upon the CO, from which only in 1971 was an appeal provided (on a point of law now to the EAT). The CO's jurisdiction is, however, a limited one. If a union has not introduced political fund rules, then any complaint about improper expenditure on political objects lies to the High Court; so also would a claim for a declaration that a union's political fund rules do not comply with the provisions of the TUA 1913. If the political fund rules, as is quite likely, deal with matters other than those required to be included by the 1913 Act, again complaint would lie to the ordinary courts in respect of breaches of these additional rules. In spite of these limitations the Registrar and his successors have played a central role in interpreting the TUA 1913 and have generally been thought to have produced, within the framework of the Act, a good balance between individual and collective interests. Whether the introduction of an appeal on a point of law to the EAT and beyond will change this assessment remains to be seen.

The operation in practice of the non-discrimination rule has proved productive of a certain amount of litigation, notably in relation to the link between the rule and qualifications stated in the union's rules for being a candidate for or elected to union office. In *Birch v. National Union of Railwaymen* [1950] Ch. 602, the controversy revolved around the exception to the non-discrimination rule, 'except in relation to the control or management of the political fund'. The union's rules required all holders of union offices which involved control or management of the political fund to be contributors to the fund. The complainant had been removed from his position as branch secretary in consequence of this provision and he sought a declaration from the High Court that the union's rules did not comply with the TUA 1913. Danckwerts J. upheld the complaint on the grounds that the effect of the rule was to exclude exempt members from more than just the control or management of the political fund, which might be only a small proportion of the functions of the office in question. An analogous problem is raised by the requirement found in some trade-union rule-books that the holders of certain offices within the union must be individual members of the Labour Party, for members of the Party must under the Party's rules, if trade-union members, contribute to the political fund of their trade union. The reason for the union's requirement is usually to enable the union officials in question to represent the union at the Party's annual conference and the condition is thus often attached to the holding of senior posts in the union.[1] In *Vaughan and National Association of Operative Plasterers* (1932) the union's national executive refused to allow the complainant to stand for the post of Assistant General Secretary on the grounds that he did not contribute to the political fund and so would not be able to attend the Labour Party Conference which he might be required to do if

[1] See now Appendix

the General Secretary were unable to attend. The Registrar denied the complaint, apparently on the basis that Vaughan had been discriminated against on the grounds of his inability to perform the functions of the office he was standing for rather than because he did not contribute to the political fund of his union. In the light of the more sophisticated notions of discrimination that have developed under the SDA 1975 and RRA 1976 (above, pp. 41–63), it is doubtful whether such a decision would be reached today. Perhaps the matter is best approached as an issue of indirect discrimination. Being a member of the Labour Party is clearly a condition that fewer exempt members can comply with than non-exempt ones, but is the requirement of being a member of the Labour Party a justifiable condition for the holding of the particular post in question?

The Green Paper, *Democracy in Trade Unions* (Cmnd. 8778, 1983), raised a number of questions about the reform of the TUA 1913, notably the question of whether a system of contracting in should replace that of contracting out contained in s.3(1)(a) of the 1913 Act. It is perhaps particularly in relation to this issue that the question raised in the Cabinet memorandum of 1924 (above, p. 686) needs to be borne in mind: is the aim to protect individuals or to weaken the financial position of the Labour Party, whose income the report of the Committee on Financial Aid to Political Parties (Cmnd. 6601, 1976) estimated to be less than half that of the Conservative Party? However, it may be that the Cabinet memorandum has not captured all the possible ways of viewing this issue. An additional aim of the contracting-in system might be to reduce the level of involvement of trade unions in the Labour Party and to try to encourage the trade-union movement along the lines of being a purely industrial movement, prepared to deal on equal terms with any elected government and having no special relationship with any particular political party. Certainly, if the aim of the legislation is perceived to be simply to weaken the financial standing of the Labour Party, then the way is opened up for an eventual riposte by way of controls upon donations by companies for political purposes, which donations go predominantly to the Conservative Party and organizations which support it. There is no equivalent legislation to the TUA 1913 controlling donations for political purposes by companies, though the outlines of such legislation would not be difficult to envisage – perhaps a requirement that donations be made from corporate funds that would otherwise be distributed by way of dividend coupled with a right for individual shareholders not to have their dividends reduced in this way. Or it might be thought at some future time that even-handed treatment of trade unions could be accomplished by simply removing the individual safeguards of the TUA 1913, leaving in place a simple reversal of the *Osborne* judgment. This, after all, is what the Labour Party of the time wished for, but it is perhaps unlikely that it would press for this today. Contracting out has become a system the unions and the Labour Party have found they can live with and which provides the necessary escape for individual consciences. It is noteworthy that the Labour government of 1945 to 1950, with a very large majority, contented itself with restoring the contracting-out procedure that the TUA 1913 had introduced but which had been replaced by a contracting-in procedure in the Trade Disputes and Trade Unions Act 1927, passed in the wake of the General Strike. The Trade Disputes and Trade Unions Act 1946, which effected this reversion (but not in Northern Ireland), thus also signified the formal acceptance by the trade unions and the Labour government that compulsory levies for political purposes were not acceptable.

Ultimately, such discussion of the government's deeper motives is at present purely speculative. In the Green Paper the case was argued purely in terms of individual rights and led to various proposals for strengthening the provisions of the TUA 1913. For example, there was said to be a 'strong case' (para. 86) that the ballot should cease to be a purely initial requirement and become instead a periodical duty, and, as we have seen, the government's document of July 1983 contained this proposal as a firm legislative commitment.[1] There was, however, no discussion in either document of the question, often raised but never satisfactorily answered in respect of the TUA 1913, of why the protection of individual rights is thought to require both a ballot and an individual right to contract out. The argument in favour of contracting in was presented in the Green Paper in terms of an alleged variation in the percentage of members of similar unions who contract out, from which it is sought to argue that the present contracting-out procedure does not work well. The statistics presented, however, may not be wholly reliable,[2] and in July 1983 the government confined itself to inviting the TUC 'to discuss the steps the trade unions themselves can take to ensure that their members are freely and effectively able to decide for themselves whether or not they pay the political levy.' Eventually, in February 1984, the TUC and the government reached an agreement whereby the government said it would not propose to introduce into the Trade Union Bill (see Appendix) any amendments to change 'the present basis of the law regarding the payment of the political levy', and the TUC agreed to issue a Statement of Guidance to its affiliated unions. In this Statement, the TUC 'strongly recommended' its affiliated unions to take steps to ensure that members were aware of their right to contract out under the provisions of the TUA 1913 and that the procedures for contracting out were operated promptly and effectively. However, this agreement did not mean the government proposed not to proceed with the Trade Union Bill, which covered issues other than contracting in.

---

[1] See now Appendix

[2] See Ewing and Rees, 'Democracy in Trade Unions – 1: The Political Levy' (1983) 133 *NLJ* 100.

6
Industrial conflict: the common law and the policy of abstention

1 Introduction – 'the right to strike'

Why not simply prohibit all strikes and other forms of industrial action? Such action usually causes loss of wages to the workers engaged in it or laid off as a result of it, loss of production to the employer in dispute and often to other employers as well, and inconvenience to the public. The simple (but important) reply might be that such a prohibition would be ineffective. In the following passage the authors suggest that there are also less pragmatic arguments against the prohibition.

Otto Kahn-Freund and Bob Hepple, *Laws Against Strikes*
(1972), pp. 4–5, 6–8

Why is it that in all democratic countries the 'freedom to strike', or, as it is sometimes put, the 'right to strike', is considered to be a fundamental freedom, alongside the freedom to organize, to assemble peacefully, to express one's opinion? Why is the strike or, better perhaps, the potentiality of a strike, that is, of an event which of necessity entails a waste of resources, and damage to the economy, nevertheless by general consent an indispensable element of a democratic society? Or, to put it the other way, why is there no one (outside a very insignificant lunatic fringe) who in countries such as Great Britain, France, West Germany, Italy and the United States would even attempt to argue that all strikes should be made illegal? Why do even communist countries, in which no freedom to strike in fact exists, find it necessary to pay at least lip service to it?

What is a strike?
To come to terms with questions such as these it is necessary to arrive at some agreement as to what one intends to mean by the word 'strike'. It is clear that the concept of a strike contains two elements; one is the cessation of work, the other is the element of concerted action. Unless there is a complete cessation of work, there is no strike. This is why in the vocabulary adopted by the Industrial Relations Act 'strike'

appears as the species of a genus 'industrial action'. There can be concerted industrial action which does not amount to a strike; go slow, work to rule, overtime ban. The point is of much more than academic importance, because there are countries, such as France, in which the freedom to strike is not understood to cover any type of action short of a complete cessation of work. Cessation of work means that those taking action leave, and stay away from, the employer's premises. Hence, even where a right to strike is recognized as a privilege granted by the constitution (as it is in France), a go slow (*grève perlée*) is unlawful as a breach of the contract of employment. The underlying thought is that those who use the right to strike should also shoulder the full risk which it involves, and that the employer should not, in addition to the loss caused by the cessation or partial cessation of the utilization of his plant, also have to undergo further sacrifice through wasted overheads.

. . . The second element of the concept of a strike is equally important; a strike presupposes concerted action. Parallel actions of isolated individuals do not amount to a strike. A number of employees, annoyed by some act of the employer, all giving notice, may do as much damage to the employer as a strike, but unless they act in agreement it is not a strike. This is generally recognized, and indeed the repressive principles which legislators and courts of law applied in the past against strikers usually fastened on this element of 'collective' action, this element of 'conspiracy' or *coalition*. Concerted action for economic purposes was obnoxious to the *laissez-faire* ideology which dominated the thinking of the middle class and therefore of the courts and the legal profession in the whole western orbit of civilization in the nineteenth century, and the spirit of the common law differs only in degree from that of the legal systems of the continent.

. . . A strike may thus be defined in terms of concerted action and of cessation of work, that is in terms of means, not in terms of ends. Men may strike in order to protest against the enactment of a statute, against an unpopular measure of foreign policy or of educational policy, against a new tax or an increase in bus fares, or in order to prevent a shipment of supplies to an unpopular government. The strike is always a phenomenon of industrial relations, but it can be used as a political weapon. However much, especially in the English speaking countries, the idea of freedom to strike is linked by tradition with the processes of collective bargaining, it would be wrong to define it exclusively in these terms. . . .

The rationale

Why, then, should the law permit the use of the concerted stoppage of work as a means of enforcing rights or their improvement? What is the justification, the rationale of the right or the freedom to strike? To this fundamental question there are at least four answers.

These are based on the equilibrium argument, the autonomy argument, the voluntary labour (or Benthamite) argument, and the psychological argument.

In the context of the use of the strike as a sanction in industrial relations, the equilibrium argument is much the most important of the four. It is simple enough, and it was, in all its simplicity, stated as long ago as 1896 by Oliver Wendell Holmes, in a classic passage of a dissenting opinion in the Supreme Judicial Court of Massachusetts. 'Combination on the one side is patent and powerful. Combination on the other is the necessary and desirable counterpart, if the battle is to be carried on in a fair and equal way . . . If it be true that working men may combine with a view, among other things, to getting as much as they can for their labour, just as capital may combine with a view to getting the greatest possible return, it must be true that when combined they have the same liberty that combined capital has to support their interests by argument, persuasion, and the bestowal or refusal of those advantages which they otherwise lawfully control.' (*Vegelahn* v. *Guntner*, 167 Massachusetts 92; 44 N E 1077 at p. 1081. Holmes had previously formulated the argument in 'Privilege, malice and intent', 8 *Harvard Law Review* (1894) 1 at p. 8.) Except in the most mechanical sense, there is nothing like parity or a possible equilibrium between an individual employer and an individual worker. The concentrated power of accumulated capital can only be matched by the concentrated power of the workers acting in solidarity. A lockout is only in appearance the act of an individual, in reality it is the exercise of a social power; as such it can be countered by the potentiality of the strike. All this is almost platitudinous, but the argument, based on the need for an equilibrium of forces in labour/management relations, derives its importance from the antithetic or polemical function it had to exercise in the history of labour law. It was this theory of countervailing power which was needed to overcome the mechanical individualism permeating the legal systems of continental countries such as France or West Germany no less than those of the United Kingdom or the United States. The argument, it may be noticed, presupposes that the pressure is directed against the employer or possibly the employers. It does not support, nor does it run counter to, the use of the freedom to strike so as to exercise pressure against the consumer or against the user of services.

The second argument, the need for autonomous sanctions, is linked with collective bargaining. Except in marginal situations, conditions of employment cannot be regulated by legislation, not even in countries such as Italy, and, in a minor way, France and West Germany, where the law governing the contract of employment is codified, much less in Britain or the United States where most of this has to be done by case-law. The rules of employment have to be made outside the framework of law-making in the technical sense, that is through collective bargaining. This need for, and existence of, a body of autonomous norms is not peculiar to labour relations (we find it in commercial relations of many kinds) but what is characteristic of labour relations is that the individual whose rights are involved does not participate in the rule-making process, hardly ever on the workers' side and frequently not on the employers' side. Moreover, it is (in some important instances at least) a continuous process of bargaining, a process of rule-making by collective entities acting through an often informal procedure which, in many cases, goes on without interruption. Nor are these rules only designed to regulate the mutual rights of individual employers and workers (such as wages, holidays, hours of work and overtime); they also govern the conditions of engagement, the labour market, the question who is to work where and to do what. Most important, they are the basis for the representation of interests on both sides, at plant level through shop stewards (at any rate in the English-speaking countries), and centrally through permanent councils and committees. They are also the basis of the procedure for the settlement of claims.

How can such rules be enforced through sanctions provided by law, through the judgments of courts and the machinery for their enforcement? It is not only desirable that those who have made the autonomous rules should also wield the sanctions, and not leave the enforcement to individuals who did not participate in the rule-making. It is far more important that the substance of many of these norms defies the use of legal sanctions. This is one reason why 'the right of workmen to strike is an essential element in the principle of collective bargaining'. (This is the way Lord Wright put it in the House of Lords in the leading case of *Crofter Harris Tweed* v. *Veitch* [1942] 1 All ER 142, at 157.) It is, in other words, an essential element not only of the unions' bargaining power, that is for the bargaining process itself, it is also a necessary sanction for enforcing agreed rules.

As a sanction the strike or the threat of a strike can be far more expeditious and stringent than any legal procedure, especially in response to a unilateral action taken by management, such as fixing a new piece rate or resorting to discipline without consultation. In such a situation the sanction is a kind of self help which the law, and often even an agreed grievance procedure, is too slow to supplant. The strike is here the equivalent of the managerial prerogative, the factual power of management unilaterally to change the conditions of work. Experience has shown in many countries that, whatever the law may say, it cannot suppress spontaneous action in response to unilateral change. The argument derived from autonomy can be put in the severely practical terms of social necessity.

The case for freedom to strike can also be put in terms of social ethics. If people may not withdraw their labour, this may mean that the law compels them to work, and a legal compulsion to work is abhorrent to systems of law imbued with a liberal tradition, and compatible only with a totalitarian system of government. . . . This argument, ultimately based on the Benthamite postulate of the freedom to dispose of one's labour, is likely to impress the legal mind more than the arguments derived from social reality.

It is, however, on closer inspection less far reaching and less persuasive. As a matter of legislative technique it is possible to forbid a strike without forcing the individual striker to go back to work and without threatening him with imprisonment if he does not. Thus, the Industrial Relations Act 1971 restricts its sanctions to those who call, organize, procure or finance a strike. This is a more credible and therefore a more powerful threat than that of fining or imprisoning the rank and file participants, because experience (for instance, in the United Kingdom during the Second World War) has shown that legal sanctions cannot be enforced against the strikers. The argument against compulsory labour, whilst superficially appealing to sentiment, is thus less than convincing because the freedom to strike can be effectively undermined without directly compelling anyone to work.

Indirect compulsion, however, may be exercised without necessarily being considered as an attack on the freedom to strike. What is the denial of unemployment benefit, of supplementary welfare payments or of tax refunds if it is not an indirect compulsion to return to work?

Yet we do not normally say that these deprivations are incompatible with freedom to strike. Thus it may be inimical to that freedom to create certain inducements not to exercise it (such as threats against the leaders), whilst other inducements in the same direction are considered differently (denial of unemployment benefit). The law can seek to suppress strikes without forcing people to work, and it can indirectly seek to induce them to return to work without suppressing the freedom to strike.

Lastly, it is now widely accepted that the strike is sometimes a necessary release of psychological tension, especially where men and women have to work under physical or psychological strain. How much weight this argument carries is a difficult question, but it cannot be neglected. To some extent, but compared with other factors perhaps only to a minor extent, it may help to explain the distribution of the incidence of strikes over various industries.

It may have something to do with the fact that the mining industries have always and everywhere been the scene of a large number of frequently spontaneous stoppages.

However, the imperative need for a social power countervailing that of property overshadows everything else. If the workers are not free by concerted action to withdraw their labour, their organizations do not wield a credible social force. The power to withdraw their labour is for the workers what for management is its power to shut down production, to switch it to different purposes, to transfer it to different places. A legal system which suppresses the freedom to strike puts the workers at the mercy of their employers. This – in all its simplicity – is the essence of the matter.

The arguments advanced by the authors in the previous extract are not arguments against *any* legal restrictions upon industrial action, but only against its restriction to the point where the 'right to strike' becomes illusory. Opinions are likely to differ as to when that point has been reached. But even when it is agreed that a particular state of the law is not such as to render the right to strike illusory, there may still be controversy as to whether the law unduly restricts or unduly permits resort to industrial action. An almost infinite range of arguments may then become relevant. Should it matter whether the strike is official (i.e. sanctioned by the union) or unofficial; whether it is in breach of the terms of a collective agreement; whether the strikers are employed in a public service; whether the strike has been preceded by a ballot of the strikers; whether the strikers are employed in an employment covered by a closed shop agreement; whether the struck employer is a primary or a secondary employer, and so on? In relation to these issues one of the authors of the extract just quoted, Professor Kahn-Freund, was in fact associated, in his writings of the 1950s in particular, with the view that the law should take a broad view of what was permitted by way of industrial action, We have already discussed in Chapter 2 (above, pp. 132–4) Professor Kahn-Freund's theory of collective *laissez-faire*. At that point the aspect of the theory that was of greatest concern to us was the explanation it provided for the general poverty of English law in terms of legal mechanisms for the positive encouragement of collective bargaining. Another aspect of the theory, and probably at that time a more important one in its author's eyes, was its explanation of how English law, as exemplified above all by the Trade Disputes Act 1906, tended very strongly towards the view that the peaceful infliction of economic harm in consequence of industrial disputes should not be restricted by the law. This was not a theory that countenanced the use of force, either to person or to property, but within the area of peaceful economic sanctions the theory suggested that the answer to the questions posed at the beginning of this paragraph should be in the negative. Writing in 1959, Professor Kahn-Freund described the existing state of English law in terms of 'this policy of withdrawing the law from the battlefield of industrial hostilities' and in terms of a public opinion that 'the courts would not intervene as long as the parties were engaged in conflicts of interest and their settlement through persuasion or pressure'. (See *Selected Writings of Otto Kahn-Freund* (1978), p. 23.)

The law of industrial conflict has a substantial history. Although it is much disputed whether it is trade unions that lead to strikes or strikes that lead to trade unions, it is clear that in a system of collective bargaining the two go hand in hand. In the particular social circumstances of Great Britain it was possible for trade unions and collective bargaining to develop and even, to a degree, to flourish in the absence (before 1971) of any general, positive, legal encouragement of them by way of recognition machineries or legal protection of the freedom of association, as we have noted already in Chapter 2. However, from the advent of trade unions and their attempts to establish collective bargaining arrangements the question had to be answered as to whether and, if so, how far the law should contain obstacles to the development of collective bargaining, in the shape in particular of restrictions upon the freedom of employees to form trade unions (discussed above, pp. 588–93) or upon their freedom to take industrial action, if the employer would not engage in collective bargaining or if collective negotiations produced no agreed resolution (the subject matter of this chapter). The history of industrial conflict law, from, say, the beginning of the nineteenth century until the passing of the Trade Disputes Act 1906 or even later, can be seen as a struggle for reflection in the law between two views representing the opposite ends of a broad spectrum. The one view was, indeed, that the right to strike should be rendered illusory (at least in legal terms) and the other was the abstentionist theory subsequently articulated by Professor Kahn-Freund. The result of this struggle was the triumph of the latter view. As Kahn-Freund put it in 1954, 'English law has . . . undergone very profound changes. Generally speaking, it has . . . moved from an attitude of suppression to one of abstention.' (O. Kahn-Freund, 'Legal Framework' in A. Flanders and H. A. Clegg (eds.), *The System of Industrial Relations in Great Britain* (1954), pp. 102–3.)

Since the Second World War, however, a rather more sophisticated challenge to the abstentionist viewpoint has increasingly been mounted in some employer circles and in Whitehall. The old debate is not dead. The embers of the fire can still be fanned into flame, as, for example, by the decision of the House of Lords in *Rookes* v. *Barnard* [1964] AC 1129, which raised again the spectre that the right to strike would become illusory. However, the legal doctrine established by that decision was quickly neutralized by the Trade Disputes Act 1965 as far as labour law was concerned (see below, p. 744). The main impact of the decision was political: it cast doubt on the extent to which the TDA 1906 had effectively embodied the abstentionist doctrine in English law and it led to the apppointment of the Royal Commission on Trade Unions and Employers' Associations, to which were made a series of more limited, but fundamental, proposals for a move away from abstentionism.

As we have noted in Chapter 2 (above, p. 137), a major risk from the point of view of the state in relying upon an autonomous system of collective bargaining to settle terms and conditions of employment is that the system may generate unacceptably high levels of industrial conflict that interfere with the attainment of other objectives that government has set itself. It is perfectly consistent with the abstentionist standpoint that government should provide facilities for third-party conciliation and arbitration for employers and trade unions to make use of in the settlement of their disputes, if they so wish. Such machinery has existed in English law since the last century and is currently the main responsibility of ACAS,[1] but rising levels of industrial conflict are likely to generate pressures for more coercive forms of intervention by the law in the settlement of disputes. For the Donovan Commission the nature and growing extent of Britian's strike problem was to be explained as an adjunct to the growth, especially in private manufacturing industry, of a disorderly system of plant bargaining conducted, on the employees' side, largely by shop stewards. Although it was true that 'from time to time this country still experiences big strikes', the most significant feature of strikes in Britain in the view of the Commission was the 'comparatively large number of stoppages [which] are of fairly short duration and do not usually involve very large numbers of people'. The number of these short stoppages (outside coal mining) was increasing quite quickly (from about 600 per year according to the official statistics in 1957 to about 1,600 per year a decade later). Nearly 95 per cent of stoppages were unofficial (i.e. not sanctioned or ratified by the union or unions whose members were on strike), and the majority were also unconstitutional (i.e. taken in breach of collectively agreed disputes procedures). It was the short stoppages that were identified overwhelmingly with unofficial and unconstitutional action; the big stoppages were likely to be both official and constitutional. (See paras. 362–77.) And it was the growing number of short, unofficial and unconstitutional strikes that created the greatest pressures to modify the abstentionist legal régime so as to reduce, in various ways, the extent of the legal protection afforded to them.

At the end of the day the Commission resisted these pressures, not, however, because they thought that there was no 'strike problem' to be dealt with, but because they doubted the likely effectiveness of the proposed legal changes in producing the results claimed for them. The main proposal before the Commission to deal with unconstitutional strikes was to make collective agreements in some way legally enforceable. The Commission preferred to recommend voluntary reform of the inadequate procedures that were seen by the Commission to be the cause of much of the unofficial and unconstitutional strike action, rather than propose to render the existing inadequate procedures legally binding. The Commission thus hoped to maintain the traditional autonomy of the collective bargaining system in the new era of plant-level bargaining by ensuring that the collective bargaining system itself provided the mechanism for the orderly resolution of conflicts of interest. It was, however, a somewhat qualified defence of abstentionism, for the Commission

---

[1] For a description of the work of ACAS in providing voluntary arbitration, mediation and conciliation services, see ACAS, *Annual Report 1978*, Chaps. 8 and 9, and Kahn-Freund, *Labour and the Law* (3rd edn, 1983), Chap. 5.

conceded the case for legal enforceability of collective agreements should the reformed procedures not secure compliance with their provisions (paras. 500–518). The Commission also considered certain proposals to deal with official strikes, conceived of as breakdowns in negotiations at national level in a particular industry. The Commission rejected the argument that British law should contain procedures, modelled upon the US Taft-Hartley procedures, to deal with large-scale disputes that led to a national emergency (see further, below, p. 868), and it also rejected the proposal that the holding of a secret ballot should be a pre-condition for a lawful strike (paras. 416–30). In part the Commission thought the proposals unlikely to be effective, but it is difficult to avoid the conclusion that they were much influenced by their finding that official strikes were 'relatively infrequent and their number shows no consistent tendency to grow' (para. 1044).

The Donovan Commission's report was thus, in large part, a defence and reassertion of the traditional virtues of the doctrine of abstentionism as far as the law of industrial conflict was concerned. Yet it was more than just that, for Kahn-Freund (who was a member of the Commission) had developed his theory at a time when the British collective bargaining system was regarded as a model way of reconciling the goals of autonomy, democracy and efficiency in the settling of terms and conditions of employment. The Donovan Commission asserted that collective bargaining was still in principle the best way to achieve these conflicting goals, but not that the British system of bargaining at that time reflected this ideal. The case for reform of the collective bargaining system was accepted by the Commission; indeed it devoted much of its report to stating that case to the public in general. The debate within and around the Commission was as to the appropriate balance between reform brought about by employers and unions themselves and reform initiated by the state, and, in respect of state reform, the appropriate role for legal intervention. The Commission recommended that the preponderance of reforming effort should come from the industrial relations parties themselves and that state intervention should not be primarily through the coercive use of the law. However, in recommending and advocating reform at all the Donovan Commission's report was a watershed and its reformist arguments provided a more difficult context in which to argue the abstentionist case than the context in which Kahn-Freund had originally elaborated his views.

It was perhaps the difficulty of combining in a convincing manner the reformist arguments about the industrial relations system and the abstentionist arguments about the law that contributed to the qualified acceptance that the Report (published in 1968) received from the then Conservative opposition and also certain sections of the then Labour government. The Labour government issued a White Paper, *In Place of Strife* (Cmnd. 3888, 1969), in part as a response to the Commission's Report, in part as a response to the failure of its incomes policies and the growing levels of industrial conflict. The White Paper accepted the vast majority of the Commission's specific recommendations, but, in a radical break from abstentionist law, also proposed that the Secretary of State should have the power to order a return to work for a period of up to 28 days in the case of a strike that was 'unconstitutional or in which for other reasons adequate joint discussions have not taken place' and which was likely to have serious consequences for other workpeople or the economy. Power should also exist for the Secretary of State to require a ballot where official action was being contemplated which would seriously threaten the economy and there was doubt whether the employees involved supported the strike (paras. 93–8). Finally, proposals for the settlement of inter-union disputes by means of an order excluding a union from recognition by an employer could also have resulted in financial penalties being imposed on a union which took industrial action contrary to the order (para. 60). These departures from the Donovan Commission's proposals were bound to be unpopular with the trade unions, but this unpopularity was much increased when the government decided not to implement all its proposals at once but to proceed first with what, it was hoped, would be a quick and short Bill containing only five proposals, two of which, however, were to be the proposals relating to unconstitutional strikes and inter-union disputes. The opposition from the TUC was fierce, the Labour Party in Parliament was split, and after a very public row among the various segments of the labour movement the proposals for 'penal clauses' were dropped.[1]

Before the Labour government could implement the Commission's proposals (shorn of the penal clauses) it was defeated at a general election and replaced by the Conservative government of Mr Heath. Before the Commission had reported the Conservative Party had published a policy document, *Fair Deal at Work* (1968), which contained a fairly comprehensive rejection of the abstentionist viewpoint, and the Industrial Relations Act 1971, enacted by the new government, reflected this policy. There were provisions for conciliation pauses and compulsory ballots in disputes that created national emergencies (IRA 1971, Part VIII); special restrictions upon unofficial action (s.96) and secondary action (s.98); and a range of prohibitions upon industrial action that might undermine machinery established by the Act (e.g. the recognition machinery) or promote practices prohibited by the Act (e.g. pre-entry closed shops). As part of this reform the TDA 1906 was repealed. As we shall discuss in more detail below (pp. 825–6) the IRA 1971 in its short life more than amply bore witness to the wisdom of the warnings of the Donovan Commission about the potential weakness of legal sanctions in industrial relations, at least when used against individual workers using traditional methods of pressure in pursuit of causes in whose justice they deeply believed. The Act proved productive more of constitutional crises than of industrial peace, and even the government that had passed it found it becoming an increasing obstacle in its attempts to reach agreement with the

[1] See P. Jenkins, *The Battle of Downing Street* (1970); D. Barnes and E. Reid, *Governments and Trade Unions* (1980), Chap. 7.

TUC over incomes policy.[1]

Accordingly, when a Labour government was elected in 1974 the scene was set for a reassertion of the traditional abstentionist framework of industrial conflict law. The demise of the IRA 1971 seemed to have discredited the arguments for restriction of the freedom to strike and, in any case, a Labour government that was seeking agreement with the TUC over the implement-ation of a 'Social Contract' no longer had any hankering after 'penal clauses'. Consequently, the Trade Union and Labour Relations Acts 1974 and 1976 swept away the IRA 1971 and returned to the policy of the TDA 1906 (if in a more sophisticated and elaborate guise). The IRA 1971 could appear in these heady times as a short-lived aberration, a momentary departure from the true doctrine of collective *laissez-faire* which had been the dominant stance of English industrial conflict law in the twentieth century. Indeed, TULRA 1974–6 are still the foundations of the law of industrial conflict, and the history of the IRA 1971 is probably still taken as demonstrating even in inter-ventionist circles the undesirability of comprehensive, root-and-branch reform of labour law introduced at one go. Nevertheless, the law of 1983 is very different from the law of 1976. Increasingly during the 1970s public attention has moved away from the large number of short, unofficial and unconsti-tutional strikes towards the small number of large, industry-wide official conflicts, often arising out of incomes policy and often as much disputes between union and government as between union and employer. There is statistical evidence to show that the average number of large stoppages per year more than doubled between the 1960s and the 1970s and that 'large stoppages accounted for the greater part of the sharp increase between the 1960s and 1970s in total working days lost in all industrial disputes, which rose from 3.6 million a year to 12.9 million'.[2] Although one is talking even in the 1970s of only four or five large stoppages per year on average, these disputes are highly visible, may be highly disruptive of the general life of the community, and easily generate political pressures for a change in the law.

It was in particular a rash of large disputes in the winter of 1978/9, coinciding with the collapse of the Labour government's Social Contract, which created the political opportunity, and even necessity, for the Conserva-tive government of Mrs Thatcher, elected in 1979, to move the law away once again from the abstentionist position. Unlike the government of Mr Heath, Mrs Thatcher's administration moved not through a single reforming measure but through a series of measures, of which the two most important ones to date have been the Employment Acts of 1980 and 1982.[3] Again unlike the IRA 1971, the EA 1980 and 1982 kept the structure of the previous law, but modified it fundamentally. The EA 1980 imposed special restrictions upon the legality of secondary action and picketing (the latter resurfacing in

---

[1] A. W. J. Thomson and S. R. Engleman, *The Industrial Relations Act* (1975), Chaps. 5 and 6; M. Moran, *The Politics of Industrial Relations* (1977), Chap. 8.

[2] 'Large industrial stoppages 1960–1979', *Employment Gazette*, (Sept. 1980), p. 994.

[3] To which must now be added Part II of the Trade Union Bill (see Appendix).

the 1970s as a topic of public concern), and the EA 1982 added a series of additional restrictions (especially in relation to the liability of trade unions as such). In a Green Paper, *Trade Union Immunities* (Cmnd. 8128, 1981), issued between the 1980 and 1982 Acts, the government put its view of the issues discussed above in the following terms:

Trade Union Immunities (1981), paras. 3–6

3. The freedom of employees to combine and to withdraw their labour is their ultimate safeguard against the inherent imbalance of power between the employer and the individual employee. This freedom has come to be accepted as a hallmark of a free society. But implicit in that acceptance is the assumption that this freedom will be used responsibly, that industrial action will be taken only with proper regard for the interests of others and of the community as a whole. In times of national emergency, for example, greater restraint is expected – and has been shown – in the use of this essentially disruptive power.

4. The importance of the freedom to combine to withdraw labour in the face of serious grievances at work is not in question. What is questioned is the readiness to threaten and deploy the strike weapon with apparent disregard for the consequences, whether for the future of the enterprises affected, for the jobs and livelihoods of their employees or for the rest of the community. Many strikes effectively repudiate agreements made by those organising them or by their representatives and the vast majority are called without reference to senior trade union officials and without their endorsement. All too often the strike or the threat of a strike is a tactic of first instead of last resort. And, when strikes occur, the degree of disruption is sometimes quite disproportionate to the grievance felt. Industrial action is extended deliberately to harm employees who have no interest in the dispute and pushed even further to inflict the maximum hardship and inconvenience on the community. Moreover, the mere threat of a strike can in some circumstances be as effective a weapon as a strike itself. The readiness to threaten industrial action has imposed serious obstacles to necessary change, greater efficiency and improved performance in many of our industries. As a result our ability to compete in home and overseas markets has seriously declined.

5. All this has led to questioning of the scope which the law permits to industrial action and to a wider debate about the role of trade unions and management in our society. These have long been a matter of controversy. For at least a hundred years there has been argument about the acceptable balance of bargaining power between employees and their employers and the duties they and their representatives owe to the nation. Industrial relations cannot operate fairly and efficiently or to the benefit of the nation as a whole if either employers or employees collectively are given predominant power – that is, the capacity effectively to dictate the behaviour of others. What the law can achieve in affecting the balance of power must not be over-estimated, but it has always been recognised as a proper role of Parliament to intervene by statute to correct manifestations – whether by employers or employees – of a disequilibrium of bargaining power.

6. A rational and informed public debate about the law and practice of industrial relations is now essential. Such a debate took place in the years following the Donovan Commission report. It must now be resumed. Many of the problems identified then have remained or intensified. Our success as a manufacturing and trading nation depends crucially on the improvement of our industrial relations.

2 Industrial conflict and the common law

One can see the history of the English law of industrial conflict in very broad terms as, first, a move from suppression to abstention and, second, a move to modify the abstentionist stance of the law on the grounds of a need to protect the community at large and the efficient functioning of the economy. The second phase is still being enacted, and it is at present unclear whether at the end of the day the policy of abstention will emerge fortified in its position as the dominant doctrine or whether the law will adopt permanently a more restrictive position and, if so, what the details of that position will turn out to be. Clearly, this debate is at the centre of current British politics, and the legal dimensions of the issue will necessarily have to occupy a good part of our discussion. However, as we now turn to the details of the current law, it is in fact necessary to revert to the first phase of the development of the law of industrial conflict. Although one may optimistically surmise that the political debate about whether there should be a non-illusory freedom to strike is long over, the legal ramifications of this matter are still with us. Even our current law still contains the potential to render the right to strike a nullity, and it is in the common law that we must seek the explanation of this surprising fact.

When in the nineteenth century courts were faced with the question of whether a particular piece of industrial action was legal, there was sometimes, especially on the criminal side, a statute which provided the answer. But generally, and especially in relation to the law of tort, the answer had to be found in the common law. The answer of the common law was generally in the negative, not because all the judges were hostile to trade unions (although some of them undoubtedly were), but because the phenomena of collective action did not and could not generally coincide with the concepts of legality established in the common law. In the introduction to his Hamlyn lectures, delivered in 1971, Professor Kahn-Freund put the point in the following way:

Labour and the Law (1st edn, 1972), p. 1

However, no one who surveys the history and structure of labour law can remain unaware of the inherent contradiction between the requirements of public welfare and the spirit and the possibilities of the common law. The evolution of an orderly and (compared with many other countries) even today reasonably well functioning system of labour relations is one of the great achievements of British civilisation. This system of collective bargaining rests on a balance of the collective forces of management and organised labour. To maintain it has on the whole been the policy of the legislature during the last 100 years or so. The welfare of the nation depends on its continuity and on its growing strength – a sentiment shared, it is believed, by all political parties represented in the House of Commons. However, the common law knows nothing of a balance of collective forces. It is (and this is its strength and its weakness) inspired by the belief in the equality (real or fictitious) of individuals, it operates between individuals and not otherwise. Perhaps one of the most important characteristics of civil litigation is that the public interest is not represented in the civil courts. This, and not only the personal background of the judiciary, explains the inescapable fact that the contribution which the courts have made to the orderly development of collective labour relations has been infinitesimal. More than that, on a number of vitally important occasions Parliament has had to intervene to redress the balance which had been upset by court decisions capable of exercising the most injurious influence on the relations between capital and labour. A series of lectures on labour law – and here is my confession – is not the best place to extol the virtues of the common law.

As Kahn-Freund indicates in the above passage, the incompatibility between collective action and common-law notions of legality was such that, in order to establish the legal freedom to strike, Parliament was eventually persuaded to intervene and to render certain common-law doctrines inapplicable in the area of industrial relations. Those acting 'in contemplation or furtherance of a trade dispute' – the 'golden formula' in Professor Wedderburn's phrase – were given an immunity against the application of certain rules of the common law that would otherwise apply to them. Since these common-law rules, especially the economic torts, have not ceased to be part of the common law but have, on the contrary, expanded their scope since the nineteenth century, it continues to be a function of the modern law of industrial conflict to exclude those rules which, if not excluded, would render the right to strike illusory. One can see that function being performed today by s.13 of TULRA 1974 (as amended). Since, moreover, the common law is not a static body of rules, statutory exclusion was not a single act of the nineteenth-century legislator, which has been bequeathed in immutable form to later Parliaments. On the contrary, statutory exclusion is, and has been, a continuing process in which developments in the common law have had to be neutralized from time to time in order to preserve a right to strike. Thus, as we shall see below, exclusion of the common-law crime of conspiracy in 1875 did not protect against the development of the tort of conspiracy, which was excluded only by the TDA 1906. This latter Act was found not to protect against the tort of intimidation, as greatly expanded by the House of Lords in *Rookes* v. *Barnard* [1964] AC 1129, and so it had to be supplemented by the TDA 1965. TULRA 1974–6 restored the policy of the TDA 1906, but in a much more elaborate form partly because of intervening common-law developments, for example, in relation to the tort of inducing breach of contract. The statutory structure established by EA 1980 to control secondary action was almost overthrown by common-law developments in the tort of interference with business by unlawful means. We shall look at these points in detail below.

Thus, the means by which statute attempts to prevent the common law from rendering the right to strike illusory have to be studied as a function of the modern law of industrial conflict, and because of the dynamic nature of the common law these means have become over time more complex and elaborate, even over-elaborate. Moreover, the pattern of common-law liability and statutory immunity provides the structure of the law of industrial conflict, within which those currently wishing to move away from the abstentionist position have chosen to work. Certainly this is true of the legislators of the EA 1980 and 1982 who attempted to modify, rather than replace, the structure created by TULRA 1974 and 1976. Hence, s.17 of the EA 1980, whose aim is to place restrictions upon the legality of certain forms of secondary action, does not operate by the simple method of declaring those forms of secondary action illegal. Instead, it says that, in respect of those forms of secondary action, the immunities against the common-law liabilities provided by s.13(1) of TULRA 1974 will not be available. There is thus created a highly complex, three-tier relationship which has to be analysed in order to find out whether a particular piece of secondary action is lawful: is the action a breach of the common-law rules; is immunity against the relevant rule provided by TULRA 1974; has that immunity been removed in respect of this type of secondary action by EA 1980, s.17? No doubt, a more simple way of legislating could be found by those who wish to move away from the abstentionist position. To some extent this was done by the legislators of the IRA 1971, who replaced the common-law liabilities within the area of industrial relations by statutory 'unfair industrial practices', although even some of these were based on common-law models. Nevertheless, the present restrictive provisions in the EA 1980 and 1982 operate as modifications of the conventional framework, and so it is necessary to begin with the common law, both in order to understand how the abstentionist position was created in technical terms and also to provide the basis for understanding how that position is being and could be modified in a restrictive direction. We shall look, successively, at the common-law doctrines of conspiracy, inducing breach of contract, intimidation, interference with business by unlawful means and duress, and at the way in which statute law responded to these doctrines.[1]

3 Conspiracy

In the first three-quarters of the nineteenth century industrial action was very likely to be held by the courts to be a criminal offence. The bases for the finding of criminality varied enormously, but the most generally used argument, as well as the most damaging one because it went to the heart of the employees' collective strength, was that action should be regarded as a crime because it was taken in combination with others, even though the act in question, if done without combination, would not be a crime. In the early days the view that strikes were criminal conspiracies was the one held by Parliament as well as by the common law. Thus, the Combination Acts of 1799 and 1800 rendered criminal all agreements to do acts in order to increase wages or reduce hours. Even the Combination Laws Repeal Act 1825 did not remove the threat of statutory illegality from combinations of workers entirely, whilst, on the other

[1] The best comprehensive account of the economic torts is to be found in *Clerk and Lindsell on Torts* (15th edn, 1982), Chap. 15 (edited by Wedderburn). For earlier developments see K. W. Wedderburn, *The Worker and the Law* (2nd edn, 1971), Chaps. 7 and 8.

hand, the doctrine of criminal conspiracy at common law became more and more accepted by the judges after 1825. Up until the 1870s industrial action was at great risk of being declared a criminal conspiracy, either by statute or at common law, because, in Professor Kahn-Freund's words, 'the element of concerted action – the essence of the strike – became the gist of the crime' (*Labour and the Law* (2nd edn, 1977), p. 229).

The situation was revolutionized as far as the criminal law was concerned by two Acts in the 1870s: the Criminal Law Amendment Act 1871 and the Conspiracy and Protection of Property Act 1875. These Acts (together with the Trade Union Act 1871, discussed above, at p. 592) represented the acceptance by the established powers in society that trade unions had a legitimate role within the state, and so the Trade Union Act sought to remove doubts about the legality of trade unions as organizations whilst the Criminal Law Amendment Act sought to remove the threat of criminal conspiracy from industrial action. However, in *R.* v. *Bunn* (1872) 12 Cox 316, Brett J. held that the doctrine of criminal conspiracy at common law had survived the 1871 Act. Workers had threatened to strike unless a colleague dismissed for union activity was reinstated. The judge held this to be a criminal conspiracy as 'an unjustifiable annoyance and interference with the masters in the conduct of their business'. Aiming to gain the vote of the newly enfranchized urban, male workers, Disraeli's government elected in 1874 passed the Conspiracy and Protection of Property Act 1875, section 3 of which provided:

An agreement or combination by two or more persons to do or procure to be done any act in contemplation or furtherance of a trade dispute . . . shall not be indictable as a conspiracy if such act committed by one person would not be punishable as a crime.

Although section 3 of the 1875 Act represented a watershed in the history of the law of industrial conflict because its formulation for giving statutory protection against common-law criminal liabilities was, as we shall see, subsequently adopted on the civil side to give protection against tort liabilities, the section itself has been repealed by the Criminal Law Act 1977 (except in Scotland where the relevant provisions of the 1977 Act do not apply). This occurred not because Parliament in 1977 wished to reverse its policy of 1875, but, on the contrary, because it wished to generalise beyond the area of industrial relations the principle of no liability for criminal conspiracy unless the act agreed upon was itself a crime. Consequently, section 5 of the 1977 Act abolishes (with a few limited exceptions) the offence of criminal conspiracy at common law, whilst s.1 of the Act creates a statutory offence of criminal conspiracy, but one defined in terms of an agreement 'which will necessarily amount to or involve the commission of any offence or offences by one or more of the parties to the agreement if the agreement is carried out. . . .'[1] The 1977 Act was mainly a response to events occurring outside the field of industrial

[1] However, there is one minor special protection for those taking industrial action, which has been carried forward from the 1875 Act. Where the offence is committed in contemplation or furtherance of a trade dispute, it is to be disregarded if it is a summary offence not punishable with imprisonment: 1977 Act, s.1(3).

relations since within that field the relevant principle was already established by the 1875 Act, but even within the field of industrial relations problems had been caused by the fact that, where the conspiracy *did* involve the commission of a criminal act, the penalty for the common-law crime of conspiracy was at large, whilst the penalty for the substantive criminal offence might be limited by statute. See *R.* v. *Jones (John)* [1974] ICR 310 (CA). Consequently, s.3 of the 1977 Act introduces limits on the penalties for statutory conspiracy which, in the case of imprisonment, means the limit applicable to the substantive offence.

Thus, by 1875 Parliament had asserted its view that criminal prohibition of the mainstream activities of trade unions was incompatible with their new-found legitimacy, and from then on the criminal law ceased to have a central place in the regulation of industrial conflict. The restriction of criminal conspiracy was accompanied by the repeal of the Master and Servant Acts, which had made simple breach of contract by an employee a criminal offence, and this repeal was expressive of the same policy. But is is important not to exaggerate what was done in 1875. It was precisely because the aim of the economic sanctions was to put pressure upon the employer that the employees' actions were criminal under the old law – they were, in Brett J.'s words, 'an unjustifiable annoyance and interference' in the employer's business. However, the new policy that rejected this view did not imply in addition that strikers should be relieved of criminal liability if they used methods that would be illegal even if used outside the context of a trade dispute. Thus, for example, strikers who commit or threaten to commit damage to person or property or whose acts threaten public order are subject to the criminal law, and in those, perhaps uncommon, situations where there is a likelihood of such behaviour, as on some picket lines, the criminal law does continue to play a prominent role. As we shall see below (pp. 842–62) the principle of imposing criminal liability in such cases is not challenged even today, though it is debated whether the criminal law as applied to picketing does not go further than is needed to secure the implementation of this principle, i.e. whether it renders in some cases even peaceful picketing a criminal activity.

The positive principle that perhaps emerges from the 1875 Act is that the stigma of the criminal law should be removed from the intentional infliction of purely economic harm upon an employer in the context of a trade dispute. Although this may sound, and no doubt in the 1870s was, a radical proposition, it is not inconsistent with the imposition of criminal liability upon strikers in certain situations even though their conduct would not, unlike the case of the violent picket, attract criminal liability if done outside the context of a trade dispute. Thus, ss.4 and 5 of the 1875 Act re-enacted in a residual form the principle of the Master and Servant Acts that a breach of a contract of employment was also a criminal offence. In s.4 it was made a criminal offence for employees in the gas, water or (after 1919) electricity industries intentionally to break their contracts of employment (either alone or in combination with other employees) if they knew or ought to have known that the result of their action was likely to be to deprive the inhabitants of a town of their supplies. Section 4 was repealed by the I R A 1971 on the grounds that it was unsatisfactory to single out these three industries for special attention, although the Donovan Commission (para. 838) had recommended that the section be neither repealed nor extended. Section 5 of the 1875 Act, however, continues on the statute book. It is of general application and provides:

Where any person wilfully and maliciously breaks a contract of service or of hiring, knowing or having reasonable cause to believe that the probable consequences of his so doing, either alone or in combination with others, will be to endanger human life, or cause serious bodily injury, or to expose valuable property whether real or personal to destruction or serious injury, he shall on conviction thereof by a court of summary jurisdiction . . . be liable either to pay a penalty not exceeding twenty pounds, or to be imprisoned for a term not exceeding three months, with or without hard labour.

The Donovan Commission was unaware of there having been a prosecution under the section and that appears still to be the case, although situations have subsequently arisen where it might have been used. Nevertheless, the Commission did not recommend the section's repeal either on this ground of desuetude or on the ground that its provisions could be avoided by giving notice to terminate the contract of employment (see below, p. 719) before engaging in the industrial action, for it was thought that repeal 'involves the risk that it might be construed as an express licence to do that which the criminal law now forbids' (para. 846).

Thus, both ss.4 and 5 of the 1875 Act contemplated the imposition of criminal liability upon employees whose industrial action resulted in a threat to life, limb or property or even (in the case of section 4) in a threat of substantial inconvenience to a section of the population, in circumstances in which it was at least not clear that under the general criminal law such action would be a crime. The Donovan Commission did not wish to disturb the structure of the law, but it is probably fair to say that it was overwhelmingly concerned with short strikes in private manufacturing industry (on which ss.4 and 5 had little bearing), whereas subsequent changes in the pattern of strikes towards more large-scale, public sector confrontations (see above, p. 702) have brought the policy question again to the fore. The Green Paper, *Trade Union Immunities*, discusses these sections in the context of a consideration of the impact of strike action upon 'the community as a whole' (see paras. 306– 38), and we shall return to this broader question below (pp. 868–86).

With the relegation after 1875 of the criminal law to a relatively minor role in the control of industrial action (other than picketing) it was perhaps inevitable that sooner or later similar policy issues should be raised before, and need to be settled by, the civil courts. In fact, this occurred in a series of cases, notably a trilogy of House of Lords decisions, around the turn of the nineteenth century, a period of intensified industrial conflict associated with the growth of unionization amongst unskilled and semi-skilled manual workers (see above,

p. 117). The main question was whether the intentional but peaceful infliction of economic harm upon an employer in an industrial dispute amounted to the commission of a tort. In formal terms, the fact that such conduct after 1875 would not usually be a crime was not dispositive of the question of whether such action was tortious. To those engaged in industrial action, however, the distinction between crime and tort was perhaps not so clear, for if the industrial action was tortious, the employer could usually obtain from the court an injunction to restrain the action. As the late Professor Kahn-Freund remarked in *Labour and the Law* (2nd edn, 1977, p. 231):

In theory there is a big difference between the criminal law and the law of tort. In practice the difference is small: it is whether you go to prison by reason of conviction for a criminal offence or by reason of contempt of court. Committal for contempt may in fact be much more serious than conviction for an offence.

However, in *Allen* v. *Flood* [1898] AC 1 the House of Lords appeared to decide that conduct otherwise not tortious would not become so because the conduct was carried out with the intention of deliberately harming the economic interests of another. In that case the defendant union official threatened to call out boilermakers employed by an employer (without any breach of contract by the boilermakers) unless the plaintiff shipwrights also employed by the employer were dismissed (again without any breach of contract on the part of the employer). The defendant acted as he did partly in order to punish the shipwrights for past misconduct. Nevertheless, the defendant was held to have committed no tort. Mere interference with the plaintiffs' employment was not tortious and the addition of an element of malice or spite did not alter the legal position. However, trade unionists' rejoicings that the courts were not going to use the law of tort to take up again the role recently removed from the criminal law were cut short by the decision of a differently constituted House of Lords in the case of *Quinn* v. *Leathem* [1901] AC 495, one of the earliest reported cases to involve secondary industrial action (though from a legal point of view nothing turned on this). The defendant union officials demanded that the plaintiff (Leathem) dismiss certain non-unionists employed by him in his fleshing business. When he refused to do so, the union approached a butcher, who was a customer of Leathem and persuaded him, under threat of a strike by his employees, not to deal with Leathem until Leathem sacked the non-unionists. Leathem sued the defendant officials in tort. It appeared that neither the dismissal of the non-unionists by Leathem nor the threatened strike by the butcher's employees nor the butcher's ceasing to trade with Leathem involved a breach of contract by any of the relevant parties. Nevertheless, the defendants were held to have committed a tort, namely the tort of conspiracy.

To some degree the results in these two House of Lords cases are simply inconsistent with one another, but *Quinn* v. *Leathem* is now generally taken to stand for the proposition that an *agreement* intentionally to inflict economic harm upon another is tortious, even where the act by which the harm is to be inflicted is not independently unlawful, whereas by virtue of *Allen* v. *Flood* an act done by an individual which inflicts economic harm upon another is not tortious. (See, for example, *Sorrell* v. *Smith* [1925] AC 700 *per* Lord Dunedin.) Thus, the element of combination was the essence of the tort and the result was in practice to overturn the decision in *Allen* v. *Flood* as far as trade unionists were concerned because, as we noted above in relation to criminal conspiracy, freedom to act collectively is the fundamental requirement of effective industrial action. After statutory criminal conspiracy and common-law criminal conspiracy the doctrine of conspiracy had reappeared for a third time to render any social right to strike illusory in legal terms. In so far as a policy rationale was offered at all in *Quinn* v. *Leathem* for the distinction that was drawn between that case and *Allen* v. *Flood*, it was that a group of people can inflict greater economic harm than a single individual. As a general proposition this is clearly unsustainable in view of the acceptance by English law of the doctrine of separate, corporate, legal personality (an acceptance confirmed by the House of Lords itself some four years before *Quinn* v. *Leathem* in the great case of *Salomon* v. *Salomon & Co.* [1897] AC 22). As Lord Diplock pointed out in the recent case of *Lonrho Ltd* v. *Shell Petroleum Co. Ltd* [1982] AC 173, it is absurd to suppose that a combination of small grocers can wield greater economic power than a single company owning a string of large supermarkets. Nevertheless, in respect of employees the perception of their lordships in *Quinn* v. *Leathem* is generally accurate, which is why the institution of collective bargaining was developed by trade unionists. Unfortunately, this contrast between the position of employees and that of capital (for which the company form provides for the process of combination to occur within a single legal person) only seems to strengthen the view that the decision in *Quinn* v. *Leathem* was arrived at precisely in order to reduce the industrial strength of the nascent union movement. This view is strengthened by the decision of the House of Lords in the third of the trilogy of cases (albeit the first in point of time). In *Mogul Steamship Co. Ltd* v. *McGregor, Gow & Co. Ltd* [1892] AC 25, the House had held that an agreement among a group of shippers to undercut a rival trader on a certain route so as to obtain a monopoly of it for themselves was not a tortious conspiracy or, if it was, the defendants had a defence of justification in that they were acting only in pursuit of their own legitimate economic self-interest.

In the TDA 1906, s.1, Parliament responded to the decision in *Quinn* v. *Leathem* by inserting a new paragraph into s.3 of the 1875 Act so as to extend the principle of that section to actions in tort. Today that provision is found in TULRA 1974, s.13(4) and it provides that:

An agreement or combination by two or more persons to do or procure the doing of any act in contemplation or furtherance of a trade dispute is not actionable in tort if the act is one which, if done without any such agreement or combination, would not be actionable in tort.

The effect was that after 1906 'simple' conspiracy or conspiracy 'to injure', where the gist of the tort was the element of combination, ceased to operate so as to frustrate the right to strike. Section 13(4) does not, however, provide any protection when the agreement is to commit an act which *would* be tortious if committed by an individual. As it is sometimes put, liability for conspiracy to use unlawful means is not excluded by s.13(4), but in that situation tortious conspiracy operates to supplement another tortious liability which in principle exists rather than to create tortious liability where none in principle exists.

The effect of the conflict between *Allen* v. *Flood* and *Quinn* v. *Leathem* was also to throw some doubt on the principle which the former case seemed to stand for. Consequently, in the second limb of s.3 of the TDA 1906 Parliament put the principle in statutory form for those acting in contemplation or furtherance of a trade dispute. As re-enacted by s.13(2) of TULRA 1974 it provided that:

For the avoidance of doubt it is hereby declared that an act done by a person in contemplation or furtherance of a trade dispute is not actionable in tort on the ground only that it is an interference with the trade, business or employment of another person, or with the right of another person to dispose of his capital or his labour as he wills.

It is important to note the limits of this principle. In *Allen* v. *Flood* itself we have seen that the interference did not involve the use of means that were independently unlawful: no breach of contract, it seems, was threatened or committed. As with the provisions of s.1 on conspiracy, it was not generally thought that the statutory enactment of the principle of *Allen* v. *Flood* in s.3 would apply if the interference did involve the use of independently unlawful means. Indeed, the decision of the House of Lords in *Rookes* v. *Barnard* (see below, p. 738) seemed to depend upon the correctness of this view. However, some incautious dicta of Lord Diplock in *Hadmor Productions Ltd* v. *Hamilton* [1982] ICR 114 suggested that s.13(2) of TULRA 1974 might apply even if unlawful means were used, and these dicta were followed by the Court of Session in *Plessey plc* v. *Wilson* [1982] IRLR 198. Here the interference consisted of an occupation by the employees of the employer's factory, an act which would seem to involve the tort of trespass (although the decision may also have turned on the Scottish rule that trespass is not actionable *per se* but only on proof of damage). The government of the day did not wait for the opportunity to arise for the House of Lords to rule upon these conflicting dicta and decisions but in EA 1982, s.19(1) repealed s.13(2) of TULRA 1974. In one sense the repeal of s.13(2) may not be thought to matter, since *Allen* v. *Flood* is today generally understood as standing for the principle that mere interference with business (without unlawfull means) is not tortious. Hence, today, the common law is seen as providing an equivalent protection to the repealed s.13(2). But the principle of *Allen* v. *Flood* has not always been accepted in recent times by judges as expressing the most desirable rule. There are supporters of the position that the law ought to be that mere interference is *prima facie* tortious, subject to a defence of justification. Consequently, now that the House of Lords is no longer bound by its own previous decisions, the principle of *Allen* v. *Flood* may not be as deeply entrenched as it seems to be.[1] Thus, after 1906 the torts of mere interference with business and conspiracy to injure were excluded from the area of industrial relations. Had they not been, any effective piece of industrial action would have been open to legal challenge. There is, however, a tail-piece to the story which consists of subsequent common law developments in the tort of conspiracy.

After the First World War and with the growth of Whitleyism (see above, p. 118) the common law of tortious conspiracy fell into line with the 1906 Act. This was done through the development by the courts of a wide-ranging defence of justification in relation to the tort of conspiracy, even for those engaged in industrial action. Thus, in *Reynolds* v. *Shipping Federation* [1924] 1 Ch. 28, Sargeant J. was faced with an agreement between a shipowners' federation and a union not to employ as seamen people who were not members of specified unions. A seaman, who was a member of a different union, brought an action alleging tortious conspiracy between federation and union, but the judge held that the claim failed because 'the motive of the exclusion was not a malicious desire to inflict loss on any individual or class of individuals, but a desire to advance the business interests of employers and employed alike, by securing and maintaining those advantages of collective bargaining and control which had been experienced since . . .' the setting up of the closed-shop arrangement. The judge explicitly conceived of himself as applying the principles of the *Mogul* case to the agreement. *Quinn* v. *Leathem* was now seen as a case where the defendants could not set up a defence of justification because they had acted out of spite, although the evidence for that factual finding in *Quinn* v. *Leathem* was rather thin and certainly was much less strong than the evidence for it in *Allen* v. *Flood*, where, however, the defendant was found not to have committed a tortious act! Nevertheless, the approach of Sargeant J. was ultimately approved by the House of Lords in another case of union and employer combination, which we set out below.

Crofter Handwoven Harris Tweed Co. Ltd v. *Veitch*
[1942] AC 435 (HL)

Millowners on the Island of Lewis, who made and sold tweed cloth, agreed to employ 100 per cent union labour if the union in question, the Transport and General Workers' Union, instructed its members employed in the port not to handle yarn which local producers imported, turned into cloth and sold at prices below those of the millowners. The local producers sued the union officials in tort for conspiracy to injure.

LORD WRIGHT: . . . The concept of a civil conspiracy to injure has been in the main developed in the course of the last half century. . . . The rule may seem anomalous, so far as it holds that conduct by two may be actionable if it causes damage, whereas the same conduct done by one, causing the same damage, would give no redress. In effect

---

[1] Thus, Lord Devlin has written extra-judicially that the decision in *Allen* v *Flood* 'damned a stream of thought that . . . would have had a beneficial effect on the law of tort' (*Samples of Lawmaking* (1962), p.11).

the plaintiff's right is that he should not be damnified by a conspiracy to injure him, and it is in the fact of the conspiracy that the unlawfulness resides. It is a different matter if the conspiracy is to do acts in themselves wrongful, such as to deceive or defraud, to commit violence, or to conduct a strike or lock-out by means of conduct prohibited by the Conspiracy and Protection of Property Act, 1875, or which contravenes the Trade Disputes and Trade Unions Act, 1927. But a conspiracy to injure is a tort which requires careful definition, in order to hold the balance between the defendant's right to exercise his lawful rights and the plaintiff's right not to be injured by an injurious conspiracy. As I read the authorities, there is a clear and definite distinction which runs through them all between what Lord Dunedin in *Sorrell* v. *Smith* calls 'a conspiracy to injure' and 'a set of acts dictated by business interest'. I should qualify 'business' by adding 'or other legitimate interests', using the convenient adjective not very precisely. . . .

As the claim is for a tort, it is necessary to ascertain what constitutes the tort alleged. It cannot be merely that the appellants' right to freedom in conducting their trade has been interfered with. That right is not an absolute or unconditional right. It is only a particular aspect of the citizen's right to personal freedom, and like other aspects of that right is qualified by various legal limitations, either by statute or by common law. Such limitations are inevitable in organized societies where the rights of individuals may clash. In commercial affairs each trader's rights are qualified by the right of others to compete. Where the rights of labour are concerned, the rights of the employer are conditioned by the rights of the men to give or withhold their services. The right of workmen to strike is an essential element in the principle of collective bargaining. . . .

It is thus clear that employers of workmen or those who like the appellants depend in part on the services of workmen, have in the conduct of their affairs to reckon with this freedom of the men and to realize that the exercise of the men's rights may involve some limitation on their own freedom in the management of their business. Such interference with a person's business, so long as the limitations enforced by law are not contravened, involves no legal wrong against the person. In the present case the respondents are sued for imposing the 'embargo', which corresponds to calling out the men on strike. The dockers were free to obey or not to obey the call to refuse to handle the appellants' goods. In refusing to handle the goods they did not commit any breach of contract with anyone; they were merely exercising their own rights. But there might be circumstances which rendered the action wrongful. The men might be called out in breach of their contracts with their employer, and that would be clearly a wrongful act as against the employer, an interference with his contractual right, for which damages could be claimed not only as against the contract-breaker, but against the person who counselled or procured or advised the breach. . . .

I have attempted to state principles so generally accepted as to pass into the realm of what has been called jurisprudence, at least in English law, which has for better or worse adopted the test of self-interest or selfishness as being capable of justifying the deliberate doing of lawful acts which inflict harm, so long as the means employed are not wrongful. The common law in England might have adopted a different criterion and one more consistent with the standpoint of a man who refuses to benefit himself at the cost of harming another. But we live in a competitive or acquisitive society, and the English common law may have felt that it was beyond its power to fix by any but the crudest distinctions the metes and bounds which divide the rightful from the wrongful use of the actor's own freedom, leaving the precise application in any particular case to the jury or judge of fact. If further principles of regulation or control are to be introduced, that is matter for the legislature. . . .

In *Sorrell* v. *Smith* the judge's view was 'that the defendants were well meaning busybodies, who intimidated third parties and so meddled with the plaintiff's business in a matter which was no business of theirs' because, as he held, they wanted a controlling decision in the dispute. The Court of Appeal and this House reversed the decision of the judge on the short ground that the real purpose of the newspaper proprietors was to promote the circulation of their papers, and that they did so by lawful means.

I think this line of reasoning applies here to answer the appellants' contention that the respondents or the union had no direct interest in the importation of yarn. On the facts found, rightly as I think, they were of the opinion that the prosperity of the industry in Harris tweed was jeopardized by the importation. It is not for the court to decide whether this opinion was reasonable or not. It was a genuine opinion. It cannot be said that it was a mere sham intended to cloak a sinister desire to injure the importers. The respondents had no quarrel with the yarn importers. Their sole object, the courts below have held, was to promote their union's interests by promoting the interest of the industry on which the men's wages depended. On these findings, with which I agree, it could not be said that their combination was without sufficient justification. Nor would this conclusion be vitiated, even though their motives may have been mixed, so long as the real or predominant object, if they had more than one object, was not wrongful. Nor is the objection tenable that the respondent's real or predominant object was to secure the employers' help to get 100 per cent. membership of the union among the textile workers. Cases of mixed motives or, as I should prefer to say, of the presence of more than one object, are not uncommon. If so, it is for the jury or judge of fact to decide which is the predominant object, as it may be assumed the jury did in *Quinn's* case, when they decided on the basis that the object of the combiners was vindictive punishment, not their own practical advantage. . . . It was objected that there could be no combination between the employers and the union because their respective interests were necessarily opposed. I think that is a fallacious contention. It is true that employers and workmen are often at variance because the special interest of each side conflicts in a material respect as, for instance, in questions of wages, conditions or hours of work, exclusion of non-union labour. But apart from these differences in interest, both employers and workmen have a common interest in the prosperity of their industry, though the interest of one side may be in profits and of the other in wages. Hence a wider and truer view is that there is a community of interest. That view was acted upon in the present case in regard to the essential matter of yarn importation. As to the separate matter of the union membership, while that was something regarded as important by the respondents it was probably regarded by the employers as a matter of indifference to them. It was, in any case, a side issue in the combination even from the respondents' point of view. I may add that I do not accept, as a general proposition, that there must be a complete identity of interest between parties to a combination. There must, however, be sufficient identity of object, though the advantage to be derived from that same object may not be the same. . . .

I need add merely a few words on the objection that the embargo was the act of the dockers for the benefit, not of themselves, but of the textile workers. It is enough to say that both sections were members of the union, and there was in my opinion a sufficient community of interest even if the matter is regarded from the standpoint of the men, as individuals, and not from the standpoint of the respondents, who were the only parties sued. Their interest, however, was to promote the advantage of the union as a whole.

VISCOUNTS SIMON, L.C., and MAUGHAM, and LORDS THANKERTON and PORTER delivered concurring speeches.

Thus, in the space of half a century the view of the House of Lords in relation to the tort of conspiracy to injure had completely changed. In *Quinn* v. *Leathem* the tort was established with apparently little prospect of a successful defence of justification being accepted, so that the law of tort had rendered the 'right to strike' as illusory as had previously the criminal law of conspiracy. In the *Crofter* case so wide a defence of legitimate protection of one's own interests was allowed as to remove the tort of conspiracy from a significant role in the regulation of industrial conflict, and this has continued to be the situation since 1942.[1] The courts have resisted the temptation to use the defence of justification so as to draw a line between what they regard as justifiable and what they regard as unjustifiable purposes so long as these purposes are in the field of industrial relations. They have, however, used the defence to distinguish between purposes within the field of industrial relations and purposes without it. As we shall see below in relation to the definition of trade disputes (pp. 795–805), this latter distinction is not an easy one to draw.

Two cases subsequent to *Crofter* indicate the problem in relation to the law of conspiracy. In *Huntley* v. *Thornton* [1957] 1 WLR 321, the defendants were members of a district committee of the Amalgamated Engineering Union. The plaintiff was a member of that union who had refused to take part in a 24-hour strike over a wage claim. The plaintiff was consequently summoned before the committee to explain his conduct. At the meeting he adopted a truculent attitude and eventually walked out, leaving the district committee to pass a resolution recommending to the executive council of the union that the plaintiff be expelled. The executive council refused to accept the recommendation. The district committee used its best efforts to secure that the plaintiff, who had resigned from his original employment, did not secure other employment in engineering shops in the district, rebuffed the plaintiff's efforts to make his peace with them and purported to expel him (though the committee was without power to do so). The plaintiff brought an action for damages for conspiracy against the defendants.

Harman J. said of the defendants' purposes after the decision of the executive committee, '. . . by this time the district committee had entirely lost sight of what the interests of the union demanded, and thought only of their own ruffled dignity'. Consequently, the defendants were held to have committed the tort of conspiracy to injure. On the other hand, in *Scala Ballroom (Wolverhampton) Ltd* v. *Ratcliffe* [1958] 1 WLR 1057 the defendant officials of the Musicians' Union organized a boycott by their members of a ballroom which applied a colour bar. The court held that the defendants had a justification for the tort of conspiracy to injure. Morris L.J. said: 'But it seems

---

[1] In *Lonrho Ltd* v *Shell Petroleum Co. Ltd* [1982] AC 173, the House of Lords was prepared to apply the defence of justification by way of pursuit of one's own self-interest even to the tort of conspiracy to use unlawful means.

to me that, if the defendants honestly believe that a certain policy is desirable and that it is the wish of their members that that policy should prevail and that there should be no colour bar discrimination, it can be said that the welfare of the members is being advanced, even though it cannot be positively translated into or shown to be reflected in detailed financial terms.'

There are two aspects of these developments in the law of conspiracy after 1906 which are worthy of note. First, as Professor Wedderburn has suggested,[1] the *Crofter* case and *Reynolds* v. *Shipping Federation* represented the acceptance by the judiciary in the inter-war period of the abstentionist position established by the TDA 1906. It was these decisions in particular that Professor Kahn-Freund referred to in the 1950s when writing about collective *laissez-faire*. In the 1960s, with the growth of plant-level bargaining and an increase in levels of industrial conflict, judicial attitudes in fact moved away from abstentionism, as exemplified by the decision in *Rookes* v. *Barnard*, but this move reflected itself in the development of economic torts other than the tort of conspiracy to injure, which has been left very much where the House of Lords left it after the *Crofter* case. This brings us to the second point, which concerns techniques of judicial law-making. It is at first sight odd that the law should have swung so rapidly from the end of the spectrum represented by *Quinn* v. *Leathem* to that represented by the *Crofter* case, without any serious attempt to try out an intermediate position. This position would be that conspiracy to injure should be tortious, but the defence of justification should be used to distinguish between acceptable and unacceptable forms of industrial action, for example, between constitutional and unconstitutional strikes. This would be a rather different use of the defence of justification from the one rejected in *Crofter*. In that case the House refused to use the defence to distinguish between proper and improper purposes for industrial action (provided that the purpose was a purpose within the field of industrial relations). However, such modified use of the defence of justification has never appealed to the judiciary, even in the 1960s and later. It might be said that, in view of the provisions of the TDA 1906 and TULRA 1974 excluding the tort of conspiracy to injure from trade disputes, such a development at common law would in any event be nugatory. However, the same reluctance to distinguish between fair and unfair methods of competition can be found in the *Mogul* case. In the Court of Appeal in that case, Fry L.J. said that 'to draw a line between fair and unfair competition, between what is reasonable and unreasonable, passes the power of the courts' ((1889) 23 QBD 598 at 625–6). Perhaps the use of the defence of justification to distinguish between fair and unfair methods of competition or fair and unfair forms of industrial action would appear to the judges to be too naked an exercise of their creative powers.

However that may be, the common law of the economic torts bears today in consequence a much more technical aspect. Instead of using the defence of justification to develop a functional relationship between industrial relations

[1] K. W. Wedderburn, 'Labour Law and Labour Relations in Britain' (1972) 10 *BJIR* 270.

concepts and concepts of legality, the common law has relied upon its own, rather esoteric notions of lawfulness. This has made the law neither easy for the layman to understand nor free from anomaly in its operation. Nevertheless, labour lawyers must study it as it is. In a recent and invaluable article[1] Patrick Elias and Keith Ewing suggest that the notions to which the common law has had recourse in determining whether a particular method of industrial action is lawful or unlawful can be placed in one or other of three categories. The courts have asked: does the action interfere with the plaintiff's pre-existing legal rights; does the action interfere with the plaintiff's interests through the use of independently unlawful means; or does the action interfere with the performance of the plaintiff's statutory duties? We now turn to consider the other economic torts in the light of this suggested categorization.

4 Inducing breach of contract

(a) Inducing breach of contracts of employment

In distinguishing between lawful and unlawful methods of industrial action it is perhaps natural to the common-law mind to ask if that action infringes any of the plaintiff's pre-existing rights. A pervasive source of such rights in society is contract and hence the importance for the law of industrial action of the tort of inducing breach of contract. The modern form of the tort has its origins in the decision in *Lumley* v. *Gye* (1853) 2 E & B 216, in which it was held tortious for the defendant to persuade a Miss Wagner to sing at Her Majesty's Theatre when she was under contract with the plaintiff to sing exclusively at the Queen's Theatre for a period of three months. The existence of the tort was confirmed by the House of Lords and applied to a typical conflict between employer and trade union in *South Wales Miners' Federation* v. *Glamorgan Coal Company Ltd* [1905] AC 239. The employees represented by the appellant union were paid on a sliding scale which varied with the price of coal. In order to maintain the price of coal the union instructed its members from time to time not to report to work. This was held to amount to inducement by the union of its members to break their contracts of employment with the respondent company, and thus the commission of a tort by the union against the company. The House rejected the argument that furtherance by the union of the interests of the workmen was a defence to the tort, and the defence of justification to this tort has subsequently remained very restricted.[2]

How great a restriction upon the legal freedom of employees to take industrial action has the development of this tort proved to be? We have seen that in *Allen* v. *Flood* and *Quinn* v. *Leathem* the employees were able to organize effective industrial action without any breach of contract apparently being threatened or committed. This was perhaps because many manual workers at

---

[1] 'Economic Torts and Industrial Action: Old Principles and New Liabilities' [1982] *CLJ* 321.
[2] Cf. *Brimelow* v *Casson* [1924] 1 Ch.302; *Pete's Towing Services Ltd* v. *Northern Industrial Union of Workers* [1970] NZLR 32.

that time were employed on terms such that they could leave or be discharged instantly or at least upon very short notice (e.g. an hour's notice). In such circumstances it was not natural to think of the strike as a breach of contract, and consequently strike organizers would not be in the position of committing the tort of inducing breach of contract. However, not all workers, even manual ones, were employed on such terms. In the *Glamorgan Coal Co.* case there was a collective agreement between the union and the employers' association, which the courts apparently treated as incorporated into the contracts of employment of the individual miners, that notice of termination, by either employer or employee, could be given only on the first day of any month to terminate on the last day of that month (see [1903] 1 KB at p. 210). The union's practice of calling one-day stoppages at short or no notice to the employers was found to be contrary to this provision, thus putting the union in the position of having committed the tort of inducing breach of contract.

As time has passed since that case, it has become more and more common for employees to be employed on terms requiring fairly lengthy terms of notice by them to terminate their contracts. We have seen above (p. 434) that by EPCA 1978, s.49(2), the length of notice required of an employee who has been employed for at least four weeks, to terminate his contract, is a minimum of one week. Often, however, provision is made in the contract of employment for longer periods, sometimes periods which are parallel to those which the employer has to observe (s.49(1)). Since the strike notice for all the employees would have to be of the length of the notice required to be given by the employee who was under the obligation to give the longest period of notice (assuming that it was desired that all the strikers should cease work at the same time), strike organizers today would have to give long periods of notice to employers if they were to have any hope of avoiding liability for inducing breach of contract. Such a development, however, might not be thought to be undesirable. On the contrary, it might be thought to make the law of industrial conflict more functional by providing a legal method for distinguishing between constitutional and unconstitutional strikes. Somewhat in this vein the Donovan Commission, for example, when recommending the retention of s.4 of the CPPA 1875, which, it will be recalled (see above, p. 708), imposed criminal liability in respect of certain strikes in breach of contract, put forward the view that 'the effect of the section is . . . to give to the employer and through him to the public previous warning of a stoppage which . . . may expose the public to danger' (para. 838).

However, the notion that strike organizers could avoid liability for inducing breach of contract by giving due notice before striking was not one that was ever strongly taken up by the common law. The exact legal status of different types of strike notice has not always been clear, but, rather ironically, in the 1960s when public disquiet over unconstitutional strikes was at its highest and when Parliament tried to distinguish between acceptable and unacceptable strikes by reference to their contractual status (see below, p. 932), the dominant trend in the courts came to be that of seeing even due notice of a strike as notice to *break* rather than as notice to *terminate* the contracts of employment of the strikers. Thus, in *Rookes* v. *Barnard* [1964] AC 1129 Lord Devlin said: '. . . the object of the notice was not to terminate the contract either before or after the expiry of seven days [the period of notice required to terminate the contract]. The object was to break the contract by withholding labour but keeping the contract alive for as long as the employers would tolerate the breach without exercising their right of rescission.' Equally, the Donovan Commission said that a strike will normally result in a breach of the contract of employment 'even if notice of the intention to strike is given, whether the notice be shorter, or longer, or the same length as the notice required by the contract for its termination' (para. 937). This result is arrived at simply as a matter of construction by the courts of notice of an intention to strike or withdraw labour. It would seem that notice which was sufficiently clearly expressed as a notice to terminate would be treated as such by the courts, but it is not the practice for such notice to be given.[1]

The above discussion has proceeded upon the assumption that for employees to go on strike is for them to break their contracts of employment unless those contracts have been lawfully terminated before the strike takes place. A third analysis would be to view the strike as the exercise of a right conferred by the contract rather than a breach of it. It is clear that the parties may come to an agreement which expressly or by necessary implication confers such a right upon the employe, but this is, of course, unusual. Although the idea that it was a generally implied term in the contract of employment that the employee was free to strike (under certain circumstances) was floated by Lord Denning in *Morgan* v. *Fry* [1968] 2 QB at p. 730, it was rejected by later cases and has not taken root in the common law; and, although a form of the idea was contained in s.147 of the IRA 1971, it had been rejected as a legislative proposal by the Donovan Commission (see paras. 936–52) and it has not found favour with subsequent legislators and so it is not part of current statute law. We shall return to this topic, however, when we discuss the employer's self-help remedies (below, pp. 913ff.). The upshot is that a strike, even after due notice, is usually analysed as a breach of the relevant contracts of employment, thus rendering the strike organizer *prima facie* liable in tort.

The position of the organizer of industrial action that falls short of a full strike is not much more favourable, although it is equally complex. To persuade employees to perform less than their full contractual duties, for example, by 'blacking' (i.e. refusing to handle) the supply of goods or services to a particular customer of the employer whilst handling supplies to all other customers in the usual way, is normally to induce them to break their contracts of employment. In some rare cases the union may negotiate with the employer for a provision which entitles the employees not to perform the full range of normal duties (e.g. a provision that drivers employed by the employer are

---

[1] See further, Hepple and O'Higgins, *Employment Law* (4th edn, 1981), paras. 494–6.

entitled to refuse to cross official picket lines established by that union or, perhaps, by any other union). In the absence of such a provision, however, blacking will be a breach of contract. So also will be a go-slow. The legality of an overtime ban will often turn upon the question of whether the working of overtime was voluntary (as it was conceded to be in *Secretary of State* v. *ASLEF (No. 2)* [1972] 2 QB 455) or was obligatory, at least as far as the employees were concerned (see above, pp. 335–8).[1] The same question can arise in relation to a wide range of employee duties, for example, in relation to the participation by teachers in lunch-time supervision or in extra-curricular activities. A work-to-rule was held to be a breach of contract in *Secretary of State* v. *ASLEF (No. 2)* [1972] 2 QB 455 (see above, pp. 269 and 309). In spite of many questionable dicta in that case, the decision itself can be supported on the grounds that the meaning of the contract was that normally given to it by both parties to it, even if that meaning departed from the literal meaning of its terms, upon which the employees were, for the period of the industrial action, insisting.

Two points seem to emerge from the above discussion of the relationship of the contract of employment to industrial action as far as the tort of inducing breach of contract is concerned. First, the tort of inducing breach emerges as *prima facie* inconsistent with a right to strike because of the wide range of circumstances in which industrial action will be a breach of the contract of employment. Second, both common law and statute law have largely renounced the opportunity to modify this result by developing the law of the contract of employment so as to make a more discriminating and functional distinction between different methods of industrial action. One can see this in regard to the legal status of strike notices, whilst the distinction between those forms of action short of a strike which are in breach of contract or those which are not is almost wholly arbitrary in industrial relations terms. However, this second development, or rather lack of development, in the law of contract of employment is, of course, consistent with an abstentionist stance on the part of the law, and so should perhaps cause us no surprise. To use the law of the contract of employment to distinguish between desirable and undesirable methods of industrial action would not be to withdraw the law from 'the battlefield of industrial hostilities' (above, p. 697) but rather to involve it more deeply in the fighting. However, abstentionism as far as the contract of employment is concerned means that the tort of inducing breach poses a very stark challenge to employees' freedom to engage in industrial action. That challenge was very quickly perceived by the legislators after the House of Lords' decision in the *Glamorgan Coal Co.* case. Whilst the Trade Disputes Bill was before the House of Commons in 1906, Sir Charles Dilke introduced an amendment to clause 3 (which previously was drafted only to provide

---

[1] See also *Camden Exhibition and Display Ltd* v *Lynott* [1966] 1 QB 555 (above, p.290), on the incorporation of provisions concerning restrictions on overtime from the collective agreement into the individual contract of employment. But cf. now TULRA 1974, s.18(4), discussed below at p.777.

statutory confirmation of the principle laid down in *Allen* v. *Flood* (see above, p. 711) so that by its 'first limb' it protected also those who, in contemplation or furtherance of a trade dispute, induced 'some other person to break a contract of employment'. As Richard Kidner has remarked, 'without that phrase the very system of unrestricted collective bargaining would have become impossible'.[1] The modern version of the protection can be found in s.13(1) of TULRA 1974, and it remains the bedrock of the legal freedom to strike, because no subsequent developments in the common law relating to inducing breach of contract have occurred which have performed for that tort what the defence of justification achieved for the tort of conspiracy.

However, it is as well to remember that while contract is the main source of rights that industrial action may interfere with, it is by no means the only source. In *Prudential Assurance Co.* v. *Lorenz* (1971) 11 KIR 78, the officials of a union who persuaded agents of the plaintiff not to remit premiums collected by them to their employer as a form of industrial action were held to have committed a tort by inducing breaches of fiduciary duty. Since the agents' fiduciary duties to their employer were held to arise independently of the contract of employment, the defendants were not protected by s.3 of the TDA 1906. The decision may be correct at a doctrinal level, but it is somewhat arbitrary that this particular form of industrial action escaped from the statutory protections.

(b) Inducing breach of commercial contracts

Our discussion so far has assumed that the tort of inducing breach of contract poses a problem to organizers of industrial action only to the extent that they are likely to induce breaches of contracts of employment by those taking the industrial action. This, however, is not so. If his employees go on strike an employer may be put in a position where he cannot fulfil his commercial contracts with his customers and (in the absence of a *force majeure* clause) is consequently in breach of them. Can either employer or customer sue the strike organizer for inducing breach of commercial contract? Perhaps surprisingly, this situation has been little discussed in the cases. Indeed, the customer might not have a cause of action at common law. Inducing breach is a tort of intention and, where the employees' dispute is with their own employer, it might be said that the customer is not a party aimed at by the strikers even if they know what the effect on the commercial contract of their taking industrial action will be.[2] The typical situation that has been considered by the courts is one where the employees of the primary employer take industrial action in pursuit of some dispute with him but that action is for some reason ineffective in securing their objectives. The organizers of the

---

[1] R. Kidner, 'Lessons in trade union law reform: the origins and passage of the Trade Disputes Act 1906' (1982) 2 *LS* 34 at 51.

[2] Cf. the rejection by the House of Lords in *Lonrho Ltd* v. *Shell Petroleum Co. Ltd* [1982] AC 173 of the principle laid down in *Beaudesert Shire Council* v. *Smith* (1966) 120 CLR 145 below, (p. 754).

industrial action then persuade the employees of another, 'secondary' employer to take some action which will increase the pressure on the primary employer. There is no independent dispute between the secondary employer and his employees, and the action of these employees typically takes the form of blacking supplies to or from the primary employer, rather than a full strike. If the action of the employees of the secondary employer produces a breach of a commercial contract between primary and secondary employer, why should not either employer sue the organizers of the action? The situation can be set out diagrammatically as follows:

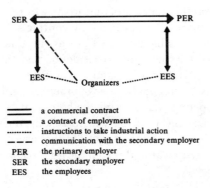

══════	a commercial contract
▬▬▬▬	a contract of employment
··········	instructions to take industrial action
– – –	communication with the secondary employer
PER	the primary employer
SER	the secondary employer
EES	the employees

For once, there is a fair degree of coincidence between the legal issue (i.e. is there liability for inducing breach of the commercial contract?) and the issue of public policy (i.e. should secondary industrial action be proscribed?). The coincidence is not complete, since secondary action which did *not* involve inducing breach of contractual relations between PER and SER would not be caught, for example, where SER is persuaded not to enter into a new contract with PER (cf. *Midland Cold Storage* v. *Steer* [1972] ICR 435). Equally, in the first example given above of primary action causing the employer to be unable to fulfil his contract with a customer, if the customer could sue for the breach of the commercial contract, the tort would be operating so as to make primary industrial action unlawful because of its secondary effects. Nevertheless, the question of whether there is or should be liability for inducing breach of commercial contracts (i.e. contracts other than contracts of employment)[1] has come to be seen as the way in Britain that the question of the legality of secondary industrial action should be dealt with. Can the secondary employer claim to be a neutral in the dispute between primary employer and his employees and so entitled to legal protection from industrial action? Is secondary action regarded as putting unfair pressure on the primary employer

[1] This is the conventional way of describing contracts that fell outside the scope of the protection of s.3 of the TDA 1906, but it means that the term 'commercial contract' is used to signify a very wide range of contracts indeed, some of which, e.g. labour-only supply contracts in *Emerald Construction* v. *Lowthian* [1966] 1 WLR 691, are analogous to, but do not amount to, contracts of employment.

so that he also can sue the organizers of the secondary action?

It might be thought that Parliament in 1906 was answering these questions in the affirmative by confining the statutory protection to the act of inducing breach of contracts of employment, especially as the potential liability of organizers of industrial action in respect of commercial contracts had been recognized in *Temperton* v. *Russell (No. 2)* [1893] 1 QB 239. However, the one matter upon which all the commentators on the confused circumstances in which the TDA 1906 was passed seem agreed is in concluding that Parliament intended to draw no such conscious and principled distinction. The Donovan Commission devoted some attention to this issue and concluded that 'it is not possible at this distance of time to say why the protection afforded by section 3 was confined to breaches of contracts of employment'. It suggested that 'it may . . . have seemed . . . at the time that this was the situation which called for some immediate action and there was no present need to go further' (para.887). Certainly, it is true that the limits of the protection afforded by s.3 did not become of practical significance until much later. The inter-war period was perhaps the highpoint of abstentionism and employers did not seem concerned to try to press home their legal rights. Only in the changed circumstances of the 1950s did the tort of inducing breach of commercial contracts reappear to threaten the legal security of the organizers of industrial action.

The first such case of importance was *D. C. Thomson & Co. Ltd* v. *Deakin* [1952] Ch. 646. The plaintiff employer lost his action, and the case can be regarded as something of a bench-mark against which to judge later developments in the common law. The Court of Appeal accepted the principle of liability for inducing breaches of commercial contract, but set a number of hurdles that prospective plaintiffs needed to surmount before they achieved success. In particular, the court stressed that the tort was a tort of intention, so that the organizers' knowledge of the existence of the contract and its terms and their intention to induce breaches of it needed to be fully proved. It also drew an absolutely crucial distinction between the 'direct' and 'indirect' forms of inducement of breach of contract and stressed that the use of independently unlawful means was an essential ingredient for liability in the indirect form of the tort.

D. C. Thomson & Co. Ltd v. *Deakin* [1952] Ch. 646 (CA)

The plaintiffs ran a non-union shop and dismissed a man who had joined a union. The union to which the man belonged (NATSOPA) sought to organize a boycott of the plaintiffs. In pursuance of this boycott the employees of Bowaters Ltd, who belonged to another union (TGWU), told Bowaters, who supplied paper to the plaintiffs, that they might not be willing to continue the supply. Consequently, Bowaters did not ask their employees to continue to handle supplies to the plaintiffs. This led to a breach of the commercial contract between Bowaters and the plaintiffs, who sued the officials of the

TGWU and NATSOPA for their part in organizing the action by the employees of Bowaters.

JENKINS L.J.: . . . The parties to this unfortunate controversy are entitled to advance their respective sides of it by any lawful means they think fit to adopt, and the sole question for the court is whether the defendants or any and, if so, which of them have, as alleged by the plaintiffs, overstepped the bounds of lawful action in the promotion of their cause or, perhaps I should say, the cause of Natsopa.

Apart from the effect of the Trade Disputes Act, 1906, the principles of law to be applied in this case are thus summarized by Lord Simon L.C. in *Crofter Hand Woven Harris Tweed Co. Ltd* v. *Veitch* [[1942] AC 435, 442]:

> First, then, apart from the effects of combination, it is clear that (1) if A is damaged by the action of B, A nevertheless has no remedy against B, if B's act is lawful in itself and is carried out without employing unlawful means. In such a case A has to endure damnum absque injuria. (2) It makes no difference to the above proposition that B in so acting had the purpose of damaging A. A bad motive does not per se turn an individual's otherwise lawful act into an unlawful one. (3) If C has an existing contract with A and B is aware of it, and if B persuades or induces C to break the contract with resulting damage to A, this is, generally speaking, a tortious act for which B will be liable to A for the injury he has done to him. In some cases, however, B may be able to justify his procuring of the breach of contract,

and the passage goes on to give an example of such justification.

In view of Mr Beyfus' [counsel for the plaintiffs] disclaimer for the purposes of the motion of any allegation of conspiracy to injure, the reference to the effect of combination, developed later in the same speech, requires no further notice here.

Lord Simon L.C.'s first and second propositions found earlier recognition in the speech of Lord Macnaghten in *Allen* v. *Flood* [[1898] AC 1, 151], where he said:

> I do not think that there is any foundation in good sense or in authority for the proposition that a person who suffers loss by reason of another doing or not doing some act which that other is entitled to do or to abstain from doing at his own will and pleasure, whatever his real motive may be, has a remedy against a third person who, by persuasion or some other means not in itself unlawful, has brought about the act of omission from which the loss comes, even though it could be proved that such person was actuated by malice towards the plaintiff, and that his conduct if it could be inquired into was without justification or excuse.
>
> The case may be different where the act itself to which the loss is traceable involves some breach of contract or some breach of duty, and amounts to an interference with legal rights. There the immediate agent is liable, and it may well be that the person in the background who pulls the strings is liable too, though it is not necessary in the present case to express any opinion on that point. . . .

Lord Simon L.C.'s third proposition refers to what may be described as the primary form of the type of wrong held to be actionable in *Lumley* v. *Gye* [2 El. & Bl. 216], and in that form commonly designated 'procuring or inducing a breach of contract.'

This type of wrong was more broadly defined by Lord Macnaghten in *Quinn* v. *Leathem* [[1901] AC 495, 510], where he said:

> Speaking for myself, I have no hesitation in saying that I think the decision was right,

not on the ground of malicious intention – that was not, I think, the gist of the action – but on the ground that a violation of legal right committed knowingly is a cause of action, and that it is a violation of legal right to interfere with contractual relations recognized by law if there be no sufficient justification for the interference.

To this should be added Lord Lindley's statement of the law in the same case [ibid., 535]:

If the above reasoning is correct, *Lumley* v. *Gye* [2 El. & Bl. 16] was rightly decided, as I am of opinion it clearly was. Further, the principle involved in it cannot be confined to inducements to break contracts of service, nor indeed to inducements to break any contracts. The principle which underlies the decision reaches all wrongful acts done intentionally to damage a particular individual and actually damaging him.

We were referred to a great many more authorities, but no useful purpose will be served by multiplying citations, as the passages I have quoted sufficiently indicate the general principles of law to be applied.

After a full and elaborate argument, I am satisfied, first, that Lord Simon L.C.'s third proposition does not exhaustively define the type of actionable wrong to which it refers, as there may, on the principles stated by Lords Macnaghten and Lindley in *Quinn* v. *Leathem* [[1901] A C 495], be an actionable interference with contractual rights where other means of interference than persuasion or procurement or inducement, in the sense of influence of one kind or another brought to bear on the mind of the contract breaker to cause him to break his contract, are used by the interferer; but, secondly, that (apart from conspiracy to injure, which, as I have said, is not in question so far as this motion is concerned) acts of a third party lawful in themselves do not constitute an actionable interference with contractual rights merely because they bring about a breach of contract, even if they were done with the object and intention of bringing about such breach.

With these two propositions in mind I turn to consider what are the necessary ingredients of an actionable interference with contractual rights.

The breach of contract complained of must be brought about by some act of a third party (whether alone or in concert with the contract breaker), which is in itself unlawful, but that act need not necessarily take the form of persuasion or procurement or inducement of the contract breaker, in the sense above indicated.

Direct persuasion or procurement or inducement applied by the third party to the contract breaker, with knowledge of the contract and the intention of bringing about its breach, is clearly to be regarded as a wrongful act in itself, and where this is shown a case of actionable interference in its primary form is made out: *Lumley* v. *Gye* [2 El. & Bl. 216].

But the contract breaker may himself be a willing party to the breach, without any persuasion by the third party, and there seems to be no doubt that if a third party, with knowledge of a contract between the contract breaker and another, has dealings with the contract breaker which the third party knows to be inconsistent with the contract, he has committed an actionable interference. . . .

Again, so far from persuading or inducing or procuring one of the parties to the contract to break it, the third party may commit an actionable interference with the contract, against the will of both and without the knowledge of either, if, with knowledge of the contract, he does an act which, if done by one of the parties to it, would have been a breach. Of this type of interference the case of *GWK Ltd* v. *Dunlop Rubber Co. Ltd* [42 TLR 376] affords a striking example.

Further, I apprehend that an actionable interference would undoubtedly be committed if a third party, with knowledge of a contract and intent to bring about its breach, placed physical restraint upon one of the parties to the contract so as to prevent him from carrying it out.

It is to be observed that in all these cases there is something amounting to a direct invasion by the third party of the rights of one of the parties to the contract, by prevailing upon the other party to do, or doing in concert with him, or doing without reference to either party, that which is inconsistent with the contract; or by preventing, by means of actual physical restraint, one of the parties from being where he should be, or doing what he should do, under the contract.

But here the acts complained of as constituting the actionable interference do not amount to a direct invasion of the plaintiffs' contractual rights. The plaintiffs' case, as regards paper, is that the defendants persuaded, induced or procured employees of Bowaters (that is, drivers employed by Bowaters Sales Company Ltd, and loaders employed by Bowaters Mersey Mills Ltd) to break their contracts of employment by refusing to drive lorries loaded with, or to load lorries with, paper destined for the plaintiffs, with the object and intention of causing Bowaters to break, or making it impossible for them to fulfil, their contract for the supply of paper to the plaintiffs; and that the defendants did in fact, by the means I have stated, produce the intended result.

I have stated the plaintiffs' case in the only form in which (if made out on the facts) it can, in my view, be maintainable in law apart from conspiracy to injure; for I reject, as inconsistent with the authorities referred to at the beginning of this judgment, Mr Beyfus' submission that it is unnecessary for him in order to make out his case to show that any acts wrongful in themselves were done by the defendants in order to bring about the breach of Bowaters' contract with the plaintiffs, provided they were done with the intention of causing and did in fact cause such breach; and, so far as I can see, the only acts wrongful in themselves, which there is any question of imputing to the defendants on the evidence, must consist in their having persuaded, induced or procured the employees concerned to break their contracts of employment.

I have not overlooked Mr Beyfus' submission that there is evidence of direct persuasion or procurement or inducement of Bowaters to break the contract with the plaintiffs, but I do not agree that this is so, and will therefore deal with that part of Mr Beyfus' argument when I come to examine the evidence.

Now the plaintiffs' case, as I have stated it, does seem to me to involve an extension of the range of actionable interference with contractual rights beyond any actual instance of this type of wrong to be found in the decided cases. Here there is no direct invasion of the plaintiffs' rights under the contract. It was no part of their contract that these particular employees, or any particular employees, should be employed by Bowaters for the purpose of effecting deliveries of paper to them. Thus the breaches by these men of their contracts of service with Bowaters (if made out on the facts) did not in themselves involve any breach of Bowaters' contract with the plaintiffs. The breaches of the contracts of service (if made out) were, so to speak, at one remove from the breach of contract complained of. Nevertheless, I think that in principle an actionable interference with contractual relations may be committed by a third party who, with knowledge of a contract between two other persons and with the intention of causing its breach, or of preventing its performance, persuades, induces or procures the servants of one of those parties, on whose services he relies for the performance of his contract, to break their contracts of employment with him, either by leaving him without notice or by refusing to do what is necessary for the performance of his contract, provided that the breach of the contract between the two other persons intended to be brought about by the third party does in fact ensue as a necessary consequence of the third party's wrongful interference with the contracts of employment.

I take this view because I see no distinction in principle for the present purpose between persuading a man to break his contract with another, preventing him by physical restraint from performing it, making his performance of it impossible by taking away or damaging his tools or machinery, and making his performance of it impossible by depriving him, in breach of their contracts, of the services of his employees. All these are wrongful acts, and if done with knowledge of and intention to bring about a breach of a contract to which the person directly wronged is a party, and, if in fact producing that result, I fail to see why they should not all alike fall within the sphere of actionable interference with contractual relations delimited by Lords Macnaghten and Lindley in *Quinn* v. *Leathem* [[1901] AC 495].

But, while admitting this form of actionable interference in principle, I would hold it strictly confined to cases where it is clearly shown, first, that the person charged with actionable interference knew of the existence of the contract and intended to procure its breach; secondly, that the person so charged did definitely and unequivocally persuade, induce or procure the employees concerned to break their contracts of employment with the intent I have mentioned; thirdly, that the employees so persuaded, induced or procured did in fact break their contracts of employment; and, fourthly, that breach of the contract forming the alleged subject of interference ensued as a necessary consequence of the breaches by the employees concerned of their contracts of employment.

I should add that by the expression 'necessary consequence' used here and elsewhere in this judgment I mean that it must be shown that, by reason of the withdrawal of the services of the employees concerned, the contract breaker was unable, as a matter of practical possibility, to perform his contract; in other words, I think the continuance of the services of the particular employees concerned must be so vital to the performance of the contract alleged to have been interfered with as to make the effect of their withdrawal comparable, for practical purposes, to a direct invasion of the contractual rights of the party aggrieved under the contract alleged to have been interfered with, as, for example (in the case of a contract for personal services), the physical restraint of the person by whom such services are to be performed.

I make the above reservations in regard to the scope of this newly propounded form of actionable interference with contractual rights for these reasons: It is now well settled that, apart from conspiracy to injure, no actionable wrong is committed by a person who, by acts not in themselves unlawful, prevents another person from obtaining goods or services necessary for the purposes of his business, or who induces others so to prevent that person by any lawful means. It follows, in my view, that (again apart from conspiracy to injure) there is nothing unlawful, under the law as enunciated in *Allen* v. *Flood* [[1898] AC 1] and subsequent cases, in general appeals to others to prevent a given person from obtaining goods or services, for that is a purpose capable of being lawfully carried out, and there can, therefore, be nothing unlawful in advocating it, unless unlawful means are advocated. The result of such advocacy may well be that unlawful means are adopted by some to achieve the purpose advocated, but that is not to say that a person who advocates the object without advocating the means is to be taken to have advocated recourse to unlawful means. If by reference to the form of actionable interference with contractual rights now propounded, general exhortations issued in the course of a trade dispute, such as 'Stop supplies to X,' 'Refuse to handle X's goods,' 'Treat X as "black," ' and the like, were regarded as amounting to actionable interference, because persons reached by such exhortations might respond to them by breaking their contracts of employment and thereby causing breaches of contracts between their employers and other persons, and because the person issuing such exhortations must be taken constructively to have known that the employers concerned must have contracts of some kind or other with other persons, and that his exhortations (general as they were) might lead to breaches of those contracts through breaches of contracts of employment committed by persons moved by his exhortations, then, the proposition must be accepted, that it is an actionable wrong to advocate objects which can be achieved by lawful means, because they can also be achieved by unlawful means; and to that proposition I decline to subscribe.

Furthermore, as the judge in effect pointed out in his judgment, almost every strike, if to any extent successful, must cause breaches of contracts between the employer against whom it is directed and the persons with whom he is doing business, the very object of the strike being to bring his business to a standstill or himself to terms. Again, many a strike embarked on in support of a strike in progress in some other concern must have had for its immediate object the cutting off of supplies to, or prevention of distribution of the products of, or the application of similar pressure upon, that other concern.

Yet we have been referred to no case in which the persons inciting a strike have been held liable for actionable interference with contractual relations between the strikers' employers and the persons with whom they deal; and in principle I do not think that the inciters of the strike could be held so liable in the absence of proof that they knew of the existence of a particular contract, and, with a view to bringing about its breach, counselled action by employees in itself necessarily unlawful (as, for example, breach of their contracts of employment) designed to achieve that end.

To hold otherwise would, in my view, be to admit not only an addition to the means whereby actionable interference with contractual rights may be compassed (which addition, as I have said, I am in principle prepared to accept), but also an enlargement of the character and scope of the tort itself (which I cannot agree to). [His Lordship then agreed with the findings of Lord Evershed M.R. that on the facts of the case the defendants had not induced a breach of contract on the part of Bowaters' employees because Bowaters did not in fact ask their employees to load paper for the plaintiffs; and that the direct contacts between the defendants and Bowaters amounted only to 'a statement of the facts as the members of the union understood them to be' and not to persuasion by the defendants of Bowaters to break their contract with the plaintiffs. See [1952] 1 Ch. at pp. 685–6.]

LORD EVERSHED M.R.: . . .In the case of *South Wales Miners' Federation* v. *Glamorgan Coal Co. Ltd* [[1905] AC 239; [1903] 2 KB 545] afterwards affirmed by the House of Lords, to which I shall hereafter refer as the *Glamorgan* case, a case in this court upon which Mr Beyfus greatly relies, the contracts broken were contracts of service between the employees of coal mining concerns and the concerns themselves.

In that case, the alleged wrongdoers had directly intervened personally between the contracting parties. They had themselves induced and procured a number of individuals, being parties to the contracts of service, to break their bargains with the other parties to the contracts, their employers.

It was suggested in the course of argument by Sir Frank Soskice and by Mr Lindner [counsel for the defendants], that the tort must still be properly confined to such direct intervention, that is, to cases where the intervener or persuader uses by personal intervention persuasion on the mind of one of the parties to the contract so as to procure that party to break it.

I am unable to agree that any such limitation is logical, rational or part of our law. In such cases where the intervener (if I may call him such) does so directly act upon the mind of a party to the contract as to cause him to break it, the result is, for practical purposes, as though in substance he, the intervener, is breaking the contract, although he is not a party to it. Such a statement of the matter I take from Pollock's Law of Torts, 15th ed., p. 251, where reference is made to Street's Foundations of Legal Liability. At any rate, it is clear that, when there is such a direct intervention by the intervener, the intervention itself is thereby considered wrongful.

I cannot think that the result is any different if the intervener, instead of so acting upon the mind of the contracting party himself, by some other act, tortious in itself, prevents the contracting party from performing the bargain. A simple case is where the intervener, for example, physically detains the contracting party so that the contracting party is rendered unable by the detention to perform the contract. The cases, as I shall presently show, contain several instances where the intervener has employed such means, being means wrongful in themselves.

An example is to be found in a recent case which came before Roxburgh J., *British Motor Trade Association* v. *Salvadori* [[1949] Ch. 556], where there was a criminal conspiracy and the party procuring the breach acted in pursuance of such a conspiracy.

The matter then proceeds to the next stage. So far I have considered only the case in which the intervener directly acts himself, either by persuasion or by some wrongful act of his own. What is the situation if he attains the same result, indirectly, by bringing his persuasion or procuration to bear upon some third party, commonly a servant of the contracting party, but possibly an independent third person? In my judgment, it is reasonably plain (and the result, as it seems to me, would otherwise be highly illogical and irrational) that, if the act which the third party is persuaded to do is itself an unlawful act or a wrongful act (including in that phrase a breach of contract) and the other elements are present (namely, knowledge and intention to do the damage which is in fact suffered), then the result is the same and the intervener or procurer will be liable for the loss or damage which the injured party sustains. . . .

In *Merkur Island Shipping Corporation* v. *Laughton* [1983] I C R 178, the Court of Appeal held that the principles of the *D. C. Thomson* case applied even where the employees, whose breaches of contracts were induced, were not employed by one of the parties to the relevant commercial contract, whose performance was interfered with. In this case the union called upon employees employed by A not to provide services to a ship owned by D. The failure to provide the services put A in breach of his commercial contract with B, a sub-charterer of the ship from C, and further caused interference with the performance of the charter between D and C. D sued the organizers of the blacking for indirect interference with the contract between D and C. The Court of Appeal accepted that such action was tortious, but stressed the need in such cases to show that the organizers of the industrial action did intend to interfere with the contract which was the subject matter of the suit and that the breach or interference did flow as a necessary consequence from the wrongful acts committed by the defendants. On appeal, the House of Lords ([1983] ICR 490) also found no difficulty in applying the tests developed by Jenkins L.J. to this, more extended, situation.

The distinction between direct inducement and indirect procurement (the middle category of direct intervention falling short of inducement is generally assimilable to the category of indirect procurement and we will not discuss it separately) is important, not only because of the need to prove the use of unlawful means in the latter category of case, but also because of the impact of the distinction upon the question of who has a cause of action arising out of the defendants' activities. In the case of direct inducement it seems to be accepted that only the other party to the contract can sue. The person upon whom the persuasion is exercised should resist and, if he does not, he cannot subsequently sue. See, for example, *Boulting* v. *ACTT* [1963] 2 QB 606, 639–40 per Upjohn L.J. Whatever the merits of this argument, it seems not to be applicable to cases of indirect procurement, where the contracting party is put in a position such that, willy nilly, he cannot perform his contractual obligations. In such cases it seems likely that both parties to the contract can sue the defendant.

The limits on the tort of inducing breach of contract postulated in the *D. C. Thomson* case had a somewhat chequered career in the 1960s, especially in the hands of Lord Denning, who, on the one hand, was more concerned than some of his judicial colleagues to preserve the integrity of the statutory protection against liability for inducing breaches of contracts of employment, but, on the other, was concerned to extend the tort of inducing breach of commercial contract. In *Daily Mirror Newspapers Ltd* v. *Gardner* [1968] 2 QB 762, he suggested that the indirect form of the tort of inducing or, perhaps better, procuring a breach of contract could be committed even in the absence of independently unlawful means. In *Torquay Hotel Co. Ltd* v. *Cousins* (1968) (below), however, he repudiated this view when it became clear how far it would restrict the right to strike. It is interesting that the example he gave of this consequence was one of primary action being rendered unlawful because of its secondary effects rather than an example of secondary action as such. Having become convinced of this view, he was not prepared to let it be circumvented by the argument that the inducement of breaches of contracts of employment, for which by virtue of s.3 of the TDA 1906 the defendants could not be liable, would nevertheless constitute unlawful means for the purposes of indirect procurement of the breach of the commercial contract. The general issue of whether acts declared 'not actionable' by statute could nevertheless count as unlawful means for the purposes of establishing liability in tort had a long history and was eventually settled in favour of Lord Denning's 1968 view by the House of Lords in *Hadmor Productions Ltd* v. *Hamilton* [1982] ICR 114 (see below, p. 747), by which time, however, Lord Denning had changed his view.

The need for the plaintiff to prove unlawful means would be removed if the court regarded the tort as having been committed in its direct rather than its indirect form. In practice the organizers of industrial action are likely to approach both the employees of the secondary employer in order to persuade them to black the primary employer (which suggests the indirect form of the tort) and the secondary employer himself. If the approach to the secondary employer is merely in order to give information, then the *D. C. Thomson* case suggests that this does not turn the tort into the direct form; some element of persuasion of the secondary employer is required for that result to follow. However, in *Stratford & Sons Ltd* v. *Lindley* [1965] AC 269 (HL) some doubt was cast upon this view by the speeches of some of their lordships, who seemed to regard the giving of information as sufficient to turn the tort into the direct form. In *Torquay Hotel*, Lord Denning seemed to wish to maintain the approach of the Court of Appeal in *D. C. Thomson*, but, confusingly, only where there was a trade dispute. Although the existence or otherwise of a trade dispute is relevant to the question of whether the defendants can claim the protection of the statutory immunities, it is difficult to see its relevance to the essentially factual question of whether the defendants have acted directly or indirectly. The point is still an open one.

On the other hand, in the *Torquay Hotel* case, Lord Denning (following dicta in the *Thomson* case) achieved a great expansion of the tort of inducing breach by holding that it included interference with contractual relations falling short of breach of contract. Although the other judges in the case based their decisions on different reasoning, his view seems to have gained acceptance as time has passed. It was eventually confirmed at the highest level by the House of Lords in *Merkur Island Shipping Corp.* v. *Laughton* [1983] ICR 490. In effect, this view reduces the area of operation of the principle of non-liability established in *Allen* v. *Flood* and increases the area of liability flowing from the decision in *Lumley* v. *Gye*.

Torquay Hotel Co. Ltd v. *Cousins* [1969] 2 Ch. 106 (CA)

The officials of the TGWU were conducting an organizing campaign among hotel staff in the Torquay area. After the refusal of the management of the Torbay Hotel to recognize the union, that hotel was picketed. The manager of the Imperial Hotel (owned by the plaintiff company) made remarks supportive of the stand of the local Hotel Association against recognizing the TGWU, and in consequence that hotel was also picketed, although no members of the union were employed there. The district official of the union telephoned the local depot of the Esso Petroleum Co. with whom the plaintiffs had a contract for the supply of fuel oil, and informed them that there was an official dispute at the Imperial Hotel and that members of the union employed by Esso would not deliver oil to the Imperial. The contract between the plaintiffs and Esso contained a *force majeure* clause to the effect that neither party would be liable if fulfilment of any term of the contract was hindered by labour disputes. The plaintiffs eventually obtained fuel supplies from Alternative Fuels Ltd, who delivered at night, but an official of the union contacted Alternative and warned of 'serious repercussions' if supplies continued. The Court of Appeal held there was a trade dispute at the Torbay Hotel but not at the Imperial (on this point, see below, p. 795).

LORD DENNING M.R.: . . .

The principles of law

The principle of *Lumley* v. *Gye* (1853) 2 E & B 216 is that each of the parties to a contract has a 'right to the performance' of it: and it is wrong for another to procure one of the parties to break it or not to perform it. That principle was extended a step further by Lord Macnaghten in *Quinn* v. *Leathem* [1901] AC 495, so that each of the parties has a right to have his 'contractual relations' with the other duly observed. 'It is,' he said at p. 510, 'a violation of legal right to interfere with contractual relations recognised by law if there be no sufficient justification for the interference.' That statement was adopted and applied by a strong board of the Privy Council in *Jasperson* v. *Dominion Tobacco Co.* [1923] AC 709. It included Viscount Haldane and Lord Sumner. The time has come when the principle should be further extended to cover 'deliberate and direct interference with the execution of a contract without that causing any breach.' That was a point left open by Lord Reid in *Stratford (J. T.) & Son Ltd* v. *Lindley* [1965] AC 269, 324. But the common law would be seriously deficient if it did not condemn such interference. It is this very case. The principle can be subdivided into three elements:

First, there must be *interference* in the execution of a contract. The interference is not confined to the procurement of a *breach* of contract. It extends to a case where a third person *prevents* or *hinders* one party from performing his contract, even though it be not a breach.

Second, the interference must be deliberate. The person must know of the contract or, at any rate, turn a blind eye to it and intend to interfere with it: see *Emerald Construction Co.* v. *Lowthian* [1966] 1 WLR 691.

Third, the interference must be *direct*. Indirect interference will not do. Thus, a man who 'corners the market' in a commodity may well know that it may prevent others from performing their contracts, but he is not liable to an action for so doing. A trade union official, who calls a strike on proper notice, may well know that it will prevent the employers from performing their contracts to deliver goods, but he is not liable in damages for calling it. *Indirect* interference is only unlawful if unlawful means are used. I went too far when I said in *Daily Mirror Newspapers Ltd* v. *Gardner* [1968] 2 QB 762, 782 that there was no difference between direct and indirect interference. On reading once again *Thomson (D. C.) & Co. Ltd* v. *Deakin* [1952] Ch. 646, with more time, I find there is a difference. Morris L.J., at p. 702, there draws the very distinction between '*direct* persuasion to breach of contract' which is unlawful in itself: and 'the intentional bringing about of a breach by *indirect* methods involving wrongdoing.' This distinction must be maintained, else we should take away the right to strike altogether. Nearly every trade union official who calls a strike – even on due notice, as in *Morgan* v. *Fry* [1968] 2 QB 710 – knows that it may prevent the employers from performing their contracts. He may be taken even to intend it. Yet no one has supposed hitherto that it was unlawful: and we should not render it unlawful today. A trade union official is only in the wrong when he procures a contracting party *directly* to break his contract, or when he does it indirectly by *unlawful means*. On reconsideration of the *Daily Mirror* case [1968] 2 QB 762, I think that the defendants there interfered directly by getting the retailers as their agents to approach the wholesalers.

I must say a word about unlawful means, because that brings in another principle. I have always understood that if one person deliberately interferes with the trade or business of another, and does so by unlawful means, that is, by an act which he is not at liberty to commit, then he is acting unlawfully, even though he does not procure or induce any actual breach of contract. If the means are unlawful, that is enough. Thus in *Rookes* v. *Barnard* [1964] AC 1129 (as explained by Lord Reid in *Stratford* v. *Lindley* [1965] AC 269, 325 and Lord Upjohn, at p. 337) the defendants interfered with the employment of Rookes – and they did it by unlawful means, namely, by intimidation of his employers – and they were held to be acting unlawfully, even though the employers committed no breach of contract as they gave Rookes proper notice. And in *Stratford* v. *Lindley* [1965] AC 269, the defendants interfered with the business of Stratford – and they did it by *unlawful means*, namely, by inducing the men to *break their contracts* of employment by refusing to handle the barges – and they were held to be acting unlawfully, even in regard to *new business* of Stratford which was not the subject of contract. Lord Reid said, at p. 324:

> The respondents' action made it practically impossible for the appellants to do any new business with the barge hirers. It was not disputed that such interference is tortious if any unlawful means are employed.

So also on the second point in *Daily Mirror* v. *Gardner* [1968] 2 QB 762, the defendants interfered with the business of the 'Daily Mirror' – and they did it by a collective boycott which was held to be *unlawful* under the Restrictive Trade Practices Act, 1956 – and they were held to be acting unlawfully.

This point about unlawful means is of particular importance when a place is declared 'black.' At common law it often involves the use of unlawful means. Take the Imperial Hotel. When it was declared 'black,' it meant that the drivers of the tankers would not take oil to the hotel. The drivers would thus be induced to break their contracts of employment. That would be unlawful at common law. The only case in which 'blacking' of such a kind is lawful is when it is done 'in contemplation or furtherance of a trade dispute.' It is then protected by section 3 of the Trade Disputes Act, 1906: see *Thomson (D. C.) & Co. Ltd* v. *Deakin* [1952] Ch. 646, 662, 663 by Upjohn J.; for, in that event, the act of inducing a breach of a contract of employment is a lawful act which is not actionable at the suit of anyone: see *Stratford* v. *Lindley* [1965] AC 269, 303 by Salmon L.J., and *Morgan* v. *Fry* [1968] 2 QB 710, 728 by myself. Seeing that the act is lawful, it must, I think, be lawful for the trade union officials to tell the employers and their customers about it. And this is so, even though it does mean that those people are compelled to break their commercial contracts. The interference with the commercial contracts is only indirect, and not direct: see what Lord Upjohn said in *Stratford* v. *Lindley* [1965] AC 269, 337. So, if there had been a 'trade dispute' in this case, I think it would have protected the trade union officials when they informed Esso that the dispute with Imperial was an 'official dispute' and said that the hotel was 'blacked.' It would be like the 'blacking' of the barges in *Stratford* v. *Lindley* [1965] AC 269, where we held, in the Court of Appeal, at pp. 276–307, that, on the basis that there was a 'trade dispute,' the defendants were not liable.

APPLYING THE PRINCIPLE IN THIS CASE

Seeing that there was no 'trade dispute' this case falls to be determined by the common law. It seems to me that the trade union officials deliberately and directly interfered with the execution of the contract between the Imperial Hotel and Esso. They must have known that there was a contract between the Imperial Hotel and Esso. Why otherwise did they on that very first Saturday afternoon telephone the bulk plant at Plymouth? They may not have known with exactitude all the terms of the contract. But no more did the defendants in *Stratford* v. *Lindley*, at p. 332. They must also have intended to prevent the performance of the contract. That is plain from the telephone message: 'Any supplies of fuel-oil will be stopped being made.' And the interference was direct. It was as direct as could be – a telephone message from the trade union official to the bulk plant.

Take next the supplies from Alternative Fuels. The first wagon got through. As it happened, there was no need for the Imperial Hotel to order any further supplies from Alternative Fuels. But suppose they had given a further order, it is quite plain that the trade union officials would have done their best to prevent it being delivered. Their telephone messages show that they intended to prevent supplies being made by all means in their power. By threatening 'repercussions' they interfered unlawfully with the performance of any future order which Imperial Hotel might give to Alternative Fuels. And the interference was direct again. It was direct to Alternative Fuels. Such interference was sufficient to warrant the grant of an injunction quia timet.

The third area of debate about the tort of inducing breach of contract in the 1960s concerned the degree of knowledge of the contract in question and the type of intention the defendants needed to be shown to have possessed in order to be liable. In *Emerald Construction* v. *Lowthian* [1966] 1 WLR 691 (CA), the defendant officials of the Amalgamated Union of Building Trade Workers put pressure on the main contractors on a building site (Higgs & Hill Ltd) to terminate a 'labour only' contract (see above, p. 94) between the plaintiffs and Higgs & Hill. The defendants obviously knew of the existence of the contract but did not know, at least initially, its terms. The defendants argued that, in the absence of such knowledge, it could not be said that they intended to procure a breach of it. The Court of Appeal rejected the argument. Lord Denning said:

If the officers of the trade union, knowing of the contract, deliberately sought to procure a breach of it they would do wrong: see *Lumley* v. *Gye*. Even if they did not know of the actual terms of the contract, but had the means of knowledge – which they deliberately disregarded – that would be enough. Like the man who turns a blind eye. So here, if the officers deliberately sought to get this contract terminated, heedless of its terms, regardless whether it was terminated by breach or not, they would do wrong. For it is unlawful for a third person to procure a breach of contract knowingly, or recklessly, indifferent whether it is a breach or not. . . . Suffice it that if the intention of the defendants was to get this contract terminated at all events, breach or no breach, they were *prima facie* in the wrong.

The evidence at present before us points in this direction. The object of the defendant officers was plain. It was to get Higgs & Hill Ltd to terminate this 'labour only' sub-contract; and the evidence suggests that they did not care how it was terminated, so long as it was terminated. The two letters of ultimatum contain an unequivocal demand. They did not inquire what were the terms of the contract. They did not request that it be terminated by lawful notice. They made the straight demand that it be terminated within the time limit – or else there would be a strike. When Higgs & Hill Ltd refused the demand, the defendants called a strike and did their best to get the contract terminated by that means. Even when they or their advisers got to know of the terms of the contract, they still continued the strike. All goes to show that they were determined to bring this contractual relationship to an end if they could, regardless of whether it was done in breach or not.

Thus, by the end of the 1960s the tort of inducing breach as applied to contracts other than contracts of employment constituted a considerable threat to the legality of industrial action, especially secondary industrial action. The distinction between the direct and indirect forms of the tort had been preserved, together with the need for independently unlawful means in the latter case, but courts were increasingly willing to see the tort as having been committed directly. The requirements of knowledge of the contract had been reduced, and Lord Denning seemed about to succeed in extending the tort to include interference with contractual relations falling short of breach. Much of this extension was due to the activities of the Court of Appeal. Lord Denning later put it extra-judicially in the following terms when referring to his judgments of this period. 'The first way in which the law about "inducing a breach of contract" was extended was by stretching the "knowingly" part of it. . . . The second way in which the law about "inducing a breach of contract" was extended was by stretching the "breach" part.' (*The Discipline of Law* (1979), pp. 178 and 179.) However, the activities of the Court of Appeal at this time seemed fully in line with the attitudes of the judiciary generally and the House of Lords in particular. In *Stratford* v. *Lindley*, the only opportunity the House had for a major consideration of the tort in this period, the judgments of their lordships also favoured expansion of the tort, especially in relation to the requirements of knowledge and the scope of the direct form of the tort.

Consequently, it is not surprising that the Donovan Commission devoted some consideration to this tort (see paras. 878–94). They regarded the current state of the law as uncertain and irrational and recommended that clarity be obtained by extending the statutory protection to inducing breach of all types of contract (although the majority inclined to restrict the extended protection to official action). The legislators of the IRA 1971, far from following this recommendation, used the tort of inducing breach of commercial contracts as a model for the statutory unfair industrial practice created by s.98 of that Act, the side-note to which read: 'Industrial action against extraneous parties'. The Labour government, elected in 1974, wished to restore an abstentionist framework for industrial dispute law and so took up the Commission's recommendation (but without the restriction to official action). However, because in 1974 that government did not command a majority in the

Commons, it had to accept an opposition amendment which restricted the protection of s.13(1) of TULRA 1974 to contracts of employment (following s.3 of the TDA 1906). Only with the enactment of TULRA 1976 was the protection of s.13(1) extended to all contracts. The opportunity was also taken in TULRA 1976 to rewrite s.13(1) so that it became wide enough to catch interference with contract falling short of breach (assuming such was tortious). Consequently, after 1976 s.13(1)(*a*) of TULRA 1974 read, and still reads, as follows:

An act done by a person in contemplation or furtherance of a trade dispute shall not be actionable in tort on the ground only – (*a*) that it induces another person to break a contract or interferes or induces any other person to interfere with its performance. . . .

The enactment of TULRA 1976 aroused great controversy, both in Parliament and without. Lord Denning remarked in *BBC* v. *Hearn* [1977] ICR 685 that: 'Trade unions and their officers – and, indeed, groups of workmen, official or unofficial – are entitled to induce others to break their contracts – not only contracts of employment but other contracts as well – they are entitled to interfere and prevent the performance of contracts by others – all with impunity'. There then followed a series of decisions in the Court of Appeal which restricted the scope of TULRA, not, however, by developing the common law of inducing breach, but by narrowly construing the statutory definition of trade dispute (see below, pp. 816–17). With the return of a Conservative government in 1979 there was speculation that TULRA would again be amended so as to revive the provisions of s.3 of the TDA 1906, but in the end this was not done. Instead, in s.17 of EA 1980 the protection of s.13(1) of TULRA is removed when certain forms of secondary action result in inducement or procurement of breaches of commercial contracts. This is both a more limited amendment of the law than a simple return to the original provisions of TULRA 1974 would have been and an attempt to bring the law into a more functional relationship with the social phenomena of industrial action. We shall look at these provisions in more detail in the next chapter. The provisions of s.17 of EA 1980 are supplemented, however, by those of s.16 of EA 1980, which removes all protection against liability for inducing breach of contract (including contracts of employment) from those picketing other than at their own place of work (see below, pp. 850–53); and by the complex provisions of s.14 of EA 1982 relating to insistence upon the use of union labour to do work or provide services (see below, pp. 862–8). The combined effect of these new provisions is to give some considerable scope for the operation of the tort of inducing breach of contract in the present framework of the law.

5 Intimidation

The developments during the 1960s of the tort of inducing breach of contract have proved in the long run to be of the greatest significance. At the time, however, they were overshadowed by the development by the House of Lords in the case of *Rookes* v. *Barnard* (see below) of the tort of intimidation. The significance of this case was threefold. It was the first occasion in the post-war period when the House of Lords had the opportunity to consider a major industrial conflict case and the attitudes of the judges showed a readiness to move decisively away from the abstentionist position which had generally been thought to be embodied in the TDA 1906 and in the House's decision in the *Crofter* case (above, p. 713) some twenty years earlier. As we have already noted (above, p. 698), the case was a watershed in the development of the law in the post-war period and it led indirectly to the establishment of the Donovan Commission. Second, the decision in the case was innovative at a doctrinal level to a greater extent than any of the decisions concerning the tort of inducing breach of contract. The essence of the tort of intimidation is that A threatens to commit an act that is unlawful *vis-à-vis* B, unless B acts (lawfully or unlawfully) to the disadvantage of C. Can C sue A in tort? There was old authority to the effect that C could sue A if A had threatened violence against B. The novelty of the decision of the House in *Rookes* v. *Barnard* consisted in its extending the range of unlawful threats so as to include threats of peaceful (but unlawful) acts, notably a threat to break a contract of employment. Third, the consequence of this development was that it threatened to render the legal freedom to strike illusory, in a way that the development of the tort of inducing breach did not. So long as s.3 of the TDA 1906 gave protection against liability for inducing breach of contracts of employment and so long as the judges were aware of the need to restrict the tort of inducing breach *vis-à-vis* commercial contracts so that it did not impinge upon the legality of primary action (cf. the remarks of Lord Denning in the *Torquay Hotel* case, above, p. 733), this tort would operate principally so as to render secondary action unlawful. But there was no such restriction upon the tort of intimidation. *Rookes* v. *Barnard* itself was a case of primary industrial action. Moreover, if the tort of intimidation could arise where only two parties were involved, i.e. A threatens an unlawful act against B unless B acts to his own disadvantage (cf. *D & C Builders Ltd* v. *Rees* [1966] 2 QB 617), then the spectre arose of an employer suing trade-union officials in tort where, for example, in response to a threat that a strike would be organized in breach of the employees' contracts of employment, the employer had conceded a bigger wage increase to the employees than he would otherwise have wished.

Rookes v. *Barnard* [1964] AC 1129 (HL)

The design office of the British Overseas Airways Corporation was subject to a closed-shop agreement between the Corporation and a trade union called the Association of Engineering and Shipbuilding Draughtsmen (AESD). The plaintiff (appellant), an employee of BOAC in the design office and a former active member of the union, resigned from the union. The other employees in the office threatened to strike unless the plaintiff was removed from the office, and the Corporation in consequence first suspended the plaintiff and then terminated his contract on due notice. (There was no unfair dismissal law in operation at this time.) By virtue of the collective agreement made by the National Joint Council for Civil Air Transport (of which both the Corporation and AESD were members) it was provided that no strikes should take place and that disputes should be dealt with through the NJC machinery with eventual reference of unresolved issues to arbitration. It was conceded by defendants' counsel that this provision of the collective agreement had been incorporated (see above, p. 281) into the individual contracts of employment of the employees in the design office. The defendants were Barnard, chairman of the local branch of the union, and Fistal, a shop steward, who were both employees of the Corporation, and Silverthorne, a local full-time official of the union, who was not, of course, employed by the Corporation.

LORD DEVLIN: My Lords, on March 16, 1956, the appellant's employment, which has lasted nine years with BOAC, was lawfully determined by notice. The reason why it was terminated was because on January 10, 1956, the members of the AESD, a trade union to which the appellant belonged and from which he had resigned, served notice on BOAC 'that if the non-unionist Mr D. E. Rookes is not removed from the design office by 4 p.m. Friday, January 13, 1956, a withdrawal of labour of all AESD membership will take place.' On January 13 the appellant was suspended from his employment and the strike thereby averted; and thereafter notice terminating his employment altogether was given to him, as I have said. The three respondents were officials of the union and two of them were employed by BOAC.

It is not disputed that the notice constituted a threat of breach of contract by the members of AESD. It is true that any individual employee could lawfully have terminated his contract by giving seven days' notice and if the matter is looked at in that way, the breach might not appear to be a very serious one. But that would be a technical way of looking at it. As Donovan L.J. said in the Court of Appeal, the object of the notice was not to terminate the contract either before or after the expiry of seven days. The object was to break the contract by withholding labour but keeping the contract alive for as long as the employers would tolerate the breach without exercising their right of rescission. In the second place, there was an agreement in force between AESD and BOAC in which the former undertook that no strike of its members would ever take place; and it is admitted that the term formed part of the contract of service of each member with BOAC. I agree with the submission made by Mr Silkin for the appellant that a strike means a concerted withdrawal of labour in furtherance of a trade dispute, whether or not the withdrawal is effected after proper notice has been given. It is common ground that the issue whether a non-unionist should continue to be employed creates a trade dispute.

It is not therefore denied that the service of the notice was an infringement of BOAC's rights. But the question is whether the respondents thereby infringed any right of the appellant. Since all that the respondents did was admittedly done in the furtherance of a trade dispute, it is idle to inquire what possible causes of action there are available to the appellant at common law without inquiring at the same time to what extent they are curtailed by statute.

Conspiracy, which suggests itself at once as a possible cause of action, is covered by section 1 of the Trade Disputes Act, 1906. There are, as is well known, two sorts of conspiracies, the *Quinn* v *Leathem* [[1901] AC 495] type which employs only lawful means but aims at an unlawful end, and the type which employs unlawful means. Section 1 of the Act contains the formula which negatives the first type as a cause of action where there is a trade dispute. In the latter type, which in my opinion is not affected by the section, the element of conspiracy is usually only of secondary importance since the unlawful means are actionable by themselves.

Section 3 provides a second barrier for the appellant to surmount. It grants immunity in respect of certain acts which include, it is said (I shall have later to examine carefully the language in which the immunity is granted), an inducement of 'some other person to break a contract of employment' and 'an interference with the trade business or employment of some other person'.

The appellant's choice of remedies being restricted in this way, the only wrong which he asserts as having been committed by the respondents is the tort of intimidation. On this the respondents say, first, that there is no such tort; secondly, that if there is, the respondents did not commit it; and thirdly, that if they did commit it, they are given immunity by section 3 because the intimidation resulted in an interference with the employment of the appellant by BOAC.

My Lords, in my opinion there is a tort of intimidation of the nature described in chapter 18 of Salmond on the Law of Torts, 13th ed. (1961), p. 697. The tort can take one of two forms which are set out in Salmond as follows:

(1) *Intimidation of the plaintiff himself*
Although there seems to be no authority on the point, it cannot be doubted that it is an actionable wrong intentionally to compel a person, by means of a threat of an illegal act, to do some act whereby loss accrues to him: for example, an action will doubtless lie at the suit of a trader who has been compelled to discontinue his business by means of threats of personal violence made against him by the defendant with that intention. . . .
(2) *Intimidation of other persons to the injury of the plaintiff*
In certain cases it is an actionable wrong to intimidate other persons with the intent and effect of compelling them to act in a manner or to do acts which they themselves have a legal right to do which cause loss to the plaintiff: for example, the intimidation of the plaintiff's customers whereby they are compelled to withdraw their custom from him, or the intimidation of an employer whereby he is compelled to discharge his servant, the plaintiff. Intimidation of this sort is actionable, as we have said, in certain classes of cases; for it does not follow that, because a plaintiff's customers have a right to cease to deal with him if they please, other persons have a right as against the plaintiff to compel his customers to do so. There are at least two cases in which such intimidation may constitute a cause of action:-
(i) When the intimidation consists in a threat to do or procure an illegal act;
(ii) When the intimidation is the act, not of a single person, but of two or more persons acting together in pursuance of a common intention.

As your Lordships are all of opinion that there is a tort of intimidation and on this point approve the judgments in both courts below, I do not propose to offer any further authorities or reasons in support of my conclusion. I note that no issue on justification was raised at the time and there is no finding of fact upon it. So your Lordships have not to consider what part, if any, justification plays in the tort of intimidation.

Your Lordships are here concerned with the sort of intimidation which Salmond puts into the second category, and with the first of Salmond's two cases. The second case is, so Salmond later observed, 'one form of the tort of conspiracy.' That form is the *Quinn* v *Leathem* [[1901] AC 495] type, so that it is no use to the appellant here. He relies upon 'a threat to do or procure an illegal act,' namely, a breach of contract. Doubtless it would suit him better if he could rely on the procuring of a breach of contract, for that is a tort; but immunity from that is guaranteed in terms by section 3. So he complains only of the threat to break the service contracts and the breach would undoubtedly be an act actionable by BOAC though it is neither tortious nor criminal. He does not have to contend that in the tort of intimidation, as in the tort of conspiracy, there can be, if the object is injurious, an unlawful threat to use lawful means. I do not think that there can be. The line must be drawn according to the law. It cannot be said that to use a threat of any sort is per se unlawful; and I do not see how, except in relation to the nature of the act threatened, i.e., whether it is lawful or unlawful, one could satisfactorily distinguish between a lawful and an unlawful threat.

This conclusion, while not directly in point, assists me in my approach to the matter to be determined here. It is not, of course, disputed that if the act threatened is a crime, the threat is unlawful. But otherwise is it enough to say that the act threatened is actionable as a breach of contract or must it be actionable as a tort? My Lords, I see no good ground for the latter limitation. I find the reasoning on this point of Professor Hamson [Prof. C. J. Hamson, *Cambridge Law Journal*, November 1961, pp. 189, 191] (which Sellers L.J. [[1963] 1 QB 623, 666] sets out in his judgment though he does not himself accept it) very persuasive. The essence of the offence is coercion. It cannot be said that every form of coercion is wrong. A dividing line must be drawn and the natural line runs between what is lawful and unlawful as against the party threatened. If the defendant threatens something that that party cannot legally resist, the plaintiff likewise cannot be allowed to resist the consequences; both must put up with the coercion and its results. But if the intermediate party is threatened with an illegal injury, the plaintiff who suffers by the aversion of the act threatened can fairly claim that he is illegally injured.

Accordingly, I reach the conclusion that the respondents' second point fails and on the facts of this case the tort of intimidation was committed. . . .

His lordship then considered whether s.3 of TDA 1906 provided a defence. The 'first limb' of that section (above, p. 722) was held to protect only against liability for inducing breach of contract and not against any other head of tort liability (e.g. intimidation) even if that liability arose out of the same course of conduct. The same reasoning applied to the 'second limb' (above, p. 712) but here the argument was slightly more complex because Lord Devlin was prepared to assume that interference with business without more was not a tort. Consequently, if the second limb did not operate to protect defendants when the interference took the form of, for example, intimidation, it seemed to confer no protection at all. Lord Devlin, however, was prepared to accept this conclusion on the grounds that the second limb had been passed by Parliament in 1906 when the state of the law was unclear. If mere interference was subsequently held not to be tortious at common law, then the second limb 'would be otiose but harmless; if it was, the enactment would achieve the object desired' (p. 1216). It is notable that Lord Devlin did not say that *Allen* v *Flood* had established that mere interference was not tortious, but rather he was clearly anxious to hold the point open for later consideration by the House (cf. the discussion above, p. 712, on the significance of the repeal of s.13(2) of TULRA 1974). Lord Devlin also considered s.1 of TDA 1906, which was particularly relevant to the liability of Silverthorne, who was not an employee of the Corporation, could not have threatened to break his own contract, but could perhaps be seen as a conspirator with Barnard and Fistal. However, s.1 did not save Silverthorne, because it applied only to conspiracies 'to injure' (see above, p. 712) and had no application where the act the conspirators had combined to do was actionable without the allegation of conspiracy (as the intimidation was in this case). The judgment then continued as follows:

I have therefore reached the conclusion that the true effect of section 3 is that in a trade dispute it deprives the plaintiff of any cause of action he may have on the facts for inducing a breach of contract and any cause of action he may have on the facts or in law for interference with his employment by lawful means; but that in neither case does it countenance the use of tortious means. So the appellant's cause of action in intimidation is not barred by the statute.

This leads to the conclusion that this appeal should succeed. But there is one argument, or at least one consideration, that remains to be noticed. It is that the strike weapon is now so generally sanctioned that it cannot really be regarded as an unlawful weapon of intimidation; and so there must be something wrong with a conclusion that treats it as such. This thought plainly influenced quite strongly the judgments in the Court of Appeal. To give effect to it means either that illegal means ought not to include a breach of contract; or that the statute ought to be construed as wide enough to give protection. The Court of Appeal tended, I think, to apply the argument to both points indiscriminately.

I see the force of this consideration. But your Lordships can, in my opinion, give effect to it only if you are prepared either to hobble the common law in all classes of disputes lest its range is too wide to suit industrial disputes or to give the statute a wider scope than it was ever intended to have.

As to the former alternative, I cannot doubt that the threat of a breach of contract can be a most intimidating thing. The present case provides as good an example of the force of such a threat as could be found. A great and powerful corporation submits to it at once, for it was threatened with the infliction of incalculable loss and of grave inconvenience to the public which it serves. The threat is made by men who are flagrantly violating a pledge not to strike, at least until constitutional means of resolving the dispute have been exhausted. It is not just a technical illegality, a case in which a few days longer notice might have made the difference. Because of the damage that would ensue from a strike, BOAC, no doubt in return for corresponding benefits, secured the pledge not to strike; and it is that pledge that is being broken. Granted that there is a tort of intimidation, I think it would be quite wrong to cripple the common law so that it cannot give relief in these circumstances. I think it would be old-fashioned and unrealistic for the law to refuse relief in such a case and to grant it where there is a shake of a fist or a threat to publish a nasty and untrue story.

I said that I thought it would be wrong to cripple the common law in such a case, but that does not mean that I am necessarily criticising the policy of the Trade Disputes Act. It is easy now to see that Parliament in 1906 might have felt that the only way of giving labour an equality of bargaining power with capital was to give it special immunities which the common law did not permit. Even now, when the scales have been redressed, it is easy to see that Parliament might think that a strike, whether reprehensible or not, ought not to be made a ground for litigation and that industrial peace should be sought by other means.

It may therefore as a matter of policy be right that a breach of contract should not be treated as an illegal means within the limited field of industrial disputes. But can your Lordships get that out of the words of the Act? Section 3 gives immunity from action for procuring a breach of contract but not for the breach itself. In the Court of Appeal Donovan L.J. [[1963] 1 Q B 623, 685] said with great force: '. . . if one may procure the breach of another's contract with impunity in a trade dispute it is certainly odd if one cannot even threaten to break one's own.' The section could easily have read – 'shall not be actionable on the ground only that it *is a breach of contract* or induces some other person' etc., but it is not so written. It may be that, as Mr Gardiner suggests, Parliament thought it very unlikely that an employer would resort to action against workmen individually for breaches of contract and that he would get very little from it if he did: see on this point *National Coal Board* v *Galley* [[1958] 1 W L R 16, 27; [1958] 1 All E R. 91, C A]. Or it may be that Parliament did not anticipate that a threat of breach of contract would be regarded as an intimidatory weapon. Whatever the reason, the immunity is not in the statute; the section clearly exempts the procurer or inducer and equally clearly does not exempt the breaker. It is not suggested that the House can remove the oddity by reading words into the Act that are not there.

So your Lordships cannot construe the Act to give protection in the case of a threat of a breach of contract unless you also make it wide enough to protect the threatener of physical violence. The Act was no doubt intended to give immunity for all forms of peaceful persuasion, but I am sure – and Lord Loreburn LC in the passage I have cited from *Conway* v *Wade* [[1909] AC 495, 511] says as much – that it was not intended to give protection from violent persuasion. I do not think it would be right so to construe it. It would mean that under the licence of a trade dispute one man could force another out of his job by threats of violence; and since such threats would not be actionable, I doubt if an aggrieved party could even get an injunction to restrain their constant repetition.

The essence of the difficulty lies in the fact that in determining what constitutes the tort of intimidation your Lordships have drawn the dividing line not between physical and economic coercion but between lawful and unlawful coercion. For the universal purposes of the common law, I am sure that that is the right, natural and logical line. For the purpose of the limited field of industrial disputes which is controlled by statute and where much that is in principle unlawful is already tolerated, it may be that pragmatically and on grounds of policy the line should be drawn between physical and economic pressure. But that is for Parliament to decide. What the House said in *Vacher & Sons Ltd* v *London Society of Compositors* [[1913] AC 107, 118], especially *per* Lord Macnaghten, is a very clear warning, if one be needed, against the interference of the courts in matters of policy in this branch of the law.

It was thought in some quarters in the immediate aftermath of this decision that it turned particularly upon the presence of the 'no strike' clause in the contracts of employment. However, as we have seen (above, pp. 718–20), a strike will frequently be a breach of contract irrespective of the presence or absence of such a clause in it. This became clear in *Morgan* v *Fry* [1968] 2 QB 710, which involved facts very close to those in *Rookes* v *Barnard* except that there was not a no-strike clause in the contracts of employment. The Port of London Authority operated a *de facto* closed shop. Morgan, a lockman, left the recognized union, the TGWU, to form, with others, a breakaway union. Fry, a regional organizer of the TGWU, informed the Authority that his members would not work with Morgan and the Authority then terminated Morgan's contract after due notice. However, all the members of the Court of Appeal held, upon different reasoning, that Fry had not committed the tort of intimidation, although the crucial fact upon which all the judges built the various arguments by which they distinguished *Rookes* v *Barnard* was the same, namely, that in this case the notice of the strike action given by Fry was at least as long as that needed to be given by the employees to terminate their contracts of employment. It was in this case that Lord Denning, who was overtly concerned with the impact of the decision in *Rookes* v *Barnard* upon the legality of primary industrial action, developed his notion of a strike upon due notice leading to the suspension rather than the breach of the contract of employment (see above, p. 720).

Although an interesting commentary upon conflicting judicial attitudes at this time, the decision in *Morgan* v *Fry* was of less practical importance because in 1965 Parliament had passed the TDA 1965, a short Act declaring it not to be actionable for a person acting in contemplation or furtherance of a trade dispute to threaten 'that a contract of employment (whether one to which he is a party or not) will be broken.' The Act rendered non-actionable also a threat that a person would 'induce another to break a contract of employment to which that other is a party'. In the latter case the threat would be to do something declared not actionable by s.3 of TDA 1906 and for this reason the threat might not count as a threat to do an unlawful act for the purposes of the tort of intimidation. This was certainly the opinion of the Court of Appeal in *Stratford* v *Lindley* [1965] AC 269, but Parliament perhaps thought it wise to have a statutory statement to this effect. The 1965 Act effectively neutralized *Rookes* v *Barnard* in trade disputes, but did not reverse the central doctrinal development of that case, which was to see a threat to break a contract as unlawful means for the purposes of the economic torts.

The TDA 1965 was swept away by the IRA 1971, along with the TDA 1906. When re-enacting the abstentionist framework, Parliament in TULRA 1974, s.13(1)(b), first followed the *ipsissima verba* of the TDA 1965, just as in s.13(1)(a) it followed the wording of the first limb of s.3 of TDA 1906 (see above, p. 737). After the amendments effected by TULRA 1976, however, s.13(1)(b) was altered to its present-day wording so as to include threats of interference falling short of breach and to embrace all contracts and not just contracts of employment. The present wording is:

An act done by a person in contemplation or furtherance of a trade dispute shall not be actionable in tort on the ground only –

(*b*) that it consists of his threatening that a contract (whether one to which he is a party or not) will be broken or its performance interfered with, or that he will induce another person to break a contract or to interfere with its performance.

Thus, since 1965, although the extent of the protection has varied, statute has attempted to treat liability in tort for threats and liability for acts in the same way, thus removing the special position occupied by threats in the immediate aftermath of the *Rookes* v *Barnard* decision. In the same way, the exceptions (see above, p. 737) made by EA 1980, and 1982 to the protection afforded by s.13(1) of TULRA 1974 apply equally to subsections (*a*) and (*b*), as we shall see when we examine these exceptions in greater detail in the next chapter.

6 Interference with business by unlawful means

Like the tort of intimidation the tort of interference with business by unlawful means is essentially a recent creation. Unlike, however, the tort of intimidation, which burst upon the labour law scene with the House of Lords' decision in *Rookes* v. *Barnard*, the tort of interference with business by unlawful means has established itself over a period of time without ever having been subject to sustained consideration at the highest levels. The modern development of the tort began with a series of decisions, mainly at the level of the Court of Appeal, from the 1960s onwards. In *Daily Mirror Newspapers Ltd* v. *Gardner* [1968] 2 QB 762 (not a trade dispute case), Lord Denning said: 'I have always understood that if one person interferes with the trade or business of another, and does so by unlawful means, then he is acting unlawfully, even though he does not procure or induce any actual breach of contract.' This principle was again applied in *Acrow (Automation) Ltd* v. *Rex Chainbelt Inc.* [1971] 1 WLR 1676 (CA) and *Brekkes Ltd* v. *Cattel* [1972] Ch. 105, and the existence of this head of liability was accepted without serious argument in two recent decisions of the House of Lords, *Hadmor Productions Ltd* v. *Hamilton* [1982] ICR 114, and *Lonrho Ltd* v. *Shell Petroleum Co. Ltd* [1982] AC 173.

Once articulated, however, this principle of liability seems an obvious one. It does not contradict the decision in *Allen* v. *Flood* because, as we have noted (above, p. 712), the principle of that case assumes that no unlawful means have been employed. Moreover, the general principle can be used to subsume situations in which liability has long been imposed but explained by reference to other nominate torts. For example, liability for conspiracy to use unlawful means (in contrast to conspiracy to injure (above, p. 712)), for indirect procurement by unlawful means of a breach of contract (above, p. 731), and for intimidation arising out of a threat to use unlawful means (above, p. 738) is now well recognized. Should these be regarded merely as examples of the application of the general principle of liability for interference by unlawful means? The decision in *Rookes* v. *Barnard*, especially, suggests that the answer should be in the affirmative: if it is tortious to threaten an unlawful action, should not liability be imposed for the commission of the same act?

Although this argument may seem impeccable at a doctrinal level, the extent to which it depends upon reasoning from *Rookes* v. *Barnard* should warn us about the extent to which the new head of liability is capable of rendering industrial action unlawful at common law. Take a simple example. A shop stewards' committee organizes a strike against an employer, in breach of the contracts of employment of the strikers, because the employer has refused to concede a claim put forward by the committee. Can the employer successfully argue that this is an interference with his business by unlawful means, the means being the inducement by the stewards of the employees to break their contracts of employment? If inducement of breach of contracts of employment can constitute unlawful means for the purposes of the tort of interference, a way is opened up to evade the statutory protection that has existed since 1906 against this liability. Of course, it might be thought to be too much of a sleight of hand for the employer to succeed in an action in tort by arguing that, although inducement of breach of the contracts of employment was not, as such, actionable (because of s.3 of TDA 1906), nevertheless, it could be prayed in aid as unlawful means for the purposes of the tort of interference. Suppose, however, the action organized by the committee was aimed at some other person as well as at the employer. Could that third person sue on the basis of unlawful interference? In *Stratford* v. *Lindley* [1965] AC 269 Lord Pearce had suggested that the words 'shall not be actionable' in s.3 of the TDA 1906 meant only not actionable at the suit of the employer. To accept this would be to give great significance to the generalized tort of interference by unlawful means, for it would allow the third party to build a tort action on the basis of unlawful means which were not independently actionable by him.

Another contrast between the torts of intimidation and interference by unlawful means is that, whereas Parliament reacted to the tort of intimidation only after its consequences for labour law had become clear through judicial decision, it to some extent anticipated the tort of interference in the provisions of TULRA 1974. That Act did not seek to exclude the tort from trade disputes, but it did seek to limit its operation by restricting what can be seen as the crucial aspect of the tort, namely, the range of matters that can be considered as unlawful means. In TULRA 1974, s.13(3) it was provided:

For the avoidance of doubt it is hereby declared that – (*a*) an act which by reason of subsection (1) or (2) above is itself not actionable . . . shall not be regarded as the doing of an unlawful act or as the use of unlawful means for the purpose of establishing liability in tort.

However, in EA 1980, s.17(8) Parliament repealed s.13(3) of TULRA 1974. The government of the day expressly denied any intention of reducing the legal immunity granted to primary action and claimed that the repeal of s. 13(3) was necessary to ensure that the other provisions of s.17 of EA 1980, which removed protection from certain forms of secondary action and which we shall discuss in the next chapter, operated as they were intended. Perhaps the obvious solution would have been to repeal s.13(3) of TULRA only for the purposes of s.17 of EA 1980, but the government, having effected a complete repeal, caused all the debates about the relationship between the statutory immunities and unlawful means to be revived, especially controversy about the correctness of Lord Pearce's dictum. The issue arose very quickly in the courts and was resolved by the House of Lords contrary to Lord Pearce's view, a decision which thus preserved the integrity of the statutory scheme created by the 1980 Act. It is interesting to note how close the factual situation in *Hadmor* was to that discussed under the heading of intimidation in *Rookes* v. *Barnard*.

Hadmor Productions Ltd v. *Hamilton* [1982] ICR 114 (HL)

A trade union, ACTT, had a history of being opposed to the transmission by the television companies of material produced by facility companies, i.e. companies not under the control of the television companies. The plaintiff company was a facility company but its owners thought they had obtained the approval of the union for material produced by it to be transmitted, and the company produced and sold a series of programmes to Thames Television (though Thames was not contractually obliged to transmit them). The employees of Thames, however, threatened to black the programmes after a few of them had been transmitted, and Thames thereupon withdrew the remainder. The defendants were a shop steward employed by Thames and a local full-time official of the union.

LORD DIPLOCK: . . .
Issue (i). Have Hamilton or Bould committed any tort at common law?
Since, at the time of hearing by Dillon J., there was no evidence before him that there had been any prior agreement between Thames and ACTT that films or video tapes produced by facility companies should not be transmitted without prior consultation with ACTT, the defendants' case had to be presented to him on the basis that for a member of ACTT to disobey an order to transmit a programme produced by a facility company would be a breach of his contract of employment with Thames, and thus an 'unlawful act' of which a threat to do it or procure it is capable of constituting the common law tort of intimidation discussed by this House in *Rookes* v. *Barnard* [1964] AC 1129, Dillon J. did not deal separately with this issue. He was content to assume that in the absence of any statutory immunity it would have raised a serious question to be tried. By the time that the matter came before the Court of Appeal Hadmor's case on this vital issue had been weakened by the uncontradicted evidence of the agreement between Thames and ACTT that Thames would not require ACTT's members to transmit programmes produced by facility companies except after prior consultation with the union. The extent to which terms relating to the performance of contracts of employment which have been agreed between an employer and a trade union of which

his employees are members are to be treated as incorporated in the individual contracts of employment of those members, raises interesting and difficult questions of law into which it would be inappropriate to enter upon a motion for an interlocutory injunction. I would therefore hold, although not without considerable misgivings, that Hadmor does manage to scramble over the first hurdle in its path, viz. that presented by issue (i). . . .

Issue (iii). Are Hamilton and Bould entitled to immunity from liability in tort to Hadmor under section 13 of the Trade Union and Labour Relations Act 1974? . . .

My Lords, one can leave aside the tort of conspiracy to injure a man in his trade or business. Hadmor does not rely on that for reasons that are obvious in view of the recent decision of this House in *Lonrho Ltd* v. *Shell Petroleum Co. Ltd (No. 2)* [1981] 3 WLR 33; however misguided the purpose of ACTT in threatening the blacking may have been, that purpose was not to injure Hadmor however inevitably injury to Hadmor might be one result of the blacking. As already mentioned in connection with issue (i), the tort upon which Hadmor relies is interference with its trade or business by unlawful means; and the unlawful means relied upon consisted in the acts of Hamilton and Bould in threatening that they would induce other persons, viz. ACTT members employed by Thames, to break their contracts of employment with Thames. Such an act is capable of constituting unlawful means, and if its effect is to cause damage to someone, even though he is not a party to the contract threatened to be broken, by interfering with that third party's trade or business, it is actionable as a tort to which the name 'intimidation' was attached by this House in *Rookes* v. *Barnard* [1964] AC 1129. This particular kind of unlawful act is covered by section 13(1)(b). It is the only kind of unlawful act on the part of Hamilton and Bould upon which Hadmor seeks to rely. It is the only ground on which the acts of Hamilton and Bould could be capable of being actionable in tort in the absence of section 13(1), and section 13(1) says that it shall *not* be actionable. . . .

This subsection, [TULRA 1974, s.13(3)] which does not purport to amend the existing law but merely to declare and clarify it, appears to be directed against the future acceptance by the courts, as being a correct expression of the law, of certain obiter dicta to be found in speeches of individual members of this House in *Rookes* v. *Barnard* [1964] AC 1129 and *J. T. Stratford & Son Ltd* v. *Lindley* [1965] AC 269, and, in particular, to a dictum by Lord Pearce in the latter case (where the actual decision was that there was *not* a trade dispute) in which he suggested (p. 336) that in section 3 of the Trade Disputes Act 1906 the expression 'shall not be actionable' meant only that it should not be actionable *at the suit of the employer* and afforded no protection against liability in tort to any third party who suffered damage as a result of the breach of contract of employment that had been so induced.

This dictum, which be it noted, was made in reference only to the narrow immunity conferred by the Trade Disputes Act 1906, before the additional immunity in respect of the tort of intimidation had been added by the Trade Disputes Act 1965, had by 1974 received a chequered reception by the courts, which is admirably summarised by Templeman J. in his judgment in *Camellia Tanker Ltd SA* v. *International Transport Workers' Federation* [1976] ICR 274, 285–289. In *Morgan* v. *Fry* [1968] 2 QB 710, 729, Lord Denning M.R. had rejected Lord Pearce's dictum as a correct statement of the law even under the Trade Disputes Act 1906, and Templeman J. in the judgment referred to, so far from coming down in favour of the view of Lord Pearce (as in his judgment in the instant case, Lord Denning M.R. suggested that he did), said that it had no application to section 13(1) of the Act of 1974. In reaching this conclusion Templeman J. did not find it necessary to place any reliance upon, or even mention, subsection (3). For my part I think that Lord Pearce's dictum was wrong even in relation to section 3 of the Trade Disputes Act 1906 standing alone, and a fortiori that it has no application to the wider immunity conferred by section 13(1) of the Act of 1974 in the form in which it was originally enacted; but since the immunity was then confined to acts done in relation to contracts of employment Parliament may well have thought it prudent to make assurance doubly sure by incorporating subsection (3) in section 13.

What happened next was the substitution by the Trade Union and Labour Relations (Amendment) Act 1976 of the new subsection (1) to section 13 of the Act of 1974, which increases very substantially the breadth of the immunity. Subsection (3) was left alone, although I should regard it by then as having become wholly otiose.

Lastly, one comes to section 17 of the Employment Act 1980, passed by a Conservative Government. That section provides in subsections (1) to (5) for certain exceptions to the immunity against liability in tort conferred by section 13(1) of the Act of 1974, where the acts complained of involve particular kinds of what is described as 'secondary action.' The withdrawal of immunity from these categories of acts would conflict with what was declared to be the law by subsection (3) of section 13. Subsection (8) of section 17 of the Employment Act 1980 accordingly provided: 'Subsection (3) of section 13 of the 1974 Act shall cease to have effect.'

My Lords, I see no need to seek for any other reason than this obvious one for the repeal of section 13(3) of the Act of 1974.

The judgment of Lord Denning M.R. in the instant case was the only one that dealt with the question of construction of section 13 of the Act of 1974. It was concurred in, upon this point, by Watkins L.J., O'Connor L.J., having found that there was no trade dispute existing or threatened, preferred to express no opinion. Lord Denning M.R. looked at subsection (8) of section 17 of the Employment Act 1980 in isolation, divorced from all other provisions of the section of which it formed a part. What he said was [1981] ICR 690, 710:

> I cannot think that the legislature intended by this sentence to throw us back into the era of doubt which had existed before 1974, so that we should have to decide whether Lord Pearce was right or wrong in what he said in *J. T. Stratford & Son Ltd* v. *Lindley* [1965] AC 269. I feel that the effect of section 17(8) is to take away the effect of section 13(3), so that the acts which it said were '*not to be regarded* as . . . unlawful' are now, since the Act of 1980, '*to be regarded* as unlawful.' They are 'not actionable' by the employer, but they are unlawful so as to be available as 'unlawful means' for the purpose of establishing liability in tort.

My Lords, it seems to me, with great respect, that such a conclusion could never be reached by applying any of the accepted principles of statutory construction, even if section 17(8) had stood alone as a separate section of the Employment Act 1980. Standing as it does as the last of eight subsections in a section dealing with a selective withdrawal of immunity from certain kinds of secondary action which satisfy the carefully defined requirements of subsections (3), (4), or (5), it seems to me to be quite impossible to ascribe to subsection (8) a meaning which, in the way the earlier subsections are drafted, would make them wholly ineffectual; since it would impose liability in tort for all secondary action as defined in subsection (3), including secondary action which satisfied the requirements of subsections (3), (4), or (5).

Thus, we see that in *Hadmor* the House of Lords interpreted the immunities conferred by s.13(1) of TULRA 1974 (as amended) sufficiently broadly to prevent the tort of interference by unlawful means from upsetting the careful modification of TULRA made by EA 1980, s.17. As we shall see in more detail below, (pp. 830–42), the aim of that modification is that statutory protection against the common-law liabilities mentioned in s.13(1) shall not exist in certain cases of secondary action. The essence of secondary action as defined by the statute (EA 1980, s.17(2)) is that it involves calling upon employees not employed by the primary employer to take action in breach of their contracts of employment in order to assist the employees of the primary employer. In *Hadmor*, however, it was only employees of the primary employer (Thames) who took any industrial action, and this is not secondary action within the concept of s.17, even if it happened, and was no doubt intended, that somebody (i.e. Hadmor) in addition to the primary employer would be harmed by the action. Whether such action should be called secondary action is purely a matter of semantics and whether it should be restricted or prohibited is an important question of policy, to which we shall return. Nevertheless, what is clear is that the government in enacting s.17 did not intend to remove the statutory protections from it, and it is a tribute to the revolutionary potential of the tort of interference that it seemed at one stage capable of achieving so far-reaching a result.

The decision of the House of Lords in *Hadmor* is of first-rate importance because the most obvious source of unlawful means in the area of trade disputes is the range of acts rendered not actionable by s.13(1) of TULRA 1974. However, whilst it cannot be said to be clear how long the potential list of unlawful means may be or whether the list is the same for all the torts involving the use of unlawful means, it is apparent that the list is not confined to the matters listed in s.13(1). In relation to these unlawful means the question of their impact upon trade disputes has to be faced without the aid of any statutory immunities. A crucial question is how far a plaintiff has a cause of action in tort for interference where the industrial action involves the breach of a penal statute governing the activities of the employees. The question is crucial not only at a doctrinal level, but also because in many public and quasi-public employments the employees may be subject to rules contained in or made under Acts of Parliament (public or private), and a broad recognition that infringement of these rules gives those aimed at a cause of action in tort for interference would be materially to restrict the legal freedom of public sector employees to take industrial action (see further, below, pp. 871–9).

Although it is possible to state what the significance of the issue is, it is much less easy to say what the approach of the courts is to the question of the circumstances in which breach of a penal statute is capable of giving rise to an action in tort for unlawful interference. At one end of the spectrum there is a dictum by Lord Denning in *Torquay Hotel Co. Ltd* v. *Cousins* [1969] 2 Ch. at p. 139 (above, p. 734) which would give a wide scope to the operation of unlawful means: 'I have always understood that if one person deliberately interferes with the trade or business of another, and does so by unlawful means, that is, by an action which he is not at liberty to commit, then he is acting unlawfully. . . .' This approach would suggest that any breach of a penal statute should constitute *prima facie* unlawful means so as to render the defendant liable in tort if he has deliberately used these means to inflict economic harm on the plaintiff. At the other end of the spectrum would be the approach that the unlawful means must be independently actionable, which in the case of breach of a penal statute would mean that the liability would arise only in cases in which a penal statute can be construed[1] as giving rise to a civil action in the case of breach. In brief, the same tests should be used to determine whether breach of statute can constitute unlawful means for the tort of interference with business and other torts requiring unlawful means as are currently used to determine whether breach of a penal statute can give rise to a civil action for breach of statutory duty. In effect, this is to regard liability as arising not so much from the use of unlawful means as from the interference with the plaintiff's existing rights, derived, in these cases, not from contract but from statute. In the absence of an express provision in the statute providing for a civil remedy, English courts have traditionally been reluctant to find that such an action for breach of statutory duty was intended by Parliament to be provided.

Although it is impossible to marshal all the decided cases at either end of the spectrum or at any consistent point in between, it has to be said that two recent decisions of the House of Lords have tended to favour the restrictive approach of the breach of statutory duty cases. In *Gouriet* v. *Union of Post Office Workers* [1978] AC 435 the defendant union, as part of a campaign against apartheid, called upon its members not to handle mail to South Africa for a period of a week. The plaintiff, who was for these purposes an ordinary member of the public with no particular interest in communications with South Africa, sought an injunction to restrain the proposed boycott, on the grounds that it was a breach by the union and the Post Office employees of certain sections of the Post Office Act 1953. Section 58 of the 1953 Act made it an indictable criminal offence if any employee of the Post Office 'wilfully detains or delays . . . any postal packet' and s.68 made it a criminal offence for any person to procure the doing of any offence indictable under the Act. The main argument in the case concerned the plaintiff's legal entitlement (if any) to require the Attorney General to act as plaintiff in a relator action to secure the injunction. A subsidiary point was whether the plaintiff had *locus standi* to sue even in the absence of the Attorney General, and the House of Lords held he had not. A private person could only bring an action to restrain a threatened breach of the criminal law if his claim was based on an allegation that the threatened breach

---

[1] The statute may expressly provide a civil remedy or expressly deny one (as under the Prices and Incomes Act 1966, s.16(5) or the Counter-Inflation (Temporary Provisions) Act 1972, s.5(8) (both now repealed) or HSWA 1974, s.47(1)(a)), but typically does neither thing.

would constitute an infringement of his private rights or would inflict special damage upon him.

A more important decision was *Lonrho Ltd* v. *Shell Petroleum Co. Ltd* [1982] AC 173, both because the plaintiff suffered special harm from the defendants' acts and because the House enlarged upon its concept of private rights. For the purposes of the action it was assumed that the defendants had supplied oil from their South African subsidiaries to Southern Rhodesia in breach of an Order in Council making it a criminal offence to supply petroleum products to Southern Rhodesia in the period after the unilateral declaration of independence (UDI) by that country. The plaintiffs owned a pipeline running from a port in Mozambique to a refinery in Southern Rhodesia, which was owned by, among others, the defendants. The shipment of crude oil to Mozambique for passage to the refinery ceased with the Order in Council and the plaintiffs also ceased to earn any revenue from the pipeline. The plaintiffs argued that the supply of petroleum products by the defendants from South Africa to Southern Rhodesia prolonged the period of UDI and hence the period during which the plaintiffs earned no revenue. It was held that this alleged state of facts disclosed no cause of action. Lord Diplock (with whom the other judges concurred) said:

The sanctions Order thus creates a statutory prohibition upon the doing of certain classes of acts and provides the means of enforcing the prohibition by prosecution for a criminal offence which is subject to heavy penalties including imprisonment. So one starts with the presumption laid down originally by Lord Tenterden c.j. in *Doe d. Murray* v. *Bridges* (1831) 1 B. & Ad. 847, 859, where he spoke of the 'general rule' that 'where an Act creates an obligation, and enforces the performance in a specified manner . . . that performance cannot be enforced in any other manner' – a statement that has frequently been cited with approval ever since, including on several occasions in speeches in this House. Where the only manner of enforcing performance for which the Act provides is prosecution for the criminal offence of failure to perform the statutory obligation or for contravening the statutory prohibition which the Act creates, there are two classes of exception to this general rule.

The first is where upon the true construction of the Act it is apparent that the obligation or prohibition was imposed for the benefit or protection of a particular class of individuals, as in the case of the Factories Acts and similar legislation. As Lord Kinnear put it in *Butler (or Black)* v. *Fife Coal Co. Ltd* [1912] AC 149, 165, in the case of such a statute:

There is no reasonable ground for maintaining that a proceeding by way of penalty is the only remedy allowed by the statute. . . . We are to consider the scope and purpose of the statute and in particular for whose benefit it is intended. Now the object of the present statute is plain. It was intended to compel mine owners to make due provision for the safety of the men working in their mines, and the persons for whose benefit all these rules are to be enforced are the persons exposed to danger. But when a duty of this kind is imposed for the benefit of particular persons there arises at common law a correlative right in those persons who may be injured by its contravention.

The second exception is where the statute creates a public right (i.e. a right to be enjoyed by all those of Her Majesty's subjects who wish to avail themselves of it) and a particular member of the public suffers what Brett J. in *Benjamin* v. *Storr* (1874) LR 9 CP 400, 407, described as 'particular, direct, and substantial' damage 'other and different from that which was common to all the rest of the public.' Most of the authorities about this second exception deal not with public rights created by statute but with public rights existing at common law, particularly in respect of use of highways. *Boyce* v. *Paddington Borough Council* [1903] 1 Ch. 109 is one of the comparatively few cases about a right conferred upon the general public by statute. It is in relation to that class of statute only that Buckley J.'s oft-cited statement at p. 114 as to the two cases in which a plaintiff, without joining the Attorney-General, could himself sue in private law for interference with that public right, must be understood. The two cases he said were: '. . . first, where the interference with the public right is such as that some private right of his is at the same time interfered with . . . and, secondly, where no private right is interfered with, but the plaintiff, in respect of his public right, suffers special damage peculiar to himself from the interference with the public right.' The first case would not appear to depend upon the existence of a public right in addition to the private one; while to come within the second case at all it has first to be shown that the statute, having regard to its scope and language, does fall within that class of statutes which creates a legal right to be enjoyed by all of Her Majesty's subjects who wish to avail themselves of it. A mere prohibition upon members of the public generally from doing what it would otherwise be lawful for them to do, is not enough.

My Lords, it has been the unanimous opinion of the arbitrators with the concurrence of the umpire, of Parker J., and of each of the three members of the Court of Appeal that the sanctions Orders made pursuant to the Southern Rhodesia Act 1965 fell within neither of these two exceptions. Clearly they were not within the first category of exception. They were not imposed for the *benefit* or *protection* of a particular class of individuals who were engaged in supplying or delivering crude oil or petroleum products to Southern Rhodesia. They were intended to put an end to such transactions. Equally plainly they did not create any public right to be enjoyed by all those of Her Majesty's subjects who wished to avail themselves of it. On the contrary, what they did was to withdraw a previously existing right of citizens of, and companies incorporated in, the United Kingdom to trade with Southern Rhodesia in crude oil and petroleum products. Their purpose was, perhaps, most aptly stated by Fox L.J.:

> I cannot think that they were concerned with conferring rights either upon individuals or the public at large. Their purpose was the destruction, by economic pressure, of the UDI regime in Southern Rhodesia; they were instruments of state policy in an international matter.

Until the United Nations called upon its members to impose sanctions on the illegal regime in Southern Rhodesia it may not be strictly accurate to speak of it as an international matter, but from the outset it was certainly state policy in affairs external to the United Kingdom.

In agreement with all those present and former members of the judiciary who have considered the matter I can see no ground on which contraventions by Shell and BP of the sanctions Order though not amounting to any breach of their contract with Lonrho, nevertheless constituted a tort for which Lonrho could recover in a civil suit any loss caused to them by such contraventions.

Although *Lonrho Ltd* v. *Shell Petroleum* is a case of high authority, it is doubtful whether it is the last word on the subject. There is quite general agreement that the decision was correct on the grounds that the defendants had no intention to injure Lonrho. Their lordships rejected a suggestion put forward in an Australian case, *Beaudesert Shire Council* v. *Smith* (1966) 120 CLR 145, that an action will lie where 'a person suffers harm or loss as the irresistible consequence of the unlawful, intentional and positive acts of another'. However, it is only common sense to acknowledge the attractiveness in terms of merits of a plaintiff who says he has been deliberately injured by the criminal acts of the defendant and who seeks redress in tort.[1] Indeed, Patrick Elias and Keith Ewing[2] argue that in such a case the plaintiff ought to win in an action for interference by unlawful means whether or not the breach of statute gives rise to an action for breach of statutory duty, unless his case falls within one of four categories of exceptions. Their most important exception is that the plaintiff should not succeed if it would be 'inconsistent with the intention of Parliament to treat certain breaches of statute as unlawful means'. Sometimes that intention is put expressly by Parliament. In the absence of express intention the matter would be one of construction, but, whereas the established presumption is against an answer favourable to a civil action when the question is asked whether Parliament intended breach of a statute to create an action for breach of statutory duty, they suggest that the presumption would be in favour of a civil action when the question is asked whether breach of a statute should constitute unlawful means for the purposes of liability in tort. Of course, the courts could continue to apply the same tests to answer both questions, but become more flexible about the circumstances in which they were prepared to find a breach of a private right or special damage flowing from a public obligation. Such a development would pose as many problems for labour law as the more principled suggestion of Elias and Ewing.

Thus, in the relation to breaches of penal statutes, the divide is between those who argue that the breach can constitute unlawful means only when the breach would be actionable as a breach of statutory duty and those who argue that such breaches should *prima facie* always count as unlawful means. This might suggest that there is at least agreement on the general proposition that an act which is itself actionable, e.g. any tort or breach of contract, should always be capable of counting as unlawful means, thus rendering the defendant liable for the tort of interference, subject to any statutory immunities he might have. Indeed, if such acts cannot count as unlawful means, one might wonder what would suffice. In relation to labour law, much of the sting of the proposition has been removed for the present, so far as acts actionable as torts are concerned, by the decision in the *Hadmor* case, as we

---

[1] Cf. *RCA Corporation* v. *Pollard* [1982] 3 WLR 1007 (CA), and the trenchant comments thereon by Professor Wedderburn (1983) 46 *MLR* 224.

[2] Op.cit., pp. 336–41.

have seen. But what about acts which are breaches of contract? To return to the example we considered in the preamble to the *Hadmor* case (above, p. 746) of shop stewards who organize industrial action against their employer which is in breach of the contracts of employment of the employees who take the action. Could the employer succeed in an argument that the shop stewards had interfered with his business by unlawful means, the unlawful means being the actual breaches of the contracts of employment? In *Rookes* v. *Barnard* (above), the House of Lords held that a threat to break a contract of employment could constitute unlawful means for the purposes of the tort of intimidation, and so why should not an actual breach constitute unlawful means for the tort of interference with business?

In 1974, Parliament anticipated this development by enacting in TULRA 1974, s.13(3)(*b*) that 'a breach of contract in contemplation or furtherance of a trade dispute shall not be regarded as the doing of an unlawful act or as the use of unlawful means for the purpose of establishing liability in tort'. This provision was repealed along with the rest of s.13(3) in 1980 (see above, p. 746) and, although the decision of the House of Lords in *Hadmor* case has settled that s.13(3)(*a*) was an unnecessary addition to s.13(1), the case in no way answers the question whether the liability against which s.13(3)(*b*) purported to guard was a real one or not. There is no authority in favour of the proposition that a breach of contract can constitute unlawful means and the effect of so holding in the example given above would be to turn a breach of contract into a tort; and in a case where the industrial action was aimed at someone in addition to the employer the effect would be, if that third party could successfully sue, to allow a non-party to sue for breach of a contract. Nevertheless, there is no authority directly against the argument and the analogy with *Rookes* v. *Barnard* is a strong one. This kind of potential liability acts like a time-bomb in our labour law, but no one is sure whether it will ever go off.

Before we leave the tortuous area of interference by unlawful means, there is one final issue we should look at. Two recent decisions of the Court of Appeal suggest that inducement of breach of statutory duty may be emerging as a distinct head of liability, something of a hybrid between inducing breach of contract and interference by unlawful means. In the earlier case of *Cunard Steamship Co. Ltd* v. *Stacey* [1955] 2 Lloyd's Rep. 247 (CA), statutory duties were laid upon the employees, the employer was seeking to enforce them by an action in tort, and the court asked the traditional question of whether the breach of statute gave rise to a civil action at the suit of the employer. In the recent cases, however, the duty has been laid upon the employer and the question has arisen as to whether the employer (or conceivably a third party) could bring an action in tort against the organizers of industrial action which had prevented the employer from discharging its statutory duties.

In *Meade* v. *Haringey LBC* [1979] ICR 494, caretakers of schools employed by the authority struck in pursuance of a national dispute with the local authorities. In Haringey the local authority responded by closing the schools, which the plaintiff parents argued was a breach of the authority's duty under the Education Act 1944 to provide education. The majority of the Court of Appeal were not prepared to find in an interlocutory hearing that the authority was in fact in breach of its statutory duty. Lord Denning M.R., however, thought that the evidence disclosed that the authority had acted under the influence of the local authority unions and thus unlawfully. The authority should have kept the schools open and 'moved the court for an injunction to restrain the leaders of the trade unions from interfering with the due opening of the schools' (at p. 505). Since the organizers of the industrial action were not parties to the litigation, the point was not fully argued. If it could be shown that the organizers had used unlawful means to bring about the breach of duty, then the case would fall within the categories of interference with business by unlawful means discussed above. However, Lord Denning did not suggest that proof of unlawful means was a requirement for success by the employer. Inducement of breach of statutory duty, it seemed to be suggested, was by itself tortious, and TULRA 1974, s.13 would provide no protection against this type of tortious liability. 'Now section 13 . . . gives them immunity if they induce a person to break a contract. But it gives them no immunity if they induce a local authority to break its statutory duty.' (ibid.)[1] In *Associated Newspapers Group Ltd* v. *Wade* [1979] ICR 664, Lord Denning (again without the express support of the other members of the court) took these ideas a stage further. Here, employees of certain newspapers blacked advertising copy from certain sources, including some public sector employers which were under a statutory duty to advertise appointments in the media. Lord Denning suggested that mere hindering the performance of statutory duties (without any actual breach of duty) might be enough for liability, and that liability for such action did not sound in tort at all but was an independent head of liability. This head of liability is still very much in an embryonic state, but its development would cause major problems for public sector employees and operate so as to outflank the immunities provided by TULRA 1974, even as amended by EA 1980 and 1982.

7 Duress[2]

We have seen that a major doctrinal and practical development in the common law of the economic torts in the post-war period has consisted in the imposition of liability for economic harm intentionally inflicted by unlawful means. In the field of labour law the paradigm case of unlawful means has been the threat to break or induce a breach of contracts of employment by threatening to organize or to continue some form of industrial action which

[1] Lord Denning did not raise the issue of whether the local authority could sue if it had been directly induced to break its statutory duty (cf. p. 731 above).

[2] See generally Goff and Jones, *The Law of Restitution* (2nd edn, 1978), Chap. 9.

involves a breach of their contracts of employment by those participating in it. In *Rookes* v. *Barnard* (above) such a threat was held to constitute unlawful means for the purposes of the tort of intimidation; in *Hadmor Productions Ltd* v. *Hamilton* (above) the House of Lords accepted that such a threat constituted unlawful means for the purposes of the tort of interference. Since we have suggested that the tort of interference is a generalization of the more limited principle behind the tort of intimidation, it is not surprising that the House of Lords should have held the threat to break a contract of employment to be unlawful means for the purposes of both torts. The contrast between the two cases lies in the different approaches to the further question that arises once a common-law tort based upon unlawful means has been held to be established, namely, do the existing statutory immunities provide protection against the common-law liabilities? In *Hadmor*, decided at a time when Parliament was giving active consideration to the appropriate scope of the statutory immunities, the House of Lords was clearly anxious to interpret TULRA 1974 in such a way that new common-law developments did not undermine the statutory scheme of immunities. By contrast, in *Rookes* v. *Barnard* the House (see Lord Devlin, above, at p. 742) was prepared to leave to Parliament by subsequent legislation the task of bringing the statutory immunities back into line with the newly expanded common law, if it thought fit to do so. This was at a time when Parliament had not given detailed consideration to the statutory immunities for over fifty years and when pressure was building up for a fundamental reconsideration of the relationship between common-law and statutory immunities, and their lordships seemed to see no reason not to add to those pressures.

Such is the protean nature of the common law, however, that the legal status of the threats mentioned in the previous paragraph has had to be considered recently in yet a third legal context. That context was the context of duress. It has long been recognized that a claim could succeed to have a contract avoided on the grounds that it had been entered into under duress or to recover from a defendant money paid under duress on the grounds that it was money had and received to the plaintiff's use. Rather like the early concept of intimidation (see above, p. 738), however, duress was originally conceived of as confined to actual or threatened force to the person. In the early twentieth century, certain cases of 'duress to goods' were included in the concept, but the major development, parallelling that in *Rookes* v. *Barnard*, occurred from the middle 1970s when in some commercial cases the courts developed the notion of 'economic duress'. In such cases purely economic pressure is held to amount to duress, provided the pressure applied is such as to 'overbear the will' of the person to whom it is applied.

It was no doubt inevitable that sooner or later the courts would have to consider a claim based upon duress in the context of labour relations. To return to our example of the industrial action organized by the shop stewards' committee, suppose that in the face of the pressure the employer should concede the stewards' claim. Could he, after the pressure had been removed, seek to claim back the concession on the grounds that it was made under duress? If the employer had entered into a collective agreement with the trade union as a result of the pressure, it is unlikely that he would wish to seek to have it avoided on grounds of duress, since, as we shall see below (p. 783) it is very unlikely to be legally binding upon him even in the absence of duress. On the other hand, if the employer had made a payment to the trade union in order to secure the removal of the pressure, that payment might be claimed back as money had and received by the trade union to the employer's use. This was the situation that was considered by the House of Lords in *Universe Tankships Inc. of Monrovia* v. *International Transport Workers' Federation* (below)[1]. In spite of the recent and high nature of this authority, however, it is of relatively limited guidance in mapping out the contours of duress in the area of collective labour relations and in establishing the relationship between duress and the statutory immunities, because of two crucial concessions made by counsel in the case. Counsel for the union conceded that the pressure applied to the plaintiff amounted to economic duress, so that the House did not have to consider what types of industrial action in what circumstances could amount to duress. One point of significance on this issue did emerge, however. Lord Scarman, at least, was prepared to accept that pressure could amount to economic duress even though it was not independently unlawful. 'Duress can, of course, exist even if the threat is one of lawful action: whether it does so depends upon the nature of the demand' ([1982] ICR at p. 289). The question was one of the legitimacy of the pressure applied, not of its legality. This dictum increases the range of industrial action capable of amounting to duress, so as to include, for example, industrial action which does not involve any breach of contract on the part of those participating in it, but does not by itself help to establish which types of action will be regarded as legitimate and which not.

Having established by way of concession that the industrial pressure applied amounted to economic duress, the House had to consider the relationship between duress and the statutory immunities. Here the defendants faced an apparently insuperable problem. They had induced and threatened to continue to induce employees to break their contracts of employment. Such acts were rendered by TULRA 1974, s.13(1), 'not actionable in tort', although the TDA 1906 (but *not* the TDA 1965) had stated that inducing breach of a contract of employment should simply 'not be actionable'. Since the plaintiff's claim was a restitutionary one and not a claim in tort, TULRA 1974, s.13(1), seemed to have no application. The decision taken in 1965 and followed thereafter (see IRA 1971, s.132, as well as TULRA 1974, s.13) to make an express restriction on the immunities to actions in tort was thus seen to have been of the utmost significance. However, their lordships, following the policy that appears in the *Hadmor* case, in effect reverted to the policy of the TDA 1906 and applied the statutory immunities

[1] Noted by Wedderburn (1982) 45 *MLR* 556 (an invaluable note) and by Sterling (1982) 11 *ILJ* 156.

by way of analogy in order to determine whether the economic duress imposed by the union was legitimate or not. Again, this was done by way of concession, this time by counsel for the plaintiffs, and, although the majority of their lordships seem to have thought that the concession accurately reflected the law, Lord Brandon of Oakbrook wished it to be quite clear that the House was not 'giving the seal of . . . approval' to this proposition (at p. 294). Had their lordships not applied the statutory immunities by analogy, the result might well have been precisely the one they had sought to avoid in the *Hadmor* case, namely that a new common-law liability would have substantially undermined the statutory framework of immunities established by TULRA 1974 and 1976 and modified by EA 1980 and 1982. Whatever the general arguments for judicial activism, they are clearly much less strong if Parliament is currently grappling with the relevant problem and that problem lies at the centre of national politics.

However, there was one oddity in the application by the House of the statutory immunities by analogy. The action in this case was brought against the union as such and not against officials of the union, as in the other cases so far set out in this chapter. The union, when acting in contemplation or furtherance of a trade dispute, can claim, of course, the immunities provided by s.13 of TULRA 1974 (and its predecessors). However, as we shall see below (pp. 763–5), in s.4 of the TDA 1906 an additional and broader immunity was provided for trade unions (and certain employers' associations), which was continued by TULRA 1974, s.14, until that section was repealed by EA 1982, s.15(1). The broader immunity applied whether or not the trade union had acted in contemplation or furtherance of a trade dispute and provided an immunity, with limited exceptions, against all liability in tort and not just against the specific types of tortious liability mentioned in TULRA 1974, s.13. However, their lordships were not prepared to apply s.14 by analogy, for reasons which remain unclear. Indeed, only Lord Diplock adverted to the point. Had s.14 been applied by analogy the result in the case would have been different because it would not have been necessary for the defendants to show that they acted in contemplation or furtherance of a trade dispute. Perhaps this was an example of judicial anticipation of Parliamentary repeal of s.14.

Universe Tankships Inc. of Monrovia v. International Transport Workers
Federation [1982] ICR 262 (HL)

The union was conducting a campaign against the low wages paid to crews of ships flying flags of convenience. In July 1978 the *Universe Sentinel*, registered in Liberia, owned through a Liberian company by shareholders domiciled in the United States, and having a predominantly Asian crew, arrived at Milford Haven. The ITF secured through its affiliate UK unions that the crews of tugs at Milford Haven blacked the ship in breach of their contracts of employment, so that the ship could not leave port. In order to secure the release of the ship, its owners entered into two collective agreements with the ITF, the 'special agreement' and the 'typescript agreement', by which, *inter alia*, the owners agreed to pay the crew at the ITF recognized rates rather than at the much lower rates they had previously been receiving. The owners also made certain payments to the ITF, namely $80,000 by way of back pay to be distributed to the crew; $2,800 by way of entrance and membership fees for the crew; and $6,480 as a contribution to the union's welfare fund. After the release of the ship the owners demanded repayment of the money paid to the union, but ultimately abandoned their claims to the back pay and the entrance fees, leaving only the payment to the welfare fund at issue before the House of Lords.

LORD DIPLOCK: . . . My Lords, I turn to the second ground on which repayment of the $6,480 is claimed, which I will call the duress point. It is not disputed that the circumstances in which ITF demanded that the shipowners should enter into the special agreement and the typescript agreement and should pay the moneys of which the latter documents acknowledge receipt, amounted to economic duress upon the shipowners; that is to say, it is conceded that the financial consequences to the shipowners of the *Universe Sentinel* continuing to be rendered off-hire under her time charter to Texaco, while the blacking continued, were so catastrophic as to amount to a coercion of the shipowners' will which vitiated their consent to those agreements and to the payments made by them to ITF. This concession makes it unnecessary for your Lordships to use the instant appeal as the occasion for a general consideration of the developing law of economic duress as a ground for treating contracts as voidable and obtaining restitution of money paid under economic duress as money had and received to the plaintiffs' use. That economic duress may constitute a ground for such redress was recognised, albeit obiter, by the Privy Council in *Pao On* v. *Lau Yiu Long* [1980] AC 614. The Board in that case referred with approval to two judgments at first instance in the commercial court which recognised that commercial pressure may constitute duress: one by Kerr J. in *Occidental Worldwide Investment Corporation* v. *Skibs A/S Avanti* [1976] 1 Lloyd's Rep. 293, the other by Mocatta J. in *North Ocean Shipping Co. Ltd* v. *Hyundai Construction Co. Ltd* [1979] QB 705, which traces the development of this branch of the law from its origin in the 18th and early 19th century cases.

It is, however, in my view crucial to the decision of the instant appeal to identify the rationale of this development of the common law. It is not that the party seeking to avoid the contract which he has entered into with another party, or to recover money that he has paid to another party in response to a demand, did not know the nature or the precise terms of the contract at the time when he entered into it or did not understand the purpose for which the payment was demanded. The rationale is that his apparent consent was induced by pressure exercised upon him by that other party which the law does not regard as legitimate, with the consequence that the consent is treated in law as revocable unless approbated either expressly or by implication after the illegitimate pressure has ceased to operate on his mind. It is a rationale similar to that which underlies the avoidability of contracts entered into and the recovery of money exacted under colour of office, or under undue influence or in consequence of threats of physical duress.

Commercial pressure, in some degree, exists wherever one party to a commercial transaction is in a stronger bargaining position than the other party. It is not, however, in my view, necessary, nor would it be appropriate in the instant appeal, to enter into the general question of the kinds of circumstances, if any, in which commercial pressure, even though it amounts to a coercion of the will of a party in the weaker bargaining position, may be treated as legitimate and, accordingly, as not giving rise to any legal right of redress. In the instant appeal the economic duress complained of was exercised in the field of industrial relations to which very special considerations apply.

My Lords, so far as is relevant to this appeal, the policy of Parliament, ever since the Trade Disputes Act 1906 was passed to overrule a decision of this House, has been to legitimise acts done by employees, or by trade unions acting or purporting to act on their behalf, which would otherwise be unlawful wherever such acts are done in contemplation or furtherance of a dispute which is connected with the terms and conditions of employment of any employees. I can confine myself to the kind of acts and the particular subject matter of the trade dispute that was involved in the instant case, and I use the expression 'legitimise' as meaning that the doer of the act is rendered immune from any liability to damages or any other remedy against him in a court of justice, at the suit of a person who has suffered loss or damage in consequence of the act; save only a remedy for breach of contract where the act is done in breach of a direct contract between the doer of the act and the person by whom the damage is sustained.

The statutory provisions in force when the events with which this appeal is concerned took place, and which point to the public policy to which effect ought to be given by your Lordships, are chiefly contained in sections 13, 14 and 29 of the Trade Union and Labour Relations Act 1974. The legislative history of these sections is referred to in the recent decision of this House in *Hadmor Productions Ltd* v. *Hamilton* [1982] I C R 114. In terms they are confined to bestowing immunity from liability in tort; they do not deal with immunity in any other type of action. In the case of a trade union such immunity is extended by section 14 to virtually all torts; in the case of individuals, it is extended by section 13 to defined classes of torts (which would include the blacking of the *Universe Sentinel*) which are limited, not only in their nature, but also by the requirement that what would otherwise be the tortious act must be committed in contemplation or furtherance of a trade dispute as defined in section 29.

The use of economic duress to induce another person to part with property or money is not a tort per se; the form that the duress takes may, or may not, be tortious. The remedy to which economic duress gives rise is not an action for damages but an action for restitution of property or money exacted under such duress and the avoidance of any contract that had been induced by it; but where the particular form taken by the economic duress used is itself a tort, the restitutional remedy for money had and received by the defendant to the plaintiff's use is one which the plaintiff is entitled to pursue as an alternative remedy to an action for damages in tort.

In extending into the field of industrial relations the common law concept of economic duress and the right to a restitutionary remedy for it which is currently in process of development by judicial decisions, this House would not, in my view, be exercising the restraint that is appropriate to such a process if it were so to develop the concept that, by the simple expedient of 'waiving the tort,' a restitutionary remedy for money had and received is made enforceable in cases in which Parliament has, over so long a period of years, manifested its preference for a public policy that a particular kind of tortious act should be legitimised in the sense that I am using that expression.

It is only in this indirect way that the provisions of the Trade Union and Labour

Relations Act 1974 are relevant to the duress point. The immunities from liability in tort provided by sections 13 and 14 are not directly applicable to the shipowners' cause of action for money had and received. Nevertheless, these sections, together with the definition of trade dispute in section 29, afford an indication, which your Lordships should respect, of where public policy requires that the line should be drawn between what kind of commercial pressure by a trade union upon an employer in the field of industrial relations ought to be treated as legitimised despite the fact that the will of the employer is thereby coerced, and what kind of commercial pressure in that field does amount to economic duress that entitles the employer victim to restitutionary remedies.

My Lords, ITF does not suggest that the immunity from suit in most kinds of tort conferred upon trade unions by section 14 whether or not they are committed in contemplation or furtherance of a trade dispute, point to a public policy that trade unions should be immune from a restitutionary action for money had and received. Such a suggestion would not be sustainable. If Parliament had intended to give to trade unions, simply because they are trade unions, a wider immunity from suit than that for which section 14 provides, it would have done so. What ITF relies upon is the immunity from actions for particular kinds of tort given by section 13 to every person, whether a trade union or not.

To qualify for immunity under section 13, an act, which would otherwise be actionable in tort, must be done in contemplation or in furtherance of a trade dispute; and for a dispute to qualify as a trade dispute within the meaning of section 29(1), it must be a dispute which is connected with one or more of a number of subject matters, of which the only one relied on by ITF in this appeal is: 'terms and conditions of employment' of the crew of the *Universe Sentinel*.

Lord Diplock (with whom Lords Cross and Russell agreed) then held that the payment to the welfare fund was not made in pursuance of a dispute connected with the terms and conditions of employment of the crew and so the pressure applied in this respect was not applied in furtherance of a trade dispute. Lords Scarman and Brandon dissented on this point. We shall return to it in our discussion of the meaning of trade dispute (below, p. 802).

It may be said that the *Universe Tankships* decision is of limited significance because it is not the typical outcome of a successful piece of industrial action that money is paid to a trade union. The employer may agree to pay higher wages to the employees, but this will usually be done directly and not via the union. In such a case a restitutionary claim against the union is not of much use to the employer. What he needs is an action in tort to provide a remedy for the harm the industrial action has inflicted upon him. However, it would only be a short step for a court to hold that the deliberate use of industrial action, that amounts to duress, to injure a person involves committing the tort of interference by unlawful means, although the *Hadmor* decision would probably protect the defendants if the duress consisted in the doing of acts rendered not actionable by TULRA 1974, s.13. *A fortiori*, the defendants should not be liable if the industrial action does not involve the commission of any independent illegality.

8 **Remedies**

So far we have been concerned with the substantive law. We have seen how the policy of abstention, as embodied in the TDA 1906, required the exclusion of common-law tort liabilities from the area of trade disputes; how the process of exclusion has had to be a continuing one because of the developing nature of the common law; how, perhaps surprisingly, in the modern era, when there have been two concerted attempts (IRA 1971 and EA 1980 and 1982) to move away from the policy of abstention, there has been a continuing need to exclude new common-law developments because of their potential for undermining even the current, more restrictive law; and how, at least at the level of the House of Lords, the judiciary in the most recent decisions seem to accept that common-law liabilities should be kept at bay at a time when Parliament is implementing its new, more interventionist policies.[1] To some large degree these developments in the substantive law have their parallels in the law relating to the remedies for tortious acts committed in the course of industrial disputes. The two main legal remedies available to the employer against whom tortious industrial pressure is being applied are damages and the injunction. We shall look at each in turn.

(a) **The protection of trade-union funds**

A court will make an award of damages in favour of an employer against whom tortious industrial pressure has been applied only at the end of a full trial, in which the relevant factual and legal issues have been explored. Such a trial may take many months, sometimes years, to come on, and the industrial dispute out of which the legal claim arose may long have been settled. The unwillingness of employers to rake over the embers of half-forgotten disputes, to the detriment of what are now, it is to be hoped, relatively harmonious relations with their employees and their trade unions, may go a long way to explain why very few legal actions arising out of industrial disputes are carried through to a full trial. But not all employers will be in this position. For example, in *General Aviation Services (UK) Ltd* v. *Transport and General Workers' Union* [1976] IRLR 225 (HL), a case decided under the IRA 1971 (see below, p. 829), a Canadian company had been granted a franchise by the British Airports Authority to operate at Heathrow Airport. The shop stewards' committee at the airport objected to this as a form of 'privatization', and conducted a long campaign against the company, which eventually withdrew and went back to Canada. The company sued the shop stewards' union for damages of £2 million: it had no continuing operations in the UK and so it had no relations with UK unions or employees which its legal action

---

[1] The test of judicial self-restraint would arise in its acutest form if in the future Parliament reverted to a policy of abstention. Cf. the restrictive approach of the Court of Appeal after the passing of TULRA 1976, analysed in Davies and Freedland, 'Lord Denning and Labour Law' in Jowell and McAuslan (eds.), *Lord Denning, the Judge and the Law* (forthcoming) and see below, p. 816. By the time these cases reached the House of Lords in 1979, the government had changed and was committed to moving away from abstentionism.

might prejudice and it stood to obtain a large amount of financial compensation if its legal action succeeded. It was fear of such crippling awards of damages against trade unions that led Parliament in s.4 of the TDA 1906 to grant trade unions the special and virtually complete immunity against liability in tort which we noted in the preamble to the *Universe Tankships* case (above p. 759). That immunity was removed in 1971, restored in 1974 (TULRA 1974, s.14) and removed again in 1982 (EA 1982, s.15(1)). Of course, even when s.4 of TDA 1906 and s.14 of TULRA 1974 were in force, it was always possible for the employer to sue individual union officials for damages (subject to the protection they might have in virtue of the other sections of the TDA 1906 or s.13 of TULRA 1974), but this was no doubt a less attractive option for employers than the ability directly to attack the trade union's own funds.

The special immunity for trade unions granted by the 1906 Act had often been a matter of controversy. Before the 1906 Act trade unions as such were generally regarded as immune from suit because they were (and, indeed, still are; see TULRA 1974, s.2(1)) unincorporated associations. The majority report of the Royal Commission on Labour (C. 7421, 1894) regarded this position as unsatisfactory because persons injured by trade unions 'can only proceed against the agents personally, and, whilst they may obtain verdicts against them . . . be unable to recover adequate damages'. However, in 1901 in *Taff Vale Railway Co.* v. *Amalgamated Society of Railway Servants* [1901] AC 426 the House of Lords held, in what must still be the most famous labour law case, that trade unions which had chosen to register under the Trade Union Act 1871 (which was the majority) could be sued in their own name. A local official of the union had organized a strike and picketing against the railway in response to its alleged victimization of a signalman for his trade-union activities. The union, which had somewhat reluctantly approved the action, was found to have committed the tort of conspiracy to induce breaches of contracts of employment (this was before the enactment of s.3 of the TDA 1906) and conspiracy to interfere with the company's business by unlawful means (viz. the unlawful picketing). The reaction of the rank-and-file of the trade unions was to press for legislation to restore what had previously been thought to be the position, but the union leaderships, including that of the ASRS itself, were initially less militant.[1] They thought that a complete exemption from tort liability for trade unions would be unacceptable to Parliament and even that the existence of such liability would strengthen union executives' hands *vis-à-vis* more militant local elements. They therefore wished to have legislation that rendered the union liable only for illegal acts authorized by the trade union (as in the *Taff Vale* case itself). However, opinion hardened, even among the leaderships, when the cost to the ASRS of the *Taff Vale* litigation became clear. The union paid the company £23,000 to

[1] For a general discussion of the events occurring between the decision in *Taff Vale* and the passing of the TDA 1906, see Clegg, Fox and Thompson, *A History of British Trade Unions 1889–1910* (1964), Chap. 8.

cover both damages and the company's costs and the union's own costs amounted to almost as much again. The total, £42,000, was almost two-thirds of the union's annual income at this time. Further, the Conservative government of the time rejected overtures for the passing of a bill of the type originally desired by the trade-union leaderships. Progress had to wait for the return of a Liberal government which, after some hesitation, was persuaded to restore the complete immunity in s.4 of the TDA 1906. Thus, that Act overturned three decisions of the House of Lords of the previous decade which were adverse to trade unions: the *Taff Vale* case in s.4; *Quinn* v. *Leathem* (above, p. 710) in s.1; and the *Glamorgan Coal Co.* case (above, p. 718) in s.3; and it confirmed one House of Lords decision that was favourable to trade unions (*Allen* v. *Flood* (above, p. 710) in s.3).

The Donovan Commission considered the issue only briefly. It recommended that the special immunity should remain, but that it should be confined to acts done in contemplation or furtherance of a trade dispute (see paras. 902–11). The IRA 1971 removed the immunity (although some special protection was given to official action taken by registered trade unions); TULRA 1974 restored the immunity in its full vigour; EA 1982 removed it again. Thus, we can see that in the moves away from abstentionism and towards some more interventionist stance by the law of industrial conflict, the issue of the liability of the trade union has been a central one. We shall return, in the next chapter, to the question of what goals those who favour the removal of the unions' special immunity might hope to achieve.

(b) Interlocutory injunctions

At the end of the trial a successful employer might also be awarded an injunction in order to prohibit any continuation of the unlawful conduct. However, as we have already observed, by the time of the trial the original dispute and its concomitant unlawful industrial action will probably long have been settled, so that the employer is unlikely to need an injunction at this point. That need exists when the industrial action is on foot. If the employer at that stage can obtain a court order prohibiting the continuance of the industrial action, it may be of the greatest benefit to him. Fortunately for the employer, the law can respond to his need. Unlike damages, the injunctive remedy can be awarded by the courts not only at trial but also in interlocutory proceedings. Under what is now s.37 of the Supreme Court Act 1981 and RSC, Ord. 29, r.1, the High Court can grant an interlocutory injunction at a very early stage of a legal action, and similar powers exist in the County Court. This is a general power that the courts have, not one confined to the area of labour law or of trade disputes, but there are particular problems in the area of industrial conflict that arise out of the courts' powers to grant injunctive relief before the factual and legal issues in the case have been fully investigated.

The essence of the law's dilemma with the interlocutory injunction is this: if the employer is denied relief during the course of the dispute, it may be of no avail to him, as we have seen, after the dispute has been settled. The same, however, is true of the employees' side. If the workers' economic sanctions are proscribed and the dispute is settled, in all probability on less favourable terms for the employees than if they had been able to make full use of their industrial power, then it is most unlikely that they will wish to reopen the underlying issue if a court later declares that the sanctions were not, after all, illegal. Indeed, whether they win or lose in the interlocutory proceedings, it is unusual in labour disputes for either side to bother to take the issue to a full trial (though they may appeal the interlocutory decision). The problem stems, of course, from the limited nature of the court's jurisdiction: it can enjoin the use of particular sanctions, but has no jurisdiction over the underlying dispute, being unable either to freeze the industrial relations situation until completion of the full trial or to impose a form of compulsory arbitration of the underlying dispute upon the parties.

The competing interests of the parties in interlocutory proceedings are thus clear. The employer will wish the court to issue the injunction after only cursory investigation of the legal and factual situation, stressing the harm he will suffer if the injunction is not immediately granted and it later turns out that the employees' action was illegal. The defendants will want to make the interlocutory proceedings as much like a full trial as possible, stressing the damage they will suffer if the injunction is granted and it later turns out that their actions were legal. The defendants' doubts about the fairness of the proceedings will be particularly strong if the interlocutory proceedings take what is known as the *ex parte* form. The Rules of the Supreme Court permit such a form where the case is 'urgent'. Here the plaintiff alone appears before the judge seeking an injunction, an application that competent solicitors can arrange to be heard within a few hours of being instructed to go ahead. In spite of various safeguards that exist to protect to some extent the defendant who is not present (notably the reluctance of judges to grant *ex parte* injunctions except for short periods until an *inter partes* hearing (both parties present) can be arranged), the procedure is clearly an unhappy one. Consequently s.17(1) of TULRA 1974 now places special requirements as to notice on the plaintiff seeking *ex parte* relief where the defendant is likely to claim that he acted in contemplation or furtherance of a trade dispute. The section requires the applicant to take reasonable steps to give notice to the defendant of the intended application and an opportunity of being heard in respect of it. In practice plaintiffs seem to give, and courts accept as sufficient, about 24 hours' notice.

Even if the plaintiff proceeds by way of an *inter partes* application, the defendant may have doubts about the procedural adequacy of the hearing. He is likely to have had only a day or two's notice of the hearing, evidence will usually be by affidavit and so without cross-examination, and the hearing will be a truncated one, falling far short of a full trial. The major area of debate in recent years has in fact been that of how far the court in interlocutory proceedings should go in probing the strengths and weaknesses of the plaintiff's case. The traditional test was that the plaintiff must establish a *prima facie* case, i.e. the court must be satisfied, after hearing the plaintiff's affidavit evidence, that if no further evidence were led at the trial the plaintiff would be likely to succeed on the legal and factual issues at stake. In addition, as a quite separate matter, the plaintiff must be able to satisfy the balance of convenience. This was traditionally viewed as purely a matter of comparative harm and did not relate, at least in theory, to the strength of the plaintiff's case. The court must be of the opinion that, on the assumption that the plaintiff will succeed in establishing his case at the trial, the harm he is likely to suffer in the interim if the interlocutory injunction is denied will exceed that likely to be suffered by the defendant if the interlocutory injunction is granted and it turns out at the trial that the plaintiff fails to establish his case. The balance of convenience is a necessary second hurdle because of the risk that the plaintiff's case has appeared in the truncated interlocutory proceedings in a more favourable light than it deserves. The court is willing to run the risk of granting an unjustified remedy only if the plaintiff will otherwise suffer greater harm than the defendant.

In a recent decision the House of Lords expressed some dissatisfaction with the '*prima facie* case' test because it did not very precisely indicate to the court how far it should investigate the plaintiff's case. In *American Cyanamid* v. *Ethicon* [1975] AC 396, a patent case, the House of Lords, speaking through Lord Diplock, thought that the judge in the interlocutory hearing and the Court of Appeal, on appeal from the interlocutory decision, had gone too far in hearing evidence: 'In effect what the Court of Appeal was doing was trying the issue of infringement on the conflicting affidavit evidence as it stood, without the benefit of oral testimony or cross-examination.' In order to discourage such an approach the House of Lords downgraded the '*prima facie* case' test, in particular the requirement that the plaintiff establish a *prima facie* case before the court moves on to consider the balance of convenience. In future, provided there was 'a serious question to be tried', i.e. the plaintiff's claim was not frivolous or vexatious, the court's decision whether to grant the interlocutory remedy should depend mainly on the balance of convenience. Only where the balance of convenience was in equilibrium should the court have regard to the strength of the plaintiff's case, and even then, where other factors were equal, 'it is a counsel of prudence to take such measures as are calculated to preserve the status quo.If the defendant is enjoined temporarily from doing something that he has not done before, the only effect of the interlocutory injunction in the event of his succeeding at the trial is to postpone the date at which he is able to embark on a course of action which he has not previously found it necessary to undertake. . . .'

The judgment was clearly motivated by a desire to discourage lower courts from making difficult legal and factual determinations on the basis of inadequate evidence and argument. Its effect was to make it easier for plaintiffs to obtain injunctions. There followed a lively debate in the courts, especially at the level of the Court of Appeal, which changed its mind on the matter in the course of the debate, about the appropriateness of the *Ethicon* approach in industrial disputes; Parliament intervened in the Employment Protection Act 1975 to add a new subsection (2) to s.17 of TULRA 1974; and eventually guidelines were established by the House of Lords in decisions in 1979 and 1980 which did considerably modify the *Ethicon* approach in trade disputes, but which were themselves modified by the House of Lords in 1984. There were two arguments against the *Ethicon* approach in trade disputes. First, as Lord Denning pointed out in *Hubbard* v. *Pitt* [1975] ICR 308, 320, a case concerning picketing of an estate agent's office by 'anti- gentrification' campaigners in Islington, the court could not in fact by granting the interlocutory injunction preserve the status quo until trial.

If an interlocutory injunction is granted, it will virtually decide the whole action in favour of the plaintiffs: because the defendants will be restrained until the trial (which may mean two years, or more) from picketing the plaintiffs' premises, by which time the campaign will be over. It is true that the plaintiffs will have to give an undertaking in damages, but that will be of no use to the defendants, seeing that they will not suffer any pecuniary damages, but only be prevented from continuing their campaign in this way.

Second, the balance of convenience test was traditionally applied in such a way as to take greater account of the interests of employers than of those of the organizers of industrial action. The loss of production and revenue to the employer totally overshadowed the prohibition of the industrial action, which was often seen as merely a temporary inconvenience to the organizers of it. Again, the passage of Lord Denning from *Hubbard* v. *Pitt* implicitly rejects this view.

These considerations operated upon Parliament in the debates leading up to the passing of the EPA 1975. By that Act a new s.17(2) was added to TULRA 1974, which, as subsequently amended, reads as follows:

It is hereby declared for the avoidance of doubt that where an application is made to a court, pending the trial of an action, for an interlocutory injunction and the party against whom the injunction is sought claims that he acted in contemplation or furtherance of a trade dispute, the court shall, in exercising its discretion whether or not to grant the injunction, have regard to the likelihood of that party's succeeding at the trial of the action in establishing the matter or matters which would, under any provision of section 13 or 15 above, afford a defence to the action.

Curiously, this new provision (which does not apply in Scotland) did not operate so as to confirm the Court of Appeal in the approach indicated by Lord Denning in *Hubbard* v. *Pitt*. On the contrary, as we shall see below (pp. 816–17), with the extension of the statutory immunities against tort liabilities by TULRA 1976 the Court of Appeal began to interpret the legislation, especially the notion of furthering a trade dispute, much more strictly, and this new approach was accompanied by a changed attitude towards the granting of interlocutory injunctions. In part, the Court of Appeal was helped in this approach by the vagueness of s.17(2) itself. The court was to 'have regard' to the likelihood of the defendant succeeding at the trial with a defence under ss.13 or 15 of TULRA 1974, but it was not instructed to come to any particular conclusion as a result of its having had regard. In *Star Sea Transport Corporation of Monrovia* v. *Slater* [1978] IRLR 507, another case of blacking, organized by the ITF, at an English port of a ship flying a flag of convenience, Lord Denning applied the balance of convenience test in the traditional way in the employer's favour and was willing to grant an interlocutory injunction even though it was 'very arguable' that the defendant would succeed at the trial. He said:

> ... Applying these considerations, it seems to me that there is a very arguable point of law here. It is mixed up with facts which require detailed consideration. We have to consider the balance of convenience. It seems to me that the balance of convenience is in favour of issuing an injunction to stop the blacking. On the one hand, this vessel has been held up for days. She is prevented from sailing on her lawful activities of carrying grain across the world. The owners are losing all their hire. Damage is mounting every day. Not only the owners but many others – including the public at large – are suffering damage, loss and inconvenience.
>
> On the other hand, if the injunction issues, what damage will be done to these men of the federation? They do not suffer any actual damage.They only lose a bargaining counter which is in their hands. Mr Irvine has said that the international federation are willing to give an undertaking to pay any damages that there may be. That may be, but such an undertaking does not seem to me to weigh very much in the scales when considering the balance of convenience.

Another significant development of this period was the emergence of the 'public interest' as a factor in the balance of convenience. Traditionally, the balance of convenience was strictly a matter of the competing interests of the parties to the litigation. The addition of the 'public interest' tended to weigh the scales even more heavily in favour of the employer and, indeed, combined with the downgrading of the '*prima facie* case' requirement, tended to produce a situation in which the employer was granted an interlocutory injunction irrespective of the strength of his legal claim; right and remedy were in danger of becoming completely divorced. In *Beaverbrook Newspapers Ltd* v. *Keys* [1978] ICR 582, 586–7, Lord Denning put it this way:

> So we come back to the balance of convenience. I need not go through *American Cyanamid Co.* v. *Ethicon Ltd* [1975] AC 396 once more. If it came to a matter of damages, it is quite plain that the 'Daily Express', if the orders by SOGAT were allowed to continue, would suffer enormous damages – they would lose threequarters of a million copies in one day. Mr Keys could not afford to pay the damages. If it were the other way about, if Mr Keys is restrained, it would be very difficult to see what damage he would suffer. I would do what indeed Mr Shields [counsel for the employer] invited us to do. I would look at the matters more broadly. It seems to me that the public interest is the

overriding consideration. I put on one side the damage to either party or the convenience or inconvenience to either of them.

To my mind the public should not be made to suffer at the hands of the contesting parties. Readers ought to be allowed to get a newspaper to read. The newsagents ought to be allowed to distribute them. Neither Mr Keys nor the SOGAT members should be allowed to interfere with this service to the public.

Eventually, in a trilogy of cases in 1979 and 1980, the House of Lords rejected the Court of Appeal's approach to the notion of furthering a trade dispute (see below, pp. 816–17) and at the same time their lordships rejected its most recent approach to the granting of interlocutory injunctions. The leading speech was delivered by Lord Diplock in *NWL* v. *Woods* [1979] ICR 867, yet another case of blacking by the ITF of a ship flying a flag of convenience. Although Lord Diplock suggested that what he was saying in *NWL* was consistent with his speech in *Ethicon*, the later judgment amounted to a considerable modification of the earlier and a substantial recognition of the special position of trade disputes. On the other hand, the '*prima facie* case' test was not as such restored; considerations of the organizers' possible defences were now part of a very complex calculus that the balance of convenience test had become. Nor had considerations of the public interest been entirely expelled. Lord Diplock expressly retained a residual discretion to grant an injunction in the public interest, and this point was emphasized by other judges in the trilogy, e.g. Lord Fraser of Tullybelton in *Duport Steels Ltd* v. *Sirs* [1980] ICR 161, 187. In neither case were the conditions for the exception thought to be met, but it remains part of the law and is, no doubt, capable of development. Indeed, the Court of Session in *Phestos Shipping Co. Ltd* v. *Kurmiawan* [1983] SLT 389 subsequently granted an employer an injunction almost entirely on the basis of balance of convenience considerations from which the legal issues relating to the strength of the plaintiff's claim, or of the defences thereto, were excluded. The court was particularly impressed by the fact that the defendants had in the court's eyes the alternative to industrial action of taking the underlying dispute, which was about unpaid wages, to the courts in an action for breach of contract. (See Brodie (1983) 12 *ILJ* 170.) This case may suggest that the views of the House of Lords will have less impact than might be expected upon the practice of the lower courts in granting injunctions, at least north of the border where s.17(2) of TULRA 1974 does not apply.

Lord Diplock's speech in *NWL* on the granting of interlocutory injunctions was as follows:

I turn next to the effect of section 17 (2) upon applications for interlocutory injunctions in cases of this kind. The nature and goals of industrial action, the virtual immunity from liability for tort conferred upon trade unions by section 14, and the immunity from liability for the tort of wrongfully inducing breaches of contract conferred upon all persons by section 13 where this is done in connection with a trade dispute, are three factors which, in combination, would make the balance of convenience come down heavily in favour of granting an interlocutory injunction if the usual criteria were alone applied.

In the normal case of threatened industrial action against an employer, the damage that he will sustain if the action is carried out is likely to be large, difficult to assess in money and may well be irreparable. Furthermore damage is likely to be caused to customers of the employer's business who are not parties to the action, and to the public at large. On the other hand the defendant is not the trade union but an individual officer of the union who, although he is acting on its behalf, can be sued in his personal capacity only. In that personal capacity he will suffer virtually no damage if the injunction is granted, whereas if it is not granted and the action against him ultimately succeeds it is most improbable that damages on the scale that are likely to be awarded against him will prove to be recoverable from him. Again, to grant the injunction will maintain the status quo until the trial; and this too is a factor which in evenly balanced cases generally operates in favour of granting an interlocutory injunction. So on the face of the proceedings in an action of this kind the balance of convenience as to the grant of an interlocutory injunction would appear to be heavily weighted in favour of the employer.

To take this view, however, would be to blind oneself to the practical realities: (1) that the real dispute is not between the employer and the nominal defendant but between the employer and the trade union that is threatening industrial action; (2) that the threat of blacking or other industrial action is being used as a bargaining counter in negotiations either existing or anticipated to obtain agreement by the employer to do whatever it is the union requires of him; (3) that it is the nature of industrial action that it can be promoted effectively only so long as it is possible to strike while the iron is still hot; once postponed it is unlikely that it can be revived; (4) that, in consequence of these three characteristics, the grant or refusal of an interlocutory injunction generally disposes finally of the action; in practice actions of this type seldom if ever come to actual trial.

Subsection (2) of section 17 which is said to be passed 'for the avoidance of doubt' and does not apply to Scotland, appears to me to be intended as a reminder addressed by Parliament to English judges, that where industrial action is threatened that is prima facie tortious because it induces a breach of contract they should, in exercising their discretion whether or not to grant an interlocutory injunction, put into the balance of convenience in favour of the defendant those countervailing practical realities and, in particular, that the grant of an injunction is tantamount to giving final judgment against the defendant.

The subsection, it is to be noted, does not expressly enjoin the judge to have regard to the likelihood of success in establishing any other defence than a statutory immunity created by the Act although there may well be other defences to alleged wrongful inducement of breach of contract, such as denial of inducement or that what was sought to be induced would not constitute a breach, or justification of the inducement on other grounds than the existence of a trade dispute. So the subsection is selective; it applies to one only out of several possible defences and, consequently, only to those actions which, since they are connected with trade disputes, involve the practical realities which I have mentioned.

My Lords, when properly understood, there is in my view nothing in the decision of this House in *American Cyanamid Co.* v. *Ethicon Ltd* [1975] AC 396 to suggest that in considering whether or not to grant an interlocutory injunction the judge ought not to give full weight to all the practical realities of the situation to which the injunction will apply. *American Cyanamid Co.* v. *Ethicon Ltd*, which enjoins the judge upon an application for an interlocutory injunction to direct his attention to the balance of convenience as soon as he has satisfied himself that there is a serious question to be tried, was not dealing with a case in which the grant or refusal of an injunction at that stage would, in effect, dispose of the action finally in favour of whichever party was successful in the application, because there would be nothing left on which it was in the unsuccessful party's interest to proceed to trial. By the time the trial came on the industrial dispute, if there were one, in furtherance of which the acts sought to be restrained were threatened or done, would be likely to have been settled and it would not be in the employer's interest to exacerbate relations with his workmen by continuing the proceedings against the individual defendants none of whom would be capable financially of meeting a substantial claim for damages. Nor, if an interlocutory injunction had been granted against them, would it be worthwhile for the individual defendants to take steps to obtain a final judgment in their favour, since any damages that they could claim in respect of personal pecuniary loss caused to them by the grant of the injunction and which they could recover under the employer's undertaking on damages, would be very small.

Cases of this kind are exceptional, but when they do occur they bring into the balance of convenience an important additional element. In assessing whether what is compendiously called the balance of convenience lies in granting or refusing interlocutory injunctions in actions between parties of undoubted solvency the judge is engaged in weighing the respective risks that injustice may result from his deciding one way rather than the other at a stage when the evidence is incomplete. On the one hand there is the risk that if the interlocutory injunction is refused but the plaintiff succeeds in establishing at the trial his legal right for the protection of which the injunction had been sought he may in the meantime have suffered harm and inconvenience for which an award of money can provide no adequate recompense. On the other hand there is the risk that if the interlocutory injunction is granted but the plaintiff fails at the trial, the defendant may in the meantime have suffered harm and inconvenience which is similarly irrecompensable. The nature and degree of harm and inconvenience that are likely to be sustained in these two events by the defendant and the plaintiff respectively in consequence of the grant or the refusal of the injunction are generally sufficiently disproportionate to bring down, by themselves, the balance on one side or the other; and this is what I understand to be the thrust of the decision of this House in *American Cyanamid Co.* v. *Ethicon Ltd.* Where, however, the grant or refusal of the interlocutory injunction will have the practical effect of putting an end to the action because the harm that will have been already caused to the losing party by its grant or its refusal is complete and of a kind for which money cannot constitute any worthwhile recompense, the degree of likelihood that the plaintiff would have succeeded in establishing his right to an injunction if the action had gone to trial, is a factor to be brought into the balance by the judge in weighing the risks that injustice may result from his deciding the application one way rather than the other.

The characteristics of the type of action to which section 17 applies have already been discussed. They are unique; and, whether it was strictly necessary to do so or not, it was clearly prudent of the draftsman of the section to state expressly that in considering whether or not to grant an interlocutory injunction the court should have regard to the likelihood of the defendant's succeeding in establishing that what he did or threatened was done or threatened in contemplation or furtherance of a trade dispute.

My Lords, counsel for the respondents have invited this House to say that because it is singled out for special mention it is an 'overriding' or a 'paramount' factor against granting the injunction once it appears to the judge that the defence of statutory immunity is more likely to succeed than not. I do not think that your Lordships should give your approval to the use of either of these or any other adjective to define the weight to be given to this factor by the judge, particularly as the subsection does not apply to Scotland where, as my noble and learned friend Lord Fraser of Tullybelton explains, it would be but one of several factors to be taken into consideration whose relative weight might vary with the circumstances of the case. Parliament cannot be taken to have intended that radically different criteria should be applied by English and Scots courts. The degree of likelihood of success of the special defence under section 13 beyond its being slightly more probable than not is clearly relevant; so is the degree of irrecoverable damage likely to be sustained by the employer, his customers and the general public if the injunction is refused and the defence ultimately fails. Judges would, I think, be respecting the intention of Parliament in making this change in the law in 1975, if in the normal way the injunction were refused in cases where the defendant had shown that it was more likely than not that he would succeed in his defence of statutory immunity; but this does not mean that there may not be cases where the consequences to the employer or to third parties or the public and perhaps the nation itself, may be so disastrous that the injunction ought not to be refused, unless there is a high degree of probability that the defence will succeed.

My Lords, the instant case presents no problem. On the evidence before the court at each stage of these proceedings, the defendants have a virtual certainty of establishing their defence of statutory immunity. I would dismiss these appeals.

It is not surprising that the testing time for the *Ethicon* principles concerning the granting of interlocutory injunctions should have occurred during the period when an abstentionist framework of trade dispute law had been restored by TULRA 1974–6 and before its amendment by EA 1980 and 1982. The *Ethicon* principle of relying almost exclusively on the balance of convenience, coupled with the traditional interpretation of what an assessment of the balance of convenience required, was bound to favour employers, and yet defendants would also normally be able to argue that they had a good prospect of success at trial. This conflict was ultimately resolved or, perhaps better, disguised, as we have seen, by building a consideration of the defendant's chances of succeeding with a trade dispute defence into the balance of convenience. The result is neither tidy nor clear, though the tone of the judgments in *NWL* v. *Woods* and *Duport Steels Ltd* v. *Sirs* was that courts should be very reluctant to grant an interlocutory injunction, no matter how grievous the harm the employer was suffering, if it was more likely than not that the defendant had a good defence under the statutory immunities. The cases represented a recognition, perhaps reluctant, by the House of Lords that there is in industrial conflict cases such a thing as *damnum absque injuria*: pressure applied by a group of workers to an employer is not unlawful simply because it is effective.

However, in 1984 the Lords qualified this cautious approach in cases where the trade union itself was the defendant (see the note on p. 789). In any event the overall effect of EA 1980 and 1982 is to reduce the range of situations in which harm inflicted upon an employer is given statutory protection. There will be in future a greater number of cases in which it is tolerably clear that the defendants have no trade dispute defence, and in such cases there seems no reason why the courts will not apply the original *Ethicon* principle, unrestrained by TULRA 1974, s.17(2) or Lord Diplock's speech in *NWL* v. *Woods* (cf. the approach of Griffiths J. in *Express Newspapers Ltd* v. *Keys* [1980] IRLR 247). A good example of such a situation arises in relation to picketing (see further, below, pp. 850–53). By TULRA 1974, s.15, as amended by EA 1980, s.16, the statutory immunities against tort liabilities apply only (with a few minor exceptions) to those picketing at their own place of work. It quite often happens that workers picket elsewhere (e.g. miners picketing at other pits in order to raise support for a dispute at their own pit) and it is usually (but not always) quite clear when workers are picketing other than at their own place of work. In such a case the employer's path to an injunction is likely to be pretty free of legal obstacles even on the approach laid down in *NWL*.

Whether or not an employer will seek an injunction and at what stage of the dispute he will seek it will depend largely on extra-legal considerations, notably considerations of industrial relations strategy and tactics. We cannot enlarge upon this point here, but two considerations are worth noting. First, because the English law of industrial conflict has been abstentionist during much of this century, no tradition has grown up of employers' routinely using injunctions as a method of processing industrial disputes. Whilst there is no reason to suppose that any employer, if sufficiently pressed, will not have resort to the legal process, it is likely that, at least initially, that act will be for the majority of employers a matter of last rather than first resort. Second, the likely effect of the injunction is, in any case, not an unproblematic issue for employers. Traditionally, except during the period of the IRA 1971, injunctions have been obeyed by those to whom they were addressed, but an injunction may nevertheless push the workers involved into taking more effective, but lawful, industrial action and may in particular secure for the workers in dispute the support of other groups of workers that was previously not being provided. The employer may also predict that resort to the legal process will damage his long-term relations with the trade union involved and that this may reduce the employer's ability to reach constructive agreements with his employees (including those not currently in dispute) over a wide range of issues beyond the one that is currently the *casus belli*.[1]

As we have said, these are essentially considerations of an industrial relations nature, and they are, in any event, unlikely to be so persuasive as to preclude in all cases resort by employers to injunctive relief. There is, however, one legal issue that is likely to be of relevance to these considerations, and that is the question of who is bound by the injunction issued by the court. Since the

[1] See generally S. Evans, 'The Labour Injunction Revisited' (1983) 12 *ILJ* 129.

interlocutory injunction is, at least in theory, a preliminary step in a piece of civil litigation between particular parties, it follows that those primarily addressed by the injunction are the defendants in the action. If the employer has identified and named in the writ all those taking or threatening to take unlawful industrial action against him, then the coverage of the injunction may be wide enough for his purposes. However, the process of identification is likely in fact to be an impossible one to carry out and it will in any event omit those who join or threaten to join the industrial action only after the injunction is granted. The employer may return to the court for a further injunction, but from his point of view the unwelcome prospect opens up of the employees effectively carrying on the industrial action through different groups of workers and so remaining always one step ahead of the employer's legal remedies. Again, the problem has been raised particularly in relation to picketing, where in some cases only a small number of those on strike are needed for effective picketing at, say, another plant of the same employer. If, say, 1,000 employees are on strike at Plant A and 6 pickets are enough to secure the closure of plant B, do the picket organizers have approximately 166 bites at the cherry before the employer's similar number of injunctions eventually puts them out of business?

Unfortunately from the picket organizers' point of view this prospect is a fanciful one, although there is a genuine problem hidden in the example. A wise employer will seek an injunction against the picket organizers, in addition to such of the actual pickets as can be identified. The standard form of the injunction prohibits the defendants 'by themselves or by their servants or agents' from doing certain acts, say, inducing breaches of the contracts of employment of those approaching, but turned back at, the picket line. The fact that the organizers do not themselves picket will not save them from being in contempt of court, if they continue to organize the picketing. What about the pickets, if they are not actually named in the injunction? It has been clear, at least since *Seaward* v. *Paterson* [1897] 1 Ch. 545, that the injunction embraces those who are not named in it if they aid and abet those who are named in it to do the forbidden act. In *Acrow (Automatic) Ltd* v. *Rex Chainbelt Inc.* [1971] 3 All E R at p. 1181, Lord Denning said: 'It seems to me that if a person complies with a direction of another, which he knows or has reason to know, is unlawful, then he is acting unlawfully himself. He is aiding and abetting the unlawful act.' Consequently, those who continue to act upon the enjoined organizers' instructions would seem also to be in contempt of court. However, if all those enjoined cease from further participation in the picketing or its organization but the picketing continues through other organizers and other pickets, it is difficult to see how anyone is in contempt of court. English law has not yet taken the decisive step that was taken in the USA in the early part of the century whereby all those who had knowledge of what was prohibited by the injunction came under a duty not to do the act in question, although the Code of Practice on Picketing in para. 21 perhaps gives the impression that this is also the English position. Under the American rule, provided the employer publicized the injunction widely enough, then 'a particular controversy between particular parties . . . is made the occasion for a code of conduct governing the whole community' (Frankfurter and Greene, *The Labor Injunction* (1930), p. 126). A somewhat analogous suggestion was canvassed in the Green Paper, *Trade Union Immunities*, but rejected on the grounds that the effective operation of such a provision would require extreme involvement of the police in civil remedies (paras. 175–8). See below, p. 855.

However, there have been two recent developments, one statutory and one judicial, which further improve the position of the employer seeking an injunction. First, by virtue of the removal of the union's special immunity, which we have already briefly noted and will discuss in greater detail in the next chapter, an employer may in appropriate cases seek against a union not only damages but also injunctive relief. Once the union is enjoined, it will be under legal pressure, on pain of penalties for contempt of court, to control the illegal actions of its servants and agents, at least within the limits of the rules about the vicarious liability of trade unions established by EA 1982, s.15. Second, in *M. Michaels (Furriers) Ltd* v. *Askew, The Times*, 25 June 1983, the Court of Appeal relaxed the rules relating to the bringing of representative actions. In that case the court upheld the granting of an interlocutory injunction to a furrier whose shops had been subject to illegal picketing by some members of Animal Aid, an unincorporated association. Because the furrier had had difficulty in identifying all those responsible for the picketing, he sued the local Bristol 'contact' of Animal Aid and its national organizer as representing all the members of the organization and thus obtained an injunction which, by virtue of RSC, Ord. 15, r.12(3), bound all the members of Animal Aid. The Court of Appeal was prepared to relax the previously strict requirements that all those covered by a representative action must have a common interest in the action because of the provisions of Ord. 15, introduced in 1962, that the court's order cannot be enforced against those bound by it but not parties to the action without the leave of the court, a procedure that allows such persons to come before the court and dispute their liability. Since in this case the evidence *prima facie* disclosed that Animal Aid was counselling and procuring the unlawful picketing, and the defence was a straightforward denial of the link between Animal Aid and the picketing (i.e. a defence which did not apply differently to the various members of the organization), the injunction was granted. Although Animal Aid is not a trade union and trade unions can, unlike Animal Aid, be sued in their own name (TULRA 1974, s.2), trade unions are also unincorporated bodies and a number of the cases relied upon by the Court of Appeal (notably the *Taff Vale* case) did involve trade unions. The application of the principle of this case to trade unions would be of the utmost significance because it would provide employers with a way of binding all the members of a trade union subject only to their taking steps to exculpate themselves when the court's order was enforced against them.

When an injunction has been properly served and non-compliance with its terms properly demonstrated (cf. *Churchmen* v. *Joint Shop Stewards' Committee of the Workers of the Port of London* [1972] I C R 222), the defendant will be in contempt of court. The court has powers at large to imprison or fine a contemnor, but these powers will be exercised according to the gravity of the contempt. In some cases the person enjoined will have been required, not merely to refrain from a certain act (e.g. inducing employees to break their contracts), but also to do certain things (e.g. to withdraw strike instructions). A recent example of the mandatory form of the injunction occurred in *Express Newspapers plc* v. *Mitchell* [1982] I R L R 465, where the defendant Geraghty (a branch secretary) was enjoined to do his best (although these words were not in the actual order) to withdraw strike advice and encouragement given by those concerned in the management of the union, even though he himself was not proved to have issued any such advice, and he was fined £350 for failing to take any steps in pursuance of the order.

9 Actions for breach of contract

So far we have concentrated mainly on an employer's remedies in tort arising out of industrial action taken against him. We have said something about the criminal law and a little about restitutionary claims. We have not discussed actions for breach of contract as such, although we have constantly seen how important for liability in tort is the answer to the question of whether the industrial action was a breach of the contracts of employment of those engaged in it. Since it is clear that in many cases the industrial action is a breach of contract of employment (see pp. 718–21 above), one might suppose that actions by employers against their employees for breach of contract might be a frequent source of litigation in industrial disputes. Yet this is not so. A small part of the explanation is to be found in the rule contained in T U L R A 1974, s.18(4) that no term in a collective agreement which has the aim or effect of prohibiting or restricting the right of workers to engage in industrial action shall be incorporated into the individual contract of employment unless the collective agreement is in writing, contains a provision expressly permitting incorporation, is reasonably accessible to the employee at his place of work and has been concluded only by independent trade unions. This is a statutory response to the concession made by counsel in *Rookes* v. *Barnard* (above, p. 738) that the no-strike clause from the collective agreement had been incorporated in that case, but, as we also saw, the significance of this concession was probably not very great, since the current view is that many forms of industrial action do constitute breaches of the contract of employment even in the absence of a no-strike clause, whether incorporated from a collective agreement or not.

A second small part of the explanation is that the extent of the damages awarded against any single striker is not likely to be large. In *NCB* v. *Galley*

[1958] 1 WLR 16, the defendant, a deputy employed by the Board, participated in a ban on Saturday shift-working along with other deputies employed at the mine. Because of the absence of the deputies, who performed supervisory functions, the shifts could not be worked. Galley was sued for breach of contract by his employer in respect of his absence from one particular Saturday shift and at first instance damages were assessed as his share of the £535 profit lost by the Board. On appeal, however, it was held that his liability was limited to the loss caused by his own breach of contract, even though he knew his fellow deputies intended also to break their contracts at the same time. In some technological situations the loss of output caused to an employer by an individual employee's absence from work might, of course, be considerable, but in the case of Galley, who would have been doing safety work, the loss was assessed at the cost to the employer of hiring a substitute, viz. £3 18s 2d.

As is so often the case with labour law, however, it is social reality rather than legal principle that is the more significant in understanding the use made of the legal rules. This, at least, was the opinion of the Donovan Commission when it considered why employers so rarely sue their employees for breach of contract.

Most of those participating in these strikes are, under the present law, liable to court proceedings. This is because notice of the strike is hardly ever given to the employer. . . . In this sense no legislation is needed to make unofficial strikes 'illegal'. The law can intervene at the employer's option. The point is that hardly any employer exercises that option. As the CBI stated in its evidence (paragraph 170) this is 'not so much because the measure of damages against one man might be very small compared with the cost and inconvenience of litigation and because the chance of recovering the damages was doubtful, but because the main interest of the employer is in a resumption of work and preservation of good will'. It cannot be in the employer's interest to exacerbate his relations with his own men by summoning them before a court, and to do so at a time when, in the large majority of cases, the strike will be over. Whatever deterrent effect such court proceedings may have will be outweighed by the harm they are liable to do to future relations on the shop floor, on the building site, in the office. The same would in our opinion also apply if an employer deducted from wages any amount awarded to him by way of damages, a possibility referred to by the CBI in its supplementary oral evidence. [Para. 463.]

It might be that the force of the Donovan Commission's argument would be reduced if the employer could obtain *during the course of the industrial action* an effective remedy against his employees on grounds of breach of contract, in particular if he could obtain an interlocutory injunction to restrain the breach, but in relation to the contract of employment the common law has traditionally set its face against injunctive relief (whether interlocutory or not) that would compel the employee (or employer) to perform his obligations. This common-law principle is now reflected in s.16 of TULRA 1974, which provides that no court shall by way of an order of specific performance of a contract of employment or an injunction restraining breach of such a contract compel an employee to work or attend at any place in order to do work.

An alternative source of contractual liability is the collective agreement. If industrial action is organized in breach of an express or implied undertaking – the 'peace obligation' – in a collective agreement not to take industrial action or to do so only after a particular procedure has been exhausted, can the employer sue the other party to the collective agreement (i.e. usually, the trade union) for breach of contract? An employer might be less inhibited in suing the trade union as against suing his own employees under their contracts of employment. However, although the special immunity for trade unions (until lately contained in TULRA 1974, s.14) never applied beyond actions in tort and so did not protect unions in actions for breach of contract, the law and practice in England with regard to the enforcement of the collective agreement as a contract was, until 1971 at least, as abstentionist in relation to contractual actions against trade unions as in relation to tortious ones, and the law has subsequently re-adopted its abstentionist stance. For a century s.4 of the Trade Union Act 1871 prevented the direct enforcement of, *inter alia*, 'any agreement made between one trade union and another', which included, by virtue of the then statutory definition of trade union, agreements between trade unions and employers' associations. This was the dominant form of collective agreement until well after the Second World War, and s.4 seems to have helped to set a tradition that applied to all types of collective agreement. Certainly, the enforceability of collective agreements with single employers did not squarely arise for decision by a court until 1969, when the court decided against enforceability. By this time the practice of non-enforcement seems to have operated, in a somewhat question-begging way, to support a rule of non-enforceability, although the court was clearly influenced by the imprecise nature of the agreement it might have to interpret if it decided otherwise.

Ford Motor Co. v. *Amalgamated Union of Engineering and Foundry Workers* [1969] 2 All ER 481 (QBD)

The Ford Motor Co. negotiated at company level with the unions having its employees in membership, through the medium of a National Joint Negotiating Committee. Prior to the 1969 negotiations relations between the company, the unions and the workers were governed by two basic agreements (contained in the 'Blue Book') – a mainly procedural agreement of 1955 and a mainly substantive agreement of 1967. In 1969 the company and the unions on the NJNC reached an agreement for improvements in terms and conditions of employment in return for additional restrictions upon industrial action. When news of the agreement reached the employees, it was very unpopular and unofficial strikes broke out, which the two defendant unions (AEF and TGWU) later declared official. The company obtained *ex parte* injunctions against the unions on the grounds that their action was in breach of the 1969 and earlier agreements. On a motion to make the injunctions interlocutory until trial:

GEOFFREY LANE J.: . . . Assuming for the moment that there do exist agreements in the broad sense between Fords on the one hand and the three defendants on the other, are these agreements enforceable by legal process in this court or not? There is a dearth of direct authority on the point. This is, perhaps, hardly surprising, because most cases in this branch of the law fall plainly into one or other of two categories. Either they are commercial contracts between parties at arm's length, which are obviously intended to be enforceable at law unless the parties by express provision declare that they are binding in honour only, or otherwise they are social or domestic arrangements which are equally obviously not designed to be legally binding, the type of arrangement whereby one person says to another, 'I will meet you at 7.30; you bring the food; I will bring the drink.' Neither party, of course, envisages any action in the county court if either commodity is not forthcoming, although it would presumably be possible by express provision to make even such an agreement legally enforceable. In other words, the intention of the parties is usually obvious from the surrounding circumstances or from the express terms of the contract itself.

. . . In the present case, there is no express provision by the parties to provide any assistance as to their intentions. Consequently, it is necessary to look at all the surrounding circumstances to ascertain what the intention of the parties was. This, in my view, is not a case where, without further ado, the situation falls into one or other of the categories which I have mentioned previously. Consequently, one must look at all the surrounding facts in order to discover what the intentions of the parties were. On the one hand, and this is Fords' case, there exist the foundations of legally enforceable contracts. There is, of course, ample consideration; one assumes, for the purposes of this argument, that there is or was agreement between the parties in the case of the 1955, 1967 and 1969 agreements. No one, says Fords, could describe these as domestic, social or family arrangements. They were hammered out, it is said – and I do not doubt that this is true – with great difficulty and lengthy discussions between the parties, Fords on the one hand and the unions on the other, and no doubt also between the unions themselves. They were designed, it is said, to regulate the business matters of wages, working conditions, terms, penalties, and so on. To that extent, say Fords, they are clearly commercial agreements, carrying the usual sanction with such agreements, namely, recourse to the courts should there be a breach on either side. So far there can be little quarrel with those contentions, although it should perhaps be mentioned in passing that Mr Blakeman, the protagonist of Fords, in his original affidavit and indeed in both his affidavits, remains silent as to any intention on his part or that of Fords that the agreements should have legal effect. It is fair to add that counsel for Fords, as an explanation of that silence, says that what his or Fords' intention was at the making of the agreements is immaterial, and, if not immaterial, irrelevant. However, there are other matters to be considered besides those. There is no doubt that the executive officers of Fords, Mr Blakeman in particular, must have been aware of current attitudes and developments in this field, and similarly with the executive officers of the unions – that is their job – and there is no reason to doubt that we are dealing on either side in this case with people who are in the top rank of efficiency, expertise and knowledge of their jobs and everything that goes to make up those jobs.

[Having referred to writings by Professor Kahn-Freund in (1942/3) 6 *MLR* 112 and in *The System of Industrial Relations in Great Britain* (edited by A. Flanders and H. Clegg, 1954), to the Donovan Commission's Report, para. 470 and to a Court of Inquiry into the Electricity Supply Industry (Cmnd. 2361, 1964), the judgment continues:]

From these materials, it will be clear that the climate of opinion was almost unanimous to the effect that no legally enforceable contract resulted from the collective agreements. As I say, both Mr Blakeman and the unions were obviously abreast of these developments and statements of opinion and must be credited with knowledge of the contents of the various publications or at least those of the publications which were connected with the Pearson report and also the report of the Donovan Commission.

Counsel for Fords argues that these publications are irrelevant to the consideration of this case and that no regard should be had to them. To that argument I do not accede. Where a court is endeavouring to discover the intention of the parties to an agreement, it is impossible and indeed unreal to disregard evidence of their knowledge and, accordingly, of their state of mind at the time. These documents show, to my mind, that certainly since 1954 the general climate of opinion on both sides of industry has overwhelmingly been in favour of no legal obligation from collective agreements.

No less important than a consideration of what has been called 'extra-judicial' authorities is a consideration of the terms of the agreements themselves. Counsel on behalf of the AEF puts his argument in this way. He submits that, if one looks at the terms of the 1955 and the 1967 agreements in the Blue Book, it would be possible or almost possible to argue that any contract would be 'void' for uncertainty because of the way in which a large preponderance of the clauses are drawn. He does not put his argument as high as that; indeed it might be difficult to do so in the light of the decision in *National Coal Board* v. *Galley* [1958] 1 WLR 16. What he does say is that the vague aspirational wording of many of the clauses makes it as clear as can be that the parties could not possibly have considered that these contracts would be enforceable in a court of law. One perhaps can, without going through it clause by clause, point to one or two of the clauses to which he drew my attention: cl. 3(i)(a) of the 1955 agreement (on p. 6 of the Blue Book) and cl. 4(a) (on p. 9).[1] He points out in addition that cl. 4(a), which deals with the method of complaints arising on the shop floor being taken higher and higher, so to speak, by redress of grievance procedure, could not possibly be enforced effectively at law when there are no time limits imposed for any of the steps taken. He adds in parenthesis that that was one of the matters, namely, the imposition of time limits, which was sought to be remedied by the 1969 agreement. He points further to cl. 7 and cl. 8 of the 1967 agreement (on p. 18 of the Blue Book) to cl. 22 (on p. 34 of the Blue Book), and so on.[2]

---

[1] Clause 3(i)(a) provides: '[Fords recognize] the right of the employees to have an adequate number of representatives appointed on a craft, departmental or geographical basis to act on their behalf in accordance with the terms of this Agreement.' Clause 4(a) provides: 'Any employee who wishes to raise any matter directly affecting his work shall first discuss it with his Chargehand and/or Foreman. If, in consequence of that discussion, no satisfaction results, the employee then may make a further approach to the Chargehand and/or Foreman, accompanied by his Shop Steward. If there is still no satisfaction the Shop Steward and employee may approach the appropriate Superintendent. If the matter is not resolved the Superintendent shall without delay report it to the Personnel Manager who will then arrange for a discussion between the appropriate persons concerned.'

[2] The clauses referred to are in the following terms: '7. Movement of Employees between Jobs in the New Wage Structure. The statement entitled "Agreed Policy Concerning the Movement of Employees between jobs in the New Wage Structure" is set out in Appendix 1.8. Productivity Improvements. As stated in the Agreement dated 27th July between the parties hereto, the implementation of the new wage structure was conditional upon the completion of productivity bargaining in the twenty-three designated bargaining areas. The parties to this Agreement hereby confirm their approval and ratification of the twenty-three domestically made productivity bargains. 22. The Achievement of Efficiency of Operations. The Trade Unions and [Fords] agree on the need: (i) to achieve efficient production by all reasonable means; (ii) for the introduction of labour-saving machines and methods; (iii) for [Fords] to transfer employees from one job or department to another as may be desirable having in mind continuity of employment and flow of production. It is not part of the duty of any Shop Steward whose constitution and duties are defined in the Procedure Agreement to deal with such matters in the Shop, but he may refer them for consideration by the Works Committee.'

The way that counsel for the AEF argues the matter is this. He says that the agreements, if one regards them closely, can really be divided as to their clauses into two categories. There are the specific clauses dealing with wage rates and so on on the one hand, which are drawn with sufficient particularity. There are, on the other hand, the broad aspirational clauses drawn in vague terms. He suggests that the only possible explanation of that dichotomy is that the specific terms are made in due course to be incorporated in the contract of employment between Fords and their employees, and those terms, as in *National Coal Board* v. *Galley,* will certainly be legally enforceable by or against, if necessary, the employee. So far as the vaguer terms are concerned, submits counsel for the AEF, those are the terms which are effective between the employer Fords and the unions, and one only has to look, he submits, at the nature of those terms to see that the parties cannot really have expected any court to give legal effect to matters couched in that way.

The conclusion which I have reached is this; it is necessarily a preliminary view as this, of course, is not the hearing of the action proper. If one applies the subjective test and asks what the intentions of the various parties were, the answer is that, so far as they had any express intentions, they were certainly not to make the agreement enforceable at law. If one applies an objective test and asks what intention must be imputed from all the circumstances of the case, the answer is the same. The fact that the agreements prima facie deal with commercial relationships is outweighed by the other considerations, by the wording of the agreements, by the nature of the agreements, and by the climate of opinion voiced and evidenced by the extra-judicial authorities. Agreements such as these, composed largely of optimistic aspirations, presenting grave practical problems of enforcement and reached against a background of opinion adverse to enforceability, are, in my judgment, not contracts in the legal sense and are not enforceable at law. Without clear and express provisions making them amenable to legal action, they remain in the realm of undertakings binding in honour. None of the authorities cited by counsel for Fords dissuades me from this view. In my judgment, the parties, neither of them, had the intention to make these agreements binding at law. *Ex parte injunction discharged.*

Although criticized by some commentators at the time, Geoffrey Lane J.'s judgment was in accordance with the conclusion of the Donovan Commission, especially in relation to the unwisdom of legally enforcing unreformed disputes procedures (see above, p.699). In the IRA 1971, however, the legislators convinced themselves that legal enforcement could be a positive aid to reform. That Act repealed s.4 of the Trade Union Act 1871 and by s.34 all collective agreements in writing were conclusively presumed to be intended by the parties to them to be legally enforceable, unless they contained a provision stating that the agreement was intended not to be so enforceable. It then became an unfair industrial practice for any party to the agreement to break it, and also for a trade union not to take all such steps as were reasonably practicable to prevent members of the union from doing things which, if done by the union, would have been a breach of the collective agreement (s.36). Thus, the IRA 1971 did not simply make collective agreements enforceable as contracts, but rather it coupled that step with a particularly broad form of vicarious liability. However, this part of the Act was virtually a dead letter. In its Annual Report for 1972, the CIR described what had happened after the passing of the Act:

It has been TUC policy to have an exclusion clause inserted in all new agreements and the great majority of collective agreements in companies we visited contained such provisions. In some circumstances this was the result largely of unions complying with TUC policy but this view was also held by non-TUC unions and in the majority of cases it appeared to represent a genuine distaste for the introduction of the law. . . . The almost universal use of exclusion clauses does not detract from the significance of legal enforceability. The question of legal enforceability necessarily becomes an item in each individual negotiating situation. Whether it achieves importance as a factor in the negotiation depends on whether one or other party feels strongly that it is to their advantage to have a legally enforceable agreement. We did not find any evidence that the question had become a significant bargaining issue. [paras. 110 and 114].

The IRA 1971 also contained a set of provisions, whereby, in the absence of collectively agreed procedural arrangements for handling disputes in a particular workplace, the Secretary of State could set in motion machinery at the end of which a procedure devised by the CIR would be imposed upon employer and trade union. The Secretary of State never invoked these provisions.

In 1974 the abstentionist position was restored, but now by express statutory provision. By TULRA 1974, s.18, a collective agreement is conclusively presumed not to be intended by the parties to be legally enforceable, unless it is in writing and contains a provision 'however expressed' that the parties do intend the agreement to be so enforceable. The presumption of the IRA 1971 is thus reversed. Although there is some danger that a formally drafted collective agreement might be held by a court to be intended by implication to be legally enforceable, there does not seem to have been any sustained attempt by employers to avoid the impact of s.18.[1] Given the experience with the IRA 1971 this is not surprising. Nevertheless, the issue of legal enforceability of collective agreements continues to be raised in public debate. The subject was discussed at some length in *Trade Union Immunities* (paras. 215–44). That document was a consultative document, but its general tone was one of being convinced of the potential advantages of legal enforceability on the grounds that it tends to confine overt industrial conflict to the period when the agreement is being re-negotiated and that it tends to produce agreements that are 'more comprehensive as to the rights and obligations of the parties and less likely to contain uncertainties or ambiguities which may provide grounds for disputes' (para.218). These, of course, were the arguments that underlay the 1971 Act. On the other hand, the document was sceptical about the willingness of employers and unions actually to

[1] In *Monterosso Shipping Co. Ltd* v. *International Transport Workers' Federation* [1982] IRLR 468 (CA) an employer managed to escape from the provisions of s.18 by convincing the court that the collective agreement in question was subject to Spanish, not English, law. In the *Universe Tankships* case (above, p. 759), the union's claim to enforce a collective agreement was dismissed by Parker J. at first instance, and his decision on this point was not subject to appeal. See [1981] ICR at p. 145.

operate a system of legally enforceable agreements, and about the suitability of British collective agreements for legal enforcement.

Our own experience suggests that legislation alone might be unlikely to bring about the necessary change in attitudes. If the legislation allowed the parties to collective agreements to opt out of legal enforceability (for example, by an express provision in an agreement that a person is not to be subject to legal action if he acts in breach of it) as is the case with contracts generally, the experience of the 1971 Act suggests that everyone might do so. On the other hand, to impose a compulsory system of enforceability would be to reverse the long-established principle of law that the parties can decide whether or not to make contracts legally enforceable. It could be evaded by those who were determined to do so. Trade Unions in particular might well seek to avoid legal enforceability by the simple expedient of refusing to conclude new written agreements at all and by withdrawing from existing procedure agreements. If so, the effect would be the reverse of that intended. . . .

It might be, however, that given the history and practice of industrial relations in Great Britain, the task of convincing negotiators of the value of legal enforceability is primarily an educational one and an essential pre-requisite is still the need to secure an improvement in the nature of collective bargaining and the form of agreements concluded, particularly procedure agreements. A very significant change in practice would seem to be necessary to avoid the difficulties the courts would otherwise have in establishing what were the provisions and intentions of existing agreements. Without such changes, and without an established basis of consent, it is possible that any attempt to impose legally enforceable collective agreements would be hindered by evasion of the kind described in paragraph 241 and by the difficulty the courts would face. [paras. 241 and 243].

The Green Paper did canvass, however, one proposal that would amount to indirect, rather than direct, enforcement of the collective agreement. This would be to withdraw the statutory immunities against *tort* liabilities where industrial action is taken in breach of a disputes procedure contained in a collective agreement or, possibly, is taken at all during the currency of a collective agreement. This would be to turn the breach of a non-legally binding agreement in many cases into a tort or, to put the matter slightly differently, in effect to impose a statutory peace obligation upon the parties to the collective agreement. From the point of view of those favouring legal enforcement the suggestion has the merit that it does not require the employer to decide whether to be in favour of legal enforcement during the negotiations leading to the agreement (when he may be willing to forgo its somewhat speculative advantages in the cause of obtaining an overall agreement) but only at the point when he is being subject to industrial pressure (when the advantages of the legal process may appear more compelling). The proposal also solves in part the question of who is liable for the breach of the agreement. Those who organize the industrial action will lose the statutory immunities against tort liability, whether they are parties to the agreement or not. Finally, it can be pointed out that this type of suggestion clearly has the purpose of restricting the legality of industrial action and nothing else. Since the collective agreement as such is not treated as a contract, the employer is not bound in law to any of its substantive terms, which, as we pointed out in Chapter 2 (p. 129) constitute the part of the agreement in which the trade union has the greatest interest.

10 Immunities and a legal right to strike

We began this chapter with a section which discussed 'the right to strike' and we return to that topic at the end of the chapter. It will have become clear during the course of the chapter that to refer to a 'right to strike' in relation to English law is a misnomer. English law does not provide a right to strike; it provides immunities to organizers of industrial action against the tort liabilities at common law that would otherwise, in the words of the Green Paper, *Trade Union Immunities*, 'make it virtually impossible for trade unions to exist and operate lawfully at all' (para.342). This does not mean that it is in any way improper or nonsensical to talk about a socially recognized right to strike in the United Kingdom, but as a description of the techniques of English law it is inaccurate. The reliance of English law upon immunities also operates to mark off the English system of labour law from many of the continental European systems. In these systems also the first step in the nineteenth century was to provide immunity against or to repeal repressive, usually criminal, laws that rendered illegal association of workers in trade unions. But in most Western European countries there followed a further stage in which *rights* to associate and organize and, above all, to strike were recognized in those legal systems, sometimes at the level of fundamental constitutional law and sometimes in other ways. In Britain a right to strike was never recognized in law in express terms. Why was this? Professor Wedderburn has suggested that the reasons can be found in the disparate pace of development of the industrial and the political power of the labour movement. He has put the argument as follows (see Wedderburn, 'Industrial Relations and the Courts' (1980) 9 *ILJ* 65, 70–1):

It is, of course, quite false to see the 'negative statutory protections' which exclude common law liabilities for acts done in furtherance of a trade dispute as essentially some kind of privilege. They are no more than the curious British method of affording to workers in a modern democratic society what in many other countries are positive rights. 'In substance, behind the form, the statute provides liberties or rights which the common law would deny to unions. The "immunity" is mere form.'

But why did this strange British legal pattern ever emerge? What was so *different* about Britain that no positive rights were created for trade unions? After all, British trade unions were at least as strong at the comparable point in their industrial revolution as unions in the other countries. Why did they not demand and obtain a right to organise and a right to strike?

The central reason is surely to be found in the nature of the labour movement in the *formative* period of our labour law. That period in Britain lies between 1867 (the year of the first great Royal Commission) and 1906 (when the Trade Disputes Act was passed). In that period the organic relationship between law and industrial relations was established. In just that period the nature of the British working class movement was uniquely different from its European counterparts during *their* 'formative' periods:

> The essential feature of that period was a labour movement which was relatively strong; but which was *wholly* an industrial movement. Unlike its European counterparts it had, as yet, no ideological political wing. The Labour Party was not born until 1906. It was, therefore, a movement which made pragmatic not ideological demands. And those demands registered upon bourgeois parties in Parliament as they encountered a gradual extension of the political franchise in 1867 and 1884 – although of course universal franchise did not come until after the end of this formative period. [(1978) 13 *Israel LR* 435, 437.]

Although there has been debate at many times about whether the system of immunities granted too broad or too narrow a protection to strikers, it was not until very recently that the system of immunities itself came under question. The Donovan Commission treated the question very briefly (see paras. 928–34) and saw it essentially from the point of view of the individual striker rather than from the point of view of the strike organizer, with whom we have been mainly concerned in this chapter. There are perhaps three reasons that explain why the issue has arisen in public debate in the past five years. First, the general question of whether there should be a Bill of Rights in the United Kingdom has received some publicity in this period and consideration of a right to strike has naturally been part of this discussion. Second, and somewhat ironically, those who favour restricting the legal freedom of employees to organize and engage in industrial action have sometimes proposed that the restricted area of legal freedom should, perhaps in order to make their proposals more palatable to trade unions and public opinion, be cast in terms of positive rights. However, as the authors of the Green Paper commented:

> . . . In considering the merits of a positive rights system it can be misleading to suppose that the provision of a positive right to strike would necessarily impose further restrictions on union power. Many who favour such restrictions are attracted by a legal system based on positive rights. There is, however, nothing in a positive rights system which is inherently more restrictive of trade union power than the present system. As experience of other countries shows, positive rights can accommodate a whole range of different approaches. [para.378.]

The converse of the point also follows. There is no guarantee that a system of positive rights would confer greater legal freedom upon employees to take industrial action. What, then, are said to be the advantages of a system of positive rights? This brings us on to the third contributing reason for the debate. There has been growing criticism of the technical efficiency of the system of immunities. It has been said that the system of common-law liability and statutory immunity gives rise to a very complex body of law, and this chapter can stand witness to the truth of that statement. As three distinguished writers, none of them lawyers, have commented, 'British trade union law has always been a mystery to laymen, to trade unionists, and probably to most lawyers as well' (Clegg, Fox and Thompson, *A History of British Trade Unions 1889–1910* (1964), p.305, using the phrase 'trade union law' to include the law of industrial conflict). Nothing that has happened since 1964, in relation, say, to the torts of intimidation or interference with business by unlawful means, is likely to have caused these authors to change their view. Further, it is said that the system of immunities is a very uncertain way for the legislators to achieve their policy objectives. As Professor Wedderburn pointed out some time ago: 'One of the problems inherent in this way of doing things is that the judges remain in a strategically very powerful position. For if they later decide that the common-law doctrine is, after all, rather different from what it is thought to be at the time the statute was passed, then in the light of their subsequent pronouncements as to the "true" doctrine, the statute itself may come to have a different effect from what it was meant to have – and there may even be need for a new statute' (*The Worker and the Law* (2nd edn, 1971), p.314). Again there can be nothing that has happened since 1971 that could cause a change of view about the truth of this perception. The hydra-headed nature of the common law is demonstrated by the appearance of the threat to break a contract of employment in three different legal guises in the last two decades: as intimidation, as unlawful interference and as duress. Finally, it may be said, as we have suggested above (p. 717), that the lines of legality and illegality at common law bear a not very functional relationship to the language and concepts of industrial relations.

To what extent may a system of positive rights be expected to overcome these difficulties? It is likely that positive rights could be more clearly and functionally expressed than a system of immunities, especially the present system of abstentionist immunities in TULRA 1974, modified in a restrictive direction by EA 1980 and 1982, thus creating two layers of statutory rules to be integrated with the common law. Clarity would not necessarily mean an absence of complexity. If the legislator is pursuing a complex policy, for example, in distinguishing among different types of secondary action (see below, pp. 830–42), the resulting rules will necessarily be complex. A system of positive rights ought also to be proof against subsequent common-law developments, which it would override just as it overrode those common-law liabilities existing at the date of its enactment. This would not eliminate, however, the element of judicial discretion. The courts would still have the task of interpreting the right to strike (even if that task is given to a separate system of labour courts, as the Green Paper contemplates), and, as judicial interpretation of the statutory trade dispute formula in the period 1977 to 1980 demonstrated (see below, pp. 816–17), these powers of statutory interpretation can be of enormous significance. That particular episode can give one no great confidence that a system of positive rights would give a government a more certain way of achieving its policy objectives, if it found itself pursuing objectives with which the judiciary had no great sympathy.

Finally, one may wonder whether complexity and uncertainty are necessary concomitants of the system of immunities. After all, the immunity formerly provided to trade unions by s.14 of TULRA 1974 gave rise to no complicated body of law nor was its policy objective seriously threatened by common-law developments whilst it remained on the statute book. It might have been a good idea to have applied the same approach of a blanket immunity against tort liabilities in s.13 of TULRA 1974 instead of providing protection against only a list of possible torts, since this latter approach was clearly vulnerable to later common-law developments. Such protection for individuals would necessarily have had to be confined to acts done in contemplation or furtherance of a trade dispute, but, as the Green Paper pointed out in relation to the trade union immunity, 'since trade unions have not sought to avoid liability for torts committed outside a trade dispute, the withdrawal of immunity from such torts would be little more than recognition of existing practice' (para.110). Now, of course, those who were just about to repeal s.14 of TULRA 1974 were unlikely to be impressed by a suggestion that the principle behind it should be restored and applied to all those, including trade unions, acting in contemplation of furtherance of a trade dispute. Hence, this particular method of achieving simplicity and clarity within a system of immunities is not canvassed in the Green Paper. But its existence as a theoretical possibility prompts two reflections. First, perhaps the system of immunities is capable, after all, of giving effective expression to an abstentionist view of the role of industrial conflict law, and the problems of complexity and unclarity arise particularly when it is sought to modify the abstentionist system of immunities in a restrictive way. To that extent, those who see a system of positive rights as particularly likely to accompany the movement of the law in a restrictive direction are correct. Second, the fact that Parliament in the TDA 1906 confined itself to giving individuals immunities against specific tortious liabilities which the House of Lords had recently discovered or extended – and went further in respect of trade unions in s.4 because previously it had been thought trade unions could not be sued as entities (and thus set a pattern which continues today) – suggests a reflection about what Parliament thought it was doing in 1906. Although it is no doubt true that, objectively speaking, the statutory immunities are the British equivalent of what appear in other countries as positive rights, it is much less clear that Parliament in 1906 regarded itself as giving effect to a social right to strike. It was enough for the legislators, as it was again with the TDA 1965, that, unless the common-law liabilities were excluded, trade unions would hardly be able to operate. Again, it is probably not unreasonable to view a more considered debate about a positive right to strike as the concomitant of a policy that has begun to question the wisdom of abstentionism pure and simple.

Note

In *Dimbleby & Sons Ltd* v. *National Union of Journalists* [1984] 1 All ER 751, the House of Lords, again speaking through Lord Diplock, said that the 'practical realities' listed in its decision in the *NWL* case (see the third paragraph of the quotation from Lord Diplock, above, p. 771) 'no longer apply in 1983 to a suit against a trade union'. The surprising reason for this view was that, with the repeal of the trade-union immunity, the plaintiff was provided with a substantial defendant (which a trade-union official might not be), so that the judge should not 'exercise his discretion on the assumption that the case will never proceed to trial' (at p. 755). This reason is surprising because the unavailability of the union as defendant before 1982 is given in the first and second paragraphs of the quotation from Lord Diplock as a reason *in favour* of granting the interlocutory injunction: it is an argument in favour of the plaintiff's being granted the interlocutory remedy that he may not be able to recover in full any damages eventually awarded to him. Hence the availability of the union after 1982 ought to strengthen, not weaken, the cautious approach to interlocutory remedies laid down in *NWL*. Moreover, the availability of the union as defendant would not seem to affect the 'practical realities' (except the first one listed): the grant of the interlocutory injunction is still likely to cause the end, not merely the postponement, of the industrial action. The fact that employer plaintiffs may now be more willing to proceed to a full trial in order to obtain an award of damages in no way diminishes the impact of the interlocutory injunction upon those organizing the industrial action. However this may be, the decision in *Dimbleby* clearly confirms the restoration of the *Ethicon* approach in trade dispute cases and gives employers an added reason to seek interlocutory relief against trade unions.

7
Statutory restriction of industrial action

1 **Introduction**

We have already discussed at the beginning of the previous chapter (pp. 697–703) the economic and political pressures that have caused some governments over the past fifteen years to attempt to move away, to a greater or lesser extent, from the policy of pure abstention and towards a more restrictive position[1] as far as the law of industrial conflict is concerned. In this chapter we shall look at the techniques that have been employed to this end, the current state of the law in this regard and at some possibilities for future development. If we leave on one side the Labour government's proposals contained in *In Place of Strife* (1969) which were never implemented, we are left with two exercises in reformulation of the policy behind the law of industrial conflict, that contained in the IRA 1971 and that contained in EA 1980 and 1982. The latter exercise is one that has perhaps not yet run its course, for the Green Papers, *Trade Union Immunities* (1981) and *Democracy in Trade Unions* (1983), canvass many more possibilities for legislation than either of these Acts in fact contains.[2] The IRA 1971 and the Employment Acts represent something of a contrast in styles. Obviously, the former was a single piece of comprehensive legislation, covering the whole field of labour law, whilst the latter are the expression of a piecemeal approach to the reform of labour law. From our immediate concern with industrial conflict law, however, another contrast is more pertinent. In the IRA 1971, Parliament sought to exclude the common

---

[1] For a stimulating analysis of 'restrictive' tendencies in modern labour law see. J. Clark and Lord Wedderburn, 'Modern Labour Law: Problems, Functions and Policies' in Wedderburn, Lewis and Clark (eds.), *Labour Law and Industrial Relations* (1983), to which we are indebted.

[2] See now the Trade Union Bill (Appendix).

law liabilities from trade disputes and to regulate industrial action through the creation of statutory unfair industrial practices. The legislators were, thus, not reliant upon common law concepts of legality but were free to mould their own concepts through the unfair practices. The point should not be taken too far. Because of the narrowness of their definition of trade – or rather industrial – disputes (see below, p. 793) the legislators of the IRA 1971 gave some scope for the common law torts to operate, whilst, within the area of industrial disputes, where the statutory unfair industrial practices operated alone, in some instances the statutory torts had a close relationship to the common-law ones (see, for example, IRA 1971, ss. 96 and 98). Nevertheless, in 1971 Parliament did create for itself a considerable degree of freeedom to mould the law of industrial conflict, not merely in a more restrictive way but in a restrictive way that owed relatively little to common law notions of legality.

In the Employment Acts, on the other hand, Parliament has chosen to operate within the framework of immunity created by TULRA 1974–6, whilst still aiming to achieve restrictive goals. It is true that TULRA 1974, ss.13 (2) and (3) and 14, have been repealed, as we have noted in the previous chapter, but the main burden of s.13 was always carried by s.13 (1) and that has survived intact, in contrast to the way in which the IRA 1971 simply repealed the TDA 1906 and 1965. Essentially, what EA 1980 and 82 have done has been to reduce the range of situations in which TULRA 1974, s.13, can be relied upon by the organizers of industrial action. Where s.13 can no longer be prayed in aid, the common law torts will apply in an unrestricted manner. Two immediate questions arise out of Parliament's adoption of this way of proceeding. First, by reference to which criteria has Parliament chosen to identify the situations in which the statutory immunities will no longer apply? This is the main question for this chapter, but there is also a subsidiary second question which will occur from time to time. How satisfactory is it ultimately to rely upon the common law to provide the touchstone of legality? If, as is the case, pickets picketing other than at their own place of work cannot normally now claim the protection of TULRA 1974, s.13 (see below, pp. 850–53), this does not mean that such pickets are acting unlawfully. That will be so only if, as far as the civil law is concerned, the pickets are committing a tort in the course of their 'off-site' picketing. Is it sensible to distinguish between 'off-site' pickets in this way? Would it be more rational to give employers a civil remedy against all pickets causing an employer economic loss where the pickets are not picketing at their own place of work?[1]

This point was raised by Viscount Radcliffe in *Stratford Ltd* v. *Lindley* [1965] AC 269, in the context of a case of what was in fact secondary action. In this case the Watermen's Union had been refused recognition by Bowker & King Ltd. In response the union put pressure on the plaintiff company which hired out barges and which was run by the same person as ran Bowker & King Ltd.

[1] In fact injunctions granted in such cases often purport to restrain the defendants from picketing at all rather than, as should be the case, committing torts in the course of their off-site picketing.

The union instructed its members to embargo Stratford Ltd's barges (in breach of their contracts of employment) so that existing customers could not return their barges to Stratford at the end of the hire period (in breach of the hiring contracts) and the new customers could not get hold of the barges (which probably did not involve any breach of contract but rather the prevention of the conclusion of new contracts, which was not tortious). The House of Lords thought there was no trade dispute because the union had acted for motives of 'prestige' (cf. below, p. 796); if there had been such a dispute s.3 of the 1906 Act would have protected the union's officials from liability for inducing breaches of the employment contracts but not from liability in respect of the hiring contracts. Viscount Radcliffe said:

> What puts the defendants in the wrong in legal analysis is that they have used the procuring of breaches of contract to enforce their policy of attacking Stratford. I cannot say, when I look at the facts of the case, that this strikes me as a satisfactory or even realistic dividing line between what the law forbids and what the law permits. There is a special point here about the existence of a trade dispute, but that is possibly an accidental specialty: one can see that with a small shift in the facts, which the full trial of the action may itself achieve, there could easily be a trade dispute to be contemplated or furthered. Then there would remain only the hiring contracts: and one sees again how easily a slight difference in the framing of the embargo order might have avoided incitement to breach of contract, while still achieving a virtual cessation of the plaintiff's business. I cannot see it as a satisfactory state of the law that the dividing line between what is lawful and what is unlawful should run just along this contour. The essence of the matter is that the defendants, conceiving themselves to be acting in the interests of their union, decided to use the power of their control of that union to put the plaintiffs out of business for the time being. When and upon what conditions they would be allowed to resume their business was left in the air. In my opinion, the law should treat a resolution of this sort according to its substance, without the comparatively accidental issue whether breaches of contract are looked for and involved; and by its substance it should be either licensed, controlled or forbidden.

Viscount Radcliffe thus postulates a more rational way of distinguishing between legitimate and illegitimate industrial action than the structure of common-law torts and trade dispute immunities as it existed at that time. In the ensuing years, extensive changes to statute law were to be mooted and carried out in pursuit of that goal and in response to the shifts in interpretation of the existing law. In describing these developments, we can usefully begin with the definition of trade dispute.

2 The definition of trade dispute

We saw in the previous chapter that the immunities against tort liabilities accorded to individuals, and, since the EA 1982, to trade unions, have been confined to those who acted in contemplation or furtherance of a trade dispute. This limiting phrase – the 'golden formula', as Professor Wedderburn has termed it – was first used in the Conspiracy and Protection of Property Act

1875 and was first defined in the TDA 1906, s.5(3). The IRA 1971 provided a definition of what was now termed an 'industrial' dispute that was at once more elaborate and yet more circumscribed – for example, by the exclusion of disputes between workers and workers – than that in the TDA 1906 (see s.167). TULRA 1974, s.29, reverted to the traditional phrase 'trade dispute', but retained the elaboration of the approach of the 1971 Act. More important, in 1974 Parliament rejected the restrictive elements of the 1971 definition and the opportunity was taken to bring expressly within the definition certain disputes whose previous status had been to some degree unclear, for example, recognition disputes or disputes relating to matters occurring outside Great Britain.[1] As enacted in 1974, s.29 (1)–(6) of TULRA read as follows:

Trade Union and Labour Relations Act 1974, s.29(1)–(6), as originally enacted

29.—(1) In this Act 'trade dispute' means a dispute between employers and workers, or between workers and workers, which is connected with one or more of the following, that is to say—

(a) terms and conditions of employment, or the physical conditions in which any workers are required to work;

(b) engagement or non-engagement, or termination or suspension of employment or the duties of employment, of one or more workers;

(c) allocation of work or the duties of employment as between workers or groups of workers;

(d) matters of discipline;

(e) the membership or non-membership of a trade union on the part of a worker;

(f) facilities for officials of trade unions; and

(g) machinery for negotiation or consultation, and other procedures, relating to any of the foregoing matters, including the recognition by employers or employers' associations of the right of a trade union to represent workers in any such negotiation or consultation or in the carrying out of such procedures.

(2) A dispute between a Minister of the Crown and any workers shall, notwithstanding that he is not the employer of those workers, be treated for the purposes of this Act as a dispute between employer and those workers if the dispute relates—

(a) to matters which have been referred for consideration by a joint body on which, by virtue of any provision made by or under any enactment, that Minister is represented; or

(b) to matters which cannot be settled without that Minister exercising a power conferred on him by or under an enactment.

(3) There is a trade dispute for the purposes of this Act even though it relates to matters occurring outside Great Britain, so long as the person or persons whose actions in Great Britain are said to be in contemplation or furtherance of a trade dispute relating to matters occurring outside Great Britain are likely to be affected in respect of

---

[1] For a useful analysis of these changes, see Simpson (1977) 40 *MLR* 16.

one or more of the matters specified in subsection (1) of this section by the outcome of that dispute.

(4) A dispute to which a trade union or employers' association is a party shall be treated for the purposes of this Act as a dispute to which workers or, as the case may be, employers are parties.

(5) An act, threat or demand done or made by one person or organisation against another which, if resisted, would have led to a trade dispute with that other, shall, notwithstanding that because that other submits to the act or threat or accedes to the demand no dispute arises, be treated for the purposes of this Act as being done or made in contemplation of a trade dispute with that other.

(6) In this section—

'employment' includes any relationship whereby one person personally does work or performs services for another;

'worker', in relation to a dispute to which an employer is a party, includes any worker even if not employed by that employer.

However, EA 1982, s.18, made a number of important changes in this definition, but, in the manner of the Employment Acts, without seeking to substitute an entirely new formula. The current definition is, thus, that laid down in TULRA 1974, slightly amended by TULRA 1976, and amended more fundamentally in EA 1982. One can see that the proper definition of 'trade dispute' has been a matter of concern, both to those seeking to implement a policy of abstention with regard to the law of industrial conflict and to those willing to follow a policy of restriction. In both sets of policies the definition of trade dispute has to perform the role of demarcating in legal terms the proper sphere of industrial relations, marking it off from other areas of social and economic life. This is because, as Kahn-Freund and Hepple pointed out above (p. 694), the legal tradition in the UK has been to accord the strike legitimacy as a tool of industrial relations or of collective bargaining, but not as a general political weapon. This principle is generally accepted as much by those pursuing a policy of abstention as by those committed to restriction, though these two sets of people tend to have different views as to where the line between industrial relations and other areas of activity should be drawn, as we shall see below (p. 804). However, within the area of industrial relations, once it has been defined, legislation giving effect to a policy of abstention will aim to be inclusive, to embrace all types of industrial relations disputes without exception. Legislators of a more restrictive cast, on the other hand, may well take the view that manipulation of the definition of trade dispute provides a convenient method of excluding certain types of industrial relations disputes or methods of pursuing industrial disputes from the area of legitimacy by depriving them of protection against the common law torts. The definitions in the TDA 1906 and TULRA 1974 fell into the former category; those in the IRA 1971 and EA 1982 into the latter.

A policy of restriction need not, of course, involve amendment of the definition of trade dispute. The EA 1980 made considerable modifications to the structure of law created by TULRA 1974–6 without touching the trade dispute definition. To some extent it is a matter of opportunity and elegance as to how a particular restrictive policy is implemented in the law. Between 1976 and 1979 the Court of Appeal withdrew immunity from certain types of secondary action (see below, pp. 816–17) by holding that such action was not done 'in furtherance' of a trade dispute. EA 1980, s.17 achieved the same policy result by legislative declaration that the immunities would not be available in such cases even for acts done in furtherance of a trade dispute. However, as the IRA 1971 and EA 1982 demonstrate, any extensive policy of making trade dispute law more restrictive is likely, sooner rather than later, to involve amendment to the definition of trade dispute.

We shall begin our analysis by looking at the function common to both policies, that of marking off the area of industrial relations, and we shall see how even within this common objective there can be disagreements as to how it should be achieved.

(a) **Disputes with a non-industrial objective**

This is sometimes seen as the problem of excluding political disputes from the protection of the statutory immunities. Although this is a function of the definition and a controversial one because of disagreement about what makes a dispute a political rather than industrial one, the general problem is in fact a wider one. Since the strike is seen as a legitimate weapon only of industrial relations, the use of industrial action for any non-industrial purposes is to be excluded by the definition. In fact from the beginning of the century (see *Conway* v. *Wade* [1909] AC 506 (HL)) there has been a steady trickle of cases which have been held not to fall within the definition because the action was taken in pursuance of a personal grudge rather than an industrial dispute. The goal of exclusion – whether of political or of other non-industrial disputes – is achieved by the requirements of the definition that the industrial action must be taken (i) in contemplation or furtherance, (ii) of a dispute between employers and workers,[1] (iii) which has the relevant relationship[2] with the matters listed in s.29(1) of TULRA 1974. Political disputes or action taken in furtherance of a personal grudge or any other 'non-industrial' action are not in terms excluded, but the non-industrial element in the dispute may (but need not necessarily) prevent the action from meeting one or more of these three requirements.

A good illustration of judicial application of the three requirements to a set of facts is provided by *Huntley* v. *Thornton* (below). Harman J. found that the personal element caused the defendants to be unable to satisfy either requirement (i) or requirement (iii). They could satisfy requirement (ii) as the

[1] Except between 1971 and 1974 and since 1982 a dispute between workers and workers was also included. See below, pp. 805–9.

[2] Again a relationship differently expressed between 1971 and 1974 and since 1982 than at other times. See below, pp. 802–5.

dispute was one between workers and workers, which type of dispute was included within the definitions of the TDA 1906 and TULRA 1974, though as we shall see below (p. 806) it was excluded by EA 1982. Consequently today the defendants would in fact fail to satisfy all three requirements because of the personal element. We have already mentioned *Huntley* v. *Thornton* in connection with the defence of justification to the tort of conspiracy, (above, p. 716) and, as Harman J. makes clear, there is a considerable degree of overlap between that defence and the trade dispute defence.

Huntley v. *Thornton* [1957] 1 WLR 321 (Ch. D.)

The defendants were members of a district committee of the Amalgamated Engineering Union. The plaintiff was a member of that union who had refused to take part in a 24-hour strike over a wage claim. The plaintiff was consequently summoned before the committee to explain his conduct. At the meeting he adopted a truculent attitude and eventually walked out, leaving the district committee to pass a resolution recommending to the executive council of the union that the plaintiff be expelled. The executive council refused to accept the recommendation. The district committee used its best efforts to secure that the plaintiff, who had resigned from his original employment, did not secure other employment in engineering shops in the district, rebuffed the plaintiff's efforts to make his peace with them, and purported to expel him (though the committee was without power to do so). The plaintiff brought an action for damages for conspiracy against the defendants.

HARMAN J.: . . . Two questions arise out of this: first, was this a trade dispute; and, secondly, were the actions of the district committee done in furtherance of it?

I need not reconsider here the earlier efforts to have the plaintiff expelled, for they were frustrated by higher authority and came to nothing. This issue was settled by 6 January. The facts to be considered begin on 15 January, when the first move was made to boycott or black-list the plaintiff. It was not argued that these acts were 'in contemplation' of a trade dispute, and the plea in the defence that the dispute was as to the 15 per cent increase in wages then being demanded by the union was not persisted in. Further, in my judgment the employers were in no way parties to any dispute. But was it a dispute within the meaning of the Act, and, if so, was it one between workmen and workmen? According to the defendants the contestants were the district committee on the one side and the plaintiff on the other, and the subject whether the plaintiff (a member of the union) should be allowed to earn his living as an engineer in a closed shop in the district. It was contended for the plaintiff that the members of the committee did not act in their capacity as workmen. I feel the force of this point, but on the whole feel bound to reject it. The committee consisted of elected representatives of the workmen in the district who were members of the union. There are a number of cases to show that if the plaintiff had not been a member of the union and his right to work had been contested on that ground, this would have been considered a trade dispute. A more persuasive argument for the plaintiff is that the committee embarked on a policy of embargo entirely unauthorized by the rules of the union, and that they cannot escape the consequences of a wrong which was of their own invention by labelling it a trade dispute. This is to say that there was no 'dispute' at all. It was argued nonetheless for the defendants that the words of the definition clause cover the case: it was a dispute, say they, 'as to the employment of the plaintiff' within the words of the clause. [See now TULRA 1974, s.29(1)(b).]

The plaintiff's contention derives some support from the speeches in *Conway* v. *Wade* [1909] AC 506, and in particular the speech of Lord Shaw. In that case the defendant Wade had no authority from the union to threaten the employers with a strike unless they dismissed Conway. What Wade was trying to do was punish Conway for not having paid a union fine in the past, as to which apparently no dispute at that time existed.

. . . On the whole I have come to the conclusion that this was not a trade dispute. The defendants were not asserting a trade right, for they knew they could not procure the plaintiff's expulsion from the union. The dispute, if it could be so called, had become an internecine struggle between members of the union and no interests of 'the trade' were involved. It was a personal matter.

Behind these considerations lies a more fundamental point, namely, whether the committee's actions were 'in *furtherance* of a trade dispute'. In my judgment this raises the same question as the issue of conspiracy. If, as I have held, the paramount object of the committee was to injure the plaintiff, then that was the object in furtherance of which they acted. They did not intend to further the dispute arising out of the plaintiff's refusal to strike – that was settled by higher authority; they intended to injure the plaintiff in his trade by their embargo, and it was to that end that their actions were directed. They were not furthering a trade dispute, but a grudge; the Act does not protect them.

The logic of this judgment is impeccable provided one accepts as correct its starting point, namely the characterization of the defendants' conduct as motivated by personal spite rather than by trade interests. In Harman J.'s reasoning on this point the refusal of the executive committee to expel the plaintiff plays a crucial role. This refusal deprived the district committee of the union of its claim to a 'trade interest' and turned the dispute into an 'internecine struggle between members'. A different interpretation of the facts would be that the district committee was acting upon a view of the union's best interests, albeit not the same view that the executive committee of the union had taken. Our point is not that Harman J. might have been wrong on this issue, but rather that in the application of the trade dispute definition judicial evaluation of the facts plays a critical role, as we shall often see in this section. In the instant case the evaluation tended to reduce the chances of unofficial action obtaining the protection of the statutory immunities.

When one turns to disputes that are claimed to be non-industrial disputes because of a political element, one finds that an additional difficulty about applying the requirements of the trade dispute definition is that no clear distinction exists between politics and industrial relations. The point is not simply that at a factual level the dispute may be difficult to place on one side or another of a line that is in principle clear, but rather that the line itself is very unclear. This was pointed out by Professor Kahn-Freund some thirty years ago, but, as the following passage also suggests, the necessity of drawing such a line continues to exist so long as one wishes to restrict the legitimacy of the strike weapon to the area of industrial relations.

O. Kahn-Freund, 'Legal Framework,' in A. Flanders
and H. A. Clegg (eds.), *The System of Industrial Relations in
Great Britain* (1954), pp. 126–7

There is, however, another side to this matter, and this has been the subject of one of the keenest legal and political controversies of this century. Where exactly is the borderline between a strike connected with a trade dispute, e.g. a sympathetic strike, and a political strike? Suppose an industry is subsidized by the government and, as a result, able to maintain a certain level of wages. Suppose, further, that the government decides to withdraw the subsidy, and that, in consequence, the employers in the industry announce that they will reduce the wages. If the workers declare a strike, are they striking against the employers in order to maintain their wages or are they striking against the government in order to maintain the subsidy? And if the workers in other industries come out in support of the workers concerned, are they striking in sympathy with their wage demand or in order to press the government to renew the subsidy? The reader will realize that we are now discussing the question whether the so-called 'General Strike' of 1926 was 'legal'. Nobody seems to have doubted that what the coal miners did in 1926 was lawful. They refused to assent to the modification of their wages, i.e. of their contracts of employment, on which the employers insisted, and the employers terminated the contracts. In other words: this was a lockout and not a strike. The decisive point is that, for the miners, the subsidy was only a means to an end. They did not care whether their wages came out of a subsidy or out of any other sources. They were in dispute with their employers in connection with the 'terms of their employment'. The legal controversy was about the action taken by the TUC and unions affiliated to it when they came out during the first week of May 1926. The present writer believes that this was a sympathetic strike and within the definition of a trade dispute in the 1906 Act, for the same reasons for which the dispute in the mining industry itself was a trade dispute. It is, however, undeniable that the government was involved and that the question of the subsidy cannot be separated from the motives which prompted the TUC and the unions affiliated to it. The truth of the matter is that, once again, we are faced with the 'quagmire' of mixed motives and in search of a test which would enable us to disentangle the manifold purposes that determine human action. We have once again to try to answer the question: which of a variety of purposes was 'predominant'?

. . . The definition of a 'trade dispute' in the Act of 1906 rests on a theory of society and of politics which, even in 1906, was open to grave doubt and which to-day is plainly untenable. It rests on the assumption that one can separate economic from political motives and economic action from political action. To show that the economic and the political elements cannot be kept in watertight compartments, at any rate in the sphere of life with which we are concerned, one does not have to refer to the millions of employees who are serving the state and public corporations. The problem would be the same if there was no public enterprise in this country at all. The level of wages depends to-day only partly and perhaps only to a minor extent on decisions of private employers. In all sorts of ways it depends on governmental policies. It is hardly possible to think of any major labour dispute in which the government is not somehow involved. How then can anyone, judge, juror, or private citizen, determine how far any strike is intended primarily to induce the employers to pay wages of a certain amount or the government to change its policy? The law as it stands to-day reflects the conditions of the nineteenth century. Perhaps it was then possible to draw a line between the sphere of the 'State' and the sphere of 'Society'. To-day any attempt to do so is doomed to failure. It may be possible to carry on with the present law for many years to come, but one should at least realize that its foundations are shaky. These foundations are the social and political convictions on which all law-making rests, and with them we reach the limits of the law.

Consequently, whenever the plaintiff alleges that a dispute is not a trade dispute because of a political element in it, one may anticipate that the court will have a difficult issue to decide. There is no short cut around the necessity to apply painstakingly the various requirements of the trade dispute definition to the facts of the case to see if they are all satisfied. The process is the same as with the cases arising out of personal grudges. The argument cannot be that any dispute with a political element in it is automatically excluded, because the definition in TULRA 1974 (even as amended by EA 1982) does not permit this approach. The Green Paper, *Trade Union Immunities* (1981), canvassed such a suggestion for a change in the law. It pointed out the counter arguments. 'The difficulty, however, would be in finding a generally acceptable definition of "political". Furthermore, such an approach would remove immunity from a wide range of industrial action in what would otherwise be regarded as perfectly legitimate disputes about terms and conditions of employment where Government is either the employer or the provider of money to the employer' (para. 199). Consequently EA 1982 did not take up this particular suggestion, though, as we shall see, it did enact another proposal of the Green Paper relating to 'political' disputes.

A dispute with a political element is likely to be vulnerable to the argument that the dispute is not a dispute between employers and workers or that it is not a dispute which has the correct relationship with the matters listed in TULRA, s.29(1). The court may see the dispute, for example, as a dispute between workers and government rather than between workers and employer. On the other hand, the government is the employer of many workers, and British law has always accepted the distinction between the state as employer and as a political entity. Unlike the law of many other countries, notably the USA, British law has not imposed special disabilities in the taking of industrial action upon public employees simply because they are public employees. Section 29(2) of the 1974 Act applies this principle also where the government is not the employer of the workers concerned but has a statutory power to control the settlement of the matters at issue or is represented on the bargaining committee which is considering the issues, as is sometimes the case with public-sector employees who are not directly employed by the govern-ment, e.g. university teachers.

Nevertheless, situations may arise where the industrial action is clearly aimed at the government, and the government is not the employer of the workers concerned nor does s.29(2) cover the situation. Thus, in *Associated Newspaper Group* v. *Flynn* (1971) 10 K I R 17, the judge held that a short strike organized by the defendant officials of a printing union to protest against the Industrial Relations Bill was not protected because the dispute was between workers and the government, concerning proposed legislation, albeit in the industrial relations sphere. This approach was followed in *Express Newspapers Ltd* v. *Keys* [1980] I R L R 247. In other cases it may not be easy to decide who are the parties to the dispute or what its subject matter is. In *Sherard* v. *A U E W* [1973] I C R 421 the defendant union called a one-day strike of all its members for 1 May 1973 'as a demonstration against the government's Counter-Inflation Act'. Some members of the union employed at various government establishments sought an interlocutory injunction on 26 April to restrain the union from proceeding with its strike. The Court of Appeal refused to grant an interlocutory injunction on the grounds that there was arguably an industrial dispute between the government as employers and some of its workers. 'The government as employers have decided to enforce Phase Two, which has frozen wages against the will of the workers. The men in the government employ object to this freezing of their wages. They – or some of them – are in dispute with their employers about it.' The court may also have been influenced by the fact that, even if the union and its officials were enjoined, it was clear that the majority of the members of the union would still come out on strike.

The necessity for painstaking analysis can be demonstrated by a consideration of the Court of Appeal's judgment in *Duport Steels Ltd* v. *Sirs* [1980] I C R 161. There was a dispute in the public sector of the steel industry between various unions and the British Steel Corporation over a wage claim. In order to strengthen their position the main union involved decided to call out its members employed in the private sector of the industry, who were not in dispute with their employers. The Court of Appeal analysed the dispute in the private sector as one between the union and the government, on the grounds that the union's objective in extending the strike was to increase the political pressure on the government, which was seen as the ultimate arbiter of the BSC's wages policy. In a hastily convened Saturday morning hearing the Court of Appeal granted the private sector employers an interlocutory injunction on the grounds that the dispute in the private sector was not a trade dispute. On reflection, the argument apeared so wrong that counsel for the employers did not attempt to advance it in the House of Lords (see [1980] I C R at p. 182). Even if the Court of Appeal's characterization of the dispute in the private sector was correct, it was clear to the House of Lords that it was still action taken by the union in furtherance of the dispute in the public sector, which clearly was a trade dispute, having the correct parties and the correct subject matter. In other words, secondary action is brought within the trade dispute formula, not on the grounds that there is a trade dispute with the secondary employer (that may or may not be the case), but on the grounds that it is action taken in furtherance of the primary dispute, so that the crucial question is whether the primary dispute is a trade dispute. (Of course, today, similar action would not be protected because, although taken in furtherance of a trade dispute, it fell within the scope of EA 1980, s.17 (1) and (2). See below, pp. 835–6.)

The question of whether a dispute ceases to be a trade dispute because of the presence of a political element may arise even though it is clear that the dispute is between the correct parties, i.e. it is a dispute between employer and workers and not a dispute between workers and government. In such cases the question is whether the dispute has the correct subject matter, as listed in TULRA 1974, s.29 (1) (above, p. 793). In so far as a union sees itself not as a mere 'business union' but as having purposes which go beyond improvement of their members' terms and conditions of employment, to embrace the improvement of society at large, then it may on occasion wish to use its industrial power to give expression to these wider purposes.

BBC v. *Hearn* [1977] ICR 685 (CA)

The defendant, general secretary of the Association of Broadcasting Staffs (ABS), in response to a request from the Action Committee Against Racialism and in conformity with the union's policies on racialism, informed the BBC that the union's members would take 'whatever industrial action was necessary' to prevent the 1977 Cup Final being relayed via satellite to South Africa. The threat to cut off satellite transmission would, if implemented, have deprived many other countries of transmission.

ROSKILL L.J.: . . . As Lord Denning M.R. has said, the phrase 'trade dispute' has received various definitions at different times. We are presently only concerned with the definition in the current legislation. It is, however, worth pointing out that in section 167 (1) of the Industrial Relations Act 1971, an almost identical definition of 'industrial dispute' was given as is given of 'trade dispute' in the present legislation. But – and this is to be noted – that statute, unlike the present legislation, defined the phrase 'terms and conditions of employment' as meaning: 'the terms and conditions on which one or more workers are, or are to be, required to work for their employers.' That definition was, no doubt deliberately, not included in the Act of 1974. It is not necessary to speculate as to the reason for that omission. But there is one obvious possible reason: that it was thought that, with that definition, too narrow a construction might be placed on the phrase 'terms and conditions of employment.' Accordingly, freed from the bonds of that definition, it is open to us, in this court, to give that phrase – and I think we should give that phrase – a very wide meaning, so that it embraces everything which can fairly be said to form part (to repeat a phrase I used during the argument) of the 'totality of the terms and conditions' upon which employees of particular employers are from time to time employed, such as what Lord Denning M.R. during the argument called fringe benefits. They may and often will in some trades extend to include perquisites of one form or another, perfectly legitimate and of long standing, which both sides in the particular industry have for many years treated as accepted attributes of particular contracts of employment in that industry.

But giving that phrase the widest construction that one can, one still has to ask, oneself: 'Is the instant dispute one which is connected with terms and conditions of employment?' I asked Mr Inskip this afternoon what he said the extant dispute was at the time when the BBC issued the writ. He replied that the dispute was whether it should be – and note the words 'should be' – a condition of employment that union members should transmit tomorrow's Cup Final on to the Indian Ocean satellite when they knew that was to be in pursuance of a contract to transmit to South Africa. With respect I do not think that that was the dispute at that point. I do not think that the dispute between Sir Charles Curran and the secretary of the union, Mr Hearn, had reached anything like that stage. The position was, at the time the writ was issued, no more than this, that there was an assertion on behalf of the union, in pursuance of feelings no doubt genuinely felt, that if the BBC persisted in exercising what the BBC claimed (rightly, I think) to be their contractual rights to cause this broadcast to take place tomorrow, then, to use a colloquialism, the switches would be pulled. That, in those circumstances, does not seem to me capable, as a matter of law, of being a trade dispute between employers and workers which is connected with their terms and conditions of employment.

Although a number of decisions of the Court of Appeal in areas of industrial conflict decided in the period 1976 to 1979 were subsequently overruled by the House of Lords, the decision in *BBC* v. *Hearn* was in fact subsequently approved (see *Express Newspapers* v. *McShane* [1980] ICR at 53 and 64). On the other hand, in *Universe Tankships Inc.* v. *ITF* (above, p. 759) Lords Diplock, Cross and Russell expressed doubt about the point accepted by the court in *Hearn*, namely, that there would have been a trade dispute had the employees formulated a demand to have their terms and conditions altered so that they could not be required to transmit material when it was contrary to their consciences to do so. Lord Cross stated quite baldly 'A trade union cannot turn a dispute which in reality has no connection with terms and conditions of employment into a dispute connected with terms and conditions of employment by insisting that the employer inserts appropriate terms into the contracts of employment into which he enters' ([1982] ICR at p. 280).

Although EA 1982 did not amend the definition of trade dispute so as to remove from it all disputes with a political element, in s. 18(2)(c) a change was made that will affect the chances of a dispute with a political element or, indeed, a dispute with any non-industrial element in it being brought within the statutory definition. The change was to substitute in s.29(1) of TULRA 1974 (above, p. 793) the words 'relates wholly or mainly to' for the words 'is connected with'. The latter phrase had been used in the original definition in the TDA 1906; the former in the IRA 1971. The immediate cause of the change, however, was the interpretation attached to the phrase 'is connected with' by the House of Lords in *NWL Ltd* v. *Woods* [1979] ICR 867. This was another case of blacking by the ITF in pursuance of its campaign against ships flying flags of convenience. In the Court of Appeal's decision in a previous, similar case, *Star Sea Transport Corporation* v. *Slater* [1978] IRLR 507, a rather over-sophisticated distinction had been drawn between two purposes the defendants were said to have had: to end the practice of using flags of convenience and to raise the rates of pay received by the crews of such ships. The second purpose was regarded as falling within the statutory definition; the first was not. Since the Court concluded that the first purpose was the predominant one, the defendants' action was not protected.

Before 1979 most commentators would probably have accepted that where the defendant was pursuing two purposes, one protected, the other not, the question of whether his action was covered by the immunities was to be answered by asking which was the predominant purpose. See also the similar approach to the defence of justification to the tort of conspiracy in the *Crofter* case (above, p. 713). One might nevertheless criticize the *Star Sea* decision on the grounds that the distinction drawn by the Court was an artificial one. From the defendants' point of view, did not the two purposes amount to the same thing? As Lord Diplock said in *NWL*, 'Furthermore, in a case originating in the commercial court it would be carrying judicial anchoritism too far if this House were to feign ignorance of the fact that, apart from fiscal advantages, one of the main commercial attractions of registering vessels under flags of convenience is that it facilitates the use of cheap labour to man them. So even the ultimate object of ITF's campaign is connected with the terms and conditions of employment of seamen' ([1979] ICR at p. 876). However, their lordships did not merely reject the analysis that the elimination of flags of convenience was not a purpose connected with the matters listed in s.29(1) of TULRA 1974. They rejected the predominant purpose test laid down in the *Star Sea* case, which was overruled. Consequently, even if it could be shown that the predominant purpose of the defendants in seeking to end the system of flags of convenience was not to increase the rates of pay of the crews but was, say, to put political pressure on those countries which acted as countries of registry for such ships to adopt more democratic forms of government, nevertheless the defendants' action would be protected, provided they had the subordinate purpose of increasing wages, because that subordinate purpose would be enough to establish a connection with the matters listed in s.29(1). Lord Diplock continued as follows:

Neither, in my view, does it matter that the demand is made and the dispute pursued with more than one object in mind and that of those objects the predominant one is not the improvement of the terms and conditions of employment of those workers to whom the demand relates. Even if the predominant object were to bring down the fabric of the present economic system by raising wages to unrealistic levels, or to drive Asian seamen from the seas except when they serve in ships beneficially owned by nationals of their own countries, this would not, in my view, make it any less a dispute connected with terms and conditions of employment and thus a trade dispute, if the actual demand that is resisted by the employer is as to the terms and conditions on which his workers are to be employed. The threat of industrial action if the demand is not met is nonetheless an act done in furtherance of that trade dispute.

The Green Paper, *Trade Union Immunities*, canvassed the argument that 'there should be some measurement of the importance of the trade dispute element and that a dispute should only fall within the definition of trade dispute if that element is found to be significant compared with other elements' (para. 190). It considered two methods of achieving this result: express enactment of the predominant purpose requirement or a return to the formula 'relates wholly or mainly to'. EA 1982 enacted the latter. It is not entirely easy to assess the impact of this change. Neither formula indicates very precisely the relationship that has to exist between the defendants' purposes and the statutory list of protected subject matters, though it is clear that the new formula is designed to require a closer relationship. But it is not merely a question of what the new formula is interpreted to require; it is also a question of the application of the new formula to the facts of particular cases. As the Green Paper itself pointed out, 'in many disputes it is by no means easy to separate the different elements or to decide which is predominant.'

Perhaps the best that can be done is to indicate the sort of factual situations likely to be at risk of not falling within the new formula but which have been held to fall within the old formula. In *Crazy Prices (Northern Ireland) Ltd* v. *Hewitt* [1980] IRLR 396, the Northern Ireland Court of Appeal had to consider a situation in which the TGWU had a policy of not permitting sliced loaves to be sold in Northern Ireland at more than 3p below the recommended retail price. The plaintiffs imported such bread from the Republic and sold it at 9½p below the recommended price. The defendant then instructed his members employed in the Northern Ireland bakeries not to supply any bread products to the plaintiffs. The Court held that art. 3 of the Industrial Relations (Northern Ireland) Order 1976 (identical to TULRA 1974, s.29) protected the defendant. The dispute was not directly about the termination of the employment of employees at the Northern Ireland bakeries; it was about the price of bread. However, the dispute was connected with the maintenance of employment at the Northern Ireland bakeries because the import of cheaper bread from the Republic would reduce employment opportunities in the north. 'A dispute may be connected with such matters involving industrial relations even though the connection is not immediate or proximate' (at p. 401).

The general issue raised by the case is as to the circumstances in which a group of employees can take industrial action in order to try and prevent or reverse a managerial decision which they fear will lead to redundancies, even though that decision is not itself a decision to dismiss any employees. The question is particularly likely to arise out of managerial decisions to employ outside labour in one form or another to perform tasks previously carried out by the employer's own employees. The general tradition of the courts over the last decade has been to include such action within the definition of trade dispute. Thus, in *General Aviation Services Ltd* v. *Transport and General Workers' Union* [1975] I C R 276 (C A – the point was not discussed on appeal to the House of Lords) opposition by employees at Heathrow Airport to the granting of a franchise to a Canadian company to provide handling services previously provided by the employees of the nationalized airlines was held to be included, as was a refusal to co-operate with a computer system company which offered services currently provided by health authorities' own computer departments in *Health Computing Ltd* v. *Meek* [1981] I C R 24 and the blacking of facility companies' products in *Hadmor Productions Ltd* v. *Hamilton* (above, p. 747). The first of these cases was a particularly strong one, since it was decided under the terms of the I R A 1971 and thus by reference to the phrase 'relates wholly or mainly to' and an official inquiry had found that the employees' fears of redundancy were groundless. Nevertheless, since the fears 'were genuinely and widely entertained' (per Orr L.J. at p. 294), the necessary relationship could be established. On the other hand, in *Universe Tankships Inc.* v. *I T F* (above, p. 759) the majority of their lordships held that the payment made by the employer in respect of each crew member to the union's welfare fund, established 'to provide welfare, social and recreational facilities in ports around the world for seafarers of all nations, especially those serving in flag of convenience ships' was not a payment connected with the terms and conditions of employment of the ship's crew. Lord Diplock retreated from what he had said in *N W L* v. *Woods* about the phrase 'connected with'. The phrase was a wide phrase, but not so wide as to embrace a situation where the employees' entitlement to benefits from the welfare fund did not depend upon the existence of an employment relationship between shipowner and crew. More important, in *Mercury Communications Ltd* v. *Scott-Garner* [1984] I C R 74 the Court of Appeal accepted that E A 1982, s.18(2)(*c*), had made a significant and restrictive alteration in the definition of trade dispute, notably by the use of the words 'wholly or mainly'. The question now was what the dispute was 'predominantly about' (at p. 114F.) Although the Court was prepared to accept that genuine fears of future redundancies (even when the employer had not threatened any) fell within T U L R A, s.29(1) (*b*), it held that, on the facts of the case before it, the refusal of the employees of British Telecom to interconnect the network of the private company, Mercury, to the B T network was mainly due, not to fears of job losses, but to political objection to the breaking of the monopoly of a nationalized industry.

(b) **Worker and worker disputes**
We examined in the previous section of this chapter the manifold problems that arise out of what we suggest is the inevitable function of the definition of trade dispute, namely, to mark off the industrial sphere from other spheres of social and economic activity. Of course, as we have also seen, those who favour a policy of abstention tend to approach this process of demarcation with a presumption in favour of inclusion within the industrial sphere, which those

favouring a more restrictive policy do not share. However, the major differences between the two policies show themselves most clearly within the area of industrial relations. Here those in favour of restriction are likely to wish to use the definition of trade dispute to remove the statutory immunities from certain types of dispute. In EA 1982, s.18 three amendments are made to the definition in TULRA 1974, s.29 (in addition to the insertion of the phrase 'relates wholly or mainly to' already discussed) in order to implement restrictive policies. These are the removal of disputes between workers and workers; the insistence that the dispute exist between an employer and his own workers; and an alteration relating to disputes outside the United Kingdom. We shall look at each in turn.

Disputes between workers and workers were included in the 1906 definition, excluded between 1971 and 1974, brought back within the protection in 1974 and excluded again in 1982. What is the rationale for removing such disputes from the protection of the immunities and how significant a step is it? Some members of the Donovan Commission were in favour of removing from protection 'demarcation disputes between trade unions in which the employer is neutral (that is, is indifferent as to which of the contending parties' members do the particular job). . . . The dispute . . . is not of the employer's making, he can do nothing to resolve it . . . and in these circumstances it is unjust that he should be debarred from exercising legal remedies . . .' (para. 820). The majority of the Commission rejected the proposal on the grounds that it would be difficult to identify situations in which the employer was truly neutral (in the sense defined), and the two leading cases on the point decided under the IRA 1971 tended to support the majority's view. Under the IRA 1971, as under EA 1982, the exclusion of worker and worker disputes was not confined to demarcation disputes and the decided cases in fact concerned union membership.

Cory Lighterage v. *Transport and General Workers' Union*
[1973] ICR 339 (CA)

Mr Shute, a lighterman in the Port of London where an informal closed shop operated, deliberately allowed his union membership to lapse and informed his fellow employees of the fact. The other workers employed by the plaintiffs refused to work with Shute whom the employers consequently suspended on full pay. Three months later the employers, having been refused permission by the Dock Labour Board to dismiss Shute, sought an injunction against the union restraining it from instructing its members to withhold their labour.

LORD DENNING M.R.: . . . The Act of 1971 defines an 'industrial dispute' as 'a dispute between one or more employers or organisations of employers and one or more workers or organisations of workers' where the dispute relates wholly or mainly to any one or more of several matters which are set out. This definition differs in an important respect from the Trade Disputes Act 1906, section 5 (3) of which defined 'trade dispute' as 'any dispute between employers and workmen, *or between workmen and workmen*,' which is connected with various matters there set out. The important difference is that the Act of 1971 omits a dispute between 'workmen and workmen.' The significance of this difference can only be seen by tracing the history.

In 1875 Parliament passed a statute which took strikes out of the reach of the criminal law of conspiracy. Section 3 of the Conspiracy and Protection of Property Act 1875 was in these words:

> An agreement or combination by two or more persons to do or procure to be done any act *in contemplation or furtherance of a trade dispute between employers and workmen* shall not be indictable as a conspiracy if such act committed by one person would not be punishable as a crime.

This section was obviously confined to disputes between employers and workmen. It did not extend to disputes between workmen and workmen. It was considered by the House of Lords in the leading case of *Quinn* v. *Leathem* [1901] AC 495. Leathem was a wholesale butcher who employed non-union men. Quinn was an officer of a trade union of butchers' men. They objected to Leathem employing non-union men. They threatened Leathem that they would stop his customers from dealing with him unless he dismissed his non-union men. Leathem refused to put them out on the street. He brought an action for damages for conspiracy against the officers of the union. The jury awarded him damages of £200 and their verdict was upheld in every court up to the highest in the House of Lords. Lord Lindley said, at pp. 541–542:

> I cannot myself see that there was in this case any trade dispute between employers and workmen within the meaning of section 3. I am not at present prepared to say that the officers of a trade union who create strife by calling out members of the union working for an employer with whom none of them have any dispute can invoke the benefit of this section even on an indictment for a conspiracy.

The trade unions were much disturbed by the decision in *Quinn* v. *Leathem*, just as they were with the *Taff Vale* case a fortnight earlier (*Taff Vale Railway Co.* v. *Amalgamated Society of Railway Servants* [1901] AC 426). In 1906, when Parliament gave them a charter of immunity – I refer, of course, to the Trade Disputes Act 1906 – Parliament deliberately widened the definition of 'trade dispute.' It was extended so as to include any dispute 'between workmen and workmen.' The ambit of immunity was also extended. No longer was the immunity confined to an indictment for criminal conspiracy. It was extended to a civil action for damages for conspiracy. . . .

Since that case [*White* v. *Riley*] there have been many cases in which union men have refused to work with a non-union man. They have threatened the employers that unless the non-union man is dismissed, they will stop work. It has always been accepted that a dispute on those lines as to union membership is a 'trade dispute.' Such was *Rookes* v. *Barnard* [1964] AC 1129 and *Morgan* v. *Fry* [1968] 2 QB 710. The reason is plain. It was because the dispute fell exactly within the words of the Act of 1906 as a dispute 'between workmen and workmen' which is connected with the employment or non-employment of any person.

Now among the many changes made by the Industrial Relations Act 1971, there is one very significant one. It omits the words 'between workmen and workmen.' So all the cases which rested on those words since *White* v. *Riley* [1921] 1 Ch. 1 onwards must be put on one side. A dispute as to union membership is a typical dispute between workmen and workmen. It does not fall within the new definition of industrial disputes. . . .

Mr Gibson was constrained to admit that the dispute in this case was, at its inception, a dispute 'between workmen and workmen' which was not protected by the Act of 1971. But he submitted that the employers afterwards got involved in it, so that it became a dispute between employers and workmen. I cannot accept this submission. The employers never were in dispute with the union or its officers. The employers recognized their desire for 100 per cent. membership. So the employers did not *resist* the demands of the union or its officers. They acceded to them. They ordered Shute off the tug. They told him to go home. The employers were just at the 'receiving' end of the dispute. They took the only course open to them. They had no option. The tugs had to sail. The refuse had to be collected. So Shute had to stay ashore. It is rather like passengers in a railway strike. If the trains do not run, the passengers have to walk or get a lift. The passengers may sympathise with one side or the other. They may get very annoyed with the disputants, but they are not themselves parties to the dispute.

I realise, of course, that in this very case the employers have since brought an action at law against the union and its officers. So there is now a dispute between the employers and the organisation of workers. And Shute has himself brought proceedings against the employers in the industrial tribunal. So there is now a dispute between Shute and the employers. But neither of those disputes were in the mind of anyone on October 2, 1972, and December 4, 1972. The acts done on those days were not done 'in contemplation of' these later disputes. An act is not done 'in contemplation of' a trade dispute unless it is done in expectation of and with a view to it: see *Conway* v. *Wade* [1909] AC 506.

On the evidence so far, it seems to me that there has only been one dispute in the present case, and that is the dispute between Shute on the one hand and the union and its officers and members on the other hand. It was a dispute between workmen and workmen relating to his membership of the union. All the acts done on October 2 and December 14, 1972, were done in contemplation or in furtherance of that dispute or in consequence of that dispute, and not in contemplation or in furtherance of any other dispute.

Langston v. *A UEW* [1974] ICR 180 (CA)

The plaintiff, a car welder employed by Chrysler (UK) Ltd, sought to leave the defendant union which operated a closed shop at his place of employment. His employers suspended him on full pay. Part of his claim against the union was that the union was in breach of s.96 of the IRA 1971 on the grounds that it had induced the employer to break the employee's contract of employment by suspending him (above, p. 314). Section 96 applied, however, only if the union had acted in contemplation of furtherance of an industrial dispute.

LORD DENNING M.R.: . . . [Next] Mr Harvey suggested that there was no 'industrial dispute' in existence or in contemplation. This was based on *Cory Lighterage Ltd* v. *Transport and General Workers' Union* [1973] ICR 339, where this court pointed out that the definition of 'industrial dispute' in section 167 [of IRA 1971] did not include disputes between 'workers and workers'. But we added that very often a dispute between workers and workers evolves into a dispute between employers and workers. In the present case the dispute at the beginning was between Mr Langston and his fellow workers. So long as he was employed by Chryslers at his job, he was not in dispute with his employers. But as soon as the other men went to Chryslers and said to them: 'We will not work with Langston. He must not be allowed on the plant' – then one of two things were in contemplation. On the one hand Chryslers might *refuse* the men's demands. If they did so, there would be a dispute between Chryslers and the workers. It would be a dispute as to the termination or suspension of Langston from his employment. On the other hand, Chryslers might *accede* to the men's demands. They might dismiss or suspend Mr Langston from his work against his will. If they did so, there would be a dispute between the employers and Mr Langston. It would be a dispute either as to the termination or suspension of his employment, or, at any rate, as to the terms and conditions of his employment. He claimed to have a right to work at his job. The employees would not allow him to do it. It is very different from the *Cory Lighterage* case, where Shute was only too pleased to be sent home on paid leave: see [1973] I C R 339, 351. In either event, therefore, there was in contemplation a dispute between the employers and one or more workers, and it came within the definition in section 167.

To the extent that Lord Denning's argument in the *Cory Lighterage* case depended upon the view that there was no trade dispute with the employer because the employer did not resist the union's demands, it has been weakened by the subsequent enactment of T U L R A, s.29(5) (above, p. 794), which has not been repealed by E A 1982. This subsection decreases still further the likelihood of the court finding that the employer has remained neutral in the dispute between groups of workers.

One should also note that by virtue of the definition of secondary action in E A 1980, s.17(2) (see below, p. 835), that section operates rather curiously to remove protection in respect of inducing breaches of commercial contracts from purely worker and worker disputes. Thus, one could say that E A 1982 merely completes the process of taking worker and worker disputes outside the immunities, which had been initiated by E A 1980. Although both lines of argument are now open, presumably plaintiffs will in fact rely upon the simpler and yet more far-reaching argument that worker and worker disputes are not trade disputes and so have no protection at all under s.13 of T U L R A 1974.

(c) **Disputes between employers and workers not employed by them**

By s.18(2)(*a*) of E A 1982, disputes between employers and workers are brought within the definition only so far as the dispute is between an employer and his workers. For the words 'between employers and workers' in the original version of T U L R A 1974, s.29(1) (above, p. 793), are substituted the words 'between workers and their employers' and a new definition of 'worker' in s.29(6) is provided by E A 1982, s.18(6). This is the second restriction upon the appropriate parties to a trade dispute that E A 1982 introduces, and it is not one that has previously been imposed upon the definition. Thus, in *Midland Cold Storage Ltd* v. *Turner* [1972] I C R 230 registered dock workers picketed a cold store, claiming that the jobs currently held at the store by non-dock workers should be done by them. This was held to be an industrial dispute under the I R A 1971. In the Green Paper, *Trade Union Immunities* (paras 206–13), a general and a particular argument were advanced in favour of this change. The general argument was that there was 'a right for employees to work undisturbed on terms of employment that they find acceptable and to have the protection of the law if anyone tries to stop them' (para. 208). The particular argument related to the International Transport Workers' Federation's campaign of blacking ships flying flags of convenience, which, as we have seen, has given rise to many pieces of litigation in the English courts in recent years. In most of these cases, but by no means all, the crew of the ship are not in dispute with the shipowner, sometimes because they know that if they did make a claim for higher wages their own national seamen's union would not support them and might even ensure that they obtained no further employment in international shipping (cf. the facts of *Star Sea Transport Corporation of Monrovia* v. *Slater* [1978] IRLR 507, where the Indian crew in fact refused to accept the higher wages negotiated by the ITF with the shipowner). In such cases the ITF is in effect acting on behalf of unemployed seamen of the countries in which the beneficial ownership of the ships resides, where job opportunities have been diminished by the low wages crews from the Third World are prepared or compelled to accept. The arguments against protecting such action from tort liability were put in the Green Paper as follows:

In favour of a change, it is argued that it is wrong in principle to apply British law, based on an evaluation of domestic industrial relations, to foreign ships with different industrial relations problems and which are outside the jurisdiction of British law as soon as they sail out of territorial waters. It is also said that our legislation makes it much easier to pursue a campaign of blacking in British ports than in any other Western European ports. As a result, it is argued first, that Britain's international trade and commerce will suffer because only high-cost shipping will be prepared to risk coming to our ports, and that this could put at hazard jobs in Britain which depend on international trade. Secondly, it is argued that British shipping will be exposed to similar treatment in foreign ports; and that this will put at risk British seafarers' jobs, which are heavily dependent on the preservation of the freedom of the seas.

The arguments against making the change put forward in the Green Paper were twofold. First, it was suggested that the proposed restriction would provide an incentive to employers to dismiss those who joined the union. The new definition of worker contained in EA 1982, s.18(6) attempts to catch the most blatant examples of such conduct by including within it people who have ceased to be employed by the employer but who were dismissed in connection with the dispute or whose dismissal was one of the circumstances giving rise to the dispute. The more general argument against the change, and one which EA 1982 rejects, is that the proposal depends upon the view that the primary legitimate function of a trade union is to act as the agent of discrete groups of workers and that the union has only a very limited responsibility to its members as a whole or to the labour movement as a whole. This provision of the EA 1982 expresses in effect the view that the claims of trade unions to act on a broad front should be accorded only limited recognition; it represents the polar opposite of the arguments that led the Labour government of 1974 to 1979 to include trade unions in discussions of social and economic policy at the highest levels in a 'Social Contract' (see above, p. 137).

The implementation of this policy in the EA 1982 required, however, a further amendment to the 1974 definition. In 1974, in s.29(4), a new element of the statutory definition had been introduced, which provided that 'a dispute to which a trade union . . . is a party shall be treated for the purposes of this Act as a dispute to which workers . . . are parties'. This was repealed by EA 1982, s.18(5). Clearly, without this repeal the change in s.29(1) could have been to a large degree ineffective. The ITF, for example, would have been able to continue its campaign. But the effect of the repeal is to revive a long-standing problem under the 1906 definition, which can occur even when the union has members amongst the workforce of the employer in question and even when the claim the union is pursuing is for their apparent benefit. The argument that can be raised is that in order for the union to bring its actions within the protection of the new formula it must act in order to further an already existing dispute between the employees and their employer; the union cannot initiate the dispute itself. The problem is perhaps particularly likely to arise in relation to claims for recognition, where the employer may seek to argue that the claim is put forward on behalf of the union, not on behalf of his employees. However, the argument just outlined seems not to have represented the position under the 1906 Act. Although unions were not mentioned as potential parties to trade disputes, it came to be accepted that they could be parties. Certainly, they could be parties only in a representative capacity, but that was enough to enable them to initiate disputes and no evidence of express adoption of the dispute by the members was required.[1] Presumably, the repeal of TULRA 1974, s.29(4) will cause the revival of this prior learning. There would not seem to be anything in the pre-1974 cases that would subvert the new policy of confining trade disputes to disputes between employers and their own employees, but the principles derived from those cases would enable a union to claim representative status on behalf of the employees more freely than if a requirement of a pre-existing dispute between employer and employees were developed.

An example of the significance of the point is provided by *Beetham* v. *Trinidad Cement Ltd* [1960] AC 132, where the Privy Council had to consider under a Trinidadian ordinance (identical for all relevant purposes to TDA 1906, s.5(3)) a claim for recognition by a union, which had some two hundred out of three hundred relevant employees in membership. Lord Denning said:

> But then it was said that this was not a difference between the company and *the workmen*, as the ordinance requires, but only a difference between the company and *the union*; and attention was drawn to the statement by Bennett, J., that a dispute between such bodies is not a trade dispute: see *R.* v. *National Arbitration Tribunal, Ex parte Bolton*

[1] Cf. K. D. Ewing (1982) 11 *ILJ* at p. 215.

Corpn. [1941] 2 KB at p. 421. To this their Lordships think that Lord Wright gave a sufficient answer when that case reached the House of Lords. He said: [1943] AC at p. 189 'It would be strangely out of date to hold, as was argued, that a trade union cannot act on behalf of its members in a trade dispute, or that a difference between a trade union acting for its members and their employer cannot be a trade dispute.' Accepting this statement, however, it was said that, in this case, the trade union was not acting *for its members*, but for itself. The claim for bargaining status was never authorized or approved, so it was said, by any of the members of the branch at Claxton Bay. It was done by the head office acting on its own initiative. And reliance was placed on observations in some of the cases that, if a trade union acts 'on a frolic of its own', there is not a trade dispute: see *R. v. National Arbitration Tribunal, Ex parte Keable Press Ltd* [1943] 2 All ER 633, *R. v. Industrial Disputes Tribunal, Ex parte Courage & Co. Ltd* [1956] 3 All ER 411. Their Lordships cannot accept this argument. The claim was made by the executive committee who were, by the rules, entrusted with the general management of the union; and it was clearly within the scope of their authority to put forward a claim for bargaining status. If the union were able to obtain bargaining status, it would be able to promote the interest of its members far better than if it were unrecognised. Moreover, the claim had been brought to the attention of the branch who may fairly be assumed to have approved of it. The union can, therefore, properly be considered as acting for its members; and in consequence, the difference was one 'between employers and workmen'.

This decision may be thought to have had some doubt cast upon it by the House of Lords' decision in *Stratford & Sons Ltd* v. *Lindley* (above, p. 791), where a union's claim for joint recognition was turned down by an employer, who granted sole recognition to the other union. Only 3 of the 48 employees of the employer were members of the refused union and there was no evidence that they were dissatisfied with their position. The industrial action organized by the refused union was held not to be taken in furtherance of a trade dispute. There were several strands in their lordships' reasoning, but the Donovan Commission (para. 818) (Lord Donovan having delivered one of the speeches in *Stratford* that had given rise to the doubts) explained the decision on the grounds that their lordships had not found *any* dispute to be in existence in that case: the claim for joint recognition had been made some time previously and might be thought to have lapsed and the union had not renewed its claim after it had learned of the sole recognition granted to the other union but had immediately taken industrial action.

Finally, it should be noted that the restriction of trade disputes to those between employers and their own employees is *not* an indirect way of restricting secondary action. Provided such a dispute exists, industrial action taken by employees of another employer, with whom the secondary employees have no dispute, can still be taken in furtherance of the dispute between the primary employer and his employees, and so be protected. That this is the correct analysis appears from a consideration of *Duport Steels Ltd* v. *Sirs* (above, p. 800) and the argument is strengthened by the provision in EA 1982, s.18(7) that 'the amendments made by this section do not affect the question whether an act done by a person is done by him in contemplation or furtherance of a trade dispute, whether he is a party to the dispute or not.' Secondary action is, of course, controlled by the provisions of EA 1980, s.17 (below, pp. 835–42).

(d) Disputes outside the United Kingdom

The final amendment made by EA 1982, s.18, relates to disputes outside the United Kingdom. If there is a trade dispute abroad and workers in the United Kingdom take action in furtherance of it, is their action protected? It was unclear whether such action was protected by the formulas of the TDA 1906 or IRA 1971. In 1974 the government wished simply to enact: 'There is a trade dispute for the purposes of this Act even though it relates to matters occurring outside Great Britain.' This would have covered all situations in which workers in Great Britain took industrial action in furtherance of a dispute that originated abroad or in which workers in Great Britain made a demand of their employer which required him to take action abroad (for example, to pay his South African workers higher wages, even though those employees had made no such demand). By opposition amendment, however, the qualification relating to the employees in Great Britain being likely to be affected by the outcome of the dispute was introduced (above, p. 793). That qualification was removed by TULRA 1976, s.1(d); it is restored by EA 1982, s.18(4), and the whole provision is made to refer to matters occurring outside the United Kingdom (not Great Britain).

The effect of the amendment is, once again, to strike at the legitimacy of action taken by workers in solidarity with other workers; now an element of self-interest (it is unclear how strong an element) is required on the part of those taking the industrial action in the United Kingdom to bring their action within the protection of the trade dispute formula. However, this is a general feature of the legislation passed in 1980 and 1982, and industrial action taken in the United Kingdom in support of workers employed outside the United Kingdom in, say, another part of a multinational group runs the risk of being unprotected for several reasons. If, as is likely, the multinational group operates through separate subsidiary companies in each of the countries, action taken by the employees of the United Kingdom subsidiary in support of a dispute between the employees of the Belgian subsidiary and their employer will be secondary action within the meaning of EA 1980, s.17 and so protected only if it falls within one of the gateways provided by EA 1980, s.17(3)–(5). See below, pp. 835–42. Again, a demand by employees in the United Kingdom that the UK holding company should require its South African subsidiary to pay higher wages to the employees of the subsidiary would not seem to be a trade dispute irrespective of the provisions of s.18(4). Even if the dispute can be seen as a dispute between the UK holding company and its employees (and thus a dispute 'between workers and their employer'), the dispute may not relate to 'terms and conditions of employment' (s.29(1)(a)). If that phrase is interpreted to mean 'terms and conditions of employment of workers' (which is what the wording of sub-paragraphs (*a*) to (*g*) suggests) then the new and restrictive definition of 'worker' (below, p. 815) will confine trade disputes essentially to disputes about the terms and conditions of the employer's own workers.

It may be useful to set out in full at this point s.29(1)–(6) of TULRA 1974 as amended by EA 1982.

Trade Union and Labour Relations Act 1974,
s.29(1)–(6), as amended

29.–(1) In this Act 'trade dispute' means a dispute between workers and their employer which relates wholly or mainly to one or more of the following, that is to say –

- (*a*) terms and conditions of employment, or the physical conditions in which any workers are required to work;
- (*b*) engagement or non-engagement, or termination or suspension of employment or the duties of employment, of one or more workers;
- (*c*) allocation of work or the duties of employment as between workers or groups of workers;
- (*d*) matters of discipline;
- (*e*) the membership or non-membership of a trade union on the part of a worker;
- (*f*) facilities for officials of trade unions; and
- (*g*) machinery for negotiation or consultation, and other procedures, relating to any of the foregoing matters, including the recognition by employers or employers' associations of the right of a trade union to represent workers in any such negotiation or consultation or in the carrying out of such procedures.

(2) A dispute between a Minister of the Crown and any workers shall, notwithstanding that he is not the employer of those workers, be treated for the purposes of this Act as a dispute between those workers and their employer if the dispute relates –

- (*a*) to matters which have been referred for consideration by a joint body on which, by virtue of any provision made by or under any enactment, that Minister is represented; or
- (*b*) to matters which cannot be settled without that Minister exercising a power conferred on him by or under an enactment.

(3) There is a trade dispute for the purposes of this Act even though it relates to matters occurring outside the United Kingdom, so long as the person or persons whose actions in the United Kingdom are said to be in contemplation or furtherance of a trade dispute relating to matters occurring outside the United Kingdom are likely to be affected in respect of one or more of the matters specified in subsection (1) of this section by the outcome of that dispute. . . .

(5) An act, threat or demand done or made by one person or organisation against another which, if resisted, would have led to a trade dispute with that other, shall, notwithstanding that because that other submits to the act or threat or accedes to the demand no dispute arises, be treated for the purposes of this Act as being done or made in contemplation of a trade dispute with that other.

(6) In this section –

'employment' includes any relationship whereby one person personally does work

or performs services for another;
'worker', in relation to a dispute with an employer, means –

    (*a*) a worker employed by that employer; or
    (*b*) a person who has ceased to be employed by that employer where –
        (i)   his employment was terminated in connection with the dispute; or
        (ii) the termination of his employment was one of the circumstances giving rise to the dispute.

(7) The amendments made by this section do not affect the question whether an act done by a person is done by him in contemplation or furtherance of a dispute, whether he is a party to the dispute or not.

(e) In contemplation or furtherance of a trade dispute

We have now considered all the amendments made to the 1974 definition of a trade dispute by EA 1982. We ought to consider finally what it means to act 'in contemplation or furtherance' of a trade dispute. This particular phrase has not been subject to further statutory elaboration, although it has been subject to extensive judicial interpretation. We have already seen (above, pp. 795–805) that where a trade dispute exists, but the court finds that the defendants' actions were motivated by a non-industrial objective, it may give effect to that finding by concluding that the defendant did not act in furtherance of the trade dispute but rather in furtherance of the non-industrial objective. Even when the defendant's objective is indubitably industrial, however, two arguments may be made to the effect that the defendant was not acting in contemplation or furtherance of a trade dispute.

First, this requirement may be used to disqualify from protection what the court regards as too hasty a resort by the union to industrial action. It would be wrong to say that this requirement has been interpreted by the courts so as to deprive all unconstitutional action (i.e. action taken before disputes procedures have been exhausted) from protection, but certain examples of what the courts have regarded as extreme conduct of this kind have been so treated. We have already seen that the Donovan Commission regarded *Stratford* v. *Lindley* (above, p. 812) as based on the proposition that the union's resort to industrial action without renewing its claim for recognition meant that there was no dispute at all between employer and workers. Certainly, if there is no dispute, it is difficult to see how the union can act in furtherance of it, but the courts have also built a requirement of imminence into the provision that action 'in contemplation of' a trade dispute is protected. Thus in *Bents Brewery Co. Ltd.* v. *Hogan* [1945] 2 All ER 570, a union's action in seeking information from its members prior to formulating a wage claim was held not to be protected as done 'in contemplation' of a dispute (the disclosure of information being a breach of the contracts of employment of the employees concerned).[1] On the other hand, in those cases already discussed (above, p. 804) of workers

---

[1] It is interesting to consider whether the union would be able to require the employer today to disclose the information under EPA 1975, ss.17–21. See above, pp. 205–19.

taking industrial action against managerial acts which they fear will lead to redundancies, the courts have generally been prepared to hold on the facts that the action was taken in contemplation of a dispute with the employer about the use of outside contractors and not because of 'groundless fears of remotely possible events' (i.e. the feared redundancies). See *Health Computing Ltd* v. *Meek* [1981] ICR 24.

Second, in the late 1970s the phrase 'in furtherance' of a trade dispute was interpreted by the Court of Appeal so as to remove from the protection of the immunities certain forms of secondary industrial action and certain other types of industrial action that the court found unacceptable. There was a variety of approaches used to achieve this end, but the essence of the matter was that 'furtherance' of a dispute was not interpreted as a subjective test (did the defendant genuinely, even if unreasonably, think his actions would further the trade dispute?) but as an objective one (was the action likely to achieve the defendant's goals or, even, had it done so?) and a considerable element of the court's assessment of the merits of the dispute was then injected into the application of the objective test. The flavour of the Court of Appeal's approach emerges perhaps most strongly from the judgment of Lord Denning M.R. in *Express Newspapers Ltd* v. *McShane* [1979] ICR 210. In that case the union's members were in dispute over a wage claim with the provincial newspaper employers. The provincial newspapers continued to be published, in part because of copy supplied by the Press Association. The union then called upon its members at the PA to come out on strike, but only half of them did so. To encourage the rest to join in, the union then instructed its members employed by the national newspapers to black copy from the PA. The question for the court was the legality of the industrial action at the national newspapers. Lord Denning said:

It is said on behalf of the trade union leaders that 'furtherance' depended on their state of mind. If they genuinely and honestly *believed* that the 'blacking' would advance the cause of the provincial journalists, then their acts were done 'in furtherance of' the dispute. The judge did not accept that submission. Nor do I. 'Furtherance' is not a merely subjective concept. There is an objective element in it. The *Shorter Oxford English Dictionary* defines 'furtherance' as 'the fact or state of being helped forward.' It seems to me that, for an act to be done 'in furtherance of' a trade dispute, it must be reasonably capable of doing so, or have a reasonable prospect of it in this way, that it must help one side or the other to the dispute in a *practical* way by giving support to the one or bringing pressure to bear on the other. Such as in the common case where men, who are in dispute with their employer, withdraw their labour, or 'black' materials coming to his factory, or are supported by pickets outside his gates. Those are practical measures which have an impact in *fact* on the employer. They directly damage the employer's business. Such acts have a different quality from those which do not directly damage the employer's business but serve only to improve the morale of the strikers or promote their confidence or encourage them in their efforts, or damage innocent people not parties to the dispute. If this is all they do, they are not 'in furtherance' of the dispute. In ordinary speech we draw a distinction between giving moral support to a cause and practical support to it. To be 'in furtherance of' a dispute, an act must give practical support to one side or the other and not merely moral support.

In this passage Lord Denning not only rejected a subjective test of 'furtherance', but also adopted a strong version of the objective test, namely, one requiring 'practical effects' to flow from the secondary action, and, further, rejected the proposition that improvement of the strikers' morale could qualify as a practical effect. His approach was, thus, considerably more restrictive than a simple rejection of the subjective approach might imply.

We need not pursue the intricacies of the arguments developed by the Court of Appeal during this period, because the House of Lords, in a second[1] trilogy of decisions in 1979 and 1980 restored the subjective test. See *NWL* v. *Woods* [1979] ICR 897, *Express Newspapers Ltd* v. *McShane* [1980] ICR 42, *Duport Steels Ltd* v. *Sirs* [1980] ICR 161. In consequence, the government introduced into the Employment Bill then before Parliament a clause which became s.17 of EA 1980. That section did not rely principally upon an objective test of furtherance to control secondary action but upon a simple statutory declaration that certain types of secondary action were not protected. The subjective test of furtherance, as established by the House of Lords, remains the correct approach to the interpretation of the golden formula. Two additional points only need to be made. First, the trilogy was notable for some strong expressions of opinion by their lordships at the unwillingness of Lord Denning to accept that the subjective test was the correct one. See especially *Duport Steels Ltd* v. *Sirs* [1980] ICR 161, 190. Lord Denning's desire to restrict by judicial means the legality of secondary action continued even after the enactment of EA 1980, s.17, and brought forth further criticism from their lordships in *Hadmor Productions Ltd* v. *Hamilton* [1982] ICR at pp. 129–31.[2] Second, the effect of the Court of Appeal's interpretation of the golden formula was that the Labour government's policy of abstention in the area of industrial conflict, which was not fully established until the passing of the amendments made by TULRA 1976 (see above, pp. 737 and 744), was never really implemented in practice. By the time the House of Lords came to assert the subjective view a Conservative government had been elected. That this remarkable state of affairs should have occurred may well cause any future government that wishes to implement a policy of abstention to consider very carefully not just the appropriate substantive law to be passed but also the nature of the courts to which interpretation of the law will be entrusted.

3 The liability of trade unions

We have already seen (above, pp. 763–5) that in EA 1982, s.15(1), the

---

[1] The first trilogy of House of Lords cases was composed of *Mogul Steamship Co. Ltd* v. *McGregor, Gow & Co.* [1892] AC 25; *Allen* v. *Flood* [1898] AC 1; and *Quinn* v. *Leathem* [1901] AC 495. See above, p. 709.

[2] For a fuller discussion of these developments see Davies and Freedland, 'Labour Law' in McAuslan and Jowell (eds.) *Lord Denning, the Judge and the Law* (forthcoming).

special immunities for trade unions against liability in tort were removed, thus bringing trade-union immunity into line with that provided for individuals. At the same time the immunity provided for individuals has itself been narrowed by EA 1980 and 1982; for example, by the narrowing of the trade dispute definition. In the succeeding sections of this chapter we shall look at other changes brought about by the Employment Acts in the immunities for individuals (and, thus, now for trade unions). The removal of the special trade-union immunity was one of the more dramatic changes effected in this period. Partly this was because the legal status of trade unions as far as tort liability was concerned had acquired a symbolic value, both for the labour movement itself and for those wishing to modify the abstentional stance of trade dispute law. However, what more practical goals may those in favour of the removal of this immunity be said to have had? One obvious goal would be to meet the complaint of the Royal Commission on Labour (1894) that without union liability those injured by unlawful actions in trade disputes may 'be unable to recover adequate damages' (above, p. 764). The obvious counter-argument is that unlimited exposure of trade-union funds to liability is likely to put the union out of operation as effectively as a simple prohibition upon its activities, a policy which no government has adopted in the last 100 years.

The EA 1982, s.16, attempts a compromise between these two points of view by exposing union funds to liability but by also imposing a limit upon that liability. In the case of large unions (those with 100,000 or more members) the amount that can be awarded by way of damages 'in any proceedings' in tort against a trade union (except in certain actions for personal injury or actions arising out of the use of property) is £250,000.[1] The limit does not apply to the amount that is awarded against the union by way of costs or, of course, to the costs that the union may itself incur in defending the proceedings. In the *Taff Vale* case (above, p. 765) the amount of damages awarded against the union was less than half the total amount of damages, other party's costs and own costs incurred by the union. The limit does not apply either to fines imposed upon the union for contempt of court. Thus, the limit imposed by s.16 is less of a limit than it may seem at first sight. Its impact in practice is, even within its field of operation, likely to be somewhat arbitrary. The limit applies separately to each set of proceedings commenced against the union, so that in, say, a national strike in a fragmented industry a lot will depend upon how many employers decide to sue. In *Duport Steels Ltd* v. *Sirs* [1980] ICR 161 there were 15 plaintiffs and in *Associated Newspaper Group Ltd* v. *Wade* [1979] ICR 664 there were 14.

EA 1982, s.17 imposes a further limitation as to the type of union funds against which awards of damages or costs (but not contempt fines) are to be recoverable. The most important funds thus protected are the political fund of the union (provided it is established under the TUA 1913 and is not available

---

[1] For unions with fewer than 5,000 members the limit is £10,000; for those with fewer than 25,000 members £50,000; for those with fewer than 100,000 members £125,000.

for financing industrial action) and the union's provident benefits fund (when the fund exists solely for providing provident benefits).

However, a second and more interesting goal of those who argue for the imposition of liability upon trade unions is that 'if trade unions were made financially responsible . . . they could be expected in their own interest to exert greater internal discipline over their officials and members, particularly in respect of unofficial action' (*Trade Union Immunities*, para. 112). Legally, the question is one of vicarious liability, and the issue is a critical one, since a union cannot be held liable except vicariously for acts committed by natural persons on its behalf. Socially, we are presented with a proposal for the control of unofficial action and a bold suggestion that the law can be used to alter the internal relations of trade unions so as to make unions rather more the policemen of their members' actions and rather less the means of articulating their members' wishes. It must be said that there is a certain potential contradiction between this view of the proper role of trade-union leaderships and that expressed in the later Green Paper, *Democracy in Trade Unions* (1983). See above, pp. 683–4.

Both in terms of legal and social policy the central issue becomes one of deciding for whose acts the union is to be liable. Unions employ officials at various levels within their organization (often at national, regional and local levels); there will be a much larger number of unpaid officials (shop stewards, branch chairmen etc. – 'official' is defined in TULRA 1974, s.30 widely enough to cover both categories); there will be periodic delegate meetings of the unions' membership in annual conferences and so on; the national executive of the union may consist wholly or mainly of lay members of the union; and finally there are the members themselves, individually and collectively. For which categories of people and in which circumstances is the union to be liable? In particular, can the union be liable for action taken which has not been authorized by some officially constituted body in the union?

On this issue there is an interesting contrast between the position that obtained under the IRA 1971 (when the special union immunity was also removed) and that apparently aimed at by EA 1982. In the IRA 1971 Parliament, unaccountably, did not deal directly with the question of a union's vicarious liability and in the case of unregistered unions (the majority) did not even deal with the issue indirectly through mandatory provisions in the union's rule-book. The matter had to be settled in the courts in *Heatons Transport Ltd* v. *Transport and General Workers' Union* [1972] ICR 308. In this case committees of shop stewards at Liverpool and Hull docks, which were unofficial committees in the sense that they were not provided for in the union's rule-book and had been set up on the sole initiative of the stewards themselves, instituted a campaign of blacking, at the docks, lorries operated by firms which carried on the business of packing and unpacking containers for shipment by sea. The dockers' claim was that this was a substitute for traditional dock work of loading and unloading cargo into the holds of ships and therefore ought to be carried out in the dock area by dock workers. It was the union's policy that this work should be done by dock labour, but the union's official bodies had not authorized the blacking. Although there was some evidence in Liverpool that the local union official was co-operating with the stewards' committee, in Hull the committee (which also contained stewards from another union) was clearly not supported by the local official committee of the union, which had denied before the events began that the stewards' committee had authority to negotiate on behalf of the union. The blacked employers sought injunctions against the union.

This situation was subject to two contrasting analyses in the Court of Appeal and the House of Lords, the 'dual authority' analysis of Lord Denning, which led to the conclusion that the union was not liable for the unofficial acts of the stewards, and the analysis by Lord Wilberforce of the conferment of authority 'from the bottom', which led to the opposite conclusion.

Heatons Transport Ltd v. *Transport and General Workers' Union*
[1972] ICR 308

LORD DENNING:
X. The position of shop stewards
    Until this case the position of shop stewards has never come up for consideration in the courts of law. To determine it, much useful material has been placed before us. I must describe it, but I will not go into detail. First, there is a valuable discussion in the *Report of the Royal Commission on Trade Unions and Employers' Associations* (1968) (Cmnd. No. 3623) over which Lord Donovan presided: see paragraphs 96 to 110 and 696 to 699. Secondly, there is the Industrial Relations Act 1971. It had shop stewards very much in mind: see section 167 (1), under 'official,' and Schedule 4, paragraph 10. Thirdly, there is the *Code of Practice [H.M.S.O.]* (paragraphs 99 to 129) which has received the approval of both Houses of Parliament under the Act: see section 3. It came into force on February 28, 1972, and applies not only to registered trade unions, but also to organisations of workers like this union: see the note on p. 2 of that *Code of Practice*. Fourthly, there is the Guide issued by the Trade Union Congress on *Good Industrial Relations* (1971), para. 61. Fifthly, there are the rules of this union [as amended April 7, 1971], particularly rule 11 (4) and also the full picture given in the *Shop Stewards' Handbook* (1970). Sixthly, in addition, in the port of Hull, there are most valuable documents kept by the Hull Joint Port Working Committee. That is a committee consisting of representatives of employers, work-people and of the Hull Dock Labour Board. It has minutes and agreements which throw much light on the position of shop stewards, at any rate, in that port. Seventhly, there is much evidence that, in this union, the shop stewards have been entrusted with local negotiations, as part of a policy of decentralisation.

    From all this material I deduce this. On the one hand, a 'shop steward' is the representative of his work group, that is, his fellow-workers in a particular place of work, such as a factory, depot or wharf or a section of it. He is one of them. He works alongside them. He is employed by the same employer as they are. He is their leader. He speaks for them. If any of them has a grievance with the management, he takes it up. He negotiates on their behalf with the employers on any point specially connected with that particular shop, such as, who is to do this piece of work or that, whether they should work overtime and so forth. He is often appointed by the workers unopposed, but, in case of difference, they hold an election to decide who it shall be. If there are other 'shops' with similar problems, he may join with other shop stewards in a 'shop stewards' committee' so as to present a united front in their negotiations. In all this, he is essentially the representative of his own work group. The work group is, as the Royal Commission said, at p. 27, para. 104:

> the basis of the shop steward's power. He could not of his own volition impose a limit on output or a ban on non-unionists. This can only be done by decision of the group of workers which he represents.

On the other hand, a 'shop steward' is also a representative of a trade union. He is accredited to the union. He collects the men's contributions to the union or sees that they are collected. He sees that new men join the union. He keeps his fellow-workers informed of the policy of the union and of the decisions of branches. If the union decides to take action of one kind or another, he would be responsible for carrying it out in his shop. But he is not paid by the union. He is not an 'officer' of the union. He is only an 'official.' He is paid by his employers and is the servant of his employers: but they allow him to spend part of his time – and sometimes the whole of it – on his shop steward duties. They may allow him an office and the use of a telephone. This is because he is so valuable a person in the whole set-up. I would quote the words again of the Royal Commission, at p. 29, para. 110:

> the shop-floor decisions which generally precede unofficial strikes are often taken against the advice of shop stewards. Thus shop stewards are rarely agitators pushing workers towards unconstitutional action. In some instances they may be the mere mouthpieces of their work groups. But quite commonly they are supporters of order exercising a restraining influence on their members in conditions which promote disorder.

So the shop steward has a dual role. He is at one and the same time the representative of his own work group: and also the representative of the trade union. Suppose now that he, by himself or in conjunction with other shop stewards, calls on his fellow-workers to take industrial action. Does it mean that he is acting with the authority of the union? I think not – or not necessarily. He may be acting on behalf of his own work group and under pressure by them – without any authority from the union at all. If he is to have authority from the union so as to make the union responsible for unlawful action by him, it must be found in the rules or the handbook or in the course of dealing. I have studied all these with the greatest care. I find that a shop steward, by himself or in conjunction with others, has authority to negotiate terms with his employers; but this, as I see it, does not include taking industrial action. Industrial action is not to be regarded as ancillary to or incidental to the negotiations. I find no authority in a shop steward – or in a shop stewards' committee – to take industrial action on his or their own initiative. The matter must first be put before one of the official committees of the union before it can be made responsible. It must at least be approved by the district committee of the union. That is the lowest body to which the rules permit industrial action to be delegated: see rules 3 (9) and 6 (15) and (16). It is no good getting the approval of an officer of the union. It must be by an official committee of the union. . . .

As I read the evidence in both Liverpool and Hull, the permanent officers of the union were well aware of what was going on; but they were powerless to prevent it. They did not turn a blind eye to it. They did not approve it by a nod or a wink. Some of them, indeed, did what they could to get the shop stewards to call off the 'blacking': but it was no good. The shop stewards were not acting in this regard as representatives of the union. They were acting as representatives of their own work group. But in each case their action was endorsed overwhelmingly by the mass meetings of the dock workers. I do not think the 'blacking' was within the express or implied authority of the union: nor was it ratified by the union.

XI. 'Within the scope of authority'

Accepting that the 'blacking' was not within the actual authority, express or implied, of the shop stewards' committee, the question still remains whether the union can be made responsible for it. The National Industrial Relations Court seem to have held that it can. But I cannot accept this. There is no question here of ostensible authority. The shop stewards did not profess to be acting on behalf of the union: nor did the union hold them out as having authority. The union can only be made liable if the 'blacking' was, in the time-honoured phrase, 'within the scope of the authority' of the shop stewards.

The expression 'in the scope of his authority' of an agent is comparable with the expression 'in the course of employment' for a servant. But it is very different in its effect. I do not think a principal is liable for the wrongs done by his agent which are not authorised by the principal, unless the agent is carrying out a task or duty delegated to him by the principal, and does the wrongful act – not as a casual act of his own – but as part of the very carrying out of that task or duty: see *Navarro* v. *Moregrand Ltd* [1951] 2 TLR 674, 681; *Cassidy* v. *Ministry of Health* [1951] 2 KB 343, 363–365 and *Launchbury* v. *Morgans* [1972] 2 WLR 1217, very recently in the House of Lords.

In the present case the union had at no time delegated any task or duty to the shop stewards which is of any relevance. The shop stewards did the 'blacking' on their own. The union are, therefore, not responsible for it.

In addition, the legislature has itself used the phrase 'within the scope of his authority' in this very Act: see sections 96 (1) (b) and 101 (4). It has defined it in section 167 (9) in these words:

> Any reference in this Act to a person taking any action within the scope of his authority on behalf of an organisation shall be construed as a reference to his taking that action in his capacity as an official or agent of the organisation in circumstances where he is authorised, by or under the rules of the organisation or by virtue of an office in the organisation which he holds or otherwise, to take that action on its behalf.

Apply that definition. A shop steward has no authority by the rules, or by virtue of his office, or otherwise, to call for industrial action on behalf of the union. So his action in 'blacking,' is not done within the scope of his authority. The union is not responsible for it. The shop stewards do it as representatives of their own work groups and not with the authority of the union. They may be guilty personally of an unfair industrial practice under section 96; but they do not make the union responsible for it. In this respect the case is, to my mind, not governed by the decision of the House of Lords in *Taff Vale Railway Co.* v. *Amalgamated Society of Railway Servants* [1901] AC 426 but by the later decision in *Denaby and Cadeby Main Collieries Ltd* v. *Yorkshire Miners' Association* [1906]

AC 384.

I would therefore allow the appeals against the final orders as against the union and set them aside.

LORD WILBERFORCE: . . . This argument based upon the necessity for delegation of authority by the general executive council commended itself to Lord Denning M.R. and to Roskill L.J. in the Court of Appeal. There are passages in their judgments where the words 'the union' are used so as to mean the general executive council and senior permanent officers at its headquarters. But questions of delegation from 'the top,' to use the phrase adopted by Roskill L.J. do not arise if authority to take industrial action has either expressly or implicitly been conferred directly upon shop stewards from 'the bottom', i.e. the membership of the union, whose agreement is also the ultimate source of authority of the general executive council itself. One therefore looks first at the rule book to see what kinds of action the members of the union have expressly agreed may be taken on their behalf by shop stewards.

Shop stewards are elected by the membership in a defined working place and hold office for two years. Upon ratification of their election by the appropriate district committee and regional committee they are accredited officials of the union. Their credentials may be withdrawn by the regional committee or its authorised sub-committee, but only if the shop steward is not acting in accordance with the union rules and policy.

The purpose for which shop stewards are elected is described as that of 'representing membership on matters affecting their employment.' This is a phrase which is both wide and vague. No doubt their main concern is intended to be the particular industrial interests of the members of the union in the work places for which they are shop stewards. This has given rise to the suggestion that they play a 'dual role,' in that in respect of some acts done by them they are to be treated in law as agents for the union, but in respect of others as agents only for those members of the union by whom they have been elected as shop stewards. For the latter the union is said to be not responsible in law as their principal.

This concept of duality of roles is not one which would be likely to occur to trade unionists. The rules of the Transport and General Workers' Union themselves provide that 'Shop stewards shall receive the fullest support and protection from the union.' Even upon the lowest basis of individual self-interest – and there is no reason to suppose that members of trade unions are actuated by this alone – it may well be thought that an improvement in the earnings or conditions of employment of any group of members will make it easier to achieve improvements for other groups and ultimately for all the members. There is thus no a priori reason why the members of the union should not agree that shop stewards should be authorised by *all* the members to take action to promote the interests of members employed in a particular work place.

That this is the industrial strategy of the Transport and General Workers' Union in particular is apparent from the introductory paragraph in the shop stewards' handbook issued by the union to shop stewards and from the following extract from the official journal of the union, the 'Record,' for February 1972:

> Wage increases worth hundreds of millions of pounds have been won by the TGWU in the last year – and the key to this success has been the fact that the union has involved shop stewards and members in taking decisions on agreements.

That in what they do for the purpose of representing membership in the work place shop stewards are acting on behalf of the members of the union as a whole is emphasised time and again in the Shop Stewards' Handbook.

'As a shop steward there is no doubt that the eyes of the members in your shop are upon you. You are the union as far as they are concerned. You are the agency through which come any services which our union provides for them, and through which they normally hear about us.' Again: 'Remember first of all you are an official of the union'; and again: 'As a shop steward you represent *on behalf of the union* its members in the workplace.'

That decisions by the union must be taken only at the 'top' is specifically disclaimed in the 'Record' (May 1972) where it is said:

to limit the ability of the union to act vigorously in the place of work or encouraging the idea that decisions have to be taken at the 'top' and handed down, is merely to encourage breakaways and splits that will end in anarchy in industrial relations.

The basic error which underlies the judgments of the two members of the Court of Appeal from whose conclusion Buckley L.J. ultimately did not feel he should dissent lies in their acceptance of the necessity to find some express delegation of authority from the top – a necessity which the union itself consistently and publicly disclaims.

The National Industrial Relations Court perceived clearly enough that in many contexts – including those of industrial action to keep up wages and protect working conditions, 'the union' includes shop stewards. It is hardly conceivable that a dock worker joining the Transport and General Workers' Union would be content to be represented in an industrial dispute by someone who was not in a position to call for industrial action by him and his workmates in support of their claim.

The policy of the union prior to and up to March 1972 as respects the settlement which it was at that time endeavouring to achieve of the dispute about 'container-isation' is clear. It had been laid down by a dockers delegates' conference in 1971, which it is conceded had authority to do so on behalf of the union. It was that the task of stuffing and stripping containers carried by sea should in general be reserved for dock workers. So in seeking to achieve that object the shop stewards were acting in accordance with union policy.

It is clear, furthermore, that it was union policy to seek to achieve this by industrial action, including the blacking of haulier firms and that this extended to organising at the work place. The facts, to be referred to, relating to the form of agreement sought to be imposed on hauliers at Liverpool, which was clearly in line with union policy, demonstrate this. In Hull there was official blacking of a firm handling groupage cargoes in 1971. In so far, therefore, as shop stewards decided to use industrial action in particular localities, there could be no question of their acting contrary to 'union policy and rules.' On the contrary they were promoting union policy.

The conclusion appears clear on the evidence, and was found by the court and substantially accepted by Buckley L.J., that before the events in question there was a general implied authority for the shop stewards to protect their men's wages and jobs by blacking.

[Lord Wilberforce then considered whether the union had disobeyed the injunctions granted by the NIRC:]

The final question, therefore, is whether the evidence proves that at any time after

March 23, 1972, the union withdrew from shop stewards at Liverpool or at Hull the whole or any part of their general authority and discretion to organise blacking on the union's behalf in support of its policy of reserving stuffing and stripping containers.

To be effective in law a withdrawal or curtailment of an existing actual authority of an agent must be communicated by the principal to the agent in terms which the agent would reasonably understand as forbidding him to do that which he had previously been authorised to do on the principal's behalf. One is looking therefore for some communication to the shop stewards, by some officer or committee entitled to give them instructions on behalf of the union, couched in language which they would understand as being an order by the union to stop organising the blacking by members of the union of vehicles operated by the appellant companies. . . .

The members of the court [NIRC], with their special knowledge and experience of industrial relations, took the view that 'advice,' unaccompanied by any suggestion of disciplinary action if the advice was not taken, was not sufficient to make a shop steward reasonably understand that he was forbidden to do what he had previously been doing with the authority of the union. The officials of the union explained in the proceedings upon review why they had not taken any more positive steps to withdraw the authority of the shop stewards to continue the blacking of Heatons and Craddocks and, in particular, why the withdrawal of the shop stewards' credentials in the event of their failure to follow the advice was never even suggested to the shop stewards as a step which the union might take. The court accepted that, at any rate in Hull where the local officers' attempts at persuasion were rather more positive than at Liverpool, these officers genuinely believed that, from the union's point of view, it would not be good policy to bring the question of the authority of the shop stewards to a head. But though understandable, this only serves to confirm the view of the court that there was no withdrawal of the shop stewards' authority to continue blacking communicated to them in terms which would be reasonably understood by them as forbidding them to continue.

It is not necessary to consider whether any step, short of withdrawing the credentials of shop stewards in the event of their continuing the blacking in the face of express orders, as distinct from 'advice' to stop it, given by the appropriate committee or officer of the union, would have sufficed; for no such orders were ever given.

Whilst the proceedings against the union arising out of events at Liverpool and Hull had been under way, other sets of proceedings arising out of a similar dispute in London had also been begun, but this time against the individual organizers of the unofficial action rather than against the union (see *Churchman* v. *JSSC* [1972] ICR 222; *Midland Cold Storage* v. *Turner*, ibid., 230; *Midland Cold Storage* v. *Steer*, ibid., 435). Eventually, injunctions were granted by the NIRC against some of the individuals concerned. These were disobeyed and the individuals were gaoled for contempt of court. The imprisonment occurred after the decision of Court of Appeal in the *Heatons* case, but before that of the House of Lords. The imprisonment of the dockers' leaders led to a general dock strike and widespread sympathy action from workers in other industries, and brought the TUC close to calling a general strike. On the morning of the decison of the House of Lords in the *Heatons* case, however, the National Industrial Relations Court released the dockers' leaders, although they had neither apologized for their past contempt nor promised not to repeat it, on the grounds that the primary method of enforcement of the prohibitions in the IRA 1971 should be against the funds of organizations rather than against individuals.

Two points should be made about the *Heatons* litigation. First, it is usual to discuss the removal of the unions' immunity in terms of the exposure of the unions' funds to liability for damages. This is the problem to which EA 1982, ss.16 and 17, are directed. But the removal of the unions' special protection makes it equally possible for the employer to seek an interlocutory injunction against the union. This is demonstrated by the *Heatons* litigation, and it is a consequence of the EA 1982 as much as it was of the IRA 1971. Indeed, under the IRA 1971 it was perhaps more attractive to an employer to seek an injunction against the union than against the individual, if he thought that there was any danger of the injunction being disobeyed. The union, if enjoined, had to take strong measures to end the industrial action (cf. Lord Wilberforce's remarks about the withdrawal of the shop stewards' credentials) and, if it failed to do so, it might be fined for contempt and its assets sequestrated to pay the fine, if the fine was not paid voluntarily (see *Con-Mech (Engineers) Ltd* v. *AUEW (No.* 3) [1974] ICR 464).[1] This constituted a strong form of pressure upon the union, but it carried none of the odium that imprisonment of an individual for contempt of court involves. As the Green Paper put it, perhaps somewhat cynically, 'this procedure carries the risk that individuals may be moved to seek martyrdom by deliberately ignoring an injunction, with the risk that new and emotive grounds might then be provided to widen and prolong the dispute' (para. 134). This sort of reasoning certainly seems to have influenced the NIRC in its decision to release the dockers and to encourage plaintiffs to sue unions instead.

Of course, proceeding against the union will be attractive for an employer only so far as the union is subject to a wide vicarious liability. Under the IRA 1971 the *Heatons* case established such a wide liability. This brings us to the second point about the House of Lords' judgment. It seems highly likely that it was much influenced by the events surrounding the gaoling of the dockers. The appeal from the Court of Appeal was heard very quickly; judgment was delivered only seven days after the close of argument; and Lord Wilberforce delivered a joint opinion of all their lordships. Perhaps this haste explains the awkward jump in his reasoning. Whilst it must be correct in principle to interpret trade-union rule-books in the light of customary practices, for the rule-book alone would provide only an incomplete and inaccurate guide to the union's living constitution, and whilst it is undoubtedly correct that 'there is . . . no a priori reason why the members of a union should not agree that shop stewards should be authorised by all the members to take action to promote the interests of members employed in a particular work place', the evidence in fact adduced in the judgment to show that the members had implicitly

---

[1] Cf. the fines of £50,000 and £100,000 and the sequestration of assets imposed on the NGA in late 1983 in connection with the *Stockport Messenger* dispute.

authorized the stewards to take industrial action *on behalf of the union* in pursuit of union goals has never carried much conviction. The hypothetical union member might indeed not be 'content to be represented in an industrial dispute by someone who was not in a position to call for industrial action by him and his workmates in support of their claim', as Lord Wilberforce suggested, but he might well be content, as Lord Denning put it, to know that joining the union gave him the support of his workmates without caring much whether that committed the union outside the workplace to his support. The judgment in effect imposed liability upon the union for the unofficial acts of its stewards. That might have been good policy; it certainly enabled the NIRC to get out of a tight corner; it is much less clear that in any real sense the stewards were implicitly authorized to do what they did on behalf of the union.

The scheme of vicarious liability established by EA 1982, s.15, is at once more precise and apparently more limited than the principles enunciated in the *Heatons* case. The union is made liable for a tortious act 'if, but only if, it was authorised or endorsed by a responsible person' (s.15(2)). The statute then lists five, exclusive categories of 'responsible persons', whose authorization or endorsement alone can make the union liable. In respect of some of these categories the union can control the extent of its liability by appropriate provisions in its rule-book or by speedy repudiation of the officials' unlawful act. The contrast between the two approaches can perhaps best be highlighted by keeping in mind the question, in what circumstances under the 1982 Act would the union be liable for unofficial action instituted by shop stewards in pursuance of union policies?

The categories of responsible persons are as follows. The principal executive committee and the president or general secretary of the union constitute two of the categories (s.15(3) (*a*) and (*c*)). If the union is to be vicariously liable for anyone's acts, these two categories are bound to be included as constituting the main decision-making bodies or individuals in most unions. What should be noted, however, is that the union is made liable for unlawful acts authorized or endorsed by them, even if the authorization or endorsement constituted a breach of the union's rule-book (except perhaps if the act was *ultra vires* the union). The third category is persons 'empowered by the rules to authorise . . . or endorse acts of the kind in question' (s.15(3) (*b*)). Most union rule-books are cautious about empowering officials to authorize industrial action and, in any event, the extent of the union's potential liability for persons in this category lies within the union's own hands through its control of the rule-book. The final two categories are the ones that create the greatest potential liability for unions: tortious acts authorized or endorsed by employed officials of the union (but not shop stewards, who are not employed by the union) or by 'any committee of the union to whom an employed official regularly reports' (e.g. a district committee of the AUEW but not a shop stewards' committee) (s.15(3) (*d*) and (*e*)). The union can escape liability in these last two cases either if the official or committee was prevented by the rules from authorizing or endorsing acts of the kind in question or if the executive committee of the union or its general secretary or president repudiate the act which the lower official or committee has endorsed. The Act lays down rules about the need for speedy repudiation (s.15(5)(a)); speedy communication of the repudiation to the lower official or committee (s.15(5)(b)); and the need for the union through its committees and officials to conduct itself subsequently consistently with the repudiation (s.15(6)).

No doubt, the apparent narrowness of the liability imposed upon trade unions under this scheme is in fact capable of considerable expansion under the pressure of its application to particular situations. What, for example, amounts to authorization or endorsement? Is it sufficient for endorsement that the relevant official or committee of the union knew of the industrial action and did nothing to stop it or is some more active and formal step required? Does repudiation of an unlawful act by the top officials or committee of a union necessitate the strikers being ordered to return to work or is it sufficient that the top officials dissociate the union from the action being taken? No doubt, the answers to these questions will depend to some extent upon the particular provisions of the rule-book of the union involved and its customary practice, but to the extent that passivity is held to amount to endorsement and activity is required for repudiation, judicial interpretation will reduce the gap between the practical operation of the provisions of the 1982 Act and of the *Heatons* principle.[1]

Assume, however, that the principles in the 1982 Act are interpreted in a fairly neutral way. The contrast between the impact of the Act and of the *Heatons* decision upon unions' behaviour in industrial disputes then appears to be a strong one. Under the *Heatons* principle it was very difficult for the union to escape *prima facie* liability for unofficial acts of the membership, at least if the acts were done in pursuit of agreed union policy. Pressure was then placed upon the union leadership to intervene in the unofficial dispute and to secure its resolution or, if that was not possible, to discipline those organizing the illegal action, perhaps to the point of withdrawing the credentials of the shop stewards involved (cf. the speech of Lord Wilberforce, above, p. 825). It was because the principles of vicarious liability operated under the *Heatons* doctrine so as to cause the union to intervene that the case was sometimes described as turning the union into a policeman of its members' actions. Under a strict and narrow construction of the 1982 Act, however, the pressure created by the legislation might seem to be not a pressure towards intervention in and control of unofficial action but towards the leadership's disassociation from and removal of support for unofficial action. The union's leadership will have to be careful to do nothing that is capable of being interpreted as endorsement of the illegal action and, if such endorsement is given by lower officials, they must be quickly repudiated. The union can escape liability, not only by ensuring compliance by its members with the law, but also, and perhaps more easily, by abandoning them to their own devices.

[1] For further discussion of these issues, see K. D. Ewing (1982) 11 *ILJ* 209.

Whether or not judicial interpretation of s.15 of EA 1982 will result in this strategy being effective at a technical level to avoid union liability, there must be grave doubt whether such a strategy would be compatible in the long run with the social purposes of trade unions. Members pay subscriptions to trade unions in order to have the union defend their interests, not in order to be abandoned by it. It seems unlikely that over a period of time any union leadership could consistently follow a policy of disassociation from unlawful, unofficial action without incurring great unpopularity with the membership of the union – nor indeed that it would be in the long-run interest of employers to encourage such an attitude on the part of union leaderships. It seems equally unlikely that intervention by the union leadership to negotiate a settlement of the dispute would have the confidence of the members if at the same time the union was repudiating the action of the unofficial strike leadership. Thus, one may suppose that, in a contest between legal pressures pushing the union leadership towards non-intervention and the internal political processes of the union – supported indeed by the employer's expectations of intervention derived from his collective bargaining arrangements with the union – pushing the leadership in the opposite direction, the pressures towards intervention would triumph and the union would, at least in significant cases of unofficial action, have no choice but to run the risk of legal liability.

However this may turn out, a bizarre feature of the drafting of s.15 of EA 1982 is that its scheme of vicarious liability does not apply to all situations in which the issue will have to be faced. Section 15 applies only to actions 'in tort', so that it has no application where a union is joined as a third party to an unfair dismissal claim under the provisions of the new s.26A of EPCA 1978 (inserted by EA 1982, s.11). See above, p. 655. Nor does the statutory scheme apply to all actions in tort, but only to actions based on the grounds specified in TULRA 1974, s.13(1), or conspiracy to do such acts. The scheme would thus not apply to actions for interference with business by unlawful means where the unlawful means were something other than the acts covered by TULRA 1974, s.13(1). As we have seen above (pp. 750–55), this is potentially a very large area of liability. In these cases the statute is silent as to the principles of vicarious liability that should be applied, and it might be thought that the common-law principles of the *Heatons* case would again be applicable. That the issue will have to be decided as a matter of common law is clear; it is less obvious that the *Heatons* case will be applied in an unmodified way. First, Lord Wilberforce himself in his judgment (above, p. 823) was careful to restrict his speech to vicarious liability for the unfair industrial practices of the 1971 Act. Although it may seem odd to contemplate different treatment of statutory and common-law torts, Lord Wilberforce may perhaps have been intending to indicate the extent to which his thinking about vicarious liability for the unfair industrial practices was influenced by the overall structure of the 1971 Act. Second, the *Heatons* case itself seemed to be modified somewhat by the subsequent House of Lords' decision in *General Aviation Services (UK) Ltd* v.

TGWU [1976] IRLR 225, a case decided on facts occurring during the life of the 1971 Act. In this case the union was held not to be liable for the unofficial acts of a shop stewards' committee at Heathrow. Each case had to be decided on its facts. In this case the facts indicated that, although it was union policy that GAS should leave the airport, it was also union policy that this should be achieved through the established negotiating machinery. Hence, it could not be said that the stewards had implied authority to take industrial action to exclude GAS from the airport. Thus, even if the *Heatons* case is to be applied where the statutory scheme is inapplicable, the exact processes by which in law the authority of stewards is established have still to be settled.

In July 1983 the government proposed to introduce a further set of conditions which would add to the difficulties faced by a trade union seeking to render itself free from liability in tort. The reasoning now was not based upon the desirability of a union's exercising control over its members, but upon the need for strikes, particularly national strikes and strikes in essential services, to take place only with the support of the majority of those required to take part in the action. Consequently, after canvassing various possibilities in the Green Paper, *Democracy in Trade Unions*, the government in July 1983 announced its intention to make the union's immunity in tort depend upon the support of the union members concerned being tested in a secret ballot. The requirement would be that a ballot be held, not that any particular result be achieved in the ballot. On the other hand, holding a ballot would not by itself confer complete immunity upon the union. Without the ballot the union would have no immunity; with the ballot the union would have such immunity as was conferred upon individuals. In short the ballot would be an *additional* requirement for unions to observe where they had authorized or endorsed industrial action that was unlawful at common law. Only where the industrial action was not in breach of contract would a ballot not be required. If these proposals are implemented in this form,[1] then in a short space of time the legal protection afforded to trade unions will have undergone a revolution. Until 1982 the union had a special and almost complete immunity against liability in tort – indeed a union privilege, as Kahn-Freund called it (*Labour and the Law*, 2nd edn, 1977, p. 274); the EA 1982 equated the legal protections of individuals and unions. The proposals described above would subject trade unions to special and burdensome procedural requirements as the price of the reduced immunity.

4 Secondary action

In recent years the term secondary action has generally come to mean industrial action taken by workers employed by an employer who is not a party to the trade dispute. This is a central element of the definition of 'secondary action' in EA 1980, s.17(2). Although the enactment of that section was the first occasion on which a precise definition of secondary action was provided

---

[1] See now Appendix.

by Parliament, indirect regulation of secondary action can be seen to have been an inherent feature of our labour law for some time. We have already seen (above, p. 723) how the failure of Parliament in 1906 to give protection in respect of inducement of breaches of commercial contracts came to be rationalized in the 1950s and 1960s as a way of imposing liability in respect of secondary action, although, as the Donovan Commission pointed out, this result was achieved only in a rather haphazard and unprincipled way (see paras. 888–94). Nevertheless, in s.98 of the IRA 1971 this distinction was given statutory blessing when it became an unfair industrial practice to induce a breach of a commercial contract entered into between the primary employer and another employer, unless that other employer was a party to the dispute or had 'taken any action in material support of a party to it' (s.98(2)(*b*)). TULRA 1974 repealed the IRA 1971 and restored the protection of the TDA 1906 as far as inducing breach of contract was concerned. TULRA 1976 extended the statutory protection to all classes of contract, but, as we have seen (above, p. 816), the Court of Appeal after 1976 prevented the complete achievement of the aims of Parliament in 1976 by introducing, via interpretation of the concept of furtherance of a trade dispute, a distinction between more and less remote types of secondary action, the former not enjoying statutory protection under the Court of Appeal's decisions. The Court of Appeal's interpretation of furtherance of a trade dispute was overthrown by the House of Lords in 1979 and 1980 (above, p. 817), but in a way the Court of Appeal was ultimately vindicated. The government elected in 1979 decided to legislate on secondary action once it became clear that the House of Lords was not going to relieve them of this task, and the policy they chose to embody in s.17 of EA 1980 was not that of the TDA 1906 (or the modified version embodied in the IRA 1971) but that of the Court of Appeal.[1]

Before looking at the provisions of s.17 in detail it is worth asking why secondary action should have become an object of attention for those wishing to have a more restrictive framework of industrial conflict law. It is essential to realize that secondary action (as defined above) is not always taken for the same purposes. The traditional aim of secondary action has been to supplement the pressure being brought by the employees of the primary employer to bear upon their employer and has thus been resorted to when the action taken by the primary employees has been for some reason less than fully effective *vis-à-vis* the primary employer. A good example is provided by the facts of *D. C. Thomson & Co.* v. *Deakin* (above, p. 724). The employer had followed a policy of requiring his employees not to join any trade union and of dismissing those he discovered had joined. When a particular employee was dismissed for membership, the degree of economic pressure his fellow unionists employed by the same employer could bring to bear was naturally very small, because there were so few of them. Consequently, his union appealed to their members employed elsewhere and to members of other

[1] See the Working Paper on Secondary Industrial Action, reproduced in *The Times*, 20 February 1980.

unions to boycott the primary employer by not handling supplies destined for or coming from Thomson's. The argument in favour of proscribing such secondary action is usually put in terms of the need to protect the 'neutrality' of secondary employers, who are seen as not involved in the primary dispute (cf. the arguments about the neutrality of primary employers in disputes between groups of workers). This type of argument has been the subject of a penetrating analysis by two American authors, whose views are of particular interest given the long-standing restrictions on secondary boycotts that US federal labour law contains.

> Summers and Wellington, *Cases and Materials on Labor Law* (1968), pp. 279–81

The elusive term 'secondary boycott' carries two connotations, one factual and the other legal. The factual connotation is one of indirect attack through a third person – the bringing of pressure on one person in order to exert pressure on another with whom the underlying dispute exists. The legal connotation is one of illegality, for the term is a word of opprobrium to label that which is deemed illegal. The factual and legal connotations are not necessarily coextensive and the double image of the term has blurred analysis. Moreover, inquiry often has been into whether conduct is 'primary' or 'secondary', and this in turn has often seemed to be a search for confusion in a semantic wilderness.

A good starting place for analysis is a recognition that a secondary boycott, however defined, is simply another device for bringing economic pressure on an employer with whom the union has a dispute. Like a strike, the secondary boycott is an exercise of the union's economic strength to prevent the employer from continuing operations until he reaches an agreement with the union. The very premise of free collective bargaining is that terms and conditions of employment shall be determined by the bargaining power of the parties – by their relative economic strength. To curtail secondary boycotts is to deprive unions of an element of their strength, to make them enter the economic struggle with one hand tied. This leads us to what may be the central problem and one which goes close to the heart of free collective bargaining: Why should unions be deprived of this economic device? Why should they not be free to make full use of their economic strength?

The traditional justification for restricting the use of secondary boycotts is the protection of neutrals. Though appeals in the name of innocent third persons evoke our sympathy, they do not illuminate our understanding. For in labour disputes innocent people are always being hurt. An elevator operator's strike makes innocent tenants walk, a carpenter's strike may throw plumbers out of work, and an auto worker's strike may bankrupt car dealers. These are considered part of the cost of free collective bargaining, and innocent third persons bear these costs because of the values which they, as part of the public, receive from preserving collective bargaining. Only when the strike creates a national emergency by threatening the national health or safety does the law intervene. Moreover, it it is not always clear that the secondary person against whom the pressure is directed is entirely innocent or completely neutral. A clothing store may profit from the sweatshop wages of the suit manufacturer, the trucking company, which hauls finished goods from a struck plant has a hollow claim of neutrality, and a builder who subcontracts to a non-union plumbing contractor wears a tattered cloak of innocence.

Another justification sometimes given for restricting secondary boycotts is that such restriction confines the area of the dispute in order to limit its disruptive effects – to prevent what has been graphically described as 'the metastasis of labor disputes'. (See Lesnick, 'The Gravamen of the Secondary Boycott', 62 *Colum. L. Rev.* 1363, 1415 (1962).) Senator Taft argued that if secondary action were not limited, 'there can be a chain reaction that will tie up the entire United States in a series of sympathetic strikes': 2 *LMRA* Leg. Hist. 1107. One may think in terms of quarantining the dispute or defining the area of economic competition. But the metaphor misleads for it focuses on the union's action rather than on the conflict's economic repercussions. A draymen's strike may be felt by every business man in the city, and the effects of a steel strike may radiate to remote parts of the economy, but the union's action is neither curbed nor tailored to quarantine the impact of the strike. More important, the metaphors misrepresent the function of secondary action. No matter how widely the union spreads the dispute, the purpose remains the same – to prevent the primary employer from continuing operations until he has reached an agreement with the union. Normally, all a union seeks to achieve by secondary action is the equivalent of a fully effective strike of the primary employer; and all the union asks of the 'neutral' is that he act as if the primary employer were in fact closed by a strike.

It is clear from the above passage, especially its last paragraph, that the authors have in mind the situation we have been discussing, namely, one where the sole objective of the union is to close down the primary employer's operations until some compromise is reached on the union's claim. However, over the last fifteen years or so a form of secondary action has developed, intimately associated with governments' pursuit of incomes policies, in which the unions' objectives appear to go beyond the closure of the primary employer and to embrace more general disruption of economic life in the industrial sector in which the primary employer is operating. This dramatic extension of unions' goals is explicable in those situations, usually involving public sector employers, in which the closure of the primary employer, often easily achieved, advances the union's claim very little. This is because government, in order to achieve its incomes policy targets, is prepared to direct the employer not to concede the claim and is further prepared, at least in the short term, to save the employer from the financial consequences of the industrial action. The classical pattern of collective bargaining assumes the employer is master in his own house and that economic pressure applied to him is being applied against the person taking the decision the union wishes to influence. In major public sector confrontations this is by no means always the case: the government controls the purse strings and may decide as a matter of political judgment that only a certain level of increase is acceptable. The union is then tempted to respond in a more political way, in particular by spreading the industrial dispute so as to disrupt the life of the community and create political pressure upon the government to settle. The logic of this situation could drive a union into calling for secondary action in areas wholly unconnected with the primary dispute, or even to a general strike, but in fact secondary action in such situations has tended to occur in the same or adjacent economic sectors. Thus, in 1980 the steel unions in dispute with the British Steel Corporation called out their members employed in private steel firms, irrespective of whether or not the private company was supplying steel to a customer who had previously been supplied by the BSC (see above, p. 800). In these cases, it is *not* sufficient for the neutral to 'act as if the primary employer were in fact closed by a strike'. The closure of the neutral itself is an aim of the union's pressure. Such action is clearly open to the criticism made in *Trade Union Immunities* (para. 141) that 'secondary action is being used, not for its traditional purpose of putting commercial pressure on the employer in dispute, but indiscriminately to spread the consequences of the dispute to as many people as possible, to inflict damage on the economy and to put pressure on the community as a whole'. What this criticism lacks is any explanation as to why trade unionists should engage in such apparently irrational action, and, when an explanation is provided along the lines suggested above, it becomes clear that legal restrictions upon secondary action operate not only to protect the life of the community (a topic to which we return below, p. 868) but also to secure the implementation of incomes policies, especially in the public sector.

There is a third category of secondary action, which is often referred to as sympathetic action and which is not entirely distinct from the second category. The aim of sympathetic action is to express the support of the secondary strikers for and their solidarity with the primary employees. They do not aim to disrupt supplies to or from the primary employer nor is the aim usually to produce widespread economic dislocation. Sympathetic action is essentially demonstrative in its intention, but it may, of course, affect public opinion and hence put political pressure on government to produce a settlement favourable to the employees. A good recent example of sympathy action was the planned series of 24-hour stoppages in Fleet Street in support of the nurses' wage claim in the National Health Service. No doubt, in some cases the industrial action may have elements present in it of all three of the categories mentioned above.

In all three cases discussed above – the blacking of newsprint supplies by the employees of Bowaters in the *D. C. Thomson* case, the strike action by the employees in the private steel sector in 1980 and the 24-hour stoppages by the print workers in Fleet Street in support of the health workers – the industrial action that was the subject of the litigation was secondary in the sense that we have suggested is the most common meaning attached to the phrase 'secondary action', i.e. it was action taken by employees not employed by a party to the trade dispute. As we shall see, it is the inducement of employees to take secondary action in this sense, in breach of their contracts of employment, that can lead to liability in tort as a consequence of s.17 of the 1980 Act. However, there are a number of other possible definitions[1] of what makes action secondary and one of these has become important in recent years in

---

[1] In *Hadmor Productions* v. *Hamilton* [1981] ICR 690 (CA) Lord Denning regarded as secondary industrial action taken by employees at their own place of work in a dispute with their own employer because 'it directly interferes with the business of any customer or supplier or other trader – not a party to the dispute – who suffers by it', i.e. in this case the maker of the programmes which the employees wished their employer not to transmit. See above, p. 747.

relation to one particular form of industrial action, namely, picketing. If employees who are on strike send some of their number to picket the premises of another employer, it is often referred to as 'secondary' picketing. Such picketing is said to be secondary not because of who is participating in the activity, but rather because of the place where the activity takes place, i.e. because the employees are not picketing at their own place of work. It is said to be secondary picketing even if the pickets do not succeed in involving any employees of the other employer in their industrial dispute. Indeed such a tight geographical definition of secondariness would render picketing secondary when employees picket premises of their own employer other than those at which they are themselves employed. Again, it is possible to see traditional and modern uses of secondary picketing. Uses of secondary picketing falling within the classical pattern of collective bargaining would be picketing designed to encourage employees of another employer (or lorry drivers calling at those premises) to black supplies to the primary employer or to black supplies destined elsewhere that are in substitution for supplies that would otherwise have been provided by the struck employer. A non-classical use of secondary picketing would be to spread the dispute to other employers in order to increase the political pressure on the government. The picketing by the miners of power stations, including oil-burning power stations, in pursuit of their national wage claim in 1972 or by the lorry drivers in the 'hire and reward' sector of the road haulage industry of manufacturers who ran their own transport fleets in 1978–79 probably was motivated by both a desire to close sources of substitute supply and to spread the industrial action more widely.

The legality of secondary picketing is determined, as we shall see in the next section of this chapter, primarily by s.16 of EA 1980, which contains a geographical definition of secondariness. However, because secondary picketing may often result, if it is successful, in the persuasion of employees not employed by a party to the dispute into the taking of industrial action, the general restrictions on secondary action contained in s.17 of the 1980 Act are also relevant to picketing.

With this preamble, we can now turn to examine in detail the provisions of s.17. The core case of secondary action occurs when a person induces employees of an employer who is not a party to the dispute to break their contracts of employment (s.17(2)). However, the definition is wide enough to include inducement falling short of breach (interference), threats to induce a breach or to interfere with performance, actual interference, and threats to break or interfere with performance of a contract of employment. In short, all the extensions of the common law which we discussed above under inducing breach of contract and intimidation (pp. 722–45) are covered in the definition of secondary action. For ease of reference we shall use the term 'inducing breach' to cover all these situations, unless the context otherwise requires. However, secondary action is not in itself rendered unprotected. The protection against liability for inducing breaches of contracts of employment, first laid down in the TDA 1906, is not removed. The significance of secondary action in the scheme created by s.17 is that statutory protection is removed against liability for inducing (in the broad sense) breaches of commercial contracts where the inducement of the breach of the commercial contract is brought about by secondary action. This is done by saying that in such cases s.13(1) of TULRA 1974 shall not apply to the inducement of breach of the commercial contract (s.17(1)). Thus, where a trade union official asks employees of a secondary employer to black (in breach of their contracts of employment) supplies to the primary employer, s.17 of EA 1980 creates no risk that the official will be successfully sued by the secondary employer for inducing the breach of the contracts of employment. However, if as a result of the secondary action the secondary employer is put in breach of his commercial contract with the primary employer, either secondary or primary employer[1] might sue the official for procurement of the breach of that commercial contract by secondary action. The effect of s.17 is thus to remove statutory protection from a particular – no doubt the most common – form of indirect[2] inducement or procurement of breach of commercial contract.

If section 17 stopped at this point, its effect would be to remove protection in all the three cases of secondary action discussed above, where the secondary action led to procurement of breaches of commercial contracts. The section contains, however, three gateways back to the full protection of TULRA 1974, s.13(1), of which two need to be discussed at this point. The third, relating to picketing, is discussed below (p. 853). The effect of s.17(3) and (4) is to restore protection to certain forms of the traditional type of secondary action falling within the first category discussed above, but not to provide protection for any examples of secondary action falling within our second or third categories. In relation to the first category, the policy of s.17(3) was described in the government working paper which preceded s.17 as one of continuing protection in respect of secondary industrial action taken 'by employees of those first suppliers or customers of the employer in dispute who were not themselves party to the dispute.'[3] Consequently, s.17(3) provides that secondary action is protected if its purpose is directly to prevent or disrupt the supply during the dispute of goods or services between the party to the dispute and the employer 'under the contract of employment to which the secondary action relates'. In addition the secondary action must be likely to achieve this purpose. In this context, therefore, the subjective approach of the House of Lords to the definition of purpose is reversed (see above, p. 817).

Thus, the official who asks employees of a supplier in direct contractual relations with the primary employer to black supplies to the primary employer

---

[1] On the question of who can sue for the tort of inducing breach of a contract see above, p. 731.

[2] On the distinction between direct and indirect forms of inducement see above, p. 724. The enactment of s.17 may reduce the judicial tendency to find the tort to have been committed directly because of information passed by the organizers of the action to the secondary employer. See above, p. 732.

[3] Op. cit., para. 18.

would probably continue to be protected. On the other hand, on the facts of *Express Newspapers Ltd* v. *McShane* (above, p. 816), the blacking of the Press Association copy by the employees of the national newspapers would not be protected if (as might or might not be the case) it caused a breach of a commercial contract between the PA and the national newspaper proprietors, since neither of them was a party to the dispute between the provincial newspaper employers and their employees. In the latter case the union's objective of ending the supply of copy from the Press Association to the provincial newspaper proprietors was pursued by organizing industrial action on the part of employees of too remote an employer (Express Newspapers). Consequently, the secondary action by the employees of Express Newspapers could not, should the facts be repeated today, fall within the provisions of s.17(3).

It seems clear that this is the distinction the legislators of s.17(3) intended to draw. There must be some doubt, however, as to whether it has been clearly drawn by the actual provisions of s.17, and, in particular, whether all cases of the disruption of supplies between the party to the dispute and his first suppliers or customers have been brought within the protection of s.17(3). In order to come within s.17(3), the purpose of the industrial action must be 'directly' to disrupt the supply of goods or services and 'directly' is defined in s.17(6)(b) as prevention or disruption 'otherwise than by means of preventing or disrupting the supply of goods or services by or to any other person'. This raises the problem of intermediate carriage contracts. Suppose the supplier has a contract with a haulier for the delivery of components to the primary employer and blacking by the secondary employer's workers puts the secondary employer in breach of the haulage contract or at least causes some interference with its performance. In this case it might be argued that the secondary action has disrupted the supply of haulage services between two persons, neither of whom is a party to the dispute and both of whom, therefore, could sue the organizers of the secondary action for inducing breach of the haulage contract. Moreover, the disruption of the supplies between the component maker and the primary employer has not been achieved 'directly' and so the procurement of the breach of the supply contract cannot be brought within the terms of s.17(3) either. Both component maker and primary employer could then sue the organizers of the secondary action because of its impact upon the supply contract. The acceptance of this argument would come close to destroying the 'first customer, first supplier' gateway to legality since such intermediate contracts must be common. The solution, strongly argued for by Professor Wedderburn ('Secondary Action and Gateways to Legality: A Note' (1981) 10 *ILJ* 113,115), might be to lay stress upon the opening words of s.17(3), which legalize secondary action according to its purpose or principal purpose. If the principal purpose of the action organized by the union official in the example given is to disrupt supplies between secondary and primary employers, then the action does not cease to be protected even if, as a consequence, even an intended consequence of it, the performance of other commercial contracts is interfered with. Any fanciful claims as to purpose that a union official might put forward are controlled by the requirement in s.17(3)(b) that the secondary action must be likely to achieve the declared purpose.

A similar solution might be available to the problem raised by the definition of 'the supply of goods or services' in s.17(6)(a). This is defined as the supply between two persons 'in pursuance of a contract between them subsisting at the time of the secondary action'. It might be thought that, if there is no contract between primary and secondary employers, then the organizers of the secondary action could not in any case be liable. However, it is apparent on a moment's reflection that the secondary action might bring about the disruption of some other commercial contract, the parties to which might wish to sue the organizers. Would the organizers lose the protection of s.17(3) because the supply of goods between secondary and primary employer did not take place in pursuit of a contract between them, or is it enough that the purpose of the organizers was to disrupt such a contract (thinking it existed)? In the latter case the organizers would have to prove that such was their genuine purpose (and so they would have to explain how they came to labour under a misapprehension about the relations between primary and secondary employer), but the latter solution does to some degree reduce the arbitrariness of s.17(3). However, in *Marina Shipping Ltd* v. *Laughton* [1982] ICR 215 (*The Antama*) and *Merkur Island Shipping Corporation* v. *Laughton* [1983] ICR 490, the courts seemed to reject this approach and thus to cast doubt also upon the solution to the problem raised by the definition of 'directly' suggested above.

Merkur Island Shipping Corporation v. *Laughton* [1983]
ICR 490 (HL)

The plaintiffs owned a ship, the *Hoegh Apapa*, which flew a flag of convenience. A member of the crew complained to the International Transport Workers' Federation about the low wages paid by the owners. When the ship arrived in Liverpool, the defendant official of the ITF secured that tugmen in breach of their contracts of employment refused to assist the ship to leave the port, unless the ITF's demands were met. During the period in question the ship had been time-chartered by the owners to Leif Hoegh & Co. and sub-chartered to Ned Lloyd. The court held that the contract for the supply of the tug services had been made by agents on behalf of the sub-charterers. The owners sought an injunction to restrain the interference with the performance of the time-charter between themselves and Leif Hoegh & Co. brought about by the secondary action. (The nature of the owners' claim at common law is discussed above at p. 730).

LORD DIPLOCK: . . . Section 17(1) lays down two conditions which must be satisfied in order to bring an act within the sub-species from which immunity is withdrawn. The first, in paragraph (a), is simple. The subsisting contract of which the non-performance of a primary obligation is procured must not be a contract of employment. A charterparty, whether a time charter or a voyage or consecutive voyage charter, is not a contract of employment. The second condition, in paragraph (*b*), is highly complex since it brings in also subsection (2) which in turn, for the purposes of the instant case, brings in subsection (3), which in its turn brings in subsection (6).

To start with there must be 'secondary action' as defined in subsection (2). That subsection, in effect, defines secondary action in such a way as to single out from the species of torts referred to in section 13 (1) of the Act of 1974 a sub-species in which the means of interference with the performance of a contract is to procure employees of an employer who is not a party to a trade dispute to break their contracts of employment with that employer. Withdrawal of immunity is confined to this sub-species. Subsection (3), however, then goes on to limit the withdrawal of immunity to a sub-species of secondary action that is defined by reference to its purpose and the likelihood of achieving that purpose; but the description of the purpose incorporates two phrases, 'supply . . . of goods or services' between two persons and 'directly to prevent or disrupt' such supply. The meaning of these phrases is to be found in subsection (6).

Reading into subsection (3) (*a*) the definitions of those phrases from subsection (6) the paragraph would run (inelegantly) as follows:

> (3) Secondary action satisfies the requirements of this subsection if – (*a*) the purpose or principal purpose of the secondary action was to prevent or disrupt, during the trade dispute, the supply of goods or services between parties to a contract where (i) the contract pursuant to which such services are agreed to be supplied is a contract then subsisting between the employer who is a party to the trade dispute and the employer under the contract of employment to which the secondary action relates, and (ii) the prevention or disruption of the supply of goods or services between those parties is brought about by some means other than by preventing or disrupting the supply of goods or services by or to any other person than a party to such contract.

My Lords, in the instant case the contract concerned was the charter. The employers who were parties to the trade dispute were the shipowners. The charter was a contract for the supply of services, to which the shipowners and the charterers alone were parties. The shipowners were not parties to any subsisting contract with the tugowners. The tugowners were the employers under the contract of employment to which the secondary action related. So the requirements of subsection (3) (*a*) were not satisfied; nor would those requirements have been satisfied if the contract with the tugowners had been made directly between the tugowners and the charterers pursuant to clause 8 of the charter instead of being made between the tugowners and the sub-charterers. Neither the charterers nor the sub-charterers were parties to the trade dispute, of which the subject matter was the terms and conditions upon which the shipowners employed the ship's crew and, in particular, the wages paid by the shipowners to them.

So, I agree with the Court of Appeal that in the instant case there was secondary action within the meaning of subsection (2) of section 17 which did not satisfy the requirements of subsection (3) (the only relevant subsection), with the result that the immunity from liability in tort granted by section 13 of the Act of 1974 was withdrawn by subsection (1) of section 17 of the Act of 1980. It is a very winding path that leads to this conclusion but the maze through which it winds has only one centre, which, when one reaches it, is unmistakable.

It was submitted on behalf of ITF, although counsel was at a loss to find any justification for this submission in the language of section 17 itself, that Parliament cannot have intended that the employer who was an actual party to the trade dispute should be included in the beneficiaries of the withdrawal of immunity from liability in tort from those who procured the interference with the performance of a contract to which he was himself a party. For my part, in the absence of any words expressing such a limitation upon the withdrawal of immunity for liability, I can see no reason for supposing that Parliament nevertheless sub silentio intended such a limitation to be understood. On the contrary, as a matter of legislative history, the employer who was the party to the trade dispute was the obvious plaintiff whose right of action in tort for procuring a breach of a contract of employment by his own employees was taken away by section 3 of the Trade Disputes Act 1906. There is no compelling reason for supposing that if a contract into which he himself had entered satisfied the criteria laid down in section 17 (1) for withdrawal of immunity from liability in tort on the part of anyone who procured an interference with its performance, Parliament intended to deprive the employer who was party to the dispute of the benefit of the withdrawal of that immunity.

The result in practice of these two decisions is, it must be admitted, rather arbitrary. In part the arbitrariness results, as has already been suggested (above, p. 791), from using breach of contract to define the limits between lawful and unlawful industrial action, but even within that way of proceeding it adds a refinement of absurdity to place organizers of industrial action in a position where, in order to determine their legal position, they need a degree of expertise in the analysis of commercial contractual relations that most of them do not, and ought not to be required to, possess.[1]

The gateway to legality provided by s.17(3) is supplemented to some degree by s.17(4). Here secondary action is lawful if its purpose is to disrupt the supply of goods or services between any person and, not the party to the dispute, but an associated employer of the employer in dispute, provided that the goods or services are being supplied in substitution for goods and services that would have been supplied by the party to the dispute, and provided that the secondary action involves employees of either the associated employer or the other party to the supply. The secondary action must also be likely to achieve its purpose (s.17(4)(d)). Thus, if in a group of companies one company is closed by a strike and supplies to a customer are then provided by another company in the group, it would be legitimate for a trade-union official to persuade the employees of the customer to black the new supplies. The subsection does not grant a general licence for organizers of industrial action to black substituted goods or services, however, because these supplies must come from an associated employer. Associated employer is defined (TULRA 1974, s.30(5)) in terms of one company having (directly or indirectly) control of another or where a third person (directly or indirectly) has control of both companies. The definition is not apt either for small businesses (which may not be in the form of companies) or for the governmental or public service sector of the economy. See *Gardiner* v. *London Borough of Merton* [1980] IRLR

---

[1] See now also *Dimbleby & Sons Ltd* v. *NUJ* [1984] 1 All ER at p. 758.

472 (CA).

Thus, we have seen that there is some doubt as to how far our first category of secondary action can be brought within the provisions of s.17(3) or (4) of EA 1980, although it is clear that Parliament did intend to create an area within which some types of such action could still legally take place. Our second and third categories benefit from no such concession. Purely sympathetic action would seem no longer to be protected, since its aim is not to disrupt supplies to or from the primary employer. This was the conclusion the court arrived at in the case of the sympathy action taken by Fleet Street electricians in support of the nurses (see *Express Newspapers plc* v. *Mitchell* [1982] IRLR 465, which is reported, however, more on the point of contempt of court than on the point of unlawful secondary action. Indeed, it is not clear from the report which commercial contract was interfered with by the secondary action). Secondary action aimed at spreading the disruption rather than at increasing the pressure on the primary employer would also in most cases be deprived of immunity by s.17. Thus, on the facts of *Duport Steels Ltd* v. *Sirs* (above, p. 800) the inducement of breaches of commercial contracts caused by the calling out of the employees in the private sector of the steel industry would now be protected only in so far as the aim was confined to cutting off substitute supplies to BSC's customers from private sector companies associated with the BSC (s.17(4)) or in so far as the private sector employers were providing supplies to the BSC itself (s.17(3)) – the latter being unlikely since the strike at BSC was complete. The aim of simply cutting off the supply of steel to the British market would not be protected.

One should also note the impact of s.17 upon pure 'worker and worker' disputes (above, p. 805). In these cases the employer of the workers involved is not a party to the dispute, so that for a union official to call upon such a group of workers to take industrial action would be for him to engage in secondary action, as it is defined in s.17. If, in consequence, the employer was put in breach of a commercial contract with a third party, both employer and third party might be able to sue the organizer, subject to proof of the relevant degree of knowledge and intention (above, p. 731). It seems likely, however, that after 1982 the employer will simply argue that there is no trade dispute and base his action upon the inducement of the breach of the contract of employment.

Before leaving the subject of secondary action there is one fundamental problem that needs to be noted. Section 17 of the 1980 Act, and the above analysis of it, assume that it is unproblematic to determine whether an employer is a party to a trade dispute. If this is not so, or is not always so, then it may be difficult to know whether a union official, who has induced a group of employees to take industrial action in breach of their contracts of employment, has in fact organized secondary action. The assumption of the legislation clearly is that, if a union official seeks the support of employees other than those employed by the employer against whom the claim originally giving rise to the dispute was made, he does not thereby cause the secondary employer to become a party to the trade dispute to which the primary employer is party. In general, this will no doubt be the case, but, as s.98(3) of I R A 1971 recognized, there might be a range of situations where it was arguable that the 'secondary' employer was a party to the dispute, even though the union had made no claim against him. This might include cases where the outcome of the dispute would have a direct impact[1] upon the terms and conditions of employment of the secondary employer, where the primary employer was being supported in the dispute out of a fund to which the 'secondary' employer had contributed, or where the 'secondary' employer had provided aid to the primary employer, beyond existing contractual commitments, to enable the primary employer to continue to function.

Alternatively, even where it is accepted that the secondary employer is not a party to the trade dispute with the primary employer, it might be sought to be argued that, say, the union's demand that the secondary employer cease to supply the primary employer and the secondary employer's refusal to accede to that demand created a separate trade dispute with the secondary employer. The blacking imposed by the employees of the secondary employer would then be argued to have been imposed in furtherance of the dispute with the secondary, not the primary, employer. This is by no means an unreal way to describe the nature of the relationship between the union and the secondary employer, but it probably is unreal to regard the industrial action as imposed wholly in respect of the secondary employer's refusal to stop supplies and not at all in respect of the primary employer's dispute with his employees. Section 17(2) of E A 1980 requires only that secondary action be taken 'in relation to a trade dispute' and it would be difficult to argue in this example that the blacking was not imposed 'in relation to' the primary dispute, even if it was also being imposed in furtherance of a separate dispute with the secondary employer.

5 Picketing

The social phenomena of picketing bring together a number of separate strands of legal doctrine. We have already noted (above, p. 708) that picketing is an activity in the regulation of which the criminal law plays a substantial part because of the potential threat to public order that some instances of picketing present. Unlike strikes and most other forms of industrial action, which are purely internal to the workplace, picketing typically takes place on the highway or in some place (e.g. a private industrial estate) to which non-involved persons have access, and so there is sometimes a problem of regulating the impact of the picketing upon public rights of passage. Indeed the various statutory provisions, which we shall shortly examine, have to some extent protected picketing 'at or near' premises but never picketing on land against the will of the owner. See *Larkin* v. *Belfast Harbour Commissioners* [1908] 2 I R 214, recently applied in *British Airports Authority* v. *Ashton* [1983] I R L R

[1] Cf. the meaning of 'directly interested' in the context of the trade dispute disqualification from social security benefits (below, p. 941).

287 (DC). More important, whilst the aim of some forms of picketing is purely demonstrative, in many cases the pickets wish to achieve the result that persons or vehicles do not enter the place being picketed. If those being picketed agree with the pickets' aims, then no problem of public order usually arises, but it is the potential consequences of disagreement between pickets and picketed (as illustrated by the events at the Saltley Coke depot during the 1972 miners' strike or outside the Grunwick Laboratories in London in 1976/7) that police officers, union officials and employers always have in the back of their minds. On the civil side, because the aim of pickets is often to control access to or egress from premises, there is the potentiality of the employer having a claim in nuisance against the pickets, and, of course, the economic torts discussed in the previous chapter will be applicable. Pickets who persuade lorry drivers to turn back may be as much inducing them to break their contracts of employment as a union official who persuades the drivers to black deliveries to certain premises.

Historically, the law relating to picketing has seen two periods of development. At the turn of the last century, employers responded to the unionization of unskilled workers in the 'new unions' by the extensive use of blacklegs to defeat strikes. The strikers responded by large-scale picketing of the struck premises and some violent confrontations between pickets and blacklegs occurred. There was considerable litigation, both on the criminal and on the civil side, arising out of incidents of picketing, and it was not surprising that the TDA 1906 sought to deal with the matter. S.2(1) of the TDA 1906 provided: 'It shall be lawful for one or more persons, acting on their own behalf or on behalf of a trade union or of an individual employer or firm in contemplation or furtherance of a trade dispute, to attend at or near a house or place where a person resides or works or carries on business or happens to be, if they so attend merely for the purpose of peacefully obtaining or communicating information, or of peacefully persuading any person to work or abstain from working.' The section thus provided protection, within its limits, against both criminal and civil liability by means of the phrase 'it shall be lawful', in place of the phrase 'shall not be actionable' used elsewhere in the Act. The phrase 'it shall be lawful' is perhaps the nearest the legislature has come to the statement of a positive right for those taking industrial action.

This section was not an entirely new departure on the criminal side. Section 7 of the CPPA 1875 had provided, and still provides, a final version of various statutory criminal liabilities developed by Parliament during the nineteenth century to regulate picketing. S.7 makes it a criminal offence to do various acts 'with a view to compel any person to abstain from doing or to do any act which such other person has a legal right to do or abstain from doing', including where a person 'wrongfully and without legal authority . . . watches or besets the house or other place where such other person resides, or works, or carries on business, or happens to be, or the approach to such house or place . . .' (s.7(4)). By a proviso to s.7, however, attending at or near such a place 'in order merely to obtain or communicate information' was deemed not to be a watching or besetting. S.2 of the TDA 1906 replaced this proviso. S.2, unlike the proviso, covered peaceful persuasion to work or not to work as well as the obtaining or communicating of information, and the section provided a more general protection against criminal and civil liability and not just a defence to the liabilities created by s.7. Curiously, although s.7 of the CPPA 1875 remains on the statute book, the police rarely bring charges under it, perhaps because it does not create an arrestable offence, perhaps because of a preference on the part of the police for not using specific 'picketing' charges but rather general public order charges (obstruction of the highway, obstruction of a police officer in the execution of his duty, etc.). Thus, none of the more than 500 charges brought as a result of the picketing outside Grunwick Laboratories Ltd was brought under the 1875 Act, and hence the surprise when after the civil servants' strike a prosecution was initiated in Scotland against a striker under s.7(2) on the grounds that he 'persistently follow[ed] such other person about from place to place.'[1] However, as we shall see, s.7 has played an important part in the development of civil liability for nuisance.

In the inter-war period, at least after the General Strike of 1926, which involved quite a degree of picketing, there was a period of quiescence in labour relations. Even in the aftermath of the General Strike pressures for serious amendment of the 1906 Act were resisted by government, and so s.2, along with the other sections, continued on the statute book.[2] What is more interesting is that the pressures that developed in the 1950s and 1960s for a more restrictive framework of industrial conflict law did not initially focus on the law of picketing. The Donovan Commission devoted only a small space to the topic (see paras. 855–77) and s.134 of the IRA 1971 followed the policy, if not the format, of the 1906 Act, although it did implement a recommendation of the minority of the Commission that protection should not extend to picketing of a person's home (unless it was also his place of business). TULRA 1974, s.15 returned to both the policy and the format of the 1906 Act, whilst retaining the exclusion of a person's home.

However, by this time the restoration of the 1906 formula was being justified more as a holding operation than as an expression of a conviction that that Act contained the ideal solution to the problems of picketing. Shortly after the passing of the IRA 1971 picketing re-established itself as a major weapon of industrial conflict through its use by the miners in their national strike of 1972. The picketing during this strike was largely, but not universally, peaceful, but disorderly picketing occurred during the national building workers' strike later that year. Picketing has been a feature, sometimes large, sometimes small, of many national strikes since then. It was perhaps inevitable that with

---

[1] *Elsey* v. *Smith* [1983] IRLR 292 (an unsuccessful appeal against the Sheriff's decision finding the appellant guilty). S.7 is now being more widely used by the (independent) prosecuting authorities in Scotland.

[2] See G. W. McDonald, 'The Role of British Industry in 1926', Special Study I in M. Morris, *The General Strike* (1976).

the growth of national disputes in the 1970s, as compared with the earlier post-war period (see above, p. 702), picketing should be more often resorted to by trade unionists. It is one way that unions can try to ensure the greatest support for the strike amongst the relevant employees. More important, in the case of those disputes (discussed above, p. 833) where the government is in effect determining the level of increase that the employer may offer, picketing may be one of the methods used to spread the strike so as to increase the political pressure upon the government. Again, we can note that in the latter context restrictions upon picketing activity may operate both to protect the community from the impact of the strike and to insulate the government's incomes policy from political pressure for its norms to be relaxed.[1]

It is not surprising that the developments noted in the previous paragraph caused arguments for a more restrictive approach to be developed also in relation to picketing. Since the problem was initially perceived as a problem of public order, attention was focused upon the criminal law and the role of the police. At the same time, however, the TUC put forward arguments which it had been developing over a number of years, that the criminal law and police practice did not guarantee the effective exercise of the right to picket peacefully. The particular concern of the TUC was that persons in vehicles might drive through picket lines – sometimes, indeed, with police help – without the pickets having the chance to address them and so to atempt to persuade them not to proceed. Proposals to change the law, whether in a more restrictive or a more liberal direction, made, however, very little progress before 1980. In the case of those favouring restriction it was found to be very difficult, as the following cases suggest, to identify any form of behaviour by pickets that deserved to be treated as criminal and that was not already a crime. The decided cases suggested, somewhat ironically in view of the origin of s. 15 of TULRA 1974 as a proviso to the criminal liabilities created by s. 7 of the CPPA 1875, that the statutory immunity gave no protection against criminal liabilities, or at least, against any such liabilities that the police were actually likely to enforce. This conclusion tended to strengthen the argument of the TUC that in some cases the criminal law operated so as to prevent peaceful picketing. The counter-argument was that the police in practice usually permitted such picketing, and the response that they should therefore not object to being put under a duty to stop vehicles in order for pickets to approach the drivers foundered upon difficulties of drafting such a duty and, even more, upon strong police objections to being put under a duty to one side in an industrial dispute.

---

[1] Clearly, not all the well-known incidents of picketing in the 1970s can be explained by reference to incomes policies. The Grunwick dispute was not in this category. Rather, it was an example of a long-standing, if infrequently occurring, phenomenon: a strongly anti-union employer resisting at all costs the union's claim for recognition. See also the Roberts-Arundel dispute in 1966 and the Fine Tubes dispute in 1971.

Broome v. *DPP* [1974] I C R 84 (H L)

During a nationwide building strike the appellant, a union official, unsuccessfully sought to persuade a lorry driver not to deliver at a building site. Shortly afterwards the appellant saw the driver again, asked him to draw over to the side of the road and again attempted to persuade him not to deliver. After a brief conversation with the appellant the driver attempted to proceed into the site, but the appellant, by standing in front of the lorry, prevented him from so doing. A police officer arrived and arrested the appellant who refused to move out of the lorry's path. The appellant was charged with obstructing the highway contrary to s. 121 of the Highways Act 1959, but the justices dismissed the information.

LORD REID: . . . Returning to section 134 [of I RA 1971] I see no reason to construe it in any other than the usual way. One takes the ordinary and natural meaning of the words and applies that meaning. Subsection (2) is the operative provision. In enacts that conduct described in subsection (1) shall not of itself constitute an offence under any enactment. So if the appellant is to be convicted it must be shown that this conduct at the place where the alleged offence was committed exceeded any conduct to which the terms of subsection (1) can apply.

His attendance there is only made lawful by subsection (2) if he attended only for the purpose of obtaining or communicating information or 'peacefully persuading' the lorry driver. Attendance for that purpose must I think include the right to try to persuade anyone who chooses to stop and listen, at least in so far as this is done in a reasonable way with due consideration for the rights of others. A right to attend for the purpose of peaceful persuasion would be meaningless unless this were implied.

But I see no ground for implying any right to require the person whom it is sought to persuade to submit to any kind of constraint or restriction of his personal freedom. One is familiar with persons at the side of a road signalling to a driver requesting him to stop. It is then for the driver to decide whether he will stop or not. That, in my view, a picket is entitled to do. If the driver stops, the picket can talk to him but only for so long as the driver is willing to listen.

That must be so because if the picket had a statutory right to stop or to detain the driver that must necessarily imply that the Act has imposed on those passing along the road a statutory duty to stop or to remain for longer than they chose to stay. So far as my recollection goes it would be unique for Parliament to impose such a duty otherwise than by express words, and even if one envisages the possibility of such a duty being imposed by implication the need for it would have to be crystal clear. Here I can see no need at all for any such implication.

Without the protection of the section merely inviting a driver to stop and then, if he were willing to stop and listen, proceeding to try to persuade him not to go on, would in many cases be either an offence or a tort or both, particularly if more than a very few pickets were acting together. I see no reason to hold that the section confers any other right.

The justices speak of the appellant's 'statutory right peacefully to seek to persuade'. That is not an accurate or adequate statement of the provisions of the section. And their further statement that,

> his statutory right is meaningless unless the picket places himself in such a position that the person to be persuaded is obliged to stop and listen for a reasonable length of time

is for the reasons I have given wholly erroneous.

There was a suggestion that if a picket does not have a right to stop a driver or pedestrian the same result could be obtained lawfully by a large number of pickets gathering at the same place and doing nothing. The section does not limit the number of pickets and no limitation of numbers can be implied. So if a large number assemble it will not be physically possible in many cases for a driver or pedestrian to proceed.

But if a picket has a purpose beyond those set out in the section, then his presence becomes unlawful and in many cases such as I have supposed it would not be difficult to infer as a matter of fact that pickets who assemble in unreasonably large numbers do have the purpose of preventing free passage. If that were the proper inference then their presence on the highway would become unlawful. *Tynan's* case [1967] 1 QB 91 is a good example of this.

In *Kavanagh* v. *Hiscock* [1974] ICR 282 (DC) police formed a cordon on either side of the exit from a picketed hospital in order to allow the departure of a coach carrying workers who had taken over the strikers' jobs. The defendant objected to the fact that not even the four 'official' pickets were allowed inside the cordon (there were some thirty to forty pickets in all) and so could not approach the coach driver in order to persuade him to stop. The defendant consequently attempted to break through the cordon, was arrested and subsequently convicted of obstructing a police officer in the execution of his duty contrary to s.51 of the Police Act 1964. On appeal the defendant's counsel (Lord Gifford) argued that Lord Reid's speech (above) recognized a right of pickets to approach drivers of vehicles with a view to persuading them not to cross picket lines. The court, however, held that Lord Reid meant nothing more than 'that a picket who attends within the terms of the immunity conferred by the section does not lose his immunity simply because he tries to persuade anyone who chooses to stop and listen, to listen to him' (at p. 291A). On the question of whether the police were acting in the execution of, or whether they were exceeding, their duty, Lord Widgery C.J. said (at p. 288E-G):

Was that on its face a lawful and proper act for a responsible police officer in the circumstances? On its face, and ignoring for the moment Lord Gifford's argument, it seems to me that it was. There are in fact two, indeed perhaps three, ways in which the police officer could justify the conclusion that he ought to use his men to clear a path through the crowd for the coach to reach the highway. In the first place he had reasonable apprehension that otherwise the coach would be stopped, and it is now clear that even pickets cannot stop a vehicle unless the driver wishes to stop. The police officer had reasonable apprehension that the rights of the coach driver and the passengers would be interfered with by being forced to stop. He had reasonable apprehension that there would be disorder, as the magistrate finds, and certainly there might be such language as might amount to the offence of using threatening words and behaviour. Furthermore, police officers have the general duty to regulate the use of the highway by competing users, and to make sure that everybody gets a fair share. If the driver of a vehicle wants to drive down the highway and is obstructed by others in his path, the police are within their rights, if they can, to make a path for the vehicle.

V. Craig, 'Picketing and the Law', 1975 SLT (News),
pp. 137–40

... The need for tougher laws

This argument is more easily rejected than that put forward by the other side. A glance at a few cases endorses this view. For example, in *Piddington* v. *Bates* [1961] 1 WLR 162, the power of the police and the relative impotence of a perfectly lawful picket is highlighted. A picket who disagreed with a policeman's view as to the number of pickets required, was convicted of obstruction of a police officer in the execution of his duty when he indicated an intention to join the prescribed number. Similarly in *Tynan* v. *Balmer* [1966] 2 WLR 1181, 40 pickets who formed a moving circle on an access road were obstructing the highway. Two pickets at an Edinburgh brewery who refused to leave when asked to by police were convicted of 'behaving in a disorderly manner and committing a breach of the peace'. On occasions where the law is said to be ineffectual, in reality it is not the law which is weak but the police force which is unable to match the pickets in terms of numbers. That is, the problem is one of law enforcement not law-making or reform. In reality, making the law tougher intensifies this problem by requiring more duties of an already over-stretched police force.

Changing the law cannot prevent 1,500 miners surging through a 500-strong police cordon (Longannet, 1972) and the police are forced to admit that they only make 'token' arrests.

The arguments for toughening the law are effectively countered by what one labour lawyer has said: 'Today's pickets are not so much concerned with the answer to the question "What constitutes lawful picketing?" as they are with the reply to the question "What illegalities will be allowed by the police?" '

The other side

The other view is that pickets require more immunity from prosecution, and it is frequently asserted that the added protection pickets allegedly require should take the form of a right to stop people who propose to cross the picket lines. In *Broome* v. *DPP* [1974] IRLR 26, Viscount Dilhorne suggested that: 'It may be that unless the right to picket includes and extends to stopping people against their will, pickets will be unable to exercise their powers of persuasion . . .' The TUC have demanded that the law be amended to include such a right and the present Secretary of State for Employment has stated to Parliament that the law should give '. . . a right for pickets to communicate with the occupants of vehicles so as peacefully to persuade them . . .' (1974 HC vol. 870, col. 1488).

. . . In practice, in many cases the police ensure that the vehicles are stopped. In 1972 the chief superintendent of the Suffolk police was reported as saying: 'We made sure the lorries were stopped and allowed not more than four pickets to talk to the driver.' A similar tactic was adopted by the police at Longannet power station to permit nine of the assembled 2,500 to approach and speak to drivers.

There is little evidence therefore that a *right* to stop lorries to speak to occupants would greatly improve the picket's present position. Most cases indicate that pickets fall foul of the law after they have attempted persuasion but it has failed to produce the desired effect.

. . . There is a lot of evidence that in practice – with the help of the police – pickets are placed in a position where representations can be made to drivers. However, admittedly, problems do exist with this type of remedy. Thus, in *Kavanagh* v. *Hiscock* the police cordoned off the entire picket in such a way as to prevent anyone even approaching the vehicle, and, while a right to stop would have in all probability prevented Kavanagh's arrest no other reported case indicates that pickets are prevented from even approaching those who propose to cross the line. It is perhaps relevant to mention that Kavanagh had already spoken to the driver of the vehicle and made his views known. However it is necessary for the police to co-operate with some uniformity and, to avoid the possibility of uneven treatment by police, perhaps the Home Secretary should give guidelines to chief constables in relation to picketing. This could ensure that the existing practice of some chief constables was adopted uniformly throughout the country. Such a system would eliminate the potential difficulties of allowing pickets the *right* to stop, but should also eliminate the apparent injustice of the *Kavanagh* case. Although there is no evidence of uneven treatment the Edinburgh city police leave the matter to the discretion of the senior officer on the spot – which seems neither helpful nor necessary. A simple stock instruction could well prevent conflicts and improve police relations. . . . If it is accepted that picketing is primarily a means of communication then trade unions (and other groups) should consider other means of getting the strikers' views across – as well as, or perhaps instead of, face-to-face exchanges of views. In fact the National Union of Mineworkers is already embarking on a system of inter-union communication. The effect of this is that pickets would be a secondary line of communication. At least they could presume that other unionists would have heard of their views before they arrived at the picket line and the NUM obviously hoped that their system of 'picketing' would ensure that unionized workers would not even reach the picket lines. The pickets would then, it is hoped, only be required to persuade non-unionists not to cross. Prior consultation with the police also ensures the assistance of the police for stopping vehicles, and if the police were made aware that pickets have been informed of legal 'rights' there should be less likelihood of police anticipating breach of peace, as in the *Kavanagh* case. (The anticipation itself can have important legal consequences – it can justify police action (e.g. reducing number of pickets) which might otherwise not be permissible.) . . . Although not disturbed by this point one labour lawyer seems to be prepared to concede a statutory right to stop (and, presumably, detain) for the purposes of peaceful communication without feeling any duty to suggest any limits in its exercise. It is suggested that it is dangerous to propose such reforms without apparently contemplating their consequences. Would the proposed right of a picket to stop (and detain) be exercisable by the picket or through the agency of the police force? Would third parties be under a duty to listen and, if so, for how long? Would such persons, once having listened, be deemed to have performed their duty and be immune from further 'stops' during the same dispute? Would the non-strikers have a right to stop and persuade the striking pickets? Would the right be exercisable at any other place where a person 'happens to be, not being a place where he resides?' (Trade Union and Labour Relations Act 1974, s.15.) Or would the right be available only 'at or near' the place? Would the right be available in official and unofficial disputes? Would it be exercisable by authorized pickets or by all or any of those involved in the dispute?

It is submitted that those who propose to give pickets a right to stop must provide answers to these questions before making their proposals. It is flippant to make the proposal then leave the matter up in the air.

The result of detailed analysis of the criminal law thus seemed to be, first, that the criminal law was as strict as anyone could reasonably want – perhaps even too strict – and that from the police's point of view the problem was one of law enforcement and not the lack of criminal prohibitions. Second, it seemed that the police were unalterably opposed, on grounds of the infringement of their 'neutrality', to being placed under a duty to stop vehicles. In this situation a civil legal action brought in the middle of the lorry drivers' dispute in the winter of 1978–9 seemed to open up new vistas for those favouring a more restrictive approach by the law. In *United Biscuits (UK) Ltd* v. *Fall* [1979] IRLR 110, the plaintiff manufacturers obtained supplies partly by delivery by lorries owned by outside contractors who were members of the Road Haulage Association and partly by means of lorries owned and operated by the plaintiff. In the course of a dispute between the members of the RHA and their employees, drivers of lorries owned by the plaintiffs found picket lines established by the RHA employees at one of the plaintiffs' major suppliers. There was no dispute between the plaintiffs and their employees or between the suppliers and their employees. Ackner J. granted an injunction against the organizers of the picketing on the grounds that they were interfering with the performance of the contracts of employment of the plaintiffs' employees and with the commercial contract between the plaintiffs and their suppliers. This was held not to be something done in furtherance of the dispute with the members of the RHA on the objective test subsequently rejected by the House of Lords (above, p. 816). The significance of this case in particular and of the dispute in general was that, although they may not have directly produced, they did act as a catalyst in producing the notion that the right to picket should be confined, in general, to the employees' own place of work and that greater weight in regulating picketing activity should be thrown upon the civil law. These were the ideas embodied in s.16 of EA 1980.

Section 16(1) of EA 1980 substituted a new s.15 of TULRA 1974. This follows the format of old s.15 by making it lawful to attend for the purpose of peacefully obtaining or communicating information or peacefully persuading any person to work or abstain from working, but the permitted location of peaceful picketing activity is now much restricted. An employee who is not an official of a trade union can, with but two exceptions, lawfully picket only at his own place of work. This is a highly restrictive definition of the appropriate locus of picketing. It excludes not only picketing at the premises of other employers, but also picketing at premises of the pickets' own employer other than the premises at which the pickets are employed – an important restriction in multi-plant companies. There is no exception which permits a broader range of picketing if, for example, another plant or another employer has taken over the supply of goods previously supplied from the pickets' own plant (cf. EA 1980, s.17(4), above, p. 840). S.15 permits the barest minimum that is compatible with having a right to picket at all. The two exceptions to the restrictions are that employees employed otherwise than at any one place and employees employed at a place the location of which is such as to make picketing there impracticable may picket at any premises of their employer from which the employee works or from which his work is administered (s.15(2)). An example of the former category would indeed seem to be lorry drivers employed in the 'hire and reward' section of the industry, where lorries carry loads for a large number of different customers, but the exception would allow only picketing of premises of the drivers' employer (i.e. the RHA member) and not of the customers' premises (as occurred in the *United Biscuits* case). An example of the latter category would be an oil rig; in that case the employees might picket, for example, the on-shore office of the employer which deals with the dispatching of personnel to the rigs.

An implication of the new form of s.15 is that no one who is not an employee may claim the protection of s.15. This is a new restriction; the traditional formulation has been to protect those 'acting in contemplation or furtherance of a trade dispute' whether or not they are employees. The traditional restriction is retained in s.15 but in addition the person furthering the dispute must (subject to the two exceptions noted above) be picketing at or near his own place of work. There is a relaxation in this respect in s.15(3) which includes unemployed persons whose employment was terminated in connection with a trade dispute. Such employees may picket their former place of work. Former employees who have found work elsewhere will not be able to bring themselves within the section, nor, of course, will people who have never been employed at the premises in question. The only exception to this proposition is a union official accompanying a member of the union whom he represents (s.15(1)(b) and (4)).

To what range of additional legal liabilities do the provisions of new s.15 of TULRA 1974 expose those engaging in picketing? By and large those picketing other than at their own place of work will no longer be able to claim the protection of s.15 against criminal liability, but since that protection, as we have seen, was already illusory, its further restriction cannot be of great significance. The main impact of the new provision is, in fact, in relation to the civil law. First, the protection of new s.15 will not apply to 'off-site' pickets in relation to the law of nuisance. This has caused the revival of an unsolved disagreement between two decisions of the Court of Appeal at the turn of the century over the question of whether peaceful persuasion constitutes the tort of nuisance. The two cases revolved around s.7 of the CPPA 1875, which, as we have seen, created criminal liabilities, but did so by attaching criminal penalties to acts which had been regarded as nuisances at civil law, so that the section was regarded as relevant in civil proceedings. In *J. Lyons & Sons* v. *Wilkins (No. 2)* [1899] 1 Ch. 255, the Court of Appeal took the view that peaceful persuasion not to work was a civil nuisance by virtue of being a watching and besetting and was not protected by the proviso to s.7 which referred only to the peaceful communication of information. In *Ward Lock* v. *Operative Printers' Assistants' Society* (1906) 22 TLR 327, where the pickets were peacefully persuading employees to join the union and then to come out on strike, the Court of Appeal reached the opposite conclusion by stressing that the opening words of s.7 – 'wrongfully and without legal authority' – indicated that Parliament did not take the view that all watching and besetting was a nuisance at common law, so that in the court's view picketing became a nuisance only if accompanied by some independently unlawful act.

The need for immediate resolution of the point in the context in trade disputes was removed by the enactment of s.2 of the TDA 1906 (see above), but new s.15 of TULRA 1974 has restored the significance of the point at common law, as the facts in *Mersey Dock and Harbour Co.* v. *Verrinder* [1982] IRLR 152 illustrate. Lorry drivers at Liverpool commenced peacefully picketing the entrances of two container terminals operated by the plaintiffs with the aim of restricting the categories of vehicles having access to the terminals. The drivers were not employed by the plaintiffs. The company brought an action against the organizers of the pickets in nuisance. The judge in fact granted an interlocutory injunction against the defendants on the grounds that there was a serious issue to be tried on the principles laid down in the *Ethicon* case (above, p. 767) without attempting to resolve the conflict in the early cases. The same approach had been adopted by the majority of the Court of Appeal in *Hubbard* v. *Pitt* [1975] ICR 308, a case of peaceful picketing by 'anti-gentrification' campaigners in Islington and so not a trade dispute. Only Lord Denning M.R. (dissenting) addressed the substantive issue in that case and he supported the approach in the *Ward Lock* case. 'Picketing is not a nuisance in itself. Nor is it a nuisance for a group of people to attend at or near the plaintiffs' premises in order to obtain or to communicate information or in order peacefully to persuade. It does not become a nuisance unless it is associated with obstruction, violence, intimidation, molestation or threats.'

It is submitted that this is the correct approach and that the approach of the court in *Lyons* v. *Wilkins* was but an example of the doctrine later discredited in *Allen* v. *Flood* (above, p. 710), namely, that mere interference with a person's business (without any independently unlawful means) was a tort. Thus, in *Lyons* v. *Wilkins* Lord Lindley M.R. said that peaceful picketing of a man's house 'seriously interferes with the ordinary comfort of human existence and ordinary enjoyment of the house beset.' It is but a short step to extend this reasoning to give the employer a remedy for picketing of his premises – in *Lyons* v. *Wilkins* a house was picketed because it was the residence of a home-worker employed by the company – and then the dictum of Lord Lindley would read very much like the notorious dictum of Brett J. in *R.* v. *Bunn* (above, p. 707) that combination was a criminal conspiracy where it was 'an unjustifiable annoyance and interference with the masters in the conduct of their business. . . .' The *Ward Lock* case, decided in 1906, reflected the new approach of basing illegality upon unlawful means.

Although the law of nuisance is interesting as a potential example of the survival of nineteenth-century attitudes towards the infliction of economic harm in the course of trade disputes into the 1980s, it seems likely that the economic torts will normally[1] provide the most convenient basis for a civil legal action by an employer. Here any protection afforded by s.15 of T U L R A against liability for inducing breach of contract etc. has been reduced by its restriction to picketing at the employee's own place of work. However, even before its amendment s.15 of T U L R A did not provide the main protection for pickets against the economic torts. That was provided by s.13 of T U L R A 1974 which applied to pickets as much as to anyone else acting in contemplation or furtherance of a trade dispute. It is therefore of the utmost significance for the new role of the civil law in regulating picketing that compliance with the provisions of the new s.15 of T U L R A 1974 is expressly made a condition for the access of pickets to the protections of s.13 (E A 1980, s.16(2)). Those picketing other than at their own place of work (unless within one of the exceptions) and those picketing in the right place but in the wrong way (i.e. not peacefully) or for the wrong purposes (i.e. not for communicating information or persuading people to work or not to work) cannot any longer claim the protection of s.13 of T U L R A 1974. The exposure of pickets to liability from the economic torts is thus greater than that to which those organizing secondary action (other than secondary picketing) are subject by s.17 of E A 1980. The organizers of secondary action, as we have seen (above, p. 836), are made liable where the secondary action leads to the indirect procurement of breaches of commercial contracts; pickets and picket organizers are liable when they induce a breach of any type of contract and whether they do it directly or indirectly, if they go outside the boundaries of s.15 of T U L R A 1974. Thus, it is highly likely that the employer of those turned back at a picket line, which is not in accordance with the provisions of s.15, will have an action for inducing breach of contract of employment against the pickets and picket organizers and that the owner of the business being picketed, even if he is not the employer of those persuaded not to cross, will have an action for interference with business by unlawful means.

A final point on the substantive civil liability of pickets needs to be noted. Suppose pickets are picketing at their own place of work within s.15, can they find that they nevertheless have partially lost the protection of s.13 because they are engaged in secondary action as defined by E A 1980, s.17? The answer seems to be that they might indeed find themselves in such a situation. Suppose the pickets persuade lorry drivers, not employed by a party to the dispute, to turn back in breach of their contracts of employment. That would be secondary action within s.17(2). If in consequence, the haulier employer of the drivers were put in breach of his commercial contract of carriage with a supplier, also not a party to the dispute, who regularly supplied the premises being picketed, either haulier or supplier would have an action against the

[1] In *Mersey Dock and Harbour Co.* v. *Verrinder* the plaintiffs were the port authorities and, presumably, had no contracts themselves for the supply or delivery of goods which the picketing could be said to be interfering with. On the other hand, they presumably wanted to preserve the commercial reputation of the port and an action in nuisance may have seemed the best way to achieve this end.

pickets which would fall within EA 1980, s.17(1). We have suggested above (p. 837) that in such circumstances the pickets might be able to bring themselves within s.17(3) by arguing that their principal purpose was to disrupt supplies between the supplier and the employer (a party to the dispute) whose premises were being picketed. However, s.17(5) provides a specific protection for pickets in such a case. Provided the pickets are picketing within new s.15 and are employed by a party to the dispute, they retain the protection of s.13(1) of TULRA 1974.

S.17(5) does not apply if the pickets are not employed by a party to the dispute, even if they are picketing at their own place of work. Suppose, for example, employees of a secondary employer picketed their own plant in order to persuade lorry drivers bringing supplies from the primary employer to turn back. The pickets would be acting within the provisions of s.15 of TULRA 1974, but would not be within the provisions of s.17(5) of EA 1980 and in the circumstances Parliament seems to have thought that the pickets would be exposed to liability by virtue of the provisions of EA 1980, s.17(1) and (2). But one may wonder whether this is correct and, further, whether EA 1980, s.17(5) is really necessary. S.15 of TULRA says it is 'lawful' for persons to attend at the right place and for the right purposes. Is not the implication that, if the constraints of s.15 are met, the pickets' conduct is lawful and that the provisions of EA 1980, s.17 are overridden? The somewhat ironic result would be that it would not matter if pickets persuaded employees of a non-party to the dispute to break their contracts provided they were picketing at their own place of work. However, one cannot be confident that the courts will give the phrase 'it shall be lawful' such a wide interpretation in view of the narrowness of their approach in the past to the construction of these words in criminal cases (see above, pp. 845–7 and especially *Tynan* v. *Balmer* [1967] 1 QB 91 (DC)). It will be interesting to see whether recent discussion of positive rights (see above, p. 785) which, if followed through to the point of legislation, would presumably involve extensive reliance upon phrases such as 'it shall be lawful', will encourage a more liberal approach on the part of the judiciary to s.15 of TULRA 1974.

A major question is how often employers will seek to use their new civil remedies. In the first two years' operation of the new version of s.15 of TULRA 1974 employers initiated the civil legal process for the purpose of obtaining injunctions on only some half dozen occasions, but in late 1983 and early 1984 injunctions were obtained by employers in two prominent disputes, i.e. against the NGA by the *Stockport Messenger* and against the NUM by the NCB. We have commented above (pp. 775–7) on the potential limitations upon the efficacy of the injunction from an employer's point of view. The difficulties predicted at the time when the new picketing legislation was passed, arising out of the employer's need to identify those responsible for organizing the picketing before he can bring a legal action against them, seem not to have materialized, nor have difficulties manifested themselves because of the limited range of people covered by the injunction. However, in the latter case the issue is still an open one, because the injunctions so far issued have been against either trade unions in official disputes or, in unofficial disputes, individual pickets who have not sought to avoid them. The issues of identification and enforcement were still live enough to be discussed in *Trade Union Immunities* (1981), where proposals were considered that would have involved the police in the civil legal process. The Green Paper stressed quite strongly the arguments against such an involvement, on the grounds of infringement of police 'neutrality' or, perhaps better, the maintenance of police discretion to pursue the preservation of public order in the way they think best. The attitude of the police on these issues is the counterpart of their unwillingness to be put under a duty to stop vehicles on behalf of pickets (above, p. 845). The Green Paper put the issue as follows:

173. However, it has been suggested that a faster and more certain procedure would be to place an obligation on the police to ascertain the names and addresses of pickets at the request of the employer concerned in these circumstances, and that it should be made a criminal offence for the pickets to refuse to supply their names and addresses.

174. The main objection is that this would involve a breach of what has hitherto been regarded as an important principle in relation to the conduct of picketing – namely the neutrality of the police. Provided that the pickets are peaceful and do not commit or threaten to commit criminal offences, the police do not become involved: they are impartial as between employer and picket. Their role is to see that the peace is kept, not to take sides. The police themselves attach the greatest importance to maintaining this position of neutrality. It enables them in the great majority of cases to avoid hostility and establish reasonable relations with pickets. To require the police to demand names and addresses at the request of the employer might well be seen as enlisting their services on the side of the employer.

175. It has been suggested that an alternative approach might be to provide in the law for injunctions to be taken out against 'the act of picketing' ie against unnamed persons. This, it is suggested, would also deal with the so-called rotation of pickets, ie where the pickets are changed from day to day to make it more difficult for an employer to identify them and for the courts to enforce an injunction against named individuals.

176. Such a procedure, it has been argued, would be analogous to Order 113 of the Rules of the Supreme Court which was introduced to deal with the problem of squatters. The Order provides a procedure for recovering possession of land or a building occupied by unknown persons. However, there are fundamental differences between this procedure and that proposed for proceeding against unnamed pickets. In the former case the procedure is for the repossession of private premises which belong to someone who is entitled to their recovery. In the case of picketing, which normally takes place outside the employer's premises on the highway or pavement there can be no question of recovering possession: everyone has a right of access to the highway. Again, once the Order 113 procedure has been used and the premises repossessed, there is usually no question of recurrence. In the case of picketing, however, the removal of one set of pickets might well be followed by the arrival of further pickets who in turn would need to be removed.

177. For such a procedure to be effective in the case of picketing, it would be

necessary to make provision, on the application of the employer, for defined places to be made 'no-go' areas for secondary pickets. They would then have to be kept clear by the police. Moreover, there would appear to be difficulties in applying this principle only to secondary pickets. To do so would mean the police having to distinguish between primary and secondary pickets and other people with legitimate business in the area. They are not readily in a position to do this. On the other hand, to stop everyone from entering a given area would mean creating areas where, if only temporarily, the right of passage along the highway and the right of free speech for the purposes of peacefully communicating and persuading no longer applied. Moreover, whatever the details of the proposal, it would again seem that the services of the police were being enlisted on behalf of the employer. There would also be practical difficulty in defining the geographical area to which any such procedure should apply, the length of time for which it should remain in force and who should be allowed to appear as defendant in any action, should a union or group of workers wish to contest it.

178. Abandoning the principle of the neutrality of the police could have serious implications. Without clear evidence that employers are being seriously frustrated from taking advantage of the provisions of the Employment Act 1980 by their inability to secure the names and addresses of pickets, it may in any case be thought premature at this time to consider making a change in the law of this nature.

Thus, the impact of the changes made to s.15 of TULRA 1974 has been in the area of the civil law rather than the criminal law, and the restrictions on the immunities of pickets have been far greater than those imposed upon those taking secondary action other than picketing. It is perhaps surprising that the civil law should have borne the weight of the changes made by s.16 of EA 1980, given that the government explained the need for more stringent controls on picketing as against other forms of industrial action by reference to the former's 'special connotations for public order' (Working Paper on Secondary Industrial Action (1980), para. 9). However, s.16 was not the only section relevant to picketing contained in EA 1980. By s.3 of that Act, the Secretary of State had conferred upon him the power to issue Codes of Practice and he used that power to issue a Code of Practice on Picketing, which came into force on 17 December 1980. A Code of Practice cannot change the law – failure to observe it does not itself render a person liable to any proceedings (s.3(8)) – but can it be said to have been intended to affect police practice in enforcing the criminal law?

According to para. 1 of the Code it is not addressed to the police but rather to those taking part in or organizing a picket and those affected by the picketing (whether employers, other workers or members of the public). The main aims of the Code would seem to be to explain to pickets and picket organizers what they need to do in order to remain within the law (both civil and criminal) – see sections B and C of the Code – and to persuade picket organizers to conduct the picketing in such a way as to facilitate the job of the police (e.g. by the provision of armbands to authorized pickets and by maintaining 'close contact' with the police) and to minimize the impact of the picketing upon the public in general and upon the movement of essential goods and supplies in particular (see Sections F and G of the Code). It is, thus, clearly not a Code designed to advise picket organizers how they may picket effectively whilst remaining within the law. Where the Code goes beyond describing the law, it suggests additional restraints upon the conduct of pickets. The exact legal status of these additional restraints is not always easy to determine. Formally, while non-observance of the Code is not itself unlawful, any court or industrial tribunal must take into account any provision of the Code that appears to it to be relevant to the determination of any issue before it (EA 1980, s.3(8)). Thus a court might regard a picket organizer's level of compliance with the provisions concerning liaison with the police as relevant to the question of whether or not a police officer was acting in the execution of his duty in imposing conditions upon the conduct of the picketing. A bold civil court might regard non-compliance with the Code as unlawful means for the purposes of establishing liability in tort, as Lord Denning was thus prepared to regard a breach of the European Convention on Human Rights in *Associated Newspapers Group Ltd* v. *Wade* [1972] ICR 664. However, this would come close to infringing the provisions of s.3(8) and would be an approach rather at odds with the House of Lords' views on unlawful means in *Lonrho Ltd* v. *Shell Petroleum* [1982] AC 173 (above, p. 752). Thus, the link between non-observance of the Code and legal liability is often rather indirect.

So far we have discussed the impact of the Code upon the behaviour, or at least the legal liabilities, of pickets. What of its impact upon the behaviour of the police? Although the police are not addressed by the Code as such, the Code may operate upon them in two ways. It may generate in them expectations of a new kind as to how pickets should behave and this may influence their exercise of the considerable discretion the criminal law confers upon them (above, pp. 848-9). Alternatively, or in addition, the Code may generate in outsiders expectation as to how the police will deal with pickets, notably by ensuring their compliance with the Code. There is evidence that the Code did lead some employers to expect that the police would secure compliance with the provisions concerning essential supplies and that in practice these expectations were usually disappointed. Public order remained the main concern of the police: from their point of view entirely peaceful persuasion of someone with vital supplies to turn back tends to be less of a problem than the closure through violent picketing of a factory producing something that 20 other plants in the country were continuing to produce.

How about provisions in the Code more closely connected with the police's concern with public order? Here we need to consider the controversial provisions in the Code relating to the number of pickets. In section E of the Code, headed 'Limiting number of pickets', there is contained the recommendation that 'pickets and their organisers should ensure that in general the number of pickets does not exceed six at any entrance to a workplace; frequently a smaller number will be appropriate' (para. 31). Curiously, in the preceding section D of the Code, headed 'Role of the Police', reference to a specific number of pickets does not occur. Having stressed in para. 27 that 'the police have *no* responsibility for enforcing the *civil* law' (emphasis in the original), the Code goes on to say in para. 28:

As regards the *criminal* law the police have considerable discretionary powers to limit the number of pickets at any one place where they have reasonable cause to fear disorder. The law does not impose a specific limit on the number of people who may picket at any one place; nor does this Code affect in any way the discretion of the police to limit the number of people on a particular picket line. It is for the police to decide, taking into account all the circumstances, whether the number of pickets at any particular place is likely to lead to a breach of the peace. If a picket does not leave the picket line when asked to do so by the police he is liable to be arrested for obstruction either of the highway or of a police officer in the execution of his duty if the obstruction is such as to cause, or be likely to cause, a breach of the peace.

When the Code of Practice was published in its draft form, para. 30, which later became para. 31 of the final version, was more stringently worded in its reference to the number of six and it also contained in the same paragraph some comment on the role of the police. It read as follows.

The number of pickets at an entrance to a workplace should, therefore, be limited to what is reasonably needed to permit the peaceful persuasion of those entering and leaving the premises who are prepared to listen. As a general rule, it will be rare for such a number to exceed six, and frequently a smaller number will be sufficient. While the law does not impose a specific limit on the number of people who may picket at any one workplace, it does give the police considerable discretionary powers to limit the number of pickets in any one place where they have reasonable cause to fear disorder. It is for the police to decide, taking into account all the circumstances, whether the number of pickets in the particular case is likely to lead to a breach of the peace.

That draft gave rise to the following discussion when the Metropolitan Police and the Association of Chief Police Officers gave evidence to the Employment Committee of the House of Commons in 1980. Mr Terry, Mr Gibson, Sir Philip Knights and Mr Hall were police spokesmen; their interlocutors Members of Parliament.

House of Commons, Employment Committee, Minutes of
Evidence, 29 October 1980 (HC 462 – viii)

Chairman

545. If you present your thoughts in your own way and then we will come back to that. Comment on 30 in your own way.

(*Mr Terry*) This is so tied up with a number of things, Chairman, but in paragraph 30 in the second sentence the number six is referred to. We see the value of a number as being illustrative of the scale but we do not think that six is necessarily at all the right number, but it should convey that picketing is not something which is done on a massive scale but properly, well organised and effective, and therefore if I give an example of our wording it could well be 'As a general rule it will' and then I alter what is written 'not often be necessary for the number to exceed six' and we believe that has a very different meaning. The one problem, of course, with an arbitrary number with no qualification is that it sometimes can be self-defeating. It can be misunderstood by those who are in circumstances where a greater number is very necessary and very justified, or it may convey to others who really can do an effective job at one entrance to an office or a works with only two and they think they ought to have more. So we see its value as a guide only to show the scale of picketing which is necessary. . . .

546. Why do you not use the expression 'small numbers' rather than six? Why do you, in trying to rephrase, keep in the number six? You make your point when you say it is important that the numbers be small. That is the police point of view, is it not? That is a pure police point of view, that the numbers should be so small so there is no danger to breach of the peace?

(*Mr Gibson*) I think 'small numbers' immediately creates a problem of what is 'small'? One man may have a very different proposition of what 'small' may be from someone who feels he has a justifiable case which he wants to demonstrate or picket about. We think that if we were to use the figure as it is stated in the code, six, if we were to agree that that is the number that should be quoted, as long as it was stressed that it is purely illustrative and not definitive – that, I think, is the vital factor. In other words that Parliament in its wisdom is saying that is the scale, the sort of scale we are talking about, numbers around six and not around the 600 mark. I think that is the distinction we are trying to make.

547. Around the six mark?

(*Mr Gibson*) Yes.

Mr Townend

548. Under what circumstances would you say it was acceptable that the numbers should be greater than six?

(*Sir Philip Knights*) I can think of an example –

(*Mr Terry*) Many of us can.

(*Sir Philip Knights*) – from my own area, a very large factory with a great number of entrances, many of which are wide, with a large workforce coming in early in the morning in large numbers, I would be quite prepared to see five or six on each side of the gate as long as nobody else was there interfering, because I do not believe that six necessarily would be able to achieve what they are rightly there seeking to achieve and that is trying to persuade the other people round to their point of view. In the circumstances I had in mind I could well see 10 or a dozen would not be out of place, but on the other hand I can see circumstances where more than two would be more than enough.

Mr Gorst

549. Would you say six would be adequate to picket the gate that we come into for the House of Commons, as opposed to 600?

(*Sir Philip Knights*) In my area –

Chairman

550. When we were in Birmingham!

(*Sir Philip Knights*) If 600 people wanted to get through one of your gates, having all come off a train, then I do not think six necessarily would be out of place, or indeed it might not necessarily be sufficient, but if you were coming in twos or threes and then a gap and then another four or five, two would be all that was necessary.

(*Mr Gibson*) To answer your question as posed I think six would be adequate if it was the House.

Mr Gorst

551. It would not be if there was a division!

(*Mr Gibson*) There are several entrances and they come in from all angles, so it might not be.

Mr Wickenden

552. What you are saying is that a hangar door is very different from one like that?

(*Mr Gibson*) Yes.

(*Mr Terry*) I think the code may not be clear in item 13 and where you have a factory with a number of gates I think it should be made clear that the code relates to one entrance.

Mr Townend

553. In the paragraph it says 'an entrance', I would have thought that indicated what you are saying.

(*Mr Terry*) Thank you. I withdraw on that.

(*Mr Townend*) Which is why I asked the question. I thought you were giving the impression that you thought there were occasions when you needed more than six because there were a number of entrances.

Chairman

554. The width of the gate and all the rest of it would be taken into account.

(*Mr Terry*) There are many works entrances where you have a road for vehicles coming in and out with a check in the middle and on each side a place for people coming in on foot. You need more than six in those circumstances if they need to do their job properly.

Mr Townend

555. Can you give us your view on what you think should be the absolute maximum at any one entrance?

(*Mr Terry*) I think so much has to come into this. There would be times of a day where, with discussions with the organisers, you might say the maximum number should be six, and at the busiest time when people are coming in to clock on, you might say it would go up to 10, but it depends on the location, the safety aspect of vehicles and the mix or traffic, whether pedestrian or vehicular, the proximity of a major road and so on. I think it would be absolutely impossible for me to say to policemen 'In every case the maximum is so and so.'

Chairman

556. What worries me is the formulation. This is obviously directed towards the police. The advice is directed towards the police as well as to pickets. If the formulation were in the sense that the police had complete discretion but the Government would themselves believe it reasonable if the police decided this, that or the other, that would not be such an objectionable formulation, would it?

(*Mr Terry*) I did not read, and I do not think any of my colleagues really read, this as something aimed only at the police. I believe everyone should know what is a reasonable number of people if it is going to be mentioned, so it is all concerned. But it is mentioned in No. 30 that it is for the police to decide, taking into account all the circumstances which I have just been referring to, whether the number of pickets in a particular case is likely to lead to a breach of the peace.

557. That is quite different. The difficulty of this paragraph is that there are two separate elements in it. The first element relates, as far as I can see, to the numbers reasonably needed to make peaceful persuasion. That number could be different from

those which are the numbers the police think would create a risk of a breach of the peace.

(*Mr Terry*) Chairman, I would very sincerely –

558. There are two separate elements in the paragraph.

(*Mr Hall*) Surely the major point here is that, whatever the advice as regards numbers, it must be emphasised that in the final analysis it is for the senior police officer present to make that decision. That is what we were wanting to state here.

(*Mr Gibson*) Because the circumstances at any particular point in a day could be so different – totally different.

559. What I am saying is that the paragraph leaves it with you to decide, taking account of all circumstances, whether the number of pickets is likely to lead to a breach of the peace. That is not in argument, but the restriction to six relates to the numbers reasonably needed to permit the peaceful persuasion of those entering, right? That is what the number is. As I understand it, the Government is not saying 'Look, if you have more than six you are likely to have a breach of the peace'; the Government's position is, 'Look, you limit the number of pickets to the minimum required to allow peaceful persuasion to take place.' They are two quite separate points that are being made, are they not? You could decide that you only need one peacefully to picket but a policeman could then say, 'Look, there's no chance of a breach of the peace even if there are three, four, five, six, seven'. They are separate, are they not?

(*Mr Gibson*) We suggest it should be left to the senior officer on duty at the scene to make the decision. The point which I think seems to be causing a little bit of controversy is around this magic figure of six. The whole point of our contention is that the six should be an illustrative consideration rather than a definitive number. In other words, we say it would be at that end of the scale – the six end of the scale – rather than the 600 end of the scale.

Mr Bowden

560. Is it not vital that the police have the complete flexibility necessary to ensure that the law is upheld and that is really, as I see it, what Mr Terry and his colleagues are arguing for?

(*Mr Terry*) That is correct, Chairman. Could I say that over the years when we have discussed with the organisers in a dispute putting the pickets out there are thousands upon thousands of instances over the years when there has been absolute agreement as to the sensible number of pickets on any number of entrances. The problem has not come from that; the problem has come from your demonstrators, not from the number of pickets as agreed between the policemen and the convener.

This passage demonstrates in a graphic manner the desire of the police to preserve their ultimate discretion as to how pickets should be regulated as far as the criminal law is concerned. The changes made in the Code of Practice on picketing between draft and final version constituted an attempt to reconcile this desire with the government's desire to make some fairly precise statement as to the permissible number of pickets. It remains to be seen whether pressure will not build up to give the numerical limit on pickets statutory force. This may happen if there is a series of well publicized disputes in which the police either decide or are forced to permit pickets to attend in numbers considerably in excess of six.

6 **Industrial action to secure union membership or recognition**

So far we have looked at restrictions that have been imposed upon the legality of industrial action by reference to the methods employed (picketing, secondary action), by reference to the parties to the dispute (exclusion of workers and worker disputes or disputes between an employer and employees not employed by him from the definition of trade dispute) and by reference to the geographical location of the cause of the dispute (disputes relating to matters outside the United Kingdom). We now turn to restrictions imposed by reference to the purpose of those taking the industrial action. This is an obvious enough basis upon which to restrict the legality of industrial action, if one is in favour of a more restrictive framework of law, although this way of analysing the legality of industrial action in fact played only a small role in the abstentionist framework of law. Once the tort of conspiracy to injure had withdrawn, or been withdrawn, from the field of industrial conflict, the common law based illegality upon the methods of industrial action (inducing breach of contract, interference by unlawful means etc.) and the protective statutes necessarily followed the same lines. The purposes of those taking industrial action were relevant to the question of whether they had acted in contemplation or furtherance of a trade dispute, but, so long as trade dispute was broadly defined, the defendants' purposes, provided they lay within the field of industrial relations, operated to confer statutory protection upon the action taken, rather than the reverse. See above pp. 795–805.

The IRA 1971, however, created several unfair industrial practices which turned upon the purpose of the industrial action. For example, by s.55 of that Act, where an employer had been ordered by the Industrial Court to recognize a particular trade union, it was an unfair industrial practice for any person to organize industrial action for the purpose of inducing the employer not to comply with the order. A definition of illegality by reference to purpose now occurs in the current law in s.14 of EA 1982. We have seen above, in Chapter 5, that the closed shop has been subjected in recent years to a variety of legal restraints, which relate to the fairness of dismissals by employers of employees for non-membership of the relevant union, the legal freedom of trade unions to exclude or expel people from membership in a closed shop situation, the validity of clauses in commercial contracts requiring the use of union members in the performance of the contract or the recognition of a union by a party to the contract, and the legality of various practices in the sphere of commercial contracting arising out of the same views of union membership or recognition. Throughout the protracted political debate on the closed shop there have been demands from some quarters that the closed shop should be 'outlawed'. It is often unclear what such a proposal is intended to mean, but one way of making sense of such a suggestion is to take it as a proposal to remove the statutory protections against the common law liabilities from industrial action designed to secure the creation or maintenance of closed shop agreements or arrangements. Thus, under the IRA 1971, s.5(2), it was an unfair industrial practice for an employer to dismiss an employee for non-membership of a particular or any trade union (subject to limited exceptions concerning agency shops and approved closed shops) and by s.33(3) of that Act it was an unfair industrial practice for a person to organize industrial action for the purpose of inducing an employer to do an act that would be unlawful under s.5(2). The current legislation does not entirely remove protection against the common law liabilities from industrial action designed to support the institution of the closed shop, but s.14 of EA 1982 does perform that function in relation to industrial action taken for that purpose in certain instances, and we now turn to examine the details of s.14.[1]

Section 14 falls into two parts. S.14(1) removes the protection of s.13 of TULRA 1974 from industrial action which is aimed at inducing a person to incorporate into a contract to which he is or will be a party a term which is rendered void by s.12(1) or 13(1) of EA 1982. As we have seen above (pp. 668–70), s.12(1) renders void clauses requiring union members (or non-members) to be used in the performance of contracts for the supply of goods or services, and s.13(1) does the same in relation to clauses requiring a party to such a contract to recognize a trade union or consult with the officials of a trade union. In this case the removal of protection from industrial action operates to strengthen the rather weak impact of ss.12(1) and 13(1) in declaring such clauses void, which would not necessarily result, by itself, in such clauses no longer appearing in commercial contracts. However, the real criticism of ss.12(1) and 13(1) from the point of view of those who wish to end 'union labour only' practices is that, whether such clauses continue to appear in commercial contracts or not, 'many organisations would no longer place contracts with known non-union companies or that they would require contractors to send only union labour to fulfil a contract, without actually putting such a requirement into the written contract' (*Trade Union Immunities*, para. 300). Consequently, as we have seen, ss.12(2) and 13(2) go further and render it unlawful for a person to engage in any one of a variety of contractual practices because of the likelihood of the other contracting party using non-union (or union) labour or his not recognizing a trade union or not consulting the officials of a trade union. It is the contractual practices rather than the contractual clauses that are likely to be significant in actual situations and so it is important to note that s.14(1) removes the protection of s.13 of TULRA also from industrial action which induces or attempts to induce a contractor to break ss. 12(2) or 13(2).

Thus, s.14(1) of EA 1982 operates so as to remove immunity, not from industrial action aimed to ensure that an employer enters into or maintains a closed-shop arrangement *vis-à-vis* his own employees, but from industrial

[1] We are here concerned with the tort liabilities of those organizing industrial action in support of the closed shop. The liability of organizers of such action to be joined as third parties in unfair dismissal claims arising out of closed-shop arrangements is discussed above at pp. 654–5.

action designed to persuade him to use his contracting power to impose union-labour requirements on his suppliers or customers. The use of contracting power in this way is common in a number of industrial situations. For example, employers operating large and strongly unionized establishments often require contractors, who come onto the site to erect new plant or maintain existing plant, to employ union labour. Industrial action designed to secure the continuation of this situation by putting pressure upon the employer to insert the relevant clause in the commercial contract or to engage in the proscribed contractual practices (e.g. refusing to consider tenders from non-union contractors) will lose the immunities provided by s.13 of TULRA 1974. Who, in consequence, will be able to sue the organizers of the industrial action? If the industrial action involves a breach of the contracts of employment of those participating in it, their employer (i.e. the operator of the establishment in the above example) will be able to sue the organizers as inducers: as with the provisions of EA 1980, s.16 on picketing, the loss of protection brought about by s.14(1) of EA 1982 is total and is not confined to inducing breaches of commercial contracts. In many cases, however, the site operator is happy to insist upon contractors using union labour and he is less likely to wish to sue the organizers of the industrial action than the contractor or potential contractor upon whom the requirement is being imposed. If the purpose of the industrial action is to secure that the operator breaks his contract with the contractor, the contractor will have an action for inducement of breach of the commercial contract. Even where the pressure is aimed at merely ensuring that the operator will not enter into fresh contracts with a particular contractor, the latter will probably have an action for interference with his business by unlawful means. The unlawful means will be the inducement of the breaches of the contracts of employment and the decision in the *Hadmor* case (above, p. 747) would not protect the organizers because the inducement of the breach of the contracts of employment would no longer be protected by s.13 of TULRA 1974.

The second part of s.14 of EA 1982 (s.14(2)–(4)) is also concerned with a range of situations in which industrial action is taken by employees in order to influence the employment practices of employers other than their own in so far as these practices relate to union membership or recognition. The second part of s.14 had a predecessor in s.18 of EA 1980, which is repealed by EA 1982 because its effect is encompassed within the broader provisions of the 1982 Act. Nevertheless, it helps in unravelling the provisions of s.14 to begin with s.18 of the 1980 Act. S.18 arose out of the report by Andrew Leggatt QC into *Certain Trade Union Recruitment Activities* (Cmnd. 7706, 1979), in which he found that the union SLADE had compelled employees in non-union art studios to become members of the union by organizing the blacking the work of their employers at unionized printers, even though the employees did not wish to join SLADE and there was some doubt whether the union could or would effectively represent them. The section removed the protection of s.13(1) of

TULRA 1974 from inducing breach etc. of contracts of employment or of other types of contract where inducing breach of contracts of employment was one of the facts relied upon as establishing liability. Liability was imposed where the purpose of the action was to compel workers to join a particular trade union 'or one of two or more particular trade unions', provided that none of the workers worked for the same employer or at the same place as the employees working under the contracts of employment in question. Thus, if employees of employer B blacked, in breach of their contracts of employment, work from employer A in order to achieve the forbidden purpose, employer B could sue the organizer of the blacking in respect of the breaches of the contracts of employment by his employees, and employer A could also sue if the breaches of the contracts of employment had brought about breach of a commercial contract between A and B.

In the Green Paper, *Trade Union Immunities*, it was suggested that s. 18 of EA 1980 was too narrowly conceived because it regulated only industrial action which had the purpose of compelling other employees to join a trade union. It was suggested that the section would not catch the mere refusal to handle work from non-union companies or to work with non-union labour, because the purpose of the refusal might not be to compel the non-unionists to join a union. In the latter case an additional objection to liability was that s. 18 did not apply to acts done *vis-à-vis* employees working at the same place of work as those taking the industrial action, even though they were employed by an outside contractor. (See paras. 287–94.) In s. 14(2)–(4) of EA 1982 both these restrictions on the scope of s. 18 of EA 1980 have been removed. The two defining features of the section are the purposes of the industrial action proscribed by it and the method of industrial action proscribed. The protection of s. 13 of TULRA 1974 is removed from any act which interferes with the supply of goods or services (whether under a contract or not) where one of the facts relied upon for establishing liability is that a person has induced another to break a contract of employment (or done any of the analogous acts described above (p. 835) in connection with s. 17(2) of EA 1980), where the act in question was done for any one of three reasons. Those reasons are (a) that the work to be done in connection with the supply was likely to be done by non-unionists or people who were not members of a particular trade union, or (b) that it was likely to be done by unionists or members of a particular trade union, or (c) that the supplier did not recognize a trade union or consult with officials of a trade union. In cases (a) and (b), the persons to whom the objection is taken must be employed by someone other than the employer of those taking the industrial action, and in case (c) the supplier must be someone other than the employer of those taking the industrial action.

Thus, in the example given above in relation to the operation of s. 18 of EA 1980, B and A would now be able to sue even if the refusal to handle the work was not embarked upon in order to compel the employees of A to join a union but simply out of objection to the work having been done by non-unionists. If the action taken by the employees of B did not lead to a breach of the commercial contract between B and A, A might well still have an action for interference with his business by unlawful means, as indeed might the employees of A. If the action took the form of a refusal, in breach of contract, to work alongside non-unionists brought onto a site, liabilities could arise in the same way at the suit of B, A and the employees of A, because s.14 no longer contains the restriction that the employees objected to must not work at the same place of work as the objectors. However, the objectors and those objected to must not work for the same employer. In this way, presumably, it is hoped to preserve the protection of industrial action taken by employees designed to compel their fellow employees to join a trade union.

Since s.14, in general, is concerned with industrial action aimed at the employment practices of employers other than the employer of those taking the industrial action, it may be thought that the 'outside' employer and his employees have a claim to be insulated against industrial action taken by others. The outside employer and his employees should be free to negotiate their own terms and conditions of employment. The interrelated nature of commercial life, however, tends to reduce the force of this argument. Insistence upon the employment of union members by outside contractors may be, for those taking the industrial action, a way of insisting upon the outsiders having reached acceptable standards of safety or training (important where the employees of the outside employers are to work alongside those taking the action) or a way of insisting upon the payment of proper wages and thus a protection against undercutting by the outside contractors. In some industries, e.g. the building industry, the use of non-union self-employed labour by sub-contractors may threaten the stability of the structure of collective bargaining in the industry (see above, p. 94). It is now very difficult to take lawful industrial action for the purpose of insisting that contractors or suppliers use union labour. However, it should be noted that, while industrial action for this purpose or to ensure that the outside employer negotiates with or consults a trade union may well be unlawful, s.14 does not impinge upon action genuinely designed to ensure that the outside contractor observes a certain level of terms and conditions of employment. Indeed, it has been government policy until recently to insist upon precisely this requirement through the Fair Wages Resolution and some local authorities may well continue to insert such clauses in their contracts (see above, p. 154). However, one can imagine that in particular situations it may not be at all easy to decide whether the industrial action was tainted by reason of having an unlawful purpose or not (s.14(3) appears to render the action unlawful provided one, but not necessarily the main, reason for it was an improper one). See Roy Lewis and Bob Simpson, 'Disorganising Industrial Relations' (1982) 11 *ILJ* at pp. 231–3.

Thus, s.14 of EA 1982 provides perhaps a third way of defining what is meant by secondary action. S.17 of EA 1980 restricts the legality of industrial action taken by employees not employed by a party to the dispute. S.16 of EA 1980 adopts a geographical definition to restrict the legality of picketing other than at the employee's own place of work. Typically, industrial action covered by s.14 will be taken by employees in dispute with their own employer (the dispute being over the employees' demand that their employer should ensure that his contractors use union labour or should obtain his supplies from union shops) and the industrial action (blacking or refusal to work alongside non-unionists) will occur at the place of work of those taking the industrial action. Such action would not be classed as secondary on the basis of the policies enshrined in either s.16 or s.17 of EA 1980. However, s.14 of EA 1982 makes the action illegal because its aim is to influence the employment practices of other employers. This is the third definition of secondariness: it is illegality based upon the secondary consequences (intended, no doubt) of primary industrial action.[1]

However, although the origins of s.14 in the Leggatt report and the link between s.14(1) and ss.12 and 13 of the 1982 Act clearly demonstrate that the main aim of the legislators in enacting s.14 was to reduce the legal freedom of strongly organized groups of workers to impose particular practices as to the use of union labour or the recognition of trade unions upon other employers and their employees, it may well be that s.14(2)–(4) go beyond this primary purpose. These further consequences may have been intended by the government or may simply be the unintended (but perhaps not unwelcome) consequences of the complex method of drafting which s.14 shares with s.17 of the 1980 Act. Roy Lewis and Bob Simpson suggest the following example ((1983) 12 ILJ at p.103). The union members employed by employer A make a claim for recognition of their union by A but are refused and they take industrial action. The union then asks the employees of employer B to black supplies from A until the recognition claim has been met by A. The action by the employees of B interferes with the supply of goods from A (who is continuing operation with the help of his non-union employees) and either A or B brings an action against the organizers of the industrial action taken by the employees of B. By virtue of s.14(4) the 'relevant' employer is B, i.e. the employer under the contracts of employment whose breach is being induced. The supplier of the goods is A (who is not the 'relevant' employer) and the reason for the industrial action is that A does not recognize the union. Consequently, the provisions of s.14(3)(c) are satisfied and the industrial action by the employees of B loses its immunities under s.13 of TULRA 1974. The reason why this example of unprotected activity is a surprising one is that it is not an example of the employees of B attempting to impose union recognition upon the unwilling employees of A (the non-unionists employed by A may simply be indifferent to the resolution of the recognition claim) but of secondary action being taken in support of the employees of A (at least the

[1] Cf. *Hadmor Productions* v. *Hamilton* (above, p. 747).

union members employed there).[1] If the action were judged solely on the criteria of s.17 of EA 1980, it would probably remain protected because it satisfied the requirements of the 'first customer' gateway in s.17(3). However, the action loses immunity because of the provisions of s.14(2)–(4) of EA 1982, so that s.14 in this context is not so much rendering illegal a third type of secondary action as imposing a stricter legal régime upon a form of secondary action which in principle is dealt with in s.17 of EA 1980. This example demonstrates in a particularly graphic way the reversal by the EA 1980–2 of the traditional public policy of support for collective bargaining: action taken to help other workers secure recognition is now marked out for particularly unfavourable treatment in terms of the immunities, even though the statutory procedures which could have been used for obtaining recognition without recourse to industrial action have been repealed.

7 Emergency disputes[2]

In this section we shall look at various legal provisions, actual or proposed, which restrict the legality or effectiveness of industrial disputes that give rise to an emergency. The function of these restrictive provisions is to reduce the adverse effects of a strike or other piece of industrial action upon the community as a whole, though, as we shall see, there is a wide variety of ways in which this objective may be sought to be achieved. In general the government plays a larger direct role in the operation of these provisions than it does by virtue of the provisions so far discussed in this chapter. Of course, when legislating for new laws on picketing or secondary action, for example, government sees itself as acting in the public interest, but, once enacted, these laws, as we have seen, tend to operate by conferring private rights of action upon those persons whose economic interests are harmed by the industrial action. In emergency disputes the government often appears, not merely as legislator, but also as the invoker of the legislative provisions, acting in its capacity as guardian of the general interest. This executive role of the government creates particular problems for administrations committed to a general policy of abstention in regard to industrial conflict law. Even for governments not so committed, there is often an uneasy conflict of roles as between the government as the protector of the community and the government as an interested party to the trade dispute. This is obviously the case when the Government is the employer of the workers in dispute, but the problem is much wider than that. Disputes that give rise to emergencies tend to be national disputes and, as we have noted, over the last fifteen years or so national strikes have often involved an element of challenge to the incomes

---

[1] The impact of s.14(2)–(4) is also haphazard. If B were the supplier to A, rather than vice versa, then supplier and relevant employer would be the same person and the requirements of s.14(3)(c) would not be satisfied.

[2] For a very useful survey see Gillian Morris, 'Essential Services, the Law and the Community' (1983) 12 *ILJ* 69, and see generally the essays published in Wedderburn and Murphy (eds.), *Labour Law and the Community* (1982).

policy being operated by the government of the day. It is not always easy to tell whether the government in a particular case has been more moved by the need to protect its own economic policy or by the need to preserve the essentials of life for the community.

(a) Emergency powers legislation[1]

The emergency powers legislation, which is of long standing, attempts to reduce the acuteness of the dilemma outlined in the previous paragraph by giving the government power to mitigate the consequences of the industrial action but no power to require the cessation of the action. There are two sets of statutory provisions. Under the Emergency Powers Act 1920 the government may delcare by proclamation a state of emergency where events (including strikes) threaten 'by interfering with the supply and distribution of food, water, fuel, or light, or with the means of locomotion, to deprive the community, or any substantial portion of the community, of the essentials of life' (s.1(1)). During the emergency the government may, by order in council, make regulations 'for securing the essentials of life to the community', which may confer wide powers upon the government. However, the regulations must be approved by Parliament within seven days (or else will lapse) and the regulations may not make striking or organizing a strike a criminal offence nor may they impose upon the strikers (or anyone else) any form of conscription. Under the Emergency Powers Act 1964, s.2, whether or not a state of emergency has been declared, the Defence Council may direct the use of troops in temporary work which is 'urgent work of national importance'. The Defence Council, which is chaired by the Secretary of State for Defence, may act without proclamation and so without consulting Parliament, although the Secretary of State remains accountable to Parliament, in the usual ways, for the decisions of the Council.

Powers under both Acts have been taken only infrequently, but there was, not surprisingly given the resurgence of national disputes on income policies, an increase in their use during the 1970s. Up until the end of 1982 a state of emergency had been declared under the 1920 Act as a result of an industrial dispute on some twelve occasions, of which five occurred between 1970 and 1974, and none since. Troops have been used in industrial disputes under the 1964 Act or the Defence Regulations which preceded it on some nineteen occasions since the Second World War and on five further occasions in this period during an emergency declared under the 1920 Act. If the sole step that the government decides to take is the deployment of troops, who will then use their own equipment (e.g. their own fire-engines during a strike by civilian firemen), the 1964 Act provides sufficient authority. If the government decides in addition to requisition private property for the troops to use (e.g. petrol tankers owned by the oil companies) a proclamation under the 1920 Act becomes necessary, as it also does if the government does not wish to use troops

[1] See Morris, 'The Emergency Powers Act 1920' [1979] *PL* 317.

at all but wants, for example, to ration the consumption of electricity.[1]

The most controversial aspect of the emergency powers is, no doubt, the use of troops[2] to do some or all of the work previously performed by the strikers. A recent study of states of emergency was boldly subtitled 'British Governments and Strike-breaking since 1919'.[3] There seems little doubt that at least in some cases the use of troops can seriously undermine the effectiveness of the strikers' industrial action and prevent them from achieving their goals, as with the firemen's strike in 1977/8.[4] In many cases the government has regarded that effect as desirable in itself. On the other hand, it is clearly unreasonable to expect a government not to respond to political pressures to take action if a strike is depriving the community of the essentials of life. No matter how narrowly one defines the essentials of life and no matter how rigorously one excludes from the definition of emergency situations disputes in which what is at stake is in reality the economic policy of the government of the day, there remains the possibility of situations arising in which the entirely peaceful resort by workers to industrial sanctions gives rise to a serious threat to life or property. This dilemma raises in its acutest form the question of what costs the community can be asked to bear as the price for a genuinely autonomous system of collective bargaining. In this situation, as Professor Kahn-Freund recognized many years ago, one reaches the limits of the doctrine of collective *laissez-faire*,[5] and this area is, in consequence, an obvious one for the attention of those generally in favour of a more restrictive approach to the law of industrial conflict.

However, before turning to the various ways in which the law does or might render industrial action itself unlawful in emergencies, it is worth noting that it is not only troops that have been used to perform the work of strikers. In recent years the police have been used in that role also.[6] Indeed, it might be thought to be constitutionally easier to use the police in this way than the army, but in fact this development represented something of a challenge to principle for the police. During the General Strike, Sir John Anderson, a senior official in the Home Office, had persuaded those concerned that it would be unwise to use the police to deliver medical supplies to hospitals in London because 'such action . . . would contravene the important principle that in a dispute the police did not take either side, and any impairment of police impartiality

[1] Regardless of the precise nature of the emergency the practice has developed of issuing a complete 'code' of regulations if the government decides to issue regulations at all after the proclamation of the emergency. See Morris, ibid., pp. 325–31, for an analysis of the content of these codes.

[2] There is now a considerable literature on the use of troops in emergencies, from which the statistics in this section have been extracted. See, in particular, Whelan, 'Military Intervention in Industrial Disputes' (1979) 8 *ILJ* 222 and 'State Intervention, Major Disputes and the Role of Law' in Wedderburn and Murphy (eds.), op. cit., p. 37, and Jeffery and Hennessy, *States of Emergency* (1983).

[3] Jeffery and Hennessy, ibid.

[4] In the case of other groups of workers, for example power engineers, it is doubtful if it is technically possible for troops to provide a substitute for the services withdrawn by those taking industrial action.

[5] Kahn-Freund, 'Legal Framework' in Flanders and Clegg (eds.), *The System of Industrial Relations in Great Britain* (1954), p. 124.

[6] See Morris, 'The Police and Industrial Emergencies' (1980) 9 *ILJ* 1.

would undermine their power to keep order'.[1] However, during the ambulancemen's dispute in early 1979 the police maintained an emergency service in areas where emergency cover was not being provided by the ambulancemen themselves, and the police were also used in this way during a strike by social workers during the same period. This amounts to a substantial modification of the principle of police neutrality which we discussed above in relation to picketing (see pp. 845 and 855). The police are unwilling to be put under a duty to either employers or workers (whether it be to stop lorries or to collect names for injunctions) but they are less willing or able to resist the pressures from government to help mitigate the consequences of emergency strikes. It seems likely that contingency planning by government in respect of emergency disputes, the machinery for which was re-vamped after the national miners' strike of 1972,[2] will in future count upon the availability of both troops and police in appropriate cases.

(b) Restrictions upon industrial action by specific groups of workers

A simple, but rather crude, way of dealing with the problems of disputes giving rise to an emergency would be to prohibit industrial action by employees in an essential service. We have already noted above (p.708) the special criminal liabilities imposed by s.4 of the CPPA 1875 upon strikers in the gas, water and (later) electricity industries and their repeal by the IRA 1971. This repeal was effected apparently because in 1971 the government agreed with the reasoning on this point in Mr Andrew Shonfield's Note of Reservation to the Donovan Commission's Report (the majority having recommended the retention of s.4). The logic of Mr Shonfield's view was that the liabilities imposed by s.5 of the 1875 Act should be retained and expanded beyond situations where the strike was a breach of contract, but his views on s.5 were not implemented in 1971. He said (at paras. 10 and 11 of his Note):

The existing legal framework of industrial relations is not only meagre, it is also rather too free in its application of the criminal law. The category of industrial crimes ought now to be narrowed down to the minimum that is absolutely necessary for the protection of people's lives and safety. This means that section 4 of the Conspiracy and Protection of Property Act of 1875, and its extension by the Act of 1919 . . . should be repealed. This law singles out the employees of three industries, gas, water and electricity, for criminal penalties if they engage in a lightning strike, on the ground that sudden stoppages here may pose a special threat to health and safety. This is true; but their case is not unique. It is not clear why it is a worse offence for a group of maintenance workers to shut down the supply of gas in a district which is provided with electricity and other alternative fuels than it would be, for example, for nurses in a hospital to stage a sudden walk-out. The criterion, it is clear, should not be whether workers are employed in a particular industry but what are the likely consequences of a sudden stoppage in their particular job.

This is the criterion which is applied – to employers as well as to employees – by

[1] Jeffery and Hennessy, op. cit., p. 123. [2] Ibid., pp. 234 ff.

section 5 of the 1875 Act. Indeed what section 5 does in essence is to say that actions known to be likely to endanger life, limb or valuable property, which we would recognise as criminal if done by an individual, are also a crime if done by a combination of people who break their contracts by staging a strike without proper notice.[1] I find the arguments advanced in the Report for retaining the special additional penalties under section 4 unconvincing. It does not seem to me that the narrowing of the criminal law would be construed as 'an express licence' to behave irresponsibly by workers in gas, water and electricity. . . . On the contrary, by narrowing the law to its true purpose and making it more rational it would be given more credibility and persuasive power. Moreover, the criminal penalty should apply to people who act dangerously, regardless whether they are formally breaking their contracts or not. I fail to see the difficulty . . . of punishing someone for criminally irresponsible behaviour even if this behaviour took place when he 'lawfully terminated his contract'. Indeed it would seem to be a valuable contribution to our laws to make it clear that in our kind of society, in which people are increasingly dependent on the punctual performance of services by one another, the duty to avoid doing people or property serious damage, when the risk is clearly apparent is what counts – regardless of the precise nature of the contractual obligation undertaken in one's job. Section 5 should, therefore, be elaborated to establish this principle.

Nevertheless, despite Mr Shonfield's criticisms of the principle of singling out groups of workers for special restrictions, s.4 of the 1875 Act was not the only expression of this notion to be found in the law. Throughout most of this century, including the heyday of collective *laissez-faire*, two groups of workers have been forbidden to strike – the police and the armed forces, a fact which gives a certain piquancy to the role of these bodies under the emergency powers legislation – and merchant seamen have been placed under very severe restrictions as to their participation in industrial action. The Police Act 1964, s.53(1) makes it overwhelmingly likely that an organizer of industrial action by the police would commit a criminal offence and individual striking policemen would probably commit offences under the Police (Discipline) Regulations 1977. The organizers of industrial action among the armed forces would similarly commit an offence under the Incitement to Dissatisfaction Act 1934 and individual participants a breach of military discipline. The restriction on strikes by merchant seamen probably does not fall to be classed as one motivated by a desire to protect the public but as something imposed in the interests of safety and the interests of employers. In this case, moreover, the criminal offences created in respect of seamen taking industrial action are modified by the provision of s.42(2) of the Merchant Shipping Act 1970, whereby a seaman has a positive statutory right to 'terminate his employment' (no matter what his contract may say) in contemplation or furtherance of a trade dispute, provided his ship is safely berthed in the UK and the seaman has given 48 hours' notice of leaving after the ship has been moored.

[1] In fact s.5 does apply to those acting alone as well as to those acting in combination and it is unclear that the act forbidden by s.5 would be criminal apart from that section. If it would be, then a combination of people to do the act would presumably be a criminal conspiracy, quite apart from s.5.

The Green Paper, *Trade Union Immunities*, having referred to these instances of prohibitions on resort to industrial action,[1] concluded that 'in each case, however, there are arguments of public order, security and safety which make it difficult to draw any general lessons for other industries' (para. 331). Nevertheless, the authors of the document also suggested that 'it can be . . . argued that it is not an unreasonable condition of employment in an essential service for the employee to be required to waive his right to abrogate that contract at will if the consequence is to threaten the continued function of that service with grave effects on the country' (para. 330). Although apparently cautiously formulated, this proposition could deprive employees in some industries of any right to take industrial action, and in that case the proposition would not appear inherently reasonable, unless the employees were provided with some substitute for their loss of the right to take industrial action. These substitutes, curiously not mentioned in the Green Paper, might take a number of forms, e.g. unilateral access to binding arbitration by a third party or a guarantee of a particular position in the league-table of earnings. What is clear is that a right to negotiate with one's employer is of little value unless, ultimately, a credible threat of resort to industrial action can be made. The counter-argument to the provision of a substitute for the right to strike is that the employer would be taking on a financial burden of large, but uncertain, proportions; and where, as is usually the case, the employer, directly or indirectly, is the government, that financial obligation might be or become inconsistent with its general economic policies.

The interplay between the various arguments can be seen in the two following extracts from recent Committees of Inquiry. In the case of the police a Royal Commission in 1960–2 had reviewed police pay and brought them into line with other groups. Since that time their relative position had deteriorated to the point where the police had become dissatisfied with the restrictions on their right to strike. The Edmund-Davies Committee in 1978 rejected proposals to remove the restrictions but accepted as a quid pro quo that the earnings of the police must be protected. Government acceptance of the Report did not create a legal entitlement on the part of the police to any particular level of earnings, but it did create a political commitment, which has been honoured to date, in spite of a general policy of controlling public

[1] The Green Paper might also have mentioned the particular criminal restriction upon industrial action by employees of the Post Office or British Telecom, contained in the Post Office Act 1953 and the Telegraph Act of 1863, where the industrial action involves the delay of a postal packet or telephone message. The Telecommunications Bill 1984 proposes to delete the criminal liabilities of the 1863 Act, but to create instead a statutory civil liability for inducing breach of statutory duty (*cf.* pp. 755–6 above). Where the Director-General of Telecommunications has made an order requiring a telecommunications operator to do or not do a particular thing, a duty is placed upon all persons (including trade unions) not to induce the operator to break the order or to interfere with his compliance with it, provided the act of inducement or interference 'is done wholly or partly for the purpose of achieving that result.' The purpose of the proviso is, apparently, to impose liability only where breach of the order is the object of the industrial action and not where it is an incidental consequence, albeit a foreseeable one, of industrial action (*cf.* p. 722 above). The duty is owed to all persons who may be affected by non-compliance with the order, and their remedies will be damages (to which the limits of EA 1982, s. 16, would not apply) and an injunction.

expenditure which the government elected in 1979 put into operation. The situation of the civil servants was almost the opposite. They were not restricted legally in their right to strike, but did not in practice exercise it because a Royal Commission in 1953–5 had established a comparability formula for the fixing of civil servants' pay, which in effect guaranteed the civil servants a particular relative level of earnings and came close to rendering collective bargaining a mechanical exercise. In 1981 the government itself, in pursuit of its incomes policy, refused to accept the comparability formula and a long and damaging strike ensued. The Megaw Committee set up in the wake of the strike supported the government's view that a greater degree of genuine negotiation should be built into the determination of civil service pay, but was unimpressed by proposals for specific mechanisms to avoid the breakdown of negotiations and resort to industrial conflict. In essence, their view was that such devices were inconsistent with the reasons for moving away from comparability in the first place. What the report suggests is that the initially attractive idea, both for workers and the public interested in continuous service, of restrictions on industrial action in exchange for a protected pay position is unlikely to commend itself to government on any large scale.[1]

Report of Committee of Inquiry on the Police, Cmnd. 7283
(1978), Report II, paras. 73–4, 76–8, 83–7, 257, 260–1

73.   The members of the Police Superintendents' Association, all of whom were former members of the Police Federations, have made similar submissions regarding the gravity of the consequences of a police strike. We quote:

It is essential that the police service remains independent and unfettered by any political considerations or any Trade Union. This must apply right through the law-enforcement agency, from the most junior constable to the most senior judge.

It is not difficult to imagine the problems that would arise if the service had the right to strike. Presumably, when taking such action, it would be necessary to seek the support of other unions, and, conversely, there would be occasions when the service was asked to strike in sympathy – a situation that could *not* be allowed. The Service must stand apart, or we shall quickly find ourselves compromised when policing industrial disputes and police officers' sympathies are courted.

74.   The Association of Chief Police Officers were equally forthright. They commented:

Given the right to take industrial action, the police would presumably be able, when in dispute, to refuse to render certain duties, and it is difficult to foresee to what ends this could lead. It would make ridiculous the Chief Officers' vicarious liability for the acts of his officers and the duty of the police authority to pay sums awarded in damages by a court as a result of that liability. Equally it would make nonsense of the police authority's position under the Riot Damages Act 1883. Any affiliation to other

---

[1] See, for example, also the Report of the Committee of Inquiry into the United Kingdom Prison Services, Cmnd. 7673, 1979, para. 10.48.

branches could make difficult, if not impossible, the position of police officers in dealing with some of the public order problems which arise in industrial disputes.

76.   Indeed, so uniform were the views expressed on both sides of the Police Council that the question which naturally arises is: why, then, do the Police Federation [the organization representing the lower ranks] seek the right to strike? To this they appear to give two answers, and each must be considered in its turn:

(A)   Almost all workers in the United Kingdom enjoy the right to strike, even though in many cases its exercise could create considerable disturbance; it is, accordingly, for those who would withhold a similar right from the police to justify such a differentiation.

(B)   The lack of a right to strike has greatly weakened the police forces in negotiating the conditions of their service (and particularly in the matter of pay), and they have all suffered substantially as a result.

77.   As to (A), it has to be said that the Police Federation adopt inconsistent attitudes. They readily accept the uniqueness of their role in society, and we have no doubt that they rightly take pride in it. At the same time, in the matter of the right to strike they claim to be treated on the same basis as the general body of workers. But, in fact as well as in law, they are set apart from all other workers, save for the armed forces of the Crown and the Judiciary. We have earlier referred to the virtually unique undertaking given before a magistrate by each police officer on the day he is appointed. . . . From the moment of recruitment he therefore dedicates himself to the faithful discharge of public duties of a high order. He thereby elects to place himself in a category wholly different from all other civilian workers in the land. The Association of Chief Police Officers are therefore clearly right in submitting that, '. . . to allow the police to withdraw their labour as a bargaining weapon over negotiations of pay and conditions of service would change the character of the force very much for the worse. It would make meaningless the oath which the policeman makes on his appointment.'

78.   Our conclusion as to (A), therefore, is that the Police Federation have advanced no reason which is even remotely acceptable as to why the relevant provision of the Police Act 1964, should now be repealed and replaced by others conferring upon members of the police forces of this country a right to strike. On the contrary those who oppose such a course have, in our view, conclusively established that no such right should be conferred.

83.   We do not think that it is open to doubt that the three Police Federations genuinely consider that up to the present they have been at a substantial disadvantage in negotiating on pay and other conditions of service by reason of their lack of 'industrial muscle' due to the absence of any right to strike. It is not necessary for us to decide whether this conviction is well-founded, although those representing the Official Side strongly maintained that they have at all times been at pains to safeguard the police against the risk of their being placed at any disadvantage. But, whichever side is right on this point, the contrary conviction of the Police Federations is a fact and a factor which must be taken into account.

84.   In common with all those who submitted evidence for our consideration, this Committee is satisfied that the absence of the right to strike is a serious deprivation for any worker. It is essential that the police should not suffer in pay because they are deprived of the right to strike, and that it should be put beyond doubt that they are being paid fairly.

85.   Such an important limitation on the freedom of action of members of the police force renders it even more essential (i) that the machinery for determining police pay and other conditions of service commands the confidence of all sections of the service; (ii) that the absence of any right to strike be borne in mind by both sides when negotiating and should lead to an award that does full justice to the claims of the police; and (iii) that there should be speedy arbitration at the request of either party. We sought to bear (i) and (iii) in mind when considering the future form of the negotiating machinery (see Report I, paragraphs 107 and 125). As to (ii), we have throughout had in mind the absence of such a right and emphasize that this fact has been taken into account in formulating our conclusions as to pay.

86.   It is, we think, noteworthy that the Royal Commission on Trade Unions and Employers' Associations (Cmnd. 3623, 1968) seemingly regarded it as axiomatic that no such rights should exist in the cases of the police and the armed forces of the Crown (see paragraph 245 of the Report).

87.   On such a fundamental issue as the preservation of law and order, the withdrawal of labour would be incompatible with the responsibilities of the police service and contrary to the interests of the nation. This is particularly so in relation to the maintenance of good order in emergencies (both local and national), since there are no adequate acceptable substitute arrangements which the Government could make in the event of the widespread withdrawal of police labour. Indeed, even the threat of a police strike could be very damaging to the state of law and order.

Relationship of police pay to some general index of wages or earnings

257.   There was fairly general agreement that police pay should be related to some general index, and that this should be related to earnings rather than wages. . . .

260.   The proposals by the Police Federations and the Official Side for a link at a particular level with one specific earnings index (whether non-manual male workers or all male workers) would have the effect of linking the police with one section of the community at a particular level. We have already said that the police cannot properly be compared with any other single group of workers. We therefore favour comparison with the earnings of the whole community. There is the further point that the New Earnings Survey for the groups proposed in the evidence is only available for a date in April each year, and even general results of the survey are not available till late October. This means that for a September review date the figures would not be available, and even when they did become available they would have to be up-dated by some other method, almost certainly the monthly index of average earnings.

261.   This led us to the conclusion that it would be preferable to use the monthly index of average earnings in the first place. This index has considerable advantages. It covers the whole community, and it is also available with a short time-lag of about six weeks. We therefore decided that police pay should not be linked to any particular New Earnings Survey index, but rather to the monthly index of average earnings. There are at present two series published under this index, the new series covering all employees, and the older series which does not cover the whole economy, but principally production industries. We recommend use of the new series. The salary levels which we recommend for the federated ranks and superintendents as at 1 September 1978 should therefore be updated on 1 September 1979 in accordance with changes in the index of average earnings (new series) in the previous 12 months, and similarly in subsequent years, and we recommend accordingly. (*Recommendation* 43)

Report of Committee of Inquiry into Civil Service Pay,
Cmnd. 8590 (1982), paras. 256–7, 260–1,
263–70, 273

256.   The system we propose avoids the use of set formulae in determining civil service pay. That is because a variety of factors are important and few of them, if any, can be measured exactly. Our proposals lay the emphasis upon reasoning and judgement. This inevitably, and deliberately, leaves wider scope for negotiation between Government and unions. This is a change of emphasis from the previous system, where the main determinant of the pay settlement was the results of the comparisons studies. Under our proposals the room for manoeuvre is wider.

257.   The weight we place on negotiations is not without dangers. Inevitably there is more scope for disagreement. We make no apology for this. Recent history shows that the wide measure of agreement presupposed by the Priestley system proved increasingly difficult to maintain. A new system has to reflect, not conceal, the different standpoints of the parties. However, the importance of reaching a settlement without the kind of disruption seen in 1981 is undiminished. . . .

'No industrial action' agreement

260.   A number of witnesses, notably the Ministry of Defence, have suggested that there might be scope for the introduction of 'no industrial action' agreements either into the Civil Service as a whole or for limited groups of staff engaged on particularly sensitive work. It has also been put to us that a legal liability might be introduced to deter industrial action in the Civil Service. In several democratic countries (for example the United States and the Federal Republic of Germany) civil servants are forbidden to strike. In this country the police and the armed forces are, by different statutes, effectively forbidden not to carry out their duties.

261.   We do not believe such an agreement or liability to be necessary or to be a practicable option. We do not think that it is possible to create separate groups of civil servants with publicised and enforceable 'no strike' conditions, in exchange for more favourable terms than other civil servants. It would be very hard to define the groups, and difficult to sustain the distinction in times of industrial relations tension. Neither is it a practicable option that there should be an overall declaration by the unions that all civil servants would no longer even contemplate breaking their contracts through industrial action, in exchange for some commitment by the Government to honour a future pay system. Neither side would be likely to be able to pledge itself to honour the bargain, nor would it be easy to reach a deal at a price acceptable to all parties, including the taxpayer. . . .

Arbitration

263.   The present Civil Service Arbitration Agreement, which dates from 1925, though it has been amended in various ways since, provides in theory (though not in practice for the last decade or more) for arbitration at the request of either party for claims concerning the pay of any civil servants up to the level of the Principal maximum. For grades with pay higher than this, arbitration is only with the consent of both parties.

264.   In practice, however, the Government has applied two qualifications to this agreement for unilateral arbitration. First, there is the constitutional reservation recorded in 1925: 'Subject to the overriding authority of Parliament the Government will give effect to the awards of the Court'. This qualification was made to preserve the

constitutional supremacy of Parliament and the possibility of a Government defeat there. The pledge was explained as meaning that the Government would not itself propose to Parliament the rejection of an award, once made.

265.   The second qualification on unilateral arbitration, which has been formulated more recently, has been to refuse access to arbitration on 'policy grounds'. This was explained as being necessary because the Government is responsible to Parliament for the national interest and the administration of the public service and cannot relieve itself of that responsibility or share it with any other persons or organisation , except through certain international obligations. Such refusals on grounds of policy have been extremely rare. When they have been exercised, it has almost invariably been during a period of national incomes policy. The most recent refusal of access, in 1981, was the first time a claim for arbitration had been made on behalf of the whole Civil Service (as opposed to individual unions) and the first time a claim had been refused on grounds of policy when no declared national incomes policy was in force.

266.   The parties concerned have disagreed on these 'qualifications' in the past, and it was therefore not surprising that they gave us conflicting views as to arbitration arrangements for the future. The Government stated that it 'attaches the greatest importance to ensuring that, whatever the future arrangements may be, it cannot be forced into an arbitration process with an award which it is required to implement regardless of circumstances'. The Council of Civil Service Unions, commenting on this statement, said, 'This is, of course, another variation of the "heads I win, tails you lose" attitude of the Government in their relations with their own employees. Just as no realistic collective bargaining system can include this notion, so can no acceptable form of arbitration be devised which includes this provision'.

267.   We are convinced of the value of arbitration on civil service pay. It offers an important way to avoid conflict when the two parties involved are large, monopolistic organisations where industrial action is particularly damaging and difficult to resolve. It also acts as a discipline on the parties to avoid extreme positions in negotiation which could not be sustained at arbitration. However, we think that circumstances have changed since 1925 when unilateral access to arbitration was envisaged as the norm. The Civil Service has come, within an expanded public sector, to have more impact on the economy as a whole, and the Government has therefore increasingly had to concern itself about repercussions of developments in the public sector on the rest of the economy. At the same time, changes in civil service pay arrangements and heightened concern with defending living standards in the face of inflation have made it more likely that each year the unions would wish to consider pressing claims to arbitration not just for one group of staff, but for the whole Civil Service. Moreover, arrangements for unilateral access to binding arbitration are extremely rare in other sectors of employment.

268.   The extremes to which Governments have felt obliged to go in recent years to refuse to process applications to go to arbitration, because they felt that the results might be against the wider public interest, seem to us to point to the unworkability of unilateral access in today's circumstances. Arbitration cannot be forced on an unwilling party who will find scope to avoid the most ingenious restrictions. More important, Governments cannot be expected to abdicate their duty to make judgments on what is the wider public interest and, of course, live with them and be accountable to Parliament for the consequences. For example, in times of a statutory or declared incomes policy we accept the amount of the civil service pay settlement cannot be made

subject to arbitration, and we have seen that in practice Governments have refused access to arbitration in such circumstances in the past.

269.   It seems essential to us, therefore, that the unions should be given the same right to refuse to go to arbitration. The pre-existing arrangements, and the operation of them by recent Governments, appeared to mean that the unions could always be forced to accept a third party verdict, while the Government could not. This is manifestly unfair.

270.   We therefore recommend that the present Civil Service Arbitration Agreement should be re-negotiated to make it clear that access is at the request of both parties, and either side can refuse to go. The Agreement should, however, go on to state clearly that once a reference to arbitration has been agreed both sides have committed themselves to accept its outcome whatever the problems this might create, subject always, in the case of the Government, to the overriding authority of Parliament. . . .

Breakdown in negotiations

273.   If arbitration or mediation is not employed, or if mediation fails to resolve a dispute, we think it important that industrial action should be seen to be a weapon of last resort. We recommend that in the suggested new Arbitration Agreement the parties should stipulate a period from the declaration of a breakdown in negotiations over the annual pay award during which no industrial action would take place. This period (which should in no circumstances precede the 1 April settlement date) should be sufficient to allow both sides to take stock, explain their case to the staff and make their statements available to Parliament and the public. At the end of the period the Government would be expected to announce its considered position in a Parliamentary statement, and the unions would then have to decide their reaction. The purpose of this procedure would be to give the parties a final opportunity to avoid a dispute which would do serious damage to each other and to the country.

(c) **Restrictions upon industrial action causing an emergency**

An alternative to prohibiting or restricting industrial action by specific groups of workers is to restrict the legality of industrial action according to its consequences or effects. Here, it is the fact that the industrial action has caused an emergency that triggers the legal provisions, not the fact that certain workers have resorted to industrial action. In this instance the legal provisions respond directly to the underlying policy objective of preserving the essentials of life. We have already noted (above, p. 871) that s.5 of the CPPA 1875 operates in this way by rendering liable to criminal prosecution those who (in whatever occupation employed) take industrial action in breach of their contracts of employment where they have reasonable cause to believe that the probable consequence of their action will be to endanger human life, cause serious bodily injury or expose valuable property to destruction or serious injury. We have also noted that this provision has been very infrequently invoked, perhaps because strikers taking action which is potentially of the type proscribed are usually careful to provide emergency cover on a voluntary basis (see below), perhaps because the criminal law is thought to be too blunt an instrument in such cases, and perhaps because vigorous enforcement of s.5 might well have the simple consequence that the strikers gave clear notice to terminate their contracts of employment (see above, p. 872) before the strike began. In most national strikes, notice of the impending action is not lacking; it would make little difference if the notice given ceased to be notice to break the contracts of employment and became instead notice to terminate, although a requirement to terminate might well affect the effectiveness of short stoppages or of action short of a strike.

We have also noted that the normal principles limiting the granting of interlocutory injunctions might not apply in emergency disputes (above, p. 770). However, in general the technique of restricting the legality of industrial action by reference to its consequences is not strongly represented in current labour law. This technique has the advantage over the technique of prohibiting industrial action by specified groups of workers that it does not require the legislator to define an 'essential' service. As the Green Paper noted, 'there would be great difficulty in deciding which groups of workers should be chosen and on what criteria' (para. 334). Do civil servants, for example, provide an essential service? No doubt, the answer will vary according to the branch of the civil service one is considering. However, restriction by reference to consequences brings its own definitional problems in its train. The definition of the relevant consequences in s.5 of CPPA 1875 is quite strict (at least the probability of serious injury to persons or valuable property) as is the definition of an emergency in the 1920 Act (in contrast to the much more permissive phrase, 'urgent work of national importance', used in the 1964 Act). The 1920 Act refers to the deprivation of the essentials of life by interference with the supply of food, water, fuel, light or transport. Under the emergency disputes provisions of the IRA 1971 a much broader definition of emergency was used. The Secretary of State could apply to the courts for a 'cooling off' order if the industrial action was causing or threatening to cause an interruption in the supply of goods or services that was likely (a) to be gravely injurious to the national economy, imperil national security or create a serious risk of public disorder, or (b) endanger the lives of substantial numbers of persons or expose substantial numbers of persons to serious risk of disease or personal injury (s.138(2)). In addition he could apply for a ballot to be ordered of the relevant workers if any of the above conditions were satisfied or if the action was likely to be seriously injurious to the livelihood of a substantial number of workers employed in the industry in question (s.141(2)). Writing at the time, Professor Kahn-Freund, having noted that the 1971 definition went beyond the 1875 and 1920 definitions in two respects, by including threats to national security or public order and action 'gravely injurious to the national economy', remarked in relation to the latter extension.

Labour and the Law (1st edn, 1972), p. 240

This is a gigantic expansion of the definition of an 'emergency'. It is also extremely vague. A case can be made for it in terms of the fundamental dependence of the British economy on exports, and the future legal historian may read it in the light of what his colleague, the economic historian, will tell him about the balance of payments deficit which still existed at one time, and of what the other colleague, the political historian, will tell him about the place which the balance of payments was then (at the time of the deficit) made to occupy in the public discussion. However, looking at the definition as one is forced to look at a statute, that is, forgetting its origin, one wonders how many strikes of any importance are outside that definition. Even a strike in an industry producing luxury goods or providing luxury services for the home market can gravely injure the national economy – think of the effect of an hotel strike on the tourist trade. One should not, perhaps, attach exaggerated importance to the provisions in the Act on 'emergency procedures,' but one must consider this inflation of the concept of an 'emergency' as a momentous, perhaps a portentous event.

It has sometimes been proposed that emergency provisions along the lines of those contained in the IRA 1971 should be reintroduced, even though they were used only once and then without conspicuous success. The provisions enabled the government to apply to the courts for a remedy. It is clear that in an emergency situation the government needs a remedy that lies in its own hands and should not be put in a position where it has to rely upon an employer to bring a civil action, as would be the case if the statutory immunities against tort liability were simply removed from industrial action having certain consequences. However, the history of the one occasion upon which the 1971 Act's provisions were used shows the political pressures to which governments become subject and their tendency to abuse emergency powers. Under IRA 1971, s.138, the Secretary of State could apply for a 'cooling-off' order, i.e. an injunction from the court directing named persons to cease organizing industrial action for a period of up to 60 days, not whenever there was an emergency as defined above, but only where it was also the case that 'it would be conducive to a settlement of [the dispute] by negotiation, conciliation or arbitration if the industrial action were discontinued or deferred' (s.138(1)(c)). In the case of the work-to-rule by the railwaymen in 1972, the government was attempting to operate an incomes policy. That policy had been seriously breached by the miners earlier in the year. The government was undecided what to do about its policy in the aftermath of the miners' dispute when the action on the railways over a pay claim began. Barnes and Reid (*Governments and Trade Unions* (1980), pp. 160–1) have described the government's subsequent actions in the following terms:

The choice facing the government was now exceedingly disagreeable – further inconvenience for the public and industry or a settlement and a further defeat on wages. There was, however, a new factor. As the government was not willing to make any further move to settle the dispute, it played for time by applying to the NIRC, under the provisions governing national emergencies in the Industrial Relations Act, for a 'cooling-off period' of 21 days. The union did not appear before the Court, which imposed a 'cooling-off period' of 14 days and ordered the union to instruct its members to resume normal working. The application was a gamble. There was no reason to assume, in view of the trade union policy of non-co-operation, that the unions would comply with the court order to instruct their members to return to normal working or that their members would obey the instruction. The unions did, however, comply, normal working was resumed and the ministers enjoyed a brief spell of euphoria over the success of the Act. The application for a cooling-off period could, however, be criticised as disingenuous. The purpose of 'cooling-off' was to allow moves to be made to secure a settlement, but the government was not yet ready to agree to any advance on the increases recommended by Jarratt [a mediator whose recommendations the union had rejected]. The provision in the Act, conceived to operate in a situation where industrial relations were unaffected by government policies on wages, was being used as a device for supporting what remained of the government wages policy. The time gained did not remove the dilemma.

After the 14-day cooling-off period the union reimposed the work-to-rule and overtime ban. Now the government applied to the courts for the industrial action to be ordered to be suspended whilst a ballot of the strikers was taken. The government was empowered by the IRA 1971 to apply for a ballot when there was an emergency (as defined above) and 'there are reasons for doubting whether the workers who are taking part . . . in the . . . industrial action are . . . taking part in it in accordance with their wishes and whether they have had an adequate opportunity of indicating their wishes in this respect' (s.141(1)(c)). The Court of Appeal ordered a ballot; the industrial action was suspended; 80 per cent of those voting, in a ballot in which 85 per cent of those entitled voted, cast their votes in favour of industrial action; the action was commenced for a third time; the government conceded a further 2 per cent to settle the union's wage claim. What this history illustrates is not merely the political pressures upon government to use emergency procedures, if they exist, even if the conditions for their use are not fully satisfied, but also the weakness of the control exercised by the court over the executive in such cases. Under the IRA 1971 it had to 'appear to the Secretary of State' that a cooling-off order would be conducive to a settlement or that there were reasons for doubting whether the industrial action was in accordance with the employees' wishes. In *Secretary of State* v. *ASLEF (No. 1)* [1972] ICR 7, the NIRC stressed that it was the Secretary of State's view as to the usefulness of the cooling-off period that was relevant and not the court's view. The Secretary of State had merely asserted his view on the matter and not sought to justify it. Indeed, as Barnes and Reid have subsequently made clear, it would have been difficult for him to do so since the government at the time were not prepared to allow the British Railways Board to increase its pay offer. Nevertheless, the NIRC merely concluded that 'we can see no grounds upon which the Secretary of State's view on this matter (and it is, of course, his view which matters) can be attacked' (p. 16). In *Secretary of State* v. *ASLEF (No. 2)* [1972] ICR 19, the point was considered again by the Court of Appeal on the application for a ballot. Buckley L.J. said:

There are, so far as I can see, no means for compelling the Secretary of State to explain on what grounds it appears to him that the conditions in paragraphs (*a*), (*b*) and (*c*) of section 141(1) are satisfied. This is not a case in which there is any duty imposed upon the Secretary of State to do something which the court could compel him to do by a writ of mandamus. It may well be that in the interests of good industrial relations frankness may often be a desirable policy to pursue, but if for any reason the Secretary of State chooses not to disclose his reasons I can see nothing in the section which compels him to do so.

It leaves it, therefore, to anybody who wishes to say that the Secretary of State has acted on insufficient material or with an improper appreciation of the position to establish that no reasonable man in the position of the Secretary of State could have reached the conclusions which he says he has reached without misdirecting himself in some material respect. If that were shown in evidence which satisfied the court, then I think it would be the duty of the court to proceed upon the basis that the Secretary of State was in fact proceeding upon insufficient or inaccurate material or a mistaken view of the law or whatever may be the particular aspect in which it is said that he has erred.

In consequence judicial review of the Minister's decision was, if not entirely excluded, rendered exiguous. In a case where the executive thinks there is a national emergency it is perhaps unrealistic to expect the courts to exercise greater scrutiny, if not positively invited to do so by the statute in question.

Perhaps in response to this unhappy history the Green Paper, *Trade Union Immunities*, suggests investing government with a power simply to prohibit industrial action that causes a national emergency and further suggests that the simplest way to do this would be by removing the restriction that regulations made under the Emergency Powers Act 1920 cannot make participating in a strike or peacefully persuading another to take part in a strike an offence (para. 319). In fact, experience during the Second World War suggests that prosecution of large numbers of strikes is often impractical,[1] so that the question is really whether organizing a strike should be made a criminal offence in an emergency. As the Green Paper itself notes, the proposal 'places in the hands of the executive a considerable power to restrict strikes and undermines basic liberties in a way which many would regard as unacceptable' (para. 320).

An alternative proposal would be to take the initiation of ballots out of the hands of government and also to make them a more general feature of the process of decision-making about strikes. This proposal is considered in the Green Paper, *Democracy in Trade Unions* (Cmnd. 8778, 1983). The main policy thrust of the proposal is not as a way of dealing with emergencies, but as a way of ensuring that 'important decisions are supported by a majority of the members voting in a secret ballot' (para. 56). We have already considered the implications of this proposal for the liability of trade unions in tort.[2] However, this Green Paper also notes the serious effects of strikes 'for the community as a

---

[1] See Report of the Royal Commission on Trade Unions and Employers' Associations, Appendix 6, on the results of the prosecution of strikers from the Betteshanger Colliery in 1941. Prosecution of 1,000 miners proved feasible because they agreed to plead guilty after convictions had been obtained in a few cases which the union agreed to accept as test cases. Even so, the ending of the strike had to be negotiated in gaol with the imprisoned strike leaders.

[2] And see now Appendix.

whole' (ibid.). As with the balloting provisions of the IRA 1971 the 1983 Green Paper is concerned both with protection of the community and with ensuring that strikes are not begun without strong membership support. In 1971 the former goal was perhaps the predominant one; in 1983 the latter. The Green Paper accepts that it would be impractical to require the holding of a ballot as a precondition for any lawful industrial action,[1] but considers suggestions that either a specific proportion of the union's members or perhaps even the employer in dispute should be able to call for a ballot. If no ballot were held or, perhaps, if a majority in favour of strike action was not obtained, the industrial action would no longer benefit from the statutory protections against the common law liabilities. These proposals raise a number of technical problems, but in any event, it seems unlikely that a government concerned to deal with emergency disputes would not also give itself power to call for a ballot, if it took the view that the ballot was an appropriate way to determine the legitimacy of the industrial action. Here perhaps lies the nub of the problem of compulsory ballots as a way of handling emergency disputes. Unless, contrary to experience, one takes the view that industrial action leading to emergency situations is invariably, or even usually, begun by union leaders who do not have the support of their members, it is likely that a ballot will merely demonstrate the strength of the support amongst the members for the action rather than secure its cessation, as with the industrial action by the railwaymen in 1972. At best, this dispute suggests a requirement to ballot should be imposed by government only in those situations where there is genuine ground to suppose that the dispute lacks support amongst the members and that other methods should be used to deal with emergency disputes which do not lack support. At worst, the experience of 1972 suggests government would not be able to resist the temptation to use the machinery of the compulsory ballot, if it were provided, in cases where its use would be inappropriate and even self-defeating.

(d) **Self-restraint**

In the past the potential conflict between the doctrine of collective *laissez-faire* and governments' perceived need to protect the community in emergency situations has been resolved as much by self-restraint on the part of workers in essential services as by use of the emergency powers legislation. The Green Paper, *Trade Union Immunities*, notes that 'in general workers who are in a position to endanger life or threaten security either do not go on strike, or if they do so, ensure that essential services are maintained' (para. 323). The economic conditions for the first form of self-restraint, not striking or not taking other industrial action, have increasingly ceased to obtain over the last two decades, as successive governments, of all political hues, have followed,

[1] But note that the Code of Practice on Closed Shop Agreements and Arrangements, para. 61, does apparently regard a secret ballot as in all cases a pre-condition for lawful expulsion from a trade union of a member who has refused to engage in industrial action. See above, p. 627.

especially in the public sector, incomes policies or policies of 'cash limits' of an increasingly rigorous kind. Indeed, as we saw above in relation to the civil servants, government has been driven to attack the very mechanisms (in that case the technique of comparability) that reduced the pressures for industrial action and has been reluctant to create new mechanisms that might perform a similar function. This development has thrown greater weight upon the second method of self-restraint: the maintenance of essential services even during industrial action. There has been a proliferation of codes of conduct in the essential services, sometimes issued unilaterally by the trade unions, sometimes negotiated with management, sometimes issued *ad hoc* for particular disputes, sometimes drawn up in advance. Practice was sufficiently developed for the TUC in 1979, after a rash of disputes that caused considerable difficulties for people in general, to issue some general guidance to affiliated unions on this matter. It issued a guide on the Conduct of Industrial Disputes, which put forward the following view in paras. 6 to 9:

Generally unions already recognise the need to provide emergency or essential services and to maintain plant and equipment during industrial disputes, and the TUC considers that such action is vitally necessary. It will be a matter for each union or unions to consider the action that is necessary in the light of the circumstances of the dispute. But the General Council advise that for the duration of an industrial dispute, the union(s) involved should, where necessary, make arrangements in advance and with due notice, in consultation and preferably by agreement with the employer, for the maintenance by their members of supplies and services essential to the health or safety of the community or otherwise required to avoid causing exceptional hardship or serious pollution.

Trade union members should also provide cover for the maintenance of plant and equipment essential to the functioning of the establishment and which also ensures, as far as possible, a smooth return to full production on a resumption of normal working.

Where livestock is involved, trade union members should also ensure that systems essential to their wellbeing continue to function and that supplies of foodstuffs are maintained.

Somewhat similar precepts are expressed, as we have seen above (p. 856), in paras. 37 and 38 of the Code of Practice on Picketing, issued under the Employment Act 1980, except that this contains a longer and more precise list of essential supplies and services. The question of whether to agree to and operate a voluntary code of conduct or even whether to abide by the picketing code (which, as we have seen, in paras. 37 and 38 does not seem to impinge very closely on the *legal* obligations of pickets) poses difficult issues for trade unions, but also for management. For trade unions a code of practice may be necessary to avoid the growth of public resentment against the strikers, which can, by itself, severely undermine the strikers' morale and willingness to continue with the industrial action. On the other hand, of course, the workers by imposing self-restraint may deprive themselves of the essential element of their bargaining strength. As the long-running industrial action by nurses and ancillary workers in the health service in 1982 demonstrated, the unions, by observing a code of practice which forbade industrial action which threatened the life, limb or ultimate safety of patients,[1] committed themselves to a lengthy and ultimately unsuccessful dispute with a government which saw itself as fighting for an essential element in its economic policy and which was unmoved by the hardship caused to the community by the withdrawal of non-essential medical services. Perhaps no group of workers is in so weak a bargaining position as those whose bargaining strength is too great to be capable of being deployed in practice.

Codes of conduct for the handling of disputes can also create problems for management. This perhaps seems surprising since they offer to management the advantage of reducing the impact of the strike, but they are also usually contingent upon management's adoption of a particular way of handling the dispute. The operation by the union and workers concerned of a code of conduct will normally be dependent upon management not exploiting to the full the potential pressure it could bring to bear on the strikers. It might, for example, be regarded by the workers as inconsistent with a code of conduct for the employer to refuse to pay normal wages to employees providing emergency cover, even though that cover was less than the employees' normal, full, contractual duties (see below, p. 900). Management's acceptance of a code of conduct might also be held by the workers to imply that outside contractors or volunteers would not be brought in to do the strikers' jobs or even that management would not have resort to legal remedies as a way of settling the dispute. The doing of any of these things by management might be seen by the strikers as providing the justification for departing from the rules laid down in the code of conduct, which otherwise they would have been reluctant to do. Indeed, a hardened manager might argue that codes of conduct restrict management more than workers, because codes of conduct impose upon those taking industrial action an obligation not to do things they would probably in any case be ill-advised to do. Whatever the truth of that view, it seems clear that codes of conduct can be successfully operated only with managements that are committed to negotiated settlements of disputes and to keeping open channels of communication with the strikers and their unions. As with voluntary solutions to industrial relations problems in general, success is as much the product of management attitudes and efforts as it is of those of workers and trade unions.

8 Occupations and work-ins

An occupation may be defined as a situation where the employees 'not merely down tools and remain at their places of work, but where they . . . take steps to interfere with the employer's business by seizing control of either a whole or a part of the premises in order to put pressure on the employer to concede their

---

[1] The essentials of the Code are set out in TUC Health Services Committee, *Improving Industrial Relations in the National Health Service* (1981), Chap. 10.

requests'. (Metra Oxford Consulting Ltd, *Who's in Charge? Worker Sit-ins in Britain Today* (1975), p. 9.) The seizing of control may be effected peacefully, but, even so, it is clear that the employer's property rights are being infringed. Is this sufficient to take the employees' action outside the scope of 'collective *laissez-faire*'?

As a form of industrial action the sit-in has a long, if intermittent, history. After the success of the occupation at Upper Clyde Shipbuilders in 1971 it has become a somewhat more frequently used form of pressure, usually, but not exclusively, in response to proposals by management to declare redundancies. From the employees' point of view it has the advantages that it is a much more dramatic assertion of their desire to retain their jobs, it is easier for the employees to maintain their morale than during a strike when the employees merely stay at home, and it may be more effective than a strike plus picket lines in preventing management from removing machinery and stocks of finished goods, control of which is the employees' strongest bargaining counter. Nevertheless, the employees' negotiating position is inherently weak if the employer wishes to close part of the business and occupations have rarely been successful in securing a reversal of management's decision (though they have sometimes obtained a stay of execution or enhanced redundancy payments). The TUC has described occupations as 'local level defensive reactions to decisions on investment, closure and mergers taken elsewhere' (*Industrial Democracy* (1974), para. 71). Occasionally, particular industrial and political circumstances enable the employees, having seized control of the plant, to continue to operate it. Such 'work-ins' have in some cases developed into fully-fledged worker co-operatives where the employees have been able to raise the finance, usually from the government, to buy out the previous owners, as at the Triumph plant in Meriden. Although rare, these developments have conferred a new legitimacy upon and created a new enthusiasm for worker co-operatives and the Co-operative Development Agency Act 1978 was a recognition by government of this fact. The Act creates a source of advice and co-ordination for worker co-operatives (whether arising out of occupations or not). (See further (1979) 8 *ILJ* 19.)

Although occupations have invariably been peaceful and the police have not usually thought it necessary to intervene beyond keeping themselves informed of developments, and although the increased use of the occupation in the face of economic recession and high unemployment seems to have conferred a certain social legitimacy upon it as a method of industrial action, there have been no corresponding developments in the legal status of the occupation; in fact, in procedural terms the reverse has occurred. The position is that a workers' sit-in will usually be a civil wrong against the employer and may also in some circumstances involve the employees in criminal liability. The civil wrong would be trespass, against which s.13 of TULRA provides no protection even in the context of trade disputes, for, although employees are clearly lawfully present as licensees when they are in the factory or office to perform their normal duties, their presence for other purposes may take them outside the scope of the implied licence or the employer may, after the occupation has begun, expressly withdraw the employees' implied permission to be on the premises (cf. *GLC* v. *Jenkins* [1975] 1 WLR 155 (CA)). The employer's legal problem has usually been, not to establish a basis of civil liability, but to secure an effective remedy. He may seek an interlocutory injunction under the procedures described above (pp. 765ff.), but injunctions can normally be sought only against named defendants and the employer may have difficulty in identifying all those who are in occupation or who are helping to organize the occupation. Once obtained, the injunction will bind not only the named defendants but also those who assist the named parties to disobey it, but withdrawal of the named defendants from participation in the occupation may remove the legal threat against those not named whilst not significantly weakening the occupation.

A legally more effective remedy, which, however, is not available to plaintiffs in Scotland, is the order for possession, and the Rules of the Supreme Court now contain an expedited procedure for the recovery of land.[1] This was introduced in 1970 in order to provide a speedy remedy primarily against squatters, but also against occupations by students or workers (see Rules of the Supreme Court, Order 113 as amended, and the equivalent Order 26 of the County Court Rules).[2] The standard procedure for the recovery of possession of land, like the injunction procedure, was seen not to work entirely effectively if the plaintiff could not identify all those in possession. Order 113, which applies where a person 'claims possession of land which he alleges is occupied solely by . . . persons . . . who entered into or remained in occupation without his licence or consent', allows the plaintiff to proceed by originating summons against all those in possession, whether he can identify them or not, requiring him to name in the summons only those he can identify. The summons may be served, both upon those named and those not named (*Crosfield Electronics Ltd* v. *Baginskey* [1975] 1 WLR 1135 (CA)), by fixing a copy of the summons and the supporting affidavits to the main door of the premises and, if practicable, by inserting them through the letter-box. The summons can be made returnable as a matter of urgency before a judge in a few days – any person in possession may apply at the hearing to be joined as a defendant – and the judge may at that hearing grant an order for possession. The sheriff acting under a writ of possession may evict anyone he finds on the premises, whether they were there when the summons was served or not: *R.* v. *Wandsworth County Court ex p. Wandsworth LBC* [1975] 1 WLR 1314 (DC).

The criminal liabilities for England and Wales are now mainly contained in the CLA 1977 (although, of course, deliberate destruction of the employer's property would be an offence under the Criminal Damage Act 1971).

---

[1] This procedure does not apply in Scotland, where the employer has to accept the disadvantages of proceeding for an injunction. See *Plessey plc* v. *Wilson* [1982] IRLR 198 (noted by Miller (1982) 11 *ILJ* 115).

[2] See generally Pritchard, *Squatting* (1981).

Although the Law Commission originally proposed otherwise, mere adverse occupation of premises, even after being asked by the rightful occupier to leave, is not a criminal offence, except in relation to residential premises and foreign missions. Otherwise the criminal offences are confined to resisting or obstructing an officer of a court executing a possession order obtained under the procedure described in the previous paragraph (s.10), using or threatening violence to secure entry to premises where there is someone on the premises opposed to the entry (s.6), and being on premises with a weapon of offence after having entered as a trespasser (s.8). Since most occupations take management by surprise and are not opposed by them, s.6 is more likely to be a restriction on any self-help by the latter designed to regain possession than on the initial occupation. Section 8, although limited to cases where the entry was a trespass, could have wide implications for the legality of occupations and the involvement of the police in them, since ordinary factory tools would become 'weapons of offence' if the workers formed the intention to use them for causing injury, and a reasonable suspicion on the part of the police that this was so would entitle them to enter and search the premises and to make arrests (s.11).

9 Self-help by employers

(a) The lock-out[1]

So far in this chapter, and in the previous one, we have been concerned with the situations in which industrial action taken by workers may be unlawful and with the legal remedies that an employer may be able to claim where the action is, in fact, unlawful. Such an approach leaves two sets of questions untouched. First, in what circumstances may industrial action taken by an employer or by employers be unlawful? Second, what remedies other than the institution of legal proceedings may be available to an employer who is faced by industrial action taken by workers? Both these questions are raised in a consideration of the lock-out. In many presentations of the law of industrial conflict the lock-out is viewed as the symmetrical counterpart of the strike. It is seen as a form of pressure which employers can use to persuade their employees to accept managements proposals, just as the strike is used in that way by workers. From such a perspective it is natural to ask what the counterparts are to the restrictions on the legality of industrial action by workers. In fact, however, although the law does in many ways treat the strike and the lock-out symmetrically, it must be doubted whether these two phenomena are socially equivalent. The use by an employer of the lock-out to secure acceptance of his proposals by the employees (the offensive lock-out, as it is sometimes called) is in practice a rare event, notwithstanding some noteworthy examples of its use; for example, the closure by the then owners of *The Times* for fifty weeks from November 1978.

[1] See generally Hepple, 'Lock-outs in Great Britain' (1980) 33 *Recht der Arbeit* 25.

The reasons for this situation are to be found in the fact that the employer is in a much more powerful position, legally, than his employees, even when the latter are acting in concert. The employer owns and controls the enterprise in which the workers are employed and can usually achieve the results he wishes to obtain on any matter in dispute by the exercise of the legal rights attached to his ownership and control. The employees, on the other hand, lacking those rights of control, need to influence the employer's exercise of them, by taking industrial action if the processes of negotiation are unsuccessful. Whether the initiative for change comes from management or workers, the employer can usually implement or refuse to implement the change by the exercise of his managerial powers; the employees, on the other hand, need to influence the employer's decisions. There is nothing particularly new in all this. Allan Flanders argued in the 1960s for the view that collective bargaining was best seen as a method of subjecting the otherwise unfettered discretion of management to a process of joint regulation.[1] However, a sometimes unappreciated consequence of this analysis is that the freedom on the part of the employees to take industrial action is the true counterpart of the employer's exercise generally of his legal powers of ownership and control (or his managerial 'prerogatives', as they are sometimes termed), of which the lock-out (i.e. his exclusion of the employees from the premises) is but an example and not the most important example. This is not to say that there may not well arise situations in which the employer needs to use the 'offensive' lock-out. This might happen when the employees have built up a large degree of *de facto* unilateral control of their own over the work processes (in defiance, perhaps, of the employer's legal entitlements). In such a case the employer would need to secure the consent of the employees before a change in the working practices could be instituted, and might impose a lock-out to this end. It is perhaps no accident that the most recent and notable use of the 'offensive' lock-out occurred in the national newspaper industry, where unilateral employee control of work processes is uniquely well developed.

Before leaving this point it is worth observing that another consequence of this analysis is that 'no strike – no lock-out' clauses in collective agreements do not impose symmetrical restraints upon employer and workers. Such clauses are much more restrictive of the freedom of workers to secure their ends than of management's freedom of action. From the union's point of view what is needed is a clause that controls managerial prerogatives much more broadly. In the 1970s some unions succeeded in re-drawing the boundaries of the peace obligation so that it no longer controlled only the right of the union to resort to industrial action before the procedure was exhausted but also the right of the employer to initiate change before exhaustion. See S. D. Anderman, 'The Status Quo Issue and Industrial Disputes Procedures' (1975) 4 *ILJ* 131. A good example of such a 'Status Quo' clause is that contained in the engineering industry disputes procedure of 1976. This provides:

[1] Flanders, 'Collective Bargaining: A Theoretical Analysis' in *Management and Unions* (1970), pp. 213ff.

Where any party wishes to raise a matter for resolution, there shall be discussion at domestic or national level, as appropriate. It is agreed that in the event of any difference arising which cannot immediately be disposed of, then whatever practice or agreement existed prior to the difference shall continue to operate pending a settlement or until the agreed procedure has been exhausted. In order to allow for the peaceful resolution of any matter raised by any party, there shall be no stoppage of work, either of a partial or general character, such as a strike, lock-out, go-slow, work-to-rule, overtime ban or any other restrictions, before the stages of procedure provided for in this Agreement have been exhausted. [Clause 5]

The above may help to explain the infrequency of the use of the 'offensive' lock-out by employers. The 'defensive' lock-out, or the use of the lock-out as a response to industrial action taken by employees, is more frequently found in practice. This raises the second issue mentioned at the beginning of this section, namely the question of the legality of self-help remedies available to an employer who cannot (because the employees' action is not unlawful) or does not wish to have resort to the courts for an injunction or an award of damages. An employer, who, say, is suffering from a go-slow which has severely disrupted production, may prefer to precipitate a full stoppage through a lock-out because it may considerably increase the pressures on the workers (by depriving them of wages) whilst only marginally worsening the employer's position. How does such action stand in law?

Whilst in social practice the strike and the lock-out may not be equivalents, the law tends to treat them as such, so that an employer who locks out his employees could be liable to them, in principle, either for the commission of an economic tort or for breach of their contracts of employment. Even here, the employer has certain in-built advantages. A company is in law a single person. Where it locks out its employees in breach of their contracts, it would seem to commit neither the tort of conspiracy nor the tort of inducing breach of contract. Matters might be different if the industrial action were co-ordinated by an employer's federation, but even then the defendants might well have the protection of s.13 of TULRA 1974 (as amended). The situation in which the protections of TULRA have been withdrawn by EA 1980 and 1982 are not ones likely to affect the protection of locking-out employers. In any case, as Professor Hepple has pointed out,[1] no case appears to have been made out against an employer that his lock-out was tortious.

More attention has been paid to the question of whether the lock-out is a breach by the employer of the contracts of employment of the employees locked out. It would seem that an offensive lock-out is normally a breach if the employees are ready and willing to work normally on their existing terms and conditions of employment and the lock-out has not been preceded by notice of the appropriate length (which would depend upon length of service, cf. EPCA 1978, s.49(1)) from the employer to terminate the contracts of

[1] Op. cit., p. 28.

employment of all the individuals who are to be locked out.[1] By analogy with strike notices, ambiguous notices to lock out might well be construed by the courts as notices of intention to break the contracts of employment rather than as notice to terminate (see above, p. 720).[2] By analogy with the position of strikes (see below, p. 903) an offensive lock-out is in the usual case, not merely a breach of contract, but also a repudiatory breach by the employer, entitling the employees lawfully to terminate their contracts, a course of action, however, which may well offer little advantage to them. Dismissal of strikers by an employer may be a prelude to the hiring of a replacement workforce and the resumption of production; there is no equivalent collective action on the employees' side which their ending of their contracts may permit them to do, although they may, of course, individually go to jobs elsewhere. Termination of the contract in response to the employer's repudiatory breach in locking the employees out might be a more advantageous course for the employees if it opened the way, via the concept of constructive dismissal (see above, p. 448), to unfair dismissal remedies, but, as we shall see in a moment, access to unfair dismissal claims is very much restricted where it is a lock-out that has led to the termination of the contract.

Thus, an employee's purely contractual remedies are rather limited when he is locked out by an employer as part of an offensive lock-out which has not been preceded by lawful termination of the contracts of employment of those locked out. This is perhaps no more than a reflection in a particular situation of the general weakness of the employee's remedies for breach of contract (cf. above, p. 459). Where the lock-out is used defensively, however, as will more often be the case, the employee's contractual remedies may disappear entirely. We have already seen that many forms of industrial action short of a strike amount to breaches of the contract of employment by those taking the action (above, p. 720). If, as will also often be the case, such action is regarded as repudiatory on the part of the employees, the employer may lock out those taking the action and justify the lock-out as merely acceptance on his part of the repudiatory conduct of the employees. In the following case the matter was taken a stage further, because the employers threatened to lock out not merely the employees engaged in the disruptive action but also all those who would benefit if the action were successful. The employees sought injunctions to restrain the employers from implementing their threats, but failed to obtain them. In view of the long-standing common law rule that the contract of employment is not specifically enforceable, the result is not surprising and it is unclear why the employees brought the litigation before the threats were implemented (see Freedland (1975) 3 *ILJ* at p. 181). For present purposes the interest in the case lies in the question of whether it suggests that the employer

---

[1] *Cummings* v. *Charles Connell & Co (Shipbuilders) Ltd* 1969 SLT 25 where, unusually, the employer had in effect entered into a fixed term contract of 18 months' duration with the employee, who was held entitled to recover by way of damages wages not paid to him during a two-month-long lock-out.

[2] Thus giving the employee an entitlement to damages in respect of unpaid wages. See n.1.

is contractually free to lock-out employees not engaged in the industrial action but who will directly benefit from the success of the action, at least where the employees refuse to give guarantees of 'good behaviour'.

Chappell v. *Times Newspapers Ltd* [1975] ICR 145 (CA)

The Newspaper Publishers Association were in dispute with the National Graphical Association about pay differentials of NGA members employed in Fleet Street. In order to further their claim the NGA called upon small groups of key workers in the composing rooms to take various forms of short-lived industrial action, which severely disrupted the production of some daily papers. Attempts at a settlement failed and the union announced that it would 'prosecute the dispute with all the resources at its disposal'. The NPA replied to the union that, unless it withdrew its instructions about further industrial action, the employers 'will regard all your members employed as having by action or implication accepted instruction to infringe their personal contracts of employment and thereby to have terminated their own engagements'. The plaintiffs, members of the union and employees of the newspaper publishers, sought injunctions restraining the publishers from terminating their employment.

LORD DENNING M.R.: ... The case for the men is that they should be regarded as individuals with their own individual contracts of employment. They say that they have not taken part in any disruptive action at all. They were not members of any of the groups which stopped production. They have not repudiated their contract. They have not broken their contract of employment in any way. And therefore the employers have no right to dismiss them or threaten them with dismissal. So they ask for an injunction to prevent the employers from terminating their employment.

The only point which could be taken against the men – regarded as individuals – was their refusal to give an undertaking. It arose in this way. During the hearing before Megarry J., this question was put to counsel for these men: 'Will you undertake not to engage in disruptive activities?' Each of the men by their counsel refused to give such an undertaking. Is that refusal to be taken as a breach or a repudiation of his individual contract of employment? Mr Pain said not. He referred to a passage in *Halsbury's Laws of England*, 4th ed., vol. 9 (1974), p. 377, para. 548, where it is said: 'A party is not bound before the time for performance to give a definite answer whether he intends to fulfil the contracts or not', for which is cited an old case of *Ripley* v. *M'Clure* (1849) 4 Exch. 345.

I doubt whether that old case should be regarded as an authority for that proposition. It has been overtaken by later cases such as *Hochster* v. *De La Tour* (1853) 2 E&B 678, 692 and *Mersey Steel and Iron Co.* v. *Naylor, Benzon & Co.* (1884) 9 App. Cas. 434. It seems to me that it all depends on the evidence. If the conduct of these men evinces an intention no longer to be bound by their contracts of employment, they could properly be said to be repudiating their contracts. But the failure to give an undertaking might not, by itself, be sufficient. It might be regarded as equivocal. So for present purposes I would be prepared to accept that if you look at these individual men and see what each of them has done himself – apart from what the union has done – it could well be said that they were not individually in breach of their terms of employment.

Mr Neill, for the publishers, did not rely much, if at all, on that failure to give an undertakng. His point was that we ought not to look at what each man himself had done as an individual. We ought to look at what the trade union had done on his behalf, that is, on behalf of him and all the other members of the union. He urged that, in threatening to take industrial action, the union was acting as the agent of the men and of each of them.

In considering this question of agency, I would take it in steps. First, I would consider the role of the union in negotiating with the employers. There is no doubt, I should have thought, that when a union is seeking on behalf of the men higher wages – sitting at the table, negotiating with employers – they are acting in the interests of the men and on behalf of the men.

But in this case we are not concerned simply with negotiations. We are concerned with the threat of industrial action contained in the press release of 14 January 1975. Was that done as agent for the members of the union? Some such question arose in *Heatons Transport (St Helens) Ltd* v. *Transport and General Workers Union* [1972] ICR 308. In that case the shop stewards at Hull had taken industrial action – by 'blacking' – contrary to the advice of the union officials (which was sincerely given) that they were to cease 'blacking'. In the Court of Appeal I myself expressed the view that the shop stewards had authority to *negotiate* on behalf of the union, but not to take industrial action: see [1972] ICR 308, 341. But the House of Lords held that the shop stewards had authority, not only to negotiate, but *also to take industrial action* so as to make the union responsible. This authority did not arise out of delegation from 'the top' (that is from the council of the union), but arose out of authority given from 'the bottom' (that is, given by the membership of the union). This authority was derived from the custom and practice of trade unions. It was held that the shop stewards have a general implied authority to act *on behalf of all the members* to defend and improve their rates of pay and working conditions, and may do so by negotiation *or by industrial action* at the place of work; see the opinion of the House in [1972] ICR 308, 393F–G, 395F–G, 397F–G, 405G.

If this be right – if the source of the authority of the shop stewards and of the union is derived from 'the bottom' – that is, from all the members – it seems to follow that the members themselves must be taken to authorize whatever the union or its officials do on their behalf. I mean, of course, in negotiating better terms or taking industrial action in support of them. Each member must be taken to authorize what is done in these respects on behalf of each and all of them, unless he specifically disavows it.

If this is correct, then in issuing the press release, as the NGA did (saying they were going to resume industrial action in support of their claim) it can well be argued that the union were acting on behalf of all of the men. Mr Pain sought to draw a distinction between the membership of the union as a whole and each individual within it. But that distinction did not convince me. If the press release was issued by the union on behalf of *all* the men, then each one of them must be taken to have authorised it, unless he disavowed it. None of them did disavow it. And, having been authorized by all, it can well be said that it amounted to a repudiation by all of their contracts of employment. That is indeed what Mr Neill submitted. He said that the publishers were justified in retorting, as they did, and saying: 'If the men do this and threaten industrial action in this way, they are repudiating their contracts and we are entitled to treat them, and all of them, as terminated.'

with their employers.

. . . Assume, however, that the publishers were in the wrong, and that they ought not to have said that they would regard the men as having terminated their own engagements, nevertheless the question arises whether an injunction should be granted restraining the publishers from terminating agreements. The general rule is that the courts will not order specific performance of contracts of employment. If there is a wrongful termination by one side, the remedy of the other party is in damages only. That has been the law for a very long time. It is reinforced by section 16 of the Trade Union and Labour Relations Act 1974, which says:

> No court shall, whether by way of – (*a*) an order for specific performance or specific implement of a contract of employment, or (*b*) an injunction or interdict restraining a breach or threatened breach of such a contract, compel an employee to do any work or attend at any place for the doing of any work.

An exception was created in this court in *Hill* v. *C. A. Parsons & Co. Ltd* [1972] Ch. 305, which was considered recently by Sir John Donaldson in *Sanders* v. *Ernest A. Neale Ltd* [1974] ICR 565. *Hill* v. *Parsons* was exceptional, in that both employers and Mr Hill had complete confidence in one another. Yet the employers – against their own wishes – gave Mr Hill notice of the termination of his employment. It was given under pressure from a trade union. The notice was invalid. By granting an injunction the law was vindicated and justice was done. I would not detract from anything that was said in that case; but this case is very different. If an injunction were granted here, no one could have any confidence that the employment would continue peaceably. The NGA have destroyed any expectation of peace by saying that they are going to resume industrial action. No employers can be expected to continue to employ a body of men – or any of them – who assert through their union that they intend to disrupt the business and bring losses on their employers. It may be that only a small group of the union will actually take industrial action. But that does not mean that the others (who are not actually taking the industrial action) can get an injunction. It would be quite unacceptable for the court to put such compulsion on the employers – so as to make them keep many men on at the place of work and to pay them wages – for doing nothing – while industrial action was being pursued by a small group.

There is another point which seems to me decisive. These men are saying that the publishers are about to break the contract of employment. But it is plain that they are not ready and willing to perform their own side of it. It has long been settled both at common law and in equity that in a contract where each has to do his part concurrently with the other, then if one party seeks relief, he must be ready and willing to do his part in it.

. . . In this case it seems to me impossible for any of the plaintiffs to say that he is ready and willing to perform his part of the contract when on the statement of his union, the National Graphical Association (which he has never disavowed), he may be called upon, or other members of his union may be called upon, to take industrial action so as to bring great losses to their employers. Not being ready and willing to do their part, they cannot call on the employers to continue to employ them. They are seeking equity when they are not ready to do it themselves.

The remarks of Lord Denning in the above case based upon the House of Lords' decision in *Heatons Transport* v. *TGWU* may need reconsideration in the light of their lordships' subsequent decision in *General Aviation Services* v. *TGWU* (above, p. 829), and in view of the fact that the point at issue in those cases was the liability of the union for its member's action and not vice versa. Nevertheless, the main thrust of the Court of Appeal's decision is clear. They were unwilling to hold to be a breach of contract an employer's proposed defensive lock-out where the union, by calling upon only selected groups of key workers to strike, had been able to inflict considerable loss upon the employer at relatively little cost to its own members. A rather similar point, although one with opposite implications for the employer, arises in respect of the employer's liability to unfair dismissal proceedings when he has locked out his employees. For reasons that we shall look at more fully below in relation to strikes, Parliament ever since the unfair dismissal laws were introduced in 1971 has taken the view that they should not in general be capable of being used to judge the fairness of dismissals which are effected during the course of industrial disputes. Consequently, s.62 of EPCA 1978 provides that where at the date of the dismissal the employer was conducting or instituting a lock-out, the industrial tribunal shall not have jurisdiction to consider the fairness of the dismissal – with one exception. That exception operates to give the tribunal jurisdiction if either one or more of the relevant employees has not been dismissed or one or more of the relevant employees has been offered re-engagement and the applicant has not. In short, the policy seems to be to relieve the employer who locks out of the need to justify his actions if he dismisses all the relevant employees and re-engages none of them. If, on the other hand, he treats some of the employees more favourably, the tribunal will have jurisdiction to scrutinize the fairness of the dismissals, or, if there has been selective re-engagement, the fairness of the refusal to offer re-engagement (see *Edwards* v. *Cardiff CC* [1979] IRLR 303). Of course, it does not follow from the grant of jurisdiction to the tribunal in such cases that it will necessarily find the selective dismissals or offers of re-engagement to have been unreasonable.

However, there is a problem about defining the relevant group of employees whom the employer must treat equally, if the tribunal is not to have jurisdiction. As we shall see below, the problem is not without difficulty in the case of the dismissal of strikers or those taking other industrial action, but at least in that case it is easy to see that the basic principle should be equal treatment for all those taking the action, a group which is not defined by the employer himself. But in the case of a lock-out it will not do to say that all those locked out must be dismissed or not offered re-engagement, for the employer could then build in the element of selectivity when deciding whom to lock out. He might, for example, lock out only those he regarded as the ringleaders of the dispute. Consequently, in relation to a lock-out 'relevant employees' are defined by s.62(4)(*b*)(i) of EPCA 1978 as those 'directly interested in the dispute in contemplation or furtherance of which the lock-out occurred'. The concept of 'direct interest' is one borrowed from social security law (see below,

p. 941) and would seem to embrace anyone whose terms and conditions of employment are likely to be immediately affected by the outcome of the dispute. As the following case suggests, in order to preserve his decisions from the scrutiny of the industrial tribunal the employer may have to dismiss a wider range of people than those he has actually locked out.

Fisher v. York Trailer Co. Ltd [1979] ICR 834 (EAT)

The employers sent a letter on 7 February to 34 of their employees working in a particular section of their plant, seeking an undertaking that they would work at a normal incentive pace and saying that they would be suspended from the start of the next shift if they did not give the undertaking. The next day none of the employees worked, but they held a meeting to consider the letter and, in the result, all but seven employees gave the undertaking. The seven were suspended and a few days later were given another letter which said they would be dismissed if they did not sign the undertaking by the beginning of the next shift. The seven did not sign, were dismissed on 13 or 14 February, and claimed compensation for unfair dismissal.

SLYNN J.: . . . The industrial tribunal, in this case, came to the conclusion that, at the time of the dismissals on February 13 or 14, the company was conducting a lock-out. They took the definition of 'lock-out' from the Contracts of Employment Act 1972, Schedule 1, paragraph 11 (1) [now EPCA 1978, Sch. 13, para. 24(1)]. They went to that Act because there is no definition of a 'lock-out' in the Trade Union and Labour Relations Act 1974. In the Contracts of Employment Act 1972 'lock-out' means:

. . . the closing of a place of employment, or the suspension of work, or the refusal by an employer to continue to employ any number of persons employed by him in consequence of a dispute, done with a view to compelling those persons, or to aid another employer in compelling persons employed by him, to accept terms or conditions of or affecting employment.

On the appeal to us, which is brought by three out of the six employees who were dismissed, it has not been suggested that we should do other than follow the industrial tribunal in adopting the definition in the Act of 1972. The tribunal were satisfied that what was done here, when the company refused to allow the employees to work, unless they gave the written undertaking, was done in consequence of a dispute with a view to compelling the employees to accept, as a term of their employment, the matters set out in the letter of February 7. They also came to the conclusion that the case turned upon the meaning of 'relevant employees' in paragraph 7 (5) (*b*) (i) of Schedule 1 to the Trade Union and Labour Relations Act 1974 [now EPCA 1978, s.62(4) (*b*) (i)]. Who were the employees who were directly interested in the trade dispute in contemplation or furtherance of which the lock-out occurred? Put shortly, were the relevant employees the 34, or were they the seven? The tribunal came to the conclusion that here the persons who were directly interested in the trade dispute were only the seven. They thought that the management were dissatisfied with the rate of line movement but that there was no dispute until the letter of February 7 was given, requiring the employees to sign it and some of the employees refused to sign. At the stage there was a dispute which led to the lock-out. As we read it they were saying that it was a combination of the delivery of the letter, and the refusal to sign it, that really created, or evidenced, the dispute.

The industrial tribunal obviously came to the conclusion that the relevant time, for the purpose of this decision, was the time when the employees were dismissed. At that stage the other 27 had all gone back and so they obviously were of the view that, by then, they were not directly interested in the trade dispute. . . .

We are prepared to accept that the act done should be regarded as one done in contemplation of a trade dispute as Mr Brent, in particular, has submitted. But that, it seems to us, is not conclusive of the question. One still has to go back to ask oneself the question which is posed by paragraph 7 (5) (as amended) of Schedule 1 to the Trade Union and Labour Relations Act 1974: who are the relevant employees; who are the persons in relation to the lock-out who were interested in the trade dispute in contemplation or furtherance of which the lock-out occurred? Mr Moxon Browne [counsel for the employers], to whom we are indebted for his able and concise argument, has submitted that there was only one dispute, which led to one lock-out. That did not arise until after the majority of the employees had signed the letter. Those who signed, he says, were not parties to the dispute and are not to be treated as being locked out. It is only the seven who were in dispute and only the seven who were locked out. Alternatively, he says, that we should regard what happened here as constituting two quite separate lock-outs. The first was of the 34; that came to an end when the majority signed. A new lock-out began when the ordinary shift working recommenced and that dispute, and that lock-out, related only to the seven. Now, obviously, two quite separate lock-outs might have been found to occur. It may be that if the suspension, which was threatened in the letter of February 7, had been lifted it could be really said that no lock-out began until the majority had signed. We find it quite impossible, on the findings of the tribunal and the material which we have seen, to say that that is what happened here. The letter of February 7 went out to all the 34 employees. They were all told that they would not, in effect, be allowed to work unless they signed. None of them did sign; we understand that none of them worked on February 8. It does not seem to us that we should infer from the fact that a meeting was being held in the course of February 8 that the company in some way had lifted the suspension and withdrawn the lock-out. It seems to us, on the findings of the tribunal, that there was a lock-out from the beginning, following the delivery of the letter dated February 7 and the refusal of the employees to sign and that that same lock-out continued throughout.

Then Mr Moxon Browne relies upon the reasoning of the industrial tribunal. He says that those who were directly interested in the trade dispute were only those who, at the end, refused to sign, i.e. those who refused to sign throughout. In effect what that really comes to is that it is those who were dismissed who were to be treated as directly interested in the trade dispute at the time of their dismissal. If that is right, of course, they were all dismissed; so none of them can come to an industrial tribunal to claim in respect of unfair dismissal.

At the end of the day, as we see it, the essential question in this case is whether that is right. There clearly may be said to be force in the argument that is put forward that only those who were directly interested were those who persisted in refusing to sign, and it is those who were dismissed, still persisting in their refusal, who were the only persons directly interested.

We must look, however, at the words of the legislation. We have been reminded at the change in the wording brought about by the amendment. Paragraph 7 of Schedule 1 to the Trade Union and Labour Relations Act 1974, as initially worded, provided that the dismissal of an employee by way of a lock-out should not be regarded as unfair if the employee was offered re-engagement, as from the date of resumption of work. That was to apply whether the lock-out extended to all the employees or only to some of them and whether the dismissal occurred at the beginning of the lock-out or during the course of it. The date of resumption of work is defined in paragraph 7 (4) as being the date as from which, at or after the termination of the lock-out, the other comparable employees of the original employer, or a majority of those employees, were offered re-engagement. 'Comparable employees' in relation to an employee are defined as meaning: 'such of the employees of the original employer to whom the lock-out extended as, immediately before the effective date of termination, held positions similar to that held by that employee.' That seems to limit the comparable employees to those who were actually locked out and who held similar positions. The wording of the new paragraph [substituted by EPA 1975, Sch. 16, Pt III, para. 13 and later consolidated in EPCA 1978, s.62] appears to be wider than that. It relates to employees who were directly interested in the trade dispute, which, of course, would include those who were locked out but, it seems to us, would also include a wider category who were not actually locked out.

It is of some assistance to consider the words of paragraph 7(2)(*b*). That refers to relevant employees, in relation to a strike, as employees who took part in it. The House of Lords has held, in relation to the previous words of paragraph 8 of Schedule 1 to the Act of 1974, that those words related to persons who took part in the strike action but could not be limited only to persons who have taken part, and were still taking part in the strike at the date of dismissal. Accordingly, it would seem that the relevant employees in that context are any who took part in the strike, even if they went back before the ones who persisted throughout and who were eventually dismissed. Mr Moxon Browne is entitled to say that the wording of the two paragraphs is quite different and that what the House of Lords was doing was giving effect to the literal meaning of the words and not seeking to apply, what is sometimes called, a 'purposive method of construction.' We seek to do the same in relation to paragraph 7 (1). It is clear that there are no express words which limit the employees who are to be treated as directly interested to those who remain right through to the end. That indeed might have produced, in some situations, a difficult and perhaps surprising result. Here the question has to be: who were the employees who were directly interested in the trade dispute in contemplation or furtherance of which the lock-out occurred? That, it seems to us, involves asking when the lock-out occurred and what was the trade dispute in contemplation or furtherance of which the lock-out was put into effect? Here it is clear, as we have said, that the trade dispute was as to the obligation to sign the letter and as to whether the terms of the letter reflected the terms of the contract. As the tribunal found, and as we certainly consider, the lock-out here occurred when the employees were told that they would not be allowed to work and indeed did not work on February 8. It seems to us that, at that stage, none of the 34 employees had consented to sign the letter. There was then a dispute between all of them and the company. It seems to us that all 34 were employees who were directly interested in the trade dispute at some time while that trade dispute was going on. That was a trade dispute in respect of which the particular lock-out occurred.

Accordingly, it seems to us, contrary to the decision of the industrial tribunal, that the 34 employees were all relevant employees since they were all directly interested in the dispute which led to the lock-out. Accordingly, we do not consider that the appellants are barred from pursuing their claim before the industrial tribunal. The question which will now have to be decided is whether the dismissal, which the tribunal held occurred, was fair or unfair. We have sought, we hope successfully, not to reflect any view either way as to how that matter ought to be decided. It is to be decided entirely by the industrial tribunal on the evidence which will be adduced before them. We decide no more than that these claims are not barred by paragraph 7 (2) of Schedule 1 to the Act of 1974. . . .

(b) Non-payment of wages and suspension from employment

Although interesting from the point of view of legal analysis, the lock-out, even the defensive lock-out, is not the most usual response of an employer to industrial action by his employees. The most obvious source of economic pressure that an employer can utilize against his employees is the non-payment of wages during the continuance of the industrial action. Where the action takes the form of a strike, there seems little doubt that the employees are not entitled to wages for a period when they were not prepared to and did not work, although sometimes, upon a successful conclusion of the strike, compensation for wages lost is in fact negotiated with the employer, especially when the strike is regarded as having occurred in response to some improper action of management. In the case of action short of a strike, but which is in breach of the contracts of employment of those taking it, the position is less clear. As we have noted above, it is in such cases that the employer may wish to have recourse to the defensive lock-out. On the other hand, he may regard the simple non-payment of wages to those taking the industrial action as likely to involve him in less odium and likely to be as effective a sanction as the lock-out. This issue has been a matter of some discussion in recent years. For example, in a circular issued by the Department of Health and Social Security to Area Health Authorities in 1979[1] it was argued that employees who do not perform substantially the whole of their contractual duties are not entitled to be paid at all for the relevant period and that management should pay at most an *ex gratia* sum related to the proportion of the normal duties in fact carried out.

Such strictly contractual reasoning receives some support from the decision of the Court of Appeal in *Henthorn* v. *Central Electricity Generating Board* [1980] IRLR 361.[2] Although the issue arose as a point of law on the pleadings, its resolution has a clear implication for the substantive law in this area. The plaintiffs were manual workers, employed at a power station, who took part in an unofficial work-to-rule. The defendants took the view that this action was a breach of their contracts on the part of the employees and refused to pay wages for the period of the industrial action. The employees commenced an action in the county court claiming pay for the period and in their particulars of claim asserted that they had been ready and willing to perform their contracts. An arbitrator appointed under the County Courts Act held that on the pleadings it was for the employers to begin and he eventually awarded in favour of the

---

[1] DHSS Circular HC (79) 20, 'If Industrial Relations Break Down'.
[2] See also *Miles* v. *Wakefield MDC, The Times*, 22 November 1983.

employees on the grounds that the employers had not succeeded in showing that the employees were not ready and willing to perform their contracts. In the Court of Appeal the employers were successful in having the award set aside and the matter remitted to another arbitrator on the grounds that 'when a plaintiff claims that he is entitled to be paid money under a contract which he alleges the defendant has broken he must prove that he was ready and willing to perform the contract'. In the case of industrial action short of a strike which constituted a breach of the contract of employment it would seem that a plaintiff employee would not normally be able to discharge that burden and that his claim for wages would accordingly fail. A further development of such contractual reasoning would lead to a justification for an employer who 'suspends' employees who are not prepared to work normally. The argument would be that the employer is not obliged to accept substantially less than full performance of the duties under the contract of employment and can, thus, without breach of contract on his part, reject the proffered lesser performance.[1] Indeed, it is not clear that there is a real distinction between suspension of this type and a defensive lock-out.

However, in *Bond* v. *CAV Ltd* [1983] IRLR 360 Peter Pain J. took a somewhat more flexible view of the possible contractual analyses of these situations. In this case the plaintiff, a machine setter, refused to operate one of the four machines in his charge because he and his fellow employees were in dispute with their employers about the correct method of payment for work done on certain machines. He continued to operate the other three machines in the usual way. The learned judge accepted that 'it was open to the (employers) at any time . . . to insist that the setters cease work and leave the premises if they were not prepared to work . . .' all four machines in accordance with their contracts. However, in this case the employers had in fact permitted the employees to continue to work at less than full contractual performance by supplying the rest of the machines with power, oil and raw material, and the product of the machines had been taken by the employers and processed further in other departments. In these circumstances Peter Pain J. held that the employers had waived the employees' breach of contract, and the latter's claim for wages not paid during the period of the industrial action succeeded.

(c) Dismissal of those taking industrial action

The third form of self-help by an employer that we need to consider is the dismissal of those taking industrial action. Where the industrial action takes the form of a strike it may seem that dismissal will add little to the economic pressures upon the employees because they will no longer be in receipt of wages. Indeed, *Henthorn* v. *CEGB* suggests that the employer can apply this degree of economic pressure to those taking at least some forms of industrial action short of a strike. However, the view that dismissal adds nothing where

---

[1] Such suspension is to be distinguished from suspension as a disciplinary penalty, which is not contractually justifiable in the absence of a term in the contract permitting it: *Hanley* v. *Pease & Partners Ltd* [1915] 1 KB 698.

the employer has already ceased to pay wages grossly underestimates the psychological impact of the dismissal as a weapon in the employer's armoury and also its potential long-term economic impact. As we have pointed out above (p. 720), the legal view that strike notice is usually to be construed as notice to break the contract of employment and not as notice to terminate it is grounded in the fact that strikers do not expect the strike to end the employment relationship but rather to lead to its continuance upon terms more favourable to them. The same is true even of the lock-out, offensive or defensive, except that in the case of the offensive lock-out it is the employer who is seeking to achieve more favourable terms and conditions of employment. This view is reflected also in the statutory definitions of 'strike' and 'lock-out' in Sch. 13 to EPCA 1978. As was noted by the Appeal Tribunal in *Fisher* v. *York Trailer* (above, p. 897), these definitions, curiously, are not applied in terms to the unfair dismissal provisions of s.62 of EPCA 1978 but only to the provisions for computation of the length of continuous employment (see below, p. 932), but from the present point of view that does not matter. What is significant is that both definitions are in terms of action taken with a view to compelling the employer or the persons locked out (as the case may be) to accept or not to accept terms or conditions of or affecting employment.

In this situation the announcement by an employer of the dismissal of or of his intention to dismiss the strikers can come as a bombshell, because it amounts in effect to a declaration that the employer no longer shares the expectation that the employment relationship will resume at the end of the dispute. Of course, the employer may be bluffing or, even if he is not, the employees' bargaining strength may be such that they are able to negotiate their re-employment (or even re-engagement) as part of the terms of the settlement of the dispute. But, except in those few clear cases of bluff or of overwhelming strength on the employees' side, the employer's announcement will at least be a blow to the morale of the strikers and may in fact be the prelude to their losing their jobs permanently. This may occur because the employer intends to recruit a replacement workforce and thereby resume production, or because the employer intends to close down the part of the business in which the employee was employed, or because he intends to offer a resumption of work only on terms that the employees accept more efficient working practices so that fewer jobs will be available, and so on. What, then, does the law say about the legality of the dismissal of those on strike or taking other industrial action? Technically, as with the lock-out, the matter has to be examined both from the point of view of the law of the contract of employment and from the point of view of the law of unfair dismissal. Substantively the result is that the law places few restrictions upon the legal freedom of employers to dismiss those taking industrial action, and this raises, as we shall see, another aspect of the discussion about 'the right to strike'.

We have already noted above in connection with the legality of the defensive lock-out that the courts seem to regard many forms of industrial action as not merely constituting a breach of the contract of employment but as a repudiatory breach. This is not, of course, the invariable position: a ban on voluntary overtime may not be a breach of contract at all (see above, p. 721) and the courts may well not regard a strike that is announced in advance to be a short, demonstration strike as a repudiatory breach in all cases. Nevertheless, the general tendency seems clear, and in the situation of a repudiatory breach by the employees orthodox contractual reasoning leads to the conclusion that the employer can accept the breach and terminate the contract of employment without contractual liability on his part. This result seems to be a flat contradiction to any right to strike at the individual level, but, as we have also noted above (p. 721), the courts in general have not been astute to use the technique of terms implied by law to modify this result and that, to some extent, lack of creativity in relation to the contract of employment was an aspect of the doctrine of collective *laissez-faire*, no matter how perverse its results. The issue was most recently considered *in extenso* in *Simmons* v. *Hoover Ltd*.

Simmons v. *Hoover Ltd* [1977] ICR 61 (EAT)

The employee, who had worked for the employers for ten years, was dismissed for redundancy while he was taking part in a strike. An industrial tribunal held that his right to a redundancy payment was excluded by s.2(2) of RPA 1965 (now EPCA 1978, s.82(2)) which provides that an employee 'shall not be entitled to a redundancy payment by reason of dismissal where his employer, being entitled to terminate his contract of employment by reason of the employee's conduct, terminates it' in certain prescribed ways. The question thus arose whether the employee's conduct in striking was a breach of his contract of employment so that the employer was entitled to dismiss him or whether some alternative legal analysis should be applied.

PHILLIPS J.: . . . Mr Sedley developed his first argument at considerable length, and with much supporting authority, example and detail. However, it is possible to summarize it for present purposes comparatively shortly. The vital question which arises under section 2(2) is whether in the circumstances of this case the employers were entitled to terminate the employee's contract of employment without notice by reason of his conduct. The view of the industrial tribunal was that they were entitled to dismiss him summarily because he was on strike. In paragraph 19 of their reasons they say:

> . . . we are further satisfied that so extreme a form of industrial action as a strike would certainly justify a summary dismissal as a matter of law. Whether or not such a course would be prudent or is one commonly adopted are wholly separate questions with which we are not of course concerned.

The question is whether that view is right. Plainly, it is one of substance, with potential consequences of greater importance than those flowing from this particular case alone. The question perhaps may be put like this: when an employee refuses to do the work, or any of it, which under his contract of employment he has engaged to do, is the employer entitled to dismiss him without notice? And, if so, does it make any difference that the refusal occurred during, and in the course of, a strike in which the employee was taking part?

There are, says Mr Sedley, two main ways in which strikes may be organized. First, all the workers involved may give proper notice of termination of their contracts of employment, and in the early days of industrial disputes this method was often adopted. It had the advantage of avoiding any possible illegality which might then have resulted from going on strike in breach of contract. There are, however, many attendant disadvantages. For example, today, a man who gives notice will lose any possibility of making a claim for a redundancy payment or for compensation for unfair dismissal. Secondly – and this is the modern method – the strike may be organized without any employee giving notice of termination of his contract of employment. Often, however, a strike notice will be given, that is to say a notice of the intention of the employees to withdraw their labour upon a particular date unless by that time the demands which they are making have been met. In anything except the smallest firms, and the least organized strikes, some method of this kind is almost universally followed these days. The length of the strike notice may vary, but, except in the case of a lightning strike, it is usual for some notice, though not usually a long one, to be given of the intention to strike. The system of strikes, Mr Sedley says, has now become an accepted part of industrial organization, and neither side involved in a strike – that is to say, neither the employers nor the employees – has any expectation or wish that at the end of the strike relations between them will have been severed. There is usually an agreed procedure which has the purpose of avoiding disputes and, if disputes cannot be avoided, of regulating them. He draws attention to the agreed procedure for the avoidance of disputes in force at the employers' place of business at Perivale. The last paragraph of section 2 of the agreed procedure reads:

> Failing settlement at the joint conference – that is the last stage in the procedure for the avoidance of disputes – the procedure shall be regarded as exhausted and either side will give the other at least five working days' notice of any intended action.

The whole process has become systematized, is well understood, and no one ever expects that effective dismissals will take place.

Speaking broadly, we are prepared to accept the general account given by Mr Sedley of the way in which present day strikes are organized. The question, however, is what is the effect of a strike upon a particular employee's contract of employment? Mr Sedley says that there are two possibilities: first, that the contract of employment is suspended, and that is his contention here; or, secondly, that the withdrawal by the employee of his labour breaks the contract of employment. If he is wrong in his submission that the contract of employment is suspended, he then turns to consider the effect of the breach caused by the employee withdrawing his labour, and submits that it is not a fundamental breach entitling the employer to dismiss him without notice. Whether it is or not, he submits, depends on the circumstances in each case having regard to the effect of the breach upon the contract of employment and the employer's business.

Of his principal submission that the contract of employment is suspended, Mr Sedley says that it reflects the daily experience, understanding and practice of those engaged in industrial relations. No one so engaged supposes for a minute that the effect of a strike is to terminate the contract of employment. Not only, he submits, is this well recognized in practice, but it has received judicial blessing. He cites in support of this proposition the observations of Lord Denning M.R. in *J. T. Stratford & Sons Ltd* v. *Lindley* [1965] AC 269, 285, and also Lord Denning M.R.'s observations in *Morgan* v. *Fry* [1968]

2 QB 710, 724, 725 and 728. He relies particularly heavily upon the words of Lord Denning M.R. in the latter case, at p. 728:

> The truth is that neither employer nor workmen wish to take the drastic action of termination if it can be avoided. The men do not wish to leave their work for ever. The employers do not wish to scatter their labour force to the four winds. Each side is, therefore, content to accept a 'strike notice' of proper length as lawful. It is an implication read into the contract by the modern law as to trade disputes. If a strike takes place, the contract of employment is not terminated. It is suspended during the strike: and revives again when the strike is over.

Mr Sedley cites *Wallwork* v. *Fielding* [1922] 2 KB 66, 74 and 75 and *Bird* v. *British Celanese Ltd* [1945] KB 336, 341 as practical examples of contracts being suspended, and of the consequence flowing from suspension. So, he says, there is nothing unusual, or impossible, about a contract of employment being suspended. But even if the contract is to be treated as suspended, what is the effect of the suspension? If the employer would ordinarily be entitled to dismiss without notice, is it necessary to include among the effects of suspension the loss by the employer of that right until the suspension is lifted? The question then arises in what circumstances can the suspension be lifted? Can that be the decision of the employer alone, or does it require some further agreement between the employer and the employee?

Mr Sedley draws attention to what he claims are some of the consequences which would flow in a time of industrial dispute if it were not possible for the mutual rights and obligations of the employer and employee to be suspended. For example, the employee must choose between terminating his contract himself and striking in breach of contract; if he adopts the former course, and gives in his notice, he will be without a job and on strike. Further, he will then lose the valuable benefits which have accrued during the period of his employment. If he chooses the latter course, and goes on strike in breach of contract, he is liable in damages to his employer. Those results, says Mr Sedley, will be bleak, unsatisfactory and inharmonious. In answer to questions from the appeal tribunal about the effect of suspension, he accepted the logic of his submissions and conceded, or asserted, that the time would never come when the employer could lawfully dismiss the employee while on strike merely for failing to work; that, in other words, the employer could not lift the suspension and assert his right to terminate the employee's contract of employment.

In support of his second submission that, if there is no power of suspension, it is not every strike, or withdrawal of labour in pursuit of a strike, which constitutes a fundamental breach by the employee of his contract of employment, he cites *Laws* v. *London Chronicle (Indicator Newspapers) Ltd* [1959] 1 WLR 698, 700; *Suisse Atlantique Société d'Armement Maritime SA* v. *NV Rotterdamsche Kolen Centrale* [1967] 1 AC 361, 409, 421–422 and *Harbutt's 'Plasticine' Ltd* v. *Wayne Tank and Pump Co. Ltd* [1970] 1 QB 447, and says that every strike must be judged on its merits, looking in particular at the results of the act said to constitute the breach.

We turn to consider these submissions, assisted by a most helpful summary by Mr Morison, for the employers, of the development of this branch of the law in the last 150 years.

According to Mr Sedley the suspension may continue indefinitely; continuity of employment is not broken; the employee can get another job; and in general the relationship of employer/employee can only be terminated at the instance of the party who brought the suspension into operation. It seems to us to be clear that before the decision of the Court of Appeal in *Morgan* v. *Fry* [1968] 2 QB 710, no authority is to be found for the proposition that a contract of employment is suspended in this fashion during a strike. We are satisfied that at common law an employer is entitled to dismiss summarily an employee who refuses to do any of the work which he has engaged to do: see *Laws* v. *London Chronicle (Indicator Newspapers) Ltd* [1959] 1 WLR 698 – the employee has 'disregarded the essential conditions of the contract of service'. Does it make any difference that the refusal occurs during, and in the course of, a strike?

. . . One of the matters considered at length by the Donovan Commission (Royal Commission on Trade Unions and Employers' Associations 1965/68) (Cmnd. 3623) was the effect of strikes on the contract of employment. In paragraph 943 of the commission's report there are enumerated some of the difficulties inherent in regarding the contract as suspended. In the end the conclusion was reached that it was not practicable to introduce such a conception into the law. Whether or not that be so, it was clearly the view of the commission that at common law a contract cannot be terminated unilaterally, and that if an employee refuses to carry on working under his contract of employment his employer has the option either to ignore the breach of contract and to insist upon performance of it, or alternatively to accept such a fundamental breach as a repudiation of the contract and to treat himself as no longer bound by it: paragraph 946. In our judgment this view was in accordance with general principle and supported by authority. In short, refusal to work during a strike did not involve 'self-dismissal' by the strikers, but left the parties to the contract hoping that the strike would one day be settled, and the contract be alive, unless and until the employer exercised his right to dismiss the employee.

The question then is whether the decision in *Morgan* v. *Fry* [1968] 2 QB 710 changed the law; that is, not merely by establishing that the tort of intimidation was not committed by threats of strike action, but also by changing the underlying law concerning the relationship between employer and employee.

Since the date of the decision in *Morgan* v. *Fry* the law of industrial relations has been twice revolutionized. The Industrial Relations Act 1971 (by section 147) went some way towards establishing a sort of suspension during a strike of the obligations of the contract of employment. The language which it used for this purpose was negative in character and did not seem to suggest that the legislature assumed that such a state of the law already existed. The Act has now been repealed. The enactments which have replaced it, such as the Trade Union and Labour Relations Act 1974 (and the amending Act of 1976) go to some pains to exclude the law completely from industrial disputes. And it is noteworthy that where rights are conferred, for example to claim compensation for unfair dismissal, they are severely curtailed during a strike: see, e.g., Trade Union and Labour Relations Act 1974, Schedule 1, paragraph 8 [now EPCA 1978, s.62], and the observations of the EAT [below, p. 910] in *Thompson* v. *Eaton Ltd* [1976] ICR 336. None of this is consistent with there being a generally accepted opinion that *Morgan* v. *Fry* has revolutionized the law on this subject and established it on a firm basis. Nor is such a view given encouragement by the dicta in cases decided since 1968, such as *Secretary of State for Employment* v. *ASLEF (No. 2)* [1972] ICR 19 [above, p. 269]: see Lord Denning M.R.'s observations at p. 55 or *Chappell* v. *Times Newspapers Ltd* [1975] ICR 145 [above, p. 893] or *E. & J. Davis Transport Ltd* v. *Chattaway* [1972] ICR 267, 271.

. . . We find it impossible to think that *Morgan* v. *Fry* [1968] 2 QB 710 was intended to revolutionize the law on this subject. It was a case in which, in order to avoid a particular result which would have been out of harmony with the law on intimidation, the court reached a desired result by several routes: one member (Lord Denning M.R.) was of opinion that the contract was suspended; another (Davies L.J.) gave somewhat vague support to that view, but also thought that in some sense there was a threat to terminate the contract; and the third member (Russell L. J.) founded upon a different ground and was of opinion that there was a threatened breach. It is noteworthy that Lord Denning M.R., the only member of the court unequivocally in favour of the view that the contract was suspended, although he uses the word 'suspension', does not deal with any of the problems which arise when a contract is suspended in the sense that the obligations of the parties are suspended, such as those referred to in the Donovan Commission Report, for example, paragraph 943:

The concept is not as simple as it sounds: and before any such new law could be formulated problems of some difficulty would have to be faced and solved. They include the following: (a) To what strikes would it apply? To unofficial and unconstitutional as well as to official strikes? How would strikes be defined for this purpose? (b) Would it also apply to other industrial action such as a ban on overtime in breach of contract or to a 'go-slow'? (c) Would it apply to 'lightning strikes' or only to strikes where at least *some* notice was given, though less than the notice required for termination of the contract? If so, what length of notice should be required? (d) Would the new law apply to the gas, water, and electriciy industries, which at present are subject to the special provisions of section 4 of the Conspiracy and Protection of Property Act 1875? What also would be the position under section 5 of the same Act? (e) Would the employer still be allowed instantly to dismiss an employee for grave misconduct during the course of the strike? (Note: this is the case under French law where strikes are treated as suspending the contract of employment.) If so, what kind of acts would constitute 'grave misconduct'? (f) Would 'contracting out' of the new law be permissible, e.g. in collective bargains, or in individual contracts of employment? (g) Would strikers be free to take up other employment while the contract was suspended? If so, would any obligations of secrecy in the suspended contract be suspended too? (h) If all efforts to end the strike failed, upon what event would the suspension of the contract cease and be replaced by termination?

Mr Sedley, in the course of his submissions, offered answers to all these questions. Interesting, however, as they were, none of them was founded on authority; and there is no doubt that if *Morgan* v. *Fry* [1968] 2 QB 710 has introduced into the law the concept of the suspension of a contract it is in only an embryonic form, for none of the consequences has been worked out; and it is difficult to see how this could be done except by legislation.

In these circumstances, and bearing in mind the many changes in the law of industrial relations which have occurred since the decision in *Morgan* v. *Fry*, we do not feel that we are bound by that case to hold that the effect of a strike, whether preceded by a proper strike notice or not, is to prevent the employer from exercising the remedy which in our judgment he formerly enjoyed at common law to dismiss the employee for refusing to work. We accept, of course, that in most cases men are not dismissed when on strike; that they expect not to be dismissed; that the employers do not expect to dismiss them, and that both sides hope and expect one day to return to work. Sometimes, however, dismissals do take place, and in our judgment they are lawful.

. . . We do not accept Mr Sedley's submission that, if the contract of employment was not suspended, nonetheless the employee's action in going on strike was not repudiatory of the contract. It seems to us to be plain that it was, for here there was a settled, confirmed and continued intention on the part of the employee not to do any of the work which under his contract he had engaged to do; which was the whole purpose of the contract. Judged by the usual standards, such conduct by the employee appears to us to be repudiatory of the contract of employment. We should not be taken to be saying that all strikes are necessarily repudiatory, though usually they will be. For example, it could hardly be said that a strike of employees in opposition to demands by an employer in breach of contract by him would be repudiatory. But what may be called a 'real' strike in our judgment always will be.

For completeness, it should be said that it was not contended by Mr Sedley that there was here an implied term of the contract that it was to be suspended in the event of a strike. There are obvious difficulties in the way of implying such a term: cf. *Cummings* v. *Charles Connell and Co. (Shipbuilders) Ltd*, 1969 SLT 25, which, incidentally, tends to suggest that, in the absence of an express or implied term of the contract to the contrary, an employer, according to the law of Scotland, may dismiss an employee who refuses to work because he is on strike.

The one partial attempt by Parliament to provide a doctrine of suspension was, as mentioned in the judgment, contained in the IRA 1971. Section 147 of IRA 1971 provided that an employee who struck after giving due notice of his intention to strike (i.e. notice of length equivalent to that needed to terminate the contract) was not to be regarded as in breach of his contract of employment, *inter alia*, 'for the purpose of any proceedings in contract' brought against him (s.147(2)). But s.147(2) did not apply 'to any action by an employee which is contrary to a term of his contract . . . excluding or restricting his right to take part in a strike' (s.147(3)), nor did it 'exclude or restrict any right which an employer would have apart from the subsection to dismiss . . . an employee who takes part in a strike' (s.147(4)). Professor Blanc-Jouvan wrote: 'It will be very clear that the system adopted by the Industrial Relations Act is quite distinct from the ordinary system of suspension of the individual contracts of employment: it is far from giving similar protection to strikers.' (X. Blanc-Jouvan, 'The Effect of Industrial Action on the Status of the Individual Employee' in *Industrial Conflict*, ed. B. Aaron and K. W. Wedderburn (1972), p. 204).

It is clear that the parties may agree, expressly or impliedly, that the employees should have the right to suspend the contract of employment by taking industrial action, but *Simmons* v. *Hoover* confirms the dominant judicial stance that this result does not follow as a matter of necessary implication from the court's view of the nature of the contract of employment. What, then, of the law of unfair dismissal? When this legislation was introduced in 1971, Parliament had to decide what attitude should be adopted towards dismissals of those taking industrial action. The decision taken at that time was, on this point, to bring the law of unfair dismissal broadly into line with the common law of the contract of employment (rather than to seek to modify the common law, as was the general thrust of the unfair dismissal legislation). Accordingly, s.26 of IRA 1971 provided that dismissals of those taking industrial action should in general 'not be regarded as unfair' if the principal reason for the dismissal was participation in the industrial action. An exception to this rule was created where not all those 'who took part in that action' were dismissed for taking part in it or where, of those dismissed, not all were offered reinstatement, *and* where the reason for the different treatment was that those dismissed or not offered re-engagement had exercised their 'freedom of association' rights under s.5 of the 1971 Act (above, p. 179). In this case the dismissal would be unfair. (s.5 created rights for individuals to join or take part in the activities of registered trade unions or not to join any trade union.) Although s.26 probably conferred marginally more protection upon employees than the common law on this point, because the notion of abuse of rights at common law was probably not sufficiently well developed to control the employer's differential exercise of his right to terminate the contracts of employment of strikers, nevertheless the degree of control exercised by the unfair dismissal laws was also slight, because it was only differential treatment on s.5 grounds that was caught.

These provisions were continued by T U L R A 1974, Sch. 1, para. 8, except that, by virtue of the re-drafting of the 'freedom of association' provisions in 1974 (see above, p. 179), the exception to the general rule was given a somewhat different ambit. The major changes came, however, in 1975, when Sch. 16 of E P A 1975 amended and combined the hitherto separately expressed provisions on strikes and lock-outs in a way that was later consolidated in E P C A 1978, s.62. In spite of the significance of these changes, they did not mark a move away from the principle that the law of unfair dismissal should not be used to control in any general way the employer's legal freedom to dismiss those taking industrial action. Indeed, in part, the changes of 1975 increased the employer's freedom of action; in part, they narrowed it. The narrowing consisted in the fact that a challenge to differential treatment could now be mounted, not only where the reason for the differentiation was an 'inadmissible' one, as the 1974 Act required, but whenever there was differential treatment. Of course, it could not be supposed that the employer would never be able to put forward a good reason for differential treatment and so it was necessary to give the tribunal discretion to assess the reasonableness of the employer's action on a case-by-case basis. This result was achieved technically by turning the provisions about the fairness of the dismissals of those taking industrial action into provisions which operated by conferring or not conferring jurisdiction on the tribunal to hear the complaint of unfair dismissal. If all the relevant employees were treated equally, then the industrial tribunal did not have jurisdiction to hear the complaint of unfair dismissal, which was the equivalent in effect of the provision in the I R A 1971 that such a dismissal should not be regarded as unfair. If there was differential treatment, the industrial tribunal would have jurisdiction to hear the complaint, but might not, of course, conclude that the employer had acted unfairly. This latter point is often forgotten in public debate about s.62 of

EPCA 1978. It is assumed that the conferment of jurisdiction is the equivalent to a finding of unfairness.

On the other hand, the rule as to non-liability was extended in 1975 by the enactment that non-discriminatory dismissals of those engaging in industrial action should not come within the tribunal's jurisdiction, whether or not the principal reason for the dismissal was (as the IRA 1971 required) the fact that the employees were engaging in the industrial action (see EPCA 1978, s.62(1) and (2)). The rule now is that an employee cannot have his claim adjudicated upon by a tribunal if at the date of his dismissal he was taking part in industrial action, unless, of course, he can show differential treatment of other strikers. Even in this case, however, it is not enough for him to show that other strikers were not dismissed at the time he was dismissed. He must show that by the time of the hearing before the tribunal some of his fellow strikers had not been dismissed. As *McCormick* v. *Horsepower Ltd* [1981] ICR 535 (CA) shows, if after the strike has ended but before the applicant's claim is heard by the tribunal the non-dismissed strikers are in fact dismissed for some other reason, e.g. redundancy, the tribunal will not have jurisdiction to hear the applicant's claim. Thus, the removal of any reference in s.62 to the reason for the dismissal has rendered the section rather capricious in its operation, and the change does emphasize the way in which those taking part in industrial action are in principle excluded from the pale of unfair dismissal protection. It also raises more acutely the question of what is the underlying policy rationale of s.62. As the EAT pointed out in *Thompson* v. *Eaton* [1976] ICR 336, it is at first sight odd that TULRA 1974 should have carried over the provisions of the IRA 1971 on this point, given the generally very different orientations of those two statutes towards the legality of industrial conflict. The extension of the non-liability rule in 1975 made the process even odder, because it removed the possibility, held out in *Thompson* v. *Eaton*, that the rule might not apply where the merits were wholly on the employees' side because they had struck in response to a provocative act of management, that is, management had engineered the strike. In *Thompson* v. *Eaton* the EAT had suggested that in such a case the reason for the dismissal might be said to be, not the participation of the employees in the industrial action, but the desire of the employer to be rid of the employees which had led him to engineer the strike. However, as the EAT subsequently recognized in *Marsden* v. *Fairey Stainless Ltd* [1979] IRLR 103, under the present law the tribunal is not concerned with the reason for the dismissal, if all the strikers are treated equally.

We set out below three passages which are relevant to this question of the underlying rationale of s.62. In the first a continental lawyer describes the development of doctrines of suspension of the contract of employment in other European countries and suggests that the absence of a suspension doctrine in English law – and by implication, the presence of s.62 of EPCA 1978 – are inconsistent with the right to strike. In the second extract two academic writers on industrial relations, whose standpoint is one of being generally sympathetic to the legislation contained in TULRA 1974–6, develop the notion of the employer's legal freedom to discipline his employees being a part of, not a contradiction to, the principles of collective *laissez-faire*. Finally, a well-known journalist suggests that the underlying rationale of s.62 was to exclude the industrial tribunals as far as possible from the need to consider issues arising out of industrial conflict and that this policy proved unpalatable to trade unions in practice.

> X. Blanc-Jouvan, 'The Effect of Industrial Action on the Status of the Individual Employee' in B. Aaron and K. W. Wedderburn (eds), *Industrial Conflict – A Comparative Legal Survey* (1972), pp. 178–9, 184–5

In the first stage, the law guaranteed only the freedom to resort to industrial action. This meant that strikes and lockouts were protected against the State; they could no longer give rise to criminal prosecutions; they could be ranked among civil liberties, although they were not protected against the other party to the individual relation of employment. There was no law limiting their use, but no law either limiting the resort to civil sanctions against them. This last point was particularly important. Neither the employee nor the employer could invoke any special privilege; they all remained subject to the ordinary rules of the civil law or common law of contracts. The employees on strike could be dismissed by the employer, and the employer, in case of a lockout, could be ordered to pay the normal wages to his personnel as though there had been no interruption in the work. There is no need to emphasize that such sanctions were commonly used and they constituted a very efficient weapon. The situation was undoubtedly justified at a strictly juridical level, by application of the classical principles of the law of contracts, especially to the extent that industrial action was analysed in individualistic terms: the participation in a strike or the lockout of an employee certainly was to be regarded as a breach of the individual contract of employment, giving rise to civil sanctions. But this solution also led, in practice, to very unfortunate consequences. The freedom to resort to industrial action was considerably impaired by the threat of sanctions taken by the other party, and the freedom to strike, notably, was of little interest for the individual worker who could fear to have his contract terminated and to lose his job.

All these reasons explain that the system has become more and more anachronistic and that, in a second stage of the evolution, it has been largely abandoned. This can be explained, not only by practical reasons (the necessity to assure the employee involved in labour dispute better protection against anti-union activities and, notably, a greater security of employment), but also by theoretical considerations on the true nature of industrial action. Even in the systems in which a strong emphasis is put on the employer-employee relationship, it has become progressively more obvious that such an action cannot be regarded only from the point of view of each individual engaged in it: it must rather be viewed as an action of a specific type, which has a predominantly collective character. Its effect on the contract of employment cannot therefore be defined according to the traditional scheme taken from the law of contracts; it must be determined by new, particular standards. In practically all countries, the freedom to engage in some types of industrial action has become a right. This right can be officially and expressly recognized by the Constitution itself, or it can be, more modestly, implied by the terms of some recently enacted statutes – sometimes even merely affirmed by the courts. But in any case, the idea has triumphed that it is a right, which means that it is protected not only against the State, but also against the other party to the employment relationship, in the sense that it cannot give rise on his part to any sort of civil action.

It would be, however, excessive to say that the previous system is no longer applied today. The 'right' granted by law is not – and cannot be – absolute and the protection against civil sanctions does not – and cannot – extend to all concerted activities. There are some of these activities which remain subject to the ordinary law of contracts. This is even the basis for a distinction between lawful and unlawful actions, a distinction that is quite different in each of the countries covered by this study. Naturally, this is extremely important as to the effect of the action on the status of the individual employee.

It so appears that this status is far from being as simple as it might seem at first sight. We must examine the situation, first, from the point of view of the maintenance of the employment relationship throughout the strike or the lockout, and, second, from the point of view of the consequences attached to this relationship; in fact, the rights and duties of each of the parties.

. . . In fact, it is certain that on the level of the individual employment relationship, the strongest arguments are in favour of the termination of the contract. It is only on the level of collective relations that the theory of the suspension of the contract may find a solid foundation. This is a new manifestation of the original character of labour law as compared with civil or common law. The basic idea is that the strike must be regarded as a collective phenomenon – the action of a group rather than of an individual; therefore it can only be subject to specific rules and not to rules provided for the individual employer-employee relationship. To the extent that a right to strike is officially granted by law, this right must normally be protected against the employer: this means that its exercise cannot produce as a consequence the loss of his job by the employee. Of course, this may be contrary to the ordinary law of contracts: but it is admitted that the collective right to strike given to the employees must prevail over the individual right to the execution of the contract given to the employer. The result is clear: as soon as the strike is regarded as lawful on the collective level, it can no longer be treated as a breach of contract and give rise to civil sanctions on the level of the individual relation of employment. The strike may be a non-performance of the contract, but it is not a breach of contract, because it is the exercise of a collective right. This right is an element of the legal status of the employee, to which all individual employment contracts implicitly refer. This is why it becomes impossible to claim that the contract has been broken because the right has been exercised.

Whatever is the theoretical justification for this doctrine of suspension of the contract, it is necessary to know exactly what consequences it involves from the point of view of the maintenance of the employment relationship. There can be no doubt that in case of suspension the contract is not automatically terminated as a consequence of the strike and that it cannot be terminated by the employer as a civil or disciplinary sanction (that is, without previous notice). It is certain that if the employer dismisses the employee for the only reason that he participated in a strike, he commits an unfair or abusive dismissal and he may be ordered to reinstate him or to pay him damages. But it remains a problem to know whether the employer still has the possibility to dismiss the employee on strike, after giving whatever previous notice is usually required, or to refuse to reinstate him, in spite of the fact that his contract is only suspended. There is, in that respect, a great variety of solutions. Between the systems admitting that the employer is still allowed to terminate the contract of the strikers – not as a sanction, but in application of the rule that any party to an employment contract which is not for a fixed term may, at any time and without any specific reason, terminate this contract – and those admitting that the employer cannot, under any pretext, dismiss the employees on strike, many intermediate positions can be found: it may be provided, for example, that the employer can only terminate the contract for economic reasons or in order to hire replacements. This shows that the protection granted to the strikers may be more or less complete. It is important to take into account, into [*sic*] that respect, the differences existing from one country to another – and also, in some cases, from one type of strike to another.

> W. E. J. McCarthy and N. D. Ellis, *Management by*
> *Agreement* (1973), pp. 160–1, 165

The case for comprehensive and balanced laws that regulate the use made of industrial power is a complex one that is seldom if ever fully developed. This is partly because arguments about the use of industrial sanctions, and their justifiability, are so often dominated by the case for and against the right of *workers* to withdraw their labour. At least the debate is conducted as if this were the sole or primary issue to be decided; as though trade unions and management had no particular interest in the form and content of the law in this area. Thus the implication is drawn that unions will naturally be able to exert sufficient influence over the content of collective bargaining wherever workers possess a well established and well developed right to strike. Similarly, the suggestion is made that the form taken by the right to strike will not affect management very much, so long as they retain their ultimate power to 'dispose of the capital of the business'. Thus a recent discussion of the legal limits of the right to strike in a number of countries including our own concluded that:

> ... the imperative need for a social power countervailing that of property overshadows everything else. If the workers are not free by concerted action to withdraw their labour, their organizations do not wield credible social force. The power to withdraw their labour is for the workers what for management is its power to shut down production, to switch it to different purposes, to transfer it to different places. A legal system which suppresses the freedom to strike puts the workers at the mercy of their employers. This – in all its simplicty – is the essence of the matter. [O. Kahn-Freund and Bob Hepple, *Laws against Strikes*, above, p. 693.]

... But things are also rather more complex on the management side. Management interests are not sufficiently ensured simply because they remain free, in the last analysis, to abandon production, or to change its locale or end-product. For the most part if a management feels it must respond to the threat of strike action in this way it has already lost the battle. What management requires is a series of less draconic but more gradual sanctions – which would enable them to exert a range of industrial pressures on workers, while remaining in business. And here their legal right to discipline their own employees is a central requirement.

In the first place management must retain the right to deploy the normal processes of industrial discipline in the course of an industrial dispute. This means, above all, that laws are required which safeguard their right to suspend or discharge on grounds of indiscipline, where the workers involved are contemplating or using various kinds of collective action. In the section below something is said about the need to ensure that management's right to dismiss is used within the context of a more extended law of unfair dismissal, but subject to these qualifications we would not advocate the circumscription or removal of such a right. Here we feel that the broad approach of the 1971 Act is correct. Section 26 of the Act specifically provides for lawful dismissal during and after [sic, but cf. *Heath* v. *J. F. Longman (Meat Salesmen) Ltd* [1973] I C R 407 (N I R C)] a strike where participation in strike action is given as the reason. The only qualification is that the employer must treat all the workers involved in the strike in the same way. Similarly, s.25 allows for dismissal as part of a 'lock-out'. We think the retention of such rights as these are part of the essential armoury of employers.

We also think employers must be allowed to suspend or dismiss workers who take industrial action in breach of their contract of employment – though it may be necessary to define more carefully what this means. It is also only reasonable to allow employers to include in the terms of contract an undertaking to observe established joint procedures for dealing with disputes, so long as the workers concerned agree to this. In this way strikes in breach of procedure become strikes in breach of the employment contract.

J. Rogaly, *Grunwick* (1977), pp. 137–40

One of the few loopholes in this law allows employers to sack the whole of a group of workers who are on strike, or who have been locked out, or who are taking part in other 'industrial action'. This loophole is created by the Trade Union and Labour Relations Act 1974, as amended by the Employment Protection Act 1975. If there is an 'industrial action' in progress, the law lays down, an industrial tribunal shall not determine whether the sackings were fair or unfair unless it can be shown that there has been discrimination between employees – i.e. that some have been sacked and some not, or that some have been taken back and some not.

It was this provision of the law that led the Grunwick management to decide, after taking legal advice early on in the dispute, that it would sack all who were on strike, without exception. The position was maintained by Mr Ward during the whole of the troublesome year that followed; his argument was that if he went so far as to reinstate even one of the dismissed workers he would be taken before an industrial tribunal where he would be obliged to defend the sacking of all the others.

. . . The really important point about this loophole in the law is that *it is there because the trade unions want it to be there*. The idea was to keep the law out of industrial disputes, a notion that was accepted in the Tories' 1971 Act and repeated during the passage of the 1974 Act, as well as throughout most of 1975. If a tribunal had to decide whether a sacking of people who were on strike or locked out or engaged in an official go-slow was fair, then that same tribunal might have to pass judgment on the merits of the dispute. This at any rate was the original fear. Then it was realized that if such a provision was written into the new law, employers could sack people during strikes for reasons that had nothing to do with the immediate 'industrial action'. Thus the provision was made that all those who were dismissed had to be treated alike: you could not sack some people who were on strike but not others.

If that is, as it were, trade-union-made law, then it appears that companies are expected by the new Establishment to take it in a spirit favourable to trade unions. The Scarman report [Cmnd. 6922] says of Grunwick:

By dismissing all those who went on strike they have excluded judicial review of the dismissals, but in our view they acted unreasonably in so doing. The dismissal of strikers, particularly within days of a strike starting, is extremely rare in practice, and by their own admission in evidence, they would have been willing to take some of the strikers back but refused to so do since, if they did, they would have to face proceedings by the others in an industrial tribunal in which the company would have to show in each case that the dismissal was fair. We ask – why not? Was it really unfair or unreasonable that a dismissed employee should have his individual case considered by a court or tribunal on its merits? Upon our analysis of the underlying causes of the strike the answer must be No.

This is a curious line of argument to come from a report signed by so distinguished a judge. For what it seems to say is that although the letter of the law is defective, companies are obliged to act according to the general notion of what is good industrial practice, or pay the penalty of being labelled unreasonable. In earlier chapters it has been argued that the cause taken up by APEX was a just one: the strikers needed help, and it was morally right to help them. This is also the view expressed in the Scarman report. But from the very first days of the walk-out, Mr Len Gristey [an APEX official] cognizant of the law as he was, warned that it might not be possible to get reinstatement for those who had been sacked for going on strike. We can now see that if the law is unhelpful on this point the reason is to be found in the attitude of the trade union movement to the law. As shall be shown later, there is an apparent difference between the Lord Justice Scarman who has argued eloquently about a Bill of Rights and the need to bring industrial relations within the law, and the Scarman report on Grunwick, which on the matter of unfair dismissals, appears to say, 'if the law is defective, pay heed to the established view on industrial relations policy'.

Even if the principle behind s.62 of EPCA 1978 is regarded as satisfactory and even necessary, it may be thought that the striker should not be penalized beyond the loss of his job. On this basis the result in *Simmons* v. *Hoover Ltd* is undesirable. Indeed, it seems likely that Parliament intended by s.10 of RPA 1965 (now s.92 of EPCA 1978) to take out of the scope of s.2(2) (now s.82(2)) all situations where an employee's dismissal for redundancy coincides with industrial action, but the EAT held that the wording of the section was inadequate to achieve that result where the strike preceded the dismissal for redundancy rather than vice versa. It might also be thought that the striker should not be penalized after the strike has ended (cf. *Heath* v. *J. F. Longman (Meat Salesmen) Ltd* [1973] ICR 407) a principle that would reconcile the provisions preserving statutory continuity during the strikes (below, p. 933) with the doctrine of s.62. Does the following decision offend against the suggested principle?

Cruickshank v. *Hobbs* [1977] ICR 725 (EAT)

The applicants went on strike over a pay dispute. During the course of the strike, and for reasons unconnected with it, the employer formed the view that he would have to declare five of his employees redundant. Almost immediately after the strike was settled the employer dismissed five of the six strikers as redundant, took back one of the strikers and retained all his employees (about thirty) who had not gone on strike. The applicants complained of unfair dismissal on the grounds that they had been unfairly selected as redundant.

CUMMING-BRUCE J.: The next point on behalf of the applicants is in our view more formidable. The Trade Union and Labour Relations Act 1974 imposes on the employer the duty to make a selection which is reasonable having regard to all the circumstances and having regard to equity and the substantial merits of the case. Mr Mulcahy submits that in a small undertaking at least, the statute imposes on the employer some duty to consider the situation of individual employees. One such criterion is that which the trainer mentioned to the shop steward in the rather casual conversation in 1975, 'Last in, first out,' which has a rough and ready fairness about it, is well recognized as a criterion amongst the unions and employees, and has the advantage of saving an employer from attempting to make invidious distinctions between the merits and personalities of individuals of a kind likely to stimulate jealousy and impair morale. Counsel submits that to divide the employees into two classes, the sheep who were loyal to the employer and stayed at work, and the goats who were loyal to the union and refused to work, is to approach the problem of selection quite unreasonably, because it disregards two facts. First, the employer has to do equity as far as he can having regard to the interests of the business and the interests of each and all of his employees; secondly, the men who have been absent from work were absent not out of disloyalty to their employer but out of loyalty to their union. In so far as the trainer simply applied the criterion, 'Those loyal to me shall be saved, and those loyal to the union shall be cast into the outer darkness,' he was failing to have regard to equity and the substantial merits of the case; and the fact that his motives were pure, unsullied by any vindictiveness or unkindness, is irrelevant to the reasonableness of the criterion that he decided to apply.

In our view a strike may be relevant to selection for redundancy in a number of ways, though its weight as a factor may be negligible. If the strike has caused or aggravated the redundancy, it may be reasonable to take account of the conduct of the strikers as causing the redundancy so that it is a factor that points to their selection rather than any of those who did not by their conduct reduce the number of jobs available. But that is not this case. Secondly, if the withdrawal of labour lasts long enough, the reintroduction into the reduced force of men who have been long absent may give rise to practical difficulties arising from technical or administrative changes which have occurred during their long absence. Thirdly, passions may be aroused during the strike, or incidents of abuse or violence between strikers and those remaining at work may have the effect that to sack men who stayed on and replace them with strikers may be expected to cause such friction between opposing groups on the shop floor that the morale and efficiency of the undertaking will be significantly impaired. In this situation it is not the strike itself, but the consequence of and incidents during the strike, which may be relevant to selection for redundancy. It is this third situation which the tribunal appears to describe in paragraph 21 of their reasons, and, if the evidence supports such a finding, a decision that the trainer was reasonable in giving great or paramount weight to this factor, the decision cannot be reversed on the ground that it disclosed an error of law even though we disagreed with their view. So the problem resolves itself into the question whether the evidence of the trainer can support such a finding.

[The EAT held by a majority that the trainer's evidence did support the industrial tribunal's finding.]

Thus, in 1975 the legislation concerning unfair dismissal of those taking industrial action could be thought to give the employer a greater legal freedom than had the corresponding provisions of the IRA 1971, at least when the employer treated all the relevant employees equally. Nevertheless, s.62 of EPCA 1978 (consolidating the 1975 changes) was the subject of further amendment by EA 1982, s.9, so as to confer even greater freedom of action upon employers. The main cause of this second set of amendments was a difficulty that had arisen in defining the relevant employees. S.62(4)(*b*)(ii), following the formulation of the IRA 1971 and TULRA 1974, defined the relevant employees, in relation to a strike or other industrial action, as 'the employees who took part in it'. In *Stock* v. *Frank Jones (Tipton) Ltd* [1978] ICR 347, one or two workers had returned to work during the course of the strike. The remaining strikers, who included the applicant, were subsequently dismissed. The House of Lords held that the industrial tribunal had been wrong not to entertain the applicant's complaint of unfair dismissal: some of those who took part in the industrial action had not been dismissed, even if all those on strike at the date of the applicant's dismissal had been treated in the same way. This was thought by the government unduly to restrict the employer's freedom of action[1] and in consequence s.9 of EA 1982 substitutes a new s.62(4)(*b*)(ii). This defines the relevant employees as 'those employees at the establishment who were taking part in the action at the complainant's date of dismissal'. This narrows the relevant group of employees in two ways, for it not only deals with the issue raised in *Stock* v. *Frank Jones*, but also confines the group to those employed at the same establishment as the applicant. Previously *all* the employees of the employer, no matter at which establishment employed, had to be treated equally. Thus, an employer, faced with a strike at two of his plants, might now deliver an ultimatum to all those on strike to the effect that they must return by a certain date or be dismissed. If at plant A 90 per cent of the strikers returned to work, whilst only 10 per cent did so at plant B, the employer might decide to dismiss the 10 per cent still on strike at plant A but do nothing to implement his threat at plant B, and he could not be challenged under the unfair dismissal laws.

S.9 also makes a third change in s.62, which relates to the offer of re-engagement. Under the old version of s.62 a differential offer of re-engagement made by an employer at any subsequent time would enable a dismissed striker who was not offered re-engagement to make a claim for unfair dismissal, in effect treating the non-offer of re-engagement as the act complained of (EPCA 1978, ss.62(3) and 67(3)). By virtue of the new EPCA 1978, s.62(2)(*b*), the dismissed striker can now complain that the re-engagement was not offered him only if the offer was made to another dismissed employee within three months of the complainant's date of dismissal, and a new s.67(3) allows

---

[1] To protect himself against claims by the strikers the employer would have to dismiss those who had returned to work as well, but s.62 could not be invoked against claims by the returners because they were not on strike when dismissed.

complaints of differential offers of re-engagement to be lodged with industrial tribunals within six months of the complainant's date of dismissal. The government's aim was to end the 'completely open-ended obligation [whereby] employers could never take on sacked employees again without putting themselves at risk of placing the dismissals within the jurisdiction of the industrial tribunal'.[1] The effect is to increase the employer's ability to make differential offers of re-engagement, albeit after a lapse of time, and this is particularly significant because possibilities of discriminatory treatment are already inherent in the statutory definition of re-engagement in s.62(4). Re-engagement is not defined as the same job with the same employer, but as an offer by the original employer or a successor employer or, more important, an associated employer to re-engage the employee either in the same job as he previously held or 'in a different job which would be reasonably suitable in his case'. It would seem that not all the dismissed employees need be offered re-engagement on the same terms (cf. s.62(2)(b)). Some might, for example, be offered different, but reasonably suitable, jobs by an associated employer and others their old jobs back, but all would have been offered re-engagement as defined. Moreover, it would seem it would be permissible for the employer to take account of conduct during the strike in deciding the terms of the offer of re-engagement (cf. *Cruikshank* v. *Hobbs*, above p. 915).

This latter argument is supported by the decision of the Court of Appeal in *Williams* v. *National Theatre Board Ltd* [1982] ICR 715, in which the statutory definition of 'job' was considered. 'Job' is defined in s.153(1) of EPCA 1978 as 'the nature of the work which [the employee] is employed to do in accordance with his contract and the capacity and place in which he is so employed'. The majority of the employees were offered re-engagement in their old jobs but subject to the condition that they should be treated as having forfeited their rights both to a caution and to a warning under the disciplinary procedure and could be suspended for a future breach of contract. One of the strikers, who had in fact returned to work by the time the strikers were dismissed and so would not come within the relevant group for that reason today, was also dismissed with those still on strike, but was later offered re-engagement without the condition as to disciplinary status attached. The Court of Appeal held that the condition did not touch the elements of the nature of the work, capacity and place, which are the elements mentioned in the statutory definition of 'job'. Consequently the applicants had been offered re-engagement. Moreover, the fact that one striker had been offered re-engagement on more favourable terms was irrelevant provided all had been offered what amounted to re-engagement. 'Whether in an individual case there has or has not been an offer of re-engagement is to be determined by examining the facts of *that* case. . . . Factors such as discrimination or differentiation do not enter into the problem which falls to be resolved on absolute and not on comparative considerations' (at p. 725).

[1] Official Report, Standing Committee G, 24th sitting, col. 1112 (22 April 1982).

However, the major change made by s.9 of EA 1982 was the redefinition of the relevant group to mean those taking part in the strike or other industrial action at the establishment at the date of the applicant's dismissal. This has produced something of a contrast between the definitions of the relevant group in relation to a strike or other industrial action, on the one hand, and a lock-out on the other. As we noted above (p. 896) it was not possible to define the relevant group in relation to a lock-out as those whom the employer chose to lock out and instead the definition of those directly interested in the dispute was used. *Fisher* v. *York Trailer* (above, p. 897) shows that those 'directly interested' is a broader group than those locked out at the date of the applicant's dismissal. The definition seems wide enough to embrace those who have never been locked out and those, whether locked out or not, who are employed at other establishments than the applicant's. The notion of 'direct interest' is borrowed from social security law and, as we shall see below (p. 941), its whole function there is to bring into disqualification from benefit workers other than those who are participating in the dispute, typically those non-participants whose terms and conditions of employment are likely to be affected by the outcome of the dispute. Consequently, it is a matter of some importance to those involved to know whether the employer faces a strike or a lock-out. Must he dismiss only those who are not working or also those directly interested in the dispute? The definitions of 'strike' and 'lock-out' – there is no statutory definition of action short of a strike – in Sch. 13 to EPCA 1978 are usually applied by analogy to s.62, but are not completely free from ambiguity, simply because it cannot always be clear whether sanctions are being imposed by the employees to secure compliance by the employer with their wishes, or vice versa, or, indeed, whether both processes are not occurring. Suppose an employer introduces new machinery and requires a group of employees to work it without extra payment on the grounds that its operation falls within their existing contractual duties. The employees dispute the contractual obligation and refuse to work the machinery without extra payment. The employer says that the employees need not come to work if they are not prepared to work normally. Later he dismisses them. It seems as plausible to argue that at the date of the dismissal the employees were engaging in industrial action (refusal to work the machines) as that the employer was locking them out. Yet upon the answer to this question will in turn depend the answer to the further question of whether the employer must also dismiss another group of workers for whom similar new machinery has arrived but who have not yet been asked to work it, if he is to succeed in his claim that the tribunal has no jurisdiction over the dismissals. In other words, distinguishing for the purposes of s.62 the defensive lock-out from the industrial action in response to which the employer locked out may prove a difficult, indeed unrealistic, task: it is not for nothing that what are commonly referred to as the government's strike statistics are in fact statistics about stoppages of work, which do not distinguish between stoppages caused by strikes and those caused by lock-outs.[1]

This is a problem the tribunals and the courts will have to face in the future. To date they have been concerned mainly with two other problems. What defines industrial action short of a strike and when can an employee be said to be participating in a strike? On the former point there is no statutory definition, even one to be applied by analogy, although there was a definition of 'irregular industrial action short of a strike' in s.33(4) of IRA 1971, a necessary ingredient of which was that the action should be a breach of contract on the part of at least some of those engaging in it. In *Power Packing Casemakers Ltd* v. *Faust* [1983] ICR 292, the CA rejected, rightly it is suggested, the notion that a breach of contract was an inherent part of action short of a strike in the absence of a statutory definition importing this requirement. In this case three employees were dismissed for refusing to work overtime which they, and the industrial tribunal, regarded as not obligatory upon them under their contracts of employment. The tribunal held the refusal to work overtime to have been industrial action in this case because the evidence before the tribunal was that the refusal was intended to put additional pressure upon the employer to concede a pay claim which the employees had put to the employer. The notion of concerted action designed to put pressure upon the employer to concede a demand made upon him by the employees as the essence of industrial action short of a strike (just as it is of a full strike) seems correct, and had previously been put forward as the test by the EAT in *Rasool* v. *Hepworth Pipe Co. Ltd* [1980] ICR 494. The attendance at an unauthorized mass meeting held during working hours was held not to be industrial action because the purpose of the meeting was to hear the views of the workforce and not to put pressure on the employer. This is the correct approach, although it would be wrong to define the purpose that will make concerted action industrial action too narrowly, for that, ironically, might reduce the employer's freedom of action in the case of secondary or sympathetic action or of disputes between groups of workers. Here the definition of strike in Sch. 13 to EPCA 1978 can provide guidance. That defines strike in para. 24 in terms of a concerted withdrawal of labour by workers 'done as a means of compelling their employer or any person or body of persons employed, or to aid other employees in compelling their employer or any person or body of persons employed, to accept or not to accept terms or conditions of or affecting employment'. This definition is much broader than merely concerted action by employees to put pressure on their own employer.

Thus, the courts appear to be moving towards the view that a strike or other industrial action is defined by reference to two essential characteristics. There must be concerted action and that action must be taken for a particular purpose or range of purposes connected with terms and conditions of employment. This view would include within the concept of industrial action secondary or sympathy action, but would presumably exclude action directed

[1] Department of Employment, *Strikes in Britain* (1978), p. 13.

at, say, persuading the government to change its mind, not *qua* employer, but *qua* legislator (cf. pp.795 ff. above). In the latter case the employer would be in a strong position to obtain an interlocutory injunction against the organizers of the action, but would apparently not be able to claim any particular protection if he dismissed those taking the action. However, the issue of unfair dismissal in such case has not yet arisen for decision.

Although these tests may be adequate for deciding whether the action, considered collectively, amounts to industrial action, the courts have found it difficult to decide whether they are also appropriate for deciding whether a particular individual was participating in what was, when viewed collectively, admittedly industrial action. Must the individual in question, not merely participate in the action, but also share its goals? The issue can arise in two situations. The employee who was dismissed may claim that at the time he was not engaging in industrial action, so that s.62 of E PCA 1978 does not apply in his case. Or the dismissed employee may concede that he was dismissed when engaging in industrial action but claim that some other relevant individual was not dismissed or was offered re-engagement, and the issue is whether that other relevant individual was participating in the industrial action. In either case the argument may be that the dismissed employee or the third person was not committing the necessary acts to constitute the taking of industrial action or that he did not share the purposes of the others taking the industrial action and so was not engaging in concerted activity. To date the cases before the appeal tribunal concerning dismissed employees who claimed that they were not taking part in industrial action have revolved around the question of whether they were committing the necessary acts at the time of their dismissal. In particular, it has been argued on their behalf that they could not be said to be committing the necessary acts if it was the case that, at the time of their dismissal, they would not have been at work even if no industrial action had been taking place. The appeal tribunal, however, has been satisfied with proof that the dismissed employee shared the goals of the industrial action and would have been committing the necessary acts at the time of his dismissal had the occasion arisen for him to be at work. Thus, in *Williams* v *Western Mail & Echo Ltd* [1980] I C R 366 an employee had been participating in various forms of industrial action short of a strike against his employer, but at the time he and his colleagues were dismissed was in fact at home ill. The EAT held that the employee's claim was subject to s.62 of EPCA 1978 since he had not indicated to his employer that he was abandoning the sanctions and, moreover, he would, so the industrial tribunal found, have participated in the sanctions had he attended work. Similarly, in *Winnett* v *Seamarks Brothers Ltd* [1978] I R L R 387 a group of four drivers told the managing director that they were going on strike over the dismissal of a colleague and were then sacked. The applicant was held to be subject to the predecessor of s.62 of E PCA 1978, even though he was not due on duty until the next day. (Contrast, however, *Midland Plastics* v *Till* [1983] I R L R 9 (EAT): s.62 not applicable where the employees were dismissed for having announced an intention to take industrial action but before any one of them had imposed any sanctions. See also *Naylor* v *Orton & Smith Ltd* [1983] IRLR 233. The law on this point is clearly in some disarray at the moment.)

Thus, the appeal tribunal seems to find it enough to bring s.62 into operation that the employee shared the goals of those taking the industrial action and had the intention to abstain from working or not to work normally when the occasion should next arise for him to attend work. Although one can express some unease at the possible implications of this principle, it does seem correct to argue that s.62 would become even more capricious than it already is, if the employer could dismiss only at the time when the employee was actually refraining from normal working (e.g. members of the night shift would have to be dismissed at night). However, the more interesting cases concern those who are committing the necessary acts at the relevant time (i.e. are not working normally), but of whom it is argued that they are not engaged in concerted action because they do not share the goals of the industrial action. This argument has been advanced, with rather different results, in two cases before the Court of Appeal, in situations where the dismissed employee had argued that all those engaged in the industrial action had not been treated equally and the question was whether a particular person, who admittedly was treated more favourably, was participating or not in the industrial action. In *McCormick* v *Horsepower Ltd* (above, p.910) some boilermakers (including the applicant) went on strike. Mr Brazier, who was an engineer in a different department, was on holiday at the time. When he returned to work, he initially refused to cross the boilermakers' picket line, but later did so. The boilermakers were later dismissed for being on strike, but Mr Brazier, who was now crossing the picket line, was not dismissed for his earlier refusals to work, although he was made redundant at about the time the strikers were dismissed. As we have seen, one reason for holding that s.62 applied was that by the date of the tribunal hearing Mr Brazier had, in fact, been treated in the same way as the boilermakers. The alternative holding was that Mr Brazier was not participating in the strike because he was not shown to have had a common purpose with the boilermakers. This alternative rationale caused difficulties for the Court of Appeal in a subsequent case of a refusal to go into work, where the employee in question was a member of the same grade of workers as those taking the industrial action and where her refusal to work, far from being motivated by notions of solidarity with the strikers, was attributed to her fear of social disapproval if she did work.

Coates v. *Modern Methods and Materials Ltd* [1982] ICR 763 (CA)

The employers dismissed nine employees, after the workforce had failed to produce ten volunteers for transfer to another plant. The next morning the workforce decided to meet outside the factory gate at the normal time for the commencement of work to discuss the situation. The overwhelming majority decided not to go into work until their grievance was redressed, but one or two workers went into work and were verbally abused by the rest of the workforce. Mrs Leith gave evidence that she decided not to go into work because she did not wish to face the abuse and at 10.30 she went off to see her doctor with whom she had a previously arranged appointment. She was sick for the rest of the strike and beyond. She did not draw strike pay, but did attend strike meetings. She ultimately returned to work. The applicants were dismissed for being on strike and claimed the tribunal had jurisdiction to hear their complaint because Mrs Leith had not been dismissed.

STEPHENSON L.J.: . . . Both counsel, Mr Sedley for the applicants and Mr Clarke for the employer, took something from these definitions of a strike [in Sch. 13 to EPCA] for the meaning which they submitted should be given to the words 'was taking, or took, part in a strike or other industrial action' – for they must mean the same in subsection (1)(b) and (4)(b)(ii) of section 62. Mr Sedley accepted Mr Clarke's submission that for an employee to come within the words there must be a concerted stoppage of work done as a means of compelling the employer to accede to certain demands and that there must be in existence at the time the strike is called a common purpose of compelling the employer to accede to the demand. But they differed as to what is required of the employee when there is such a concerted cessation of work or withdrawal of labour and a common purpose to put pressure on the employer. Mr Clarke submitted that the employee must support the strike by sharing the common purpose of compelling the employer to accede to the demand. Mr Sedley on the other hand contended that once there is an attempt to persuade all workers affected to join in withdrawing their labour, the individual worker affected can take part in the attempt without supporting, or even fully appreciating, the purpose or the cause. The individuals may be ignorant or confused. Their motives may be mixed. But motivation and intention are irrelevant; provided the effect of what they do adds to the pressure on the employer, they take part in the strike. Mere withdrawal of labour when or after others do so will usually contribute to achieving the object of the strike; if it does so, that is taking part in it. Mr Sedley submitted that on this interpretation of the statutory words the industrial tribunal reasonably held that Mrs Leith had taken part in the strike by withdrawing her labour and not breaking the strike on February 12, 1980. If she had been unable to go in to work because she was prevented physically or by such threats or violence as might have deprived her of her freedom of choice, she might not have taken part. But the pressure or constraint put upon her by the threat of being abused, as Mrs Jessop was, was not enough to prevent her from making a voluntary decision to stay out of the factory and so take part, however unwillingly, in the strike of those who stayed out with her. That is the view expressed in the industrial tribunal's decision. Fear of abuse was not a good reason; she had the power to decide whether or not to break the strike, she did decide not to do so and it matters not why.

On Mr Clarke's construction of the statutory words he submitted that no reasonable tribunal could have found that Mrs Leith took part in the strike without rejecting her evidence. But the industrial tribunal accepted her evidence that she did not go into the factory because of the abuse and so it was not open to them to find, and they did not find, that she supported the strike or acted in concert with the strikers or shared their purpose. On her accepted evidence she did not share in the strikers' purpose or agree with it, and acted not in pursuance of it but in apprehension of what others might say in pursuance of it. Her intention in going to work on February 12, 1980, knowing that strike action was being taken, was to work, not strike; and it was never suggested that she changed her mind that morning or indeed right up to the time when she was fit enough to return to work. Mr Clarke pointed out that nowhere does the industrial tribunal attempt to state what meaning they give to the statutory phrase nor for that matter does the appeal tribunal – and it can only be by misinterpreting the phrase and giving it an unnatural meaning that the industrial tribunal have held that it applied to Mrs Leith's actions on February 12, 1980. That is a misdirection in law which entitled the appeal tribunal to review the industrial tribunal's decision and required them to correct the decision. It would, he submitted, be most unreasonable to conclude from a strained construction of the statutory words that Mrs Leith was on strike with the others; the employer and the majority of the appeal tribunal were right to hold that she was not.

I have found this a difficult case. It ought to be easy to decide what 'taking part in a strike' means and whether on proved or accepted facts a particular employee was or was not taking part in a strike. The industrial tribunal seem to have found it easy, because they unanimously decided that Mrs Leith was taking part, and on an application for review the chairman thought the weight of the evidence showed that she was taking part and a review had no reasonable prospect of success. I know that the construction of a statute is a question of law; but the meaning of ordinary words is not, and the meaning of 'taking part in a strike' seems to me to be just the sort of question which an industrial jury is best fitted to decide. No member of either tribunal has spelt out its meaning, perhaps because it was thought unwise or impossible to attempt a paraphrase of plain words. But I should be very reluctant to assume that any of them attributed to the words an unnatural meaning which they were incapable of bearing in their context, or to differ from their conclusion that Mrs Leith took part in a strike. Only the plainest error in law would enable me to differ from them on such a finding, particularly when the majority of the appeal tribunal, whose decision convicts them of such error, appear themselves to be influenced by an erroneous conception of their power to interfere with the industrial tribunal's decision. On the other hand, I think that on the evidence without argument and reflection I should have taken the view which Mrs Leith's employer appears to have taken that she was not on strike or striking or taking part in the strike. That view takes into account her state of mind, her intention, her motive, her wishes. Some support for doing that is to be found in what Talbot J said in giving the judgment of the appeal tribunal in *McCormick* v *Horsepower Ltd* [1980] ICR 278, 283 about Brazier not being motivated by fear in refusing to cross the picket line and withdrawing his labour to aid the strikers: and also in what Lawton L. J., in the passage I have quoted from his judgment in the same case [1981] ICR 535, 541, said obiter about giving help generally and about Brazier not being shown to have had a common purpose with the striking boiler-makers. Furthermore, it seems hard on an employer who takes the trouble to investigate an employee's motives and reasons for stopping work to be told 'you were wrong to accept what she told you; you ought to have dismissed her and so prevented two other strikers from complaining to the industrial tribunal of unfair dismissal.' On the other side it was said that it would be intolerable to impose on employers the burden, which this employer undertook with one employee, of looking into the mind of every employee withholding his or her labour before deciding whether to dismiss, in order to see if each had some reason for stopping work unconnected with the object of the strike.

I have come to the conclusion that participation in a strike must be judged by what the employee does and not by what he thinks or why he does it. If he stops work when his workmates come out on strike and does not say or do anything to make plain his disagreement, or which could amount to a refusal to join them, he takes part in their strike. The line between unwilling participation and not taking part may be difficult to draw, but those who stay away from work with the strikers without protest for whatever reason are to be regarded as having crossed that line to take part in the strike. In the field of industrial action those who are not openly against it are presumably for it. This seems to be the thinking behind the industrial tribunal's decision. If the words in question are capable of bearing that meaning, they are capable of being applied to Mrs Leith's actions on the morning of February 12, 1980, though her time outside the factory gates with the strikers was short and her reason for not entering the factory was accepted. In my judgment a reasonable tribunal could give that meaning to the statutory words and could apply them to Mrs Leith. The industrial tribunal did not, therefore, go wrong in law and it was the majority of the appeal tribunal who did. I would accordingly allow the appeal, set aside the decision of the Employment Appeal Tribunal and restore the decision of the industrial tribunal.

EVELEIGH L.J.: . . . In my opinion the word 'strike' has achieved a technical meaning and it is that which appears in paragraph 24 of Schedule 13. I appreciate that we do not find it in the main body of the Act. However this legislation began by adopting the method of laying down principles which were to govern industrial relations in schedules and the schedules are of very great importance. Schedule 13 is dealing with the financial consequences of a strike to those who take part in it and I would find it strange if a strike for the purpose of section 62 was something different from a strike for the purpose of Schedule 13. The complainant, being a person who took part in a strike, is subject to certain disabilities both under section 62 and also as laid down in Schedule 13. The relevant person is also subject to the disabilities in Schedule 13. Consequently in my opinion the expression 'to take part in a strike' should be strictly and not widely construed. I remind myself that both the complainant and the relevant person are described by the same expression.

There are many different ways in which a person can be involved in a strike. There are many ways in which a person's actions may be of assistance to the strikers. It does not follow that they are taking part in a strike. In my opinion for a person to take part in a strike he must be acting jointly or in concert with others who withdrew their labour, and this means that he must withdraw his labour in support of their claim. The fact that a man stays away from work when a strike is on does not lead inevitably to the conclusion that he is taking part in a strike. This was firmly the view of the Court of Appeal in *McCormick* v *Horsepower Ltd* [1981] ICR 535, and also of the appeal tribunal in the same case: [1980] ICR 278. In the Court of Appeal two grounds for the decision were stated. The first was that it was sufficient to defeat the claim if the dismissal of the 'relevant employee' took place before the date of the hearing. The second ground was that the alleged 'relevant employee' did not take part in the same strike as the complainant because although he decided not to cross the picket line he was not acting in concert with the strikers. It is true that Templeman L.J. said that it was strictly unnecessary to determine whether the man was a 'relevant employee.' Nonetheless he and Lawton and O'Connor L.J. were unanimous in the test which they applied to determine whether or not a person was a 'relevant employee.' I regard both grounds for the decision as being of equal force. If, as has been submitted, the second ground was obiter and therefore not binding upon us, I would feel the greatest reluctance in not following it unless of course it could be shown to have been arrived at per incuriam. Templeman L.J. said, at p. 540:

> The boilermakers went on strike and agreed or were instructed to come out together and they were under a mutual obligation to stay out together and go back together. Mr Brazier did not become under any obligation to come out or stay out with the boilermakers. Mr Brazier did not take part in any sympathetic strike by the engineers or any other body of persons because there was no sympathetic strike. Mr Brazier did not agree with any other person or become under any obligation to come out or stay out with the boilermakers, the engineers or any other person. Mr Brazier was an individual who voluntarily decided not to work on October 9, 1978, because the boilermakers were on strike and voluntarily decided to resume work on November 13, 1978, although the boilermakers were still on strike.

Lawton L.J. said, at p. 541:

> He was not a relevant employee unless he took part in the same strike as the employee. The statutory words 'who took part in it' (that is, the strike) mean giving help by acting in concert with each other and in withdrawing their labour for a common purpose or pursuant to a dispute which they or a majority of them or their union have with their employers and staying away from work as long as the strike lasts. Some help by standing on picket lines or by doing organising work in committee rooms. Evidence of Mr Brazier's refusal to cross the boilermakers' picket lines even though, as the industrial tribunal found, his refusal was not brought about by fear, was not in my judgment enough to prove that he was taking part in the boilermakers' strike. He was not shown to have had a common purpose with them or any interest in their dispute with their employers. He was not acting in concert with them as was shown by the fact that he returned to his work on November 13, 1978, whilst they were still on strike. In my judgment there was evidence upon which the industrial tribunal could find, as it did, that he was not taking part in the strike and in consequence was not a relevant employee. . . .

I am unable to find in this case any route by which the industrial tribunal could have accepted Mrs Leith's evidence and none the less come to the conclusion that she acted in concert with the other strikers. I can only conclude that the industrial tribunal wrongly approached the question as to whether or not Mrs Leith took part in the strike. The industrial tribunal seems to have treated as conclusive against Mrs Leith that she was not prepared to defy the pickets and 'that she would not break the strike.' I would dismiss this appeal.

KERR L.J.: . . . Turning then to what I have referred to as the primary issue, it seems to me, for the reasons already stated by Stephenson L.J., that there was ample material on which the industrial tribunal could reasonably conclude that Mrs Leith was taking part in a strike on that Tuesday morning. Indeed, I would go further and say that I would have reached the same conclusion as the industrial tribunal as a matter of first impression, and that I remain of this view after having heard the arguments on this appeal. To this extent, accordingly, I am inclined to differ from Stephenson L.J.'s views in that regard. Since there has been so much argument and so many references in the judgments as to what constitutes 'taking part in a strike,' I propose briefly to add my own view on this question, although this is not strictly necessary for the decision of the primary issue. Whatever definition of a strike one may adopt, such as that in paragraph 24 of Schedule 13 to the Act of 1978, it is common ground that there was a strike in progress on that Tuesday morning. The only issue is whether Mrs Leith was among the persons who took part in it, and it is also common ground that in the ultimate analysis this falls to be decided by reference to the events of that morning. As to this issue, and on this basis, it seems to me – given that there was then a strike – that all those, including Mrs Leith, who chose to remain outside and not to go to work were taking part in that strike, and only those, like Mrs Jessop, who chose to go in were not taking part in it. In this connection I do not think that it would be correct, or practicable, to differentiate between those who chose to remain outside by reference to their reasons for doing so. They were all free to go in, in the sense that the gate was open and that Mr Raistrick, the managing director, was urging them to do so. The fact that they had to cross the picket line to go in, and thereby suffer some abuse at the time, and quite possibly some unpopularity, or worse, among their fellow employees thereafter, and that feelings of this kind, as in the case of Mrs Leith, may have deterred them from going in, does not appear to me to make any difference. Nor would it make any difference, in my view, that their reason for staying out was that they were in sympathy with the strike. As it seems to me, their reasons or motives cannot be regarded as relevant. Nor would it be relevant to consider whether their utterances or actions, or silence or inaction, showed support, opposition or indifference in relation to the strike. When it is necessary to determine the question whether an employee does or does not take part in a strike which is admittedly in progress, but which does not prevent the employee from going to work in defiance of the manifold pressures which the existence of the strike is bound to exert, then it seems to me that this question can in practice only be answered on the basis of his or her action by either staying out or going in. Of course, if the employee does not go to work for reasons which have nothing to do with the strike, such as illness or being on holiday, then the position would be different. But when the employee's absence from work is due to the existence of the strike in some respect, because he or she chooses not to go to work during the strike, then I think that the employee should be regarded as taking part in the strike.

If this were not so, it seems to me that section 62 would be unworkable in practice. To take one example which I mentioned in the course of the argument, suppose that there is a meeting of the workforce to decide whether there should be a strike or not, in circumstances where the employers make it clear that they hope that everyone will continue to work whatever may be the outcome and that it will be open to everyone to do so. At the meeting there are then speeches for and against, and then 60 per cent vote in favour of the strike and 40 per cent against. A strike is then declared to exist, whether official or unofficial, and then everyone goes home and no one goes back to work, with some maintaining their support, others their opposition, and many saying nothing. How is it possible in practice to differentiate between them? Or suppose that some of those opposed to the strike go back to work, but that others decide not to do so because they fear the consequences, or because they will not – or fear to – cross a picket line, but nevertheless remain opposed to the strike, with some of them perhaps expressing their opposition by action or words, while the majority do and say nothing. As it seems to me, the issue as to who takes part in the strike in such commonplace occurrences can only be determined on the basis of who stays out and who does not.

I then turn finally to *McCormick* v *Horsepower Ltd* [1981] I C R 535. Assuming that the judgments in this court are to be taken as having decided a second issue apart from the decision that the relevant time is the date of the hearing for the purposes of determining whether or not any 'relevant employee' has been dismissed, it seems to me that the judgments are only authority for the proposition that anyone who may or may not have been a 'relevant employee' must on any view have taken part in the same strike as those employees who were dismissed. This was clearly what Templeman L.J. decided at p. 539H and O'Connor L.J. agreed with him. Lawton L.J. also agreed with this conclusion at p. 541C, and I think that his remarks in that passage were directed to the issue and that they should not be treated as authority for present purposes.

For these reasons I would allow this appeal.

The result of these two decisions of the Court of Appeal is rather ironic. A man who supported the strikers' goals is held not to have participated in the strike when he refused to go into work. Whereas a woman, who was not in sympathy with the strikers' goals, is held to have participated in the strike, when she was unwilling to incur the disapproval of the strikers by going into work. The crucial factor in the latter holding seems to have been that the woman was a member of the group of employees to whom the underlying dispute related. Consequently, the Court was not prepared to regard her as a non-participant if she actually did not report for work, simply on the basis of her mental reservation about the purpose of the strike. Some greater degree of disassociation from the strike was required, although it is unclear whether anything less than reporting to work would have sufficed (e.g. informing the employer of her readiness to work if the picket line were withdrawn; cf. *Naylor v. Orton & Smith Ltd* [1983] IRLR 233). It seems that majority took this view because in large part they thought that any other approach would render the employer's task an impossible one. If a group of employees go on strike and set up a picket line, how is the employer to know which of the group are at any particular time refusing to cross it because of whole-hearted commitment to the strike, which because of fear of social ostracism or worse, and which for reasons falling somewhat in between these sets of reasons? A similar line of reasoning may also explain the apparently contradictory decision in *McCormick* v *Horsepower Ltd*. The implication of the majority's judgments, put expressly by Kerr L.J., is that those who take action in sympathy with strikers are not participating in the original strike, but this is not to say that they cannot be said to be engaging in their own and separate industrial action. In consequence, the employer can treat the two groups of workers separately for the purposes of s.62, perhaps dismissing the strikers but not those taking sympathy action, because he may expect that to cease of its own accord when the main dispute had been ended by the dismissals.

Finally, it might be thought that the 1982 amendments to s.62 will have reduced the scale of the employer's problems in the *Coates* case. In fact the reverse may have occurred. At the time of the decision of the Court of Appeal in this case the decision of the House of Lords in *Stock* v *Frank Jones* (above, p. 917) was applicable. Consequently, if Mrs Leith took part in the strike between 8.00 and 10.30 on the first morning of the strike she had to be dismissed six weeks later along with the rest of the strikers if the tribunal was to be deprived of jurisdiction to hear the claimant's case. Consequently, the Court of Appeal rightly concentrated upon what happened in that short space of time. Under s.62 as amended the question would be whether Mrs Leith was still on strike when the claimants were dismissed at the end of the six weeks. She was, of course, still sick at that time and it would be an interesting test of the principle laid down in *Williams* v *Western Mail* (above, p. 921) to have to decide whether she was nevertheless on strike. One may hazard a guess that the employer's reasons for not dismissing Mrs Leith were that they did not regard her as being on strike at the date the others were dismissed because of the length of time she had been sick.

We can thus see that s.62 has given rise to, and continues to give rise to, difficult problems of interpretation. One suspects that part of the difficulty in resolving these problems lies in Parliament's failure to provide a clear-cut and precise rationale for the section. One is struck in this area by how often the courts say that the words of the section must be given their natural meaning, not perhaps because the natural meaning provides obviously sensible results (cf. *Stock* v *Frank Jones* and *McCormick* v *Horsepower Ltd*) but because no teleological approach is obviously available which will produce more sensible outcomes to the cases. However, if one stands back from the particular problems of interpretation, some general points about s.62 and its pre-decessors emerge clearly enough. One is the commitment of the legislators in 1971 not to allow the new unfair dismissal laws to produce in relation to the employer's self-help remedies – whether by way of dismissal or lock-out – a legal régime markedly different from that which obtained as a result of common law, contractual analysis – provided, of course, the employer treated all the relevant employees equally. On this point the radical potential of the new laws was explicitly curbed. The second is the survival, and indeed reaffirmation, of this policy in the rather different legal and political contexts of 1975 and 1982. Indeed, as we have seen, it was made easier in 1975 and again in 1982 for the non-discriminatory employer to dismiss those involved in industrial action. We have suggested that this occurred because the policy of freedom to dismiss appealed, for different reasons, both to advocates of collective *laissez-faire* and to those in favour of more restrictive legislation. Collective *laissez-faire*, after all, meant that the law should not restrict resort by either side to peaceful economic sanctions in pursuit of their ends in trade disputes, and this theory could be applied to the employer as well as to the employees. This argument was strengthened in 1975 by the desire of the then government not to involve industrial tribunals more than was necessary in adjudicating upon the merits of industrial disputes.

For those in favour of restrictive legislation, encouragement of self-help remedies on the part of employers may in practice prove to be more effective than the provision of opportunities to seek injunctions against the organizers of

industrial action or damages against trade-union funds. As the history of the
IRA 1971 demonstrated, the latter is a 'high risk' strategy. More important,
perhaps, it gives management weapons they are unused to handling and of
whose potential they are unsure. The self-help remedies are already part of
managerial strategies for dealing with industrial action; the removal of the
legal doubts surrounding them is then an obvious restrictive policy. That there
is strong support for this view in employer circles is perhaps well demonstrated
by the reaction of the Engineering Employers' Federation to the government's
Green Paper, *Trade Union Immunities*.

The particular point that concerned the Federation was the employer's
liability to pay wages, not to those taking the industrial action, but to those laid
off as a result of it. The extent of the employer's right to lay off those for whom
no work is available has long been a vexed question at common law. The
nineteenth-century cases tended to grant employers a wide implied right to lay
off because of poor trading conditions. However, in 1906 the Court of Appeal
in *Devonald* v. *Rosser and Sons* [1906] 2 KB 728 refused to imply a right to lay off
in such cases because such a term would not be reasonable. The principle
established in this case was qualified by the decision of Greer J. in *Browning* v.
Crumlin Valley Collieries Ltd [1926] 1 KB 522, where an implied right to lay off
was found when a mine was temporarily closed, not as a result of recession, but
because it was unsafe. Thereafter, the issue tended to disappear from the
case-law, perhaps because of the development in the practice of collective
bargaining of 'guaranteed week arrangements' (see above, p. 359). These
arrangements, if incorporated into the individual contract of employment,
gave the employee an express entitlement to wages of a certain amount,
irrespective of whether work was available. They also usually provided for
'suspension' of the guarantee in certain circumstances, and it is usually
assumed that the suspension provisions amount to a specific agreement that
wages are not payable in such cases. Suspension is frequently provided for
where the lack of work is due to industrial action. Perhaps the most well-
known provision in this regard is that contained in the agreement between the
Engineering Employers Federation and the Confederation of Shipbuilding
and Engineering Unions, which stated that the guarantee was 'automatically
suspended' where there was 'dislocation of production in a federated
establishment as a result of an industrial dispute in that or any other federated
establishment'.[1] However, in *Bond* v. *CAV Ltd* [1983] IRLR 360, Peter Pain
J. interpreted this suspension clause narrowly and, asserting the primacy of the
principle in *Devonald* v. *Rosser*, expressed himself as not necessarily convinced
that the suspension clause would operate to defeat the common-law rights of
employees who, by virtue of EPCA 1978, s.49, were no longer hourly paid but
entitled to at least a week's notice to terminate their employment.

The Federation's proposals were clearly an attempt to clarify the law in the
direction of increasing the employer's freedom to lay off. Although the
government did not adopt the Federation's proposals in the EA 1982, they

[1] See above, p. 296.

remain evidence of the existence of a problem as perceived by employers, at least in that industry, and, perhaps more interesting from our point of view, contain a forceful statement of the view that self-help remedies are more important in practice than legal action.

Engineering Employers Federation, *Response to Green Paper on Trade Union Immunities* (1981), paras. 2–4

2. The Green Paper deals, of course, essentially with the topic of union immunities: and the Federation, in common with a very large body of opinion in the country, believes that the existing immunities of unions are too extensive for a modern industrial society. But it does not follow that the significant cutting back of those immunities is the most urgent or effective action needed to produce a fair balance in power between unions and employers in the interest of the whole community, so that their vulnerability is more evenly matched. Indeed, the Federation believes that this is not so. The reason for this lies in the realities of the British political and industrial system. Unions will not willingly acquiesce in any significant reduction in their immunities: and under the British political system it is virtually certain that immunities taken away by a government of one complexion will be at least restored by another government more sympathetic to the cause of union power. There is no merit therefore in initiating this kind of debilitating struggle in industry merely to make use of a temporary political advantage. However desirable in principle the wholesale radical reform of union immunities may seem to be, there is no advantage in attempting it unless the British political system can deliver the prospect of its durability.

3. This is the reason why in this statement of views the Federation, while accepting the need in the longer-term to restrict union immunities in certain respects, identifies certain other priority objectives for legislation in order to achieve the improved industrial performance, for which the Green Paper calls. The achievement of these other objectives would have a much more certain and significant effect in producing a reasonable balance of power between unions and employers than cutting back union immunities. It would also impose much stronger restraints on the power of unions to damage the community as a whole through the deployment of industrial action; and would command much greater public support.

4. Briefly, the type of priority objectives which the Federation wishes to see pursued are, first, those that provide a reasonable and effective counter to the increasingly-damaging deployment of selective industrial action: hence, the Federation's call (Section 2(b)(i) below) for a power to allow an employer whose business is disrupted by industrial action taken by some of his employees to lay off other employees without pay, even if their normal work is available. Second, the Federation wishes to see some curb on the ruinous economic effects of serious industrial action in key undertakings, usually in the public sector: hence, the Federation's call (Section 3H below) for legislation to enable employers to relieve themselves of the burden of having to maintain the pay of employees when large sections of the economy are paralysed by such extraneous industrial action, and when they themselves are unable to produce any goods for sale.

10 Employment protection rights, social security benefits and industrial action

The final area in which we need to examine the working out of trends towards a more restrictive framework of labour law concerns neither the law of industrial conflict itself nor the employer's self-help remedies, but rather the question of whether an employee taking industrial action is to be deprived of benefits (financial or otherwise) that he would normally be entitled to from the state. The most obvious and important example of this problem concerns entitlement to unemployment or supplementary benefit. A person out of work normally has an entitlement to one or other (sometimes both) of these benefits. Is that entitlement removed when the employee is out of work because he is on strike or has been locked out by his employer? Even more difficult, is the entitlement removed from an employee laid off because of a strike by or lock-out of other workers? There are two main competing views on this question. On the one hand, there is the argument that the state should be neutral in industrial conflict situations, helping neither one side nor the other. This is the counterpart to the theory of collective *laissez-faire*, i.e. the theory that employers and employees should be unrestricted in their peaceful use of economic sanctions in the course of trade disputes. As we shall see, however, it has proved difficult to attach a coherent meaning to neutrality on the part of the state in this context. The alternative theory is that the state should not even aspire to neutrality but rather should use the legislation conferring benefits on employees to encourage certain types of behaviour in the course of industrial disputes and to discourage others.

Although the problem can be clearly identified in relation to financial benefits provided by the state, it is not confined to these benefits. Indeed, there has been an interesting debate of this type in relation to the statutory seniority provisions. These provisions, of course, determine whether the employee has a legal claim against his employer and, in some cases, the extent of that claim. The benefits are thus provided by the employer (at least where he is solvent), but one can in another sense regard them as benefits provided by the state. The government when passing the relevant employment protection legislation requiring the employer to provide the benefits has to decide what the impact of industrial action upon the employee's entitlement to benefits from his employer shall be. The Contracts of Employment Act 1963 introduced statutory entitlement to minimum periods of notice where an employer wished to terminate a contract of employment (in the absence of conduct justifying summary dismissal). The length of the minimum period depended (and still does depend; see above, p. 434) upon the length of the continuous period of employment the employee had with his employer at the point the notice was given. Sch. 1 to the 1963 Act set out rules for computing the length of periods of continuous employment, and it dealt with the problem of strikes by providing that a period spent on strike would not count towards the period of continuous employment but neither would going on strike break the period of continuous employment, provided, in the latter case, that the strike did not amount to a breach of the contracts of employment of those participating in it. It seems clear that the Conservative government which passed the CEA 1963 saw this provision as a useful way of distinguishing between strikes embarked upon after due notice and unconstitutional strikes and as a way of putting some pressure upon employees to strike only after due notice. Unfortunately for the legislators, the House of Lords in its decision in *Rookes* v. *Barnard* [1964] AC 1129 took the view, as we have seen (above, p. 720), that most strikes, even after due notice, would be in breach of the contracts of employment of those participating in them. Thus, the contractual status of the strike ceased to be a possible way of distinguishing between (in industrial relations terms) constitutional and unconstitutional strikes, and the legislators of the 1963 Act had in fact produced a situation in which most strikes would break continuity of employment. Consequently, in s.37 of the RPA 1965 the opportunity was taken to remove the proviso from the provisions about strikes in Sch. 1 to the 1963 Act: strikes should neither count towards nor break continuity of employment, no matter what their contractual status.

However, the original policy of the 1963 Act was revived in a proposal made to the Donovan Commission. The proposal was now put explicitly in industrial relations terms rather than in terms of the contractual status of the industrial action. Industrial action which was in breach of a procedure agreed between employer and union for the handling of disputes should break the period of continuous employment, i.e. those taking the industrial action would forfeit their accrued statutory seniority, for the purposes of both the CEA 1963 and, now more important, of redundancy payments under the RPA 1965. This proposal caused the Commission to evaluate the merits of the policy originally embodied in the CEA 1963, and it had little difficulty in showing that such a sanction against unconstitutional action would operate in an arbitrary and capricious way.

> *Report of the Royal Commission on Trade Unions and Employers'*
> *Associations*, Cmnd. 3623, 1968, paras. 495–9

495. There are other reasons why such a measure would not have the effect it is intended to have. As we point out in Chapter VII unofficial strikes are most frequent in four industries. One of these is the docks, to which the Redundancy Payments Act does not apply. Another one, ship-building and ship-repairing, has a very high rate of labour turnover with the result that only a small minority of workers would be affected by the envisaged forfeiture of seniority rights. Moreover, in the 'trouble spots' where unconstitutional strikes are particularly frequent the potency of the sanction would soon evaporate. Once a worker has, through participation in an unofficial strike, lost his 'seniority', he will cease to be interested in the threatened penalty. Nothing much can happen to him, at least for some considerable time, and whatever deterrent effect the sanction may have had is now lost. This however means that where it is most urgently necessary to reduce the number of unofficial strikes, this penalty will be subject to a very fast-working 'law of diminishing returns'. After a short time it will lose its effect as a deterrent, and only the bitterness will remain. It is a penalty which, as it were, can effectively be imposed only for the first offence.

496. The sanction is intended to operate by way of delayed action: it would be felt years, possibly many years, after the event, and only by those employees who happened to be

given notice or made redundant. One must envisage the situation at the time of the termination of the employment which, but for the strike, would have given rise to a claim for notice under the Act of 1963 and to a claim for a redundancy payment under the Act of 1965. By that time the unofficial strike for which the employee is now to suffer the penalty may be and is indeed likely to be forgotten. The employer will often have an interest in letting sleeping dogs lie and in not stirring up new trouble by reviving the memory of ancient battles. He may find it, at that moment, invidious to discriminate between those about to lose their jobs. He is likely to 'condone' the 'offence', to waive the penalty and to treat the employees to be discharged as if the strike had never occurred. This is what many employers can be expected to do and what many people, including strikers, will expect them to do – in so far as in the heat of the moment the thought of the amount of their notice and redundancy pay enters their consciousness at all. For this reason too the deterrent effect of this sanction is likely to be illusory.

497. There is of course nothing in the law to prevent an employer from 'condoning' the offence by giving to the employee the full notice and the full redundancy pay to which he would have been entitled but for the strike. He will not, however, be able to recover the 'rebate' payable to him out of the Redundancy Fund for more than an amount calculated on the basis of a seniority shortened by the strike; the Department of Employment and Productivity has no power to pay a rebate for more than what the employer owes as a matter of law. In such a situation it is the employer and not the striker who is penalised; instead of recovering the larger amount of the redundancy pay from the Fund he pays it all out of his own pocket.

498. Since both employers and employees can be expected to foresee this situation, it is all too probable that they will agree, if they can, not to allow the news of the strike to become too widely known and above all not to come to the notice of those administering the Redundancy Fund.

499. For the older workers, and especially the most steady workers with long records of employment, that is for the most responsible workers who are least in need of a 'deterrent', the threat would be drastic indeed – far more drastic than the payment of damages or of a fine. To gauge its magnitude one must see the offence and the penalty in perspective. The offence would be participation in a strike, or a go-slow, or a work to rule, or an overtime ban. This may be action taken on the spur and in the heat of the moment, and it may last only for a short time – many unofficial strikes are over in a few hours. It may and often will be action taken by a group of men under some real or imagined provocation, and action in which only a person of unusual strength of character can refuse to participate. It is true – and this is claimed as one of the merits of the proposal – that it would enlist the interest of the older and more thoughtful men who may succeed in persuading their younger colleagues from taking rash and sudden action. But the burden it imposes on these men is perhaps more than an ordinary individual of no more than average strength of personality can be expected to bear. For the risk involved to the older men may be almost intolerable: it may be the risk of losing an expectation to payments amounting to up to £1,200 and acquired through decades of work for an employer, and losing it through inability to dissuade one's fellows from ill-considered action and inability to dissociate oneself from it. The fruits of a life-time's work may thus be lost in five minutes and through participation in an action which may be over in an hour. The history of our law – especially of our criminal law – shows that where the penalty is too harsh it will not be imposed. Those making this proposal suggest that an appellate body should have jurisdiction to mitigate the penalty. It

would soon do so in a radical way and to the extent of making the threat completely unreal. There must be some proportion between means and ends. This is out of proportion.

The Donovan Commission Report was accepted on this point and the provisions of the RPA 1965 were not changed. They are currently codified in para. 15 of Sch. 13 to EPCA 1978. On the whole they have been implemented fully by the courts.

Bloomfield v. *Springfield Hosiery Finishing Co. Ltd* [1972]
ICR 91 (NIRC)

In July 1969 the employees went on strike in breach of contract and the employer dismissed them. Later the strike was settled in the employer's favour and the employees were taken back. In late 1970 the employees were dismissed on grounds of redundancy. The industrial tribunal dismissed their application for redundancy payments on the grounds that they did not have two years' continuous service prior to the date of dismissal.

SIR JOHN DONALDSON: . . . Basing themselves upon this paragraph [EPCA 1978, Sch. 13, para 15], the employees submit that for purposes of continuity they are entitled to count the whole period between 7 July when they went on strike and 21 July when they were re-employed, or, in the case of one of them, are deemed to have been re-employed. The employers' answer to this contention is that the strike ended when the employees were dismissed, that thereafter their relations with the employers were not governed by any contract of employment, thus excluding paragraph 4 [EPCA 1978, Sch. 13, para. 4] and that there was no 'temporary cessation of work' within the meaning of paragraph 5(1)(*b*) [EPCA 1978, Sch. 13, para. 9(1)(*b*)], these words having been construed *per* Lord Upjohn in *Fitzgerald* v. *Hall, Russell & Co. Ltd* [1970] AC 984, 1002 [above, p. 572], as describing a situation in which the employer no longer had work available for the employee personally. In this case, the employers say, there was ample work available to the employees if only they were prepared to undertake it upon the employer's terms.

A 'strike' is defined in paragraph 11 of the code [EPCA 1978, Sch. 13, para. 24] as meaning:

. . . the cessation of work by a body of persons employed acting in combination, or a concerted refusal or a refusal under a common understanding of any number of persons employed to continue to work for an employer in consequence of a dispute, done as a means of compelling their employer or any person or body of persons employed, or to aid other employees in compelling their employer or any person or body of persons employed, to accept or not to accept terms or conditions of or affecting employment.

Mr David submits that once the contract of employment is terminated by dismissal, the strikers cease to be 'a body of persons employed' and their action ceases to be a strike. Although this argument is superficially attractive, it is, in our judgment, wholly fallacious. It is true that under section 8(1) of the Act of 1963 [EPCA 1978, s.153] it is provided that 'employee' means an individual who has entered into or works under a contract with an employer . . . and cognate expressions shall be construed accordingly'.

However, if this definition were applied narrowly, paragraph 5 of the code could not apply to a break in employment such as occurred in *Fitzgerald's* case, because during the break there was no contract with the employer and the workmen would not, therefore, have been employees. The House of Lords held that paragraph 5 can apply in such a situation and it follows that the word 'employee' in the code is to be given a wider meaning.

In paragraph 5 of the code 'employee' must mean a person who, but for and during the continuance of one of the specified circumstances (sickness, temporary cessation of work, etc.) would be an employee. Similarly, in our judgment, 'persons employed' in the definition of a strike must be read as extending to include persons who, but for their action in ceasing or refusing to continue to work, would be employees. The fact that the employer terminates their contracts of employment does not take them outside this category, unless and until he engages other persons on a permanent basis to do the work which the strikers had been doing or he permanently discontinues the activity in which they were employed. Similarly the fact that the striker takes other temporary employment pending the settlement of the dispute does not prevent him claiming that he is taking part in a strike.

In fact in the present case none of the employees took other employment and all were re-employed. In our judgment, the employees were taking part in a strike from 7 July until 21 July 1970, unless their return to work was in some way delayed in order to achieve a phased resumption of work. In the latter case the period of delay would be covered by paragraph 5(1)(b) of the code as being, for the reasons given in *Clarke Chapman–John Thompson Ltd* v. *Walters* . . . [1972] ICR 83, an absence from work on account of a temporary cessation of work within the meaning of that paragraph. In relation to the issue of continuity, it matters not which paragraph applies and on the facts of this case it is unlikely to affect the amount of the redundancy payment to which the employees are entitled, although in theory it could.

Two of the strikers were never re-employed. We do not have to decide exactly when they ceased to be on strike, but in principle this occurred either when they took other employment without an intention of returning as soon as possible to their former employment or when the employers engaged other replacement employees on a permanent basis, whichever occurred first.

Some argument was directed to the question of whether or not the employees could successfully contend that they were absent from work by reason of a lock-out and rely upon paragraph 8 [EPCA 1978, Sch. 13, para. 15(4)] of the code which provides that:

> The continuity of the period of employment is not broken by a week which begins after this schedule comes into force and which does not count under this schedule, if in that week or any part of that week the employee is absent from work because of a lock-out by the employer.

It is a commonplace that one man's strike is another man's lock-out and it will, we think, suffice to say that similar considerations apply to the definition of 'lock-out' as to the definition of 'strike'. The only effect of dismissal as part of a lock-out is that paragraph 4 of the code ceases to apply and the locked-out workman must rely upon paragraph 8 to maintain his continuity of employment for purposes of the Act of 1965.

In *McGorry* v. *Earls Court Stand Fitting Ltd* [1973] ICR 100 (NIRC), the court held that para. 5(1)(b) could be used to maintain continuity for an employee dismissed on grounds of redundancy during a strike but re-engaged some three weeks later.

Thus, in the context of the statutory seniority provisions, neutrality has come to mean neither penalizing a person on strike by depriving him of accrued seniority nor enabling him to count periods spent on strike towards his statutory seniority, a result which has some title to be called a neutral one. In other areas of non-financial benefit the legislators have also tried to disengage facilities provided by the state from their use by one side or the other in a trade dispute. Thus, it has long been the policy of our social security legislation that the facilities of the public employment exchanges (now termed job centres) should not be available to an employer in dispute who seeks to recruit strike-breakers. Equally, those unemployed should not be under any financial pressure from the state to act as strike-breakers. S.20(4)(*a*) of the Social Security Act 1975 provides that in relation to suitable employment, refusal of which may disentitle an unemployed worker from receiving benefit, 'employment in a situation vacant in consequence of a stoppage of work due to a trade dispute' shall be deemed not to be suitable. See also EPCA 1978, s.47(5), concerning a woman's right to return to work after pregnancy or confinement.

However, there is no doubt but that it is in relation to financial benefits provided by the Social Security System to employees that the issue of neutrality has aroused the greatest controversy. We need to look separately at unemployment benefit and supplementary benefit.

(a) Unemployment benefit

Unemployment benefit is in principle, though the principle had been somewhat undermined in recent years, the product of an insurance system. Employers and employees make compulsory contributions to a fund, out of which benefits are paid to workers who become involuntarily unemployed. The 'involuntary unemployment' principle has always been applied so as to disentitle strikers themselves (or workers locked out) from receiving unemployment benefit. In this respect the British system of unemployment benefit follows the pattern of most other countries, and it has always been treated as axiomatic in public discussion that those actually on strike or locked out should not be entitled to unemployment benefit. However, as Ogus and Barendt point out,[1] the involuntary unemployment principle does not well explain why those locked out are not entitled to benefit, and, even in relation to strikers, it can be argued that the principle of involuntary unemployment ought to give way if the employees have a good cause for going on strike (just as in other contexts 'good cause' qualifies the voluntary unemployment principle), but in fact no such qualification is made for strikers. The principle of neutrality is equally difficult to apply: either the benefit is paid and the employees' ability to remain on strike is arguably increased or the benefit, to which they would otherwise be entitled, is not paid because being on strike is the cause of the unemployment, and the employer's position arguably is strengthened. Perhaps the real principle that emerges is an unwillingness to involve the social security system in an assessment of the merits of industrial disputes: employees on strike or locked out are not entitled to benefit no matter whether the merits of the dispute lie with the employees or the employer.

In consequence of the view taken about those on strike or locked out, the public debate has concentrated on the issue of how far those laid off by stoppages should also be disqualified. At first sight it may seem that being laid off by a stoppage in which one is not participating is a clear example of involuntary unemployment. It may be said on the other hand that those laid off may have an interest in the success of the strike and, indeed, that without the disqualification the union might be tempted so to arrange its industrial action as to call out only a small number of key workers in pursuance of a claim relating to a much larger group (cf. *Chappell* v. *Times Newspapers*, above, p. 893), with the consequence that the national insurance fund would be used to insulate the majority of the interested workers against the financial consequences of strike action. Because of arguments of this type the debate has been not about whether those laid off should in some circumstances be disqualified, but about what those circumstances should be.

When the unemployment benefit scheme was introduced in its new form after the Second World War the trade dispute disqualification was phrased (as consolidated in s.19(1) of the Social Security Act 1975) as follows:

A person who has lost employment as an employed earner by reason of a stoppage of work which was due to a trade dispute at his place of employment shall be disqualified for receiving unemployment benefit so long as the stoppage continues, except in a case where, during the stoppage, he has become bona fide employed elsewhere in the occupation which he usually follows or has become regularly engaged in some other occupation; but this subsection does not apply in the case of a person who proves –

(a)   that he is not participating in *or financing* or directly interested in the trade dispute which caused the stoppage of work; *and*

(b)   *that he does not belong to a grade or class of workers of which, immediately before the commencement of the stoppage, there were members employed at his place of employment any of whom are participating in or financing or directly interested in the dispute.*

As a result of the recommendations of the Donovan Commission the words italicized in the above section were repealed by s.111 of the EPA 1975. The Commission could find no adequate justification for the 'grade or class' provision (s.19(1) (b)) or for the disqualification on grounds of financing. The result of the change made in 1975 was a considerable narrowing of the disqualification. The Commission did not accept a proposal from the CBI (see paras. 970–2) that the 'place of employment' restriction should be broadened so as to include all those laid off by a dispute with their employer, albeit a dispute between the employer and workers in another plant of a multi-plant company. The 'place of employment' provision has thus remained in the section.

Report of the Royal Commission on Trade Unions and Employers' Associations, 1968, paras. 974–5, 983–5

974. The principle underlying the grade or class provision is thus stated in the evidence of the Ministry of Social Security:

Principle of the grade or class provision

The grade or class provision considers the position of workers in relation to a particular trade dispute, not according to whether they are personally involved in the dispute in the sense that they are individually participating in, financing or directly interested in the dispute, but according to whether they belong to a group of workers containing workers who are personally involved. It assumes that a group of workers doing much the same kind of work in the same place and under the same conditions and circumstances have a corporate identity and a special relationship one with another – a 'community of interest' – quite apart from their position in relation to any particular trade dispute. The argument runs that just as members of a particular grade or class are treated alike in so many other aspects of their working life in the factory so they should also be treated alike for purposes of the trade dispute disqualification. Thus if any member of the grade or class is personally involved in the dispute as participating, financing, or directly interested in it, all the other members of the grade or class are deemed to be involved by virtue of their corporate identity as members of the same grade or class, and cannot therefore escape disqualification. In some cases, a high proportion of the grade or class will be personally involved. In others this proportion will be small. The principle of treating the whole grade or class alike however applies irrespective of the proportion of members personally involved.

The Ministry goes on to say:

The grade or class provision does not assume that workers disqualified under it are in fact 'interested' in the *dispute* in the same way and to the same extent as workers personally involved as participating, financing or directly interested in the dispute may be regarded as having an 'interest' in the dispute. It operates on the principle that members of a grade or class have a mutual 'interest' *as members of that grade or class* which justifies treating them alike for unemployment benefit purposes in trade disputes.

And later the Ministry comments:

The present law was based on the assumption that this special relationship, or community of interest, between a group of workers identified as a grade or class is a reality of sufficient importance to justify treating them all alike in the matter of entitlement to unemployment benefit where work is lost as a result of a trade dispute. Whether this assumption is valid in modern industrial conditions may be open to doubt and certainly there is evidence that its validity is not generally recognized or accepted by those who are adversely affected by it.

975. In our view the reasoning thus said to underlie the grade or class provision is fallacious. In order to ascertain whether a class of persons has a common interest

simply because it is a class one needs to know what common attribute it is which marks such persons off as a class. This the law makes no attempt to do. It simply assumes, apparently, that if a group of workers in the same place of employment can by some means be identified as a 'class' or 'grade' then automatically they possess a common interest as such: and no investigation is required to disqualify them from receiving unemployment benefit beyond discovering whether there is at least one of the class participating in the trade dispute, or financing it, or directly interested in it. This seems to us not so much the recognition of an interest as the invention of it. The capricious results which the provision can and does produce are themselves some indication of the invalidity of the assumption which underlies it. If for example the process workers at a particular works go on strike on an issue which concerns them alone and one member out of a total of 100 maintenance workers strikes in sympathy, the remaining 99 if laid off will all be disqualified from receiving unemployment benefit, though they have no interest in the strike and indeed are hostile to it.

As to 'Financing'
983. It may be wondered how a person who is out of work and wishes to claim unemployment benefit is able at the same time to 'finance' a trade dispute. The answer lies in the interpretation which has been placed on the relevant statutory provision. It is construed as disqualifying from unemployment benefit any person who is unemployed as the result of a trade dispute at his place of employment if he is a member of a trade union which is paying strike pay to other members being participants in the dispute. 984. It is regarded as immaterial whether such a claimant is continuing, while unemployed, to pay his usual contributions as a member to such trade union; and a decision to this effect has, in fact, been given by the Insurance Commissioner. It is also regarded as irrelevant that the funds from which the trade union is paying strike pay are funds to which the claimant has contributed in the past, and may, if he keeps up his subscription while unemployed, still be contributing. The theory upon which the disqualification is based is that the act of the union in paying strike benefit, and thus financing the trade dispute, is the act of each and every one of its members. As members of an unincorporated association of individuals bound by a common contract providing *inter alia* for financial support for fellow-members on strike, all must be regarded as involved in the act individually as well as collectively. Expressed in another way, the union acts as agent for its members.
985. There is clearly logic in such an interpretation. But the logic squares very uneasily at times with reality. It must be obvious beforehand in most cases that a strike in one department at a place of employment is likely to throw out of work employees in another department who may have no interest in the dispute whatever. If one of the employees in this other department is a member of the union supporting the strike, it is again a little unreal to treat him automatically as a party to the union's action if he knows full well in advance that the result will be to bring considerable financial hardship upon himself, and also perhaps upon his family. Of course, such a man may be willing to accept such hardship in the interests of union solidarity; on the other hand he may regard the strike as quite unjustified and unworthy of support. At the present time he is penalized whatever view he takes.

Thus, in relation to those laid off by a stoppage of work the main test has become whether they were directly interested in the trade dispute which caused the stoppage. The attitudes of the National Insurance Commissioners on the meaning of this phrase have varied over time. The factual question has often been whether the settlement of the strike would have an impact upon the terms and conditions of employment of those laid off. Up until the middle of the 1960s the Commission seemed likely to impose disqualification if the settlement of the strike was likely to lead to changes in the terms and conditions of those laid off. In more recent decisions the Commissioners have placed greater stress upon the word 'directly' and have seemed to require virtually an automatic link between the dispute and the changes in the terms of employment of those laid off. The *locus classicus* of this approach was the decision of a Scottish Commissioner, Mr H. A. Shewan, in R(U) 13/71, in which he said:

Without attempting to define precisely what is meant by 'direct interest', I think that a claimant should not be regarded as having a direct interest in another person's dispute . . . unless there is a close association between the two occupations concerned and the outcome of the dispute is likely to affect the claimant, not at a number of removes, but virtually automatically, without further intervening contingencies.

This approach was endorsed by the Court of Session in *Watt* v. *Lord Advocate* 1979 SLT 137, and again by the House of Lords in *Presho* v. *Department of Health and Social Security* [1984] IRLR 74.

Mrs Presho was a machine operator and a member of USDAW. The employers also employed maintenance engineers who were members of the AUEW. In the course of a pay dispute between the engineers and the employers, the machine operators were laid off because the machines were not being repaired. USDAW and the AUEW negotiated separate collective agreements with the employers, but the Commissioner found as a fact that the employers' practice was to apply to all manual employees a wage increase conceded to one group. The House upheld the Insurance Officer's view that Mrs Presho was disqualified from receiving unemployment benefit. The disqualification was to be brought into play where the result of the dispute would be applied to those laid off either as a result of a collective agreement to that effect or, as in this case, where it was the custom and practice of the workplace for the employer automatically to extend the settlement to the laid-off group. This approach confines the 'directness' test within narrow limits, although not within limits as narrow as those proposed by the Court of Appeal in this case ([1983] IRLR 295). That court had seemed to require a collective or individual agreement that the result of the dispute would be extended to those laid off before the disqualification would bite.

(b) Supplementary benefit
Supplementary benefit is a non-contributory benefit payable where the head of the household is unemployed and the family's income falls below what is needed to maintain the minimum standards of living specified in the

legislation. Since the legislation provides only a 'safety net', a rock-bottom minimum below which no family should be allowed to fall, supplementary benefit claims cannot usually arise in respect of short strikes. Thus, employees are customarily paid a week in arrears and, if those arrears are paid by the employer before the strike begins, any claims will be postponed for a week. (See R. v. *Manchester Supplementary Benefit Appeal Tribunal ex parte Riley* [1979] 1 WLR 426.) Further, the supplementary benefit authorities will expect higher-paid employees to make their wages stretch over longer periods than normal (up to two weeks for each week's pay) and will refuse to entertain claims in respect of such periods.

On the other hand, once these sums are exhausted and there are no other sources of income for the household, it is less easy for the legislature to impose a trade dispute disqualification as broad as that for unemployment benefit. This is because the state has a positive policy of ensuring every member of the community a minimum living standard. To maintain a balance between this policy and a policy of not 'financing strikers', s.8 of the Supplementary Benefits Act 1976 imposes a disqualification upon strikers and those laid off in the same circumstances as s.19 of the Social Security Act 1975 (as amended) but confines the disqualification to the striker or the person laid off. Supplementary benefit is payable to meet the rent (or mortgage interest) and the needs of wives and dependent children.

The compromise has proved satisfactory to few people. On the one hand it can be said that the state is countenancing for strikers' households a fall below the minimum standards fixed for the rest of the community. On the other it can be argued that by paying out benefit at all the state is subsidizing strikers since they will undoubtedly receive some of the benefit of the payments made in respect of dependants. The amounts paid in some recent years to strikers have been substantial (nearly £5 million in 1974; £2.5 million in 1979) and they are much higher than in the 1960s (in 1964 the amount was £49,413, though there are quite large fluctuations from year to year). However, the empirical studies that have been conducted suggest that the amounts paid have been determined by the increasing number of long, official strikes over incomes policy in recent years rather than that the availability of supplementary benefit has influenced significantly the nature and duration of strikes (see J. Gennard, *Financing Strikers* (1977), Ch. 7).

There is a complex interrelationship between supplementary benefit and strike pay. Unions pay strike pay only, of course, in official strikes (i.e. those sanctioned by the relevant union body, usually the executive council). Under the rules of some unions strike benefit at a certain level must be paid in all official strikes, in others the amount of the benefit and whether it is to be paid at all is determined in each dispute by the executive. Because of the generally low subscriptions to British trade unions, the level of strike benefit is usually also low (see Gennard, op. cit., Ch.4 for more detail). There is a feeling in some quarters that, if strikers are to be financed at all, more of the burden ought to be borne by trade unions and less by the state.

In order to achieve this the Social Security Act 1971 abrogated the rule that strikers could have income from other sources (e.g. tax rebates or strike pay) up to the level of the supplementary benefit they would have been entitled to, if not disqualified, before the amount paid in respect of dependants was reduced. The 1971 Act allowed only £1 of this income to be disregarded in assessing the household's resources though the 1976 Act raised the figure to £4. Paradoxically, but not surprisingly, the Act had the opposite effect, if anything, from that intended by its drafters. Before 1971 unions were encouraged to make strike payments in order to lift the household to the supplementary benefit level; after 1971 the inducement to them was to reduce strike payments and use the money available to further the dispute in other ways.

Consequently, it was not unexpected when in 1980 the Conservative government, besides passing the Employment Act 1980, returned to the issue of the relationship between social security payments to strikers' dependants and the payment by unions of strike pay. By s.6 of the Social Security (No. 2) Act 1980 three changes were made, designed to produce an effective set of rules for the transfer of more of the burden of financing strikes from the social security system to the trade unions. First, the general disregard of income from other sources, which was raised to £4 in 1976, was completely removed. This, by itself, would not, of course, encourage unions to pay strike pay. This policy was most strongly expressed in the second change, which was that the supplementary benefit payable in respect of the dependants of those themselves disqualified should be reduced by £12 (now increased to £15[1]) from the level it would otherwise be set at. This reduction applies whether or not the person disqualified is in fact in receipt of strike pay: hence the pressure on the union to make such payments. However, that incentive might seem to be removed by the first change: if the union actually pays strike pay, will not the actual payments reduce the entitlement from the state even further? This problem is solved by regulations[2] which re-introduce a special disregard for strike pay, up to the amount by which the entitlement is automatically reduced, thus restoring the incentive. However, the union has no incentive to pay more than £15, unless the amount paid will be greater than the total entitlement from the social security system, for amounts paid over £15 reduce the supplementary benefit on a pound-for-pound basis. Thus, a person disqualified, who would otherwise be entitled to £45 for his dependants, will receive £30 from the social security system, plus whatever strike pay his union pays up to £15. If the union pays more than £15, the figure of £30 will be reduced. The person disqualified will benefit from his union's generosity only when the payment by the union exceeds £45.

This process of deeming employees to be in receipt of strike pay whether

---

[1] Social Security (No. 2) Act 1980, Specified Sum Order 1983 (SI 1983 No. 1433).

[2] Supplementary Benefit (Trade Disputes and Recovery from Earnings) Regulations 1980 (SI 1980 No. 1641), Reg. 12.

they actually were or not, had been suggested on several previous occasions. It had previously foundered on the difficulty of distinguishing between official and unofficial strikes, for it was thought not to be fair to deem unofficial strikers to be in receipt of strike pay, since unions could hardly be expected to support action of which they did not approve. However, the 1980 Act imposes a general reduction, and in the case of unofficial strikers the Act operates not so much as an incentive for unions to pay strike pay as a financial penalty for striking unofficially. Indeed, the reduction applies to all those disqualified as a result of a stoppage of work at their place of employment from having their own needs taken into account. As we have seen, this includes not only strikers but also those locked out and even those laid off, provided they have a direct interest in the dispute. It may be unrealistic to expect unions generally to pay strike pay to those laid off (who may be represented by a different union from the strikers) and in such a case the reduction of the supplementary benefit entitlement will presumably increase the pressure on the strikers from those laid off for a resumption of work.

The third change made in 1980 was, however, the one that is perhaps capable of operating most harshly. It follows from the rule that the needs of those without work because of a stoppage of work due to a trade dispute at their place of employment are to be ignored in assessing entitlement to benefit that single persons can make no claim to benefit at all, because they will have no dependants whose needs can be taken into account. However, by s.4 of the 1976 Act the authorities had an overriding discretion to make payments even to single persons in case of 'urgent need'. The categories of urgent need which the authorities in practice recognized were never very generous, but the 1980 Act and regulations[1] made under it now specify a much more restricted set of circumstances in which such payments can be made to those disqualified by a trade dispute. In particular, there is no general power to make a payment because the person is destitute. One can thus see, not only in relation to urgent needs payments but also in respect to the £15 reduction, that the policy of shifting part of the burden of financing strikes from the social security system to the trade unions goes only some of the way towards explaining the provisions of the 1980 Act. Another prominent theme is a reassertion of a function that the social security system, historically, has often fulfilled, viz., the exercise of industrial discipline, in this case against strikers. It is perhaps to be expected that such a development in the field of social security should coincide with the movement of the law of industrial conflict proper towards a more restrictive position.

[1] Ibid., Regs. 3–11.

APPENDIX: THE TRADE UNION BILL

In this Appendix we deal briefly with the provisions of the Trade Union Bill which, at the time of writing, is before Parliament. We refer to the Bill as passed by the House of Commons, i.e. as it stood at the end of April 1984. The numbers in the margin of the Appendix refer to the pages in the main text of the book in conjunction with which the various parts of this Appendix should be read.

684   Part I of the Trade Union Bill implements the proposals for the election of members of the governing bodies of trade unions which the government had announced in July 1983 (*Proposals for Legislation on Democracy in Trade Unions*). It is provided that it shall be the duty of all trade unions (except for trade-union federations which have no individual members) to ensure that voting members of the union's principal executive committee are elected to their positions and are re-elected at least every five years. In the case of members of the executive who hold their positions *ex officio*, the election requirement is applied to the office by virtue of which they are voting members of the executive. The statutory duty of the trade union to secure elections overrides anything to the contrary in the trade union's rules or, in the case of employed officials, in the terms of their employment.

The duty upon the trade union is capable of enforcement by the members of union by way of application to the High Court (or Court of Session). The applicant must be a member of the trade union at the date of the application and, in the case of complaint about a past election, at the date of the election. The application is for a declaration that the union has not complied with its duty and, if the court makes such a declaration, it shall normally also make an enforcement order requiring the union to take or not take specified action. In the case of non-compliance by the union with the order, any member who was also a member when the order was made may bring proceedings to enforce the order, non-compliance with which would be a contempt of court. The above procedure is declared to be the sole method for remedying the union's breach of duty and, in particular, non-compliance with the duty is stated not to affect the validity of anything done by the executive.

The nature of the election that the union must hold in order to comply with its duty is specified in some detail in the Bill. Although certain classes of member may be excluded from voting provided all the members of the class are excluded (unemployed members, members in arrears, apprentices, trainees, students and new members), and although the right to vote in a particular election may be restricted by the rules of the union to certain classes of member (members in particular trades, geographical areas, or sections of the union), nevertheless the general principle laid down in the Bill is that of equal entitlement to vote for all members of the union. All those entitled to vote must be able to do so without 'interference or constraint', be given a 'fair and convenient' opportunity to vote and be allowed to vote 'without incurring any direct cost'. The method of voting must be by the marking of a ballot paper, which must be supplied or made available in a convenient way to all those entitled to vote, in a ballot which is secret and whose result 'is determined solely by counting the number of votes cast directly for each candidate at the election by those voting', and the votes cast must be fairly and accurately counted.

There are, however, certain relaxations of the above requirements. First, a person elected to the executive in the five years before the commencement of Part I (which will be a date appointed by the Secretary of State) may remain a member of the executive for five years from the date of his election without the union being in breach of its duty, whether or not the election satisfied the requirements set out in the previous paragraph. Second, a limited category of full-time employees of the union is exempted from the requirement of re-election once they come within five years of retirement. Third, a period of grace of one year is afforded to new unions, including unions formed by amalgamation, and there is an analogous provision in relation to transfers of engagements (see p. 682).

Finally, in one respect the Bill goes beyond what was envisaged in July 1983. Following the guiding principles of the IRA 1971, s.65(4)(a) (see p. 680), the Bill makes it part of the duty of the union to ensure that no member of the union is unreasonably excluded from standing as a candidate at the election (except by virtue of his being a member of a class all of whose members are excluded by the rules from standing), and *690* in particular membership of a political party may not be made a requirement for standing.

688 Part III of the Trade Union Bill makes a number of alterations in the law relating to the political fund as presently contained in the TUA 1913. Among the more important of them is that a resolution under s.3 of the 1913 Act approving the adoption of political objects shall cease to have effect after ten years, so that the political fund requires a positive resolution for its continuance at least once each decade. A resolution in force on the commencement date (31 March 1985) is deemed to have been passed nine years before that date, so that the union in such a case will have until 31 March 1986 to secure the passing of a new resolution. If a ballot for a new resolution is held, but is unsuccessful, then the existing resolution is treated as rescinded as from two weeks after the date of the ballot, even if the ten-year period has not in fact expired at that point.

Where a resolution has ceased to have effect because of the expiration of the ten-year period or the holding of an unsuccessful ballot within that period, the union comes under a duty to discontinue as soon as is reasonably practicable the collection of contributions to the political fund. On application by a member, the union must refund to him contributions collected after the date of the cessation; otherwise such contributions may be paid into the non-political funds of the union. Any member may apply to the High Court (or Court of Session) for a declaration that the union has failed to discontinue the collection of contributions, and the court may make an order requiring the union to take steps to fulfil its duty. An application to enforce the order may then be made by any member who was also a member when the order was made.

As for the political fund itself, once a resolution has ceased to be in force no further property may be added to the fund 'other than that which accrues to the fund in the course of administering the assets of the fund' (e.g. interest), and the union may (but need not) transfer the whole or any part of the fund to another fund of the union. However, once the resolution ceases to be effective, any payments out of the fund for political purposes would be unlawful under the TUA 1913, and so the union is in effect forced to transfer the assets of the political fund to non-political purposes if it wishes to make any use of them at all. This approach is emphasized by the provision that, even if a new resolution is passed in the future, the new political fund may not take over the sterilized assets of the old one. There is, however, one qualification to the above: if a resolution has ceased to be effective because of the holding of an unsuccessful ballot for renewal of the resolution, the union may make payments out of the fund for political purposes for a further six months from the date of the unsuccessful ballot.

A second major change is the re-definition of 'political objects', which is achieved by the insertion of new sub-sections 3 (3)–(3C) into the TUA 1913. This modernized statement makes it clear that 'any contributions to the funds of. . . a political party' and the expenditure of money on the 'provision of any service or property for use by or on behalf of any political party' are within the regulatory scheme, but this probably does not reflect any change in the law. 'Political office' is re-defined so as to include membership of the Assembly of the European Communities. The most controversial change has been the re-definition of old s.3(3)(e) so as to include expenditure 'on the production, publication or distribution of any literature, document, film, sound recording or advertisement which, taken as a whole . . . seeks to persuade any person to vote or, as the case may be, not to vote for a political party or candidate'. It seems that the aim of the re-definition was to bring within the regulatory scheme 'anti-cuts' campaigns run by certain unions before the General Election of 1983. In so far as unions contemplating running such schemes do not have political funds (as is the case, for instance, with NALGO or the AUT), the re-definition will, where it applies, prohibit such expenditure by these unions, rather than merely require the expenditure not to be made out of the general funds of the union.

692   In spite of its agreement with the TUC, the government came under pressure from its own backbenchers at the Report stage to change the legislation so as to substitute contracting in for contracting out and to prohibit the checking off by employers of contributions to the political fund. This pressure was resisted by government ministers, but one concession was made. This was an undertaking to introduce a new clause in the House of Lords making it unlawful for a employer to whom the employee had given notice that he was contracted out to continue to make deduction of the political levy from the employee's pay. This may involve some modification of the results of *Reeves* v. *TGWU* (p. 689), or of *Williams* v. *Butlers Ltd* [1975] ICR 208, where it was held an employee could effectively bind himself to a procedure whereby notification had to be given via the union.

830   Part II of the Trade Union Bill confers no rights upon trade-union members, but rather specifies a further set of situations in which the immunities provided by TULRA 1974 are removed. The protection removed is that provided by s.13 of TULRA against liability for inducing breach of a contract of employment or inducing breach of a commercial contract where one of the facts relied upon to establish liability is that there was inducement of a breach of a contract of employment or interference with its performance. (The Bill is notable for statutory use of the term 'commercial contract' – defined to mean a contract other than a contract of employment. The term is much used by commentators in this sense, but this appears to be the first example of its statutory use.) This protection is removed in respect of acts 'done by a trade union without reference to a ballot', i.e. where the act of inducement occurs during a strike or other piece of industrial action in respect of which the union has not held a ballot. In such a case the trade union will lose its immunity against liability for inducing breach of contract. Of course, such liability will arise in the first place only if the union has authorized or endorsed the act of inducement within the meaning of s.15(2) of EA 1982 (see p. 827), which is why Part II of the Bill is sometimes said to apply only to 'official' strikes. However, s.15 of EA 1982 (see pp. 827 ff.) is capable of operating rather more broadly than that.

Moreover, the immunity against inducement is removed, not only *vis-à-vis* the union but also in respect of individuals. Consequently, the individual whose act of inducement is the act of the union will also lose the immunity of TULRA 1974. This may have surprising results. Suppose a shop steward is organizing an unofficial strike by his fellow employees at a particular plant over a pay claim. The steward is protected by s.13(1) of TULRA against liability to his employer for inducing breach of contracts of employment and would have been so protected by s.3 of the TDA 1906 between 1906 and 1971. If, however, the general secretary of the union expresses the union's support for the steward's actions in such a way as to endorse the inducement of the breach of contract, the shop steward will lose his immunity unless the endorsement has been preceded by a ballot. Thus, the absence of a ballot is capable of removing protection against a very basic form of tortious liability in even a typical piece of primary industrial action.

In order to avoid removal of immunity (for both trade union and individual), the ballot must meet certain standards. One thing, however, that is in law irrelevant is, surprisingly, the result of the ballot: 'an act shall not be taken to have been done without reference to a ballot solely on the ground that it is inconsistent with the result of ballot'. As to timing, the ballot must take place before the first authorization or endorsement by the union of any act of inducement done in the course of the action and in the case of authorization the ballot must also precede the act. In practice, therefore, the ballot will have to precede any official strike or the declaring official of any unofficial strike. On the other hand, the holding of a ballot in respect of a piece of industrial action does not give the union (or individual) unlimited protection against the removal of the immunities, for the first authorization or endorsement of the act of inducement must occur within four weeks of the ballot. If this does not happen, a fresh ballot will have to be held or else the authorization or endorsement will cause loss of immunities. The requirements as to timing seem likely to inject a further element of complication into at least some national negotiations between employers and trade unions.

Who must be balloted? In principle it is all members of the union who it is reasonable for the union to suppose at the time of the ballot will be called upon to participate in the industrial action. However, this principle is qualified by a restriction which underlies the whole concept of the provisions on strike ballots. It is only those whose participation in the industrial action is likely to involve (or continue to involve) them in breaches of their contracts of employment or interference with their performance of them who are to be balloted. Indeed, those whose participation is not likely to be in breach of their contracts of employment must not be included in the ballot. Apart from the practical difficulties this may cause because of the obscurity surrounding the contractual status of many forms of action short of a strike – see pp. 720–21 (imagine the difficulties of knowing which members of the union in a multi-employer industry are likely to be in breach of their contracts if they participate in an overtime ban) – the Bill's approach is curiously at odds with that of s.62 of EPCA 1978, where contractual considerations are now thought to be irrelevant (see p. 920). The practical difficulties for the union are increased by the provision that if a member is denied entitlement to vote (say because it is not reasonable to suppose at the time of the ballot that he will be called upon to strike in breach of his contract), but he is later induced by the union so to act, then the ballot will no longer operate to restore the immunities.

The question to be asked in the ballot, in line with the legislators' underlying perceptions, is whether the member is prepared to take part in industrial action in breach of contract. Where the question is asked of willingness to participate in a strike, the union may subsequently organize action short of a strike, but not vice versa. The results of the vote must be communicated as soon as is reasonably practicable to those entitled to vote. The other requirements as to the conduct of the ballot are the same as those laid down in Part I of the Bill.

Finally, we may note in relation to the whole Bill that the provisions of ss.1 and 2 of EA 1980 (see p. 684) may be applicable to many ballots held in discharge of duties imposed by the Bill.

INDEX